Dictionary of Literary Biography

1 *The American Renaissance in New England*, edited by Joel Myerson (1978)

2 *American Novelists Since World War II*, edited by Jeffrey Helterman and Richard Layman (1978)

3 *Antebellum Writers in New York and the South*, edited by Joel Myerson (1979)

4 *American Writers in Paris, 1920–1939*, edited by Karen Lane Rood (1980)

5 *American Poets Since World War II*, 2 parts, edited by Donald J. Greiner (1980)

6 *American Novelists Since World War II, Second Series*, edited by James E. Kibler Jr. (1980)

7 *Twentieth-Century American Dramatists*, 2 parts, edited by John MacNicholas (1981)

8 *Twentieth-Century American Science-Fiction Writers*, 2 parts, edited by David Cowart and Thomas L. Wymer (1981)

9 *American Novelists, 1910–1945*, 3 parts, edited by James J. Martine (1981)

10 *Modern British Dramatists, 1900–1945*, 2 parts, edited by Stanley Weintraub (1982)

11 *American Humorists, 1800–1950*, 2 parts, edited by Stanley Trachtenberg (1982)

12 *American Realists and Naturalists*, edited by Donald Pizer and Earl N. Harbert (1982)

13 *British Dramatists Since World War II*, 2 parts, edited by Stanley Weintraub (1982)

14 *British Novelists Since 1960*, 2 parts, edited by Jay L. Halio (1983)

15 *British Novelists, 1930–1959*, 2 parts, edited by Bernard Oldsey (1983)

16 *The Beats: Literary Bohemians in Postwar America*, 2 parts, edited by Ann Charters (1983)

17 *Twentieth-Century American Historians*, edited by Clyde N. Wilson (1983)

18 *Victorian Novelists After 1885*, edited by Ira B. Nadel and William E. Fredeman (1983)

19 *British Poets, 1880–1914*, edited by Donald E. Stanford (1983)

20 *British Poets, 1914–1945*, edited by Donald E. Stanford (1983)

21 *Victorian Novelists Before 1885*, edited by Ira B. Nadel and William E. Fredeman (1983)

22 *American Writers for Children, 1900–1960*, edited by John Cech (1983)

23 *American Newspaper Journalists, 1873–1900*, edited by Perry J. Ashley (1983)

24 *American Colonial Writers, 1606–1734*, edited by Emory Elliott (1984)

25 *American Newspaper Journalists, 1901–1925*, edited by Perry J. Ashley (1984)

26 *American Screenwriters*, edited by Robert E. Morsberger, Stephen O. Lesser, and Randall Clark (1984)

27 *Poets of Great Britain and Ireland, 1945–1960*, edited by Vincent B. Sherry Jr. (1984)

28 *Twentieth-Century American-Jewish Fiction Writers*, edited by Daniel Walden (1984)

29 *American Newspaper Journalists, 1926–1950*, edited by Perry J. Ashley (1984)

30 *American Historians, 1607–1865*, edited by Clyde N. Wilson (1984)

31 *American Colonial Writers, 1735–1781*, edited by Emory Elliott (1984)

32 *Victorian Poets Before 1850*, edited by William E. Fredeman and Ira B. Nadel (1984)

33 *Afro-American Fiction Writers After 1955*, edited by Thadious M. Davis and Trudier Harris (1984)

34 *British Novelists, 1890–1929: Traditionalists*, edited by Thomas F. Staley (1985)

35 *Victorian Poets After 1850*, edited by William E. Fredeman and Ira B. Nadel (1985)

36 *British Novelists, 1890–1929: Modernists*, edited by Thomas F. Staley (1985)

37 *American Writers of the Early Republic*, edited by Emory Elliott (1985)

38 *Afro-American Writers After 1955: Dramatists and Prose Writers*, edited by Thadious M. Davis and Trudier Harris (1985)

39 *British Novelists, 1660–1800*, 2 parts, edited by Martin C. Battestin (1985)

40 *Poets of Great Britain and Ireland Since 1960*, 2 parts, edited by Vincent B. Sherry Jr. (1985)

41 *Afro-American Poets Since 1955*, edited by Trudier Harris and Thadious M. Davis (1985)

42 *American Writers for Children Before 1900*, edited by Glenn E. Estes (1985)

43 *American Newspaper Journalists, 1690–1872*, edited by Perry J. Ashley (1986)

44 *American Screenwriters, Second Series*, edited by Randall Clark, Robert E. Morsberger, and Stephen O. Lesser (1986)

45 *American Poets, 1880–1945, First Series*, edited by Peter Quartermain (1986)

46 *American Literary Publishing Houses, 1900–1980: Trade and Paperback*, edited by Peter Dzwonkoski (1986)

47 *American Historians, 1866–1912*, edited by Clyde N. Wilson (1986)

48 *American Poets, 1880–1945, Second Series*, edited by Peter Quartermain (1986)

49 *American Literary Publishing Houses, 1638–1899*, 2 parts, edited by Peter Dzwonkoski (1986)

50 *Afro-American Writers Before the Harlem Renaissance*, edited by Trudier Harris (1986)

51 *Afro-American Writers from the Harlem Renaissance to 1940*, edited by Trudier Harris (1987)

52 *American Writers for Children Since 1960: Fiction*, edited by Glenn E. Estes (1986)

53 *Canadian Writers Since 1960, First Series*, edited by W. H. New (1986)

54 *American Poets, 1880–1945, Third Series*, 2 parts, edited by Peter Quartermain (1987)

55 *Victorian Prose Writers Before 1867*, edited by William B. Thesing (1987)

56 *German Fiction Writers, 1914–1945*, edited by James Hardin (1987)

57 *Victorian Prose Writers After 1867*, edited by William B. Thesing (1987)

58 *Jacobean and Caroline Dramatists*, edited by Fredson Bowers (1987)

59 *American Literary Critics and Scholars, 1800–1850*, edited by John W. Rathbun and Monica M. Grecu (1987)

60 *Canadian Writers Since 1960, Second Series*, edited by W. H. New (1987)

61 *American Writers for Children Since 1960: Poets, Illustrators, and Nonfiction Authors*, edited by Glenn E. Estes (1987)

62 *Elizabethan Dramatists*, edited by Fredson Bowers (1987)

63 *Modern American Critics, 1920–1955*, edited by Gregory S. Jay (1988)

64 *American Literary Critics and Scholars, 1850–1880*, edited by John W. Rathbun and Monica M. Grecu (1988)

65 *French Novelists, 1900–1930*, edited by Catharine Savage Brosman (1988)

66 *German Fiction Writers, 1885–1913*, 2 parts, edited by James Hardin (1988)

67 *Modern American Critics Since 1955*, edited by Gregory S. Jay (1988)

68 *Canadian Writers, 1920–1959, First Series*, edited by W. H. New (1988)

69 *Contemporary German Fiction Writers, First Series*, edited by Wolfgang D. Elfe and James Hardin (1988)

70 *British Mystery Writers, 1860–1919*, edited by Bernard Benstock and Thomas F. Staley (1988)

71 *American Literary Critics and Scholars, 1880–1900*, edited by John W. Rathbun and Monica M. Grecu (1988)

72 *French Novelists, 1930–1960*, edited by Catharine Savage Brosman (1988)

73 *American Magazine Journalists, 1741–1850*, edited by Sam G. Riley (1988)

74 *American Short-Story Writers Before 1880*, edited by Bobby Ellen Kimbel, with the assistance of William E. Grant (1988)

75 *Contemporary German Fiction Writers, Second Series*, edited by Wolfgang D. Elfe and James Hardin (1988)

76 *Afro-American Writers, 1940–1955*, edited by Trudier Harris (1988)

77 *British Mystery Writers, 1920–1939,* edited by Bernard Benstock and Thomas F. Staley (1988)

78 *American Short-Story Writers, 1880–1910,* edited by Bobby Ellen Kimbel, with the assistance of William E. Grant (1988)

79 *American Magazine Journalists, 1850–1900,* edited by Sam G. Riley (1988)

80 *Restoration and Eighteenth-Century Dramatists, First Series,* edited by Paula R. Backscheider (1989)

81 *Austrian Fiction Writers, 1875–1913,* edited by James Hardin and Donald G. Daviau (1989)

82 *Chicano Writers, First Series,* edited by Francisco A. Lomelí and Carl R. Shirley (1989)

83 *French Novelists Since 1960,* edited by Catharine Savage Brosman (1989)

84 *Restoration and Eighteenth-Century Dramatists, Second Series,* edited by Paula R. Backscheider (1989)

85 *Austrian Fiction Writers After 1914,* edited by James Hardin and Donald G. Daviau (1989)

86 *American Short-Story Writers, 1910–1945, First Series,* edited by Bobby Ellen Kimbel (1989)

87 *British Mystery and Thriller Writers Since 1940, First Series,* edited by Bernard Benstock and Thomas F. Staley (1989)

88 *Canadian Writers, 1920–1959, Second Series,* edited by W. H. New (1989)

89 *Restoration and Eighteenth-Century Dramatists, Third Series,* edited by Paula R. Backscheider (1989)

90 *German Writers in the Age of Goethe, 1789–1832,* edited by James Hardin and Christoph E. Schweitzer (1989)

91 *American Magazine Journalists, 1900–1960, First Series,* edited by Sam G. Riley (1990)

92 *Canadian Writers, 1890–1920,* edited by W. H. New (1990)

93 *British Romantic Poets, 1789–1832, First Series,* edited by John R. Greenfield (1990)

94 *German Writers in the Age of Goethe: Sturm und Drang to Classicism,* edited by James Hardin and Christoph E. Schweitzer (1990)

95 *Eighteenth-Century British Poets, First Series,* edited by John Sitter (1990)

96 *British Romantic Poets, 1789–1832, Second Series,* edited by John R. Greenfield (1990)

97 *German Writers from the Enlightenment to Sturm und Drang, 1720–1764,* edited by James Hardin and Christoph E. Schweitzer (1990)

98 *Modern British Essayists, First Series,* edited by Robert Beum (1990)

99 *Canadian Writers Before 1890,* edited by W. H. New (1990)

100 *Modern British Essayists, Second Series,* edited by Robert Beum (1990)

101 *British Prose Writers, 1660–1800, First Series,* edited by Donald T. Siebert (1991)

102 *American Short-Story Writers, 1910–1945, Second Series,* edited by Bobby Ellen Kimbel (1991)

103 *American Literary Biographers, First Series,* edited by Steven Serafin (1991)

104 *British Prose Writers, 1660–1800, Second Series,* edited by Donald T. Siebert (1991)

105 *American Poets Since World War II, Second Series,* edited by R. S. Gwynn (1991)

106 *British Literary Publishing Houses, 1820–1880,* edited by Patricia J. Anderson and Jonathan Rose (1991)

107 *British Romantic Prose Writers, 1789–1832, First Series,* edited by John R. Greenfield (1991)

108 *Twentieth-Century Spanish Poets, First Series,* edited by Michael L. Perna (1991)

109 *Eighteenth-Century British Poets, Second Series,* edited by John Sitter (1991)

110 *British Romantic Prose Writers, 1789–1832, Second Series,* edited by John R. Greenfield (1991)

111 *American Literary Biographers, Second Series,* edited by Steven Serafin (1991)

112 *British Literary Publishing Houses, 1881–1965,* edited by Jonathan Rose and Patricia J. Anderson (1991)

113 *Modern Latin-American Fiction Writers, First Series,* edited by William Luis (1992)

114 *Twentieth-Century Italian Poets, First Series,* edited by Giovanna Wedel De Stasio, Glauco Cambon, and Antonio Illiano (1992)

115 *Medieval Philosophers,* edited by Jeremiah Hackett (1992)

116 *British Romantic Novelists, 1789–1832,* edited by Bradford K. Mudge (1992)

117 *Twentieth-Century Caribbean and Black African Writers, First Series,* edited by Bernth Lindfors and Reinhard Sander (1992)

118 *Twentieth-Century German Dramatists, 1889–1918,* edited by Wolfgang D. Elfe and James Hardin (1992)

119 *Nineteenth-Century French Fiction Writers: Romanticism and Realism, 1800–1860,* edited by Catharine Savage Brosman (1992)

120 *American Poets Since World War II, Third Series,* edited by R. S. Gwynn (1992)

121 *Seventeenth-Century British Nondramatic Poets, First Series,* edited by M. Thomas Hester (1992)

122 *Chicano Writers, Second Series,* edited by Francisco A. Lomelí and Carl R. Shirley (1992)

123 *Nineteenth-Century French Fiction Writers: Naturalism and Beyond, 1860–1900,* edited by Catharine Savage Brosman (1992)

124 *Twentieth-Century German Dramatists, 1919–1992,* edited by Wolfgang D. Elfe and James Hardin (1992)

125 *Twentieth-Century Caribbean and Black African Writers, Second Series,* edited by Bernth Lindfors and Reinhard Sander (1993)

126 *Seventeenth-Century British Nondramatic Poets, Second Series,* edited by M. Thomas Hester (1993)

127 *American Newspaper Publishers, 1950–1990,* edited by Perry J. Ashley (1993)

128 *Twentieth-Century Italian Poets, Second Series,* edited by Giovanna Wedel De Stasio, Glauco Cambon, and Antonio Illiano (1993)

129 *Nineteenth-Century German Writers, 1841–1900,* edited by James Hardin and Siegfried Mews (1993)

130 *American Short-Story Writers Since World War II,* edited by Patrick Meanor (1993)

131 *Seventeenth-Century British Nondramatic Poets, Third Series,* edited by M. Thomas Hester (1993)

132 *Sixteenth-Century British Nondramatic Writers, First Series,* edited by David A. Richardson (1993)

133 *Nineteenth-Century German Writers to 1840,* edited by James Hardin and Siegfried Mews (1993)

134 *Twentieth-Century Spanish Poets, Second Series,* edited by Jerry Phillips Winfield (1994)

135 *British Short-Fiction Writers, 1880–1914: The Realist Tradition,* edited by William B. Thesing (1994)

136 *Sixteenth-Century British Nondramatic Writers, Second Series,* edited by David A. Richardson (1994)

137 *American Magazine Journalists, 1900–1960, Second Series,* edited by Sam G. Riley (1994)

138 *German Writers and Works of the High Middle Ages: 1170–1280,* edited by James Hardin and Will Hasty (1994)

139 *British Short-Fiction Writers, 1945–1980,* edited by Dean Baldwin (1994)

140 *American Book-Collectors and Bibliographers, First Series,* edited by Joseph Rosenblum (1994)

141 *British Children's Writers, 1880–1914,* edited by Laura M. Zaidman (1994)

142 *Eighteenth-Century British Literary Biographers,* edited by Steven Serafin (1994)

143 *American Novelists Since World War II, Third Series,* edited by James R. Giles and Wanda H. Giles (1994)

144 *Nineteenth-Century British Literary Biographers,* edited by Steven Serafin (1994)

145 *Modern Latin-American Fiction Writers, Second Series,* edited by William Luis and Ann González (1994)

146 *Old and Middle English Literature,* edited by Jeffrey Helterman and Jerome Mitchell (1994)

147 *South Slavic Writers Before World War II,* edited by Vasa D. Mihailovich (1994)

148 *German Writers and Works of the Early Middle Ages: 800–1170,* edited by Will Hasty and James Hardin (1994)

149 *Late Nineteenth- and Early Twentieth-Century British Literary Biographers,* edited by Steven Serafin (1995)

150 *Early Modern Russian Writers, Late Seventeenth and Eighteenth Centuries,* edited by Marcus C. Levitt (1995)

151 *British Prose Writers of the Early Seventeenth Century,* edited by Clayton D. Lein (1995)

152 *American Novelists Since World War II, Fourth Series,* edited by James R. Giles and Wanda H. Giles (1995)

153 *Late-Victorian and Edwardian British Novelists, First Series,* edited by George M. Johnson (1995)

154 *The British Literary Book Trade, 1700–1820,* edited by James K. Bracken and Joel Silver (1995)

155 *Twentieth-Century British Literary Biographers,* edited by Steven Serafin (1995)

156 *British Short-Fiction Writers, 1880–1914: The Romantic Tradition,* edited by William F. Naufftus (1995)

157 *Twentieth-Century Caribbean and Black African Writers, Third Series,* edited by Bernth Lindfors and Reinhard Sander (1995)

158 *British Reform Writers, 1789–1832,* edited by Gary Kelly and Edd Applegate (1995)

159 *British Short-Fiction Writers, 1800–1880,* edited by John R. Greenfield (1996)

160 *British Children's Writers, 1914–1960,* edited by Donald R. Hettinga and Gary D. Schmidt (1996)

161 *British Children's Writers Since 1960, First Series,* edited by Caroline Hunt (1996)

162 *British Short-Fiction Writers, 1915–1945,* edited by John H. Rogers (1996)

163 *British Children's Writers, 1800–1880,* edited by Meena Khorana (1996)

164 *German Baroque Writers, 1580–1660,* edited by James Hardin (1996)

165 *American Poets Since World War II, Fourth Series,* edited by Joseph Conte (1996)

166 *British Travel Writers, 1837–1875,* edited by Barbara Brothers and Julia Gergits (1996)

167 *Sixteenth-Century British Nondramatic Writers, Third Series,* edited by David A. Richardson (1996)

168 *German Baroque Writers, 1661–1730,* edited by James Hardin (1996)

169 *American Poets Since World War II, Fifth Series,* edited by Joseph Conte (1996)

170 *The British Literary Book Trade, 1475–1700,* edited by James K. Bracken and Joel Silver (1996)

171 *Twentieth-Century American Sportswriters,* edited by Richard Orodenker (1996)

172 *Sixteenth-Century British Nondramatic Writers, Fourth Series,* edited by David A. Richardson (1996)

173 *American Novelists Since World War II, Fifth Series,* edited by James R. Giles and Wanda H. Giles (1996)

174 *British Travel Writers, 1876–1909,* edited by Barbara Brothers and Julia Gergits (1997)

175 *Native American Writers of the United States,* edited by Kenneth M. Roemer (1997)

176 *Ancient Greek Authors,* edited by Ward W. Briggs (1997)

177 *Italian Novelists Since World War II, 1945–1965,* edited by Augustus Pallotta (1997)

178 *British Fantasy and Science-Fiction Writers Before World War I,* edited by Darren Harris-Fain (1997)

179 *German Writers of the Renaissance and Reformation, 1280–1580,* edited by James Hardin and Max Reinhart (1997)

180 *Japanese Fiction Writers, 1868–1945,* edited by Van C. Gessel (1997)

181 *South Slavic Writers Since World War II,* edited by Vasa D. Mihailovich (1997)

182 *Japanese Fiction Writers Since World War II,* edited by Van C. Gessel (1997)

183 *American Travel Writers, 1776–1864,* edited by James J. Schramer and Donald Ross (1997)

184 *Nineteenth-Century British Book-Collectors and Bibliographers,* edited by William Baker and Kenneth Womack (1997)

185 *American Literary Journalists, 1945–1995, First Series,* edited by Arthur J. Kaul (1998)

186 *Nineteenth-Century American Western Writers,* edited by Robert L. Gale (1998)

187 *American Book Collectors and Bibliographers, Second Series,* edited by Joseph Rosenblum (1998)

188 *American Book and Magazine Illustrators to 1920,* edited by Steven E. Smith, Catherine A. Hastedt, and Donald H. Dyal (1998)

189 *American Travel Writers, 1850–1915,* edited by Donald Ross and James J. Schramer (1998)

190 *British Reform Writers, 1832–1914,* edited by Gary Kelly and Edd Applegate (1998)

191 *British Novelists Between the Wars,* edited by George M. Johnson (1998)

192 *French Dramatists, 1789–1914,* edited by Barbara T. Cooper (1998)

193 *American Poets Since World War II, Sixth Series,* edited by Joseph Conte (1998)

194 *British Novelists Since 1960, Second Series,* edited by Merritt Moseley (1998)

195 *British Travel Writers, 1910–1939,* edited by Barbara Brothers and Julia Gergits (1998)

196 *Italian Novelists Since World War II, 1965–1995,* edited by Augustus Pallotta (1999)

197 *Late-Victorian and Edwardian British Novelists, Second Series,* edited by George M. Johnson (1999)

198 *Russian Literature in the Age of Pushkin and Gogol: Prose,* edited by Christine A. Rydel (1999)

199 *Victorian Women Poets,* edited by William B. Thesing (1999)

200 *American Women Prose Writers to 1820,* edited by Carla J. Mulford, with Angela Vietto and Amy E. Winans (1999)

201 *Twentieth-Century British Book Collectors and Bibliographers,* edited by William Baker and Kenneth Womack (1999)

202 *Nineteenth-Century American Fiction Writers,* edited by Kent P. Ljungquist (1999)

203 *Medieval Japanese Writers,* edited by Steven D. Carter (1999)

204 *British Travel Writers, 1940–1997,* edited by Barbara Brothers and Julia M. Gergits (1999)

205 *Russian Literature in the Age of Pushkin and Gogol: Poetry and Drama,* edited by Christine A. Rydel (1999)

206 *Twentieth-Century American Western Writers, First Series,* edited by Richard H. Cracroft (1999)

207 *British Novelists Since 1960, Third Series,* edited by Merritt Moseley (1999)

208 *Literature of the French and Occitan Middle Ages: Eleventh to Fifteenth Centuries,* edited by Deborah Sinnreich-Levi and Ian S. Laurie (1999)

209 *Chicano Writers, Third Series,* edited by Francisco A. Lomelí and Carl R. Shirley (1999)

210 *Ernest Hemingway: A Documentary Volume,* edited by Robert W. Trogdon (1999)

211 *Ancient Roman Writers,* edited by Ward W. Briggs (1999)

212 *Twentieth-Century American Western Writers, Second Series,* edited by Richard H. Cracroft (1999)

213 *Pre-Nineteenth-Century British Book Collectors and Bibliographers,* edited by William Baker and Kenneth Womack (1999)

214 *Twentieth-Century Danish Writers,* edited by Marianne Stecher-Hansen (1999)

215 *Twentieth-Century Eastern European Writers, First Series,* edited by Steven Serafin (1999)

216 *British Poets of the Great War: Brooke, Rosenberg, Thomas. A Documentary Volume,* edited by Patrick Quinn (2000)

217 *Nineteenth-Century French Poets,* edited by Robert Beum (2000)

218 *American Short-Story Writers Since World War II, Second Series,* edited by Patrick Meanor and Gwen Crane (2000)

219 *F. Scott Fitzgerald's* The Great Gatsby: *A Documentary Volume,* edited by Matthew J. Bruccoli (2000)

220 *Twentieth-Century Eastern European Writers, Second Series,* edited by Steven Serafin (2000)

221 *American Women Prose Writers, 1870–1920,* edited by Sharon M. Harris, with the assistance of Heidi L. M. Jacobs and Jennifer Putzi (2000)

222 *H. L. Mencken: A Documentary Volume,* edited by Richard J. Schrader (2000)

223 *The American Renaissance in New England, Second Series,* edited by Wesley T. Mott (2000)

224 *Walt Whitman: A Documentary Volume,* edited by Joel Myerson (2000)

225 *South African Writers,* edited by Paul A. Scanlon (2000)

226 *American Hard-Boiled Crime Writers,* edited by George Parker Anderson and Julie B. Anderson (2000)

227 *American Novelists Since World War II, Sixth Series,* edited by James R. Giles and Wanda H. Giles (2000)

228 *Twentieth-Century American Dramatists, Second Series,* edited by Christopher J. Wheatley (2000)

229 *Thomas Wolfe: A Documentary Volume,* edited by Ted Mitchell (2001)

230 *Australian Literature, 1788–1914,* edited by Selina Samuels (2001)

231 *British Novelists Since 1960, Fourth Series,* edited by Merritt Moseley (2001)

232 *Twentieth-Century Eastern European Writers, Third Series,* edited by Steven Serafin (2001)

233 *British and Irish Dramatists Since World War II, Second Series,* edited by John Bull (2001)

234 *American Short-Story Writers Since World War II, Third Series*, edited by Patrick Meanor and Richard E. Lee (2001)

235 *The American Renaissance in New England, Third Series*, edited by Wesley T. Mott (2001)

236 *British Rhetoricians and Logicians, 1500–1660*, edited by Edward A. Malone (2001)

237 *The Beats: A Documentary Volume*, edited by Matt Theado (2001)

238 *Russian Novelists in the Age of Tolstoy and Dostoevsky*, edited by J. Alexander Ogden and Judith E. Kalb (2001)

239 *American Women Prose Writers: 1820–1870*, edited by Amy E. Hudock and Katharine Rodier (2001)

240 *Late Nineteenth- and Early Twentieth-Century British Women Poets*, edited by William B. Thesing (2001)

241 *American Sportswriters and Writers on Sport*, edited by Richard Orodenker (2001)

242 *Twentieth-Century European Cultural Theorists, First Series*, edited by Paul Hansom (2001)

243 *The American Renaissance in New England, Fourth Series*, edited by Wesley T. Mott (2001)

244 *American Short-Story Writers Since World War II, Fourth Series*, edited by Patrick Meanor and Joseph McNicholas (2001)

245 *British and Irish Dramatists Since World War II, Third Series*, edited by John Bull (2001)

246 *Twentieth-Century American Cultural Theorists*, edited by Paul Hansom (2001)

247 *James Joyce: A Documentary Volume*, edited by A. Nicholas Fargnoli (2001)

248 *Antebellum Writers in the South, Second Series*, edited by Kent Ljungquist (2001)

249 *Twentieth-Century American Dramatists, Third Series*, edited by Christopher Wheatley (2002)

250 *Antebellum Writers in New York, Second Series*, edited by Kent Ljungquist (2002)

251 *Canadian Fantasy and Science-Fiction Writers*, edited by Douglas Ivison (2002)

252 *British Philosophers, 1500–1799*, edited by Philip B. Dematteis and Peter S. Fosl (2002)

253 *Raymond Chandler: A Documentary Volume*, edited by Robert Moss (2002)

254 *The House of Putnam, 1837–1872: A Documentary Volume*, edited by Ezra Greenspan (2002)

255 *British Fantasy and Science-Fiction Writers, 1918–1960*, edited by Darren Harris-Fain (2002)

256 *Twentieth-Century American Western Writers, Third Series*, edited by Richard H. Cracroft (2002)

257 *Twentieth-Century Swedish Writers After World War II*, edited by Ann-Charlotte Gavel Adams (2002)

258 *Modern French Poets*, edited by Jean-François Leroux (2002)

259 *Twentieth-Century Swedish Writers Before World War II*, edited by Ann-Charlotte Gavel Adams (2002)

260 *Australian Writers, 1915–1950*, edited by Selina Samuels (2002)

261 *British Fantasy and Science-Fiction Writers Since 1960*, edited by Darren Harris-Fain (2002)

262 *British Philosophers, 1800–2000*, edited by Peter S. Fosl and Leemon B. McHenry (2002)

263 *William Shakespeare: A Documentary Volume*, edited by Catherine Loomis (2002)

264 *Italian Prose Writers, 1900–1945*, edited by Luca Somigli and Rocco Capozzi (2002)

265 *American Song Lyricists, 1920–1960*, edited by Philip Furia (2002)

266 *Twentieth-Century American Dramatists, Fourth Series*, edited by Christopher J. Wheatley (2002)

267 *Twenty-First-Century British and Irish Novelists*, edited by Michael R. Molino (2002)

268 *Seventeenth-Century French Writers*, edited by Françoise Jaouën (2002)

269 *Nathaniel Hawthorne: A Documentary Volume*, edited by Benjamin Franklin V (2002)

270 *American Philosophers Before 1950*, edited by Philip B. Dematteis and Leemon B. McHenry (2002)

271 *British and Irish Novelists Since 1960*, edited by Merritt Moseley (2002)

272 *Russian Prose Writers Between the World Wars*, edited by Christine Rydel (2003)

273 *F. Scott Fitzgerald's* Tender Is the Night: *A Documentary Volume*, edited by Matthew J. Bruccoli and George Parker Anderson (2003)

274 *John Dos Passos's* U.S.A.: *A Documentary Volume*, edited by Donald Pizer (2003)

275 *Twentieth-Century American Nature Writers: Prose*, edited by Roger Thompson and J. Scott Bryson (2003)

276 *British Mystery and Thriller Writers Since 1960*, edited by Gina Macdonald (2003)

277 *Russian Literature in the Age of Realism*, edited by Allyssa Dinega Gillespie (2003)

278 *American Novelists Since World War II, Seventh Series*, edited by James R. Giles and Wanda H. Giles (2003)

279 *American Philosophers, 1950–2000*, edited by Philip B. Dematteis and Leemon B. McHenry (2003)

280 *Dashiell Hammett's* The Maltese Falcon: *A Documentary Volume*, edited by Richard Layman (2003)

281 *British Rhetoricians and Logicians, 1500–1660, Second Series*, edited by Edward A. Malone (2003)

282 *New Formalist Poets*, edited by Jonathan N. Barron and Bruce Meyer (2003)

Dictionary of Literary Biography Documentary Series

1 *Sherwood Anderson, Willa Cather, John Dos Passos, Theodore Dreiser, F. Scott Fitzgerald, Ernest Hemingway, Sinclair Lewis*, edited by Margaret A. Van Antwerp (1982)

2 *James Gould Cozzens, James T. Farrell, William Faulkner, John O'Hara, John Steinbeck, Thomas Wolfe, Richard Wright*, edited by Margaret A. Van Antwerp (1982)

3 *Saul Bellow, Jack Kerouac, Norman Mailer, Vladimir Nabokov, John Updike, Kurt Vonnegut*, edited by Mary Bruccoli (1983)

4 *Tennessee Williams*, edited by Margaret A. Van Antwerp and Sally Johns (1984)

5 *American Transcendentalists*, edited by Joel Myerson (1988)

6 *Hardboiled Mystery Writers: Raymond Chandler, Dashiell Hammett, Ross Macdonald*, edited by Matthew J. Bruccoli and Richard Layman (1989)

7 *Modern American Poets: James Dickey, Robert Frost, Marianne Moore*, edited by Karen L. Rood (1989)

8 *The Black Aesthetic Movement*, edited by Jeffrey Louis Decker (1991)

9 *American Writers of the Vietnam War: W. D. Ehrhart, Larry Heinemann, Tim O'Brien, Walter McDonald, John M. Del Vecchio*, edited by Ronald Baughman (1991)

10 *The Bloomsbury Group*, edited by Edward L. Bishop (1992)

11 *American Proletarian Culture: The Twenties and The Thirties*, edited by Jon Christian Suggs (1993)

12 *Southern Women Writers: Flannery O'Connor, Katherine Anne Porter, Eudora Welty*, edited by Mary Ann Wimsatt and Karen L. Rood (1994)

13 *The House of Scribner, 1846–1904*, edited by John Delaney (1996)

14 *Four Women Writers for Children, 1868–1918*, edited by Caroline C. Hunt (1996)

15 *American Expatriate Writers: Paris in the Twenties*, edited by Matthew J. Bruccoli and Robert W. Trogdon (1997)

16 *The House of Scribner, 1905–1930*, edited by John Delaney (1997)

17 *The House of Scribner, 1931–1984*, edited by John Delaney (1998)

18 *British Poets of The Great War: Sassoon, Graves, Owen*, edited by Patrick Quinn (1999)

19 *James Dickey*, edited by Judith S. Baughman (1999)

See also DLB 210, 216, 219, 222, 224, 229, 237, 247, 253, 254, 263, 269, 273, 274, 280

Dictionary of Literary Biography Yearbooks

1980 edited by Karen L. Rood, Jean W. Ross, and Richard Ziegfeld (1981)

1981 edited by Karen L. Rood, Jean W. Ross, and Richard Ziegfeld (1982)

1982 edited by Richard Ziegfeld; associate editors: Jean W. Ross and Lynne C. Zeigler (1983)

1983 edited by Mary Bruccoli and Jean W. Ross; associate editor Richard Ziegfeld (1984)

1984 edited by Jean W. Ross (1985)

1985 edited by Jean W. Ross (1986)

1986 edited by J. M. Brook (1987)

1987 edited by J. M. Brook (1988)

1988 edited by J. M. Brook (1989)

1989 edited by J. M. Brook (1990)

1990 edited by James W. Hipp (1991)

1991 edited by James W. Hipp (1992)

1992 edited by James W. Hipp (1993)

1993 edited by James W. Hipp, contributing editor George Garrett (1994)

1994 edited by James W. Hipp, contributing editor George Garrett (1995)

1995 edited by James W. Hipp, contributing editor George Garrett (1996)

1996 edited by Samuel W. Bruce and L. Kay Webster, contributing editor George Garrett (1997)

1997 edited by Matthew J. Bruccoli and George Garrett, with the assistance of L. Kay Webster (1998)

1998 edited by Matthew J. Bruccoli, contributing editor George Garrett, with the assistance of D. W. Thomas (1999)

1999 edited by Matthew J. Bruccoli, contributing editor George Garrett, with the assistance of D. W. Thomas (2000)

2000 edited by Matthew J. Bruccoli, contributing editor George Garrett, with the assistance of George Parker Anderson (2001)

2001 edited by Matthew J. Bruccoli, contributing editor George Garrett, with the assistance of George Parker Anderson (2002)

2002 edited by Matthew J. Bruccoli and George Garrett; George Parker Anderson, Assistant Editor (2003)

Concise Series

Concise Dictionary of American Literary Biography, 7 volumes (1988–1999): *The New Consciousness, 1941–1968; Colonization to the American Renaissance, 1640–1865; Realism, Naturalism, and Local Color, 1865–1917; The Twenties, 1917–1929; The Age of Maturity, 1929–1941; Broadening Views, 1968–1988; Supplement: Modern Writers, 1900–1998.*

Concise Dictionary of British Literary Biography, 8 volumes (1991–1992): *Writers of the Middle Ages and Renaissance Before 1660; Writers of the Restoration and Eighteenth Century, 1660–1789; Writers of the Romantic Period, 1789–1832; Victorian Writers, 1832–1890; Late-Victorian and Edwardian Writers, 1890–1914; Modern Writers, 1914–1945; Writers After World War II, 1945–1960; Contemporary Writers, 1960 to Present.*

Concise Dictionary of World Literary Biography, 4 volumes (1999–2000): *Ancient Greek and Roman Writers; German Writers; African, Caribbean, and Latin American Writers; South Slavic and Eastern European Writers.*

Dictionary of Literary Biography® • Volume Two Hundred Eighty-Two

New Formalist Poets

Dictionary of Literary Biography® • Volume Two Hundred Eighty-Two

New Formalist Poets

Edited by
Jonathan N. Barron
University of Southern Mississippi, Hattiesburg

and

Bruce Meyer
University of Toronto School of Continuing Studies

A Bruccoli Clark Layman Book

Detroit • New York • San Diego • San Francisco • Cleveland • New Haven, Conn. • Waterville, Maine • London • Munich

Dictionary of Literary Biography
Volume 282: New Formalist Poets

Jonathan N. Barron
Bruce Meyer

Advisory Board
John Baker
William Cagle
Patrick O'Connor
George Garrett
Trudier Harris
Alvin Kernan
Kenny J. Williams

Editorial Directors
Matthew J. Bruccoli and Richard Layman

© 2003 by Gale. Gale is an imprint of The Gale Group, Inc., a division of Thomson Learning, Inc.

Gale and Design™ and Thomson Learning™ are trademarks used herein under license.

For more information, contact
The Gale Group, Inc.
27500 Drake Rd.
Farmington Hills, MI 48331-3535
Or you can visit our Internet site at
http://www.gale.com

ALL RIGHTS RESERVED
No part of this work covered by the copyright hereon may be reproduced or used in any form or by any means—graphic, electronic, or mechanical, including photocopying, recording, taping, Web distribution, or information storage retrieval systems—without the written permission of the publisher.

For permission to use material from this product, submit your request via Web at http://www.gale-edit.com/permissions, or you may download our Permissions Request form and submit your request by fax or mail to:

Permissions Department
The Gale Group, Inc.
27500 Drake Rd.
Farmington Hills, MI 48331-3535
Permissions Hotline:
248-699-8006 or 800-877-4253, ext. 8006
Fax: 248-699-8074 or 800-762-4058

While every effort has been made to ensure the reliability of the information presented in this publication, The Gale Group, Inc. does not guarantee the accuracy of the data contained herein. The Gale Group, Inc. accepts no payment for listing; and inclusion in the publication of any organization, agency, institution, publication, service, or individual does not imply endorsement of the editors or publisher. Errors brought to the attention of the publisher and verified to the satisfaction of the publisher will be corrected in future editions.

LIBRARY OF CONGRESS CATALOGING-IN-PUBLICATION DATA

New formalist poets / edited by Jonathan N. Barron and Bruce Meyer.
    p. cm. — (Dictionary of literary biography ; v. 282)
"A Bruccoli Clark Layman book."
Includes bibliographical references and index.
    ISBN 0-7876-6819-2
    1. American poetry—20th century—Bio-bibliography—Dictionaries.
    2. Poets, American—20th century—Biography—Dictionaries.
    3. Literary form—Dictionaries. I. Meyer, Bruce, 1957–
II. Barron, Jonathan N. III. Series.

PS325.N49 2003
811'.509'03—dc21
                                      2003009338

Printed in the United States of America
10 9 8 7 6 5 4 3 2 1

For Ellen, Kerry, Liana, Raphael, and Katie.

Contents

Plan of the Series xv
Introduction xvii

Dick Allen (1939–) 3
   T. L. Ponick and F. S. Ponick

Julia Alvarez (1950–) 16
   Kathrine Varnes

Rafael Campo (1964–) 24
   David Caplan

Jared Carter (1939–) 31
   T. L. Ponick and F. S. Ponick

Alfred Corn (1943–) 41
   Ernest J. Smith

Dick Davis (1945–) 50
   Charles Martin

Tom Disch (1940–) 59
   Robert McPhillips

Michael Donaghy (1954–) 67
   Catherine Tufariello

Rhina P. Espaillat (1932–) 78
   Len Krisak

Frederick Feirstein (1940–) 83
   T. L. Ponick and F. S. Ponick

Annie Finch (1956–) 91
   Jonathan N. Barron

John Gery (1953–) 102
   Sonny Williams

Dana Gioia (1950–) 112
   Bruce Meyer

Emily Grosholz (1950–) 123
   Meg Schoerke

R. S. Gwynn (1948–) 132
   David Mason

Marilyn Hacker (1942–) 144
   Jennifer Factor

Rachel Hadas (1948–) 152
   Ernest J. Smith

Andrew Hudgins (1951–) 160
   Daniel Anderson

Mark Jarman (1952–) 165
   Terri Witek

Paul Lake (1951–) 173
   Jonathan N. Barron and Sonny Williams

Sydney Lea (1942–) 182
   D. Creason Bartlett

Brad Leithauser (1953–) 188
   Steven P. Schneider

Phillis Levin (1954–) 195
   Jason Schneiderman

Charles Martin (1942–) 201
   David Yezzi

David Mason (1954–) 207
   H. L. Hix

Robert McDowell (1953–) 216
   Mark Jarman

Bruce Meyer (1957–) 223
   T. L. Ponick and F. S. Ponick

Marilyn Nelson (1946–) 233
   Paul A. Griffith

Molly Peacock (1947–) 241
   Carolyn Meyer

Wyatt Prunty (1947–) 253
   N. S. Thompson

Kay Ryan (1945–) 258
   Paul Lake

Mary Jo Salter (1954–) 265
   R. A. Benthall

Gjertrud Schnackenberg (1953–) 272
   Kymberly Taylor Haywood

Vikram Seth (1952–) 279
   Robert McPhillips

Timothy Steele (1948–) 286
   Joseph O. Aimone

Frederick Turner (1943-) 293
   Sonny Williams

Anthologizing New Formalism. 305
   David Caplan

The Little Magazines of the
   New Formalism 309
   April Lindner

The New Narrative Poetry 315
   Sonny Williams

Presses of the New Formalism
   and the New Narrative 325
   April Lindner

The Prosody of the New Formalism 333
   Thomas Cable

Younger Women Poets of the New Formalism 338
   April Lindner

Books for Further Reading 347
Contributors 349
Cumulative Index 353

Plan of the Series

... Almost the most prodigious asset of a country, and perhaps its most precious possession, is its native literary product—when that product is fine and noble and enduring.

Mark Twain*

The advisory board, the editors, and the publisher of the *Dictionary of Literary Biography* are joined in endorsing Mark Twain's declaration. The literature of a nation provides an inexhaustible resource of permanent worth. Our purpose is to make literature and its creators better understood and more accessible to students and the reading public, while satisfying the needs of teachers and researchers.

To meet these requirements, *literary biography* has been construed in terms of the author's achievement. The most important thing about a writer is his writing. Accordingly, the entries in *DLB* are career biographies, tracing the development of the author's canon and the evolution of his reputation.

The purpose of *DLB* is not only to provide reliable information in a usable format but also to place the figures in the larger perspective of literary history and to offer appraisals of their accomplishments by qualified scholars.

The publication plan for *DLB* resulted from two years of preparation. The project was proposed to Bruccoli Clark by Frederick G. Ruffner, president of the Gale Research Company, in November 1975. After specimen entries were prepared and typeset, an advisory board was formed to refine the entry format and develop the series rationale. In meetings held during 1976, the publisher, series editors, and advisory board approved the scheme for a comprehensive biographical dictionary of persons who contributed to literature. Editorial work on the first volume began in January 1977, and it was published in 1978. In order to make *DLB* more than a dictionary and to compile volumes that individually have claim to status as literary history, it was decided to organize volumes by topic, period, or genre. Each of these freestanding volumes provides a biographical-bibliographical guide and overview for a particular area of literature. We are convinced that this organization—as opposed to a single alphabet method—constitutes a valuable innovation in the presentation of reference material. The volume plan necessarily requires many decisions for the placement and treatment of authors. Certain figures will be included in separate volumes, but with different entries emphasizing the aspect of his career appropriate to each volume. Ernest Hemingway, for example, is represented in *American Writers in Paris, 1920-1939* by an entry focusing on his expatriate apprenticeship; he is also in *American Novelists, 1910-1945* with an entry surveying his entire career, as well as in *American Short-Story Writers, 1910-1945, Second Series* with an entry concentrating on his short fiction. Each volume includes a cumulative index of the subject authors and articles.

Since 1981 the series has been further augmented by the *DLB Yearbooks,* which update published entries, add new entries to keep the *DLB* current with contemporary activity, and provide articles on literary history. There have also been nineteen *DLB Documentary Series* volumes, which provide illustrations, facsimiles, and biographical and critical source materials for figures, works, or groups judged to have particular interest for students. In 1999 the *Documentary Series* was incorporated into the *DLB* volume numbering system beginning with *DLB 210: Ernest Hemingway.*

We define literature as the *intellectual commerce of a nation:* not merely as belles lettres but as that ample and complex process by which ideas are generated, shaped, and transmitted. *DLB* entries are not limited to "creative writers" but extend to other figures who in their time and in their way influenced the mind of a people. Thus the series encompasses historians, journalists, publishers, book collectors, and screenwriters. By this means readers of *DLB* may be aided to perceive literature not as cult scripture in the keeping of intellectual high priests but firmly positioned at the center of a nation's life.

DLB includes the major writers appropriate to each volume and those standing in the ranks behind them. Scholarly and critical counsel has been sought in

*From an unpublished section of Mark Twain's autobiography, copyright by the Mark Twain Company

deciding which minor figures to include and how full their entries should be. Wherever possible, useful references are made to figures who do not warrant separate entries.

Each *DLB* volume has an expert volume editor responsible for planning the volume, selecting the figures for inclusion, and assigning the entries. Volume editors are also responsible for preparing, where appropriate, appendices surveying the major periodicals and literary and intellectual movements for their volumes, as well as lists of further readings. Work on the series as a whole is coordinated at the Bruccoli Clark Layman editorial center in Columbia, South Carolina, where the editorial staff is responsible for accuracy and utility of the published volumes.

One feature that distinguishes *DLB* is the illustration policy–its concern with the iconography of literature. Just as an author is influenced by his surroundings, so is the reader's understanding of the author enhanced by a knowledge of his environment. Therefore *DLB* volumes include not only drawings, paintings, and photographs of authors, often depicting them at various stages in their careers, but also illustrations of their families and places where they lived. Title pages are regularly reproduced in facsimile along with dust jackets for modern authors. The dust jackets are a special feature of *DLB* because they often document better than anything else the way in which an author's work was perceived in its own time. Specimens of the writers' manuscripts and letters are included when feasible.

Samuel Johnson rightly decreed that "The chief glory of every people arises from its authors." The purpose of the *Dictionary of Literary Biography* is to compile literary history in the surest way available to us–by accurate and comprehensive treatment of the lives and work of those who contributed to it.

The *DLB* Advisory Board

Introduction

English-language poetry for more than a century has been transformed by the rebels, "experimentalists," and liberators, who have long held that breaking with the concept of "poetry as a tradition" was an act of renewal and revitalization for the art. Literary history has suggested that vers libre was the leading edge of the art since it freed poetry from the constraints of form in order to create a fresher, more genuine poetry. The Modernists and mid-century free-verse writers argued that if traditional prosodic values were the status quo, then the status quo had to be challenged. To remain vital, poetry had to change, and change meant that traditional poetics had to be dispensed with in order to free the voice of the poet. What evolved, in its initial stages, was good for poetry. The art was refreshed. No sooner had the ink dried on this new work, however, than it, too, became a status quo. The art of poetry demands constant refreshment, renewal, and change.

In England, poets in the late 1970s—such as James Fenton, Andrew Motion, Blake Morrison, and Craig Raine—published *The Penguin Book of Contemporary British Verse* (1982). In that work Motion and Morrison suggested that if poetry were to remain a vital art, it was the duty of a poet to "make the familiar strange." By then, the strange meant returning poetry to its lyric roots in meter. Poets such as Fenton, Motion, and Raine (and Seamus Heaney, who was reluctantly included in the anthology) recognized that making the familiar strange meant making poetry both lyrical *and* accessible. They based their notion of accessibility on the idea that lyricism (the use of meter and other traditional formal techniques) could thrive in a contemporary idiom—that poetry could sing, tell stories, and entertain without losing either its audience or its power. This anthology highlighted a British poetry in what might be called the Thomas Hardy tradition, whose last exemplars were the Movement poets, the generation of British voices from the 1950s and such poets as Philip Larkin, Donald Davie, and Elizabeth Jennings. Poets such as Motion and Wendy Cope were successful in returning poetry to its rightful place as a popular art that people read, discussed, and incorporated into their daily lives.

In an independent, though parallel, phenomenon, many young American poets of the 1970s and 1980s made the same rebellious assertion: poetry should once more claim its roots in meter and other traditional techniques of lyricism. Like their British counterparts, they, too, turned to the poets of the 1950s—Americans such as Richard Wilbur, Donald Justice, Elizabeth Bishop, and Anthony Hecht. In those poets' work young American poets found the kind of compositional and aesthetic guidance that would connect them to the longstanding, pre-Modernist traditions of English-language poetry. Rather than deny form in favor of free verse, they embraced the complexities and challenge that tradition posed to them. In their hands, a sestina or a villanelle was not an academic exercise but rather a means of making language clear, accessible, and beautiful to a broad audience that had become wary of poetry. Likewise, narrative poets in the 1970s and 1980s revived the traditions of Robert Frost and Edwin Arlington Robinson that had been so popular in the nineteenth century—not because they thought nineteenth-century poetry was better, but because they foresaw the possibility that twentieth-century poetry could be improved. In the conclusion of his essay "Notes on the New Formalism" from his much-discussed book *Can Poetry Matter?* (1992), Dana Gioia (himself one of the young poets experimenting with traditional prosodic techniques) suggested that the point of the return to such forms, this new experiment, was to get people talking about poetry again. For Gioia, poetry needed resuscitation because it had ceased to hold its rightful place in the cultural awareness of Americans. For Gioia, poetry was not a contest between free and formal verse but rather an art of constant struggle. Every poet, said Gioia, must challenge the assumptions and ideas of the art form he or she inherits. Otherwise, it will be an art stalled in a neutral gear. According to Gioia,

> ten years from now the real debate among poets and concerned critics will not be about poetic form in the narrow technical sense of metrical versus nonmetrical verse. That is already a tired argument, and only the uninformed or biased can fail to recognize that genuine poetry can be created in both modes. How obvious it should be that no technique precludes poetic achievement, just as none automatically assures it (though

admittedly some techniques may be more difficult to use at certain moments in history). Soon . . . the central debate will focus on form in the wider, more elusive sense of poetic structure. How does a poet best shape words, images, and ideas into meaning? How much compression is needed to transform versified lines—be they metrical or free—into genuine poetry? The important arguments will not be about technique in isolation but about the fundamental aesthetic assumptions of writing and judging poetry.

Quite simply, the young American poets of the late 1970s and early 1980s took the position that fixed forms offered a new sense of freedom because those forms proved a need to reassess what poetry could do. Gioia and this younger group of poets foresaw that an expanded and expansive poetic range could improve the art as a whole and free it from the dangers that it faced—"the debasement of poetic language; the prolixity of the lyric; the bankruptcy of the confessional mode; the inability to establish a meaningful aesthetic for new poetic narrative; and the denial of musical texture in the contemporary poem." They perceived themselves not as conservatives or rearguard traditionalists but as poets who were providing a necessary step in the evolution of the art of poetry. For their love of form, narrative, and the elements of song inherent in the contemporary idiom, they were broadly grouped under the title New Formalism.

The term "New Formalism" expresses an array of various approaches to poetry. On the one hand, the metrical lyricists—such as Timothy Steele, Alfred Corn, or Charles Martin—rest their claims upon their intelligent and astute abilities to marry technical exactness to directness of diction and voice. The freer lyric poets—such as Molly Peacock, Annie Finch, Rhina Espaillat, and Bruce Meyer—use traditional forms and metrical structures, but only when those elements serve the purpose of the poem. Others, such as Kay Ryan, experiment with form, often including the aspects of rhyme and meter within totally new and surprising arrangements. Narrative poets—such as David Mason, Mark Jarman, Robert McDowell, Frederick Turner, and Jared Carter—have turned to the traditional elements of short fiction in order to restore poetry to the status of public storytelling. Still others—such as John Gery, Dana Gioia, R. S. Gwynn, Mary Jo Salter, Brad Leithauser, and Paul Lake—work in what is best described as a mixture of mediums, forms, and approaches in order to expand the horizons of what poetry can do. So broad is the term "New Formalism" that it has also been referred to by critics such as Frederick Feirstein, R. S. Gwynn, and Kevin Walzer as "Expansive Poetry." Whatever name is applied to this gathering of poets, one point is clear: contemporary poetry needs to embrace a wide range of styles, approaches, forms, and ideas in order to grow and remain important to readers.

Looking back from a perspective of nearly twenty-five years, one can say that, at its best, the New Formalism did succeed in once more planting some fundamental elements of poetry in the American soil. The New Formalists consciously sought to challenge the status quo. In such critical commentaries as Gioia's *Can Poetry Matter? Essays on Poetry and American Culture* (1992) their challenge did spark debate. In fact, the debate began when Gioia published the title essay in *The Atlantic Monthly* (5 May 1991). At that time he evoked a hostile response from many quarters. Who exactly were these young poetic upstarts to challenge the assumptions that had been so dearly fought for and mightily won by preceding generations of free-verse poets? And why should these New Formalists attack what was perceived to be the heart of American poetry—the traditions of the liberated voice celebrated by Walt Whitman and others for more than a century?

At their worst, New Formalists did not just revive forgotten techniques of the art of poetry: they went so far as to reject and even to deny the existence and ideas of free-verse poetry, confessional poetry, and even Modernism itself, rejecting their poetic claims altogether. In other words, some defenders of the New Formalism wanted to eradicate free verse itself, labeling the use of it an arch literary sin. This vituperative polemical spirit reigned in the 1980s and did so most notoriously in two essays by Leithauser. One of those essays, "Metrical Illiteracy" (*The New Criterion,* January 1983), even went so far as to claim that ignorance of the metrical tradition was, for a poet, "functional illiteracy." Adding the weight of science to this New Formalist defense of meter and to its assault on free-verse poetry, Frederick Turner, working with linguist Ernst Poppel, published "The Neural Lyre" (1985), declaring that meter is, in fact, part and parcel of the chemistry in the brain for language acquisition. To go against meter, in short, was to go against biology.

This tendency to privilege the elements of the New Formalism over and above competing poetic traditions did lead to some provocative scholarship, such as Timothy Steele's history and defense of meter and Wyatt Prunty's history and defense of poetic symbols. On the whole, however, the antagonistic polemics of the 1980s resulted only in giving to the New Formalism the aura of a reactionary cultural movement; poets such as Diane Wakoski and others were quick to tie New Formalist poetics to a conservative political and cultural agenda. While poets in this movement, as in most movements, claim many different political ideologies, the public impression left by the polemics was that the New Formalism, particularly in the 1980s, was nothing more than the literary arm of a neoconservative political ideology. The reality, however, is far from this philosophy. The poetry of the New Formalism has had little to do with overt political agendas or direct political statements. The poets themselves, who reside under this broad, critical umbrella, come from a diverse range of political backgrounds. What they all share in common is a love and an appreciation of the potentialities inherent in poetic language. But having caught hold of the association of the New Formalism with conservative politics, the detractors of the new poetics presented a significant red herring that for years deflected the argument from poetics and on to other issues. Two elements fostered this inaccurate reading of what the New Formalists were about. First, many of the more unforgiving of the essays from the 1980s that supported the New Formalism were first published in conservative literary magazines such as *The New Criterion,* edited by neoconservative intellectual Hilton Kramer. The politics implicit in such critiques led many critics to dismiss and vilify the New Formalism as nothing more than an ideological tool of right-wing politics. Many of the chief polemicists, moreover, were white Anglo-Saxon men, and, as it happened, the poetry they denounced and many of the examples they selected for critique were most often written by ethnic minorities, feminists, and gay and lesbian poets. The presence among the New Formalists of poets such as Rafael Campo, Alfred Corn, Rhina Espaillat, or Marilyn Nelson makes this claim against the New Formalism ridiculous. The New Formalism has presented such a broad spectrum of poetic personalities and approaches that to limit it to either an argument for or a critique against any social or political position simply does not hold up. If any certainties about the New Formalism and its practitioners exist, they are that, as a poetry by poets who are in love with poetry and who value the art in its broadest possible context, it refuses to ignore the possibilities that tradition, literary heritage, and language have to offer.

In *DLB 282: New Formalist Poets,* then, the editors hope to put the ideological association of the New Formalism with neoconservatism, at last, to rest. As the following entries will attest, the movement has always had within it a far more generous and inclusive spirit. For all of its commitment to meter, fixed rhyme schemes, and poetic forms, it has also always been an eclectic movement, even if it has sometimes been a movement in tension with itself. No doubt its more conservative and sometimes more vocal elements have long been in debate with its more liberal adherents. But these liberal voices have always been a fundamental part of the movement.

From the outset, for example, poets such as Annie Finch have insisted that New Formalist ideas be added to an already vibrant poetic mix bubbling with the energy of free-verse poetics. Rather than replace a free verse that has proved itself useful to so many poets, Finch, in both her critical work *The Ghost of Meter* (1993) and her anthology of New Formalist poems from women, *A Formal Feeling Comes* (1994), argues for the utility, even the necessity, of older forms, and of meter, even as she refuses to denounce alternative measures and forms. A similar spirit of generosity defines the work of the chief arbiter of the New Formalism, poet and polemicist Gioia. Indeed, in his essay "Notes on the New Formalism," Gioia succinctly explains why the movement emerged at all: "Free verse, the creation of an older literary revolution is now the long established, ruling orthodoxy; formal poetry, the unexpected challenge."

What has been too often lost in debates about the New Formalism is that its adherents share a love and interest in meter and fixed forms, not in political ideology. In fact, political ideology did not bring any of these poets together, nor did a shared political view create this movement. In truth, the New Formalists never did nor could have held to a particular ideological, ethnic, or even nationalist line.

As this *DLB* volume makes clear, the New Formalism is too disparate and diverse to be understood only in ideological terms. The movement includes gay and lesbian poets as well as some of the most important feminist voices in contemporary English language poetry, such as Annie Finch and Marilyn Hacker. At the same time, these poets do share a movement with a poetics of machismo and even occasional misogyny. Similarly, the entries in this *DLB* volume also give the lie to the claim that this movement is only for angry white males. In the New Formalism one finds Jewish, Latino, and African American poets, and, more dramatically, in the New Formalism one also finds an end to, or a moving beyond, merely national poetics. The movement, after all, includes such poets as Dick Davis, Bruce Meyer, Michael Donaghy, and Vikram Seth, whose backgrounds embrace the knowledge and traditions of Canadian, Irish, British, and Indian poetry. The poetry of these four, for example, testifies to the broad international scope of the movement and its ability to cross national boundaries. The scope of the New Formalism can be perceived not merely in its current practitioners but in its roots and origins also.

The New Formalism began as a concerted effort, a movement, to force what was perceived to be a poetic establishment exclusively favoring free verse to accept a set of poetic conventions that had fallen into serious disrepute. One might have thought that working in meter and traditional rhyme schemes would not cause much of a stir, and certainly poets throughout the 1970s were working in formal traditions. But a distinct generational politics was at stake. On the one hand, a generation of poets born in the 1910s and 1920s had established a solid body of poetry derived from fixed forms and meter; among them were Anthony Hecht, Richard Wilbur, John Hollander, Howard Nemerov, James Merrill, Robert Hayden, Elizabeth Bishop, and Robert Fitzgerald. On the other hand, by the 1970s the literary establishment that had given license to those older poets to continue their formal poetry had effectively disallowed such work for younger poets as somehow irrelevant to the contemporary age. A double bind awaited young poets born in the 1950s who were just coming into their own careers in the 1970s. Unwilling to mimic and write a "high style" of their elder, formalist mentors and equally unwilling to cultivate the new free-verse aesthetic then in vogue, such poets as David Mason, Dana Gioia, Mark Jarman, Frederick Feirstein, and Robert McDowell formed a movement, not initially called the New Formalism, but rather Expansive poetry. The movement even established its own magazines and presses (most famously *The Reaper,* edited by Robert McDowell and Mark Jarman). Out of this original circle of poets from the late 1970s, the New Formalism emerged, a group united by their interest in poetry and a particular poetics. But the New Formalism grew beyond the constraints of what could be called a movement, as movements have been defined in twentieth-century literary history. The term was soon applied to questions of practice rather than issues of polemics.

The use of traditional form and narrative in American poetry began to gain impetus in New York during the late 1970s. Many young poets—some under the tutelage of such older formalists as Richard Howard, Richard Wilbur, Donald Justice, Elizabeth Bishop, or Anthony Hecht—began to defy the free-verse conventions of the times by publishing poetry that was formal or narrative. Soon after, in the 1980s, a series of special issues of literary magazines appeared, particularly *The Kenyon Review, Crosscurrents,* and *The Missouri Review*. By 1990 Robert McPhillips edited an issue of *Verse* in which he noted that "a literary movement was capable of redirecting the course of American poetry."

Not only was the poetry highlighted in the literary press of the 1980s, but also a dedicated group of poets committed to the use of meter began to polemicize there, too. In *The Georgia Review* (Winter 1981), for example, Richard Moore declared there was "a new way for poetry to go: the old way that it has always gone" (1981). The polemics seemed necessary because even though the original group of New Formalists had published in the late 1970s a few books—such as Charles Martin's *Room for Error* (1978) and Timothy Steele's *Uncertainties and Rest* (1979)—they had not made any serious inroads into the literary establishment. The older generation of formalists (those born in the 1910s–1920s) apparently had been granted poetic license to practice their forms because of their stature and because they had inherited such ideas as part of the legacy of their teachers—Allan Tate, John Crowe Ransom, Yvor Winters, and W. H. Auden. The younger poets (born in the late 1940s and early 1950s) were not granted such permission because, from a generational perspective, they seemed to be twice removed from the so-called "high style" of meter and traditional prosody. To them, such traditional aspects of the craft needed to be challenged and questioned, if not refuted. The first reaction against the New Formalists, was one of shock, if not outright condemnation. The younger generation writing in such a manner seemed, as William Wordsworth would have said, to be "out of tune with the age." They were deemed to be retrograde, to be, in a word, mannered, particularly when compared to free-verse poets of the same generation. The question was, were the New Formalists a reactionary backlash against the new freedoms of contemporary poetry, or were they attempting to discover their own sense of freedom by revisiting ideas and approaches that had been neglected or completely cast aside?

The intervention of the New Formalists in the poetry world of the 1980s proved to be dramatic, because that literary scene was decidedly committed to the anecdotal free-verse lyric poem of personal experience. To be a young poet in that decade and to try to publish anything in meter was to dig one's own literary grave. The only corrective to such a situation proved to be precisely the sort of rhetorically violent denunciations that soon began regularly to appear in the literary press. By the 1990s, what emerged were not merely volumes of poetry but a whole series of books that reexamined meter and form—Alfred Corn's *The Poem's Heartbeat* (1997); Mary Kinzie's *A Poet's Guide to Poetry* (1999); Timothy Steele's *All the Fun's In How You Say a Thing* (1999); and David Baker's *Meter in English* (1996). Whatever service these books provided in defense of the New Formalism, their greater contribution was in reawakening a broad awareness of prosody as an essential element in English-language poetry.

This debate about prosody and a further exploration of its possibilities continued in the West Chester Conference on Form and Narrative in American poetry, an annual event organized by Gioia and Michael Peich, the publisher of Aralia Press. The West Chester Conference was not only an opportunity for New Formalist poets to gather and share their craft with students but also a rare occasion when a new generation of critics—many of them contributors to this volume—emerged to make a conscious attempt to debate and discuss essential poetic issues.

At the core of the New Formalism has always been a spirit of debate and discussion. Robert McDowell and Mark Jarman made a significant contribution to the New Formalism with the publication of the little magazine *The Reaper*. In "Navigating the Flood" in *The Reaper* (1981), they made a statement that is as close to a polemical manifesto as any piece of writing of the early days of the New Formalism—that contemporary poetry had ten "non-negotiable demands":

1. Take prosody off the hit list.
2. Stop calling formless writing poetry.
3. Accuracy at all costs.
4. No emotion without narrative.
5. No more meditating on the meditation.
6. No more poems about poetry.
7. No more irresponsibility of expression.
8. Raze the house of Fashion.
9. Dismantle the Office of Translation.
10. Spring open the Jail of the Self.

Regardless of the headiness of these statements and their literary/revolutionary zeal, one matter was clear: the new generation of poets born in the 1950s, raised in the 1960s, and publishing in the 1970s and 1980s could no longer cooperate with the norms of American verse that they had inherited.

Narrative poets such as McDowell and Jarman were even more strident than the more formal writers, who took a more conciliatory view of the ways in which the new poetry could extend and enhance the principles of the old poetry. In an attempt to elevate the standards of narrative verse, McDowell and Jarman published a second essay/manifesto in *The Reaper*, "How to Write a Narrative Poem," which attempted to present a semblance of a poetics by which poets could better the art. The narrative poem, they suggested, should follow ten principles:

1. A beginning, a middle, and an end.
2. Observation.
3. Compression.
4. Containment.
5. Illumination of private gestures.
6. Understatement.
7. Humor.
8. Location.
9. Memorable characters.
10. A compelling subject.

In their essay they used the example of Jared Carter's poem "The Gleaning," an understated yet highly visual, if not cinematic, rendering of the death of a farm worker killed when the belt of his threshing machine flies off. The private gestures, the shaving of the dead man by the local barber, and the final trimming of the lamp in the parlor, abide not only by the principles printed in *The Reaper* but also by the elements that make poems memorable. What the declarations of *The Reaper* tried to achieve was not the revolutionary stance of poets seeking to overthrow the art, but the reformers' stance of artists who simply wanted to see the art better served by its artists.

The stance of the rebel, however, has always been readily associated with the New Formalists and was taken a step further when David Mason and Jarman published their landmark anthology, *Rebel Angels: 25 Poets of the New Formalism* (1996). This anthology put to rest the idea of overthrowing the dominance of free-verse American poetry. Instead, the New Formalism made its case for a dramatic breadth of possibilities in the contemporary poetic idiom. The purpose of the poetry included in the anthology was not so much a critique of what had gone before but a demonstration of what was now possible:

> If we make a special claim for the New Formalists, it is that there is more variety in their approach to form and subject than in some of the work of previous generations.... In their poems there is an audible discovery of something lost, a sense of recasting from scrap, of reinventing the wheel, of new forms exploding from old ones.... Because they are formalists, they give a new vernacular life to ancient forms, but they also invent new forms of their own. Surely this is a function of that innate revolutionary bred into the American character.

In taking this broad stance, Mason and Jarman connected the New Formalism not only to the traditions of English poetry, but also to the character of the American consciousness. In their anthology Jarman and Mason explained why their work was a "new Formalism." "These younger poets grew up in the era of rock music, the Viet Nam War, the Civil Rights Movement, birth control, drugs, and feminism." While all twenty-five poets were united in their commitment to meter, they were also united by their invocation of the age through the techniques afforded by meter. Rather than merely revive the old ways, they refreshed and reinvigorated in the anapest, or, as is the case with Julia Alvarez, such forms as the sonnet.

Rebel Angels demonstates a principle at work in the New Formalism: the more poetry could embrace in terms of range, form, style, and directness, the better the art would become. Each New Formalist poet, therefore, undertook the duty to do as much with poetry as he or she could possibly muster through a mastery of the craft.

In the essay "Can Poetry Matter?" from the prose collection of the same title, Gioia suggested a list of principles that poets ought to observe if they wished to serve the art of poetry:

1. When poets give public readings, they should spend part of every program reciting other people's work.
2. When arts administrators plan public readings, they should avoid the standard subculture format of poetry only.
3. Poets need to write prose about poetry more often, more candidly, and more effectively.
4. Poets who compile anthologies—or even reading lists—should be scrupulously honest in including only poems they genuinely admire.
5. Poetry teachers, especially at the high-school level and undergraduate levels, should spend less time on analysis and more time on performance.
6. Finally, poets and arts administrators should use radio to expand the art's audience.

From Gioia's perspective, the duty of this new generations of poets was to guarantee that the art of poetry would survive into the next century by keeping it in the forefront of cultural discourse. This broader view, one of engendering debate by challenging the norms and conventions of the poetic medium and the contemporary idiom, earned Gioia a chorus of hecklers. But the important result of his ideas, moderate though they were, was that poetry was suddenly called back to the forums of both the academy and the public consciousness.

In *DLB 282: New Formalist Poets* the editors present a representative catalogue of the New Formalism that they hope will serve as a guide to future students and scholars who investigate and debate the poetry of this era. Although this volume offers a broad spectrum and a wide and diverse range of poets and poetries associated with the New Formalism, it is still not inclusive. Students and critics of the New Formalism should also investigate the poetic works of Bruce Bawer, Elizabeth Alexander, Robert B. Shaw, Kim Addonizio, Cynthia Zarin, Rachel Wetzsteon, Roseanna Warren, Aga Shahid Ali, Jacqueline Osherow, and Greg Williamson. This volume does, however, include significant essays on the major poets of the New Formalism as well as critical overviews of the main literary/historical and biographical aspects of the period.

A final connection to note is that the New Formalism not only embraces both sides of the Atlantic—claiming adherents in the United States, Ireland, and the United Kingdom—but it also crosses a major historical boundary as well, reconnecting the American idiom to the traditions of poetic practice that date back to ancient Greece. By restoring prosody not only as a serious subject for debate but also as a major issue in the composition of poetry, this gathering of poets has effectively broadened the range of what poetry can do and made an old art and its fundamental principles new again. In short, the New Formalists continue to innovate and experiment within a centuries-old tradition. Collectively, they sing the music of their age, and, in so doing, they bring the art of metrical poetry with its roots deep in English-language literature into the twenty-first century.

Bruce Meyer
University of Toronto School of Continuing Studies

Jonathan N. Barron
University of Southern Mississippi, Hattiesburg

Acknowledgments

This book was produced by Bruccoli Clark Layman, Inc. Penelope M. Hope was the in-house editor. She was assisted by Patricia Hswe and Tracy Simmons Bitonti.

Production manager is Philip B. Dematteis.

Administrative support was provided by Ann M. Cheschi and Carol A. Cheschi.

Accountant is Ann-Marie Holland.

Copyediting supervisor is Sally R. Evans. The copyediting staff includes Phyllis A. Avant, Caryl Brown, Melissa D. Hinton, Philip I. Jones, Rebecca Mayo, Nancy E. Smith, and Elizabeth Jo Ann Sumner. Freelance copyeditor is Brenda Cabra.

Editorial associates are Amelia B. Lacey, Michael S. Martin, Catherine M. Polit, and William Mathes Straney.

In-house prevetting is by Nicole A. La Rocque.

Permissions editor and database manager is Amber L. Coker.

Layout and graphics supervisor is Janet E. Hill. The graphics staff includes Zoe R. Cook and Sydney E. Hammock.

Office manager is Kathy Lawler Merlette.

Photography supervisor is Paul Talbot. Photography editor is Scott Nemzek.

Digital photographic copy work was performed by Joseph M. Bruccoli.

Systems manager is Donald Kevin Starling.

Typesetting supervisor is Kathleen M. Flanagan. The typesetting staff includes Patricia Marie Flanagan, Mark J. McEwan, and Pamela D. Norton. Freelance typesetters are Wanda Adams and Rebecca Mayo.

Walter W. Ross did library research. He was assisted by Jo Cottingham and the following other librarians at the Thomas Cooper Library of the University of South Carolina: circulation department head Tucker Taylor; reference department head Virginia W. Weathers; reference department staff Brette Barron, Marilee Birchfield, Paul Cammarata, Gary Geer, Michael Macan, Tom Marcil, Rose Marshall, and Sharon Verba; interlibrary loan department head John Brunswick; and interlibrary loan staff Robert Arndt, Hayden Battle, Alex Byrne, Bill Fetty, Marna Hostetler, and Nelson Rivera.

Dictionary of Literary Biography® • Volume Two Hundred Eighty-Two

New Formalist Poets

Dictionary of Literary Biography

Dick Allen
(8 August 1939 -)

T. L. Ponick
Washington Times

and

F. S. Ponick
Music Educators National Conference (MENC)

BOOKS: *West Is Up* (Philadelphia: Dorrance, 1961);

Anon and Various Time Machine Poems (New York: Delacorte, 1971);

Science Fiction: Jules Verne to Ray Bradbury, by Allen and Lori Allen (White Plains, N.Y.: Center for the Humanities, 1974);

Twentieth-Century Fiction: Alienation and Self Discovery, by Allen and Lori Allen (White Plains, N.Y.: Center for the Humanities, 1975);

Regions with No Proper Names (New York: St. Martin's Press, 1975);

Overnight in the Guest House of the Mystic (Baton Rouge: Louisiana State University Press, 1984);

Flight and Pursuit (Baton Rouge: Louisiana State University Press, 1987);

Ode to the Cold War: Poems New and Selected (Louisville, Ky.: Sarabande Books, 1997);

The Day Before: New Poems (Louisville, Ky.: Sarabande Books, 2003).

OTHER: "When I First Read," in *SF 12,* edited by Judith Merril (New York: Delacorte, 1968), pp. 288-289;

Science Fiction: The Future, edited by Allen (New York: Harcourt Brace Jovanovich, 1971; revised edition, 1982);

"Westport Girls," "Oh, Rousseau, Rousseau," and "Theory of the Alternate Universe," in *The Modern Age,* edited by Leonard Lief and James Light

Dick Allen on the University of Bridgeport campus, 1979
(courtesy of the author)

(New York: Holt, Rinehart & Winston, 1972), pp. 687–688;

"Podunk, 1941" and "To a Woman Half a World Away," in *Contemporary Poetry in America,* edited by Miller Williams (New York: Random House, 1973), pp. 164–165;

"Backward, into Beasts Evolving," in *The 8th Annual Best SF: 74,* edited by Harry Harrison and Brian Aldiss (New York: Bobbs-Merrill, 1974), p. 172;

Detective Fiction: Crime and Compromise, edited by Allen and David Chacko (New York: Harcourt Brace Jovanovich, 1974);

"Rethinking a Children's Story," in *Myths and Motifs in Literature,* edited by Frederick Lapides (New York: Free Press, 1974), p. 312;

Looking Ahead: The Vision of Science Fiction, edited by Allen and Lori Allen (New York: Harcourt Brace Jovanovich, 1975);

"Staying Married," "The Writer's House," "Depression," "An American Gothic," "Normal Lives," and "The Present," in *Flowering After Frost: The Anthology of Contemporary New England Poetry,* edited by Michael McMahon (Boston: Branden Press, 1975), pp. 64–70;

"Letter from the Colonies," in *Discover America,* edited by Nils Peterson, John Galm, and Naomi Clark (San Jose, Cal.: San Jose Studies, 1976), p. 21;

"Anon Visits the House of Heroes," in *Humor in America,* edited by Enid Veron (New York: Harcourt Brace Jovanovich, 1976), pp. 205–211;

"Mr. Gorsline's Town," in *The Best of the Cimarron Review,* edited by Neil J. Hackett (Stillwater: Oklahoma State University/Cimarron Review, 1981), p. 163;

"Theory of the Alternate Universe," "The Perpetual Motion Machine," "Hyperspace," "Canto Ten," and "To an Astronaut Visiting a Japanese Garden," in *The Umbral Anthology,* edited by Steve Rasnic Tem (Denver, Colo.: Umbral Press, 1982), pp. 47–56;

"Young Poet's Lament," in *Light Year, 1984,* edited by Robert Wallace (Cleveland, Ohio: Bits Press, 1984), pp. 154–155;

"Stealth," in *Light Year, 1985,* edited by Wallace (Marceline, Mo.: Walsworth, 1985), pp. 83–84;

"The Clergyman's Wife Composes a Spring Letter" and "If You Visit Our Country," in *Contemporary New England Poetry,* edited by Paul Ruffin (Huntsville, Tex.: Sam Houston State University/Texas Review Press, 1987), pp. 8, 10;

"Barge Lights on the Hudson" and "The Postmaster," in *Anthology of Magazine Verse/Yearbook of American Poetry,* edited by Alan F. Pater (Beverly Hills, Cal.: Monitor Books, 1988), pp. 9–11;

"The Flutist," in *Contemporary New England Poetry,* edited by Ruffin (Huntsville, Tex.: Sam Houston State University/Texas Review Press, 1988), II: 2;

"The Forest for the Trees," in *Expansive Poetry: The New Narrative and The New Formalism,* edited by Frederick Feirstein (Santa Cruz, Cal.: Story Line Press, 1989), pp. 77–84;

"The Adventure into Someone Else's Life," "Meditation," "A Refusal, Like Hers," "Doing Mazes," and "Mime," in *The Hampden-Sydney Poetry Review Anthology, 1975–1990,* edited by Tom O'Grady (Hampden-Sydney, Va.: Hampden-Sydney Review, 1990), pp. 33–37;

"Autobiography," in *Contemporary Authors Autobiography Series,* edited by Mark Zadrozny (Detroit, Mich.: Gale Research, 1990), pp. 1–23;

"The Emperor's New Clothes," in *Poetry After Modernism,* edited by Robert McDowell (Brownsville, Ore.: Story Line Press, 1991), pp. 71–99;

"Night Driving," in *An Introduction to Poetry,* edited by X. J. Kennedy (New York: Little, Brown, 1991), pp. 276–277;

"Talking With Poets," in *The Best American Poetry: 1991,* edited by Mark Strand (New York: Collier/Macmillan, 1991), pp. 9–10;

"Breaking the Truth," in *After the Storm: Poems on the Persian Gulf War,* edited by Jay Meek and F. D. Reeve (Washington, D.C.: Maisonneuve Press, 1992), p. 7;

"For This, For Everything," in *The Night Lifted Us* (Monterey, Ky.: Frankford Arts Foundation, Larkspur Press, 1992), pp. xi–xvi;

"Only When Love and Need Are One," in *My Poor Elephant: 27 Male Writers at Work,* edited by Eve Shelnutt (Atlanta: Longstreet Press, 1992), pp. 325–340;

"Parents' Support Group," in *Articulations: The Body and Illness in Poetry,* edited by Jon Murkand (Iowa City: University of Iowa Press, 1994), pp. 223–224;

"A Short History of the Vietnam War Years," in *The Best American Poetry: 1994,* edited by A. R. Ammons (New York: Scribners, 1994), pp. 1–2;

"Sonnet," in *Formal Introductions,* edited by Dana Gioia (West Chester, Pa.: Aralia Press, 1995), p. 1;

"Rethinking a Children's Story," "SF," "The Folk Ballad of Neil Armstrong," and "Optometrist and Poet," in *The Random House Treasury of Light Verse,* edited by Louis Phillips (New York: Random House, 1995), pp. 20–22, 80, 149–152, 256;

"The Cove," in *The Best American Poetry: 1998,* edited by John Hollander (New York: Scribners, 1998), pp. 28–29;

"The Canonical Hours," in *The Best Spiritual Writing: 1998,* edited by Philip Zaleski (San Francisco: Harper, 1998), pp. 1–5;

"The Selfishness of the Poetry Reader," in *The Best American Poetry: 1999,* edited by Robert Bly (New York: Scribner, 1999), pp. 33–34;

"Cities and Empires" and "The People through the Train Window," in *The Yellow Shoe Poets: 1964–1999,* edited by George Garrett (Baton Rouge: Louisiana State University Press, 1999), pp. 6–7;

"'The Forest for the Trees': Preliminary Thoughts on Evaluating the Long Poem," in *New Expansive Poetry: Theory, Criticism, History,* edited by R. S. Gwynn (Ashland, Ore.: Story Line Press, 1999, revised edition), pp. 199–203;

"Janes Avenue," in *Learning by Heart: Contemporary American Poetry about School,* edited by Maggie Anderson and David Hassler (Iowa City: University of Iowa Press, 1999), p. 72;

"Ode to the Cold War" and "A Short History of the Vietnam War Years," in *Scanning the Century: The Penguin Book of the Twentieth Century in Poetry,* edited by Peter Forbes (London: Viking, 1999), pp. 171–175, 202–203;

"The Back of God," "Lord, Who Gives Me," "I Want Fast Answers," "He Had Been Here," and "You Let This Happen," in *The Bible of Hell* (New York: Pendragon, 2001), pp. 70, 162–163;

"Lost Love," in *The Penguin Book of the Sonnet,* edited by Phillis Levin (New York: Penguin, 2001), p. 370;

"Below Hoover Dam," "The Day Before Yesterday," "Quiet, Quiet Now," and "Wire Tap at Century's End," in *Photographers, Writers, and The American Scene: Visions of Passage,* edited by James L. Enyert (Santa Fe: Arena Editions, 2002), pp. 300–302;

"Veterans Day," "Cities of the Fifties," "Being Taught," "Lost Love," "The Cove," "Then," "Dignity," "Still Waters," and "Allen on Form Poetry and Natural Speech Patterns," in *Contemporary American Poetry: Behind the Scenes,* edited by Ryan Van Cleave (New York: Longman, 2003), pp. 9–20.

SELECTED PERIODICAL PUBLICATIONS–UNCOLLECTED: "Of Exhibitionist Poetry, Redwoods, and the Fluid Narrative Dramatic," *Antioch Review* (Summer 1965): 265–280;

"Thoughts on Midcentury American Poetry," *Mad River Review,* 2, no. 2 (Winter–Spring 1967): 43–48;

"Poetry: The How and Why," *Writer's Digest* (August 1967), 22, 24, 26, 28–30;

"The Poet Looks at Space–Inner and Outer," *Arts in Society,* 6, no. 2 (Summer–Fall 1969): 184–193;

"Science, Space, Speculative, Fantasy, Fiction," *Yale Alumni Magazine* (January 1971): 7–11;

"Reviewing Poetry: The Why and the Howl," *Prairie Schooner* (Fall 1973): 244–246;

"After the Avant-Garde," *Counter/Measures,* 3 (1974): 201–203;

"The Poet in the Gray Flannel Suit," *Coda,* 2, no. 7 (June–July 1975): 22–23;

"What Rough Beast: SF-Oriented Poetry," *Extrapolation,* 17, no. 1 (December 1975): 8–11;

"The Poet's Descent and Crossing: Charon's Cosmology," *Manassas Review: Essays on Contemporary American Poetry,* 1, no. 2 (Winter 1978): 55–61;

"Passion and the Modern Poet," *Writer,* 98, no. 2 (February 1985): 17–19;

"Fire Burning in the Rain," *Hudson Review* (Fall 1986): 135–140;

"Pop Goes the Sestina" (on James Cummins), *American Book Review,* 9, no. 2 (March–April 1987): 21;

"Poetry Chronicle: Shrinkages and Expansions," *Hudson Review* (Fall 1987): 507–516;

"Poetry on the Slopes," *American Book Review,* 9, no. 6 (January–February 1988): 19;

"A Longing to Breathe Free," *Hudson Review* (Summer 1988): 409–415;

"Poetry Chronicle: Storytellers and Mystics," *Hudson Review* (Summer 1989): 221–229;

"Transcending the Self," *Crosscurrents,* 8, no. 2 (1989): 5–10;

"Inventions and Conventions: Form and Narrative," *Poetry Society of America Newsletter,* 32 (Winter 1990): 16–17;

"Acute Specificity," *American Book Review,* 11, no. 6 (January–February 1990): 21;

"On the Poetry of Daniel Hughes," *Academy of American Poets: Poetry Pilot* (March 1990): 3–4;

"Questions of Control," *American Book Review,* 12, no. 3 (July–August 1990);

"The Signs by Which We Must Seek," *Hudson Review* (Autumn 1990): 509–520;

"The Door Has a Creaking Latch," *Mississippi Review,* 19, no. 3 (1991): 9–11;

"At the Dead Center of All Alone," review of Isabella Gardner's *The Collected Poems, American Book Review,* 11, no. 3 (December 1991–January 1992): 21;

"My Foe Outstretched beneath the Tree," review of Philip Appleman's *Let There Be Light, American Book Review,* 13, no. 6 (February–March 1992): 25;

"Bad, Better, Best: Poetry Chronicle," *Hudson Review* (Spring 1992): 319–330;

Richard Sanders Allen, Dick Allen, and Doris Bishop Allen at Richard Allen's gas station in St. Johnsbury, Vermont, 8 February 1940 (courtesy of the author)

"Intersecting Worlds," review of John Allman's *New and Selected Poems, American Book Review,* 7, no. 5 (June–July 1996): 18;

"On the Difference in Poets and Others," "On the Personal Element in Poetry," and "On Surrealism in Poetry," *Countermeasures,* 5 (1996–1997): 5–16, 17–18;

"Looking On *Looking On,*" *Urbanus* (Spring–Summer 1997): 21–25;

"Letters to the Editor," *Hudson Review* (Summer 1997): 182, 184;

"Metaphysical Synesthesia," "Empathy," and "Sophistry," *Countermeasures,* 6 (1997): 9, 13–14, 19;

"Narrative Thrusts and Spillages," *American Book Review,* 19, no. 2 (January 1998–February 1998): 27;

"Confidence," "Well, Like, Maybe, But Probably Not," and "An Elliptical Praise of Closure," *Countermeasures,* 7 (1998): 13, 17–18, 23–24;

"Here It Is, Here We Are," *Hudson Review* (Winter 1998–1999): 781–786;

"When Poems Rise from the Pages" (on Alfred Corn and Carl Phillips), *American Book Review,* 20, no. 3 (March–April 1999): 37;

"The Path to Expansive Poetry," *Pivot,* 46 (2000): 2–11;

"Sherlock Holmes' Lesson," *Word & I* (June 2000): 316–327.

Think of him as always facing left or right,
like a book page,
sometimes lingered on, more often turned from sight,
leaving only this edge.

(from "Profile," an uncollected poem by Dick Allen)

A link to the past and a guide to the future, Dick Allen is the leading "transition generation" Expansive poet in America. His work has consistently focused on recording and exploring life in the fin-de-siècle decades at the end of the second millennium and the dawn of the third. A principal founder of the Expansive poetry movement, he helped reestablish subject-oriented and narrative poetry as an alternative to the confessional, autobiographical, free-verse lyric that came to dominate American poetry in the latter half of the twentieth century. Ranging from free verse to formal verse, Allen's substantial poetic oeuvre crisscrosses international borders from East to West, encompassing Surrealism and Realism while spanning the wildly conflicting philosophies of the Beat Generation and the Silent Generation. Many of his poems contrast high-end science and technology with the meadows, fields, and forgotten small towns of a vanishing America.

Allen characteristically writes what he calls the "narrative lyric" or "narrative-meditation." In recent years he has also created a form of narrative poetry he calls "Randomism." If his poetry can be classed as New Formalism, it is a flexible New Formalism, merging loosened traditional verse patterns, meter, and slant rhyme with contemporary and even futuristic subject matter. His is a highly imagistic poetry of synthesis, frequently fusing his love for America with a near-mystical Zen Buddhist joy.

Born in Troy, New York, on 8 August 1939, Richard Stanley Allen moved with his family to St. Johnsbury, Vermont, and Saratoga, New York, before they settled in Round Lake Village, New York, in 1942. His father, Richard Sanders Allen, worked various jobs after dropping out of Cornell University, eventually landing a position as Round Lake's postmaster. The elder Allen became a well-known amateur historian with a special interest in regional Americana, including the histories of covered bridges, iron furnaces, and early aviation. Although never rising much above working-class wages, Allen's father won a Guggenheim Fellowship, was appointed director of the New York State Bicentennial Commission, and wrote seven books on various topics.

Allen's mother, the former Doris Bishop, was a year older than his father and possessed of a totally different frame of mind. Strong and domineering, she actually ran the Allen household, maintaining a strong sense of decorum and a strict fiscal discipline that enabled the family to assume the appearance of gentility while frequently living at the poverty line. Like Allen's father, she, too, was a college dropout, failing to graduate from Cobbleskill Agricultural and Technical College, where she majored in education. Nonetheless, she maintained a strong interest in literature, particularly in poetry, frequently reciting from memory works by such poets as Henry Wadsworth Longfellow, John Greenleaf Whittier, Edna St. Vincent Millay, and Robert Frost to Dick and his younger brother, Robert, born in 1942. When Allen's father was drafted into the United States Army Air Force in 1944, his mother became the postmistress of Round Lake, serving in that capacity until the senior Allen returned to reclaim his job in 1946.

Round Lake in the 1940s and 1950s was primarily a collection of summer cottages built outside of Albany, New York, on property that once housed a Methodist church campground. People generally leased the houses for ninety-nine years at reasonable rents. Primitive roads served the village, and most of the citizens of Round Lake had little money. The Allens were no exception, although Dick's parents took great pains to cover up the fact to outsiders. Nonetheless, new clothing was a rarity for the Allen youngsters, and Christmas presents could be a sometime thing.

Dick was enrolled in a tiny Round Lake school that had two grades per room. Encouraged by his mother, he also studied on his own, reading his way through the local public library, encountering for the first time the works of William Shakespeare, Michel Eyquem de Montaigne, and Nathaniel Hawthorne. The work ethic was strongly encouraged in the Allen household, and Dick learned early on to reason things out and plan ahead. While family members socialized intensely with each other, they rarely did so with the outside world. As a result, Dick became something of a bookish loner, although he did participate enthusiastically in the Cub Scouts and the Boy Scouts.

His life began to change, however, when he enrolled at Shenendehowa Central High School, some distance from Round Lake. Shenendehowa Central was a larger school and a different world, filled with a variety of activities, not all of which involved books and study. Athletically built, Dick soon joined the cross-country track team, played varsity basketball and tennis, and helped manage the baseball team. Not one to leave his literary endeavors behind, he also wrote for the school newspaper, edited the yearbook, and wrote the senior skit. His extensive readings widened to include Dante, Walt Whitman, Henry David Thoreau, and Ralph Waldo Emerson. He also found himself increasingly attracted to works of science fiction. Of all he read, Emerson's essay "Self Reliance" resonated the most for him during this period, inspiring him to embrace religious nonconformism and to seek out alternatives to traditional Methodism and Christianity, including Unitarianism and Buddhism. Dick managed to find time to write poetry in high school, although he imagined that he would eventually become a working journalist. He began to explore philosophy as well, avidly devouring William James Durant's popular volume *The Story of Philosophy* (1926) and the more difficult works of Georg Wilhelm Friedrich Hegel and Immanuel Kant.

Upon graduation in 1957, Allen enrolled in Syracuse University, the cost of which was largely paid by a four-year New York State Regents Scholarship and a Syracuse University full tuition Citizenship Education Scholarship—one of four awarded in statewide competition. He quickly joined the staff of the school newspaper, *The Daily Orange,* and surrounded himself with literary friends. During this time he began to discover the American Beat poets, thrilling to Allen Ginsberg's *Howl* (1956). Inspired by Jack Kerouac's *On the Road* (1957), Allen began to tour the country bit by bit, starting in the summer of 1958—a tradition he tried to maintain throughout his adult life. Distracted by these heady pursuits and by an increasing involvement in political activism, he saw his grades plummet. Quickly realizing what was at stake, he managed to stay on the dean's list

Dust jacket for Allen's 1975 collection, which marks his break from confessional poetry (courtesy of the author)

throughout his remaining years at Syracuse, even though he remained heavily involved in extracurricular and political activities.

He continued to write poetry at Syracuse and tried his hand at writing a novel, a task he later abandoned. At this time he came under the influence of Arthur Hoffman, a Syracuse English professor and a leading practitioner of the New Criticism, which was then at its peak of influence. Hoffman went to great lengths to force his students to focus on the text of a poem itself, removing names and dates of publication from the poems the class studied and encouraging lengthy, written explications of each poem. The result was, for Allen, an opportunity to study poetic technique under a microscope, greatly aiding him in developing his own craft and sense of the language. Other influences on Allen in this period included Walter Sutton, who served as adviser for his honors project on the Beats, and Harlan Bro, with whom he studied religious and mystical theory.

In 1959 Allen met senior English major Lori Negridge, an independent young woman who also aspired to a career in writing. They were instantly and intensely attracted to each other, and by the spring semester they were officially engaged. They were married on 13 August 1960. Allen was, perhaps, reflecting on the great depth of their relationship in his poem "To a Woman Half a World Away":

Now you are dressed
and walk around the house with your blood pressure up,
looking for something, anything, not in its place.

The mailman comes, and this letter
of course is not there.
You worry just a little as you close the door.

And then you turn, and your face
is just so beautiful it makes me stop
and wonder why I thought I would remember your body.

Here, you will remember, I am in night
beside a river that seems to flow through every field,
learning I am sentimental past my wildest fears.

(from *Anon and Various Time Machine Poems*)

Allen in 1986 (courtesy of the author)

Around this time Allen began to reconsider his drive to become a famous journalist and a Big Man on Campus. He was troubled that his journalism and political activism were having a negative impact on his artistic writing, and he resolved to devote more attention to this aspect of his career. Soon, he published poems in *Syracuse 10* magazine, co-edited by Joyce Carol Oates, who had, perhaps coincidentally, been Lori Allen's roommate. He published "The Death of Adam" in *The New York Times* in 1960, a poem that gave voice to his increasingly powerful antinuclear sentiments. His mother, moreover, subsidized publication of a short science-fiction narrative poem sequence called *West Is Up* (1961), although he eventually disavowed the book.

Not everything went his way at Syracuse, however. Upon reading a manuscript of Allen's poems during a campus visit, noted poet W. D. Snodgrass ruthlessly tore into it, criticizing both its content and lack of technique. Snodgrass's disconcerting critique shook Allen, forcing him to realize that he had been verbose and digressive in his poems. He resolved to work, like William Butler Yeats, for greater compression and attention to detail.

By the time Allen was awarded his bachelor's degree in English composition/creative writing in 1961, he had decided to become a college professor himself and enrolled in the prestigious graduate school of Brown University to continue his literary studies. Brown initially proved to be a difficult experience. Allen discovered that his English professors expected all papers they received to be of publishable quality, an expectation that put considerable pressure on all the graduate students. In addition, the Allens lived, like most married graduate students, in near-abject poverty. Their burden was lightened somewhat in 1962 when Dick Allen was awarded a teaching assistantship and Lori Allen took a job at Kelly Girl (now Kelly Services). She finally landed a more appropriate job as a junior-high-school teacher in Pawtucket, Rhode Island.

Allen was promoted the following year to the position of teaching associate, gaining the opportunity to work with Daniel Hughes in modern poetry and later with John Berryman when Hughes fell ill. In 1962 Brown awarded Allen the Academy of American Poets Prize, and in 1963 he became a regular book reviewer for *The Providence (Rhode Island) Sunday Journal*. In that year, the Allens' son, Richard Negridge Allen, was born in Providence—a joyous event that also complicated the young couple's already tenuous financial situation. Not long after their son's birth the couple decided that in

*Lori, Richard, Tanya, and Dick Allen at Richard's ordination as a Methodist minister,
University of Bridgeport, spring 1986 (courtesy of the author)*

order to make ends meet, Dick Allen should take one of the many available teaching positions being advertised around the country before he concluded his degree work at Brown. As a result, Allen, who had been awarded his M.A. in English and American literature in 1963, left Brown in 1964–just three courses short of completing his Ph.D. requirements–to assume an instructorship in creative writing at the newly opened Wright State University in Dayton, Ohio. He never returned to Brown.

Allen plunged into his work at Wright State with gusto, cofounding and serving as poetry editor of *The Mad River Review,* soon a nationally recognized literary magazine. His partner in the venture, faculty member Bernard Strempek, was killed in an automobile accident in 1964, and Allen took over the editorship of the magazine.

Editing the review had its pluses and minuses, but the most startling part to Allen was the surpassingly poor quality of the poetry he received over the transom from the United States and around the world. He was struck with the poor craftsmanship and self-indulgence of much of this poetry, as well as the nearly obsessive overuse of the pronoun *I*. He began to feel a need to return to the kind of craftsmanship and outer-directedness that had once given poetry its mass appeal as well as its universal acceptance.

Allen's time at Wright State was exciting and productive. He wrote fiction and poetry, and through his involvement in *The Mad River Review* he met and befriended many fellow poets, including James Dickey, Donald Hall, Gwendolyn Brooks, Steven Spender, Thomas Kinsella, and Judson Jerome, who was for many years the influential poetry columnist in *Writer's Digest*. Nonetheless, both Dick and Lori Allen had grown homesick for the East Coast. As a result, he turned down an offer of tenure from Wright State and took a position as an assistant professor of English and director of creative writing at the University of Bridgeport in Connecticut, commencing in 1968. He also assumed the directorship of the Visiting Writers Lecture and Reading Series. This position gradually brought him

Postcard advertising Allen's 1997 collection, in which his poems advocate a peaceful way of life (courtesy of the author)

into contact with an expanded list of writers ranging from old acquaintances Donald Hall and Snodgrass to established and rising stars such as X. J. Kennedy, Mary Jo Salter, Brad Leithauser, Rachel Hadas, and Richard Hugo.

Building on his continuing interest in science fiction, Allen created and taught what soon became a popular seminar on the subject. He also edited an anthology of science fiction titled *Science Fiction: The Future,* which was published in 1971. The book was a popular and critical success, and he followed it with another, *Detective Fiction: Crime and Compromise* (1974), capitalizing on a newly rekindled interest in this original American genre.

In conjunction with his science-fiction efforts, he had begun writing what eventually became a book-length sonnet sequence, "The Space Sonnets," in which he yokes the traditional poetic form in service to ideas of the present and the future. Many of the sonnets have been published, but the entire sequence has not yet appeared in book form. His first commercially published book of poems, *Anon and Various Time Machine Poems,* appeared in 1971. Expanding his outlets, he also began to review books for *Poetry* magazine and *The Hudson Review.*

As a result of his increasing distaste for free-verse, confessional poetry, Allen had begun to break with literary Modernism, finding himself drawn back to received forms for inspiration. He began to experiment with meter and rhyme, toying with formal structures in an attempt to get them to fit modern speech patterns more closely while not going back into free verse. Simultaneously, he sought to expand the subject matter of modern poetry beyond the inscape of the poet himself, refusing to cede such territory forever to novelists and short-story writers.

Riding out the tumultuous campus events of the late 1960s, including the occupation of campus buildings by students protesting the Kent State University shootings, Allen was taken aback by the contrast between his tranquil existence at Bridgeport and the violence of Vietnam and the nationwide protests that denounced the unpopular war. Convinced that the United States, in the aftermath of the assassinations of Martin Luther King Jr. and the Kennedy brothers, John and Robert, would never be the same again, he resolved that his poetry would become more fully involved in his own times, attempting to steer his country toward a more peaceful way of life. He strongly questioned the American pursuit of the Vietnam War in these surrealistic stanzas from "A Short History," contrasting the Tet Offensive with the peacefulness of Buddhism, and, in the final two lines, with the uncomprehending mindset of President Lyndon Johnson:

> That was when hope was a temple bell, a bleeding eye,
> A circle of books around the lovers' bed
> As the soldiers looked on. Mai Lai fell half-asleep
> Under the full thrust moon. On bruised hands and knees,
> Tet advanced along the shadowed railroad ties
> And the deltas awoke and flooded Washington.
>
> We will drift to Cambodia, the lovers said,
> Dance in People's Park, burn incense tapers
> At Buddhist shrines. The house wrapped its black arm-
>   band
> Over the lovers as they lay entwined.
> And if you listened, you could hear the mortar fire
> Walking up the valleys like an old blind man.
>   (from *Ode to the Cold War: Poems New and Selected*)

But Allen's spiritual side would not allow his vision of a peaceful American future to be disrupted, and he explored this belief in his poem "Waiting for the Year 2000":

> All will incredibly change. Neither the eyes
> of cameras nor the words of the Bible
> in this universe I call "The Honeycomb"
> can predict rightly. We matter to ourselves
> and stand, head-deep/ in the air
> of a planet spun round.
>
> Which is glorious—like living in
> a village where nothing truly ever happened
> more important than birth,
> or archipelagoes with a cargo religion
> at that very moment when/ the rainforest shakes,
> Americans walk out like God.
>   (from *Regions with No Proper Names*)

Both poems mark a clean break with the short confessional lyric still strongly prevalent in the 1970s. The meter is relatively free. But the strong, engaged, intellectual content of what was soon called Expansive poetry clearly differentiates these poems from the narcissism that by this time had overwhelmed American poetry while sweeping away its popular audience.

Allen was made an associate professor in 1971 and was promoted to a full professorship in 1974. As a result of this increased financial security—and to provide room for their expanded family, which now included daughter Tanya Angell, born in 1971—the Allens moved from their rental home to Trumbull, Connecticut, and an idyllic cottage on tranquil Thrushwood Lake where they have remained since. Allen's second volume of poems, *Regions with No Proper Names*, was published in 1975.

As a result of complications from phlebitis and a variety of other health problems stemming from a near-diabetic condition, Allen suffered an onslaught of seemingly intractable health problems in 1977 that caused a serious depression. Put on a strict diet to control his blood sugar and blood pressure, his health slowly returned to normal, but he was effectively unable to write for five years. Balancing out the health problems somewhat was Allen's award in 1978 by the University of Bridgeport of the Charles A. Dana Endowed Chair of English. Receipt of this honor added to the family's security and helped Allen regain some of his confidence as a creative artist.

Around this time, Allen made the acquaintance of Frederick Turner, who had been appointed editor of the newly revived *Kenyon Review*. Dick and Lori Allen met with Turner and Frederick Feirstein—a New York poet, playwright, and psychoanalyst—in Minetta Tavern in New York in 1981. All found themselves in nearly complete agreement in rejecting Modernism, the confessional free-verse lyric, and poetic narcissism. At this crucial meeting they decided to champion a new American poetry that would draw on its metrical heritage to reengage with the world and encompass those narrative and dramatic elements that once gave poetry its humanity. This nascent movement—dubbed "Expansive Poetry" by Wade Newman—caused a revolution in the closed, almost exclusively academic world of American poetry. Not long after the Minetta Tavern meeting, the New York–area Expansivists began to discover many fellow travelers, including Dana Gioia, Charles Martin, Richard Moore, Timothy Steele, and Robert McDowell, as well as old acquaintances such as Mary Jo Salter.

Allen's volume of poetry *Overnight in the Guest House of the Mystic* was published in 1984 and was nominated for a National Book Critics Circle Award. Adding to his growing string of honors during this time was his 1984–1985 National Endowment for the Arts Fellowship in poetry writing. With the aid of an Ingram-Merrill Poetry Writing Fellowship he was able to complete his next book, *Flight and Pursuit* (1987). By this

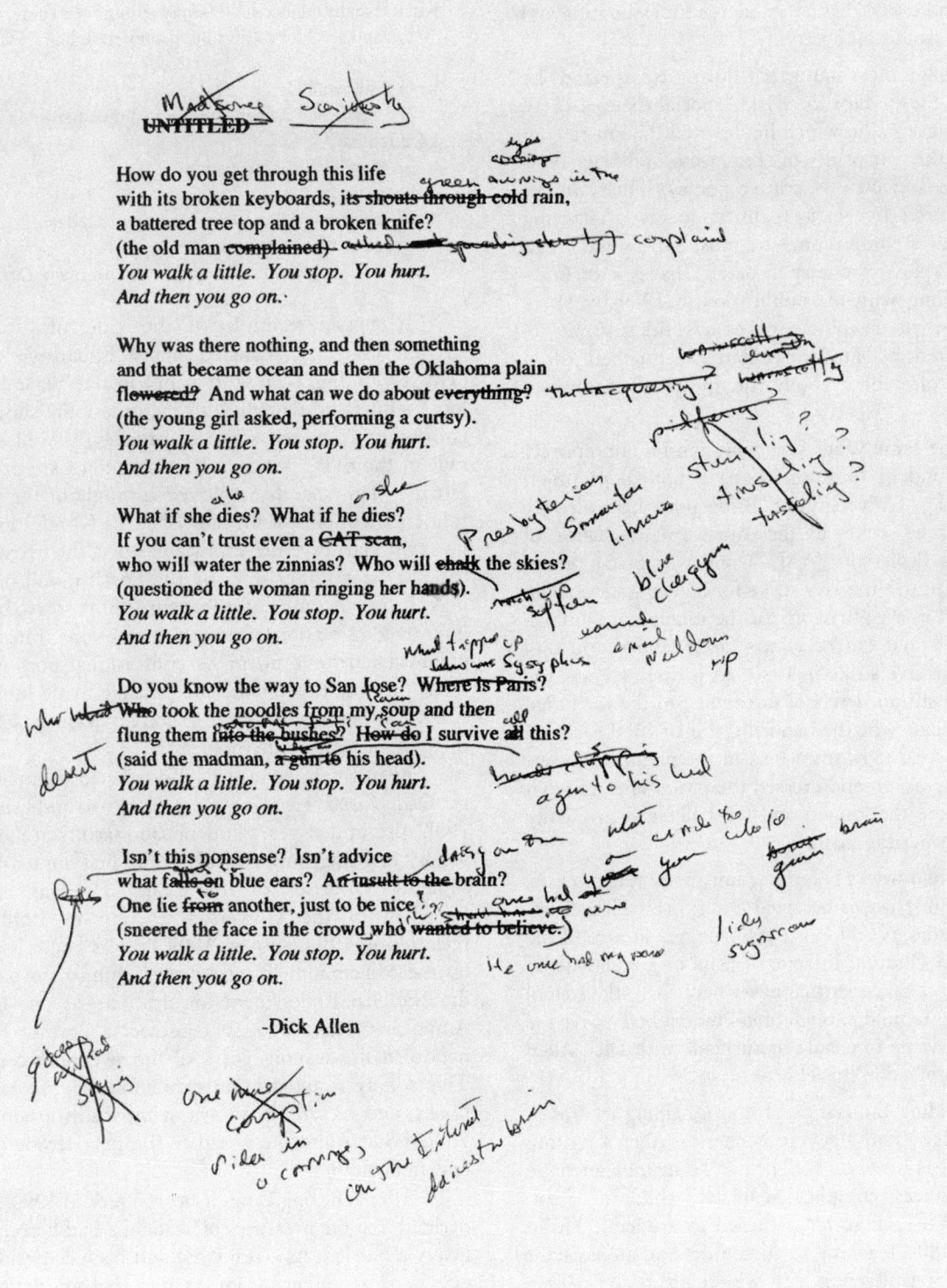

Working draft for "A Complaint," forthcoming in the spring 2004 issue of *The Hudson Review* (courtesy of the author)

time, Allen had increasingly, though not entirely, left free verse behind him, at the same time demanding, in reviews and essays, higher standards for evaluating and reviewing American poetry.

Perhaps most important during this period, he served as guest editor for a 1989 special issue of *Crosscurrents* magazine, in which he devoted the entire contents to the offspring of Expansive poetry, New Formalism and New Narrative poetry. This January issue featured five essays, thirty poems of varying length, and a symposium—the most substantial treatment of Expansive poetry to date. This issue of *Crosscurrents*, along with the publication in 1989 by Story Line Press of a volume of essays titled *Expansive Poetry*—edited by Frederick Feirstein—touched off a firestorm of debate about the future of American poetry.

In the same year, Allen's life ran into an entirely different kind of firestorm. Long a hotbed of union activity, the University of Bridgeport had already endured three strikes by the American Association of University Professors (AAUP) and was being threatened by a fourth massive strike for higher wages. Allen tried to act as a go-between for the union and administration. His and others' efforts failed, and the faculty called a massive strike in 1990. As a consequence, the financially strapped school threatened to file for bankruptcy. Allen, who had initially joined in the strike, became increasingly suspicious of the political motivations of the union and crossed the picket lines of what soon became the longest and most bitter such faculty action in American history.

Just two weeks before the university was to close, the board of trustees accepted a surprise bailout from the Professors World Peace Association, an arm of the Unification Church. In spite of fears of a takeover by the church—a takeover that never happened—the school was able to rebuild enough of its student body over the next three years to ensure its survival, with Dick Allen heavily involved in this effort.

Spending thousands of hours helping to "save" the university had a severe impact on Allen's writing life as well as his fiscal well-being. To help balance the family finances, complicated by two children of college age, Lori Allen had returned to academic life in the late 1980s, teaching as an adjunct and an assistant professor at Bridgeport and winning a *Writer's Digest* Grand Prize for her fiction. With his wife's help, Allen was able to restore some semblance of balance to his writing life, although he mourned the loss of his mother during this period. Strong-willed to the end, she had not gone easily, as Allen describes chillingly in "Heart Condition":

"You would take their side!" my mother screamed
    at my father
when the ambulance he'd finally summoned came,
    and she kicked and bit as they took her

from Aspinwall Drive
    where she'd been trying to compel her heart back,
keep it alive
    on a diet of carrot sticks

and her famous will power. Tied down, sedated,
    eight hours later, she died.

(from *The Day Before*)

A classic example of the kind of "sprung" rhythm that has attracted many Expansive poets, "Heart Condition" is written not in free verse but in loose iambs and dactyls with the occasional short line conveying an added sense of urgency as well as the rage of the dying woman. Rhyming lines are present, but the plain speech employed throughout the poem renders them almost invisible. "Heart Condition" is a powerful narrative driven by the story, the event, and the character rather than by the poet's mood or feelings. It has the aura of an intense short story, but its intense compression of powerful emotions transforms it into a narrative poem. A confessional poet would focus on how this pivotal life passage made him feel. Allen allows the story itself to convey feelings, leaving the judgment up to the reader.

Allen's volume of new and selected poems *Ode to the Cold War: Poems New and Selected* was published in 1997. Also in that year, students and faculty at the University of Bridgeport voted him the first annual "Outstanding Professor of the Year." He was elected President of the University Faculty in 1998 and reelected in 1999. Also in 1999 he was commissioned by the Millennium Survey Project—funded in part by the National Endowment for the Arts—as one of the American writers to help construct a portrait of the nation in the waning years of the twentieth century. This survey resulted in an exhibition of photographs, books, and recordings shown at museums around the United States and the world in the first decade of the new millennium.

After suffering a minor heart attack in 1999, Allen decided that the pressures of academia had become too heavy a burden. As a result, he and his wife decided to take early retirement from the university in the spring of 2001. To honor his work at the school, the University of Bridgeport trustees appointed him Charles A. Dana Endowed Chair as Professor Emeritus of English in May of that year.

Allen has devoted his active retirement exclusively to poetry and poetry-connected activities. He and his wife plan annual, Kerouac-inspired motor-pilgrimages across the United States in search of America and new poetic ideas–one of which, "The Dusk Traveller," exploits the traditional villanelle to describe the wandering life of a latter-day Beat poet.

> When the highway's almost empty and the mist is thin,
> This trilogy of joy is what I want:
> Black Honda, banjo music, and a Red Roof Inn . . .
>
> Let me sleep cheap beyond the daily din.
> Cut down my life to one straight forward plot
> (When the highway's almost empty and the mist is thin),
> Black Honda, banjo music, and a Red Roof Inn.
> <div align="right">(from <i>The Day Before</i>)</div>

In Allen's collection *The Day Before: New Poems* (2003), he experiments with lyric-narrative and lyric-meditative poems in the form Randomism, which consists of a loosened iambic base, usually employing a short anecdote as a foundation for random improvisations (as in jazz) that return to the main theme at the close. He is also writing a series of linked essays on contemporary poetry and is planning at least two new book-length poems in the future.

Dick Allen continues to pursue his studies of Eastern religion, especially Zen Buddhism, which inspires him to compose carefully crafted poems that extol the American landscape and mindscape. Allen still emphasizes the importance of subject-oriented, rhymed, and metrical Expansive poetry in American arts and letters. His poems have won increasing acceptance and have been read by Garrison Keillor on "Writer's Almanac" (PBS). Work by his former students has appeared in more than two hundred publications.

Interview:

Hill-Stead Museum and *Hartford Courant's Northeast Magazine, Dick Allen at the Sunken Garden Poetry Festival, 23 July 1997*–includes poetry reading.

References:

Frank Allen, "Antennae of the Race," *American Book Review* (May–June 1998): 24;

Floyd Collins, "Memory, Perception, and Language: Three Poets for the New Millenium," *West Branch*, 47 (Fall 2000): 101–119;

Henry Hart, "Five Poets in Search of a Zeitgeist," *Michigan Quarterly Review* (Summer 1989): 417–436.

Julia Alvarez
(27 March 1950 -   )

Kathrine Varnes
University of Missouri–Columbia

BOOKS: *The Housekeeping Book* (Burlington, Vt.: Vermont Council of the Arts, 1984);
Homecoming: Poems (New York: Grove, 1984); revised and enlarged as *Homecoming: New and Collected Poems* (New York: Plume, 1996);
How the García Girls Lost Their Accents (Chapel Hill, N.C.: Algonquin, 1991);
In the Time of the Butterflies (Chapel Hill, N.C.: Algonquin, 1994);
The Other Side: El Otro Lado (New York: Dutton, 1995);
¡Yo! (Chapel Hill, N.C.: Algonquin, 1997);
Seven Trees, text by Alvarez, lithographs by Sara Eichner (North Andover, Mass.: Kat Ran Press, 1998);
Something to Declare (Chapel Hill, N.C.: Algonquin, 1998);
In the Name of Salomé (Chapel Hill, N.C.: Algonquin, 2000);
The Secret Footprints (New York: Knopf, 2000);
How Tia Lola Came to ~~Visit~~ Stay (New York: Knopf, 2001);
A Cafecito Story (White River Junction, Vt.: Chelsea Green, 2001);
Before We Were Free (New York: Knopf, 2002).

OTHER: *Old Age Ain't for Sissies*, edited by Alvarez (Sanford, N.C.: Crawl Creek Press, 1979);
"Housekeeping Cages," in *A Formal Feeling Comes: Poems in Form by Contemporary Women,* edited by Annie Finch (Brownsville, Ore.: Story Line Press, 1994), pp. 16–18.

PERIODICAL PUBLICATION–UNCOLLECTED: "Noah's Ark Choices," *Library Journal,* 125 (1 September 2000): 168–171.

Julia Alvarez (photograph from the dust jacket for ¡Yo!, *1997; Richland County Public Library)*

Julia Alvarez is a highly regarded writer and winner of many awards and fellowships, including the PEN Oakland Award, a National Endowment for the Arts Grant, and a Yaddo residency, with novels named as American Library Association Notable and National Book Critics Circle Award finalists. Published in such high-profile venues as *The New York Times Magazine, Allure,* and *The New Yorker,* Alvarez has written a range of books for adults and, more recently, for children. Of her eleven books, just two are full-length collections of poetry, printed eleven years apart, but her poetry remains largely unconsidered. Although most critics view her solely as a novelist, Julia Alvarez began her career with poetry–as an anthology editor of senior-citizen poetry, with *Old Age Ain't for Sissies* (1979), as a chapbook author, with *The Housekeeping Book* (1984), and then more prominently as the author of a longer collection, *Homecoming: Poems* (1984). A full seven years later a novel–

How the García Girls Lost Their Accents (1991)—was responsible for catapulting Alvarez into the spotlight. The novel became an international best-seller and won her a PEN Oakland Award and a notable book designation with the American Library Association and *The New York Times*. Despite the passage of time, though, substantial critical attention to Alvarez's abiding poetic interests remains scant. Even while writing prose, Alvarez shows her love of poetry, often as an important part of a character's life, whether in Yoyo's discovery of Walt Whitman in *How the García Girls Lost Their Accents,* or in Minerva's love of poetry in *In the Time of the Butterflies* (1994), or in the narrative of her latest novel, *In the Name of Salomé* (2000), in which the main character Camila mourns the loss of her mother, Salomé Urena, a poet whom Alvarez describes as the Emily Dickinson of the Dominican Republic. Alvarez's largely autobiographically based poetry in the two versions of *Homecoming* and in *The Other Side: El Otro Lado* (1995) uses the pleasure of poetic form as a way of understanding, perhaps fixing for a moment, the identities of immigrant, daughter, author, divorcée, woman, sister, lover, friend, and character. Leery of tokenism, Alvarez resists describing herself with political or aesthetic labels, a decision that makes claiming her difficult for any group, but her poetic project to merge exalted traditional forms with the drudgery of housekeeping, for instance, certainly dovetails with the stated desires of both feminist and New Formalist critics.

Born in New York City, Julia Altagracia Alvarez grew up in the Dominican Republic until the age of ten, when in 1960 her father and the rest of the family escaped the country after supporting a rebel faction trying to oust dictator Rafael Trujillo. Her father (who often recited poems and ended each evening by announcing that El Doctor was heading to bed) established a medical practice in Brooklyn while her mother, born Julia Tavares, attended to their four daughters. Alvarez attended Connecticut College for two years, graduated summa cum laude from Middlebury College in 1971, earned her master's degree at Syracuse University in 1975, and in 1986 attended Bread Loaf Writers' Conference, the director of which later assisted with the publication of Alvarez's first poetry book. She married Bill Eichner, a doctor from Nebraska with two grown daughters, on 3 June 1989. The couple lives in Vermont, where she has been teaching at Middlebury College since 1988 and is now writer-in-residence.

Julia Alvarez's poetic voice comes across as both plainspoken and cagey, an appropriate choice for negotiating borders, whether personal, national, lingual, or prosodic. She uses lines of meter and free verse alike with an easy hand, incorporating figurative language, wordplay, and other pleasures without letting them tangle the narrative or lyric thrust of the poem. For this reason, her work might be read less carefully than it merits, especially in a period when highly textured language that announces its technique enjoys critical favor. Nevertheless, Alvarez's subtle craft and imagination, woven with her frequently domestic subjects, achieve the kind of poetry that celebrates daily living and finds ritual where others see the mundane. By centering her poetry on such accessible material, Alvarez remains available to readers on many levels—understandable to beginners as well as rewarding for more sophisticated readers.

Alvarez wrote her first book, the full-length poetry collection *Homecoming,* while teaching at the University of Vermont and living in a ground-floor apartment in Burlington. Much of the book was composed when she was thirty-three, roughly eight years after she earned her master's degree in creative writing from Syracuse University. As she explains in *Something to Declare* (1998), she married and divorced twice before turning thirty, setting aside her writing each time, believing, as she had been told by the women in her family, that she could (and should) write later. The second divorce had the unexpected effect, however, of freeing her to do as she wished; having failed traditional expectations, she enrolled in a fiction workshop and accepted a temporary teaching position that afforded her time to write.

Appropriately enough, *Homecoming* introduced, as Alvarez herself describes in the afterword of the second edition, a writer coming into her "woman's voice." The book opens with the title poem, set at Alvarez's cousin Carmen's wedding in the Dominican Republic—where, perhaps mirroring the cultural marriage in Alvarez's own intellect, Carmen weds a Minnesotan who answers to the quintessentially American name of Dick. In this poem, in a free-verse line with a heavy iambic pentameter backbeat, Alvarez lays out a crucial framework for the rest of the collection, a preoccupation with the importance of money—how it is handled (as when Carmen's father arranges for an armored truck to hold the wedding guests' jewelry as they swim); how it creates uneven relationships (her description of her uncle, who while dancing, was "fondling my shoulder blades beneath my bridesmaid gown / as if they were breasts" as he says "all this is yours!"); and where it comes from (the ever-present workmen and maids as part of the opulent landscape—carrying trays of food, tending to the melting wedding cake decorated like a miniature *rancho* until, as if staging a small-scale revolution

Paperback cover for the enlarged edition (1996) of Alvarez's 1984 collection, her first commercially published book. The sonnet series "33" increases from forty-one to forty-six poems in the later edition (Richland County Public Library).

against the already stuffed guests, the workers eat the cake in the morning "with their fingers from their open palms / windows, shutters, walls, pillars, doors, / made from the cane they had cut in the fields"). The poems that follow, on housekeeping and writing, benefit from this meditation on invisible labor, because it offers a wider political frame for the interior sketches and because it reminds the readers that the three positions—worker, homemaker, and writer—share a kind of interminability. They are, as the saying goes, like "woman's work"—never done.

The lyrical "Housekeeping" poems reveal a tension between mother and daughter, as well as the troubling traditional conflation of woman, home, and identity. Cleaning house becomes a metaphor for love and its substitutes, for the fierce martyrdom of motherhood that Alvarez both admires and rejects, as in "Dusting," when she writes, "She erased my fingerprints / from the bookshelf and rocker, polished mirrors on the desk / scribbled with my alphabets. . . . But I refused with every mark / to be like her, anonymous." The struggle between mother and daughter (in "Folding My Clothes," the mother would "fold / the arms in and fold again where my back / should go until she made a small / tight square of my chest") becomes emblematic—not just of familial conflict but also of the larger problem of a young woman searching for a comfortable position in the world and realizing that her mother, whose role is to teach her daughters traditional skills, may be unable to provide all the answers.

In her struggles for independence, the speaker of these housekeeping poems transforms each chore into something new, as in "Ironing Their Clothes," when she presses her "excess love" into the family's clothing, ironing "the yoke, / the breast pocket, collar and cuffs, / until . . . the shoulders shrugged off / the world, the collapsed arms spread for a hug." This generous vision sees love in ironing, that most irksome and boring of jobs before permanent press. In the delicious lists of "Naming the Fabrics" this view appears to be shared by both daughter and mother. Beginning with the daughter's invocation for the mother to "dress the world in vocabulary: broadcloth, corduroy, denim, terry," the second section of the poem is written in the mother's teasing bravura as she names the fabrics for each family member. Representing a joyful mother-daughter game, the poem also brings to mind reconciliation through the intimacy of handling—even creating—each other, through cloth. Possible recriminations ("My husband blames that sheer chiffon / for our four girls he sowed as sons") soften in the off-rhymes and playful polysyllabic matches such as "satin-stitch" and "handkerchiefs" or "skittish and British."

Just as Alvarez works her identity into the disciplines of housework, so she approaches poetic form, explaining in "Housekeeping Cages," collected in *A Formal Feeling Comes: Poems in Form by Contemporary Women* (1994), that "My idea of traditional forms is that as women much of our heritage is trapped in them. But the cage can turn into a house if you housekeep it the right way." Alvarez applies this concept to writing formal verse most apparently, with sestinas, villanelles (which she characterizes as useful for a "nagging" subject), and especially with sonnets, in which she replaces the image of women as "love objects" with a woman's voice. In "Charges"—a sestina with the teleutons "free," "paid," "job," "fees," "sweep," and "house"—the daughter's enterprising scheme to bill her mother for various chores ("a dime for dusting, a nickel to sweep / the yard") instigates weeks of maternal scorn. What starts as an amusing anecdote accrues meaning in the same way the end-words gather momentum: from the literal "I charged too high for the job" in the second stanza, the poem moves to the metaphorical "You should have seen her face—it was a job / to look at her" in the third stanza, to the conditional "as if my job / were to maintain her love for me dirt-free" in the sixth stanza and back again to the envoy's tough literal "Her love should have been free, not swept away / as a fee for the hard job of being my mother." While the speaker pins her adult reluctance to accept payment for work on this incident, the poem also infers something about the mother's difficult position. The daughter, after all, requested mere nickel-and-dime payment for a large portion of her mother's daily activity, an insult next to the "hard job" for which no one could recompense her mother. The collection continues to build in formal intensity, moving from the sestina immediately to two villanelles, "Mother Love" and "Women's Work," with relaxed refrains that perhaps rebel in their writerly way against a rigorously disciplined mother figure. In the first villanelle, exploring the downside of her mother's discipline, the daughter discovers that "only her mother love went bad," but in the second villanelle she admits to being "my mother's child: a woman working at home on her art, / housekeeping paper as if it were her heart." Surely, an appreciation of the poems must acknowledge the mother's inspiration for them. The balance exemplifies a particular strength in Alvarez's poetry that can air damaging character details while ultimately claiming redemption for all, despite flaws.

The *rancho grande* of *Homecoming: New and Collected Poems* is "33," a sonnet series that grew from forty-one to forty-six poems in the revised version of the book. The series probes the speaker's struggles with love, as well as family, religion, and the business of writing. Alvarez herself calls them free-verse sonnets (a bit of a misnomer), as a way of addressing her loose pentameter, heavy enjambment, and varying slant rhymes; yet, the lines stay near a regular syllabic count of ten, often keep to regular meter, and experiment with innovative schemes. One sonnet, rather than employing the traditional rhymes, ends each line with words that begin with *w*. Another sonnet is dashed out of a breezy "He" and "She" dialogue ("He: Statistics say I'll probably die first. / She: Statistics say most couples get divorced"). Yet another, which begins, in characteristic understated devastation, "I met a man at a self-improvement / weekend," repeats the words *sad* or *sadly* seven times in fourteen lines. Further innovation comes with her subjects, little songs of herself (complete with allusions to Whitman) that consider what it means to turn thirty-three, or any age, through birthday calls, flirtations with the UPS man, heartfelt chats with friends ("My friend Carol says aging evens out / the advantage of beautiful women / over plain ones"), intruding memories of past lovers, critiques of the reasons—"trifles," in the poem—that she fell for each past lover, even (in the later edition) a broadening of the scope of the series by considering atrocities cultural (one begins as a primer: "A is for Auschwitz, B for Biafra") as well as personal.

The final ten sonnets of *33* start by revisiting a precipitous drive down mountain roads from a writer's conference, where despite being warned by best-selling authors "against giving our characters / our own predictable, excessive lives" and despite her manuscript's having suffered a difficult reading by a "kind," W. H. Auden–quoting critic who drinks wine before noon, the narrator seems, slowly, to settle into herself as a writer. Of the first five sonnets in this sequence, that four include the phrase "driving down the mountain" (with the ever-lingering threat of plunging through the guardrail) suggests that the mountain is a metaphor for risk, perhaps toward ambition, ventured and survived. While at times *33* might seem an apology for the autobiographical lyric, the verbal play, patterning, and repetition suggest both that Alvarez is not sorry for writing it and that she has something more formal in mind. For ultimately it is the writer's perpetual project—not life per se—in which the speaker takes her momentary solace, noting that "Sometimes the words are so close I am / more who I am when I'm down on paper." Opening with that perfect writer's gesture, the final sonnet also winds to a close with an allusion to Emma Lazarus's famous sonnet quoted on the Statue of Liberty ("Those of you lost and yearning to be free") and adapts its final line from Whitman's *Leaves of Grass* ("Who touches this poem, touches a woman"). It is safe to say that the writer's gesture dominates this final word of *33*, not those excessive details of life all readers know better than to want.

In the years between publishing *Homecoming* in 1984 and *The Other Side: El Otro Lado* in 1995, Alvarez found an agent who won her a contract with Algonquin Books for her first novel, *How the García Girls Lost Their Accents*. The novel was republished two months after Alvarez's forty-first birthday. At this time, she also put an end to her itinerancy by accepting a teaching post at Middlebury College in 1988 and marrying Eichner—an ophthalmologist who recently published *The New Family Cookbook* (2000)—with whom she built a house on eleven country acres in Vermont. She earned tenure in 1991 and was pro-

Dust jacket for Alvarez's 1991 novel, winner of the PEN Oakland Award (Richland County Public Library)

moted to full professor in 1996. While she considers receiving praise after so many years of work wonderful, Alvarez has mentioned in interviews and autobiographical essays how difficult it was for her to field questions that assumed her life exactly mirrored that of her characters. Perhaps reacting to that difficulty as well as to her family's disgruntled response to characters based on them, her second novel, *In the Time of the Butterflies,* centers on the historical Mirabal sisters of the Dominican Republic. Appearing just one year before her second book of poems, *In the Time of the Butterflies* necessitated research (an extension of her annual trip to the Dominican Republic) that likely triggered a great deal of the material in her poetry as well.

As Alvarez explains in an interview, once her first two novels gained her a large and appreciative audience, the people at Plume, according to Maria Garcia Tabor, realized that to print the poetry collection *The Other Side: El Otro Lado* would be to their advantage in order to "keep" Alvarez "happy." And despite so much acclaim almost exclusively going to her novels, Alvarez not only wrote this second book of poems but also revised her first collection for an almost simultaneous release. The second collection continues to explore the feeling of being caught between two cultures, including how language can transmit as well as occlude insight, how stories lie but are necessary. Less overtly traditional in form, the poetry still retains the context of an iambic line and is more often traditionally metered than not. In six parts, the collection begins and ends with single-poem sections. The first is "Bilingual Sestina," which recalls learning words at the apron strings of women ("Gladys, Rosario, Altagracia") who helped to run the busy household. With the rhythms and pitch of a prayer, the sestina invokes Alvarez's earliest memories of language as one might invoke a muse. Balancing the end words (and their variations: said/say/saying, English/*en inglés,* closed/close, words/world, *nombres*/numbering/names, Spanish), she remembers when "the world was simple and intact in Spanish— /*luna, sol, case, luz, flor,* as if the *nombres* / were the outer skin of things." This verbal juggling act announces the primary concerns of the collection—the loss of early security and a desire for a difficult-to-attain adult intimacy with language, with others, or with the immediate world. As Richard Vela explains, when one is caught between two languages, the failure of language to represent faithfully "is either doubled, or halved." Representative of this communicative conflict, too, is the final poem in the collection, "Estel," a poem written for a mute child, who with beneficent interference eventually attends school. The implied narrative of the collection suggests the limitations of either language, especially when the speaker in "Estel," misunderstanding the child's mother, accidentally teaches the girl described as "out there beyond the reach of words I love" and whose actual name is *Esther* to recognize *Estel* as herself in writing. Although, in the poem, she tells Esther/Estel that "there will always be this sheerest gap / between the world and the word," she means the message for herself as well as for her readers, and it functions as a modest, writerly apology for what the poems may not have accomplished.

Between the two bookend poems are four middle sections also focused on loss, loosely ordered in an autobiographical chronology: "The Gladys Poems," "Making Up the Past," "The Joe Poems," and *The Other Side: El Otro Lado.* The Gladys Poems, written in three- and four-beat lines vaguely reminiscent of hymnal and ballad patterns, pay homage to a young woman who cleaned house for the family in the Dominican Republic and who taught the speaker to sing, talk, and play when she was a young girl. In "Mami and Gauguin," the narrow-lined poem reminiscent of Elizabeth Bishop's "In the Waiting Room" explores her mother's decision to hang "the berry-red titties / of the Tahitian girls" in the dining room where Gladys served dinner and glanced at "the young women her color." Eventually she discerns from her mother that desire, while restrained in dining-table formalities, is permitted in art—a distinction for which we understand Gladys would not fall. As if foreshadowing her loss of the homeland, Gladys, too, disappears in a poem titled "Abandoned," a word with multiple meanings.

The next section, titled "Making Up the Past," does just what it promises, filling in the gaps of memory and knowledge with stories from her girlhood in New York. In one poem, "Papi Working," the speaker tells her readers that her father's immigrant patients "often . . . came only to hear him / say *nada* in their mother tongue. / *I found nothing wrong.*" Still looming large in the poems, loss now has fanned out to trouble the community around her. The poems of "Sound Bites," while personal, take on the larger issue of adapting to a new culture and language, noting that "There were no words for his smell / or the taste of his sweaty skin . . . / in the *American Heritage Dictionary* / my parents gave me," but she gives herself over to the experience anyway. Presented in fragments, the poem suggests that only as an adult writer is she able to recall in the appropriate words "what was happening in silence / in my *cuerpo* and his heart, / in his *corazón* and my body." Because the cultural and familial pressures to assimilate must ease before she can remember this material or realize its value, only as an adult can she reclaim the lost language of her youth and its unvoiced past and make it up again.

Performing an emotional balance similar to *33*, "The Joe Poems" are a long series, most with epigrams from Jalāl ad-Din ar-Rūmī, that span nearly fifty pages and chronicle the dissolution of a love affair that was only barely held together by language. In an early poem, for example, the speaker calls from an airport phone because "*I've lost a word*," and her lover correctly guesses "touchstone," a word "*for a stone / you hold things to / to see if they are genuine.*" But the poem repeats that word so often, even in the title, that it begins to empty out its meaning. In "Monkey Business," he sends her an issue of *National Geographic* with an article about male baboon mating behavior that suggests "*The males who got the females were / the slow and patient ones, who practiced guile*"—perhaps as a coy, yet disingenuous, explanation for his distance, including that telltale encouragement to date others. Likewise, "You Remember the Definitions, Not the Words" shows a couple exchanging language as a substitute for love, but even the substitution "the poems of our trying / to talk ourselves in love" is incomplete. Formally, the Joe Poems rely mostly on patterns of indentation to heighten the relationships between efficient lines of free verse. While the landscape in this poem is largely interior, it remains more philosophically ambitious than in her earlier work—reaching into science as well as biblical allusions to transform frustrations into something more meditative.

The penultimate section of *The Other Side: El Otro Lado,* the twenty-one-part title poem, narrates a return to the Dominican Republic for a writer's residency, which, much like Alvarez's return to her first language, constitutes a search for herself, a place where she belongs. Populated at first with other artists—"a Parisian working with large canvases," a German "with her young lover and vegetable juicer," a punk New Yorker, and a Seattle printmaker—the poem quickly takes the narrator and Mike, "arriving with dope and an amorous proposal," into the town of Boca, where they are regaled with stories by and about the local characters. Searching for purpose, since she "bypassed the other stories afraid of their golden cages," Alvarez sorts out the fantasy of returning to live in her homeland from the life she left and the life she desires in what she calls the "portable homeland"—language. Each character—the dubious mayor, the begging children named for saints, the schoolgirls and -boys learning their times tables, the wronged women, the wise and tired wives, the generous shop and restaurant owners, the fishermen, the *gringa* (female foreigner, usually derogatory term for white speakers of English) who arrives pregnant and seduces a local man, and others—serves as an Ancient Mariner, with Alvarez as a variably willing Wedding Guest. Finally, the love affair and her fantasy both come to an end when she departs in a boat "across the watery darkness / to the shore I've made up on the other side." Alvarez's poetic voice has the clarity of prose.

Comparing the revisions from the 1984 to the 1996 version of *Homecoming* proves an instructive exercise when considering the development of Alvarez the poet, both in her small changes (a judicious decision to excise what had been an overabundance of ellipses, for instance) and in her large additions, which had the effect of widening her vision, adding more-conspicuous outward glances to what might first have been more easily understood as mere inward gaze. The revisions also make a more overt claim to her heritage by replacing all occurrences of "mother" and "father" with "mami" and "papi." In a similar vein, the new heroine poems (one titled "Against Cinderella") reveal a willingness not only to

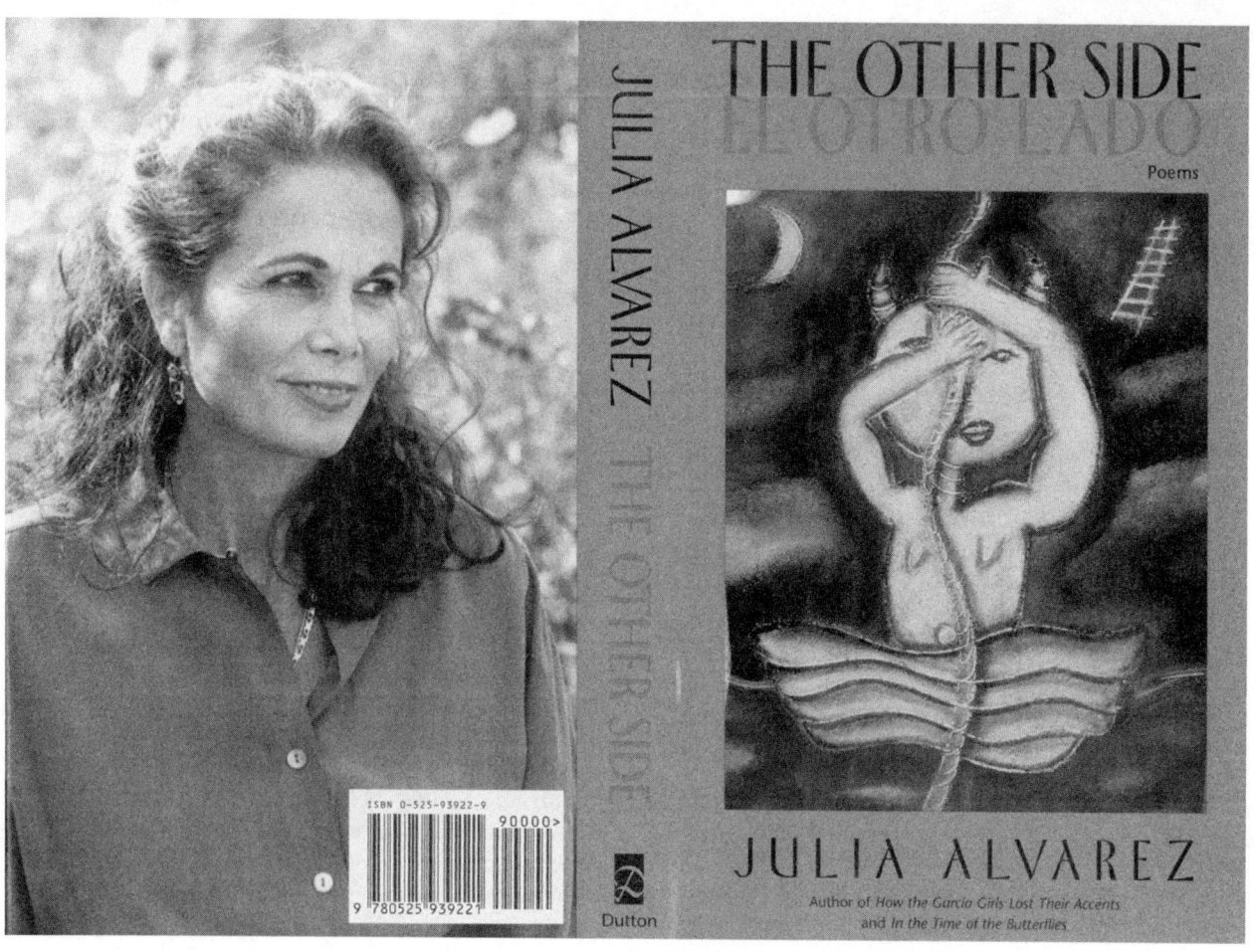

Dust jacket for Alvarez's second volume of poetry, published in 1995, which includes the autobiographical twenty-one-part title poem about a visit by the author to her homeland, the Dominican Republic (Bruccoli Clark Layman Archives)

speak for and about herself but also to draw bolder connections between herself and others. A series of ten Redwing Sonnets, most of which were likely written in the same period as the poems in *The Other Side: El Otro Lado,* add a mature confidence to the collection. Serving as a fitting *ars poetica* (art of poetry) to close the second edition, which claims not just her woman's voice, not just her writer's voice, but her poet's voice, the Redwing Sonnets rhapsodize from a bird's song to considering human song, from individual words to the many objectives of human talk ("in all tongues / there are at least a dozen words for talk: / the heart-to-heart, the chat, the confession, / the juicy gossip, the quip, the harangue") to the reasons for writing.

After earning tenure in 1991 and a full professorship in 1996, Alvarez, in order to spend more time on her writing, did what many would find unthinkable: she gave up her full-time post in 1998, although retaining her relationship with Middlebury College as a writer-in-residence. Since her second collection of poems, the prolific Alvarez had published two more novels, *¡Yo!* (1997) and *In the Name of Salomé* (2000), in addition to a collection of autobiographical essays, *Something to Declare* (1998), the short *A Cafecito Story* (2001), about growing coffee with sustainable agriculture (drawn from her own shade-grown coffee farm/literary center in the Dominican Republic), and two children's books, *The Secret Footprints* (2000) and *How Tia Lola Came to ~~Visit~~ Stay* (2001). She published a young adult's book, *Before We Were Free,* in 2002, about a twelve-year-old's life under and flight from oppression in the Dominican Republic. Her considerable influence has resulted in many elaborate websites compiled by her readers in addition to a full-length critical study with a chapter by Silvio Sirias devoted to each of her novels, although none, unfortunately, on her poetry.

Writing anecdotally in *Something to Declare,* Julia Alvarez tells how she found her voice at Yaddo. Tucked away in her room, she froze at the sound of surrounding typewriters and at the thought of adding something "important" to the canon–until she heard the sound of the vacuum in the hallway. Before long, she had struck up a conversation with the woman outside her door, and together they went down to the kitchen, where the words of the cook and her cookbook sparked Alvarez: "Twenty years after learning to sing with Gladys, I was reminded . . . that my voice would not be found up in a tower, in those upper reaches or important places, but down in the kitchen among the women who first taught me about service, about passion, about singing as if my life depended on it." Perhaps the kitchen, where everyday words move from recipe to nourishment, is an ideal place to transform ordinary language into magical stories and songs.

Interviews:

Jonathan Bing, "Julia Alvarez: Books That Cross Borders," *Publishers Weekly,* 241, no. 51 (December 1996): 38–39;

Heather Rosaria-Sievert, "Conversation with Julia Alvarez," *Latin American Literature and Arts Review,* 54 (1997): 31–37;

Maria Garcia Tabor, "The Truth According to Your Characters: Interview with Julia Alvarez," *Prairie Schooner,* 74 (Summer 2000): 151–156.

References:

Langdon Hammer, "Poetry in Review," *Yale Review,* 83, no. 1 (June 1995): 121–141;

Fred Muratori, "Traditional Form and the Living Breathing American Poet," *New England Review and Bread Loaf Quarterly* (Winter 1986): 231–232;

Silvio Sirias, *Julia Alvarez: A Critical Companion* (Westport, Conn.: Greenwood Press, 2001);

Luz Maria Umpierre, "Sexualidad y metapoesia: Cuatro poemas de Julia Alvarez," *Americas Review: A Review of Hispanic Literature and Art of the USA,* 17, no. 1 (1989): 108–114;

Kathrine Varnes, "'Practicing for the Real Me': Form and Authenticity in the Poetry of Julia Alvarez," *Antipodas,* 10 (1998): 67–78;

Richard Vela, "Daughter of Invention: The Poetry of Julia Alvarez," *Postscript: Publication of the Philological Association of the Carolinas,* 16 (1999): 33–42.

Rafael Campo
(24 November 1964 -   )

David Caplan
Ohio Wesleyan University

BOOKS: *The Other Man Was Me: A Voyage to the New World* (Houston: Arte Público Press, 1994);
What the Body Told (Durham, N.C. & London: Duke University Press, 1996);
The Poetry of Healing: A Doctor's Education in Empathy, Identity, and Desire (New York & London: Norton, 1997); republished in paperback as *The Desire to Heal: A Doctor's Education in Empathy, Identity, and Poetry* (New York & London: Norton, 1997);
Diva (Durham, N.C. & London: Duke University Press, 1999);
Landscape with Human Figure (Durham, N.C.: Duke University Press, 2002).

OTHER: *Rebel Angels: 25 Poets of the New Formalism*, edited by Mark Jarman and David Mason (Brownsville, Ore.: Story Line Press, 1996)—includes selections by Campo.

Rafael Campo (photograph © Miriam Berkley; courtesy of the author)

Rafael Campo's poetry extends many traditions. It belongs to the large community of gay and lesbian poetry and the growing body of Latino literature written in America. A physician-poet, he is the heir of both William Carlos Williams and John Keats. He also writes from the perspective of a Catholic struggling to reconcile his faith with the conservative positions of the Catholic Church on issues such as homosexuality and birth control. Finally, Campo's expertise in such verse forms as the sonnet, the heroic couplet, and the villanelle earn him the label of "new formalist." Despite the reservations he has expressed about the movement, he did not decline inclusion of his work in the 1996 anthology *Rebel Angels: 25 Poets of the New Formalism*.

Campo's poetry, like his life, is drawn from diverse influences. He was born on 24 November 1964 in Dover, New Jersey. His Cuban American father was a businessman, and his Italian American mother taught learning-disabled children in the elementary school that Campo attended. He grew up in what he called the "bland suburban wasteland" of New Jersey and in Venezuela, where he remembers first glimpsing widespread poverty and social injustice. His truly impressive academic career has consistently sought and earned the most grueling honors. The remarkably low acceptance rate of students into Amherst College attracted him to the school. When enrolled, he discovered a conservative and occasionally homophobic culture and endured the extreme rigors of a premed major. Yet, Campo's time at Amherst was not wholly unhappy. He met his partner, Jorge Arroyo, a fellow premed major and son of Latin immigrants, and studied with Eve Kosofsky

Sedgwick, a leading figure in the academic discipline known as queer studies. Campo completed his medical education at Harvard Medical School and the University of California, San Francisco Medical Center, two world-class facilities.

While at Harvard Medical School, he received a scholarship to study creative writing at Boston University, where his teachers included Robert Pinsky and Derek Walcott. In a later poem, "A Poet's Education," collected in *Diva* (1999), Campo remembers Walcott's intimidating yet inspirational classroom presence. On the first day, Walcott "outlined what his expectations were, / And warned us if we didn't read, his rage / Would be exacted on our timid verse, / Which, by the way, we would not read in class." Campo's time at Boston University was extremely productive, as he produced more poems than his first manuscript could include. After he finished his medical training, Harvard University recruited him to teach general internal medicine at the medical school and to practice that specialty at Beth Israel Deaconess Hospital. Teaching at the medical school that he had attended and at times despised, Campo has tried to change what he sees as its antihumanist culture. He has worked to revise its curriculum, encouraging the doctors he trains to consider the potential of literature to help patients understand their illnesses and achieve an emotional peace. He also encourages his patients to write about their experiences. Campo lives with Arroyo on a tree-lined street near Beth Israel Deaconess Hospital. They have an adopted son.

To date, Campo has been remarkably productive. Before turning forty, the age when American poets are no longer considered "young," he had published four poetry collections and one book of essays, even while pursuing an impressive career in medicine. The many awards that Campo has received include a Lambda Literary Award for memoir (for his 1997 *The Poetry of Healing: A Doctor's Education in Empathy, Identity, and Desire*), a Lambda Literary Award for poetry (for his 1996 *What the Body Told*), and a National Book Critics Circle Award nomination (for *Diva*).

Gloria Vando selected Campo's *The Other Man Was Me: A Voyage to the New World* (1994) for publication in The National Poetry Series. The collection displays several of the characteristics that mark Campo's later work. The title of the book suggests two of his most important subjects—homosexuality in America and the second-generation Latin American experience.

Cuba fascinates Campo because it represents the end point of self-knowledge, a place he has never visited that somehow constitutes an important part of his identity. The distant father who inhabits Campo's poetry embodies this paradox; he remains unknowable because the poet can only imagine the country and the culture that helped to form his character. In "San Fernando" the speaker's struggle to understand his father is also the struggle to understand himself. The speaker declares to his father, "I know / Almost the knife of your exile." The telling qualification "Almost" acknowledges the limits of the son's experience, of his knowledge and self-knowledge. The speaker desperately wants to understand his father because his father's "exile" offers more clues into his own estrangements. The poem insists on this point: "I save the parts of you / You let me have, like shards of pottery, // Like fragments of my own puzzle."

One large piece of the "puzzle" that Campo seeks to solve is his difficult relation to Latino culture. In another poem in *The Other Man Was Me,* the speaker visits Café Pamplona in Cambridge, Massachusetts, an American coffeehouse. Despite his denials, he fantasizes that he has traveled to "Santander / before the war," where he might come to terms with his father and thus himself. "I know this really isn't Spain," the speaker admits. "But still, / You'd think I'd find my father here." Of course, the speaker does not find his father; his daydream returns him to the attitudes that separate them. Even in an imaginary conversation, the father voices his reactionary politics and homophobia. By the end of the poem, the speaker finds himself almost wholly alienated from Spanish culture. The patrons of the imagined café and Café Pamplona agree on one point: no one identifies with the speaker. "You think they'd guess / I'm Spanish," he laments, "since it's clear I can't forget."

The Other Man Was Me also shows Campo discovering verse forms appropriate to his subjects. The middle section of the collection presents four sequences of sixteen sonnets of sixteen lines each. These works achieve an effect similar to that of a carefully ordered family scrapbook, as each sonnet presents a kind of snapshot off which the next sonnet plays. Campo's poems in this form also draw upon the love-sonnet tradition. Two of Campo's subjects—homosexual life and the second-generation Latin American experience—combine into one, love in its various forms and with its various difficulties.

Campo formulates this idea more precisely in his second book, *What the Body Told*. "No knowledge is more powerful / Than knowing love," he declares; then he revises this notion later in the same poem to say "All I know is this: I'm gay // And knowledge is less powerful / Than love." The cover of the book introduces this devotion to the powers of love. A detail of Joan R. Fugazzi's painting *Eros*—a mustached, dark-haired male nude—faces the reader, his hands over his head, his eyes darkly shaded and perhaps closed. The colorful

Dust jacket for Campo's second poetry collection, which includes sonnets that have been compared to photographs from a family scrapbook (Richland County Public Library)

background emphasizes the long expanse of his naked flesh. The cover crops the painting so the title, *What the Body Told,* appears over the figure's groin. As featured on the cover, the painting presents a moment of erotic contemplation or gratification, suggesting that desire makes these two pleasures indistinguishable.

What the Body Told shows Campo returning to and building upon the explorations of his first book. Like *The Other Man Was Me, What the Body Told* includes several sixteen-line sonnet sequences. In the most striking of these sequences, "Ten Patients and Another," Campo presents patient histories in the sonnet form. Drawing upon the language of internal medicine, Campo's specialty, these sonnets transcend the fantasy of the physician as a benevolent caretaker. Instead, they show a physician often appalled, confused, and disgusted by his patients. The speaker's clinical posture often gives way to a grim impatience. In "F. P.," the speaker describes "Another AIDS admission" with self-protecting irony: "This one's great: / They bring him in strapped down because he threw / His own infected shit at them—you better bring your goggles!—and a mask, we think he's got / TB."

The attitude that this sonnet sequence most frequently expresses, though, is a tempered outrage over the cruelty that the patients endure. The characters that the sonnets present include a twelve-year-old girl impregnated by her father, a night nurse attacked after work because his assailants mistakenly thought he was gay, and a wife beaten by her husband who impatiently waits for the physician to finish stitching the wound. The clinical, ironic tone of each poem works to offset the potential melodrama of these situations. "Tommy," for example, describes a man shot while buying drugs. The immediate medical problem is his refusal to give informed consent for surgery. The terse language of the poem remains professionally unemotional, while the poetic line beautifully modulates its caesuras: "He states he'd rather die than be / Dependent on his family for care. / They're questioning his competence, of course. / They're waiting on his folks. His wife just stares."

When writing from the perspective of a physician, Campo often explores the issue of empathy or, more precisely, the limits of empathy. The doctor understands the physical damage that the bullet wound inflicts but not the desperation that motivated Tommy to endure the dangers of buying and using illegal drugs. For this reason, the doctor can read nothing in the wife's blank stare.

"Song before Dying" also explores the limits of medical empathy, except from the opposite perspective. This sequence describes a particularly fearful moment in Campo's life, when a routine exam suggested he might have cancer. The sonnets present the doctor as patient; his expertise does not exempt him from the various humiliations, confusions, and fears that modern health inspires. "Just the Facts" follows the same strategy of many of Campo's other sonnets about medicine: it employs the deliberate language of a pathology report in order to describe a life-and-death condition. Yet, the "twenty-six-year old, still healthy, with / A history of trauma to / The right arm," the patient struggling with the indifference of a medical establishment to his concerns, is the physician-poet.

In a sonnet sequence dedicated to Eve Kosofsky Sedgwick, Campo shows his former teacher's influence. "The Fat Lady Sings" is a dramatic monologue written in Sedgwick's voice. The voice summarizes several of her most influential ideas, including her belief in the fluidity of sex. In the words of the poem, "'identity' is merely fiction– / Think of it we're more than men or women."

Published a year after *What the Body Told*, *The Poetry of Healing: A Doctor's Education in Empathy, Identity, and Desire* (republished in paperback as *The Desire to Heal: A Doctor's Education in Empathy, Identity, and Poetry*) collects ten essays that range from literary criticism, cultural critique, and autobiography to analysis of the health-care system. At least half the essays previously appeared in leading literary journals and in *The New York Times Magazine*; several explore the relation of poetry to the body and the consolations it offers in an age of AIDS. In the essays most directly relevant to his own poetry, Campo frequently asserts a biological grounding to meter. He describes, for instance, the experience of reading Thom Gunn's elegy *Lament* (1985) to a patient as the two hear the patient's "respirator functioning in the plunging up-and-down iambics." Some of Campo's poems praise meter for the opposite reason, however, celebrating its artificiality, comparing the "adornment" of a rhyme and meter to a drag queen's performance.

Campo's book *Diva* continues the investigations by his earlier works of gay and Latino culture, but with a slightly different emphasis. The poetic forms that Campo chooses signal this shift. While Campo's earlier snapshots of familial and cultural life favored the sonnet form, the ten-section "Baby Pictures" turns to the prose poem. The first section, "Imaginary," starts, "Now that we are mostly in our early thirties, it seems that so many of my friends from medical school are rushing to get pregnant and have babies–while all I have given birth to these past three years is utterly imaginary." As this passage suggests, the prose poem allows Campo access to a wide range of rhetorical effects. This sentence opens with a breezy colloquial tone–the speaker's friends "are rushing to get pregnant"–and closes with an intimate disclosure expressed more formally–"all I have given birth to these past three years is utterly imaginary." As a sonneteer, Campo often writes conversational, narrative verse. The prose-poem form inspires a greater expansiveness. Instead of compressing a portrait into fourteen iambic pentameter lines, the prose-poem form allows a greater opportunity for digression and exposition.

This desire for digression and exposition also informs Campo's decision to write heroic couplets and his handling of this unfashionable metrical form. "Philadelphia" retells the story of the movie of the same name:

> A homophobic lawyer takes his case;
> When someone spots a lesion on his face.
>
> The character Tom Hanks plays is abruptly fired
> By the firm that made him partner. What he desires
> Is more than acceptance (he is gay);
> He wants respect, he wants to make them pay
>
> A million dollars. . . .

This nearly straightforward plot summary might strike some readers as "unpoetic," as it almost blandly recounts the story line of a popular movie. Yet, this cautious rhetorical style is strategic. Hailed as the first mainstream motion picture to discuss AIDS, *Philadelphia* assiduously avoided presenting gay sexuality. Campo's poem does not avoid it. Tom Hanks's

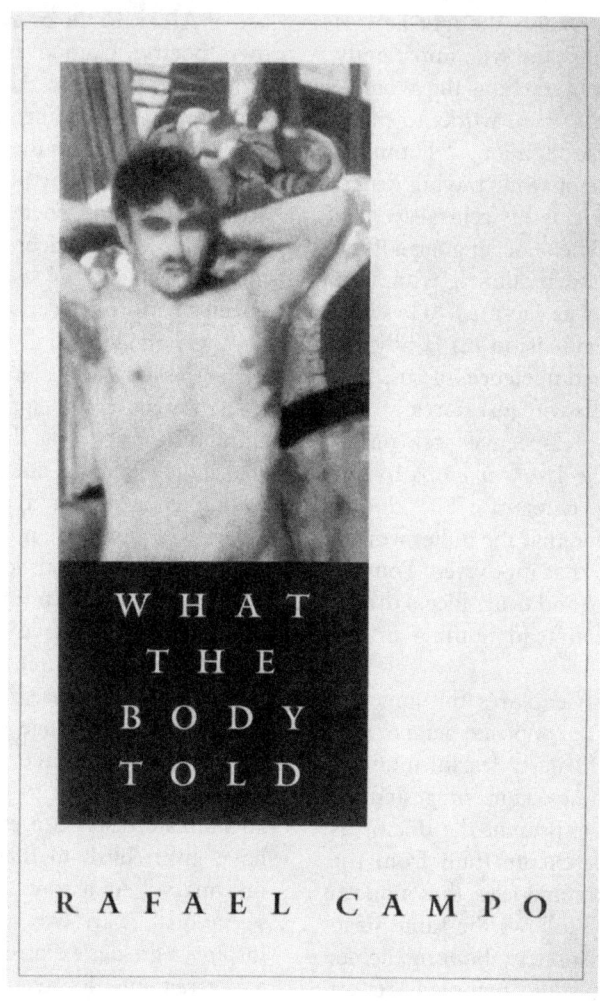

Paperback cover for Campo's 1996 book, which includes a sonnet sequence describing the histories of his patients (courtesy of the author)

movie appealed to a mass-market audience by making the characters asexual. The subtlety of Campo's poem highlights the cost of this decision. Drained of eroticism, the motion picture allows itself only platitudes; Hanks's character "is gay," "wants respect," and "wants to make them pay." Unlike "the movie neither of us liked," "My movie," the speaker declares, "would be sexy, passionate." Campo's poem declares the need to celebrate sexuality in the age of AIDS and to create works of art out of this celebration, not the pretense that AIDS makes gay sexuality unmentionable.

"Philadelphia" is one of three poems in *Diva* that considers recent movies. While in Campo's previous volumes he expressed a lively interest in the contemporary moment, in *Diva* he uses current events and pop culture as inspiration. The poems quote tabloid headlines read in line at the Lil' Peach and articles from *The New York Times;* its cast of characters includes Doctor Kevorkian, Susan Sarandon, and Oprah Winfrey. The title poem exemplifies this tendency. With campy, self-deprecating awe, it names no fewer than four MTV pop stars, who inspire a teen trapped in suburbia to "turn diva in my bathroom mirror."

In addition to his own new poems, *Diva* also features Campo's translation of Federico García Lorca's "Sonetos del Amor Oscuro" as "Sonnets of Dark Love." Campo's note on his translation amounts to a statement of his own poetic principles as Campo describes the affinities he discovered between García Lorca's work and his own. Describing why he admires "their [the sonnets'] use of the form as a way to engender delicious frictions which themselves convey meaning," Campo writes:

> Throughout these difficult poems, Lorca's desire refuses to be contained, always full of the possibilities and uncertainties of the times in which he lived and

Dust jacket for Campo's 1997 collection of essays, which includes literary criticism as well as a critique of the health-care system (Bruccoli Clark Layman Archives)

created them. As a gay man facing the next new millennium, one which has been ushered in by the brutal murder of a young gay person in my own nation's heartland, one which sees still threatened the basic human rights to love and to live freely, and with its arts community still facing censorship, the urgency of this project was all the more clear.

These translations circle back to Campo's earlier explorations of Latino culture. In *The Other Man Was Me,* even in death Lorca endures homophobic dismissals, loathing rooted in reactionary politics and hatred: "All / These people reading Lorca would disgust him. / Communists and homosexuals, he'd say." Campo's translations pay homage to an indomitable spirit. They celebrate Lorca less equivocally and less tragically—as a diva, a poet of the erotic, transcendent and triumphant.

Several other poems consider frictions of a different sort, arising from the conflict of agape, not eros. "Last Rites" reworks an anecdote from Campo's essay "Like a Prayer" in *The Desire to Heal.* "Like a Prayer" recounts Campo's interactions with a terminal AIDS patient. "Hey, doc, when you get to church this morning, pray for me," the patient tells him, then snarls, "Yeah, you must be a real good fucking Catholic with a name like that." This moment inspires the meditation in the essay on Campo's difficult relationship with Catholicism. Set a few years later, in Boston, not San Francisco, "Last Rites" considers a gentler version of this harsh challenge, as another patient confides, "I pray," then asks the physician-speaker, "Do you believe in Christ?" The final stanza describes the moment after the patient bleeds to death:

The clots that lingered in his mouth were slick

As cherry candies on his startled tongue.
He looked at me, as pale as I was dumb,

And faded to his final peace. With God?
I searched the skyline for his wisp of smoke,
But night had rendered it invisible.

This conclusion insists upon the inexpressibility of what occurs; just as the patient's clotted "tongue" cannot speak, the doctor is also made speechless. The two silences rhyme: the patient's lifeless "tongue" and the doctor struck "dumb." If the soul departed ascends to heaven, it does so invisibly, hidden by the night that surrounds it. God's presence is a two-word, unanswered question. Death's only sweetness is utterly grotesque: the clots on the tongue "slick // As cherry candies on his startled tongue," a repulsive reworking of the sacrament.

While the poem expresses severe spiritual doubt, it also extends a prayer, heartfelt and needful enough to admit the extremity of its own turmoil. As the title suggests, the poem offers a version of the last rites priests perform. Earlier in the poem, the speaker admits, "I didn't pray–I had forgotten how," as if prayer were primarily the product of religious education and doctrinal knowledge. The death he witnesses, though, teaches that spiritual need cannot be forgotten.

Rafael Campo's poetry fits uneasily into the broad rubric of New Formalism. None of the most famous New Formalists have written about his work; discussions of the movement commonly pay Campo only cursory attention, if any at all. As New Formalism turns into an historical movement, not a rallying cry, the critical focus may shift to include this writer of large ambition and vision, a poet, essayist, and physician who has produced an impressive body of work before celebrating his fortieth birthday.

Interview:

Katerina A. Christopoulos and Schuyler W. Henderson, "Where Poetry and Medicine Meet: A Conversation with Rafael Campo," *MSJAMA* (6 October 1999) <http://www.ama-assn.org>;

References:

David Abel, "Treating Illness with Literature: Doctor Urges Patients to Heal Their Souls through Reading, Writing," *Boston Globe,* 4 January 2000, p. B1;

David Caplan, "Contemporary Verses Bristle with Immediacy," *Columbus Dispatch,* 19 February 2002, p. D8;

Davis Courtney, review of *The Other Man Was Me: A Voyage to the New World, Literature and Medicine,* 14, no. 2 (1995): 258–263;

Suzanne Gordon, "Try a Little Tenderness," *Washington Post,* 9 February 1997, p. X7;

Susan Reynolds Salter, "Reconciling His Many Selves," *Los Angeles Times,* 24 January 1997, Home Edition, p. 4;

Jerry W. Ward, "Poetry," *Washington Post,* 12 March 2000, Final Edition, Book World, p. X6.

Jared Carter
(10 January 1939 -)

T. L. Ponick
Washington Times

and

F. S. Ponick
Music Educators National Conference (MENC)

BOOKS: *Early Warning* (Daleville, Ind.: Barnwood Press, 1979);
Work, for the Night Is Coming (New York: Macmillan, 1981);
Fugue State (Daleville, Ind.: Barnwood Press, 1984);
Pincushion's Strawberry (Cleveland, Ohio: Cleveland State University Poetry Center, 1984);
Millennial Harbinger (Philadelphia: Slash & Burn Press, 1986);
The Shriving (Tuscaloosa: Duende Press, 1990);
Blues Project (Indianapolis: Writers' Center Press, 1991);
Situation Normal (Indianapolis: Writers' Center Press, 1991);
After the Rain (Cleveland, Ohio: Cleveland State University Poetry Center, 1993);
Les Barricades Mystérieuses (Cleveland, Ohio: Cleveland State University Poetry Center, 1999).

RECORDINGS: "Jared Carter," read by Carter, Amherst, Mass., WFCR, 1986;
"Jared Carter," read by Carter, Brockport, Writers Forum Videotape Library, 1 April 1987;
"Jared Carter," read by Carter, Kansas City, New Letters, 1993;
"After the Rain," read by Carter, Amherst, Mass./Madison, Wis., Wisconsin Public Radio, 1994.

SELECTED PERIODICAL PUBLICATIONS–
UNCOLLECTED:
FICTION
"The Sorcerer," *In But Not Of* (December 1970): 2;
"A Blue Willowware Tale," *Indiana Writes*, 1, nos. 3–4 (1976): 106–133;
"The Shoat," *Long Story*, 3 (1985): 96–126;
"Disclosure," *People's Culture*, new series nos. 24–25 (1994–1995): 2–3;

Jared Carter, 1986 (photograph by Ed Breen, Fort Wayne Journal Gazette; *courtesy of the author)*

"Nine Panels in Acrylic," *No Exit*, 9 (Summer 2002): 23–29;
"Epiphany," *One Trick Pony*, 8 (Fall 2002): 12–15.
NONFICTION
"Poetry Chapbooks: Many Are Called," *Georgia Review*, 38, no. 4 (1984): 881–890;
"Poetry Chapbooks: Things Invisible to See," *Georgia Review*, 39, no. 2 (1985): 432–443;

"Poetry Chapbooks: Back to the Basics," *Georgia Review*, 40, no. 2 (1986): 532–547;

"Hesiod: Poet and Peasant Overtures," *Chicago Review*, 37, no. 1 (1990): 89–112;

"Journey of Darkness," *The Long Story*, 19 (2001): 5–10.

Before Expansive poetry and its offshoots, New Formalism and New Narrative poetry, coalesced as an identifiable movement, Jared Carter had already established a small but important body of work that differed to a large extent from the prevailing Modernist and postmodernist crosscurrents in American poetry. Whether employing free verse or traditional meters, Carter's verse has been distinguished by its strong narrative line and its attention to minute detail. In addition, Carter has been unafraid to abandon the prevailing confessional lyric, and he frequently knits an entire short story in verse should his subject require it. In this respect, he eventually proved to be one of the unsung innovators in American poetry as the twentieth century wound to its uncertain close. Born and reared in the American Midwest, Carter was strongly influenced by the region of his birth. A significant body of his work explores the life and history of this geographical area, which he recast as the mythical Mississinewa County, Indiana. In this creation, he shares two characteristics with other such strongly regional poets as Robert Frost and Edgar Lee Masters, or with regional novelists such as William Faulkner and Thomas Wolfe: Carter's sensitive work conveys a powerful sense of place as well as a respect for human eccentricities and the small triumphs and tragedies that go along with them. By virtue of his solid background as a journalist and editor and his continuing fascination with the rapidly vanishing techniques of traditional, old-school printing and photography, Carter has been obsessed throughout his career with getting his stories and his characters right and true. In his frequently "plain style" poetry he strives to create a recognizable small-town world that is accessible to all readers yet is somehow different enough to seem exotic. The knowledge of character, for Carter, depends on the gradual accretion of particulars and background. His characters are discovered, not explained, and his narrative poetry shares a great deal of territory with the finest realistic novels and short stories of the twentieth century.

Jared Carter was born on 10 January 1939 in Elwood, Indiana, a small town roughly forty miles northeast of Indianapolis. His father, Robert, also born in Elwood (in 1910), was a general contractor as Jared's grandfather, Tom, had been. Jared's mother, born Cleva Hackett in 1913, kept her husband's books and managed his payroll. In addition to Jared, the Carters had three other children: Michelle Anne (born in 1932), Richard Dee (born in 1934), and Candace Kyle (born in 1951).

Of many family members who were early influences on Carter's literary background, few were as important as his paternal grandmother, Effie Hinshaw Carter, Tom Carter's wife, who was born in 1878. Jared Carter's grandmother read to her grandchildren endlessly, nearly always from what she regarded as the modern classics—John Greenleaf Whittier's *Snow-Bound* (1866), Andrew Lang's *Blue Fairy Book* (1889), and Nathaniel Hawthorne's *The House of the Seven Gables* (1851). But she also introduced the children to the works of the ancient Greeks, including Homer's stirring epics, as well as Jonathan Swift's *Gulliver's Travels* (1726), and a host of other tales. She appears and is commemorated in "Shaking the Peonies," a poem in Carter's first book, and one of her stories concerning her own childhood crops up in an altered form in "Foundling," a poem that appears in Carter's second book.

Carter first discovered the fascinating worlds of journalism and printing in high school. Working on his high-school newspaper, he became acquainted with two job printers who set type in the old-fashioned way—by hand. Their storefront shops—the kind that have now vanished from the American landscape—were crowded with wooden trays of type, stacks of dusty books, and ornate cast-iron presses. Carter gradually grew to understand that these men were practicing a skilled craft that had not changed in many ways from the era of Johannes Gutenberg some five hundred years earlier. Carter's association with these printers and his befriending by a young reporter who worked for the town newspaper combined to ignite his lifetime passion for the arts of printing and publishing, strongly influencing his eventual career choices as well as the subject matter of many of his later poems and works of fiction.

Carter graduated from high school in 1956, and in the fall of that year he enrolled at Yale University, where he had been given a scholarship and where he majored in English literature. He worked odd jobs in Elwood during the summer to earn tuition money but chose to drop out of Yale in the spring of his junior year, finding work as a reporter for a daily newspaper in Huntington, Indiana—a position that had been arranged for him by his reporter friend back home. In 1960 Carter made one more stab at finishing his education at Yale, but he did not graduate. His literary skills, however, continued to mature, and he managed to win Yale's Academy of American Poets Prize in the spring of 1961 before he left the school for the second time. It seemed as if Carter were beginning to realize that one's skill as a writer does not necessarily depend on a college degree.

Carter on his front porch, Indianapolis, 1976 (photograph by Roger Pfingston; courtesy of the author)

Carter was married in December of 1961 to a young woman who had graduated from Bennington College. (The marriage produced one daughter, Selene, in 1969 but ended in divorce in 1974.) After a brief move to San Francisco, Carter was drafted into the United States Army in 1962 and was sent to France, where his wife eventually was able to join him. Carter was stationed in Fontainebleau, although he resided for three years in the village of By-Thomery, which overlooked the Seine. After leaving the army in 1965, Carter traveled throughout Europe, including France, Italy, Greece, Spain, and the United Kingdom.

Always a Midwesterner at heart, he returned once again to his hometown in Indiana and spent the next four years there making a living doing various odd jobs and writing poetry and short stories whenever he could. As he perfected his craft both as a poet and a fiction writer, his work began to build on the promise he had shown at Yale earlier in the decade. His first published work, a group of ten poems, appeared in an anthology, *Indiana Sesquicentennial Poets,* in 1967. At this time Carter decided to finish college. He enrolled in an experimental nonresident program at highly untraditional Goddard College in Vermont and eventually received a B.A. from that institution in 1969.

Unlike many poets of the current generation, however, the independent-minded Carter resisted the obvious perks accorded the increasing number of poets who served as instructors and writers-in-residence on college campuses across the United States. Relocating to the larger city of Indianapolis, he established a residence in Woodruff Place—an historic neighborhood on the near east side of the city—and took advantage of an opportunity to work at Bobbs-Merrill, an old-line book publishing firm. By 1973 he had risen to become managing editor of the textbook division of the firm. Once again, Carter was able to work in the fast-paced publishing environment that he loved, taking a big step up at this nationally known firm that boasted of putting out a book a day year-round. His division alone turned out one book a week, and, as managing editor, he supervised manuscript editing, interior design, and the actual manufacture of the books, whether perfect-bound or case bound. During this time, his division published several anthologies of serious contemporary poetry, and he was able to work with prominent poets,

Dust jacket for Carter's first poetry book, winner of the Walt Whitman Award in 1980 (courtesy of the author)

translators, and scholars from around the country, an opportunity that provided him with valuable insights into the literary business to which he still aspired.

Carter was restless, however, and he considered leaving the firm. Around this time he met Barbara Diane Haston, a teacher and part-time college instructor, who proved instrumental in persuading him to follow his instincts and strike out on his own as a freelancer in order to devote more time to his own work. Carter finally left Bobbs-Merrill in 1976 and became an independent contractor, copyediting manuscripts and designing books. To help make ends meet, he also taught in a prison, served as a field interviewer for an ethnomusicology project, and worked as a pianist in a local tavern. During this time he also relocated to Windsor Park, a smaller neighborhood slightly to the north of his old residence.

Carter began to concentrate on poetry and to send out more work to an increasing number of publications. This latest spurt of energy soon reaped large dividends. In 1976 *The Nation* published one of his poems, and additional acceptances in other publications quickly followed. Carter and Haston were married 21 June 1979. In the spring of 1980, he received word that his poetry manuscript, "Work, for the Night Is Coming," had been selected by Galway Kinnell from among 1,200 manuscripts as winner of the 1980 Walt Whitman Award for a first book in a competition sponsored annually by the Academy of American Poets. The prize was a generous $1,000, and the book was scheduled for publication by the major publishing house Macmillan. Carter was also invited to read from his work at the Donnell Library in Manhattan.

Carter was a relatively advanced forty-two years old when his first collection was actually published in the spring of 1981. (He had published a short chapbook, *Early Warning*, in 1979.) *Work, for the Night Is Coming* was well received, with poet and critic Henry Taylor calling it "one of the clearest and strongest first books to have appeared in recent decades." The book is still in print, currently by the Cleveland State University Poetry Center, and has now sold approximately ten thousand copies.

Carter's strong, unapologetic regionalism is perhaps the most striking characteristic of his first collection. Breaking with a generation of contemporary poets who only find significance in big cities and in tortured, complex ideas and theories, Carter believes in the primacy of people and place and thrives on the different, perhaps less hackneyed, ways in which Midwesterners view their lives and their environment. As Timothy J. Deines (in an unpublished thesis) astutely observes, in Carter's poetry the reader is interested in "the ways that human beings interact with their environment, and the wisdom to be gleaned from patient observation of events."

With his background as a journalist and his fascination with the minutiae of editing, typesetting, and bookmaking, Carter as a poet has proven himself a master of the kind of small, seemingly insignificant clues that provide substantial insights into the human condition. Deines observes that reading Carter's poetry "is like visiting a small town that he has built with his own hands, wandering along its streets, in and out of its houses, talking with its people, listening to the rumors, reminiscences, and stories that are told on front porches and in its soda shops." In "Walking the Ties" (collected in *Early Warning*), the reader finds an "old woman who ate canned dog food," "the red wagon she pulled through the alleys," "the boys who shouted and threw things" at her, and "the bar where she went each night to sit."

Carter's late-blooming career now began to take off in earnest. During the 1980s he spent a good deal of his time traveling around the country to campuses, museums, art galleries, and community centers to give readings of his poems, and on two occasions he was invited to teach courses as a writer-in-residence at nearby Purdue University. He was in demand at other colleges as well, and the Purdue connection led to his being invited to travel overseas as a guest of the University of Hamburg and the United States Information Service (USIS) in 1986. The following year, he read poetry and visited with students at universities in Rio de Janeiro while on travel in Brazil. He has remained popular as a public reader of his poetry, at least in part because he commonly recites his poetry from memory, a habit that enables him to focus on his delivery rather than on laborious and embarrassing fumblings with the printed page–a common and maddening affectation that has severely limited the audience for contemporary poetry readings.

Carter's parade of honors and awards continued to lengthen during the 1980s, including a scholarship to Bread Loaf, a National Endowment for the Arts (NEA) Grant, a Guggenheim Fellowship, and an award by the governor of Indiana. Other honors and opportunities followed, including a stint on the NEA's literature advisory panel (1985–1986). Carter soon began to publish poetry in prestigious magazines such as *The New Yorker, Poetry,* and *The Iowa Review.*

In spite of his increasing literary fame and his introduction to modern computer technology, Carter still found the time to indulge his fascination with traditional publishing methods, such as handmade paper, monotype, handset type, and hand sewing and binding. As a result of his continuing interest in this area, he reviewed, for a time, poetry chapbooks for *The Georgia Review,* a journal the typesetting and traditional production methods of which he admired greatly. He also became more interested in photography, something that had intrigued him since his early newspaper days. He studied the craft with several Indiana photographers, including Darryl Jones, Roger Pfingston, Chris Minnick, Seldon Bradley, and Richard Pflum. Carter's ongoing interest in photography surfaced in his most recent long narrative poem, "Glass Negatives," which appeared in *The Edge City Review* (April 2001), in which the nighttime obsessions of the town eccentric are chronicled in fascinating and telling detail.

Carter's description of the protagonist–the third-person narrator's grandfather–is a brilliant example of the use of plain-style language focused into greater sharpness by a fairly regular blank verse line:

> He was an atheist,
> you understand? Back in that little town.
> He didn't give a damn for God, and said so,
> every chance he got. He was the scourge,
> the socialist, the troublemaker, all
> the other things they didn't like, rolled
> into one. If you grew up in any sort
> of place that's off the beaten track, you know
> the score. Each town, each neighborhood must have
> some misfits in the cast, or else the drama
> can't be acted properly.

Crank though he is, Carter's protagonist earns his living as a photographer, a visual chronicler of First Communions, graduations, and the like. But he has a dark secret; at night, he persuades young women to doff their clothes in the name of art:

> he never touched them, never made advances.
> They shifted, took up different poses now
> and then, but didn't act lascivious.
> In those days people still believed in art–
> or what they thought was art, if that would mean
> that they were beautiful. He promised them
> the lens could see that beauty, could reveal
> the truth within, make them immortal. Sure,
> and when you're young, you'll live forever, too.

But this is not Hollywood. There will be no police, no sensationalism–indeed, no improper discoveries. And this is not a man (indeed, not a town) that is caught up in abstract art and postmodernism. While certainly prim, proper, and circumspect, as are most small-town people, Carter's Midwesterners are progressive in their own way. They "still believed in art" if the human beings portrayed within that art "were beautiful." In Carter's world, the world of the small town and the kept secret, things rarely get out of hand. No one talks; no one ever knows until the narrator discovers the incriminating set of glass negatives years later–scheduled to be shipped to a landfill–and needs to make a decision as to their disposal. These small, important tidbits, the hallmark of Carter's poetry, not only reveal the character of the old man; they also serve to chronicle the life and attitudes of a small town and the reticence of the narrator to allow those timeless patterns to change or to evolve.

Carter displays a peculiar journalistic ability to get extraordinarily close to his subject in this poem–and indeed, in all of his work–while remaining detached. As he himself stated in an interview with David Lee Garrison, "Years ago I heard Robert Bly speak, and he said something I've always remembered. He said that poetry has to 'come up close to its object.' That made a great deal of sense to me–coming up close. I'm a great believer in careful observation, along with extensive background study."

During the 1980s and early 1990s, Carter published several small-press chapbooks, and he received a second NEA Grant in 1991. Although his second collec-

Carter in his Indianapolis office, 1982 (photograph by Chris Minnick; courtesy of the author)

tion, *After the Rain,* was a long time in the making, it was finally published by the Cleveland State University Poetry Center in 1993. Poet and critic Dana Gioia, writing for *The Washington Post,* found the collection to be "extraordinary . . . A dark, haunting book in the tradition of Frost." It was subsequently awarded the Poets' Prize for 1995.

Deines commends the title poem in this collection for cleverly juggling traditional and contemporary techniques of enjambment in order to make its formality less obvious, citing the poem's opening eight lines:

> After the rain, it's time to walk the field
> again, near where the river bends. Each year
> I come to look for what this place will yield–
> lost things still rising here.
>
> The farmer's plow turns over, without fail,
> a crop of arrowheads, but where or why
> they fall is hard to say. They seem, like hail,
> dropped from an empty sky.

Deines also comments favorably on the continuing evolution of Carter's sparkling, yet not always obvious, plain-style language by observing that this poem "is essentially a lyric, but its colloquial language is so strong throughout that it gives the impression of storytelling." Carter is indeed, first and foremost, a storyteller. But, like the storytellers of ancient times–those whose stories were first read to him by his grandmother–he finds telling his stories in sharply etched and memorable lines of poetry most effective.

Carter's third collection of poems, *Les Barricades Mystérieuses,* was published in April 1999 by the Cleveland State University Poetry Center. This volume constitutes an interesting departure from the poet's previous books. "There are no stories or dialogue here," writes Garrison in his review of the book, "but things happen. Things as simple and subtle as the change in light and shadow against a wall created by the shift of a log in the fire, the sound of a door swinging open in the wind, or peonies that reveal an old pathway through an orchard. This is a book about 'the murmuring of things. . . .'"

An extended poetic sequence, *Les Barricades Mystérieuses* consists of thirty-two villanelles arranged in four sections of eight poems each–an audacious virtuoso experiment with an old form that constitutes a clear challenge to anti-Formalist poets. The locale of most of the sequence—the American Midwest—is familiar to readers of Carter's earlier books.

In *Les Barricades Mystérieuses* the hallmark of each poem is its unusual, hypnotic repetition of lines. These lines are frequently re-formed in different grammatical structures, but the words are invariably the same. The first line of "Ford," which is one of the two lines repeated throughout the poem, is an especially good example of this variation:

> A place of crossing over, where the river (line 1)
> a place of crossing. Over where the river (line 6)
> a place of crossing over. Where the river (line 12)
> a place of crossing over, where the river (line 19)

But the poems in *Les Barricades Mystérieuses* are not idle wordplay as is the fashion with those contemporary poets who seem to thrive on riddling or obscuring the meanings of their poems. Even in this robust formalistic excursion, Carter works to ensure that words and phrases, the meanings of which may be less than obvious, are understood by the average reader, whose perspective he is able to stretch without condescension.

Reviewers in his home state especially praised Carter's new poems. "This stuff is work," said Jay Harvey in *The Indianapolis Star,* "and only accomplished poets need apply." It is "poetry I think you'll truly enjoy reading," wrote Jim Powell in *Nuvo News Weekly.* "An enormous accomplishment," said David Hackett in the *Daily Journal.*

Carter regularly reads his work to audiences around the country and is perhaps as well known for his public presentations as he is for his well-received poetry collections. He is working on a fourth collection of poetry.

Ultimately, it is difficult to pigeonhole Carter's work in terms of a particular contemporary "movement." He continues to write in free verse, traditional forms, and even, on occasion, experimental modes, such as the recent long, postmodernist poem "Nine Panels in Acrylic" published in *No Exit,* intended as homage to the German objectivist painter Max Beckmann.

In fact, Carter's connections with New Formalism are somewhat tenuous and primarily result from his acquaintance with two of its proponents, Gioia and Robert McDowell, during the years before the movement began to pick up steam in the late 1980s. He has never been invited to New Formalist gatherings or had work included in their anthologies, although he has on occasion published in a few of their magazines, chiefly *The Formalist, Edge City Review,* and *Iambs & Trochees.* He has at the same time managed to place sonnets, villanelles, and sestinas in less specialized poetry magazines such as *Poetry, The Iowa Review,* and *New Letters.*

It is safe to say that New Formalist commentators have respected his work in traditional forms and that he has appreciated their encouragement. But he is considered by many of these critics as part of an older, "transition" generation, and someone neither central to their concerns nor significant in their pantheon. In turn, toward New Formalism and its adherents he maintains a quiet impartiality, believing that there is a considerable difference between a literary movement, such as that of the Beats or the Parnassians, and a literary style, such as Romanticism.

Carter's poetry is likely to be regarded as the work of a permanent outsider and sometime visionary, following in the tradition of certain solitaries and mavericks in American art before him—Albert Pinkham Ryder, for example, or Edward Dahlberg, or Jelly Roll Morton. They, too, for most of their careers, were regarded as "local colorists," "regionalists," outcasts, or downright cranks, until later interpreters began to understand that each of them had something quite different to offer—something apart from the prevailing aesthetic assumptions of their times.

Carter himself believes he will be thought of as a minor poet, like many of the "minor" writers he most admires—Walter Savage Landor, John Clare, Sarah Orne Jewett, Edgar Lee Masters, Edwin Arlington Robinson, and John Horne Burns. Yet, he has studied a diverse list of masters—Friedrich Hölderlin, Gustave Flaubert, Franz Kafka, Jorge Luis Borges, Louis Sullivan, Thomas Eakins, Scott Joplin, Flannery O'Connor—and has attempted to borrow something from each.

He is eclectic and takes his influences where he finds them. His remarkable close-up realism, noted earlier, accords ultimately with Mies van der Rohe's wry pronouncement "God is in the details," and he has learned far more about description from the brooding photographic starkness of Eakins and of Walker Evans than from any literary predecessor.

Jared Carter's narrative force comes not from the formulas of the academic workshop but from having punched out stories and met deadlines, his plain style not from committee-meeting banter but from years of blue-penciling the manuscripts of others, his notions of structure and proportion not from abstract discourse about "theory" but from having as a young man helped his father build bridges and erect warehouses. Carter remains independent, unattached, and, for the most part, without official patronage from any quarter. For him, academic writing programs, poetry slams, ideological culture wars, and the assorted shouts and cries of

3rd draft (3)

He had only known hard work on the farm

And in the fields since he was a boy.

All his life he had tried to understand

Cattle, and dogs, and the weather

And the way things grow. Standing

By the barn he could hear the dogs

Talking to each other as they brought

The cattle in. It was the clearest thing

He knew. That night he shot them both

And then himself. The purpose of poetry

Is to tell us about life.

4th draft (4)

He had only known dirt under his nails

And trips to town on Saturdays since

He was a boy. All his life he had been

Around cattle, and dogs, and the earth. ~~things that~~ grow.

Standing by the barn he could hear the dogs

Talking to each other as they brought

The herd ~~cattle~~ in. And the cows answering them.
~~Them.~~
~~The dogs~~. It was the clearest thing he knew.

That night he shot them both and then himself.

The purpose of poetry is to tell us about life.

Early drafts for the final stanza of "The Purpose of Poetry," collected in Carter's 1993 book,
After the Rain (courtesy of the author)

5th draft

He had only known dirt under his nails

And trips to town on Saturday ~~afternoons~~ mornings

Since he was a boy. Always he had been around

Cattle, and dogs, and land near the river.

Evenings
~~Standing~~ by the barn he could hear the dogs

Talking to each other as they brought

The herd in; / And the cows answering them.

It was the clearest thing he knew. That night

He shot them both and then himself.

The purpose of poetry is to tell us about life.

6th draft

purpose/two

He had only known dirt under his fingernails

in the pick-up
And trips to town on Saturday mornings

Since he was a boy. Always he had been around

crops
Cattle, and ~~dogs~~, and land near the river.

Evenings by the barn he could hear the dogs

Talking to each other as they brought

The herd in; and the cows answering them.

It was the clearest thing he knew. That night

He shot them both and then himself.

The purpose of poetry is to tell us about life.

(end)

contemporary American poetry all constitute a single "road not taken." Set apart from all that, he eschews labels and goes his own way.

Interviews:

Patricia Lieb and Carol Schott, "Interview with Jared Carter," *Pteranodon,* 5 (1981): 13–18;

Alberta T. Turner, "Jared Carter: *Mourning Doves,*" in *45 Contemporary Poems: The Creative Process,* edited by Turner (White Plains, N.Y.: Longman, 1985), pp. 24–33;

George Fish, "An Interview with Jared Carter," *IndiAnnual,* 3 (1987): 5–23;

Harry Humes, "Landscape and Literary Ancestors," *Yarrow,* 8, no. 1 (1987): 5–18;

Lenny Emmanuel, "A Conversation with Jared Carter," *New Laurel Review,* 20 (1998): 78–94;

David Lee Garrison, "An Interview with Jared Carter," *Edge City Review,* 15 (April 2001): 17–20.

References:

Timothy J. Deines, "The Gleaning: Regionalism, Form, and Theme in the Poetry of Jared Carter," M.A. thesis, Cleveland State University, 1998;

David Lee Garrison, "The Murmuring of Things," *Southern Indiana Review,* 7, no. 1 (Autumn 2000): 84–87;

Dana Gioia, "Jared Carter," in *Can Poetry Matter? Essays on Poetry and American Culture* (Minneapolis, Minn.: Graywolf Press, 1992), pp. 188–190;

Robert Hosmer, "Meditative Gazing: On Contemporary Poetry," *Southern Review,* 30, no. 3 (Summer 1994): 631–640;

Roland John, "Miniature Stories," *Poetry Nation Review,* 26, no. 4 (March/April 2000): 58–59;

Joseph S. Salemi, "A Dainty Thing," *Iambs and Trochees,* 1, no. 2 (Fall/Winter 2002): 102–107;

Henry Taylor, "Work, for the Night is Coming," in *Magill's Literary Annual 1982,* volume 2, edited by Frank N. Magill (Englewood Cliffs, N.J.: Salem Press, 1982), pp. 968–971;

Helen Vendler, "Adrienne Rich, Jared Carter, Philip Levine," in *The Music of What Happens: Poems, Poets, Critics* (Cambridge, Mass.: Harvard University Press, 1988), pp. 374–378.

Alfred Corn
(14 August 1943 -)

Ernest J. Smith
University of Central Florida

See also the Corn entries in *DLB 120: American Poets Since World War II, Third Series* and *DLB Yearbook: 1980.*

BOOKS: *All Roads at Once* (New York: Viking, 1976);
A Call in the Midst of the Crowd: Poems (New York: Viking, 1978; Harmondsworth, U.K.: Penguin, 1978);
The Various Light (New York: Viking, 1980);
The New Life, twelve sections from a work in progress (New York: Albondocani Press, 1983);
Notes from a Child of Paradise (New York: Viking, 1984; Harmondsworth, U.K.: Penguin, 1984);
The Metamorphoses of Metaphor: Essays in Poetry and Fiction (New York: Viking, 1987; London: Viking, 1987);
An Xmas Murder (New York: Sea Cliff Press, 1987);
The West Door (New York: Viking, 1988);
Autobiographies: Poems (New York: Viking, 1992);
An Encounter with Flannery O'Connor and "Parker's Back," Bell Lecture Series (Tulsa, Okla.: University of Tulsa, 1992);
Present (Washington, D.C.: Counterpoint, 1997);
Part of His Story (Minneapolis: Mid-List Press, 1997);
The Poem's Heartbeat: A Manual of Prosody (Brownsville, Ore.: Story Line Press, 1997);
Stake: Poems, 1972–1992 (Washington, D.C.: Counterpoint, 1999);
Aaron Rose: Photographs, photographs by Rose, text by Corn (New York & London: Harry N. Abrams, 2001);
Contradictions: Poems (Port Townsend, Wash.: Copper Canyon Press, 2002).

OTHER: *Incarnation: Contemporary Writers on the New Testament,* edited by Corn (New York: Viking, 1990);
Marcel Proust, *L'indifférent,* translated by Corn (New York: Sea Cliff Press, 1991);
Aristophanes, *The Frogs,* translated by Corn (Philadelphia: University of Pennsylvania Press, 1999);
James Haug, *Walking Liberty,* edited by Corn (Boston, Mass.: Northeastern University Press, 1999).

Alfred Corn (photograph © Robert Giard; from the dust jacket for Present, *1997; courtesy of the author)*

Since the publication of his first volume of poetry in 1976, Alfred Corn has increasingly distinguished himself as one of the most accomplished, musical, and versatile poets of his generation. He is a master of the lyric form, and several of his books have included long poetic sequences; one, *Notes from a Child of Paradise* (1984), is a book-length narrative poem structurally modeled on Dante's *Divina Commedia* (circa 1307–1321). He has also published one novel; a highly praised manual of prosody; a collection of essays; translations of poetry and drama; critical writing on art, music, and the theater; and a collection of essays on the New Testament, which he edited. While he has never been identified, or identified himself, as one of the core group of New Formalist poets, he has served as a faculty member at the West Chester Writer's Conference for three consecutive years and is adept at writing poetry in a wide range of fixed forms, structured stanzas, and various metrical patterns, as well as free verse.

Alfred DeWitt Corn III was born 14 August 1943 in Bainbridge, Georgia, to Grace Lahey Corn and Alfred DeWitt Corn Jr. The youngest of three children, his sisters were Zola Marie (Zoe, born in 1935) and Margaret Eve (born in 1941). Shortly after his birth, his father was mustered into the United States Army, assigned to the Army Corps of Engineers, and stationed in the Philippines. On 14 August 1945, Alfred's second birthday, his mother died as a result of complications following a burst appendix. The children were kept first by friends, then by their father's sister Jon and her husband, Fred Schroer, on their farm near Ray City, Georgia, until May 1946, when the elder Alfred Corn was discharged from the army. For a year, the family lived with the father's parents in Valdosta, Georgia, before setting up their own household in the same town. In August 1948 the father married a young war widow, Virginia Whitaker MacMillan. As early as second grade, Alfred Corn III was singled out as a strong student, and by 1953 he had been told that his learning abilities were three years ahead of his age. That same year his younger sister Virginia was born; she died just a year later from complications related to meningitis.

After graduating as salutatorian from his junior high school, Corn entered Valdosta High School. By his own account, the years 1956–1961 were years of "religious fervor" for Corn, who announced his desire to become a Methodist minister. Around the same time, however, he became aware of his variant sexual orientation, though he dated female classmates in the hope that he was going through a temporary phase. He began to write poems and a few short stories, composed a senior thesis on James Joyce and stream-of-consciousness narration, scored in the 790s on both the mathematics and English portions of the SAT, graduated as class valedictorian, and was accepted by Columbia, Emory, Harvard, Princeton, and Yale Universities. In 1961 he entered Emory as a French major and during his junior year was able to travel abroad through a summer program. During this trip to France in 1964 he met Ann Rosalind Jones, whom he married three years later. After graduating from Emory summa cum laude, Corn was accepted into the graduate programs in French literature at Columbia, Harvard, Princeton, and Yale and ultimately chose Columbia "because of its excellent French department and because it was located in New York City. The City then was on a steady rise. There were opportunities to see performances, films—I did it all and was still able to handle all the reading."

Corn's graduate student days and his travel abroad during this period are presented most fully in his fifth volume, *Notes from a Child of Paradise,* which chronicles his relationship with Jones, but New York City pervades every volume of Corn's poetry. His first volume, *All Roads at Once* (1976), pays homage to one of his major forebears and influences, American poet Hart Crane, in "The Bridge, Palm Sunday, 1973." In this poem the speaker and a companion set out on a "pilgrimage" to find 110 Columbia Heights, "Where Hart Crane once lived." Discovering that the address no longer exists, they decide that "The only / Available tribute was to read his poem / there on the Promenade in sight of the theme." Crane's evocation of Brooklyn Bridge as a symbol of aspiration and connection, and his attempt to transcend the boundaries of time and space to join with Walt Whitman prompt the speaker to ponder the nature of the connection between him and his friend, as well as that between himself and all of humanity. He calls on the spirit of Crane and his poem to help him "overlook / Distance, shrug off time" and forge at least a temporary connection with the "brother" at his side. Even with this goal, suggested in the epigraph of the poem, from Walt Whitman's 1856 "Crossing Brooklyn Ferry" ("It avails not, time nor place–distance avails not"), the poem touches on the essential loneliness at the heart of much of Corn's poetry. Many of his poems also deal with the theme of mutability, as in "At the Brooklyn Botanic Garden," written in iambic pentameter, or the nine-section free-verse sequence "Pages from a Voyage," an autobiographical poem that parallels a period in the poet's own life with some of Charles Darwin's impressions and experiences as recorded in *The Voyage of the Beagle* (1839). This sense of movement, both literal and psychological, threads together the poems in this first volume, its title taken from a line by the Russian poet Marina Tsvetayeva in her "A Prayer"–"I long for all roads at once." In addition to free verse, *All Roads at Once* offers poems in fixed forms, such as the sonnet, and the poet's own nonce forms created for individual lyrics. He favors the five- and six-line stanza and often works off an undergirding of iambic pentameter. Again and again the poems demonstrate an interest in how the thinking, feeling mind works. In the sequence "An Oregon Journal" the poet remarks that love and memory are the two things that make life worth the trouble, and he concludes that "The best / themes are the moving ones."

Corn's second book, *A Call in the Midst of the Crowd: Poems* (1978), takes its title from Whitman's "Song of Myself" (1855) and is highlighted by the title poem, a poetic sequence subtitled "Poem in Four Parts on New York City," which presents scenes of New

THE CANDLELIGHT BURGLARY

Open the vacation house after a winter's absence
And always some surface or hidden damage lies in wait,
~~~~~~~~ to confirm the adage, still not obsolete, [which]
That nothing really ever lasts but Time itself.
This year, it took the form of a second-story man;
Amateur, a detective also amateur would judge
From simple clues: a punched-in glass pane and (power
Was off) quick recourse to a candle-end, abandoned
On the mantel first by host and then by visitor—
This marble-pale wand, guttered, with a black wire
At its core. Wouldn't anyone have thought to bring
A flashlight? Well, a stand-in was near and apropos,
Provided by the absentee. "Through all her kingdoms,
Nature insures herself." True, and someone has to make
An inventory: <u>landscape with boy angling in rushing
Stream; music system, more or less new; a chiming clock;
A Federal mirror</u>.... Portable, negotiable,
They were what attracted his quick sleights of hand.
(At least the silver knew enough to stay in hiding.)
I'm sure this place was only one of several targets;
And then, effects not used nine months a year, we can
Obviously live without, hence may not have a right to....

But look, now the hindered title, at one stroke,
Breaks free: mine—the law $275.50—if stolen from me.
(As losses help the gambler own up to what he lacks?)
In each drawer jerked open, a starry splash of marble,
Tears spilled over things taken, or rather those
Left behind for me to try to have and hold.... Imagine
The scene in eerie chiaroscuro that sprang into life
For that carpenter ant typing his way across the sill,
Who, how many nights ago, paused, antennae extended
At a blocklike grain of sugar, saw its quartz sparkle
In the glow and waver of invasive light, and then
A distant, crouching prowler, almost giant as his shadow.
A witness so marginal could hardly identify
Or think valuable what was spirited away
On the spread wings of cupidity-with-mind-made-up....
Nor have followed the implications of a psyche's forcing
The issue, fear of discovery, of loss, the curious
Unconsidered spilling of light (and burning wax)
On all that's truly worth having. Worth having, that is,
When we keep, among other uninsurables, our word—
Goods possessed, for the most part, courtesy of darkness,
Which keeps things secret and doing so keeps them.

Emerson, "The Poet"

Alfred Corn

Revised typescript for "The Candlelight Burglary," collected in Corn's 1988 book, The West Door *(courtesy of the author)*

York in each of the four seasons. The poem sits distinctly in a line of long American poems of place, particularly the city, beginning with Whitman's evocations of New York in "Song of Myself" and "Crossing Brooklyn Ferry" and including Crane's *The Bridge* (1930) and William Carlos Williams's *Paterson* (1946–1951). It is most reminiscent of *Paterson* in its use of prose excerpts from various sources, which document the history, development, and social and literary observations of New York. Among the prose sources sprinkled between individual poems are news accounts of events in the city from *The New York Times;* encyclopedia entries on New York; magazine articles; personal letters and historical documents concerning the acquisition of the land and early days of the city in colonial times; and letters and memoirs from literary figures such as Crane, Henry James, Herman Melville, Frank O'Hara, Edgar Allan Poe, Wallace Stevens, and Whitman. While some reviewers were critical of these sources, finding them mundane and not as interesting as those Williams used in *Paterson,* the general critical consensus was that the poem succeeded. Harold Bloom commented that the poem "is an extraordinary and quite inevitable extension of the New York tradition of major visionary poems." Amid the grounding sources are several strong odes to the city within the title poem, such as "Earth: Stone, Brick, Metal"; "April," which recalls Crane's "The Harbor Dawn"; "Declaration, July 4"; "Fifty-Seventh Street and Fifth"; and "Short Story: A Covenant." But Corn's subject is not merely the city; it is every bit as much the self in the city. As he asks in "January," the opening poem of the title sequence, "How to sustain it, the doubtful subject / Of a self . . . ?" The self's ongoing struggle to connect with the city and find personal connections within it is what binds the poem together.

Among the lyrics in the first part of the book, preceding the title poem, many deal with the gradual, often surprising revelation of forms of knowledge. One of the best of these is "Darkening Hotel Room," which uses dream and memory to deal with the theme of the passage of time. A three-part poem, sections one and three use regular stanza forms, while section two, the dreamscape, is irregular. Other poems also employ regular stanza forms, such as the quatrains of "Return," while the invocation piece, "*To a Muse,*" is in iambic tetrameter. However, the use of meter and regular stanzas, as in most of Corn's work, is not constantly adhered to throughout the book.

With his third volume, *The Various Light* (1980), Corn presents a varied array of poems in the lyric mode, ranging from sonnets and pantoums to elegies and other poems of roughly forty to fifty lines not broken into stanzas. Many of the poems in the book with regular stanzas employ the quatrain: "November Leaves" and "Oxygen" are brief eight-line lyrics, the first using a variable iambic meter and rhyme scheme *(aabb, cdcd)* to evoke seasonal change, the second offering an almost Dickinson-like riddle in iambic tetrameter with rhyme *(abcb, defe).* "Interior" is another brief, almost Imagistic lyric consisting of four quatrains, while "Cornwall," a longer (seventy-four-line) poem of place, makes use of slant rhyme in its four-line stanzas. Some of these brief, perfectly made lyrics reflect the influence of James Merrill's early work in *Braving the Elements* (1972) and *Nights and Days* (1966), not only in their use of form, but also in Corn's ability to transform the everyday, ordinary observation into a deep metaphysical meditation, while also delighting in the sheer play of language. This element of delight in language also recalls Stevens, a distinct influence in this volume with "At the Grave of Wallace Stevens," an elegy that in its language and attitude evokes the earlier poet's philosophical and metaphorical approach to the external world, and "Gloze," which takes its stanza form and much of its language from Stevens's "The Death of a Soldier" (1931). In fact, every word of the Stevens poem appears in "Gloze," in order. Corn has said, "Why did I do it? To see if I could, and what the result would be. If I didn't like it, I could always throw the poem away, but I ended up publishing it." In a particularly insightful review of *The Various Light* in *The Nation* (8 November 1980), Robert B. Shaw noted the Stevensian trace in Corn's new work and also compared Corn with Andrew Marvell, the seventeenth-century poet whose "The Garden" (circa 1650–1652) provided Corn the title of this volume. Marvell and Corn share "urbanity, wit, authoritative phrasing and an exciting tension between skeptical intelligence and mystical intuition." In *The Hudson Review* (Winter 1980–1981), Dana Gioia called this book Corn's "finest," one that "shows a consistency of concentration and inspiration unmatched in the earlier books."

Bracketing the impressive collection of lyrics in *The Various Light* are two autobiographical narratives, "Moving: New York–New Haven Line" and "The Outdoor Amphitheater," two of the best poems in the book. The first presents the poet-speaker on a train as he moves from one city to another to join a lover and impressively portrays the dynamics between change, temporality, emotional uncertainty, and the anchor that love provides. The perspective on the fleeting, exterior landscape as the train moves northward is used to parallel the flux of time and memory, and the underlying ghost of meter, with many eleven-syllable lines playing off the iambic pentameter, reinforces the themes of moving and the wavering assertions and hesitancies of personal emotions. "The Outdoor Amphitheater" is a memory of the poet's childhood in the rural South and the summer social center of his hometown, where "Easters or / Summer afternoons, when people, whole families, / their friends and distant relatives, / Went to the outdoor amphitheater." This poem is the longest in the volume, running to twelve pages with long, irregular stanzas, chronicling the many local productions and traveling troupes that came through the town, including musical choirs, vaudeville acts, and fire-and-brimstone revivals. The amphitheater also served as the setting for the poet's high-school graduation and his own valedictory address, as well as his sister's crowning in a beauty pageant. This poem, in the autobiographical mode, even more than the long form of "A Call in the Midst of the Crowd," anticipates the form of the personal narrative, which comprised the entirety of Corn's next volume.

The twists and turns of Corn's relationship with Jones are perhaps typical of a youthful romance, but that does not make *Notes from a Child of Paradise* less interesting or accomplished. The social and political climate of the 1960s and the two young lovers' being so intellectually and socially engaged make the poem much more that a chapter in the poet's autobiography. In its own way, *Notes from a Child of Paradise* stands as a particularly unusual social document, the only long poem in American letters that records a history of intellectual life and the counterculture movement in America during one of the most turbulent decades of the country. Although this aspect of the poem has been largely neglected by commentators—Alan Williamson's review in *The New Republic* is one exception—in favor of attention to the personal revelations of the poem (held in balance by its remarkable formal virtuosity), as time goes by, *Notes from a Child of Paradise* may begin to be considered as an important historical poem, even if that was not the poet's primary intention in writing it.

A book-length narrative poem structurally modeled on Dante's *Divina Commedia*, *Notes from a Child of Paradise* is divided into three parts of thirty-three cantos each, with a dedicatory letter as introduction. In part 1, the cantos consist of three ten-line stanzas; in part 2, two stanzas of fifteen lines; and in part 3, ten stanzas in tercets. The first part or canticle is written in syllabics, ten per line, at times moving into iambic pentameter. In part 2, all sections can be scanned as pentameter, with substitutions and hypercatalexis. The final part of the poem is fairly free, with many sections written in iambic hexameter, which, Corn has commented, "may well be a more American measure than pentameter." Corn's relationship with Jones is the subject, with Jones sometimes paralleled with Dante's Beatrice. In addition, the Northwest Passage of Lewis and Clark is woven into the poem by occasional cantos chronicling that journey.

Dust jacket for Corn's 1997 book, which prompted a reviewer to call Corn "one of our finest living poets" (courtesy of the author)

In the tenth canto of part 2, Corn offers a helpful passage on how these threads of the poem run concurrently: "For those voyages of discovery– / The slowly unfurling story of Ann and Alfred, / Or tracking the sources of the great Missouri, / Or Dante's autobiographical / And catechistic narrative–all strike / The keynotes of a cyclic canon, call / It 'Pilgrim Achieves a Soul through Steep Progression / Toward Revelation.'"

The "voyage of discovery" of Alfred and Ann encompasses their initial meeting, romance, cohabitation, marriage of convenience in July 1967 to enable her to accompany him on a Fulbright scholarship to Paris, involvement while abroad in *Comités de base,* a French group opposing the United States presence in Vietnam, travel to Italy, subsequent return to the United States, cross-country trip by car across America, and, finally, the decision to separate. (The couple finalized their divorce in 1972, amicably, not long after Corn had met and moved in with Walter Brown.) A reader cannot help but be engaged by the personal narrative recorded in the poem, but again, what ultimately might be more compelling is the way in which it captures the spirit of the age, the growing political disillusionment of two young intellectuals coming of age in the 1960s. In canto 30, part 1, Corn powerfully evokes the way in which first Auschwitz, then Hiroshima, and ultimately "The War for Peace in Southeast Asia" shadowed "Millions of postwar childhoods." Throughout the poem, the poet presents himself as politically sympathetic with the counterculture movement of the 1960s but increasingly impatient with the glamorized public displays and commodification of the movement. Ultimately, political fervor lessens as academic interests take precedence for the couple. Personal friendships also make their way into the poem, particularly with the writer Edmund White, whose *Forgetting Elena* (1973) he shares with the couple, chapter by chapter, as he is writing it. During this time, Alfred is also trying his hand at fiction, moving toward abandoning his dissertation, and beginning to write poetry for the first time since high school. Corn has noted that when asked about the motivation to write narrative poetry, he has frequently offered as reply the names Homer, Dante, and Geoffrey Chaucer. In a 1995 symposium on narrative, he observed that because narrative "asks for reader *identification,* appropriation of a character's experience," it has become an important form for poetry "in a period when the question of identity and difference stands in the forefront of contemporary cultural debate."

In commenting on the earlier poem "The Outdoor Amphitheater," from *The Various Light,* G. E. Murray noted how Corn's task in that poem is "transgressing time so as to arrive at a psychological place in which to fix assessment and perspective." This endeavor is what *Notes from a Child of Paradise,* Corn's only book-length narrative poem to date, shares with many of his shorter poems, both before and since. Noting that telling the story of this poem is at times "Painful as anything / I've ever done," he recognizes that "I'd assumed, wrongly, / These subjects for the most part would have lost / Their power to hurt." The poet's ability to face both the pain and joy of memory, and to render these personal feelings in a carefully woven form, makes *Notes from a Child of Paradise* one of the more interesting long poems of its day.

In 1987 Corn published *The Metamorphoses of Metaphor: Essays in Poetry and Fiction,* his only book of critical writing to date, although he has published some critical articles on the arts in magazines and journals. Dedicating the book to his teachers, he comments in the preface that "I have always been interested in criticism nearly as much as in imaginative writing in general. The two projects seem related: poets must discover critical faculties within themselves in order to test their first efforts at articulation, and critics, in order to write well about their subjects, must have at their disposal some of the gifts of poets, chiefly imagination and an availability to subtle, partly conscious responses." In many ways the poets who are subjects of these essays stand as some of Corn's chief influences: Stevens, John Ashbery, Eugenio Montale, Robert Lowell, Elizabeth Bishop, and Crane. But in his preface he identifies two long-standing traditions that he finds himself returning to in critical discourse: "the Dantean legacy, central for English and American poetry since the Romantic period," and "the Symbolist movement in all its transformations, which continue even into the present." Certainly some of the density of imagery and language in Corn's shorter lyrics may suggest the influence of the Symbolist legacy, and his description of Dante's poetic endeavor, "a vision at once autobiographical, aesthetic, and theological," could easily stand as a characterization of his own body of poetry to date. Some of the other figures treated in these essays suggest the breadth of Corn's reading, such as the Russians Boris Pasternak and Andrey Bely, the Greek writer C. P. Cavafy, and the Anglo-Irish novelist Elizabeth Bowen.

In 1990 Viking published *Incarnation: Contemporary Writers on the New Testament,* a book edited by Corn, which includes responses to specific biblical texts by twenty-three contemporary authors. In his own essay, on the second epistle of Paul the Apostle to the Corinthians, Corn speculates on the effect of his extensive reading of Scripture as a youth: "First, I became aware that there are several kinds of language and that unaccustomed ways of putting things are often the most memorable and powerful. . . . The second lesson was that reading, engagement with texts, directed and shaped human life. The Bible's importance prepared me to see other texts as important also." Later in the essay, Corn recounts the episode of his own adult conversion from atheist to Christian while listening to a Johann Sebastian Bach fugue during a walk through a cemetery, a feeling of "complete certainty that the world and everything in it was a Creation." He chose to be confirmed in the American Episcopal denomination, he explains, because it is one in which "the inherited strands of Catholicism and Protestantism both are active and in fruitful dialogue."

Corn's interest in themes pertaining to religion and his wide range of reading both become more evident in the volume of poems *The West Door* (1988). Of this book, he has said, "If *Notes from a Child of Paradise* was in the mode of ascent, then *The West Door* is in the mode of descent, many of the poems concerned with incarnational themes. To go out of the west door of the sanctuary is an entry into the world of physicality, of suffering and death. The book is dedicated to David Kalstone, critic and teacher, who died of AIDS in 1986." In the poem "Dogwood," Corn works off of the theological legend of the dogwood, the tree from which the Cross was supposedly cut, while "*Navidad,* St. Nicholas Ave." presents a brief scene of a couple in Harlem, home with a new infant, in language that suggests a parallel with the birth of Christ. The great tradition of poetry is represented by four translations, the first ever included by Corn in a volume of his own verse, with poems by Eugenio Montale, Rainer Maria Rilke, Pablo Neruda, and Sappho appearing in the middle of the book. In addition, Corn includes his first "shape" poem, "The Column"; poems in fixed forms, such as "From the United Provinces, 1632–1677"; paired sonnets on Benedict de Spinoza and Jan Vermeer; "A Little Lower than the Angels," a somewhat whimsical poem in couplets, about a conversation while seated next to a businessman on a plane; and "Tercina: Winter in Vermont." More than any of his previous volumes, *The West Door* also includes poems in other voices: "Home Thoughts in Winter, 1778" is a dramatic monologue in the voice of an ancestor who fought in the American Revolution; "Letter to Teresa Guiccioli" is another dramatic monologue, in the form of a letter from George Gordon, Lord Byron; and the centerpiece of the book, "An Xmas Murder" (separately published the previous year by small publisher Sea Cliff Press), a dark narrative in the mode of Robert Frost's longer blank-verse poems. This poem marks something of a departure for Corn. In the poem a country doctor in Vermont relates to the poet and a companion, new to the region, the story of a local farmer's murder at the hands of jealous, narrow-minded locals. During the course of the poem, the doctor's own homosexuality is revealed, as he recounts his trial testimony as the only witness to the crime. Superb in its technique and authenticity of voice, this poem further broadens the variety of forms in which Corn has worked.

With his 1992 volume, *Autobiographies: Poems,* Corn continues to investigate the possibilities of voice and personal stories in verse. The final poem of the book–and Corn's longest to date other than the book-length *Notes from a Child of Paradise*–is "1992," a seventy-five-page poem in twenty numbered sections, each titled for an individual year from the past. Each section begins with a scene from the poet's life, then concludes with a scene from the life of another person or persons, representing a cross section of life in America. He has people dealing with issues related to ill or aging parents, troubled relationships, frustrated artistic ambitions, substance abuse, homelessness, and other problems. In the

*Paperback cover for Corn's 1997 book on prosody
(Richland County Public Library)*

final section of the poem, the story of each person written of earlier is brought up to date in a short prose passage, each of which ends in a partially completed sentence, suggesting the process of ongoing lives. The range and authenticity of the characters' thoughts and feelings, related in language close to their own consciousness, is remarkable. Balanced by the poet's bittersweet reflections on his own autobiography, this poem is one of Corn's strongest and most revealing, reminiscent of Whitman in its attention to the lives of ordinary citizens and in its awareness of the dignity of individual and collective struggle; it is similar to some of Adrienne Rich's longer poems, such as "An Atlas of the Difficult World" (1991). Among the poems leading up to the long title sequence, Corn presents an imagined dialogue between a lone pine tree and its surrounding granite landscape; a meditation on the soul's love of travel; a poem in the voices of Anthony Trollope's mother and a friend; and more playful poems on the letter *k* in contemporary culture and a woman being slowly courted

Dust jacket for Corn's 1999 selection of poems from the first twenty years of his career (courtesy of the author)

to death by a vampire-count figure. The volume opens with "A Village Walk Under Snow," one of Corn's perfectly made lyrics, in rhyming quatrains.

In 1997 Corn published three books: the novel *Part of His Story,* the highly-praised prosody manual *The Poem's Heartbeat,* and another volume of poems, *Present.* Since these books are in three different genres, that each book had a different publisher is not surprising, but that *Present* marks a break between Corn and Viking, longtime publisher of his poetry, is significant. *Present* was published by Counterpoint, founded by Jack Shoemaker, former head of the influential small house North Point Press. In her review of *Present* for *The Nation,* Grace Schulman wrote, "Alfred Corn is one of our finest living poets. He works in the visionary tradition of Whitman and Crane, and makes bold new use of classical and European influences. Besides artistry, *Present* contains urgent lessons for our time: presence, care, visibility—all related, I think, in the code of this gay writer, to the wisdom of coming out." This volume is as varied as any Corn has published, in terms of both forms and subject matter. Among its opening pieces are a powerful and disturbing poem about the homeless; a sustained, moving elegy for the poet's stepmother; and a nine-page autobiographical memoir of childhood, "A Goya Reproduction," in its placement and function recalling Robert Lowell's prose piece "91 Revere Street," from *Life Studies* (1959). Music, dance, places, objects, and love inspire other poems. The longest piece in the book is a fourteen-part sequence titled "Musical Sacrifice," a stylistic tour de force, an homage to the genius of Bach and Franz Kafka, with the poet's prose reminiscence of his initial discovery of each artist included as a section of the poem. "Choreography" pays tribute to both George Balanchine and Mikhail Baryshnikov, depicted dancing to the choreography of Mark Morris. "Wonderbread" is a whimsical send-up of the product named in the title; "Conch" is another shape poem; "Two Greek Subjects" includes a poem in sapphics; "A Marriage in the Nineties" and "Insertion Arias," love lyrics, conclude the volume.

Part of His Story is a significant contribution to contemporary AIDS-related literature. In the novel, a young American playwright goes to London in an attempt to move through the process of mourning his deceased lover. The setting of the American abroad, his social interactions, and the focus on the psychological mind-set of this protagonist at times recall Henry James.

What is most compelling about the novel, however, is the focus on the survivor through his own first-person narration, as Avery Walsh reflects on his own experiences and emotions and comes to the realization, at the end of the novel, that he is HIV-positive. The novel was widely praised in reviews, termed a "quiet, honorable novel" by *The Nation,* "insightful, elegant" by *The New York Times Book Review,* and, "a graceful and sensitive mix of art and insight, compassion and intelligence" by the novelist Mary Gordon.

Corn's prosody manual, *The Poem's Heartbeat,* published by Robert McDowell's Story Line Press, the cornerstone press of New Formalism, has been one of the best-selling books for the company. Dedicating the book to his students, Corn begins by exploring the connections and differences between verse and music, concluding that "the differences between poetry and music outweigh the similarities." One of the most interesting insights in the text is Corn's assertion that while verse is scanned by marking "stressed" and "unstressed" syllables, in actuality all syllables carry some degree of stress, lest they be inaudible. So, after introducing scansion via the standard model of scanning for stresses or beats, he goes on to propose a numbering system, whereby a reader can register degrees of stress, by marking syllables with numerals one to four. *The Poem's Heartbeat* testifies to Corn's highly tuned ear as well as his keen awareness of the tradition of poetry, illustrated by many examples of poems from across the centuries to illustrate meters and verse forms.

Corn's career as a poet began auspiciously, his early volumes garnering high praise from some of the best-known critics and reviewers of contemporary poetry, but his later books have undoubtedly enhanced his reputation, as he continues to expand the range of his work, in terms of theme, form, and genre. His book of selected poems, *Stake: Poems, 1972–1992* (1999), which surveys the first twenty years of his career, affords readers a chance to gauge the progress of a distinguished and ongoing career.

Corn's ninth volume of poems, *Contradictions* (2002), contains poems dealing with travel, memory, art, and sexuality. New York City is again the setting for several strong poems, including "My Last June in Chelsea" and "New York Three Decades On." Corn addresses the AIDS pandemic in "Long-Distance Call to a Friend Who Lived with AIDS As Long As He Could" and "To a Lover Who Is HIV-Positive." The volume concludes with "Seeing All the Vermeers," a longer poem that serves as something of a travelogue, tracing the speaker's interaction with Vermeer paintings seen in various locales over the past five decades. As varied in types of poems as any of his preceeding volumes, *Contradictions* confirms Alfred Corn's place as one of the most versatile poets working in the United States.

References:

Richard Aboritz, "The Traveler: On the Poetry of Alfred Corn," *Kenyon Review,* 15, no. 4 (1994): 204–216;

Brian Henry, "On Alfred Corn," *Iowa Review,* 28 (1998): 183–188;

Robert K. Martin, *The Homosexual Tradition in American Poetry* (Austin: University of Texas Press, 1979), pp. 208–217;

G. E. Murray, "In the Place of Time," *Parnassus: Poetry in Review,* 11, no. 1 (1983): 277–285.

Papers:

The manuscripts and papers of Alfred Corn are in the Beineke Rare Book Library at Yale University and The Henry A. and Albert W. Berg Collection, New York Public Library.

Dick Davis
(18 April 1945 -)

Charles Martin
Queensborough Community College, CUNY

See also the Davis entry in *DLB 40: Poets of Great Britain and Ireland Since 1960.*

BOOKS: *Shade Mariners,* by Davis, Clive Wilmer, and Robert Wells, edited by Gregory Spiro (Cambridge: Spiro, 1970);

In the Distance (London: Anvil Press, 1975);

Seeing the World (London: Anvil Press, 1980);

Visitations. 6 Poems (Colchester, U.K.: Ampersand Press, 1983);

Wisdom and Wilderness: The Achievement of Yvor Winters (Athens: University of Georgia Press, 1983);

The Covenant (London: Anvil Press, 1984);

What the Mind Wants (Florence, Ky.: Barth, 1984);

Four Visitations (West Chester, Pa.: Aralia Press, 1984);

Lares (Omaha, Neb.: Cummington Press, 1986);

Devices and Desires: New and Selected Poems, 1967–1987 (London: Anvil Press, 1989);

A Kind of Love: Selected and New Poems (Fayetteville: University of Arkansas Press, 1991);

Epic and Sedition: The Case of Ferdowsi's Shahnameh (Fayetteville: University of Arkansas Press, 1992);

Touchwood: Poems, 1991–1994 (London: Anvil Press, 1996);

Belonging: Poems (Athens, Ohio: Swallow Press / Ohio University Press, 2002; London: Anvil Press, 2002);

Panthea's Children: Hellenistic Novels and Medieval Persian Romances (New York: Bibliotheca Persica Press, 2002).

Dick Davis (photograph by Bruce Meyer)

TRANSLATIONS: Farid od-Din 'Attar, *The Conference of the Birds,* translated, with an introduction, by Davis and Afkham Darbandi (Harmondsworth, U.K. & New York: Penguin, 1984);

Natalia Ginzburg, *The City and the House,* translated by Davis (Manchester, U.K.: Carcanet, 1986);

Let Them Be Changed, translated by Davis (Florence, Ky.: Barth, 1989);

Borrowed Ware: Medieval Persian Epigrams, translated by Davis (Florence, Ky.: Barth, 1990; London: Anvil Press, 1996; enlarged edition, Washington, D.C.: Mage, 1997);

Ferdowsi, *The Legend of Seyavash,* translated by Davis (London & New York: Penguin, 1992);

Iraj Pezeshkzad, *My Uncle Napoleon, A Novel,* translated by Davis (Washington, D.C.: Mage, 1996);

Ferdowsi, *The Lion and the Throne,* translated by Davis (Washington, D.C.: Mage, 1998);

Ferdowsi, *Fathers and Sons,* translated by Davis (Washington, D.C.: Mage, 2000).

Dick Davis was born in Portsmouth, England, on 18 April 1945, to Daniel Cambridge and Marie Truscott Cambridge. He took the surname of his stepfather, Roy Davis, when he was sixteen. After being educated at various state schools, he did his undergraduate work at Kings College Cambridge, where he read English. He received his B.A. degree in 1966 and an M.A. in 1970. From 1966 to 1968 he taught English in Italy and Greece; from 1968 to 1970 he was Lecturer in English Literature at Margaret McMillan College in Yorkshire, England. Anvil Press Poetry published his first book of poems, *In the Distance,* in 1975.

From 1970 to 1978 Davis lived in Iran, and there he met Afkham Darbandi, a nurse who saved his life during a serious illness, and whom he subsequently married. They left Iran for England at the beginning of the Islamic Revolution in 1978, where their daughters Mariam and Mehri were born in 1982 and 1984.

In the early 1980s Davis worked as a freelance writer in England, publishing his poems widely and contributing, by his own estimate, about 170 reviews and essays to such journals as *TLS: The Times Literary Supplement, The Listener, P.N Review,* and *The Spectator.* In 1980, *Seeing the World,* his second book of poems, appeared from Anvil Press, which also published *The Covenant,* his third book of poems, in 1984. In 1988 he took his Ph.D. in Medieval Persian Literature at the University of Manchester; after several visiting professorships in England and the United States, he accepted an appointment at the University of Ohio, where he is now professor of Persian.

Davis is a prolific scholar and publishes critical essays and translations in his field. Readers of his poetry will also be interested in *The Conference of the Birds* (1984), a translation with Afkham Darbandi from the Persian of Attar, and *Borrowed Ware: Medieval Persian Epigrams* (1990), a collection of Davis's translations of more than 150 poems. Since relocating to the United States, Davis has continued to publish poetry in the United States and England. His most important collections have been *A Kind of Love: Selected and New Poems* (1991), *Touchwood: Poems, 1991–1994* (1996), and *Belonging: Poems* (2002).

His poetry and scholarship have been rewarded with many prizes, awards, and fellowships from early on in his career. He has received grants and awards from the Arts Council of Great Britain, the Poetry Society, a Fulbright travel scholarship, an Ingram-Merrill Foundation Grant, and a Guggenheim Fellowship.

Poets seldom look back from the vantage point of their mature work to comment on their earlier efforts, perhaps because, when they do, they offer an irresistible opportunity for the critic. Davis takes such a vantage point, however, in a poem called "Déjà Lu" from his latest collection, *Belonging:*

> I read my first book through again,
> The poems of my messy twenties:
> The stench of misery rose up,
> Every last stanza stank of it.
>
> And at the time I thought I'd been
> So circumspect, impersonal,
> Threading my way through myths and meters . . .
> I'd never do that now of course.

The reader may suspect that the last line is to be taken ironically: the latter part of Davis's canon includes many poems in which the reader feels that a similar refrain is to be followed by an unspoken, "Yeah, sure." But the mess and misery so apparent to the mature author in his earliest work likely went unnoticed by the readers, past and present, of his impressively accomplished first book of poems, *In the Distance.* Those readers would have found (and continue to find) the work of a young poet making his way with skill and assurance through those "myths and meters," creating poems that display the strengths that Davis has explored and built upon in eight later collections of verse.

Because of his British origin, Davis has not been considered as a New Formalist, even though his work has much in common with the poets of this movement. The most obvious shared characteristics are his devotion to the metrical tradition and his avoidance of the trendier "schools" of contemporary verse practice, such as confessionalism and Surrealism. Moreover, the direction that Davis took in earlier poems was affected by his enthusiasm for the poetry of Yvor Winters, who, as poet and critic, was also important for several of the American New Formalists. Davis repaid in full whatever debt he may have owed Winters when he wrote *Wisdom and Wilderness: The Achievement of Yvor Winters* (1983), still the best book on the older poet's work and one that, by peeling away the layers of misinformation (and critical disinformation) that had gotten attached to his poetry, did much to influence its rediscovery both in the United States and abroad.

Winters's poetry, not his criticism, interested Davis. As Davis says in the introduction to *Wisdom and Wilderness,* he discovered Winters's *Collected Poems* (1952) as an undergraduate and, with no knowledge of Winters's criticism, "could value the poetry simply for itself," impressed by its "tone of deeply affectionate love–almost reverence–for the poems' subjects. . . ." The poems revealed to Davis "an author far more interested in the world about him than in himself, whose language hardly ever drew attention to itself, whose verse seemed visionary but never eccentric, intense but

Paperback cover for Davis's first poetry collection (1975), which includes poems that explore the mental distances between the present and the ancient past (Bruccoli Clark Layman Archives)

never self-obsessed. Yet, paradoxically . . . the poems did exude a definite character: they never seemed anonymous or simply ordinary; they implied a specific personality." Since, as Davis also says in his introduction, "men frequently find in literature what they are looking for," and since poetic influence is both benign and effective, the reader should not be surprised that the qualities and characteristics Davis found in Winters are those found in Davis's own work.

Davis is a poet for whom the world is present, and what he writes about is, for the most part, what he loves, except when he is writing about himself, in which case (as the reader may have gathered from "Déjà Lu") he is apt to take a fairly hard line on his subject. The concerns of Davis's poetry begin at home, with his wife, his family, and his friends; they extend to his late brother, a suicide at the age of nineteen; to women sleeping (a subject that, visited often over the years, has become a kind of subgenre of his poetic activity); to the idea of travel and the people and scenes that present themselves to the poet when he is traveling or thinking about traveling; and, in later poems, to the Persian language and the poets whom he has read in it, translated out of it, or (as in a poem about the hell reserved for scrupulous translators) left undone. The subjects of his verse seem more interesting to Davis than the kind of exploration of the poetic psyche so common in contemporary verse, especially in the United States.

The language in which he writes his poems is for the most part the language of everyday life, language that rarely calls attention to itself, though it is always heightened by the kind of emphasis that only meter can give it. Like J. V. Cunningham (with whom he shares an enthusiasm for epigrams) Davis sees poems as compositions in metrical verse. Though he has from time to time occasionally turned to W. H. Auden, Robert Browning, or Edward FitzGerald to borrow a meter, Davis regularly employs standard English prosody.

Likewise, he uses standard forms; he is one of the best contemporary epigrammatists, and his epigrams most often do their work in a rhymed couplet or quatrain; quatrains, and poems consisting of several quatrains, abound in all of his collections. Davis has also written many distinguished sonnets and at least three villanelles, but he has so far avoided the other elaborate French fixed forms. Though the means are ordinary, the effect is not, and, as with Winters, an intense though not idiosyncratic vision produces an impression of poetry that is powerfully personal—that is to say, it yields a voice that is the expression of a powerful personality.

Though Winters was an important poet for the young Davis in much the same way (and for many of the same reasons) that Thomas Hardy was important for the young Auden, clearly, from the beginning of *In the Distance* Davis is writing his own and no one else's poems:

The Diver
For Michaelis Nicoletséas

The blue-cold spasm passes,
And he's broken in.
Assailed by silence he descends
Lost suddenly

To air and sunburned friends,
And wholly underwater now
He plies his strength against
The element that

Slows all probings to their feint.
Still down, still losing
Light he drifts to the wealthy wreck
And its shade-mariners

Who flit about a fractured deck
That holds old purposes
In darkness. He hesitates, then
Wreathes his body in.

If the diver is the poet's surrogate, then it is significant that readers encounter him first as an almost entirely physical presence in the world, suddenly made speechless, and deprived in the underwater silence of the kind of figures poetic speech normally can count on: "blue-cold spasm" is the only figure used, and a lean one. The physicality of the experience is also emphasized in the second and third stanzas, in which the diver loses his mobility until he is carried down to "the wealthy wreck / And its shade-mariners"; up to this point, the poet has been resolutely avoiding any temptation to make the experience an allegory, but with the ghosts of its old crew, and with its "fractured deck / That holds old purposes / In darkness" in the next stanza, the altogether convincing description of a physical experience is turned toward the possibilities of allegory; the poet as diver can perhaps be seen as a kind of submarine archaeologist, who will attempt to rediscover, to put back together again, the motives of the past. Yet, "He hesitates," says Davis, granting him in the next to last line of the poem the only consciousness that he shows; the diver's last gesture is one of graceful physicality; careless of all thought, he "Wreathes his body in." But into what? The gesture is wonderfully ambiguous, for if the wreck is meant to be the past itself, the diver's action presents him at the end of the poem as one who enters and becomes one with the past, not as a consciousness divided from that past, attempting to reconstruct its lost order.

If this poem is an allegory, then it is one that insists to the end on its character as physical description; it succeeds in its figurative expression by its simultaneous insistence on describing the experience of the dive. That emphasis on physicality and on specific detail at the expense of abstraction and generalities in thought and language, evident in this poem and throughout Davis's work, is his own, as is the openness to experience that both the subject and its treatment convey—not something that he could have learned from Winters.

Many of the poems in Davis's first book explore the mental distances between the present and the archaic or mythological past, as well as the physical distances involved in travel. In the most interesting of these poems, the order of the mythic past is unrecoverable: time abrades and eliminates the context of the present in the process of making the past. The archaic speaker of "A Mycenaean Brooch" still beats out "useless / Bronze to fend off history" but understands that there is no way to return to the age and culture that have been shattered by iron and that his future is one of exile and diminishment, a conclusion that links him to other "traditional modernists," such as Robert Frost and Seamus Heaney. In "Scavenging after a Battle," a poem built out of Imagistic particulars and firm meter, the speaker imagines one who "picks his way among corpses," dismantling the present tense of the battlefield:

Diligently he
Severs gold, hacks the stones free

Of their rusting heraldic moulds—
Rubies; sapphires; emeralds.

Colour cupped in his hand; the sea
And the clouds cold grey.

Both knowledge of the past and the artisan's skill in setting that knowledge are lost, and the different kinds of gems are reduced to a handful of nameless colors.

Davis in London, circa 1980 (photograph by Nigel Gray)

Other poems—such as "Among Ruins," "Byzantine Coin," and "The Art Historian"—explore the relations between the "unhoused mind" of the present and the fragments of the past that it encounters. The most striking of these poems (and the only one in which the influence of Winters seems at all apparent) is "The Bond Slave," in which the poet begins from a frankly confessed desire to rediscover and reconstruct the order of the past:

> Among shards and the names of wars
> I sought a sane cold thing
> I could examine for its laws
> And found a random pain
>
> Anarchic, dark and old; and now
> That I have raised this shade
> Of woe I cannot find out how
> It may again be laid—

The bits and fragments that the speaker comes across do not cohere; what one discovers in them is the pain of the unjustified and unjustifiable repression that propped up the formal order, and that, once found, cannot be put to rest or right. The consequences for the speaker of the poem are poignant:

> And it has overthrown my brain
> That wanders in its service
> Like a dumb bond slave, half-insane
> With known injustice.

Like many poets of his generation, Davis turned to mythological subjects to express his feelings. But if the past refuses to yield a credible order to guide the poet in the present, then such mythological excursions can be little more than scenes in which sacred time and space abruptly spill onto one's unconsecrated grounds. As a result, despite their formal accomplishment—Davis from the beginning has been incapable of writing a slack line—a certain predictability in his treatment of mythological themes has crept in. In "The Expulsion from Eden," the first parents "descend / To worlds they cannot comprehend"; "Diana and Actaeon" ends with an awakening as "through the dream / He feels the gash of pain." The eponymous subject of "The Virgin Mary," moreover, has endured

> Her days indifferently,
> And waited vaguely for
> One slight contingency
> That would resolve them all.

St. George, confident that he has dispatched absolute evil absolutely, is ignorant of what the villagers know—"that other beasts / Would come when he had gone."

Even the Savior, in "Jesus on the Water" envies Peter for "Rock and weight and / All his sea-drenched hair."

Another group of poems takes up the theme of travel. One of the features of many of Davis's books has been a poem near the end that is raised and explored more fully in the next book. "The Socratic Traveller" and "Pilgrim" together seem to perform that function in *In the Distance,* the former offering an exploration and defense of the skeptic's position, and the latter an emblem of the traveler's unhoused, questing life:

> The road continues to a second town:
> He searches for a place where he can pause
> And eat: the low room offers shade and food
> And company: he puts the money down,
> Half-listens, speaks, is partly understood.
> An hour. What is it that he seeks? He knows
> It is not here. He rises and he goes.

This kind of question is often raised before travel, but the actual experience of traveling, the subject of many of the best poems in Davis's second book, *Seeing the World,* renders it moot, since the traveler's concern for what he seeks is replaced by an intense curiosity about what he finds. This curiosity, modified by a restraint that seems to come from Davis's imaginative sympathy and tact, is illustrated beautifully in the first major poem of his second book, "Desert Stop at Noon":

> The house is one bare room
> And only tea is served.
> The old man, mild, reserved,
> Shuffles into a gloom
> Where mattresses are laid.
> I sip, grateful for the cool shade.

Travel teaches what will suffice: tea provided by a minimal family (the old man and his son) in a minimal landscape:

> I know that thirty miles
> Without a house or tree
> Surround their crumbling shack.

Davis's brilliant and restrained description of the situation of the old man and his son makes the question posed in "Pilgrim"—"What is it he seeks?"—seem altogether unreal. His questions now are far more modest: "Water? And the boy's mother? / Both seem impossible . . ." "And love? Impertinence / To ask." The traveler inserts himself gently into the situation that he finds and tries to imagine what living in their circumstances would be like. Rather than the answers to the large questions, the speaker is grateful for an hour or so in the shade before setting out again.

The poems of *Seeing the World* are similar in formality to those of *In the Distance*—Davis is not one to make great stylistic leaps from book to book, though he demonstrates a steady development in terms of craft and a continuing thematic broadening and renewal. From the first poem in the book, a pair of epigrams called "Travelling," Davis lets the reader see that the large questions are to be disarmed with provisional answers, and the universals are to be seen as particulars; "Reason," he says, "is a small boy who throws stones, sends / His yapping dog . . . to guide the errant flock." "Marriage as a Problem of Universals," whether seen either as an epithalamium or as the best seventeenth-century poem written in the twentieth, elegantly and wittily defines the local, the provisional, and the particular as all humans know and need to know of universals:

> Marriage is where
> The large abstractions we profess
> Are put gently in their small place—
> The holist's stare
> In love with Man has managed less
> Than eyes that love one aging face.

Seeing the World illustrates both the formal and the thematic richness of Davis's work, from epigram to epithalamium, with poems on love, death, and much in between, including the unsettling visions that often manifest themselves during night journeys by train. "The City of Orange Trees" and "Syncretic and Sectarian" open new areas of exploration for the poet. Both poems deal with the relationship between civilization and barbarism; "The City of Orange Trees" is a meditation on the proverb,

> 'The city filled with orange trees
> Is lost,' which, interpreted, meant
> All conspicuous luxuries
> Augur ruinous punishment.

The one who meditates is one who, at the end of the poem, closes his book and goes forth to parley with Tamburlaine at the gates of his city; as Davis reminds the reader, he is one "Who, barbarous, impatient, vain, / No vows or presents could placate." "Syncretic and Sectarian," set in seventeenth-century India, offers an equally ironic view of the quarrel between fundamentalist religious purity and liberal notions of tolerance and brotherhood; while one brother translated Hindu scriptures into Persian, the other sharpened his sword against heresy. The ironic balance that Davis establishes might seem, especially in an age when irony is often thought to equal evasion, an avoiding of responsibility; but this notion is simplistic: irony for

Dust jacket for Davis's 1991 collection of epigrams and occasional poems about the Middle East, travel, exile, and life in suburban America (Bruccoli Clark Layman Archives)

Davis is hardly neutral or uncommitted. As he says in "Opening the Pyramid,"

> Irony, like the free air and sunlight,
> Crumbles the mummy of each simple creed.

And an epigram on Maximilian Kolbe, the Polish priest at Auschwitz, who, Davis says in a note, "voluntarily took upon himself the death sentence passed on another prisoner" reminds the reader that the conflict Davis has been speaking of has been one that devastated Europe within his lifetime, and whose effects are still felt.

That conflict between fundamentalism and tolerance is one that involves irony and aesthetics. Resistance to totalitarian evil can be regarded as a moral issue, but that is only because people today have separated aesthetics from morality; someone in occupied France might be moved to hide Jews from the Nazis as much by a horror of Nazi music and uniforms as by a detestation of its political aims. The two expressions of Nazi culture, the aesthetic and the political, are inseparable. "Fräulein X," the first poem in Davis's third book of poetry, *The Covenant,* is an emblem of the values of aesthetics and irony in the struggle between racial hatred and liberal values. It begins with a quotation from the Diary of Reck-Malleczewan for December of 1938: *"And it turned out that with her thanks for the poison, Fräulein X had still one more request: would the friend sing Brahms's 'fier ernste Gesänge' before they parted."* Having decided to commit suicide, Fräulein X, who is Jewish, wishes to hear sung one last time Brahms's settings of Martin Luther's translation of four of the Psalms of David. Luther's anti-Semitism is one of the roots of her present dilemma, but her life, in the poet's reconstruction, has been one of aesthetic quietism. In her room, she displays, to "friendship's gentler eye,"

> Views of the Rhine and of the Holy Land,
> Deep vistas of the spirit's need and rest:
> Frail on glass shelves Venetian glass stand,
> The keepsakes of a life secure and blessed.

The album of watercolors and the Venetian glassware, though imperiled, stand—at least until the *Kristallnacht* (Night of Broken Glass—that is, the night of 9–10 November 1938, when Nazi youth gangs ran through the streets breaking windows and looting in Jewish neighborhoods). The privileged life offers no defense against the forces of barbarism; indeed, like the city of orange trees, it is the natural target of barbarism. Nevertheless, the aesthetic life has a moral value that must be reasserted:

> Now, in this last desire, she redeclares
> Old faith in what is hers—Judaic psalms,
> The German tongue: that heritage she shares,
> Immutably—with Luther and with Brahms . . .

The value of that heritage is one that represents the covenant of Davis's title, and that value is what survives beyond defeat.

The Covenant, like Davis's other books, is impressively diverse in its themes and impressive also in the accomplishment of its verse; focusing on one poem, even though it is one of his best, necessarily scants his thematic and formal developments in this book. But the struggle between fundamentalism and tolerance and the assertion of aesthetic, moral, even ironic value persisting into exile and death are underlying presences in his second book and constant threads running through many of the poems in *The Covenant* and into future poems.

In its faith in the persistence of the covenant forged by aesthetic and moral values, "Fräulein X" shows a certain optimism. A more pessimistic view is shown in "Near Coltishall," in which the poet meditates on the maneuvers of fighter-bombers taking off from a Royal Air Force (RAF) airbase near the little village where he is spending an evening reading the works of Michel Eyquem de Montaigne. The possibility of total annihilation raised by the fighters is one undreamt of in Montaigne's philosophy; a humanistic notion of the value of the individual and the private life may already be dead, but Davis's address to Montaigne seems to affirm both values, as well as that of philosophical skepticism:

> Which would you choose, my lord—
> The cant of government,
> The smug cant of dissent?
> Or would you turn toward
> Your book's long argument
>
> That wisdom is to know
> How blindly we descend
> To where no arms defend
> Our ignorance from no
> Imaginable end?

After the publication of *The Covenant,* Davis produced a chapbook, *Lares,* in 1986 and then paused to collect himself in *A Kind of Love: Selected and New Poems,* which appeared in 1991. With a few important exceptions, the new work in these books tends toward the epigrammatic and the occasional; these poems carry the poet's themes of travel, exile, and life in the Middle East to suburban America, where Davis began teaching at this time. One has the feeling that Davis's muse took a fair bit of time settling in and that the period of adjustment was not always comfortable. Nevertheless, from these two collections, "Chebutykin," "The Departure of the Myths," "Lady with a Theorbo," and "On the Iranian Diaspora" are important additions to the Davis canon, either for their subject, their accomplishment, or both.

A problem with the short poem is that in aggregate it displays what Cunningham, who also loved it, called "the defect of brevity," which could be mitigated, he said, in two ways: one is by interleaving short poems with prose, in the manner of Dante's *La Vita Nuova* (written in the period between 1290 and 1294), and the other is by stringing short poems together into a poetic sequence. Davis has not yet tried Cunningham's first solution, but in *Touchwood,* his first collection of verse since the selected poems appeared in 1991, there is an informal sequence of short poems dealing with domestic life, his children, and his own childhood, in which he discusses, poignantly, the effects of its brutality on his life and on that of his brother, who committed suicide at the age of nineteen.

Davis has never been a "confessional poet" in the contemporary American fashion, and in "Pragmatic Therapy" and the title poem, he expresses heartfelt skepticism about the value of the confessional. Nevertheless, these poems are among the most intense and moving in the book, the more so for their formal and psychological restraint.

In addition to the unnamed sequence, memorable poems deal with the tribulations of middle age and poems celebrating Edgar Bowers, Suzanne Doyle, and Auden—the last of these written in the meter Auden employed for his "Paradise Island." But the major departure in *Touchwood* is the presence of "Esther," a long poem that is, in effect, a lyric sequence. This form

Dust jacket for the 2002 collection of Davis's poems that includes a dramatic monologue spoken by a seventeenth-century Persian woman who is married to an Englishman (Richland County Public Library)

allows Davis to avoid the "defect of brevity" by gathering together short poems (and some prose) while helping him to avoid the narrowness of poetic monologue; different voices and different perspectives, including the poet's own, are easily encompassed within this casual narrative form. The poem explores the biblical story of Esther, taking off from the modern currency of the story in the Middle East via a quotation from Freya Stark's autobiography and then retelling it from the varied perspectives of its characters. The form allows digressions on European orientalism, the Medieval pogrom at York, and the survival–for worse rather than better–of tribalism into the present time. Its pessimistic "Envoi" is well earned.

Belonging: Poems is distinguished more for the variety than for the thematic consistency of its contents. In it the poet goes wherever he will, writing whatever he is pleased to write, whether the erotic playfulness of its opening poem, "A Monorhyme for the Shower"; the poignant sonnet to his aunts, "Duchy and Shinks"; or the wisdom of "A Bit of Paternity," which celebrates an underappreciated aspect of fatherhood. Perhaps the most impressive poem in the book is a dramatic monologue called "Teresia Sherley" (in the meter of Browning's "A Toccata of Galuppi's"), a seventeenth-century Persian woman's account of her marriage to an Englishman. Those qualities so abundant in Davis's work, of tact and imaginative sympathy, help him to create an unforgettable portrait of a woman distant, exotic, but credibly real. This collection adds some important poems to the Davis canon.

Since the 1970s Dick Davis has shown that the metrical tradition is alive and well. While so occupied, he has created a body of work that includes some of the best poems that anyone has written in English during that time.

Interview:

"Dick Davis in Conversation with Clive Wilmer," *Between the Lines,* new series 1 (2003).

Tom Disch
(2 February 1940 -)

Robert McPhillips
Iona College

See also the entry on Disch in *DLB 8: Twentieth-Century American Science-Fiction Writers*.

BOOKS: *The Genocides* (New York: Berkley, 1965; London: Whiting & Wheaton, 1967);

Mankind under the Leash (New York: Ace, 1966); republished as *The Puppies of Terra* (London: Panther, 1978; New York: Pocket Books, 1980);

One Hundred and Two H-Bombs: And Other Science Fiction Stories (London: Roberts & Vinter, 1966); republished with a new arrangement of stories as *White Fang Goes Dingo and Other Funny S. F. Stories* (London: Arrow, 1971);

The House that Fear Built, by Disch and John Sladek as Cassandra Kaye (New York: Paperback Library, 1966);

Echo Round His Bones (New York: Berkley, 1967; London: Hart-Davis, 1969);

Black Alice, by Disch and Sladek as Thom Demijohn (Garden City, N.Y.: Doubleday, 1968; London: Dobson, 1969);

Camp Concentration (London: Hart-Davis, 1968; Garden City, N.Y.: Doubleday, 1971);

Under Compulsion (London: Hart-Davis, 1968); also published as *Fun with Your New Head* (Garden City, N.Y.: Doubleday, 1969);

The Prisoner (New York: Ace, 1969; London: Dobson, 1979);

Highway Sandwiches, with Marilyn Hacker and Charles Platt (Privately printed, 1970);

The Right Way to Figure Plumbing (Fredonia, N.Y.: Basilisk Press, 1972);

334 (London: MacGibbon & Kee, 1972; New York: Avon, 1974);

Getting into Death: The Best Stories of Thomas M. Disch, (London: Hart-Davis, MacGibbon, 1973); republished with a new arrangement of stories as *Getting into Death and Other Stories* (New York: Knopf, 1976);

Clara Reeve, as Leonie Hargrave (New York: Knopf, 1975; London: Hutchinson, 1975);

Tom Disch (photograph by Jerry Bauer; from the dust jacket for the 1995 U.S. edition of The Priest; *Richland County Public Library)*

The Early Science Fiction Stories of Thomas M. Disch (Boston: Gregg Press, 1977);

On Wings of Song (London: Gollancz, 1979; New York: St. Martin's Press, 1979);

ABCDEFG HIJKLM NOPQRST UVWXYZ (London: Anvil Press in association with Wildwood House, 1981);

Neighboring Lives, by Disch and Charles Naylor (New York: Scribners, 1981; London: Hutchinson, 1981);

Fundamental Disch, edited by Samuel R. Delaney (London: Gollancz, 1981; New York: Bantam, 1982);

Burn This (London: Hutchinson, 1982; revised edition, Patchogue, N.Y.: Wiseacre Books, 1995);

The Man Who Had No Idea (London: Gollancz, 1982; New York: Bantam, 1982);

Orders of the Retina: Poems (West Branch, Iowa: Toothpaste Press, 1982);

Here I Am, There You Are, Where Were We? (London: Hutchinson, 1982);

Ringtime: A Story (West Branch, Iowa: Toothpaste Press, 1983);

The Businessman: A Tale of Terror (New York: Harper & Row, 1984; London: Cape, 1984);

Torturing Mr. Amberwell (New Castle, Va.: Cheap Street, 1985);

The Brave Little Toaster: A Bedtime Story for Small Appliances (Garden City, N.Y.: Doubleday, 1986; London: Grafton, 1986);

The Tale of Dan De Lion (Minneapolis: Evening Coffee Editions, 1986);

The Silver Pillow: A Tale of Witchcraft (Willametic, Conn.: Ziesing, 1987);

The Brave Little Toaster Goes to Mars (Garden City, N.Y.: Doubleday, 1988);

Yes, Let's: New and Selected Poems (Baltimore & London: Johns Hopkins University Press, 1989);

The M.D.: A Horror Story (New York: Knopf, 1991; London: HarperCollins, 1992);

Dark Verses and Light (Baltimore & London: Johns Hopkins University Press, 1991);

The Priest: A Gothic Romance (London: Millenium, 1994; New York: Knopf, 1995);

The Castle of Indolence: On Poetry, Poets, and Poetasters (New York: Picador, 1995);

A Child's Garden of Grammar (Hanover, N.H.: University Press of New England, 1997);

The Dreams Our Stuff Is Made Of: How Science Fiction Conquered the World (New York: Free Press, 1998);

The Sub: A Study in Witchcraft (New York: Knopf, 1999);

The Castle of Perseverance: Job Opportunities in Contemporary Poetry (Ann Arbor: University of Michigan Press, 2002).

OTHER: "Thomas M. Disch," in *Contemporary Authors Autobiography Series* (Detroit: Gale, 1986), IV: 143–157;

"Ballade of the New God," in *Rebel Angels: 25 Poets of the New Formalism,* edited by Mark Jarman and David Mason (Brownsville, Ohio: Story Line Press, 1996);

"The Prisoner," in Disch, David McDaniel, and Hank Stine, *The Prisoner Omnibus* (London: Carlton, 2002).

Polymath poet Tom Disch is also one of the most talented of the "New Wave" of science-fiction writers who emerged in Great Britain (where Disch lived for a time and where he published much of his early fiction and all of his early poetry) in the 1960s. (Others in the group included J. G. Ballard, Brian W. Aldiss, and Michael Moorcock.) This group, along with such American writers of the period as Samuel R. Delany, Ursula K. Le Guin, and Joanna Russ, all treated science fiction as a serious genre that enabled them to confront subjects ranging from ecology through amorphous gender roles in a postmodernist nuclear age. As a novelist, Disch has written such critically acclaimed volumes as *Camp Concentration* (1968), *334* (1972), and *On Wings of Song* (1979), a novel set in a futuristic Iowa that nonetheless reads something like Disch's own portrait of the artist as a young man growing up gay and Catholic in the Midwest. Under the pseudonym Leonie Hargrave, Disch had his best sales for a book that was written in the style of a nineteenth-century Gothic novel, *Clara Reeve* (1975). With his partner, Charles Naylor, Disch wrote a well-reviewed historical novel focusing on Victorian England, *Neighboring Lives* (1981). *The Businessman: A Tale of Terror* (1984), a brilliant Gothic tale set in St. Paul (where Disch spent much of his youth) focusing on, among other things, the poet John Berryman, who leaped to his death from the Washington Avenue Bridge in Minneapolis, initiated a trilogy of literate contemporary Gothic novels rounded out by *The Priest: A Gothic Romance* (1994) and *The Sub: A Study in Witchcraft* (1999). He achieved renown, as well, as a children's author with *The Brave Little Toaster: A Bedtime Story for Small Appliances* (1986), which was turned into a popular Disney animated feature. Yet, Disch has also lived a seemingly parallel existence as a poet, whose emergence in the United States did not become fully apparent to most American readers until the belated publication by Johns Hopkins University Press, in 1989, of *Yes, Let's: New and Selected Poems,* a collection that includes much of Disch's verse that had been in print in England for a decade. This belated American debut, however, came about at a not unpropitious time for Disch, corresponding, as it did, with the emergence in the United States of the New Formalism, a group with whom his witty, colloquial, formal verse bore a strong affinity. *Yes, Let's* was reviewed in the Winter 1990 special issue of the Scottish American journal *Verse,* edited by Robert McPhillips, devoted to "The New Formalism in American Poetry"; and a substantial selection from his poetry was included in the first anthology of poetry devoted to New Formalism, *Rebel Angels: 25 Poets of the New Formalism* (1996), edited by Mark Jarman and David Mason. With R. S. Gwynn and Charles Martin, Disch joined the forefront of the satirical wing of the New Formalist school.

Thomas Michael Disch was born in Des Moines, Iowa, on 2 February 1940 to Felix and Helen Gilbertson Disch and grew up in St. Paul and rural Minnesota. His father was a traveling salesman; his mother grew up on a farm in southern Minnesota, and Disch divided his childhood between stints living in the Twin Cities, in smaller Minnesota towns, and, for a brief, idyllic period, on the family farm. He attended Catholic schools, including the Cretin Military High School. Disch has credited these experiences, in the 1986 article he wrote for *Contemporary Authors Autobiography Series* (CAAS), with providing him with the ability "to diagram sentences and sit behind a desk for hours at a time, essential skills for any writer" as well as a lifelong skepticism toward authority.

Shortly after high school in the late 1950s Disch embarked for Manhattan, where, through the mid 1960s he worked as an extra at the Metropolitan Opera; ushered at a Broadway theater; joined the army, from which he went AWOL in New Orleans, leading to a stay in a mental institution in lieu of imprisonment; studied at Cooper Union and New York University (the latter of which he dropped out from shortly before graduation); clerked at bookstores; and worked as a copywriter for the advertising firm of Doyle Dane Bernach. During the 1960s, Disch befriended such writers as Delany and the poet Marilyn Hacker, the former of whom has written a book-length study of one of Disch's short stories, the latter with whom Disch collaborated on his first, privately published chapbook of verse. With John Sladek, Disch traveled through northern Africa and Europe and co-authored several books. In 1969 Disch met Naylor, with whom he has shared an apartment on Union Square in Manhattan and a summer cabin in the Catskills ever since. Of this relationship, Disch wrote in *CAAS*, "Not that my poetry is particularly diaristic or confessional, but among the poems in the four collections of poetry between 1981 and 1984 and the two more assembled and waiting in the wings [poems included in *Yes, Let's*], the circumstances of our lives together are pretty thoroughly documented." Disch has supplemented his income derived from his fiction and poetry as a literary and theater critic for such publications as *Playboy*, *The Nation*, and *The New York Daily News*. *The Castle of Indolence: On Poetry, Poets, and Poetasters* (1995), Disch's collection of his essays on poetry, was a finalist for the National Book Critics Circle Award for criticism.

While Disch is recognized as one of the finest science-fiction writers of his generation, were he less talented and ambitious, his poetry—for a long time known only to a small group of British and American readers of five books of poetry in Great Britain and the United States, among them Donald Davie, who praised *Burn This* (1982) in his article "Prize Poems" in *The London Review of Books* (1–14 July 1982), saying "It's a long time since I

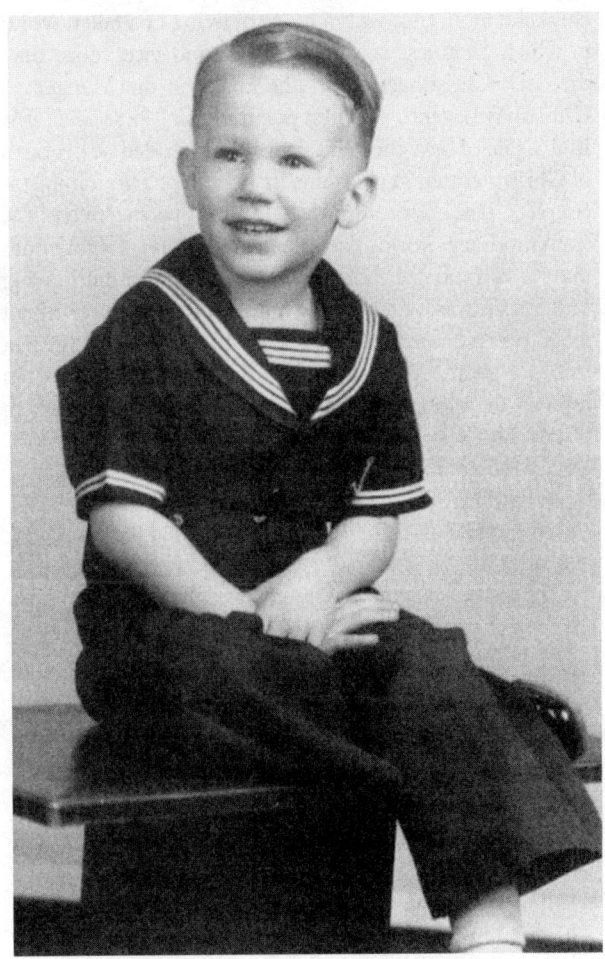

Disch at age four (from Adele Sarkissian, ed., Contemporary Authors Autobiography Series, *volume 4, 1986)*

read a book of verse so consistently entertaining and intelligent," before its 1995 introduction to a wider American audience—would, in itself, establish Disch as a first-rate literary talent. His poems—collected in *Yes, Let's* and the subsequent *Dark Verses and Light* (1991), in addition to a 1995 enlarged American edition of *Burn This* and his earlier children's book in verse, *The Tale of Dan De Lion* (1986)—include "A Bookmark," a pointed critique of the longueurs of Marcel Proust's *Remembrance of Things Past* (1913–1927); a satire, "The Rapist's Villanelle" (decidedly politically incorrect); as well as more personal lyric satires, "Entropic Villanelle" and the self-deifying "Ballade of the New God." In general, his poetry is animated by a satiric venom often paradoxically combined with a child-like innocence and sense of wonder, seemingly generated from Disch's existence as a gay lapsed Catholic in a fallen world with the hope of salvation seemingly absent for him.

Perhaps no poem better exemplifies the light and dark aspects of Disch's satiric verse, the combination of child-like innocence with a sense of living in a fallen world in which goodness is a mask of evil and vice versa, than the dark Christmas fable "The Snake in the Manger: A Christmas Legend," the first poem in *Dark Verses and Light*. In this tale of how the animal world responded to the birth of Christ, written in quatrains that combine two four-stress couplets, Disch writes from the "fallen" perspective of the contemporary world, parodying the decay of Christmas into a commercial holiday concerned with gift giving rather than spirituality, as the appealingly demonic serpent plots to present the newborn Christ with the best present from the members of the animal kingdom. Animals from around the globe, espying the star that led the Magi to Christ, finally arrive at Bethlehem:

> At last they got where they were going
> On a cold dark night with the North Wind blowing,
> And if sleet wasn't sleeting, then snow was snowing.
> And lo! in the night a lamp was glowing,
>
> And three Wise Men were kneeling down
> Before a Fair Lady in a blue gown,
> And in the Lady's arms a Child
> Cooed and burbled and wriggled and smiled.
>
> "The darling! the treasure!" declared a cow.
> "I wish I had a camera now!"
> "Just look at Him," an old hen clucked.
> "If he's not God, then I'll be plucked."

Disch's artfully simple voice, presenting Jesus "in the Lady's arms" in clichéd and fawning language echoed by the cow and the hen, combined with the anachronistic mention of a camera and weather appropriate to a modern image of Christmas as winter holiday associated with snow and sleet–the "White Christmas" cliché–but totally inappropriate to the Middle Eastern landscape where the event actually occurred, comically masks Disch's darker vision of his subject. Indeed, one of the most subversive elements in the poem is his characterization of Mary–initially presented as a Lady associated with the medieval courtly tradition (an association that is a convention of the English medieval lyric, secular imagery used within religious lyrics)–who is presented as an ungracious hostess to the well-intentioned serpent:

> "A snake!" the Lady screamed. "A snake!
> Joseph, kill it, for Heaven's sake!"
> "Now, Mary dear, don't be upset:
> The thing's behaving like a pet."
>
> "Crush it! Smash it! Drive it away!
> To think I've lived to see the day
> When snakes should curl about the head
> Of our dear Jesus in his bed."

The serpent, after all, is merely trying to please Jesus with a gift, though his own biological makeup, God given within the Christian mythos of the poem, frustrates him in this attempt. Thinking that a pelican's egg would be a perfect gift, the serpent is furious that his body had devoured it during his journey with it to the manger: "The pelican's Egg had been digested, / And all it could give was the broken shell. / 'God send,' it hissed, 'all fowl to hell!'"

Not to be dissuaded, the snake decides to find another gift, deciding upon the perfect gourd to serve as a rattle for the infant. Once again, though, transportation of the gift proves problematic, and when the snake arrives at Jesus' crib, the gourd rattle has been digested, ending up in the snake's tail. This time, the snake is so enraged that it decides to bite and thus murder the infant, though this intention leads to the poem's wickedly ironic denouement:

> Its evil intent so thrilled the snake
> That its swollen tail began to shake,
> And at the sound of the hollow gourd
> The Child awoke (though His folks still snored)
>
> And clapped His infant hands with glee
> And snapped the snakeskin rattle free.
> "Why, thank you, Snake. Is this for Me?
> Come here and sit upon my knee
>
> "And let me stroke each shining scale
> And help regenerate your tail."
> The snake complied with snakish blushes
> And joined the Child in His bed of rushes.
>
> "*Your* gift, bright Snake, was dearest of all–
> Not just your brutish wherewithal,
> But something to suit a baby's whims
> Better than a hundred hymns."

In a seemingly innocent yet subversive scene, not without homoerotic implications, the infant Jesus himself, as the Romantics often claimed of Milton, is really part of Satan's crew, establishing an unholy alliance with him while the decent Joseph and the censorious Mary are asleep, turning the serpent into a rattlesnake and assuring him "'The Son of Man / Needs you for His eternal plan.'" By the final two stanzas of the poem, Disch annihilates the possibility of salvation in a fallen world by presenting an image, at once child-like and appalling, of Christ and Satan united as one, sin and love eternally intertwined:

> "Now go in peace. My Mother's stirring.
> We don't want another scene occurring."
> The serpent's tongue met the infant's lips
> Like the first taste of potato chips.

And the Child knew Sin, and the snake knew Love,
And in the heavens high above
The angels sang of Peace on Earth
And the wonder of the God-Child's birth.

In the strongest of his other poems, Disch is given to satiric self-portraits, from the humble "Entropic Villanelle" to the mock-heroic "Ballade of a New God," dealing in their own ways with existing in a fallen universe, and poems that skewer contemporary aesthetics, especially poetry and its critics. These latter poems include parodies of such contemporary poets as A. R. Ammons, Robert Bly, Robert Creeley, and James Merrill and a critique of critic Marjorie Perloff's defense of avant-garde poetry. In "'Ritin': A Manifesto," Disch presents a down-home defense of the unfashionable poetry of Robert Service—and, in a broader sense, of pleasure in general.

In "Entropic Villanelle," Disch employs the hypnotically repetitive French form of the villanelle to celebrate a fallen world in which "Things break down in different ways." These things include the poet's own body: "I have had heartburn several days, / And it's ten years since I've been thin. / Things break down in different ways." Yet, despite that "melanomas graze / Upon the meadows of the skin," as well as that lesser disasters occur, such as spoiled fruit, decayed meat, and eroding teeth, Disch cannot evade celebrating the world—as Frost did—for what it is:

> The odds still favor croupiers,
>   But give the wheel another spin.
> Things break down in different ways:
> We can't, for that, omit their praise.

By contrast to the vision of "Entropic Villanelle," Disch declares, with mock megalomania, in "Ballade of the New God" that "A new religion starts tonight!"—and that its god is none other than Disch himself. The poem opens with the bold assertion: "I have decided I'm divine," and goes on to instruct potential followers of his church:

> No booze, no pot, no sex, no swine:
> I've decreed them all taboo.
> My words will be your only wine,
> The thought of me your honeydew.
> All other thoughts you will eschew.
> You'll call yourself a Thomasite
> and hymn my praise with loud yahoo.
> A new religion starts tonight.

These two satiric poems by Disch illustrate two personal versions of his response to living in a fallen world.

In the majority of his other poems, Disch critiques the state of present-day culture. One of the most devastat-

Dust jacket for the 1989 volume that marked Disch's debut as a poet in the United States. Most of the poems had been published in England more than a decade earlier (Bruccoli Clark Layman Archives).

ing of these satires is "The Rapist's Villanelle," originally published in *ABCDEFG HIjKLM NOPQRST UVWXYZ* (1981), Disch's second book of verse published in Great Britain, and reprinted in *Yes, Let's*. The horror is evoked in Disch's poem in an inverse fashion from Robert Browning's "My Last Duchess." In Browning's dramatic monologue readers slowly discover that the Duke speaking of a painting of his late wife has, in fact, murdered her; in Disch's poem, the horror is evoked by the title, for, without it, the reader would likely remain in the dark about why the poem's speaker "had to laugh" as he obsessively observes (stalks, one realizes from the poem's title) her "spend her money with such perfect style." The first five tercets of this villanelle can be seen as a gently satiric portrait of a wealthy woman ("my darling of the avenues")—the Belinda of Alexander Pope's *The Rape of the Lock* transported to the tony upper East Side of contemporary Manhattan—concerned narcissistically with

Disch, circa 1991 (photograph by Jamie Spracher; from the dust jacket for The M.D.: A Horror Story, *1991; Richland County Public Library)*

adding more chic clothing ("Her blouse was from Bendel's, as were her shoes") to her extensive wardrobe. The concluding quatrain of the villanelle, however, horrifies as the reader recognizes that the speaker in this poem is far more dangerous than Pope's angry aristocrat who symbolically rapes the self-absorbed Belinda by cutting off a lock from her luxuriant hair—*rape,* in Pope's time meaning "to seize" as well as its current meaning. Disch's character is a literal rapist, and the poem becomes a double-edged satire on the close proximity in society between the conspicuous spending and implied amorality of the wealthy in society and the amorality of a violently pathological criminal:

> I couldn't help myself. I had to smile.
>
> At how she never once surmised my guile.
> My heart was hers—I'd nothing else to lose.
> She spent her money with such perfect style.
> I couldn't help myself. I had to smile.

That the rapist's strongest emotion here seems to be his need to "smile," a gesture that no doubt hides the "guile" through which he designs to assault all that the woman's "style" has come to stand for to the rapist, makes the reader eerily understand the banality of evil that seems so prevalent in so many levels of society.

Disch's literary satires are less shocking than "The Rapist's Villanelle," but they are savagely incisive and funny as well. One of his best is "A Bookmark," which comments on the tedium that often accompanies a reading of Proust's *Remembrance of Things Past* in its entirety. But Disch is of most interest as a satirist of contemporary poetry. In "High Purpose in Poetry: A Primer" he skewers Ammons's eschewing of the human in his abstract meditations on "nature" (his best and most representative being, perhaps, "Corson's Inlet"), for

It's best for affirmation to be limited to those objects in

Nature that can't reply: for imagine if a murderer
Or even the loan application examiner at your local bank,
Finding himself affirmed, were to decide that your Yes
Was insincere or failed to do justice to his condition–

Disch goes on, as Ammons often seems to go on, interminably. Robert Creeley's minimalist verse is parodied in "Really," in *Burn This,* as is the otherworldly element of James Merrill's epic *The Changing Light at Sandover* in "Conclusive Evidence" in the same volume. But perhaps the funniest poetic parody from *Burn This* is "A Letter to Robert Bly," a response to Bly's statement in the April 1980 *Poetry Project Newsletter* that "If plants wrote poetry, you know, they'd write prose poems. . . . Plants are just not interested in a Miltonic style." The letter is written in the voice of a rose disagreeing with Bly's hilarious aesthetic assumption. It begins:

Dear Mr. Bly,
    I would like to deny
Your theory that plants prefer prose.
In my experience as a rose
I've noticed that the best poems spring
From a light loam of meter and rhyme.

Disch goes on to parody Bly's assumptions that meter and rhyme reflect political conservatism: "My reply, Mr. Bly, must be, Alas– / A rose will never be a leave of grass." Disch in this poem wrote a critical defense of formalism in poetry before the existence of the New Formalism had yet been recognized.

But Disch continued this aesthetic argument when such academic critics as Perloff began scoffing at what she perceived to be the reactionary status of contemporary poets who depended upon "a light loam of meter and rhyme" to create their poems. "Orientating Mr. Blank," dedicated, tongue-in-cheek, to Perloff, indicts what Disch sees as academia's institutionalization of mediocrity in contemporary American poetry. In "By themselves," the speaker, a professor welcoming "Mr. Blank" to his new job at his university, asserts, "A dozen mediocrities amount to nothing, but put them together / And you have a department." Against the wittily bleak (and all-too-accurate) portrait of the aesthetic landscape of most mainstream contemporary poetry, Disch, in another poem, presents an alternate aesthetic in which the sheer pleasure to be gotten from a certain type of poetry is more important than the M.B.A. held by the poet who writes it.

The poem "'Ritin': A Manifesto" concerns the academically unspeakable poet, Service, who has always appealed to a general audience that cannot make heads or tails of the more elitist poetry that has

Paperback cover for Disch's 1991 collection, which opens with the dark fable "The Snake in the Manger: A Christmas Legend" (Bruccoli Clark Layman Archives)

been praised by professors since T. S. Eliot and Ezra Pound arrived on the poetic scene in the second decade of the twentieth century. Written deliberately in the exaggerated working-class voice that Service affected in his poems of the common folk, Disch both satirizes and defends Service, even as he wittily dismisses the pretension and tedium of most twentieth-century poetry. Assuming this voice has the effect of disarming criticism:

Now I am not braggin', jest speakin' out plain,
But most of the 'ritin' I see is insane.
The prose is all 'ritten for someone age five,
An' the poetry, dammit, there's none that's alive.

Ultimately, if Service is the immediate source of Disch's praise here, the significance of this poem is more general in its emphasis on the qualities, lacking in so much contemporary poetry, that make it—however unsophisticatedly—"alive": a gift for meter and rhyme put to the use of telling a good story:

> Now yer snow is a killer, an' so are some men,
> An' old Bobby Service, why, he knew 'em when.
> He knew 'em in New York, he knew 'em in Nome,
> And he stuck every one of 'em into a poem!
>
> An' Bob did it, I'll betcha, by seeing things square,
> Then settin' 'em down with not one word to spare,
> Like a good line of rivets, or a tol'rance so true
> You knew that his stories could happen to you.
>
> So that's why I say of all 'riters there are,
> The best of the lot was Bob Service by far,
> An' all of you eggheads up there on Parnassus
> Should do jest like he did an' get up your asses.

Behind the mask of this persona—a character far from its Manhattan-dwelling creator (but perhaps less far from his outsider's soul)—Disch makes it clear that for him, as for the New Formalists collectively, poetry, and "'ritin'" in general, is too vital to be left to the "eggheads."

In his poetry, Tom Disch has created a body of satirical verse that establishes him as one of the finest poets in America. Combined with his work as a novelist as well as a critic, he is perhaps one of its most unusual contemporary men of letters as well.

References:

Thomas DePietro, Review of *Yes, Let's: New and Selected Poems, Verse,* 7, no. 3 (Winter 1990): 72–74;

Dana Gioia, "Tom Disch," in *Can Poetry Matter? Essays on Poetry and American Culture* (St. Paul, Minn.: Graywolf Press, 1992), pp. 193–196;

Kevin Walzer, "The Sword of Wit: Disch, Feinstein, Gwynn, Martin," in *The Ghost of Tradition* (Brownsville, Ore.: Story Line Press, 1998), pp. 152–184;

David Yezzi, "Thomas M., Meet Tom," *Parnassus: Poetry in Review,* 22, nos. 1–2 (1995): 389–400.

Michael Donaghy
(24 May 1954 -   )

Catherine Tufariello

BOOKS: *Slivers* (Chicago: Thompson Hill, 1985);
Machines: A Poem (Guildford, U.K.: Circle Press, 1986);
Shibboleth (Oxford & New York: Oxford University Press, 1988);
O'Ryan's Belt (Madison, Wis.: Silver Buckle Press, 1991);
Errata (Oxford & New York: Oxford University Press, 1993);
Wallflowers: A Lecture on Poetry with Misplaced Notes and Additional Heckling (London: Poetry Society, 1999);
Dances Learned Last Night: Poems 1975–1995 (London: Picador, 2000);
Conjure (London: Picador, 2000).

PRODUCED SCRIPT: *Habit,* motion picture, Momentum Video, 1996.

RECORDING: *The Poetry Quartets: 6,* includes poems by Donaghy, British Council/Bloodaxe, 2000.

OTHER: Poems by Donaghy in *The New Poetry,* edited by Michael Hulse, David Kennedy, and David Morley (Tarset, U.K.: Bloodaxe Books, 1993), pp. 206–209;
"Reliquary," in *Real Cool,* edited by Niall MacMonagle (Dublin: Martello Books, 1994), p. 121;
"Caliban's Books," in *Emergency Kit: Poems for Strange Times,* edited by Jo Shapcott and Matthew Sweeney (London: Faber & Faber, 1996), p. 216;
Poems by Donaghy in *Penguin Modern Poets 11: Michael Donaghy, Andrew Motion, Hugo Williams* (London: Penguin, 1997), pp. 3–40;
"The Tuning" and "Caliban's Box," in *The Firebox: Poetry in Britain and Ireland after 1945,* edited by Sean O'Brien (London: Picador, 1998), pp. 414, 416;
"Shibboleth," "Liverpool," and "Reliquary," in *The Penguin Book of Poetry from Britain and Ireland since 1945,* edited by Simon Armitage and Robert Crawford (London: Penguin, 1998), pp. 374–376;

Michael Donaghy (courtesy of the author)

"My Report Card," in *Strong Words: Modern Poets on Modern Poetry,* edited by W. N. Herbert and Matthew Hollis (Tarset, U.K.: Bloodaxe Books, 2000), pp. 423–424;
"Machines" and "My Flu," in *Staying Alive: Real Poems for Unreal Times,* edited by Neil Astley (Tarset, U.K.: Bloodaxe Books, 2000), pp. 81, 200.

SELECTED PERIODICAL PUBLICATIONS–
UNCOLLECTED: "Criticism and Hedonism," review of Dana Gioia, *Can Poetry Matter? Poetry Review,* 83, no. 2 (Summer 1993): 75–76;
"A Defence of Breathing," review of *A Formal Feeling Comes,* edited by Annie Finch, *Poetry Review,* 85, no. 1 (Spring 1995): 69–70.

Michael Donaghy has been called the best-kept secret in American poetry. Though his work is little known in the United States, where he was born and lived until the age of thirty, Donaghy is one of the most original, influential, and respected younger poets in England. Sean O'Brien, poetry critic for the London Sunday *Times* (1 May 1994), has called him "one of the half dozen contemporary poets whose work is essential reading." Donaghy's stature derives in part from his versatility: he has shown equal facility with the techniques of formal and free verse, and lyric and dramatic poetry.

The son of Patrick and Eveline Sheehy Donaghy, Michael John Donaghy was born in the Bronx, New York, on 24 May 1954. His father was a machinist in a factory that made printing presses, and his mother worked as a hotel maid before leaving her job to care for Michael and his sister, Patricia. Both parents grew up in Ireland–his father in Belfast and his mother in Tralee. They immigrated to the South Bronx in 1949. The family returned to Ireland when Michael was one year old and lived there for three years in his parents' native cities but eventually moved back to New York. The part of the South Bronx where the family lived had once been predominantly Irish, and in the 1920s and 1930s, the heyday of Irish traditional music, it was known as the "Reel Factory." But during Michael's childhood the area was a poor African American and Puerto Rican neighborhood, and the family was part of a small white minority.

Violence was commonplace, and sometimes it touched people Michael knew. He survived, he has said in interviews, by keeping his head down and staying off the streets. In the poem "A Repertoire," Donaghy describes the South Bronx in the 1960s and 1970s as a place where "every night the skies were pink with arson." Such an environment seems unlikely to inspire the controlled and elegant formal verse for which Donaghy later became known. Yet, some of his best poems are set in the South Bronx in its most dangerous, crime-ridden era, recalling with sympathy and without melodrama or sentimentality the people Donaghy knew there as a child and adolescent. In an interview with composer John Wall in 1996 (published in *Verse* in 1997), more than a decade after he immigrated to England, Donaghy remarked that he still dreams about the Bronx, and indeed his poems set there have a haunting dream-like quality.

Though neither parent had much formal education (his father left school at fifteen), the Donaghy home was a cultured one. There were always books around the house, including anthologies of poetry in which Michael remembers first encountering the works of such poets as Dylan Thomas. Michael's autodidact father enjoyed reciting poetry. In addition, both parents played Irish music, and his mother sang. Michael's twin passions for poetry and music thus were nurtured early. Many of his poems, particularly in his second collection, *Errata* (1993), center on music–Irish music, blues, and Greek folk music–and he has worked for many years as a musician, performing both Irish traditional music and jazz. While his study and performance of music have not influenced the form of his poems in any direct way, the musician often appears in his work as a metaphor for the artist, who attempts to render a chaotic world in a way shapely and true. In discussing his poems, Donaghy often reaches for musical analogies; in a 1998 interview with Conor O'Callaghan, Donaghy explained his use of metrical substitutions, for example, by comparing a roughening of poetic rhythm to "the way that a drummer 'drops a bomb.'" And he has observed that both traditional music and formal poetry rely on traditional structures–the jig, for instance, or the sonnet–that impose certain constraints on their composers while simultaneously inciting the imagination and leaving room for infinite variation.

Donaghy received his B.A. in English at Fordham University in 1976 and entered the Ph.D. program in literature at the University of Chicago in 1977, receiving an M.A. two years later. But his skeptical intelligence and independence made him something of an outsider, and he left without completing work for a doctorate. Donaghy quickly grew disillusioned with literary theory when he realized that many of his colleagues in the doctoral program hated literature and were actually contemptuous of living writers. (In his interview with Wall he commented that saying he started a Ph.D. in English because he loved poetry "is like saying I studied vivisection because I loved dogs.") Perhaps Donaghy's most valuable experience during this time was serving as editor of the *Chicago Review*. He enjoyed the excitement of discovering new talent and becoming acquainted with the full compass of contemporary poetry.

Donaghy immigrated to England in 1985. Since 1986 he has lived in north London with his partner, Maddy Paxman, working as a musician and a teacher. A chapbook, *Slivers,* appeared from Thompson Hill in Chicago in 1985, but Donaghy's three full-length collections have all been published in England. Since 1988 he has held part-time positions as a tutor at several universities, including Birkbeck College, University of London, and City University, London.

Donaghy's Irish ancestry, his American birth, and his immigration to England give him access and claim to three major and potentially conflicting literary traditions. He defined his heritage in the 1997 *Verse* interview as "Irish, proletarian, and Catholic," noting that these three facets of his background are inescapable. He expresses admiration for Irish poets, from William But-

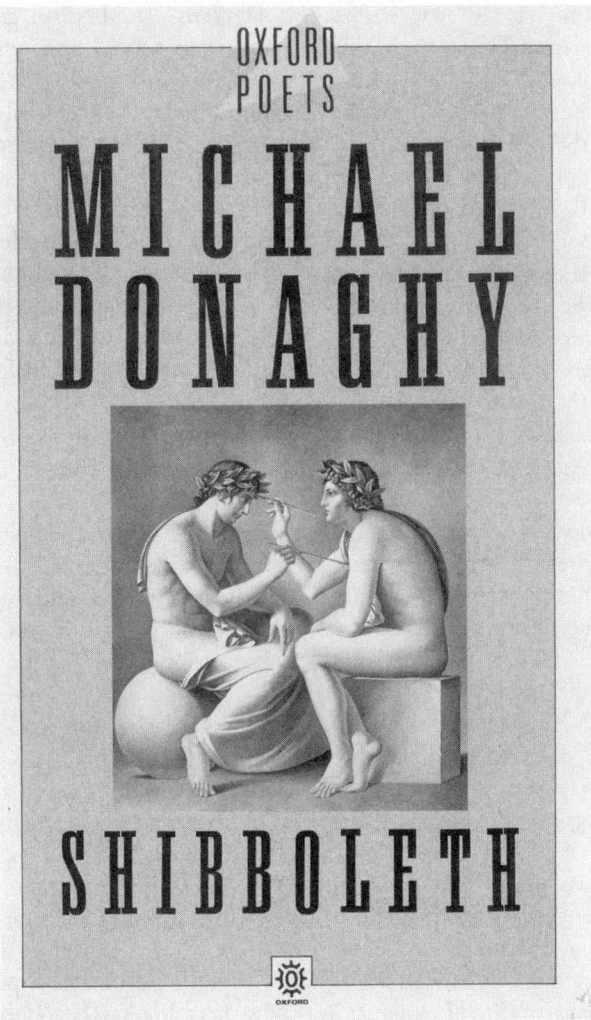

Paperback cover for Donaghy's first book-length collection of poems; the title poem won second place in the 1987 National Poetry Competition in England (Thomas Cooper Library, University of South Carolina)

ler Yeats to Seamus Heaney, Derek Mahon, and Paul Muldoon, and describes their influence as liberating. Yet, he is resistant to nationalism in any form, and he has never pursued an Irish poetic identity for himself in any programmatic way. Similarly, Donaghy has never aspired to be the next "New American Voice," and he seems relieved to have escaped, via immigration, some of the pressures of American literary nationalism. According to his *Verse* interview, his mixed heritage makes Donaghy feel "a bit of a trespasser everywhere," yet it also fosters personal and artistic independence. Donaghy's aesthetic freedom is reflected in the healthy eclecticism of his verse, which is open to a variety of competing influences and which experiments with diverse forms (from the prose poem to the villanelle, for example) and genres (from the traditional love lyric to the dramatic monologue).

Donaghy's first full-length collection, *Shibboleth,* was published by Oxford University Press in 1988. The previous year, the title poem had taken second place in the National Poetry Competition. Although almost all of the poems were lyrics, the book showed that, like his new countryman James Fenton, Donaghy had the rare ability to write both astute, sharp-witted political poems and fresh, affecting love poems. By any measure, the book was an impressive debut, winning both the prestigious Whitbread Poetry Prize and the Geoffrey Faber Memorial Prize for poetry. In general, critics were favorably impressed. In *Poetry Review* (Spring 1989) poet Glyn Maxwell praised Donaghy's "skill with exact and surprising perceptions," calling *Shibboleth* "an exercise in chilled and nervy precision" that included "wild successes," even as Maxwell found some fault with the formal poems in the book.

In *TLS: The Times Literary Supplement* (1–7 December 1989) Bernard O'Donoghue praised Donaghy's "telling, unhectoring political parables" and his willingness to take on large subjects. Although O'Donoghue felt that in the end the book did not fully plumb its ambitious themes and evaded some of the ethical and personal concerns that it raised, he called *Shibboleth* a debut of "much promise."

The personal lyrics and the political parables in *Shibboleth* are connected by their concern with the power—at once perilous and miraculous—of language. The book includes many poems concerned with the nature of art and the role of the artist. The opening poem, "Machines," which became one of Donaghy's most quoted, establishes this theme, which is explored with variations throughout the book. "Machines" begins with an unexpected analogy, reminiscent of the love poems of John Donne, between courtly music and a modern machine: "Dearest, note how these two are alike: / This harpsichord pavane by Purcell / And the racer's twelve-speed bike." Donaghy implicitly attributes to the poet as well the "agility, desire, and feverish care" of bicyclist and harpsichordist, "Who only by moving can balance, / Only by balancing move." The remarkable love poem "Pentecost" is another *ars poetica* of sorts. "Though we command the language of desire," the speaker tells his lover, "The voice of ecstasy is not our own"—lines that sum up Donaghy's poetics, which depends for its effects both on the difficult balancing act of careful, precise craft and the exhilarating momentum generated by surrender to form. In "Pentecost," the literal "gift of tongues" enjoyed by two lovers—their intelligible words replaced with inarticulate cries of desire—is identified with the "amethyst uraeuses of flame" that descended on the apostles in Galilee, allowing them to speak languages they had never learned and reversing the curse of Babel. The uraeus—the sacred asp or cobra of ancient Egypt—is an apt image for the organ of language, the tongue, one that conveys both the sacredness and the danger of words.

Other poems—"Shibboleth" and "Analysand," for example—explore the ways in which language can betray and even kill. The former is spoken by a GI who memorizes American pop cultural trivia, such as baseball statistics and the first names of the Andrews sisters, to prevent being mistaken for an infiltrator. The latter has as its epigraph "Judges 12: 5–6," the verses to which the book title *Shibboleth* alludes. When the Israelites suspect a soldier of being an enemy Ephraimite in disguise, sent across the Jordan as a spy, they test him by making him say the code word "shibboleth," which Ephraimites cannot correctly pronounce. "Analysand" relates a dream about "Ephraim Herrero," a Mexican gang leader whom the speaker knew in school and whom he once both feared and admired but finally betrayed: "It was a kick to see him so afraid," he remembers having felt at the older man's trial. In the dream he is himself a fugitive, wading across a frozen stream. Trapped in a police searchlight, he finds himself stricken mute, as the ghostly shadow of Ephraim Herrero steps between him and the light. As O'Donoghue noted in his review, Donaghy's unifying theme throughout the book, reflected in this poem, is "the way language works as a system of acceptance or exclusion."

"Herrero" is Spanish for "blacksmith," linking "Analysand" with another of the strongest poems in the collection, "'Smith.'" The speaker begins by questioning why "a forger's nerve" seems required to develop a natural-seeming signature, recalling the way a nun had scorned his ornate childish scrawl as "affected." In the end, he remembers having brought a girlfriend to a hotel one blistering August night when he was twenty and having signed the register with names "practiced into spontaneity"—the comical, unlikely "Mr. and Mrs. Smith":

Dear friend, whatever is most true in me
Lives now and forever in that instant,
The night I forged a hand, not mine, not anyone's,
And in that tiny furnace of a room,
Forged a thing unalterable as iron.

"'Smith'" introduces a preoccupation that resurfaces in his later books. Throughout, Donaghy's work shows a fascination with "forging," both in the sense of making something—a signature, a name, an identity, a work of art—and of faking or counterfeiting. If our own real signatures or true identities are merely "a trick we learn to do consistently," while a fraudulent signature can "forge a thing unalterable as iron," then forging and forgery are not so different as they seem. Indeed, as Michael O'Neill has observed, this poem conveys Donaghy's belief that "the truest poetry may be the most feigning."

Donaghy's interest in the power of language to counterfeit as well as create is not always handled seriously. He is a poet of unusual tonal range, capable of writing tender love lyrics, acerbic political poems, and humorous verse. He confesses to a lifelong fascination with hoaxes, literary and otherwise. As a college student he once convinced a chapter of the Jung Society that North African gnostics believed all physical beings were three-dimensional hieroglyphics in an infinite divine text; he was delighted when this fabrication later appeared as sober fact in one of the papers of the society. *Shibboleth* includes one of Donaghy's earliest and most successful literary forgeries: a sequence of seven short poems purporting, in an elaborate mock-scholarly headnote, to be translations of the thirty-syllable *englynion* of "Sion ap Brydydd (d. 1360)," an unjustly neglected medieval Welsh poet. While the form—a kind of Welsh haiku—is a real one, Donaghy invented the poet and poems. He succeeded in convincing some critics that the poems were genuine translations and even won praise for them. Donaghy's *englynion* and his pleasure in jokes and spoofs reflect his tendency to view poetry as a game, and a spirit of playfulness lightens even his darkest and most philosophically challenging poems.

The poems in *Shibboleth* are unusually varied in form as well as in style, tone, and genre. The book includes several skillful, even virtuosic, poems in traditional fixed forms. One of the best of these is the villanelle "Khalypso," which features a repeated line modulated with unusual subtlety. The villanelle's first refrain—"Cast off old love like substance from a flame"—begins as the nymph's imperative to Odysseus to forget Penelope and his old life in Ithaca. But by the end, this line evolves into an acknowledgment that Khalypso herself is among all that Odysseus, her "old love," has "cast off" in preparing to embark again for home. The book also includes two deft sonnets, "Auto da Fé" and "The Present," the form of the latter disguised by being printed in nonrhyming two-line stanzas. But the collection includes many free-verse poems as well, and—probably the largest category—poems in nonce forms or poems that draw on formal elements but not in a thoroughgoing and consistent way. "Cadenza," for example, is mainly but not entirely loose blank verse, and the antiheroic "Remembering Steps to Dances Learned Last Night," which presents Odysseus's return from the perspective of a young Ithacan goatherd, begins in dactylic pentameter—"Massive my heart, the heart of a hero, I knew it"—but then modulates into strongly rhythmic free verse. Donaghy has claimed Richard Wilbur and Anthony Hecht as influences, and his affinities with them are obvious in the wit and gracefulness of his poems and in their concern with the poet as maker and conscious shaper of language. Yet, Donaghy's forms and meters are rougher, his surfaces less elegantly polished, than those of older formalists of the mid twentieth century, reflecting his fascination with colloquial language and with presenting the minds and voices of ordinary people.

Because he is known for his facility with form, Donaghy is often asked whether he considers himself a "New Formalist." This question is reasonable, because, like Donaghy, the American New Formalists tend to be interested in popular as well as high culture and to use accessible, colloquial diction. Although in his criticism he has written appreciatively of the chief practitioners of New Formalism—Dana Gioia and Timothy Steele, for example—Donaghy has never identified with the American return to form and narrative. Just as he resists declaring allegiance to any single literary tradition, he also refuses to align himself with any literary schools, which he regards both as arbitrary public-relations ploys and as constraints on any serious poet's creative freedom. In addition, Donaghy's expatriate status fosters his sense of detachment from New Formalism. Because free verse has never enjoyed the sort of hegemony in the British Isles that it has in America since the 1960s, writing formal verse does not have the force in England of a conscious act of defiance or rebellion, as it does in the United States; and the American New Formalists have largely defined themselves as rebels against the free-verse establishment.

Finally, Donaghy regards his poetic practice as distinct from, and perhaps incompatible with, New Formalism. In his interview with Wall, Donaghy argued that he is "trying to do something very different with form." He explained that he sees himself as being more concerned than Gioia, Steele, and other New Formalists with "the unconscious effect of form on the poet." Whereas New Formalist manifestos have tended to stress the importance of an apprentice poet's mastering form and craft, Donaghy views the same relationship in terms of negotiation and often—on the poet's side—of surrender: "You have to compromise what you originally intended to say—which is always more likely to be full of self-deception, prejudice, and cliché—and it's in that negotiation that discovery takes place." In an article for *Poetry Review* (Spring 1995) on the anthology *A Formal Feeling Comes,* edited by Annie Finch, Donaghy noted that American women poets working in form are the poets who have placed special emphasis on the pleasures and rewards involved in accommodating to the demands of a form—on form as serendipity rather than mastery. In adjusting their original ideas and intentions to the requirements of a resistant medium, poets discover deeper truths than they knew existed and experience what once was called the presence of the Muse. To the extent, then, that Donaghy feels sympathy with New Formalism, it is primarily with the poetics of the female practitioners of the school.

Donaghy's second collection, *Errata,* appeared in 1993, also from Oxford University Press. The book shows the poet extending his already impressive formal and thematic range. *Errata* includes poems of even greater lyric grace than those in *Shibboleth*—for example, "Cruising Byzantium," an elegant love poem in rhymed iambic pentameter, and the opening poem, "Held," which alternates lines of dactylic pentameters and tetrameters:

Paperback cover for Donaghy's 1993 collection of poems, many of which show the influence of his experiences as a musician (Thomas Cooper Library, University of South Carolina)

> Not in the sense that this snapshot, a girl in a garden,
> Is named for its subject, or saves her from ageing,
> Not as this ammonite changed like a sinner to minerals
> Heavy and cold on my palm is immortal,
> But as we stopped for the sound of the lakefront one morning
> Before the dawn chorus of sprinklers and starlings.

The poem contrasts four tangibles that symbolize love and promise to suspend time—a photograph, a stone, a hieroglyph carved in lapis lazuli, and an Irish ring—with two finite moments shared by the speaker and his lover, moments that quickly passed and yet felt "held" (the title suggesting as well a suspension of breath, perhaps an embrace). In the final lines, he recalls a day that they "stood at the window together, in silence, / Precisely twelve minutes by candlelight waiting for thunder"—the twelve minutes reflected in the poem's twelve lines, half of them twelve syllables, and also suggestive of the hours on a clock face. The poem, like the remembered moments, at once marks and defies the passage of time, as do the delicately suspended feminine line endings, which defer a sense of closure.

But *Errata* is most significant in marking Donaghy's movement away from lyric into other modes. Formally traditional, measured and somewhat mannered in its diction, "Held" contrasts starkly with the most structurally experimental poem in the book, "True," a palimpsest of quotations—some taken verbatim from historical accounts, some "trued," or invented by the poet—on the subject of Captain Franklin's ill-fated expedition to find a Northwest Passage. Donaghy's development beyond the lyric is also shown in some fine narratives, particularly "City of God," a quietly affecting poem about a mentally ill young man who fails out of seminary and returns to the Bronx, consumed with the past and insisting that the real reason he has returned is to find "the secret order of the world." Walking through familiar streets, he associates each place he passes with the memory of someone or something gone, as once he had memorized the order of the Mass by associating its elements with the columns, statues, and transepts of a church:

> Here was Bruno Street where Bernadette
> collapsed, bleeding through her skirt
> and died, he had heard, in a state of mortal sin;
> here, the site of the bakery fire where Peter stood
> screaming on the red hot fire escape,
> his bare feet blistering before he jumped;
> and here the storefront voodoo church beneath the el
> where the Cuban *bruja* bought black candles,
> its window strange with plaster saints and seashells.

Donaghy's experiments with dramatic verse, however, proved the most inventive and exciting of the collection. *Errata* includes an impressive variety of ambitious dramatic monologues, including "Ovation," spoken by Adolf Hitler in hell as he recalls his final days on Earth; "The Incense Contest," a blank-verse monologue addressed by an aristocrat of the imperial Japanese court to her foreign lover; "The Commission," set in Renaissance Rome and spoken by a metalsmith, hired by Pope Clement, who recalls how he avenged the murder of his brother; and "Signifyin' Monkey," spoken by the supervisor of a Chicago security firm who has a bizarre experience on his lunch break one day. Perhaps no other contemporary poet is as interested in giving, much less able to give, voice to men and women in such disparate personal and historical circumstances. Strongly influenced by Robert Browning, Donaghy's monologues often employ a loose, colloquial blank verse that has a distinctive texture for each speaker. "Are you awake, my sweet barbarian?" begins the courtly lady of the Heian dynasty. "Why you look as though you'd seen a ghost!" How completely different is the voice that addresses the reader in the equally arresting opening lines of "Signifyin' Monkey":

> O.K., I'll tell it, but only if you buy lunch.
> One summer I worked nights for Vigil-Guard,
> the Chicago security firm. The work was easy. . . .

This poem is particularly clever and fun, a disguised sestina (one with the usual stanza breaks elided) that uses its end words in unpredictable ways and as different parts of speech, managing to make this often-attempted but rarely mastered form look effortless.

Finally, *Errata* is notable for including an entire section of poems, titled "O'Ryan's Belt," on music and musicians. Especially memorable and moving is "A Repertoire," an elegy for an old Irish fiddler named Tom, who owned a Bronx bar called The Blarney Stone and who knew a seemingly inexhaustible store of melodies—whether traditional or invented ones, the speaker is never certain:

> "Play us one we've never heard before,"
> we'd ask this old guy in our neighborhood.
> He'd rosin up a good three or four
> seconds, stalling, but he always could.

One Easter Sunday, Tom suddenly insists that the speaker and his friends tape everything he can play: "'I gave you these. Make sure you put that down,' / Meaning all he didn't have to say." By the end of that summer, Tom has sold the bar to Puerto Ricans and has died soon after of cancer, but his songs have been preserved. As in "City of God," Donaghy manages to avoid either sentimentalizing or overdramatizing life in the neighborhood where he grew up. He depicts the Bronx vividly, grittily, and with touches of humor:

> All that summer we slept on fire escapes,
> or tried to sleep, while sirens or the brass
> from our neighbor's Tito Puente tapes
> kept us up and made us late for mass.
> I found our back door bent back to admit
> beneath the thick sweet reek of grass
> a nest of needles, bottlecaps and shit.

Two other poems in "O'Ryan's Belt"—"The Hunter's Purse" and "A Reprieve"—also center on the importance of recording and remembering Irish traditional tunes. "A Reprieve," a companion poem to "A Repertoire," recalls a Chicago police chief, Francis O'Neil, who cuts an unconventional deal with certain suspects. A flutist named Nolan, arrested for assault, who is willing to "play three jigs / slowly, so O'Neil can take them down," is allowed to go free. In the end O'Neil is seen in his "lamplit cell . . . / scratching in his manuscript like a monk / at his illuminations." Both Chief O'Neil and fiddler Tom—tough, streetwise, yet susceptible to beauty and lovers of art—can be seen as figures for the poet himself. Waiting until his second book to publish these poems was a wise decision, one that allowed Donaghy to attain some distance from the music and culture of his childhood and youth before transforming them into his own verbal art. Although some of the poems in *Errata* have autobiographical elements, the connection between the poet's life and his work is complex, its nature kept continually in question. While they draw in various ways on experience, his poems are never "confessional." In "Acts of Contrition," Donaghy satirizes the poets who offer up personal revelations and the readers who seek them: "There's you, behind the red curtain, / Waiting to absolve me in the dark . . . / I'm working on my confessional tone."

After the publication of *Errata,* Donaghy was awarded generous grants from the Ingram-Merrill Foundation and the Arts Council of England, and in 1994 he was among twenty poets under forty years old selected for the controversial "New Generation Poets" promotion. This collaboration involved various poetry publishers and a London public relations firm, Colman-Getty, to increase sales of contemporary poetry by giving younger poets heightened media exposure. Although Donaghy has since expressed ambivalence about his participation—and his energetic reading and teaching schedule made him less in need of the extra attention than were some of the other poets chosen—the associated publicity probably did gain him new readers. But *Errata* did not win any of the big poetry prizes, and although its reception was mainly favorable, this second collection received less notice from critics than the first. Michael Hulse, in *Poetry Review* (Summer 1993), speculated that Donaghy's active reading schedule was coarsening his verse, arguing that some poems in *Errata* seemed calculated to elicit the immediate gratification of audience laughter or applause. But he commended the energy, wit, and eloquence of the best poems in the book, singling out "City of God" for special praise. One of the most appreciative reviews appeared in *TLS* (2 July 1993), in which Tim Dooley wrote, "The delicate balances displayed here—between tradition and innovation, between improvisation and formal structure, between notions of art reflecting or rising above its surroundings—all serve to make the once-fashionable debate in American poetry between 'the raw' and 'the cooked' look rather trite. At his best, Donaghy has both the musicality of Richard Wilbur and the engagement with experience of George Oppen."

The stylistic range that favorably impressed some critics struck others, however, as evidence of capriciousness or immaturity. Neil Powell, writing on Donaghy in *The Oxford Companion to Twentieth-Century Poetry in English* (1994), observed that "a poet who tries on so many suits of clothes is always in danger of looking like a coat-hanger"; and in an introduction to a selection of Donaghy's poems, *Poetry Review* (Spring 1994) similarly noted that Donaghy's "restless trying on of styles between the poles of streetlore and ornate, mannered narrative" had been censured by some critics. Donaghy himself echoed this recurrent criticism in another of his forgeries. Several times, in interviews and in writing, he has cited the judgments of a hostile critic of his own invention, "Florence Olsen." In a prose piece titled "My Report Card"—in the anthology *Strong Words* (2000)—he quotes Olsen as having disparaged, in a made-up journal called *Hierophant,* "a fidgety affectation of style after style which suggests that unlike more mature poets of his generation, Donaghy has not yet found his voice." By ventriloquizing this critical judgment, Donaghy at once humorously accepts the criticism and questions its premises. His entire body of work to date is an interrogation and a sly undermining of the notion that all poets are, or should be, on a perpetual quest for a single, "authentic" voice.

Donaghy's first two books allowed him to launch and develop an unusually active career as a freelance teacher and reader of his work. Though his witty, philosophically subtle poems appeal to highly educated readers—in 1999 he had the honor of being made a Fellow of the Royal Society of Literature—Donaghy is the antithesis of an "academic" poet in the American sense. He has never held a permanent position on a university faculty, and he has reached out to a general audience in a way that most of his American contemporaries, placed in a ghetto within the academy, can only envy. He has taught graduate workshops in poetry writing, as many poets in the United States do, but he has also designed poetry workshops for school librarians and for dyslexic children. In his position as Creative Reader-in-Residence for the Poetry Society in 1998-1999, he organized discussions of poetry designed to revive its appeal and pleasure for people whose enjoyment of the art had been tainted by the overly cerebral approach taken in schools. In the same capacity he produced an unconventional Poetry Society monograph, *Wallflowers: A Lecture on Poetry with Misplaced Notes and Additional Heckling* (1999), in which he invites his audience to a fresh consideration of his art through such diverse means as digressions, anecdotes, quotations from a wide range of canonical and contemporary poetry, photographs, marginal commentaries in which the reader interrupts the text, and diagrams of Irish dance steps, sign language, poem structures, and mathematical principles.

Donaghy's goal as an advocate for poetry—his own and that of others—is to lift it from the page, giving it life in the voice and body of the reader, much as Irish traditional dancers incarnate the music to which they move. He is a charismatic reader of his own poems, which he recites from memory, and his performances often combine music and poetry. In addition to his work as a musician—he has recorded a CD with the jazz band Lammas and another with composer John Wall—Donaghy has worked in nonprint media in other ways. In collaboration with director Miranda Pennel and actress Fiona Shaw, he made a short film, *Habit,* which was awarded first prize at the 1997 Festival Internacional de Cine i Video in Valencia, Spain. He also frequently comments on poetry for a variety of BBC Radio literary programs, and he has made television appearances on such programs as BBC2's "The Late Show" and "Poetry Nation." He thus enjoys an influence and an audience well beyond the confines of the universities where he often reads and teaches.

Donaghy's third collection, *Conjure*, published in 2000, simultaneously deepens and extends both his work in the lyric mode and his experiments with narrative and drama. Formally, the book marks a shift away from rhymed metrical poems toward unrhymed free verse, though Donaghy's free verse is always carefully crafted and often, like T. S. Eliot's variable meter, approaches and retreats from an iambic pentameter norm. *Conjure* is at once Donaghy's most narratively and dramatically ambitious collection and his most personal book.

Conjure opens with an epigraph from William Shakespeare, Horatio's words to Hamlet upon seeing the ghost of King Hamlet: "It beckons you to go away with it / As if it some impartment did desire / To you alone." Donaghy thus immediately introduces the two interrelated central themes of the book. The speaker's search for his lost father is a running motif that unifies and frames the book, from the opening group of poems to the final ones. In addition, the book is concerned with the ways in which a poet, like a magician, uses language to summon spirits from the past. In "Not Knowing the Words" the dead father is an old priest of sorts, one who "magicked his blood to bourbon and tears" after his wife's death and who has left his son an old overcoat redolent of his stifling grief and his inability to share it: "Am I talking to him now, as I get it out / And pull its damp night down about my shoulders? / Shall I take up the task, and fill its tweedy skin?" In the long narrative poem "Mine," the speaker is a contemporary Theseus who enters the labyrinth of an abandoned coal mine to confront, in its center, a once fearsome monster now decrepit and blind, confined to "an airless room of baby food and wheelchairs / where the nurse arrives through muslin-filtered light / to hoover, plump, switch off Columbo, / and bring to the ancient bullheaded bastard its bedpan." In the speaker's final nightmare vision, the father-minotaur refuses to recognize him as his son, ordering him to return to the upper world, where no Ariadne—reader, or lover—holds the other end of the "diver's air hose" he has unreeled behind him.

Perhaps the most impressive of the poems exploring father-son relationships is "Caliban's Books," in which the speaker attempts to call up his father's ghost by the spell of a beloved old family story. The son imagines the time his father was chosen, at age fourteen, to play Caliban in the school play—chosen for this role because, as he liked to say with deadpan humor, "I was the handsomest boy at school." To re-create this memory is not easy, the speaker notes with similar wry wit, as he is in possession of only half of the spell "and I won't be born for twenty years." Holding his father's yellowed old paperbacks, each a "seachanged bouquet" covered with marginalia, he makes two false starts, but as in a fairy tale, the third time proves the charm. The resolution of the poem is both unexpected and affecting, as the spell calls up not a schoolboy playing Caliban but the creature himself, belowdecks on a ship pulling into the port of Naples but "dreaming of a distant island":

> The moment comes. It slips from the hold
> and knucklewalks across the dark piazza
> sobbing *maestro! maestro!* But the duke's long dead
> and all his magic books are drowned.

By a surprising and effective reversal, in the end the son implicitly assumes the role of Caliban, mourning for his lost master and the master's books of magic, their spells unrecoverable after all. The combination of humor and emotional power—the first not deflecting, as sometimes in his earlier poems, but deepening into and enhancing the second—is characteristic of Donaghy's most mature work.

In "Haunts," the final poem of the volume, when a father again addresses his son, his message this time is an unexpectedly consoling one: "Don't be afraid, old son, it's only me," a line also quoted in the epigraph of the book. In the context of the earlier poems, "Haunts" seems to summon the poet's lost father from the dead and give him voice. No longer either pitiable or monstrous, he now speaks with a matter-of-fact domestic intimacy and love. But the poem can also be read as addressed from the poet to his own son, Ruairí Tomas, who was born to Donaghy and Maddy Paxman in 1996 and to whom *Conjure* is dedicated. "Haunts" thus brings the volume full circle—from a preoccupation with filial memories, duties, regrets, and griefs to an identification with the paternal role—and effects a satisfying sense of closure. The poems sound a more personal note than Donaghy had struck in his first two books, plumbing emotional territory he had before evaded. But as in the past, his mastery of craft allows him to handle challenging autobiographical material in a way that transcends the merely confessional.

Conjure also continues Donaghy's exploration of the possibilities of the contemporary dramatic monologue, including speeches by one carnival performer to another ("Celibates"), a prisoner to a hospital orderly ("Timing"), a guest to his hostess at a party ("Black Ice

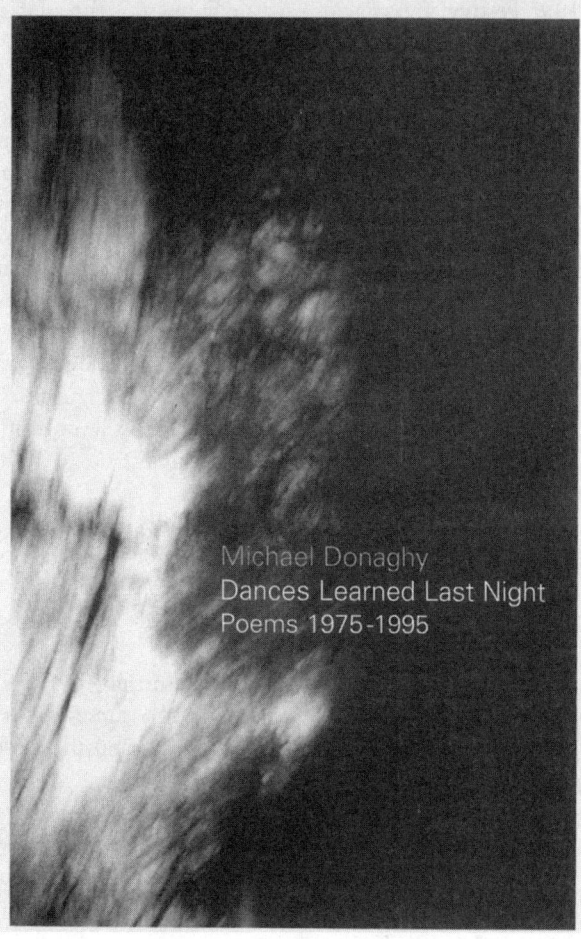

Paperback cover for Donaghy's retrospective collection, published in 2000 (Bruccoli Clark Layman Archives)

and Rain"), a damned soul to a newcomer to hell ("Quease"), an ascetic monk to God ("Irena of Alexandria"), and a loquacious, irreverent Upper East Side doorman to an anonymous passerby ("Local 32B"). These poems offer all the familiar pleasures of the dramatic poems in *Errata,* each presenting a distinct, fully realized character. Though Donaghy's subjects are often dark—journeys to the underworld, for example, are a common motif, and elegies abound—the poems are enlivened throughout with the poet's distinctive sleight of hand and his humor.

In "Irena of Alexandria" a jealous ascetic resentful of the saintly Irena makes a sarcastic prayer thanking God for having humbled him and praising Irena's "miracles": "May sparrows continue to litter her shoulders, / children carpet her footsteps in lavender, / and may her martyrdom be beautiful and slow." In "Local 32B" a highly literate doorman—his short speech quotes or alludes to lines from F. Scott Fitzgerald, Yeats, and John Milton—recalls having hailed a taxi for Luciano Pavarotti,

getting no tip for his trouble but exacting this comic revenge: "Yessir, I put the tenor in the vehicle. / And a mighty tight squeeze it was." This monologue was probably less of an imaginative stretch than the others for Donaghy, who worked as a doorman in New York while he was in college—excellent training in psychology and sociology, one would think, for a future poet.

Unlike Donaghy's first two collections, *Conjure* was not published by Oxford University Press. In 1999 he had lost his publisher when Oxford, in a controversial and much-lamented move, jettisoned its entire poetry department. But Donaghy was able to place *Conjure* with Picador Press, and it has turned out to be his most celebrated collection yet, winning the Forward Poetry Prize—at £10,000 Britain's biggest contemporary poetry award—as the best volume of poetry published in Great Britain in the previous twelve months. In addition, *Conjure* was the Poetry Book Society choice for autumn 2000, was selected by Andrew Motion as his Book of the Year for the *London Financial Times,* and was a finalist for both the 2000 Whitbread Poetry Award and the T. S. Eliot Award. The early reviews have been correspondingly enthusiastic. The Forward Poetry Prize judges wrote of their choice: "These dark and magical poems wear their depth lightly–Donaghy draws you in with the skill of a conjuror to reveal something much more profound and dangerous." Writer and broadcaster Melvyn Bragg, commenting on *Conjure* for *The London Observer* (26 November 2000), offered lavish praise, saying that it includes "poems which are as deeply structured, as lucid, witty, and moving as Auden at his best." In the same *Observer* feature, novelist Helen Dunmore wrote, "It's seven years since Michael Donaghy last published a poetry collection. Here, after a magical interval, is *Conjure,* his best book yet. *Conjure* takes all the Donaghy virtues–wit, clarity, breathtaking control of rhyme and rhythm–and adds a new intensity of feeling."

In a time when the imperative to "find a voice" too often means that poets learn what they can do well and are satisfied to repeat the same performance again and again, Michael Donaghy has been willing to extend himself, to take on philosophical and aesthetic challenges, and to risk both vulnerability and failure. Given his range of achievements to date, one cannot predict how Donaghy's work and his career will continue to unfold. But they will certainly bear and reward watching. His diverse talents for formal and free verse, and for lyric, drama, and narrative; his ability to reach out to a broad audience via his teaching, reading, and musical careers; and his varied connections to the poetic traditions of both the United States and the British Isles make him an exceptionally important and influential poet, one who eludes the ready-made categories of the contemporary poetry world. One also hopes that eventually this expatriate American poet will win a large United States readership.

Interviews:

John Wall, "Michael Donaghy in Conversation with John Wall," *Verse,* 14, no. 1 (1997): 64–70;

Andy Brown, Interview with Michael Donaghy, in *Binary Myths* (Exeter, U.K.: Stride Publications, 1998), pp. 59–63;

Conor O'Callaghan, "Interview with Michael Donaghy," *Metre* (Ireland), no. 4 (Spring/Summer 1998): 75–84.

References:

Peter Forbes, "Talking About the New Generation," *Poetry Review,* 84, no. 1 (Spring 1994): 4–6;

Michael Hulse, review of *Errata, Poetry Review,* 83, no. 2 (Summer 1993): 67–68;

Michael O'Neill, "Michael (John) Donaghy," *Contemporary Poets,* edited by Thomas Riggs (Detroit: St. James Press, 1996), pp. 267–268;

Neil Powell, "Michael Donaghy," in *The Oxford Companion to Twentieth-Century Poetry in English,* edited by Ian Hamilton (Oxford & New York: Oxford University Press, 1994), p. 131.

Rhina P. Espaillat
(20 January 1932 -   )

Len Krisak
Stonehill College

BOOKS: *Lapsing to Grace: Poems and Drawings* (East Lansing, Mich.: Bennett & Kitchel, 1992);

Where Horizons Go (Kirksville, Mo.: New Odyssey Press, 1998);

Mundo y Palabra (The World and the Word), in *Walking to Windward: 21 New England Poets,* edited by Cicely Buckley (Durham, N.H.: Oyster River Press, 2001);

Rhina P. Espaillat, Greatest Hits: 1941-2001, edited by Jennifer Bosveld (Johnstown, Ohio: Pudding House, 2002);

Rehearsing Absence (Evansville, Ind.: University of Evansville Press, 2002).

OTHER: "The Pigeons," in *Riverside Poetry, 1953: Poems by Students in Colleges and Universities in New York City,* selected by W. H. Auden, Marianne Moore, and Karl Shapiro, introduction by Stanley Romaine Hopper (New York: Association Press, 1953);

Landscapes with Women: Four American Poets, edited by Gail White (Canton, Conn.: Singular Speech Press, 1999)–includes poems by Espaillat.

TRANSLATION: César Sánchez Beras, *Trovas del mar: Troves of the Sea,* translated by Espaillat and Len Krisak (Santo Domingo: Editora Búho, 2002).

Rhina P. Espaillat (photograph by Bryan Eaton, The Daily News, *Newburyport, Massachusetts)*

Rhina P. Espaillat occupies an unusual position in the movement generally designated as New Formalism. Like that of other, better-known formalists–such as Richard Wilbur, Anthony Hecht, James Merrill, X. J. Kennedy, and Donald Justice–Espaillat began her publishing career in the 1940s well before the New Formalist movement began. Her early work, though achieving considerable success in periodicals and occasionally gaining recognition for prize-winning individual poems, did not figure as a presence in American poetry until her first collection appeared in 1992. Her more or less continuous formalist career does refute the common misconception that free verse and other nonmetrical forms so dominated the period from roughly 1960 to 1990 that the only major work in meter and/or rhyme was being written by a handful of better-known "academic" poets. In this sense, she worked on, not alone, but quietly, while such academic or formalist verse as did manage to appear showed the public face of formalism.

Espaillat also represents a singular phenomenon in formalist practice. Alone among metrical poets, she is recognized for her true bilingual comprehension of the English- and Spanish-language poetic traditions–that is,

Dust jacket for Espaillat's second collection of poetry, which won the T. S. Eliot Prize (courtesy of the author)

she not only writes in and translates Spanish verse into English, but she also works in her native Spanish, creating original poems. Perhaps few poets among the figures of the New Formalism could be expected to have translated touchstone pieces by Robert Frost, for example, into another language, carrying over his expressive phonic qualities in English while at the same time creating independently successful Spanish versions.

Espaillat's belated recognition for work in book form, as for example her receiving the T. S. Eliot Prize (1998) and the Richard Wilbur Award (2001), along with her influential work on the West Chester University Poetry Conference faculty—a position crucial to the maintenance and promulgation of the New Formalism—has helped to place her in the forefront of a movement she never had to "join." She never "left" it.

Rhina Polonia Espaillat was born 20 January 1932 in Santo Domingo, Dominican Republic, to Homero and Dulce Maria Espaillat. Her father was secretary of the legation of the Dominican diplomatic mission in Washington, D.C., in the 1930s, and when his family was exiled by the Rafael Trujillo regime, he relocated to New York in 1939.

Espaillat's first five years in the Dominican Republic constituted a fundamental introduction to Spanish verse. She recalls, for example, composing her first poems in Spanish at the age of five, and in English by the age of eight. A particularly strong influence was her grandmother, herself a poet, who read to Espaillat and to other members of the extended family and to friends, inculcating a love of verse and music.

Moving to New York in 1939 and living on West Sixty-fifth Street in Manhattan, Espaillat absorbed English rapidly, a time recounted in her influential essay "Bilingual/Bilingüe," published in *Where Horizons Go* (1998). She was soon so proficient at verse that her high school English teachers sent off, unbeknownst to their pupil, some poems composed outside of class.

They were promptly accepted by *The Ladies' Home Journal* in 1947. At only sixteen, Espaillat was accepted for membership into the Poetry Society of America—an organization that later bestowed on her three separate prizes in their national competitions, in 1986, 1989, and 2000.

An uncollected piece from her juvenilia, "The Pigeons," was quoted in a feature article, "Teen-Age Poet Wins Honors," in the *New York Sun* (4 January 1950) and reprinted along with "The Pigeons" in *Riverside Poetry, 1953* (1953), an anthology of prize-winning college work. "The Pigeons" shows her characteristic metrical facility, domestic subject matter, detached yet sympathetic tone, simple diction, workable scale, semantic playfulness (in the pun on "scans"), and perennial themes of the necessity for love and the sanctity of family:

> A lady, proud in poverty,
> Fine but underfed,
> With wary and disdainful eye,
> Scans my gifts of bread.
>
> A cautious hop from sill to sill,
> A peck, a warning note—
> Love draws the lady back to fill
> Two small and raucous throats.

On 28 June 1952 Espaillat married World War II veteran and industrial arts teacher Alfred Moskowitz, and in 1953 she graduated from Hunter College, City University of New York (CUNY), with a B.A. in English literature. She then taught junior high school English from 1953 to 1954 and began to raise a family in 1954. A son, Philip, was born in that year, and a second son, Warren, in 1957. A third (foster) son, Gaston W. Dubois (born in 1952), joined the family in 1968.

Espaillat reentered the academic world by attending graduate school in education at Queens College, CUNY, from 1964 to 1965, taking her M.S.E. in 1965. Following receipt of this degree, she taught high school English at Jamaica High School, Queens, from 1965 to 1980.

Much of her poetic activity slowed or even ceased altogether in this period, but she ended her teaching career in 1980 and began to renew her engagement with verse by helping found the Fresh Meadows Poets (Queens), conducting adult poetry workshops and teaching poetry classes for retired teachers at the United Federation of Teachers Outreach Center. With this renewed activity came more periodical publication and recognition. Her work began appearing in anthologies from 1990 on.

In 1990 Espaillat and her husband moved to Newburyport, Massachusetts, and in 1992 her first collection, *Lapsing to Grace: Poems and Drawings,* appeared. It includes work in both English and Spanish. It deals, moreover, with what must be considered typical themes and characteristic subject matter, usually in meter and often in fixed forms, such as sonnets and villanelles.

Espaillat's work shows a remarkable continuity from her first book to her most recent, *Rehearsing Absence* (2002). The homely domestic details of a life lived through the kitchen window, in the garden, at the family reunion, or by the observation of the modestly scaled, constantly yield vivid metaphors, colloquial syntax counterpointed off traditional meters, and a fairly resilient, if somewhat careful, affirmation in the face of metaphysical doubt and earthbound despair.

Espaillat's work does not shrink from the world. In "Incident" (a villanelle about a subway panhandler), the speaker seeks "escape," but only to a seat slightly farther away. When "dare not" struggles with "ought," the result is a moment of distress disguised as equipoise:

> and what there is to think, God knows I've thought.
>
> A stranger asked me for a coin today;
> I took another seat and looked away.

In "Slum Church" a descriptive sonnet settles into meditation, as a gray granite angel feeds a dove (one of the ubiquitous pigeons of the city slum, dressed up in religious nomenclature), "as if remembered love / warmed" you. The "Maker's grace" flows through the human mason's hand to create compassion—but a stony compassion.

With "Miscarriage," human loss disappears as the speaker speculates on the "pure alien form" of the soul let loose. The speaker in "Winter Beach" reaches much the same conclusion when a couple questions their "oddly tinged" joy at what remains whole (some shells), while lovers, still "clenched" and "pulsing life," stand in for all that the universe will eventually "shatter."

Critical commentary on Espaillat is not yet extensive, so assessment must proceed primarily on a small number of periodical pieces or casual reviews. With *Where Horizons Go,* her second collection, one must remain content to begin with the considered reflection of X. J. Kennedy, the judge who awarded the book the T. S. Eliot Prize: "common experience" is examined with "keen intelligence," again with the metrical and rhyming mastery of the work affirmed. It is perhaps a sign of Espaillat's difficulties in receiving critical attention that Bill Christophersen's brief review of *Where Horizons Go* in *Poetry* (September 1999) mentions the work as her "first collection." However, he goes on to say that "she enriches it [English] with every line she

Paperback cover for Espaillat's 2002 collection of poems, praised by some critics for their technical mastery (courtesy of the author)

writes" and that behind banal titles "fireworks" lurk. He praises her "unsentimental empathy" and ability to leverage "simple images and lackluster situations into epiphanies."

Where Horizons Go represents an extension of the concerns in *Lapsing to Grace*, with perhaps a slightly more tentative stance on religious acceptance. In her signature form of the villanelle, Espaillat ends "Song," which employs a fluid alliteration and assonance miming a woman's Alzheimer's-induced ideational slippage, with a reference to "dark forgiving waters [that] wait." But the perspective of the speaker suggests forgiveness through blessed oblivion, not forgiveness of human weakness or fault or sin.

In *Landscapes with Women* (1999) Espaillat comments subtly on the pressures felt by a poet resigned to draw her themes and subjects from the mundane elements of life—family, home, chores, and "rehearsing the absence" of the living. That the poem "Workshop" should have provided Espaillat with the title of the collection that won her the Wilbur Award in 2001 is not surprising when one sees the pertinent line in context. The speaker has been responding to an imagined questioner about where she has been:

> I've been setting the table for the dead,
> rehearsing the absence of the living,
> seasoning age with names for the unborn.
> I've been putting a life together, like
> supper, like a poem, with what I have.

But the wit of such work—"seasoning" age, for example—is no guaranteed defense against the charge of a cleansed world made too easy to accept and affirm. With Espaillat's fourth book, *Rehearsing Absence,* came the charge that in her work she eschewed the violent and the degrading, the disquieting and the evil. In Joseph Salemi's attack, "The Poetry of Nicey-Nice," he accuses Espaillat of being too "subjective," "emotionally revelatory," and attuned to the "tentative and the provisional." Salemi's charges of the elision of "serious conflict or contestation," of an evasion of anything "not in a tentative soft-focus," have been strongly countered by David Berman in "A Review of Joseph Salemi's Review of Rhina Espaillat's *Rehearsing Absence.*" Berman responds by accusing Salemi of misconstruing tone and failing to recognize disquieting and disturbing subject matter in the book. He points out Espaillat's technical mastery and charges Salemi with irrelevant biographical explanations of her work.

Espaillat's poetry continues to invest and enliven New Formalism with a true bilingual energy and with a high standard of intelligence, wit, sympathy, and technical mastery of prosody. In demonstration of this fact, her manuscripts continue to claim prizes: "Playing at Stillness" won the 2003 National Poetry Book Award sponsored by Salmon Run Press and Texas A&M University, and "The Shadow I Dress In" won the 2003 Stanzas Prize sponsored by David Robert Press. Her persisting pedagogical influence, as evidenced by work on the faculty of New Formalism's premier proselytizing forum at West Chester University, will undoubtedly contribute to the invigoration of the movement.

References:

Peter Berkrot, "Waltzing Towards Art," *Merrimack Valley Sunday,* 27 September 1992, pp. 12–14;

David Berman, "A Review of Joseph Salemi's Review of Rhina Espaillat's *Rehearsing Absence,*" *Able Muse* (8 March 2002) <http://www.ablemuse.com>;

Bill Christophersen, "Spruce but Loose: Formalism in the Nineties," *Poetry* (September 1999): 345–351;

"Couple Relocate Portable Careers," *Newburyport Daily News,* 26 April 1991, p. B1;

Joseph Salemi, "The Poetry of Nicey-Nice," *Expansive Poetry & Music Online* (March 2002) <http://www.n2hos.com/acm/>;

Silvio Torres-Saillant and Ramona Hernández, *The Dominican Americans* (Westport, Conn.: Greenwood Press, 1998).

Frederick Feirstein
(2 January 1940 –   )

T. L. Ponick
Washington Times

and

F. S. Ponick
Music Educator's National Conference (MENC)

BOOKS: *The Family Circle* (London: Davis-Poynter, 1973);
Survivors (New York: David Lewis, 1974);
Walking Away (Advent, 1975);
Manhattan Carnival: A Dramatic Dialogue (Woodstock, Vt.: Countryman Press, 1981);
Fathering. A Sequence of Poems (Cambridge, Mass.: Applewood Books, 1982);
Family History, in *QRL Poetry Series*, volume 26, edited by Theodore and Renée Weiss (Princeton, N.J.: Quarterly Review of Literature, 1986);
City Life (Brownsville, Ore.: Story Line Press, 1991);
Ending the Twentieth Century, in *QRL Poetry Series*, volume 34, edited by Weiss and Weiss (Princeton, N.J.: Quarterly Review of Literature, 1995);
New and Selected Poems (Brownsville, Ore.: Story Line Press, 1998).

PLAY PRODUCTIONS: *Simon and the Shoeshine Boy*, New York, Chelsea Theater Center, 1966;
Harold and *Sondra*, New York, Provincetown Playhouse, 1967; *Sondra*, revised as *John Wayne Doesn't Hit Women*, New York Theater Ensemble, March 1972; *Harold*, revised as *The Family Circle*, Los Angeles, Theater Rapport, 1974;
The Exhumation and Installation of Robert E. Lee Haines, New York, Actors Studio, 1971;
Masquerade, Washington, D.C., A.S.T.A., April 1974;
The Children's Revolt, book and lyrics by Feirstein, music by Gregory Sandow, Milwaukee, Theater X, Spring 1976;
Dr. Rush Pays a House-Call, Massachusetts, Berkshire Theater Festival, Summer 1976;
Manhattan Carnival, New York, The Medicine Show, 1985;
The Psychiatrist at the Cocktail Party, New York, The Medicine Show, 1991;

Frederick Feirstein (from Mark Zadrozny, ed., Contemporary Authors Autobiography Series, *volume 11, 1990)*

Innocence, book and lyrics by Feirstein, music by Gershon Kingsley, New York, Pulse Ensemble Theater, 1998.

PRODUCED SCRIPTS: *Midway* and *Regensburg/Schweinfurt*, television, *G. I. Diary*, CBS, 1978.

OTHER: "The Anti-Life," in *Contemporary Poetry,* edited by Theodore Weiss and Renée Weiss (Princeton: Princeton University Press, 1976);

"The Boarder" and "'Grandfather' in Winter," in *New York Poems,* edited by Howard Moss (New York: Avon, 1980);

"L'Art," in *Strong Measures: Poetry in Traditional Form,* edited by Philip Dacey and David Jauss (New York: Harper & Row, 1986);

"Celebrating," in *Arvon Foundation 1985 Anthology* (England: Southeby's and Duncan & Lawrie, Ltd., 1987);

Expansive Poetry: Essays on the New Narrative & The New Formalism, edited by Feirstein, introduction by Feirstein and Frederick Turner (Santa Cruz, Cal.: Story Line Press, 1989);

"Frederick Feirstein," in *Contemporary Authors Autobiography Series,* volume 11, edited by Mark Zadrozny (Detroit: Gale, 1990), pp. 73–86;

"Psychoanalysis and Creativity," in *Poetry After Modernism,* edited by Robert McDowell (Ashland, Ore.: Story Line Press, 1991);

"The Rune-Maker," "Mark Stern Wakes Up" (an excerpt from *Manhattan Carnival*), and "Mark Stern" (an excerpt from "The Psychiatrist at the Cocktail Party"), in *Rebel Angels: 25 Poets of the New Formalism,* edited by Mark Jarman and David Mason (Brownsville, Ore.: Story Line Press, 1996), pp. 30–35;

"Rhyme," in *Poetry After Modernism,* revised and expanded edition, edited by McDowell (Ashland, Ore.: Story Line Press, 1998);

"Psychoanalysis and Poetry," in *After New Formalism,* edited by Annie Finch (Ashland, Ore.: Story Line Press, 1999), pp. 179–187.

SELECTED PERIODICAL PUBLICATIONS—UNCOLLECTED: "The Comedy: Dreams, Associations, and Waking," *Shenandoah,* 20, no. 3 (Fall 1971): 56–66;

"From *Manhattan Carnival,*" *Kenyon Review,* new series, 2, no. 4 (Fall 1980): 1–13;

"From *Family Matters,*" *Ontario Review,* 15 (Fall–Winter 1981–1982): 65–72;

"Siddhartha Dove," *Salmagundi,* no. 55 (Winter 1982): 131–132;

"The Other Long Poem," *Kenyon Review,* new series (Spring 1983): 52–56;

"Blackout Holiday," *Ploughshares,* edited by Seamus Heaney, 10, no. 1 (Spring 1984): 65–66;

"From *To The Storm's End,*" in *Ploughshares,* edited by M. L. Rosenthal, 11, no. 1 (Spring 1991): 48–54;

"The Magic Kingdom," "Spectacle," "Manhattan Elegy," "Fin de Siecle," "Gravedona," "Stresa," "The Revolution," and "Peasant Carts," *Quarterly Review of Literature, 50th Anniversary Anthology,* edited by Theodore Weiss and Renée Weiss, 32–33 (1995) <http://www.princeton.edu/~qrl/poetry series.html>.

One of the founders of the Expansive poetry movement, Frederick Feirstein has championed the reestablishment of formal verse, verse narrative, and verse satire in American poetry–just the prescription, he feels, for bringing poetry back to the people and tearing it out of the rarified climate of academia where it has languished, self-referentially, for half a century. His own poetical works focus on the postmodern beauty and brutality of his native New York City, the obsessively sexual orientation of classic New York–style psychoanalysis, and the problem of Jewishness in American identity. His sense of outrage sets his work apart from the poetry of his quieter, more introspective academic colleagues in the New Formalist movement. Indeed, although he is considered one of America's foremost and most original New Formalist poets by those in the movement, Feirstein objects strongly to the ascendancy of that term over the broader intent of Expansive poetry. Feirstein, and earlier founders of the Expansive poetry movement such as Dick Allen, Frederick Turner, and Wade Newman, prefer the word "expansive" to describe a vigorous new poetry that not only employs traditional verse forms such as the sonnet and heroic couplet but also encourages a wide-ranging freedom of subject matter and promotes the creation of longer narrative poems, a former staple of English and American poetry. Feirstein has insisted on a clear and revolutionary break with establishment schools of academic poets who have rigidly enforced the notion that real American poetry could only be written in free verse that emphasized esoteric language and the primacy of the poet's sensations and personal feelings over the world outside. Feirstein wants to turn poetry outward once again, "expanding" it by abandoning the narcissistic obsessions of confessionalists and Language poets who typically prefer not to deal with the concerns of the public at large.

Of Eastern European Jewish stock, Frederick Feirstein was born on 2 January 1940 in New York City, the son of Arnold and Nettie Feirstein. His early years were spent growing up in a crowded cooperative apartment building in a teeming, multiethnic neighborhood on the Lower East Side of New York City. His boisterous extended family consisted of nine individuals with radically different personalities, including his pugnacious grandfather, a Polish immigrant. The colorful and sometimes violent stories they told one another deeply influenced Feirstein's later development as a playwright and a narrative poet.

As a child Feirstein was precociously artistic. A talented violinist, he played professionally in his teens with the Brooklyn All-City Orchestra and the Queens Symphony. He attended New York University (NYU) from 1956 to 1958, transferring to the University of Buffalo, where he earned a B.A. degree in English in 1960. Returning to NYU, he earned his M.A. in 1962. He married Linda Bergton in New York City on 9 June 1963.

When Feirstein was appointed an instructor in English at the University of Wisconsin–Milwaukee that year, the newly married couple relocated to the Midwest, remaining in Milwaukee until 1965. While in Wisconsin, Feirstein's interest in both poetry and theater grew—two threads that later united in his dramatic and satirical narratives. During this period, Feirstein began composing free-verse poetry, which was the current fashion, but also experimenting with meter and rhyme. In addition, he wrote several drafts of his first play, *Simon and the Shoeshine Boy,* which was eventually produced at the Chelsea Theater Center in New York in 1966.

To get closer to the pulsating New York theater scene, the Feirsteins next moved to Philadelphia, where Feirstein was appointed assistant professor of English at Temple University from 1965–1970. As a prolific poet and dramatist, Feirstein grew disenchanted with the English faculty, which seemed to him to disdain active creative writers, preferring to view the academic critic as significantly more important than the artist. Leaving Temple, Feirstein retreated to New York, driven by his love for the theater. He lectured on theater at the Continuing Education Division of New York University as well as the New School for Social Research, and he cofounded a theater for playwrights at the Manhattan Theater Club. His play *Harold* was produced at the Provincetown Playhouse in 1967 along with *Sondra,* a companion piece.

But to his dismay Feirstein found the New York theater scene as discouraging as the academic life he was leaving behind. Just as literature professors viewed the work of a creative writer as mere grist for the scholarly mill, the imperious theater directors of New York increasingly regarded the work of a playwright as scaffolding upon which to hang increasingly exotic directorial "interpretations" that usurped the author's original vision. Feirstein noted that directors and actors had a tendency to equate literary style and structure with authoritarian politics, viewing carefully honed language and plots as reactionary and oppressive. An advocate of formal dramatic structures, Feirstein was hitting a brick wall. Critics and directors were opposed to plot and the

Feirstein with his father, Arnold Feirstein, in Tompkins Square Park, New York City, circa 1943 (from Zadrozny, ed., Contemporary Authors Autobiography Series, *volume 11, 1990)*

dramatic line, just as professors and critics were becoming hostile toward the metrical line in poetry.

Feirstein was politically influenced at this time by his direct involvement with the American Committee to Keep Biafra Alive, which flourished during the Nigerian civil war. He was dismayed to see how the personal and the political were connected. This realization gave him a caustic perspective on political hypocrisy, including showy New York benefit parties, the main aim of which, it seemed to him, was to allow rich, shallow leftists to parade their beneficence in public while people continued to die halfway around the globe. Novelist Tom Wolfe dubbed this phenomenon "radical chic," and it was this kind of hypocrisy that Feirstein eventually satirized in his narrative poem "The Psychiatrist at the Cocktail Party."

During the early 1970s Feirstein realized that neither teaching nor working as a playwright would enable him to support a family. He and his wife decided to become psychotherapists, since psychotherapy was an area in which they had long held a deep interest. After a rigorous course of study, both eventually developed

Dust jacket for Feirstein's first book of poems, published in 1974 and selected by Choice, the magazine of the American Library Association, as one of two outstanding books of poetry for 1975–1976 (Bruccoli Clark Layman Archives)

successful practices. But during their long and extensive training Feirstein pressed on with playwriting and poetry, living on the financial edge, piecing together a living by writing film and television scripts and winning an occasional grant, including a Guggenheim Fellowship.

In 1973 *Harold* and *Sondra* were revised and published as *The Family Circle*. During this period Feirstein also began to write poetry in earnest, and his first book of poems, *Survivors*, was published in 1974. A collection of dramatic and narrative poems in meter, *Survivors* was selected by *Choice*, magazine of the American Library Association, as one of two outstanding books of poetry for 1975–1976. In this collection he first began to experiment with reviving the heroic couplet, a form he had begun to favor for narrative satirical poetry.

By the late 1970s Feirstein was building on his success, abandoning theater to concentrate entirely on poetry and eventually building his psychotherapy practice. He began to compose some of his major poetic works in this decade, including *Manhattan Carnival: A Dramatic Dialogue* (1981) and *Family History* (1986). Combining meter and rhyme with rough, colloquial diction, he dusted off the old forms favored by poets as diverse as Geoffrey Chaucer and Alexander Pope and revived them by giving them a modern spin. Theatricality, meter, rhyme, and the harsh thrust of satire united to give Feirstein's mature poetry an edginess frequently lacking in the university-workshop atmosphere.

Feirstein had believed that he was a lonely voice in the poetry world, but his feeling of isolation did not last. In 1979 he discovered that Frederick Turner and Ron Sharpe, who supported the work of poets writing in form, were reviving the venerable *Kenyon Review*. He contacted Turner, who was enthusiastic about the New Yorker's work. As a result, most of *Manhattan Carnival* was published in 1980 in the *Kenyon Review* (volume 2, number 4).

One of the earliest examples of Expansive poetry, *Manhattan Carnival* proved that the long narrative was still a robust vehicle for artistic expression and social commentary. In this narrative Feirstein mounts an open rebellion against Modernism, postmodernism, and confessional poetry, selecting a mock epic of 533 rhyming heroic couplets as his weapon of choice. It was a pathbreaking, satirical work, almost without precedent in the latter half of the twentieth century, a deliberate gesture of contempt toward what Feirstein viewed as the narcissistic, academic, confessional/free-verse establishment.

Feirstein's narrative unfolds in a series of apparently freestanding short lyrics well matched to the quick-cut lifestyle of New York. The gradual accretion of detail and the focus of Feirstein's camera lens derive from contemporary cinematic technique. But the concision imposed by the form distinguishes this poem from its longer fictional cousins.

Through the central intelligence of the hapless Mark Stern, the comic antihero of the poem, Feirstein criticizes the social excesses of New York eccentrics and their single-minded obsessions with self and sex–obsessions he later demolishes completely in "The Psychiatrist at the Cocktail Party."

Although it is a satire, *Manhattan Carnival* is filled with bravura passages, such as Stern's homage to New York City, which describes Manhattan in loving and telling detail:

> I need the antiseptic house next door,
> Its plastic shrubs, its missing thirteenth floor,
> Its glass door with its wooden coat of arms,
> Its lobby with its European charms;

Its French Provincial chairs, its Spanish chest,
Its walls with scenes of gypsy Bucharest,
Its German pewter mug and washing bowl;
Its elevators playing Barcarolle,
Its terraces where crones play solitaire
Or paint their toes and set their platinum hair,
Its rows of built-in air conditioning vents,
Its windows mirroring the tenements
Across the street, ruins of a better Spring,
Less lonely, rootless, modern, maddening.

In spite of his savage portrayal of New Yorkers in *Manhattan Carnival*, Feirstein's passion for his city shines through, further intensifying the ironic juxtaposition of joy and misery set in a conversational poetic language that any reader can easily understand.

Feirstein traces his involvement in what eventually became known as the Expansive poetry movement (a term attributed to poet Wade Newman) to 1981, when he, his new friend Frederick Turner, Dick Allen (a poet and writer), and Allen's writer-wife Lori met at the Mineta Tavern in New York to discuss what appeared to be the coalescing of a new direction in contemporary American poetry. Feirstein, Turner, and the Allens championed a return to form and endorsed narrative poetry over confessional free verse. The reclamation of narrative and exposition in poetry was in many ways more important to them at the time than the return of poetry to its metrical roots.

As the 1980s unfolded the Mineta Tavern group joined forces with Dana Gioia and poets in other parts of the country who shared similar interests. Although some disputed its working title, the new Expansive poetry movement proved to be a kind of umbrella that eventually encompassed the poets who became known as the "New Formalists," who supported a return to traditional meters and rhyme schemes while encouraging innovations within those forms and the creation of new forms; and "New Narrative" poets, who were attempting to reclaim the power and subject matter of narrative poetry, a tradition of medium-to-longer-length poems largely supplanted in the twentieth century by the confessional free-verse lyric.

Gioia introduced Feirstein to Robert McDowell and Mark Jarman, founders of *The Reaper,* a little magazine that polemicized in favor of formal poetry. That operation evolved into Story Line Press, a small publishing house devoted to the same cause. Story Line Press in 1989 published the first edition of a seminal collection of essays defining the new movement, titled *Expansive Poetry: Essays on the New Narrative & The New Formalism,* edited by Feirstein with an introduction by Feirstein and Turner. Part criticism, part polemic, and part manifesto, this volume set out to encourage the hoped-for revolt against Modernism and postmodern-

Feirstein and his son, David, in 1979 (from Zadrozny, ed.,
Contemporary Authors Autobiography Series,
volume 11, 1990)

ism, which held the American poetry establishment in an iron grip. Feirstein thought that Expansive poetry would create a new body of poetic work that would open up or "expand" into the world with a broad vision to differentiate it significantly from the currently prevailing type of poetry—primarily the inward turning, confessional free-verse lyric—encouraged in the academy to the exclusion of all other possibilities, save equally exhausting experiments, such as Language poetry.

During the 1990s Feirstein continued to publish his own hard-edged narrative and lyric poetry. In addition to *City Life* (1991), his *Ending the Twentieth Century* appeared in the 1995 *Quarterly Review of Literature* series, and *New and Selected Poems,* a retrospective anthology also including new poetry, was published in 1998.

Feirstein's narrative "The Psychiatrist at the Cocktail Party," taking up much of his *City Life* volume and subtitled "A Dramatic Poem," is a closet drama, going far beyond Mark Stern's adventures in *Manhattan*

Feirstein and his wife, Linda Bergton Feirstein, in 1987 (from Zadrozny, ed., Contemporary Authors Autobiography Series, *volume 11, 1990)*

Carnival. "The Psychiatrist at the Cocktail Party" carefully observes the unities of time, place, and action. The radical chic parties pioneered by the type of liberals whose hypocrisy had rankled Feirstein for years loosely inspire its meticulously constructed plot. The cocktail party of the title is an airily stupid upper-class bash held to raise funds for a Latin American leftist thug who would happily turn on his oblivious backers if he found them on his own turf. Feirstein's wickedly brilliant satire is a compelling hybrid that mates Rabelaisian bawdiness with the wit and concision of a Chaucer, a Pope, or a Jonathan Swift.

Feirstein's poem—actually an interlocking series of monologues—takes place at a Manhattan party thrown by Larry, a forty-something leisure-suit liberal. The sections of the poem are written in four- to six-line stanzas employing varied rhyme patterns, including but not limited to heroic couplets. The prevailing rhythm is iambic, but Feirstein mixes his forms to suit each character: the gold-digging former cheerleader locked in a loveless marriage with the obese but wealthy sausage maker; Leisure-Suit Larry, putting off his decent fiancée, Joyce, while eyeing up the "Meat King's" wife; the bogus generalissimo, in town trolling for money from rich closet leftists while romancing Joyce's drug-addicted son; and various other characters and hangers-on. The older and presumably wiser Mark Stern makes a cameo appearance. All dip and sway in a ghostly dance of death, a boozy, Pan-Cake made-up nightmare of loneliness and meaninglessness in which espousing a cause or embracing a way of life does not mean one has to believe in it or make a commitment.

Fear of commitment is the thread that connects the disparate elements of the narrative. In "The Psychiatrist's Epilogue" Ben, the psychiatrist, and Joyce, Larry's fiancée, consider running away to start a new life where they left off so many years before—before each married someone else and before the widowed Joyce fell into an increasingly shallow relationship with Larry. Ben raises the unanswered question of his generation:

> . . . last night, another life ago,
> We swore that we'd be young and simply go.
> But now that seems a gesture we have to make,
> Therapeutic, for our soul's or psyche's sake.
> You feel the same—to leave or not to leave,
> To rock and roll the moment that we grieve,
> Or else to find your son and me my wife,
> Return to an irrevocably altered life.
> What shall we do? says The Mentor to his Joyce:
> Be old or young again? What's your choice?

For Ben Struthers, the word "young" is synonymous with recklessness, with putting off choices and endlessly deferring maturity. "The Psychiatrist's Epilogue" is a poignant reminder that the Woodstock Generation, hardwired for hedonism and irresponsibility, remains frozen in time, unable to make commitments or life choices. Feirstein's partygoers are modern Hamlets, incapable of committing to anything unless disaster overtakes them—and then only reluctantly.

In the 1990s a narrative poet such as Feirstein had increasingly few comfortable options for publication. Most magazines, large and small, remained hostile to the long poem. As a partial response to this problem, Feirstein began to turn to the poetic sequence, a construct that was gaining in popularity as the last decade of the twentieth century drew to a close. (Indeed, Feirstein had already experimented with using the sequence back in his early volume *Survivors.*) Feirstein's *Ending the Twentieth Century,* published in the softbound poetry series of the *Quarterly Review of Literature,* is actually a pair of "sequences," a term favored by modern poets to describe a series of thematic poems strung together without the benefit of a linear narrative. *Ending the Twentieth Century* mourns the loss of 1960s idealism and innocence and anticipates an uncertain, somehow more brutalized future. The mood of these lyrics is elegiac and contemplative. "Song of the Suburbs," for example, begins with a declaration tinged with irony and doubt:

Paperback cover for Feirstein's 1991 volume, much of which includes his long narrative poem "The Psychiatrist at the Cocktail Party" (Bruccoli Clark Layman Archives)

> The prospect of an automatic life:
> Working from nine to five, dinner, then bed,
> Maybe a night or two with the wife;
> Watching t.v. or visiting the dead . . .
> That's what we rebelled against in youth.
> We were going to fix the world, set social trends
> In conscript dungarees. We possessed the truth.

The poet is ruefully aware of the falsity of these sentiments, realizing that all too quickly the rebellious youth of the 1950s and 1960s had become part of the problem, not the solution.

> Adolescents see things clearly, simply . . .
> Though we protest, we really are the enemy
> Like our parents. Truth is, we depress them . . .

While Feirstein, or his virtual protagonist, rebelled against and presumably escaped "the suburbs" of his childhood, he is now trapped in the suburbs of the mind numbed and compromised by the inevitable necessity of adapting to the way life always is. The problem is not that youth is wrong so much as that its idealism can never be fulfilled before it is defeated by an entropic sameness.

If there is an overarching fixation in Feirstein's poetry, it is his belief that the human species is highly resistant to long-term improvement. Given a chance, many people will return to beasthood at the least provocation, whether through a pogrom in Russia; genocide in Biafra, Cambodia, or Kosovo; religious and social conflict in Belfast or the Middle East; or tribal ethnic warfare in Manhattan. In "Mosaic," which appeared for the first time in his *New and Selected Poems*, characters from the Jewish and African American communities of New York City are at violent loggerheads over a racial incident that results in murder. The last lines of this four-part narrative poem sum up their confused attitudes succinctly in a monologue delivered by a pacifist Jewish character:

My father's eyes say *Shutup* but I can't
Help but be the future generation
And make good come from evil. I know it must,
Eventually. My books say so. Israel from Auschwitz.
You tell your demagogues, your hypocrites
What's stamped on every cent of this scared nation:
E Pluribus Unum, In God We Trust.

The abrupt line break between "must," and "Eventually" is telling. It forces the reader to pause between the two words and undercuts the pacifist's forced optimism. He tries again by declaring that his "books say so." But the reader can tell that even he is no longer entirely convinced by his own argument. Things fall apart in "Mosaic."

The remainder of *New and Selected Poems* is cobbled together from Feirstein's earlier books—some long out of print—including *Survivors, Manhattan Carnival, Family History, City Life,* and *Ending the Twentieth Century,* in addition to new poems such as "Mosaic." This book is the most comprehensive sampling of his work to date.

As the twenty-first century begins, Frederick Feirstein continues to defy the free-verse, purely lyric undertow that is beginning to reclaim some of the academic New Formalists. Never wholly a creature of the university system, Frederick Feirstein defies categorization in his work but also lacks the champions that an academic environment can create for a poet. Nonetheless, he has survived without them. He creates in his verse an unusual, teeming, urban world of eccentric characters, urban neuroses, and angst that crackles on the page as academic confessional verse cannot. His poetry asks many hard questions but answers few of them. In Feirstein's morally gray universe, some certainties and neatly resolved crises do not play a significant part. As a result he remains among the prickliest and most vital of the Expansive/New Formalist poets and the only twentieth-century poet who has had the courage to stake nearly his entire reputation on the dramatic satirical monologues in which he excels.

Interview:

Claudia Gary Annis, "An Interview with Frederick Feirstein," *Edge City Review,* 3, no. 1 (October 1997): 3–7.

References:

Dick Allen, "The Path to Expansive Poetry," *Pivot,* no. 46 (1998);

Christopher Clausen, "Explorations of America," *The Moral Imagination: Essays in Literature and Ethics* (Iowa City: University of Iowa Press, 1986), pp. 154–176;

Dana Gioia, "Poetry Chronicle," review of *Manhattan Carnival, Hudson Review,* 35, no. 4 (Winter 1982–1983): 641–653;

Arthur Mortensen, "Review of *New and Collected Poems,*" *Edge City Review,* 4, no. 2 (April 1998): 37–41;

Wade Newman, "Crossing the Boundary: The Expansive Movement in American Poetry," *Crosscurrents,* 8, no. 6 (1989): 142–153;

T. L. Ponick, "Manhattan Carnival of the Damned– The Urban Nightmares of Frederick Feirstein," *Edge City Review,* 3, no. 1 (October 1997): 11–17;

Frederick Turner, "The Carnival Revolution," *Ontario Review,* no. 16 (Spring–Summer 1982): 93–97;

Kevin Walzer, *The Ghost of Tradition: Expansive Poetry and Postmodernism* (Ashland, Ore.: Story Line Press, 1998).

Annie Finch
(31 October 1956 –)

Jonathan N. Barron
University of Southern Mississippi

BOOKS: *The Encyclopedia of Scotland* (Amherst, Mass.: Caribou Press, 1982);
The Ghost of Meter: Culture and Prosody in American Free Verse (Ann Arbor: University of Michigan Press, 1993);
Catching the Mermother (West Chester, Pa.: Aralia Press, 1996);
Eve (Brownsville, Ore.: Story Line Press, 1997);
Marie Moving: An Epic Poem (Brownsville, Ore.: Story Line Press, 2002);
Season Poems (Los Angeles: Calliope Press, 2002);
Calendars (Dorset, Vt.: Tupelo Press, 2003).

OTHER: *A Formal Feeling Comes: Poems in Form by Contemporary Women,* edited by Finch (Brownsville, Ore.: Story Line Press, 1994)—includes poems by Finch;
"Metrical Diversity: A Defense of Non-Iambic Meters," in *Meter in English: A Critical Engagement,* edited by David Baker (Fayetteville: University of Arkansas Press, 1996), pp. 59–74;
"A Rock in the River: Maxine Kumin's Rhythmic Countercurrents" and "Zaraf's Star," in *Telling the Barn Swallow: Poets on the Poetry of Maxine Kumin,* edited by Emily Grosholz (Hanover, N.H.: University Press of New England, 1997), pp. 22–31, 178–179;
After New Formalism, edited by Finch (Brownsville, Ore.: Story Line Press, 1999);
Carolyn Kizer: Perspectives on Her Life and Work, edited by Finch, Johanna Keller, and Candace McClelland (Fort Lee, N.J.: CavanKerry Press, 2001);
An Exaltation of Forms: Contemporary Poets Celebrate the Diversity of Their Art, edited by Finch and Kathrine Varnes (Ann Arbor: University of Michigan Press, 2002).

SELECTED PERIODICAL PUBLICATION– UNCOLLECTED: "The Sentimental Poetess in the World: Metaphor and Subjectivity in Lydia Sigourney's Nature Poetry," *Legacy,* 5, no. 2 (Fall 1987): 3–18.

Annie Finch (photograph by Michael Pleasant, courtesy of the author)

Poet, translator, librettist, playwright, theorist, and editor Annie Finch challenges the various orthodoxies of contemporary American poetry. In the general climate of realism and autobiographical confession, Finch's work engages mythic and magical traditions rather than the plain-speech, sharply defined anecdotal incident. In an age of free verse that associates "free" forms with feminism and a particular kind of American nationalism, Finch rejects such claims, finding her femi-

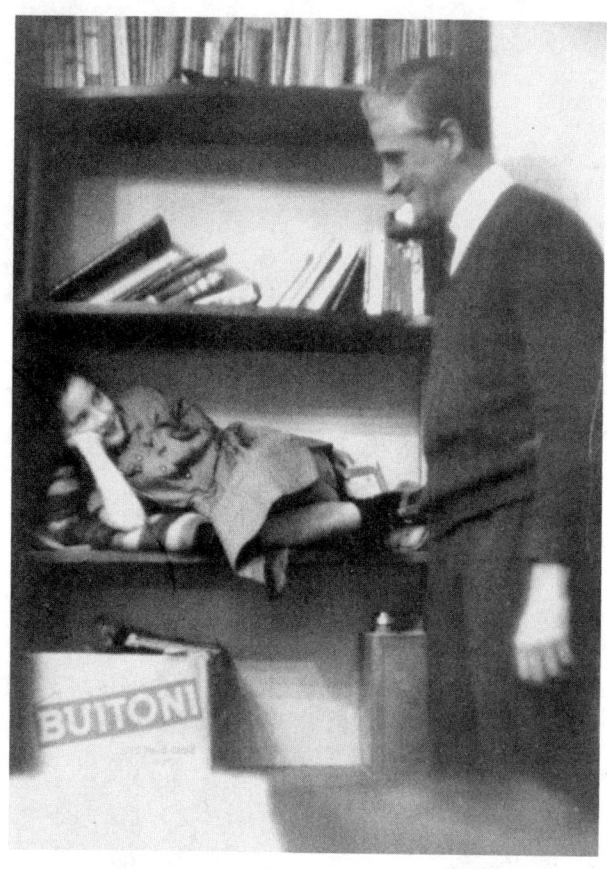

Finch with her father, Henry Leroy Finch Jr., in Kitissia, Greece, 1963 (courtesy of the author)

nism and American identity in the traditional forms of an eclectic, multicultural poetry. In a milieu shaped by the boundaries between avant-garde, narrative, formal, and performance poetics, Finch brings together all of these traditions in her poetry, anthologies, and theoretical work. Finch calls herself "the first postmodern formal poet" because her poems combine virtuosity of poetic patterning with a contemporary understanding of language and identity. Uniting all of Finch's work is a conception of poetry as essentially incantatory, performative, speaking to the body as much as, if not more than, to the mind.

Annie Ridley Crane Finch was born on 31 October 1956 in New Rochelle, New York, the fourth of five children, and grew up in a home lined with books from floor to ceiling, in an artistically and politically engaged household. Her mother, Margaret Evelyn (Rockwell) Finch, a doll artist and poet, is the niece of Jessie Wallace Hughan, founder of the pacifist War Resisters League (WRL). Her father, Henry Leroy Finch Jr., a philosophy professor and scholar of Ludwig Wittgenstein and comparative religion, was a conscientious objector during World War II and director of the WRL during the 1960s. One of her sisters, who loved to read poetry to her as a child, became an artist and sculptor; another is a painter, dancer, and actress; her brother became a musician, screenwriter, and film director. During her father's 1963–1964 sabbatical, the family traveled in Europe and the Middle East for a year, often camping out of their Volkswagen van. That year was a formative period in her life. She recalls, "I was hearing a half-dozen unfamiliar languages, one after the other, over a period of 15 months. I never heard English the same way again."

For high school, she went to Simon's Rock Early College, a school known for a curriculum encouraging creativity and intellectual experiment. For college, Finch went to Yale (1974–1979), where she majored in English. At Yale she was particularly influenced by John Hollander, one of the principal formalist poets of the second half of the twentieth century. As the student of Penelope Laurens, she was also given encouragement in her feminist studies. In 1986 Finch obtained an M.F.A. in poetry writing from the University of Houston. While there, she published her first chapbook, *The Encyclopedia of Scotland,* a performance poem for voices, costumes, and bagpipe (1982). Her interest in poetic drama was also incorporated into her first play, *The Mermaid Tragedy* (1986), also performed in Houston. In both works Finch's interest in female archetypes, traditions, and the rhythmic music inherent in language depend on free-verse techniques. On 6 December 1985, while working on her M.F.A., Finch married Glen Brand. They have two children, Julian Hughan (born 14 November 1990) and Althea Margaret Crane (born 21 December 1998).

In 1991 Finch obtained her Ph.D. in English from Stanford University. Her dissertation became her first book, *The Ghost of Meter: Culture and Prosody in American Free Verse* (1993). At Stanford, Finch not only pursued intellectual, scholarly, and theoretical interests but also developed her editorial talents. From 1987 through 1991, she edited the literary magazine *Sequoia,* which had become one of the major New Formalist magazines in the United States. Sponsored by the creative-writing and English programs at Stanford, *Sequoia* had in the 1970s been transformed into a national magazine under the editorship of Dana Gioia. Even as Finch was becoming involved with the formalist milieu of the poetic community at Stanford, she was at the same time cultivating friendships with the free-verse avant-garde, the Language poets. She also became more and more attracted to the African American poetic tradition. Of her mentors at Stanford, Finch particularly singles out two—Ntozake Shange and Diane Middlebrook.

WATCHING THE WHALE

Her gray fin's hard wave walks out first on the water
thickening to part open, alive to encounter.
Long-formed ocean bodies are twisting to find
motion around her. The luminous wake wakes our eyes.
It is her footprint. We rush to the side where a railing
stops the salt spray with round beads on the white metal.

Darkening down the green path nine knots give water,
she leads us through twenty-six fathoms. We shadow her
into and out of the light in the depth that has spun
her shadowy body. It measures our absence in green,
till each of the six-foot-deep green women grows fertile.
She muses in her low winter. Lulled with her krill,

[stanza break]

Draft for "Watching the Whale" (courtesy of the author)

Finch in 2002 (courtesy of the author)

At Stanford, these friendships across the boundaries of contemporary American poetry affected not only her scholarship and her editorial commitments but her poetry as well. Their influence is particularly evident in the exploratory imagery and language of the two poetic plays she had performed in her Stanford years: *The Moon and the Snake* (1989) and *Life by the Ocean* (1990). Increasingly, then, Finch turned to drama—eventually acting, producing, and directing plays for the Magic Theater of San Francisco.

Finch's first academic job was as poet-in-residence and assistant professor of English at the University of Northern Iowa (1992–1995). In these years, she gained notice as an editor and a scholar of New Formalist poetics, publishing two groundbreaking books—*The Ghost of Meter* and *A Formal Feeling Comes: Poems in Form by Contemporary Women* (1994). She also continued writing poetry based on the dramatic, vocal qualities of words, and of the Jungian archetypal meaning of the feminine and of women. This interest in sound ultimately led to the composition of a song cycle, *The Furious Sun in her Mane,* performed in 1994, and a cantata, *Cantata for My Daughter,* performed in 2001.

In 1995 Finch left Northern Iowa for a new position at Miami University of Ohio. In 1997, having already made her mark as a theorist and editor on the poetics of New Formalism, Finch published her first book of poetry, *Eve*. An advance glimpse of this book first appeared in 1996 when twelve of its poems, titled *Catching the Mermother,* were published by Aralia, a New Formalist fine-arts press. The poems of *Eve,* Finch's first major collection, were divided into nine sections, each introduced by a poem to a different goddess from a variety of traditions and cultures across both time and space. Altogether, *Eve* carved out a new poetic arena for New Formalist poetry in particular but also for women's and American poetry in general. In *Eve,* Finch demonstrates that one can write of the mysteries, of the soul, and of "the goddess" in a skeptical age. She also offers an example of how one can write in a variety of structured forms even while retaining a progressive, feminist sensibility.

Although Finch has always defined herself first and last as a poet, she initially made her mark as a result of her theoretical and editorial work in *The Ghost of Meter* and *A Formal Feeling Comes*. Both books were controversial when they were published. In *The Ghost of Meter,* for example, Finch argued for the existence of a "metrical code." She made a case for the use of meter even in free-verse poetry, and in so doing, her book, along with Timothy Steele's *Missing Measures* (1990), became another defining New Formalist statement on the enduring power and importance of meter in American poetry. Unlike Steele, however, Finch did not divorce free verse from metered poetry—rather she read a "metrical code" in free verse itself, establishing a continuum, not a dichotomy, in American poetics. Describing her book in a 1994 interview for *Poetry Flash,* she says, "I was having an identity crisis as a poet who had been raised on free verse and was finding herself irresistibly drawn towards writing in meter." This crisis was particularly serious, because to fall in love with meter in the late 1980s was nothing less than heresy. As Finch says, "One is trained out of meter." Despite an intellectual training away from meter, she was unwilling to deny her experience as a poet: "as a poet I love meter . . . sound repetitions, physical repetitions. This is something I have felt as part of my body, part of my ear, part of my psyche since I was a child. The hate was—that as a sophisticated, over-educated, literary person who had been trained to believe that meter was wrong . . . I hated it intellectually."

Although Finch was taught an intellectual disdain for meter, the education had a particularly political visceral consequence: "As a woman I think I had an extra measure of hate or suspicion towards meter; I associated it with the patriarchal tradition. . . . What I didn't anticipate was that there was a whole other rhythmic pattern in Dickinson and other poets—the triple rhythms, the dactylic rhythms, I call them." In short, Finch's discovery of the "metrical code" was a way to excuse or explain not only her own attraction to meter as a poet but also its existence in otherwise feminist poets such as Dickinson. *The Ghost of Meter* reconciled Finch's love of "formal music" with a feminist suspicion of the obviously patriarchal heritage of meter.

The impact of the book on New Formalist poetics was pronounced: it was the first serious feminist defense of meter. Briefly summarized, Finch's book explained how a wider, more generous understanding of meter as a repetitive sonic structure required one to accommodate triple rhythms and dactyls in any prosodic study. She argues that women were the poets to use such meters most frequently. Therefore, Finch's study offered to women a metrical tradition that had been effectively silenced for more than one hundred years. Indeed, hints of this defense of a feminine metrical tradition were already introduced in her influential 1987 article on the nineteenth-century American poet Lydia Sigourney.

In the *Poetry Flash* interview she explains the importance of this expanded definition of meter:

> The poets I looked at were . . . writing in free verse or at least in metrically variable verse during the 19th century when metrical patterns were much more flexible than they had been previously. And I found that for these poets, metered metrical patterns themselves had *meanings*. Metrical patterns signify in a physical, unconscious way different attitudes toward cultural traditions, different attitudes toward literary traditions, and different attitudes, perhaps, toward gender. What was particularly fascinating, if not surprising, was that similar patterns appeared in poets from Walt Whitman to Audre. . . . The iambic pentameter was associated with patriarchal cultures, society, traditional ways of doing things, and the dactylic with a much freer, more immediate, more unconscious, perhaps more subversive attitude towards identity and towards culture.

The importance of this argument was recognized immediately. The reviewer for *The Virginia Quarterly Review* wrote, "As the rift in literary scholarship between cultural studies and Formalist criticism appears to widen, this brave book sets itself the ambitious task of reconciling the two sides." In the theoretical journal *Style,* Timothy Morris wrote that Finch's book

> is a watershed in the study of the relation of form to meaning. Finch's theory of the "metrical code," which "implies that meter in a metrically organic poem can function like a language," enables her to argue that meter enacts meaning not just situationally or tactically, but at the larger relational level of cultural intertextuality. Finch's key insight is that iambic pentameter, which carries such a heavy baggage of patriarchal institutions in education and the high tradition of English poetic diction, can best be studied at the moment of early free verse in English, when the grip of pentameter on verse was becoming unclenched.

Finch's treatise has since gone into a second edition.

When *The Ghost Of Meter* was published, many readers were surprised to learn that it was written by a poet. Nonetheless, as Finch says in *Contemporary Authors,* "poetry has been the focus of my inner and outer life since I was about nine years old." Like Marianne Moore, and her own personal hero, Emily Dickinson, Finch does not rush her poetry into print. She often keeps it to herself, refining, reworking, often taking years to perfect just one poem. Also, Finch was not convinced the literary community was ready to hear the sort of poetry she had begun to write.

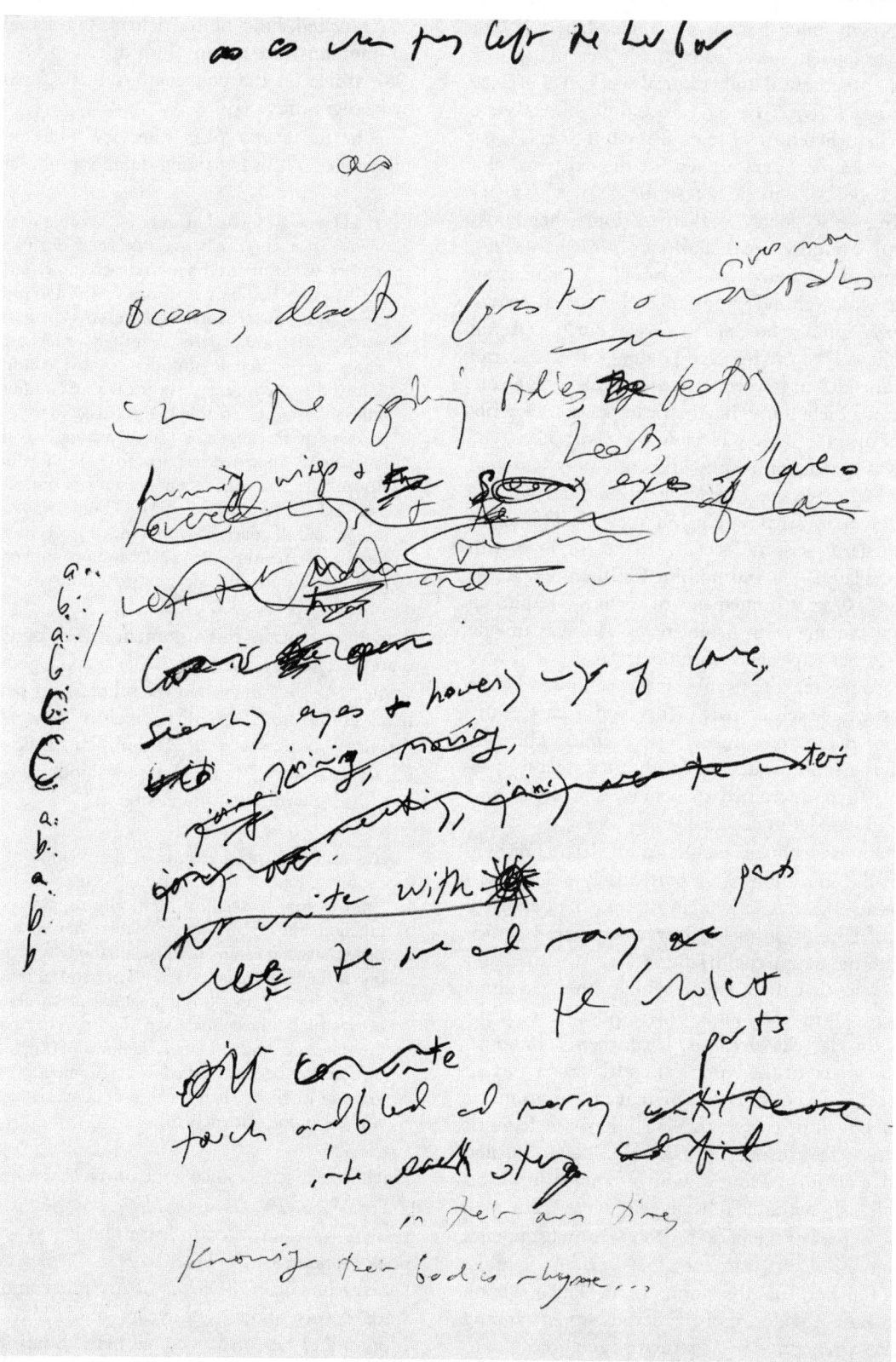

Front and back of a leaf from a draft for "A Wedding on Earth" (courtesy of the author)

In order to create a context and community for her own work then, her second book, *A Formal Feeling Comes* (which takes its title from a poem by Dickinson), is an anthology of formal poetry by sixty contemporary women poets, including Finch herself. Each poet is represented by a selection of poetry and her own commentary on her experience with form in poetry. The anthology established a vital link between the present and the past in terms of formal traditions for women poets. It also proved just how many contemporary women were currently engaged in the problems raised by the association of form and gender, form and nation, and form and voice.

Also significant was the publisher of the anthology, Story Line, the publishing "house" of New Formalism. By producing this book Story Line proved that, as a movement, New Formalism would not accept the charge that theirs was an exclusively male, patriarchal, conservatively grounded countertradition associated with American conservative politics. As Finch says in *Contemporary Authors:* "At a time when formalism is widely associated with reactionary conservatism, I am proud to have acted as a bridge-builder to broaden the definition of form and to demonstrate the value of form to poets who might not have felt comfortable with it otherwise." If *The Ghost of Meter* offered the literary community a theoretical and historical justification for New Formalism in women's poetry by expanding the idea of form, *A Formal Feeling Comes* introduced to the poetic community a lively and diverse group of women already engaged in New Formalist poetic issues. In the interview with *Poetry Flash,* Finch says of both books:

> I was looking for form in a place where a lot of people wouldn't look for it.
> In *The Ghost of Meter* I looked for form and meter in free verse, and in *A Formal Feeling Comes* I found form in poems that some people would say were not formal. And in both cases I was trying to find a place for myself as a poet. . . . I felt that formal verse was extremely powerful in a way that reached into the roots of human need, and my politics are all about returning to human need. . . . I wanted to corral the power of formal verse and open it up for purposes other than just the conservative maintenance of whatever power hierarchies exist. I started out feeling as if I were the only woman poet around who was a feminist writing in form. By the time I finished the book, I found that there has been a real grassroots shift towards formalism among women poets. . . .

A Formal Feeling Comes met with an immediate welcome, as well as with controversy. At the Associated Writing Programs Annual Conference in 1994, a special session was held to discuss the anthology. The sense at the conference was of general relief that at last women's poetry, particularly feminist poetry, would not have to find its voice solely in the narrow orthodoxy of free verse. Writing a review in the *Eugene Weekly,* Alice Evans expressed the general feeling:

> I confess a bias toward free verse, and so I read *A Formal Feeling Comes* with what was at first a sense of hesitance, even alarm. This was writing of a kind I had tried to murder in myself, having absorbed the in-vogue dictum of the 1970s and 1980s that said formal poetry, particularly poetry rhymed and strictly metered, is something modern poets must evolve beyond.
> But here are 60 modern women poets, including such stars as U.S. Poet Laureate Rita Dove and Pulitzer Prize–winner Carolyn Kizer, singing the praises of form, giving testimony to its lasting beauty. Ground once considered overworked has gained new topsoil. . . . Plants are not only growing once again, they have been growing all along.

By contrast, Langdon Hammer, writing in *The Yale Review,* could barely contain his skepticism at the broad definition of form in the anthology, or even by the suggestion that form and gender were intimately connected: "A Native American poet who writes in traditional Native American forms is not a formalist, surely, in the same sense that a woman who writes in rhyme and meter is." The all too easy assumption behind this "surely" was precisely what both *The Ghost of Meter* and *A Formal Feeling Comes* meant to challenge. In an unpublished interview, Finch explained that for her, form is about repeated verbal and sonic structure in a poem: it is not limited to particular culturally determined repetitions familiar in the Western tradition. That Hammer would reject the association between structure and form only highlighted the controversial impact of Finch's prosodic theories. As she told *Contemporary Authors,* "I found no ready acceptance for my particular poetic blend of passion, music and female sensibility. Through my critical studies of the female poetic tradition and the complexities of metrical interaction, as well as through editing projects that have expanded the definition of formal poetry . . . I feel I have finally been able to create a literary context in which my own poetry can make sense." Yet, as Hammer's review indicates, even that context would be hard to win.

For all her theoretical and editorial work expanding New Formalist poetics in order to allow for a more diverse community of poets and for progressive political concerns, Finch is, above all else, a poet herself. To understand the impetus behind her first two works, one must attend to her poetic sensi-

Paperback cover for Finch's collection of poems that was a finalist in the 2000 National Poetry Series (courtesy of the author)

bility. After publishing her first two books, Finch released *Eve* (1997). This collection, also published by Story Line, includes a brew of music, female sensibility, magic, myth, and diverse forms. *Eve* was recognized as a singular poetic effort. It was a finalist in three national competitions—the Yale Series of Younger Poets, the National Poetry Series, and the Great Lakes Writers Award.

The reviews proved that Finch's first books had established a critical context for her own poetry. This outcome, however, was double-edged. Writing in *The Georgia Review,* Judith Kitchen singled out the formal concerns of the collection as if they were far more important than the thematic ones. One suspects that because the publisher, Story Line, and Finch herself had defined themselves chiefly as advocates of formal approaches to poetry, Kitchen had been unduly influenced. As she said, "One senses that content is of secondary interest to her—that her interest is form itself." By contrast, C. L. Rawlins, writing in *The Bloomsbury Review,* stated,

> Though noted as a scholar, Finch is a poet in her bones, and *Eve* is the most delightful and original poetry I've run across in years. Starting with nine ancestral goddesses, she composes for each a section-opening poem that reflects not only the content but the style of the original; for instance, "Inanna" adopts from Sumerian hymns a four-beat accentual line, divided into two parts. . . . From its mythic starting point, each section diverges in startling ways. For instance, following "Inanna" is a poem about fishing in San Francisco Bay that, in a way altogether stranger than Elizabeth Bishop's "The Fish," becomes an encounter with the very depths of inspiration. For instead of a fish, what surfaces is a "mermother."

Similarly, Kizer, writing in *The Michigan Quarterly Review,* responded primarily to the way Finch integrated her themes with her forms:

Eve, by Annie Finch, was eagerly anticipated, as publishers love to say, but it certainly was, by some old formalists, new formalists, and just plain poets like me. We had been struck by her poems in literary journals and by her anthology, *A Formal Feeling Comes*. We liked the use of myth in modern contexts; we loved the wild energy held in check by form. In an ecstatic review the poet C. L. Rawlins said, her "rhyme and meter isn't just a formerly fashionable sort of bondage . . . but is instead a bio-acoustic key to memory and emotion, which existed prior to the written word." She does indeed abolish linear time: past fables and present events coalesce. Einstein might have accompanied her on his violin.

Particularly striking about *Eve* was the way it managed to join so many oppositions: male and female, spirit and matter, myth and science, imagination and logic, music and speech, free verse and meter, triple meters and double meters. Free-verse poems such as "Another Reluctance" make even regular spoken diction musical:

> Chestnuts fell in the charred season,
> fell finally, finding room
> in air to open their old cases
> so they gleam out from the gold leaves
> in dust now, where they dropped down.

All of the lyrics in the book concern the female experience either from a cultural or a personal perspective. In "My Raptor" Finch considers pregnancy and her baby as the poem explores the mysterious fact of pregnancy. The poem explores all that is not rational, logical, or medical:

> my mind learned not to care
> whether thoughts I felt he noticed with no fear
> were mine alone—or whether he could hear.

By contrast, other poems engage the patriarchal aspects of the English tradition. In "Tribute," Finch turns to Dickinson to laud a woman in an overwhelmingly male canon, while in "Coy Mistress" she has the subject of poet Andrew Marvell's "coy mistress" offer a poetic retort of her own. This poem is also a retort to the whole tradition of the courtship sonnet. Its final couplet reads, "You've praised my eyes, forehead, breast: / you've all our lives to praise the rest."

Of the many poems invoking female myths, "No Snake" demonstrates how myth can become an active agent in one's lived experience:

> Inside my Eden I can find no snake.
> There's not one I could look to and believe,
> obey and then be ruined by and leave
> because of, bearing children and an ache.

Commenting on the rhyme of this stanza and its subtle play against the meaning, one reviewer wrote, "English, unlike Italian or Spanish, is poor in end-rhyme, tending to figures like alliteration and stress. This makes rhyme a considerable challenge, one that most poets duly strain to meet. . . . But Finch strains not at all, taking to formal verse as her namesake bird takes to air." Finally, the focus in the book on the feminine includes the image of the goddess, a thread that connects the nine sections of the book. As a poetic debut, *Eve* impressed its reviewers. They noted its command of technique, maturity of vision, and other hallmarks unusual in first books of poetry.

Since publishing that first collection, Finch has continued her various interests, but increasingly she has begun to question the New Formalist movement even as she has continued to be an advocate for the association of structure with form. As if to announce such a distance, she published, through Story Line, her fourth book, a collection of critical essays by poets, *After New Formalism* (1999). The key word "after" in the title implies that, for Finch, the impulse behind New Formalism, that prosodic issues were of central importance to contemporary poets, had been won.

The anthology is divided into three sections—"Traditions," "Poetics," and "Directions." Combined, the essays tackle questions of gender, voice, nationalism, and literary history and are meant to push New Formalism out of an increasingly narrow corner defined by conservative politics, predominantly male poetic traditions, and increasingly traditional literary as opposed to experimental literary concerns. As Finch said in an unpublished interview with Kristina Emick, her own theoretical concern with formalist—that is, structured—poetry had three goals: to prove that "formalism can be very diverse," to prove that formalism "can be theoretically compelling," and finally, "to show that formalism is not necessarily politically reactionary." In *After New Formalism*, she and the poets whose essays she includes make a case for all three positions.

At about the same time, Finch began a vigorous dialogue with poets from the American experimental avant-garde concerning her ideas of form. This dialogue ultimately produced another anthology, one that illustrates Finch's expanded ideas of poetic form. That book, *An Exaltation of Forms: Contemporary Poets Celebrate the Diversity of Their Art* (2002), co-edited with Kathrine Varnes, brings together male and female poets from a variety of backgrounds and traditions. Each poet offers an historical survey and discussion of a form as well as many poetic examples. Sixty poets altogether discuss sixty verse forms, including a variety of metrical, stanzaic, and avant-garde structures.

Continuing her explorations of the intersections between traditional and exploratory poetics, Finch is co-editing with avant-garde poet Susan Schultz another book of essays, "Multiformalisms: Postmodern Poetics of Form," which will collect essays on traditional and avant-garde poetics by poets from across the aesthetic spectrum.

Finch completed another book of poetry, *Calendars,* a National Poetry Series finalist (2000), which was published by Tupelo Press in Spring 2003. *Calendars* is a collection of lyrics on mortality, human relationships, and nature, including several ritual chants for different seasons, a long elegy for Finch's father, and an epithalamium in an invented form combining elements of Sapphic and Spenserian stanzas. She has also begun work with composer Deborah Drattell on an ambitious trilogy of operas, "Three Mothers," which explores the sometimes tragic conflicts between motherhood and creativity in women's lives. Finch has also finished a translation of the complete poems of French Renaissance poet Louise Labé for the University of Chicago Press—the first translation to copy exactly the rhyme schemes of the original sonnets—and has begun to translate the poems of another key Renaissance woman poet, Pernette du Guillet. Another project, *Marie Moving: An Epic Poem* (2002), is written in dactyls and tells the mythic tale of a woman undergoing a rape, an abortion, and a spiritual apprenticeship to seven different goddesses in various human and other guises.

Annie Finch's combined talents as poet, theoretician, and editor have, more than those of any other New Formalist poet, brought some of the most difficult and most necessary issues to the forefront of contemporary poetic debate. What, she demands, do poets mean by the word *form?* Do the answers to that question depend on gender assumptions? Are there implicit political ideologies in such definitions? Is there room in theoretical discourse for the mystery and passion of poetry? Asking such questions in her prose, and often answering them in her poems, Finch has become one of the central figures in contemporary American poetics.

Interviews:

Tomma Lou Maas, "Interview with Annie Finch," *Poetry Flash* (September 1994) <http://www.users.muohio.edu/finchar/biography/interview1.html>;

Marilyn Hacker, "Marilyn Hacker: An Interview on Form," *American Poetry Review,* 25, no. 3 (May/June 1996): 23–27.

John Gery
(2 June 1953 –)

Sonny Williams
University of New Orleans

BOOKS: *Charlemagne: A Song of Gestures* (Cerrillos, N.M.: Plumbers Ink, 1983);
The Burning of New Orleans, with an introduction by Gery (Bakersfield, Cal.: Amelia, 1988);
Three Poems (West Chester, Pa.: LeStat, 1989);
The Enemies of Leisure (Brownsville, Ore.: Story Line Press, 1995);
Nuclear Annihilation and Contemporary American Poetry: Ways Of Nothingness (Gainesville: University Press of Florida, 1996);
American Ghost: Selected Poems (bilingual edition), translated into Serbian by Biljana D. Obradović (Merrick, N.Y.: Cross-Cultural Communications, 1999);
Davenport's Version (New Orleans: Portals, 2003);
A Gallery of Ghosts (Ashland, Ore.: Story Line Press, forthcoming 2004).

OTHER: Poems by Gery, in *Immortelles: Poems of Life and Death by New Southern Writers,* edited by Thomas Bonner Jr. and Robert E. Skinner (New Orleans: Xavier Review Press, 1995);
Poems by Gery, in *Uncommonplace: An Anthology of Contemporary Louisiana Poets,* edited by Ann Brewster Dobie (Baton Rouge: Louisiana State University Press, 1998), pp. 87–89;
Hmayyag Shems, *For the House of Torkom,* translated by Gery and Vahé Baladouni (Merrick, N.Y.: Cross-Cultural Communications, 1999).

SELECTED PERIODICAL PUBLICATIONS–UNCOLLECTED: "The Paradox of Form," *Verse,* 7 (1990): 40–41;
"Form Follows Faction: New Formalism and the Lyric," *Proceedings of the Philological Association of Louisiana* (1990): 1–11;
"The Anxiety of Influence," *Verse,* 8 (1991): 28–32;
"Subversive Parody in the Early Poems of Gwendolyn Brooks," *South Central Review,* 16 (1999);
"'Mocking My Own Ripeness': Authenticity, Heritage, and Self-Erasure in the Poetry of Marilyn Chin,"

John Gery (photograph by John Cook; from the paperback cover for The Enemies of Leisure, *1995; Richland County Public Library)*

Literature, Interpretation, Theory: Lit., 12 (2001): 25–45.

Writing in traditional forms and composing stories in verse, John Gery appears to display all of the aesthetic affiliations of a New Formalist and a New Narrative poet. Two of his poetry collections have been published by Story Line Press, whose founders were instrumental in establishing the Expansive poetry movement. He also attended Stanford University, a school with a long line of formalist graduates such as Dana Gioia, Paul Lake, and Vikram Seth. Gery exists precariously, however, on the fringes of the Expansive

Lee Harvey Oswald on tape

They thought I had a plan, but I was lonely,
living each afternoon without a job.
You wouldn't know. So when this fat guy—well,
he wasn't really fat, just wealthy, only
he wore a baggy suit—white—like a slob
might wear. He told me all about Fidel
the day I met him down on Magazine,
invited me to stop by at Canal
to read some literature, but when I got there
he wasn't there. Instead, this fairy queen,
who hated loiterers, gave me a scowl,
then started filling the place with this hot air
about "the revolution." What the fuck—
did I care? I was out of work, not jargon.
For half an hour I listened to that liar
and would've left, except this pick-up truck
pulled up. The driver offered me a bargain
so trembling like those rats trapped on the high wire,
I stood on Bourbon Street to hand out leaflets
to all the derelicts and tourists. Well,
not tourists. They ignored me. But it's always
for me been that way. Always. You're the chief, it's
quite obvious and I can go to hell
for all you care. Walking down these hallways
to be transferred to another jail—
You watch. They won't ignore me any more.
But back then in New Orleans you could pay me
to do or say most anything, and I would fail
or move along, and quietly ignore
that no one noticed. Now no one can slay me
by telling me they can't recall my name
and what my crime is. Since my crime is theirs
I have the full protection of the law.

You wouldn't know. That's been my
all along. I'm ready. Let's go downsta
Now that you've grilled me,
let's show a little

Manuscript for a poem in A Gallery of Ghosts, *forthcoming in 2004 (courtesy of the author)*

Paperback cover for Gery's 1983 collection of poems
(courtesy of the author)

poetry movement, for he has not aligned himself officially with any contemporary poetry camp. Although he writes formal and narrative poems, Gery is just as comfortable composing free verse poems.

Born John Roy Octavius Gery on 2 June 1953 in Reading, Pennsylvania, Gery is the second son and fourth child of Malcolm R. Dougherty, a United States diplomat and cutlery businessman, and Eugenie Gunesh (Guran) Gery, a homemaker and language teacher, herself the daughter of a Turkish physician father and Russian mother. He took his stepfather's name in 1955 when his mother married Addison Harbster Gery Jr., a jazz musician and business executive. Malcolm Dougherty died when his private plane crashed on 1 January 1958. Gery grew up in Lititz, Pennsylvania, with his brother and five sisters. He received a B.A. with honors from Princeton University in 1975. Afterward, he attended the University of Chicago, receiving an M.A. in 1976, and then went to Stanford University on an Edith Mirrielees Fellowship in creative writing, from which he received another M.A. in 1978. After holding various jobs as a journalist, a maintenance man, a sales clerk, and an encyclopedia salesman, Gery became a lecturer of English at Stanford University and San Jose State University from 1977 to 1979. In 1979 he accepted a position as an instructor at the University of New Orleans where he later became, from 1986 to 1990, the coordinator of creative writing. In 1991–1992 he held a Visiting Associate Professor position at the University of Iowa. As of 2003, he is a Research Professor of English at the University of New Orleans. Also, since 1990 he has served as the founding director of the Ezra Pound Center for Literature at Brunnenburg Castle, Italy, home of Pound's daughter, Mary de Rachewiltz, and her son's family. Gery is married to Serbian poet Biljana D. Obradović; the couple have one son, Peter Malcolm Obradović Gery, born 31 March 2003.

Gery's initial influences range from the Greek lyrics of Sappho to the urban contemporary poems of John Ashbery and Adrienne Rich, as well as to Ezra Pound and the Latin poet Horace. As he asserted in his candidate statement for nomination to the research professorship at the University of New Orleans, "My earliest poems, in fact, primarily consist of formal imitations of my mentors, poetic exercises in which I consciously adopted others' voices, or *personae*." His first collection of poems, *Charlemagne: A Song of Gestures,* appeared in 1983 and received the Plumbers Ink Poetry Award. The collection is a linked sequence of poems inspired by the history and legends of the medieval figure of Charlemagne, the famous "King of the West." Gery explains in the same candidate statement, "Rather than only create *personae* poems set in Charlemagne's time, though, I decided to transport this Frankish monarch, via a transatlantic jet, into a modern American landscape. As part of my apprenticeship, my Charlemagne poems depict the old king in incongruously American situations, such as a cross-country car trip with the poet, an elevator ride up the Sears Tower in Chicago, and a movie premiere in Hollywood—until king and poet finally face each other in a gunslinging showdown in Texas."

Although incongruity becomes a recurring element in Gery's future poetry, one can sense congruous, formal elements at work in *Charlemagne* in the poem "Monk's Compleynt," for example. Lines such as "my fingers / curl from dipping styluses in india ink" are clearly iambic, and other lines, which appear in "The Organ in Aachen Cathedral," another poem from *Charlemagne,* echo the music of John Donne with their easy cadence and alternating line lengths.

> I ask you–do you apprehend
> what purpose music serves for thought
>   or feeling? Listen how
>
> those booming tones reverberate below
>   clattering the walls,
> till suddenly the organist
> will lift his fingers, close the stops
>   and clinch in a twist
> the air of angels! It enthralls
> this old man's heart–until it drops
>   because I want to know
>
> if it is dangerous to think about
>   other worlds than ours,
> when I am subject to a song,
> what, if invisible these pleasures
>   do move me, is wrong
> with granting this machine its powers
> to change my mind by aural measures
>   it leaves me still in doubt.

Indeed, Gery's lines reverberate like a cathedral organ. He is questioning himself, however, about the pleasure of those aural measures of metrical verse; they evoke the air of angels and enthrall his heart, but their use still leaves him in doubt.

After *Charlemagne,* Gery concentrated on short lyrics and long narrative poetry. In 1988 *The Burning of New Orleans* was published after it had won the 1987 Charles William Duke "Long Poem" Award. This poem, which tells of life in New Orleans during the Civil War, is a portion of a much longer work of narrative verse, in five books, titled *Davenport's Version* (2003), and its aesthetic surface departs from that of Gery's other poetry. In the introduction to the poem Gery states, "It concerns the life of Bressie LaRouche, a young Creole widow who at the start of the war becomes involved with a Cavalry officer in the Confederate army, Colonel B. Trosler White. After the Union occupation of the city, however, [a Union Captain David] Davenport is assigned to escort Bressie back to New Orleans from her exile along the Bayou Teche, and their encounter initiates a relationship between them." *The Burning of New Orleans* begins with the invasion of the Union army after they have broken the Confederate blockade at the mouth of the Mississippi. General Mansfield Lovell, who commands all Confederate troops in New Orleans, orders his troops' evacuation. As a result, many New Orleans civilians flee the city. As narrated by Davenport himself in trochaic pentameter, the story possesses a downward, tragic tone indicative of the falling rhythms in the poem. The invocation to the Greek Furies at the beginning of the poem enhances further its tragic mood:

> O blessed Euminides, please
> warm me, hold me, quench my longing, leave me
> kindly looked on when I die. I praise you–
> cruel Megaera, casual Alecto,
> indiscriminate Tisiphone–
> only so you won't forget me, later,
> nor through this weak try at invocation
> do I mean to flaunt belief. I'm trying,
> simply to remember things–

The epic language then changes as the story begins. Gery adroitly handles the trochaic line, so that at moments it may impart grandeur or sound natural as common speech. The climax of the poem occurs when the troops actually enter New Orleans. Gery's phrasing rushes the reader headlong in anticipation:

> So when we slipped by their sleeping cannons
> on the evening of the 27th,
> past Chalmette, we sailed into New Orleans
> as though sailing into Hell: the levees,
> stacked with bales of cotton, burned on both banks,
> shooting flames like comets through the night sky
> from two blazing walls of red and yellow.
> Seven warships cut loose their moorings,
> masts ablaze, their tops in flames, their bows black,
> like held candles at an evening worship
> floated aimlessly into the river–
> which itself seemed scorched, a bed of lava
> or pool of molten lead–as screams from women,
> shrill and urgent cries from men lamenting,
> burst forth from behind that flaring curtain
> in an orgiastic chorus, moaning
> for their gods, in their abandonment there
> where the white smoke billowed full of anger
> and the red flames danced and fell.

The storytelling in this poem is both exciting and harrowing. Because Gery provides accurate historical information and intimate details, readers can follow the characters easily and feel as if they are participating in the action. Instead of emulating his mentors–such as Pound, William Carlos Williams, and Ashbery–and writing elusive collages in which symbols and associative meanings dominate, Gery uses traditional narrative techniques to produce a compelling and memorable story. Indeed, much of the longer poem, *Davenport's Version,* owes its genesis to Geoffrey Chaucer's *Troilus and Criseyde* (circa 1385).

As the Expansive poetry movement began to establish itself, Gery contributed an essay, as well as poems, to an important issue of *Verse* (Winter 1990) devoted to New Formalism in American poetry.

Manuscript for the title poem in Gery's 1999 book (courtesy of the author)

Revealing in the essay "The Paradox of Form" his compulsion to write in both traditional forms and free verse, he states: "In my own writing, I continued to experiment, often unsuccessfully, with as many different forms as possible, and a dozen years later I am still experimenting, still playing with a variety of rhythms, voices, and syntactic patterns found in middle-class American English." In 1990 he also contributed an essay titled "Form Follows Faction: New Formalism and the Lyric" to *Proceedings of the Philological Association of Louisiana*. Gery deflates the debate between the New Formalists and the "organic" or "free verse" poets by calling it "the most dynamic and the least compelling new controversy to occur in American poetry in the last twenty-five years." Because of these kinds of essays and his continued publication of free-verse poems in well-known journals such as *Chicago Review*, *The Iowa Review*, and the *New Orleans Review*, poets and critics alike continue to have difficulty aligning Gery with any particular poetry group or movement.

Gery spent the next several years concentrating on writing traditional poems—particularly sonnets, rhyming quatrains, sexains, and villanelles—many of which were published in major journals across the country, including *Paris Review*, *Southwest Review*, *Kenyon Review*, *Cumberland Poetry Review*, *Piedmont Literary Review*, and *Verse*. He continued to experiment with a variety of free-verse forms and voices as well. Eventually, he collected these poems in *The Enemies of Leisure*, his first book published by Story Line Press, in 1995. *Enemies of Leisure* received much praise and was honored by *Publishers Weekly* as a Best Book of 1995 in poetry as well as by a Critics' Choice Award from the *San Francisco Review of Books*. While many formal poems are presented in the collection, a major portion of the poems are free verse or prose. As Alan Golding notes in the journal *Louisiana Literature*, "In fact, over half the book's forty poems are written in free verse, and in many cases even the more 'traditional' elements emerge only on repeated reading, unobtrusive amid the book's variety."

Revealing a social and spiritual vision of American culture, *The Enemies of Leisure* encompasses poems about relationships, sex, love, death, childhood, loss, regret, work, and idleness. Divided into four parts, with each part introduced by an epigraph defining it, it is a book of contradictions in which Gery struggles with leisure and work, being and nonbeing, and certainty and uncertainty. His vision of the world is one that is indeterministic—a world in which there is little that is concrete. The personae of his poems wander through relationships and American culture in an attempt to discover meaning. Yet, this search is what makes Gery's work compelling, as he seeks form and patterns in an otherwise chaotic world.

Paperback cover for the 1999 Serbian-English selection of Gery's poetry (courtesy of the author)

Predominately concerned with relationships, both adolescent and adult, the first section begins with an epigraph by Sappho ("I confess I love that which caresses me") and includes some of Gery's finest poems. Golding observes, "Gery writes piercingly of adult love, its moments of grace, its missed and savored opportunities, its declines and losses." Indeed, the sonnet "Love's Myriad Alterations" is a poem about love in decline and begins resignedly, "Fine." The narrator then lists several disagreements between himself and his lover. Instead of resolving their conflict, he decides to move out, take "the other odds / and ends of independent life," and says he will "take up the sextant, worship roving Gods" in an oblique allusion to William Shakespeare's Sonnet 116. Another poem of lost love, "Photograph from the Gulf Coast" tells "of two hearts drowning in the open air." It begins with a couple on vacation—which happens to be their last together—and a man is taking their photograph. The reader already apprehends the doom of the relationship as the photographer has "caught these smiles," after the couple has been arguing for hours. There is "the smell of silences, the dearth of laughter," and the photo reveals the truth about their feelings: "my frozen eyes, glazed over, vague and bored, / your rigid mouth constricted to a grin." Gery provides telling details and portrays the boredom and lack of concern that sometimes befall relationships.

The second section continues the theme of relationships. As Golding observes, "Key poems of part 2 then recall defining moments in earlier friendships with other young men that also become moments, in retrospect, of an emerging political consciousness." Yet, it is a "self-deprecating political poetry." In "The Arbitrary Edge" the poet meditates on his languid youth spent stealing peaches from the neighbor's grove with his friends, smoking, and drinking. One of his friends, Charlie, who is older, fights in the Vietnam War. At fourteen the poet dreams of the Viet Cong surrounding his house and contemplates:

> Why,
> I wondered, had they no knapsacks, no food,
> no radios, no family, no way
> of feeling as at home as I did there
> where I knew every tree by name. They crouched
> and when I peered down at them from my bedroom
> they fired in quick bursts. I jerked awake.

The next day, he watches as his neighbor carefully mows his lawn up to the edge of his yard ("that arbitrary edge") and stops. Sixteen years later, as the same neighbor is driving home drunk, "he drove his old gray Buick over the edge / and into our Dutch elm." The verse ends as the poet is saved from combat in Vietnam, and he says, "how fortunate we are to be alive, / too young for the last war, too old for the next." Here, Gery studies the arbitrary borders that exist between individuals, communities, and countries. For him, these borders are the direct cause of conflict and disruption of lives, but, paradoxically, the borders of age prevent him from going to war.

The third section begins with an epigraph by J. M. Coetzee, in which "he was learning to love idleness, idleness no longer as stretches of freedom reclaimed by stealth here and there from involuntary labor . . . but as a yielding up of himself to time." However, in the title poem, "The Enemies of Leisure," the poet is beset by troublesome individuals who invade his leisure time: "the enemies of leisure sat down on a park bench / to plot their strategy against my turgescent idleness." One of these "enemies" has green skin; one has red scrubbed hands; one is dressed in a black cape; and yet another wears a brown three-piece suit. The seven enemies carry the dark political persona of demon Internal Revenue Service (IRS) auditors who leave "tracks of purpose" and who are "making small entries on a clipboard." Gery's aesthetic in this poem echoes Archibald MacLeish's "Ars Poetica" (published in *Streets in the Moon,* 1928) in which MacLeish concludes, "A poem should not mean / But be." Gery, too, questions whether poetry should have a purpose—a utilitarian, practical use. The poet implores the reader,

> I repeat, I am dying, S. O. S.,
> Come to me quickly, you're my only chance, I will save
>   for you
> The tracks of purpose and warm wine. Abandoning ship.
> This may be the last letter you receive from me
> That has no point to it.

Must poetry have a point, Gery asks, and is poetry a product that must be labeled and have a marketable purpose? Gery also questions the more general, American conception that idleness is equivalent to laziness. For poets, moments of idleness or—according to some—moments of indolence during which they meditate enable them to "hear" the lyrics that they will write. Poets have become ghosts in the American conscience, however, and may as well not exist because of their apparent absence in the capitalist, free-market landscape. Gery attempts to come to terms with this conception of laziness and the uses of poetry, and he even concedes that he will save some purpose for the reader, with hopes that poetry will have some relevance to the polis.

The fourth section of the book begins with an epigraph by Ashbery: "Our passing is a façade. But our understanding of it is justified." The poem "The Shape of Sadness," a particularly forlorn sonnet, appears in this section, and in it Gery compares sadness to a dying evergreen. The dying condition of the tree is barely noticeable, for "It will not tear its roots from underground." Instead, the tree takes years to expire, but its "slow descent claims all." One may not notice that the tree is dying because of its familiar façade; it still gives shade and leaks sap, and a bird inhabits its branches. However, the reader learns, "Only, the shade may somehow seem less cool, / the bark less pliable, the sap not so clear, / the lark's shrill call less gentle, and then, cruel." Although loss, sadness, and regret dominate the spirit of the book, it ends on a hopeful note—with an epithalamion in which Gery speaks of "this comfortable journey" and "the welcome embrace of your loved ones," giving the reader a final respite from death, doom and "the hours of darkness." Gery's purpose is to construct a more humane world through poetry. He believes that poetry is necessary and provides beauty in a world where so much of it is lacking. As Golding concludes, Gery's poetry is that of scope and delicacy.

In 1996 Gery's highly acclaimed critical study, *Nuclear Annihilation and Contemporary American Poetry: Ways of*

Gery reading at the Belgrade International Meeting of Writers, October 1990 (courtesy of the author)

Nothingness, was released. It looks across the spectrum of American poetry since 1945 and analyzes the role that poets have begun to play in the nuclear age. The book examines four distinct poetic approaches to nuclear culture—protest poetry, apocalyptic lyric poetry, psychohistorical poetry, and the poetry of uncertainty. For Gery, poetry embodies the contemporary experience of an individual's sense of human continuity and survival contrasted with a sense of impending annihilation. Laurence Goldstein in the *Michigan Quarterly Review* (1999) states,

> Gery's premise is that all thinking about nuclear weapons is symbolic thinking, since only a miniscule percentage of the world's population has any experience of or contact with such weapons and their catastrophic consequences. The real work of the creative imagination cannot be the roller-coaster ride of anxiety and relief provided by action movies and trashy best-sellers, but the 'reconstructive' labor, performed by the culture's acknowledged experts in symbol-making, of credibly imagining a future in which the nuclear threat is radically diminished as an obsession.

Gery asserts that poets use poetry—both its lyric and dramatic forms—to explore the threat of nuclear annihilation, or ways of nothingness, in order to help readers think about such a devastating presence. Margaret Moran in *American Literature* (1997) states, "This book forcefully demonstrates the rich diversity of contemporary American poetry on the theme of nuclear annihilation . . . these readings pay an impressive tribute to the multifaceted and life-affirming response poets have made to this grimmest of all topics."

In 1999 *American Ghost: Selected Poems* was released. A bilingual selection of verse in English and Serbian (translated by Biljana D. Obradović), this book includes poems from previous collections, new poems, and poems that appear in *A Gallery of Ghosts* (forthcoming in 2004). As in his earlier volumes, in *American Ghost* Gery shows a mastery of form combined with a smooth, natural speech. Loss, regret, and uncertainty are again the dominating themes.

In the section titled "Gallery of Ghosts," the poem "The Day After Labor Day" is one of the more agonizing compositions. The pun in the title lays bare the painstaking, daily labor of relationships, as well as the labor involved in creating poetry. The sweet ache of longing,

Gery reading from the works of Desanka Maksimovic at her grave site in Brankovina, Serbia, October 2000 (photograph by Biljana D. Obradović; courtesy of the author)

regret, and loss in the poem is intensified by the pastoral, tranquil ocean scene and the attention given to otherwise ignored details: "adjust her baby's strap," "unwrap the towel from her thighs," and the "flap- / flap in the ocean sounds." One feels the narrator's desire, with his obsessive repetition of "her." He is also pained by the quiet torture of memory:

> —I swear
> if I could bring her back now, bring that beach
> into this room, I'd make up for my breach
>
> of faith that afternoon, and wouldn't lie
> like this, hands clutched between my knees,
> blanched, June
> past memory, the blue days of July
> as distant as the promise of the moon,
> September's seagulls calling, *not so soon so soon!*

The excellent enjambment produces several interpretations and mirrors the confusion and uncertainty in the narrator's mind. The use of the word "lie" denotes the narrator's position, as well as the lie that he is telling himself. In addition, the enjambment of "blanched" combined with "June" leaves one wondering if June or he is blanched? The poem ends with a chorus of seagulls calling, "not so soon so soon!" and the swooning *O*s impart a yearning for the summer not to end. The pathos of the poem is deepened with the mellifluous lines and exact rhymes, reminding the reader of an earlier melancholic poem, "The Shape of Sadness."

Another formal poem, "The Empty Staircase," is foreboding and cynical. The poet guides the reader through his dilapidated mind, as if it were a condemned building: "Here is the empty staircase in my head. / Rather than push you through the dark, / I'll light this switch," and he warns the reader, "Beware that red / glowing behind you." The tour of his psyche ends as he tells the reader, "Mine / has collapsed. It's been posted with a sign. / It reads, CONDEMNED: ABANDON HOPE." For Gery, the world is seen as ghostly, empty, and transparent. In "Old Ghosts the Best," a poem about his father's ghost, his "mind yields nothing concrete," and the sonnet "Bachelor of Arts" ends "I'm like a bird that crashes into glass: / I can see through but I can't pass." In the same section of the book, Gery presents three poems from a sequence of ten poems, titled "A Pack of Lies." These poems focus on dubious historical claims and question what is to be believed, such as

Frances Osgood's claim of sleeping with Edgar Allan Poe; the claim that Francis Parkman almost died on the Oregon trail; and the claim that Felix Mendelssohn-Bartholdy died mourning his wife's death. Some hope does exist, however, in Gery's world. The poem "Your Average Piecework," for example, evokes a connection to the rest of the world. It begins with an epigraph by Emerson, "All are needed by each one; Nothing is fair or good alone." The poet muses on how people would perceive him if his personality were surgically detached. He then realizes that all of humanity is "a casual combination of / divine wet meat," and the poem ends, "when really, universally, / we're all things each and never alone."

American Ghost is a diverse collection both in content and in music, and it provides the reader with a substantial look at the development of Gery's voice. Although he moves easily from formal to free verse, his free verse is never watered down, nor is it an excuse for sloppiness. He possesses deft control, and his lines, effectively, are tightly compressed or loose. The diction is conversational, coupled with an earnest Latinate formality. The poem "Promiscuous Spirit" discloses Gery's intent: "I round out various sounds you say and lay them / at your feet like beads, in hope you won't notice / other than the gentle muscle of my need."

Gery is concerned with the past and how one derives one's identity. Moreover, he addresses sadness, regret, and—as he states in "The Panthers of Worry"— "things undone, things unsaid." In addition, nothingness and inevitability pervade his poetry, themes ordinarily suggesting that poetry is an art form that is unnecessary or useless. Gery notes in *Contemporary Authors* (volume 52, 1996), however, that "poetry is essential to our very survival, as it stubbornly reminds us of the significance of each human being (no matter what dangers our 'global' perspective may lead us into), and how necessary it is to nurture the spirit."

Unlike Frederick Turner, an Expansive poet who has written extensively on cultural universality, Gery is interested in typically postmodern themes such as otherness, identity, gender, and race. His poetry consists of pushing the boundaries of knowledge, and it has both a denseness of language and imagery and a compressed, elliptical expression that can prove difficult to the reader. Indeed, uncertainty and disorientation are prevalent in his work. Gery continues with these themes in a collection of poems in progress titled "Have at You Now!" which includes telling titles such as "Grief" and "English is Dying." His poetry is paradoxical, even contradictory, in its congruity and incongruity. While some poets and critics are not certain of Gery's placement in the Expansive poetry movement, the variety of forms and subjects that he treats can truly be called expansive.

Interview:
Anne Giovingo, "An Interviw with John Gery," *Ellipsis* (University of New Orleans), 21 (1992): 11–28.

References:
DeWitt Clinton, "A Guide to Historical/Epic Poems Published in English 1980–1985," *Salthouse,* 14–17 (1986): 1–27;

Walter Kalaidjian, "Nuclear Criticism," *Contemporary Literature,* 40, no. 2 (Summer 1999): 311–318;

Dave Mason, "Where Does This Music Take Us?" *Nebo,* 2 (Fall 1984): 48–49;

Martha McFerren, "Easy Does It," *New Orleans Times-Picayune,* 30 June 1996, pp. E6–E7;

Robert McPhillips, "The New Formalism and the Revival of the Love Lyric," *Verse,* 7 (Winter 1990): 22–27;

Frederick Turner, "The Birth of Natural Classicism," *Wilson Quarterly,* 20 (Winter 1996): 27–33;

Sonny Williams, "Stratford-on-Teche," review of John Gery's *Davenport's Version, New Orleans Times-Picayune,* 24 November 2002;

Don Zimmerman, "When Hamlet Meets the Bomb: The Poetry and Criticism of John Gery," *War, Literature & the Arts,* 10 (Spring/Summer 1998): 187–200.

Dana Gioia
(24 December 1950 -   )

Bruce Meyer
University of Toronto School of Continuing Studies

See also the Gioia entry in *DLB 120: American Poets Since World War II, Third Series.*

BOOKS: *Two Poems* (New York: Bowery, 1982);

Daily Horoscope (Iowa City: Windhover, 1982; enlarged edition, St. Paul, Minn.: Graywolf, 1986; Calstock, U.K.: Peterloo, 1991);

Letter to the Bahamas (Omaha: Abattoir, 1983);

Summer (West Chester, Pa.: Aralia, 1983);

Journeys in Sunlight, with etchings by Fulvio Testa (Cottondale, Ala.: Ex Ophidia, 1986);

Words for Music (Tuscaloosa, Ala.: Parallel, 1987);

Planting a Sequoia (West Chester, Pa.: Aralia, 1991);

The Gods of Winter (St. Paul, Minn.: Graywolf, 1991);

Can Poetry Matter?: Essays on Poetry and American Culture (St. Paul, Minn.: Graywolf, 1992);

Interrogations at Noon (St. Paul, Minn.: Graywolf, 2001);

Nosferatu: An Opera Libretto (St. Paul, Minn.: Graywolf, 2001);

Barrier of a Common Language: An American Looks at Contemporary British Poetry (Ann Arbor: University of Michigan Press, 2003).

OTHER: *Sequoia: Twentieth Anniversary Issue: Poetry, 1956–1976,* edited by Gioia and others (Stanford, Cal.: Associated Students of Stanford University, 1976);

Weldon Kees, *The Ceremony and Other Stories,* edited, with an introduction, by Gioia (Port Townsend, Wash.: Graywolf, 1984); enlarged as *Selected Short Stories of Weldon Kees* (Lincoln: University of Nebraska Press, 2002);

Kees, *Two Prose Sketches,* with an introduction by Gioia (West Chester, Pa.: Aralia, 1984);

Poems from Italy, edited by Gioia and William Jay Smith (St. Paul, Minn.: New Rivers Press, 1985);

Eugenio Montale, *Mottetti: Poems of Love,* translated, with an introduction, by Gioia (St. Paul, Minn.: Graywolf, 1990);

New Italian Poets, edited by Gioia and Michael Palma (Brownsville, Ore.: Story Line, 1991);

Dana Gioia, 1995 (photograph by Star Black; courtesy of the author)

Formal Introductions: An Investigative Anthology, edited by Gioia (West Chester, Pa.: Aralia, 1994);

An Introduction to Poetry, edited by Gioia and X. J. Kennedy (New York: HarperCollins, 1994; revised, New York: Longman, 1997; revised, 2001);

An Introduction to Fiction, compiled by Gioia and Kennedy (New York: HarperCollins, 1995; revised, New York: Longman, 1999; revised, 2001);

Literature: An Introduction to Fiction, Poetry, and Drama, compiled by Gioia and Kennedy (New York: HarperCollins, 1995; revised, New York: Longman, 1999; revised, 2000; revised, 2001; revised, 2003);

Seneca, *The Madness of Hercules (Hercules Furens),* translated by Gioia, in *Seneca: The Tragedies,* volume 2, edited by David R. Slavitt (Baltimore: Johns Hopkins University Press, 1995);

Certain Solitudes: On the Poetry of Donald Justice, edited by Gioia and William Logan (Fayetteville: University of Arkansas Press, 1997);

"Fallen Western Star: The Decline of San Francisco as a Literary Region," in *The "Fallen Western Star" Wars: A Debate about Literary California,* edited by Jack Foley (Oakland, Cal.: Scarlet Tanager, 2001), pp. 7–26;

Longman Anthology of Short Fiction, compiled by Gioia and R. S. Gwynn (New York: Longman, 2001);

Longman Masters of Short Fiction, edited by Gioia and Gwynn (New York: Longman, 2002).

Among the poets of the New Formalism, none has been more active as a force of organization and encouragement than Dana Gioia. Amid the chorus of New Formalist poets, Gioia's voice has been one of the clearest and most profound; he communicates with beauty, grace, and engagement the importance of prosody in the expression of the contemporary idiom. His three principal collections of poetry, *Daily Horoscope* (1982), *The Gods of Winter* (1991), and *Interrogations at Noon* (2001) are significant contributions not only to the renewal of formal and narrative poetry in America but also to the contemporary English-language idiom. *The Gods of Winter* was chosen as a "Main Selection" of the Poetry Book Society of Great Britain—recognition that his talents among his contemporaries are held in the highest esteem. *Interrogations at Noon* brought Gioia an American Book Award for poetry in 2002. Nonetheless, Gioia's poetry has often been overshadowed by the critical debates in which he has been engaged, especially in defense of form and tradition in contemporary American poetry. His best-selling collection of essays, *Can Poetry Matter?: Essays on Poetry and American Culture* (1992), the title essay of which first appeared in *The Atlantic Monthly* in May 1991 and provoked an international response, did much to establish Gioia's reputation as a major voice in contemporary letters, a position already recognized in the mid 1980s when *Esquire* magazine selected him as one of the leading cultural figures of his generation. This claim was confirmed on 10 January 2003 when Gioia was named by President George W. Bush to be the chairman of the National Endowment for the Arts. His thorough and sensitive knowledge of business, literature, art, music, opera, and the artistic communities that comprise the contemporary cultural scene made him the ideal candidate to guide American arts through a crucial period in their evolution.

As the chief poet-critic of the New Formalism, Gioia has argued for a recognition, if not a rebirth, of the craft and values of traditional poetics. Indicted by his critics and celebrated by his supporters, he has achieved one of his most important goals as a contemporary poet—namely, to bring the discussion of poetics to the forefront of current compositional debates. His informed, pragmatic, and often irreverent approach has encouraged an active awareness of the possibilities of both tradition and meaningful innovation in contemporary poetry. His insistence that today's poets owe more than lip service to the accomplishments and examples of past masters places him not only among the front ranks of the New Formalists but also among the chief champions for the lasting values of literary heritage.

Gioia's poetry is tied closely to his life and experiences, to the extent that he can be considered an elegist of the changing self. His poems reflect the stages of life that he has experienced, the places where he has lived, and the observations that he has drawn from both experience and literature. Michael Dana Gioia was born 24 December 1950 in Los Angeles to Michael Gioia, a cab driver, and Dorothy Ortiz Gioia, a telephone operator. Although Gioia grew up in a working-class home, he was surrounded by the books, records, and musical scores that had been left in his parents' care by his Mexican maternal uncle, Theodore Ortiz, who was serving in the merchant marine. In the elegy "Night Watch," from *The Gods of Winter,* Gioia recalls his uncle:

> There are so many ways to waste a life.
> Why choose between these icons of unhappiness,
> when there is the undisguised illusion of the sea,
> the comfort of old books and solitude to fill
> the long night watch, the endless argument of waves?

Gioia perceives Ortiz as more than a drowned Lycidas: his uncle is someone who could have opted for a different life—safe, at home, and certain—rather than that of an Odyssean wanderer. For Gioia, there is a certainty, if not a refuge, that resides in literature. His uncle's books were passed on to him not only as heirlooms but also as repositories for tradition when Ortiz died in a plane crash in 1955. In many respects the absent uncle became the first ghost of tradition in Gioia's life, and the books, their content, and the potential for what one could do with literature offered him a vision of life quite distinct from the rough and raw world that he saw around him.

Paperback cover for Gioia's 1982 poetry collection, which celebrates places and experiences in idiomatic language (courtesy of the author)

and music as a neglected and often disparaged literary form in English literature:

> If a poet wishes to write a libretto seriously, however, he or she must accept that opera is not considered primarily a literary form. The poet may remain a necessary partner in creating a new opera, but he or she is indisputably a subordinate one, and poetry itself is secondary to other literary concerns in a libretto. "The job of the librettist," wrote W. H. Auden, "is to furnish the composer with a plot, characters and words: of these, the least important so far as the audience is concerned, are the words." There is nothing to stop a writer from filling a libretto with superb poetry.... How then does one judge the quality of an opera libretto? Is it to be read as poetry or drama? Need it have any genuine existence as a verbal work of art?... The true test of a libretto is ultimately how well it operates in the finished work of art.

Nosferatu, which is based on F. W. Murnau's 1922 silent movie, re-creates the Dracula story as a poetic overlay of words and music. When *Nosferatu* was completed with music by composer Alva Henderson, the verse play at the core of the libretto included arias crafted from rhyme quatrains and duets where passages of blank verse counterpointed each other. From Gioia's perspective, music and poetry are so closely related as to be almost synonymous as foundations for works of art. Indeed, the world itself for Gioia is a combination of words and music.

The scholarly yet defiant young Gioia was constantly confronted by a world that fused daily existence, music, and poetry while growing up in 1960s California. Both nostalgic and lightly elegiac of the lost ethos of the 1960s, "Cruising with the Beachboys" (from *Daily Horoscope*) paints the portrait of a young man driving his father's car "down to the beach to park" where he walks "along the railings of the pier." Like the personae in the poems of Philip Larkin, Gioia's figure in this poem is both isolated and engaged; he observes the "waves monotonous against the shore," the "darkness and mist, the midnight sea," and "the flickering lights reflected from the city." This moment in the poem is, essentially, Matthew Arnold's "Dover Beach" (1867) meeting up with the epiphany scene from James Joyce's *A Portrait of the Artist as a Young Man* (1916). The moment is transforming yet nostalgic, as years later in recollection the persona laments: "I thought by now I'd left those nights behind, / Lost like the girls that I could never get, / Gone with the years, junked with the old T-Bird."

Music itself recalls the moment of sad, lonely, youthful clarity during a "lovesick summer" when singing along to a pop song meant "a primal scream in croaky baritone." Writing in *The Ghost of Tradition: Expansive Poetry and Postmodernism* (1998), critic Kevin Walzer comments that "Cruising with the Beachboys" is full of "ironic self-mockery," which the poem utilizes

Gioia's education, aside from what he achieved for himself through the books, classical recordings, and musical scores that were left to him, was not out of the ordinary during his early years. He attended a parochial school run by the Sisters of Providence in Hawthorne, California, and an all-male Catholic high school run by Marianist brothers in Gardena. He took piano and theory lessons from the age of eight and eventually learned to play a wide variety of instruments. There is a natural musicality in Gioia's lines, an elegance that comes from apprehending how words and music can coalesce into a moving artistic unity. In his essay "Sotto Voce: Notes on the Libretto as a Literary Form," which serves as an afterword to *Nosferatu: An Opera Libretto* (2001), Gioia explains the relationship between words to "undercut the sentimentality of the poem's theme." Walzer notes that little separates this poem from hundreds like it that are produced in creative-writing workshops in which poets are asked to reflect on nostalgic moments in their lives. What makes Gioia's poem so different, Walzer adds, is its clarifying sense of irony and its ability to strip away the illusions of the self—particularly evident in the last line of the poem, in which Gioia explains that the whole remembrance brings "on tears shed only for myself." Gioia, the classical-music enthusiast, reduces the music of the 1960s to a "primal scream," a cry of internal pain that lacks the duende or power of expressive intensification that great artistry provides. Memory is not just personal: it can become universal when properly conveyed through art. Gioia reminds the reader in his poetry that form—the music of language—is a means for art to rise above the cacophony of life.

Walzer notes in the same essay that Gioia's poetry, especially the poetry in which he comments on his early years, is "probing beneath the surface of middle-class life." Walzer adds: "By itself, of course, this is not a unique subject; it has been a staple of American poetry since Confessionalism, and practically become dogma in the first-person, free-verse workshop lyric." But what makes Gioia's commentary on the experiences of the self so important is that the traditions, either formal or thematic, always seem to rise above the individual voice. In "Cruising with the Beachboys" the music is a pathway to the memory by which the poet becomes choked up over the self that he once was that is lost forever:

> But one old song, a stretch of empty road,
> Can open up a door and let them fall
> Tumbling like boxes from a dusty shelf,
> Tightening my throat for no reason at all
> Bringing on tears shed only for myself.

Beneath the layers of memory and nostalgia, Gioia's poetry is haunted by the speculation of what might have been and by the endless possibilities that did not happen because one chose another route in life. In "Summer Storm" (from *Interrogations at Noon*) he speculates on how a chance meeting with a woman, years before at a wedding, could have changed the course of both their lives:

> There are so many *might-have-beens*,
> *What-ifs* that won't stay buried,
> Other cities, other jobs,
> Strangers we might have married.
>
> And memory insists on pining
> For places it never went,
> As if life would be happier
> Just by being different.

Throughout Gioia's poetry the persona constantly confronts himself, forcefully questioning and reevaluating his experience on several levels in order to comprehend just where he stands. In the title poem from *Interrogations at Noon* Gioia depicts a doppelgänger situation, in which the speaker is confronted and interrogated by the better self that he has failed to become:

> Just before noon I often hear a voice,
> Cool and insistent, whispering in my head.
> It is the better man I might have been,
> Who chronicles the life I've never led.
> He cannot understand what grim mistake
> Granted me life but left him still unborn.
> He views his wayward brother with regret
>
> And hardly bothers to disguise his scorn.

Beneath the gothic aspects of a man confronted by his other self—not unlike those presented by Joseph Conrad in his doppelgänger novella, *The Secret Sharer: An Episode from the Coast* (1910)—exists a much larger question than can be explained either through irony or dark fantasy. There is the question of how poetry becomes a search for order and understanding, presupposing that such order and understanding starts with the venture into the labyrinth of the self. In "Maze without a Minotaur" (from *The Gods of Winter*) Gioia ventures a poem on the theme of the story of Theseus and his journey into a labyrinth constructed for King Minos by the artificer Daedalus in ancient Crete. The labyrinth is both the self and the art that the voice must confront, a series of complexities and puzzles that if solved provide the solution to the question of personal identity:

> If we could only push these walls
> apart, unfold the room the way
> a child might take apart a box
> and lay it flat upon the floor—
> so many corners cleared at last!
> Or else could rip away the roof
> and stare down at the dirty rooms,
> the hallways turning on themselves,
> and understand at last their plan—
> dark maze without a minotaur,
> no monsters but ourselves.

Gioia concludes the poem with yet another comment of reflexive irony, though it is far more profound in its psychological meaning and impact: "we / can only pray that if these rooms / have memories, they are not ours." As the old Socratic maxim suggests—"the unexamined life is not worth living"—Gioia's poetry is spared from the self-defeating confessionalism of a life

Gioia in 1985 (photograph by Jan Carp; courtesy of the author)

overly examined through his use of narrative. His poems usually tell a story, even when they appear to be lyric and autobiographical, and this underlying narrative structure helps make even his most difficult works accessible. The other side of the Socratic maxim, however, is that the overly examined life can become unbearable. Gioia attempts to strike a balance in his poetry between the examination of the internal world of his personae while at the same time celebrating the life that is both thrilled (in the Burkean sense) and horrified by what it encounters.

In 1969 Gioia entered Stanford University with plans to become a composer. A year later, while studying German and music in the Stanford-in-Austria program, he decided to become a poet, and returning to America, he switched his major to English. He also edited the Stanford literary magazine, *Sequoia,* and won a prize for the best English honors essay (an analysis of the doppelgänger motif in the short stories of Edgar Allan Poe) in the English department. Following his graduation from Stanford in 1973, he received a fellowship to Harvard University to study toward a doctorate in comparative literature, and there worked with the famed translator Robert Fitzgerald, the poet Elizabeth Bishop (whose brilliance with form and language became a key inspiration to Gioia in his development as a poet), and the Canadian literary critic Northrop Frye (who was a visiting professor at Harvard while on leave from the University of Toronto). In "The Example of Elizabeth Bishop" (from *Can Poetry Matter?*) Gioia notes that what she did as a poet had a profound impact on his own view of writing poetry. Bishop, unlike her contemporaries, was a private poet, unaccustomed to public performances and extraliterary props such those used by other major poets writing in the 1970s such as Robert Bly and Allen Ginsberg. To Gioia, Bishop's importance rests solely on her focus on craft:

> Young writers not only need to learn their craft well. They must also shape their values and aspirations to resist the manifold temptations to write cheaply or dishonestly in the fashionable ways. They need to develop a character strong enough to withstand both failure and success. . . .
>
> But a writer can also choose to remain invisible. Bishop was a poet who existed publicly only in her work. Yet how clearly one saw her values in the poetry. It reflected a modest woman who prized honesty, clarity, and exactitude. The voice was personal, even intimate, but never forward or indecorous. While speaking openly, it also asserted that some things needed to remain private.

Gioia's admiration for Bishop is, in many ways, a description of what he strives to achieve in his own poetry. Like Bishop, Gioia is a dedicated practitioner of the traditional values of craft, as evidenced in his tight and graceful control of blank verse—the prosodic form of public utterance. Also like Bishop, Gioia uses free verse when it seems appropriate. He embraces tradition without excluding innovation and experiment.

One way in which Gioia has sought to cultivate a public voice for poetry is through narrative verse. Making common cause with New Narrative poets such as Robert McDowell, Mark Jarman, and David Mason, Gioia has developed a contemporary idiom for telling stories in poetry that is accessible and remarkably individual. Poems such as the film noir "The Homecoming" (published in *The Gods of Winter*), which tells the story of a young man who is released from prison and shows up at the home of his biological mother to kill her, owe much in their construction and pacing to Hollywood movies. What lies at the root of this impetus toward storytelling is the belief that part of the accessibility of modern poetry comes from the ability of the poet to adapt his or her own vision to the artistic modes that society finds most seductive. Popular

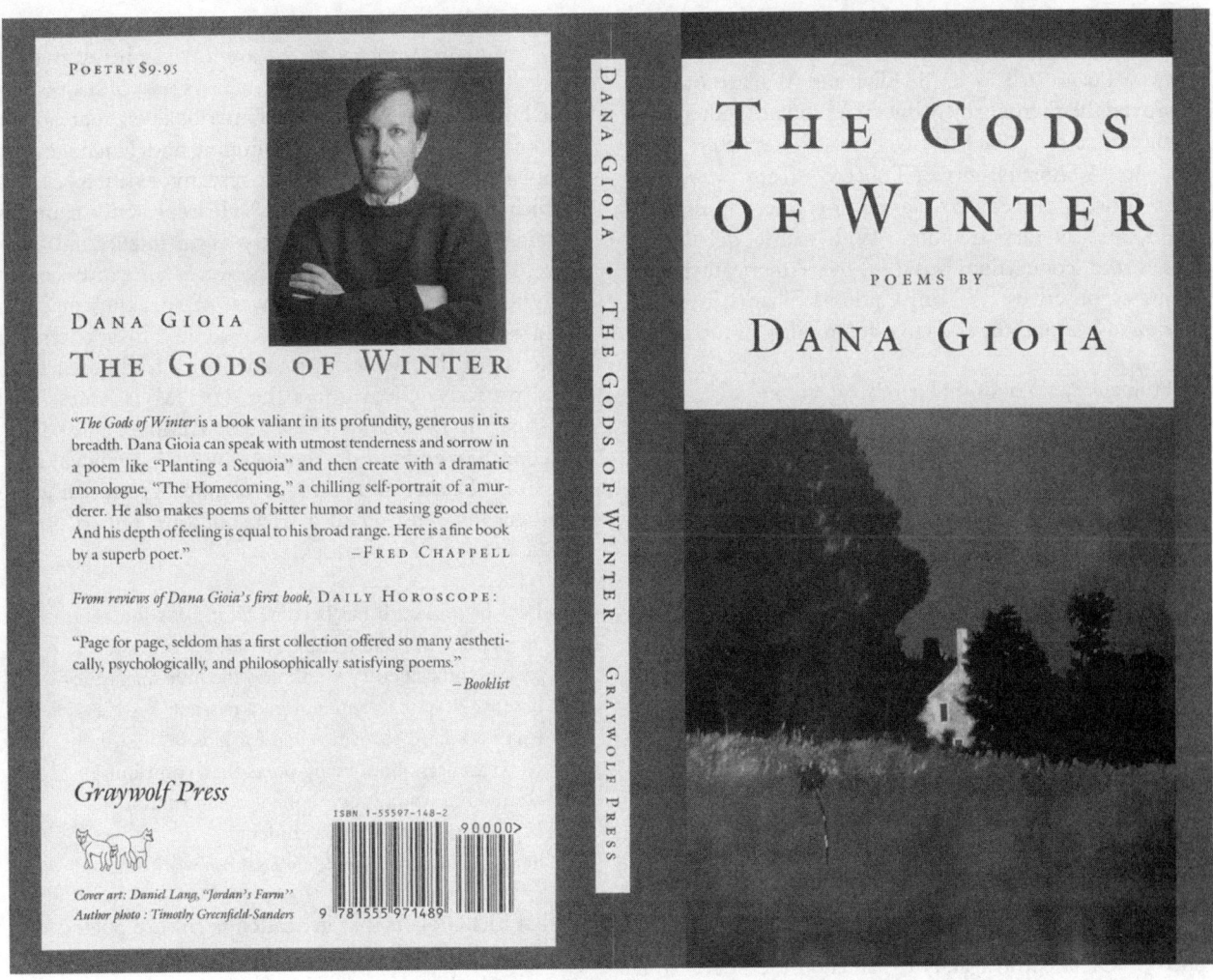

Paperback cover for Gioia's 1991 poetry collection, which includes poems about exploring the outer world as a means of finding the self (courtesy of the author)

culture, Gioia believes, has much to teach the serious poet. For Gioia, there is an inextricably close relationship between the world inside each poem and the world in which one lives. The job of the poet is to link the two, not to avoid their interplay.

The combination of Gioia's natural artistic inclinations and his noted teachers had a definite impact on his poetry. The makings of a poet who later displayed an understanding, if not a mastery, of both poetic form and literary knowledge, appear to have shown their first inklings during this period. Yet, by 1975, when he had completed all the course work for his Ph.D., Gioia abandoned academia for a different career. He left Harvard and returned to his native California, where he completed an M.B.A. at the Stanford Graduate School of Business. This turn toward business marked a major shift in direction in his life, a change that had a profound impact on his poetic career in later years.

In his influential essay "Business and Poetry" (from *Can Poetry Matter?*) Gioia recognized that American poetry includes a tradition of poets who worked in professions other than teaching or writing and who were able to fuse the two lives into a creative symbiosis:

> At present, most American poetry has little in common with the world outside of literature–no reciprocal sense of mission, no mutual set of ideas and concerns, no shared symbolic structure, no overlapping feeling of tradition. Often it seems that the two worlds don't even share a common language. At its best our poetry has been private rather than public, intimate rather than social, ideological rather than political. . . . For many reasons–some of them compelling–most of our poets have rejected the vernacular of educated men and tried to develop conspicuously personal and often private languages of their own.

The poet Marianne Moore said, Gioia points out, that poetry should not "discriminate against business documents." Poets such as T. S. Eliot and Wallace Stevens improved their writing by maintaining contact with a community other than that exclusively related to poetry.

In "A Short History of Tobacco" (from *Daily Horoscope*) Gioia is exceedingly playful in connecting money, greed, and literary tradition. With satiric delight he makes the connection between the American poetic idiom espoused by William Carlos Williams in *In the American Grain* and the addictive commodity of tobacco:

> Profitable, poisonous, and purely American—
> it was Columbus who discovered it
> on reaching China, noticing the leaves
> in a canoe. He sent his men ashore
> to find the Great Khan's palace. They returned
> to tell of squatting natives who drank smoke.

Tobacco, like poetry, is a "gift from God," a vatic perception of something that allows a vision of two worlds at once—this world and the next. The bitter irony in this dualistic vision of the here and the hereafter is that as he explains the curative powers of the leaf, the reader is aware of the great damage it can wreak if one overindulges in it.

In an attempt to express the experience of American life through the vehicle of American poetry, Gioia borrows some of his own words from "Business and Poetry" for the playful free verse poem "Money" in *The Gods of Winter*. Taking up Stevens's comment that "Money is a kind of poetry," Gioia extravagantly expands on the notion in a catalogue of American financial slang:

> Chock it up, fork it over,
> shell it out. Watch it
> burn holes through pockets.
>
> To be made of it! To have it
> to burn! Greenbacks, double eagles,
> megabucks and Ginnie Maes.
>   . . . .
> Money breeds money.
> Gathering interest, compounding daily.
> Always in circulation.
>
> Money. You don't know where it's been,
> but you put it where your mouth is.
> And it talks.

The word "money," in this context, could easily be replaced with the word "poetry." What strikes Gioia is the fact that money, like poetry, is generated by other money—an idea that was often presented (in the context of poetry, at least) by his Harvard teacher, the critic Frye.

Gioia's public message, delivered in *Can Poetry Matter?*, is that poetry as an art form is being overindulged, mishandled, and misused. As part of his respect for both tradition and craft, Gioia believes that poetry should express a unity of emotion and language and not merely an exercise for creative-writing classes which he refers to as "mills." He repeatedly cautions against viewing form in poetry as an intellectual exercise. Poetic form, as he perceives it, is an expression of physical pleasure, a special way of speaking that can add layers of delight and accessibility to a poem. In defense of the beauty and sanctity of traditional form and prosody, Gioia offers the wry "My Confessional Sestina" in *The Gods of Winter*. The complex and beautiful dance of end words—evolved by such medieval masters as Dante and Arnaut Daniel—should not be bathetically reduced to a trick question put to undergraduates as an assignment:

> Let's be honest. It has become a form for students,
> an exercise to build technique rather than taste
> and the official entry blank into the little magazines—
> because despite its reputation, a passable sestina
> isn't very hard to write, even for kids in workshops
> who care less about being poets than contributors.
> Granted nowadays everyone is a contributor.
> My barber is currently a student
> in a rigorous correspondence school workshop.

What irks Gioia is that in academic culture poetry as an art form is reduced to a pedantic assignment, an exercise made less for artistic expression than as a step toward an institutional credential. He dislikes the poseur status of amateurs.

While studying for his M.B.A. at Stanford in 1976, Gioia met Mary Hiecke, a fellow M.B.A. student. They married in 1980 and had three sons: Michael Jasper (who died of Sudden Infant Death Syndrome at four months old, in 1987), Theodore Jasper, and Michael Frederick. Gioia's wife assisted him greatly on his various literary projects throughout the 1990s and the following decade. A closeness to family is an important feature in Gioia's poetry. The home of his childhood, a triplex in Hawthorne, California, was next door to his Sicilian grandparents, aunt, uncle, and cousins. In his later life he lived close to his parents' home in Sonoma County, California. Familial closeness is key for Gioia because he perceives that the Latin tradition is not only a literary matter but also a personal one. In the elegy "Planting a Sequoia" (from *The Gods of Winter*), written on the death of his firstborn son, Gioia acknowledges the importance of cultural tradition and family ritual as a means of remembering and celebrating one's personal community:

Paperback cover for Gioia's 1992 collection of essays on poetics (courtesy of the author)

In Sicily a father plants a tree to celebrate his first son's
   birth–
An olive or a fig tree–a sign that the earth has one more
   life to bear.
I would have done the same, proudly laying new stock
   into my father's orchard,
A green sapling rising among the twisted apple boughs,
A promise of new fruit in other autumns.

"Planting a Sequoia" is a poem that owes much to Virgil's *Georgica* (37–30 B.C.), in that it is about life in the countryside–how to tend to that life and how the practice of keeping the land enriches the sense of who and what one is. Rather than being a fruit-bearing tree, the sequoia that is planted is as tall and stately as the young man that the father had hoped the child would become. Unlike the olive or the fig, the sequoia has a much longer life in store for it, and it is intended to become a monumental life, even in the face of death, long after the entire family has vanished. At its roots, the tree holds the traces of the child's life:

> But today we kneel in the cold planting you, our native
>   giant,
> Defying the practical custom of our fathers,
> Wrapping in your roots a lock of hair, a piece of an
>   infant's birth cord,
> All that remains above earth of a first-born son,
> A few stray atoms brought back to the elements.

Memory for Gioia, in this instance and throughout his poetry, is a matter of giving. As a writer who has a healthy respect for tradition and continuity both in life and literature, Gioia is more than an apologist for custom. He believes that tradition is what reinforces and strengthens life and literature.

While pursuing his M.B.A. at Stanford, Gioia sat in on an eighteenth-century poetry class conducted by Donald Davie. A renowned British poet and critic, Davie was a member of "The Movement," a gathering of poets in Britain during the 1950s that included Larkin, Kingsley Amis, John Wain, and Elizabeth Jennings. Their stance, as articulated by Robert Conquest in his introduction to the groundbreaking anthology of The Movement, *New Lines* (1956), was that Davie's generation of poets had rejected the extraliterary poseur stance in favor of a new verse that was "anti-phony, anti-wet." In many respects, the New Formalists—as they have evolved under Gioia's influence and critical guidance—have practiced this stance in America. Gioia is often criticized for being elitist in this stance, and his desire to protect and nurture form and traditional prosody can be explained in part by his teacher Davie. Like the poets of The Movement, the New Formalists have taken up the Hardy lyric (a tightly wrought lyric stanza that consciously avoids overly poetic diction in favor of direct, common speech, in the manner of Thomas Hardy) as one of their chief idioms of expression. Davie's classes in eighteenth-century poetry and the writing workshop that Gioia took with Davie introduced Gioia to a new generation of American poets who were beginning to experiment with form, narrative, and traditional prosody. This group included Vikram Seth and John Gery.

During the 1980s Gioia's career in business led him to New York, where he worked in product management for General Foods. Living mostly in Hastings-on-Hudson, he frequented many literary gatherings with young New Formalist poets, who included Charles Martin, Tom Disch, Phillis Levin, and Frederick Turner. What emerged during those years became the material for the raison d'être behind the New Formalism. In the essay "Notes on the New Formalism" (from *Can Poetry Matter?*) Gioia brings together the various aspects of his personal life, his views on art and literature, and his approach to the practice of his craft. His statements have become more than a personal credo about poetry: they represent some of the guiding principles behind the rise of the New Formalism as both a significant movement in and a considerable contribution to American literature. As perceived by Gioia, form is not to be feared. It is a means for expanding the capabilities of what poetry can do as a vital art form—an argument that has given rise to the other name for the New Formalism, Expansive Poetry:

> I suspect that ten years from now the real debate among poets and concerned critics will not be about poetic form in the narrow technical sense of metrical versus nonmetrical verse. That is already a tired argument, and only the uninformed or biased can fail to recognize that genuine poetry can be created in both modes. How obvious it should be that no technique precludes poetic achievement, just as none automatically assures it. . . . Soon, I believe, the central debate will focus on form in the wider, more elusive sense of poetic structure. How does a poet best shape words, images, and ideas into meaning? How much compression is needed to transform versified lines—be they metrical or free—into genuine poetry?

What Gioia has attempted to do is to spark debate and renew interest in the art of poetry in general. What may come of that debate remains to be seen, but his point is well taken. Poetry demands that readers and writers engage in the art form from an informed and vital perspective, because at the root of the art are the necessary human values that sustain us.

In January 1992, five years after the death of his son, Gioia quit his job at General Foods and dedicated himself full-time to the vocation of writing. His assiduous work as a critic, editor, translator, teacher, and anthologist has led to the creation of such events as the annual conference on narrative and form in American poetry held annually at West Chester University in Pennsylvania and the "Teaching Poetry" conference in Santa Rosa, California. As an anthologist, his work in editing numerous literary textbooks has been instrumental in keeping the knowledge of diverse poetic traditions alive in the classrooms of America. But his return to California in 1996 represents far more than just a relocation or even a change of vocation; it has allowed him to reconnect with the personal traditions and geography that played such a distinct role in shaping his poetry on the page.

In "Planting a Sequoia," that the deceased son is returned to the family's land in the poet's native landscape of California is of no small significance in Gioia's life and work. Deeply rooted in the region where he grew up and now lives, Gioia works a close identification between the internal landscape and the external one. In "Los Angeles after the Rain" (from *The Gods of Winter*) the adult who had grown up in California and moved away returns to his native city:

> Back home again on one of those bright mornings
> when the city wakes to find itself reborn.
> . . . .
> It is a morning snatched from Paradise,
> a vision of the desert brought to flower—
> of Eve standing in her nakedness,
> immortal Adam drunk with all
> the gaudy colors of the world,
> and each taste and touch, each
> astounding pleasure still waiting to be named.

What lies at the heart of this epiphany is the rediscovery of the place of origin, a first state comparable to Eden, where the persona grapples with the ethereal beauty of a new day in a place that has become unfamiliar through time. At the end of the poem Gioia concludes that it is "A day to . . . look up / old friends, and dream / of quiet love, impossible resolutions." Yet for all its splendor, the California of the past remains a paradise lost, a place that it is almost impossible to return to because it represents the lost choices one once had.

Gioia sums up this loss of choices, the "what-ifs" of a life that might have been different had one made other choices, in "The Lost Garden" from *Interrogations at Noon*:

> If ever we see those gardens again,
> The summer will be gone—at least our summer.
> Some other mockingbird will concertize

Among the mulberries, and other vines
Will climb the high brick wall to disappear.

What connects the past to the present—and indeed paradise to this fallen world, in Gioia's view—is the power of memory. Just as St. Augustine in *Confessiones* (The Confessions, written 397–401) argues that memory is the path of beholding the eternal, if not some minor comprehension of God, so, too, does Gioia insist on the redemptive nature of memory. At the conclusion of "The Lost Garden" he reminds his reader:

The trick is making memory a blessing,
To learn by loss the cool subtraction of desire,
Of wanting nothing more than what has been,
To know the past forever lost, yet seeing
Behind the wall a garden still in blossom.

The past is lost, Gioia argues, only if one fails to make memories poignant enough to be worth preserving. Poetry provides one means to that renewal; from his perspective, poetry is something that must be created as a work of art. In "A California Requiem" (from *Interrogations at Noon*) Gioia celebrates the power of his native state and his first home, to be both the material for memories and the power that can summon them forth:

"Become the voice of our forgotten places.
Teach us the names of what we have destroyed.
We are like shadows the bright noon erases,
Weightlessly shrinking, bleached into the void.

"We offer you the landscape of your birth—
Exquisite and despoiled. We all share blame.
We cannot ask forgiveness of the earth
For killing what we cannot even name."

More than simply a cry for environmentalist reform, the poem is also a call for the recognition of what place contributes to an individual. For Gioia, California has a rich, though often overlooked, poetic tradition. His work with the Robinson Jeffers Tor House Foundation (an effort to preserve both the poetry and the home of a twentieth-century Californian poet) is more than mere historical conservatism. What Jeffers captured in his poetry—indeed what Gioia seeks to discover in his own work—is the genius loci, the spirit that is invested in a place that shapes the individual. In the true Virgilian tradition, care for the landscape and its ethos is ultimately the process of caring for what made one and what continues to influence the individual identity.

Gioia's long essay "Fallen Western Star: The Decline of San Francisco as a Literary Region" (published in *Hungry Mind Review* and later republished in *The "Fallen Western Star" Wars: A Debate about Literary*

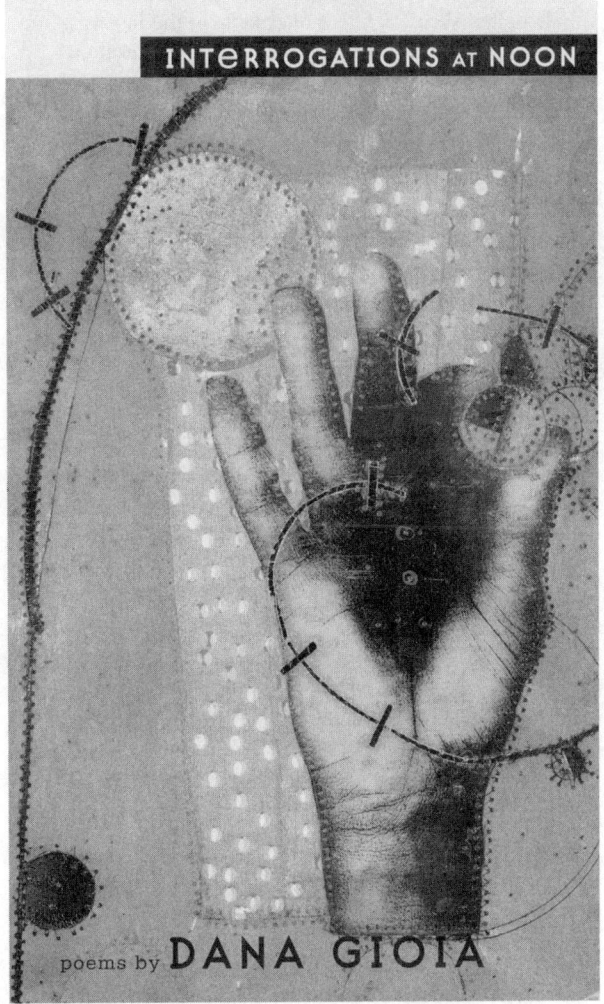

Advertisement for the work that received an American Book Award from the Before Columbus Foundation in 2002 (courtesy of the author)

California, 2001) provoked a broad, ongoing, at times vicious public debate about California literary culture and identity. He presents the case that San Francisco has ceased to contribute to the national literature because it has ceased to provide a complete and vital literary milieu for writers. He laments the loss of the dynamic traditions established by earlier California poets, such as Jeffers, Kenneth Rexroth, and Yvor Winters. In "Fallen Western Star" Gioia establishes the importance of place to poets such as himself and others in his tradition:

Western literary life, by contrast, tends to be private and individualistic. Writers live far apart, and there are few occasions that bring them together in significant numbers. A California writer is more likely to see local colleagues in a Manhattan publisher's office than near home.... Solitary and reflective, the Western writer is also often skeptical about the merits of the intrinsically social acts of criticism and institutional organization.

Gioia perceives the Western writer as someone who is often isolated and lacks the artistic and intellectual communities that one finds in Northeastern urban centers. As a result, he suggests that Western writers are naturally introspective–loners who are obliged to turn their gaze both inward and outward in order to write successfully about their context and their place in the world.

In "California Hills in August" (from *Daily Horoscope*) Gioia offers what appears at first to be a surface description of the individual who encounters the place to which he feels a close connection:

> I can imagine someone who found
> these fields unbearable, who climbed
> the hillside in the heat, cursing the dust,
> cracking the brittle weeds underfoot,
> wishing a few more trees for shade.

As the poem progresses, the description is transformed by the witness, an Easterner who feels displaced in the arid hills–who would "hate the bright stillness of the noon / without wind, without motion," where the only other living thing is a hawk "suspended / in the blinding, sunlit blue." The perception shifts dramatically in the final stanza. The persona of the poem suddenly recognizes that the California hills are living things to those who are familiar, both physically and spiritually, with the place. As in the Irish *dinnseanchas* tradition, in which a poet is able to read and express the spirit or genius of a particular place, Gioia captures the ethos of that which the poem strives to express:

> And yet how gentle it seems to someone
> raised in a landscape short of rain–
> the skyline of a hill broken by no more
> trees than one can count, the grass,
> the empty sky, the wish for water.

The job of the poet, Dana Gioia argues throughout his works, is to find life within the actual places and situations that he experiences; and "the wish for water" amounts to the quest for that life that the poet educates himself to find. In reestablishing the important connection to his personal past through his return to the West, Gioia has found what makes poetry worth writing. In "Speaking of Love" (from *The Gods of Winter*) he writes what may be the key lines in his entire opus, articulating the need to treat language with the dignity that it deserves to the point where language itself leaps into the anagoge of the inexpressible:

> And so at last we speak again of love,
> Now that there is nothing left unsaid,
> Surrendering our voices to the past,
> Which has betrayed us. Each of us alone,
> Obsessed by memory, befriended by desire,
> With no words left to summon back our love.

Interviews:

Robert McPhillips, "Dana Gioia," *Verse* (England), 9 (Summer 1992): 9–27;

Isabelle Cartwright, "Dana Gioia," *Irish Review* (Ireland), no. 16 (Autumn/Winter 1994): 109–122;

Gloria Glickstein Brame, "Poetry: Paradigms Lost, Interview with Dana Gioia," parts 1 and 2, *ELF* (Spring 1995): 34–40; (Summer 1995): 34–38;

Raúl Peschiera, "America and the Culture of Poetry," *The Review* (Canada), (Summer 1997): 87–99;

Lequita Vance-Watkins, "Interview with Dana Gioia," *Caesura* (Winter 1998): 4–7.

Bibliographies:

Michael Peich, *Dana Gioia and Fine Press Printing: A Bibliographic Checklist* (West Chester, Pa.: Kelly/Winterton, 2000);

Jack W. C. Hagstrom and Bill Morgan, *Dana Gioia: A Descriptive Bibliography with Critical Essays* (Jackson, Miss.: Parrish House, 2002).

References:

Robert Conquest, Introduction, in *New Lines*, edited by Conquest (London: Macmillan / New York: St. Martin's Press, 1956);

Frederick Feirstein, ed., *Expansive Poetry: Essays on the New Narrative and the New Formalism* (Santa Cruz, Cal.: Story Line, 1989);

R. S. Gwynn, ed., *New Expansive Poetry: Theory, Criticism, History* (Ashland, Ore.: Story Line, 1999);

April Lindner, *Dana Gioia*, Western Writers Series (Boise, Id.: Boise State University Press, 2000);

David Mason, "Dana Gioia's Case for Poetry," in his *The Poetry of Life and the Life of Poetry: Essays and Reviews* (Ashland, Ore.: Story Line, 2000);

Lewis Turco, "Dana Gioia," in *Dictionary of Literary Biography*, volume 120, edited by Gwynn (Columbia, S.C.: Bruccoli Clark Layman, 1992);

Kevin Walzer, "Still Waters: Gioia, Mason, McDowell, Salter," in his *The Ghost of Tradition: Expansive Poetry and Postmodernism* (Ashland, Ore.: Story Line, 1998).

Papers:

Some of Dana Gioia's papers can be found in The Henry A. and Albert W. Berg Collection, New York Public Library.

Emily Grosholz
(17 October 1950 -   )

Meg Schoerke
San Francisco State University

BOOKS: *The River Painter: Poems* (Urbana: University of Illinois Press, 1984);
Shores and Headlands (Princeton & Guildford, U.K.: Princeton University Press, 1988);
Cartesian Method and the Problem of Reduction (New York: Oxford University Press, 1991; Oxford: Clarendon Press, 1991);
Eden (Baltimore & London: Johns Hopkins University Press, 1992);
Leibniz's Science of the Rational, Studia Leibnitiana Sonderheft, 26, by Grosholz and Elhanan Yarika (Stuttgart: Steiner, 1998);
The Abacus of Years (Boston: Godine, 2002).

OTHER: *W. E. B. DuBois on Race and Culture: Philosophy, Politics, Poetics,* edited by Grosholz, Bernard W. Bell, and James B. Stewart (New York & London: Routledge, 1996);
Telling the Barn Swallow: Poets on the Poetry of Maxine Kumin, edited by Grosholz (Hanover, N.H. & London: University Press of New England, 1997);
The Growth of Mathematical Knowledge, edited by Grosholz and Herbert Breger (Boston: Kluwer, 2000; Dordrecht, Netherlands & London: Kluwer, 2000);
The Legacy of Simone de Beauvoir, edited by Grosholz (Oxford: Oxford University Press, 2003).

SELECTED PERIODICAL PUBLICATIONS—
UNCOLLECTED: "Miłosz and the Moral Authority of Poetry," *Hudson Review,* 39, no. 2 (Summer 1986): 251–270;
"Marriages and Partings," review of six books of poetry, *Hudson Review,* 40, no. 1 (Spring 1987): 156–164;
"Hope and Illusion in a Late Age: The Poetics of Yves Bonnefoy," *Hudson Review,* 42, no. 2 (Winter 1988–1989): 667–674;
"Class and Poetry on the Outskirts of Philadelphia," *New England Review,* 12, no. 2 (Spring 1993): 19–22;

Emily Grosholz (photograph by Leland Monroe; courtesy of the author)

"Poetry and Science in America," *Princeton University Library Chronicle,* 55, no. 3 (Spring 1994): 532–552;
"Distortion, Explosion, Embrace: The Poetry of Alice Fulton," *Michigan Quarterly Review,* 34, no. 2 (Spring 1995): 213–229;
"Leibniz and Plato against the Materialists," *Journal of the History of Ideas,* 57, no. 2 (April 1996).

Paperback cover for Grosholz's first collection of poems (1984), many of which are about her experiences of city life and country excursions in Europe (Thomas Cooper Library, University of South Carolina)

Many contemporary American poets earn their livings by university teaching, most often by teaching creative writing; Emily Grosholz, however, has distinguished herself by teaching philosophy and by crafting four books of poetry that explore her philosophical concerns. Yet, her poetry is not philosophical in any conventional sense, for it does not depend upon pithy sententiae or abstract meditations on Being. Grosholz aims for what she describes in an essay on Czesław Miłosz as "the delicate enmeshment of universal and particular." In *Cartesian Method and the Problem of Reduction* (1991), articles such as "Leibniz and Plato against the Materialists" (1996) and her frequent essays and reviews on poetry, Grosholz has consistently opposed reductionism and charted the tensions between subjectivity—"the unity of thought that confronts matter and tries to represent it"—and the pull of the external world. While not eschewing subjectivity, she stresses that poets and philosophers should be conscious of themselves as contingent beings, shaped by "the sensual imperfect abundance of experience." Because "experience" includes not only the material variety of the world but also the complexities of human relationships—among family, friends, and community—Grosholz argues that poetry and philosophy are profoundly moral endeavors, responsive to human interchanges and the pressures of history and culture. In her poetry, therefore, although she often writes about personal experiences—such as her travels in Europe, childhood memories, marriage, and motherhood—she qualifies these experiences by focusing on the stubborn details of the phenomenal world and the welcome otherness of family members, friends, and the cultures she encounters abroad. The poetry thus develops a flexible middle ground between the extremes of a radical subjectivity and an equally radical objectivity that, as she points out in "Leibniz and Plato against the Materialists," implicates the writer as an agent, but not the sole agent, of world-construction. While she does not scant the difficulties of contemporary social and political life, her poetics, like the ideals she attributes to Yves Bonnefoy in "Hope and Illusion in a Late Age: The Poetics of Yves Bonnefoy" (1988–1989), arise from a temperament whose optimism "rests on a belief that a deep, universal order still remains 'in place, in nature and in us.' So it is the poet's task not only to remember and to hope, but to make manifest what is already there, a presence hidden by the dissociations and alienations of modern culture."

Grosholz's emphasis on finding a middle ground, coming to terms with incongruent variables, and maintaining hope stems in part from a childhood precariously balanced between the emotional and economic hardships incurred by her father's alcoholism and her family's sustaining commitment to books and education. Emily Rolfe Grosholz was born on 17 October 1950 in Bryn Mawr, Pennsylvania, and grew up in Strafford, Pennsylvania, in an old corner house beside a Catholic church. She was an only child until the age of eight when the first of her two younger brothers was born. Her father, Edwin DeHaven Grosholz, a graduate of Haverford College, owned and operated a small printing press but lost it because of his drinking; he eventually found work as a traveling salesman. Grosholz's mother, Frances Skerrett Grosholz, received a B.A. degree from Pembroke College, earned her living as a civil servant in Washington, D.C., during World War II, and then became a homemaker after her marriage. To help the family survive, she worked as a teacher in a private primary school; late in her life, she earned an M.S.W. degree and then did social work for two years before her death from cancer in 1975 at the age of fifty-two.

In an autobiographical essay, "Class and Poetry on the Outskirts of Philadelphia" (1993), she describes the tension between her family's "*Petit bourgeois* [life] and *haut bourgeois* pretensions," particularly the blindness to "the differentiations of class and its imposed burdens" that allowed the family, despite its poverty, to think of itself as above its working-class Irish and Italian neighbors. What she calls "the remnants of family affluence"—summer vacations at the Jersey Shore at the homes of an aunt and a grandmother; attending concerts, theater, and museums; her family's emphasis on books and education—were privileges that nourished Grosholz yet incited a wish to escape: "when I was seventeen, the world I wanted was Baudelaire's Paris, Bernini's Rome, Socrates's Athens, and nobody I knew at home could take me there." College provided one means of escape: she attended the University of Chicago on a scholarship and graduated with honors in Ideas and Methods. Travel gave her another, equally significant opportunity: a gift of $3,000 from relatives made possible two summers in Europe when she was twenty and twenty-three, and until her mid thirties she took every chance she could find to spend time in Europe, especially France, Italy, and Greece. During her twenties she studied philosophy at Yale University and received her Ph.D. in 1978; she also read philosophy at the University of Muenster from 1976 through 1977. Since 1979 she has taught philosophy at Pennsylvania State University, achieving the rank of full professor in 1993; her research and publications on rationalism and the philosophy of science have been furthered by grants from the American Council of Learned Societies (1982–1983; 1997), the National Endowment for the Humanities at the National Humanities Center (1994–1997), and a Visiting Fellowship at Clare Hall, University of Cambridge (1997–1998). While at the National Humanities Center in North Carolina, she met a medievalist, Robert R. Edwards, whom she married on 2 January 1987. After enduring the strains of a commuter marriage, Grosholz and Edwards settled in University Park, Pennsylvania, to raise their four children: Benjamin, born in 1989; Robert, adopted in 1993; William Jules-Yves, born in 1995; and Mary-Frances, adopted in 1995.

Grosholz's life, as she notes in "Class and Poetry," has come full circle, from fleeing the complexities of family relationships to seeking them. Yet, the often autobiographical poetry of her two most recent books, *Eden* (1992) and *The Abacus of Years* (2002), registers not a complacent dwelling in family life but a full engagement with its tensions and rewards. Applying the story of Odysseus's travels and return to her own life and poems, Grosholz closes "Class and Poetry" by envisioning a poetry in which divergent experiences converge and complicate one another, for Grosholz the poet is not a passive recorder of experience but a maker in the classical sense of shaping the world through naming it: "We need a poetry that knows it is not just representing, but constituting and revising the social reality it sets upon the stage of life. So my poems, as I hope, will lead other young women *inter alia* to travel far away, like Odysseus, like me, and also to come home not by compulsion but by choice, to find the old world still stubbornly entrenched in all its divisions and communities, and yet still somehow new." Characteristically, Grosholz draws together oppositions yet respects their distinctiveness—between self and community, in this case a community of women writers; between journeying abroad and at home; and between the old world and the new—as realms that she refuses to separate in conventional ways, because for her the "old world" is not Europe but home, an American family life that is made new through her encounter with its "stubborn particulars" that defy classification.

That Grosholz's poetry and criticism only loosely conform to being classified as New Formalist is not surprising considering her own commitment to resisting reductive classifications. Although her poetry has been included in two defining anthologies, *A Formal Feeling Comes* (1994) and *Rebel Angels* (1996), and she has published frequently in *The Hudson Review,* where she has served as an advisory editor since 1984, her approach to form is distinctive, for she writes primarily in iambic measures yet plays with frequent metrical substitutions, often changes her line lengths within a poem, and, when she adopts rhyme, favors slant rhymes. These strategies are a welcome departure from the tendency in much New Formalist work toward metrical norms that are so strict that they can become monotonous and predictable full rhymes. Similarly, whereas some New Formalists adhere to a severely plain diction and syntax that edges into prosaism, Grosholz varies her diction and syntax. Unlike many New Formalists, Grosholz, as she says in "Distortion, Explosion, Embrace: The Poetry of Alice Fulton" (1995), sees poetic meter not as reflecting an iambic norm inherent in the English language, but as a distortion that attests to the vital subjectivity of poetry: "All poetry distorts language. Formal patterns wrench it from its everyday cadences, and figures from its accustomed ways of referring. . . . In art, distortion is expressive as well as inescapable. Indeed, the studied distortions of art are not only meaningful, they play an essential role in the way we make the world mean, which is often how we make the world *tout court*. In fact, undistorted repre-

The Play of Light

The tentative and fluid rainbows
on the nacreous surfaces
of shells, on peacock feathers
and ~~soap~~ bubbles, ~~are explained~~ may be elucidated
~~by the way in which~~ by thinking: incident light
refracts and reflects off the nether
and upper surfaces
of ~~thin~~ delicate films: one wave train
tagging after the other,
like a little brother.
~~Destructive~~ So interference!
(I want to play with the big guys,
go find some kids your own age),
which, for a given thickness
of film, will only let one color through.
So, on the peacock's wing,
here it is royal purple,
there it is blue;
the displacements of luminous children
in the long ~~deserted~~ recess
of ~~time and~~ space.
(Across, of ~~time~~ and space, the endless recess.)

Emily R. Grosholz
October 1984

Draft for a poem that appeared in Grosholz's first collection (courtesy of the author)

Rhyme of the (ancient) Physics Major

The time integral of force, which is impulse,
measures the change of momentum
in a system;
the displacement integral of force,
which is work,
measures the system's change of energy.

Systems upon which
no external force is acting
(like the universe)
are governed by the two great principles
of conservation:
energy and momentum.
(Angular momentum is also conserved).

This observation tends
to render Newton's ghostly forces
even more spectral; indeed
they may be disappearing altogether.

Emily R Grosholz
October 1984

Draft for a poem by Grosholz parodying Samuel Taylor Coleridge's "The Rime of the Ancient Mariner"
(courtesy of the author)

sentation is just as impossible as meaningless experience." And yet, like the New Formalists, Grosholz criticizes contemporary poets—as she does in "Poetry and Science in America" (1994)—who "retreat into poetry that is relentlessly subjective, hermetic, and fragmentary." Thus, for her, as she says in "Miłosz and the Moral Authority of Poetry" (1986) writing in form is a moral choice based on the urgent need to reach readers: "Prudential wisdom must be eloquent to be effective. And part (but not all) of eloquence is an attention to form: balanced periods, colorful figures, symmetry of argument and counter argument." But, because achieving prudential wisdom is by no means a simple process, Grosholz opposes writing that oversimplifies; the balance she attains in her best poetry—between the demands and distortions of form, the pulse of the pentameter and the unruliness of everyday cadences, and the tensions of argument and counterargument (however symmetrically arranged)—harmonizes with her insistence on the moral obligation of poetry both to address the complexity of human experience and to move readers; as she says in "Marriages and Partings" (1987) "we should strive to be both difficult and clear. Difficult, because no important human problems can be resolved by any simple appeal to univocal principles; clear, because to be effective, a voice must be comprehensible and persuasive."

Grosholz's first book of poetry, *The River Painter: Poems* (1984), gains momentum from the exuberance of her discoveries, both of Europe and of her voice as a poet. The poems catalogue an abundance of city life and country explorations, and also of form, for Grosholz's iambs feel effortless, yet sometimes hurried, as if she could barely keep up with the cascade of experiences she sought to register. The book was praised by James Finn Cotter, in his article "Poetry Marathon" in *The Hudson Review* (Autumn 1984), for her ability to "capture . . . setting and situation, not as a passing tourist but as a person involved with others in place and time." That involvement, however, gains urgency from the poet's consciousness of change. Thus, meditation tempers the exuberance of the poems, for the speakers are often solitary and, even in the midst of detailing lush particulars or addressing friends in letter poems, contemplate loss and the passage of time. The two sections of the book, "The Voyage" and "The Return," although concerned, respectively, with sojourns in Europe and returns to the United States, complement one another, for the poems of the first section often consider domestic life abroad, and the poems of the second section examine the displacements of home and the attractions of "the world" that "resumes the place left empty" ("Ithaka"). Like the Chinese river painter in the title poem, Grosholz aims both to "recollect" herself and, through travel and the discipline of writing, empty out the self to the dispersion of the world.

The tension between recollection—the wish to stop time and somehow solidify the self through memory—and the ceaseless changes of the world is beautifully detailed in "The Gold Earrings," the lead poem of her next collection, *Shores and Headlands* (1988). Revisiting the Pacific coast, she imagines meeting her mother, with whom she may have first seen the place years ago:

> I thought that I would meet you here.
> You stood on the pavilion beside *Nepenthe*
> Where the view is still the same.
> Nepenthe, you told me, means forgetfulness.
> You reminded me to notice the body of earth
> so often that our exchange
> melts back into a hundred other occasions.
> Surely we admired the cliffs together
> descending and descending to the horizon
> south of San Luis Obispo; singular pines;
> the blue Pacific arrested in a motion
> so vast and tranquil it resembles staying.
> Forgetfulness pours through the enormous veins
> that bind and furrow the world,
> the ancient rivers of Acheron and Lethe. . . .

The poem embodies Grosholz's gift for throwing "argument and counter argument," universals and particulars, in tension with one another, for she accedes to mutability and the inevitability of forgetfulness; yet, she works against forgetfulness through her precise delineations of the scenes she describes. On the other hand, those scenes, despite their sharp particularity, become universals: as the poem develops, the Pacific is associated with Acheron and Lethe; a souvenir shop is quite literally equated with memory; and the earrings, loved and lost, remind the poet not only of her mother, also loved and lost, but also of her own changes over time. Grosholz demonstrates how memory and forgetfulness, normally considered opposites, are not so readily separable, a paradox that she underscores at the conclusion of the poem by casting doubt on whether she and her mother ever viewed the coast together.

The title of the book, *Shores and Headlands,* establishes the metaphor of boundaries. Throughout the collection, Grosholz both demarcates and blurs boundaries—between the past and present in the first section, "Exchanges," a group of poems about family and friends; between the self and European landscapes and cultures in the second section, "Vagabondage," a series of loosely rhymed sonnets, and also in the fourth section, "Italian Elegies"; in the epistolary

Dust jacket for Grosholz's second collection, in which she deals with the conflict between attempts to stop time through memory and the inevitable passing of time (courtesy of the author)

poems of "Exile," in which long-distance lovers mourn their separation and contemplate their different cultural and political circumstances in the United States and Argentina; and between philosophical configurations of subjectivity and objectivity in the fifth season, "Philosophers." Grosholz closes the book with "Prothalamia," nine love poems for her husband that detail the rewards of "gratified desire" ("Open Secrets") instilled not only by the joys of physical love but also by the landscapes that Grosholz perceives as analogues for the relationship. Unlike the Pacific headlands describes in "The Golden Earrings," these cliffs do not oppose human love and memory but embody them through the subjective power of the poet's words.

Boundaries also dominate *Eden*, particularly the line between innocence and knowledge that Grosholz dramatizes in poems about childhood and marriage. She writes not only of childhood innocence, lost or defiantly maintained, in poems about her own childhood ("Boundaries," "Secret Places of Forrest Lane," and "The Neolithic Revolution of 1956") and that of her son ("The Shape of Desire" and "Eden") but also of adult innocence that falls into knowledge of the rewards and difficulties of marriage and parenthood ("Commuter Marriage," "Pilgrims," "Thirty-Six Weeks," "Rain or Shine," and "The Pot of Basil"). As in her previous books, Grosholz refuses to oversimplify. The boundaries she traces are never sharp, for the poems often include multiple perspectives on the experiences they consider. Contrasting her own position as poet and mother with that of male artists whose creations were made possible by the domestic labors of women, she admits:

> The world of culture slants away from me,
> I fit its shelves and don't. Whom should I speak for?
> Those wives and maids and models
> used to speak for themselves sharply enough
> in the case of an ailing child or a boney chicken

Grosholz's household in 1996. Back: Grosholz's husband, Robert R. Edwards, and Helena Izquierdo, a student who was living with the family, holding William Jules-Yves Grosholz Edwards. Front: Benjamin Grosholz Edwards, Emily Grosholz holding Mary-Frances Grosholz Edwards, and Robert Grosholz Edwards (photograph by Olan Mills Studios; courtesy of the author).

> or beauty's indecent tariff,
> although they are silent now,
> and never devised a poem or drew a face.
> . . . .
> I have to weave two lines in all I say:
> recorded tenor, evanescent alto;
> fixed trellis, quick and immemorial vine.

The "two lines" attest to the symmetry Grosholz achieves in the book between domestic experience, often quick and chaotic like the vine, and the controlled domain of art that has been celebrated when claimed by men and evanescent when developed by women.

Her most recent collection, *The Abacus of Years*, also calls on public and private realms in poems that chart the intimate world of her experience as a mother and meditate on the humanities. In a note at the end of the book, Grosholz adopts philosophical terms to describe the arrangement of the poems:

> the first three sections are full of births and deaths, and exist in the realm of becoming, to use Plato's terms; the last two sections hover in the realm of being. But the fourth section speaks of the arrested time of neurotic repetition, while the fifth section speaks of the overarching time of history, philosophy, art, and science, which is somehow fruitful. Each section departs and goes far away (England, France, Israel, Germany, a patchwork of elsewheres) to return home at the end, and thus also to give the being in the last two sections a chance to touch down in becoming.

As in her first three books, Grosholz is concerned with journeys abroad and at home, in the external world and in the mind. But these journeys are often fused. Thus, in "Rondo, Andante," the balanced patterns of Wolfgang Amadeus Mozart's piano music become analogues for thought and also resonate in complex relations with Grosholz's domestic life in the past and present:

> Crisscross bayberry lattice, rhododendron
> starred, right angles on the oak,
> the tumbled arches of forsythia,
> piano music Mozart simplified
> so children may repeat him, and their mother
> who never played at all until this year.
> . . . .
> . . . . Relationship
> makes elements complex
> therefore estranging them from what they were
> as elements. . . .

The orderly patterns of music fuse with those of the plants and the mother and children's shared task of learning to play the piano. Because of the complexity of these relationships, the individuals change. Grosholz closes the poem by remembering her mother listening to Mozart and by depicting herself standing "all alone at the front door / watching the maples flicker against the horizon. . . ." In her many analogies for change, Grosholz creates complex interweavings—of past and present, philosophical knowledge and lived experience, objectivity and subjectivity.

Overall, Grosholz's agile iambic measures, her goal of communicating with an audience, and her insistence that the poet bears a moral responsibility to explore the complexities of human experience link her to the New Formalist poets. Yet, her emphasis on flexibility—whether in the liberties she takes with form or in her acceptance of difficult and ultimately unresolvable problems and experiences—differentiates her from New Formalists who value order and unmediated clarity, whether in verse technique or in their approach to the world. Striking a difficult middle ground between clarity and difficulty, formal order and dissonance, Grosholz achieves a poetry of intellectual, emotional, and moral complexity.

References:

Stephen Behrendt, "Varieties of Romanticism: The Tradition Lives," *Prairie Schooner,* 58 (Winter 1984): 102–104;

Fred Chappell, "Purple Patches, Fuddle, and the Hard Noon Light," *Georgia Review,* 43 (Summer 1989): 390–391;

James Finn Cotter, "Poetry Marathon," *Hudson Review,* 37 (Autumn 1984): 496–507;

Mary Kinzie, "Among the Shades," *American Poetry Review,* 13 (March 1984): 41–44.

R. S. Gwynn
(13 May 1948 –   )

David Mason
Colorado College

BOOKS: *Bearing and Distance* (New Braunfels, Tex.: Cedar Rock, 1977);

The Narcissiad, with drawings by Ramderanius (New Braunfels, Tex.: Cedar Rock, 1981);

The Drive-In, A Breakthrough Book, no. 50 (Columbia: University of Missouri Press, 1986);

The Area Code of God (West Chester, Pa.: Aralia, 1993);

A Toast from Cana (West Chester, Pa.: Aralia, 1994);

If My Song: Poems and Translations (Black Mountain, N.C.: Lisle, 1999);

No Word of Farewell: Poems 1970–2000 (Ashland, Ore.: Story Line Press, 2001);

The Voices of the Poet, Distinguished Faculty Lecture Series (Beaumont, Tex.: Lamar University, 2001).

OTHER: *Eating the Menu*, edited by Bruce Edward Taylor, with a contribution by Gwynn (Dubuque, Iowa: Kendall/Hunt, 1974);

Body Bags, in *Texas Poets in Concert: A Quartet*, by Gwynn, Jan Epton Seale, Naomi Shihab Nye, and William Virgil Davis, Texas Poets Series, no. 2 (Denton: University of North Texas Press, 1990);

Dictionary of Literary Biography 105: American Poets Since World War II, Second Series, edited by Gwynn (Detroit: Gale Research, 1991);

Dictionary of Literary Biography 120: American Poets Since World War II, Third Series, edited by Gwynn (Detroit: Gale Research, 1992);

Drama: A HarperCollins Pocket Anthology, edited by Gwynn (New York: HarperCollins, 1993);

Fiction: A HarperCollins Pocket Anthology, compiled by Gwynn (New York: HarperCollins, 1993);

Poetry: A HarperCollins Pocket Anthology, edited, with an introduction, by Gwynn (New York: HarperCollins, 1993);

The Advocates of Poetry: A Reader of American Poet-Critics of the Modernist Era, edited, with an introduction, by Gwynn (Fayetteville: University of Arkansas Press, 1996);

R. S. Gwynn (photograph by Bruce Meyer)

Fiction: A Longman Pocket Anthology, edited by Gwynn (New York: Longman, 1997);

Poetry: A Longman Pocket Anthology, edited by Gwynn (New York: Longman, 1997);

New Expansive Poetry, edited, with an introduction, by Gwynn (Ashland, Ore.: Story Line Press, 1999);

Drama: A Pocket Anthology, edited by Gwynn (New York: Penguin, 2001);

Fiction: A Pocket Anthology, edited by Gwynn (New York: Penguin, 2001);

Poetry: A Pocket Anthology, edited by Gwynn (New York: Penguin, 2001);

The Longman Anthology of Short Fiction: Stories and Authors in Context, edited by Gwynn and Dana Gioia (New York: Longman, 2001);

The Longman Masters of Short Fiction, edited by Gwynn and Gioia (New York: Longman, 2002).

SELECTED PERIODICAL PUBLICATIONS–UNCOLLECTED: "Wilbur's Techniques of Translation," *Sewanee Review,* 92 (Fall 1984): 644–649;

"Double Agents," *Sewanee Review,* 96 (Spring 1988): 297–305;

"Labors of Love," *Hudson Review,* 47 (Autumn 1994): 483–489;

"What the Center Holds," *Hudson Review,* 46 (Winter 1994): 741–750;

"Runaway Cannons: At War with Dickey and Bly," *Sewanee Review,* 102 (Winter 1994): 152–160;

"Poetry Chronicle," *Hudson Review,* 49 (Summer 1996): 341–351.

R. S. Gwynn is one of the best writers of his generation. Yet, until 2001, when *No Word of Farewell: Poems 1970–2000* came out, his poetry was little known; before that year he had published only one full-length collection, *The Drive-In* (1986). In the fifteen years between these two books, Gwynn published chapbooks, edited critical volumes, and was a prolific reviewer of poetry. But to some readers the sheer bulk and excellence of his verse seemed a well-guarded secret, even though his work had appeared in periodicals such as *Poetry, The Hudson Review, The Sewanee Review,* and *New York Quarterly.* Among poets associated with New Formalism, Gwynn–whose next book was continually and eagerly awaited–became something of a cult figure.

What distinguished Gwynn's work almost from the start was not only a pitch-perfect command of meter and rhyme but also a broad intellectual and emotional range. While his best-known poems were satirical, he also wrote narratives and dramatic monologues, elegies, light verse, and lyrics of great tenderness. In some ways Gwynn's poetry resembles that of François Villon, the fifteenth-century French poet whose verse Gwynn has sometimes translated and imitated. His work most resembles that of contemporary American poets such as Richard Wilbur, Anthony Hecht (in the latter's darker modes), and X. J. Kennedy. The Australian poet A. D. Hope was also an influence. Gwynn came of age in the Vietnam War era, however, and his writing reflects the particular disillusionment of his time–a disillusionment that might have found a kind of dark affirmation when he began to read the work of Weldon Kees. Gwynn's irreverence toward cultural icons, his openness to pop-culture subjects, and his deep experience of the American South also distinguish his work. A comparison of Gwynn to other Southern writers reveals that he is more disciplined than Robert Penn Warren and fiercer and earthier than Allen Tate. Though very much a writer of his time and place, Gwynn is potentially a poet for the ages.

Robert Samuel Gwynn (informally known as Sam) was born on 13 May 1948 to Dallas Edmund Gwynn and Thelma Howe Gwynn–married since the late 1930s–in Leaksville (now Eden), North Carolina. The middle of three sons, Gwynn is partly named after his paternal stepgrandfather, Samuel Henry Jamerson, who ran a clothing store. His maternal grandfather, William Howe, was superintendent of the Leaksville Woolen Mill. Gwynn's older brother, Dallas Edmund Gwynn Jr., was born in 1943, and Andrew Howe Gwynn, his younger brother, was born in 1957. Their father attended the University of North Carolina but left before graduation to join the Army Air Corps as a flying cadet. Once again, he did not graduate; he "washed out" after suffering a heat stroke–the subject of Gwynn's poem, "Randolph Field, 1938" (published in *Body Bags,* 1990). Gwynn senior returned to Leaksville, trying several jobs, and then joined the merchant marine in 1943; during World War II he sailed primarily to the Mediterranean.

After the war Gwynn's father went into a business partnership and ran several movie theaters–first the Henry (a "colored" theater) and then drive-in theaters. The Eden Drive-In opened on 14 May 1948, one day after the poet's birth. A photograph taken that day, showing a beaming Gwynn senior in front of the ticket booth for his new theater, later graced the cover of *The Drive-In.* After leaving the movie-theater business in 1954, Gwynn's father worked as a salesman for Industries for the Blind in Greensboro, North Carolina, and retired in the early 1980s as sales manager. Thelma Gwynn worked as a kindergarten teacher and day-care worker into the mid 1980s, by which time she and Gwynn senior had been divorced for many years.

Gwynn attended John Motley Morehead High School in Eden, North Carolina, graduating at age seventeen in 1965. He received a B.A. in English from Davidson College in Davidson, North Carolina, in 1969 and then entered the University of Arkansas, from which he received an M.A. in 1972 and an M.F.A. one year later. During high school he worked for W. T. Combs, a land surveyor and civil engineer. Gwynn's summer job during his college years was as an overhauler in the Spray Cotton Mills. In both high school

The Classroom at the Mall

by R.S. Gwynn

Some higher-up who deemed it would be good
For Learning (even better for P.R.)
To make the school "accessible to all"
Rented the shut-down bookstore at the Mall
A few steps from Poquito's Mexican Food
And Chocolate Chips Ahoy. So here we are—

Four housewives, several solemn student nurses,
Ms. Washington, well-dressed and very dark,
Pete Fontenot, who teaches high-school shop
And is besides a part-time private cop
Who leaves his .38 among the purses,
And I, not quite as thin as Chaucer's Clerk—

Met for our final class while Season's Greetings
Echo subliminally with calls to buy
Whatever this year's taste deems necessary
For Joy and Happiness. The Virgin Mary,
Set up outside to audit our last meetings,
Adores her infant with a glassy eye.

Invoke the Musak: hail to thee, World Lit!
Hail, Epic ("most of which was wrote in Greek")
And hail three hours deep in Dante's Hell
(The occupants of which no one could spell)—
As much as the tight schedule might admit
Of the Great Thoughts of Man—one dose per week.

I've lectured facing towards the esplanade,
Through plate-glass windows on such irony
As Helen's face ("that launched a thousand ships")
Blooming with pimples from the chocolate chips.
Nobody got the joke. Rapt on a grade,
They put it in their notebooks. They face me.

One night near Hallowe'en I filled the board
with notes on *Faust*. A woman with blue hair
Stood writing at the window, looking in

And copying my scrawl with a tight grin
That threatened she'd be back with flaming sword
To corner me and Satan in our lair.

Tonight, though, all is calm. They take their quiz
While I sit calculating if I've made
Enough for the kids' presents. From my chair
I watch the Christmas window-shoppers stare
At what must seem a novelty, and is,
The Church of Reason in the Stalls of Trade.

Like the blond twins who press against the door,
Accompanied by footsore, pregnant Mummy,
Who tiredly spells out for them the reason
I am not price-tagged as befits the season,
Explaining what is sold in such a store
With nothing but this animated dummy

Who rises, takes the papers one by one
With warm assurances that all shall pass
Because "requirements have been met," because
I am an academic Santa Claus,
Because mild-mannered Pete's strapped on his gun.
Ms. Washington declares she has enjoyed the class:
"They had some thoughts, those old guys," she begins,
Then falters for the rest. And I agree
Because, for once, I've nothing left to say
And couldn't put it better anyway.
I pack the tests, gather my grading pens,
And fumble in my jacket for the key,

With time to shop and promises to keep
And no epiphany to end the tale
Except the drifting, circulating teens
With Daddy's plastic pulsing in their jeans
Who wander by in search of something cheap,
Or something, surely, soon to go on sale.

SEPTEMBER 1989/23

Gwynn's proof corrections of a poem published in Chronicles: A Magazine of American Culture *(courtesy of the author)* and college Gwynn played football. At Davidson he won a partial scholarship for athletics and lettered in his sophomore year. During spring practice in 1967, however, a knee injury both ended his college football career and disqualified him from advanced ROTC. Writing in the second of three sonnets about the Vietnam War era (the sonnets were published collectively as *Body Bags*), Gwynn refers to these events:

> . . . A scaled-down wild man, though,
> Like Dennis "Wampus" Peterson, could haul
> His ass around right end for me to slip
> Behind his blocks. Played college ball a year—
> Red-shirted when they yanked his scholarship
> Because he majored, so he claimed, in Beer.
>
> I saw him one last time. He'd added weight
> Around the neck, used words like "grunt" and "slope,"
> And said he'd swap his Harley and his dope
> And both balls for a 4-F knee like mine.
> This happened in the spring of '68.
> He hanged himself in 1969.

Like many young people of his generation, Gwynn was not immediately aware of the attractions of poetry. In high school he had written movie reviews for the school paper. He also read the works of W. Somerset Maugham and James Joyce, but not until college did he become actively interested in poetry. The first creative-writing class that he took was taught by George Core, who later became editor of *The Sewanee Review*. Gwynn served as assistant editor of Davidson's literary magazine, *The Miscellany*, and won the Vereen Bell Award for creative writing in 1968 and 1969. The latter award was judged by George Garrett, who more than a decade later chose Gwynn's first poetry collection for publication by the University of Missouri Press.

Gwynn's initial publications were in *Coraddi* (a literary magazine at the University of North Carolina at Greensboro), *The New Orleans Review* (edited by Miller Williams), and *The New England Review*. Translations of three Villon ballades appeared in the Autumn 1971 issue of *The Sewanee Review* (then edited by Andrew Lytle); there Gwynn is identified as Robert S. Gwynn, "studying in the imaginative writing program at the University of Arkansas." These three ballades are notable not just for the deftness of Gwynn's translations but also because a refrain from one of them—"And this the wind will bear away"—is later echoed in the final line of "Cléante to Elmire," one of Gwynn's richest poems, published in *No Word of Farewell* (2001).

Gwynn was not only publishing early but also actively acquainting himself with the literary world in other ways. In 1968 he attended the Bread Loaf Writers' Conference on a waiter's scholarship; he returned the following summer to take courses from Robert Pack and Wylie Sypher at the Bread Loaf School of English. While a graduate student at the University of Arkansas, Gwynn met poets such as Leon Stokesbury, Ralph Adamo, John A. Wood, and Frank Stanford (who committed suicide in 1977). He also studied with poets Williams and James Whitehead. During these years Gwynn published poems in *Shenandoah, Poetry Northwest,* and *Eating the Menu* (1974), an anthology edited by Bruce Edward Taylor. In short, Gwynn's early mastery of traditional verse and the easy erudition displayed in his essays and reviews are grounded in these apprentice years.

He took his first teaching job in 1973 as an instructor at Southwest Texas State University, located in San Marcos. There he met writer B. H. Fairchild and began producing a poetry column for *Cedar Rock,* a literary quarterly. Through this association he became acquainted with Judson Jerome, who wrote for both *Cedar Rock* and *Writer's Digest. Cedar Rock* published Gwynn's first two chapbooks, *Bearing and Distance* (1977) and *The Narcissiad* (1981). In 1976 Gwynn began teaching at Lamar University in Beaumont, Texas, where he has taught ever since. He was named University Professor in 1997.

Gwynn married Martha Faye LaPrade in 1969, and they were later divorced. In 1977 he married Donna Kay Simon, who had two sons, Jason and Dustin, from a previous marriage. The couple also had a son together, William Tyree Gwynn, born in 1978.

If indeed American poetry of the 1970s and 1980s was dominated by the free-verse confessional lyric, then Gwynn's poetry must have seemed an anomaly from the start. Not only were his early poems in meter, but they were also bitingly satirical and often attacked the contemporary scene. In *The Narcissiad* Gwynn employs heroic couplets reminiscent of Alexander Pope—hardly the most fashionable poet at the time—and applies the societal diagnosis made by Christopher Lasch (in Lasch's *The Culture of Narcissism* [1978]) to contemporary American poetry. Epigraphs for the poem are from writings by Lasch, Pope, John Dryden, and George Gordon, Lord Byron; later Gwynn added another epigraph from a work by W. H. Auden. After a survey of poetry for which Apollo and Dionysus served as deities, Gwynn writes,

> Enough of that. The two gods served us well,
> But now, today, we hear a different bell
> Whose jangling clatter flabbergasts the nerves
> In zig-zag tones outside harmonic curves,
> And ushers in, immortal in his way,
> Our Boy, the god who rules the present day.
> From the jacuzzi, wreathed in scented foam,
> He steps with his blow-dryer and his comb
> To face that altar where all things are clearer,
> To wit, his dressing table and his mirror.

```
Two Views from a High Window: 1971-1991

Above a Midas-trove of golden leaves
And, by his reckoning, on a higher plane
Than other mortals, under peeling eaves
In a drab third-floor office in Old Main,
The teaching fellow shuts his Blake again,
Turns to the window and the perfect day,
And scrapes his nails against a dusty pane
To etch a mandala.  Not far away,
Cheers echo when a marching band begins to play.

Below him, late already for the game,
A carmine-clad alumnus tries to show
His family where the sidewalk bears his name.
His wife and two teenagers urge his slow
Progress along with tugs, then finally throw
Their hands up in despair and hurry on,
Leaving him in his reverie, bent low
Over the concrete.  When he finds his own,
He waves and calls, stumbles, and finds himself alone.

Almost alone, that is, for as he gets
His wind and balance, he becomes aware
Of movement high above his head and lets
His eyes ascend the bricks to meet a pair
Of steel-rimmed glasses and a cloud of hair
And tangled beard, framing a pale, pinched face.
For one long moment they exchange a stare --
Two aliens crossing paths in outer space
Trying to ascertain which is the lesser race.

It's best to leave them thus, shifting the scene
Forward two decades, though the splendid view,
Observed through windowpanes that now are clean,
Changes little.  The carpet may be new,
But the two men there seem familiar too.
The younger doodles mandalas upon
A scratch pad while leafing through
A sheaf of papers, pulls out one
```

Corrected typescript for a poem written by Gwynn on the occasion of the rededication of the Old Main building at the University of Arkansas, 1991 (courtesy of the author)

In the course of the poem Gwynn skewers the reputations of periodicals such as *The American Poetry Review,* as well as an array of "prominent" poets. *The Narcissiad* received more attention than is typically given to poetry chapbooks, including praise from Kenley Smith in *The Hollins Critic* (October 1982) and Jerome in *Writer's Digest* (December 1980).

Poems from his first chapbook, *Bearing and Distance* (a title derived from his land-surveying experience), were reprinted in Gwynn's collection *The Drive-In,* which was no. 50 in the Breakthrough Book series from the University of Missouri Press. The back cover of the book had lengthy and glowing blurbs from Garrett and Kennedy, the latter commenting, "Open the book to 'Among Philistines' and you're helpless in the hands of a poet not quite like any other now practicing. Verse so strictly crafted is rare, yet Gwynn is no mere tinkering formalist: his work has equal parts of passion, energy, and outrageousness. Poem after poem reads like a tightly corked explosion." Kennedy also remarks on the mixture of dark and light emotions in the collection and notes the maturity of its technique and its vision.

"Among Philistines," which first appeared in *Poetry* (March 1983) in the days of John Frederick Nims's editorship, is the opening poem of *The Drive-In* and introduces Gwynn's satirical mode in full stride. Written in fifteen pentameter quatrains, the poem revisits the biblical story of Samson and Delilah—yet this time the hero is a handsome, contemporary man, and Delilah is a movie actress whom he sees on television:

> Unbearable, he thought, and flipped the switch,
> Lay sleepless on the bed in the bright room
> Where every thought brought back the pretty bitch
> And all the Orient of her perfume,
>
> Her perfect breasts, her hips and slender waist,
> Matchless among the centerfolds of Zion,
> Which summoned to his tongue the mingled taste
> Of honey oozing from the rotted lion.

Reduced to the catatonia of a couch potato, Samson can at least summon up his anger at the crassness of the modern world:

> Such were his thoughts; much more severe the dreams
> That sped him through his sleep in a wild car:
> Vistas of billboards where he lathered cream,
> Gulped milk, chugged beer, or smoked a foul cigar,
>
> And this last image, *this,* mile upon mile:
> Delilah, naked, sucking on a pair
> Of golden shears, winking her lewdest smile
> Amid a monumental pile of hair
>
> And headlines. . . .

The lines are packed and various, the meter driven by a righteous anger that climaxes in Samson's prayer to the "Lord God of Hosts, whose name cannot be used / Promotion-wise. . . ." Yet, in the end the weakened hero chooses blindness rather than his vision of the American wasteland:

> So, shorn and strengthless, led through Gaza Mall
> Past shoeshop and boutique, Hallmark and Sears,
> He held his head erect and smiled to all
> And did not dignify the scene with tears,
>
> Knowing that God could mercifully ordain,
> For punishment, a blessing in disguise.
> "Good riddance," he said, whispering to the pain
> As searing, the twin picks hissed in his eyes.

To find another late-twentieth-century American poem as fierce as this one without looking at the work of a master such as Hecht would be difficult. *The Drive-In* begins as stunningly as any book yet produced by a poet of Gwynn's generation.

Pop-culture imagery occurs as well in "M. Magus," the sonnet that follows "Among Philistines." The title "M. Magus" references the famous blind cartoon character Mr. Magoo (blindness is a major theme in *The Drive-In*). A biblical allusion also surfaces—this time from the New Testament—as the reader perceives that Magus is in some sense one of the Magi, who tries to follow the star to the birth of Jesus. Like several poems by Eliot and Auden, Gwynn's "M. Magus" mixes up chronology, but the allusion to television cartoons distinguishes his work generationally. This sonnet is more than a joke, however, and it ends with a fine sestet:

> Too many years of study by the dim
> Glow of the midnight oil have left these eyes
> Two cloudy windows on a clouded mind.
> Now I wonder at the meaning of the hymn
> That lifted up our thoughts to touch the skies.
> Wonder and wander. The blind shall lead the blind.

Gwynn is a kind of magus himself, one who can make forms do his bidding. Two pages after "M. Magus" is another sonnet, "Iago to His Torturers," that can be read as a hilarious sadomasochistic monologue in miniature. Just as William Shakespeare is often thought to have enjoyed writing Iago's part more than Othello's, Gwynn reminds us of perverse pleasures one might have missed this side of Robert Browning, well known for his love of violent characters. The difference between Shakespeare and Gwynn is that the latter's cartoonish treatment of madness is almost hallucinogenic, not unlike what happens in the second half of Vladimir Nabokov's *Lolita* (1955). In "Horatio's Philosophy," the poem that follows "Iago to

His Torturers," a kind of literary situation comedy unfolds in which the late Hamlet's university chum wrestles with the dictates of his dead friend. Here the conceit seems not unlike that used by Tom Stoppard in his *Rozencrantz and Guildenstern Are Dead* (1967), although all the action in the poem takes place after the curtain has fallen on the play. Poem after poem in *The Drive-In* begins in some whimsical literary conceit, but Gwynn pushes beyond his original impulse to find some startling insight into human character–especially the desires and losses that people can suffer, or their metaphorical blindness.

The Drive-In also proves something about Gwynn that is borne out in his later work: he is one of the best sonneteers of his generation. Six of the poems in this book are sonnets or sequences of sonnets, each of them distinguished by the apparent care with which Gwynn moves within such tight formal structures. "Parenthetical" could be compared to Auden's "Who's Who" (1936), while the sonnet sequence "1916" movingly evokes the generation of Rupert Brooke. The often anthologized "Scenes from the Playroom" casts a cold eye on the viciousness of certain children and the indifference of some parents. "Untitled" plays on the prefix of his title to become a little meditation on absence and loss. By the time he was thirty-eight years old, Gwynn had joined the ranks of such sonnet masters as Edwin Arlington Robinson and Robert Frost.

The book is still more various, however, and includes wild Surrealist poems such as "The Decline of the West"; a good concrete poem titled "Rubbers"; and the cynical epigram, "*Ars Poetica*," which runs as follows: "Sweet music makes the same old story new. / That is a lie, but it will have to do." "A Short History of the New South" reads like verse Flannery O'Connor, while "Anacreontic" begins "You drink to piss it all away," and spends the next thirty-one lines playing related tetrameter riffs on mortality. One lyric, "Our Hearts Were Growing Up," borrows its title (randomly chosen) from a 1946 movie starring Brian Donlevy, while the exquisite "Mimosa" borrows a stanza of Paul Valéry's "Palme," which was duplicated in James Merrill's translation, "Palme," published in the 18 March 1982 *New York Review of Books*.

The actor Donlevy makes another appearance, albeit obliquely, in "The Drive-In," an autobiographical poem in tetrameter couplets (this time not used to comic effect as in Samuel Butler's *Hudibras*, 1663, 1664) about the family movie theater. The motion picture that follows a slapstick cartoon on the outdoor screen is *Union Pacific* (1939), Cecil B. DeMille's dramatization of the building of the first transcontinental railroad. The movie pits Joel McCrea against Donlevy, but the poem seems more concerned with the theme of union: communication between family members, one's own memories of childhood, and the strange way in which movies reflect so powerfully one's sense of experience and the passage of time. At the end of the poem Gwynn writes,

I fall asleep. The night is cold.
And waking to the seat's chill touch
I hear the last car's slipping clutch,
As on the glass a veil of frost
Obscures the childhood I have lost.
The show is over. Time descends.
And no one tells me how it ends.

This fine personal meditation is followed by another, "Three Views of the Young Poet," which reads like an expertly crafted short story in verse. Perhaps the best distillation of the fallen world surveyed by Gwynn in *The Drive-In* is the final poem, fittingly titled "The Denouement":

Who were those persons who chased us?
They were the last of the others.
. . . .
What is the word for this place?
No one has ever used it.

When shall I hear the word?
Never, until it is spoken.

Who were my father and mother?
Trust me to keep your secret.

What is the mark on your forehead?
What is the mark on your cheek?

One might think that, having produced a volume as strong as *The Drive-In*, Gwynn would be recognized throughout the poetry world as a major new talent, but such an outcome did not happen. The book won no awards and was not widely reviewed. One of the best reviews it received, by Fred Chappell writing in *The Greensboro News and Record*, noted, "*The Drive-In* is a bitterly witty book, tough and funny. It is a joy and a victory." Yet, even so perceptive a critic as Chappell pegged Gwynn as primarily a satirist–perhaps because satire is the most uncommon element in the book–and paid scant attention to the rest of his range. A much longer review by R. C. Reynolds appeared in *The Bloomsbury Review* and summed up the qualities of the collection: "*The Drive-In*, by R. S. Gwynn, demonstrates that poetry can be emotional without sentimentality, disciplined without banality, intellectual without pedantry, and personal without self-pity. In fact, this slender volume offers a wonderful collection of verse that is unique in its strict attention to craft, original in its approach to art, and delightful in its revelation of the

Paperback cover for Gwynn's 2001 collection (courtesy of the author)

outrageous reaches of the poet's imagination." Reynolds concludes by calling Gwynn "a major and powerful voice," but one still wishes that more critics had been able to hear that voice. Floyd Collins, in the *Lamar Journal of the Humanities,* also contributed a thoughtful reading of the book, aptly comparing Gwynn to Hecht. Dabney Stuart, writing in *Tar River Poetry,* ventured that "five or six" poems in the book were "as fine as anything being published anywhere." Despite this praise and notice in a few other journals, one can say only that *The Drive-In* did not find quickly the praise it deserved.

Fifteen years (and the end of the millennium) passed before Gwynn published another major collection. In the meantime two chapbooks whetted the appetites of his readers, who were growing in number. *Body Bags* was one of four short collections published in *Texas Poets in Concert: A Quartet* (1990); the other collections were by the poets Jan Epton Seale, Naomi Shihab Nye, and William Virgil Davis. Gwynn's selection encompassed ten poems and two translations (Gwynn translated a poem by Heinrich Heine and another by Karl Haushofer). Among the "lighter" poems, "Snow White and the Seven Deadly Sins" is much in the mode of "Among Philistines," though without its bitter fury. "Two Songs: From *Notes & Queries: An Academic Operetta,*" on the other hand, is hilarious. The first part, "Terminal Song," alternates between *Asst. Prof.* and a *Chorus of Beards* locked in a battle over tenure. The second, "The Professor's Lot," is another academic satire, and Gwynn sometimes sings it in a baritone voice to its Gilbert and Sullivan tune. These songs are followed by a tour de force, "Approaching a Significant Birthday, He Peruses *The Norton Anthology of Poetry,*" in which each line of the seven-pentameter quatrains is quoted from some canonical poem by such authors as John Milton, John Keats, Percy Bysshe Shelley, William Wordsworth, Alfred Tennyson, William Butler Yeats, Dylan Thomas, and Eliot. This poem is the ultimate New Critical joke, because its meditations on mortality are turned into an academic guessing game in which one attempts to name all the authors represented.

As the title of the chapbook suggests, thoughts of mortality are rarely absent from these poems. "Randolph Field, 1938" is about the illness that prevented Gwynn's father from finishing flight school in the Army Air Corps, while "West Palm" is a dramatic monologue in the voice of a draft-board doctor who protests his official duties:

> Sometimes I'd listen with the stethoscope
> Until I half convinced myself I heard
> A murmur. Hell, nobody questioned me
> As long as every bus to camp was filled.

As good as this poem is, it does not compare with Gwynn's much later monologue "Cléante to Elmire" for emotional impact. Yet, that his war poems are usually about men who never went to war is interesting. In the three sonnets of *Body Bags,* he considers the impact of Vietnam on his generation, and the passage of time since that war makes each situation more poignant. Here is an excerpt from the final sonnet, which concludes the chapbook:

> Jay Swinney did a great Roy Orbison
> Impersonation once at Lyn-Rock Park,
> Lip-synching to "It's Over" in his dark
> Glasses beside the jukebox. He was one
> Who'd want no better for an epitaph
> Than he was good with girls and charmed them by
> Opening his billfold to a photograph:
> Big brother. The Marine. Who didn't die.

Critic Jonathan Holden noted the successes of this sonnet in his essay, "The Public Nature of End-Rhymed Poems."

Increasingly and subtly, Gwynn becomes a poet of spirit—or yearning for spirit—as well as a poet of human dust. One could see signs of it in Samson's prayer in "Among Philistines," and one finds a muted spirituality in Gwynn's 1993 chapbook, *The Area Code of God.* This booklet also displays Gwynn's comedic talents in full force. The title comes from "1-800," a poem about home shopping in which materialism is a substitute for spiritual connection. "The Classroom at the Mall" constitutes another academic satire and is followed by two strong sonnets. The final poem of this collection, however—the curtal sonnet titled "Release" (begun some twenty years before it was published)—proves the greatest success of the chapbook:

> Slow for the sake of flowers as they turn
>   Toward sunlight, graceful as a line of sail
>   Coming into the wind. Slow for the mill-
> Wheel's heft and plummet, for the chug and churn
> Of water as it gathers, for the frail
>   Half-life of splaylets as they toss and spill.
>
> For all that lags and eases, all that shows
>   The winding-downward and diminished scale
>   Of days declining to a twilit chill,
> Breathe quietly, release into repose:
>   Be still.

What sailors mean by "coming into the wind" would produce a flapping sail, not a graceful one. Gwynn probably means a sail just as the wind catches and fills it. Perhaps the meditative quietude here comes from the effort to imitate Gerard Manley Hopkins, but this poem is much closer to a whisper than Hopkins's "Pied Beauty" (1877).

In 1995 Gwynn's father died. "Randolph Field, 1938" was read at a family service in his memory. Another poem dedicated to Gwynn's father is the rondeau "A Box of Ashes," one of the many new poems he includes in *No Word of Farewell.* In another rondeau, called "Bone Scan," the poet alludes not only to his father's death but also to his own recent struggle against prostate cancer:

> Shadows surround me, building in the air
> Like clouds, were I inclined here to compare
> My kingly state to portents in the sky.
> I could say the expected: I could lie,
> Claiming our long-term forecast will be fair.
> . . . .
> The night my father died, I moved my chair
> Close to his bed to touch his meager hair
> While shadows gathered in his room that I
> Might gather I was not too young to die.
> Now, circuits close. A tunnel beckons where
>   Shadows surround me.

A villanelle titled "The Dark Place" takes a Larkinesque view of things and concludes, "In this dark place where I have come to piss, / Where none of us deserves a death like this." Another poem, "Train for Ill," is written in the stanza of Tennyson's "Lady of Shalott" (1832).

Still, a great many of Gwynn's poems since the mid 1980s are notable for their humor. There is rueful comedy in "My Agent Says"; satire in the *pantoum* (a Malaysian poetic form) "Black Helicopters"; narrative humor in "The Ballad of Burton and Bobby and Bill"; and sublime silliness in both the villanelle "Why They

Love Us" and the epigrammatic sequence "Versions for the Millennium." Gwynn also includes his backward villanelle, "Ellenalliv for Lew [Turco]: On His Retirement," and the Villon parody titled "Ballade of the Yale Younger Poets of Yesteryear."

Among the most substantial new poems Gwynn has collected are the sonnets in "Two Portraits," a lyric titled "1969," and the dramatic monologue "Cléante to Elmire." The last piece in part pays homage to Wilbur–it is written in the couplets that Wilbur used for his translations of Molière–but it is more than just praise for another poet. Gwynn's experiences of hospitals and the artist's life in provincial towns have given him an entry into the mind of a dying man. This man is a homosexual, dying of AIDS and thinking of a friend, Cara, with whom he acted in a local production of *Tartuffe*:

> Lord, twenty years have passed and still each line
> Smacks tartly on the tongue like a good wine
> Heady with epigram and foiled seduction.
>
> It was the Coastal Players' great production–
> Rhymed verse they said our audience could not
> Make much of, let alone digest the plot–
> Yet how we triumphed, I the *raisonneur*
> Cléante and you the faithful spouse, the pure
> Elmire, the model of a perfect wife.

Gwynn pulls us into a world where role-playing and the heightened clarity of art are partial compensations for these two people's more ordinary secrets. The speaker, by "coming out" in a small town, is finally able to drop one role he had played, while Cara's attempt to move on to a professional career in acting ends, horribly, in her murder by a drug-ravaged boyfriend. All of this narrative is spoken to Cara's spirit, which comes to mind now because of hurricane season; the hospital will be evacuated to save its patients' lives–an irony not lost on the doomed speaker. The other irony is that the storm has been given a woman's name, Cara.

> Corny? You know me, Cara, for I am
> The same as you, eternally a ham
> Who holds out hopes of One who can explain,
> A *raisonneur* of happiness and pain,
> Who proves for us that love is possible
> And need not climax in so great a fall
> As what we've suffered . . .

What left Gwynn's Samson in a state of righteous rage in "Among Philistines" leaves this narrator in a somewhat sadder place, and the emotional riskiness of the poem pays huge dividends of memorable feeling. "Cléante to Elmire" is arguably not only Gwynn's best dramatic monologue but also one of the best poems by any American poet of the twenty-first century. It is about forgiveness in a world where people must try to write their own benedictions and about the weight of reality countering all the fantasy in art and in the human mind.

Gwynn's editorial work is distinguished by his extensive classroom experience–which has helped him produce several successful textbooks–as well as his wide and sympathetic reading. For five years, from 1987 to 1991, he wrote "The Year in Poetry" for the *Dictionary of Literary Biography* (*DLB*) *Yearbook.* That work, in which he reviewed nearly every new collection of poems published in the United States, amply displayed some of Gwynn's virtues as a critic. In the 1989 volume, for example, he surveyed the controversy that had erupted following the publication of Joseph Epstein's essay "Who Killed Poetry?" (1988) and began with an accurate survey of what Epstein had actually said. He also noted the special issue of *Crosscurrents,* edited by Dick Allen, which announced New Formalism as a movement; with such gestures Gwynn continued the description of New Formalism that had been partly instigated by his predecessor in "The Year in Poetry," Lewis Turco. Another controversy enlivened Gwynn's 1990 essay, in which he examined a public feud between poet Louis Simpson and David Fenza, editor of *The Writer's Chronicle,* over the awarding of the Pulitzer Prize to the prose poems of Charles Simic; Simpson had pointed out that the prize should be awarded to an author for a book of verse. In both of these cases Gwynn's calm, accurate recounting of the arguments that were involved is superb. He also proves that he appreciates writers of various kinds; he offers high praise for new books by Rodney Jones, Marilyn Nelson (Waniek), and Hecht.

Gwynn can also be an amusing critic in his reviews (he credits movie critic Pauline Kael as one of his strongest influences). In a "Poetry Chronicle," for *The Hudson Review* (Summer 1996), he referred to "The Fame Factory, where public reputations of all sorts are manufactured. The reader begins in the malodorous sub-basement with politicians and ascends past movie and rock stars and National Endowment of the Arts–funded performance artists to the thirteenth floor, where in a cobwebbed cubicle a shape with Helen Vendler's body and the head of Bill Moyers presides over the Big Board of Poetic Futures." Such humor risks alienating powerful figures in the poetry world, but Gwynn's integrity as a critic and his distaste for cultural sham are welcome aberrations in a climate where publicity triumphs over artistic virtue.

Gwynn does not appear to be a critic with a broad vision of the art or its cultural position. He does not work from an apparent theory or statement of

Gwynn in 2002 (photograph by Ty Gwynn; courtesy of the author)

principles. Though he has written overviews of the poetry scene, he seems most comfortable when addressing the specific example of a given poet's work. One case in point is his essay-review "Wilbur's Techniques of Translation," published in *The Sewanee Review* (Fall 1984). Building on his experiences as a reader as well as a translator, Gwynn begins with a succinct and thoughtful overview of the problems involved in translating poetry. "Translating poetry is a task of such supreme difficulty," he writes, "that one wonders why poets continue to attempt it." But his subsequent close reading of Wilbur makes it amply clear how great an accomplishment these translations are, and how other poet-translators have fallen short of the mark. In other words, Gwynn is a critic from whom one can learn not because of his sweeping vision but because of his precise attention to detail and his quiet understanding of context.

As an editor, in addition to his textbooks and *DLB* surveys, he has published two important books, *The Advocates of Poetry: A Reader of American Poet-Critics of the Modernist Era* (1996) and *New Expansive Poetry* (1999). *The Advocates of Poetry* includes reprints of essays by figures such as John Crowe Ransom, Kenneth Burke, Louise Bogan, Robert Hayden, Randall Jarrell, and John Ciardi. Gwynn's well-written introduction reminds the reader not only how much valuable criticism these poets contributed but also how far literary criticism has moved from such values–how only a few good poet-critics have resulted in the decades after Ransom, Burke, Bogan, and the others were writing. *New Expansive Poetry* arose from a more difficult and controversial assignment: the revision of an earlier book called *Expansive Poetry,* which had been edited by Frederick Feirstein (with Frederick Turner). The earlier book was a flawed attempt to announce the arrival of a movement defined in broader terms than those implied by the New Formalism. It featured essays by figures such as Dana Gioia and Timothy Steele–as well as Turner's controversial essay "The Neural Lyre"–but its preface resembled a hollow manifesto: the movement had simply not produced enough good writing to justify the claims of the book. Gwynn refined and expanded *Expansive Poetry*. In his revision, Gwynn cut weak essays, added stronger ones, and introduced a broader social range to the book than might have been possible for its earlier incarnation. One can only hope that Gwynn's sensible revision of this book will help readers make a serious appraisal of the claims and accomplishments of the movement.

Ultimately, what matters is that the best poems of a generation be read and recognized. R. S. Gwynn has demonstrated the contemporary validity of fixed forms such as the sonnet and has written some of the most sophisticated comic and satirical verse available in American poetry. Part of that sophistication lies in the seriousness of his spiritual and social concerns. His work, its range and accomplishment, is ripe for more recognition.

References:

Bruce Bawer, "Born Ceaselessly into the Past," *Hudson Review* (Autumn 2001): 513–519;

Jonathan Holden, "The Public Nature of End-Rhymed Poems," *Writer's Chronicle,* 32 (December 1999): 10–14;

Allan M. Jalon, "Texas Poet Skewers American Pop Culture," *San Francisco Chronicle,* 26 August 2001, 79;

Dave Oliphant, "The New Formalism in Texas," *Texas Observer,* 3 August 2001;

Leon Stokesbury, "As If the Ax Man's Sorrows Were His Own," *Sewanee Review* (Winter 2001): xxiii–xxv;

Kevin Walzer, *The Ghost of Tradition: Expansive Poetry and Post Modernism* (Ashland, Ore.: Story Line Press, 1998).

Papers:

A collection of R. S. Gwynn's papers (dating from 1976 to 1994) can be found in the Southwest Writers Collection at Albert B. Alkek Library (Special Collections), Southwest Texas State University, in San Marcos, Texas. This collection consists of materials relating to Gwynn's first two chapbooks of poetry, *Bearing and Distance* and *The Narcissiad,* as well as his first full-length volume, *The Drive-In.*

Marilyn Hacker

(27 November 1942 –   )

Jennifer Factor

See also the Hacker entry in *DLB 120: American Poets Since World War II, Third Series.*

BOOKS: *The Terrible Children: Poems* (New York?: Privately printed by Samuel R. Delany, 1967);
Highway Sandwiches, by Hacker, Tom Disch, and Charles Platt (N.p., 1970);
Presentation Piece (New York: Viking, 1974);
Separations (New York: Knopf, 1976);
Taking Notice (New York: Knopf, 1980);
Assumptions (New York: Knopf, 1985);
Love, Death, and the Changing of the Seasons (New York: Arbor House, 1986; London: Onlywomen, 1987);
Going Back to the River: Poems (New York: Random House, 1990);
The Hang-Glider's Daughter: New and Selected Poems (London: Onlywomen, 1990);
Selected Poems, 1965–1990 (New York & London: Norton, 1994);
Winter Numbers: Poems (New York & London: Norton, 1994);
Squares and Courtyards (New York & London: Norton, 2000);
Desesperanto: Poems 1999–2002 (New York: Norton, 2003);
First Cities: Collected Early Poems, 1960–1979 (New York: Norton, 2003).

Edition: *Love, Death, and the Changing of the Seasons* (New York: Norton, 1995).

OTHER: *Quark,* 4 volumes, edited by Hacker and Samuel R. Delany (New York: Paperback Library, 1970–1971);
Ploughshares, poetry issue, edited by Hacker, 15 (Winter 1989);
"Meditating Formally," in *A Formal Feeling Comes: Poems in Form by Contemporary Women,* edited by Annie Finch (Brownsville, Ore.: Story Line Press, 1994);
Ploughshares, poetry and fiction issue, edited by Hacker (Spring 1996);
"A Few Cranky Paragraphs on Form and Content," in *Dwelling in Possibility: Women Poets and Critics on Poetry,* edited by Yopie Prins and Maeera Shreiber (Ithaca, N.Y.: Cornell University Press, 1997), pp. 193–201;
"Journals," in *Living on the Margins: Women Writers on Cancer,* edited by Hilda Raz (New York: Persea Books, 1999);
"The Sonnet," in *An Exaltation of Forms,* edited by Annie Finch and Kathrine Varnes (Ann Arbor: University of Michigan Press, 2002).

TRANSLATIONS: Claire Malroux, *Edge* (Winston-Salem, N.C.: Wake Forest University Press, 1996);
Malroux, *A Long-Gone Sun* (River-on-Hudson, N.Y.: Sheep Meadow Press, 2000);
Vénus Khoury-Ghata, *Here There Was Once a Country* (Oberlin, Ohio: Oberlin College Press, 2001);
Khoury-Ghata, *She Says* (St. Paul, Minn.: Graywolf Press, 2003).

SELECTED PERIODICAL PUBLICATIONS–UNCOLLECTED: "The Classic Poem: Rukeyser's 'Nine Poems for the Unborn Child,'" *Poetry Review* (London) (Fall 1997);
"What's American about American Form?" *HeART Quarterly,* 3, no. 1 (Summer 1999): 10–14.

Marilyn Hacker reads and writes with an ear cocked toward living language. Her diction takes in the raunchy, down-home language of street corners as well as the lyrical richness of a metric line and the punctuated earnestness of a good conversation with a friend. This authentic sense of language lends an urgent modernity to Hacker's voice. Hacker also offers a vivid, original eye for detail in the material world and tends to populate poems with complex people in uneasily characterized relationships; she then brings these skills to a tremendous gift for unanticipated rhymes and obscure poetic forms. While Hacker's poetry is formally

Marilyn Hacker (courtesy of the author)

demanding, it is also topically accessible and ultimately political.

Born in the Bronx on 27 November 1942, Hacker grew up as the only child of working-class Jewish parents, Albert Abraham Hacker (a management consultant) and Hilda Rosengarten Hacker (a teacher), who had been the first in their respective families to attend a university. Her engagement with poetry began in her youth. In 1958, at the age of sixteen, Marilyn Hacker left home and the Bronx High School of Science for an early acceptance to New York University. By 1961 she was living and working in near-poverty conditions and contributing to the youthful, artistic countercultures of the East Village of New York, then San Francisco and London. She married Samuel R. Delany on 22 August 1961, and in 1964 she finished her B.A. degree at New York University. Faking her age for an employment application, Hacker first worked as an editor at the science-fiction imprint Ace Books. Later, while attaining her earliest public poetic recognition, she performed whatever work was available–from post-office worker to employment counselor to textbook writer. For several notable years, 1971–1976, Hacker earned her living as an antiquarian bookseller in London. She and Delany had one child, Iva Alyxander Hacker-Delany, born in London in 1974. During that same year the couple separated, though they did not formally divorce until 1980.

Hacker's playful literary friendships with artists and writers from Tom Disch to Delany leave a paper trail of the type of energy she brought into the lives of those around her. In fact, in her early and late twenties, Hacker attracted rare favorable notice from W. H. Auden (who issued her an invitation to tea and later came to dinner) and the then-already-established poet, editor, and critic Richard Howard. Howard, then at the helm of *The New American Review,* provided Hacker with her first important poetic breakthrough. His response to her work went beyond enthusiasm. He offered to take all of the poems she had sent and asked her to send more. Shortly thereafter, a small sample of these poems won the prestigious Discovery/*The Nation* Award.

The special energy of these early years foreshadows the career that has followed. Hacker's awareness of the work of young and highly original writers, her engagement with the ideas of critics, other writers, and political dissidents and nonconformists, and her eclectic tastes have marked editorial tenures at the helms of the journal *City* (1965–1969), *The Little Magazine* (1977–1980), the feminist *13th Moon* (1982–1986), and the *Kenyon Review* (1990–1994). Her degree in Romance languages and literature presaged her later work translating such French contemporary poets as Claire Malroux, Hédi Kaddour, Marie Etienne, Vénus Khoury-Ghata, Guy Goffette, Andre Velter, Habib Tengour, and Amina Said. Hacker also served as a guest editor for a special double issue on contemporary French poets for *Poetry Magazine* (October–November 2000) and two issues of *Ploughshares* (1989, 1996). Currently, Hacker lives half the year in Manhattan and the other half in Paris, and teaches at the City College of New York.

The poems of her first poetry collection, *Presentation Piece* (1974), trace an immense variety of human interactions, witnessed and lived through in the youthful countercultures of San Francisco, London, and the East Village during a time of widespread sexual and intellectual discovery. Hacker depicts this quotidian with tremendous compassion and humor; an eye for the precise, telling detail; and a penchant to get the grit of the actual onto the page. She usually writes in exacting meter with inventive rhyme and in such forms as the villanelle, the sestina, and the sonnet. "She Bitches about Boys" is an example of strong multisyllabic rhymes and humor:

> Girls love a sick child or a healthy animal.
> A man who's both itches them like an incubus,
> but I, for one, have had a bellyful
> of giving reassurances and obvious
> advice with scrambled eggs and cereal[.]

As personable as this adapted terza rima is, the diction in other poems from *Presentation Piece* is cool, detached, and skillfully highbrow. This segment from the long saga "The Navigators" is an example of this tone:

> Trackless and lost between piss-colored walls,
> she huddles on the bench arm, hides her face,
> shakes with sobs or dry retching. The intern calls
> names in a bored voice. People shift in place.
> Clocks sweep toward morning and she hides her face.

The scene, a hospital emergency room, is both precise and contemporary ("piss-colored walls," "The intern calls names in a bored voice") but is also sonorous and atemporal, filled with the devices readers expect from a poetry trying to sink roots into literary tradition (the dramatic repetition of "she hides her face," the long and elegant phrases that seem, effortlessly, to pass through their rhyme-stitching and then metrically onward, the unsurprising but imposing rhymes). One hears Auden in the line about the clocks, but there is also, importantly, a modern young woman writing the poem. The speaker has brought a woman to the hospital out of necessity, although they are not friends: "I am a stranger whom she cannot trust"; but she concludes, "Since she must / feel some hand on her sickness and her fear, / my hand is on her shoulder; we are here."

Presentation Piece is filled with these partial narratives delineating relationships that feel, in the end, unsatisfied and unfinished: between two male lovers, between two men and a woman, between a mother and a daughter, between a daughter and a displaced father, and between a woman and her male lover. Usually, these narratives are curtailed at the moment of highest intensity, as if the interchange the author wishes to hold up to the light will gain resonance from being left a little detached, a bit incomplete.

Presentation Piece also presents the seed of a surreal, nonformalist poet into whom Hacker does not, ultimately, develop.

> We are asleep under mirrors. What do I
> look like? Your mouth
> opens on a dream of altered landscapes. ("Before the War")

However, the interest in myth, the willingness to launch into a surreal image, the ability to travel along the nerve endings of a sensation toward a truth (practiced responses to the work she admired by Jack Spicer) echo into all her subsequent work in traditional forms. The ability to render an external and internal consciousness simultaneously and to bridge the humor and cacophony of city life with human pathos is reminiscent of the New York School poets.

Presentation Piece became both the Lamont Poetry Selection and the recipient of the National Book Award in 1975—the latter a highly unusual honor for a debut volume. The next year, combining new work with poems left out of *Presentation Piece,* Hacker published *Separations* (1976), her second book, which also received critical acclaim. In Hayden Carruth's review of *Separations* in *The New York Times* (25 July 1976), he focuses on Hacker's formal mastery and the "adultness" of her subject matter.

These two initial entries into the world of published volumes of poetry secured a widespread respect for Hacker's craft. In interviews and speeches at this time, Hacker revealed herself to be a mostly serious young woman intensely focused on the life of poetry, its readership, and its relevance, and extremely aware of herself as a woman poet, with all the contradiction that entails. Hacker's National Book Award acceptance speech in 1975 provides an uncanny example of her seriousness of purpose, and her propensity to recognize political implications to everyday subjects (foreshadowing foci and concern her poetry soon began to own):

Dust jacket for Hacker's 1974 collection of poems about a variety of relationships she had during a period of sexual and intellectual exploration in London, New York City, and San Francisco (Richland County Public Library)

I wonder if that traditional inaccessibility of poetry isn't becoming a physical, not an intellectual, problem. Books of poetry . . . are simply not visible where those readers can find them, or priced so those readers can buy them. I'd like to see books of poetry you could afford . . . on a student's budget, or a bus driver's or an unsupported mother's. And I'd like to see those books, cheap and attractively packaged, distributed and displayed where students and mothers and bus drivers could see them.

Then in the late 1970s, living and teaching in Washington, D.C., and in New York City, Hacker began to write a book that signaled a sea change. The poems of *Taking Notice* (1980) are loosely narrative–with humor, craft, and no shortage of formal challenge (from official forms such as pantoums, canzones, and rhymed syllabics to one poem, "Huge Baby Blues," written under the invented construction of using only those letters printable on an LED display board)–toward a self-discovery with the weight of epiphany.

If the speaker of Hacker's first two volumes seems to be an extraordinary and visceral observer, one who records, with a fine degree of resolution, the nature and character of her responses, the speaker in *Taking Notice* is no longer merely observing the world as she moves through it. The speaker of these poems has learned who she is and what she wants; and with these revelations, Hacker's voice suddenly takes action, gaining humanity, vulnerability, and, above all, muscularity. These poems have the engaged, delighted presence of a person involved in her own life.

I'll tell you what I don't want: an affair,
love, by appointment only, twice a week . . .
. . . When it's easier to speak
about than to you, when I think of you
more than I'm with you, more anxious than tender,
I feel less than a friend. There's work to do.
Artist, woman, I love you; craft and gender . . .

In *Taking Notice* Hacker turns her thematic attention toward relationships between women, as her lovers and her friends. Also, she is now the single mother of her own Black-Jewish toddler daughter. "Iva's Pantoum," one of two memorable examples of this form in

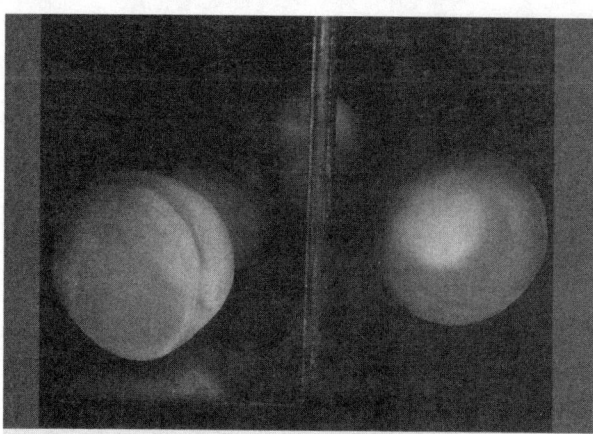

Paperback cover for Hacker's retrospective 1994 collection (Richland County Public Library)

Taking Notice, covers the real and fluid relationship between mother and daughter, as parent and child, and as woman and woman:

> We pace each other for a long time.
> I packed my anger with the beef jerky.
> You are the baby on the mountain. I am
> in a cold stream where I led you.
>
> I packed my anger with the beef jerky.
> You are the woman sticking her tongue out
> in a cold stream where I led you.
> You are the woman with springwater palms....
>
> ... Our friend gives you a sharp knife,
> shows how the useful blades open.
> Was any witch's youngest daughter
> golden and bold as you? You run and
>
> show how the useful blades open.
> You are the baby on the mountain. I am
> golden and bold as you. You run and
> we pace each other for a long time.

Taking Notice receives its title from a sonnet sequence, the endpoint in the apparent arc of this book, tracing the desires and intricacies of the speaker's relationship with another woman. From *Taking Notice* onward, lesbian and feminist politics become an important aspect of Hacker's creative energy. But unlike lesbian-feminist poet Adrienne Rich, Hacker sees no reason to dismiss poetic forms as "patriarchal" at the time her content changes. Rather, Hacker uses the shapeliness of her poems to hold her excursion into personally unknown space to rhythmically and formally comfortable paths easier for her readers to follow. With *Taking Notice,* Hacker's already sophisticated and facile use of iambs becomes more interesting; her two-syllable pairings often include a chain of higher-level stresses (almost spondees). Her rhymes continue to vary from cleverly rhymed multisyllabics to elegant single-syllable rhymes, knitted seamlessly into a continuous fabric.

In the creative flowering of Hacker's work following *Taking Notice,* her narratives more often move beyond the portrait of a moment typical of her previous work and into fully realized anecdotes, then later into verse novels (*Love, Death, and the Changing of the Seasons,* 1986).

Hacker now places even greater trust in the universality of specificity, telling her speaker's complete story and leaving the reader to identify with its intimacy and detail, the way one would identify with a good friend's letter. In fact, many poems in the books following *Taking Notice* are epistolary; and the friends whom Hacker names sometimes recur from volume to volume.

Toward this created community that includes other friends who are poets—such as Marie Ponsot, Carruth, Julie Fay, Kim Vaeth, and Eavan Boland—the speaker's diction is warm and funny, personal and engaged. While readers know what wine the people in the poems drank at dinner, they also know where their thoughts were, what they talked about, and how the food became a part of that interaction. Hacker's usage returns lived experience to each label, whether a political label (such as "queer") or a commercial product (such as "Land Rover"). Her astutely observant mind often draws philosophical conclusions from these interactions and juxtapositions. These gifts make her an ideal poet to explore the paradoxes transecting a personal experience at the point where its resonance is also political. In this process, Hacker's formal dexterity, her decisions to challenge herself to speak in complex meters, rhyme schemes, and cleverly manipulated refrains, make each observation, no matter how modern or immediate, resonate with historical and metrical weight.

Throughout the next decade of Hacker's work, every book–every poem practically–becomes an extension further out into the territory of what can be said. *Assumptions* (1985), Hacker's fourth book, explores mothers and daughters–in her own experience as daughter to a smart, shrill, diabetic, widowed mother, as mother to Iva, and in the multigenerational relationships and observed lives of her friends. *Assumptions* closes with an important feminist rewriting of Hans Christian Andersen's myth of the Snow Queen. Adopting different viewpoints and voices, this story of Gerda and the Little Robber Girl echoes lines and poems from other parts of the modern feminist canon. This excerpt, for example, employs psychologically intense blank verse and decasyllabics:

Gerda in the Aerie

> Then the robber girl put her arm round Gerda's neck and slept. But Gerda was much too afraid to close her eyes.
>
> –H. C. Andersen, "The Snow Queen"

I almost love you. I've wanted to be you
all my life. You are asleep in the straw
with my story, your arm thrown across
my neck. . . .
   . . . Do you have a story?
. . . .
You wrapped yourself for sleep in the soft shawl
I had unknotted. Your breasts asked, like eyes.
A girl looks at another girl's breasts
covertly, thinking, we should be alike,
we are the same kind. But we are not.
Fear tethers me to the fire. I was raised afraid
of strange men, sudden noises, groups of men
in the square, isolate men on the road. . . .

. . . .
You aren't listening. You're asleep
in your adventure, which I probably
won't know, maybe take part in. I won't know
what part. . . .

Love, Death, and the Changing of the Seasons extends Hacker's talent for narrative, characterization, and formal skill into a poem of 260 sonnets, novel-sized. Telling the story of an affair between a writing student and her teacher, *Love, Death, and the Changing of the Seasons* is, among other things, a watershed in the use of the sonnet. Arranged in small sequences and full crowns, with unexpected rhymes and extraordinary twists of coronastyle refrain, sonnets become similar to the still shots of a photo album. Turns of phrase far outlast the read:

. . . Hug; hug; this time I brushed my lips
   just across yours, and fire down below
      in February flared. . . .

Imagery, object, emotion, and philosophy speak out in a sort of counterpoint. The diction, from carnal to cerebral, funny to tender, becomes striking:

How can you love me with the things I feel
that scare me crashing on the window glass?
How can you love me when I'm such an asshole (sometimes) I can't take hold of what's really there and use it, let you take the wheel
and put my head back as the truck-stops pass?

There is also philosophic Pope-ish humor:

Until they made the Iliad about it,
nobody would have seen a fit of pique
as quintessentially *geste heroique*.
Is indecision epic? If you doubt it,
look at the texts. Where would they be without it.

From June 1990 through June 1994 Hacker lived in New York and Paris, and published two new volumes of poetry–*Going Back to the River* (1990) and *Winter Numbers* (1994). In form and theme, *Winter Numbers* is the more challenging book. It includes no fewer than twenty-two pages in falling meters: six poems in sapphics and three in alcaics, an extraordinary example of their relevance to modern English. The poems in *Winter Numbers* follow a biographic arc that includes the speaker's breast cancer diagnosis and treatment. The poems in it, however, seem to reach far beyond issues of the self to dwell on the poet's context as expatriate and Jew, citizen and woman (in the fiftieth anniversary year of the Holocaust). For instance, a double crown of sonnets with a complicated use of refrain detailing the speaker's experience with breast cancer is set beside "August Journal," a poem whose title echoes the fine World War II–era sequence of Louis MacNeice and closes the book:

If I'm one of the victims, who survives?
If I'm–reach for it–a survivor, who
are the victims? The heroic dead,
the ones who died in despair, the ones who died
in terror, the exhausted ones who died
tired? . . .

. . . It *is* exceptional to die in bed
at ninety-eight, not having been gassed, shot
wrung dry with dysentery, drowned at birth
in a basin for unwanted girls.
The unexceptional beg on the street
outside the Red Apple, outside Monoprix. . . .

Dust jacket for Hacker's 2000 collection, which ends with a sequence of unmetered, rhymed poems that form a personal chronology (Richland County Public Library)

Winter Numbers won the Lenore Marshall Prize for poetry from the Academy of American Poets in 1995 and a Lambda Literary Award. Hacker's *Selected Poems, 1965–1990* (1994) won the Poet's Prize in 1996.

In 1999 Hacker finished a new volume of poetry, *Squares and Courtyards* (2000). In 2002 she finished *Desesperanto: Poems 1999–2002* (2003), which reenters some of the Surrealist territory of *Presentation Piece,* now laced with the structure and syntax of some of the contemporary French poetry Hacker has translated.

Each of these books scores formal surprises, such as "Paragraphs from a Day-Book," the stunning closing chapter of *Squares and Courtyards,* which consists of forty-five "paragraphs"–a fifteen-line rhymed, unmetered short form invented and utilized by the poet Carruth. Interlacing scenes and images from Europe and the United States over the past fifty years with philosophical and semantic analyses of love and a running observation of a pair of homeless women, these poems also take on personal chronology. The paragraphs give startling treatment to the vivid, memory-saturated details of the speaker's own early childhood and the loss of her grandmother. Because of their total thematic and object-symbol unity and complexity, the "paragraphs" move with cadence, color, and completeness. Readers experience the collage of thought and image, story by story, pane by pane, as viewed alternately through the lenses of experience and interpretation.

"Squares and Courtyards," the title poem and a sonnet crown whose eighth sonnet brilliantly utilizes the linking lines of each preceding sonnet, also shows Hacker's astonishing syntactic versatility; the opening stanza meanders like a fine sentence or a perambulation through the *place* and then comes to a terse and high-impact end:

> Across the Place du Marché Ste-Catherine
> the light which frames a building that I see
> daily, walking home from the bakery,
> white voile in open windows, sudden green . . .
> . . . is such a gift of the quotidian,
> a benefice of sight and consciousness,
> I sometimes stop, confused with gratitude,
> not knowing what to thank or whom to bless,
> break off an end of seven-grain baguette
> as if my orchestrated senses could
> confirm the day. It's fragrant. I eat it.

Hacker's work has been heralded for its contribution to the New Formalism. Hacker writes in "Meditating Formally," the introduction to her work in Annie Finch's *A Formal Feeling Comes: Poems in Form by Contemporary Women* (1994): "The choice or use of a fixed or structured form–whether I learned it or invented it–has always been, for me, one of the primary pleasures in writing poetry. I have no political or aesthetic rationale for it, except that I like it."

Her refusal to enter some sort of poetry debate on the relative virtues of poetic "forms and freedoms" gets further play in her speech to a panel of the Poetry Society of America in November 1998, "What's American about American Form?"; it was reprinted by *HeART Quarterly* (Summer 1999):

> American poets writing in English . . . stand at an intersection of many formal traditions, including the indigenous poetries of Native Americans, the call-and-response forms enslaved Africans brought with them to this continent, which they married to English ballad and hymn forms to create both spirituals and the blues, the continual proximity of Latin American poetry, and, of course, the variegated English language prosodic tradition and its antitheses which came to this continent with the English settlers. . . . American poets seem to have a propensity to invent forms; and our very characteristic contentiousness on the subject . . . is also the sign of an extreme attention. Dickinson's secular transformation of hymnal measures was as deliberate a ges-

ture of prosodic innovation as Whitman's rolling cadences. . . .

Hacker's own words, including her "new formalism," do, in fact, arguably have a political relevance, even though that may not be her driving motivation. As editor and writer, she owns her antecedents; she pays tribute to the writers she admires by adopting their forms as well as referencing their messages. And in speaking to the Poetry Society of America symposium in November 1998, she shows how rhyme can indeed make disparate parts of American diction cohere to one another:

> And that is one thing, in a personal parenthesis, which makes the writing of metered and rhymed poetry in English such a pleasure—the juxtaposition of those Latinate, Anglo-Saxon, and other-flavored words, "chickenshit" and "hematocrit," "morose" and "Mykonos," "contextual" and "transexual," "marathon" and "macron," "dental floss" and "meshugass."

The creation of cohesion in language can clearly be seen as a counterpoint to the creation of cohesion in reality.

"Political" is a term by which many critics would denounce someone's poetry. The difficulty is to explain accurately what is "political" to Marilyn Hacker, whose work never generalizes, even as it deals in an idea, a political label, or an abstraction. Hacker has had the courage and the heart to say what she knows, however contradictory. Out of that honesty, over a two-and-a-half-decade-long career, backed by an extraordinary lyric and formal gift, a trajectory has developed. Hacker has expanded the possible use of several difficult forms and pieces of prosody. She has also spoken with a relevant and courageous willingness to own a message or a contradiction. By this self-possession in the midst of a forward-looking, soul-searching modernity, she makes her place.

Interviews:

Annie Finch, "Marilyn Hacker: An Interview on Form," *American Poetry Review* (May/June 1996);

Suzanne Gardinier, "An Interview with Marilyn Hacker," *AWP Chronicle,* 28, no. 5 (1996).

References:

Rafael Campo, "About Marilyn Hacker: A Profile," *Ploughshares,* 22, no. 1 (Spring 1996): 95–100;

Lynn Keller, "Measured Feet in Gender-Bender Shoes," in *Forms of Expansion: Recent Long Poems by Women* (Chicago: University of Chicago Press, 1979), pp. 155–186;

Joan Larkin, "Women's Poetry: Once More with Form," *Ms.* (March 1981);

Janet McCann, "Review of Marilyn Hacker's *Squares and Courtyards,*" in *Magill's Literary Annual* (Englewood Cliffs, N.J.: Salem Press, 2001), pp. 796–800;

Stanley Plumley, "Lyricism, Verbal Energy, the Sonnet, and Gallows Humor," *Book World,* 2 (November 1980);

Grace Schulman, "Chiliastic Sapphic," *Nation,* no. 259 (7 November 1994);

Melissa F. Zeiger, "Chapter 6: Against Elegies: Women's Breast Cancer Poems," in *Beyond Consolation: The Changing Shape of Elegy* (Ithaca, N.Y.: Cornell University Press, 1997), pp. 159–165.

Papers:

Papers and correspondence of Marilyn Hacker are held by the Beinecke Library of Yale University.

Rachel Hadas
(8 November 1948 -)

Ernest J. Smith
University of Central Florida

See also the Hadas entry in *DLB 120: American Poets Since World War II, Third Series.*

BOOKS: *Starting from Troy* (Boston: Godine, 1975);
Slow Transparency (Middletown, Conn.: Wesleyan University Press, 1983);
Form, Cycle, Infinity: Landscape Imagery in the Poetry of Robert Frost and George Seferis (Lewisburg, Pa.: Bucknell University Press, 1985);
A Son from Sleep (Middletown, Conn.: Wesleyan University Press, 1987);
Pass It On (Princeton, N.J.: Princeton University Press, 1989);
Living in Time (New Brunswick, N.J.: Rutgers University Press, 1990);
Unending Dialogue: Voices from an AIDS Poetry Workshop, by Hadas and others (Boston & London: Faber & Faber, 1991);
Mirrors of Astonishment (New Brunswick, N.J.: Rutgers University Press, 1992);
Other Worlds Than This: Translations (New Brunswick, N.J.: Rutgers University Press, 1994);
The Empty Bed (Hanover, N.H. & London: Wesleyan University Press/University Press of New England, 1995);
The Double Legacy: Reflections on a Pair of Deaths (Boston & London: Faber & Faber, 1995);
Halfway Down the Hall: New and Selected Poems (Hanover, N.H. & London: Wesleyan University Press/University Press of New England, 1998);
Merrill, Cavafy, Poems, and Dreams (Ann Arbor: University of Michigan Press, 2000);
Indelible (Middletown, Conn.: Wesleyan University Press, 2001);
Laws (Lincoln, Neb.: Zoo Press, forthcoming 2004).

OTHER: "Rachel Hadas," in *Contemporary Authors Autobiography Series,* volume 23, edited by Shelly Andrews (Detroit: Gale, 1996), pp. 117–132.

Rachel Hadas (photograph by Jack Mitchell; from the dust jacket for The Double Legacy: Reflections on a Pair of Deaths, *1995; Richland County Public Library)*

The appearance of Rachel Hadas's *Halfway Down the Hall: New and Selected Poems* in 1998 allowed readers to survey the development of a skilled and imaginative poet in midcareer. From the beginning, Hadas's poems have been marked by intelligence, acute perception, attention to craft and form, and a constant sense of the ability of time to both illuminate and transform the past. Birth, family, friendship, death, and the power of language itself have been among her recurring themes, with individual volumes tracing varied subjects such as her son's childhood years and her work leading an

Paperback cover for Hadas's 1998 collection, a finalist for the Lenore Marshall Poetry Prize (Richland County Public Library)

AIDS poetry workshop. But Hadas's major theme is memory, how the past continues to re-present itself, both raising and answering questions about how humans define themselves through their lived and imagined experiences. Although she has never aligned herself with any particular poetry movement in either prose or interviews, she has most often been associated with the New Formalists. Her poetry has been included in anthologies associated with the movement, such as *A Formal Feeling Comes: Poems in Form by Contemporary Women* (1994) and *Rebel Angels: 25 Poets of the New Formalism* (1996). However, she has termed various methods of categorization of poets, and affiliation with styles or movements, as "reductive" and "irrelevant to the quality of poetry."

Rachel Chamberlayne Hadas was born on 8 November 1948 in New York City, the daughter of Elizabeth Chamberlayne Hadas and Moses Hadas. She has one sister, Elizabeth, born in 1946. Her father was a highly respected translator, scholar of classics, and professor at Columbia University, and her mother also taught Latin at the prestigious Spence School in Manhattan. Rachel Hadas attended the Riverdale Country Day School in the Bronx and went on to major in classics at Radcliffe College, earning a B.A. and graduating magna cum laude in 1969. She also took a poetry-writing class with renowned translator, poet, and classicist Robert Fitzgerald. In 1966, when Hadas was seventeen, her father died suddenly, a loss that haunts much of her early poetry. After Radcliffe, she traveled to Greece on a fellowship, where she met W. H. Auden as well as the poets Alan Ansen and James Merrill, two major influences on her work.

While in Greece, Hadas met Stavros Kondylis, whom she married in 1970. The couple lived on the Greek island of Samos between 1971 and 1975, running an olive-oil press. In 1974 Hadas was indicted, tried, and ultimately acquitted of the charge of arson in connection with a fire that largely destroyed the press. Hadas returned to the United States, and in 1977 she earned an M.A. from the poetry-writing program at Johns Hopkins University. In 1978 she divorced Kondylis and married the composer George Edwards, a music professor at Columbia, and in 1982 she earned a Ph.D. in comparative literature from Princeton University. Her dissertation was revised and appeared as the book *Form, Cycle, Infinity: Landscape Imagery in the Poetry of Robert Frost and George Seferis* (1985). Hadas and Edwards have one son, Jonathan, and live in New York City and Vermont. During the academic year Hadas teaches at the Newark campus of Rutgers University, where she is a tenured professor.

Hadas's first volume, the chapbook *Starting from Troy* (1975), is dedicated to her father, and the spirit and absence of Moses Hadas are felt throughout the book. Two of the strongest poems in this short collection, "That Time, This Place" and "Daddy," deal directly with the aftermath of his death. "That Time, This Place" uses classical history and myth in comparing the loss of the father with that of other "departed heroes," the poem beginning and ending with the figure of a house without a patriarch. "Daddy" is a more directly personal treatment of the theme, focusing specifically on a daughter's emotional state after her father's death: "Let me write elegies at least, / I said, and then wrote nothing down. // But no forgetting. Elegies / were all around me." "Daughters and Others" is another poem that presents the feelings, emotions, and words of daughters responding to fathers' deaths, with Lucia Joyce and Sylvia Plath prominently featured. The words of Joyce serve as the refrain: "They buried father, but he's not dead. / He's watching us all."

Other poems use classical figures and legend, such as the opening poem, "The Fall of Troy," which presents Aeneas leaving Troy to found Rome. The first line, "Sing now the heavy furniture of the fall," echoes the opening of *The Aeneid,* and the poem proceeds in iambic pentameter with intermediate couplets. Several additional poems are set in Greece. There are no poems in specific fixed forms, though several use regularly structured stanzas, ranging from couplets, tercets, and quatrains to longer-lined stanzas of five or seven lines, as in "The Color-Blind Raspberry Picker," which employs a fairly regular syllable count for corresponding lines from stanza to stanza. This volume shows a clear attraction to the classical subject and to traditional meters and stanza forms, though Hadas exhibits a great deal of lyrical variety from poem to poem.

Like many of her subsequent volumes, Hadas's second book, *Slow Transparency* (1983), is divided into three parts. The poems in part 1 are set in Greece, described in one poem as "Eden, oasis, exile, island, desert." Another poem, "The Trial for Arson," uses rhyming couplets to tell the story of Hadas's trial and acquittal, while "The Lesson of the Elements," which meditates on air, water, earth, and fire as metaphors for the transfiguring power of time, moves from terza rima to rhyming quatrains and then back to terza rima. "Forgetting Greek" and "Island Noons" are among several striking poems treating the theme of the poet's interaction with the Greek language, culture, and people. The latter evocatively presents the landscape: "No mirrors but the water and the sky / No verticals except the granite mountain / to punctuate the landscape. Shuttered houses / huddled together—still in fear of pirates?" Later in the volume, the subject of poetry is addressed in "On Poetry" and "Kaleidoscope," the latter of which takes the title object as a metaphor for poetry. Hadas has written that "Often in my work, if I have no particular incident to chew over, I turn to contemplate the ever-present and ever-enigmatic medium itself: language," and these two poems demonstrate that tendency. Beginning with "Pantoum on Pumpkin Hill," the third part of *Slow Transparency* consists of rural poems set in Vermont. "Five September Hours" is typical of the mood of these poems, focusing on lyrical yet frozen moments, achieving a still-life effect.

A Son from Sleep (1987) centers on the birth and infancy of Hadas's son, Jonathan, born on 4 February 1984. The title of the volume is taken from a phrase in "The Dream of Severing," a brief lyric that admits to the fear attending the literal separation—the severing of the umbilical cord—of mother and child. Meditations on the various acts and thoughts involved in parenting predominate, from nighttime nursing to fear of the child's fragility. Other poems encompass larger themes prompted by the birth of a child, such as "Philemon and Baucis," which explores feelings toward aging parents, and "Amnesia Changes," which concerns the ongoing process of recovering the woman/self who existed preceding the baby's birth. "Succession" has an almost fairy-tale feel as it enters into speculation on successive generations of male swimmers near the shore. Throughout the volume, in what are largely personal poems, Hadas continues to exhibit a mastery of regular forms, semimetrical verse, and free verse. The prevailing meters are iambic trimeter and pentameter, with at least one poem in syllabic verse.

Pass It On (1989), Hadas's fourth volume of poems, displays a more varied array of both subject matter and formal dexterity than any of her previous volumes, often in poems of significant length. The book begins with a thirteen-part poetic sequence, "The Fields of Sleep (Summer)," the first of four consecutive poems that use each of the seasons as a mood evocation or setting. The third of these, "Fix It (Winter)," explores various approaches to both the sonnet form and the power of intricately repeated end words within the line.

Glimpses of family life, the daily moment, and personal insight thread through these poems, with several continuing to explore the rhythms and activities associated with motherhood. A handful of poems cluster around the theme of the child's acquisition of language, while "Pass It On I" and "Pass It On II" concern tradition, the legacy of writing and translating passed down to Hadas from her father.

Living in Time (1990) is made up of prose pieces on various subjects, bracketing Hadas's longest single poem, "The Dream Machine," a poem of some sixty-five pages in fourteen numbered sections, prompted by a question from the poet's son about the nature of stories and language. This theme is at the heart of section 13, "Our Need for Stories." While the long poem is in free verse, with an iambic pentameter undergirding, it does include smaller embedded poems in form, such as the sonnet "In the Hammock" and "Always Afternoon," written in quatrains with slant rhyme. Combining biography and what poet Alfred Corn in his review for *Poetry* (December 1991) termed "metaphysical speculation," the poem "The Dream Machine," despite its length and breadth, is typical of Hadas's best work in the way it revolves around memory, literature, loss, family, and the overall sense of community and continuity. The prose pieces include essays on such subjects as time, reading, the poet's years in Greece, and, in "The Lights Must Never Go Out," her poetry workshop for people with AIDS.

Hadas had lost friends such as the critic David Kalstone to AIDS, and she responded by deciding to teach poetry writing to HIV-positive patients. In 1991 Hadas published a book about this workshop, *Unending Dialogue: Voices from an AIDS Poetry Workshop*, with eight male co-authors who participated in the class at the Gay Men's Health Crisis Workshop in New York City between early 1988 and early 1991. The volume opens with Hadas's essay "The Lights Must Never Go Out"; the middle section of the book consists of forty-five poems by the workshop members; and the final section offers sixteen poems by Hadas that grew out of her work with the group. These final poems are offered within surrounding prose commentary that gives them context. In the opening essay, Hadas compares her involvement in the workshop group with the years she spent on the Greek island of Samos, describing her role in terms of "the privileged status of the outsider who not only observes but who can also minimally participate in the action." Within the discussion of her motivations and hesitancies in starting the workshop, which began with only two participants, Hadas speculates on the role of poetry within specific contexts, including the range of complex emotions experienced by the workshop members. In addition, this teaching and writing experience allows the range of Hadas's reading to speak to her in new ways. For instance, Czesław Miłosz's remarks on the "detachment" often necessary to create art have a specific pertinence to the situation of writing about AIDS and the teacher's challenge of enabling the men in her class to write "on material that could be so overwhelming as to be either incommunicable or, of all things, banal." Hadas's experience in writing elegiac poems on the death of her father comes into play in this work, and she admits that one of her reasons for conducting the workshop may have been "to fill the gap still left by my father's death."

One result of the workshop was a great friendship between Hadas and Charles Barber, the first member of the group. Barber's eventual death in 1992, along with the death of Hadas's mother the same year, became the impetus for the prose work *The Double Legacy: Reflections on a Pair of Deaths* (1995). Barber is also the central figure in Hadas's poems in the final section of *Unending Dialogue*. Speaking of how her sixteen poems retain the "charge" of the context that prompted them, Hadas offers a useful summation of how memory and the past compel her work: "Looked *through:* does the visible but opaque carapace of things grow transparent, then, with time? In poem after poem, my 1983 book *Slow Transparency* affirms exactly that. I now think the answer is both yes and no. We look at things until we can see through them, but in this world the things themselves are still there."

The dust jacket to Hadas's 1992 volume of poems, *Mirrors of Astonishment,* notes that the poet has described this collection "as a triptych and as a hall of mirrors." The book again falls into three parts: the first and third sections each consist of five poetic sequences, and the middle section offers shorter lyrics. "Art" is the opening poem, a sequence of eleven sections with eleven lines each, exploring the endeavors of poetry and the general process of making art. As with several other poems in this book, "Art" finds the poet opening herself to the varied materials and responses that can prompt poetry, concluding that "Shakespeare wrote 'eternal lines to time.' / Particular and universal, / elegy, artifact, intrusion: / nothing to do but join the dots I saw." Another of the sequences in part 1, "On Poetry," approaches the same subject in a slightly more lighthearted tone. This poem has three sections, each consisting of six quatrains with an underlying meter of iambic pentameter. Section 1, "Lyric," offers a somewhat barbed critique of what a critic would say a lyric is and is not allowed to do, while section 2, "Trivia," balances part 1 in suggesting the vast materials that poetry might include. Time, mutability, and memory are the abiding themes in the sequences of section 1, with regular stanza forms predominating. The final poem of this

Pages from two drafts for a 2003 poem, "Hermes" (Collection of Rachel Hadas)

Hermes... a connector, messenger, veteran of command

1/4/03 Hermes is the one [god] told off to go down to tell Calypso the unwelcome news she must release Odysseus from her nowhere island.

Having told her this,
he gets to {zoom/speed} back up to Mt. Olympus,
leaving her to mop up [the] human mess:
(grief, loss,) must or the picked dilemma of Olympus who loves a mortal.
and face the puzzle of mortality.

He puts her face to face with her forlorn lover, and vanishes. zooms back up to

Word Wide Web; neural net;
facilitator of chatrooms, message boards,
listservs, who { brings [nest] adoptees to their parents,
{ helps adoptees find their [who were] birth parents —

(lover to lover = the) buzzing dark
and steps lightly out of the resulting tangle / knot
into the { a radiance of neutrality
         { neutral radiance
a neutral roomy. of immortality
(a radiance) our only realm of disappointment

section, "Cupfuls of Summer," is a powerful evocation of both place and the passage of time. The second section of the poem opens with lines that are typical of Hadas's attitude toward experience: "The rhythm here is not so much recurrence / as slow accumulation. Things stand still / and using them we measure how we've grown. / Who last came here a child no longer sleeps alone."

Most of the lyrics of part 2 of *Mirrors of Astonishment* employ regular stanza forms, whether the rhyming quatrains of "Roadblock," the regular ten-line stanzas with variable rhyme in "Visiting the Gypsy," or the fifteen-line stanzas of "Genealogies," a poem dealing with the legacy of Hadas's father as a teacher. Part 3 of the volume includes "Desire," a poem in eleven sections using several stanza forms, including the sonnet; and the final poem, "Love," returns to the form of the eleven-line stanza used in "Art." Overall, *Mirrors of Astonishment* displays the work of a writer in command of both her lyric and formal skills, branching into poetic sequences in the meditative mode.

Hadas's volume of translations, *Other Worlds Than This* (1994), consists largely of translations from the French–Victor Hugo, Charles Baudelaire, Stéphane Mallarmé, Jean-Nicolas-Arthur Rimbaud, and Paul Valéry–with additional translated poems from Tibullus, Seneca, and the modern Greek poet Konstantine Karyotakis. Hadas's own work has always demonstrated the importance of world literatures and poetry in languages other than English, particularly "the Greek and Latin classics." In her introduction to this volume she describes Baudelaire as "a crucial poet for me" and professes that the poems in *Les Fleurs du mal* (Flowers of Evil, 1857) "could and should be made to rhyme in English." Later in this introduction she addresses the artistry of translation, comparing lines, stanzas, and poems to "riddles," each "a problem I could solve without shattering it only if I moved gently."

The Empty Bed, published in 1995, is dominated by elegies for friends and family members such as Hadas's mother, several of the poets from the Gay Men's Health Crisis Workshop, and Kalstone. "Upon My Mother's Death" begins with the phrase taken as the volume title and moves through rhyming tercets exploring response to the loss of the mother. Beginning with the sense of both the absence of the dead and the loneliness of the surviving, the poem traces "the gradual process" of becoming "her who was gone." The poet retrieves first the mother's belongings and ultimately the mother's body, ferrying her away from the "pristine dominion" of the hospital. Although brief, this lyric, like many others in the volume, follows the movement of the classical elegy, broadening its focus from individual loss to larger, more philosophical reflection on loss in general: "Love lorn live lose lone: need we really choose?" Ultimately, the poem finds an ironic affirmation in death. While the human capacity for grief is "limitless," the poem concludes that the very breadth of that emotion "blurs the limits of mortality."

Many of the poems in *The Empty Bed* are written in form, employing rhyming couplets, tercets, and quatrains, regular stanza forms and line patterns, and sophisticated metrical variations. The intricacies of craft offer Hadas the opportunity to control pace, tone, and emotion. "Passage" uses iambic lines to bracket stanzas consisting of recurring trimeter and three-syllable lines, shaping a "thin song" out of "the bleak debris of cancelled things." "Lullaby II" uses looser, irregular rhyme and a line of refrain to move the volume toward conclusion, offering night, sleep, memory, and "tomorrow's possibility" as stays against the emptiness of loss. Other poems not using regular formal patterns, such as the powerful "Peculiar Sanctity," explore the functions of language, silence, and elegy in an era of AIDS.

The Double Legacy, published the same year as *The Empty Bed,* is in some ways its prose companion. In the foreword, Hadas identifies the deaths of her mother and Barber as the central events around which the short prose pieces of the book revolve. Her themes, she notes, are "the rhythms of grief and mourning, the odd moments of consolation and oblivion, the forms memory takes, the humdrum yet uncanny changes wrought by time." But at the same time, the book is something of an *ars poetica,* for there are several passages in which Hadas reflects on her artistic process, the inspirations and motives for her art, and her reading; in addition, she offers comments on several of her individual poems. In the longest piece, "Word by Word, Page by Page," Hadas remarks: "When I was younger, I snatched poems from experience before it could get away from me. . . . Later on, I began to compose poems long after the fact, piecing together fragments of experiences that I had recorded at the time but that were too painful to combine into a single picture until years had passed." Elsewhere, Hadas explores the relationship of loss to language, casting light on the poems in *The Empty Bed,* a volume that established her as one of the major elegists of her generation.

Halfway Down the Hall includes more than thirty new poems, essentially constituting another volume in Hadas's career. The book was a finalist for the Lenore Marshall Poetry Prize. One of the new poems, "The Red Hat," written in rhymed couplets and broken into two stanzas, traces first the literal act of parents–Hadas and her husband–walking along the opposite side of the street from their son as he goes to school in the morning. Then, in the shorter second stanza, the poem explores the charged emotions of the parents as they respond to their child's growing sense of independence. Hadas's son also figures in "The Blue Bead," a poem about the legacy of poet James Merrill for a younger generation of poets such as Hadas. A casual gift from Merrill to her son is the catalyst for a recognition of Merrill's gift to the world of poetry. Reflections on Merrill's art and legacy are also at the center of *Merrill, Cavafy, Poems, and Dreams* (2000), a collection of some of Hadas's prose pieces that had appeared over the previous ten years. In an essay originally published in May 1991 in the *AWP Chronicle*, "The Ark of What Has Been: Elegiac Thoughts on Poetry," Hadas responds to poet and critic Ira Sadoff's 1990 polemic against the New Formalists, "Neo-Formalism: A Dangerous Nostalgia," published in the *American Poetry Review*. Although Hadas has never identified herself as a New Formalist poet, her reply to Sadoff is a noteworthy defense of crafted language. As opposed to Sadoff's apparent preference for poems "that tell us exactly what they're doing," Hadas calls for "poems of greater tension and complexity, which make demands on us but also offer rewards." Hadas thus offers an apt description of her own poetry, a body of work continued in her 2001 volume, *Indelible*.

Indelible showcases the variety of Hadas's poetry, including narrative poems, free-verse lyrics, and several poems in regular stanza forms, particularly the quatrain. Poems such as "Change Is the Stranger," "Love and War," and "The Seamy Side" work with rhymed quatrains to examine themes such as memory, reading and writing, love, and mutability. Hadas describes the mystery, growth, and exploration of a twenty-year marriage in "The Crust House," and in "The Banquet" she relates in long-lined sentence stanzas a dream about her father. *Indelible* also includes many references to the Greek classics, another of Hadas's hallmarks.

Now in midcareer, Rachel Hadas is important to American poetry as a writer interested in exploring the resources and possibilities of craft, a strong voice dealing with the intersections of dreams, desire, love, literature, and death. Hadas is also an important translator of both Greek and French literature, and her *Unending Dialogue* is an early and essential text in the literature of AIDS.

Interview:

Gloria Glickstein Brame, "The Poet's Life: An Interview with Rachel Hadas," *ELF: Eclectic Literary Forum* (Spring 1997) <http://gloria-brame.com/glory/rachel.htm>.

Bibliography:

Ann Vreeland Watkins, "Rachel Hadas, Poet and Essayist: A Bibliography, 1965–1993," *Bulletin of Bibliography,* 51 (June 1994): 161–168.

Reference:

Anita Helle, "Elegy as History: Three Women Poets 'By the Century's Deathbed,'" *South Atlantic Review,* 61 (Spring 1996): 51–68.

Papers:

Manuscripts of Rachel Hadas are collected at the Alexander Library of Rutgers University in New Brunswick, New Jersey.

Andrew Hudgins
(22 April 1951 -)

Daniel Anderson
The University of the South

See also the Hudgins entry in *DLB 120: American Poets Since World War II, Third Series.*

BOOKS: *Saints and Strangers* (Boston: Houghton Mifflin, 1985);
After the Lost War: A Narrative (Boston: Houghton Mifflin, 1988);
The Never-Ending: New Poems (Boston: Houghton Mifflin, 1991);
Praying Drunk (New York: Dim Gray Bar Press, 1991);
The Glass Hammer: A Southern Childhood (Boston: Houghton Mifflin, 1994);
The Glass Anvil (Ann Arbor: University of Michigan Press, 1997);
Babylon in a Jar: New Poems (Boston: Houghton Mifflin, 1998);
The Waltz He Was Born For: An Introduction to the Writing of Walt McDonald (Lubbock: Texas Tech University Press, 2002).

OTHER: *The Best American Poetry* (New York: Collier, 1995)–includes selections by Hudgins;
The Best American Poetry (New York: Collier, 1998)–includes selections by Hudgins.

Andrew Hudgins (photograph by Erin McGraw; from the dust jacket for The Glass Hammer: A Southern Childhood, *1994; Richland County Public Library)*

When Andrew Hudgins was thirty-five, his first collection of poetry, *Saints and Strangers* (1985), was a runner-up for the 1986 Pulitzer Prize. (The recipient that year was Henry Taylor, who won for *The Flying Change* [1985].) In the time that has elapsed since then, Hudgins has published four other books of poetry and a collection of essays. His third book of poems, *The Never-Ending: New Poems* (1991), was a finalist for the 1991 National Book Award. He has received fellowships from the National Endowment for the Arts, the Poet's Prize, the Witter Bynner Award of the American Academy and Institute of Arts and Letters, has twice appeared in *The Best American Poetry* (1995 and 1998), and has served as an Alfred Hodder Fellow at Princeton University. While Hudgins is widely recognized as a poet who traditionally works in meter, he has also built a reputation as a representative voice of the American South. Both classifications–formalist and regional poet–may ultimately be somewhat shortsighted, however, when one considers the work of Andrew Hudgins. These elements are integral parts of his poetry, but equally important to his work are concerns that transcend what some might perceive as mere aesthetic agendas. His vast imaginative scope, his curiosity in matters of narrative voice, and his shrewd sense of both dramatic and comic timing distinguish his poetry from that of many poets of his generation.

Dust jacket for Hudgins's 1985 collection of poetry (Bruccoli Clark Layman Archives)

Andrew Leon Hudgins Jr. was born on 22 April 1951 in Killeen, Texas. His parents, Andrew Leon Hudgins Sr., a career air force officer who served in the United States Navy during World War II and later graduated from West Point, and Roberta Rodgers Hudgins, a housewife, moved the family from one military base to another during many of Andrew Jr.'s formative years. Over the years their addresses included New Mexico, Ohio, England, North Carolina, California, and France. They ultimately settled in Montgomery, Alabama, in 1966, where Andrew graduated from Sidney Lanier High School in 1969.

After earning his B.A. degree in 1974 from Huntingdon College, with a double major in English and history, Hudgins married Olivia Hardy and taught sixth grade for one year at Carver Elementary School in Montgomery, Alabama. He returned to school to earn his M.A. degree from the University of Alabama, which he received in 1976. He then enrolled in the Ph.D. program at Syracuse University in the fall of 1976, where his wife attended law school. Hudgins withdrew from the program at Syracuse in 1978, after having completed twenty-four hours of study toward his doctorate degree. The couple moved back to Alabama, where they lived from 1978–1981. Hudgins taught as an adjunct instructor at Auburn University in Montgomery and worked odd jobs during this time. His marriage ultimately ended in divorce, and he enrolled in the M.F.A. program at Iowa in 1981. (He had originally applied to but was rejected by Iowa in 1976.) He finished his degree and left the Writers' Workshop in 1983, and taught as a lecturer at Baylor University. In 1985 he took a position at the University of Cincinnati as Distinguished Research Professor in English. In the spring of 1992 Hudgins married fiction writer Erin McGraw, with whom he teaches at Ohio State University.

Much of Hudgins's poetry is set in the South, and the traditional touchstones associated with Southern literature–religion, race, and violence–are often thematic focal points of his poems. His work also has a recurring preoccupation, particularly in his first four books, with narrative concerns. *Saints and Strangers* includes monologues in the voices of John James Audubon, Jonathan Edwards, Zelda Sayre, and Sidney Lanier, the figure who was the narrator for his second book, *After the Lost War: A Narrative* (1988). "On the page and in real life," Hudgins remarked in a 1995 interview later published in *The Glass Anvil* (1997), "I'm fascinated by the movement of the voice as the speaker . . . reveals and hides, evades and confesses, dissembles and tells scorching truths—all the while wanting to be liked and respected, to get rich, to get laid, to keep from suffering[.]"

In the preface to *After the Lost War,* a book-length narrative in the voice of Georgia-born poet, musician, and Civil War soldier Sidney Lanier, Hudgins acknowledges his loose employment of Lanier's persona. He writes, "I'd like to thank Lanier for allowing me to use the facts of his life—more or less—to see how I might have lived if it had been mine. And, in too many ways, I suppose it has." As he admits, the narrative is not intended as a factual re-creation of Lanier's life or his times, and Hudgins concedes that the character he has invented would "horrify the historical Sidney Lanier."

But *After the Lost War,* as a means of metaphorical self-exploration, is of particular interest when considered in conjunction with *The Glass Hammer: A Southern Childhood,* which was published in 1994. *The Glass Hammer* is a collection that Hudgins calls an autobiography in verse. In these sixty-five poems about growing up in the South during the 1950s and 1960s, Hudgins curiously claims for his book that which seems to go largely unstated—but is assumed—about much of American poetry written in the last four decades; the poet's subject is himself. But Hudgins diverges from the multitude of poets who have given in to the impulse to write about themselves through the relentless, sometimes comic, and often dark self-study that is characteristic of much of his poetry. The reader consistently senses that the speaker of a Hudgins poem, whether an individual who resembles the real-life Hudgins or a voice of an assumed persona, is not only concerned with scrutinizing the world around him but also engaged in an exercise explaining (or revealing) his own human shortcomings.

The Glass Hammer takes on, in many ways, the Wordsworthian task of tracing the development of the poet, as well as the person behind the art. In "Begotten," Hudgins begins:

> I've never, as some children do,
> looked at my folks and thought, *I must*
> have come from someone else–

Dust jacket for Hudgins's 1988 book-length poem, in which the narrator is a fictional version of Civil War soldier-poet Sidney Lanier (Bruccoli Clark Layman Archives)

> rich parents who'd misplaced me, but
> who would, as in a myth or novel,
> return and claim me. Hell, no. I saw
> my face in cousins' faces, heard
> my voice in their high drawls.

But there is little Romanticism in the poetry of this book. For Hudgins, childhood (and the self that sprang from it) is part fascination, part revulsion. The book, on occasion, acknowledges a happiness in the past it recreates, but it is always tempered with fear and awe, insecurity, too—a wicked self-consciousness that is inspired by the likely, and sometimes not so likely, experiences that shape the speaker. In "Begotten," Hudgins concludes, "I never had to ask, What am I? / I stared at my blood kin, and thought, / So *this,* dear God, is what I am." But even comprehending one's origins,

Dust jacket for Hudgins's 1994 "autobiography in verse" (Richland County Public Library)

as the poem suggests, does not guarantee a knowledge that will save one from oneself, and this notion is a frequent point of reflection in much of Hudgins's poetry.

From as far back as his first collection, he has warded off the emotional trappings that many poets fall prey to when writing about their lives—the very vulnerabilities that can make poetry sheer self-indulgence. "Sentimental Dangers," from *Saints and Strangers,* is a narrative in which Hudgins explicitly rebukes the human tendency to wallow in personal sorrow. It opens, "When out of work and fierce with self-pity / I'd walk until the fierceness left my feet / and I broke down." The poem is about the speaker's failing marriage and how, one day, he finds that his wife has brought home a stray dog. The narrator makes the stray into a figure for himself—pathetic, undesirable, and ultimately destined for an unpleasant end.

> I'd sit outside all afternoon and talk
> to him, to the hard knowledge in his face
> that she'd leave me when I was well enough
> to be left.

The wife would "tell her friends, / *He's out of work. He thinks he is that dog.*" The poem, though, turns away from self-pity when the speaker admits that "she was right." It turns further away when, in the end, the speaker hands the stray dog over to the pound: "I felt I was signing myself away," he confesses, "An illusion, sure, but one that lasted months. / I thought of this today when I crossed the bridge / and the river smelled like a wet, unwanted dog."

In his fifth and most recent collection, Hudgins demonstrates, in some ways, a restlessness with the narrative and formal practices that dominate his first four books. While a majority of the poems in the earlier collections are written in either blank verse or unrhymed tetrameter, he has moved away from meter, or at least obvious measure, in many of the poems in *Babylon in a Jar: New Poems* (1998). In some instances he has shortened the individual lines and, as Hudgins calls it, "stair-stepped" them, as in "Dragonfly":

> Book says "most predacious." Book
> says "fastest
>   flying insect," says
> it eats its body weight in half an hour.
> Mother called it
>   The devil's
> darning needle. Book
>   adds "darner"
> and "devil's arrow."

This poem is a lyric that mediates on the description of a dragonfly in a book, and the speaker's dependence on the book for knowledge. The poem uses the shorter lines, in part, to simulate the dragonfly's spastic flight, but the clipped lines also facilitate an unfolding sense of discovery as the book informs the speaker that what he's always called

> a dragonfly is really,
>   with its
> long
>   slender body, a
>   damselfly
> that strafes the pond clabber, soars,
> swoops,
>   hovers, sideslips, loops
>   and twists[.]

The quick lines of the poem achieve the same sense of speed that hinders the narrator from witnessing the damselfly's tireless, predatory task of "cracking gnats / out of the air[.]" In the end, he must "trust / Book, Book, / the goddam book because / [he] cannot see the hunting."

In "One Threw a Dirt Clod and It Ran," Hudgins uses a longer line to accomplish a similar mimetic effect. In this short poem about a group of boys who taunt a horse, chase it down, then kill it, the lines range from five to seven beats. They are often measured accentually, but when the lines fall into regular iambic rhythm, the poem creates the sense of the horse's long, lovely stride, particularly at the close of the poem, after the boys have escalated their mischief to murder.

>   Gasping for breath,
> they stared at one another, dropped the post, the stones,
>   the sticks.
> They nudged the huge corpse and waited for it to rise,
> to rise and gallop over rutted, fenced-off fields
> as if there were no nuts, no mudholes, scrub brush, wire
> so they could follow it forever, weeping and hurling stones.

Both "Dragonfly" and "One Threw a Dirt Clod and It Ran" represent narrative departures for Hudgins as well. The former is a pure lyric that perpetuates itself largely through its brief cascading lines; prior to *Babylon in a Jar*, the poems, specifically the longer narratives, are often driven rhythmically headlong through the stories that they tell. While the latter is a narrative, the absence of a conspicuous first-person speaker is something rare in a Hudgins poem.

This new direction, for a poet who has spent much of his career writing in iambic pentameter and tetrameter, is something to ponder. In an interview published in *The Glass Anvil*, he acknowledges that his initial use of meter allowed him to energize the content of his poetry: "I began to use more dialogue, more humor, and I began to include sharp tonal shifts and leaps of logic. The pulse of the meter gave me confidence that it could carry those things without collapsing into prose." But an inventive mind must always find new ways to express itself. One may read Andrew Hudgins and hear an indelible voice–his voice–in all five of his volumes of poetry, but what is remarkable is that each separate collection may be viewed as a singular project with an awareness of the book that precedes it. This consciousness, and the progression that has resulted from it, is something that seems to matter a great deal to Hudgins, and it is the mark of a poet who is driven to be different. He has shown the reader, in this moment when there is a renewed interest in formal poetry, that meter need not stiffen the lines of poetry, a statement that cannot be made about many of the so-called New Formalists. But the poetry of Andrew Hudgins is an affirmation of Emerson's observation that "it is not meters, but a meter-making argument that makes a poem–a thought so passionate and alive that like the spirit of a plant or an animal it has an architecture of its own, and adorns nature with a new thing."

Reference:

Clay Reynolds, "Crossing the Line of Poetic Biography: Andrew Hudgins' Narrative of the Life of Sidney Lanier," *Journal of the American Studies Association of Texas*, 20 (October 1989): 27–40.

Mark Jarman
(5 June 1952 -)

Terri Witek
Stetson University

See also the Jarman entry in *DLB 120: American Poets Since World War II, Third Series.*

BOOKS: *Tonight Is the Night of the Prom: Poems* (Pittsburgh: Three Rivers, 1974);
North Sea (Cleveland: Cleveland State University Poetry Center, 1978);
The Rote Walker (Pittsburgh: Carnegie-Mellon University Press, 1981);
Far and Away (Pittsburgh: Carnegie-Mellon University Press, 1985);
The Black Riviera (Middletown, Conn.: Wesleyan University Press, 1990);
Iris (Brownsville, Ore.: Story Line Press, 1992);
The Reaper Essays, by Jarman and Robert McDowell (Brownsville, Ore.: Story Line Press, 1996);
Questions for Ecclesiastes: Poems (Brownsville, Ore.: Story Line Press, 1997);
Unholy Sonnets (Ashland, Ore.: Story Line Press, 2000);
The Secret of Poetry (Brownsville, Ore.: Story Line Press, 2001);
Body and Soul: Essays on Poetry, Poets on Poetry Series (Ann Arbor: University of Michigan Press, 2002).

OTHER: "Robinson, Frost, and Jeffers and the New Narrative Poetry," in *Expansive Poetry,* edited by Frederick Feirstein (Brownsville, Ore.: Story Line Press, 1989), pp. 85–89;
"Poetry and Religion," in *Poetry After Modernism,* edited by Robert McDowell (Brownsville, Ore.: Story Line Press, 1991);
"Mark Jarman," in *Contemporary Authors Autobiography Series,* volume 22 (Detroit: Gale Research, 1996), pp. 89–106;
Rebel Angels: 25 Poets of the New Formalism, edited by Jarman and David Mason (Brownsville, Ore.: Story Line Press, 1996).

SELECTED PERIODICAL PUBLICATIONS–UNCOLLECTED: "Where Poems Take Place," *Tennessee Quarterly,* 1, no. 1 (Spring 1994): 5–23;

Mark Jarman (photograph by Rebecca Walk; courtesy of the author)

"Slip, Shift, and Speed Up: The Influence of Robinson Jeffers' Narrative Syntax," *Jeffers Studies,* 3, no. 4 (Fall 1999): 10–23.

Mark Jarman's ideas about poetic movement provide the subtext of eight books of poems and a significant body of criticism. While taking on the technical challenges of both Robinson Jeffers's long narratives and John Donne's sonnet sequences, Jarman offers a metaphysic of poetic movement that challenges his readers' ideas about the relationship between lyric and narrative impulses.

Jarman's biography might have predicted that movement would be a motif in his work. Born on 5 June 1952 as the eldest of three children and only son, Jarman was forced to move during his early childhood as his father's ministerial career required. Jarman was born in Mount Sterling, Kentucky, during his father's training at what is now the Lexington Theological Seminary; the family relocated to Santa Maria, California, when Mark was two; to Kirkcaldy, Fife, Scotland, when he was six; and to Redondo Beach, California, when he was nine. This sense of multiple landscapes and the distance to be traveled between them is keenly felt in Jarman's early work—*North Sea* (1978), *The Rote Walker* (1981), and *Far and Away* (1985). *The Black Riviera* (1990) makes the distance most literal by revisiting the Redondo Beach area where the poet lived until he graduated from high school and lets adolescence provide the first biological push into the larger world—a movement Jarman later called, in *Questions for Ecclesiastes: Poems* (1997), "the ground swell." While *Iris* (1992) converts the question of movement into a particularly American journey for his protagonist, *Questions for Ecclesiastes* negotiates distances structurally by juxtaposing what had become a signature narrative style with a persuasive group of sonnets. A lyric exploration of belief becomes metaphysical landscape in Jarman's *Unholy Sonnets* (2000), and book manuscripts of "For the Green Man," to be published by Sarabande Press in 2004, and "Epistles," slated for publication by Story Line Press in 2005, promise work that is arguably the most lyrically complex of his career.

The arc of Jarman's poetic education mirrors that of his generation's best poets. He left Redondo Beach for a distinguished undergraduate career at the University of California, Santa Cruz, where he earned a B.A. degree in English with highest honors, received the Joseph Henry Jackson Award for Poetry from the San Francisco Foundation, and published a chapbook, *Tonight Is the Night of the Prom: Poems* (1974). He studied both with Raymond Carver and, most important for his later career, with George Hitchcock, editor and publisher of *kayak* magazine. Jarman's work with Hitchcock and his friendship with fellow undergraduate Robert McDowell prepared him to found, with McDowell, *The Reaper* (1981), a journal dedicated to narrative poetry, whose rambunctious essays McDowell later reprinted at Story Line Press as *The Reaper Essays* (1996). At Santa Cruz, Jarman also met soprano Amy Kane. They married on 28 December 1974 and have two daughters, Claire (born on 15 May 1980) and Zoë (born on 16 December 1982).

Jarman began work on an M.F.A. degree at Iowa Writers' Workshop just before the Expansionist phase of creative-writing programs in American universities; he is one of a cadre of illustrious Iowa graduates of the era and worked as a teaching/writing fellow with such notable poets and teachers as Donald Justice, Charles Wright, Stanley Plumly, Sandra Macpherson, and Marvin Bell. Jarman's early career moves include teaching positions at Indiana State University, Evansville (1976–1978); the University of California, Irvine (1979–1980); Murray State University, Kentucky (1980–1983); and a 1983 appointment at Vanderbilt University, where he has helped build a notable creative-writing faculty. His poetry has been honored by many awards: he has received three National Endowment for the Arts grants (1977, 1983, and 1992) and a Guggenheim Fellowship for 1991–1992. *The Black Riviera* won the 1991 Poets' Prize, and *Questions for Ecclesiastes* was a finalist for the 1997 National Book Critics Circle Award for poetry, winning the 1998 Lenore Marshall Poetry Prize from the Academy of American Poets and *The Nation* magazine.

Productive and distinguished as a poet, Jarman has also published more than three dozen articles about poetry and as many reviews. His service to poetry includes several editorial stints: he founded and edited *The Reaper* with McDowell from 1981 to 1989, and with McDowell he was copublisher of Story Line Press from 1985 to 1987 (he served as advisory editor from 1987 to 1989). With David Mason, Jarman edited the influential poetry anthology *Rebel Angels: 25 Poets of the New Formalism* (1996) and currently edits Poet of the Month for the website *PoetryNet*. A collection of Jarman's essays, *The Secret of Poetry,* was published by Story Line Press in 2001, and another collection, *Body and Soul: Essays on Poetry,* was published in 2002 in the University of Michigan's Poets on Poetry Series. He has taught at many summer writing conferences, including Sewanee, Bread Loaf, The RopeWalk Writers Retreat, and the West Chester University Poetry Conference.

While Jarman has had an exemplary career for a poet of his generation, the development of his poetry has been surprising to readers who thought they had him pegged early. That many still think of him first as a poet of the New Narrative movement is a result not only of his own early development but also because of the republication of such essays as "How to Write Narrative Poetry: A *Reaper* Checklist." That he is profoundly interested in New Formalism as well is attested to not only by his editorship of the *Rebel Angels* anthology but also by his use of such forms as the sonnet. Of the connection between New Narrative poetry and New Formalism, Jarman has said that he has always considered narrative "a form" (while noting that *The Reaper* published mostly free-verse narrative poems). His poetic Epistles (which he calls "prose poems") reissue a challenge to those trying to categorize his work. To describe Jarman's poetry simply as either New Narrative or New Formalist is to miss the essential drama of his choices concerning poetic movement over the course of his career.

Iris

I

The woman sat on the bus, her daughter's head in her
    lap, and read the one college text
She had saved, the paperback of poems, by Robinson
    Jeffers, and, as always, talked back to him
Whom she considered her poet. The bus crossed the
    two lakes, and the land between them,
Like stages of warning, glare of water, shadow of close
    dense trees, glare again.
Then entry into the isolated flat land she had left,
    married, pregnant, unhurt,
And not yet in thrall to this stranger between limp pages,
    who spoke of an end to the continent
She had to imagine, had to summon up even more strenuously
    coming back here
To western Kentucky, a mother, estranged, abused and
    wounded, hiding a black eye behind dark glasses.
Her daughter curled up her legs on the hard vinyl seat;
The windbreak oaks dangled their pea green April flowers,
    and winter wheat a field flashed a green facet of
    winter wheat.
Iris read about granite and spray and poppies and said to
    her poet, "What is a ground swell?
Why do you envy hardness? My mama has gotten hard. Oh
    what will she say when she sees us?"

When Iris came home, she saw the new Chevy truck, with
    camper top, and Hoy and Rice, her brothers,
Standing back to smell its newness, like part of the spring
    air, fat Hoy like a friar,
His black hair shining like a wallet with greaseless hair
    oil and his twin, Rice, like the after-picture
from the diet ads, thin as a hoe handle, his hair, too,
    slick with the same stuff.

Page from the revised typescript for Jarman's 1992 novel in verse (courtesy of the author)

Dust jacket for Jarman's 1997 collection, published by Story Line Press, which Jarman and Robert McDowell founded in 1984 (Richland County Public Library)

Jarman's first full-length book, *North Sea,* uses predominantly free-verse strategies to capture the movement of memory. While the dwellings in *North Sea* seem to want to provide a domestic stay against the patterned sway of surrounding water, the earth itself "is a wave that will not set us down" ("Lullaby for Amy"). Even the houses seem to want to stay in motion: in "Foreigners," flues "blew out their gags of newspapers," while in the central domestic space, the kitchen, "The open honey jar is clotted with wasps." This sense of the interpenetrating movements of inside and outside is acknowledged by the colluding visitors: "But we keep the window open." In these poems, the persona seems to feel that despite the cost, he and his must carry their wandering with them; in recompense, they become adept at dwelling on land that moves like the sea. This skill provides more than literal rewards. When, in the last poem of the book ("Lullaby for Amy") he arrives "at another provisional town" and smells the cod of a town from sixteen years before then claims "I have never been back," readers are assured that waves of memory, like lines of poetry, do carry people back, though the journey is unpredictable and the sense of arrival is itself undermined by unstoppable motion.

The Rote Walker makes the movement of memory mostly a matter of male lineage. For Jarman, that means reconsidering both his preacher father and his preacher grandfather, newly deceased. The conflicted grandson watching his grandfather's exit and rethinking his father through the lens of inherited faith presages his own use of faith and language as twin engines to drive poetry. In "Glossolalia," Father and Grandfather disagree about a young speaker in tongues: they "swear and counterswear, flinging / faiths into separate heavens." The son, however, listens as the "conchlike" glossolalist does to these "attributed voices belonging to others." That he learns "there are both ecstasy and the word against it" not only demonstrates the characteristic tug in Jarman's poetry between belief and doubt but also suggests that by being able to speak at least doubly the poet and the glossolalist share fundamentally similar talents.

Much of the ironic yet hopeful stance toward God that fuels Jarman's later work is given its first full treatment in *The Rote Walker*. The querying of Christian ritual is also a way of using its strategies: the title poem builds a series of "Blessed are's," for example, much as the later "Questions for Ecclesiastes" uses its earlier "attributed voice." The title "Lower Rooms" is a turn on "the upper room" of the Last Supper just as the later *Unholy Sonnets* reconsider Donne's "Holy Sonnets." And when the poet takes on Satan in "Address to the Devil," his alternately irritated, amused, and finally respectful stance is one he will employ again when directly addressing his difficult God.

While *The Rote Walker* moves along the poet's male and Christian lineage, *Far and Away* is, if anything, even more wave-driven than the earlier *North Sea.* Whether waves are viewed aerially–"From that height they still look frail and frozen, / full of simple sweetness and repetition" ("The Supremes")–or close up in a surfer who "used the calms to lie still" ("The Face of the Wave"), tidal movement is regarded as at once essential, symbolic, and melancholy. "Growing up is all vacillation," Jarman claims in "Classmates." Many different creatures join the perennial shoreline stirring of *Far and Away:* the men who sleep under the pier and "blow into town, beg money, blow out again" ("By-Blows"), bees fixed in salt ("Bees at the Tide Line"), a rower in "Two Rivers," and the young father who lets his daughter ride his shoulders as he once rode the surf: "I am a good horse," he notes wryly.

While the poems of these earlier books are notable for a gathering, spill-down-the-page narrative power, they also offer glimpses of what will develop in Jarman's work of a decade later. *North Sea* includes "Three Gods Share Their Past," a triptych in which Neptune, Mercury, and Vulcan each are allotted a sixteen-line space that offers a sonnet-like turn between lines nine and ten. *The Rote Walker* also offers several mostly free-verse fourteen-line poems. One of the most intriguing entries in *Far and Away* is "Half Sonnets," nine seven-line poems that are early, free-verse examples of the swell of meditative "arriving and leaving" that later characterize the poet's sustained lyric sequences.

In *The Black Riviera,* Jarman authoritatively weds his sense of narrative sweep to assured, metrically regular iambic lines. By now the sense of landscape as what is both outside and inside seems signature: "Sometimes I feel the whole coast in my body," he proclaims in "Human Geography." This identification now lets him take *The Black Riviera* into ever stranger and more beautiful places: he has learned to "drive back into a story / Any I choose." Jarman's confidence in the rhythms that have brought him lead him into newly strange urban neighborhoods and into familiar-seeming but almost hallucinatory countries. In the tour de force "Liechtenstein," Jarman expands a literal postage stamp into a complex double narrative of a family whose parents take different paths to learning the language: the man who stays in with a stomachache and the woman who walks out of the hotel into adventure are equally convincing, a truth that suggests that Jarman has learned to move as confidently among his imaginary characters as he has across remembered landscapes. Interestingly, his most intriguing new characters are women, particularly the kidnapped girl who speaks "The Gift" and Miss Urquhart of "Miss Urquhart's Tiara." That men and women may not only meet on equally shifting ground in Jarman's poems but also have the same rights as survivors is made clear in "Between Flights," in which the poet and his sister, baby in tow, consider "the black box / Recorded with the last message of childhood." Such equivalent motions provide the best effects in *The Black Riviera*. The drug dealer's car in "The Black Riviera," which inspires adolescent boys in love to "sink in their little bathyspheres" until kisses drag them up "like bursts of bloody oxygen," is perhaps the most startling example of the way Jarman's sense of double movement has rounded into something else; the burning tire of an overturned and finally transcendent bicycle of "The Shrine and the Burning Wheel" is another. Even the simple dramatic situation of the "Days of '74" wheels back on itself: the silences of lovers in two different rooms becomes the movement of sex over time, when a man and woman

> . . . felt that slowness
> that the best days begin with
> turn into the speed with which they fly.

Jarman's most complex version of the movement between men and women occurs in the 1992 book-length *Iris,* in which the title character drags herself, her daughter, her mother, and finally a female hitchhiker (she bears Jarman's maternal grandmother's name, Nora) across country in a prototypical American journey that is part discovery literature, part captivity narrative. That Jarman's own biographical loop is rewritten by *Iris* is no accident: the poet who was born in Kentucky, moved to California, and returned to the South as a married adult with children propels Iris from Kentucky to California in violence-inspired gold-rush fashion, though to achieve her dream (arrival at Robinson Jeffers's Tor House) she has to leave a second husband and her by now grown-up daughter. Jarman has written of a typical Robert Frost strategy that

> Frost's narrator is rarely central, but usually along for the walk or the ride. . . . This is an appealing role for the contemporary narrative poet who cannot, as Frost rarely could, completely dispense with himself or herself in a narrative poem. (*The Secret of Poetry*)

This particular narrative stance is given a complex and ambitious treatment in *Iris*. In his foreword to the book, Dana Gioia has argued of the protagonist that "In a better world she would have been an artist." More metaphorically, she is an artist: by splitting an imaginative identity between Iris and Jeffers (a woman and "her poet") and offering himself as the poet behind both, Jarman has managed to catch adroitly both Jeffers's wavelike lines and narrative sweep and the psyche of a woman who finally does not agree with him. Jarman thus creates for Iris's true "other" poet a compassionate enactment of the drama of identity that is as moving as the silent sex of the couple in "Days of '74" and a treatment of female lineage even more ambitious and risk-taking than his querying of male ancestry in *The Rote Walker*.

Jarman's increasingly assured manner of doing at least two things at once is made structurally literal in *Questions for Ecclesiastes,* which the poet opens with a reminder of where his particular rhythms began:

> Yes, I can write about a lot of things
> Besides the summer that I turned sixteen.
> But that's my ground swell. I must start
> Where things began to happen and I knew it.
>   ("Ground Swell")

The poems that return to those "things" and their rhythms surround twenty sonnets at the core of the

Unholy Sonnet

Have healed the flesh ~~with prayer~~ and changed the weather,
Have girdled [desert peaks] with lightning flashes,
Have turned the rose when it began to wither,
Have drawn to inside straights and royal flushes—
With prayer, that gesture out into the blankness,
Beyondness, nothingness, the shaftless mine
~~Of prayer-answering, which makes its thankless~~
Miracles for certain lucky men
And women who believe in the power of prayer.
Have not, however, ended poverty
Or hatred (we will always hate the poor)
Or ~~found~~ a chamber in the busy heart
To love the world away from making war
Or ~~take~~ to ~~should be~~ what things always were.

Draft for one of the series of sonnets in which Jarman responds to John Donne's "Holy Sonnets" (courtesy of the author) book, which query God the way Iris queries Jeffers. The swing poem in this case is the title poem of the book, in which the poet's "What if" frames a tale of domestic tragedy within the tale of a minister who travels out to it and then back into his own home. This narrative situation is complicated enough, but that Jarman situates it within a series of unanswerable questions demonstrates the complex pulls in his poetry toward both narrative and lyric even as the poem spills down the page like an antiphonal reading at church or an Old Testament list. By claiming that

> . . . God who shall bring
> every work into judgement, with every secret thing,
> whether it be good or whether it be evil, who could
> have shared what he knew with people who needed
> urgently to hear it, God kept a secret.
> ("Questions For Ecclesiastes")

the poet acknowledges the way silence organizes human experience as surely as does the forward rush of event. This reminder is then enacted at the heart of the book, section three of five, in which the poet's efforts to think about and talk to God directly are given sonnet form.

Jarman's "Unholy Sonnets," twenty of which appear in *Questions for Ecclesiastes* and forty-eight of which structure his 2000 collection, *Unholy Sonnets,* offer a heartfelt response to Donne's "Holy Sonnets." The twentieth-century poet, who is a preacher's son and grandson, wrestles with different angels from those of the early-seventeenth-century preacher-poet Donne. But the lyric power of Jarman's sonnets, their philosophical thirst, is as profound (and often more disquieting) than his most vivid narrative effects. This combination of modes was powerful enough to launch *Questions for Ecclesiastes* into the National Book Critics Circle Award competition.

Jarman's "unholy sonnets" subsume their occasional narratives into the philosophical argumentation of the sonnet form, often to wry effect. While the television stays off in Sonnet 17, the "gray" living room of memory hosts another visitation:

> A sudden apparition in a chair
> Who flares up like the vision of a god
> And blinds them, and intones, "This is my son,
> In whom I am not pleased."

In Sonnet 27, the persona crowds into a taxi in which the occupants are "talking food" and, in weird communion, begin discussing internal organs:

> That's when an idea froze inside my head,
> While they yakked on, the giblet-loving crew,
> And I knew that this was hell and I was dead.

Dust jacket for the 2000 collection of forty-eight of Jarman's philosophical meditations (Richland County Public Library)

Sometimes readers are given particular instructions, as hard to follow as it is to find replies to certain of Jarman's questions. When the thief in Sonnet 11 "pulls a nylon stocking over his head," readers are instructed to "Look for the sacred face inside that face." In such poems Jarman makes clear that ideas about God remain as disturbing as ever and, in unanswerable moments parallel to a turn of the sonnet, drive some of Jarman's best work.

The poet's wedding of narrative and lyric strategies presents a bigger challenge still in the new "Epistles." Whereas Jarman sends his readers back to Donne in his "Unholy Sonnets," the Epistles deliberately offer readers the apostle Paul. But the resemblance, as it was in the poem "Questions for Ecclesiastes," is mostly structural. Jarman offers lavish biblical rhythms, especially repetition, in work that looks like prose and simultaneously offers some of his most lyric effects:

> What are we living for? Isn't it finally to make a rhythm
>   we can live with daily,
> that will stress pleasures like bars of melody, strike and
>   hold the note of our contentment as claims about the
>   real and unreal pass through it, thick thread
> through the eye of the whole truth?
>
>   ("I have always thought")

Like Jarman's earlier poems, the Epistles also provide memorable characters; now, like Walt Whitman's, they inhabit a landscape of connection that covers all this world and perhaps some of the next. This strategy leads to some intriguing reuse of the poet's own poetic past. At the same time, it offers such metaphysical sweep—for example, the Epistle beginning "I have always thought" also provides a sly return to the image of the young poet/father who played horse with his daughter in "Poem in June" of *Far and Away*. Now he offers his own roving, compassionate eye embedded in the eye of another:

> And you ask me if I mean to provide counsel and consola-
>   tion. Someone else
> could embody all I am saying in a horse. He would see it
>   through the animal's
> coffee clear eye, as it stood between traces on cobble-
>   stones, pained by a growth
> above its right fetlock—a soft, gray, carrotlike protrusion.
>   There is a vegetable cart
> with its meager bounty. There are women leaving houses.
>   The horse looks
> between smokestacks at the sea, the taint of linseed fumes
>   in its whiskered nostrils,
> the cold sun hanging in a gray emulsion of cloud cover.
>   The growth on its leg is
> untended by the horse's owner, the vegetable seller, who is
>   himself covered with
> moles and wens, a melon-headed, straw-bodied effigy in a
>   great coat and flat cap.
> The life funnelled though the horse's eye is one of motion
>   and rest, pain and less
> pain, cut by rocking figures of gulls, diluted by rain or a
>   gift pressed up against the
> lips, in the damp palm of a girl.

When Jarman scrupulously observes in a particular moment the becalmed horse decked in growths like flowers, the news he provides is perennial "motion and rest," "pain and less pain."

As Andrew Hudgins has said of *The Black Riviera*, "the range of these poems—geographically, emotionally, poetically—is astonishing." What persists within that range is a belief in the power of poetic movement as it pulls characters away from the familiar and back, as it pulls the eye toward and away from what is difficult to watch but essential to see, and as it pulls poets into ever deeper philosophical waters with increasingly subtle poetic skills. To Mark Jarman's great credit and the discreet flummoxing of his critics, he has continued to develop new strategies to meet the perhaps unanswerable questions he insists on considering. As he continues to take the measure of the ineffable, in the decades to come Jarman is sure to surprise readers again with his choices about matters of poetic "motion and rest."

Interviews:

J. M. Spalding, "Mark Jarman," *Cortland Review* (January 1999) <http://www.cortlandreview.com/features/99/01>;

Mary Flinn, "An Interview with Mark Jarman," *Blackbird: An Online Journal of Literature and the Arts*, 1 (Fall 2002) <http://www.blackbird.vcu.edu/v1n2/features/jarman_m_120202/jarman_m.htm>.

Reference:

Jason Schneiderman, "The Holy Forms of Mark Jarman," *Frigate*, no. 2 (November 2000–September 2001) <http://www.frigatezine.com/review/poetry/rpy02sch.html>.

Paul Lake
(5 August 1951 -   )

Jonathan N. Barron
University of Southern Mississippi

and

Sonny Williams
University of New Orleans

Paul Lake (courtesy of the author)

BOOKS: *Bull Dancing: Poems,* New Poets series (Baltimore, 1977);

Catches (Florence, Ky.: Barth, 1986);

Another Kind of Travel (Chicago: University of Chicago Press, 1988);

Among the Immortals: A Vampire Mystery (Brownsville, Ore.: Story Line Press, 1994);

Walking Backward (Ashland, Ore.: Story Line Press, 1999).

OTHER: "Toward a Liberal Poetics," in *Expansive Poetry: Essays on the New Narrative and the New Formalism,* edited by Frederick Feirstein (Santa Cruz, Cal.: Story Line Press, 1989);

"The Archetypal Gesture: Myth and History in the Poetry of George Oppen," in *George Oppen: Man and Poet,* edited by Burton Hatlen (Orono, Me.: National Poetry Foundation, 1991), pp. 113–122;

"The Malady of the Quotidian," *Wallace Stevens Journal,* 17, no. 1 (Spring 1993): 100–109;

"Rhythm and Truth: The Future of Expansive Poetry," *Hellas,* 4, no. 1 (Spring/Summer 1993): 93–95;

"Of Powers and Principalities, Poems and Incipient Angels," *Hellas,* 4, no. 1 (Spring/Summer 1993): 95–104;

Rebel Angels: 25 Poets of the New Formalism, edited by Mark Jarman and David Mason (Brownsville, Ore.: Story Line Press, 1996)–includes poems by Lake, pp. 122–127;

"Disorderly Orders: Free Verse, Chaos, and the Tradition," *Southern Review,* 34 (Fall 1998): 780–803;

"The Shape of Poetry," in *Poetry After Modernism,* revised second edition, edited by Robert McDowell (Ashland, Ore.: Story Line Press, 1998), pp. 278–306;

"Return to Metaphor: From Deep Imagist to New Formalist," in *New Expansive Poetry,* edited by R. S. Gwynn (Ashland, Ore.: Story Line Press, 1999), pp. 134–147;

"Verse that Print Bred," in *After New Formalism,* edited by Annie Finch (Ashland, Ore.: Story Line Press, 1999);

"The Enchanted Loom: A New Paradigm for Literature," *Southwest Review,* 87, nos. 2–3 (2002): 355–381.

Born on 5 August 1951 in Baltimore, Maryland, to Paul S. Lake and Barbara Hull Lake, poet Paul Lake grew up in a close family with two brothers, James and Stephen, and one sister, Melody. Remaining in his home state of Maryland, Lake, between 1969 and 1971, attended Harford Community College. Before graduating in 1971, he moved to California. Enchanted by the West, Lake next traveled to Portland, Oregon, where, also in 1971, he married artist Tina Selanders, whom he had met earlier in Maryland. Eventually, the couple returned to Maryland. There, Lake worked as a pipeline construction inspector as he continued part-time college work toward completion of his degree. Ultimately, Lake graduated in 1975 from Towson State College (now Towson University) with a degree in English. He then taught eighth- and ninth-grade English for two years at an inner-city junior high school in the public school system of Baltimore.

Already publishing his poetry in many of the magazines of the era, Lake was also unusual in his commitment to fixed forms, particularly in an era almost universally opposed to such poetry. In a 1977 symposium, "Freedom and Form: American Poets Respond," Lake published one of his first essays on the topic, "Cheated." In it he said that "far from feeling that free-verse is the only legitimate contemporary verse form, I feel as if I have been cheated out of a literary heritage by two or three generations of free verse apologists." He then admits that "All of the poems I have published to date have been in free verse, although much, perhaps most, of my best work is in traditional meters with stanzas and rhyme." Still an unknown twenty-five-year-old apprentice poet, Lake made a prophetic and public declaration: "I will continue to work in the older prosody, risking the anonymity of the unpublished, because I love the sound, and the way it affects the sense, of metrical, rhymed poetry." This statement shows that almost from the beginning of his publishing career, Lake was attracted to the more formal aspects of poetry.

He had already begun sending his apprentice work to the dominant literary journals of the day. In 1977 he won the Mirrielees Creative Writing Fellowship in poetry from Stanford University, which enabled him to return once more to California. At Stanford, Lake earned an M.A. degree in creative writing and English in 1979. While at Stanford, he was influenced by Donald Davie, a poet-critic interested in both literary formalism and Modernism. After earning his degree, Lake taught English and creative writing for two years at the University of Santa Clara as an adjunct lecturer. From there, he and his wife moved to San Francisco, where she finished her M.F.A. degree.

In the summer of 1981, Lake was offered a position at Arkansas Tech University in Russellville, Arkansas. Since 1981 Lake, his wife, and their two children, Rachel and Alex, have made Russellville their home. Not long after arriving at Arkansas Tech, Lake became editor of *Nebo,* the literary magazine of the school, which he soon transformed into one of the first and liveliest outlets for narrative and formal verse. Throughout the 1980s, Lake was known to the poetry community not only as editor of *Nebo* but also as a poet of distinguished essays and poems. His poems were first collected in book form in 1986 when R. L. Barth published Lake's chapbook, *Catches.* This chapbook received little notice, but its poems eventually achieved significant attention when they were published in Lake's first full-length collection, *Another Kind of Travel* (1988). This first book won the Porter Fund Award for Literary Excellence in 1988 and attracted quite favorable reviews.

Written in three parts–"The Age of Terror," "Heartland," and "Travelers in Space and Time"–the book effectively asserts a set of dominant themes that persist in all of Lake's poetry to date. These themes are at once philosophical and dramatic, exploring and dramatizing violence and aggression even as they engage the deeper problems of time and space. This interest in space and time applies to both of his poetry collections, in which Lake often walks the fine line between higher physics and philosophy. Turning to the first section of his first book, for example, one is thrown into the violent world of a 1970s inner city. Drawing on his experience as a white man teaching junior high school in the African American inner-city "ghetto" of Baltimore, Lake produces powerful poems that engage problems of racism. In particular, the poems confront the political facts of colonization and the unequal distribution of power that it produces. Referring to Joseph Conrad's novel *Heart of Darkness* (1902), Lake's first poem, "The Heart of Darkness," does not initially lament, as Kurtz does, "the horror, the horror." Instead, the persona of the poem merely utters, "'I'm tired, I'm tired." The exhaustion, however, is, in the context of the poem, a hopeless sense of cultural failure. For the persona, a teacher, can already predict the future of his students: that their lives have already been determined, predestined for failure and misery, both depresses and indicts and implicates him. If he is a teacher, what is he to teach? Escape? Illusion? Is he more problem than benefit? In the poem, he says he is tired "of watching, as fleet-footed Donna Henson / waltzes on tiptoe like a boxing champ / into a hopeless future." Eventually, the poem does echo Kurtz's famous dying words, "the horror, the horror." When it does, the words refer to the failure of the nation to offer a life of possibility to all of its citizens:

> *The Horror!*
> Yes, the horror–
> Not of my short two-year commute
> Into the heart of darkness, but
> Of those mean streets I'd visit after work
> Where a generation grows up fatherless
> In violence and in squalor
> And where nearly one in twenty
> Men's lives will be cut short
> In bloody nightmare–

These lines depend on the typically racist assumption that the American inner city is a black "heart of darkness." Given that assumption, Lake neatly reverses the metaphor in order to locate the darkness back into its more appropriate cultural and political frame of reference: the heart of darkness is a power structure that creates such inequities in the first place.

Maintaining his intense focus on the world of inner-city Baltimore, Lake writes about an industrial area in "South of the City" where everything is gray and featureless:

> gray, fog-colored men
> move through an iron thicket,
>   pruning with blow torches
> the barbed tendrils
>   of wire, cutting and rooting up the rust-brown
> unblooming flowers
> of metal, petal and stem.

Like the previous poem, this poem also reverses a conventional poetic metaphor. The detritus of bedsprings, sheet metal, and engine blocks are compared to the flowers and plants of a garden. This metaphorical association asks readers to see this harsh environment as a genuine scene of pastoral comfort. In the final lines, such comfort is undermined when readers are shown the stacks of abandoned car batteries, "their acids draining / into the neutral ground."

In the second section of the book, Lake moves to the traditional pastoral locale of the American "Heartland"–in this case, rural Arkansas. This section is also where Lake reveals his ongoing interest in narrative and storytelling. In "The Boat" Lake offers readers a dramatic monologue told in blank verse about a married woman who is having "troubles." The woman remembers an old love and, in the poem, tells the story while her husband and children are away hunting for deer. In the course of the narrative, she describes her tanned Yankee boy and their excursion on his father's boat:

> I wish now, when I wish for anything,
> To have spent that day, instead, without the sailing.
> But there are no insteads. I've learned that much
> From piling one instead on top another,
> Thinking how that day might have turned out different
> If Jack, at first thought of turning back,
> Hadn't brushed his hand so lightly against my thigh
>   And left it there. . . .

In a twist typical of so much of Lake's poetry, a moment of potential joy and bliss leads immediately to ruin and death. The small gesture of love causes the boat to capsize. As the couple attempt to pull the boat to shore, Jack grows tired, disappears into the water, and drowns. But even this turn does not conclude the poem. For no sooner has the woman recounted the death of her lover than her husband and children return: "our husbands clattering down the road / With the tailgate down and hungry for their supper." The poem ultimately becomes a meditation on fate, even on time itself, as the woman realizes that her present domestic bliss is purchased out of that former loss. No one, says the woman, "can / sense the lives they've missed."

Rather than gain solace by viewing her present happiness as somehow compensatory for the past, the poem achieves rare power by rejecting just such easy clichéd ideas about the power of time to heal. The poem rejects the idea that fate works to the best, offering people the best rather than the worst outcome in their lives. Says this woman about her past: "I feel mine / Always below me, like a sunken deck, / Hauling its nightmare tonnage of dark water." This woman's pain will not be appeased even by a loving husband and vibrant children.

Problems of space and time are also taken up in the third section of the volume. In such poems as "Crossing America by Bus," Lake investigates the philosophical implications of travel. He asks what it might mean to be always in transit, lacking any roots to a specific place. Beginning in a bus station, the poem introduces the reader to bums, drunks, beggars, and pimps. Lake says, "Though the law defines them / wishfully as transients, it is truly / we who, lumbering past them, are transients." Just this sort of reversal of cultural cliché and meaning is what makes this volume so engaging. For, indeed, the characters of this bus station have nowhere to go and remain fixed to this transient place while the customers with money (itself a mobile

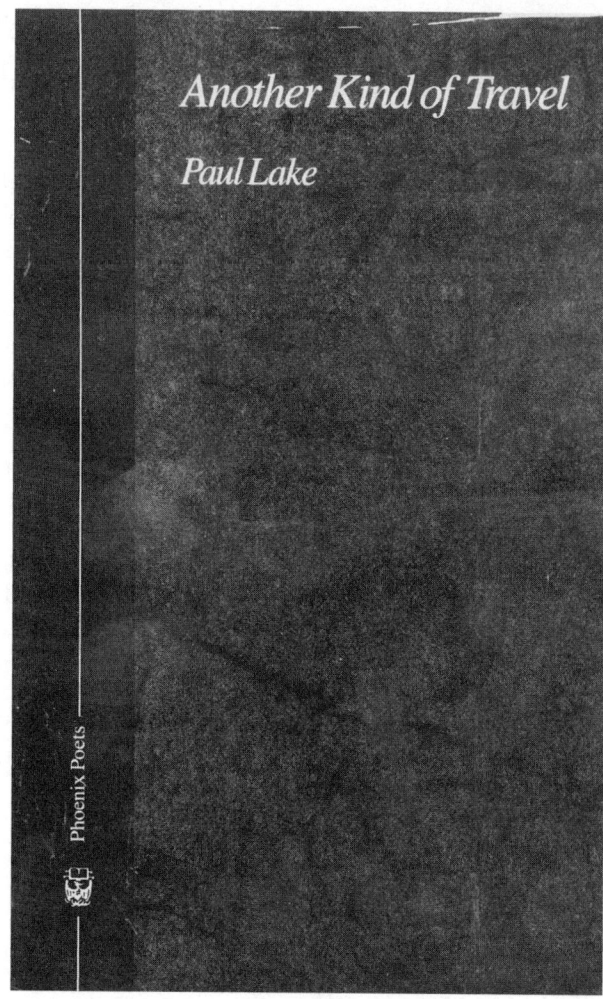

Paperback cover for Lake's first book-length poetry collection, published in 1988, which won the Porter Fund Award for Literary Excellence (Bruccoli Clark Layman Archives)

vehicle of a world economy) are forever in transit through the station.

Eventually in this poem, Lake returns to a literary source in order to reveal the pain involved for all transients: "And sea-tossed Odysseus, / his name become synonymous with journey, / knew that travail and travel had one root." The poem, in fact, takes place on a bus, and by its end, when the bus stops, the reader is compared to another literary traveler:

> we enter empty-handed
> and swollen-footed, like Oedipus, into a strange city
> with all the weight of time and distance on us
> like a tragic curse, but which is merely
> the condition we call human,
> cured by a long sleep.
> Which is another kind of travel.

The mention of Oedipus, who was fated to kill his father and marry his mother, is particularly astute: for travel as he might, Oedipus would never defeat or influence time and history. The bus may well have gone from one place to another; it may well have crossed from one time to another; but if the bus traveler is compared to Oedipus, then the fate that awaits him at the end of the road will be no different from what it was at the beginning. The poem plays with both the classical tradition and contemporary physics; in so doing, Lake deftly shows how the ancients have far more in common with moderns than many might have guessed.

For all his exploration of the dark side of experience, Lake's first collection nonetheless does end on a hopeful note with the poem "Summer Revisited." This poem has a portentous beginning: "Like an approaching storm, / time gathers, thickening the air." Yet, the threat represented by this storm becomes instead a release allowing a burst of life and joy. Such pleasure also becomes an impossible moment of timelessness: "for one moment, nature seems suspended / above its laws, / and the seconds hang / like flung gravel in mid-air."

In the story of the poem, the speaker shovels gravel from the back of a truck. The stones pause before falling to the ground, creating a continuous galaxy caught in a motionless instant, and, once again, time stands still. Comparing this sense of time stopping to the eye of a storm, Lake adds,

> But time is a storm
> and after its eye passes
> the merciless seconds
> are blown in our eyes
> like fine dust off stone
> and no amount of weeping
> can clear them from our vision.

These lines summarize the collection as a whole. Combined, the poems of Lake's first collection are like the dust of these relentless seconds—once in the reader's vision, they demand attention.

Reviewing this collection in *The Arkansas Democrat*, Wes Ziegler wrote that "Lake is not content with simply being precise and original with his descriptions. He possesses another gift of the poetic mind: the ability to make his images, his simple scenes, resonate with meaning." Similarly, reviewers in the national literary press were equally enthusiastic. Mark Jarman praised the collection in a review for *The Hudson Review* (Winter 1989) as did John Gery in *The Chicago Review* (nos. 3–4, 1989) and David Mason in *The Sewanee Review* (Winter 1989).

Following that success, Lake, although he continued to publish individual poems, next published *Among the Immortals: A Vampire Mystery* (1994). This novel marked a new direction for the poet. Yet, even this horror novel about vampires shared much with Lake's poetry. Whether he is writing in prose or poetry, Lake explores the "dark side" of human nature in stories of threat and violence. Like his poetry, the novel remains fixed and rooted in a poetics of place where the reader is made to feel every scene, each locale.

In this novel, a modern Gothic romance based on the Faustian dangers and futility of literary ambition, one Derek Hill, an aspiring poet and Berkeley graduate student, attempts to unravel the mystery shrouding the murder of his Stanford professor, a specialist in the English Romantic poets. During Hill's investigation, Romantic poets of the past, such as George Gordon, Lord Byron, and Percy Bysshe Shelley, appear as vampires. Hill wonders if the Romantic poets are still walking the earth in order to assure their continued study in universities and so their immortality. The allegory to the contemporary poetry scene, both witty and penetrating, parallels vampirism with a contemporary career in poetry, often ruefully referred to as "pobiz" by those disgusted with the triumph of marketing over art.

This venture into the world of genre fiction proved successful: the novel was selected for the *Year's Best Fantasy and Horror* list. In *Publishers Weekly*, the reviewer noted, "Not since Ken Russell's film *Gothic* has so enthusiastic an eye been cast toward the mythopoetic relationship among the Romantic poets and their role in the evolution of our horrific imagination." The reviewer concluded, "Although the final doppleganger theory doesn't quite track, readers will thrill to the plot's literary intrigue and author's elegant skewering of the dark side of the poetic sensibility."

In 1999, when Lake released his third book and second collection of poems, *Walking Backward,* eleven years had passed since the publication of his first collection. Aside from his novel and a regular presence of individual poems in the major literary magazines of the era, Lake had also spent those eleven years building his reputation as both critic and polemicist. His many essays from this period had a decisive impact on New Formalist poetics.

Almost from its inception, the New Formalism movement sparked the ire of many poets, not on aesthetic terms merely but rather on ideological grounds. By the 1980s, formal poetics had become associated with conservative, even right-wing, political views. This argument had been used by three powerful critics of New Formalism—Ira Sadoff, Diane Wakoski, and Wayne Dodd—all writing in influential literary journals: *American Poetry Review, American Book Review, Caliban,* and *The Ohio Review*. Against that ongoing assault, Lake issued, in *The Threepenny Review* (1988), a full-blown ideological polemic, "Toward a Liberal Poetics." The essay was subsequently included in the first anthology of New Formalist criticism, *Expansive Poetry,* edited by Frederick Feirstein (1989). In this article, Lake takes to task those who compare New Formalist principles to ideological concerns:

> The very term "the new formalism," which is used most often by its opponents, is misleading. It implies that formalism is new, when it fact it has been with us all along. . . . No, what is unprecedented and new about the new formalism is the fact that the best young poets in America . . . have rejected the limitations imposed by that rather circumscribed and exhausted poetics to explore richer prosodic fields—the greener pastures of formalism.

Lake then argues that the New Formalists are diverse in both style and theme and that more often than not their poetry espouses the same liberalism their detractors accuse them of denying. To argue that point, Lake singles out Charles Martin's poem "Easter Sunday, 1985," which he says "no one can accuse of Reaganism." Lake reaches his most strident and polemical pitch when he declares, "We don't need a House Committee on Un-American Poetic Activities in this country; we need good poems. The new formalists, as they seem destined to be called, are writing them."

More than merely a polemicist, however, Lake is equally at home in the more measured forms of the literary essay. His skill in this form became evident when he published "Return to Metaphor: From Deep Imagist to New Formalist" (originally published in *The Southwest Review*, 1989). In that essay, Lake defends the aesthetic principles of New Formalism. Specifically, Lake compares the way two poems from two distinct poetic movements use metaphor. He chooses a free-verse, deep image poem by Charles Wright and a formal poem in rhymed quatrains by Gjertrud Schnackenberg. In a careful analysis of each, Lake reveals the many pleasures, nuances, and skillful play formal poetry encourages. Through this close reading, Lake demonstrates the strengths and possibilities inherent in New Formalist poetry even as he reveals his own astute capacity as a critic. So convincing did this essay prove to be that when R. S. Gwynn was charged with the task of revising and polishing Feirstein's *Expansive Poetry* (1989) for a second edition published as *New Expansive Poetry* (1999), he cut "Toward a Liberal Poetics" and replaced it with "Return to Metaphor."

By the end of the 1980s, then, these two essays had joined the chorus of attack and counterattack on the meaning, use, and need for formalism in contemporary poetry. Often the attack against the New Formalism was based on the assumption that literary devices such as meter and rhyme implied a bookish, retrograde, fusty poetics. This view was contrasted to the more living dynamism and speech-based practice of free verse. In his essay "Verse that Print Bred" (originally published in *The Sewanee Review*, 1991), Lake confronted that view directly by providing a close reading of the poet Charles Olson's foundational defense of contemporary free-verse poetics—the essay "Projective Verse" (1950). In so doing, Lake argues that, ultimately, the tradition of free-verse poetry Olson's essay inaugurated and encouraged actually depends far more deeply on the mind's eye, on the act of reading, and on mental acts of decoding print on the page than on some organic conception of the breath and the body. Lake makes this point in order to defend more-traditional poetic practices such as the use of meter and rhyme and to assert further that both meter and rhyme depend on a fundamentally populist and oral culture, especially song. Ultimately, he asserts, "Formal poetry is not an elitist but a popular art form." More than a defense of New Formalism, this essay was, finally, a defense of traditional forms themselves. By this point Lake had, in three successive essays, argued that fixed forms were grounded in a liberal ideology, made exacting and complex use of figurative language, and were far more grounded in the body and organic ideas of culture than were their free-verse counterparts.

Building on this ongoing defense, Lake published "The Shape of Poetry," which claimed that both meter and rhyme ought to be understood best in terms offered by the natural sciences. Addressing all those who "can not believe there's anything natural about poems being coaxed into existence by metrical rules and formal procedures," Lake says such formal poems are like natural systems that produce "the biomorphic shapes of trees and leaves." In other words, for all those who defend free-verse forms as somehow more natural because less subject to rules, he argues, by referring to feedback theory and fractal geometry, that, in fact, nature itself is subject to rules. "We now know," he says, "that the shapes of trees and leaves are not the sums of 'rulelessness' . . . but the result of a rule-governed process dictated by their DNA and feedback from the environment as they adjust themselves in an endless feedback loop." Using the poetry of Gerard Manley Hopkins and the contemporary New Formalist Charles Martin, Lake then illustrates his views. He concludes that "symmetrical forms," "regular meter," and rhyme all function "through a process of iteration and feedback" in a "natural process" and not through some "dull mechanical ticking." In his conclusion Lake speaks of Hopkins, but the reader also senses that he may just as well have been speaking for himself, when he declares that Hopkins "believed that natural forms are produced by chance combined with natural law." This essay, like the others, also found a second life in book form when it was included in the second revised edition of Robert McDowell's critical anthology, *Poetry After Modernism* (1998).

Added to these assaults on the assumptions of antiformalist poets, Lake, in another essay, "Disorderly Orders: Free Verse, Chaos, and the Tradition" (*The Southern Review*, 1998), examined the central premise against all attacks on form—the seemingly arbitrary and unnecessary fact of having rules in so lovely and natural a form as poetry. Finding in the contemporary Language poets a suitable foil, Lake in this essay argues that their major mistake is the belief that poetry could exist in spatial or geometrical terms without regard to time. They assume that language can function in space like an actual thing, an object. Using the linguist Stephen Pinker's work, Lake claims that

Individual words, syntax, and meaning are, then, inextricable from one another; and in poetry they are even more intimately intertwined and unified by metrical rhythm. Attempts to fragment, defamiliarize, and deconstruct poetic language are therefore doomed to failure or, at best, only partial success.

According to Lake, the Language poets "illustrate this dilemma" because they cannot fully detach language from its "flow," from its connotations and denotations in meaning: "Linguistic research tells us that language cannot be broken down to strings of atomized sounds." In fact, few, if any, Language poets claim to be doing any such thing. But that polemical dimension to his work is, ultimately, far less important than his major insight: "For the idea that the poet is eternally progressive and forward-looking we will have to substitute a more recursive and evolutionary model of growth." Having already established that poetry needs rules just as natural flora does, he next makes the case that even the most exacting of avant-garde poets in the free-verse tradition needed and used fixed form. To make that case, Lake returns to the work of Walt Whitman and Ezra Pound in order to show that theirs was never a free verse but rather was itself constructed out of the artful use of particular metrics and fixed forms. Rules, he shows, have always been of the essence of poetry, even in its most avant-garde forms.

When Annie Finch compiled her important critical anthology *After New Formalism* (1999), she included "Verse that Print Bred," making Lake one of the central critical voices of the New Formalism, with essays in three of its major critical texts. Lake's reputation as a promising new poetic voice was becoming somewhat overshadowed by his role as an important critic. This situation changed when he published his second collection, *Walking Backward*, to positive reviews and an expanded audience attuned to his critical voice. This second collection includes much more formal variety—sapphics, blank verse, quatrains—than did his first. But for all of its formal distinctiveness, it also shares a great deal with that first collection. Both have similar themes as well as a three-part structure. And although the three parts of this collection—"Interrogations," "Seeing the Elephant," and "Salt"—include the same dark themes as found in the earlier volume, gender now seems to be of far more interest than in the previous collection. In these poems, such masculine themes as militarism, courage, and strength are brought into the foreground to be explored and dramatized in narratives and lyrics alike. Ultimately, the volume itself becomes an exploration of the meaning of "masculinity." This theme is particularly apparent in the nine poems of the first section, each of which, with the exception of "Antigone," explores some masculine characteristic, often set in a military context. Of these, "Inspectors," "Walking Backward," and "Interrogations" are particularly notable because they are as committed to a narrative form as they are to their masculine themes.

In the title poem, "Walking Backward," the narrator describes a local man who, for years, has been walking backward. He "Explained it with a biblical directness. / He said his life had gone so poorly forward, / He'd try the other way now for a change." This figure becomes a symbol through which the narrator can explore the meaning of such masculine virtues as courage and responsibility in contemporary times. After describing the backward man, the narrator next recalls how, by a freak ability to raise his blood pressure consciously, he failed his medical exam and escaped going to the Vietnam War. At first, he feels lucky to have missed "that foul war." But on reflection, he also understands that his "weakness" only meant someone less lucky but perhaps braver went in his place. The war itself becomes, like the backward man, a point, a moment one returns to again and again, as if walking forever backward into an abyss. As the poem says,

If I had done things differently–stood up
And borne the consequences at some cost
To peace of mind or body, I'd feel better–
Different at least–though I'm not so naive
As to believe the wheels of that machine
Which gobbled up and crushed all those young bodies
Would boggle up its cogs on my account.
No wonder we keep turning back to it
In memory and television screenplays:
We want to give those times another ending[.]

The second section, "Seeing the Elephant," consists of a single long narrative. Based on a narrative by Elizabeth Reed Murphy, the poem is a dramatic monologue told by an old woman who survived the westward migration of the ill-fated Donner Party. Lake provides a note that refers to *The Gentle Tamers* (1958) by Dee Brown: "Seeing the elephant meant going west with one's eyes wide open, expecting to find marvels and wondrous fortunes only to be monstrously defrauded in the end." With this meaning in mind, the reader follows the Donner Party as the old woman recounts the despair, hunger, death, and cannibalism of its members.

Many years later, she encounters an old acquaintance and, not knowing what to say, asks, "Have you seen it, Donny Jackson? Have you seen the elephant?" In response, he tells the riddle of the blind men and the elephant: a group of blind men each feel a different part of the elephant and so each constructs a different ani-

Paperback cover for Lake's second collection, published in 1999, in which many of the poems reflect on the meaning of masculinity (Bruccoli Clark Layman Archives)

mal from the others. Hearing this riddle, the old woman understands its meaning:

> I suppose,
> that's when it came to me–
> how there I lay, an old woman
>   at the end of a long full life,
> whose every day, every minute
>   since Donner Lake–no, since
> first setting out from Springfield–
> was a touch of the elephant
> no one can see but those
> who have walked through snow-covered mountains
> hungry, burying their dead
> under powder with their own two hands
> among neighborly cannibals.
> Every hour, every second of
> the rest of your life depends
> on the next impossible step.

In effect, the masculine themes explored in the first section, and the grim despair and determination of the characters there, are rewritten in this second section so that they can be approached from the perspective of a woman.

In the final section of nine poems, titled "Salt," the reader encounters some of Lake's bleakest poetry. In "The Century Killer" a murderer confesses to a hitchhiker whom one suspects he is also about to kill. In "In a Parking Lot," a truck driver describes various joyriding moments of near death and mayhem, moments that ended when he could not stop his truck and so killed an entire family: "You see, / With all that weight behind you, you can't stop, / Not when you're pushing eighty, eighty-five. / I think sometimes, though, of that family." In "Two Hitchhikers" Lake describes how two young college students looking for beer and fun come frighteningly close to becoming accessories to a murder-robbery and victims themselves.

This last section also includes complex lyrics, which, when mixed with the narratives, add to the overall philosophical meditative quality of the book. In such lyrics as "Additions" and "The Gift," Lake explores the meaning of cruelty, hatred, and violence that his own narratives often dramatize.

The reviews of this book were, like those for his first, both positive and plentiful. The reviewer in *Midwest Book Review* stated, "Paul Lake's poetry reflects a blending of artful language with imaginative expression to present a lucid, articulate imagery that is as impressive as it is memorable." And Jarman noted in a blurb for the cover of the book that in "formal lyrics and dramatic monologues as fine as any being written today, Lake captures the tragedy and farce of human motive and action." Ray Olson of *Booklist* said, "The moral texture of life is his ground theme, and fitting common speech to meters with the apparent ease of Robert Frost, he reflects on it so engagingly, that he is probably writing permanent literature." The reviewer in *Kirkus Reviews* thought "Lake's plain-talking speakers often have interesting stories to tell, and rely on easygoing rhythms."

After publishing *Walking Backward,* Lake continued to publish both essays and poems. Of that work, the most interesting turn occurs in his essay "The Enchanted Loom: A New Paradigm for Literature" (2002). The title itself indicates that Lake's concern with the battle between free verse and formalism may be drawing to a close as he extends his critical acumen to literature as a whole. In this essay, Lake argues that the understanding of literature, both fiction and poetry, requires a new paradigm beyond the postmodern idea that still engages most literary intellectuals. Lake says that such a paradigm is best expressed in the work of Jacques Derrida. But, according to Lake, "In creating his deconstructive philosophy, Derrida duplicates two fundamental errors. . . . He believes words can be reduced to their constituent elements, and he believes these elements are actual things. Unfortunately for his system, recent developments in science suggest that language cannot be reduced to a linear chain of signifiers strung out like dice on a wire." Bringing a vast array of learning from cognitive science, information theory, and linguistics to bear on this project, Lake argues that "Meanings don't reside within individual words any more than human memories reside within individual neurons." As a result, "In focusing on the printable and reproducible elements of linguistic forms, deconstructionists are committing an error that scientists in the fields of complexity and artificial intelligence call 'level confusion'—an idea with particular relevance to the art of writing." A focus on the material fact of sound and printed marks on a page, says Lake, is a focus on but one level of meaning creation. One must do more—and this "more," says Lake, must be a new paradigm. This new paradigm, he argues, will return to a principal mystery of all literature:

> Somehow, writers pack four dimensions of space-time implicated with human meaning into two-dimensional strings of letters on a page, which readers must then unpack, using built-in procedures they share with the writer. A further complication is that in order for this process to work, the writer must first model the minds of prospective readers to predict how they'll respond. To satisfy and subvert reader expectation, he must continuously refer to his own internal model of the reader's mind and adjust the writing process to accommodate it. Because both writer and reader share a language, a culture, and certain universal human experiences, their mental maps of the world share similar patterns. The full context of any text must include this large, recursive mapping process.

Having announced this new paradigm, Paul Lake probably will, in future collections, bring even more of his knowledge of contemporary science to his poetry, creating works that may find ever new and surprising shapes out of the old rules. As he declares in this essay, "writers who avoid closure, preferring a poetics of endless process, misunderstand the nature of creativity. Poems and stories can no more achieve perfection than people can. A 'totalizing system' is a chimera. However, by submitting to conventional constraints, writers can create works of infinite depth and complexity." Readers look forward to such works from Lake as he enters the next stage of his career.

Sydney Lea

(22 December 1942 -   )

D. Creason Bartlett
University of Texas at Dallas

See also the Lea entry in *DLB 120: American Poets Since World War II, Third Series.*

BOOKS: *Searching the Drowned Man* (Urbana & London: University of Illinois Press, 1980);

Gothic to Fantastic: Readings in Supernatural Fiction (New York: Arno, 1980);

The Floating Candles (Urbana & London: University of Illinois Press, 1982);

No Sign (Athens: University of Georgia Press, 1987);

A Place in Mind (New York: Scribners, 1989);

Prayer for the Little City (New York: Scribners, 1990);

The Blainville Testament (Brownsville, Ore.: Story Line Press, 1992);

Hunting the Whole Way Home (Hanover, N.H. & London: University Press of New England, 1994);

To the Bone: New and Selected Poems (Urbana: University of Illinois Press, 1996);

Pursuit of a Wound (Urbana: University of Illinois Press, 2000).

OTHER: *Richard Eberhart: A Celebration,* edited by Lea, M. Robin Barone, and Jay Parini (Hanover, N.H.: Kenyon Hill, 1980);

The Bread Loaf Anthology of Contemporary American Poetry, edited by Lea, Parini, and Robert Pack (Hanover, N.H.: University Press of New England, 1985);

The Burdens of Formality: Essays on the Poetry of Anthony Hecht, edited by Lea (Athens & London: University of Georgia Press, 1989);

Fiction, Flyfishing and the Search for Innocence, edited by Annie Proulx (Delhi, N.Y.: Birch Brook Press, 1994—includes a story by Lea);

"The Feud," "The Wrong Way Will Haunt You," "Telescope," "At the Flyfisher's Shack," "Clouded Evening, Late September," and "Insomnia: The Distances," in *Rebel Angels: 25 Poets of the New Formalism,* edited by Mark Jarman and David Mason (Brownsville, Ore.: Story Line Press, 1996), pp. 127-151;

Sydney Lea (photograph © 1988 by John Karol; from the dust jacket for Prayer for the Little City, *1990; Bruccoli Clark Layman Archives)*

Constance Warloe, ed., *From Daughters and Sons to Fathers: What I've Never Said,* preface by Lea (Brownsville, Ore.: Story Line Press, 2001).

SELECTED PERIODICAL PUBLICATIONS—
UNCOLLECTED: "On 'The Feud,'" *Kansas Quarterly,* 15, no. 4 (1983): 97-103;

"Eighty Percenters: Reflections on Grouse and Grouse Dogs," *Gray's Sporting Journal* (Fall 1986): 121-129;

"Fact, Dream, and Labor: Robert Frost and the New England Attitude," *Writer's Chronicle,* 35, no. 4 (October/November 2002): 4-10.

Sydney Lea is a critic, editor, essayist, novelist, short-story writer, and teacher, but he is best known for his poetry. He has been a past recipient of a Guggenheim Fellowship in poetry, a Rockefeller Foundation Fellowship, and a Fulbright Foundation Fellowship; he was also a finalist for a 2001 Pulitzer Prize in poetry. In 1977 Lea founded the *New England Review,* which he edited for thirteen years. Though the journal has published highly regarded writers such as Robert Penn Warren and Anthony Hecht, it has largely consisted of little-known writers and remains open to unsolicited material. With his poetry Lea has garnered attention for his varied and often relaxed formalism, his narrative style, and his lyrical language. Highly regarded for his use of narrative as well as elegy, Lea typically writes in a commonplace voice about commonplace people.

The oldest of five children, Sydney Longstreth Wright Lea Jr. was born in Chestnut Hill, a Philadelphia suburb, to Episcopal parents Sydney L. W. Lea and Jane Jordan Lea on 22 December 1942. The young Lea's enthusiasm for nature developed on his uncle's farm near Ambler, Pennsylvania. Lea attended the private, all-male Chestnut Hill Academy and later earned his B.A. in 1964 in history and arts and letters, his M.A. in 1968 in American studies, and his Ph.D. in 1972 in comparative literature, all from Yale. While attending Yale, Lea played hockey and pool, belonged to an intellectual fraternity, and wrote short stories and poems, though he remained distant from the literary circle on campus. In 1980 his brother Mahlon died of a brain aneurysm at the age of thirty-five. This death serves as the focus of many of Lea's poems dealing with familial relations and loss. Lea has taught at Yale, Wesleyan, Middlebury College, Dartmouth, the National University of Hungary, the University of Siena, and Vermont College. He has five children: Creston and Erika from his marriage to Carola Bradford, which ended in divorce; and Amico Jordan, Catherine Margaret, and Sydney Portia, with his second wife, lawyer Margaret Robin Barone. Lea and Barone married on 9 July 1983. A nature enthusiast and outdoorsman, Lea hunts, fishes, guides, runs sporting dogs, and writes largely of the Vermont, New Hampshire, and Maine regions. Lea's poetry and prose teem with wildlife and often mourn the destruction of nature in the wake of progress. Lea respects hunting as a near-spiritual act and therefore displays a sense of irritation with those who express antihunting sentiments but ignore the destruction of nature by commercial development.

In Lea's writing, and his poetry specifically, one sees the combination of a sentimental romantic, a mystic, and a realist who finds beauty in the bleak. William Wordsworth and Robert Frost are Lea's most obvious influences. Lea often takes for his subjects nature, family, loss, love, mood, and thought, as well as the use of language to form concrete understanding out of abstract emotion. The beauty of many of his poems derives from his struggle to use language to make meaning out of objects. Often these objects are either physical, personal items or natural, drawn from the land and region; sometimes Lea's objects are memories called into question. While Lea's poems regularly deal with deeply personal matters–his brother's death, a lost time capsule, his children–his work also expands beyond mere confession, reaching for more-universal appeal. Lea believes that poetry has alienated readers by avoiding universal concerns and appeals such as plot, character, history, or social issues. Like Wordsworth and Frost, Lea draws upon narrative values and argues in favor of poetry that allows the first-person "I" to develop as a character rather than simply to represent the poet. Internationally respected for his lyrical ear, his eye for detail, and his emotional and spiritual sensibilities, Lea writes in a range of formal styles but generally remains relaxed and accessible. He avoids flighty lyrical passages, often employs an irregular internal rhyme scheme, and in later years has written in a new style of verse blocks and prose poetry.

In his first collection, *Searching the Drowned Man* (1980), Lea's primary concerns throughout his body of work become apparent: family, place, memory, and language. Lea draws upon personal and gritty reality in this collection of poems, many of which are elegies or cite dedicatees. Actual events make up the subjects of many of these poems. The title poem is one in which the speaker has joined a search party, though he seeks something more than the dead man's body: "I who had joined the search in my young / man's search of ideas." What the speaker finds in the simplicity of the man's face, however, resists high-minded ideas: "Whatever I'd thought, / it wasn't this." Lea's characters and speakers throughout the collection find themselves facing grim realities that challenge their expectations.

Yet, Lea consistently resists using overtly figurative language, favoring instead a natural language that avoids flowery interpretation and refuses to forcibly bestow great significance upon events and objects. In "Drooge's Barn," for example, Lea insists upon a direct presentation of objects: "Look if you like / through the roof beams; / but don't compare them to ribs." A few lines further, he maintains:

> Yet of course you insist
> on listening. And what you hear is a hound,
> ragging the same white hare by moon
> that he ragged all day by day.
> His voice is a chop–like a hound's voice,
> not an ax, a hoe, an adz.

The poems in *Searching the Drowned Man* acknowledge that language is necessary for seeking significance, simple and minor though it might be, in otherwise bleak situations.

Lea's next poetry collection, *The Floating Candles* (1982), shows more variety in its technique and yet more darkness in its vision. Again, Lea draws upon personal matters as well as regional and natural settings, and again many of the poems have dedications. Finding meaning in patterns such as the stars that form the Orion constellation takes on a central role in this collection. People create patterns to contest isolation, and words are manipulated into expressive patterns that attempt to direct insight. In "Dirge for My Brother: Dawn to Dawn," Lea's first few lines demonstrate the concern with using language to handle real and even threatening situations: *"Why like a sentence that qualifies itself / to forestall the inevitable period, did I want your dying / protracted?"* Yet, Lea's somber tone takes a lighter turn in poems such as "Bernie's Quick-Shave," in which barbers in the 1960s—a time of long hair—lament the loss of something central to their lives. Balancing Lea's adeptness for emotional impact with a playful humor, "Bernie's Quick-Shave" closes out the first section of the collection.

Perhaps the best-known and most critically regarded poem of *The Floating Candles* is the blank-verse narrative "The Feud." Praised for its authentic-sounding yet poignantly descriptive language, "The Feud" demonstrates simplicity, realism, and directness. Composed in quatrains, the poem is narrated by a man who becomes involved in a cycle of revenge when the Walker family leaves a pile of deer guts to rot near his house. After a series of retaliatory acts such as slashing tires, bashing mailboxes, and poisoning hogs—which results in the narrator falling ill while wading home through an icy brook—the narrator comes to understand the consequences of judging others according to one's own views. He observes that "Maybe fate is notions / that you might have left alone, but took instead." The feud builds until the narrator's son dies in a house fire, probably arson, and the narrator comes to realize that "No man can find revenge for a thing like this." Lea realized, and portrayed through "The Feud," the pettiness of allowing differing values to direct one's life and actions.

Critically, "The Feud" is a poem about poetry. Its central issue, the devastating effects of maintaining absolute views, makes a larger statement about the limited nature of poetry that stakes out absolute stances and resists venturing into others' perceptions. In an appendix to the original publication of the poem in the *Kansas Quarterly* (1983), Lea says that the participants of

Dust jacket for Lea's 1987 collection, which concludes with a sequence of twelve sonnets tracing the cycles of a year (Bruccoli Clark Layman Archives)

the feud are "moral bullies" who "feel suited to pass righteous judgment on others' moralities and perceptions." Further in the essay Lea compares morally absolute lyric poets with the characters in his poem. Lea's poetry, and "The Feud" specifically, takes on personal issues for the author but also reaches beyond merely confessional matters.

Death, memory, and loss reappear as central issues in Lea's next collection, *No Sign* (1987), though the pensive mood steers away from despair and settles more upon gentle acceptance. Acquiescence to "what is" directs the overall mood of this collection, as in "Telescope," in which the speaker ponders "the inexact science of memory" while looking through a telescope. He knows that "there will be a lens which, pointed back / to earth, may show us all our past, / even to our creation." Yet, the speaker closes with the knowledge of

Paperback cover for Lea's 1992 collection of poems that tell stories about New England life, including one about a man killed by a falling cow (Richland County Public Library)

how little it seems it would have taken
to change the times I now imagine
in which a now quiet man or woman,
myself included, would come off better.
But all these moments are fixed forever,
and such a lens no more effective
than memory, no more corrective.

As with "Telescope," most of the poems in the collection rely more upon directness than upon figurativeness in their reflection and narratives. Lea's directly stated acceptance develops further in "Fall" when the speaker wonders at lost things:

We're good at this thing we do,
but for each bird that falls,
three get by us and go
wherever the things that get by us go.

The equanimity throughout the poems of this collection demonstrates a Christian ideology that begins to emerge in Lea's work; a Congregationalist deacon, Lea calls himself a "Deepwoods Christian."

The final poem in *No Sign,* "Annual Report," is dedicated to Lea's wife. Consisting of twelve irregular sonnets, the poem works its way through the months, starting in May, the month "that marks the twelve gone by since our son's late birth." The cycles of life and death transform through the year until in March the speaker notes awareness of "such tiny signs of life / against all odds" and finally settles on acceptance that his "dreams / of piercing through the gray of mystery / on earth seem idle. Now, the year's full circle . . . what is hope if not futility / for moments stood on end?" Overall, Lea combines formal accomplishment with directness to create moving moods ranging from resigned, almost satisfied acceptance to gloomy brooding.

In *Prayer for the Little City* (1990) Lea's reflective focus upon place, people, and loss continues. Christian images and references arise throughout the collection, as in the opening title poem, in which the "little city" of ice-fishermen's shacks on a frozen pond is compared to Bethlehem, Christ's birthplace. The men of this fishing village joke and curse but ultimately find that "The dullness is pure. No signs, no wonders, no mystery . . . / except it be the care with which all night men linger, / as if in prayer." The dichotomy of worldly and spiritual matters and the interconnectedness of these two realms course throughout the poems in *Prayer for the Little City*. Spirituality further appears in the wordplay of poems such as "Pietà," in which direct Christian connotations arise. In other poems, such as "At the Flyfisher's Shack," Lea seeks revelations in objects. The speaker scrutinizes an old fisherman's nature by considering the items in the man's shack:

> I find a blue-dun hackle neck he used,
> some orange fur he pilfered from a kitten,
> a tying bobbin hanging by its thread there,
> a vise that held his hooks, the verdigris
> collecting now where silver plate once was.
> A cap. A pair of boots. Impressions, these,
> of his career, or were they first suggestions
> of its end?

Formally, Lea makes use of irregular internal rhyme scheme and pentameter to propel the voice through the detailed images of this poem. Another poem in the collection, "Over Brogno," draws attention for its stanza patterns that approximate the speaker's desire to climb in his search for "a higher order."

The Blainville Testament (1992) continues Lea's focus on the New England landscape, moral judgment, and the use of language to form meaning from daily life incidents. The development of narrative and the need for interpretation stand at the center of the title poem, in which Mark, a young man, dies when a dead cow falls onto him in the grave he has dug for the animal. Recounted in the words of Billy, who even at age seventy-nine gets accused by the town of pushing the eight-hundred-pound animal into the grave, the tale weaves its way through captivating landscape and natural beauty. At the heart of the poem, though, stands the need to reject judgment, simply tell a story, appreciate nature's splendor, and ultimately remember: "I write to hear the voice of Billy, / to watch the landscape quicken as I listen." Vengeance returns to the elements of Lea's poetry in "Spite: Her Tale," in which a blind old woman broods over what she believes was a spiteful act. Her son and daughter-in-law cut down the "twisty beech" that the speaker had invested with so much importance. She had come to define herself through the tree, though it had "no earthly use, not even for a shade." Still, the speaker knew her place by that tree: "And once I fitted out the shape again . . . / then I felt I knew where I belonged / in all this universe." Throughout *The Blainville Testament* Christian imagery arises, but overall Lea's attention to moral ambiguity overwhelms any particular faith, while the roles of place, narrative, and reflection continue to stand out in his poetry.

Cowinner of the 1998 Poet's Prize, Lea's next collection, *To the Bone: New and Selected Poems* (1996), assembles some of the best poems from his previous collections and adds to them sixteen new poems. The emotional title poem, dedicated to the "memory of Earl Bonness, / and for Susan Kennedy, R.N. / who did the right thing," tells of a chainsaw injury and the ensuing morphine-induced memories that occur to the speaker while he recovers, weaving through the events, people, and places that have moved him throughout his life. As with Lea's other work, friendship, familial relations, outdoorsmanship, landscape, language, and the act of writing itself come together in "To the Bone." Personal crises from Lea's own life, including the deaths of family members and friends, appear throughout the poem; yet, the speaker insists upon universal meaning rather than merely personal confessions: "I'm speaking rather / of the sorts of signs that any body gathers / in the lifelong effort to make a life cohere / and give it worth." The poem portrays Lea's desire to hold things together even in the face of great loss. *To the Bone* includes work written over a period of fifteen years, and the collection demonstrates not so much a progression of talent as a development of range in form and vision.

A finalist for the 2001 Pulitzer Prize in poetry, *Pursuit of a Wound* (2000) presents nearly prosodic narrative poems that delve deeper into Lea's desire to find beauty in loss. The prevalent "wound" that Lea pursues is the paradoxical condition of a sentimental poet who wants to form powerful and affirming meanings from the crises of a world filled with death, pain, and hardship. Hence, in "Yoked Together," the first poem of part 1, Lea closes with "a famous poet's phrase about things being 'yoked together by violence.'" Showing the connection of poetic creation to real-life crises, "Reasons to Hate Poetry" tells of a boy's life-threatening accident and of a poet's mastery of the situation:

> Our sensitive poet puts Jim in a nearby clinic, a tangle of I.V. tubes
> in his body, sedated because it gets violent because he's got no notion of Fate,
> is not like us–o childhood! o innocence! And though we won't say it,
>
> a part of us breathes: a poem! a poem!

In part 2, "Local Story," Lea further pursues loss through the subjects of cancer tests, friends' deaths, his own loss of hearing, disasters such as the 1996 crash of TWA Flight 800, and suicides. In "Poor Fool Blues" a town plants a tree in memory of a young man who hanged himself. Lea finds significance in the ironic but good intentions of the town: "We fools keep on. We look for meaning and form. / If patterns and breaches of pattern wear out our words, / We still mean to do some good before we die." The final poem of the collection, "Phases," offers several pages of quatrains in which Lea addresses the effects of the mood-altering medication Zoloft. The emotional costs of loss, the ability to maintain hope, the concern for the dead, and all the various struggles of life ultimately lead the speaker to affirm that beauty and terror are indeed connected: "And I vowed to wander, in proper wonder, this valley of the shadow of death."

Known for his ear for language, Lea heightens the musicality of his poetry in this collection. Flowing along through internal rhyme and assonance, the voice in "Phases" describes wondrous images of life:

> Hard down on the pond, the ragged white pine hedge,
>   while just overhead
>   A fish hawk hen fights hard to gather yards of hurtled
>   air and then
>   Plunges entirely and thrillingly true to her target in
>   water
>   –trout or dace–with a fractional adjustment of
>   wing.

The sound of many of Lea's poems echoes the beautiful, sentimental, yet often bleak images and reflections. "How little it took to turn me sentimental," muses the speaker in the title poem. "How little it takes me still." Lea's emotional power lies in his direct acceptance of limitations—of life and of words.

Lea's narrative tendency has also led him to write a novel, *A Place in Mind* (1989), about friendship, time, and nature, as well as a collection of personal essays, *Hunting the Whole Way Home* (1994), about hunting, fishing, dog training, relationships, and memory. Pro-

Paperback cover for Lea's 2000 collection, a finalist for the 2001 Pulitzer Prize in poetry (Richland County Public Library)

foundly personal yet universally appealing, his prose and poetry constantly strive to commemorate lives and places lost and to re-create lives and places remaining. Lea has just completed an eighth collection of poems, forthcoming, called *Ghost Pain,* and he is at work on a second novel, with the working title "Each Last Lake." Story Line Press will publish a nonfiction book, *A Little Wildness: Some Notes on Rambling.*

Brad Leithauser
(27 February 1953 -)

Steven P. Schneider
University of Texas Pan American

See also the Leithauser entry in *DLB 120: American Poets Since World War II, Third Series.*

BOOKS: *Hundreds of Fireflies: Poems* (New York: Knopf, 1982);

Equal Distance: A Novel (New York: Knopf, 1985; New York & London: Penguin, 1990);

A Seaside Mountain: Eight Poems from Japan (New York: Sarabande, 1985);

Cats of the Temple: Poems (New York: Knopf, 1986);

Between Leaps: Poems, 1972-1985 (Oxford & New York: Oxford University Press, 1987);

Hence: A Novel (New York: Knopf, 1989);

The Mail from Anywhere: Poems (New York: Knopf, 1990);

Seaward: A Novel (New York: Knopf, 1993);

Penchants and Places: Essays and Criticisms (New York: Knopf, 1995);

The Friends of Freeland: A Novel (New York: Knopf, 1997);

The Odd Last Thing She Did (New York: Knopf, 1998);

The Arachnid's Triumph (West Chester, Pa.: Aralia Press, 1999);

A Few Corrections: A Novel (New York: Knopf, 2001);

Darlington's Fall: A Novel in Verse (New York: Knopf, 2002).

OTHER: *The Norton Book of Ghost Stories,* edited by Leithauser (New York: Norton, 1994);

No Other Book: Selected Essays, edited by Leithauser (New York: HarperCollins, 1995).

SELECTED PERIODICAL PUBLICATIONS-
"Metrical Illiteracy," *New Criterion,* 1 (January 1983): 41-46;

"The Confinement of Free Verse," *New Criterion,* 5 (May 1987): 4-14.

Few American poets have had such auspicious beginnings as Brad Leithauser. His first collection of poems, *Hundreds of Fireflies: Poems* (1982), was greeted

Brad Leithauser (photograph by Bruce Meyer)

with resounding critical acclaim. Not since Robert Lowell's *Lord Weary's Castle* (1946) had a first book by an American poet met with such widespread and immediate success. Major reviews of the book appeared in *The New York Review of Books, Poetry,* and *Time.* Leithauser became known as one of the leading New Formalist poets, and in two important critical essays published in *The New Criterion,* he argued against the pitfalls of "metrical illiteracy" and suggested that free-verse poets had exhausted nonmetrical poetry.

Leithauser, born on 27 February 1953 in Detroit, Michigan, is the son of Harold Edward Leithauser (a lawyer) and Gladys Garner Leithauser (a children's writer and college professor). Leithauser, a 1975 graduate of Harvard University, went on to earn a law degree from Harvard Law School in 1980. After his marriage to poet Mary Jo Salter on 2 August 1980, he began a three-year residence as a research fellow at the Kyoto Comparative Law Center in Kyoto, Japan. Leithauser has won much recognition for his writing, including an Amy Lowell Traveling Scholarship in 1981, a Guggenheim Fellowship in 1982, and a MacArthur Foundation research fellowship from 1983 through 1987. He and his wife currently live in Massachusetts, where they are professors at Mount Holyoke College. They have two daughters.

Heralded as one of the first and most important collections of New Formalism, *Hundreds of Fireflies* marked a conscious return to form and craftsmanship in American poetry after two decades of dominance by free-verse poets. In several ways the volume signaled a change in the cultural and literary climate of America. Keenly conscious of the dominant free-verse tradition of American poetry, Leithauser tried to distance himself from it, much in the same way that Richard Wilbur and other members of his generation tried to distance themselves from the dominance of Modernist aesthetics that preceded them.

Hundreds of Fireflies is predominantly a collection of lyrics, although the volume also includes a long narrative poem titled "Two Summer Jobs" as well as several witty and engaging epigrams. Leithauser's favorite subject in *Hundreds of Fireflies* is the natural world. The volume features a series of poems about animals—including bats, tortoises, and ants—complemented by a set of poems on natural scenes. The collection, however, is most distinguished by Leithauser's careful attention to craft, manifested in intricately formed poetic stanzas and subtle patterns of rhyme.

Some of the best poems in *Hundreds of Fireflies* evoke the precision of a naturalist. In his poem "Giant Tortoise" Leithauser describes its features and evolutionary success in elegantly crafted five-line stanzas. The shell of the giant tortoise in itself is remarkable:

> Never glimpsed his own patterned back,
> the stucco clustered pigments there.
> But carried it everywhere,
> a lived-in relic: calendar stone
> with muddy undeciphered zodiac.

In this and other poems, Leithauser invents new stanzaic structures and experiments with varied and elaborate rhyme schemes, much as did Marianne Moore, whose lines from her poem "What Are Years?" serves as the epigraph to Leithauser's collection. The distinct physical features of this giant tortoise are rivaled only by its evolutionary success.

> Older than whales,
> elephants, even some
> tall forests, and grown secure
> in an arrived-at wisdom:
> only the self-contained at last endure.

In this poem Leithauser moves from natural history to wry commentary and uses the rhymes to discover fresh insights. In addition to his attentiveness to the animal kingdom, Leithauser includes many poems that record his experiences of memorable natural scenes, such as "Canoeing at Night," "The Return to a Cabin," "Birches," and "Duckweed."

"The Return to a Cabin" is reminiscent of E. B. White's famous essay, "Once More to the Lake," in its description of a ritual return to a summer retreat. Leithauser's poem describes the first night upon returning to the cabin.

> Cool suddenly,
> your first night, and so queer
> at once to discover
>
> how many things
> you'd forgotten or concealed:

The poet then registers an array of impressions from past times spent at this cabin, both joys remembered and frights forgotten.

> You retained the joys
> of a sunset here – cloud
> and birch-clump dyed
> the same watery pink
> and the day's last light
> bundled off the river

In these two stanzas, he demonstrates his characteristic strengths as a poet, discovering a striking visual correspondence between the clouds and a clump of birch trees, and linking the sunset to the birches in his choice of the verb "bundled." His precise control is reflected not only in his careful selection of language but also in his finely tuned ear, which weaves natural things together through alliterative phrases. In many of Leithauser's best poems, there is a resonant silence between the stanzas and the rich verbal textures of description.

Dust jacket for Leithauser's first collection (1982), which includes several poems about animals and nature (Richland County Public Library)

Like other New Formalists, Leithauser has made a conscious effort to reclaim the short, witty poem for contemporary American poetry. "Astronomical Riddles" is composed of eleven epigrams, devoted to the planets and to other celestial bodies. The third of these epigrams, "Venus," turns description into a compelling meditation on the nature of passion.

> I am tempestuous, hot and cloudy.
>   I pay no mind.
> Love was intended to be rowdy,
>   Torrid and blind.

The personification of the planets and the rhymes deliver pleasure. Each poem becomes a miniature observatory; the viewer is treated to a new lens of consideration. In these epigrams Leithauser draws upon the tradition of Anglo-Saxon riddles and teases the reader into a reengagement with the heavens. In "Mars," for example, the reader is asked to reconsider the planet:

> Chill, frail, friendly . . . I've been misunderstood
> My color shows a love of warmth, not blood.

The centerpiece of *Hundreds of Fireflies* is a long, narrative poem titled "Two Summer Jobs." A single poem running fourteen pages in length, it accounts for two summer jobs the poet held, as an eighteen-year-old tennis instructor for a Michigan town and as a twenty-six-year-old law clerk in New York City.

The first section describes his teaching tennis to a group of women the summer prior to his entering Harvard. One of the women, Mrs. Shores, is extremely pretty, and the narrative is sustained by the tension felt between the young tennis instructor and the attractive married woman, who hosts a party at the end of the summer. There, the poet learns that he can drink beer, though he hates its taste, and discovers in the form of Mrs. Shores "a solicitude that's graceful, wise, / and impenetrably feminine."

In the second section, the poet discovers that he is not suited to work in a Manhattan law firm. He spends his time daydreaming and trying to write parodies, "caught in the trap- / pings of a Wall Street lawyer." By the end of the summer he realizes that despite the power lunches, an offer to join the law firm, and an attractive salary, he will leave this life behind "for good."

Both narratives, however, lack the heightened drama of Robert Frost's best narrative poems and the tragicomic vision of Louis Simpson's post–World War II suburban narratives. Frost and Simpson have been heralded by the New Formalists as masters of the narrative poem, and Leithauser falls short of their standards in these debut poetic narratives.

Helen Vendler, in her review of *Hundreds of Fireflies* in *The New York Review of Books* (23 September 1982), suggests "there is a welcome lightness and sweetness in Leithauser recommending him to readers whose tastes bring them to Herbert and Schubert." Vendler praises Leithauser's nature lyrics and epigrams but considers "Two Summer Jobs" too derivative of James Merrill, and though "expertly done," she says that these "are finally poems finding no stylization beyond what is offered by Merrill." Sven Birkerts, writing in the *New Boston Review* (June 1982), notes the collection "is marked by extreme control, personal reticence, and a calm, confident virtuosity that makes us think of Elizabeth Bishop or Wilbur himself." Critical reception of the volume was mostly favorable, although a few critics, notably Jay Parini, complained that the poems read like "exercises in descriptive poetry." However, the book was nominated for a National Book Critics Circle Award.

Hundreds of Fireflies was followed by a second collection, *Cats of the Temple: Poems* (1986). Between the publication of these two volumes, Leithauser wrote and published an influential essay that became a kind of manifesto for many New Formalist poets. In his essay "Metrical Illiteracy," first published in *The New Criterion* in January 1983 and later collected in R. S. Gwynn's anthology, *New Expansive Poetry* (1999), Leithauser argued that "we are not living in a golden age of poetry, and that mediocrity prevails in the periodicals and on bookstore shelves."

He goes on to lament that few young poets writing in English today work in form, despite an increasing number of poets. Much of the essay addresses four overlapping conditions that have created, in Leithauser's opinion, a decline in post–World War II American poetry: "diffusion, perceived mediocrity, the eschewal of form by the young, and an ever expanding number of poets."

To counter the lamentable state of contemporary poetry, Leithauser proposes a return to the practice of poetic form. He praises the work of several poets whose careers began in the 1940s and 1950s when formalism prevailed as a major force in American poetry, including the poems of Anthony Hecht, James Merrill, W. D. Snodgrass, and Richard Wilbur. Leithauser suggests that poets who have not gone to school on the great practitioners of the sonnet and other poetic forms will have critical faculties that are "truncated." The generally "diminished role verse now plays in the lives of the general populace," according to Leithauser, "can be attributed to the loss of familiarity and practice of formal technique by poets themselves." In the conclusion of the essay, Leithauser makes his most contentious point: "we fail to recognize that metrical illiteracy is, for the poet, functional illiteracy." While the essay "Metrical Illiteracy" won praise from the New Formalists, the article drew criticism from several free-verse poets who saw its arguments as culturally conservative and reactionary.

The publication of *Cats of the Temple* in 1986 further established Leithauser's reputation as a leading New Formalist poet. In the author's note to the volume, he describes his second book as a "sibling companion" to his first. The subject matter is similar, with many poems devoted to natural landscapes ("On the Lee Side," "On a Seaside Mountain") and animals ("A Stuffed Tortoise"). Most of the poems in the third section of the book appeared in a 1985 chapbook titled *A Seaside Mountain: Eight Poems from Japan* and were written while Leithauser was living and teaching in Japan.

The structure of the book is also similar to *Hundreds of Fireflies*, with many intricately patterned lyrics, a long narrative poem, and several intriguing epigrams clustered under the heading "Minims." In "On the Lee Side," the poet takes pleasure from the wind blowing offshore, nestled as he is in "a hip-sized hollow / on the lee side of a low / but broad-boled pine." He had been out hiking, when he decided to rest and wait out the windstorm after pursuing "the peninsula's roundabout Point." The sheer sound and motion of the wind gives him pleasure, providing the source of his inspiration in this poem.

> And what a pleasure,
> to hear the wind pitch still higher, to know
> the waves swell and fall in answer
>
> blindly to feel
> the whole sky blackening!

His excursions invariably lead him to a heightened appreciation of the senses—auditory as in "On the Lee Side," or visual as in "On a Seaside Mountain." In the latter poem, he guides the reader up a seaside mountain on a Japanese island. Like Elizabeth Bishop, Leithauser has a deft sense of place and renders it in painterly detail.

> Yet as we climb
> from the coast, slips of color filter through –
> a red swatch of earth, freshly torn, a green red-
> berried bush, green-gold clumps of bamboo –
> and the waves' gentle papery crash . . .

Through mist and fog, up terraced hills "where rice was grown by hand," the poet climbs until rounding a bend, he discovers "a horse, a chunky tan palomino / with milky mane and a calm, discerning / fix to the eyes." This horse leads the poet and his companions up the mountainside, where they discover nine other horses munching clover: "It's so quiet we can hear their surf-like breathing." Leithauser's precise description of the natural landscape culminates in a sense of mythic discovery.

Leithauser's senses of humor and irony are most keenly felt in his shorter poems. In "Poet's Lament," he makes fun of the poet who finds employment a sorrowful turn of affairs.

> Why must gainful
> Employment be so painful?

Short poems such as this one are balanced by the longer narrative poem "Two Incidents on and off Guam."

Dust jacket for Leithauser's 1998 collection of poems about family and history, landscapes, and masculinity (Richland County Public Library)

Critical reviews of *Cats of the Temple* were more mixed than the nearly unanimous acclaim for *Hundreds of Fireflies*. Vendler, writing in *The New York Review of Books* (23 October 1986), criticizes the poems in Leithauser's second volume as being too derivative of Marianne Moore. She writes, "If Leithauser did not adopt Marianne Moore's manner so strenuously one would read him in a less distracted way. One is often made so conscious of the perfectly mimicked model that the poem begins to seem a form of ventriloquism." D. J. Enright, writing in *The New Republic* (27 October 1986), also sees the influence of Moore in this collection, but not in the heavy-handed manner suggested by Vendler. He notes, "While there is something of Marianne Moore's tartness and teacherliness in the tone and the movement of the verse, its greater relaxation and more palpable humor help the poet to speak well, apparently without deliberation but with authority, about landscape and seascape, and artifacts too."

The year after the publication of *Cats of the Temple*, Leithauser published a second important essay in *The New Criterion*, "The Confinement of Free Verse." Once again he attacks the practice of free verse, suggesting that as a mode of writing it has exhausted itself. After asserting that he wished to be thought of as a formalist poet, he suggests "that free verse, its energies having peaked some time ago, is now looking rather peaked." Leithauser sees the formlessness of free verse as "the norm" and laments its "prosodic bankruptcy." The essay contrasts the enduring strength and rich complexity of formal poetry with "the running impoverishment of a genre whose prosody is limited to enjambment." This essay, like the earlier essay "Metrical Illiteracy," won praise from New Formalist poets and critics and scorn from free-verse poets.

While Leithauser's career is distinguished by his work as a poet and critic, he has also written several novels and a memorable collection of nonfiction. His published novels include *Equal Distance* (1985), *Hence* (1989), *Seaward* (1993), *The Friends of Freeland* (1997), and *A Few Corrections* (2001). In *Penchants and Places: Essays and Criticisms* (1995) Leithauser collects fifteen years of essays and reviews devoted to such topics as computer chess, ghost stories, and utopian novels, as well as pieces devoted to his experiences living in Japan and Iceland.

Leithauser's third collection of poetry, *The Mail from Anywhere* (1990), bears the postmark of a world traveler, with many of its poems situated in the distant cities he has traveled to: Reykjavík, Bangkok, and Kyoto. Several of the most striking poems in the volume describe his experiences in Iceland, when he taught on a Fulbright Fellowship in 1989. Like Elizabeth Bishop, to whom he has been compared often, Leithauser has made the most of travel and geography in his work. The poet's third collection is divided into three sections. The first of these, "The Mail from Anywhere," is poems of travel and discovery; the second section, "You and Them," is poems of the natural world. In the concluding section, "A Peopled World," the poet visits the lives of those closest to him.

The title poem of the volume speaks to the isolation of the traveler, separated by ocean from friends and relatives. It is an account of receiving mail, which would often take weeks in arriving, and which for Leithauser took on a ritualistic significance.

Mail from pretty much anywhere was nearly
A month in crossing the seas and climbing that island's
Burning hillside.

Much of the poem describes in intricate detail the landscape of that island where "sunsets were jarring, uncontrolled events" and at night "the air would cool, grow rich with massed / exploratory scents, and the thoroughfare / of the Milky Way unroll like an open road." Yet, for all the intensity of sunsets and night skies, the poet-traveler reserves his greatest joy for "another sort of light," that of a "sky / blue envelope," which meant that "*a few weeks ago, / someone was thinking of me.*" In "Reykjavik Winter Couplets" the poet evokes what it is like to live in a place where one discovers "waking at dark / the promise of dark / for hours yet."

While the poems in the first two sections of *The Mail from Anywhere* are concerned with landscape and travel, the third section opens up in a way that will foreshadow Leithauser's preoccupation with the social world in his fourth collection, *The Odd Last Thing She Did* (1998). "A Peopled World" includes "Your Natural History," an account of how one of his daughters was conceived; "First Birthday," which celebrates the child's discovery of language; and "Old Bachelor Brother," who views a wedding march "from his prominent but thankfully / uncentral position at the head of the church." These poems open up a new dimension in Leithauser's work, one that takes the pulse of human life more intimately. He concludes "Your Natural History" with the image of fire, the warmth of which lights this and other poems in the concluding section: ". . . I piled the fireplace high, / And struck a match, wresting a flame, your flame, / From ice. By just such miracles you came."

Most reviewers of *The Mail from Anywhere* see the collection as an important achievement. Henri Cole's comments in *The Nation* (15 April 1991) reflect this view. Cole notes, "this third collection by Leithauser is an achievement equal to his first two volumes . . . which when published began to exert an influence on contemporary poetic practice; many poets were hungry for a language more concentrated and a prosody less generic than the dominant 'plain style' of the 1960s and 1970s." Cole describes the poems in *The News from Anywhere* as "ruminative, elaborately syntaxed poems."

Phoebe Pettingell, writing in *The New Leader* (11 March 1991), notes that "this book's character sketches—some of his strongest work to date–reveal a hitherto unapparent sense of compassion." She admires especially the poem "Uncle Grant," about an eccentric uncle whose dreams of inventions remind the poet "of the alchemist's lead-fueled notion / of a lasting conversion to glory." Robert McDowell, however, writing in *The Hudson Review* (Winter 1991), complains that "a lot of writing here has produced only an awkward approximation of a valuable emotional insight." McDowell especially dislikes the "travelogues conveying the impression that the indolent traveler has energy enough only to scratch surfaces."

In the eight years since the publication of *The Mail from Anywhere*, Leithauser had written and published many more family poems, and the first section of *The Odd Last Thing She Did* is composed of some of these poems. The collection opens with "A Honeymoon Conception (1952)," a poem that accounts for his parents' honeymoon trip by train through the snow from New York City to Quebec, Canada. Another family poem in this section is titled "1944: Purple Heart," the story of a couple, presumably the poet's parents, who ride a streetcar together. The poem hinges on the male partner, wounded from the war, insisting that his wife-to-be take a seat offered to them by an old man on the crowded streetcar.

This entire first section of poems is marked by touching moments, and the most affectionate are found in three love poems for the poet's wife. In "Small Waterfall: A Birthday Poem" Leithauser compares his wife to a waterfall, "a thing that flows and goes / and stays, self-propelled and -replacing." Like the water, she nourishes all that comes into contact with her, most especially the couple's two daughters. Her power, like the waterfall, exceeds the poet's grasp, yet links disparate elements of creation.

> Your reach exceeds my grasp, happily,
> for yours is the river's power
> to link with liquid, unseen threads
> the low, far, moon-moved sea
> and the sun's high-lit headwaters.

In the middle section of poems in the volume, Leithauser returns to his obsession with natural scenes, and the opening and closing poems of this section are triptychs. The first of these describes a marsh in March; the second, three scenes from the tropics. Between these two longer poems are several shorter lyrics, characterized by grace, elegance, and wit. In "Clouds in Winter: Dusk," the speaker meditates on the clouds of the upper atmosphere, which "escape our seasonal vagaries."

The concluding section is devoted to "Men and Men." These are poems that address conventional male subject matter, such as hunting and warfare. This section includes a poem for Malcolm Lowry, whose "discriminating taste" the poet admires, another poem about a male friendship turned sour, and a strong, moral poem ("Not on Speaking Terms") about not being consumed by past resentments and betrayals. "Shiloh, 1993" describes the re-creation of a Civil War battlefield, ending with the wry observation that the "patches" and "shadows" of blue and gray will not come to a halt until "their shades of difference disappear / in the uncontainable outpour / of another spill of red."

In a review of *The Odd Last Thing She Did* in *The Hudson Review* (Summer 1999), Sam Gwynn worries that Leithauser's work "has been characterized by some rather too soft love poems and some rather too picturesque landscape work." On the other hand, Gwynn writes that "Leithauser has consistently handled family history with verve." He admires "Death of the Family Archivist" and the long, narrative title poem of the collection. Bill Christophersen, writing in *Poetry* (September 1999), also praises Leithauser's narratives in *The Odd Last Thing She Did*. According to Christophersen, these "narratives—full of tragedies, flukes and family yarns—coax and compel our attention." He notes, "in this family scrapbook, urgency and craft collaborate from the start."

Brad Leithauser's career has spanned three continents, and the body of his poetry reflects the observations and wry commentaries of an itinerant. His later work, however, shows him opening up to that which is closest to home, friends and family. Leithauser, who began his career as a noted observer of natural phenomena in the tradition of Marianne Moore, may become best known for his explorations of the heart. Subject matter, however, is subsumed by formal concerns in Leithauser's work, and his place as a New Formalist poet seems both secure and significant.

Phillis Levin
(18 May 1954 -   )

Jason Schneiderman
Hofstra University

BOOKS: *Temples and Fields* (Athens & London: University of Georgia Press, 1988);
The Afterimage (Providence, R.I.: Copper Beech Press, 1995);
Mercury (New York: Penguin, 2001).

OTHER: "The Ransom," in *The Best American Poetry 1989,* edited by Donald Hall (New York: Collier, 1989), pp. 103–104;
"Embracing Fate," "Citizens and Sky," "Dark Horse," and "Planting Roses," in *A Formal Feeling Comes: Poems in Form by Contemporary Women,* edited by Annie Finch (Brownsville, Ore.: Story Line Press, 1994), pp. 147–151;
"The Shadow Returns," "A Meeting of Friends," "The Lost Bee," and "Night Coach," in *Rebel Angels: 25 Poets of the New Formalism,* edited by Mark Jarman and David Mason (Brownsville, Ore.: Story Line Press, 1996), pp. 159, 160, 162, 164;
"Note on Brief Bio," in *Instructor's Manual to Accompany An Introduction to Poetry,* compiled by X. J. Kennedy, Dana Gioia, and Dorothy Kennedy, ninth edition (New York: Longman, 1998), pp. 68–69;
"Face to Face," in *How Poetry Works,* compiled by Phil Roberts, second edition (New York: Penguin, 2000), p. 261;
The Penguin Book of the Sonnet: 500 Years of a Classic Tradition in English, edited by Levin (New York: Penguin, 2001; abridged, London: Penguin, 2001).

Phillis Levin (photograph by Sheila McKinnon; courtesy of the author)

Phillis Levin has published three books of poetry, received many awards and fellowships, edited and written a forty-page introduction to a major anthology of sonnets, and taught literature and creative writing at various institutions. She has received praise from voices as diverse as John Hollander, Jean Valentine, James Merrill, William Matthews, J. D. McClatchy, Richard Howard, and Tomaž Šalamun. Translations of her poetry have been published in Peru, Argentina, Slovenia, Poland, Hungary, Russia, China, and Israel. Levin does not identify herself as a New Formalist, nor does she identify with any poetic movement. However, she has been claimed as a New Formalist, though a great many of her poems are in free verse; she has been anthologized in *A Formal Feeling Comes: Poems in Form by Contemporary Women* (1994) and *Rebel Angels: 25 Poets of the New Formalism* (1996). Across her three books, Levin's poetry emerges as deliberate and carefully planned. Her lines embody a creative tension between the rhythm of natural speech, the freedom of the mind in meditation, and the architectural pattern of the line on the level of syntax and sound.

Phillis Marna Levin was born on 18 May 1954 to Charlotte Shirley Engel Levin and Herbert Louis Levin and raised in Paterson, New Jersey, in the home of her maternal grandmother. Her maternal grandparents were involved in the silk trade, and her paternal grandparents were makers and restorers of furniture. Levin's father is a retired mechanical and electrical engineer who holds several patents; her mother, a homemaker, taught elementary school before her marriage. Levin has one younger brother, Phillip, a lawyer. She grew up watching her father design things, and what she called her earliest poems were in fact drawings. She later turned to language "in an attempt to make words fly." Levin began writing poetry seriously at the age of twelve, under the self-assigned pseudonym Kamal Amara. Her juvenilia has not been published, but it is an extensive collection of three hundred pages of poetry and three plays, maintained by the author.

Levin attended The Kimberley School in Upper Montclair, New Jersey, for the first two years of high school; she then attended and graduated from Ramapo High School. In her first year at Kimberley she was introduced to the work of Jorge Luis Borges and Octavio Paz at a formative moment; other early influences include Samuel Beckett, Wallace Stevens, and Franz Kafka. Levin entered Sarah Lawrence College in 1972 and graduated in 1976 with a B.A. concentrating in writing, philosophy, and psychology. In 1976 she entered the Johns Hopkins Writing Seminars as a teaching fellow, receiving an M.A. with honors in 1977. In the summer of 1977 she received a fellowship from the Johns Hopkins University Ancient Language Institute. Levin stayed in Maryland for another year as a humanities instructor teaching comparative literature at the Community College of Baltimore.

In 1978 she moved to New York and began teaching as an adjunct lecturer in the Department of English at Queens College in Flushing, where she taught until 1985. During this time, Levin received fellowships at the MacDowell Colony (August 1982) and the Virginia Center for the Creative Arts (January 1984). In 1985 Levin began teaching at Baruch College, where she stayed until 1989. Also in 1985 she became one of the founding editors of *Boulevard*, with which she remained editorially affiliated until 2000. In 1986 she received an Ingram-Merrill Foundation Grant in poetry. MacDowell granted her three additional fellowships, and in June 1988 she was a fellow in poetry at the Wesleyan Writers Conference at Wesleyan University.

In *A Formal Feeling Comes* each contributor was asked to write a brief statement about his or her relationship to form. Levin's statement describes her discovery in college that she wrote primarily third-person poems in free verse and first-person poems in form: "Perhaps I needed—and continue to need—formal elements in order to create a ritualized experience that would allow me to exist in the bounds of the poem (a field of play) instead of the bounds of life, to enter an altered state, a heightened relation to the temporal." Levin broke from form after Galway Kinnell pointed out this split in her first- and third-person work; she worked against rhyme and meter until she studied at The Graduate Center of the City University of New York with Christopher Ricks, who asked her why she was not allowing her music to sound. About her return to form, Levin says, "For me embracing form is a form of embracing fate, of simultaneously accepting and resisting, absorbing and shaping the forces of language and life, the interplay of the arbitrary and the given with the shaped and the chosen." The texture of the poem embodies the meaning of the poem. Levin also discusses her relationship to form in a note published in Dana Gioia, Dorothy Kennedy, and X. J. Kennedy's *Instructor's Manual to Accompany An Introduction to Poetry* (1998). In that essay she talks specifically about her 1995 poem "Brief Bio" (published in *The New Yorker* and included in *The Afterimage,* 1995). The poem is an acrostic for the word "butterfly," and Levin talks about setting in place the constraint of a vertical axis before starting the poem. Levin talks about form as a sort of riddle, the acrostic setting up a problem to be solved. The idea of poem as riddle influences much of her formal work and its playfulness.

Levin had begun publishing her work in periodicals such as *Pequod* (1976), *Virginia Quarterly Review* (1980), *Shenandoah* (1983), *Antioch Review* (1984), *Paris Review* (1985), *Grand Street* (1986), and *Partisan Review* (1987). In 1988 her first book, *Temples and Fields,* was selected by the poet Bin Ramke for publication by the University of Georgia Press. John Hollander then selected the published book to receive the Norma Farber First Book Award from the Poetry Society of America. The poems in *Temples and Fields* alternate between metered and free verse, often employing internal and off-rhymes. The work is divided into five sections. *Library Journal* (January 1999) called the book "an impressive first collection by a poet . . . with a high verbal gift." Richard Moore, in his review in the May–June 1990 issue of *American Book Review,* discussed Levin's dual strategies of explaining everything and explaining nothing as she evokes "the evanescence of our experience, forever on the point of achieving the permanence of meaning, forever sinking back into the 'shade of incoherence.'" Cynthia Kramen, in the August 1989 issue of *Poetry Flash,* placed Levin within a tradition of nature poetry reaching back to William

Paperback cover for Levin's collection of alternating metered and free-verse poems, published in 1988, which received the Norma Farber First Book Award from the Poetry Society of America (Bruccoli Clark Layman Archives)

Wordsworth, John Keats, and Gerard Manley Hopkins. Kramen lamented that "we have come, then, to a point where most poets, like most people, are bored with nature, or are unaware of it. . . . Phillis Levin has walked in fields. For this poet, fields, like the temples of her title, are sacred places." Phillip Miller's review in the Winter 1990 issue of *New Letters* mentioned Levin's poetry in the context of "the so-called 'new formalism'" and grouped her with Molly Peacock and Robert McDowell–although Miller broadens his claim for Levin's aesthetic: "Levin's work is formal, not only when its metrical stanzas rhyme, but whenever it consciously accommodates its conventions to the demands of the poem rather than the personality behind the poem. Yet her work as often chooses the conventions of free verse, carefully placing formal and free styles into counterpoint, allowing open forms to close, and closed forms to open unexpectedly." Lee Upton's review in *Denver Quarterly* (1989) declared, "Unlike writers who sentimentalize childhood, Levin invents speakers who reach toward adulthood."

The poem "A.D.," which follows two lovers on a train trip from France to Italy, is in quatrains of off-rhyming couplets. The first stanza ends with the couplet "The sky distilled, the earth grew redder, / My love and I could love no better." The poem is simple and precise–the rhyme creates a feeling of inevitability and also of play. However, the rhyme is also quite serious in its directness. The poem follows the couple on their journey, comparing them to other passengers, in particular a woman from an older couple who sits beside them: "She sank in the only seat that was free, / Squeezing together my lover and me." Levin rarely complies with the rhyme pattern in fully expected ways. By the end of the poem, the lovers on the train are arriving in Rome at dawn: "We were wound in the wheels of the holy city / By the time the train pulled into anno Domini."

In "The Ransom," Levin likewise places her speaker into the ebb and flow of history. In this poem the speaker is unexpectedly "selected as the go-between / To bring a ransom set upon the head / Of one I didn't know and never would." Taking her duty quite seriously, the speaker is shocked to discover that she is in fact an extra in a movie, and that she has been replaced. The speaker finally surrenders and meditates on the arbitrariness of being replaced ("A change that came to pass not for anything"). The speaker finally puts forth the resolution "To drink the bitter draught of history, / I'll hail the tragic muse; then drain the glass, / And put out all the lights and watch the news." The serious metamorphoses into the absurd, then back again.

In "After a Summer of Ancient Greek," which falls in tercets, two of the three lines usually rhyme, although some tercets have no rhymes, and two tercets rhyme all three lines. The poem "Night Coach," which is anthologized in *Rebel Angels,* alternates the rhyme schemes of its stanzas between envelope, alternating, and ballad quatrains. In this way, Levin sets up the formal construction of a poem as external scaffolding. Instead of the expectation of form—a rigidity demanding where the next rhyme will fall—Levin sets up a hope of form, a delight as the rhyme does or does not come.

Following the release of *Temples and Fields,* Levin accepted a position as assistant professor at the University of Maryland. In 1989 she was the Margaret Bridgman Fellow in poetry at the Bread Loaf Writers' Conference. In 1991 she received the Outstanding Teacher Award at the University of Maryland's *Celebrating Teachers* program. That same year, she was the Walter E. Dakin Fellow in poetry at the Sewanee Writers' Conference at the University of the South. In 1993 she began teaching at the Unterberg Poetry Center of the 92nd Street Y, where she continues to teach a workshop every spring. She was promoted to associate professor at the University of Maryland in 1995.

That same year, her second book, *The Afterimage,* appeared from Copper Beech Press. James McCorkle's essay "Elizabeth Bishop's Embracing Gaze: Her Influence on the Poetry of Sandra McPherson, Phillis Levin, and Jorie Graham" (1999) discusses the title poem, which details the speaker's memory of staring into a *jahrzeit* candle (in Jewish custom, lit on the anniversary of a loved one's death) and carrying the etched image of the flame with her around the house and into her bed. McCorkle comments, "Levin's affinities with Bishop derive from shared metaphysical sources and sensibilities."

Robert Schultz's review in the Autumn 1996 issue of the *Hudson Review* praised the volume: "Phillis Levin's *The Afterimage,* her second book, suggests to me a possible definition of grace, in an almost theological sense. Grace in this work is a responsiveness to the world, such that even a random street incident or coincidence can open the possibility of meanings." *Publishers Weekly* (27 November 1995) also praised the book, quoting heavily from the text: "Meticulously observant, she captures the paradox of our connection with and distance from others." Eric LeMay commented in the Summer 1996 issue of *Boston Review:* "Lyrical, austere, and formally adept, the ensuing poems present a speaker who refuses half-trusts and evasions as she re-creates herself out of this absolute negation." In a 1995 issue of *Library Journal,* Steven Ellis said that "Levin's second book of poetry serves a reminder that the classical themes of love, family, God—with references to the Bible, Homer, and Shakespeare—still have power when cast in a language that is sure of itself."

The Afterimage includes a few poems that address poetry and its construction. "The Happy Poet" argues against the notion of the poet as the Rumpelstiltskin of pain—one who turns personal agony into poetic gold. "There must have been a trauma, / We assume," Levin writes, pushing against a poetry of witness, offering herself as an example of a poet whose drive is not a therapeutic or obsessive exploration of personal pain. In this poem can perhaps be found the greatest formalist claim to her work: "All of us witness, some of us sing." Bearing carefully crafted witness constitutes poetry; depth of feeling is not enough. The poem ends with a couplet that argues for the power and independence of the nonconforming, Dionysian poet: "Dangerous, adoring, arrogant, absurd, / The happy poet struggles with a word."

The final poem of the collection, "Entry," places its speaker in a triangulation of identification between trees, flowers, and clouds. The poem begins with the realization that the domesticated, indoor flowers the speaker waters are delicate because they are removed from their natural space, and that trees in the forest are strong from belonging there. A sudden leap follows: "I wanted to be like a tree, / More like a tree than a flower." As the speaker explores her similarity to trees and flowers, she remembers that she feels most at home in the clouds. The question becomes one of roots and rootlessness: "And weren't my roots my thoughts / The stars my stones?" The speaker finally identifies with trees, but the flower quietly becomes the poetry. In this *ars poetica,* the poet's stability and roots allow her to become the gardener, nurturing the beauty readers encounter as poems.

Levin spent the year 2000 living in Italy, first in Florence, then in Rome as an Amy Lowell Poetry Traveling Scholar; in the spring of 2000 she spent a month as a fellow of the Bogliasco Foundation at the Ligura Study Center for the Arts and Humanities in Bogliasco, Italy. There she wrote new poems and completed her introduction to *The Penguin Book of the Sonnet: 500 Years of a Classic Tradition in English,* which appeared in 2001. In the same year, her third collection of poems, *Mercury,* which she had completed as a fellow at Yaddo in 1996, was published. In late January 2001 Levin began teaching at Hofstra University, where she is currently professor of English and poet-in-residence.

Mercury was received well by the critics. Bruce Bawer's article in the Autumn 2001 issue of the *Hudson Review* discusses this collection, touching on Levin's nebulous standing as a formalist: "Though Levin is sometimes counted among the New Formalists and is the editor of a forthcoming anthology of sonnets, *Mercury*–her strongest collection–consists almost entirely of free verse." As he observes, "the poems in *Mercury* mediate repeatedly between heart and mind, faith and science, the domain of ideas and the physical world." The poem "Final Request" is an unrhymed sonnet that combines elements of Judaism, Christianity, and Greco-Roman mythology. The beliefs of all three of the philosophical groundings of the poet's world–the mainstream Christianity of America, the classical foundation of Western Civilization, and the Judaism of her household–meet in the speaker's death and in her love. In the poem, the speaker is carried to the afterlife on a cross and finds herself facing a former lover in front of the river Lethe. Upon seeing the departed lover weep at having entered the afterlife that neither of them believed in, the speaker says, "my arms will be / So cruel. Whether or not / They hold him, whether or not / I want to / They will want to." The convergent strains of conflicting cultures are channeled into desire and loss.

Two of the most interesting poems in the book are "Conversation in an Empty Room" and "Table Manners," both dialogues between two unidentified but strongly characterized voices. The poems are mysterious and take place outside of time. "Conversation in an Empty Room" ends with the revelation that the poem takes place at the end of the world. "Table Manners" begins with the question, "What do you need?" and the response, "a knife, a fork, a spoon." Those three iambs suggest the careful deliberation of the respondent. The voices discuss the function of each piece of silverware, finally coming to the spoon. The spoon is deemed superfluous, and the questioning voice says, "But it isn't necessary." The respondent answers, "I can do without it, I can do without / almost anything, if necessary." The niceties of manners are stripped, and the poem contracts to basic need.

The final poem in the collection, "Meditation on A and The," makes explicit the interest in language that underlies the entire book. Elizabeth Macklin's essay in *By Herself: Women Reclaim Poetry* (2000) discusses how this poem "squiggles back and forth, intent and playfully observant, from 'a' thing to 'the' thing and vice versa." The poem ends with the creation of the world.

The Penguin Book of the Sonnet was a demanding undertaking that has established Levin as a scholar. In her introduction–which is replaced with a preface in the slimmer British edition (which has 450 sonnets while the American edition has 650)–Levin makes an expansive claim for form by pushing the boundaries of what constitutes a sonnet. Eschewing rhyme, meter, and line count as the only identifiers of a sonnet, and focusing on the "volta," she writes: "though a sonnet typically has fourteen lines, fourteen lines do not guarantee a sonnet: it is the behavior of those lines in relationship to each other–their choreography–that identifies the form." Levin discusses the history of the sonnet, including various theories as to the origin of the octave/sestet split, and the variations on the form. Written while she was living in Italy, Levin's introduction demonstrates great insight into the transition of the sonnet from Italian to English. She explains the contrast between the languages:

> so many Italian words end in the same cluster of syllables, the same pattern of consonants and vowels, a function of grammatical formations as well as the fact that every noun possesses a gender with which every related article and adjective, and in many cases the verb must agree (mamma mia is a far cry from my mother). . . . Since an Italian sonnet has four or five rhymes, whereas the English variety has seven, that alone was sufficient cause for many poets to abandon the Italian model.

Levin was invited to London in late 2001 to speak about the sonnet with Sir Frank Kermode and Jonathan Bate on the program *In Our Time,* a weekly broadcast hosted by Melvyn Bragg on BBC Radio 4. *The Penguin Book of the Sonnet* features a large contingent of twentieth-century authors and perhaps undermines the "newness" of the "new formalist" claim. Unexpected authors such as Frank Bidart, Louise Glück, Billy Collins, Bishop, and Valentine appear as sonneteers alongside some of the major innovators of the form, such as Robert Frost, Edna St. Vincent Millay, E. E. Cummings, and William Butler Yeats. Shana C. Fair concluded her review in the 1 June 2001 *Library Journal* with the statement that "No recent publication on sonnets has included such a broad spectrum of sonnet writers or attempted to present so complete a history of the sonnet. Recommended for all libraries."

In 2001 Levin began teaching in the graduate creative-writing program at New York University. In 2003 she was awarded a Guggenheim Fellowship. She spent four weeks in the summer of 2003 as a visiting artist at the American Academy of Rome. Her poems have been included in the Poetry Society of America's "Poetry in Motion" project and in poet laureate Collins's "Poetry 180: A Poem a Day for American High Schools" project.

Phillis Levin is a prominent poet whose accomplishments have earned increasing praise as her career has progressed. Her reputation has been solidified by her editing of *The Penguin Book of the Sonnet,* a work of scholarship that acknowledges the author's fascination with the freedom of formal constraint while articulating an inclusive and expansive sensibility. While her historical and aesthetic interest in the possibilities of rhythm and pattern has grown over the years, her own poetry has become freer with each successive volume.

References:

Bruce Bawer, "Borne Ceaselessly into the Past," *Hudson Review,* 54 (Autumn 2001): 513–519;

Elizabeth Macklin, "It's a Woman's Prerogative to Change Her Mind," in *By Herself: Women Reclaim Poetry,* edited by Molly McQuade (St. Paul, Minn.: Graywolf Press, 2000), pp. 9–29;

James McCorkle, "Elizabeth Bishop's Embracing Gaze: Her Influence on the Poetry of Sandra McPherson, Phillis Levin, and Jorie Graham," in *In Worcester, Massachusetts: Essays on Elizabeth Bishop, from the 1997 Elizabeth Bishop Conference at WPI,* edited by Laura Jehn Menides and Angela G. Dorenkamp (New York: Peter Lang, 1999), pp. 259–270;

Phillip Miller, "Formal and Informal," *New Letters* (Winter 1990).

Charles Martin
(25 June 1942 -)

David Yezzi

See also the Martin entry in *DLB 120: American Poets Since World War II, Third Series.*

BOOKS: *Room for Error* (Athens: University of Georgia Press, 1978);
Passages from Friday (Omaha: Abattoir Editions, University of Nebraska at Omaha, 1983);
Steal the Bacon (Baltimore: Johns Hopkins University Press, 1987);
Catullus (New Haven: Yale University Press, 1992);
Past Closing Time (Edgewood, Ky.: R. L. Barth, 1995);
What the Darkness Proposes (Baltimore: Johns Hopkins University Press, 1996);
Ferryboat (New York: CUNY, 2000);
Starting from Sleep: New and Selected Poems (Woodstock, N.Y.: Overlook Press, 2002).

OTHER: *Fulvio Testa: Watercolors, March 6–31, 1990*, text by Martin (New York: Claude Bernard Gallery, 1990);
The Poems of Catullus, translated by Martin (Omaha: Abattoir Editions, University of Nebraska at Omaha, 1979; revised, Baltimore: Johns Hopkins University Press, 1990).

SELECTED PERIODICAL PUBLICATIONS– UNCOLLECTED: "Poetry's Place," *Parnassus: Poetry in Review* (Spring/Summer 1982): 254–263;
Ovid, "From *Metamorphoses* 7," translated by Martin, *Arion,* third series 6, no. 3 (Winter 1999): 68–83;
"Five Poems from the French of Christine de Pisan," translated by Martin and Johanna Keller, *Hudson Review,* 52, no. 2 (Summer 1999).

Charles Martin (photograph by Bruce Meyer)

Charles Martin's poetry defies the popular notion that traditional forms can no longer adequately express contemporary life and speech in all their brawling multiplicity. Even a cursory glance at his work shows that he can make a line of metrical verse sonorous or playful, elegiac or mercurial. Martin demonstrates, through deep feeling and an often acid wit, the enduring ability of formal verse to perform feats of maverick virtuosity within a seamlessly modern idiom.

Of German and Irish extraction, Charles Frederick Martin is a native New Yorker, born on 25 June 1942 in the Bronx to Charles Justus Martin, a salesman, and Kathleen (née McCormack) Martin. He has one sister, Marilyn, born in 1948. Educated in Catholic schools as a boy, he later attended the Jesuit-run

The Lost Children

One of them picture books would no doubt show
The two lost children wandering in a maze
Of anthropomorphic tree limbs: the crow
Following them feasts on specks of dropped corn,
Tolerant of the error of their ways.
Hand in hand they stumble into the story.

Bright-eyed with the onset of fever, scared
Half to death, yet never for a moment
Doubting the outcome that had been prepared
Long in advance: Gretel saves brother from oven,
Wicked witch dies in appropriate torment,
Newfound wealth buys them their parents' love.

"An ending as happy as any fable
Can provide," the crow crows, who had expected more:
Delicate morsels from the witches' table.
And we, familiar with the modern version,
Might find ourselves waiting impatiently for
A different ending, as the television

Cameras focus on the corpsed bear
Beside the plaster ukelele, shattered
In a fit of rage; the lost children and
Found when only we would think to go looking
For them: under fallen leaves, the scattered
Pages of a lost childrens' picture book....

But the happy ending's a necessity,
Rather than merely a sentimental ploy:
For without the happy ending there would be
No one to tell the story but the witch,
And the story is clearly meant for the girl and boy
~~[illegible strikethrough]~~
[Now just about to step into her kitchen.

Page from a draft for the poem that was published as "A Happy Ending for the Lost Children" in Martin's 1987 collection, Steal the Bacon *(courtesy of the author)*

Fordham University, where he earned an A.B. in English in 1964. An early interest in the relationship between the classic and the modern was reflected in his dissertation for the State University of New York at Buffalo (M.A. 1984, Ph.D. 1987), which charted the influence of Latin poetry on the work of Ezra Pound. In 1965 he married Leslie Barnett, with whom he has two children, Gregory and Emily. They were divorced in 1998. Martin began his teaching career in the late 1960s at Notre Dame College on Staten Island, and since 1970 he has taught at Queensborough College. From 1988 to 1994 he also taught in the Johns Hopkins University Writing Seminars, and he has given poetry workshops at the Sewanee Writers' Conference, the West Chester Conference on Form and Narrative, and at the Unterberg Poetry Center of the 92nd Street Y in New York City. He resides in Manhattan's Washington Heights neighborhood with his wife, the poet and editor Johanna Keller, whom he married in 2001.

Martin has become one of the most eminent translators into English of the caustic and passionate poems of Catullus, beginning with a 1979 collection that was revised in 1990. In 1992 Martin also produced an important monograph on the Latin poet, part of the Hermes Books series edited by the distinguished classical scholar John Herington. As the classicist and critic Bernard Knox has noted, Martin describes Catullus both as a poet of "unimpeded spontaneity and uninhibited self-expression" and as "a masterful ironist practicing a highly sophisticated art." To a certain extent this balance of opposites—between what Knox calls "spontaneity" and "artifice"—characterizes Martin's sensibility as well.

As the poet and critic Robert McPhilips has observed, the influence of Catullus on Martin may be detected from the outset, with his first book, *Room for Error* (1978), and especially in "Calvus in Ruins," which McPhilips notes is "based upon a few extant fragments by one of Catullus's closest friends." In contrast to the formal unity of the poem, Martin employs an ironic tone that helps to create an undercurrent of ambiguity. The first stanza describes the mundane predictability of fate:

> Whatever is likeliest to happen, does:
> the maiden in the orchard is deflowered;
> the drunken husband, home from brothel-hopping,
>   finds his wife in bed
> with Caesar & a few of Caesar's cronies; . . .

In opposition to this acceptance of a sort of Murphy's Law, Martin describes "the distant provinces" where believers, who seem to prefer deception over grim realities, "fancy poets." The list of archetypal scenarios lends the poem its "public" tone; yet, Martin understands that the public must always relate to the personal in an immediate way.

Martin's early poems mine the present as productively as they do the past. In a series of poems set in Buffalo, New York, the tension that Martin achieves between public utterance and private recollection lends that famously unlovely city a patina of nostalgia reminiscent of Donald Justice's sepia-toned idylls of Florida in the 1950s, except that Martin is decidedly darker in tone. As "Leaving Buffalo" suggests, it is not a place the poet revisits fondly:

> "Our lives went wrong," their old people thought:
> "But speak of Progress, how it all gets better,
> And when it doesn't, how it doesn't matter.
> Why should we tell them it was all for naught,
> When what will last of us are our manners?"
> They called abhorrent what was merely lewd,
> But dreamt of applebreasted women: nude,
> Bronze-skinned lovelies of the far savannas. . . .

The final section of the collection begins with a return to Martin's hometown. In "Sharks at the New York Aquarium" the speaker is drawn fancifully through the glass of a shark tank and sees himself "swimming among them." A scene of bloody feeding intrudes on the reverie as the sharks turn the water from clear to red. The poem concludes on a cautionary note: "Children almost never tap on the glass." Even in his chosen city, "home" affords no safety.

His second collection, *Passages from Friday* (1983), envisions the Robinson Crusoe story through the cannibal's eyes. Crusoe, who required that Friday call him master, has died, and Friday is left to tell the story:

> Often I try'd, but never succeeded,
> in awakening them; that Enterprise
> was doom'd, for What my Europeans needed
> was not my dancing, but a Shipps Supplies;
>
> more Hats & Cloathes & shiny buckl'd Shoes,
> more Axes, Muskets, Cannon & Gun-Powder,
> more of sutch Goods than they cou'd ever use;
> ownly such Abundance cou'd have rows'd them.
>
> I danc'd about & summon'd them to dance
> but they ignor'd my importunate Commotion;
> fix'd in ther Places as tho' in a Trance,
> staring with painted Eyes at the great Ocean.

The central irony of the poem lies in the fact the European, civilized Crusoe proves singularly unfit to cope with his island environment, while Friday, whose beliefs and rituals are disparaged by Crusoe, survives. Part of the pathos (and the comedy) of the poem stems from the fact that Friday nevertheless haltingly attempts

7/

So what is done then is all mine to do,
And likewise mine, the reward, the glory,
Since, after all, it's *me* telling *your* story
And not you telling mine; I'm happy to,
I really am, and happy in my role
As residential existentialist,
To stand before your thought-stained palimpsest
And swipe occasionally at your soul;

8/

You will live on, in rooms I'll leave forever,
Confronting, with your reservoir of patience,
The rise of Provosts and the fall of Nations,
Equally present to the dull, the clever,
The hopeful, the hapless, and the bored, bored, bored;
Even for you, deaf oracle and dumb,
Milky-eyed seer, a time will surely come
When you will have passed on to your reward:

9/

Tell us, before you leave, before the earth
Possesses you again in shards and orts,
Whether there is an answer that supports
These whetherings, whatever they are worth;

—Charles Martin

Last page of the corrected typescript for "To the Blackboard," included in Martin's 2002 volume Starting from Sleep: New and Selected Poems *(courtesy of the author)* to emulate his master's form of speech. As the poet and critic Daniel Hoffman writes of the poem: "Martin's Friday, so like his master in his reasonableness, is a wholly successful characterization. His plain speech and plebeian misspellings, his notional capitals and italics comprise no mere eighteenth-century pastiche but a style that realizes and projects the speaker's character, a *tour de force* in which style embodies vision."

With *Steal the Bacon* (1987), Martin displays his ironic wit with the title poem, a wry rumination on mice attempting to abscond with bits of pork from a trap. The sense of the inexorable workings of fate, glimpsed in the Calvus poem, returns with a vengeance. Similarly, Martin reasserts the suspicion that there is no safe harbor in life, introducing a note of nervous laughter into the poem:

> Far from the muzzy warmth of the nest, that supportive nexus
> Of sensual mouselife. Those are x's
> That were his eyes, or hers. And doesn't anyone notice
> A cherished aunt or uncle's sudden
> Vanishing act? "Let's see now . . . Flossie disappeared one
> Night last week . . . was she the first? Was Sean?
> Mousebrain! Why can't I keep them in order? I only know this:
> That one by one we seem to be drawn
>
> Forward against our wills, tho' scampering brightly
> Toward that narrow strip of light we
> All of us fear. . . ."

Martin gives full rein to linguistic playfulness, which, while already abundant in his first collection, provides a whole new range of effects in this volume. Such coinages as "mouselife" and "mousebrain" provide a disarmingly sweet counterpoint to the carnage at the core of the poem, which only makes it more terrifying. The whole poem relies on a tongue-in-cheek corollary between the plight of mice—named, with an eerie quaintness, Flossie, Moe, and so on—and the plight of humans, all drawn "against their wills" toward an ultimate end.

Martin's poems continually show the ways in which form can remain inclusive, expansive, and anything but closed. As he writes in "On Epigrams" from *Past Closing Time* (1995), his preference is often to avoid the thud of closure, that finality that William Butler Yeats famously likened to a box clicking shut:

> Some poets only write the ones that close
> Debate off once they've made their argument;
> I'm occasionally fond of those,
> But much prefer the kind that keeps on playing
> Past closing time: after the blade's descent,
> The lopped head, lifted, says, "As I was saying. . . ."

Dust jacket for Martin's 2002 collection, in which he continues to explore the themes of innovation and mortality (Richland County Public Library)

Martin's enjambment of "close / Debate off" prevents even the first line of this passage from "closing" with a heavy end-stop, lending the verse a flowing movement. As the image of decapitation attests, Martin can incorporate into his measured and rational utterances the well-timed pratfall of comic surprise.

What the Darkness Proposes (1996), Martin's third full-length collection, continues to broaden his often literary frame of reference. (Like *Steal the Bacon*, the book received a nomination for the Pulitzer Prize in poetry.) In contrast to the starkly visceral and ominous comedies of his earlier volumes, *What the Darkness Proposes* takes on a more stately and contemplative cast. The long sequence "A Walk in the Hills above the Artists' House" is part writer's daybook, part philosophical inquiry into the nature of writing. Though the speaker confronts "The nothingness that seems to be / An endless, unmodulated roar / Our voices must accompany," the poem ends on a note of acceptance: "I bless the powers that sustain / Us" and "bless the darkness that extends / Beyond the darkness and proposes what / We will all come to, no doubt but." While Martin faces the same hard fact of mortality that concludes "Steal the Bacon," he does so in an entirely different mode.

Central to Martin's engagement with literary tradition is the notion of palimpsest, of writing over previous writing, of creating something new on top of something old. His reworking of Daniel Defoe's Crusoe is merely one example of this activity, the Calvus poem another. Elsewhere, Martin parodies Philip Larkin's "This Be the Verse" (1974): "They tucked you in your mum and dad; / They really weren't all that bad." Lot's wife provides her own apologia ("When tourists asked me why I turned, I'd say / I had no choice, since I was picked by Lot"). Pretonius Arbiter is given a chance to speak. In the case of such varied persona monologues, Martin succeeds in giving history a voice.

For Martin, innovation and tradition are inextricably linked. As he writes in "Against a Certain Kind of Ardency," from *Starting from Sleep: New and Selected Poems* (2002), citing Horace:

> ". . . If innovation
> Had been abhorred by the Greeks to the same extent
>   That it is by the citizens of our nation,
> There'd be no ancients for us now to read;
> Where, in what trackless wasteland, would we be?
> No ancients without moderns, is my creed."

The idea of innovation endlessly overwriting prior innovation is treated explicitly in "To the Blackboard," which Martin envisions as a "thought-stained palimpsest." The extended address of the poem leads again to Martin's recurrent theme of mortality, of brief lives bracketed by nonexistence. Martin, the lifelong teacher, speaks directly to this fixture of the classroom:

> But you'll live on in rooms I'll leave forever,
> Confronting with your reservoir of patience
> The rise of provosts and the fall of nations,
> Equally present to the dull, the clever,
> The hopeful, the hapless, and the bored, bored, bored;
> Yet even for you, deaf oracle and dumb,

> Milky-eyed seer, a time will surely come
> When you will have passed on to your reward:
> Tell us before you leave, before the earth
> Possesses you again in shards and orts,
> Whether you know an answer that supports
> This whethering of mine, for what it's worth:
> Whether, beyond us, there is aught to wonder
> At what the meaningful was meant to mean,
> At what can happen here, between
> The momentary lightning and the thunder.

While the blackboard will long outlast the speaker, even it will eventually "leave," bequeathing to history its many broken pieces. Such fragments recall the scraps of classic texts. The poem then questions the purpose of inquiry with a final ambiguity: the speaker asks if there is "aught" to wonder at, but doubt shows an even darker side in the additional meaning of "aught," which can also be read as "nothing."

The anthology *Rebel Angels: 25 Poets of the New Formalism* (1996) included Martin among the ranks of such accomplished metricists as Timothy Steele, Tom Disch, Greg Williamson, and Marilyn Hacker. Martin remains distinguished not for his prosodic excellence in an age of versified prose so much as for his excellent poems, distinguished for any age. Translation is itself a form of palimpsest, and Martin has been working on a version of Ovid's *Metamorphosis*. The excerpts that have appeared in periodicals show it to be as fluent as his celebrated Catullus. Like all exceptional poets writing in received forms, Martin makes his poetic inheritance (both ancient and modern) fresh and original.

References:

Daniel Hoffman, "Wings of a Phoenix?: Rebellion and Resuscitation in Postmodernist American Poetry," in his *Words to Create a World: Interviews, Essays, and Reviews of Contemporary Poetry* (Ann Arbor: University of Michigan Press, 1993), pp. 287–292;

Bernard Knox, "Passion and Playfulness," in his *Backing into the Future: The Classical Tradition and Its Renewal* (New York: Norton, 1994), pp. 85–105.

David Mason
(11 December 1954 -   )

H. L. Hix
Cleveland Institute of Art

BOOKS: *The Buried Houses* (Brownsville, Ore.: Story Line Press, 1991);
The Country I Remember (Brownsville, Ore.: Story Line Press, 1996);
Land without Grief (Colorado Springs: JonesAlley, 1996);
The Poetry of Life and the Life of Poetry (Ashland, Ore.: Story Line Press, 2000);
A Walk in the Park (West Chester, Pa.: Aralia Press, 2001).

OTHER: *Rebel Angels: 25 Poets of the New Formalism*, edited by Mason and Mark Jarman (Brownsville, Ore.: Story Line Press, 1996);
Western Wind: An Introduction to Poetry, fourth edition, edited by Mason and John Frederick Nims (New York: McGraw-Hill, 2000).

SELECTED PERIODICAL PUBLICATIONS–UNCOLLECTED:
POETRY
"Two Poems by Yiorgos Chouliaras," translated by Mason, *Grand Street*, 42 (Summer 1992): 147–150;
"Three Poems by Yiorgos Chouliaras," translated by Mason, *Poetry*, 162, no. 3 (June 1993): 136–137;
"Two Poems by Yiorgos Chouliaras," translated by Mason, *Modern Poetry in Translation*, 6 (Winter 1994–1995): 170–173;
"Three Poems by Yiorgos Chouliaras," translated by Mason, *International Quarterly*, 2, no. 1 (Spring 1995): 89;
"Nine Poems by Yiorgos Chouliaras," translated by Mason, *World Literature Today*, 71, no. 3 (Summer 1997): 521–522;
"Poems from Greece," *Hudson Review*, 50, no. 3 (Autumn 1997): 391–399;
"The *Century* Closes Down," *River Styx*, 53 (1998): 41;
"A Meaning Made of Trees," *New Criterion*, 16, no. 7 (March 1998): 32–33;
"The Collector's Tale," *Pivot*, 48 (Spring 1999): 60–64;

David Mason (photograph by Anne Lennox; courtesy of the author)

"The Picketwire," *Shenandoah*, 49, no. 4 (Winter 1999): 85;
"Dear John," *Poetry*, 175, no. 2 (December 1999): 138;
"Three Poems from India," *Hudson Review*, 55, no. 2 (Summer 2002): 222–224.

FICTION
"The Man on the Back of the Train," *North Dakota Quarterly*, 54, no. 4 (Fall 1986): 248–257;

207

"No One Is Ever Lost," *Seattle Review,* 10, no. 1 (Spring 1987): 137–154;

"The Kalamatiano," *Aegean Review,* 8 (Spring 1990): 57–63;

"The Altar in the Woods," *North Dakota Quarterly,* 61, no. 3 (Summer 1993): 49–60;

"Boys' State," *American Fiction,* 8 (1996): 68–86.

NONFICTION

"Letter from Greece," *Hudson Review,* 50, no. 2 (Summer 1997): 188–197;

"The Lotos-Eaters: A Memoir," *Hudson Review,* 51, no. 3 (Fall 1998): 501–514;

"Chatwin's Ashes," *Mondo Greco,* Premier issue (Spring 1999): 15–27;

"Letter from Turkey," *Hudson Review,* 55, no. 2 (Summer 2002): 182–193.

As a poet, essayist, and anthologist, David Mason has played a prominent and formative role in the development of New Formalism. His two volumes of poetry exemplify the attention to meter, rhyme, and narrative on which New Formalism has staked its identity. His essays, by defending the relevance of poetry to life outside of an academic environment and by attention to such poets as W. H. Auden, Robert Frost, Edwin Arlington Robinson, and Robinson Jeffers, offer some of the clearest and most vigorous articulations of New Formalist concerns. The anthology of New Formalist poetry that he and Mark Jarman edited, *Rebel Angels* (1996), has prompted intense, ongoing debate.

David James Mason was born on 11 December 1954 in Bellingham, Washington, where he lived through his childhood. His father, James Cameron Mason, worked as a naval officer, then as a pediatrician and psychiatrist. His mother, Evelyn Peterson, worked as a professor of psychology at Western Washington University. Though both parents were born in Colorado, they met in San Francisco when she was a student at Mills College and his ship was being repaired after action at Iwo Jima.

Mason graduated in 1978 from Colorado College with a B.A. in English, marrying Jonatha Heinrich on 1 April of that year. After completing his undergraduate degree, he spent some time away from school, working as an estate caretaker in Rochester, New York, and as a screenwriter in Los Angeles, and living for a year in Greece. Mason then entered graduate school at the University of Rochester, earning an M.A. degree in English in 1986 and a Ph.D. in 1989. Mason and Heinrich divorced in 1987, after a period of separation. On 16 October 1988 Mason married photographer Anne Lennox. They have a daughter, Darcy, by Lennox's first marriage. For the first nine years after earning his doctorate, Mason taught English at Moorhead State University in Minnesota. He was promoted to Associate Professor in 1993 and in 1994 received recognition from the Carnegie Foundation for the Advancement of Teaching and the Council for Advancement and Support of Education as the Minnesota Professor of the Year. Mason spent the spring semester of 1997 in Greece on a Fulbright Artist-in-Residence Fellowship. In 1998 he returned to the English department of his alma mater, Colorado College, where he currently teaches.

Mason's first book of poems, *The Buried Houses* (1991), was a cowinner of the 1991 Nicholas Roerich Prize. Allen Hoey writes that its poems "probe emotional life with genuine insight and feeling, rather than for the sake of the verse itself." Three narrative poems anchor the collection, each about an unconsummated love between two people brought together by circumstances but prevented by other circumstances from staying together.

"The Nightingales of Andritsena" is a dramatic monologue spoken by "Mrs. Finn, translator, / tour guide, sadly middle-aged," who lives in a room in Greece, "on Skyros facing the sea, a single bed." Her story interweaves her relationships with three men—her father, her husband, and a young student—each relationship finally unsatisfying. She continues to suffer from the abrupt ending, many years before, of her relationship with her father: "I read long books alone," she says, "just as I did / that night in Chicago many years ago / they came to tell me that my father was dead." The effect of that death is still so strong that her concluding self-definition depends on it: "I am a woman whose father committed suicide / in Chicago in 1939." Her relationship with her husband proves equally unfulfilling, though for different reasons. Her father destroyed his relationship with her by committing suicide; her husband destroyed his relationship with her by leaving her in order to chase "the body / of a girl he hardly knew, someone met / at work, a plaything he later bored."

Those two relationships are called to mind, though, by Mrs. Finn's fascination with Ross, a student in a tour group for which Mrs. Finn serves as translator and guide. Though Ross is younger than Mrs. Finn's youngest child, she is drawn to him not only by his beauty but also because, just as she "wanted words / to guide me by the solid things they stood for," so he "was the only student on the bus / who wanted lessons" in Greek. With his girlfriend, Angela, who is motivated by her interest in him, Ross takes lessons with Mrs. Finn each morning at breakfast. When the two students join Mrs. Finn one evening to listen to the nightingales,

Mason (far left) with his father, James Mason, and brothers Doug and Don, on Puget Sound in the 1960s (courtesy of the author)

We listened for the life inside each note,
or rather the children did, Ross leaning
out as if resisting an urge to fly;
Angela, her sense of possibility
untarnished, smiled like an archaic statue.

For me it had all gone flat.

Mrs. Finn recalls a line from the Greek poet George Seferis, "The nightingales won't let you sleep in Platres," and realizes the futility of her fondness for Ross and the finality of her loss of youth. She recognizes that the insatiability of her desires arises from her own nature: "Because of who I am, who I've always been, / I know the nightingales won't let me sleep."

The second "anchor" poem of *The Buried Houses* is "Spooning," a poem that, by recounting a boy's encounter with a famous actress his grandfather knew, manages simultaneously to address growing up and growing old. The boy's parents dismiss it as merely the fantasy of an infirm old man when the grandfather tells the boy he knew Lydia Truman Gates "'back when she was plain old Lydia Carter / down on Water Street. One time her old man / caught us spooning out to the railroad tracks.'" When the wealthy actress returns to the small town to receive an award from the mayor, the boy seizes his chance to validate his grandfather's story. Waiting with his brother in the alley by her limousine, the boy blurts out as the actress passes, "Our grandpa says hello." She hears and asks, "And who's he?"

"George McCracken," I said, "the one you spooned with
down by the railroad tracks."
                    "George McCracken."
She straightened, looked up at the strip of sky.
"Spooned. Well, that's one way to talk about it."
She laughed from deep down in her husky lungs.
"Old Georgie McCracken. Is he still alive?
Too scared to come downtown and say hello?"
She reached out from her furs and touched my hair.
"Thanks for the message, little man. I knew him.
I knew he'd never get out of this town.
You tell your grampa Hi from Liddy Carter."

The boy leaves the encounter with a more mature and independent outlook, and the grandfather with a measure of the respect due his age.

In "Blackened Peaches," the third long narrative in the book, a woman named Sally recounts events from her life. Though some of the events include her husband, Jim, they center on the doctor from her small town, a widower she calls Doctor Hale. She first met Doctor Hale when he was called to help her through a fever; she was a child, and her father had died recently. After the doctor learned her favorite fruit was peaches, he brought her a peach one visit and nicknamed her "Sally Peaches." Twice he tried to propose to her—once on her sixteenth birthday when "Doctor Hale and I sat in the kitchen, / him with his hands on his knees, looking shy," and the other time apparently not more than a year later, when "Mother left us alone / and Doctor Hale stood awkwardly and looked / down at me through his lenses." Both times, though, he failed to ask. The second attempt ended with his saying, "I'm wishing you good luck, good health . . . all good," but according to Sally, "each word he spoke then seemed to weaken him, / and when he drove away I sat there crying / though I couldn't tell my mother what it meant."

Years later, when Jim was sick, Doctor Hale came to help but was hurt to learn that Sally had let someone else call her "Sally Peaches," Doctor Hale's pet name for her. Doctor Hale died soon after, when his "horse took a fright / out on Mountainview Road, pulled his buggy / off a bridge, and threw him into the river," but Sally saw him one more time, when her husband was suffering through a long terminal illness. After she had prayed for her husband not to die,

> . . . the room changed.
> I knew I wasn't alone any more.
> I turned and saw a man beside the door,
> knew him by the wire rims of his glasses,
> his smile peaceful though he was covered with rain.
> heard his voice with so much gentleness:
> "Sally, all of our illnesses will end."

The "visit" from Doctor Hale helps Sally reconcile herself to Jim's death, allowing her in the end to leave "the window open for his soul to go."

In addition to the three narrative poems, *The Buried Houses* includes several shorter lyrics. The title poem meditates on the discovery of an ancient village on the Northwest coast, using it as a correlative for lost family unity, and ending with an observation that serves also as a lamentation: "Much is known by now about the buried houses, / less about the people who uncovered them." The most powerful lyrics of the book memorialize the poet's older brother, Doug, who died at the age of twenty-eight in a mountain-climbing accident. The sequence of poems includes "At the Graves of Castor and Pollux," "The Mountain Climber," "Dry Granite," and "An Absence." The last lines of "Small Elegies," spoken from the point of view of Mason's younger brother, Don, encapsulate the grief expressed in the whole sequence. In the helicopter that came to rescue him, the speaker says, "I watched the darkened snow. / My hands still felt, from earlier that day, / the tension of my brother's weight on the rope."

The significance of Mason's second book of poems, *The Country I Remember,* published in 1996, has been widely recognized. Its title poem, a long narrative in the voices of two of Mason's ancestors, won the 1993 Alice Fay Di Castagnola Award from the Poetry Society of America. Samuel Jay Keyser, writing in the *Harvard Review,* says that "The Country I Remember" reads "like a latter-day 'Our Town,' a Yankee 'Under Milkwood.'"

Though the long title poem dominates *The Country I Remember,* shorter lyrics retain a place, just as they do in *The Buried Houses.* They confirm Mason's gifts as a storyteller, for even in his lyrics, narrative lends the poems their force. "The Summer of Love," for example, tells a story, and even "In the Northern Woods," which depicts a single, more static scene, depends on narrative. The shadow cast by the very *absence* of narrative is what darkens the poem: the tragedy lies not in the poet's own grief, but in the fact that the girl's story will never be told, that she will remain as "anonymous as leaves along the shore."

The long title poem, though, defines the book. Told in seven-line blank-verse stanzas with a single line at the end of most sections, it consists of a series of monologues in the voices of Lieutenant John Mitchell, a Civil War veteran, and his daughter, Maggie Mitchell Gresham. The twelve chapters of the poem alternate between the two voices. The first, "How We Came This Far," gives Mrs. Gresham's version, recalled "two years before her death in 1956," of the family's move by train from Illinois to the Washington Territory in 1880. The move marks a pivotal transition in Maggie's life, away from her childhood contentment in familiar surroundings and from her childish naiveté. During the train ride she laments her lost security: "I was the happiest child when we had left / the farm, but now I prayed / the night would destroy us like the lost." Later, though, after they have lived for some time on the ranch Lieutenant Mitchell bought near Pomeroy in the Blue Mountains, Maggie realizes that she has changed: "We came this far, and maybe I could go / farther on my own." The effect of the train ride on her childish naiveté is more immediate and introduces the subject of Lieutenant Mitchell's monologues to follow. Maggie overhears her father talking to a fellow passenger, Mr. Kress.

> The war that made my Papa look so old
> happened in Tennessee and in Virginia
> long before my sisters and I were born.
> War had taught my Papa to stand up straight.
> War gave him his heavy cough each winter,
> but we had never heard the things I heard
> intended for the ears of Mr. Kress.

Subsequent chapters relate other incidents from the lives of father and daughter. Lieutenant Mitchell's monologues are spoken "shortly before his death at

Mason's wife, Anne Lennox, in Chautauqua, New York, shortly before their marriage in 1988
(photograph by David Mason; courtesy of the author)

Pomeroy, Washington, in 1918." The first, "Cobb's Orchard," tells a set of adventures related to securing food for a hungry traveling army. Lieutenant Mitchell recounts the time he sent Charley, "my colored man," to get food for the regiment, and that memory leads him to recall Charley's later death: "When we got whipped at Chickamauga, Charley / had no place left to run. He just stood still / and waited for the Rebs to get a rope." Two days after Charley's successful food run, Lieutenant Mitchell leads a small group in search of food and finds an orchard full of ripe peaches, a corn crib full of white corn, a family farm with hogs, and some beehives. Though the trip included a skirmish with Confederate soldiers, Lieutenant Mitchell and his men return safely, with food for all, but the recollection is dark nonetheless, because "we were on our way to Chickamauga," and because "supplies were never sent to that old couple" who let the soldiers take their hogs. For all its symbolic associations (with Christ's feeding of the five thousand, for example, and with the story of Philemon and Baucis), Mason keeps "Cobb's Orchard" firmly planted in the soil of description and the lived experience of the narrator.

Lieutenant Mitchell's other chapters retain that emphasis. "Acoustic Shadows" tells of a conflict on Sand Mountain, near Chattanooga; "Boyish War" recounts the defeat at Chickamauga; "Sojourners" recalls Mitchell's fighting with the Oregon Mounted Dragoons in 1856; "Rat Hell" tells of Mitchell's imprisonment in Libby Prison and how he helped lead a prison break in which, because of illness, he was unable to participate. "Eighty Acres" summarizes:

> This is an account of my experience,
> though much is left out: the end of the war
> and sorry death of Mr. Lincoln, months
> in hospitals spent getting my strength back,
> return to Edgar County, Illinois,
> where Mrs. Mitchell, who had had no news
> for quite a time, was glad to see me home.

Mrs. Gresham's chapters tell of an independent woman making her own way in a West still wild. "All Houses Are Haunted" tells of her childhood on the ranch, dutifully reading Henry Wadsworth Longfellow to her father "when his war-damaged eyes / no longer focused on the page," but also suffering wanderlust: "No one knew how often I left the ranch / and walked alone out to the luminous fields . . . / before the day I really left for good." "Leaving Pomeroy" focuses on the effect her decision to leave had on her parents; "The Country I Remember" tells of her finding work in Portland and then leaving after turning down the hotel keeper's marriage proposal; "The Blacksmith" tells of her marriage to Howard Gresham, a dry-goods store owner in Santa Rosa, California, and of her return to Pomeroy for her mother's funeral; and finally, in "The Children's Hour," Mrs. Gresham reflects on her life without children, and—made nostalgic by a visit from her niece Alyssa and Alyssa's two young daughters—Mrs. Gresham reports, "I was moved by everything that moved."

Though Mason is a poet first and foremost, so that "The Country I Remember" represents the major achievement by which his work to date can be measured, he also has created notable work as an anthologist and essayist. *Rebel Angels,* the 1996 anthology that Mason edited with Jarman, has proven controversial, receiving from reviewers and critics responses that range from lavish praise to virulent condemnation. Writing in *TLS: The Times Literary Supplement* (13 March 1998), N. S. Thompson calls *Rebel Angels* important "not only for the coherently framed window it provides for twenty-five significant poets, but for the part it plays in the debate about the question of form, which has recently been a subject of fierce contention again in the United States." In contrast, Greg Glazner, writing in *Poetry International* in 1997, contends that the revolutionary rhetoric of the introduction to the book contrasts with the generally "tidy, polite, nostalgic verse" collected in the book. Glazner argues that "the maneuvering here—the inclusion of so much weak work because it meets the formalist litmus test, the exclusion of more adventurous formal poems such as Richard Kenney's 'The Hours of the Day,' or of any of Denis Johnson's sonnets . . . , the inflated claims for the formalist movement, and, importantly, the movement's 'revolutionary' pose—suggest not so much a love of poetry as a desire to be elected." The controversy itself has been viewed by some critics as an argument in favor of the book: Will Clemens wrote in *The Review* in 1997 that "the debate the book causes is its tremendous success."

Jarman and Mason modestly exclude their own poems from the collection, even though they are appropriate for inclusion, and—according to Glazner—"even though their work is stronger than most of what they have selected." Its inclusions, though, have helped to solidify, out of the many poets writing verse in traditional forms, a group from whose poems New Formalism has been willing to fly its standard. The featured poets include many who have been identified with New Formalism from its beginnings—for example, Dana Gioia, Emily Grosholz, Brad Leithauser, Molly Peacock, Mary Jo Salter, and Timothy Steele—but also newer poets included on the basis of a first book, as for example, Elizabeth Alexander, Rachel Wetzsteon, and Greg Williamson. The popularity of *Rebel Angels* makes it a candidate for ongoing revision in future editions, maturing as New Formalism itself matures.

Of Mason's books, *Western Wind* (2000), a textbook aimed at college students and designed as an introduction to poetry, is least directly his own. John Frederick Nims edited the first three editions and invited Mason to join him as co-editor for the fourth edition. In addition to revisions, Mason's responsibilities included preparation of the instructor's manual, the essay assignments, and the appendices on "Poetics" and "Writing about Poetry." The appendix on "Poetics" displays Mason's characteristic modesty: after briefly suggesting that poets' talk about poetry is as natural as carpenters' talk about carpentry, Mason presents instead of his own words a miniature anthology of incisive statements about poetry from sources that include ancient standards such as Plato's *Ion* (written in 380 B.C.) and Aristotle's *Poetics* (written 350 B.C.), English-language touchstones such as Percy Bysshe Shelley's "A Defence of Poetry" (1821) and John Keats's letters, and contemporary views such as Gioia's *Can Poetry Matter?* (1992) and Alice Fulton's "Of Formal, Free and Fractal Verse: Singing the Body Electric" (1986).

The appendix on "Writing about Poetry" addresses student concerns about writing critical essays by suggesting that "no matter how long you labor in this field, the same questions arise." Three of those questions, "What will I write about?" "What will I say?" and "Who am I writing for?" serve as section headings for Mason's discussion. The appendix includes two sample essays by students from Mason's classes at Moorhead State University and ends with a short section on "Some Technical Matters," giving students basic advice about matters such as documentation, and encouraging students to "learn to take pleasure in writing and revising." The instructor's manual to *Western Wind* consists primarily of Mason's personal reflections on the poets and poems included in the text, ranging from one-sentence comments suggesting possible approaches to some of the individual poems, to more-extensive meditations on some of the featured poets, such as William Butler Yeats, Frost, and Wallace Stevens. Mason's reflections include information ("'The Man He Killed' appeared in Hardy's 1902 volume, *Time's Laughingstocks*"), critical perspective ("'Adam's Curse' represents a modernization of Yeats's voice"), and personal response ("He [A. E. Housman] seems to me one of the purest lyric poets in the language"). Since Nims's death in 1999, Mason has assumed full editorial responsibility, and as *Western Wind* continues to develop, future editions will bear his mark more and more distinctively.

The Poetry of Life and the Life of Poetry (2000), collects many of Mason's essays about poetry. The subjects of

Left: John Mitchell, one of Mason's ancestors, and his daughters, who are the subjects of the long narrative title poem in Mason's 1996 volume The Country I Remember; right: Mitchell's gravestone in Pomeroy, Washington
(courtesy of the author; photograph on right by Anne Lennox)

the essays range widely. Several of the essays examine the work of contemporaries, including Gioia, Ellen Bryant Voigt, and Seamus Heaney. Others consider the work of poets from earlier generations, including Frost, Anne Sexton, and Auden. Still others are more topical: "American Poetry in the Nineteenth Century," "Irish Poetry at the Crossroads," "The New Formalism and the Audience for Poetry," and "Other Lives: On Shorter Narrative Poems." The preface of the book clearly states Mason's ambitions: "I want to convey a passion for learning matched by an interest in life. Criticism is creative to the extent that it is stubbornly independent. My purpose in these essays and reviews has been to stand as an individual. . . ." But the preface, by asserting that "the chief advantage of an active intellectual life lies in being taken out of ourselves, listening to voices other than our own," also suggests a connection between Mason's critical work and his poetry, since his poetry so often adopts personae, on the premise (stated in his essay "Other Lives") that "empathy, the act of inhabiting a stranger's experience, is a civilizing process."

The title essay articulates the theme common to the various essays and serves as the best representative of the whole collection. It is divided into four sections, each inhabited by two presiding spirits who are brought into relation one with the other. In keeping with the title of the essay, each pair includes one presiding spirit from the poetry of Mason's life and the other from the life of twentieth-century poetry. The first section of the essay, "Forms of Memory," moves from Mason's father's experience to Frost's words. The experience occurred a decade before Mason's birth, when his father was "twenty-four, a red-haired Naval lieutenant on the bridge of a destroyer, the USS *Terry,* patrolling the waters off Iwo Jima," though his father kept the story to himself until he was in his seventies. When the ship was hit in an attack from artillery hidden in caves on the island, many of the sailors were killed or wounded. "The memory of the dead and wounded

Mason with Greek poet Yiorgos Chouliaras, whose work Mason has translated, circa 1990 (photograph by Anne Lennox; courtesy of the author)

boys has never left my father." The ship returned for repairs to San Francisco, where Mason's father and mother met at a dance, an occurrence that has made Mason feel "that I was part of a story, and that I had a sacred duty to transcribe as much of it as I could." Out of chaos, form: so poetry functions, as Frost says, as "a momentary stay against confusion."

The second section, "The Old Philosophers," conjoins Mason's former neighbor Patrick Leigh Fermor and the poet Stevens to make the case that "theorists who hold life and art completely separate are killing the thing they supposedly love." Fermor, who had walked from Holland to Constantinople as an "alternative to a college education," and who had been involved with the Cretan resistance during World War II, "represented a literary ideal, the intellectual and physical life melded into one Byronic personality." The weight of that ideal derives from, as Mason says, that "life appears on occasion to have form, and to borrow its form from poetry even as poetry borrows from life," so that even so abstruse and opaque a poet as Stevens argues that poetry "helps us live our lives."

In the third section, "The Impersonal Poet," an unidentified poet, treated impersonally, is set against the great advocate of impersonality in poetry, T. S. Eliot. "Once at a literary gathering," Mason says, "a poet asked me whom I enjoyed reading." When Mason named Eliot, "the poet turned on one heel and marched away from me in righteous indignation. To admire Eliot was, in certain circles, tantamount to admiring an impersonal royalist snob. Worse, it was like admiring the dessicated corpse of the Western tradition." Mason argues, though, that Eliot's distinction between "the man who suffers and the mind which creates" is misinterpreted when treated as an absolute separation, and that the two, though distinct, are intimately related, so that even though "poetry is not quite bread" and "does not feed the refugees," it *is* "an awareness, a verbal precision that offers flashes of lucidity."

The concluding section, "My Mother's Secret," recounts an occasion when Mason's mother pointed out to him some lines from Yeats. The experience occurred on one of Mason's trips home when he was in college. His parents had been divorced, and his mother was dating "a man who had taught me to play chess years before, and who took an active interest in my love of reading." After dinner, while the three of them talked about Yeats, the youthful Mason, busy trying "to show off my knowledge to her indulgent friend," was brought up short when his mother passed him his copy of Yeats's selected poems, open to her favorite poem, "A Deep-Sworn Vow." Only later did Mason realize that "she was talking to me through Yeats, using the poem to explain her life to me," to say "that she still loved my father, despite all the hell they put each other through." The ability of the poem to be specific to Yeats's own "life, his loves and prejudices," and yet to speak to and for other lives, including that of Mason's mother, represents what Mason sees as the ultimate power of poetry. He concludes that "the poetry of life and the life of poetry mean that reality alone is no place to live."

In all his work, whether (as an essayist) in his prose statements about poetry and life, or (as an anthologist) in his selections from the poetry of others, or (as a poet) in poems that speak through the voices of others as often as through his own, David Mason attempts to inhabit that space in which "reality" and "imagination" speak of and to each other, each revealing the other more clearly.

References:

Angus Calder, "Reflections on Scotland and America," *Dark Horse* (Scotland) (Summer 2000): 138–143;

George Core, "Procrustes' Bed," *Sewanee Review* (Winter 1994): xv–xviii;

Core, "Procrustes' Bed," *Sewanee Review* (Winter 2001): ii–viii;

Michael Donaghy, "Crashing the Devil's Party," *Poetry Review* (Summer 1997): 72–73;

Fred Eckman, "Minnesota Poets Offer Collections," *Star Tribune,* 6 September 1992, p. F9;

Jack Foley, "David Mason, The Poetry of Life and the Life of Poetry" <www.alsopreview.com/foley/jfd-mason.html>;

Jon Griffin, "To Have and to Hold," *Bookpress* (September 1993): 5;

R. S. Gwynn, ed., *The New Expansive Poetry* (Ashland, Ore.: Story Line Press, 1999);

Cynthia Haven, "Why Can't Poetry Be Fun?" *San Francisco Chronicle,* 6 February 2000, pp. 6, 11;

Judith Kitchen, "The Subjective Correlative," *Georgia Review* (Summer 2000): 367–368;

April Lindner, *New Formalist Poets of the American West,* Western Writers Series, no. 149 (Boise, Idaho: Boise State University, 2001);

Keith Maillard, review of *Rebel Angels, Antigonish Review* (Spring 1997): 37–40;

N. S. Thompson, "A Question of Form," *TLS: Times Literary Supplement,* 13 March 1998, p. 24;

Kevin Walzer, *The Ghost of Tradition* (Ashland, Ore.: Story Line Press, 1998);

Mark Royden Winchell, "A Picturesque, Unprofitable Craft," *Chronicles* (December 1997): 29–31.

Robert McDowell
(8 April 1953 –)

Mark Jarman
Vanderbilt University

BOOKS: *At the House of the Tin Man* (Wollastan, Mass.: Chowder Chapbooks, 1983);
History, Hardware, & Romance (New Harmony: Indiana State University at Evansville/New Harmony Art Gallery, 1984);
Quiet Money (New York: Holt, 1987);
The Diviners (Calstock, U.K.: Peterloo Poets, 1995);
The Reaper Essays, by McDowell and Mark Jarman (Brownsville, Ore.: Story Line Press, 1996);
Sound and Form in Modern Poetry, second edition, by McDowell and Harvey Gross (Ann Arbor: University of Michigan Press, 1996);
On Foot, in Flames (Pittsburgh & London: University of Pittsburgh Press, 2002).

OTHER: Ota Pavel, *How I Came to Know Fish,* translated by McDowell and Jindriska Badal (Brownsville, Ore.: Story Line Press, 1989; New York: New Directions Paperback, 1990);
Poetry After Modernism, edited by McDowell (Brownsville, Ore.: Story Line Press, 1991; revised and expanded, Ashland, Ore.: Story Line Press, 1998);
Cowboy Poetry Matters: From Abilene to the Mainstream: Contemporary Cowboy Writing, edited by McDowell (Ashland, Ore.: Story Line Press, 2000).

SELECTED PERIODICAL PUBLICATION–UNCOLLECTED: "Recovering E.A.R. and the Narrative of Talk," *New England Review and Bread Loaf Quarterly,* 8 (Autumn 1985): 62–69.

Robert McDowell (photograph by Tony Hayden; courtesy of the author)

One of the founders of the New Narrative movement in contemporary poetry, Robert McDowell has been one of its most devoted practitioners, telling stories in both free and formal verse about ordinary Americans in extraordinary circumstances. When his book of narrative poems, *Quiet Money,* appeared in 1987, it was hailed, by Louis Simpson and other critics, as a sign that poetry was leaving the academy. It also represented one of the first major achievements of the return to storytelling in American poetry. Eight years later, with the publication of his book-length poem, *The Diviners,* written in blank verse, McDowell's poetry showed the coming together of the New Narrative and New Formalist movements, while still focusing on the unpoetic lives of Americans who work for a living. Since then, his poetry has taken a turn toward the lyric, especially the formal lyric, such as the sonnet. Although this turn appears to indicate a further change in this poet's development and an interesting comment on his historical place, the fact is that early in his career, while a graduate student at Columbia University in the mid 1970s, he was already experimenting with formal structures.

Robert Allan McDowell was born on 8 April 1953 in Alhambra, California, and the smog-wrapped, semi-arid landscape at the base of the San Gabriel Mountains provides the background for many of his poems. His father, Gordon McDowell, a New Yorker, disappeared when McDowell was five years old. His mother, Rita Terese (née Grum) McDowell, born in Austria, died when McDowell was still in his twenties. His poetry shows a striking lack of sentimental, autobiographical reminiscence of family life. In fact, until the births of his own children, his poetry was almost devoid of any autobiographical focus, making him an exception among his contemporaries.

McDowell's poetic gift first became evident when he was a freshman at the University of California, Santa Cruz, in 1971. In a poetry-writing class with George Hitchcock, the Surrealist poet and artist and publisher of *kayak* magazine, McDowell showed the ability to write a poem of absurdist wit and mordancy in the style of James Tate. One of his first published poems, "What We Do With Ourselves," which appeared in *The Ohio Review* while he was still an undergraduate, shows his skill at the surreal satire of middle-class life, which characterizes so much poetry of the late 1960s and early 1970s:

> It's all she can do to push
> The stroller around the block.
> The child bears a paternal resemblance,
> That hulk of blue cobwebs,
> Inside, a face the size of an orange.

Another influence is Raymond Carver, whose creative-writing courses McDowell took at the University of California, Santa Cruz. Carver's interest in ordinary people, at least in his short stories, had an effect on McDowell's future poetry. In any event, influenced by his reading of W. B. Yeats and Theodore Roethke, McDowell quickly outgrew the surreal mode of writing. At Columbia University, as a student respectively of Richard Eberhart, William Jay Smith, and Mark Strand, McDowell showed a decided interest in metrical composition. Though Eberhart and Smith were encouraging, McDowell encountered resistance in his class with Strand. Still he persisted, deepening his understanding of poetic form and the verse line. When he graduated from Columbia, though he had published poems in national magazines such as *Poetry* and *kayak* and recorded his poems on tape for The Black Box series from Word Works, he had yet to discover his subject. The lines in "What We Do With Ourselves" about the exhausted young mother, however, hint at what his subject eventually became: how common, everyday people live their often stressful lives.

After graduate school, McDowell lived for two years in Palmdale, California, teaching part time at Antelope Valley Community College. These years proved to be formative. In Palmdale he wrote the poems that went into his chapbook *At the House of the Tin Man* (1983) and a few of the poems that he later included in his first full-length collection, *Quiet Money*. Living in the high desert, along the margins of agrarian and urban communities, among people who often had chosen to live there because of desires to be alone, McDowell discovered the connection between people and landscape, person and place, at a level that cannot be called cultural as much as social. The people he met formed a society of oddballs, uninfluenced by notoriety, class, or common background. So perhaps it is not surprising that, at this time, the dramatic monologue emerged as one of McDowell's favorite poetic forms. His attention to Robert Frost's sense of vernacular poetry is evident in the title poem of *At the House of the Tin Man*:

> But why tin, you ask—
> Because you can beat hell on it
> And still get it back to a useful shape.
> What with the storage sheds out back,
> When a big wind comes up
> We're inside quite a concert!
> We like to sit by the fire and listen
> To all that tin make like bells;
> Not church bells, mind,
> But them that could fit in your pocket
> Or the palm of your hand.
> It might make you anxious to leave
> If you don't have an ear for music.

The poems in *At the House of the Tin Man* reveal McDowell's ear for American speech and a gift for mimicry. In these poems, objects as various as Joshua trees and horseshoe poles speak in direct American fashion, poetic almost by accident. One can see that the lines are written by someone who has worked closely with iambic meters but has relaxed his approach. Nevertheless, McDowell's fascination with the larger possibilities of form, extending beyond traditional verse, can be seen in a poem such as "Test Pilot," perhaps his best and most daring lyric from this period.

McDowell in 2002 (photograph by Robert Jaffee; courtesy of the author)

I came here from a Kansas farm
    but now I can't feel it.
The whole world is mosaic,
And God a piece of the iris breaking off.
The sun makes flares

    out of tin roofs
    out of wings

The cockpit is a bell.

The play of lineation, form, and tone of voice, as the dramatic monologue erupts in lyric exclamation, all portend McDowell's intense interest in the capacity of poetry to tell a story in a compressed space.

In 1976 McDowell married Patricia Lynn McDowell, a distant cousin; the marriage ended in divorce three years later. In 1978 McDowell joined the English department of Indiana State University at Evansville (now the University of Southern Indiana) and began writing the poems that make up his first full-length collection, *Quiet Money*. Living in a working-class neighborhood and teaching students who were often commuters with full-time jobs, McDowell found a rich variety of quiet desperation, plus an echo of his own blue-collar background in southern California. In "After the Money's Gone," a man who has lost his job and his wife looks for ways to console himself:

His wife was worth half a dozen jobs.
That's how many he lost before she left him.
"Plant yourself," his buddy told him over beer.
"Hug your swatch of earth
Like it's your own skin.
That's what a woman wants in her man."
Hector knew if he went home he'd stay up
Watching reruns of shows he didn't care for.
He thought of going to church,
But the air in church was bad. He knew
If he thought of his wife he'd begin to cry.

In "The Cop from Traffic Accident Control" McDowell creates the voice of a police officer who has been suspended for killing a suspect in his partner's murder:

> During my suspension I had time
> To play back every illusion I'd swallowed whole—
> How I dreamed of squad cars sweet as magnolias
> Shuttling down to comfort city streets,
> Cells for the truly needy, keeping the cold out,
> Nightsticks no worse than a loving father's slap.
> At sixteen, hurling the javelin past the sun,
> I never imagined the look I'm wearing now.

In 1980 McDowell's friend and college classmate Mark Jarman came to Murray, Kentucky, to teach at Murray State University, only three hours from Evansville by car. Partly because of this proximity, McDowell suggested that they start a magazine. He believed correctly that his school would support an inexpensively produced literary quarterly, and McDowell and Jarman successfully applied for an Indiana Arts Council grant to help get the magazine under way. Thus, *The Reaper* was born. Because of his experience with Hitchcock, McDowell had a good idea of how a little magazine such as *kayak* was edited and produced. Hitchcock's *kayak*, because of its reviews and parodies, had been something of a gadfly, and it was one of the only places in the 1960s where poets working in experimental surreal and political poetry could publish their work. The aim of *The Reaper* was to attack the status quo in American letters and to clear ground, primarily the ground of contemporary poetry, although it published fiction as well as poetry throughout its ten-year run. When McDowell and his co-editor surveyed American poetry at the end of the 1970s, they saw the scene dominated by formless free-verse meditations with a watered-down, postconfessional bent, influenced by the poetry of John Ashbery and the criticism of Harold Bloom. They set about to criticize these influences and propose another way to write.

The Reaper became a voice for narrative poetry in a larger movement that had advocates in several parts of the country. Its first issue began with a manifesto, "Where *The Reaper* Stands," which included the statement:

> *The Reaper* maintains that both the accurate image and the narrative line, two determining factors of the poem's shapelessness, have been keenly honed and kept sharp by the poets included here, whereas many of their counterparts, forgetting these necessities, have wandered into a formless swamp where only the skunk cabbage of solipsistic meditation breeds, with its cloying flowers.

In collaboration with Jarman, McDowell wrote essays on the poetry of Frost and Simpson, both of whom he admired, and an essay on the poetry of Wallace Stevens, whose influence he believed was leading American poetry astray. Along with its serious criticism, *The Reaper* also ran satirical pieces, such as an interview with a fictional married couple who were writers, and a series of responses, by nonexistent readers, to a pair of recent anthologies of young American poets. In one issue, McDowell and Jarman, writing in their persona as The Reaper, printed a list of "nonnegotiable demands," the first of which was to "take prosody off the hit list." They also produced a series of letters between Homer and Dante in which the two epic poets argued the strengths and weaknesses of each other's narrative poetry. Throughout its ten years, *The Reaper* sought to publish contemporary narrative poems. Though it was not always successful in finding such poetry, by the end of its career it had published important narratives by Rita Dove, from her Pulitzer Prize–winning sequence *Thomas and Beulah* (1986); Andrew Hudgins, from *After the Lost War* (1988); Garrett Hongo, from *The River of Heaven* (1988); and Sydney Lea, from *The Blainville Testament* (1992).

Editing the magazine both confirmed McDowell's direction in his own poetry and gave it added incentive. Reading Frost closely and Edwin Arlington Robinson even more closely (he wrote a major essay about Robinson in 1985 for a symposium on narrative poetry in *The New England Review and Bread Loaf Quarterly*), McDowell began working increasingly, though not exclusively, in blank verse. The dramatic monologue continued to be a mode he preferred, but with the intimate sense, derived from Robinson and Frost, of a first-person narrator speaking to a single listener. A good example is the opening of "How Does It Look to You," a poem from *Quiet Money*:

> Listen, friend. I saw him use a Bic
> To light his pipe. We'd just climbed in the car,
> I looked over and poof! He'd lost his face.
> That damn thing going off in a closed car
> Took me back to popguns we'd packed in school,
> But there he was, thirty, burning up!

The frustrating isolation of life in southern Indiana and the feeling that he was battling obscurity as he attempted to find an audience for his poetry led McDowell to a profound understanding of frustration and obscurity in others, especially those who had done extraordinary things but appeared to the world to be ordinary and beneath notice. This understanding led to the composition of the title poem of *Quiet Money*, which is not only one of McDowell's best poems but also a major work in a tradition of American literature that includes the poems in Frost's *North of Boston* (1914), F. Scott Fitzgerald's novel *The Great Gatsby* (1925), and

Tennessee Williams's play *The Glass Menagerie* (1945). It also shares some of the historical context of these works.

"Quiet Money" is the story of a bootlegger who flies solo across the Atlantic Ocean before the flight of Charles Lindbergh. Built into his achievement is the necessity that only those closest to him, such as his wife, should know of it. The character—whose name is Joe, as in Average Joe—has a subsequent career as a pilot, and when the Lindbergh baby is kidnapped, he even assists the investigation, as he later tells his nephew, flying for the police to track down false leads. The poem creates the tension and excitement of flying the Atlantic Ocean alone and the dramatic irony of seeing Lindbergh on his way to Paris, even as Joe himself is returning to America:

> He comes to long enough to focus
> On a silvery image before him, skimming the sea.
> *Bird,* then *dolphin* occur to him. Then *plane.*
> That can't be, so he tells himself *reflection*
> And conjures the creature from an old story
> That snatches plane and pilot
> If they fly too close to water.
> "That can't be anyone but me," he says.
> The image below him fades, heading the other way.

Evoking the tragedy suffered by the Lindberghs, with the kidnapping and death of their child, the poem becomes a cautionary tale about celebrity in America and a comment on Fitzgerald's famous observation that there are no second acts in American lives. The poem ends with Joe's mature and bittersweet reflection on the bitch-goddess success:

> "Son, you have to lose to win.
> That notion settled in with us
> And we passed it on to you.
> Thank God. You know what it meant to me?
> My daughter safe, first of all,
> And all of it, really.
> I spent so many nights in her room
> Just watching her sleep,
> Convincing myself no gang would take her
> From me—ex-flyboy, average businessman—
> And suddenly I was happy.
> My life's course felt fair.
> I thought of fame and money, and still do,
> How what we do to get them can make us sorry...."

In 1984 the Nicholas Roerich Museum in New York City approached McDowell about starting a book-publishing venture. Proponents of this idea were Frederick Morgan and Paula Dietz, editors of *The Hudson Review,* who were then and continue to be supporters and publishers of McDowell's work (*The Hudson Review* had originally published "Quiet Money"). The Nicholas Roerich Museum proposed that it would fund the production of two books of poetry a year, and McDowell and Jarman, as editors of *The Reaper,* would provide their editorial and production skills to choose and publish the books. This proposal came at a propitious time for McDowell. He had met Lysa Howard, an artist and designer, who became his wife in 1985, and he had stopped teaching at Indiana State University at Evansville and decided to return to California. Amid the upheaval of moving to a new home and job, Story Line Press was born. Jarman, who had taken a position at Vanderbilt University in Nashville, Tennessee, served as co-editor and publisher for the first five years of the press, then resigned. McDowell and Howard settled in Santa Cruz, California, and set about making Story Line a successful small press that publishes serious literature.

Since its creation, Story Line Press has gone from publishing two books of poetry a year to publishing more than a dozen titles a year in poetry, fiction, and nonfiction. McDowell's vision has been solely responsible for this growth. He has published novels by Fred Viebahn and Maxine Kumin, collections of short fiction by Barbara Haas and Terence Winch, and a verse play by Rita Dove, along with helpful writers' guides and aids to writing by Michael J. Bugeja, Beth Baruch Joselow, and Alfred Corn. Yet, poetry has remained the primary focus of Story Line Press. Especially through the Nicholas Roerich Poetry Prize, which includes publication of a first book of poetry, McDowell has encouraged younger poets who work in narrative and/or traditional verse forms. Such emerging young poets as Daniel Anderson, Kate Light, Amy Uyematsu, and Greg Williamson owe publication of their first books to McDowell. He has also published books by older poets such as Sydney Lea and Paul Lake, associated with the New Narrative and New Formalist Movements. McDowell has also initiated a series of anthologies and critical books that have made a mark on the current scene. With anthologies such as *A Formal Feeling Comes: Poems in Form by Contemporary Women* (1994) and *Rebel Angels: 25 Poets of the New Formalism* (1996) and collections of essays such as *Expansive Poetry: Essays on the New Narrative & the New Formalism* (1989) and *Poetry After Modernism* (1991), Story Line Press has helped to define the various ways in which American poets are returning to traditional forms. McDowell, as publisher and editor, has motivated and kept going some of the most interesting strains in American poetry after Modernism.

Becoming a full-time editor and publisher, while moving the press three times over the course of fifteen years (McDowell now resides in southern Oregon, in the city of Ashland, with his wife and three children), McDowell still managed a prodigious amount of his

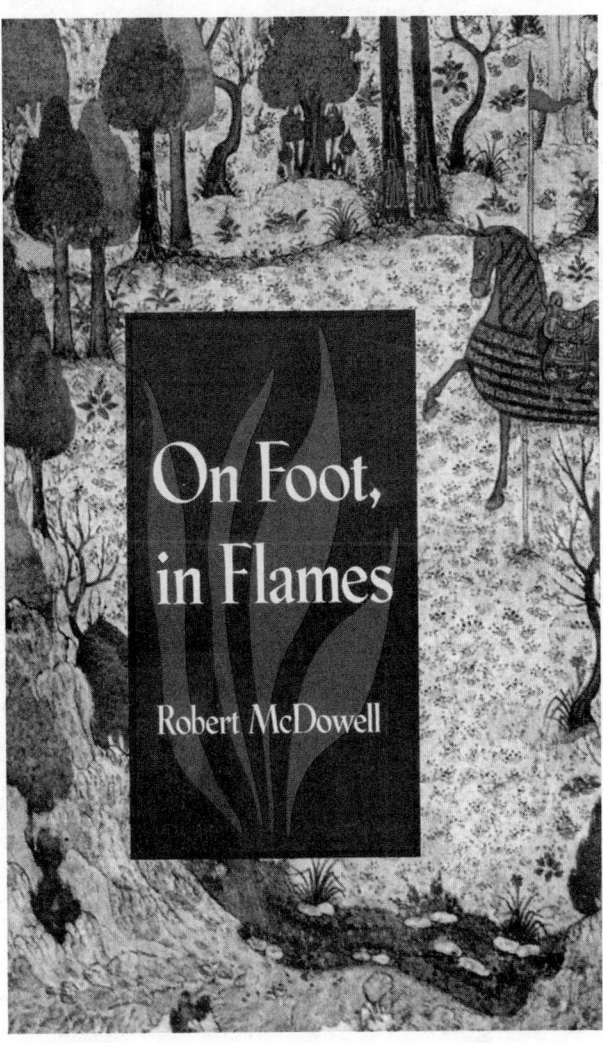

Paperback cover for McDowell's 2002 collection of narrative poems, including "Red Foxes," about a dispossessed farm family (Richland County Public Library)

own work. Holt published *Quiet Money* in 1987. It collected more than ten years' worth of poetry, mainly in the narrative mode, and the reviews that greeted it recognized both the emphasis on storytelling and the choice of subjects; parallels were drawn to Carver's fiction as well as to Frost and Robinson. In 1989 Story Line Press published *How I Came to Know Fish,* a translation from the Czech by McDowell and Jindriska Badal of the stories of Ota Pavel; New Directions published a paperback version a year later. McDowell edited *Poetry After Modernism,* which assembled essays by various authors on subjects ranging from business to religion, all in relation to poetry; McDowell also contributed an essay about the audience for poetry. The University of Michigan approached McDowell to revise Harvey Gross's classic 1964 text, *Sound and Form in Modern Poetry.* This extensive project was finally published in 1996. Meanwhile, the editor and publisher continued to write his own poetry, resulting in the publication of a book-length poem, *The Diviners,* in 1995.

The Diviners follows the lives of an American family—a mother, father, and son—through five decades. Divided in five sections titled respectively, "The Fifties," "The Sixties," "The Seventies," "The Eighties," and "The Nineties," the poem focuses especially on the son, Tom, a modern Telemachus, estranged from both parents; his mother, Eleanor, an unfaithful Penelope who dies of cancer; and his father, Al, "Boss," a bullying Odysseus whose wandering is confined to the limousine that carries him back and forth to work. The poem is entirely in blank verse, a form McDowell employed for only a few of the narratives in *Quiet Money.* At times there is a quality to the rhythm and the imagery, a kind of glaring brightness and bluntness reminiscent of the landscape of McDowell's childhood, that disguises the mythic features of the poem in ways that recall television. Parts of *The Diviners* read as if Homer had returned to direct the television show *The Wonder Years*. The morning conversation that begins "The Sixties" is a good example:

> "Just tell me what to say in my report,"
> Says Tom. Al swirls the coffee in his Answer Cup
> And tables his spoon.
>   "Ok," he says, "what class?"
>
> "It's history again," Tom sighs. "I'm stumped."
>
> He feels most like a grain of cereal.
> "I hate the subject," says the shrinking boy
> As Eleanor walks in with a photo album.
>
> "What subject do you hate?" she wants to know,
> Then focuses on glossy 8 X 10s.
> Al rubs his jaw and asks
>   "What period?"
>
> "The Forties. Shoulder pads," says Eleanor.
>
> "You mean," Al says, "those styles that hide the fact
> A woman's got no build beneath the tent."
>
> "The concept works for fat men, too," she says,
> A bit too cheerily. Al rubs his gut.

This scene is one of unusual harmony. Tom and his parents form a dysfunctional family, to say the least, but to paraphrase Leo Tolstoy, it is dysfunctional in its own way. The most moving passages in the book include Eleanor's and Al's individual descents into the underworlds of psychosis and alcoholism, respectively, and death. In a reversal of American history, Tom returns to his family's roots, in Ireland, with his wife, Elaine, an African American writer. The conclusion of the poem suggests that *The Diviners* is an epic in reverse, in which the hero disowns his birthright as an American in order to remake his identity. Strangely, Tom's disavowal of his past reflects the American desire to transcend history. The poem ends with Tom and Elaine in Wales, the night before they are to cross to Ireland:

> In bed Tom lies awake to watch the moon,
> And sees the great migrations circling back,
> The children home in lands their elders fled,
> Back home among their births and burials.
> The town clock strikes the hour. It's nearly dawn.
> Tom hears the sheep and cattle in the fields,
> The blacksmith strike his anvil, the whisk of brooms
> On cobbled streets of slowly rising steam.
> *We're old but we've forgotten nothing,* he thinks.
> Asleep, Elaine moves close. He breathes her in.
> The ferry for Dun Laoghaire sails at seven.

The challenge to the reader in the final line—to pronounce *Dun Laoghaire*—enacts in a small way the challenge of the entire poem: to see the American quest for identity as a willful return to an alien place of origin, which one chooses to make familiar once more.

McDowell's later poetry, which has been published in journals and limited editions and collected in *On Foot, in Flames* (2002), includes medium-length narratives such as "Red Foxes," a story of a family removed from its home on a farm, and "The Pact," about a wife's betrayal of her husband and their collusion to hide the death of her lover. The settings of these poems reflect McDowell's residence in rural Oregon for more than ten years, and the poems have about them some of Robinson Jeffers's sense, derived from Thomas Hardy, of the uneasy correspondence between people and place. McDowell has also been working, for the first time in twenty years, in the short, formal lyric. Many of the poems in *On Foot, in Flames* celebrate his wife and children and their attempt to live close to the earth. One of the most moving of these is "Elegy in August," a poem for his sister, who died by her own hand nearly twenty years earlier: "Sleep, little sister, far from pain. / Water smooths out stones in the river / As memory calms the chaos / You left behind." In its formality and imagery, this elegy displays the lyricism Robert McDowell has rediscovered in his poetry.

Papers:

Correspondence and manuscripts from *The Reaper,* a periodical edited by Robert McDowell and Mark Jarman between 1980 and 1989, are held by the Stanford University Library.

Bruce Meyer
(23 April 1957 -)

T. L. Ponick
Washington Times

and

F. S. Ponick
Music Educators National Conference (MENC)

BOOKS: *The Tongues between Us* (London, Ont.: Southwestern Ontario Poetry Press, 1981);

The Aging of America (Toronto: Aloysius Press, 1982);

Steel Valley, by Meyer, James Deahl, and Gilda Mekler (Toronto: Aureole Point Press, 1984);

In Their Words: Interviews with Fourteen Canadian Writers, by Meyer and Brian O'Riordan (Toronto & Buffalo, N.Y.: Anansi, 1984);

Profiles in Canadian Literature: Leonard Cohen (Toronto: Dundurn Press, 1986);

The Open Room (Windsor, Ont.: Black Moss Press, 1989; Buxton, U.K.: Aquila, 1989);

Lives and Works: Interviews with Canadian Writers, by Meyer and O'Riordan (Windsor, Ont.: Black Moss Press, 1991);

Profiles in Canadian Literature: Frank Prewett (Toronto: Dundurn Press, 1991);

Profiles in Canadian Literature: Robert Service (Toronto: Dundurn Press, 1991);

Radio Silence (Windsor, Ont.: Black Moss Press, 1992);

Goodbye Mr. Spalding (Windsor, Ont.: Black Moss Press, 1996);

The Presence (Windsor, Ont.: Black Moss Press, 1999; Ashland, Ore.: Story Line Press, 1999);

Anywhere (Toronto: Exile Editions, 2000);

The Golden Thread: A Reader's Journey through the Great Books (Toronto: HarperFlamingo, 2000);

The Spirit Bride (Toronto: Exile Editions, 2002).

OTHER: *Poetry Markets for Canadians,* edited by Meyer and James Deahl (Toronto, 1983; revised, Toronto: League of Canadian Poets, 1987);

Arrivals: Canadian Poetry in the Eighties, edited by Meyer (Greenfield, N.Y.: Greenfield Review, 1986);

Bruce Meyer (photograph by John Reeves; courtesy of the author)

Frank Prewett, *The Selected Poems of Frank Prewett,* edited by Meyer and Barry Callaghan (Toronto: Exile Editions, 1987);

Separate Islands: Contemporary British and Irish Poetry, edited by Meyer and Carolyn Meyer (Kingston, Ont.: Quarry Press, 1987);

Peter Stevens, *Swimming in the Afternoon: Selected Poems of Peter Stevens,* edited by Meyer (Windsor, Ont.: Black Moss Press, 1992);

The Stories: Contemporary Short Fiction Written in English, edited by Meyer (Toronto: Prentice Hall, 1997);

The Reader: Contemporary Short Fiction and Writing Strategies, edited by Meyer and Carolyn Meyer (Toronto: Prentice Hall, 2001);

We Wasn't Pals: Canadian Poetry and Prose of the First World War, edited by Meyer and Callaghan (Toronto: Exile Editions, 2001).

Bruce Meyer has been the chief Canadian champion of New Formalism, having aligned himself with the movement since the late 1980s. He is also one of the few New Formalists with a firm grounding in the tradition of the English lyric and has relied upon this background to break the mold of what Canadian poetry had been in the latter half of the twentieth century. In fact, he regards his work in prosody as an act of defiance against the status quo of poetry in Canada, resolutely forging ahead with traditional English forms as his guideposts in a literary context that has forgotten what tradition is. His poetry has been closely aligned with poets Molly Peacock and Dana Gioia. Canadian identity and experience, history, storytelling, family, love, the play of form, and playfulness with form—all these are hallmarks of his verse. He strives to discover the music in a life that otherwise can be prosaic, in a country that is prosaic, and in a Canadian language that has lost its sense of what good prose and poetry should be. Today he serves as the northernmost voice of New Formalism.

Bruce Miller Meyer was born in Toronto, Canada, on 23 April 1957. His mother is Margaret Ann Miller Meyer, and his father is George Homer Meyer. He has one sister, Carolyn Margaret Meyer, with whom he co-edited a textbook in 2001. He became interested in literature at an early age, teaching himself to read by the age of four, making his first attempts at writing poetry when he was six, and publishing his first poem professionally at the age of twelve. He was educated in the Toronto public school system, but his family was perhaps the greatest influence on his eventual career path.

Meyer's maternal grandfather, William Miller, loved the poems and ballads of Robert Service and recited many of them to his grandson from memory. Grandfather Miller was a sports enthusiast as well, instilling in his grandson the Canadian national passion for ice hockey and his own love for baseball, taking his grandson many times to Maple Leaf Stadium to witness the summertime heroics of Toronto's International League Triple A team.

Ida Evelyn Miller, Meyer's maternal grandmother, frequently read poetry to her grandson, constantly reminding him that one could have no higher calling in life than to be a poet. She particularly liked the poetry of Henry Wadsworth Longfellow and took her grandson through the American poet's house on a tour of Cambridge, Massachusetts, when Meyer was about ten. Ever practical, Grandmother Miller also became fluent in Chinese in order to teach Sunday school to Chinese children, an accomplishment that later served as an inspiration for the second part of her grandson's poem, "Speaking Chinese." Meyer's mother, Margaret, was a poetry aficionado as well, reading to him great quantities of the poetry of William Wordsworth from her cherished John Drinkwater anthologies.

Meyer's paternal grandfather, American Ernest Meyer, had a knack for business. He founded the first washing-machine company in Canada, although it went out of business in 1929 along with many other Canadian businesses. As a result he went into the laundry supplies business, a related area where he once again tried to make ends meet. He found he had to learn Chinese in order to be able to converse with his main clientele in Toronto. His story is told in the first part of "Speaking Chinese" (published in *The Presence,* 1999), as he

> . . . taught himself Chinese,
> traded goods for cash and Chinese cash,
> and gradually rebuilt the family business
> in bluing and buttons and collar starch,
> haggling in tongue with Chinese launders
> and out-talking them in kind. As an old man,
> who'd seen his fortunes rise and fall and rise
> again, he dressed each morning in a clean shirt,
> buttoned his waistcoat and white kid spats
> and carried a Chinese dollar, just in case–

Ernest Meyer's wife, Kathleen Kerr Meyer, was a devotee of William Shakespeare, and her grandson eventually inherited her well-worn, leather-bound volumes of Shakespeare's works. Meyer never knew his paternal grandparents, however, as both had died before he was born.

By the time he reached college age, Meyer had determined that literature and literary study would be his life. His mother, an alumna (1950) of Victoria College of the University of Toronto, had once asked him, "Do you want to go here some day?" In 1976 he decided that he did, enrolling as an English major. At Victoria he earned his bachelor of arts degree, majoring in honors English and Renaissance studies, the first time this particular degree path had been offered at the school. During his course of studies he continued to

Paperback cover for Meyer's 1992 collection, which includes "The Death of Grass," about an aging baseball player observing the introduction of Astroturf (courtesy of the author)

write free-verse poetry, accumulating enough work to send out twenty submissions to various magazines after his first year at the university. Upon returning with his parents from a family trip to England, he found twenty rejection slips awaiting him in the accumulated mail. Nonetheless, these rejections did not discourage him, nor did the initially negative opinions of one of his professors, Jay Macpherson, a protégée of British poet and novelist Robert Graves. Macpherson had won the Governor General's Award the year Meyer was born and had been a major influence on poet and writer Margaret Atwood nearly two decades previous. Upon reading some of Meyer's work, Macpherson informed the young poet that his verse was "lucid and intelligent, but possessed the meter and rhythm of prose." She was convinced he could do better.

Around this time Macpherson initiated a series of Friday prosody classes as an adjunct to her course on Romantic literature. During the prosody class, classic poems of Wordsworth, Percy Bysshe Shelley, and the other English Romantics were dissected and examined for craft and meaning, and Meyer found the class to be a revelation. While his family had schooled him in the tradition of the classics, it had never occurred to Meyer or to most other aspiring Canadian poets of the time to imagine writing poetry in anything other than free verse. Indeed, the only other Canadian poet at that time writing in meter and rhyme was Richard Outram. In Canada, meter and rhyme were almost like forbidden speech. Academic orthodoxy dictated that there was no real tradition of metrical poetry in Canada, no demonstrable connection between Canadian verse and the poetry of Edwardian and twentieth-century Georgian England. However, Meyer was intrigued by what he was learning in Macpherson's class and began to experiment with adding metrical and rhyming elements to his own poetry.

Meyer also studied extensively with Northrop Frye, perhaps the most important literary scholar of Canada and also a teacher of Gioia. Frye offered a graduate course in "Literary Symbolism" that really turned out to be a course in close literary reading. This course served as a foundation for Meyer's developing capabilities as a scholar and a critic in his own right.

Meyer and other younger Canadian poets at this time were being stymied in their efforts to gain a reading public by the rigorous gatekeeping of the League of Canadian Poets. Without becoming a member, a poet had difficulty marketing a book manuscript to Canadian publishers. But unless he had already published a book manuscript, a young poet could not become a member of the league. Meyer offered to found an associate membership branch for the league. He was taken up on his offer, and he made a permanent success of this junior branch, serving as its leader from 1980 to 1983.

By the time he was awarded his bachelor's degree in 1980, graduating with distinction, Meyer had also won the prestigious E. J. Pratt Gold Medal in 1980 for his poem "By Wood and Wire," later published in *The Open Room* (1989), bringing the medal back to Victoria College after a twenty-year absence. It had last been won by distinguished Victoria alumna Atwood. Meyer was awarded the medal a second time in 1981 as he worked on his master's degree.

During the summer of 1981 Meyer made another literary pilgrimage to England, this time with nearly disastrous consequences. While staying at a hotel in Tunbridge Wells, he and many other guests contracted typhoid fever, apparently because of improper food handling. Several of the victims died. Meyer himself almost succumbed to the disease at Westminster Hospital but eventually recovered. He left England in a severely weakened state, however, with his weight having plummeted to 110 pounds. For many months after his return to Canada he required assistance in order to attend his classes. He eventually achieved a full recovery and in 1982 was awarded his master's degree by the university, with a focus on modern poetry and literature.

Unbowed by his near-death experience and eager to continue his research on English prosody and the work of contemporary English poets, Meyer cashed in his life savings and a small inheritance from his maternal grandparents in 1983 to make an extended literary pilgrimage to Great Britain. During this sojourn he spent considerable time with such poets as Peter Redgrove, D. M. Thomas, Charles Tomlinson, George Szirtes, and Andrew Motion and contemplated doing a book of interviews.

At this time poets Richard Howard and Szirtes reinforced Macpherson's belief that Meyer's future in poetry would be considerably enhanced were he to achieve greater mastery of meter and rhyme. Szirtes himself frequently wrote in regular quatrains, and under his influence Meyer's verse began to acquire greater polish and professionalism. North American literary magazines continued to display a reflexive hostility toward this type of poetry. While Meyer continued to submit his poetry to these markets, he largely failed to achieve any recognition for his work, eventually amassing more than three hundred rejections.

Returning to Canada, Meyer enrolled in 1985 in the doctoral program at McMaster University and decided to write his dissertation on Howard Sergeant, a well-known and respected English literary editor and a godfather to many contemporary British poets. Sergeant, a onetime lover of writer Muriel Spark, turned out for Meyer to be a fountain of literary information as well as a substantial figure in his own right. A frequent guest at Sergeant's house, Meyer had ample opportunity to quiz the famous editor on all manner of literary news. During one of these conversations Meyer brought up the name of Canadian poet David Wevill, whose poem "Birth of a Shark" Meyer had initially discovered and admired in A. Alvarez's popular anthology, *New Poetry* (1962). Wevill's most notorious brush with fame had been his inadvertent involvement in the Sylvia Plath/Ted Hughes marital whirlwind. Wevill seemed to have disappeared from the scene after its denouement, and Sergeant was no longer certain where Wevill was.

Looking into the matter, Meyer discovered that Wevill had been teaching in relative obscurity at the University of Texas in Austin. Shortly thereafter, the two met almost by chance when the older poet was visiting Toronto. They struck up a friendship immediately, with Wevill taking on the role of mentor to the younger poet, teaching him how to handle emotion in poetry as well as the process of seeking and finding the truth in the image. Not long after this meeting Meyer received a call from Barry Callaghan, Wevill's Canadian editor. Callaghan needed help in editing a book of Wevill's selected poems, a difficult project that had already caused two previous poet editors to withdraw. For Meyer the daunting task was almost like the "sword in the stone," a pivotal moment in discovering and mastering the holistics of image, meaning, and form. The book was eventually retitled *Other Names for the Heart: New and Selected Poems, 1964–1984* (1985).

Manuscript page for a poem by Meyer. South Baymouth is on the southern coast of Manitoulin Island, Ontario (courtesy of the author).

In a 1985 letter to Meyer, American poet Richard Howard had written "There is no right or wrong way to write: there is only your way; but try taking your poems apart and using meter, rhyme and form." Inspired by this encouragement, Meyer kept honing his poetic output but continued to lack a publisher for the kind of work he was producing. By late 1985 he had essentially completed the manuscript that became his first book of poetry, *The Open Room,* but it was going nowhere. Providence intervened in the form of two of his teachers, Canadian poets Milton Acorn and Gwendolyn MacEwen. Acorn was one of the few more-established Canadian poets who was willing to take an unprejudiced view of helping out younger poets—even younger poets such as Meyer, who were inclined to go against the prevailing free-verse, Modernist vein that was sanctioned in Canadian poetry and in the academy. Acorn sat down with Meyer on many occasions and helped him hammer out the music in a problem line, training the younger poet's ear much in the way that McPherson had done in Meyer's undergraduate years.

Taking advantage of graduate scholarships and travel fellowships in 1986, 1987, and 1988, Meyer again began to travel, mostly to England, but occasionally to Texas to consult with Wevill and to use the extensive manuscript collection at the Harry Ransom Humanities Research Center. At this time also Meyer and Callaghan began to collaborate on an exciting project to revive the literary fortunes of Frank Prewett, a Canadian poet who had ended up in England as a result of his combat in World War I. Graves had urged Callaghan to look into the matter of Prewett, and both Callaghan and Meyer were startled to discover in this poet the "missing link," which was thought not to exist, between Canadian poetry and twentieth-century Georgian poetry. Intriguingly, Prewett had been fast friends with Siegfried Sassoon, and the Canadian's highly metrical rhyming war poetry and pastoral poetry were admired by Sassoon and others throughout literary England. The publication of Prewett's selected poems, under the editorship of Meyer and Callaghan, in 1987 not surprisingly caused a ruckus throughout Canadian academe, since it upset the current Modernist orthodoxy. This controversy further convinced Meyer of the correctness of his own poetic direction and of his attempts to reconnect Canadian poetry to its English literary roots.

Meyer continued work on his doctorate while he taught composition and Canadian literature at McMaster in 1987–1988. Meyer was awarded his Ph.D. in 1988, having completed his doctoral dissertation, "Sergeant of 'Outposts': One Editor's Role in Post-War British Poetry," on the life and work of Sergeant. The focus of the dissertation was Sergeant's role in shaping various aesthetic movements and promoting the work of the new poets who participated in them and were associated with his quarterly literary magazine. The Social Sciences and Humanities Research Council of Canada awarded Meyer a postdoctoral fellowship in Canadian literature in the years 1988–1990.

In the late 1980s MacEwen pushed Meyer's first book at Black Moss Press in Windsor, Ontario, eventually convincing the press to publish it. Meyer's book was accepted at the press a week after MacEwen's death. *The Open Room* includes two poems—"A Cold Cutting Stone" and "The White Flower"—that are posthumously dedicated to Acorn and MacEwen respectively.

In his elegy to Acorn, Meyer compares his mentor to the ancient Indian cutting implement Acorn had discovered, a carved stone whose weathered outline conjured up for the older poet a life whose stories and songs still sing beyond the ages. The memory of this stone has had the same effect upon Acorn's student:

. . . I can't believe you are dead.

An old Indian woman carved her grief.
The granite lives to pay the cost
And like granite you offered up relief.
One good story or we are lost.

In a poem dedicated to the memory of MacEwen, Meyer imagines her as holding a white flower "waiting to be pressed like a poem among the pages," a flower/poem that, like the spirit of MacEwen, radiates a soft moonglow of memory, passing it on to another generation:

Starlight, starbright, I knew a woman who sang
Of the plucked moon blooming on an August night.
She gave me the white flower in her hand.

While Meyer can be gentle in his elegies, he also stands witness to the harshness of the world. In "Blind at Dieppe" (from *The Open Room*) he recalls in rough, accentual lines and plain speech the experiences of a Canadian soldier who lost his sight in World War I:

. . . Be still
they said as a dozen hands
probed my body for photographs.
An arm led me somewhere,
Soft hands of a Hamilton girl
Caressing me at Wasaga Beach.

I went into Dieppe with my eyes open,
A truck driver from Stoney Creek.
I came out in darkness and damn
Those who tell us what our history is.

Paperback cover for Meyer's 1999 collection, which includes poems about his wife and daughter (courtesy of the author)

Meyer took a position at the University of Windsor, near Detroit, Michigan, where he began to teach a course in creative writing in addition to offering courses in Canadian literature and Canadian fiction. He returned to the University of Toronto in 1991, teaching in the School of Continuing Studies, where he added courses in poetry and the Great Books to his repertoire. At this time he also began his groundbreaking work in developing the then-new field of distance education. He continued to teach at the various colleges in the University of Toronto system and at various campuses of Seneca College throughout the 1990s, broadening his scope into modern fiction, drama, and British literature. In 1996 he was given the University of Toronto School of Continuing Studies Excellence in Teaching Award, and in that same year he taught a course at Skidmore College on the Great Books.

During all this time Meyer retained his active interest in baseball, becoming an avid fan of the Toronto Blue Jays. His own amateur baseball playing days had ended on the McMaster graduate school team when he tore a rotator cuff, but this mishap never diminished his enthusiasm for the sport. Marty Gervais, his publisher at Black Moss, bet him a hot dog that he could not come up with a poem about Astroturf. He won the hot dog for his poem "The Death of Grass," devouring his prize during a game at Tiger Stadium in Detroit. The poem eventually found its way into his second collection, *Radio Silence,* which was published in 1992. The title of the volume, with its strong allusion to protective measures undertaken during both world wars, is also meant by the poet as an ironic reference to his countrymen who live in a twilight zone, lacking a national identity and fearing to discover one. Perhaps one of these Canadians is the appropriately anonymous major leaguer in "The Death of Grass," a kind of Tennysonian Ulysses, having led a life of glory and adventure but wondering now if it is finally time for him to hang up his spikes.

As a young lad, the ballplayer yields easily to the heroic temptations of the baseball diamond, his field of dreams:

> You can believe anything you want
> they told him on his way up to the show:
> he chose to believe in grass—the green sea
> that washes over time when a pop fly hangs
> like a lover's promise in an arc through centre;
> the continent of pain when inches give way
> to miles on the tip of a glove; the reach
> that will always be bigger than a man;
> the cool green smell of life itself
> smiling up at the innings of August heat,
> and the green that shone beneath the lights
> like a sea of emeralds awash in voice.

Like the grass, the young ballplayer is pliant and alive, stretching his talents each day toward the shining sun, forever flowing and young. But not really forever:

> and then like a lover who suddenly leaves
> that season when you swing and miss,
> swing again and whiff again, error in the ninth
>
> on a pop fly, slip on a misplayed catch
> and watch from the bench as age prevails.
> And then came the season they laid the rug,
> "for a more even game" the owners said—
> but the death of grass was the death of belief.

Astroturf replaces the grass and marks the passing of time. The game has changed and so has the player. The game may again be new; the hitters more empowered by the harder surfaces; but he himself is no longer young. Meyer's poetic powers have taken a great stride toward maturity in this poem. He is still employing plain speech, accentual rather than regularly iambic lines. But, unlike so many free-verse, Modernist poets, he employs visual techniques for a purpose, not randomly. As the player "whiffs again, error in the ninth," the stanza breaks to the next line, and the reader feels the error "on a pop fly." Perceptually, metaphorically, and in actuality, the player is now a second-stringer slouching toward retirement. Like the grass, his time is past, but he still wants to believe:

> . . . There are no certainties
> in this game—only believers who swing
> at something hurled split-fingered out of forever,
> and sunlight on grass as green as last year.

In this poem Meyer clearly demonstrates his adherence to the developing tenets of Expansive/New Formalist poetry. His poetry is outer directed, a narrative—a story that, however, is tightly compressed, making it different from short fiction. The meter is rough, not regular as in Victorian poetry, and the speech, while pursuing an extended metaphor, is plain and down-to-earth, as befits a ballplayer with simple aspirations. The poet, moreover, never makes an appearance. In "Death of Grass" and other poems in *Radio Silence,* Meyer is breaking his own "silence," declaring in each poem his clean break with the tired literary Modernism of Canada.

Hockey also is a subject in *Radio Silence* in the poem "Road Hockey." Meyer visits the national pastime of Canada once again in "Minors," a poem in his fourth collection, *Anywhere* (2000). The central character in "Minors" is a stand-in for the "dying god" archetype in ancient Greek literature. But modern heroism and defeat occur on a lower plane. In "Minors," the young man has just been cut from a minor-league hockey club and trudges home with only memories of imagined glory:

> . . . numb as two minutes frozen in time.
> *Someday,* he'd vowed, *I'll skate with the stars.*

In his sports poems Meyer again offers an alternative to the *I*-dominated personal lyric so characteristic of the free-verse confessional poetry that had held America and Canada in its thrall since at least the 1950s. Meyer's sports poetry proves to be "expansive" in the best sense of the word by once again making available to poets the subjects of everyday life as opposed to the crabbed introspection of the Modernist introvert. Meyer's "I" in "Minors" is clearly a persona, a protagonist who is not the poet, although the poet might have experienced similar travails. By standing outside the narrative rather than within it, Meyer exploits his talent as a storyteller and places his craft in the service of his readers rather than confining it to narrow personal ends.

By the early 1990s Meyer's poetry had begun to attract greater attention both north and south of the Canadian border. He had learned of the Expansive/New Formalist movement in the United States and had become friends with Gioia and Peacock, both of whom influenced his work. As a result of his new friendship with Gioia, Meyer arranged to travel to the annual West Chester University Poetry Conference in West Chester, Pennsylvania, in 1997. At this conference Gioia and other noted New Formalists held court, teaching a new generation of poets the art and craft of formal verse, and Meyer easily made new friendships in the growing movement.

Meyer was awarded the Ruth Cable Memorial Prize for poetry in 1997. In March 1998, he was invited to give a poetry reading and present a lecture on Canadian poetry at the University of Southern Mississippi in Hattiesburg, Mississippi. In May of that same year he served as the representative for the University of Toronto at the opening in London of Canada House, once the lavish Canadian Embassy in Trafalgar Square, but now rehabilitated to serve as a cultural gateway for Londoners to Canada and

Paperback cover for the 2000 collection in which Meyer explores ideas about heaven (courtesy of the author)

North America. Meyer was instrumental in creating content for revolutionary, state-of-the-art Web kiosks designed by the teaching/learning subsidiary of Bell Canada to enable interactive, walk-through cyber tours in English and French.

In addition to his own work Meyer continued to champion the work of other Canadian writers and poets, some of them neglected for decades. He worked with Claude Lemoine at the National Library of Canada to create a special manuscript collection of the works of Prewett. This project finalized the work Meyer had begun in the 1980s and ultimately resulted in the retrieval and publication of a missing decade in Canadian literature, chiefly the literature of the "trench" writers of World War I. Meyer continued promoting these writers to win for them their rightful place in Canadian history in the 2001 collection *We Wasn't Pals: Canadian Poetry and Prose of the First World War*, which he co-edited with Callaghan.

In 1999 Meyer was awarded the position of writer-in-residence at the creative-writing program of the University of Texas at Austin during November. In the same year Story Line Press published Meyer's third book of poems, *The Presence*. He also began to work with the Canadian Broadcasting Corporation (CBC) to develop and air a radio series based on his Great Books courses. An immediate hit, the programs were packaged into a boxed series, becoming the network's number one best-selling audiocassettes. Building on their success, Meyer spun off a book on the same subject—*The Golden Thread: A Reader's Journey through the Great Books*, published by HarperFlamingo in Toronto in 2000. It became an instant Canadian national best-seller. Meyer's approach in *The Golden Thread* was greatly influenced by the work of his onetime mentor Frye. But the younger writer attempted to create a less opaque popular work, more accessible to the general reader. As in his poetry, Meyer sought in his prose to increase the appetite of the public for literary works.

Meyer married Kerry Johnston, a CBC journalist, on 21 May 1994. The couple's daughter, Kathleen Charlotte, was born on 18 October 1997. Meyer commemorated both events in "Mavety Street," from *The Presence*.

> When moonlight stole like guilty cats
>   and summer owned the air
> I kissed your lips on Mavety Street
>   and tousled your starlit hair.
>
> Grave windows on the darkened rows,
>   the abandoned dairy's shell
> cast off their grimy prose of life
>   and wished two lovers well . . .
>
> And moonlight stole the years away
>   and summers drank the air,
> I thirst for that kiss on Mavety Street
>   and the starlight in your hair.

Dedicated to his wife, "Mavety Street" is a celebration of the magical emotion surrounding a new and passionate romance. Yet, in the developing New Formalist/New Narrative tradition, the poet distances himself and uses a persona to convey the wonder of young love as seen from the perspective of an older man who has left something in the past. Meyer creates a true narrative poem rather than a conventional confessional-style lyric.

The short lyric sequence the poet dedicated to his young daughter is more personal. The first three lyrics celebrate the mystery of her new life and its innocence. But the fourth, titled "The Intercession" (from "Four Lullabies for a Newborn Daughter" in *The Presence*), is a modern Song of Experience:

> I will not let the stranger in the door;
> The hour is late, my child is sleeping
> And the shadows on the cold street pour
> Their grieving hearts out. I am keeping
> Watch over a promise my parents made
> One night in the summer before my breath,
> And with their sighs shield those afraid
> Of life from the reckless courage of death.

The poet-father's responsibility as a knight-protector suddenly reveals itself, and the lighter tone characteristic of the earlier lyrics in the sequence changes abruptly. A warm bed, a secure life, the carefree happiness of a gurgling and cooing infant are always threatened by what lies outside the nest, those "shadows on the cold street" from which the new father, "watching over a promise" of new life, in the tradition of his own parents, must now protect his newborn. The poem is a somber ending to the sequence, an appreciation of a father's responsibilities and of the yin and the yang of the complexities of life, not unlike the somber musical postscript that concludes Robert Schumann's piano suite, "Scenes from Early Childhood" ("Kinderscenen").

Meyer served as director of the Writing and Literature Program at the University of Toronto School of Continuing Studies, where in January 1997 he founded Canada's largest creative-writing program, which he ran until 2003 when his desire to return to teaching convinced him of the need to return to the classroom. He is also National Literary Advisor to Leacock House in Orillia, Ontario, Canada's most visited literary tourist site, and is a regular summer teacher at Athol Murray Notre Dame College in Willcocks, Saskatchewan, where he offers an annual Great Books week.

Bruce Meyer remains somewhat unusual among Canadian poets. He persists in writing formal and loosely formal verse in a country whose poets, on the whole, are postmodernists working only in free verse. Meyer has tried to demonstrate, in such projects as his efforts to bring attention to the metrical verse of Prewett, that Canadian poetry has viable connections with English verse forms of the nineteenth century. Meyer himself is far more familiar to his countrymen for his popular work on Great Books than for his highly personal and individualistic poetry. His poetical works have, however, become better known in the United States, where he is recognized and honored as a valued member of the New Formalist community.

References:

Douglas Fetherling, "Books that Built a Civilization," *Ottawa Citizen,* 5 October 2000, p. C14;

Maureen Harris, "Prewett and Meyer: The Direction of Their Gaze," *Vic Report* (Toronto), 19, no. 12 (Winter 1990–1991): 14;

Andrew Mills, "Building Cultural Capital," *National Post* (Toronto), 22 August 2002, p. A13;

Neville Newman, "The Interview as a Literary Genre," *Brantford Expositor,* 20 June 1992, p C4.

Marilyn Nelson
(26 April 1946 -   )

Paul A. Griffith
Lamar University

See also the Marilyn Nelson Waniek entry in *DLB 120: American Poets Since World War II, Third Series.*

BOOKS: *For the Body,* as Marilyn Nelson Waniek (Baton Rouge & London: Louisiana State University Press, 1978);

The Cat Walked through the Casserole and Other Poems for Children, by Nelson, as Waniek, and Pamela Espeland (Minneapolis: Carolrhoda Books, 1984);

Mama's Promises, as Waniek (Baton Rouge & London: Louisiana State University Press, 1985);

The Homeplace, as Waniek (Baton Rouge & London: Louisiana State University Press, 1990);

Partial Truth, as Waniek (Willington, Conn.: Kutenai Press, 1992);

Magnificat, as Waniek (Baton Rouge & London: Louisiana State University Press, 1994);

The Fields of Praise: New and Selected Poems (Baton Rouge & London: Louisiana State University Press, 1997);

Triolets for Triolet (Willimantic, Conn.: Curbstone Press, 2001);

Carver: A Life in Poems (Asheville, N.C.: Front Street, 2001);

She-Devil Circus (West Chester, Pa.: Aralia Press, 2001).

OTHER: "The Space Where Sex Should Be: Toward a Definition of the Black American Literary Tradition," *Studies in Black Literature,* 6 (Fall 1975): 7–13;

"A Black Rainbow: Modern Afro-American Poetry," by Nelson, as Waniek, and Rita Dove, in *Poetry After Modernism,* edited by Robert McDowell (Brownsville, Ore.: Story Line Press, 1990), pp. 171–217;

"Marilyn Nelson," in *Contemporary Authors Autobiography Series,* volume 23, edited by Shelly Andrews (Detroit: Galc, 1996), pp. 247–267;

Rumors of Troy, edited by Nelson (Boston: Pearson Custom Publishing, 2001).

Marilyn Nelson (photograph by Fran Funk; courtesy of the author)

TRANSLATIONS: Pil Dahlerup, *Literary Sex Roles* (Minneapolis: Minnesota Women in Higher Education, 1975);

Halfdan Rasmussen, *Hundreds of Hens and Other Poems for Children,* translated by Nelson, as Waniek, and Pamela Espeland (Minneapolis: Black Willow, 1982);

Euripedes, *Hecuba,* in *Euripides, 1: Medea, Hecuba, Andromache, The Bacchae,* edited by David R. Slavitt and

Palmer Bovie, Penn Greek Drama Series (Philadelphia: University of Pennsylvania Press, 1998).

SELECTED PERIODICAL PUBLICATION–UNCOLLECTED: "Aborigine in the Citadel," *Hudson Review*, 53 (Winter 2001): 543–553.

Skillfully handling narrative and lyric forms, poet Marilyn Nelson evokes complex visions of life through a simple style, colloquial language, and functional allusions that often carry charming humor and ironic power. Nelson's sensibility is essentially religious; the speaking voice, often probling the interior life, is preoccupied with enduring spiritual ideals. The poet's "double-consciousness"–the dual awareness of African and American ancestry–impacts her search for poetic forms, as evident in her efforts to weave their literary traditions into a kind of collage. Her art also suggests her sense of the artist as mythmaker, reinterpreting the modern American ethos in light of traditional folk forms and values. Thus, metrical and formal elements of Euro-American traditional modes of expression–sonnets, villanelles, blank verse–and African American rhythmic praise-songs are fused into a medium that underlines the poet's sense of the complexity of her Americanness: her diverse personal and cultural mixture. Simultaneously, Nelson validates the cultural and aesthetic importance of African American folk forms such as the blues and the chanted sermon by weaving their racy vernacular expressions, imagery, and worldviews into both free verse and Western traditional forms.

Marilyn Rae Nelson was born in Cleveland, Ohio, on 26 April 1946 to Melvin M. Nelson, a United States Air Force officer, and Johnnie Mitchell Nelson, a teacher. She has a sister, Jennifer, and a brother, Melvin Jr. Her early life was spent on different military bases. In her essay for *Contemporary Authors Autobiography Series* (1996) she writes of her father, a navigator, that "my childhood was splendid with pride in the fact that he flew"; she adds that her mother, "with her proud stories of her family," gave her roots. She began writing while in elementary school and credits her sixth-grade teacher, Dorothy Gray of Kittery Point, Maine, with fostering her literary talents. Nelson earned her B.A. degree from the University of California, Davis, in 1968; her M.A. from the University of Pennsylvania in 1970; and a Ph.D. from the University of Minnesota in 1979. Her doctoral thesis was "The Schizoid Nature of the Implied Author in Twentieth-Century American Ethnic Novels."

Nelson served as a lay associate in the Lutheran Campus Ministry program at Cornell University between 1969 and 1970. She married Erdmann F. Waniek (pronounced Vonyek), a German graduate student she met at the University of Pennsylvania, in September 1970. For the next two years, Nelson taught at the Lane Community College in Eugene, Oregon, and at Reed College. The following year she and her husband spent in Denmark, teaching at Nørre Nissum Seminarium. Nelson began teaching English as an assistant professor at St. Olaf College in Northfield, Minnesota, but in 1978 she moved to the University of Connecticut at Storrs. Her first volume of poetry, *For the Body,* was published in that same year.

For the Body is dedicated to reconstituting the self, to unifying the fragments that structure the poet's consciousness. The synecdochic assemblage of parts and "bodies" chronicles pain, frustrations, pleasures, attainments, experiences, and values that conflict, shape, and sustain the self. Nelson says the poems celebrate not only the heart–"the most desperate organ"–but also the feet, belly, and legs, "all the working class / of the body."

Other bodies Nelson celebrates in this book are family, community, and the abstract body of faith. Such images and motifs thematically, stylistically, and structurally integrate *For the Body*. The three sections of the book, "Driving Home," "The Ice Cream Woman," and "The Language We Speak Is Not the One We Dream," cohere around the poet's engagement with metaphysical, ethical, and aesthetic subjects. In "My Grandfather Walks in the Woods" images of binary oppositions–life/death, winter/spring, black/white–relate concerns about ancestry and identity and probe a mythic interest in the human relationship to an enigmatic cosmos. Nelson's maternal grandfather, John Mitchell, had lost his family as a child when night riders attacked their farm; he was raised by a white family, but the sense of roots and family continuity was truncated. In the poem, the grandfather asks the trees, "are you my father?" In response, "They answer / with voices like wind / blowing away from him." Questions of belonging, of finding roots in the American landscape, have produced puzzling answers for many Americans of African ancestry.

Other expressions of this question of belonging are rendered in wryly ironic tones in "The American Dream" and "Home." The latter poem, recalling "I, Too" by Langston Hughes (1925), explores African American social exclusion. Nelson's speaker recalls being greeted, on her first day at school, by a sixth-grader who "aimed his eyes carefully, / and shot me with / america."

Poems such as "Other Women's Children" and "Churchgoing" validate spiritual living over the sterile and meaningless social and religious rituals the poet detects in American life. The speaker in "Churchgoing" fears that in white churches, Christian worship is being reduced to the "ruins" of a "dying cult" and "empty words we moderns merely chant." She has "come bearing the cancer of my doubt," but when the congregation finally sings a spiritual, its "simple melody, though sung all wrong / captures exactly what I think is faith." The speaker concludes:

> I sit alone, tormented in my heart
> by fighting angels, one group black, one white.
> The victory is uncertain, but tonight
> I'll lie awake again, and try to start
> finding the black way back to what we've lost.

"The Diet" shifts from ethical commitment to a musing on the relationship of art to life. The speaker ambivalently considers the visionary capacity of the poetic imagination, wondering if it is not an exercise wherein the "brain will eat itself." Ultimately, she acknowledges that art is both life-giving and life-denying. On the one hand, memory is a source of redeeming power; on the other hand, the poet warns, the artist eschews the solid food of reality for a spare "diet" of dreams. In "The Writer's Wife" the poet further examines this danger of abandoning life for art. Her ultimate position, however, is that the aesthetic imagination discovers spiritual truths that affirm, not substitute for, life.

In section 3, juxtaposing the language of speech with that of dream, "The Gloved Poet" and "Fish Poem" also examine the relationship between art and reality. The artist's imagination, compared to the cyclic force of nature, is endowed with a capacity for regenerating new and vital images of life, as in "Twist the Thread":

> Spring again.
> The same birds whistle
> their sweet marriages,
> the same trees
> weave out loops
> of the same new green.

If the poet can "knit the children right," she will have "The life complete in recollection, / The perfect past."

In 1979 Nelson divorced Erdmann Waniek and married Roger R. Wilkenfeld; she continued to publish under the name Marilyn Nelson Waniek, however, through 1995. *Hundreds of Hens and Other Poems for Children* appeared in 1982, a translation with Pamela Espeland from the works of Danish poet Halfdan Rasmussen. During that year, she also received a National Endowment for the Arts Grant. In 1984 and 1985, Nelson published *The Cat Walked through the Casserole and Other Poems for Children* (another collaboration with Espeland) and *Mama's Promises*.

Paperback cover for Nelson's 1990 collection of poems inspired by family history (Bruccoli Clark Layman Archives)

The children's book *The Cat Walked through the Casserole and Other Poems* is both entertaining and didactic. "If I Could Do Whatever I Wanted" humorously inverts adult authority and values from a child's perspective. "History" raises issues about the freedom of the imagination. Other poems seek to disarm common fears among children, such as the anxieties stemming from being adopted, or the torments of loneliness.

In her autobiographical essay, Nelson writes that she "hoped *Mama's Promises* would be read as a book of black feminist theology." Celebrating the figure of the mother, the work draws on patterns of imagery that invoke mythic suggestions of birth, life, and death. Archetype as well as cultural symbol, the mother is the source of promise in life and enduring values. In her notes to *The Fields of Praise: New and Selected Poems*

(1997), Nelson says, "I had originally intended 'Mama' of my second book . . . to be not only myself, my mother, and other mothers . . . but also the Divine Mother, the feminine face of God." The simple style and colloquial language function as vehicle for the humble but enduring folk spirit. The mother figure is an image also of the poet's larger vision of human creative resilience, as seen in "Wild Pansies" and "My Second Birth." "Cover Photograph" conveys these ideals of simplicity, strength, and creative endurance:

> I want to be as familiar
> as the woman in the background
> when the heroine is packing
> and the Yankee soldiers come.
> . . . .
> I want to be remembered
> with a simple name, like Mama:
> as an open door from creation,
> as a picture of someone you know.

"The Marriage Nightmare" and "Levitation with Baby" speak about escaping the stifling conditions of domesticity, adopting an ironic perspective on life. In "The Century Quilt" Nelson pays tribute to the visionary tradition from which the poet's creative consciousness originates: "Perhaps under this quilt / I'd dream of myself, / of my childhood of miracles, / . . . / of my mother's ochre gentleness / Within the dream of myself / perhaps I'd meet my son / or my other child, as yet unconceived."

Within black folk consciousness, biblical myths served as arenas of hope to oppressed lives. Nelson's long poem "I Dream the Book of Jonah," adopts this mythic tradition by reinterpreting the Old Testament story. Readers can see an association between Jonah and the peripatetic African American blues singer, a social castaway of the late nineteenth and early twentieth centuries who survives by his indomitable will and creative talents. He peers into the folk past while also looking upward toward divine inspiration. Nelson's imagination thus brings together the homely and the visionary.

Nelson, who was promoted to full professor at the University of Connecticut in 1988, has had other brief teaching appointments at New York University, Vanderbilt University, and the United States Military Academy. In 1990 she was granted a second National Endowment for the Arts Grant. Her next book of poetry, *The Homeplace* (1990), made the National Book Award list of finalists for 1991 and won the Anisfield-Wolf Award for Race Relations in 1992.

"The Homeplace" and "Wings," the two sections that make up *The Homeplace,* offer montage vistas on history and myth. In her autobiographical essay, Nelson notes that the first section in particular "was much influenced by my earlier work with fixed forms." Celebrating memory and tradition as constituents of identity, the section titles are thematically connected. Section 1, poems about Nelson's mother's family, promotes "home" values, featuring her ancestors' tenacious will to survive with pride and dignity. "The House on Moscow Street," about a home that had been in the family since 1872, is emblematic: in "a long sunny kitchen" Nelson's great-grandfather's wife "measured cornmeal / dreaming through the window / across the ravine and up to Shelby Hill / where she had borne their spirited, high-yellow brood."

The first sequence of poems in *The Homeplace* describes the relationship of Nelson's great-great-grandparents: Diverne, a slave, and Henry Tyler, a young white man. "Diverne's Waltz," "Annunciation," and "Chosen" continue to explore the familial past as a composite of history, human mores, and myths. Diverne's "waltz" is a wry and parodic analogue of Cinderella's ball:

> Taking her hands, Henry Tyler gives her a twirl
> and off they waltz. He swirls Diverne so fast
> her head kerchief unknots itself. He smiles
> down at Diverne's embarrassment, and gasps:
>
> *They blush!* Hearing the whispers from the walls,
> he sees men grin. His father shakes his head.
> But (*that dark rose . . .*) he dances.

The sonnets "Annunciation" and "Chosen" recall, as in William Butler Yeats's "Leda and the Swan," tales of the gods' sexual visitations to "chosen" mortals. The poet further suggests that the event is not about an ethical struggle between good and evil: "And it wasn't rape. / In spite of her raw terror. And his whip."

The vigor of Nelson's black dialect is remarkable. In the sonnet "Balance," for example, the colloquial expressions "*He watch her like a coonhound watch a tree*" and "*That hoe Diverne think she Marse Tyler's wife*" open and close, respectively, this traditionally formal structure and render it rather folksy. Diverne runs a gauntlet between black society and the white man whose mistress she is—a conflict that the folk and formal expressions underline. The poet seeks to reconcile these dichotomies, to balance, via her art, past and present, the African American folk and Western traditions of consciousness she inherits.

Section 2, "Wings," includes poems inspired by Melvin Nelson's experiences as a pilot in the air force; it is also a tribute to a pantheon of heroic pioneers, the Tuskegee Airmen, World War II pilots whose aspirations and successes challenged attitudes about African Americans as a subordinate social caste. "Porter" dramatizes this new arena of social and psychological freedom while lightly satirizing a social conscience that insists on seeing the ethnic community only as a servant class.

Disarming irony is typified in "Alderman," with images that defuse the grim reality of bigotry politically ambitious blacks had to circumvent. Similar wit and play inform "The Ballad of Aunt Geneva." The simple ballad measure, which emphasizes sound and rhythm, is an appropriate vehicle for Aunt Geneva's rather libertine, nonconformist lifestyle and her impossible relationship with the man who is her true love.

The Homeplace received favorable notice in *The Kenyon Review;* highlighting the variety of Nelson's themes and forms, Leslie Ullman remarked that the collection is "anecdotal and deeply affectionate." She adds that Nelson gives "individual dimension to the characters by shaping their stories" into traditional verse forms such as the sonnet, the villanelle, and the ballad. Nelson's "easy movement between poems in form and seemingly 'found' dramatic monologues," according to Ullman, "suggests that her own background as African American poet is a rich patchwork of traditions, and that her clearly organic sense of self and family history has moved her neither to embrace nor eschew current Formalist concerns." The fact that Nelson takes pride in her experiments with blank verse and terza rima further highlights this attitude.

Perhaps Nelson's most disturbing evocation of intense situations and states of mind, *Partial Truth* (1992) is a sonnet sequence about a marriage in crisis. "Recurring Dream," a resolution to the tensions, shows that the poet is at her best when she focuses on her two favorite themes: ancestry (her sense of the fateful intertwining of history, culture, and identity); and love as the spiritual foundation for living. To rescue the speaker from her surreal world, her father returns "in dreams in which he lovingly / explained that he'd returned to be my guide / through the important shadows." Awaking from nightmare to a confident new self, she assures her spiritual guide, "I'm grown up. I don't need you any more." Her father symbolizes not only an expression of fulfilling love but also a tradition of enduring courage that helps her triumph over a dark night of the soul and affirm life as creative possibility: "Last night I had another visitor: / Love's ghost as though compelled by need, as though / it knew the way. My love, I'm grown. Let go."

The sonnet form allows the poet to go deeply into her moods and perceptions while ordering and controlling the intensity of spiritual anguish. She balances honest feelings and rational judgments. The octet of "Ice Maiden" raises the muted but moving cry of passionate lament, while the cryptic images in the final "Whip" rationally but also sardonically review such suffering. These sonnets creatively channel potentially overwhelming emotions through ironic shifts in tone and structure.

In the four sections of *Magnificat* (1994), love as divine union and erotic desire come into conflict. Ambivalent about the decision of a former beau who has become a monk, the poet ponders human intense longing for fulfillment through God, while she simultaneously laments the ascetic's renunciation of life: "At what cost do they will to keep their peace?" she wonders. Her friend Abba Jacob is now, she thinks, "a man whose sole desire is to detach / himself from self and secret sin, / who wills his lifetime to become / a great zero, filled with the purest prayer." Peace, a state of completeness in itself, also becomes a state of "desert," a death-like emptiness, where the self is tested.

Such ambiguous images in *Magnificat* suggest the interdependence of the circles of life. The poems raise questions about the ways in which the intertwining and conflicting imperatives of people's daily activities and spiritual aspirations influence their choices. The speaker suggests that life ought to be affirmed as a whole entity—sensual/divine, male/female: "I could love God through him; / he could love God through me." Flesh is offered not as an impediment to spiritual fulfillment but as its potential channel. Sensual passion may also inspire divine zeal: "I hoped you'd echo my desire / to stand up naked, soul to soul, / in one flash changing nothingness to fire." David Sofield, reviewing the volume in *America,* criticized the poet's handling of the tensions between sensual desire and divine transcendence.

Section 1, "Lost and Found," includes a sequence of prayers that, as Nelson explains in her autobiographical essay, were "intended to demonstrate a development from humor to seriousness, from selfish requests and gratitude for personal blessings to awe at the mysteries of time and death, and finally to compassion." Brief, unadorned, and simplified poems such as "Incomplete Renunciation," "Prayer on the Wing," and "Psalm" parody hypocrisies, self-deceits, and misplaced values in the modern materialist ethos: "Please let me have / a 10-room house adjacent to campus / . . . / And let it pass / through the eye of a needle" ("Incomplete Renunciation"). In such poems the gentle spoofing tone is orchestrated through the layered, ironic shifts of the texts. The brevity, the spare, skeletal stanza forms, and the simple, unrhymed lines all heighten the pithy epigrammatic effects.

The poems in the section titled "A Desert Father" are based on anecdotes from Nelson's first visit to her friend's hermitage. The section is less philosophically engaged–taking, instead, a moralist's look at the inconsistencies in human lives and the multiple contradic-

Dust jacket for Nelson's 2001 collection of poems celebrating the achievements and experiences of George Washington Carver (Richland County Public Library)

tions implicit in modern culture. Critical insights, ambiguity, and irony are still evident, but without the symbolic multiplicity of section 1. Some of these poems treat the stock themes of wealth, sin, and salvation; of the human requirement for material comfort and the soul's search for highest spiritual virtues. Abba Jacob's messages attempt to reconcile these dichotomies: "Miracles happen all the time. / We're here, / aren't we?" Of killing insects, "Abba Jacob says: Well, at least I don't call them / brother / and then kill them. / But I do / ask God's pardon."

A feature of human life has always been the quest for utopian spiritual community, and Abba Jacob, a visionary figure combining messianic, humanist, and socialist overtones, directs such questers. Further suggestive of Nelson's creative yoking of the visionary and the homely, Abba Jacob's voice, in rhapsodic as well as contemplative free verse, rises in lyric and prophetic sentiments. His teachings intuit visions of wholeness symbolized through Christ: "The world balanced / on impossible truth." His life-vision embraces harmonies of spirit and flesh, divine and human—a symbiosis "Union Apprehended" reinforces: "Your breath, the universe: / Where does one end and the other begin? Close your eyes. *Ascend into yourself.*" The Abba Jacob poems, filled with such maxims, carry a distinctly old-fashioned ring. These apothegms are linked to a tradition of wisdom literature that is as old as the biblical Book of Proverbs.

Nelson traveled to France on a Fulbright Teaching Fellowship in 1995. She published *The Fields of Praise* in 1997 and a translation of *Hecuba* in the *Euripides, 1* volume of the Penn Greek Drama Series in 1998. The orchestration of poems in *The Fields of Praise* suggests that the balancing act recognized in *Magnificat* has always been fundamental to the poet's sensibility. Reconfiguring past poems under related subheadings, this book more clearly defines the representational and expressive forms that typify Nelson's work. These subheadings reveal the unifying treatment of subject matter and mood within her poetic world: a world of restrictions and promises, frustrations and satisfactions. The volume includes Nelson's notes on the poems. The title of the collection is illustrative of the dominant tone: life is the greatest of miracles, its arenas of trial balanced by "fields of praise." This attitude, art as a celebration of life, is fundamental to Nelson's aesthetic.

Among the new poems in the book, the crown of sonnets called "Thus Far by Faith" chronicles the events leading up to the founding of a black church in Hickman, Kentucky, in 1866. Incongruously mundane experiences such as plowing cotton fields, loading lumber, and toiling over the washtub combine with racy speech rhythms associated with folk delivery, running counter to the tendency in traditional sonnets toward hyperbolic elaboration and formal heightening of romantic passion. The two traditions coalesce and conflict, making Nelson's art a vehicle for cultural tensions. The content, playing against the traditional form (as in John Donne's *Holy Sonnets,* circa 1609), nevertheless emphasizes sober realities of black life in America.

The Fields of Praise gained favorable critical attention. In *African American Review,* Miller Williams praised the "simple wisdom and straightforward, indelible stories." Edward J. Ingebretsen's review in *America* named salient themes in the book: "Domesticity's various delights and its occasional comedies and consubstantial terrors." Although Ingebretsen described the poet's treatment of memory as somewhat "heavy handed," he praised the "sly, epigrammatic, irreverent" Abba Jacobs poems, which reveal Nelson's "ear for the cadences of this stylized and modern holy man." Judith Kitchen, commenting in *The Georgia Review,* also admired Abba Jacobs and the orchestration of the volume. In *The Hudson Review,* R. S. Gwynn remarked that while some of the poems lose force by being removed from their original contexts, the book is remarkable for its "impressive range of subjects and techniques." He also liked Abba Jacobs, whom he called "a kind of saintly schlemiel" and a "likeable Everyperson."

In 1998 Nelson divorced Wilkenfeld, with whom she has a son, Jacob, and a daughter, Dora. A year later she was awarded an ACLS Contemplative Practices Fellowship. In 2001 she received a Guggenheim Fellowship and published three books of poetry: *Triolets for Triolet; Carver: A Life in Poems;* and *She-Devil Circus.*

Shifting to a new political and aesthetic arena, *Triolets for Triolet* focuses on the African diaspora and is sharply critical of continuing imperialist exploitation in a distant colonial outpost, a village called Triolet (Mauritius): "Walk through the winding streets of Triolet, / who see you, too. Who know you steal their life." The poet protests the encroachment of a Eurocentric cultural monolith, modern capitalism and its machinery of selfishness and greed: "Trying to stop, screeching toward Triolet, / the Twentieth Century Express / . . . / Trying to stop, screaming toward Triolet, / your selfishness." This eight-poem sequence of triolets (eight-line poems using a double refrain in the pattern ABaAabAB) presents a traditional poetic form that Nelson adopts to celebrate the subjected people's demands for their own authentic cultural survival.

Carver, returning to American themes, is a celebratory biography of legendary African American scientist George Washington Carver. The tribute to an intellectual ancestor recalls the folksy brand of humility and heroic attainment already seen in *The Homeplace.* This series of poems from the perspectives of Carver and people who knew him offers a mix of statement-like and Imagist verses and evokes the intense states of mind of a sensitive, spiritual being. "The Last Rose of Summer" is illustrative: "The paper shakes so / the words are hard to read, / but what good is a singing range / . . . / if *Jim* / *your brother* / *smallpox.*" This poem (similar to "A Charmed Life," "Called," and "Goliath") is about quiet creative resilience, about a monument of lasting beauty carved from a potentially suffocating environment: "When you get your grip / on the last rung of the ladder / and look over the wall / . . . / You know / you will not die."

In stylistic contrast are the surrealistic images of "The Perceiving Self." The gothic images of a lynching suggest the scientist's awareness of the grim reality of violence against which he must define his own humanity: "Then he squealed, a field mouse taken / without wingbeat, / with no shadow. / . . . / The icedrift of silence. / Smoke from a torched deadman, barking laughter / from the cottonwoods at the creek."

The verse styles channel the intensity with which Carver continues to live in the vision of the poet, who clearly identifies with the vital will of the scientist and artist. Central to the inspiring leader's legacy, Nelson affirms, is his "Walking our people / into history." *Carver* was a finalist for the 2001 National Book Award; it also received the Boston Globe–Horn Book Award and the Flora Stieglitz Straus Award from the Bank Street College of Education in 2001 and a Coretta Scott King Honor Award and a John Newbery Medal in 2002. Cathryn M. Mercier, in her review in *Horn Book,* commented that "Nelson fills in the trajectory of Carver's life with details of the cultural and political contexts that shaped him even as he shaped history." Herman Sutter's review in *Library Journal* described the poems as "simple, sincere, and . . . honest statements of pure, natural truths."

She-Devil Circus returns in style and sentiment to the anguish expressed in *Partial Truth.* This footnote to the past carries a tone that is less conciliatory: "I learned to be a nice, deceitful fool– / deceiving with each smile I used to hide / the Armageddon of my rage. That's why / it took so fucking long to say goodbye" ("Nice Girl"). The haunting emotional pain about the past exists in tension with the poet's efforts to order and control it through art.

Also in 2001 Nelson edited *Rumors of Troy,* a collection of modern poems about the events in Homer's *The Iliad,* commissioned by the United States Military Academy at West Point to be used as a textbook in the freshman English course. The diverse cultural and poetic interests of Nelson, who in 2002 became the Poet Laureate of the state of Connecticut, are further reflected in the articles she has published on the African American aesthetic, on Jewish American novels, and on Native American literature. Since 2002 she has been a professor of English at the University of Delaware.

Marilyn Nelson's work as artist, thinker, and educator speaks of the challenges that define her consciousness and moral commitment. The image of "a strange beautiful woman" unveiled by her poetry affirms the integrity of self and a resilient faith in human potential. Her art explores her complex history and nature as well as her sense of the worldly and spiritual ideals to which human beings have always aspired.

References:

Allison Murray Cummings, "'The Gender on Paper': Women in American Poetry Movements, 1975–1995 (Free Verse Mainstream, Language Poetry, New Formalist Poetry)," dissertation, University of Wisconsin–Madison, 1995;

Rodney Franklin Dick, "Creative and Constructive Tensions: A Discussion of the Poetry of Marilyn Nelson (Waniek)," M.A. thesis, University of Louisville, 2000;

Jeannine Nicole Mizingou, "A Religious Poetics in Contemporary American Poetry: Resituating Notions of God, the Other World, and the Self in Christian Faith," dissertation, Duquesne University, 2001;

Leslie Ullman, "Solitaries and Storytellers, Magicians and Pagans: Five Poets in the World," *Kenyon Review,* new series 13 (Spring 1991): 179–193.

Papers:

Manuscripts and other archives related to Marilyn Nelson's career are included in the Kerlan Collection, University of Minnesota.

Molly Peacock
(30 June 1947 -)

Carolyn Meyer
University of Toronto School of Continuing Studies

See also the Peacock entry in *DLB 120: American Poets Since World War II, Third Series.*

BOOKS: *And Live Apart* (Columbia & London: University of Missouri Press, 1980);
Raw Heaven (New York: Random House, 1984);
Take Heart: Poems (New York: Random House, 1989);
Animals at the Table, text by Peacock, illustrations by Anne Jope (Lewisburg, Pa.: Press of Appletree Alley, 1995);
Original Love (New York & London: Norton, 1995);
Paradise, Piece by Piece (New York: Riverhead Books, 1998; Toronto: M&S, 1998);
How to Read a Poem . . . and Start a Poetry Circle (New York: Riverhead Books, 1999);
Cornucopia: New & Selected Poems, 1975–2002 (New York: Norton, 2002; Toronto: Penguin, 2002).

OTHER: "What the Mockingbird Said," in *Conversant Essays: Contemporary Poets on Poetry* (Detroit, Mich.: Wayne State University Press, 1990);
"Attempting a Villanelle," in *The Practice of Poetry,* edited by Robin Behn and Chase Twichell (New York: HarperCollins, 1992);
"One Green, One Blue: One Point about Formal Verse Writing and Another about Women Writing Formal Verse," in *A Formal Feeling Comes: Poems in Form by Contemporary Women,* edited by Annie Finch (Brownsville, Ore.: Story Line Press, 1994);
Poetry in Motion: 100 Poems from the Subways and Buses, edited by Peacock, Elise Paschen, and Neil Neches (New York & London: Norton, 1996);
Michelle Boisseau, *Understory,* introduction by Peacock (Boston: Northeastern University Press, 1996);
"From Gilded Cage to Rib Cage," in *After New Formalism: Poets on Form, Narrative and Tradition,* edited by Finch (Ashland, Ore.: Story Line Press, 1999);
The Private I: Privacy in a Public World, edited by Peacock (St. Paul, Minn.: Graywolf Press, 2001).

Molly Peacock is a poet of raw grace, metaphysical impulse, and daring confessional candor who courts complexity both in the supple bending of closed forms and in the complex emotional states those forms allow her to express. Dense, sensuous, intimate, frankly conversational, explosive in their subject matter, and inventively resonant in their sound patterns, her poems are propelled by what she calls "the drive for what is real, deeper than the brain's detail—the drive to feel" (from "Desire," in *Raw Heaven* [1984]). The problems of expressing human desire in words, of articulating love in its various forms, and of understanding the meaning of that experience constitute the core, but by no means the limits, of Peacock's imaginative reach. By turns questing and questioning, the narratives and meditations that make up Peacock's complex poetic world are ones that glory in sex and the animalism of human nature, in the provocative interplay between physical landscapes and interior ones, and in the accommodation of ambivalence and ambiguity. Laid end to end through her four collections, they map out and occasionally redouble a redemptive journey of self-revision from an underworld of childhood domestic violence, abuse, and neglect to a paradise of adult love and self-love that is both that childhood's consequence and its miraculous exception. The journey is one of self-actualization, obeying psychoanalytic imperatives where darkness, loneliness, and pain must be confronted to be overcome, an undertaking accomplished in poetic terms through illustrative images and affirmations of the powers of uninhibited perception and articulation. Influenced by an elder generation of confessional poets, Peacock identifies herself as not only a formalist poet but what she terms a "personal" one. She is a practitioner of what she calls the "unbandaged poem," which strips away the psychological overlay—the bandaging that impedes understanding—from the experiential wound out of which the poem arises. Many of her poems work from detailed image to definition, aphorism, or idea in a technique reminiscent of the elaborate conceits and extended metaphors of the metaphysical poets. Peacock's admiration

Molly Peacock (photograph by V. Tony Hauser; courtesy of the author)

for the kind of formally controlled poem she had read at school–those of her favorite poet, George Herbert, among them–inspired the conscious choice of her own formalist agenda.

Peacock's reasons for embracing traditional versification are as deeply rooted in psychological need as they are in her artistic and feminist imperatives. For a poet who grew up in a situation in which nothing was delivered as promised, the comforting boundaries of received forms amount to a kind of contract by which all that is promised is satisfyingly delivered. Where all is flux and chaos, verse forms operate as emblems of order, and to this end formalist procedures assuage Peacock's desire for order. The supposition of security in, for example, the flexible rigidity of the sonnet paradoxically allows for playful daring and shocking honesty. Peacock calls prosodic scheme "a net over which to perform, in safety, on the high wire of poetry. The wire is no longer a rigid code to follow under penalty of 'death.' The safety net *is* the formal structure. The wire is the truth we step out on!" By her definition, fixed form functions not as an imprisoning "gilded cage" but as a container constituted of the contained, a structure to be inhabited, a body formed of both skeleton and skin that together embody the emotion of the poem. Peacock's formalist impulse, in fact, comes to the aid of her confessional mode since, as she explains in her essay "From the Gilded Cage to Rib Cage" (1999): "formal verse often makes impossible emotions possible" and provides a safe refuge from which to explore taboo or controversial subjects. Peacock's sonnets, villanelles, quatrains, and terza-rima-like triplets do not simply inscribe a female-speaking subjectivity but accommodate the suppressed specificity of female experience: menstruation, masturbation, pregnancy, abortion, menopause, lingering joy in the postcoital moment, and the quasi-maternal burdens of both filial responsibility and sisterhood. This kind of subject orientation has deservedly earned Peacock, along with

Sharon Olds and Linda Pastan, the designation of "Earth Mother" in *The New York Times Magazine* Poetry Pantheon. But also through her use of formal devices Peacock takes on what she calls "a certain linguistic power" once denied women outside the traditional canon. Formalism and feminism are, for her, not mutually exclusive but mutually supportive and complementary.

While women poets by no means have a monopoly on formal experimentation, Peacock looks to a female poetic heritage, to the examples of Marianne Moore, Edna St. Vincent Millay, and especially Elizabeth Bishop, when exercising her own license to break form or bend it to her purposes. Irregularity, inexactitude, fluctuation, and imperfection are part of Peacock's aesthetic and are valued for what they mirror and teach her about the emotion of the poem. Her playful rebellion against the tyranny of form finds expression in the metapoetic heroic sonnet "Good Girl" in *Take Heart: Poems* (1989), in which self-rebuke at forever having to be the perfect "good girl" overflows in an additional four lines. What spills over the strict parameters of the sonnet is a pressure from within, the anger of someone unable to restrain herself. Typical of Peacock's poetic procedures in general, the poem itself encapsulates and emphasizes the struggle of form to include what lies beyond inclusion and files notice of Peacock's own refusal, as she writes her essay "One Green, One Blue" (1994), to be "a good girl to the sonnet." Peacock retracts and expands the form at will, sometimes encasing a sonnet within a longer poem—for example, "Sunny Days" in *Raw Heaven*. The template for even her fifteen-to-eighteen-line "exploded" variants of the sonnet is still the Shakespearean sonnet, the final couplet of which seems tailor-made for her epigrammatic conclusions. Any sense of predictable "regularity," though, is offset by frequent rhyme between the inner halves and ends of lines as well as by long enjambed sentences that subsume end-rhyme within labyrinthine and occasionally wrenched syntactical structures rich in their own sound clusters of alliteration, assonance, and word repetition. While Peacock's end-rhymes tend to stabilize her lines, internal rhyme both destabilizes and adds intensity. Because they are, as critic David Lehman refers to them in a review of *Raw Heaven* in "Book World," in *The Washington Post* (2 September 1984), "agents of invention" rather than laws to be observed, Peacock's rhyme schemes are often variant—modified to meet certain psychological urgencies, to lend rough grace to the perfect surface of a form, or to surprise through unexpected semantic connection. In playing on her favorite paradoxes of containment and freedom, Peacock even suggests, in *How to Read a Poem . . . and Start a Poetry Circle* (1999), that rhyme schemes can be "keys to secrets in a poem, since rhymes are often like padlocks at the ends of lines."

Her verse, with the exception of her fourth collection, is not strictly metrical. This fact alone, however, does not explain why the label of "low" New Formalist has been applied to her. Defying easy categorization, Peacock's diction is both plain and playful—on the one hand, unadorned, familiar, and spiked with an occasional four-letter word in an effort to make pain palpable, on the other hand, elegant and inventive in such serendipitous coinages as "disiridescence" ("Dear Heart"). Most likely, though, the out-and-out eroticism of her poetry, her public flirtation with the forbidden, coupled with a love of the low-art subject, accounts for her "low" New Formalist status among the Expansive poets. She excels at bringing irreverence and humor to subjects most experience but few discuss. This lively wit is equally apparent in such word games as the acrostic "Prayer" and "The Spell" (*Take Heart*), the latter putting a telestich alphabet to phonetic use so that "spelling masks meaning"—a formalized metaphor for the masks, disguises, and duplicities of the self. The titles of the poems, too, allude to the original mysticism of the acrostic and use in the oral transmission of sacred texts. But in "Prayer," in particular, Peacock invokes this convention only to deflate it by establishing an ironic tension between spirituality and budding adolescent sexuality. A similar degree of whimsical, even gleeful, subversion of formal conventions is found in "She Lays" (*Raw Heaven*), Peacock's paean to auto-eroticism. The recumbent "she" in its initial sonnet-like stanza at first evokes the voiceless beautiful figures of that genre in object position, but the woman in this case is not a voyeur's love object denied agency but an empowered character in a story of self-love and self-recognition that becomes "world-love." The palpable sense of release—both sexual release and release from the cage (form) of the sonnet—is conveyed in the syntactically linked overflow of the next ten lines. Slow, delicately detached description rich in physiological detail builds to a simultaneous sexual and structural climax in the white space that cuts between stanzas, reinforcing formally the ecstatic loss of self—"This is lost I'm"—that the poem celebrates. Peacock exploits both the tensions that arise out of the historicism of her chosen forms and the tension created when the form appears to work in opposition to the feeling of the poem, a dynamic that has the paradoxical result of making the feeling both approachable and explorable. Gestures of form and feeling at first seem oddly mismatched in a poem such as "Say You Love Me" (*Take Heart*), which uses light, interlocking triplets to recount the horrifying fear and mortification to which she was subjected by her violent, alcoholic father. The lines have a strong forward impetus that contrasts sharply with the sense of entrapment the poem instills; yet, it is by virtue of that forward impetus that words for such painful experience can be found at all.

Born on 30 June 1947 in Buffalo, New York, Molly Peacock grew up before her time as the firstborn child in a dysfunctional working-class family. The uncertainty and instability of her early years are conveyed through the seismic shifts of the opening lines of "Those Paperweights with Snow Inside" *(Raw Heaven)*: "Dad pushed my mother down the cellar stairs. / Gram had me name each plant in her garden. / My father got drunk. Ma went to country fairs." Responsibility for the household and her younger sister fell to Peacock in early adolescence as her hard-drinking, bullying father (Edward Frank "Ted" Peacock) drifted toward alcoholism and her sober Baptist mother (Pauline Wright "Polly" Peacock) drifted away from her children because of her deepening depression and long hours spent tending her small grocery store. Peacock's escape from her father's physical threats and psychological torments—survival—meant anything that embodied order: the familiar routine of summers spent at her grandmother's house in the country while attending local Bible school, the parenting voice of her favorite authors, and the sense of "going that extra mile" that accompanied the writing of her first poem at age ten.

Not until Peacock studied under Milton Kessler as an undergraduate at the State University of New York (SUNY) at Binghamton did she realize her chaotic family life could be put in perspective through the ordering capacities of poetry. Peacock graduated magna cum laude with a B.A. from SUNY–Binghamton in 1969 and thereafter spent several years as an academic administrator at her alma mater and as coordinator of the New York State Poets-in-the-Schools program in Binghamton. Her first marriage was to Jeremy Benton, from 1970 to 1976. After they divorced, she went on to graduate school as a Danforth Fellow at Johns Hopkins University, furthering her creative-writing studies under the instruction of Cynthia MacDonald and later Richard Howard. Howard was the person who encouraged the formalist tendencies for which she had been casting around while a fellow at the MacDowell Colony in 1975. He advised her to count syllables and to search for anchoring underpinnings for her poetry in the event its emotional fever pitch failed her. Earning her M.A. with honors in 1977, she spent two years as coterminus writer-in-residence for the Delaware State Arts Council and director of the Wilmington (Delaware) Writing Workshops.

Peacock moved to New York City in 1981, teaching for more than a decade at the Friends Seminary while also holding posts as visiting poet, poet-in-residence, and/or lecturer at Columbia University, Hofstra University, Sarah Lawrence College, the 92nd Street Young Men's and Young Women's Hebrew Association (YM/YWHA) Poetry Centre, New York University, and Barnard College. More recently, she has taught at Bucknell University, Juniata College, Salem College, Pacific University, Lebanon Valley University, the University of Western Ontario, the University of California (Riverside) and again at the 92nd Street Poetry Centre. Her on-line projects included *The Spoken Word* for oxygen.com and Molly Peacock's Poetry Circles at the Learning Network. She is poet-in-residence of the Poet's Corner at the Cathedral of St. John the Divine. She was on-line lecturer at the University of Toronto School of Continuing Studies until 2002, and contributing writer for *Conde Nast House & Garden* until 2000. A product of the workshop system, she has been a resident at Yaddo, the Virginia Center for the Arts, and the MacDowell Colony, also serving as president of the fellows' organization of the latter. Peacock has been awarded fellowships from the Ingram-Merrill Foundation, the New York Foundation of the Arts and the National Endowment for the Arts, and is a five-time Woodrow Wilson Fellow. She has also served as panelist/judge for many prestigious awards and committees, including the Loft Poetry Prize and the Pulitzer Prize in poetry. From 1989 to 1995 she was president of the Poetry Society of America and oversaw its successful Poetry in Motion program responsible for bringing poetry to the masses on the subways and buses of the nation. Out of this project came her co-edited anthology *Poetry in Motion: 100 Poems from the Subways and Buses* (1996).

Peacock is married to James Joyce scholar Michael Groden, whom she married on 19 August 1992; he was her first love and high-school sweetheart with whom she reunited after nineteen years when he chanced upon a review of her second collection, *Raw Heaven*. They now divide their time between New York and Toronto, having lived for some years in London, Ontario, where Groden teaches at the University of Western Ontario.

No account of Peacock's life is complete without mention of her "hybrid memoir" *Paradise, Piece by Piece* (1998), which blends real and invented characters to document her early encounters with motherhood and the decisive moments in her life, culminating in her pregnancy and abortion at age thirty-eight and her subsequent tubal ligation, which reaffirmed her early resolution not to have children. *Paradise, Piece by Piece* is a coming-of-age story in which the passage to maturity lies not in giving birth to a child but in a metamorphic giving birth to the self through the gradual discovery of the decision that having children would not define who she is. Though sparing in feminist rhetoric and ideolog-

Paperback cover for Peacock's 1995 collection, which traces the maturation of mother love into an adult love (courtesy of the author)

ical argument, Peacock's memoir looks to her own life and the web of relationships with friends and relatives to clarify important distinctions between motherhood and womanhood, between parenthood and adulthood. With the same honesty and lucidity that mark her poetry, Peacock recasts the marginalized subject of voluntary childlessness as a narrative of the constructed self finding wholeness in radical refusal and dedication to art, not as a story of incompletion.

Peacock's first volume, *And Live Apart* (1980), aims for Herbert's brand of "monastic truth," as the title-page epigraph from Herbert makes clear: "Surely if each one saw another's heart . . . all would disperse, And live apart" *(Paradise, Piece by Piece)*. Separation, the thematic bedrock of the collection, is, as she later wrote in "Cut Flower" *(Raw Heaven)*, "a power I could wield"; yet it also upholds the promise of the holiness of a new life, a promise realized gradually over Peacock's next three collections: "To live apart was a way of having heaven, a calm place, or at least a way of avoiding hell, a jammed place" *(Paradise, Piece by Piece)*. At issue in *And Live Apart* are what critic Robert Phillips, writing for *The Hudson Review* ("Poetry Chronicle: Some Versions of the Pastoral," 1981), describes as "the reversals of love, the inescapability of fate, the inevitabilities of inheritance." Poems such as "Nightwake," "In Native Tongues," "Alibis and Lullabies," and "Anno Domini" introduce Peacock's concern for the vicissitudes of childhood and family, for their recriminatory fallout of love and hate. The price the artist is forced to pay for filial duty is explored in "The Life of Leon Bonvin," an implicit historical analogue to Peacock's self-abnegating role of dutiful daughter. With its unsentimental soundings of the past, lucid detail, grammatical complexity, and visceral feel for the emotional nuances of conversation, "Peacock's Superette," a poem about the family grocery store, comes closest to anticipating her later verse.

And Live Apart is an ambitious testing ground, not only in terms of its imaginative terrain but also in its crossover from free verse to traditional versification by way of Peacock's experimentation with many different meters and stanzas. The impulse that leads her to write a villanelle ("Walking Is Almost Falling") and embark on a formalist enterprise comes out of her need for a therapeutic poetic, as she explains in *Paradise, Piece by Piece*: "those geometric boundaries that might have chafed others felt as good as tight bandages on a broken limb. If I was broken, the lines set the bones, then acted as a cast. Art was not like life–it was the way to life. Inside a poem, I could mend." Though the poems of *And Live Apart* lack the characteristic concision and sharpness of vision of Peacock's later verse, in their melancholic softness and intelligence they make way for the emergence of a mature voice.

Raw Heaven represents a great leap forward both in the forcefulness of its perceptions–its "drive for what is real"–and its technical virtuosity, as expressed through rhyme and a skillful rehabilitative wielding of the sonnet and other forms. The assuredness of the fifty-two poems of the volume is that of a poet who has found the underpinnings with which to anchor her highly charged emotional content. She is freed, as she writes in "Berries Which Are Berries," "as a metronome saves times / by measuring." Rhyme, like the tour-de-force end-rhyme echo chamber of "The Distance Up Close," with its twenty-two consecutive *o* sounds, has the effect of guiding and liberating Peacock's fertile imagination rather than constricting it. The title of the volume, which grew out of Peacock's desire to make "the holiness of my new life sensuously palpable," exposes the paradoxes that animate *Paradise, Piece by Piece* as a whole. Simultaneously tough and tender, raw and elegant, the poems explore the extremities of sexuality and spiritual longing–of wildness and corporeality on the one hand and tameness and domestication on the other. More often than not, however, Peacock transposes the valuation of those terms, so that the house becomes a place of recollected family violence, chaotic and fearful, while recognitions of humans' animal nature affirm what is most essentially and vitally human. In "The Lull" the graphic opening image of a possum lying on train tracks "fully dead" is realized unflinchingly and with such exactitude that it seems to radiate Peacock's conviction that "description becomes knowledge" *(How to Read a Poem . . . and Start a Poetry Circle)*:

> It was big and white with flies on its head,
> a thick healthy hairless tail, and strong, hooked
> nails on its racoon-like feet. It was a full-
> grown possum. It was sturdy and adult.
> Only its head was smashed.

While the poet's companion recoils in disgust, what Peacock's feeling of kinship with the creature allows her to see is the animal's strength and health. Seizing upon this strange encounter, she fashions from it a manifesto-like statement of her defining reality, her "Pax / Peacock, with the world" made flesh: "Dreams, brains, fur and guts: what we are." The recognition that humans are indeed animals resonates not only in Peacock's raw declaration but also in the eponymous bird for which her bargain is named. Animal imagery is equally prevalent in "Just about Asleep Together," a celebration of intimacy, in which lovers drifting into post coital slumber groom themselves with swells of "monkey-like" tenderness and settle into the "softness known only to rabbits / and sleepers." Their "foetal" posture not only conflates adult and infantile sexuality but also speaks of what is inchoate and primal about both. A similar blurring of boundaries is evident in the earlier "A Kind of Parlance" *(And Live Apart)*, in which the reconnoitering calls of penguins in a zoo are echoed by those of human lovers–lovers who ultimately act upon their desires by reprising the parent-child roles of sick little penguin and consoling zookeeper. Just as speech fails the lovers at the end of the poem, "desire," in a poem by the same name, is likewise something that cannot be expressed in words–"It doesn't speak and it isn't schooled." Instead, Peacock characterizes it through primal images–"a small foetal animal" with "wettened fur," a blunt paw, a "pet who knows you / and nudges your knee with its snout." In the sonnet "Petting and Being a Pet," the pet–a paradigm of wildness domesticated–becomes a fleshy vehicle for Peacock's meditation on the human need to touch and be touched, to both *be* by being caressed and to plumb the depths of being through this darker sense. Added to the menagerie of "Dogs, lambs, chickens," the "pets of all nations," to which Peacock issues an initial rallying cry, are "women," equal in their need, not to be kept but to be caressed. Relishing the tactile, the language of the body, for the way "touch makes being make sense," Peacock also foregrounds the equally primal sense of smell for what it conjures of the past and confirms about the unifying core of human experience. Her characterization of desire as "an eyes-shut, ears-shut medicine of the heart / that smells and touches endings and beginnings," also applies to the sensory-based location of her subjects in "When You Were a Baby Girl" and "Smell," the first addressed to her sister, whose recollected baby smell unleashes a vortex of accumulated and conflicted sibling emotion:

> I loved your smell when you were a baby
> high above me lying in your bassinet
> amid cotton, flannel, and rubbery
> talc. . . .
> . . . I catch the tender
> Spark of the faint comet of your infant
> smell, still, and am shocked and won't surrender

and then do—it is all the years have meant,
the damp baby smoke of rivalry unfurled
beyond the salt and oil of the practicing world.

Similar to "the damp baby smoke of rivalry," the "smoky smell of menses" exerts an animal attraction that is by turns earthy, impure, and repellent.

> . . .Years
> of months roll away what each month tells:
> God, what animals we are, huge of haunch,
> Bloody and wise in the stench of bosk.

The sensuous feel for language evident in the clustering of *m* and *s* sounds of the heroic sonnet helps to rescue a taboo subject, like the dead animal in "The Lull," from the silent margin to which it has been socially consigned. Peacock's daring is to make the transgressive inclusive and reflective of the larger rhythms and commonalities of the phenomenal world.

The dialectic of the wild and the tame also finds expression in the lawns, gardens, and gardening metaphors of "Cutting Tall Grass," "The Burnt Lawn," "A Garden," and "Sweet Time." The effort to control nature in "Cutting Tall Grass," a love poem to lawns that prosaically extends the conventional subject matter of the sonnet, ends poised in the paradigmatic space between life and death: "the old grass spewn in the bleak shadows, / the new grass smelling of wet and slight rot, / to love to live between what is and is not." Its companion poem, "A Garden," extols the place as "the highest of civilizations, a bed in the earth," a bulwark against the fear of "dirt nature"—"the lesioned earth," "The swamp's spilled stomach." With the final, dogmatic disclosure that "a garden is a rhyme," the formal movement of the sonnet is shown to be a metaphor for the taming of the natural world. Against the backdrop of uncontrolled ("spilled") nature, gardening, like rhyming, offers a therapeutic time "seized to be eased." "Sweet Time," with its complex opening simile, celebrates what Lehman calls "the sexuality at the heart of nature": "The largest bud in creation travels / up the swollen stem of the amaryllis / like a ship in a womb up a river." Patience in the pleasure of its slow ecstatic unfolding is a virtue, forcing the bloom—prying it "out before its time"—a sin. Peacock's versification reinforces the lesson of the poem with its unforced and unpunctuated ending and tangled syntax that patiently conveys the complexity of the emotion it harbors:

> Something will try
> to surface: it is all about surfaces shed,
> discovered, it is all about what wells up
> in its own sweet time as sinless and sudden
> and unfathomed as an old bad word in the cup
> of the lips. . . .

In poems such as "The Distance Up Close," "Old Roadside Resorts," "Island in Our Eyes," "Next Afternoon," and "Among Tall Buildings," landscapes—natural, man-made, and fantasized—function as objective correlatives of emotional states, characterizing "the worlds inside you" Peacock alludes to in "Sky Inside." In the paired sonnets of "Old Roadside Resorts," the triangulated imagery of the chartreuse mountains mirrors the tangled history and pain of a love triangle of which Peacock herself is the dismayed and observant "hypotenuse." In "Mental France" a landscape of vicarious literary experience—"a hut at dusk where two lovers lay / swathed in orange light"—is appropriated and absorbed by the speaker's new reality—"my hut / in France in this apartment of flesh"—as the present finally fulfills the past longing of love. Peacock's objectifying impulse—her practice of first presenting a scene or image—is also at work in the jaunty "Squirrel Disappears," in which the small animal's erratic comings and goings oddly but aptly dramatize the emptiness and plenty of the intermittence of love. The source of much aesthetic delight in poems of this kind is Peacock's mismatched, as much as her matched, pairing of vehicle and tenor. In explaining her poetic strategies, Peacock has said in a 1994 interview with Alice Friman and Charlotte Templin that she is an inheritor of Emily Dickinson in two ways: in the way she habitually defines and in her attempt to characterize psychological states. "Desire," which combines these approaches, works by way of negative definition, positive definition, and analogy. Metaphorically dense, "Loneliness," in its abbreviated evocation of the sonnet form, reinforces its emotional content through its structural paucity.

Though the acuity of Peacock's recorded perceptions is, for her, a way of achieving heaven, it is also a way of understanding, if not necessarily exorcising, the hellish childhood that haunts her. Poems such as "Afraid," "No Earthly Reason," and the classroom confessional "Our Room" stake their imaginative claim in sorting through "the junk of childhood" to see, as she writes in her exploded sonnet "Those Paperweights with Snow Inside," "how the heart and arms were formed on its behalf." The contrapuntal movement of the poem from scenes of wife abuse to the Edenic bliss of naming garden plants contributes to an overwhelming sense of uncertainty and instability. Even the parents' identities are curiously shifting— Ma / mother, Dad / father—as though the children themselves are uncertain of who their parents are. The family's pet chameleon—"warden / of the living-room curtains where us kids / stood waiting for their headlights to turn in"—is a fitting emblem of flux and unpredictability, though in its prison-like policing of little authority over the potential menace of the head-

Paperback cover for Peacock's "hybrid memoir," published in 1998 (courtesy of the author)

lights. The negations of "not to carry" and "not to see" momentarily lift the burden of childhood grief that survives into adulthood, but along with it they deny insight into its shaping influence. Peacock's technique in this case highlights the oppressive necessity and obligation of the burden. "I can't put the burden down," Peacock confesses, nor does she allow herself to do so over the course of her next two collections.

Take Heart consolidates the achievements of *Raw Heaven*, but it also in certain respects represents a departure. Peacock courts riskier subjects–the pivotal events of her father's death and the posttraumatic memories it evokes, her brief pregnancy and subsequent abortion, even her miscalculation in buying a fake fur coat she cannot afford–and inhabits roomier forms that bring greater freedom. An understated religious feeling is found in the metaphors of the collection, in its pursuit of spiritual solace, in its *Commedia*-inspired terza-rima rhymes, and in the provenance of its prescriptive and consoling title: "In my head I invented a liturgy. Instead of *Kyrie eleison*, I said, *Take comfort*, and instead of *Christie eleison*, I said, *Take heart*" (*Paradise, Piece by Piece*).

Peacock's quest for self-awareness and understanding intensifies, foregrounding acts of articulation ("The Valley of the Monsters," "Blank Paper," "Anger Sweetened") and modes of perception, from the decipherings of "The Spell" and "A Hot Day in Agrigento" to the fantasizing-scrutinizing of "The Valley of the Monsters." Her ongoing process of self-revision, which constitutes the foundation of the collection, finds formal expression through incorporation of typescript revisions in "The Valley of Monsters" and "ChrisEaster." In the latter, a poem about her abortion, Peacock tries out metaphors of Christ's nativity, Crucifixion, and Resurrection–"in the manger, on the bald hill, near the tomb"–until finally settling on "at home," a choice that places the poem firmly back in the orbit of Peacock's private passion and rebirth but nevertheless brings to it the accumulated weight of the excised options. What the reader is privileged to see is the process of a poem, as well as a self, in its becoming.

In Peacock's previous collection the near-total absence of stanzaic divisions created the effect of a single unified sequence. By contrast, *Take Heart* encompasses a range of sonnets (even terza-rima sonnets), acrostics, and stanza types: the couplets of "The Valley of Monsters," the narrow ten-line stanzas of "A Simple Purchase," and the slender yet tightly constructed dimeter and trimeter quatrains of "Joy," "Dream Come True," and "How I Come to You." Of the last, Jay Parini in "Bright Shards and Solid Pottery" in *The New York Times Book Review* (22 October 1989) has said its meter and rhyme "cut reality into sizable chunks, the sense of the poem spilling from line to line, breathlessly." Precipitous in their movement, the thin rhymed lines of the poem break apart its grammatical structures, creating a formally apt metaphor for the broken and smashed self who presents herself, purged and transformed, to her lover.

Technically, *Take Heart* is dominated by triplet and tercet poems such as "Commands of Love," "Say You Love Me," "Putting a Burden Down," "Blue and Huge," "A Hot Day in Agrigento," "The Surge," "How I Had to Act," "Instead of Her Own," "The Worm," and "There Must Be." Occasionally, their rhyme falls into the pattern of regular terza rima, but even when it does not, it is still evocative of the stanza of Dante's *Divina Commedia*. Peacock's choice of form becomes a strangely appropriate one for her encounters with the ghosts (and demons) of her childhood—her father in his demand for proof of love, her sister in her casual power to mortify—and for the imaginative enactment of her own self-aware self-redemption. The forward impetus of the interlocking rhyme has the effect of leading out of darkness toward understanding; yet, as Peacock observes of Elizabeth Bishop's "Pink Dog," triplets have a lightness that both "works against the depth of the poet's complex feeling" and makes the expression of it possible ("From Gilded Cage to Rib Cage"). In "Say You Love Me," Peacock exploits the multiple implications of terza rima—the form not only enabling her to recount a hellish domestic scene in which articulation becomes an aberration but also accommodating long sentences with elaborate syntax that propel the narrative to its final, desolate conclusion. For the daughters who must "say they love" their drunken, violent father there is neither help nor escape, only the knowledge that "There was no world out there" and that they must remain "completely alone." The energy and free movement of the fifteen stanzas of the poem serve to underscore the speaker's profound sense of hopelessness, isolation, and entrapment. Form combats the overwhelming darkness of the poem but does not entirely overcome it.

"The Worm" and "The Surge," likewise written in triplets, also feature final quatrains that emphasize formally the emotional gestures of the poems. The near-triple rhymes of the opening stanzas of "The Worm" draw attention to themselves in a way that heightens the social embarrassment the speaker feels in the presence of her gauche and voluble sister. The final four-line stanza swells with the anger and resentment the speaker has suppressed throughout the poem: "I was twenty-two and dead then, slain by the fiend / of motherhood and sisterhood, the earth infirm / about my turning corpse, riddled by the worm." The final stanza destabilizes the central image of the poem and dispels its ambiguity. The mescal worm on which her sister had fixated becomes a metaphor for a spiritual death supplanting the speaker's mere "social death" and mortification in the earlier stanzas. The title of Peacock's aubade, "The Surge," a praise poem to her lover's morning erection, alludes to the welling up of both the flesh and the spirit in the recognition of love's mutual, almost existential, acceptances: "there is nothing I need do to please but be." About its final stanza Robert McPhillips comments, it "swells to a rhymed quatrain . . . reemphasizing the inward swelling of love represented by the outward swelling of the erection" ("The New Formalism and the Revival of the Love Lyric," in *After New Formalism*).

Poems such as "Buffalo," "Say You Love Me," "Dream Come True," and "Unexpected Freedom" indicate that though Peacock's father has died, he cannot entirely be laid to rest: "Her father who lies there / will be her nightmare." The function of these poems is not to elegize but to put into some semblance of perspective the denials and disinheritances that defined her relationship with her father—to console herself not for her paternal loss but for the loss of self that her father precipitated. The mood of these poems is rueful, pained, and resentful, relieved rather than grief-stricken. In the narrative "Buffalo" Peacock recalls the "enforced darkness" of mandatory afternoon excursions with her father to local bars. The life she describes is one of entrapment, voiceless rage, and servitude to her father's alcoholism, for in essence she is like the circumspect bartenders, who "shrink / from any conversation to endure / the serving, serving, serving of disease." The frozen emotion of her unarticulated anger finds its objective correlative in "the wide / endlessly horizontal vistas" that "rage / with sun and snow," which she cannot see from behind the bar blinds. However, this exponentially expanding world lies beyond—"Buffalo, gleaming / below Great Lakes. Behind bar blinds we were caged, / some motes of sunlight cathedrally beaming"—and brims with the potentiality of freedom and escape.

Peacock's pregnancy and abortion form the core of a second group of poems within the collection. "Merely by Wilderness," "ChrisEaster," "On the Street," and "The Ghost" are not only central to Peacock's personal mythology but also groundbreaking in their meditations on the taboo subjects of female experience: a pregnancy and its prospect of single motherhood that is not cause for celebration but for anxiety over a potential loss of self; an abortion that is truly a spiritual trial in rolling metaphors of Christ's nativity, Passion, and Resurrection all into one; ambivalent retrospection on both the medical procedure and its emotional and spiritual ramifications. "On the Street," which describes the procedure in clinical detail, provokes by the brutal power of its opening analogy—"A curette has the shape of a grapefruit spoon"—through its association of the unspeakable and the mundanely everyday. The shock of this pairing unleashes a torrent of emotion, which Peacock's rhyming couplets can barely contain. In "The Ghost," Peacock encounters the ghost of her pregnancy; the terms of parent and child are transposed, as is her practice in many earlier poems—"When I let it surround me, the embrace is / more mother than baby." Not only alarmed but comforted, parented, and restored by this fetal ghost, Peacock once again invokes the primal sense of touch as a precondition to and agency of self-knowledge: ". . . the brief pregnancy showed us, / its father and me, these choices, not shriveling / but choice alive with choice. . . ."

Original Love (1995) is in many respects the highwater mark of Peacock's poetic art. By far it is the most well orchestrated and rigorously organized of her collections, though she has always shown awareness of relationships that arise out of textual placement. The three movements of the collection—"first love," "mother love," and "another love"—accrete in a final realization of self-love through narratives of midlife courtship and marriage, conflicted daughterly love for a dying mother, and the search for a spiritual redemption that has been brought about by past trauma. Always an audacious surveyor of boundaries, Peacock not only meditates on the divisions between body and spirit, life and afterlife, animal and human, the comic and the serious, male and female, mother and daughter, but also attempts to mediate their strict oppositions. In fact, by this time Peacock has come to regard poetry as taking place in what she calls "the shimmering verge" because, as she says, "the light of the mind shines on both categories at once, trying to distinguish between them" *(How to Read a Poem . . . and Start a Poetry Circle)*.

Altogether, the three sections of *Original Love* represent stages in Peacock's metamorphosis toward an apotheosis of the self—mature poems marking the attainment of personal maturity. Her poems register the "sharp changes" of love and death, the instigators of the "entrée into maturity" that, in Peacock's words, "bring us face-to-face with what we thought life was but now must revise" *(Paradise, Piece by Piece)*. The question raised by the title is how original love—mother love—can be remade into mature love. The quest to answer this question involves the need to articulate what one reviewer of *Original Love* (in *Library Journal*, 15 February 1995) has called "the difficulties with familial, interpersonal, and sexual relationships." In the prefatory "Why I Am Not a Buddhist," an exposition that interweaves the themes, subjects, and concerns of the volume, Peacock explains her philosophy of desire: ". . . I love the things I've sought— / you in your beltless bathrobe, tongues of cash that loll / from my billfold—and love what I want: clothes, / houses, redemption." The "rags of love" Peacock offers up for use at the end of the poem not only recall the Yeatsian "rag and bone shop of the heart"—a place of the desolation and purgation of love—but also refers to the rag paper of the texts that embody her anatomy of love.

If anything, Peacock since her last collection has become bolder in her explicit eroticism, more daring in the surprising and funny provocations of her headline-like titles ("Have You Ever Faked an Orgasm?" "Panties and the Buddha," and "My College Sex Group") and more adventurous in her use of fixed forms. "The Purr," one of many poems celebrating the joys of marital sex, converts lovemaking into both a feline pas de deux and a cat-like pursuit of bird prey—". . . I . . . / tread / catlike myself behind you. . . ." The animal magnetism of attraction and sexual hunger the sonnet depicts is emphasized formally by the purring sounds of three almost identically rhymed quatrains (*abcd abcd abcd dc*).

Peacock's formal impulse also leads her to write sonnet variants—some with seventeen lines ("Baubles after Bombs," "Interrupted Elegy," and "Vogue Vista"), others with fifteen lines ("Floral Conversation" and "Forgiveness"). Peacock sometimes even superimposes one form on another, as she does in "Unseen," a sonnet that, in its stanzaic divisions, has the effect of an overlay of terza rima in its irregularly rhymed tercets. She also writes double sonnets—"The Scare" and "The Wheel"—the first minus a couplet in its final lines, as if to defy the finalization of rhyme and, by extension, to defy the closure represented by the possible recurrence of her new husband's cancer. "The Wheel," a betrothal poem, is a tour-de-force twenty-eight-line sentence, a continuous syntactical circuit evocative of the titular wheel. The encompassing reach of the form is Peacock's way of reinforcing her realization that "my childhood romance had become an adult love, that there was no turning back, and no reason to, since the love *now* contained the love *then*" *(Paradise, Piece by Piece)*. Peacock's formal repertoire in *Original Love* also includes quatrains, such as "Have You Ever Faked an Orgasm?" and "Lullaby," the latter featuring two stanzas of envelope rhyme that formally suggest the cozy security of "a circle of light / under our own big comforter" where Peacock and her husband lie gossiping. The urgent repetitions of the villanelle supply Peacock with the formal gestures necessary to convey the pressures of promises and perfectionism in "Waking Up" and the frenzied "hummingbird-hearted schedule" the happily espoused transcend in "Little Miracle."

Part 2 is taken up in the painful contemplation of a mother's dying, or, as Peacock calls it, "the shimmering verge between life and death" *(How to Read a Poem . . . and Start a Poetry Circle)*. Peacock's mother, Polly, in the needs of her illness and in the unnurturing neglectfulness of her children, stirs feelings of guilt and ambivalence, of hatred, of love (feelings her daughter tries hard to kill), and of fear at the possibility of being like her. Early in part 2, scenes from Peacock's youth implicate her mother as the root source of lasting trauma and neuroses, while later poems, such as "The Fare," address the guilt and darkness that follow her mother's death and the dread of not being able to let her go. The initially playful mood of "The Fare," created in part through the popping *p* sounds of its opening lines, is gradually dispelled by the appearance of the mother's ghost, come to demand the removal of the painful clip-on earrings she was adorned with for her burial. Peacock has said what the poem talks about is her "inability to conceive" of her mother without "a living body" as evinced by her wish for her mother to be "dead in comfort" *(How to Read a Poem . . . and Start a Poetry Circle)*. The title of the poem alludes to the coins required in payment for the dead to be ferried across the River Styx to Hades, a motif Peacock conflates with the images of subway tokens and, of course, the earrings to ensure her mother, by one means or another, will be dispatched, "return fare fallen to the pit / of a coat's satin pocket." The long, unrhymed, overflowingly emotional lines of the poem dwindle at the end to dimeter as Peacock finally lets go and her mother is laid to rest.

Just as Peacock earlier found heaven and hell in a flower-market bouquet ("A Simple Purchase," in *Take Heart*), she seeks in part 3 to find what is spiritually immanent in the everyday. "Subway Vespers," a prayer of thanks for deliverance from the hellish confines of a delayed subway car, uses triple-rhymed tercets to reinforce the connection between the underground subway tunnels of New York City and a Dantean underworld. For her, the subway has long been "an urban Hades, the place of the dead" *(How to Read a Poem . . . and Start a Poetry Circle)*. Peacock's experience is not simply a rush-hour inconvenience but a spiritual harrowing. The comic effect of the triple rhymes corroborates the understated humor in Peacock's gratitude ". . . that the man with whiskey breath and / bloodshot eyes, business suit, plus monogrammed / cuffs (likely to behave) is significantly / taller than I am. . . ." Yet, the insistence of the rhymes also allows for the expression of the fears she harbors–"Thank you . . . / . . . that we are not naked in a cattle car."

Dust jacket for Peacock's 2002 collection, in which the new poems are influenced by fantasy and legend as outlined by folklorist James Stephens (courtesy of the author)

Part 3, in fact the collection as a whole, is steeped in the language of liturgy and religious practice, continuing a trend already established in the latter poems of *Take Heart*. Abutted against part 2, in which Peacock buried her mother, part 3 begins with the religious instruction that upholds the prospect of a substituting "Heavenly Parent," a chance for her to unorphan herself in the pursuit of spiritual wholeness. Through poems reflecting on the act of transubstantiation ("Simple"), on simple acts of kindness, on "the city of a human-made Eden" ("Matins"), Peacock pursues grace, drained of life until restored "by the circles of converging city streets, / multipaned as insect eyes, or well-cut gems, or Keats, / who could talk. Found comfort" ("All

Her Life That Bra Strap"). For Peacock, the end of *Original Love* is not a case of paradise regained but of hard-won paradise attained.

In "The Land of the Shi: New Poems (2002)," in *Cornucopia* (2002), Peacock's selected poems, she continues in her groundbreaking explorations of the margins of experience, making the logical progression to that last of female frontiers—menopause—and to the world of fantasy and legend as inspired by the writings of Irish Literary Revival luminary and folklorist James Stephens. Peacock appropriates Stephens's narrative, named for the *sidhe*—the land of the fairies and the forever young in Irish mythology—and "transmogrifies" it "through the Land of the City," adapting its combined fantasy (including the occasional shape-changing and the odd leprechaun-nosed grocer) and reality to a contemporary New York setting. Ancient heroes, such as the Irish Fionn and the Scottish Fergus, share space with modern-day heroes, such as Peacock's husband and even the poet herself, who saves a woman from death by choking in a local grocery store. With the appropriative influence of legendary narratives comes a shift, or rather expansion, in Peacock's style—a feeling of graceful orality in long, unrhymed, loose-lined narrative poems and free-verse experiments. This new development sets in relief the elegant syntactical structures of the sonnet ("A Love Koan," "Conversation," "The Parsley Ship," and "Refusal"), a form Peacock mastered long ago. In particular, "A Love Koan" displays Peacock's particular talent for poising the emotional and syntactical weight of a poem on pivotal words such as "like" and "as if." Thematically, Peacock continues in her concern for the sacrifices and solaces of love, for the processes of art and understanding ("Repair" and "Diary of Our Day in Painting Titles"), for the trials and transubstantiations of the self, and for the oppositions—"solid thought" and "liquid thought," the organic and the inorganic, the acts of creation and destruction—that define her world.

How to Read a Poem . . . and Start a Poetry Circle, which features illuminating close-reading discussions of fourteen of Peacock's favorite "talismanic" poems, from Li Ch'ing-chao's "To the Tune 'Cutting a Flowering Plum Branch'" to Margaret Atwood's "Asparagus," serves not only as a barometer of her intuitive critical acuity but as an indispensable guide to her poetic procedures and eclectic literary influences.

Interviews:

Martha Serpas, "Interview with Molly Peacock," *New Delta Review*, 5, no. 1 (Spring 1988);

Alice Friman and Charlotte Templin, "An Interview with Molly Peacock," *Poets and Writers Magazine*, 22, no. 1 (January–February 1994): 34–41;

Paula Deimling, "Interview with Molly Peacock," in *1995 Poets Market* (Oxford & New York: Oxford University Press, 1994);

Kevin Walzer, "An Interview with Molly Peacock," *AWP Chronicle*, 29, no. 1 (October–November 1996): 1–6.

Wyatt Prunty
(15 May 1947 –   )

N. S. Thompson
Christ Church, University of Oxford

BOOKS: *Domestic of the Outer Banks* (Phoenix: Inland Boat Press, 1980);
The Times Between (Baltimore & London: Johns Hopkins University Press, 1982);
What Women Know, What Men Believe (Baltimore & London: Johns Hopkins University Press, 1986);
Balance as Belief (Baltimore & London: Johns Hopkins University Press, 1989);
"Fallen from the Symboled World": Precedents for the New Formalism (New York: Oxford University Press, 1990);
The Run of the House (Baltimore & London: Johns Hopkins University Press, 1993);
Since the Noon Mail Stopped (Baltimore & London: Johns Hopkins University Press, 1997);
Unarmed and Dangerous: New and Selected Poems (Baltimore & London: Johns Hopkins University Press, 2000).

OTHER: "Donald Justice," in *American Writers V*, edited by Jay Parini (New York: Scribner, 2000), pp. 115–130;
Sewanee Writers on Writing, edited by Prunty (Baton Rouge: Louisiana State University Press, 2000).

SELECTED PERIODICAL PUBLICATIONS–
UNCOLLECTED: "The Figure of Vacancy," *Shenandoah*, 46 (Fall 1996): 38–55;
"Horseradish and Roast," *Southern Review*, 36 (Spring 2000): 395–405;
"Donald Justice and the Plain Style," *Writer's Chronicle*, 34 (Fall 2001): 54–61.

Wyatt Prunty *(photograph © Miriam Berkley; courtesy of the author)*

While rightly included in the anthology *Rebel Angels: 25 Poets of the New Formalism* (1996), the work of Wyatt Prunty is less of a conscious attempt to call out from the platform of New Formalism than a reflection of a literary inspiration that has been a constant in postwar American poetry since the emergence of formalists such as Richard Wilbur, Anthony Hecht, Howard Nemerov, and Donald Justice. Indeed, Prunty's formalist roots are grounded even further back in a Southern tradition of order and method that is the flip side to Southern flamboyance, dash, and glamour. At its heart is the rigor of such poets as the Fugitive group of John Crowe Ransom, Allen Tate, and Robert Penn Warren. Each of these poets was also a formidable critic; and during his career in academia, Prunty has assumed the critical role with the same dedication. In addition to his volumes of poetry and his regular essays and reviews, he has produced perhaps the most significant work of criticism to emerge from the New Formalism movement, namely *"Fallen from the Symboled World": Precedents for the New Formalism* (1990). This work clearly defines the immediate poetical background to New Formalism, locating its readings of poets and poetry in a sophisticated, philosophical view of language and realism and providing a valuable series of benchmarks by which the multiplicity of voices in New Formalism may be judged. In Chapter 2, "Emaciated Poetry and the Imaginative Diet," Prunty refines his 1985 *Sewanee Review* essay that was an early rallying cry for New Formalism, in which he showed how many free-verse techniques employed in the name of freedom and authenticity were merely bogus and "mechanical." And with the publication of *Unarmed and Dangerous: New and Selected Poems* (2000) Prunty has shown that he is a significant individual voice.

Born in Humbolt, Tennessee, on 15 May 1947, Eugene Wyatt Prunty spent his youth in Athens, Georgia, but he and his two sisters enjoyed rural vacations in his native state, where his maternal grandparents owned a farm. His father was Merle Charles Prunty of Missouri, a geography professor at the University of Georgia; his mother was Eugenia Wyatt, from a family of prosperous farmers and businessmen in Newbern, Tennessee. The novelist Peter Taylor was a cousin of hers. At the Newbern farm, part of which was pre–Civil War, Prunty remembers history as a palpable lesson; he was allowed to handle the Colt .32, still in its Confederate-issue holster, with which his great-grandfather fought during the Civil War. Other memorabilia gathered in the "plunder room" gave Prunty a rich impression of family history.

While serving in the navy during World War II and teaching meteorology to pilots in Athens, Georgia, Merle Prunty had been invited by the president of the University of Georgia to found a geography and a geology department there. Breaks from young Prunty's grammar-school education were provided as he accompanied his father on field trips over the South, but there were also visits to Athens by Robert Frost to inspire a young reader already interested in poetry. Prunty went to study for his B.A. at the University of the South (Sewanee), majoring in English. In Prunty's final year, Tate (a former editor of the *Sewanee Review*) came back to Sewanee to teach and generously offered to look at the young poet's work, which he pronounced as "publishable" to Andrew Lytle, then current editor of the *Sewanee Review*. The journal had already published one of Prunty's poems ("Monument in the Square") in its Autumn 1968 issue, and a further eleven followed in the next few years. On graduating from Sewanee, Prunty served in the United States Navy as a gunnery officer on the USS *Wright* and the USS *Spiegle Grove*, with tours of duty in the Mediterranean, the Caribbean, and even a trip in the South Atlantic as part of the Apollo 14 mission. Once discharged, he was able to resume his academic education, earning an M.A. in poetry at Johns Hopkins University; about this experience, he wrote in a 30 July 2001 e-mail: "At Hopkins in the fall of 1972 I was the only formalist, the only one who had served in the military and thus had short hair, and the only one with a Southern accent. What I got from being that different was a tug to be less formal and to let the subject, narrator or controlling image direct where the poem went more than my determination to write in ottava rima, say."

From Hopkins, at the suggestion of John T. Irwin, friend and future editor at the university press, Prunty then applied to join the Ph.D. program at Louisiana State University (LSU), where Donald Stanford and Lewis P. Simpson were then editing the *Southern Review* and attracting many bright students to the program. One of the attractions of LSU was the fact that Peter Taylor and Robert Lowell had studied there a generation earlier, when Robert Penn Warren and Cleanth Brooks edited the review. Completing his dissertation on modern poetics in 1979 under Stanford's guidance, Prunty taught his first courses as an instructor at LSU, subsequently taking employment as assistant, then full professor at Virginia Tech (1979–1988), teaching poetry writing at the Bread Loaf Writers' Conference and the Bread Loaf School of English during his summers, and spending a year as writer-in-residence at Washington and Lee University. Then, holding the Elliott Coleman Chair at Hopkins, in 1989 he accepted the Ogden D. Carlton Chair at Sewanee, where he teaches literature but is better known as the founder and director of the Sewanee Writers' Conference and also as editor of its offshoot, the Sewanee Writers' Series, in association with Overlook Press of New York. He was awarded a Guggenheim Fellowship and a residency at Bellagio on Lake Como, Italy, courtesy of the Rockefeller Foundation, in 2002. On the domestic front, he married Barbara Heather Stell in 1973, and they have two children, Heather and Ian.

The stability and closeness of family life are vital elements in the poet's life and poetry. His usual subjects are perhaps found more often in novels: scenarios in family life that bind individuals into the greater warp and weft of existence are contrasted with the converse, as individuals become alienated from these ties. The treatment of such subject matter is, however, unquestionably poetic and suggestive, opening up ironies and ambiguities in the manner of a poem rather than a novel. In general, Prunty's poetry is local and domestic, and it features flying (the poet often pilots his own plane to engagements) or fishing as often as it does family events such as deaths and births. As might be expected from a geographer's son, it also exhibits a reverence for natural landscapes, seasons, and seasonal weather. A useful starting place for considering the formal aesthetic that underpins his poetry is the work that has its roots in his doctoral dissertation at LSU, the critical study *"Fallen from the Symboled World."*

The title is taken from a poem by Nemerov, "The Loon's Cry" (1958): "For I had fallen from / The symboled world, where I in earlier days / Found mysteries of meaning, form, and fate / Signed on the sky." From this poem, in which Nemerov's persona envies past ages rich in symbolic semiosis, Prunty generalizes to the state of American poetry post–World War II, using as a guide the particular example of Robert Lowell, whose postwar loss of faith turned his poetry from one of Christian symbolism and meaning to a personal, factual kind that was purely "realist," devoid of any ulterior systematic metaphysics. The loss of a world of faith and meaning had, of course, been anticipated by T. S. Eliot in "The Waste Land" (1922) and, in a lighter vein, in Wallace Stevens's "Sunday Morning" (1923), where order reverts to "an old chaos in the sun." But as Prunty observes, Lowell's example for a war-torn generation–some of whom found or maintained their faith, most of whom lost it–once again dramatized "the difficulties faced by a generation of poets skeptical about the tradition's ability to represent truth." The "tradition" means not only Judeo-Christian belief itself but also the symbols, allegories, and tropes rooted in that metaphysical world. In this age of doubt, some writers continued writing a poetry of faith regardless, finding new signs and symbols, but the main practice of the new generation of poets in the 1950s was to "turn away from the hierarchies of tradition, as our language hands it down, in order to focus on an individual's isolated experience, then turn back to language in order to apply tropes to that experience." Out of this epistemological crisis, with no higher authority to sanction symbol and allegory, poets turn to tropes based on similitude, a hypothesis Prunty puts to the test in his examination of poets ranging from Wilbur and Nemerov to Elizabeth Bishop and Mona Van Duyn.

It must be said that this work is not written from the detached position of critical observer alone but as a poet and believer who has adopted the physical and social world around him as the basis for his work. If Prunty sees patterns of similitude as the formative basis for his predecessors' poetry, he is wary of metaphorical tropes himself. *"Fallen from the Symboled World"* sets out the basis for defining "poems that sing" and "poems that speak." The former category represents a purely lyric utterance that tends "to rely less on experience and more on connotation and figurative thought, as well as baggage from past cultural experience," one that enables the poet to encompass more than the "here and now"; in contrast, the latter category is narrower but more mimetic of normal experience: "Poems that speak create a *sense* of realism. They tend to move from one fact to the next in a rational sequence. They also have the convincingness of an eyewitness news account provided by a prudent and reasonable person."

Prunty's emphasis on "sense" is an important reminder that any artistic creation, no matter how realist or realistic, is still the product of artifice; nor are the two categories absolutely discrete, he says, as there can be crossovers. Nevertheless, Prunty belongs to the second realist camp; many of his short narrative poems are excursions in the "witness" mode of the realistic novelist who is writing as if the experiences he encapsulates were truly observed. A corollary is that his language is "realist," consisting of plain speech rather than metaphoric, or observationally metaphoric rather than the intellectual play of the conceit. Like the work of Robert Frost, Prunty's poetry possesses a confidence and a security about it that stand out in a chaotic age. His use of poetic form and his poetic language rooted in particulars also derive from this stance.

If rightly associated with New Formalism, Prunty's work demonstrates a softer approach to form than what may be termed ideological rigidity. Unlike the poets he admires such as Nemerov and Justice, or New Formalist contemporaries such as Dana Gioia and R. S. Gwynn, he does not attempt repetitive forms such as the sestina, villanelle, or pantoum, preferring what might be called emergent form to shape his lines and stanzas. On the other hand, his poetic language has a toughness and rigor that neatly counterbalances the lack of formal structures, his work often employing metrical variations of blank verse as its core.

As a whole, then, Prunty's poetry is rooted in the observed world around him and related in an accessible, truthfully observed manner. It also encapsulates a Gerard Manley Hopkins–like reverence for created nature as God made manifest in the world, at the same time as the poet's sympathy for suffering humanity is expressed against the potential for witnessing "God's grandeur."

What ultimately shines through this work grounded in the events of self and family, domestic worlds, and everyday experience is the poet's sympathy with, and confidence in, the quotidian and his feeling blessed with the small epiphanies afforded him by life. But, as with Robert Browning's skeptical narrator in "Bishop Blougram's Apology" (1855), he also has an interest in "the dangerous edge of things," that strange, paradoxical balance of

> The honest thief, the tender murderer,
> The superstitious atheist, demirep
> That loves and saves her soul in new French books–
> We watch while these in equilibrium keep
> The giddy line midway: one step aside,
> They're classed and done with.

Dust jacket for Prunty's 2000 collection, praised by Donald Justice, X. J. Kennedy, Alice McDermott, Mark Strand, and Richard Wilbur (Richland County Public Library)

He realizes, however, that only from a position of certainty can one look meaningfully over the edge into the experiental abyss of others. Only thus is he able to make sense of the act of a suicide whom he addresses in "The Jumper," praising

>   your skill,
> your sudden thrust and cleared fall
> made as you threw yourself
> out of bounds, beyond our rules
> more absolute than we like to think.

This poem, from Prunty's first volume, *The Times Between* (1982), is not in fixed form in terms of rhyme and meter; but he uses iambic lines of differing length to express the paradoxical balance in the activity of "The Kite," which opens the volume:

> The single master of a vacant lot,
> By pulling down it rises up,
> This craft of putting fragile things aloft,
> Of letting go and holding on at once.

Events such as this one, with the epiphanies they produce, constitute the major element of Prunty's earlier work, the dangerous edge of other lives becoming an increasingly larger element in each successive volume. The two coincide in "Rooms Without Walls," a poem from his next volume, *What Women Know, What Men Believe* (1986), again in loose iambic lines of differing length. In this poem the speaker is a child walking through snow in a deprived neighborhood near his home; his steps are brought to a standstill by "cracking sounds" as a father beats his daughter into a silence as deep as the surrounding snow, and the twelve-year-old boy realizes that rooms and houses are no real separation, that people are bound together by their cruelty as much as by their common humanity.

In Prunty's next collection, *Balance as Belief* (1989), rhymed quatrains emerge in such poems as his reflection on the state of America, "To Be Sung on the Fourth of July," which again points to the fact that one needs opposing positions and viewpoints in order to gain a clear vision of life, and "The Hand-Me-Down," about the loss and gain of bereavement. As in so much of his work, Prunty is saying that one has to have black in order to understand white, and wrong in order to understand right. More gently—as in the opening poem, "Learning the Bicycle"—a loss can also paradoxically be a gain: teaching his daughter how to ride on two wheels, he learns "That to teach her I had to follow / And when she learned I had to let her go."

Formal quatrains appear with greater frequency in *The Run of the House* (1993), as in "Letter for the End," an elegy for Nemerov; but generally Prunty makes the most of local landscapes and familiar settings of his own experience, as well as telling stories about others. Prunty evinces a particular sympathy for older generations, celebrating their quirks, foibles, stoicism, and survival. If this affinity has its roots in his experience of family life, it also extends to the wider world. "The Taking Down" gets its title from the name its protagonist gives to the quiet time after Christmas and New Year's Day when the seasonal decorations are taken down. This long meditative poem of 174 lines explores the connections that Mrs. Gilbert, a volunteer worker in a geriatric ward and a senior citizen herself, finds with the patients. What Prunty creates, beyond the feelings of sympathy, is a reminder of the common links of humanity that make people ultimately responsible for each other. Elsewhere, he creates humor and irony from this position, but it is a fundamental, if unstated, moral position stemming from his own Christian belief. The theme of age recurs in "New Territory" when a new retiree suddenly notices the cruelty in nature among a group of starlings, and the reader wonders what mercy—or lack of it—this lady will find among her human group as she advances in years. Other poems give portraits of more feisty elderly characters, as in "Miss Lucy" and "Elderly Lady Crossing on Green," the latter written in neatly fashioned quatrains.

Since the Noon Mail Stopped (1997) continues the theme of time and change, and reflections on these, in a series of domestic and other scenarios. The seasons are traditional points of reference in the passing of time, addressed directly in poems such as "Seasons," "Four Winter Flies," "This," "Late Fall, Late Light," "Cold," "Pictures from January," and "Driving the Christmas Lights." In many poems throughout his work, the attention to weather felt and observed is a noticeable adjunct to emotion. This tendency may have its roots in his father's meteorology, also recollected in the family ritual of reading out loud from the newspaper in "Reading before We Read, Horoscope and Weather":

> My father laughing over the morning paper
> Where the written world fell open on the funnies,
> Manic sports, stalled politics . . . and where
> The Horoscope said, "now," the Forecast, "sunny,"
>
> He couldn't laugh enough, so skipped a page,
> Then another, till the back door shut,
> An engine turned, and I woke up his age
> In the mirror of a gray no-scissors cut.

Although he modestly finds his own performance less amusing, he repeats the ritual with his children, raising the same laughter as his father:

> telling how
> We bend, break, wires shorting, knotting and strange;
> Never as the Horoscope's predicted "now,"
> But as the weather comes, fresh and ignorant of change.

For all the warmth and ritual of family life, people are seen as vulnerable elements of nature in the near metaphors of "break" and "bend," and even as mechanical constructions of electrical wires that can short-circuit. And not everything in families runs smoothly; sometimes there is a lack of peace, as in the comic story of "The Tent," in which a father pitches a tent on the lawn in order to gain a little peace from his noisy children. Less happy lives are detailed in "The Pyromaniac" and "The Sorrows of Lester Buster" and less happy thoughts in the elegy of "The Razed House." If people value a peaceful life, they are also reminded of the fact that it is owed to an earlier generation who fought so that they could enjoy it. The innocent play of "A Baseball Team of Unknown Navy Pilots, Pacific Theater, 1944" is set starkly against their obedience to duty and the cost it entailed ("Went up when told, came home or not"). Play also surfaces as a subject in "Grown Men at Touch," where again such play is only understood by what it contrasts with—the extent of time beyond the brief respite of a game beside a barn ("Play only means because it ends"). Playfulness is further evoked in two poems ("Coach" and "Dog, Dog, Object, Object") about man's best friend, one spoken by the dog itself.

Selections from Prunty's previous books were collected with ten new poems in *Unarmed and Dangerous*, the cover of which quoted accolades from Donald Justice, X. J. Kennedy, Alice McDermott, Mark Strand, and Richard Wilbur; and reviewers repeated the favorable remarks accorded each individual volume when the collection came out. Now that he also has become the editor of a series, having already edited a collection of essays, *Sewanee Writers on Writing* (2000), this poet of deep human sympathy and clear-eyed affirmation will be extending his influence in the wider cultural arena.

Kay Ryan
(21 September 1945 -)

Paul Lake
Arkansas Tech University

BOOKS: *Dragon Acts to Dragon Ends* (Fairfax, Cal.: Taylor Street Press, 1983);

Strangely Marked Metal (Providence, R.I.: Copper Beech Press, 1985);

Flamingo Watching (Providence, R.I.: Copper Beech Press, 1994);

Elephant Rocks (New York: Grove Press, 1996);

Say Uncle (New York: Grove Press, 2000);

Believe It or Not! (Fairfax, Cal.: Jungle Garden Press, 2002).

SELECTED PERIODICAL PUBLICATIONS–UNCOLLECTED: Review of *The Selected Letters of Marianne Moore,* edited by Bonnie Costello, *Boston Review* (Summer 1998) <http://bostonreview.mit.edu/BR23.3/ryan.html>;

"Do You Like It?" *Zyzzyva,* 15 (Winter 1998): 171–173;

"Notes on the Dangers of Keeping Notebooks," *Parnassus: Poetry in Review,* 23, nos. 1–2 (1998).

Kay Ryan (photograph by Sydney Goldstein; courtesy of the author)

Coming from a working-class family, far from the centers of American literary culture, Kay Ryan is a genuine literary maverick. Unlike so many of her contemporaries who teach creative writing in universities, Ryan has spent her adult life working in the trenches of academe, teaching basic writing at the College of Marin and, for a stint, at San Quentin Prison. As her poems attest, however, working outside the literary and academic mainstream has its advantages. During the eleven years between the appearance of her first book, *Dragon Acts to Dragon Ends* (1983), and her breakthrough 1994 collection, *Flamingo Watching,* Ryan intertwined two main strands of modern American poetry to create her own distinctive style. In her mature poetry, Ryan fuses lines haunted by what T. S. Eliot called the "ghost of meter" with short-lined free verse. Rhyme is as central to her poetics as to that of a sonneteer. A dense, if often irregular, pattern of end-rhyme and internal rhyme provides the formal architecture of her poems.

One source of Ryan's distinctive vision may be her desert childhood. She was born Kay Pedersen on 21 September 1945 in San Jose, California. Her father, Kay Richard Pedersen, was an oil driller. Her mother, Bessie Barrett Pedersen, raised Kay and her older brother, Jon Pedersen, in the unfashionable interior valley and desert of southern California. Ryan graduated from Antelope Valley High School in Lancaster, California, in 1963. She received both her B.A. (1967) and M.A. (1968) in English literature from the University of California at Los Angeles and later did some work toward a Ph.D. in literary criticism at the University of California at Irvine but did not take the degree. In "Discovering Kay Ryan" (Winter 1998–1999), the first published essay on Ryan's work, Dana Gioia notes the influence of southern California on her poetry and observes, "Something of Ryan's harsh and hard-worked native terrain is reflected in her luxuriant minimalist aesthetic."

In "A Certain Meanness of Culture," from *Flamingo Watching*, Ryan describes the spartan aesthetic enforced by a desert economy:

> You can get an appreciation
> for why a donkey is
> fussy about books
> since she has to carry them.
> You start to value culture
> like you would water. . . .
> . . . .
> . . . You like winches
> and pulleys, picks and khakis,
> and the rare sweet grass you can
> find for your donkey.

Raised in such a bleak and unforgiving environment, Ryan learned early how to adapt and survive. Though her education and literary inclinations led her from her native terrain, not until she was thirty did Ryan fully accept her vocation as poet. In a short 1998 essay in *Zyzzyva* titled "Do You Like It?" she describes the moment when she answered her calling:

> In 1976, at the age of thirty, I was bicycling across the United States. I had been feeling all the tell-tale symptoms of the poetic calling for a number of years, but was resisting it because I didn't like the part about being utterly exposed, inadequate, foolish, and doomed. Still, poetry kept commandeering my mind. So the bicycle trip was four thousand miles to say yes or no to poetry.
> For a long time it didn't seem to be working.
> Then came a morning, many hundreds of miles into the rhythm of riding, going up a long, high pass in the Colorado Rockies, when I felt my mind simply lose its edges. The pines swept through my mind, my mind swept through the pines, not a bit strange. All at once I no longer had to try to appreciate my experience or try to understand; I played with the phrase *the peace that passeth understanding* like turning a silver coin in my fingers. And with the peace-beyond-the-struggle-to-understand came an unprecedented power to think.

Ryan says she became a poet at the moment when she answered her own unvoiced question about poetry–*Do you like it?*–in the affirmative.

Working in relative isolation, Ryan wrote the poems of *Dragon Acts to Dragon Ends,* her first book. A self-published volume, *Dragon Acts to Dragon Ends* was the inspiration of Ryan's longtime partner, Carol Adair, who financed publication through a subscription by friends. The poems in this volume are varied in style. Some show the influence of late-twentieth-century imagism. Others, such as "Wind," "Didactic," and "Kiwi," are more densely textured and display the earmarks of Ryan's later style. In the best poems in this book, hidden internal rhymes provide a loose structural scaffolding for short free-verse lines that play against the syntax, as in these opening lines of "Didactic":

> The Titanic
> meant to be didactic
> somewhere other than
> the North Atlantic.
> It did not mean to speak
> of Vanity
> or scuttle Humanity's
> faith in Steel . . .

Ryan's next book, *Strangely Marked Metal* (1985), was in many ways a continuation of her first. The didacticism of "Didactic" continues in "New Truth," which begins: "Only a new truth / can bring us closer / to our innocence." The poems of these two early volumes display the playful wit and stylistic cunning of later books but often lack their sureness of tone and more tightly woven structure. Though "Brooklyn Bridge" foreshadows a later poem, "Blandeur," in both style and sentiment ("Unbuild the / Brooklyn Bridge / unspan the river / return travel to water . . ."), it is less bold and original in the way it coins words and distills meaning down to essences. Published by a small press (Copper Beech) and by a relatively unknown poet, *Strangely Marked Metal* produced hardly a ripple upon publication. The appearance of her next book, *Flamingo Watching,* however, was preceded by the publication of her poems in some of the leading American literary journals: *American Poetry Review, The Atlantic, The American Scholar, The New Republic,* and *The Paris Review*. Ryan also received a small degree of support and some local recognition from the Marin Arts Council. As a result, *Flamingo Watching* was Ryan's first book to garner a review, in this instance by George Bradley in the *Yale Review* (July 1995).

By the time Ryan published *Flamingo Watching* in 1994, she had fully assimilated her influences and fashioned her signature style. Less "free" than the mainstream free verse of her contemporaries, the poems of Ryan's mature style combine the trimeter and tetrameter lines of the English lyric tradition with the more syncopated free-verse line of the Ezra Pound–William Carlos Williams–Black Mountain school. Combining occasional end-rhyme and regular meter with free verse, the poet compensates for the increased irregularity of her method by enriching the aural texture of the poems with frequent internal rhymes and thick assonance.

In some poems (such as "Spring") Ryan's formalism dominates; in others, free verse prevails. But in her

Paperback cover for Ryan's 1994 collection, the volume that attracted critical attention to her work (courtesy of the author)

most distinctive poems, the two forms merge, as in "No Rest for the Idle":

> . . . The waters
> of idleness are borderless
> of course and must always
> be plied. Relief is foreign
> on this wide and featureless
> ocean. There are no details:
> no shores, no tides, no times
> when things lift up and then
> subside, no sails or smokestacks,
> no gravel gathered up and spit back,
> no plangencies, no sea birds startled;
> the weather, without the Matthew Arnold.

Ryan creates formal verse even free-verse poets can admire, and free verse for which formalists can feel a warm consanguinity. In achieving such a fusion, Ryan has made her work thoroughly modern without employing the usual Modernist and postmodernist strategies. Instead of fragmentation, obscure allusions, and sterile verbal tricks, her poems surprise readers with their playfully shifting patterns and densely concentrated meanings. The occasional difficulty with her verse results not from the poet's disdain for the bourgeois reader but from her determination to follow Emily Dickinson's injunction to tell the truth, but tell it "slant."

Though her poems are loaded with images, Ryan is not an imagist of any modern school. Nor does she follow Pound's injunction to "Go in fear of abstractions," but rather seems to revel in them. The tables of contents in her books are litanies of lofty abstractions–

Draft for one of the poems in Ryan's 2000 collection, Say Uncle *(courtesy of the author)*

"Age," "Insult," "Hope," "Relief," "Force," "Emptiness"—yet from these vague immensities, Ryan wrings pathos, ironic insights, and heartfelt wisdom.

Ryan's best poems are suffused with an almost medieval religious sensibility. Saints, the cabala, virgin births, reliquaries, and other religious subjects appear in her lines with surprising frequency. The world in her poems often seems a complex allegorical tapestry, filled with secret emblems and occult correspondences. Though often writing with a naturalist's eye for details, Ryan is not a nature poet but an allegorist. Animals in particular often appear less as biological entities than mysterious emblems bearing a wealth of hidden meanings. One poem from *Flamingo Watching* called "Turtle" typifies Ryan's method: "Who would be a turtle who could help it? / A barely mobile hard roll, a four-oared helmet, / she can ill afford the chances she must take / in rowing toward the grasses that she eats." Ryan's unheroic little turtle is, among other things, an emblem of the poet, who quietly mastered her art while slogging through years of teaching basic English, "Never imagining some lottery / will change her load of pottery to wings." Ryan has commented, in an author's note in *An Introduction to Poetry* (1997) edited by X. J. Kennedy, on the genesis and method of this poem:

> "Turtle" came out of an extended time of the most terrible and absolute frustration. That's why it's so giddy. Everything in it is compressed, image and rhymes jammed too tight, threatening to explode. But it can't explode, because all the pieces are twisted together, and twisted again.
>
> "Turtle" was written in a single morning as almost all of my poems are. I began with the first line, "Who would be a turtle who could help it?" It's mysterious how a poem develops out of its beginnings; right now I am thinking it is like lighting a fuse that came into existence by its own burning, creating the dynamite that it explodes. But now I'm thinking, maybe the dynamite doesn't explode; maybe it just forever threatens. That's even better.

Schooled in humility and patience, Ryan's poetry, like her humble turtle, offers lessons in endurance and survival. Unlike her turtle, however, Ryan's literary excursions are sustained by more than one type of levity; irony and a wry sardonic wit lighten the burden of her moral fables.

For all her hermetic religiosity, Ryan is a thoroughly modern writer, her worldview shaped by science as much as by her own hard-won experience. As might be expected of one who grew up "living at the wrong edge / of the arable," where the impersonal mechanisms of nature are most visibly evident, she is a sharp-eyed and unsentimental observer of the natural scene, with a vision permeated by Darwinism. Frequently, both strains of her vision intertwine, as in "The Hinge of Spring," where naturalistic description is infused with metaphoric significance:

> Rabbits are one of the things
> coyotes are for. One quick scream,
> a few quick thumps,
> and a whole little area
> shoots up blue and orange clumps.

In another poem, about a remark by Charles Darwin ("I Marvelled at How Generally I Was Aided"), Ryan gives her evolutionism a more optimistic slant, suggesting that "Perhaps not chance, / but need, selects; and desperation / works upon giraffes until their necks / can reach the necessary branch."

Constrained by a hard-nosed skepticism, Ryan's faith in the meaningfulness and dignity of life is, like her turtle, well-grounded. Though she believes, like Gerard Manley Hopkins, that there lives "a dearest freshness deep down things," her optimism does not depend on transcendental hopes or supernatural aspirations but is rooted in a thoroughly American pragmatism. Faith and hope are true not because they are underwritten by religious codes or divine revelations, but because they work—physically, morally, psychologically.

Ryan's idiosyncratic faith is not rigidly orthodox but "flexible to the point / of oddity." The poet looks at things from odd angles and reexamines old ideas and opinions, refusing to settle into orthodoxy—a process she describes with remarkable brevity in "Spring":

> I see the yellow maculations spread
> across bleak hills of what I said
> I'd always think: a stippling of white
> upon the grey: a pink the shade
> of what I said I'd never say.

Ryan's poems tease the imagination with wordplay and sudden reversals, yielding richer implications with each reading. Sometimes compressed to the point of obliquity, her lines make readers dig deep to descry their meanings. New tangents often hinge on a single word, as in the title poem of *Flamingo Watching,* in which the poet takes a sly jab at stiff-necks who fail to appreciate her emblematic flamingo's disconcerting flamboyance:

> ... The natural elect,
> they think, would be less pink,
> less able to relax their necks,
> less flamboyant in general.
> They privately expect that it's some
> poorly jointed bland grey animal
> with mitts for hands
> whom God protects.

Paperback cover for Ryan's 2000 collection; the title poem depicts a writer's struggle with an inner voice of defeat (Richland County Public Library)

The poems of Ryan's next volume, *Elephant Rocks* (1996), appeared with some frequency in *The New Yorker* prior to their publication in book form. When the book appeared from Grove Press, it was reviewed by Andrew Frisardi in *Poetry* (May 1997) and Laura Miller in "Poetry for the Rest of Us" in *Salon.com,* one of the most widely read Internet journals of that era. In *Elephant Rocks,* Ryan continues to develop many of the same themes. In "Doubt" she shows that hope is often the most pragmatic, and therefore true, method of achieving one's desires and purposes by demonstrating the inefficacy of its opposite:

> A chick has just so much time
> to chip its way out, just so much
> egg energy to apply to the weakest spot
> or whatever spot it started at.
> It can't afford doubt. Who can?
> Doubt uses albumen
> at twice the rate of work.
> One backward look by any of us
> can cost what it cost Orpheus. . .

Perhaps more than any other quality, Ryan's near-religious faith in the ability of poetry to illuminate experience sets her apart from her contemporaries.

In contrast to her postmodern peers, who try to show how unstable words are by cutting the ground out from under them, Ryan digs down to their dusty roots to reinvigorate old meanings. Or she coins new words, making them mean just what she means them to, as in "Bestiary":

> A bestiary catalogs
> bests. The mediocres
> both higher and lower
> are suppressed . . .
> . . . .
> Best is not to be confused with *good*–
> a different creature altogether,
> and treated of in the goodiary–
> a text alas lost now for centuries.

In *Say Uncle* (2000) she continues to invent new words to suit her purposes, as in "Blandeur," which unfolds like an oddly off-key prayer:

> If it please God,
> let less happen.
> Even out Earth's
> rondure, flatten
> Eiger, blanden
> the Grand Canyon.

Like Ryan's preceding two volumes, *Say Uncle* attracted attention from major journals; it was included in group reviews by Rachel Hadas in *Yale Review* (April 2001) and by David Yezzi in *Poetry* (May 2001). Paul Lake's review, "Telling It Slant," appeared in *Threepenny Review* (Summer 2000). Ryan's primary allegiance is to the poem, not politics, fashion, or ideology. Though often suffused with a wily if understated feminism, her poems are too diverse and self-questioning to espouse ideas single-mindedly. Seemingly small in compass, her poems open to sometimes vast and always curious perspectives. In seeking comparisons to her poetry, one looks not to Ryan's better-known contemporaries but to such writers as Marianne Moore, Elizabeth Bishop, or Dickinson.

Coming to sudden prominence when she was almost fifty, living on the West Coast, and being largely unconnected to the academic network that nurtures writing careers, Ryan has received practically no critical attention beyond a few reviews. The fact that her poetry does not fit conveniently into any established "school" of contemporary verse is surely one cause of this situation. Yet, despite the lack of helpful commentary, Ryan's poetry has begun to draw a large audience since the late 1990s, when it began to appear with some frequency in *The New Yorker* and other leading journals. It has also garnered several major awards—a circumstance no doubt relished by this onetime literary outsider. Ryan has received a National Endowment for the Arts Fellowship, the Maurice English Poetry Prize, the Union League Poetry Prize, the Ingram-Merrill Award, two Pushcart Prizes, and inclusion in *Best American Poetry* in 1995 and 1999 and *Best of the Best American Poetry 1988–1997*. However it fares in the contemporary literary marketplace, Ryan's work is sure to be represented in any future "bestiary" of American poetry.

Interview:

Greg Giles, "An Interview with Marin Poet Kay Ryan," 5 September 2001 <http://www.oliversbooks.com/localauthors.html>.

Reference:

Dana Gioia, "Discovering Kay Ryan," *Dark Horse,* no. 7 (Winter 1998–1999): 6–9.

Mary Jo Salter
(15 August 1954 -   )

R. A. Benthall
University of North Carolina at Chapel Hill

See also the Salter entry in *DLB 120: American Poets Since World War II, Third Series.*

BOOKS: *Henry Purcell in Japan: Poems* (New York: Knopf, 1985);
Unfinished Painting: Poems (New York: Knopf, 1989);
The Moon Comes Home (New York: Knopf, 1989);
Sunday Skaters: Poems (New York: Knopf, 1994);
A Kiss in Space: Poems (New York: Knopf, 1999);
Open Shutters: Poems (New York: Knopf, 2003).

OTHER: *The Norton Anthology of Poetry,* edited by Salter, Margaret Ferguson, and Jon Stallworthy (New York: Norton, 1996; abridged, New York: Norton, 1997);
Amy Clampitt, *The Collected Poems of Amy Clampitt,* foreword by Salter (New York: Knopf, 1997).

SELECTED PERIODICAL PUBLICATIONS—
UNCOLLECTED: "Puns and Accordions," *Yale Review,* 79 (Winter 1990): 188–221;
"A Poem of One's Own: What, If Anything, Is a 'Woman Poet'?" *New Republic,* 204 (4 March 1991): 30–34;
"Thick-skinned," *New Republic,* 207 (6 July 1992): 42;
"Poets and Parents" (Elegies for James Merrill and Amy Clampitt), *New Republic,* 212 (6 March 1995): 46;
"Paper Doll Poetry," *Oxygen.com: The Read* (9 November 1999) <http://www.oxygen.com/read/archive/essay/991109essay.html>;
"But I Digress," *Oxygen.com: The Read* (24 February 2000) <http://www.oxygen.com/read/archive/essay/000224essay.html>;
"A Room (#9) Of One's Own: Meeting the Muse at a Cheap Motel," *Oxygen.com: The Read* (8 June 2000) <http://www.oxygen.com/read/archive/essay/000608essay.html>.

Known for her mastery of traditional forms as well as free verse, Mary Jo Salter has emerged as one of

Mary Jo Salter (photograph © Jerry Bauer; courtesy of the author)

the most versatile and distinctive American poets born after 1950. In addition to demonstrating her technical acumen, her poems display the workings of a keen intellect and show a remarkable eye for detail. These details are drawn from quiet domestic settings as well as the more expansive vistas of biography and history. Whether she writes about family relationships, her travels in Japan and Iceland, the fortunes of Robert Frost, or the life of Helen Keller, Salter's poems dramatize a mind and sensibility aware of loss, always in search of illumination.

Salter was born on 15 August 1954 in Grand Rapids, Michigan, and grew up in Detroit and Baltimore. Her father, Albert Gregory Salter, fought in World War II, returned to go to college on the G.I. Bill, and eventually became an advertising executive. Her mother, Lormina Paradise Salter, was a commercial artist for *The New York Times* as well as a painter. Although Salter's father appears only in her late work, her mother, by contrast, appears in many poems, early and late.

Salter received her B.A. degree cum laude from Harvard University (where she met her future husband, poet Brad Leithauser) in 1976 and her M.A. from Cambridge University with first-class honors in 1978. After returning to the United States, she taught at Harvard from 1978 to 1979 and worked as staff editor at *Atlantic Monthly* until August 1980. She and Leithauser were married on 2 August 1980 and immediately embarked for Japan, where Leithauser worked as a research fellow for the Kyoto Comparative Law Center, and Salter taught conversational English.

Although their stay in Japan lasted three years, Salter returned to the United States briefly in 1981 when she was named poet-in-residence for the Robert Frost Place. This honor was followed by her winning the Discovery Prize from the *Nation* (1983) and a National Endowment for the Arts Grant (1983–1984). In addition to Japan, Salter has lived in France, Italy, and Iceland, having made most of her travels with her husband. She has written poems set in all of these places, leading some readers to see her as a first-rate travel writer.

"Journeys to foreign places," Salter has said, "have always served me as both inspiration and insulation" (Oxygen.com, 8 June 2000), providing a place where she can harvest new perceptions of the world and find the anonymity to sit and write. Her love of contrasting American with European, and European with Eastern cultures is evidence of a deeper intellectual and artistic drive. She is a poet who thrives on sharp contrasts and uncanny similarities. William Wordsworth wrote in the preface to the second edition of his *Lyrical Ballads* (1800): "the perception of similitude in dissimilitude . . . is the great spring of the activity of our minds, and their chief feeder," concluding that "upon the accuracy with which similitude in dissimilitude, and dissimilitude in similitude are perceived, depend our taste and our moral feelings." When Henry Taylor praised Salter's third volume, *Sunday Skaters: Poems* (1994), for its "effortless observation . . . backed up by a strong and deep moral sense," and Alfred Corn noted that "a powerful ethical dimension is active everywhere in this book," they were both drawing attention to Salter's keen powers of visual and psychological perception and her commitment to seeing both dimensions clearly.

This desire for illumination through juxtaposition is fully voiced in Salter's first book of verse, *Henry Purcell in Japan: Poems* (1985), the title of which suggests cultural contrast. In the first poem of the book, "For an Italian Cousin," the speaker's devoutly Catholic cousin gives her a tour of a church, despite the fact that the speaker's faith, if she has any, is "*protestante*." Although the latter word is rhymed ironically with the Catholic "Dante," the speaker still desires to connect with her cousin, saying "I'd show you, *cugina*, a world I've pieced / together with a kind of faith at least." Although the poem is composed in loose iambic tetrameter, the lines verge on iambic pentameter, precariously enjambed with a terminal verb, as the rhymes suggest the speaker's efforts to bring order to her own fragmented world. The poem ends with an image of "San Marco in Venice, where you've never been," and where "A puzzle of figures floats on the walls / and in golden domes, and you have the feeling / this heavenly gold is not a ceiling– / but space itself, from which no one falls." The image recalls the gold mosaics at the end of William Butler Yeats's "Sailing to Byzantium," which also depicts a transcendent world, suspended by artifice.

Following a similar strategy of cultural and religious contrast, "Henry Purcell in Japan," the title poem, portrays a Westerner's sense of mystification at a Japanese funeral, at which the mourners' perception of death is different from her own. The speaker encounters the silent beauty of the written Japanese characters that name the dead, along with the Japanese funeral bell, contrasting these elements with a choir she later hears singing the music of Purcell. Whereas the Japanese letters bespeak a silent resignation to mortality, and the bell a "spirit more austere," Purcell's music typifies the Western penchant for "the antiquated light / of drafty English chapels and the comfort / of harmonies layered against the cold." As she meditates on these cultural differences, the speaker becomes aware that the "foreign country of the dead" is really much more foreign than either the Japanese or American cultures are to one another. By facing this unfathomable gulf, a fragile bond arises, bridging cultural gaps, allowing the speaker to add her own Western voice to those of the Japanese mourners by singing a single line of Purcell's, "Again I say rejoice."

Reviews of Salter's first book were somewhat mixed. M. L. Rosenthal remarked that the poems were "playful, chilly, and convoluted and always slightly too long for their subject" (*The New York Times Book Review*, 7 April 1985). Corn, however, said in *The New Republic* (8 April 1985) that "Mary Jo Salter's first book places her squarely among the new breed of poets who seem to be charting a direction for American poetry in this decade." "What first strikes us with Mary Jo Salter," he says, "is the achieved tone and fine-grained diction." He goes on to say of the Japanese poems that "these brilliant and searching poems are the best in the volume."

Dust jacket for Salter's 1999 collection, in which the title poem is about astronauts on the Mir *space station (Richland County Public Library)*

The manuscript of Salter's second volume, *Unfinished Painting: Poems* (1989), was the 1988 Lamont Poetry Selection of the Academy of American Poets, an award given specifically for an American poet's second book. Salter went on to win the Witter Bynner Foundation Poetry Prize in 1989 and to win a grant from the Ingram-Merrill Foundation. The title poem of *Unfinished Painting* shows Salter's characteristic impulse toward *ekphrasis* (highly visual poetic thought). The speaker describes the painting of a mother, most likely Salter's, who has tried to paint her son but has been called away from her art by the demands of real life: "It seems that bringing / the real boy up had taken time / away from painting him." The incompleteness of the painting embodies the idea that the mother's art has been sacrificed, forming a pointed commentary on the female artist's predicament. Salter remarked in an on-line essay for Oxygen.com (9 November 1999) that her mother "had given up Everything for motherhood," and this theme of artistic loss returns in later poems, also treated in the subject of the poet's frustrated mother. Even so, the painting still bespeaks the mother's love as, years later, the son inspects the painting and sees that the "finished head conveys / still to him how, sought in a crowd, / a loved one stands apart—he's taller / comes in a different shade."

In addition to its psychological poise between grief and affection, "Unfinished Painting" also displays Salter's formal flexibility and skill, consisting of five-line stanzas, the first four lines of which are tetrameter, followed by a trimeter. This metrical abbreviation in the last line may rhetorically underline the reflection on incompleteness in the poem. Moreover, the rhythmically "unfinished" last line rhymes at random with one of the preceding lines, often imperfectly, as in the "crowd / shade" rhyme above, giving the poem additional aural subtlety.

Although *Unfinished Painting* is dedicated to Salter's biological mother, it also acknowledges at least one poetic mother. The book includes two poems about Emily Dickinson, as well as one about Salter's elder daughter, born in 1983, and also named Emily. "Reading Room" is set in the Williston Memorial Library at Mount Holyoke College, where Dickinson matriculated and where Salter has taught since 1984. Salter eventually had a second daughter, named Hilary, in 1988.

Reviews of *Unfinished Painting* were generally more positive than those for *Henry Purcell in Japan*. Phoebe Pettingell, writing in *The New Leader* (10 July 1989), compared Salter's first and second books, saying that "her new book avoids the pitfall of overloading a small poem with disproportionately large emotional freight that her first occasionally fell into–like drawing the Crucifixion on a lady's fan, or writing a popular ballad about the Holocaust. The elegiac themes of *Unfinished Painting* are well-suited to Salter's playful profundity."

Salter won the Peter B. Lavan Award from the Academy of American Poets in 1990 and a Guggenheim Fellowship in 1993. These honors were followed by the publication of her third collection, *Sunday Skaters*, which was nominated for a National Book Critics Circle Award, in which she sets several poems in Iceland. The title poem begins by noting that "These days / the sky composes promises / and rips them to pieces," briskly using the pathetic fallacy to set an elegiac tone, which Salter employs in many other poems. The poem then describes a frozen pond in the distance, where children and adults skate on a Sunday afternoon in March. Halfway through, the poem takes an unexpected psychological turn as the speaker describes a small boy's face as "Stock still at the clock's center, / the pin that everything hinges on," a description that leads her to exclaim "It's all / about time, about time!" The skaters then become an index for the passage of time, as they inscribe lines in the ice that will surely melt.

Sunday Skaters also includes work of a more personal and domestic nature, including "Lullaby for a Daughter," which consists of four lines:

> Someday, when the sands of time
> invert, may you find perfect rest
> as a newborn nurses from
> the hourglass of your breast.

One of the more innovative poems in the book, "Poppies," characteristically begins by describing a Renoir painting but spirals back in time to describe a scene of childhood illness and a flickering black and white television movie, both of which form a backdrop for recounting the terror of abandonment at the premature loss of the poet's mother. Robert B. Shaw said of "Poppies" (*Poetry*, May 1995) that "the strands are so closely woven in this web of reminiscence" that the poem qualifies as "certainly one of Salter's finest poems." He also praises *Sunday Skaters* in general, saying that "poets grow in different ways, some in skill, others in range. From her first publications, Salter has been an accomplished stylist, one of those in her generation who have made the New Formalism more than a fad. As technically adept as ever, it is by expanded versatility that her recent work marks its advance. A wider array of themes and tones distinguishes this book from its forerunners." Salter's third book is marked by a tone of increasing confidence and authority. Shaw notes that "Rootless," for example, a poem about the plight of writer Salman Rushdie, "in its final stanzas, takes on a voice of Yeatsian authority," and Judith Hall observed of Salter in *The Antioch Review* (Winter 1995) that a "reader, relaxing in the unflinching authority of her voice, may forget how rare it is in American poetry for a woman to claim this power."

Sunday Skaters also pays homage to poet Robert Frost in "Frost at Midnight," a masterful blank-verse meditation on the more telling episodes of Frost's life. Samuel Taylor Coleridge's blank-verse poem of the same title, with its abstruse musings on the strange fabric of childhood memory, forms the perfect fulcrum. Like Robert Lowell's sonnet "Robert Frost" (1969), which begins "Robert Frost at midnight," Salter's poem also examines Frost's darker side, while still paying tribute to "the Yank from Yankville." The poem begins with a thirty-eight-year-old Frost sitting, like Coleridge, by the fire at midnight, all others asleep but he, except that Frost is writing not a poem but a letter to literary editor Susan Hayes Ward of *The Independent* (a New York periodical with national circulation) to inquire about publishing his first book of poems. Salter describes Frost weeding out his own work, tossing inferior poems on the fire, so that "the ones he saved could shine the brighter." She then considers an alternative: "Or it may be, as the curling pages turned / brilliant a fierce instant, then to ash, / he was thinking of the sallow leaves that fell / indifferently outside, beyond the laurel, / and was terrified of their unwritten message." The irregularity of the meter embodies the ominous flutter as each burning poem turns "brílliant a fíerce ínstant, thén to ásh." Touches such as these set up a metrical and allusive resonance between the two poems that makes the whole seem greater than the parts. Salter comments in the end that Frost never "lost his knack, even in prose, / for giving truth the grandeur of a cadence," an evaluation that also describes her own style at its best.

Salter served as poetry editor for *The New Republic* from 1992 until 1995 and as an editor for the fourth edition of *The Norton Anthology of Poetry* in 1996 and the abridged version in 1997. These tasks, however, did not distract her from producing her own original work. Salter's genius for juxtaposing two quite different historical templates, as in the case of Coleridge and Frost, and watching poetic moiré patterns form is even more boldly expressed in her fourth poetry collection, *A Kiss in Space: Poems* (1999). Like Salter's previous collections, this one includes poems about private domestic situations as well as outward-looking travel scenarios, several of which are set in France. In "A Leak Somewhere," for example, the speaker and her husband watch the 1953 television movie *Titanic*, in which Clifton Webb and Barbara Stanwyck play two unhappily married passengers, whose problems soon enough seem trivial aboard the doomed ship. Although the high melodrama is hard for the speaker to take seriously, the poem turns sharply in the end from the grand subject of the *Titanic* to the precariousness of private domestic life, as speaker and spouse "sense / that hidden in the house a fine / crack—nothing spectacular / only a leak somewhere—is slowly / widening to claim each of us / in random order, and we start to rock / in one another's arms." This ability to shift suddenly from a comprehensive narrative to an intensely private, lyrical gesture has become one of Salter's trademarks.

Both of Salter's parents are the subjects of "Home Movies: A Sort of Ode," which deals with her father's penchant for making home movies. After recounting his shots of children and the occasional close-up of a rose, the poem alludes to his troubled marriage to the speaker's mother. "What happened between him and her / is another story," the speaker says, and although "we have no movie of it," a hint survives on film in the "unforgiving scowls she gave / through terrifying, ticking silence / when he must have asked her (no / soundtrack) for a smile." The poem ends by recollecting a shot of the mother, happily teaching the children to dye Easter eggs. The stoneware mixing bowl is still in the speaker's possession, having become "a Grecian / urn of sorts near which—a foster / child of silence and slow time / myself—I smile because she does / and patiently await my turn." As in *Unfinished Painting*, the sufferings of Salter's mother, as well as her artistic influence, continue to speak out of the poet's past.

Strikingly, *A Kiss in Space* begins and ends with poems about people floating above the earth, wondering what to make of the world beneath them. The first poem, "Fire-Breathing Dragon," recounts a hot-air balloon ride in France, where Chartres creates a "double puncture" in the distant horizon. As the balloon itself resembles a dragon, the poem drifts into a meditation on the power of myths, religious symbols, and the power of belief: "Once / people believed in dragons— // as we began to, an hour ago, / drifting to such a height the tinted / interlocking shapes of crops / became a story in stained glass / our shadow could fall into." The beauty of the speaker's perspective makes belief seem possible, for a moment, but the ride is soon over, the balloon scraping along the ground for a landing, and the pilot deflating the balloon like St. George killing the dragon. In the end, the residue of the will to believe persists only whimsically, in a glass of champagne "whose balloons by the hundreds rise."

If "Fire-Breathing Dragon" looks backward in time to an age of belief, the last poem of the book, the title poem, "A Kiss in Space," is forward looking. The poem builds on a photo in *The New York Times*, which captured the kiss of American astronaut Norman Thagard and Russian cosmonaut Yelena Kondakova aboard the *Mir* space station. The speaker in this poem reflects on how such divergent cultures can meet in such an unlikely space, and how their kiss will be remembered even after their return "back home—or // to whatever Earth has become." As in her first book of poems, Salter continues to spotlight unlikely convergences. Although she repeatedly shows how a fragile human bond is often the only real connection between persons or events, Salter manages to convey a sense of the power of that bond, despite its fragility.

The most ambitious study in contrasts, divergences, and emergent meanings occurs in "Alternating Currents," in which Salter brings together not two but three historical templates and conjures meaning from the eerie similarities that emerge between them. The poem recounts the lives and adventures of Sherlock Holmes, Alexander Graham Bell, and Helen Keller. Both Holmes and Bell had keen, resourceful minds, and both had assistants named Watson. Bell spent much of his life trying to help the deaf, and Keller was blind and deaf. Keller discovered language through cascading water, and Holmes, at the hand of his creator, Sir Arthur Conan Doyle, perishes over a waterfall, only to be resurrected by the author. The connecting thread in the poem is the mystery of language: "Bell to Watson: 'Come here, I want / to see you.' Holmes to Watson again: 'Come at once if convenient; / if not convenient, come all the same.' / And this: "Come, Watson, the game's afoot!' // And what's the game? Something about / taking a message."

Salter has never been attracted to the confessional school of poetry or been fully committed to free verse. Her formal discipline and virtuosity, as well as her desire to render carefully the details of experience and to explore how those details ramify, tend to cool the kind of pyrotechnic emotionalism that characterizes many of the confessional free-verse poets. Some critics have read Salter's coolheadedness as "chilly" and even suspicious. In a frustrated review for *The New Criterion* (June 1999), William Logan said that *A Kiss in Space* "is full of honest, dutiful poems a housewife would write, if there were such a thing as a housewife anymore; they revel in domestic certitudes. . . ." Like Rosenberg writing in 1985, Logan remarks on a "chilliness she probably doesn't even notice." He then seizes on the phrase

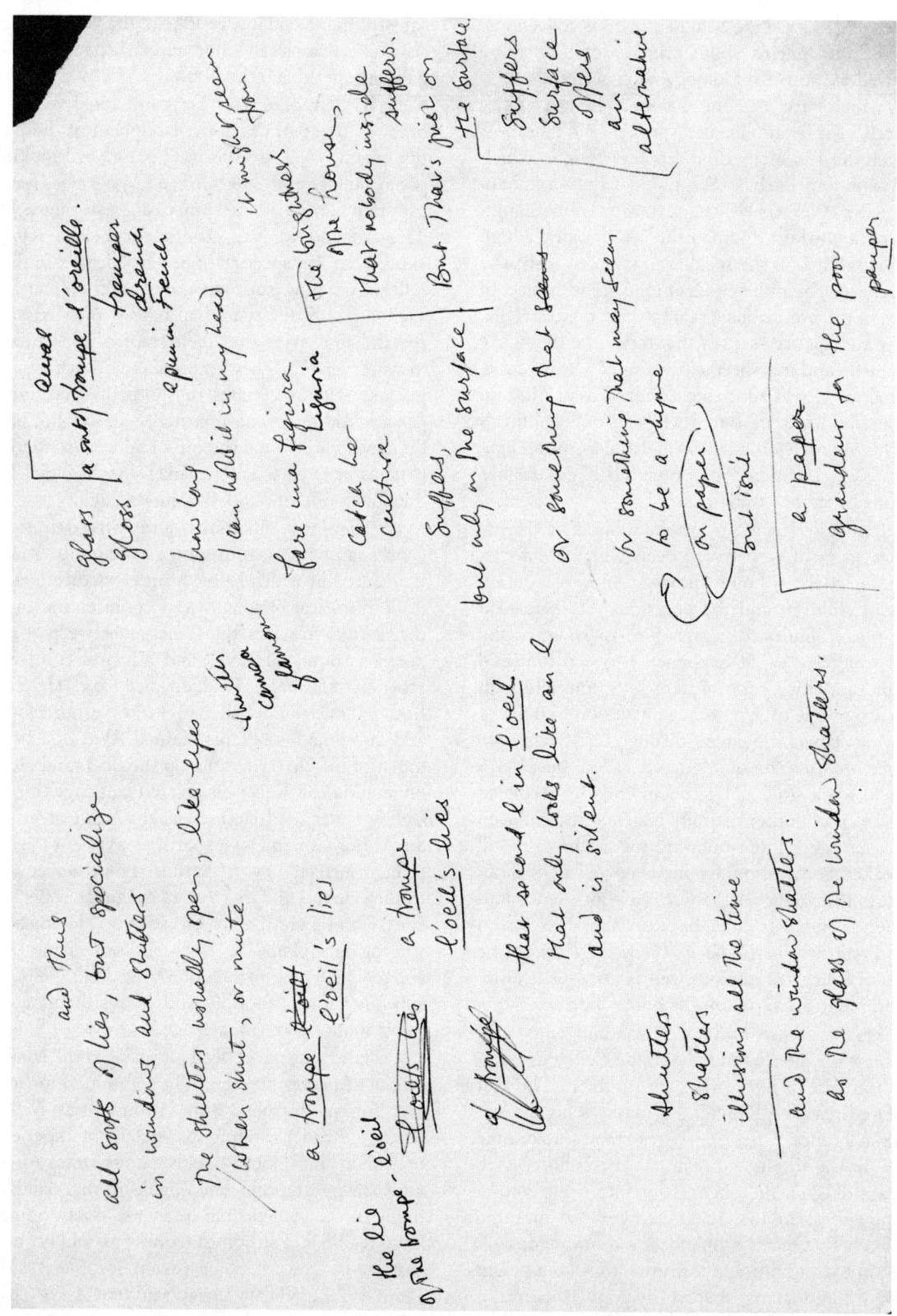

Draft for "Trompe l'Oeil," written on the back of a train schedule in Italy in December 1998. A later version of the poem was published in a 2003 issue of The Kenyon Review (courtesy of the author).

"feigning normality" from the poem "Distance," a meditation spoken by a person who has suffered an excruciating loss some time ago and has compensated by acting normal. "Feigning normality," he says. "Suddenly all that white-knuckled normalcy is explained." Logan concludes by saying that Salter is concealing "something unmentionable, and I wish she'd let it out."

Most other reviews of *A Kiss in Space,* however, have been positive, seeing virtues precisely where Logan saw vices. Barbara Hoffert called these poems "dainty but tough," concluding, "what a delight to read a poet who doesn't focus relentlessly on the long-suffering 'I'" (*Library Journal,* 15 April 2000). Although David Yezzi found that the poems in the first section of the book occasionally "lack juice," he found the rest of the volume a success, especially those poems that "play in a minor key, the sonorities of which keep the poems well clear of sentimentality. Verses as poised, lapidary, sonically lovely, and pleasingly acute as Salter's seem sweetest when cut with a bit of salt" (*Poetry,* April 2000). William Pritchard found *A Kiss in Space* "a valuable extension of the combination of writerly craft and human expressiveness evident in her earlier books." He sees the book as a volume "in which tenderness is inwoven with humor, and where impressive technical ability exists at the service of imaginative sanity" (*Commonweal,* 3 December 1999).

In addition to writing her poems, Salter contributed regularly to Oxygen.com, a women's website on which a now discontinued weekly column, "The Read," published personal essays by women writers, on a variety of topics. Salter published seven essays, three of which deal specifically with poetry. In these short essays, Salter discusses Sylvia Plath and Marianne Moore in the same breath with women's fashion and the art of daydreaming, admirably bridging the perceived chasm between poetry and popular culture. Many of the essays also include personal reflections by Salter on family life, the creative process, and the relationship between the two.

Mary Jo Salter's combination of technical virtuosity, perceptiveness, and intellectual vigor continues to produce poems of remarkable depth and subtlety, and has given readers one of the most unusual voices in late-twentieth-century American poetry. Just as her ability to extract profundity from tiny details harks back to Wordsworth, one of Salter's seldom-remarked poetic benefactors, so also her clear and quiet voice resounds with an authority all its own. Coleridge could recognize his friend Wordsworth's style so well that he once remarked of a particular passage, "had I met these lines running wild in the deserts of Arabia, I should have instantly screamed out 'Wordsworth!'" The power and singularity of Salter's style, with its carefully crafted negotiations between the general sweep of history and the private domestic sphere, or between different segments of history, continue to be recognizable anywhere.

References:

After New Formalism: Poets on Form, Narrative, and Tradition, edited by Annie Finch (Ashland, Ore.: Story Line Press, 1999);

Henry Taylor, "Faith and Practice: The Poems of Mary Jo Salter," *Hollins Critic,* 37 (February 2000).

Papers:

Mary Jo Salter's letters to Amy Clampitt can be found in the Clampitt archive in the Henry A. and Albert W. Berg Collection, New York City Public Library.

Gjertrud Schnackenberg

(27 August 1953 -   )

Kymberly Taylor Haywood
University of Notre Dame

See also the Schnackenberg entry in *DLB 120: American Poets Since World War II, Third Series.*

BOOKS: *Portraits and Elegies* (Boston: Godine, 1982; revised edition, New York: Farrar, Straus & Giroux, 1986; London: Hutchinson, 1987);
The Lamplit Answer (New York: Farrar, Straus & Giroux, 1985; London: Hutchinson, 1986);
A Gilded Lapse of Time (New York: Farrar, Straus & Giroux, 1992; London: Harvill, 1995);
The Throne of Labdacus (New York: Farrar, Straus & Giroux, 2000);
Supernatural Love: Poems 1976-1992 (New York: Farrar, Straus & Giroux, 2000);
Supernatural Love: Poems 1976-2000 (Tarset, U.K.: Bloodaxe Books, 2001).

OTHER: "Supernatural Love," in *The Direction of Poetry: An Anthology of Rhymed and Metered Verse Written in the English Language since 1975,* edited by Robert Richman (Boston: Houghton Mifflin, 1988);
"Prefaces: Five Poets on Poems by T. S. Eliot: Gjertrud Schnackenberg: 'Marina,'" *Yale Review,* 78 (Winter 1989): 210-215;
"The Epistle of Paul the Apostle to the Colossians," in *Incarnation: Contemporary Writers on the New Testament,* edited by Alfred Corn (New York: Viking, 1990), pp. 189-211.

Gjertrud Schnackenberg, 1985 (photograph by Skyla Irving)

Gjertrud Schnackenberg's first three books reveal a mastery of formal verse forms. Her debut chapbook, *Portraits and Elegies* (1982), won exceptional critical acclaim and stimulated the appetite of Americans hungry for a major new voice. A poetic triptych including formal poems of great power, *Portraits and Elegies* departed from the literary fashion of the 1980s in its historical subjects and reliance upon meter and rhyme instead of the free-verse confessional poem. However, far from revisiting the aesthete, sometimes sterile, dry academicism of the 1950s, Schnackenberg used verse forms as a whetstone to hone her own distinct voice. Her poems, dense and musical, echo traditions inherited from British poetry and early Modernists such as T. S. Eliot, William Butler Yeats, and Wallace Stevens in their concern not only with history but also with philosophy, classicism, Christianity, and metaphysics. An artistic versifier, Schnackenberg can write in flawless meter, shifting from Stevensian pentameter to Dantian terza rima with ease. In later years, her tightly meshed rhymes and rigorous metrics relaxed into loosely knit variations of meter and a powerful free verse. The seeds of Schnackenberg's historical scope, intellectual passion, and talent for the long poem, sown in *Portraits and Elegies*, bore fruit in her second book, *The Lamplit Answer* (1985). Most critics agreed that this book confirmed her meteoric rise, prompting Geoffrey Stokes to note in "Modern Necromancers" for the *Voice Literary Supplement* (7 May 1985) that her "genius, the term is not too strong, is precise, playful, and necromantic" and to proclaim Schnackenberg "the most gifted American of her generation." Seven years later, her eagerly awaited third book, *A Gilded Lapse of Time* (15 November 1992), revealed a poet whose long sequences had evolved into poems of increasing structural sophistication, formal innovation, and epic proportion. Though the book drew some criticism for its sometimes dizzying digressions and lush diction, it nonetheless prompted hard-won praise from critic and poet William Logan. In a review of *A Gilded Lapse of Time* for *The New York Times Book Review*, "Angels, Voyeurs and Cooks" (1992), Logan pronounced Schnackenberg "the best poet writing today under 40." After a silence of almost eight years, Schnackenberg's dual release of a new book-length poem on the Oedipus myth, *The Throne of Labdacus* (2000), and *Supernatural Love: Poems 1976–1992* (2000), which collects most of the poems within her first three books, assures her a distinguished place within the canon of American poetry.

Gjertrud Cecilia Schnackenberg, the daughter of Walter Charles and Doris Ione Strom Schnackenberg, was born on 27 August 1953 in Tacoma, Washington. Of Norwegian descent, she was raised a Lutheran with three sisters, Ann, Mary, and Dikka. Her father graduated from Saint Olaf College in Northfield, Minnesota, and taught Russian and medieval history at Pacific Lutheran University, a college founded by Norwegian immigrants in Tacoma. The recipient of many major prizes and prestigious fellowships, Schnackenberg received an honorary doctorate from Mount Holyoke College in 1985. She has lived in Italy, Tacoma, and Cambridge, Massachusetts, and currently resides in Boston. She married Robert Nozick, a Harvard philosophy professor, on 5 October 1987. He died in 2002.

Schnackenberg began publishing and winning awards for her poems while attending Mount Holyoke College from 1971 to 1975. Following in the footsteps of predecessors such as Sylvia Plath, Robert Lowell, and James Merrill, she won prestigious Glascock Awards for poetry in 1973 and 1974. One well-known poet of her generation who knew her in these youthful years commented on her legendary quality: "Trudy was an incredible talent, a luminous presence of astounding beauty who, when reading her poetry aloud, was mesmerizing." A professor who knew Schnackenberg at Mount Holyoke agreed: "Trudy was everyone's golden girl." He added that most were aware that she had exceptional talent and was headed for a stellar career. He explained that no one minded that she was dating one of her professors, Paul Smyth. Indeed, this was common in the prefeminist climate of the early 1970s. However, when Schnackenberg, who graduated summa cum laude in 1975, married Smyth, he said many were worried that "he would clip her wings." However, Gjertrud Schnackenberg Smyth continued to write with a passion perhaps born of pain. In the lines from the following uncollected poem, "Laughter in the Well," she writes about a middle-aged Florentine architect outraged when losing a coveted prize commission for "The Doors of Paradise" to the twenty-one-year-old prodigy Lorenzo Ghiberti:

> A living legend in his rotting boots,
> He walks zigzag into the Tuscan hills
> And as he walks he cries, he cries until
> He starts to laugh, he laughs until he hoots,
> . . . .
> A middle-aged and stocky self-exile,
> His laughing face behind despairing hands.
> He's drawn black water, bitter in the pail,
> But sends his laughter down into the well.

The departure of this elegant poem from its meticulous rhyme scheme in the final ironic couplet, where black water is replaced by a laugh destined to die unheard, recalls Yeats in its fluid intensity, an intensity brilliantly checked by Schnackenberg's formal and emotional control.

Her marriage to Smyth fell apart, and in the early 1980s Schnackenberg returned to her alma mater and a protective cadre of mentors. She soon published her chapbook *Portraits and Elegies* with Godine. At this time, Schnackenberg, increasingly focused on writing in traditional forms, was relatively well known outside of Mount Holyoke and circulated within the literary circles of Boston and Cambridge. Her poems caught the eye of Harvard poet Robert Fitzgerald. A classicist and poet, Fitzgerald in the 1970s mentored Timothy Steele and Dana Gioia as well as other poets increasingly focused on writing in classical forms. Schnackenberg's peers writing in fixed forms at this time also included Marilyn Hacker, Mary Jo Salter, Elizabeth Spires, Amy Clampitt, and Pamela Alexander. Godine's prestigious limited-edition chapbook series in which *Portraits and Elegies* appeared launched her officially. Schnackenberg's gift for interleaving history, myth, minutiae, and metaphysics is set forth in these poems of absorbing lyric grace built upon deft combinations of rhyme and meter. In this small book Schnackenberg reveals her grief over her father's death in 1973. Two poem

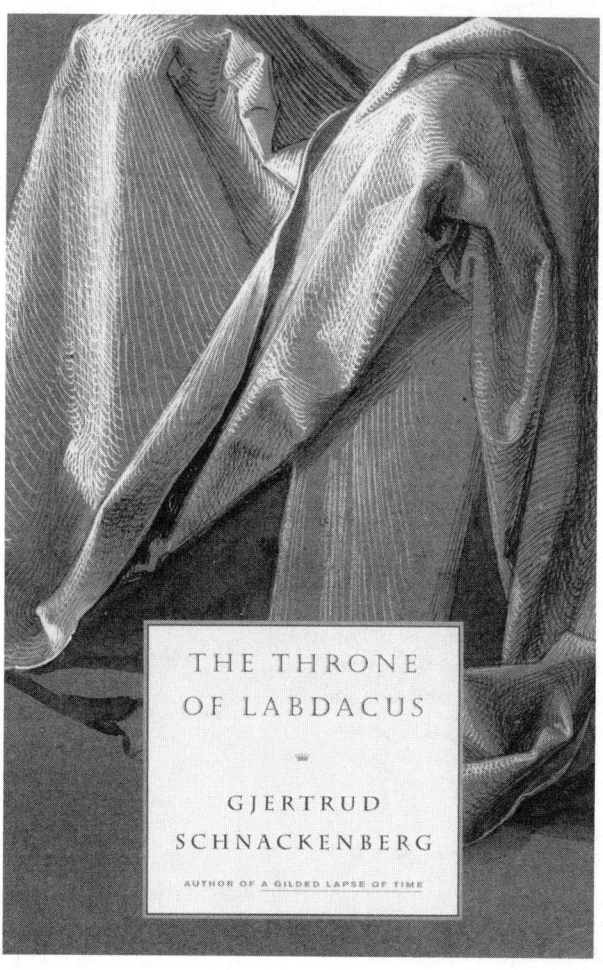

Dust jacket for Schnackenberg's 2000 book-length poem, the story of Oedipus retold by Apollo and the shepherd who rescued Oedipus as an infant (Richland County Public Library)

sequences, elegies to her father, are arranged around a centerpiece poem, a portrait of Charles Darwin in 1881, not long before his death in 1882.

In "Laughing with One Eye," the opening sequence of the book, meticulously crafted iambics convey affectionate remembrance and mourning. The elegant inclusion of primarily rhymed octaves in the poem "Walking Home," in which Schnackenberg connects a small incident of a bird defecating on her father and her memory of him in the hospital with a failing heart, is both humorous and poignant; at the same time it builds distance into a potentially overwhelming emotional scene:

> You walked, and overhead some pipsqueak bird
> Flew by and dropped a lot of something that
> Splattered, right on the good professor, splat . . .
> You bowed to improve my view of what you wore,
> So luckily, there on the center of your head.
> Man is not a god, that's what you said

After your heart gave out, to comfort me
Who came to comfort you but sobbed to see
Your heartbeat zigzagging on a TV overhead.
You knew the world was in a mess . . .
. . . and yet I never knew
A man that loved the world as much as you,
And that love was the last thing to let go.

Schnackenberg masterfully broadens her private grief over her father's death by following this sequence with the historically based poem "Darwin in 1881." The poem conjures up an abundance of literary, historical, theatrical, and scientific ghosts. In many passages, the elderly Darwin seems to personify Schnackenburg's own father. Another fascinating layer lending texture and wit to this piece is her comparison of the aging Darwin to Prospero, who at the end of William Shakespeare's *The Tempest* (written circa 1611) relinquishes his power. The book concludes with a final sequence about Schnackenberg's memories of her family's home, "19

Hadley Street," and the imagined lives of previous inhabitants. In this section one of Schnackenberg's greatest poems appears. Recalling Robert Frost's poetry in its spare music and Stevens's in its connotative force, Schnackenberg's "The Paperweight" observes a miniature toy family's fragile peace within a snowy globe. The twenty-line poem, in almost flawless meter and rhyme, presents multiple perspectives on reality, simultaneously reflecting humanity's deepest questions and darkest fears:

> . . . she serves him tea
> Once and forever, dressed from head to foot
> As she is always dressed. In this toy, history
> Sifts down through the glass like snow, and we
> Wonder if her single deed tells much
> Or little of the way she loves, and whether he
> Sees shadows in the sky. Beyond our touch, . . .
> Beyond our lives, they laugh, and drink their tea.
> We look at them just as the winter night
> With its vast empty spaces bends to see
> Our isolated little world of light,

In 1983, following the publication of *Portraits and Elegies* in 1982, Schnackenberg was given the prestigious Lavan Younger Poets Award from the American Academy of Poets; the judge was Fitzgerald of Harvard. That same year she was the recipient of the Rome Fellowship in literature from the American Academy and Institute of Arts and Letters, an award allowing her to reside in Italy from 1983 through 1984. She also won an Amy Lowell Fellowship for 1984–1985, enabling her to extend her stay in Italy for two more years.

Her second book, *The Lamplit Answer,* is more ambitious in scope than *Portraits and Elegies* and reflects a maturing talent. A marvel of great conceptual intrigue, the volume continues Schnackenberg's fascination with history and myth in imaginative reflections on the lives of Frédéric François Chopin, Simone Weil, and Sleeping Beauty. The opening sequence of the book, "Kremlin of Smoke," is an amazing eight-part evocation of Chopin as he reflects upon the 1831 fall of Warsaw. Composed in blank verse, the rhythms of the poem are more relaxed than the flowing, perfectly cadenced iambic quatrains used in Schnackenberg's first book. In fact, blank verse breaks into occasional rhyme adding welcome, if not always controlled, variations. This poem is followed by "Imaginary Prison," a metaphysical parable and variation of "Sleeping Beauty." With triplets and straightforward syntax, the poem describes a garden wall overgrown with brambles that slowly strangle to death and carry off all lovesick suitors who attempt to climb them. The dark atmosphere of this poem continues Schnackenberg's threnody, as it visits the chasm between being and nonbeing:

> Peacocks patrol the garden's sleeping borders
> Malicious as a troop of evil fairies
> Who pace and lash the brickwork with their feathers'
> Opalescent hems, and pacing screech
> How perilous is purity of heart.
> And briars tentatively hoist their thorn
> Across the dizzying ledges schisms form
> Where being and non-being break apart.

The poem dismantles the romantic ideal of rescue by a heroic prince. Instead, the poem suggests that men are weak, that love is mostly pathos and doomed to die, because fate, rather than the individual, is in control. In the following lines, a young kitchen maid learns that her betrothed, a humble woodcutter, has been impaled upon evil briars still holding the remains of "failed princes," who, like him, "became entangled and bled to death or starved."

> For she must wake from momentary rapture
> into grief approaching lunacy
> to learn, among the skeletons of princes,
> a humbler man has long since lost the struggle
> and witnessed to the end the work of briars
> As, blooming through his slowly loosened fingers,
> They carried off his ax as if it were
> A weightless toy among the waves of roses . . .

Poems in part 3 of the book depart from historical or mythical conjecture and instead are narrated in the first person to a lover. In his review of *The Lamplit Answer,* Stokes, though praising the book overall, noted that these poems represented a "falling-off" from the rest of the book and wondered whether Schnackenberg "needs the cold-eyed distance of history to write compellingly about contemporary life." About her series of love poems he wrote, "One senses her going on like a speechifying Hubert Humphrey, manic logorrhea overriding the quiet inner voice saying, 'For God's sake, *shut up!*'" However, other critics praised "Love Letter" for its humor and formal metaphysical wink in its use of the jaunty rhyme royal of George Gordon, Lord Byron's *Don Juan* (1819–1824). Though faulting some of the book for its high diction and lulling iambics, J. D. McClatchy said in "Three Senses of Self," his review in *The New York Times Book Review* (26 May 1985), that the poems on "soured love" were the most memorable for they called up "the most affecting memories and the most bitter circumstances."

Still mourning the death of her father, Schnackenberg published in this book her tour de force, "Supernatural Love," in which as a child of four she observed her father searching in a dictionary for the definition of

Paperback cover for the 2000 volume that collects most of the poems from Schnackenberg's first three books (Richland County Public Library)

carnation. As he shares its etymology with her, she finds her own childish instinctual musings about Christ's death and human suffering affirmed. Overall, her second book did not disappoint, prompting the majority of critical opinion to agree with McClatchy's assessment: "*The Lamplit Answer* is a book that shines throughout with a luminous craft and wise reflective sense of culture and its claims on human feeling."

During the next seven years, Schnackenberg published little and appeared in public less and less, though many were aware of her passionate association with Nobel Prize–winning poet Joseph Brodsky. Schnackenberg, eschewing the usual publicity whirl following publication, did allow her poem "Supernatural Love" to appear in Robert Richman's *The Direction of Poetry: An Anthology of Rhymed and Metered Verse Written in the English Language since 1975* (1988). The anthology coincided with the rising force of the New Formalists, whose best poems are free of high Modernist rhetoric and refresh the craft of meter and rhyme. Her other writings include a short essay on Eliot in the *Yale Review* in 1989 and an essay on Paul's Epistle to the Colossians for a book including essays by poets on the New Testament, edited by Alfred Corn (1990).

Thus, Schnackenberg's third book, *A Gilded Lapse of Time,* was greeted eagerly by readers. They were not disappointed. The volume established Schnackenberg as a leading poet of her age, prompting Logan to proclaim her talent. In this masterpiece she, like Eliot in "The Wasteland," meditates upon the degeneration of culture, in which the annihilated human sometimes becomes the repository of the divine. Occasionally appropriating a loose version of Dante's terza rima, she acknowledges her debt by beginning the book at Dante's grave in Ravenna, Italy. Though the work was criticized by some for being "too highbrow," Rosanna Warren in *The New Republic* (13 September 1993) affirms how expertly Schnackenberg apprenticed herself to Dante's "blizzards of rhyme" and how her work "manages to bind within the compass of its will a formidable range of diction, weaving 'crud' and 'Ostrogothic dusk' with quotations from St. Augustine, and never entirely losing sight of the small, modern person 'stranded in the aftermath.'" The poetic journey is, at some level, the poet's personal pilgrimage; yet, it also draws its life from the philosophies and agonies of such luminaries as not only Dante, but also God, Aeneas, St. Augustine, Josephus, Eusebius, Tacitus, Piero della Francesca, and Osip Mandel'shtam.

Composed during or gathered from Schnackenberg's travels abroad while supported by grants from the Guggenheim Foundation and the National Endowment for the Arts, this book draws its dense imagery from cathedrals, museums, and European soils where blood was shed, and great poets buried. Schnackenberg's increasingly labyrinthine digressions and overabundance of classical allusion were disappointing to some readers, who missed the straightforward syntax of her earlier work. However, Logan, echoing the critical consensus, proclaimed *A Gilded Lapse of Time* "her darkest and yet most radiant book . . . divided into three poetic sequences so enraptured, so lost in annunciations and resurrections, that they might be called visions."

At this point in her maturation, Schnackenberg's devotees remained faithful, trading clarity for passages of breathtaking beauty and sustained philosophical inquiry as evidenced by a section in the opening sequence of the volume, titled "At Dante's Tomb":

> In English world is an isolated sound,
> with unmistakable, audible, inward whirl,
> tilted on a hum that rhymes with itself
> revolving when we speak it, then ceasing to spin . . .
>   though if we say worldworldworldworldworld
> We can feel it beginning to spin around
> its axis, then brake to a halt
> When we turn our attention away. You believed
> We intuit the sound of the spheres, Dante,
> When God touches our ears. Ephphatha. Be thou opened.

Thus, the dual release at long last of *The Throne of Labdacus* and her collected poems in *Supernatural Love* invite assessment of Schnackenberg's complete oeuvre. When read side by side, they reveal an inexhaustible and formidable talent. In *The Throne of Labdacus,* Schnackenberg attempts her greatest conceptual orchestration. Drawing from Greek folktales, myth, legend, history, drama, and religion, she retells the Oedipal tragedy primarily from the viewpoints of Apollo, the god of music, and of a humble slave.

Apollo is ordered to set to music Sophocles' play *Oedipus Tyrannus,* soon to premiere in Athens in the 420s B.C. Through this remarkably self-reflexive medium of a book-length poem about a god obeying orders to restage this infamous drama musically, Schnackenberg lets the formal mechanism of playwriting—its concurrent layers of music, language, and symbol—mirror the eternal philosophical debate over whether human destiny is controlled by fate or by free will. The reader, with Apollo, finds riddle upon unanswered riddle and a tale within a tale about how a household slave disobeys the almighty oracle (or did he?) and rescues the maimed infant Oedipus from a gruesome death. Fearing an oracle that predicted that Oedipus would kill his father and marry his mother, "the parents pierced their three-day-old baby's ankles with an iron pin" and ordered a slave to leave him in the wilderness to die. In free-verse couplets, Schnackenberg, at the height of her gifts, conveys metaphysical reasoning through precise details:

> And a childbirth bed in an ancient palace
> And an infant maimed and left for dead,
>
> An orphan king abandoned on a mountain,
> A mountain we can visit to this day,
>
> And from the start the story had
> the god's name fastened like a worm
>
> to its heart the way the worm appears
> Out of nowhere and fastens itself
>
> To the mortal ones, with a message
> Unintelligible beyond itself
>
> Simply a making known—
> Making known *what is.*
>
> *What is:* a leaking-through of events
> From beyond the bourn of right and wrong;
>
> *What is:* a sequence of accidents
> Without a cause,
>
> Or from which the cause
> Is long-lost, like a ruthless jewel
>
> Missing from an archaic setting's
> Empty, bent, but still aggressive prongs.

In her meticulous endnotes Schnackenberg writes, *"The stuff of Greek religion is the myths, communicated in poetry; the myths are not dogmatic, but are mutable and multivalent, sculpted in water rather than carved in stone."*

Though Schnackenberg's notes reveal her careful readings of translations of many seminal texts, including those of Homer, Aristotle, and Artemidorus, one wishes that the material at times would transcend its elusive fragmentary meaning. The weaker sections in the book occur when there is too much pondering about absence, emptiness, and what is unintelligible and invisible. In lines such as "The oracles coming true, but in the past; / And not to fulfill a law. There is no need. / The laws are there, fulfilled or unfulfilled," the narrative thread is lost and the reader must flounder in water that holds no shape but instead becomes a sea of sounds.

However, the rapturous midsection, "A Shepherd Speaks," more than makes up for earlier meandering as the reader learns how the poor shepherd defied the king's orders to rescue the dying child:

> From the shroud came
> The gaze an infant bestows,
>
> In untouchable, wavering, radiant waves;
> Like a god's gaze, found in solitude.
>
> An infant maimed and left for dead. I stood
> In the shrinking snows. I knew the oracle . . .
>
> At the sight of the infant's gaze
> I was riveted, chosen, beguiled.
>
> I knew what the oracle said.
> And I rescued the child.

The final sections of the book build upon the shepherd's simple yet striking voice. With clarity and lyric grace, the power of fate reigns superior. In this double-edged tour de force, the stage is life, and history and myth are intertwined within an infinite preordained pattern. The simple shepherd who tended the infant child has become (or was he already?) a god. In the ultimate section, "The Premier of Oedipus," earlier passages repeat but change in meaning. Other details, once clear, become opaque. This strategy, with oblique shifting beauty, ensures that the overarching concept driving the tale remains clear: humans' destinies and what controls them are unknowable.

Together, the two volumes are oddly complementary. Their symmetrical music and passionate fragments emit their own frisson. *Supernatural Love* (2000), in which are collected all of the poems in her first three books, with the exception of "Love Letter," seems poised and precise. *The Throne of Labdacus,* with its allusions and high drama, is expansive, for the most part riveting in its rhymes and syntax. Logan praises the book overall in the *New Criterion* (December 2000) but adds that *The Throne of Labdacus* manifests Schnackenberg's "depths but not her passion." Most critical opinion concurs with Adam Kirsch's assessment in "All Eyes on the Snow Globe," for *The New York Times Book Review* (29 October 2000) that this book "is a very rare achievement in contemporary poetry–a philosophical idea treated, not glibly, obscurely or melodramatically, but with due seriousness and real intelligence. . . . If one feels that 'The Throne of Labdacus' is not yet that perfect balance, it is only because even more satisfying and impressive poems will surely follow it."

That her talent is still present and growing is indisputable. Gjertrud Schnackenberg in her works shows a powerful imagination, takes many risks, and tackles ambitious material. Clearly, her volumes confirm her as an important late-twentieth-century and early-twenty-first-century voice.

Reference:

Rosanna Warren, "Visitations," *New Republic* (13 September 1993): 37–41.

Vikram Seth
(20 June 1952 -)

Robert McPhillips
Iona College

See also the Seth entries in *DLB 120: American Poets Since World War II, Third Series* and *DLB 271: British and Irish Novelists Since 1960*.

BOOKS: *Mappings* (Saratoga, Cal.: Vikram Seth, 1980; Calcutta: Writers Workshop, 1981; New Delhi & London: Viking, 1994);

From Heaven Lake: Travels through Sinkiang and Tibet (London: Chatto & Windus, 1983; New York: Vintage, 1987);

The Humble Administrator's Garden (Manchester, U.K.: Carcanet, 1985; New Delhi: Viking, 1994);

The Golden Gate: A Novel in Verse (New York: Random House, 1986; London & Boston: Faber & Faber, 1986);

All You Who Sleep Tonight (New York: Knopf, 1990; London: Faber & Faber, 1990);

Beastly Tales from Here and There (New Delhi & New York: Viking, 1992; London: Phoenix House, 1993);

A Suitable Boy: A Novel (1 volume, New Delhi: Viking, 1993; London: Phoenix House, 1993; New York: HarperCollins, 1993; 3 volumes, London: Phoenix House, 1995);

Arion & the Dolphin: A Libretto (London: Phoenix House, 1994; New Delhi & New York: Penguin, 1994);

Arion and the Dolphin (London: Orion, 1994; New York: Dutton Children's Books, 1995);

Riot at Misri Mandi: From "A Suitable Boy" (London: Phoenix House, 1996);

An Equal Music (New Delhi: Viking, 1999; New York: Broadway Books, 1999; London: Phoenix House, 1999).

Collection: *The Poems, 1981-1994* (New Delhi & New York: Penguin, 1995).

TRANSLATION: *Three Chinese Poets: Translations of Poems by Wang Wei, Li Bai and Du Fu* (London: Faber & Faber, 1992; New York: HarperPerennial, 1992).

Vikram Seth (photograph by Erwin Schenkelback; from the dust jacket for the U.S. edition of An Equal Music, *1999; Richland County Public Library)*

SELECTED PERIODICAL PUBLICATION—UNCOLLECTED: "Forms and Inspirations," *London Review of Books*, 10 (29 September 1988): 18-20.

Vikram Seth is an Anglo-Indian writer perhaps best known for his monumental, nearly 1,500-page novel on domestic and political life in mid-twentieth-century India, *A Suitable Boy* (1993). But it was as the author of *The Golden Gate* (1986), his novel in verse, written while he was still at Stanford, that Seth first made a name for himself. The publication of *The Golden Gate* in the United States also brought the broader literary public the unexpected news that younger poets were not only once again writing in formal rhyme and meter but also were doing so with ease, vitality, and narrative dexterity.

Vikram Seth (pronounced "sate") was born on 20 June 1952 in Calcutta, India, the first of three children of Premnath Seth, a business consultant, and Laila Seth, a lawyer who became the first woman chief justice in India. Seth was educated at the exclusive Doon School, the preparatory school for India's elite; he also studied philosophy and the social sciences at Oxford University's Corpus Christi College, earning a B.A. in 1975. He came to Stanford University in California to work on a doctorate in Chinese economics and demography (and completed an M.A. in 1979). In a 1993 *New York Times Magazine* profile, Seth told Richard B. Woodward that he found Stanford "a very tolerant place" where "for the first time in my life I found that I could enjoy myself" and where he learned "how to have fun." He was becoming increasingly interested in poetry, and he took a year off from his economic studies when he received a Wallace Stegner Fellowship in creative writing (1977–1978). He also began an informal independent biweekly tutorial in poetry writing with Timothy Steele. Seth credits Steele for making him realize "that it was possible for a poet of my own generation to write about contemporary concerns in rhyme and meter." At Stanford, while he was studying with Steele and Donald Davie–both, in their own ways, carrying the torch of the formalist aesthetic of Yvor Winters and the Stanford School–Seth's poetic voice emerged.

Not only was *The Golden Gate* conceived of and written while Seth was at Stanford, but so were his first two volumes of poetry, *Mappings* (1980) and *The Humble Administrator's Garden* (1985), and his travel book, *From Heaven Lake: Travels through Sinkiang and Tibet* (1983). *Mappings,* first privately published in a limited, signed edition of 150 copies while Seth was residing in Saratoga, California, is apprentice work that establishes Seth's alliance to the controlled metrics of the Stanford School. It also introduces much of the subject matter that preoccupies his later poems: his family in India ("Panipat" and "Rakhi"); the landscape and custom of his adopted homelands ("Home Thoughts from the Bay" and "Sea and Desert"); and rueful reflections on lost loves and friendships ("To a Fellow Traveller" and "Sonnet"). "Quaking Bridge" is one of Seth's sonnets that combines his interests in form, landscape, memory, and loss.

Seth's narrative as well as his lyric verse is represented in this early volume. The autobiographical narrative "Departure Lounge," presenting the leave-taking in Boston's Logan Airport between an Indian student in the United States and his visiting father, dramatizes a problematic parental relationship in which can be found the seeds of the more elaborate *The Golden Gate* and his Indian family saga, *A Suitable Boy.* "From the Memoirs of Babur, First Moghul Emperor of Hindustan" signals Seth's interest in the history and myths of Asia that also animate his volume of children's verse, *Beastly Tales from Here and There* (1992). Finally, *Mappings* includes a translation from the Chinese of Du Fu's "Thoughts While Travelling at Night" (768 A.D.) as well as from the Hindi of Suryakant Triphalhi Nirala's "Stump," both accompanied with handwritten transcriptions of the poems in their original characters, indicating an interest that culminated in Seth's volume of translations from the Tang Dynasty, *Three Chinese Poets: Translations of Poems by Wang Wei, Li Bai and Du Fu* (1992).

Seth's first two books published by mainstream publishers, *From Heaven Lake* and *The Humble Administrator's Garden,* appeared in England and failed to receive attention in the United States before the subsequent publication of *The Golden Gate* created an interest in them. *From Heaven Lake* chronicles Seth's successful attempt to make his way home to India via Nepal and Tibet–rather than flying from Shanghai via Hong Kong, for which he had a ticket booked–after a year of doctoral research while in residence at Nanjing University. While primarily an engaging prose narrative, it is interspersed with brief lyric poems in the tradition of the wandering Chinese poets he was translating as well as of the Japanese haiku and tanka traditions.

From Heaven Lake and the poems collected in the first section of *The Humble Administrator's Garden,* "Wutong," in conjunction with his Chinese translations, are the only results of Seth's field work for his never-to-be-written dissertation. Seth's research technique–which he told Woodward came in handy when working on *A Suitable Boy*–is dramatized in "Research in Jiangsu Province," yielding in seventeen quatrains to a portrait of domestic life in the Nanjing area along the Yangtze River. The poem begins with the demographer's rote questions:

> From off this plastic strip the noise
> Of buzzing stops. A human voice
> Asks its set questions, pauses, then
> Waits for responses to begin.
>
> The questions bore in. How much is
> The cost and area of this house?
> I see you have two sons. Would you
> Prefer to have had a daughter too?
>
> And do your private plots provide
> Substantial income on the side?
> Do you rear silkworms? goslings? pigs?
> How much per year is spent on eggs?
>
> How much on oil and soya sauce
> And salt and vinegar? asks the voice.

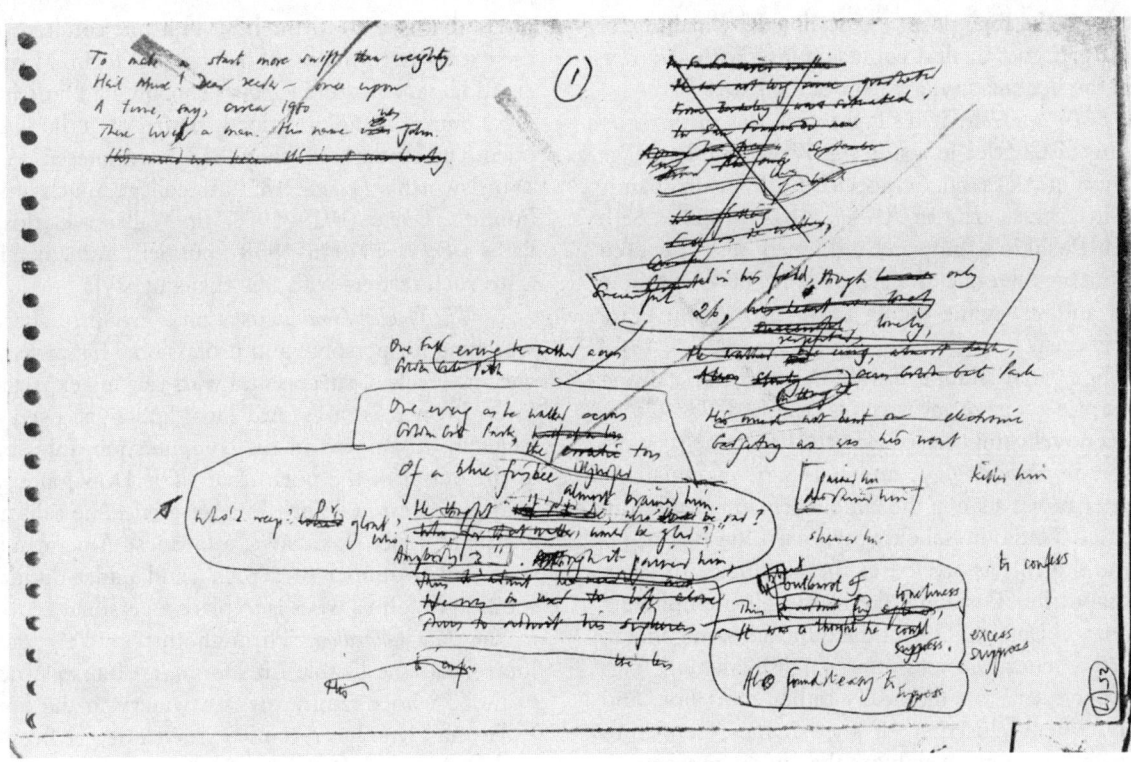

Page from an early draft for Seth's 1986 verse novel, The Golden Gate (courtesy of the author)

Seth half-jokingly hopes that the "facts" elicited from his questions will "Reveal the Grand Design to me, / Flotilla of my PhD," though he recognizes that a larger truth eludes them:

> I switch the tape off. This to me
> Encapsulates reality,
> Although the beckoning plum-trees splayed
> Against the sky, the fragrant shade,
>
> Have something tellable, it seems,
> Of evanescence, light and dreams,
> And the cloud-busy, far-blue air
> Forms a continuous questionnaire
>
> And Mrs Gao herself whose voice
> Is captive on my tape may choose
> Some time when tapes and forms are far
> To talk about the Japanese War,
>
> May mention how her family fled,
> And starved, and bartered her for bread,
> And stroke her grandson's head and say
> Such things could not occur today.

This section of *The Humble Administrator's Garden* also includes several sonnets—such as the title poem of the volume; "The Great Confucian Temple, Suzhou"; "The North Temple Tower"; and "Nanjing Night"— that paint a more colorful and human portrait of China's Jiangsu Province than could have emerged in the poet's aborted dissertation.

The other two sections of *The Humble Administrator's Garden,* "Neem" and "Live-Oak," are devoted, respectively, to poems about India and about the San Francisco Bay area. Of particular interest among the Indian poems are "The Comfortable Classes at Work and Play," a narrative that could well be about Seth's family—the mother, for instance, like Seth's, is a judge— and "From the Babur-Nama: Memoirs of Babur, First Moghul Emperor of India." The latter, the longest poem in the volume, is a total revision of the similarly titled poem from *Mappings,* now a five-part narrative that emphasizes the emperor's homosexuality. Of the California poems, "Abalone Soup" lovingly depicts the practice of diving for, cooking, and eating abalone. This section also includes two epigram-like poems focused on love, depression, and sex. "Love and Work" suggests that work would be more tolerable with love to balance it, but that work itself provides a stay against the despair of lovelessness: "There is so much to do / There isn't any time for feeling blue. / There isn't any point in feeling sad. / Things could be worse. Right now they're only bad." This poem strains a bit to achieve its wit and ultimately fails to avoid sentimentality. More successful is the final poem, "Unclaimed," which, quite differently, argues against confusing love with sex, reveling in the hedonistic enjoyment of the latter.

The Golden Gate, Seth's first novel, was inspired by a reading of Charles Johnston's 1977 English-language translation of Aleksandr Sergeevich Pushkin's romantic novel in verse, *Evgenii Onegin* (1825-1833). Seth adopted Pushkin's intricately rhymed and metered stanza for his own tale of a group of twenty-something yuppies and struggling young artists in the San Francisco Bay area.

The *Onegin* stanza has fourteen lines, causing many critics to have incorrectly identified *The Golden Gate* as a novel composed of sonnets. Its rhyme scheme, however, is *ababccddeffegg;* and it is written in iambic tetrameter rather than in the iambic pentameter used in the sonnet. Vladimir Nabokov, who in 1964 first translated the novel, has scoffed at the possibility of accurately capturing Pushkin's literal meaning employing this stanza in English. One of the difficulties, in general, that such a stanza presents to an English-language narrative poet is that the metrically rather short line, and the subsequent closeness of the rhymes, serves to emphasize the rhyme even more than in the more traditional iambic pentameter used in most English-language narrative poetry, from William Shakespeare to Robert Frost to the New Formalists—including blank verse, where rhyme is not a technical concern. But Seth, assuming the humorous and sometimes satirical tone of George Gordon, Lord Byron, has fun with the stanza from the outset of the poem:

> To make a start more swift than weighty,
> Hail Muse, Dear Reader, once upon
> A time, say, circa 1980,
> There lived a man. His name was John.
> Successful in his field though only
> Twenty-six, respected, lonely,
> One evening as he walked across
> Golden Gate Park, the ill-judged toss
> Of a red frisbee almost brained him.
> He thought, "If I died, who'd be sad?
> Who'd weep? Who'd gloat? Who would be glad?
> Would anybody?" As it pained him,
> He turned from this dispiriting theme
> To ruminations less extreme.

Seth alternates end-stopped lines with enjambment to create a tone at once relaxed and clever, and mixes rhymes such as across/toss with more thematically predictable ones such as sad/glad. Moreover, in this first stanza he establishes several features of the narrative: a witty respect for tradition, in his invocation to the Muse and address to his "Dear Reader"; the San Francisco setting; the personality of one of the central characters; and the colloquial language—distinctly of its time and place—that is used throughout in ironic counterpoint to the excessive formality of the stanzaic form. Most readers of literary fiction in 1986 probably had little interest in attempting the imagined rigors of a book-length poem, particularly if they had encountered William Wordsworth's *Prelude* (1850) in college, much less Ezra Pound's *Cantos* (1919-1970) or William Carlos Williams's *Paterson* (1946-1958); but Seth immediately disarms such readers with this engaging style.

The Golden Gate focuses on a group of characters searching for personal and professional happiness, with varying levels of success and with varying expectations. John Brown is a WASP—his father is even from England. Enamored of his computer job, John broods at the outset of the poem that "The Dow-Jones of my heart's depressed." For romantic advice, he calls an old girlfriend, Janet Hayakawa, a Japanese American sculptress and drummer in a rock band. Janet decides the solution to John's woes is to place a personal ad for him in the *Bay Guardian.* Through this unlikely method, John meets the likable Liz Dorati, an Italian American Catholic whose family owns a winery in the Sonoma Valley and who has recently earned a degree from Stanford Law School. Liz seems ready to settle down, particularly when she learns her mother is suffering from liver cancer and would like to see Liz marry before she dies. Things go well enough initially. The couple moves in together; but the condition of Liz's mother causes Liz to become more aware of temperamental differences, more serious about her choice of a completely compatible husband.

In the meantime, Seth introduces another major character, John's closest friend from Berkeley, Phil Weiss, a recently divorced father with sole custody of his son, Paul. Jewish, balding, and liberal, Phil has undergone a crisis of conscience which has forced him to quit his job at Datatronics and become an antinuclear activist. Abandoned by his well-heeled Protestant wife, Claire, Phil is also in search of romantic solace, which he finds, unexpectedly, in Ed Dorati, Liz's younger brother. Or almost does: though he clearly loves Phil, Ed is racked with Catholic guilt about homosexuality. Impatient with Ed's endless meditations on the superiority of the soul to the body, as both he and Liz become increasingly bothered by John's conservative politics, Phil sparks a romance with Liz at an antinuclear demonstration, and they are the ones who end this comedy of manners married and living, presumably, happily ever after.

The novel is replete with set pieces—the party that John and Liz throw, at which Phil meets Ed (and the reader meets, briefly, a young Indian graduate student, Kim Tarvesh, Seth's double; Seth also appears later as "Mr. Seth"); Thanksgiving weekend at the Dorati vineyard; the antinuclear demonstration. Some of the more memorable characters in the book are pets: Liz's cat, Charlemagne (who is not fond of John); Janet's pair of Siamese cats, Cuff and Link; and most exotically, Ed's green iguana, Arnold Schwarzenegger. And things do not turn out happily for everyone. On the rebound from Liz's marriage to Phil, after a series of one-night stands, John begins to date Janet again. Janet's first exhibit of sculpture is severely criticized in the press; but when she is killed in a car accident on the way to a party she and John are throwing, the critics have a change of heart about her sculpture:

> *Such startling sureness and maturity*
> *And sense of form for one so young*
> *(Which braved long years of sad obscurity*
> *And the crude taunts detractors flung)*
> *Leave us no doubt that Hayakawa*
> *Will rank with Moore and Kurosawa,*
> *Or even—this is hard to gauge—*
> *With Pollock, Ashbery, and Cage.*

Perhaps the subject that most seriously engages Seth in *The Golden Gate* is the morality of homosexuality. Though he ultimately marries Liz, Phil's philosophical-religious debates with Ed on the subject are quite extensive. Ed insists, although they made love the first evening they met, that their feelings are best left platonic:

> "I love you, Phil—but my desire
> Goes beyond sex. Lovers indeed
> Must shed more than their clothes. They need
> To shed their bodies. Flesh and fire
> Can meet but can't merge. It's a state
> Only our souls can consummate."

Clearly, Seth rejects this postulation and sides with Phil's critique of Catholicism:

> "Why, Ed? These aren't the Middle Ages.
> This is the twentieth century.
> What facet of our love outrages
> Your puritanical purity?
> Your church itself is strict or lenient
> According to what's convenient—"

Phil urges Ed to "'Defer to that strong love instead / Of spectral voices in your head,'" but Ed cannot. At this point Phil leaves Ed, eventually to marry Liz, with whom he is able to share both a passionate dedication to secular humanism as well as a fully sexual relationship. Seth's insistence that such an ideal relationship can be either heterosexual or homosexual alienated at least one conservative critic, namely Carol Iannone, who reviewed *The Golden Gate* in the journal *Commentary* (September 1986).

Much of the action of the novel is highly melodramatic. Phil's sexual identity—the ease with which he fluctuates between hetero- and homosexuality—seems psychologically unconvincing. Janet's sudden death seems contrived and arbitrary. In these instances, *The Golden Gate* seems dangerously close to soap opera. But on the whole, the historical significance of *The Golden Gate* makes these quibbles seem minor. Seth's exuberant revival of a seemingly moribund poetic genre makes this work representative of New Formalism as a whole.

As central as *The Golden Gate* is in defining the New Formalist aesthetic and galvanizing national attention for it, Seth's novel-in-verse is not his only connection to the movement. *All You Who Sleep Tonight* (1990) was Seth's first volume of lyric poetry to be published in the United States—by Knopf, no less—four years after the appearance of *The Golden Gate*. While notable for giving most American readers their first glimpse of Seth's shorter poems, the volume is quite similar to his two earlier such books in both technique and subject matter. The emotional range of Seth's shorter poems is rather narrow, once again deriving from the virtue of rational clarity balancing emotional excess inherent in the plain style; but the best of them approach the kind of depth that the poet associates with Wolfgang Amadeus Mozart—a musical presence throughout Seth's prose and poetry—as in one of his *ars poeticae*, "Adagio":

> We listen to
> The adagio of the Clarinet Quintet; if
> We see the abyss, as who can not, who can
> Resist the enveloping tranquility
> Drawn from the heart of 1789
> In the clear supple lilt of one who like
> The nightingale, his breast against the thorn,
> Sang jubilantly in sorrow, who defied
> The immobility of childhood fame
> To work this web of tenderness between
> The freedom of a child and a man's power
> Two years before the endless requiem.

Seth attains a depth of resonance, for instance, in "A Doctor's Journal Entry for August 6, 1945," a narrative spoken in the voice of a Japanese doctor slowly making sense of the horrific disaster of the atomic attack on Hiroshima. After being "startled" by "A strong flash, then another," he discovers the "weird" fact that "My drawers and undershirt had disappeared," that

> A splinter jutted from my mangled thigh.
> My right side bled, my cheek torn, and I
> Dislodged, detachedly, a piece of glass,
> All the time wondering what had come to pass.

In this narrative, from the section of the book titled "In Other Voices," Seth's focus on the small details of indi-

Dust jacket for Seth's 1986 verse novel, inspired by Charles Johnston's 1977 English translation of Aleksandr Sergeevich Pushkin's Evgenii Onegin (Richland County Public Library)

vidual lives effectively evokes, through synecdoche, the larger catastrophe. This technique is less successful in evoking the Holocaust in two poems, "Work and Freedom" and "Lithuania: Question and Answer," the former spoken by a German commander at Auschwitz, the latter by a rabbi whose wife has been raped by German soldiers and who must decide whether or not she welcomed such an attack.

Perhaps the most successful poem in the volume is "Soon," spoken to a lover by a man dying from AIDS—"I shall die soon I know. / This thing is in my blood. / It will not let me go." He asks from the lover that impossibility that the male persona of the sonnet traditionally offers confidently to his mistress, immortality:

> Stay with me by my steel ward bed
> And hold me where I lie.
> Love me when I am dead.
> And do not let me die.

While subtly playing with the conventions of the love lyric, Seth manages to express deep sorrow all the more powerfully through the restraint of his plain style. In a review of *All You Who Sleep Tonight* in the journal *Verse* (Winter 1990), Bruce Bawer admires the "brief, wistfull, Housman-like poems of love and longing" that are "pure and strong and deceptively simple."

If the modest but genuine virtues of *All You Who Sleep Tonight* seemed overshadowed, in the public mind, by the more original, vivid, novelistically appealing *The Golden Gate,* Seth's later volumes of poetry—his translations from the Chinese and his children's verse tales—were similarly overshadowed by the multimillion-dollar hoopla surrounding the publication of *A Suitable Boy*. (On the other hand, in the United States at least, these books were published by a major commercial press, HarperCollins, because of that same novel.) Yet, all of these books are equally connected to a central impulse of the New Formalist movement in general: to reconnect with an audience of "common readers" through the return to narrative and poetic techniques and genres deemed obsolete by the Modernists. In many ways, *A Suitable Boy* represents the artistic antithesis of Salman Rushdie's Booker Prize–winning *Midnight's Children* (1981), in every sense the postmodernist, postcolonial Indian novel in English, employing the techniques of magic realism to chronicle the generation of Indians—Rushdie's and Seth's generation—to be born after India gained its independence from Great Britain in 1948. Seth chooses to tackle the same subject matter but to emulate Jane Austen, Anthony Trollope, and Leo Tolstoy rather than James Joyce, William Faulkner, and Gabriel García Márquez. The question underlying Woodward's article in *The New York Times Magazine* was whether or not a "great" contemporary novel could be written using such traditional techniques. The failure of *A Suitable Boy* to be short-listed for the Booker Prize in England seemed implicitly to answer negatively, but the critical controversy that this slight generated parallels the critical brouhaha generated by the New Formalism in the United States.

Beastly Tales from Here and There engages Modernism through its resemblance to T. S. Eliot's least modernist work, *Old Possum's Book of Practical Cats* (1939). Seth's witty verse adaptations of Asian folktales fit squarely within the New Formalist aesthetic outlined in Dana Gioia's essay "The Dilemma of the Long Poem," which calls for a contemporary poetry that makes use of all the genres that have been historically available to poets but rendered obsolete by Modernism. *Three Chinese Poets,* on the other hand, represents a direct challenge to one of the canonical texts of modernism, *Cathay* (1915), Pound's beautiful but notoriously inaccurate translations from Li Po. Seth, unlike Pound, is fluent in Chinese, and he addresses this difference in his introduction: "The famous translations of Ezra Pound, compounded as they are of ignorance of Chinese and valiant self-indulgence, have remained before me of what to shun. I have preferred mentors who . . . admit the primacy of the original and attempt fidelity to it." For Seth, rhyme is a crucial element to Chinese poetry, an aspect that he refuses to lose in translation (though he admits that rhyme is much more natural in Chinese than in English). His volume of translations from the Tang Dynasty poets Wang Wei, Li Bai (Li Po), and Du Fu (Tu Fu) is an enduring contribution to the tradition of English-language translations of Chinese poetry and reflects a New Formalist's sensibility. Du Fu seems to be a particular favorite of Seth; his translation of "Travelling at Night" first appeared in *Mappings,* while that of "To Wei Ba, who has Lived Away from the Court" was included in *All You Who Sleep Tonight*. This latter poem engages one of the prevalent themes of Chinese poetry, the special importance of friendship, as it recounts the meeting of two friends long separated. It is a lyric that encapsulates two lifetimes, an extraordinary example of the concision of Chinese poetry which Seth's iambic-tetrameter, rhymed couplets capture as well as they can in English. Expressing wonder at having met his friend after a twenty-year separation, the speaker at once fills in these years during which "Old friends have died," presents the sensual details of their "rare," treasured meeting, and points to its temporal fragility:

> When last I left, so long ago,
> You were unmarried. In a row
> Suddenly now your children stand,
> Welcome their father's friend, demand
> To know his home, his town, his kin—
> Till they're chased out to fetch wine in.
> Spring chives are cut in the night rain
> And steamed rice mixed with yellow grain.
> To mark the occasion, we should drink
> Ten cups of wine straight off, you think—
> But even ten can't make me high,
> So moved by your old love am I.
> The mountains will divide our lives,
> Each to his world, when day arrives.

Seth followed these works with another novel, *An Equal Music* (1999), a disappointingly sentimental love story centered on a string quartet and set in England, Vienna, and Venice. For some, Seth's turn to prose fiction marked a defection from the poetic ranks. For others, his return to India and England, both as domiciles and as settings for his work, makes *The Golden Gate* his sole claim to membership in the New Formalism category—a membership that Seth does not particularly relish. The fact is, however, that even without these full-length narratives, Seth's lyrics and short narratives, forged to a considerable degree at Stanford under the aegis of Davie and Steele, show him to be one of the most notable contemporary practitioners of the Stanford School. *The Golden Gate* established him as a significant figure of New Formalism. *A Suitable Boy* extends the aesthetics of that movement from poetry to literature in general, establishing Seth as a major figure in contemporary world literature and placing New Formalism within the context of a shift in literary values that extends beyond the boundaries of the American poetry in which it arose.

References:

Bruce Bawer, "Pushkin by the Bay," in his *Prophets & Professors: Essays on the Lives and Works of Modern Poets* (Brownsville, Ore.: Story Line Press, 1995), pp. 333–339;

Jay Curlin, "'The World Goes On': Narrative Structure and the Sonnet in Vikram Seth's *The Golden Gate*," *Publications of the Arkansas Philological Association,* 22 (Fall 1996): 13–26;

John Hollander, "Yuppie Time in Rhyme," *New Republic,* 194 (21 April 1986): 39–47;

Bruce King, "Postmodernism and Neo-Formalist Poetry: Seth, Steele, and Strong Measures," *Southern Review,* 23 (Winter 1987): 224–231;

Marjorie Perloff, "'Homeward Ho!': Silicon Valley Pushkin," *American Poetry Review,* 15 (November–December 1986): 37–46;

Richard B. Woodward, "Vikram Seth's Big Book," *New York Times Magazine* (2 May 1993): 32–38.

Timothy Steele
(22 January 1948 -   )

Joseph O. Aimone
Santa Clara University

See also the Steele entry in *DLB 120: American Poets Since World War II, Third Series.*

BOOKS: *Uncertainties and Rest* (Baton Rouge & London: Louisiana State University Press, 1979); republished in *Sapphics and Uncertainties: Poems 1970–1986* (Fayetteville: University of Arkansas Press, 1995);

The Prudent Heart (Los Angeles: Symposium Press, 1983);

Nine Poems (Florence, Ky.: Barth, 1984);

On Harmony (Omaha: Abattoir Editions, University of Nebraska, 1984);

Short Subjects (Florence, Ky.: Barth, 1985);

Sapphics against Anger and Other Poems (New York: Random House, 1986); republished in *Sapphics and Uncertainties: Poems 1970–1986* (Fayetteville: University of Arkansas Press, 1995);

Beatitudes (Child Okeford, U.K.: Words Press, 1988);

Missing Measures: Modern Poetry and the Revolt against Meter (Fayetteville: University of Arkansas Press, 1990);

The Color Wheel (Baltimore: Johns Hopkins University Press, 1994);

Sapphics and Uncertainties: Poems 1970–1986 (Fayetteville: University of Arkansas Press, 1995);

All the Fun's in How You Say a Thing: An Explanation of Meter and Versification (Athens: Ohio University Press/Swallow Press, 1999).

OTHER: "Charles Gullans," in *Contemporary Poets*, 4th edition, edited by James Vinson and D. L. Kirkpatrick (London: St. Martin's Press, 1985), pp. 331–333;

"Prayer" *(Pater Benigne, Summa Semper Lenitas)*, translated by Steele, in *Samuel Johnson: Latin Poems Translated by Various Hands,* edited by R. L. Barth (Florence, Ky.: Barth, 1987), p. 3;

"For Charles, on his Sixtieth Birthday," in *The Music of His History: Poems for Charles Gullans on His Sixtieth Birthday,* edited by Steele (Florence, Ky.: Barth, 1989), p. 16;

"Tradition and Revolution: The Modern Movement and Free Verse," in *Expansive Poetry,* edited by Frederick Feirstein (Santa Cruz: Story Line Press, 1989), pp. 124–157;

"The Superior Art: Prose, Verse, and Modern Poetry," in *Conversant Essays: Contemporary Poets on Poetry,*

Timothy Steele (photograph by Barian; courtesy of the author)

edited by James McCorkle (Detroit: Wayne State University Press, 1990), pp. 120–131;

"Fountain in the City," in *Order in Variety: Essays and Poems in Honor of Donald E. Stanford*, edited by Rebecca Crump (Newark: University of Delaware Press, 1991), p. 182;

"Edgar Bowers," "Thom Gunn" and "Vers Libre," in *The Oxford Companion to Twentieth-Century Poetry*, edited by Hamilton (Oxford: Oxford University Press, 1994), pp. 62–63, 201–203, 558–559;

"Havens," in *Havens: An Intimate Collection of Exclusive Photographs of Celebrities and Their Favorite Rooms*, edited by Michael McCreary (Los Angeles: General Publishing Group, 1995), p. 13;

"Staunch Meter, Great Song," in *Meter in English: A Critical Engagement*, edited by David Baker (Fayetteville: University of Arkansas Press, 1996), pp. 221–247;

J. V. Cunningham, *The Poems of J. V. Cunningham*, edited, with introduction and commentary, by Steele (Athens: Ohio University Press/Swallow Press, 1997).

SELECTED PERIODICAL PUBLICATIONS– UNCOLLECTED:

POETRY

"October Dusk" and "September Noon," *Southern Review*, 8 (Winter 1972): 170–172;

"For One Who Worked Polk Street," *Counter/Measures*, 2 (1973): 79–80;

"Murder Mystery," "Border Tramp," and "From the Point," *Southern Review*, 15 (Fall 1979): 1003–1006;

"The Shortcut" and "Coming Now," *Canto*, 3 (May 1980): 73–75;

"Sunday Supplement," *Gramercy Review*, 4 (Spring 1980): 3–6;

"Last Words on the Subject" and "Estrangements," *Occident* (Winter 1981): 43–44;

"Guessing Game," *Triquarterly*, 58 (Winter 1984): 133–134;

"Sage Counsel," *Nebo*, 2 (Spring 1984): 24;

"Ethics," *Poetry*, 145 (February 1985): 262–263;

"UCSB Pastoral," *Daily Nexus*, 16 (23 May 1986): 7A;

"Once," *Spectator* (3 February 1990): 31; *Epigrammatist*, 1 (April 1990): 22–23;

"Jerusalem Delivered" and "Joseph and His Brothers," *Epigrammatist*, 1 (April 1990): 22–23;

"On His Cooking," *Lullwater Review*, 1 (Spring 1990): 14;

"One Binary Star Talking to Another," *Epigrammatist* (April 1992): 22;

"Just as Well," *Hellas*, 3 (Fall 1992): 50–52;

"Ars Poetica" and "Curriculum Vitae," *Classical Outlook*, 70 (Fall 1992): 20;

"For Wesley Trimpi," *Hellas*, 7 (Fall/Winter 1996): 13;

"For Victoria, Traveling in Europe" and "Charley," *Pivot*, 45 (1997): 24;

"Going," *Poetry*, 171 (September–October 1997): 81–82;

"Toward the Winter Solstice," *Poetry*, 177 (December 2000): 204–205;

"Starr Farm Beach" and "Snow," *New Criterion*, 19 (January 2001): 37–38;

"Faustina," *Poetry*, 177 (March 2001): 370;

"Champlain Evening," *Smartish Pace*, 4 (Spring/Summer 2001): 40;

"The Sweet Peas," *Southwest Review*, 86 (Fall 2001): 510–511;

"Didelphis Virginiana," *Bayou*, 38 (Winter 2002): 66–67;

"In the Memphis Airport," *ZYZZYVA*, 18 (Spring 2002): 177;

"The Middle Years," *Poetry*, 181 (October–November 2002): 82–83;

"Gym Evenings," *Iambs and Trochees*, 1 (Fall 2002): 12–13.

NONFICTION

"Keeping the Angels in Line," review of Mary Baron, *Letters for the New England Dead*, *Counter/Measures*, 3 (1974): 191–193;

"Sunbelly," review of Kenneth Fields, *Sunbelly*, *Southern Review*, 11 (Spring 1975): 482–486;

"Curving to Foreign Harbors," review of Turner Cassity, *The Defense of the Sugar Islands*, *Southern Review*, 17 (Winter 1981): 205–213;

"The Structure of the Detective Story: Classical or Modern?" *Modern Fiction Studies*, 27 (Winter 1981–1982): 555–570;

"Matter and Mystery: Neglected Works and Background Materials of Detective Fiction," *Modern Fiction Studies*, 29 (Autumn 1983): 435–450;

"The Dissociation of Sensibility: Mannered Muses, Ancient and Modern," *Southern Review*, 19 (Winter 1983): 57–72;

"Conversations with Novelists," review of Christopher Bigsby and Heide Ziegler, *The Radical Imagination and the Liberal Tradition: Interviews with English and American Novelists*, and of Dianna Cooper-Clark, *Designs of Darkness: Interviews with Detective Novelists*, *Modern Fiction Studies*, 30 (Summer 1984): 423–425;

"Let Thy Words Be Few: Remembering J. V. Cunningham," *Sequoia*, 29 (Spring 1985): 104–108; revised and expanded, *Verse*, 7 (Winter 1990): 33–37;

Review of *The Oxford Book of Children's Verse in America*, edited by Donald Hall, *Los Angeles Times Book Review*, 29 March 1985, pp. 3, 6;

Review of *Stevie Smith: A Selection,* edited by Hermione Lee, *Los Angeles Times Book Review,* 26 May 1985, p. 7;

"Tradition and Revolution: The Modern Movement and Free Verse," *Southwest Review,* 70 (Summer 1985): 294–319;

"J. V. Cunningham: An Introduction and an Interview," *Iowa Review,* 15 (Fall 1985): 1–24;

"Janet Lewis and the Untranslatable Heart," *Los Angeles Times Book Review,* 3 November 1985, p. 2;

Review of Frederick Crews, *Skeptical Engagements, California Magazine,* 12 (January 1987): 80–81;

"Writing in Meter," *Crosscurrents,* 8 (Winter 1989): 101–104;

"Excerpt from *Missing Measures,*" *Formalist,* 1 (Autumn 1990): 37–39;

"On Meter," *Hellas,* 1 (Fall 1990): 289–310;

"Pattern and Substance in the Life and Work of Janet Lewis," *Numbers,* 4 (Winter 1990): 79–90;

"The Forms of Poetry," *Brandeis Review* (Summer 1992): 28–33;

"On Edgar Bowers," *La Fontana,* special issue (March 1994): 44–45;

"Boundless Wealth from a Finite Store: Meter and Grammar," *Michigan Quarterly Review,* 36 (Winter 1997): 161–180.

Among the poets who began the now widely recognized revival of interest in work in meter, Timothy Steele is the most stylistically stringent and also the most highly regarded for his broadly appealing poetry. Though New Formalism may not be a movement in any strict sense of the term—that is, with common principles and allegiances shared by all its principal figures—Steele is clearly a New Formalist. He is also a principal exponent of what may be the clearest and most straightforward version of its poetics, both as exemplified in his poems and as explained in his prose, which addresses the milieu of the literary historian and the teacher of poetry, and common readers with no academic sanctions.

Timothy Reid Steele was born on 22 January 1948 in Burlington, Vermont, to Edward William Steele, a teacher, and Ruth Reid Steele, a nurse. Vermont is clearly Robert Frost territory, and Steele encountered Frost's poetry while growing up and going to school there. The stylistic similarities between the two poets are obvious enough: Frost upheld traditional forms of versification against free verse, while Steele defends traditional forms in an era that is only just now learning again how to hear them well. But the rationales and the personalities of the two poets are quite different. Steele lacks Frost's instinct for self-promotion, and he performs his work when reading aloud with more restraint and sobriety, even in humor. Both poets reach for the profound within a world of diminished subjects, but while Frost thought he was in fact the most revolutionary of Modernist poets and reveled in a grandiose role as a national figure, Steele seems content to be simply another citizen, albeit a sensitive, thoughtful, and eloquent one. He has a certain modesty, both civic and private, that invites his readers more gently to "come too" and to learn not to discard the pleasures of an old and polished art; he sees in the well-worn rules of poetry a precise applicability to contemporary life, in its anxieties and its joys.

Steele is a scholar and a teacher, in life as much as in his poetry and prose. He studied at Stanford University, earning his B.A. in 1970. In those years the idiosyncratic but undeniably compelling Yvor Winters's influence at Stanford had not waned. Winters's turn away from the free verse of his youth and his long career of insistent and argumentative opposition may have offered Steele what seemed a model of how not to win a friendly reception for a revival of interest in traditional forms of versification. At any rate, the patient and cheerfully reasonable tone of Steele's prose writing on such issues seems quite opposite from Winters's. Steele completed his Ph.D. at Brandeis University in 1977 under the direction of J. V. Cunningham, another eminent formalist poet and critic, one of Winters's former students, though certainly not cut from the same cloth as Winters. Cunningham's emotionally intense, laconic, and strictly fashioned poems, as well as his ingenious and highly formal critical writing, may also have made an imprint on Steele, who wrote a dissertation on the history and conventions of detective fiction. Cunningham also read some of Steele's work and commented (Steele recalls) "with his characteristic and supportive brevity." Steele returned to Stanford in 1975 as Jones Lecturer in Poetry. From 1977 on, he has taught English in California, first at UCLA, and for many years now at California State University, Los Angeles, with a brief stint as visiting lecturer at the University of California, Santa Barbara, in 1986. Steele's literary associates have included Janet Lewis, widow of Winters and widely known as the author of *The Wife of Martin Guerre* (1941); poet and fine-press publisher Charles Gullans; and poets Thom Gunn, Edgar Bowers, Alan Stephens, Dick Davis, John Ridland, and Vikram Seth, who credits Steele with improving his metrical writing and who dedicated to Steele the remarkable novel in verse *The Golden Gate* (1986).

Uncertainties and Rest (1979), Steele's first volume, collects ten years of publishing against the tide of editorial taste. The volume is written with control that yields an impression of the effortless and casual—sonnets worldly enough to assert that "Velveeta cheese suffices

Paperback cover for Steele's 1986 book, poems on topics such as posterity, history, harmony, and epistemology (Bruccoli Clark Layman Archives)

here for quiche"; epigrams mordant enough to skewer overly demanding friends and arts foundations; plain tetrameter quatrains rhymed in strict alternation yet free enough to allow loose feet to reverse and run "Evenly uphill as I hit my stride"; heroic couplets brave enough for effortless enjambment and the considerable claim that "One morning, rubbing the windowpane, / He grows coherent." John M. Miller in the *Chowder Review* (Spring–Summer 1980) described Steele as making a certain "genteel withdrawal into elegant, decorous sensations," but this summation is hardly fair to a poet who is willing to define culture as "an ingredient used in making / Pineapple yogurt, Gothic cathedrals," and such. By contrast, J. D. McClatchy in the *Partisan Review* (1980) proclaimed that *Uncertainties and Rest* had given him "more pleasure than any other first book I have read this year." Steele is not just clever, but sometimes deeply lyrical, as in a poem about the Maine coast:

This is the summer's course,
The natural becoming by
Returning to its source,
Its presence always on the edge
Of endless afternoons,
Wind in the eelgrass and salt sedge,
Wildflowers in the dunes.

Uncertainties and Rest nevertheless took years to attract notice. In 1986 Random House published *Sapphics against Anger and Other Poems*. Though the book collected many poems previously printed in small and limited editions, it is ambitiously forthright and philosophical, striving to instruct "the prudent heart." Topics include posterity, history, harmony, epistemology–even "Chanson Philosophique," in which the poet allows "the nominalist in me" to argue irresolvably with "the realist," concluding paradoxically with his "identity clear and blurred." And as for nearly all philosophic poets, for Steele ethics are primary—an example is the final admonition from the title poem, in which the poet meditates upon the possibility of a marital quarrel finding the course of restraint.

> For what is, after all, the good life save that
> Conducted thoughtfully, and what is passion
> If not the holiest of powers, sustaining
> Only if mastered.

Yet, the book is clearly on the side of "passion . . . the holiest of powers," and more openly erotic, because of, one speculates, Steele's marriage (on 14 January 1979) to Victoria Lee Erpelding, a librarian. In "Aubade" the poet attends to observing his beloved make her morning ablutions, recalling the "salty sweetness" and "leggy warmth" of the night before. This frank satisfaction in the wholesome carnality of the marriage bed allows the poet, in "Love Poem," the reassurance that "If, like poor Pierrot, I've anxiously / Dwelt in my life, the spell is broken."

The Color Wheel (1994), still as much involved in the philosopher's contemplations as those of the lover, is more serene and often subtler. In the opening poem the poet hopes for only that one "goddess," in an elaborate conceit of beginnings and consciousness,

> Awaken, then. Vouchsafe
> Ideas to resume.
> Draw back the drapes: let this
> Quick muffled emphasis
> Flood light across the room.

In an apostrophe another goddess, the "bewildering genetrix" in "Pacific Rim," in another conceit, is asked rhetorically the impossible question of responsibility for mortal matters:

> . . . Merciful,
> Do you accompany our mortality
> Just as, low to the water, the pelican
> Swiftly pursues his shadow down a swell?

The answer is necessarily in the affirmative, as cause must follow effect (though preceding it, as the shadow does the bird). Readers are left pondering how the mercy that made humans, its shadows, pursues them, or how it, like the shadow and human mortality, accompanies humans, with the difference between the shifting figure of the shadow on the water and the swift, solid figure of the bird taking on this play of significance. Braced by such resolute profundity at either end, the encounters with love come up again and again against the inevitable suffering love inflicts on the heart, while retaining an awareness of its sheer sublimity and its affinity with the more ethereal infinites of the mind:

> This is pain. This is power that comes and goes.
> This is as secret as the fresh clean snows
> Which, destitute of traffic to confess,
> Will serve at dawn as witness to a sky
> Withdrawing to its high blue faultlessness.

Yet, the inner leaves of the book still carry the more worldly traces, though perhaps at once more soberly and equally wryly, the "many fancying that cars and Uzis / Are proper instruments of self-expression." The joggers and jump shots, the "soda which, on opening, erupts" and other icons of quotidian late-twentieth-century Los Angeles life are still there, as is the natural world, the "old prankster" sea lion, and the worker bee on the jade plant still indifferent to "The gap between the longed for and the real." Formally the poems seem, if anything, less concerned with their still meticulously crafted structures of rhythm and rhyme. The feeling is one of the effortlessness of idiom, having endeavored "to enlist / Support from what had power to resist."

As the "poetry wars" are long over, or at least have simmered down, the question of Steele's "position" on the revival of interest in traditional form is less important for the assessment of his work than is his work itself. He seemed to weigh in early in such conflict in a 1989 symposium, reported in *Cross Currents:* "My keenest pleasure in reading poetry has from the beginning been bound up with the metrical experience; and I write in meter because only by doing so can I hope to give someone else the same degree of pleasure that the poetry I most love has given me." Yet, also absent is a context of argument in which an opponent would have to claim that the phrase "the same degree of pleasure" implied judgment as to the universal superiority for metrical poetry. Steele clearly holds his views as subjective but shareable. To conclude that his purpose is to denounce the presence of free verse is a leap. Further, Steele may reasonably be construed to be explaining his own sense of limits for himself as a writer. Richard Wilbur, a much senior poet, who always makes similar, even more-careful distinctions between his claims for the value of his work and claims about how poetry "ought" to be written, calls Steele "one of the very best young poets now writing," praising him for his "easy, unforced mastery of form [and] that truth and warmth of feeling which is sometimes denied to the formalist." Gunn, a Movement poet who, with Donald Davie, sought out and then broke the traces of the Winters orthodoxy many years ago, has also found Steele's orthodoxy compelling rather than simply gestural, and his allegiance bound to enforcing a careless "return" to

Paperback cover for Steele's 1999 book, a discussion of the forms and traditions of English poetry (Richland County Public Library)

form: "I never feel he has chosen to [write] in meter for any other reason than that by doing so he can make his speech more forceful."

Steele's first critical book, *Missing Measures: Modern Poetry and the Revolt against Meter* (1990), offers a revision of a common simplification of the history of modern poetry. That simplification is troublesome when stated baldly: "After the advent of modernism, usually dated at some point near the end of the First World War, traditional forms of metrical poetry were obsolete and permanently unusable, with rare exceptions." The normalization of American poetry around this simplification took place through publication biases and the proliferation of creative-writing workshops at colleges and universities employing poets to teach how to write poetry. Steele's concern is principally to explain, rather than denounce, how subsequent Modernist poets in English have, under the banner of Ezra Pound and T. S. Eliot, followed, "by rote and habit, a procedure of writing, and breaking up into lines, predictably mannered prose." Certainly, serious poets who write free verse, and their advocates, may easily take umbrage at that pronouncement, but few can deny that it has a grain of truth, especially from the 1970s through the mid 1980s, exactly when Steele was schooled and first began to publish his poems. Poets of quite different persuasions, such as Language poets and performance poets, and even poetry slammers often enough voice agreement about that trend. In differentiating himself from it, Steele has said,

> This preference is personal and aesthetic, however; I have never imagined that it provided me with access to cultural or spiritual virtue. And despite allegations to the contrary about *Missing Measures,* I have never said

that *vers libre* is somehow wrong and immoral or that meter is somehow right and pure. The experimental school of Pound, Eliot, Lawrence, and Williams has its own beauties and achievements.

Steele's book seems to have contributed to the erosion of that stylistic hegemony, without harboring the intention to dismiss the work of the Modernist revolution.

Steele's second book of prose, *All the Fun's in How You Say a Thing: An Explanation of Meter and Versification* (1999), shows the signs of coming after the most fractious period of the slow shift toward an eclectic poetic universe was nearly over. It offers a thorough catalogue of the forms and traditions of English poetry, with a constant concern for elucidating how formal devices create pleasure in the reader. Theorists of form and meter may not find anything especially new in Steele's account, at least as far as fact or principle goes, but a reader will find a different attitude from the usual in a tract on meter and prosody, especially one deeply concerned with a long history of poetic form: the attitude is genial, even playful. The writing is not highly technical, and it is utterly clear, if not flawless.

Timothy Steele's honors include a Guggenheim Fellowship, a Peter I. B. Lavan Younger Poets Award from the Academy of American Poets, the Los Angeles PEN Center's Literary Award for poetry, a California Arts Council Grant, and a Commonwealth Club of California Medal for poetry. Readers of poetry with a feel for formal verse can already find an interesting and gratifying wealth of invention in Steele's three volumes of poems. Those who care for explanations of versification and poetic history will find his two volumes of prose useful and readable. Those arbiters of and reporters on shifting tastes will have to take him as a reference point to orient any serious discussion of the renascent strains of traditional verse in American poetry. Steele has already left his mark.

References:

Charles B. Gullans, *A Diatribe to Dr. Steele* (Los Angeles: Symposium Press, 1982);

R. S. Gwynn, "Second Gear," *New England Review and Bread Loaf Quarterly,* 9 (Autumn 1986): 111–121;

Gordon Harvey, "Illusions Not Illusions Any Longer," *Sequoia,* 28 (Spring 1984): 91–98;

Mary Kinzie, "The Overdefinition of the Now," *American Poetry Review,* 11 (March–April 1982): 13–17;

Paul Lake, "Toward a Liberal Poetics," *Threepenny Review,* 8 (Winter 1988): 12–14;

Robert McPhillips, "What's New about the New Formalism," *Crosscurrents,* 8 (1989): 64–75.

Frederick Turner
(19 November 1943 -   )

Sonny Williams
University of New Orleans

See also the Turner entry in *DLB 40: Poets of Great Britain and Ireland Since 1960.*

BOOKS: *Deep-Sea Fish* (Santa Barbara: Unicorn Press, 1968);
Shakespeare and the Nature of Time: Moral and Philosophical Themes in Some Plays and Poems of William Shakespeare (Oxford: Clarendon Press, 1971);
Between Two Lives (Middletown, Conn.: Wesleyan University Press, 1972);
The Water World (Santa Barbara: Christopher Books, 1972);
Counter-Terra (Santa Barbara: Christopher Books, 1978);
A Double Shadow: Fiction (New York: Berkley, 1978; London: Sidgwick & Jackson, 1979);
The Return (Woodstock, Vt.: Countryman Press, 1979);
The Garden (Algonac, Mich.: Ptyx Press, 1985);
The New World: An Epic Poem (Princeton, N.J.: Princeton University Press, 1985);
Natural Classicism: Essays on Literature and Science (New York: Paragon House, 1985; Charlottesville & London: University Press of Virginia, 1992);
Genesis: An Epic Poem (Dallas & New York: Saybrook, 1988);
April Wind and Other Poems (Charlottesville: University of Virginia Press, 1991);
Beauty: The Value of Values (Charlottesville: University of Virginia Press, 1991);
Rebirth of Value: Meditations on Beauty, Ecology, Religion and Education (New York: State University of New York Press, 1991);
Tempest, Flute, & Oz: Essays on the Future (New York: Persea, 1991);
The Culture of Hope: A New Birth of the Classical Spirit (New York & London: Free Press, 1995);
The Ballad of the Good Cowboy (Eagle Pass, Tex.: Maverick Press, 1997);
Hadean Eclogues: Poems (Ashland, Ore.: Story Line Press, 1999);

Frederick Turner (courtesy of the author)

Shakespeare's Twenty-First-Century Economics: The Morality of Love and Money (New York & Oxford: Oxford University Press, 1999).

OTHER: William Shakespeare, *Romeo and Juliet,* edited by Turner (London: London University Press, 1972);

"Introduction," by Turner and Frederick Feirstein, *Expansive Poetry: Essays on the New Narrative & the New Formalism,* edited by Feirstein (Santa Cruz, Cal.: Story Line Press, 1989);

Miklós Radnóti, *Foamy Sky: The Major Poems of Miklós Radnóti,* translated by Turner and Zsuzsanna Ozsváth (Princeton, N.J.: Princeton University Press, 1992; slightly enlarged edition, Budapest: Corvina, 2000).

Rebel Angels: 25 Poets of the New Formalism, edited by Mark Jarman and David Mason (Brownsville, Ore.: Story Line Press, 1996)—includes poems by Turner;

Biopoetics: Evolutionary Explorations in the Arts, edited by Turner and Brett Cooke (Lexington, Ky.: ICUS, 1999);

Attila József, *The Iron-Blue Vault: Selected Poems,* translated by Turner and Ozsváth (Newcastle upon Tyne, U.K.: Bloodaxe Books, 2000).

SELECTED PERIODICAL PUBLICATIONS–UNCOLLECTED: "Escape from Modernism: Technology and the Future of the Imagination," *Harper's Magazine* (November 1984): 47–55;

"Only Man's Presence Can Save Nature: Towards a Truer Understanding of the Environment," *Harper's Magazine,* 280 (1990): 37–48.

Frederick Turner is a founder of and a spokesman for two movements in poetry, the New Formalism and the New Narrative, sometimes known collectively as the Expansive movement. However, his approach and methods are distinct from those of the other members of the movement. Turner's philosophy is interdisciplinary, crossing and combining the matrix of global human experience. In his poetry and his criticism, he explores the theories and new discoveries of such sciences as comparative anthropology, neurobiology, sociology, ethnology, evolutionary biology, and paleoanthropology as well as space exploration, to refound a notion of the human and what is common among all human beings. Turner's concern is one for the future. He believes, as he says in *The Culture of Hope: A New Birth of the Classical Spirit* (1995), that the new millennium will bring about a new cultural history that will "rejoin artist with public, beauty with morality, high art with low, art with craft, passion with intelligence, art with science, and past with future." As Turner also says, "There is what I am calling a 'natural classicism' in human arts that is based on culturally universal art forms and genres."

Turner was born in East Haddon, Northamptonshire, England, on 19 November 1943 to anthropologists Victor Witter Turner and Edith Davis Turner.

After spending several years among the Ndembu in central Africa, where his parents conducted field research, Turner attended Oxford University (1962–1967), where he obtained the degrees of B.A., M.A., and B.Litt. in English language and literature. He was naturalized as a United States citizen in 1977. He has been married since 25 June 1966 to Mei Lin Turner Chang and has two sons, Daniel Frederick and Victor Benjamin. Turner has held academic positions at the University of California at Santa Barbara (assistant professor 1967–1972), Kenyon College (associate professor 1972–1985), and the University of Exeter in England (visiting professor 1984–1985). Since 1985 he has been the Founders Professor of Arts and Humanities at the University of Texas at Dallas.

While at Oxford University, Turner began to develop his ideas about the interrelationship between science and literature in his dissertation, "Shakespeare and the Nature of Time," which closely analyzes William Shakespeare's poems and plays to reveal that the belief in an entropic and deterministic universe is at odds with human moral purposes. Turner's philosophical tendencies also began to reveal themselves in his poetry. He published his first full-length book of poetry in 1972. Though he wrote much of his early work in *Between Two Lives* (1972) and *Counter-Terra* (1978) in the free-verse autobiographical lyric that was predominant during the late 1960s and throughout the 1970s, he wrote some shorter narratives and lyrics in formal meter.

Turner gained recognition as a faculty member at Kenyon College, where he reestablished *The Kenyon Review,* of which he was editor between 1978 and 1982. With this periodical, Turner, along with Ronald Sharp, created one of the first forums for the New Formalism and the New Narrative. An editorial in volume one, number 1 of the winter 1979 issue states, "We invite the further development of new forms and innovative contributions in the old forms. We want to question the current conception of literature as a narrow specialization or expertise, and broaden its definition to include many types of writing not usually thought of as literature." In 1985 Turner published *The Garden,* a little-known book but one that is highly interesting. *The Garden* describes an idyllic period in Turner's life while he was in Ohio awaiting the birth of his son Victor Benjamin. Turner spent time planting a garden and doing extensive research in the sciences, theology, and philosophy. The book is divided into three parts: Pan, Yahman, and Sperimenh. In "A Theological Taxonomy," Turner provides classifications for the three parts.

Turner at Lake Geneva, Lausanne, Switzerland, 1963 (from Mark Zadrozny, ed.,
Contemporary Authors Autobiography Series, *volume 10, 1989)*

Pan is the past, Yahman the future, and Sperimenh the present. *The Garden* includes lyric poems, a philosophical excursus on language, natural aphorisms, economic aphorisms, moral aphorisms, a moral theology, prose political tracts, and a sermon upon the nonexistence of God. Many of Turner's core ideas on cosmology, evolution, and philosophy of a moral universe were first explored here. Because the book rejects the then-popular poststructuralist theory, a friend, Edwin Watkins, published it, partly at his own expense.

Turner is considered one of the most innovative and interdisciplinary of the members of the Expansive movement. For instance, his essay "The Neural Lyre"—included in *Natural Classicism: Essays on Literature and Science* (1985), the first of many prose statements of his philosophical principles—written with the psychophysicist Ernst Pöppel, argues that poetic meter is a universal human activity. His argument is based on scientific research in the field of brain evolution and its information-processing system.

> The radically interdisciplinary nature of this essay is not simply a consequence of the need to seek explanations across the boundaries of different fields. It represents also a commitment and a belief on the part of its authors. "We are convinced not only that this type of study will cast light on its specific subject (poetic meter), but also that the scientific material will be reciprocally enhanced in value, taking its place within a framework which gives it greater predictive power; and we further believe that 'understanding' itself consists in just such a union of detailed knowledge with global significance."

The essay, which appeared in *Poetry,* won the magazine's prestigious Levinson Prize in 1983.

Turner received wide attention during the middle to late 1980s with the publication of two epic poems—*The New World* (1985) and *Genesis* (1988). What is distinctive about these particular poems is that, instead of being set in a mythopoetic past, they are situated in the more modern science-fictional future. By imagining an alternative universe, Turner is given freedom to critique the present, as with the depiction in *The New World* of caste structures and humanity's rush toward self-destruction in a nuclear Armageddon. *The New World* is written in an unrhymed line of five stresses.

Turner is not providing an answer to how to stop humanity's destruction of itself, nor does he endorse the world he depicts. Instead, he is playing out an alternative historical scenario to apocalyptic destruction. *The New World* is a giant metaphor that suggests the characteristics humans must have if there is to be a viable future for them—love, self-sacrifice, and a concern for the world. As Kevin Walzer notes in *The Ghost of Tradition* (1998), ". . . James sacrifices his honor—in some ways more precious to him than his own life—in attacking Simon, to save his son's life and avenge Ruth. Such quality is essential to leadership, Turner suggests. More fundamentally, such nobility—admittedly an idealized

Turner with his wife, Mei Lin Turner Chang, and sons, Daniel and Benjamin, 1982 (from Zadrozny, ed., Contemporary Authors Autobiography Series, *volume 10, 1989)*

quality—is characteristic of the Free Counties' large vision, a vision that Turner argues is crucial to the future survival of humanity."

Yet, *The New World* has its problems. Turner's long philosophical digressions interrupt the flow of the narrative, and the oracle called Kingfish is annoying and comical. The work is, as Thomas M. Disch notes in "The New World" in *The Castle of Indolence* (1995), more of a utopian romance than an epic. Despite its problems, Disch remarks, "As a long narrative poem *The New World* has few equals in the English poetry of recent times, and as a work of science fiction there can be no dispute that it possesses an epochal significance."

In *Genesis,* which is about the future terraformation of Mars, Turner's philosophy of natural classicism, a panhuman and culturally universal world, is fully articulated. When Turner moved to Dallas, Texas, in 1985 and became the Founders Professor of Arts and Humanities at the University of Texas at Dallas, he was struck by the desolate and vast landscape of Texas; he imagined it to be much like the one on Mars. The hardscrabble, flat background of Texas gave Turner inspiration for this innovative epic. It is a poem of social, cultural, and moral import. One of the most significant debates of the twentieth century is the one between those who would abandon technology for the sake of the survival of the planet and those who would use technology for the progress of humanity. According to Turner, technology will eventually save the planet. In fact, he provides a note on the science of *Genesis,* a science that has become entirely plausible. NASA is now doing many of the things that Turner suggested in his poem for the terraforming and possible future colonization of Mars. *Genesis* is a story that covers the major historical events of the period from approximately 2015 to 2070.

Genesis has the narrative drive *The New World* lacks, and the philosophy works within the narrative framework so that it reads as easily as a novel. One of the most exciting moments occurs when the Achillean Tripitaka prepares for battle in the Olympic Wars. Instead of masses of people being killed, a certain number of soldiers who represent the population engage in battle:

> And Tripitaka, stripped down to the waist,
> His hair tied back, his sword glittering,
> Is like the motion of a running stream,
> The rainbow trout within it, and the liquid
> Running in the creature's arteries.
> No weapons touch him.

One of the many beautifully lyrical moments of the poem is Turner's description of the Sybil, a religious leader born on Mars. She is comparable to the religious prophets Isaiah, Jesus, Buddha, and Muhammad from Earth. Turner gives her ephemeral, angelic qualities:

> Her voice, they say, was of all voices ever
> In the world, the loveliest: it held
> Shell within shell, all timbres that have rung
> The purity of the simple crystalline,
> Aeolian tremors of the questing wind,
> The fluting overtones of calling birds,
> The sweet hoarse naivety of the beasts,
> The noble close intent of human speech,
> Frank shy intelligence of the consciousness,
> And something still angelic, like an eye
> Winged, with wet lashes, come to comfort us.

Turner is elastic—able to create lines that move quickly where needed to create tension and to move slowly where reflection is intended. He deftly controls the blank-verse line without its becoming too stiff and rigid. The poetics of *Genesis* is as complex as its science, much of it based on the ideas of chaos theory. As Turner notes, "The scientific and technological material of the poem constitute not only a large part of the content but also a gigantic metaphor of its very structure and form." The story is told in the persona of a poet who will not be born until more than a hundred years from the present. It is exactly ten thousand lines, in five acts, each with five scenes, each of four hundred lines. This poetic pattern represents the great branching, forking tree of evolution, story, and the universe itself, a world of fractal geometries and collapsing wave functions. In comments that appear on the back of the book, Pulitzer Prize winner James Merrill states that *Genesis* is "Grand" and "glowing," and Amy Clampitt writes, "You inspire me to read . . . all the epics of the past, whose roots you've shown to be so much alive."

Turner's ideas are usually too capacious to work well in the short, lyrical mode. Yet, he is able to compress rich imagery and symbolism into a surprisingly small space. In *April Wind and Other Poems* (1991) he expresses poetically what scientists express mathematically. For instance, in the poem "Self-Similarity," he provides an example, though not exact, of fractal scaling, which is defined as the same object displaying self-similarity on different scales:

> I listen to Bach's resonant concerto
> For organ, oboe, strings, continuo,
> As the car dives past stands of winter trees
> Whose branches branch cascades of smaller
>   V's.
> The same disorder ordered into scales
> Inheres within the cells, in the details
> Of oaks and chinquapins, as in these naves
> Of ribbed and vaulted sound, these mortised
>   waves.

Some New Formalists, such as Paul Lake, have joined Turner in using chaos theory and contemporary evolutionary theory to create new ways of regarding and analyzing poems. They believe that the laws governing the evolution of living things and other natural forms are the same laws that govern the creation of poetry. For example, in this short but richly woven poem the V-shaped branches, which are themselves self-similar, are compared to "ribbed" and "mortised waves." Johann Sebastian Bach's continuo is music, which is composed of grooved and slotted sound similar to the slotted growth of the tree branches. The scaling goes even deeper in the lines: "The same disorder ordered into scales / Inheres within the cells." The trunk of a tree is divided into heartwood, sapwood, the cambium, the phloem, and the bark, all of which are composed of cells that over time ordered themselves into a tree. But, to be more specific, the "disorder" spoken of in the poem is the fluid movement of water and nutrients, which is ordered by growth of other layers through cell division. Through this division the xylem (more commonly, wood) cells are formed, and they are what keep the trunk of the tree vertical and give it an "ordered"

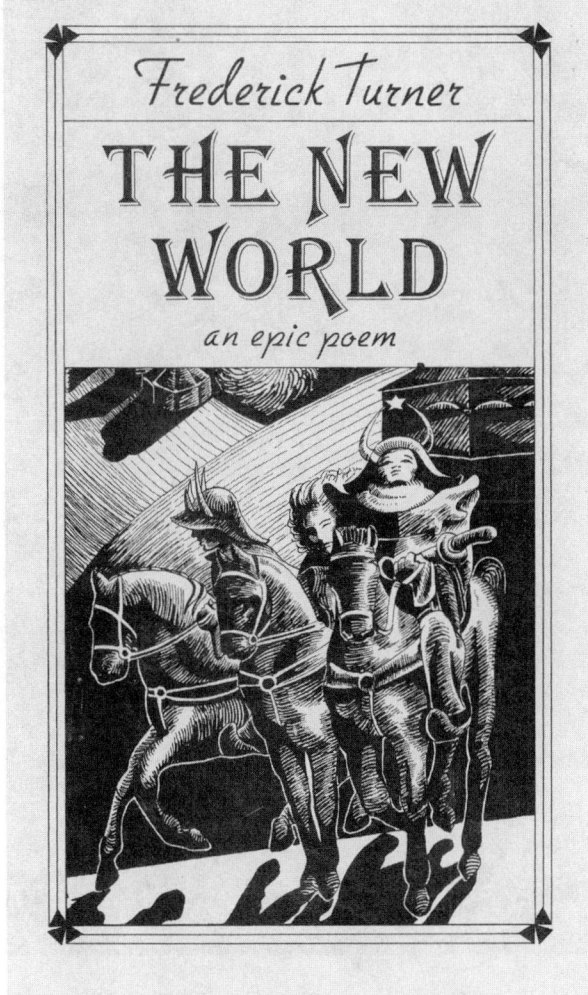

Paperback cover for Turner's 1985 science-fiction epic, about a future civilization and its rush toward nuclear Armageddon (Bruccoli Clark Layman Archives)

shape. Hence, the ordered disorder is found within the cells where the fractal scales inhere.

The composition of the poem itself is one of self-similarity and feedback. Once the scattered phrases begin to phase-lock (a natural process that occurs when many individual oscillators shift from a state of collective chaos to beating together and resonating in harmony), a recognizable meter, to which every subsequent line is similar, begins to form. When the first several lines of a poem are created, the poet refers—an organic feedback system—to the previous lines in order to create the next lines. If the meter begins to sound too regular, the poet allows some random variations to occur, such as inserting a trochaic foot in place of an iambic one, or, as Turner does in the third line of his poem, "As the car dives past stands of winter trees," place several strong stresses in a row to create a desired effect.

Dust jacket for the 1991 collection in which Turner's poetic language describes concepts that scientists express mathematically (Bruccoli Clark Layman Archives)

Rhyme also contributes as a feedback process in the formation of poems. Instead of a poet ending a line with an arbitrary word, rhyme adds an element of randomness—the way weather influences the growth of a tree—but it is also integral to the meaning of the poem. Once a rhyme scheme is established, it affects the arrangement and development of future lines. Rhyme becomes a self-interfering knot, just as human beings are knots of interwoven space-time.

Many of the poems in *April Wind* reveal this type of science—for example, "On Gibbs' Law," "Flying by Greenland," and "The Blackness of the Grackle." "The Cave at Zhoukoudian" has an elaborate scheme in which six six-line hexameter stanzas are followed by five five-line pentameter stanzas, four four-line tetrameter stanzas, three three-line trimeters, and then back to four, five, and finally six again, according to the preface, "to complete a chiastic, labyrinthine, concentric structure appropriate to its subject, the cave."

Throughout his career Turner has continued to write many books of cultural criticism, in which he presents a comprehensive view of aesthetics, religion, human culture, and the future of humanity, all of which are based on scientific discoveries in chaos theory, evolution, neurobiology, and his own poetry. This criticism has been essential in developing the theoretical and practical ideas upon which much of the New Formalism and the New Narrative are based. *Rebirth of Value: Meditations on Beauty, Ecology, Religion and Education* (1991) presents a mélange of essays that discuss such topics as evolution and chaos theory as a basis for aesthetics, environmental and ecological restoration, performative pedagogy, and social and historical studies. The work was originally titled "Reconstructive Postmodernism." One of Turner's most significant books of criticism is *Beauty: The Value of Values* (1991). Robert Kellogg of the University of Virginia is quoted on the front flap of the book as saying, "This is a radical book. It brings science and logic to bear in contradicting much of contemporary thought in the humanities.... From his assumption that there is such a thing as human nature, universal nature, essences, hierarchy, progress, comes his thesis that beauty is a fundamental reality, going beyond the subjective itself." The book delves into the biological basis of beauty, arguing that human response to beauty is culturally universal and is an evolutionary development, and that forms of art, such as storytelling, cannot be arbitrary but must be rooted in our biological inheritance.

At about this same time Turner translated the poems of the Hungarian Jewish poet Miklós Radnóti, who was shot by a Hungarian soldier at the dam near Abda around 8 November 1944. With Zsuzsanna Ozsváth, herself a Holocaust survivor and a professor at the University of Texas at Dallas, he was able to create masterful translations in classical forms. Radnóti was writing harrowing formal poetry during the chaos and terror of World War II and the German concentration camps. For Turner, this fact confirmed that classicism in the arts had absolutely nothing to do with totalitarianism and politics. In fact, even as the Nazis rose to power, Radnóti was able to write "Love Poem" in October of 1939:

The sun delays in those frothy and ruffling skies,
waves coolly, and lapses away.
And here, through a sprinkle of pearly and delicate sun-
rays
shimmers the infinite blue of your eyes.
Gold is the grass in the pathways,
thick and dead where it lies!
It's Fall. They're beating the hazelnuts down; in the halls
the stillness seeps from the walls.

When asked about his interest in Radnóti, Turner says, "To discover this poet was to find a kindred spirit from an era when modernism was the thing." *Foamy Sky: The Major Poems of Miklós Radnóti* (1992) received Hungary's highest literary honor, the Milan Fust Prize.

After his translations of Radnóti, Turner wrote his ambitious book *The Culture of Hope*. Edward O. Wilson of Harvard University is quoted on the back cover of the book as saying, "*The Culture of Hope* takes us past the wreckage of postmodernism to revive the dream of the unification of science and the humanities–and hence of culture. Frederick Turner is an articulate spokesman for the small band of visionaries who know enough, and care enough, to make that dream realizable." *The Culture of Hope* is a daring combination of literary and cultural criticism in which Turner contends "that our 'high' or 'academic' or 'avant-garde' culture is in a state of crisis . . . that threatens to destroy our society." However, Turner's complaint is not one from a conservative "blue-nosed bourgeois." On the contrary, he finds political correctness to be suffocating to the arts as well. Instead, Turner argues that a new cultural and artistic future may be envisioned based on findings in contemporary science. Walzer notes in *The Ghost of Tradition*, "To be sure, Turner's work as a theorist is significant. Turner's theoretical work shows the breadth of his interests–in science, in philosophy, in cultural history. From these diverse strands he has fashioned a coherent vision of humanity and the role of the arts and sciences in guiding humanity."

In 1997 Maverick Press of Eagle Pass, Texas, published 150 copies of *The Ballad of the Good Cowboy* as part of the Southwest Poets Series. This long narrative poem is a somewhat anomalous creation by Turner. Though the poem is occupied with cosmology and religion, it is dealt with in quite a different manner. Told in a Texas dialect, it is a mixture of medieval romance and Texas tall tale, a synthesis of Clint Eastwood and Sir Galahad. *The Ballad of the Good Cowboy* is the story of three cowboy-knights who are on a quest to rescue an imprisoned Christ. The tale is told in unrhymed quatrains of iambic pentameter and opens in a bar in Abilene when Jack McCall, the killer of Wild Bill Hickok, stumbles through the doors:

> It was a bar in Main Street, Abilene.
> The barkeeper had set us up when who
> Should stumble through the doors but Jack
>   McCall.
> Now Jack, you may recall, shot Wild Bill
>   Hickok
> In Deadwood City, South Dakota; Bill
> Was holding what we call a dead man's hand,
> Bulls over eights. He shot him from behind:
> Seemed a mite safer than the other side.

Paperback cover for Turner's 1999 collection, poems about Texas in the tradition of Theocritus and Virgil (Richland County Public Library)

Jack is feeling suicidal, so Gabby Salvador, known for spinning yarns, tells him the story of the Good Cowboy. Tex Galahad, Red Boyce, and Jesse Passaval are employed as cowpunchers, a group that is counterpart to Jesus' disciples, Arthur's Round Table, and Robin Hood's Merry Men. While out on the range they encounter a Mexican boy who unrolls a cope, which contains the image of an imprisoned Christ, in whose eyes is painted the face of a woman, the veiled Sister of the Good Cowboy. After a miracle they are inspired to look for the "shanghied Christ." So begins their quest to find the Good Cowboy and, ultimately, the search for their own salvation. Turner mixes Mexican folklore, Native American legend, and chivalric romance and creates a strange cosmology where there is nothing east of Chicago, where San Francisco sits on the Gulf of Mexico, and where "Horizons didn't bend as they do now." The structure of the poem is also one of numerology based on the powers of two: two to the power of ten lines altogether, two to the power of three sections each containing two to the power of five stanzas of two to the power of two lines each. The story evokes the strange, surreal world of the spaghetti Western and traditional cowboy poetry, yet this is no typical cowboy poem.

Turner's fascination with Texas and the myth of the West continued with *Hadean Eclogues: Poems* (1999), which presents what Turner titles "Texas Eclogues," along with shorter lyrical and philosophical poems in a variety of forms. The eclogues draw from the classical pastoral or bucolic tradition of Theocritus and Virgil, or as Turner calls the poems, a *dejeuner sur l'herbe* (a picnic in words). He envisions North Texas as a hellmouth, a gateway between the living and the dead. In his preface Turner says, "On this side of those gates the landscape is especially strange and beautiful; often it is a valley on the slopes of a volcano, like Virgil's Avernus in the shadow of Vesuvius, or the vale of Enna beneath Mount Etna that Milton compared to Paradise . . . in the desert, the Alps, the Lake District, the exotic lands of Abyssinia or Xanadu." Again Turner is questioning the future of humanity by asking where the hadean arcadia of the twenty-first century is located. For Turner it is in the savannahs and artificial lakes of North Texas:

> I walk by Lavon Lake in the Indian summer,
> By the satiny-silver bones and skulls of the trees.
> Where I find half-buried in crumbly sable gumbo
> The great greenblack shell of a dead snapping turtle,
> A tiny convolvulus, violet-throated, enweaved
> In its gaping orifice; a foam-rubber cushion choked
> With the lake-silt, bearing a miniature garden of clubferns,
> An ant's-nest, a gauzewinged azure surefooted dragonfly!

These lines have the flowing cadences of Walt Whitman combined with the sprung rhythm of Gerard Manley Hopkins. One can hear "My tongue, every atom of my blood, form'd from this soil, this air" mixed with the compound Anglo-Saxon words "dapple-dawn-drawn" and "bow-bend."

The longest piece in the collection is "Field Notes." Turner uses a combination of verse and prose for this first-person account of Jesus' life: "I had devised a form of verses for these scholia, these field-notes that you have asked me to record, for this science is one that will ask all the depth of poetry." The poem is a series of reflections by Jesus divided into six parts beginning with "The Temptation in the Desert," followed by "The Transfiguration," "Gethsemane," "Golgotha," "The Harrowing of Hell," and ending with "The Sea of Tiberias." It is a story revealing Jesus as both human and divine.

Also in this collection is a "Death Mass" written in rhyming quatrains in which the failures of the twentieth century are revealed:

> This is the ugliest death: dishonesty.
> I would bring down the temple in my rage:
> I'm sick enough with our stupidity
> To crush the prisoner as break his cage.

Other poems—such as "Villanelle on the Oregon Coast," "Geysers in Yellowstone," "North Sea Storm," and "Pinatubo Summer"—are pastoral places where the cultivated mingles with the uncultivated. Just as environmental restorationists are re-creating extinct ecosystems, Turner is taking old, sometimes forgotten forms, re-creating them, and forming new structures with fractal depth. For Turner the formal meters of these poems are the medium of his conversation between the living and the dead from every corner of the world. In 1999 Ray Olson of *Booklist* wrote, "Best of all, there is in every poem the combination of wit and sagacity also found in such classical and classicist poets as Horace, Dryden, and Pope. Brilliant."

One of Turner's latest critical works is a return to an old interest, Shakespeare. However, this time Turner uses Shakespeare's poetic terms to reveal a more humane economic future. In *Shakespeare's Twenty-First-Century Economics: The Morality of Love and Money* (1999), Turner argues that a new economy was envisaged centuries ago in poetic terms by William Shakespeare. Turner himself states,

> As Shakespeare shows, buried within our existing language of finance and business are the living meanings that we seek. Such words as "bond," "trust," "goods," "save," "equity," "value," "means," "redeem," "redemption," "forgive," "dear," "obligation," "interest," "honor," "company," "balance," "credit," "issue," "worth," "due," "duty," "thrift," "use," "will," "partner," "deed," "fair," "owe," "ought," "treasure," "sacrifice," "risk," "royalty," "fortune," "venture," "grace," preserve within them the values, patterns of action, qualities, abstract entities, and social emotions that characterized the gift and barter exchange systems upon which they are founded.

Turner also translated another collection of Hungarian poetry, poems by Attila József, again with Ozsváth, *The Iron-Blue Vault: Selected Poems* (2000). A writer for *The Kirkus Review* stated in 2000, "József is arguably the greatest Hungarian poet of this century," and his poetry has "the power of extruded molten steel taking shape under the most extraordinary pressure." József, born in 1907, abandoned by his father at an early age and sent to foster families by his destitute mother, first attempted suicide at the age of nine and finally suc-

Draft for a poem published in the February 2002 issue of Scriptorium *(courtesy of the author)* ceeded in 1937. He wrote poems of love and poems of personal despair that gloried in sound, in rhythm. A review in *Booklist* in 2000 noted that József "wrote with an adroitness of rhythm and rhyme that Turner, one of the best U.S. formalist poets, is probably especially responsible for reproducing in English."

Frederick Turner is a prolific writer, and he has created a body of work unlike any other poet of the Expansive poetry movement. He has produced books of literary and cultural criticism as well as multiple collections of lyric poetry, narrative poetry, epic poetry, and translations of poetry. His concerns lie beyond the self, but he does consider the individual in society, the world, and the universe. This point of view allows Turner to create highly imaginative stories with intellectual complexity and formal skill. In *The Ghost of Tradition* Walzer observed that Turner's "major work has earned him a place among the significant poets of the twentieth century," and his influence has extended into the twenty-first century.

Interviews:

Wade Newman, "Interview with Frederick Turner," *Southwest Review,* 71, no. 3 (1986): 337–356;

Paul Lake, "An Interview with Frederick Turner," *Hellas,* 4, no. 1 (Spring 1993): 95–104.

References:

Curtis Carbonell, "The Beautiful as Tragic Affirmation: An Approach to Frederick Turner's *Genesis: An Epic Poem,*" M.A. thesis, Clemson University, 1996;

Thomas M. Disch, "The New World," in his *The Castle of Indolence* (New York: Picador, 1995), pp. 95–104;

John Gery, *Nuclear Annihilation and Contemporary American Poetry: Ways of Nothingness* (Gainesville: University Press of Florida, 1996), pp. 98–100, 104, 124, 129–134;

Gayle Golden, "Universal Poet," *Dallas Morning News: Dallas Life Magazine,* 2 (September 1990): 10–21;

Jeff Gorvetzian, "Beauty Secrets," *Daily Texan: Images,* 4 October 1990, pp. 14–15;

R. S. Gwynn, "When Professor Turner Takes the Stage . . . ," *A Quarterly of Light Verse,* no. 31 (Winter 2000/2001): 53–54;

Frederick Hart, "Beauty: A Dialogue with Frederick Turner," *American Arts Quarterly* (Winter 1993): 8–15, 32–36;

Jane Amanda Hawkhurst, "Beauty, Classicism, and Dancing to Meter," *Ellipsis,* 18 (1990): 60–64;

Paul Lake, "An Interview with Frederick Turner," *Expansive Poetry and Music Online,* 1996 (28 August 2001) <http://www.n2hos.com/acm/index.html>;

Judith de Luce, "Genesis: an Epic Poem: Interventionist Ecology in Iambic Pentameter," *Restoration Ecology* (November–December 1983);

Daniel Marowski and Roger Matuz, *Contemporary Literary Criticism,* 48 (1988), pp. 398–402;

Wade Newman, "Crossing the Boundary: The Expansive Movement in American Poetry," *Crosscurrents,* 8, no. 2 (1989): 142–153;

Gerry O'Sullivan and Carl Pletsch, "Inventing Arcadia: An Interview with Frederick Turner," *Humanist,* 53, no. 6 (November/December 1993): 9–18;

Kevin Walzer, "Chapter 4: Bold Colors," in his *The Ghost of Tradition* (Ashland, Ore.: Story Line Press, 1998), pp. 110–121.

Appendix

Anthologizing New Formalism

David Caplan
Ohio Wesleyan University

"Anthology" derives from the Greek *anthos* and *logia,* meaning a gathering of flowers. This rather serene etymology, however, is far removed from the combative stances that contemporary poetry anthologies strike. Instead of the scabrous pamphlets of the eighteenth century, the twentieth-century literary scene favored polemical anthologies. There are several reasons for this situation: anthologies of contemporary poetry attract critical attention, redress canonical oversights, and establish group identities. They also offer relatively attractive commercial opportunities to committed publishers of poetry and, not coincidentally, convenient texts to literature and creative-writing courses.

Like other twentieth-century poetry movements, the New Formalists published several anthologies. The three major anthologies are Robert Richman's *The Direction of Poetry: An Anthology of Rhymed and Metered Verse Written in the English Language since 1975* (1988), Annie Finch's *A Formal Feeling Comes: Poems in Form by Contemporary Women* (1994), and Mark Jarman and David Mason's *Rebel Angels: 25 Poets of the New Formalism* (1996). Significantly, Story Line Press, a major supporter of New Formalist poetry, criticism, and scholarship, published the two latter books.

A fourth anthology, *Formal Introductions: An Investigative Anthology* (1994), remains important largely because of the people and organizations involved in its publication. Dana Gioia edited the volume, and Aralia Press published it. Aralia Press has been particularly active in the New Formalist movement. Its printer, Michael Peich, has helped to run the annual Exploring Form and Narrative Conference at West Chester University, where Peich teaches and where Aralia Press is headquartered. The press has also published several limited-edition works written by poets associated with the New Formalist movement. As Gioia's introduction to the anthology notes, "various personal and practical reasons" delayed publication from 1986 to 1994. In the intervening years other anthologies had performed many of the tasks that *Formal Introductions* set for itself. The slim, forty-page anthology includes the work of many writers already known to readers of contemporary poetry.

The canon wars that raged during the 1980s called attention to the ways that even self-professed "comprehensive" editorial projects promote certain aesthetics to the exclusion of others. As if in acknowledgment of this truth none of the New Formalist anthologies feigns a disinterested posture. Instead, they self-consciously take part in the contentious debates about versification, the politics of poetic form, and the cultural marginalization of poetry. By doing so, these anthologies also highlight important differences between the various poets associated with New Formalism, a group too often discussed as if it were monolithic.

The full title of Richman's book captures its unequivocal tone. Poets who "have an ambivalent attitude toward meter . . . have been excluded," he declares. In a similar spirit the editor's note asserts:

> This anthology contains the work of poets sharing a similar aesthetic perspective. It does not intend to be entirely representative of the times. It celebrates the work of a particular group of poets—the most important group to have emerged in the last fifteen years.

The introduction expands upon these grand claims. As in almost all of the New Formalist manifestos, Richman calls for a more accessible poetry capable of appealing to a larger audience. The main strategy he proposes is a "return to musicality." Coupled with "pleasure giving" imagery, this musicality invites a general readership repulsed by "two decades of obscure, linguistically flat poetry."

According to Richman, accentual-syllabic verse offers a possible means to these goals. Thus, he anthologizes only "formal verse" defined as "verse written in metrical feet." Metrical feet are also strictly defined: "The permissible substitutions for an iambic foot proposed by George Saintsbury in *Historical Manual of English Prosody* (1910) still apply to poets writing in meter today," he asserts. At such moments Richman

Paperback cover for the 1994 anthology whose editor attempts to "contradict the popular assumption that formal poetics correspond to reactionary politics and elitist aesthetics" (Richland County Public Library)

advocates pre-Modernist strategies for contemporary dilemmas. While few prosodists would deny Saintsbury's continued influence, even fewer would contend that metrical practice has not changed substantially since 1910. Contemporary writers of accentual-syllabic verse characteristically adhere only loosely to identifiable rules of permissible substitutions. In fact, Richman concedes as much when he condemns the "free verse orthodoxy" that "has insinuated itself so deeply into our respective poetic cultures that the entire conception of form has been corrupted."

Richman's rhetoric suggests he intended to provoke an argument; if so, he succeeded. In the January–February 1990 issue of *American Poetry Review,* Ira Sadoff published the most widely noticed critique of New Formalism, "Neo-Formalism: A Dangerous Nostalgia." Citing Richman's anthology as its prime evidence, Sadoff's critique charged the New Formalist poets with political and aesthetic conservativism: "Their narrow-minded appreciation of cadence and music unconsciously creates a kind of cultural imperialism." Sadoff asserted that "the true enemies of neo-formalism" are "democratic relativism and subjectivity." As support for this claim Sadoff compared a passage from Richman's introduction and Allan Bloom's *The Closing of the American Mind* (1987). By doing so, Sadoff sought to highlight a shared conservative agenda, involving a distaste for the perceived deterioration of civilization, an impatience with non-Anglophile conceptions of culture, and a resistance to social and literary change. As further evidence Sadoff also cited Richman's position as poetry editor of *The New Criterion,* a conservative arts journal.

Even if one accepts Sadoff's individual points, his argument rests upon two problematic assumptions. Sadoff assumes not only that *The Direction of Poetry* represents New Formalism but also that Richman's introduction accurately summarizes the group's shared views. Unlike most articulations of New Formalism, however, *The Direction of Poetry* presents an international, cross-generational movement. Thus, the anthology includes Americans Richard Wilbur and Mary Jo Salter alongside Irish, West Indian, British, and Commonwealth poets. In this respect *The Direction of Poetry* significantly differs from landmark essays such as Gioia's "The Poet in an Age of Prose" (1992), which defines the movement as consisting solely of younger American poets. Though expressing respect for the achievements of Anthony Hecht, Donald Justice, and Wilbur, Gioia declares the New Formalists' ambitions to be "in many respects irreconcilable" with these senior poets' work.

The most persuasive counterargument to Sadoff's dismissal of contemporary metrical verse as "a dangerous nostalgia" appeared in the form of another anthology. *A Formal Feeling Comes* seeks, as editor Finch says, to "contradict the popular assumption that formal poetics correspond to reactionary politics and elitist aesthetics." A central figure in *A Formal Feeling Comes* is Marilyn Hacker, whose influence several other contributors acknowledge. Hacker's sonnet sequence, sapphic verse, and ballads express the perspective of a leftist, feminist lesbian; only a dogmatic misreading could interpret such works to be politically conservative.

In the introduction Finch argues that the works she anthologizes reclaim a vital, female-based poetic tradition. Scorned by modernists, metrical verse forms such as the sonnet embrace the populist modes of much nineteenth-century poetry written by women. Finch argues that while women poets earlier in the twentieth century generally renounced and repressed that tradition, many contemporary women poets seize it as their inheritance.

Complications arise, however, when Finch explains what she means by "formal" poetry. She writes that she is defining formal poetry as "poetry that foregrounds the artificial and rhetorical nature of poetic language by means of conspicuously repeated patterns." As she acknowledges, Finch's definition is quite broad. In fact it could almost function as a definition of poetry itself, which tends to emphasize "the artificial and rhetorical nature" of its language "by means of conspicuously repeated patterns." For this reason it is difficult to see how the definition Finch proposes excludes almost any particular poem written by a contemporary woman. To cite only one famous example, Lyn Hejinian's book-length prose poem *My Life* (1987) consists of forty-five sections of forty-five sentences apiece, one for each year of the author's life.

A brief comparison between *A Formal Feeling Comes* and *The Direction of Poetry* reveals the substantive differences between the two New Formalist anthologies. Befitting its title, which declares *"The,"* not *"A," Direction of Poetry,* Richman's anthology is proudly partisan, organized according to a rather severe conception of poetic form. His justifications, however, are often questionable. Though Richman strongly implies that rhymed, metrical verse possesses a "musicality" superior to free verse, one need not look farther than the books of the poets he anthologizes to find evidence to the contrary: Justice's "Variations on a Text by Vallejo" (1979) and Derek Walcott's "A Sea-Chantey" (1969), for example, demonstrate the ability of free verse to convey incantatory rhythms. In contrast Finch wishes to include a diversity of poetics under the rubric of New Formalism. Especially when compared to *The Direction of Poetry,* which features the work of only thirteen women (compared to forty-four men) and, as Sadoff points out, extremely few persons of color, Finch presents a fairly broad, multicultural range of poetry by women. Her anthology achieves inclusiveness, however, at the cost of some organizational coherence.

Rebel Angels marks another stage in the development of the movement. More retrospective than either *The Direction of Poetry* or *A Formal Feeling Comes, Rebel Angels* follows nearly a decade of New Formalist poetry and controversies about it. Like its bibliography of critical works about New Formalism, *Rebel Angels* self-consciously frames a movement already familiar to many of its readers.

The preface displays the editors' keen awareness of the various claims and counterclaims made about New Formalism. The editors spend considerable space addressing what they call "One of the most notorious attacks upon poets who have the effrontery to use rhyme and meter": Diane Wakoski's May–June 1986

Paperback cover for the 1996 anthology whose editors describe New Formalism as a rejection of the "sentimental notion that meter is un-American" (Bruccoli Clark Layman Archives)

American Book Review article, "The New Conservatism in American Poetry." The nationalistic and, at times, xenophobic rhetoric Wakoski employed suggested that free verse was somehow more "American" than accentual-syllabic verse forms.

The preface to *Rebel Angels* declares that the New Formalists reject this "sentimental notion that meter is un-American." Discrediting Wakoski's position is crucial to Jarman and Mason because they define New Formalism as an American movement. The preface opens:

> Revolution, as the critic Monroe Spears has observed, is bred in the bone of the American character. That character has been manifest in modern American poetry in particular. So it is no surprise that the most significant development in recent American poetry has been a resurgence of meter and rhyme, as well as narrative, among large numbers of younger poets, after a period when these essential elements of verse had been suppressed. . . . These poets represent nothing less than

a revolution, a fundamental change, in the art of poetry as it is practiced in this country.

As in the preface as a whole, the central trope in this passage is rebellion. The "rebel angels" whom Jarman and Mason present are "younger" (born in 1940 or later); unlike the senior generation of metrical writers, they learned to write poetry during an era generally unreceptive to metrical verse.

Like Wakoski's attack upon New Formalism, however, the argument Jarman and Mason put forth rests upon essentializing myths of America and American identity. Though their tone is far milder than Wakoski's, their argument curiously accepts her terms. The shared standard judges poets on the basis of their perceived Americanness. By implication contemporary poets disinclined to write rhymed, metrical, or narrative verse shirk their national responsibilities to the "revolution" and thus contest "the American character."

The other major claim the preface makes for the New Formalist poets is "that there is more variety in their approach to form and subject matter than in some work of the previous generation." The editors' commitment to "variety" manifests itself in the diverse group they present; unlike the almost defiantly white and male *The Direction of Poetry*, *Rebel Angels,* though limited to twenty-five authors, includes the work of Hacker, Elizabeth Alexander, Julia Alvarez, Rafael Campo, and Marilyn Nelson. The second poem in the anthology begins:

> Colored cowboy named Nat Love,
> they called him Deadwood Dick.
> A black thatch of snakes for hair,
> Close-mouthed. Bullet-hipped.

The second-to-last poem ends:

> From a pool of syllables, words hover
> With rich potential, then spill across the lip
> And rifle down the page, for better or worse,
> Making their chancy trip,
> Becoming sentences as they discover
>   (Now flowing, now seeming to stammer)
>   Their English channels, trickling over
>   The periodic pauses of its grammar.

The styles, forms, language, and rhetoric of these works differ strikingly. With such heterogeneity New Formalism progresses past the initial stages of group formation and declarations. After *Rebel Angels* the need for another New Formalist anthology no longer remains pressing. Instead of more polemics and attempts to define the group's characteristics, careful readings of individual poets' work are needed. The critical question shifts from which poems exemplify New Formalism to which are distinctive.

The Little Magazines of the New Formalism

April Lindner
Saint Joseph's University

In the 1970s, when poets interested in form and narrative worked in relative isolation from each other and from the poetry establishment, a handful of little magazines enabled these poets to reach an audience and define their practices. The poet X. J. Kennedy and his wife, Dorothy, founded *Counter/Measures* in 1971, when most literary magazines had turned their backs on meter and traditional form. Though the magazine folded after only three issues, it made a strong statement against the prevailing orthodoxy of the neo-confessional, free-verse lyric poem. In "Fenced-In Fields," an essay featured in the first issue, the editors wrote:

> To deny poetry any of its possibilities is mistaken, we believe. We could quote a long, depressing catalogue of recent pontifications by critics and poets to the effect that meter and rime are worn out and don't matter. It isn't that we greatly mind seeing these patterns attacked by people who couldn't scan a nursery rime if they tried. What saddens us still more is that the attack has been carried on by many skilled, literate poets who, in the act of turning from their earlier fondness for pattern, have thought it necessary to preach the destruction of the entire metrical tradition—like suicides who want to take along the whole airliner.

In addition to poetry and reviews, *Counter/Measures* featured translations and song lyrics. Among its contributors were W. D. Snodgrass, John Hollander, Mona Van Duyn, James Merrill, Ted Kooser, and Kelly Cherry. *Counter/Measures* provided sustenance for a generation of poets interested in received forms.

Another early magazine to provide a safe haven for formalists was *Sequoia* at Stanford University, which, despite its formalist tradition, had not published formal poetry for years when undergraduate Dana Gioia became editor in 1972. Gioia included formal poetry and worked to build a general readership for what had been strictly a campus literary magazine. He helped boost circulation to approximately 2,500, briefly making *Sequoia* the best-selling small literary magazine on the West Coast. *Sequoia* published the work of several young poets working in form—Timothy Steele, Timothy Dekin, Alan Shapiro, Michael B. Stillman, Robert B. Shaw, and Dick Davis. A twenty-five-year *Sequoia* poetry retrospective in 1976 showcased formal work as Stanford's distinctive style, at a time when to do so was to flout literary fashion. Although not himself a Wintersian, Gioia used the anthology to celebrate the heritage of the late Yvor Winters, who had taught at Stanford for nearly forty years. Gioia also coined the term "the Stanford style" for the plain, formal manner adopted by Winters's followers.

Stanford University launched the careers of several key New Formalist figures, including Steele, Vikram Seth, and Paul Lake. In 1982 Lake assumed editorship of *Nebo,* the literary magazine of Arkansas Tech University, and refocused the publication on formal poetry. *Nebo* featured poems and criticism by Gioia, David Mason, Mary Jo Salter, and Jack Butler well before New Formalism had coalesced as a movement. Lake edited the publication for seven years and still serves as advisory editor. Almost two decades later, *Nebo* remained a welcoming venue for formal poetry.

While some publications were founded and others were reconfigured with the explicit purpose of restoring formal verse to its place in the contemporary pantheon, other journals were not expressly New Formalist in intent but resisted the dictates of literary fashion. These magazines showcased poems the editors admired, regardless of whether they were written in form or free verse. Two of the most respected American literary magazines made room in the 1970s and 1980s for formal verse. *The Kenyon Review,* arguably the most important American literary magazine of the 1940s and 1950s, was revived in 1979 by Frederick Turner and Ronald Sharp. (Originally founded by poet/critic John Crowe Ransom, *The Kenyon Review* had featured the work of Robert Lowell, Robert Penn Warren, Delmore Schwartz, and Mark Van Doren but had fallen on hard times and ceased publication in 1969.) The new *Kenyon Review* nourished formal and narrative verse by publishing the literary debuts of Emily Grosholz and Frederick Feirstein. In June 1990 the quarterly hired the formalist

Cover for the first issue of the revival of one of the important literary magazines of the 1940s and 1950s (Thomas Cooper Library, University of South Carolina)

Marilyn Hacker as its first full-time editor. David Lynn took over editorship in 1994.

The Hudson Review provided another early forum for the New Formalists. Founded in 1948 by Frederick Morgan and Joseph Bennett, *The Hudson Review* always has featured the work of important writers; the debut issue featured work by Wallace Stevens and E. E. Cummings, as well as W. S. Merwin's first published poem. A longtime supporter of emerging writers, *The Hudson Review* published early poetry and prose by key New Formalist figures, including Gioia, Grosholz, Mark Jarman, Charles Martin, Alfred Corn, Andrew Hudgins, and Robert McDowell. "Notes on the New Formalism," the essay in which Gioia set the terms of the movement, first appeared in the pages of *The Hudson Review*, as did a third of the essays that were eventually collected in Gioia's first volume of collected prose, *Can Poetry Matter?* (1992).

Support of New Formalism and its goals was characteristic of the aptly named *Eclectic Literary Forum (ELF)*, which expressly promoted traditional literary values while featuring a wide range of poetry as well as short fiction, art, and criticism. Founded in 1991 by C. K. Erbes and discontinued in 1998, *ELF* contributed most strikingly to the New Formalism via its reviews, interviews, and essays. *ELF* published a series of essays by critic Kevin Walzer that later evolved into the first full-length critical study of the movement, *The Ghost of Tradition: Expansive Poetry and Postmodernism* (1998). It also published Gloria Glickstein Brame's interview with Gioia and reviews of books by Marilyn Nelson, Sam Hamill, and Annie Finch and has consistently provided fertile ground for commentary on Expansive poetry.

Among the mainstream journals that have provided a safe haven for formal verse, *Italian Americana* is atypical in that it is not a literary magazine per se. A cultural and historical review, it features poems along with short stories, reviews, and essays on Italian American life. Before 1993, when Gioia was named poetry editor, the journal had featured an undistinguished selection of poetry. Under Gioia's guidance, *Italian Americana* has published a diverse selection of poems and consistently has included formal work by writers such as Salter, John Ciardi, Jay Parini, Samuel Maio, and Gabriella Mirollo.

Like the New Formalists, who hoped to win back a general audience for poetry through a return to accessibility and musicality, a group of poets in the early 1980s began to argue that poetry should offer the entertainment value—characters and a gripping plot—that readers might find in good fiction. The New Narrative movement, like New Formalism, wanted nothing less than to restore the lost cultural relevance of poetry. Though the similarity in mission and method between the two movements seems self-evident today, this affinity was less obvious in the early 1980s, when the first seeds of the New Narrative were sown.

In 1981 poets Jarman and McDowell founded *The Reaper,* the scathingly satirical journal that eventually grew into Story Line Press. Reacting against the ubiquitous neo-confessional lyric poem of the 1960s, 1970s, and early 1980s, *The Reaper* argued for the return of storytelling in poetry. As the critic Meg Schoerke pointed out in her introduction to Jarman and McDowell's *The Reaper Essays* (1996), "By the late 1970s, a number of critics had begun to attack the excesses that they saw in contemporary poetry, but *The Reaper*'s editors were the first to propose narrative as an alternative and *The Reaper* became the only little magazine of the 1980s—even of the century—to focus on narrative poetry and to develop a sustained argument in favor of its vitality."

In the first issue Jarman and McDowell spelled out their editorial stance: "The Reaper is the great deleter, the one who determines when the story ends. Most contemporary poets have forgotten him. Navel gazers and mannerists, their time is running out." Claiming that poets, editors, and critics were not "listening to their language anymore," Jarman and McDowell decried the "favorite gods" of the current poetry mainstream, "inaccuracy, bathos, sentimentality, posturing, evasion." Central to the philosophy of *The Reaper* was its list of "Non-Negotiable Demands":

1. Take prosody off the hit list.

2. Stop calling formless writing poetry.

3. Accuracy, at all costs.

4. No emotion without narrative.

5. No more meditating on the meditation.

6. No more poems about poetry.

7. No more irresponsibility of expression.

8. Raze the House of Fashion.

9. Dismantle the Office of Translation.

10. Spring open the Jail of the Self.

Finding poetry that met these standards proved difficult, however. *The Reaper,* which met its demise in 1989, is remembered less for the poetry it published—much of which failed to live up to the "demands" of the publication—than for its caustic commentaries, which provided marching orders for the New Narrative movement.

While *The Reaper* was making plans for the future of narrative poetry, a 1986 issue of the *New England Review/ Bread Loaf Quarterly* explored its past. This issue collected essays on American narrative tradition by a diverse group of practicing poets. According to guest editor Jarman, the goal of the special issue was not to come up with "an actual definition of narrative poetry" but instead "to establish a foundation of precedents or tradition or even . . . non-tradition upon which further arguments could be based."

In 1989 the journal *Crosscurrents* linked the New Formalist and New Narrative movements for the first time. The special issue titled *Expansionist Poetry: The New Formalism and The New Narrative* was the first full-length consideration of the New Formalist movement and provided the combined movements a broader and more accurate name: Expansive poetry. This ambitious volume offered the first comprehensive collection of Expansive poetry, showcasing poems by Salter, Martin, Turner, Gioia, Steele, Brad Leithauser, and Molly Peacock. It also featured several landmark essays. In "Transcending the Self" guest editor Dick Allen defined the differences between a new generation of formalist poets and the academic formalists of the 1950s and 1960s:

> We bring experimentation to form. We follow natural speech patterns, use colloquial diction, in our formal poetry sometimes do not adhere to strictly measured iambic lines and exact form. Our content often ranges wider than that of Academic formalists, and, unlike Beat Poetry, contains more affirmation than protest. We treat contemporary culture as a given rather than as something to be despised. We may quarrel with our age, but we do not pretend to be separate from it.

In a symposium on form, Leithauser called for "new forms—new patterns of expectation and, in time, new ways of subverting those patterns" and defended the iambic line, arguing that "anyone who loves poetic form, and has worked hard within it, knows that the iambic line is still a loded gold mine. We may choose to board it up, but we cannot for a moment pretend it is exhausted." In "Iambic in the 80s" David Dooley, a free-verse poet who was the winner in 1988 of the first

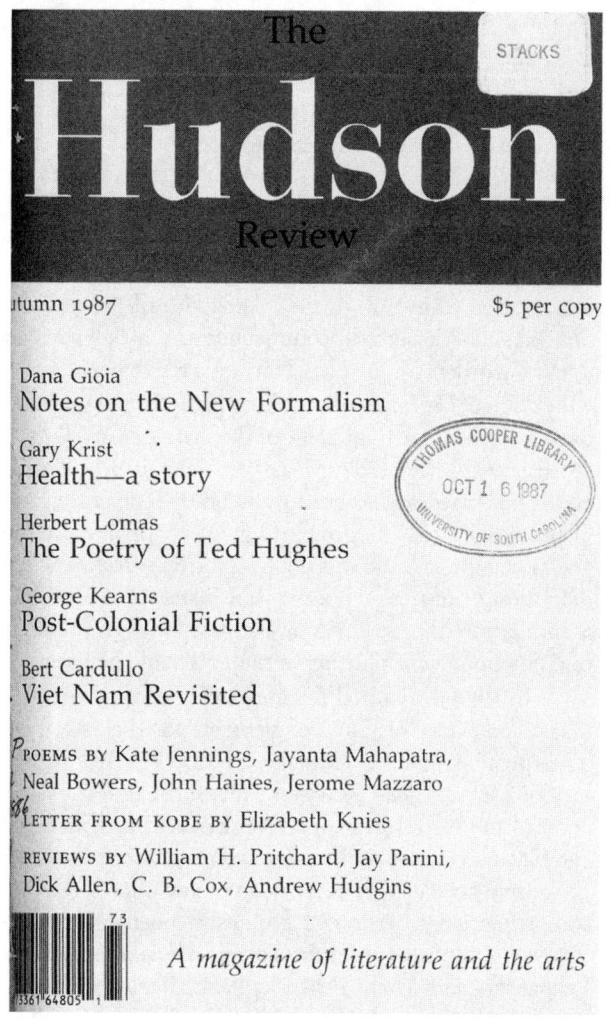

Cover for an issue of the literary magazine, founded in 1948, that provided an early forum for the New Formalist poets (Thomas Cooper Library, University of South Carolina)

Nicholas Roerich Poetry Prize from Story Line Press, struck a conciliatory note in arguing for the merits of traditional form:

> Free verse and metered verse are not enemies, are not even rivals, but are complementary kinds of knowledge.... The free verse poet, no less than the poet who writes in strict meter, is concerned with clustering and spacing of accents, end-stopping, positioning of caesuras, accommodation of speech rhythms and verbal music, and incorporation of local effects into an overall flow. It is impossible to imagine a writer of good free verse unconcerned with such matters.

Despite the conciliatory note struck by *Crosscurrents,* many mainstream poets reacted with mistrust, and even hostility, to the poetry and polemics of the Expansive poets. A literary climate hostile to formal verse ultimately helped to galvanize the Expansive poets and gave rise in the late 1980s and early 1990s to several specialized magazines devoted to actively promoting a return to tradition. The strongest of these is *The Formalist,* which, as its name suggests, exclusively publishes formal, metrical verse, which editor William Baer refers to as "the mainstream of English-language verse." Since its inception in 1990, *The Formalist* has remained a remarkably consistent product, both in its mission and its appearance. Encased in an understated cream cover printed with burgundy ink, each issue includes a distinctive mix of serious and light verse, translations, and satirical stabs at postmodern poetics and academic culture. Baer publishes no reviews and stresses the continuity between the older and newer generations of formal poets, thus promoting formal poetry while steering clear of the polemics that have surrounded New Formalism. *The Formalist* features poets from both sides of the Atlantic and encompasses academic formalists (including Kennedy, Howard Nemerov, Donald Justice, and Richard Wilbur) and a newer generation of poets (among them Peacock, Hudgins, and Rachel Hadas). Each issue includes a section of poems titled "From the Tradition," which features such canonical mainstays as W. H. Auden, William Butler Yeats, Alexander Pope, and William Shakespeare. *The Formalist* also regularly reprints definitive critical essays by such major figures as Peter Levi, Paul Fussell, Philip Larkin, and John Frederick Nims and features interviews with the best of the 1950s formalists, including Justice, Nims, and Maxine Kumin. The advisory board of the publication over the years has boasted Wilbur, Van Duyn, Douglas Dunn, Anthony Hecht, Arthur Miller, John Updike, and Derek Walcott. Before his death in 1991, Nemerov served as advisory editor for two issues. In his honor, *The Formalist* established its Howard Nemerov Sonnet Award.

Sparrow: The Yearbook of the Sonnet, like *The Formalist,* is wholly dedicated to promoting traditional form and has been instrumental in the revival of the sonnet. One of the oldest ongoing American literary magazines, founded in 1954, *Sparrow* originally was greatly influenced by William Carlos Williams, who had been a friend and mentor to its founding editor, Felix Stefanile. The journal, however, was reborn in its fifty-ninth issue when Stefanile proclaimed it "The REVENGE of the Sonnet." Stefanile, a literary contrarian who sees the little magazine as "a vision of excellence founded upon prejudice," set out to disprove the notion that no serious contemporary poet would write a sonnet. He defends the sonnet against critics who see inherent fascism in the form itself, and he points to rap and country music as evidence that rhyme and meter are not essentially elitist. The roster of authors whose work has appeared in *Sparrow* is an impressive list of the best of

Expansive poets and editors at Wade Newman's apartment in New York City on 1 September 2001: Art Mortensen, T. L. Ponick, Newman, Dick Allen, Frederick Feirstein, Frederick Turner, and Joseph Salemi

two generations of formalists. *Sparrow*, again like *The Formalist*, features metrical translations and has published work by Johann Wolfgang von Goethe, Anna Akhmatova, Li Po, and Petrarch. *Sparrow* also has published musical settings for poetry, including the full libretto of *Nosferatu*, with lyrics by Gioia and music by Alva Henderson; Henderson's setting for Edna St. Vincent Millay's "Love Is Not All"; and Claudia Gary Annis's setting for Shakespeare's Sonnet 18. Stefanile is committed to promoting younger poets through book reviews as well as through the *Sparrow* sonnet prize. Founded in 1992, the prize has been awarded to Finch, Tim Murphy, Gerry Cambridge, and Thomas Carper. The sixty-fifth issue of *Sparrow* (September 2000) was its last.

Another specialized magazine, *The Epigrammatist*, yielded only six volumes between 1991 and 1995 because of the scarcity of good, serious epigrams. R. L. Barth founded the publication in 1990 and handed it off in 1994 to Nancy Winters, the daughter-in-law of Yvor Winters and Janet Lewis. *The Epigrammatist* featured work by Kennedy, Snodgrass, Nims, Steele, Suzanne Doyle, and James Cummins. Two noteworthy special issues were produced by Nancy Winters, the first devoted entirely to the work of Kennedy, and the second a tribute to Barth.

Two other specifically formalist magazines are small-scale endeavors on the radical fringes of the New Formalism, in one case aesthetic, and in the other, political. *Hellas*, which first appeared in 1990, is an aesthetically reactionary journal. Editor Gerald Harnett promotes a "New Classicism" that opposes high Modernism and postmodernism alike, denouncing the work of T. S. Eliot and his contemporaries as "unfinished and obscure." Issues of *Hellas* usually feature Harnett's column (titled "Ex Cathedra") and his long, digressive polemics. The journal, however, has a strong commitment to the Greek and Roman classics and has published many translations as well as strong, original poetry by Steele, Finch, A. E. Stallings, Warren Hope, Timothy Murphy, and David Rothman. Despite widespread rumors that *Hellas* has ceased production, Harnett maintains that he will continue to publish. Issues of *Hellas* last appeared in 1999.

The irreverent *Edge City Review (ECR)*, on the other hand, defines itself as a culturally conservative alternative to what editor T. L. Ponick calls the "literary dross being churned out by the academic mills." Founded in 1991 as *The Reston Review* and renamed in 1994, *ECR* openly and often abrasively opposes what it views as the oppressive "political correctness" of academia. Often wildly irreverent in tone, *ECR* mixes iconoclastic political commentary with generally strong poetry and literary criticism by key New Formalist poets. *ECR* frequently publishes major interviews with New Formalist figures. It also has an extensive and regularly updated website: <http://www.edge-city.com/>.

Another trend in the little magazines of the New Formalism has been internationalization. The oldest and most established international magazine to seriously address the New Formalism, *Verse,* receives support from both the Scottish Arts Council and the College of William and Mary in Virginia. Founded in 1984 by Henry Hart, Robert Crawford, and David Kinloch, the journal is noteworthy both for its international scope (special issues have been devoted to Canadian, Australian, Scottish, and Welsh poets) and for its systematic exploration of the different movements and styles of contemporary poetry. Guest edited by Robert McPhillips, the issue on American New Formalism appeared in 1990 and featured essays and poems by, and reviews of, several noteworthy New Formalists, including McPhillips, Seth, Gioia, Peacock, Gwynn, Mason, and Steele. Other special issues of *Verse* have been devoted to critical analysis of Justice, Merrill, Weldon Kees, and Elizabeth Bishop.

In the wake of *Verse,* several formalism-friendly poetry journals sought to improve communication across borders. Peruvian/Canadian poet Raúl Peschiera, editor of *The Review* in London, writes, "More than ever, contemporary metered verse and free verse have become more like nationalities that wave over the heads of poets, or are used to serve as vigorous testaments to a poet's progressiveness. . . . but poetry is beyond identity. All good poets know this, and know what rules is not the color of one's flag, but the integrity of one's art." Founded in 1995, *The Review* features free and formal verse by poets from both sides of the Atlantic. A kindred effort, *Janus: A Journal of Literature,* appeared in 1996 and showcased poetry and essays by international writers and often featured translations. During its five-year lifespan, in which five major issues appeared, *Janus* emphasized meter and narrative poetry and featured several American formalists, including Kennedy, Mason, Martin, McDowell, Murphy, Louis Simpson, and Kate Light. It also published Maio's important essay-review of *Rebel Angels: 25 Poets of the New Formalism* (1996), the definitive anthology of New Formalist poetry. Founding editor David Livewell intended his publication to reach across the border that separates academia from the common reader as well as across political borders. Also international in scope, *The Long Poem Group Newsletter* provides a forum for discussion of what editor William Oxley calls "arguably the major literary art form, namely, the long poem," a form of narrative poetry that tends to be tied to the metrical line. In addition, two issues of *Oxford Poetry* (1998–1999) have explored American New Formalism: one issue features an essay on the topic by N. S. Thompson; the other features poems by five American formalists. In 1999 New Formalism reached beyond the English-speaking world when Denmark's *Den Bla Port* (The Blue Gate) featured a translation of Gioia's groundbreaking essay "Notes on the New Formalism."

The strongest of the international literary magazines of the New Formalism is Scotland's *The Dark Horse,* founded and edited by Gerry Cambridge. (Gioia serves as the United States editor.) In addition to its first-rate literary criticism, *The Dark Horse* features poems in both Scots and English by Scottish poets such as Edwin Morgan and Kirkpatrick Dobie as well as work by a range of British and American poets. While *The Dark Horse* favors formal poetry, it does not turn away good free verse. In its catholic tastes as well as its internationalism, *The Dark Horse* is typical of New Formalist literary magazines founded in the second half of the 1990s.

The history of the little magazines of the New Formalism mirrors the gains made over the last two decades by the Expansive poetry movement. In the late 1990s, as mainstream literary magazines have begun to include poetry in regular forms, the newest little magazines of the New Formalism have responded in kind by publishing occasional free-verse poems among the villanelles and sonnets. This new inclusiveness comes at a time when these magazines are working to consolidate the Expansive poetry movement across national boundaries. Both trends indicate that editors fighting for the health of narrative and traditional form no longer are on the defensive.

The New Narrative Poetry

Sonny Williams
University of New Orleans

The New Narrative poetry, a subgenre of Expansive poetry, is considered one of the most interesting and controversial movements of the 1980s and the 1990s. Robert McDowell states in his essay "The New Narrative Poetry," first published in *Crosscurrents* in 1988, that "the current flowering of narrative marks the boldest and most unexpected innovation in our poetry since the work of the great Modernist poets in the early decades of this century." Indeed, after the temporary decline of narrative poetry during the Modernist era and the decades that followed, the revival of narrative poetry represents one of the most significant developments in contemporary verse. Although narrative poetry has generally been disregarded and unheralded, it has resurfaced as an important, viable, and necessary alternative to the dominant poetic modes of the twentieth century. R. S. Gwynn explains, in his introduction to *New Expansive Poetry*, published in 1999, "In recent years narrative poems—both book-length and shorter—by Robert McDowell, Dana Gioia, Mark Jarman, Sydney Lea, David Mason, Marilyn Nelson, and others have found enthusiastic critics and audiences eager to read poetry of the type that has been virtually extinct in the second half of our century." An historical perspective of American poetry will help readers to understand why narrative poetry first fell into disfavor and why the New Narrative movement has taken place.

One of the best places to begin examining tendencies and developing a perspective of American poetry is with the anthologies. As Gioia states in his essay "Can Poetry Matter?", "Anthologies are poetry's gateway to the general culture." Anthologies of poetry provide readers with an opportunity to sample many authors and styles, and these anthologies exist as a form of poetic barometer. Since no one can read every anthology on American poetry that has been published, examination will be limited to a few better-known titles and editors. A study of their contents illustrates an obvious and indisputable trend—that narrative is a particular area of poetry that is oddly absent from most anthologies of American verse.

During the last one hundred years, few anthologies have devoted themselves solely to narrative poetry, which seems strange considering the number providing only lyric poetry. The few anthologies of narrative poetry that do exist are international in scope. One of the most notable is *Rising Early: Story Poems and Ballads of the Twentieth Century,* first published in Great Britain in 1964 and edited by Charles Causley, himself a fine narrative poet. *Rising Early* is an important collection written by such diverse poets as Donald Hall, John Betjeman, Bertold Brecht, and Edith Sitwell. In his introduction, Causley asks, "What makes poets still write in these forms today?" Indeed, many poets and critics are still asking this question more than thirty-five years later. *The Poet's Tales: A New Book of Story Poems,* edited by William Cole and published in 1971, is another important anthology. It encompasses a wide range of poets, including the American poet Stephen Vincent Benét and the Australian poet Judith Wright. Another significant narrative anthology, *The Oxford Book of Narrative Verse,* edited by Iona and Peter Opie and published in 1986, focuses mainly on nineteenth-century narrative poetry and ends with W. H. Auden. George Teter's *One Hundred Narrative Poems,* published in 1918, was edited for school use and is a wonderful assemblage of many forgotten nineteenth-century stories in verse, both English and American.

Despite these few exceptions, the more popular and widely used anthologies reveal the preference for the lyric mode, especially those anthologies published after the 1960s. *The Norton Anthology of Poetry,* published in 1970 and edited by Arthur M. Eastman, claims to represent the grand sweep of poetry in English. Eastman's book includes the requisite narratives by Geoffrey Chaucer, Edmund Spenser, and the popular ballads. William Shakespeare's long narrative poems, however, such as "Venus and Adonis" and "The Rape of Lucrece," are never included, even in collections devoted entirely to English literature, such as *The Norton Anthology of English Literature,* fifth edition (1986). The latter part of the book is distinctively sparse in narrative poetry and includes no narratives by American poets.

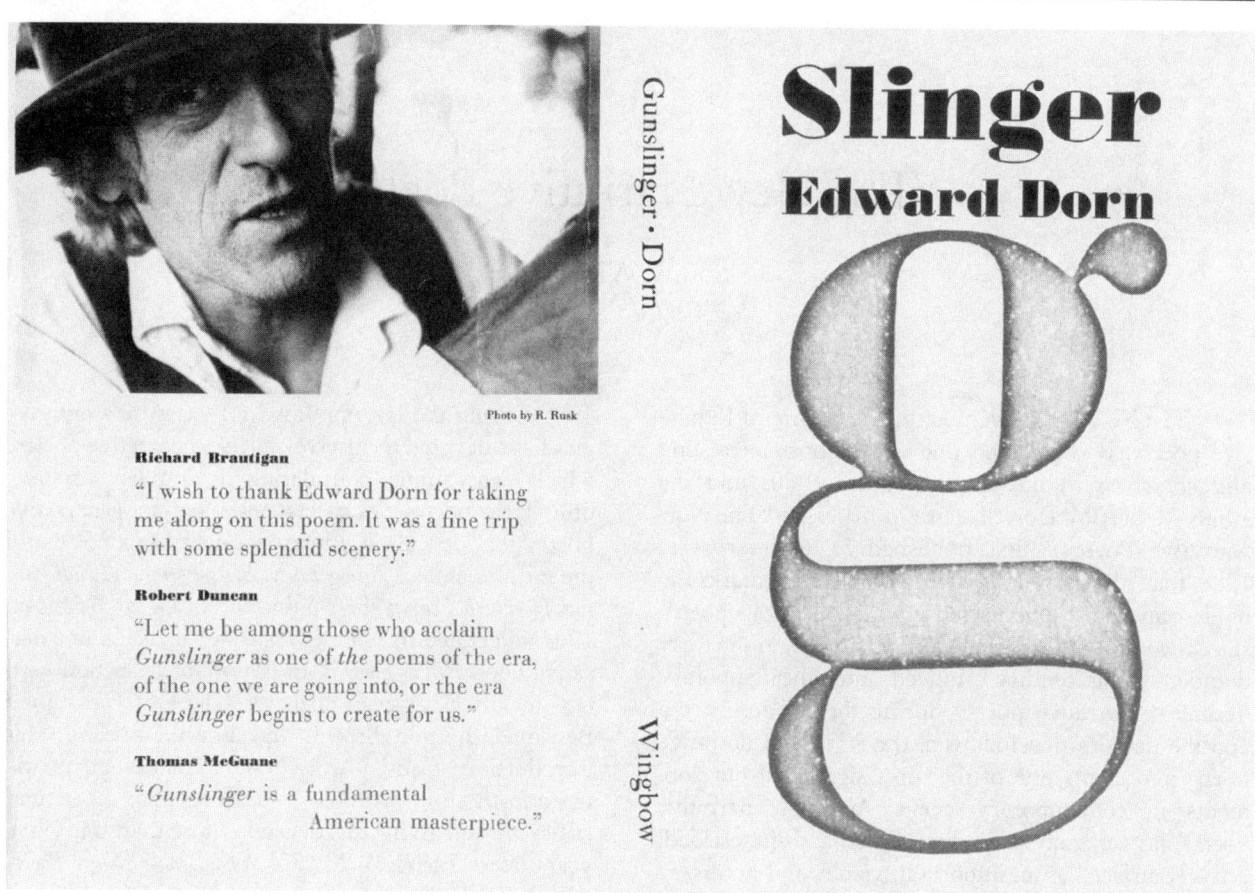

Dust jacket for a 1975 work by a Black Mountain poet that one critic calls a "fractured (anti) narrative" (Bruccoli Clark Layman Archives)

Henry Wadsworth Longfellow and Robert Frost spent a great deal of time writing in the form.

The Norton Anthology of Modern Poetry, published in 1973 and edited by Richard Ellman, presents the previous seventy-five years of poetry in English. Though the vast majority of the anthology is lyric poetry, Ellman does include some narrative poems by Randall Jarrell, Etheridge Knight, and Gwendolyn Brooks. Yet, in a remarkable statement in a short biographical note on Frost preceding his poetry, Ellman states, "Aside from long meditative poems and two masques, he wrote only lyrics." Even as he says this, Ellman includes "The Witch of Coös," certainly deciding it must be a long meditative poem. One can only assume that such poems as "The Death of the Hired Man," "Home Burial," and "'Out, Out–,'" all of which Ellman excludes, are to be considered meditative as well.

The Harvard Book of Contemporary American Poetry, published in 1985 and edited by Helen Vendler, includes many poets, from Wallace Stevens and Langston Hughes to Rita Dove and Jorie Graham. In the introduction Vendler states, "The social genres–drama and the novel–preserve our life with others; the private genre, lyric, preserves our inner life." Vendler thus gives the impression that poetry is not to be considered a social genre that deals with others. Instead, poetry is a private conversation with the poet's self. She continues to claim that "The lyric poet has had to evolve new strategies of representation in order to become a social voice," suggesting that the lyric is the only mode of expression available to the poet. Strangely enough, Vendler includes a few narrative poems by Elizabeth Bishop and Jarrell. One supposes she considers these stories in verse "new strategies of representation." Other masters of contemporary narrative poetry–Anthony Hecht, Louis Simpson, and James Dickey, for example–are conspicuously absent from her book.

As can be seen by these few examples, narrative poetry has been improperly defined or ignored altogether. The contemporary poetry scene has been dominated by free-verse lyrics and anecdotes, which, according to the poets of the Expansive poetry movement, narrows the range of possibilities for poets. The concept of narrative verse has become unrecognizable and impossible to specify, and, when it is included, editors have the curious tendency to call it something else.

Narrative poetry has been seen as something from the past, stuck in the mud of tradition like an archaeological artifact, to be studied but not used.

Historically, American poetry has had a rich tradition of storytelling in verse. One need only look back to the nineteenth century to Longfellow, Oliver Wendell Holmes, John Greenleaf Whittier, the long forgotten Joaquin Miller, Herman Melville, and even Walt Whitman. While these poets were successful at domesticating European subject matter and meters, they also wrote verse narratives with a distinctively American flair. They wrote of important American subjects in galloping, anapestic meters in such poems as "Paul Revere's Ride" and "The Defense of the Alamo." "Kit Carson's Ride" by Miller, for instance, is a story about the legendary hunter, trapper, and scout written in tetrameter lines that sprawl across the page in as many as thirteen syllables a line, evoking the expansive landscapes of New Mexico and California, where Carson and Miller both spent much of their lives. These anapestic lines, along with the varying rhyme schemes, provide the heart-pounding intensity of fleeing on horseback across the wide plains of the American West. Many scholars today regard the works of these poets as aesthetically inferior to poetry of the Modern period, but to ignore the haunting music that pervades the American subconscious in such lines as Longfellow's "Listen, my children, and you shall hear / Of the midnight ride of Paul Revere" is difficult.

Yet, even in the nineteenth century, antinarrative sentiments abounded. Edgar Allan Poe felt that the raison d'être or the "feeling" of poetry was best expressed in the lyric poem and that the long poem did not exist. Even the English essayist Walter Pater trumpeted the lyric poem as supreme. By the turn of the century, even as Ezra Pound and T. S. Eliot were writing deliberately skewed and fragmented narrative poems, narrative no longer held a respectable place among the High Modernists. For them, narrative was best left to prose fiction writers.

Modernists considered the lyric to be the highest and purest form of poetry. Symbolism and, later, Imagism became the dominant movements. Although important elements for creating powerful poetry, symbols and images in themselves are not conducive to the loose, capacious style of traditional narrative verse. Pound's *The Cantos* (1919–1970), William Carlos Williams's *Paterson* (1946–1958), Eliot's *The Waste Land* (1922), and Hart Crane's *The Bridge* (1930) are considered to be some of the great long poems in modern American literature. Though some of these poems have dramatic movement, and their authors were able to reach beyond the inward perspective of the lyric, none of these poems can be called a narrative. *The Cantos* and *Paterson* are long imagist lyrics. *The Waste Land* has a thin thread of narrative running through it, but it is more of an apocalyptic vision. *The Bridge* has sections that could be considered narrative, but the poem as a whole lacks unity. Lynn Keller reveals this view in her essay "The Twentieth-Century Long Poem," in which she describes Pound's *Cantos* as a "collage" and says that "Pound himself . . . struggles with his inability to 'make it cohere.'" She considers Eliot's *The Waste Land* "paratactic" in form and sees an "uneasy coexistence of Eliot's longing to impose the once viable organization of a unified perceiving consciousness or a coherent narrative and his desire to represent the chaos of a botched civilization." Williams's *Paterson* "is held together largely by symbolic patterns" and Crane's *The Bridge* "asks the reader to follow the associations in the poet's mind" and employs "multifaceted symbols as ordering devices." By definition, Modernism was predicated upon challenging the readers' expectations of coherence, experimenting with conventions, and dwelling on ambiguity and uncertainty. Coupled with the tenets of Imagism, the High Modernist poets were unable or unwilling to write complete, coherent stories. Even so, a few poets continued to write narratives.

Edwin Arlington Robinson, Benét, Frost, and Robinson Jeffers are the most important twentieth-century contributors to the American tradition of verse narrative. None of these poets took part in articulating the Modernist aesthetic, though they dealt with distinctively modern themes. Robinson, Benét, Frost, and Jeffers followed many of the precepts of Modernism, using layered meanings and sophisticated rhythmic effects, but unlike their modern counterparts, they wrote linear and coherent narratives as opposed to spatial and fragmented ones, as was the fashion of the day. They did not feel the need to form a narrative movement nor to write a manifesto, because narrative was not yet completely banished from the realm of American poetry.

In the mid twentieth century the prevailing poetic mode became the short free-verse autobiographical lyric, and the writing of narrative poetry became anathema. By the 1960s the great narrative light of Frost was but a glimmer, and the narrative poem in the twentieth century was thought to have gone the way of the madrigal and the masque in the seventeenth century. In movements such as Beat, Black Mountain, Confessional, and Deep Image, long poems did dominate, from Allen Ginsberg's "Howl" to Charles Olson's "Maximus." But narrative poems, understood as plot-driven stories, usually gave way to increasing self-obsessiveness, self-referentiality, social withdrawal, and psychological curiosity. Poets such as Ed Dorn did write story-like poems, as with *Slinger* (1975), but it was, according to Keller, a "fractured (anti) narrative." Olson wrote *The*

Maximus Poems, the first ten published in 1953 and the final ones published posthumously in 1975; yet, this work, in Keller's words, is also "elliptical and allusive" and "has no plot or guiding plan." Despite the current fashion, some poets continued to turn to narrative to express their ideas, finding the short lyric too confining. Poets such as Robert Penn Warren, Bishop, Simpson, and Donald Justice wrote narrative poetry and, with varying influence, shaped the ideas of the poets yet to come.

Though a handful of poets wrote narrative poems during the 1960s and 1970s, few of these poems were published in literary journals, and no forum existed in which to discuss their aesthetics. The turn of taste was a long, gradual, and largely independent one. It began with such influential venues as Robert Fitzgerald at Harvard and Miller Williams at the University of Arkansas. In 1979 Robert McDowell and Mark Jarman started *The Reaper,* a literary journal that promoted narrative poetry. Later, McDowell and Jarman began Story Line Press, one of the few literary presses devoted to publishing narrative poetry. X. J. Kennedy at *Counter/Measures* and Frederick Morgan at *The Hudson Review* also provided important outlets for poets writing narrative poetry. Gioia published short to mid-length narrative poems in *Sequoia* in the mid 1970s, as did Frederick Turner at *The Kenyon Review.* By the mid 1980s, full-length books in verse began to appear in rapid succession. Frederick Feirstein with his New York love story *Manhattan Carnival* (1982), Frederick Turner with his science fiction epic poems *The New World* (1985) and *Genesis* (1988), Vikram Seth with his yuppie soap opera *The Golden Gate* (1986), Frederick Pollack with his afterworld journey *The Adventure* (1986), Rita Dove with her African American family history *Thomas and Beulah* (1986), Andrew Hudgins with his Civil War saga *After the Lost War* (1988), Brooks Haxton with his action adventure *Dead Reckoning* (1988), and a host of others began to reclaim much of the ground ceded to the novel almost a century before. This movement toward narrative poetry was first labeled as the New Narrative, sometimes associated with the New Formalism; it is now generally known as the Expansive movement, though some of these poets do not wish to be categorized in such a fashion. Some work in traditional forms and some do not, and many desire to rejuvenate poetry by expanding the acceptable forms and resources of poetry beyond the short free-verse autobiographical lyric. In addition, they have sought to revive traditional storytelling, which had been pushed to the fringes during the middle decades of the twentieth century. Worth noting is that at the same time as these poets began having an intense interest in form and narrative poetry, an interest for Cowboy poetry arose. Paul Zarzyski in his essay "The Lariati Versus/Verses the Literati: Loping Toward Dana Gioia's 'Dream Come Real'" writes that "The western renaissance began in 1985 with the first Cowboy Poetry Gathering" in Elko, Nevada. Cowboy poetry has "range rhymes and bunkhouse ballads written and recited by buckaroo bards and cowpuncher poets." The narrative poems written by these diverse poets—such as Donald Hall, Wallace McRae, Maxine Kumine, and Linda McCarriston—naturally thrive from the tradition, hence their apparent connection to the New Narrative poetry.

As Feirstein and Turner state in the introduction to *Expansive Poetry,* published in 1989, "The reason to use narrative and meter and rhyme is not to be fashionable but to open worlds of reality and imagination to the poet which might otherwise be shut off." For some, articulated by Gioia in his essay "Can Poetry Matter?", writing narrative poetry is an opportunity to give poetry cultural significance, a significance that was perceived as lost. David Mason succinctly expresses both of these concerns in his essay "Other Lives: On Shorter Narrative Poems," which was included in a special issue of *Verse* edited by Robert McPhillips:

> There are at least two good reasons why contemporary poets might use verse to create characters and tell stories. One reason is that it can rejuvenate their art by compelling them to reevaluate the subjects they write about, to look more closely at lives usually deemed insufficiently flashy or spectacular. By involving us in the nuances of social and individual problems, narrative poetry can address issues beyond the narrow confines of the poet's life, or it can focus emotions too painfully personal to be revealed directly in a lyric. It is also possible that the line has advantages lacking in prose, the chief one being that it contributes to memorability, helping to sustain a literary culture most of us would agree is in danger of extinction.

Unlike their predecessors—who looked to the English masters such as George Crabbe, William Wordsworth, Robert Browning, and Thomas Hardy—these young writers had no available contemporary tradition from which to draw. Modernism had repudiated the American examples of Longfellow, Whittier, and Miller, and the short story and the novel had completely taken the place of narrative verse. Those interested in narrative poetry had to explore the neglected past of Robinson, Frost, and Jeffers in order to develop the beginnings of a narrative aesthetic. Their central questions were: How does one write compelling narrative verse without becoming prosaic? What forms and styles must be used or invented to tell these stories? What kind of narrative verse should be written after such movements as Modernism, the rise of the motion picture, two world wars, and the cultural upheaval of the 1960s? Simply to tell a story in poetic form was not good enough. They realized a complex dynamic exists in the use of language, form, and drama. How does one tell a memorable story that maintains the evocative compression and intensity of the lyric?

The answers to these questions are revealed through the narrative poems that have been written over the last twenty years. Most of the popular and critical attention has been given to book-length stories in verse. Two of the more recent successes are *Iris* (1992) by Jarman and *Jimmy and Rita* (1997) by Kim Addonizio. However, these and many other contemporary authors write short and middle-length narratives as well, and these shorter narratives deserve a closer study, with examples from Lea's "The Feud," Nelson's "The Ballad of Aunt Geneva," and Gioia's "Homecoming."

Lea's "The Feud" first appeared in *The Kansas Quarterly*, was later included in his collection *The Floating Candles* (1982), and was again reprinted in the anthology *Rebel Angels: 25 Poets of the New Formalism* (1996). "The Feud" is a story told in 101 quatrains of iambic pentameter. A story of revenge and its consequences, set in a small rural community, it is reminiscent of the feud between the Hatfields and the McCoys. The first-person narrator begins forebodingly: "I don't know your stories. This one here / is the meanest one I've got or ever hope to." The nameless narrator encounters the troublesome Walker gang and attempts to be affable toward them:

> I waved at them from the porch—they just looked up—
> and turned away. I try to keep good terms
> with everyone, but with a crowd like that
> I don't do anymore than necessary.

However, tensions rise, as does the heat. The narrator values common sense and a certain amount of decorum. His wife and children have gone to the pond to get cool, but he warns, "That made some sense. It's the last that will." The reader then meets the odd characters of the Walker gang:

> I peeked out quick through the window as the Walker's
> truck ripped past, and said out loud, "Damn fools!"
> The old man, Sanitary Jim they call him,
> at the wheel, the rifles piled between
>
> him and Step-and-a-Half, the crippled son.
> In back, all smiles and sucking down his beer,
> Short Jim and the deer. Now Short Jim seems all right.
> To see his eyes, in fact, you'd call him shy.

The conflict begins when the Walker crew leave their deer guts to cook in the sun, a thoughtless act that

Dust jacket for a 1986 series of narrative poems about an African American family (Bruccoli Clark Layman Archives)

produces an awful smell. The narrator has an intense dislike for the Walkers and thinks the gang "A worthless bunch." He rakes up the deer guts, strews them in the Walkers' dooryard, and signs his actual name. He realizes the senselessness in such an action and meditates on his beliefs:

> . . . I've lost most of my churching,
> but don't believe in taking up with feuds.
> I usually let the Good Lord have His vengeance.
>
> Nothing any good has ever grown
> Out of revenge.

He remembers a particular instance in his childhood when he slapped Lemmie Watson for breaking a little mill the narrator had built at the brook: "And so I learned . . . and I've been different ever since." The reader also learns that the leaving of the deer guts is not the Walker gang's first infraction. They have bothered the narrator in the past with a number of offenses, first by digging up his mailbox, or so the narrator assumes: "At least I don't know who in the hell beside them / would have done it." His wife advises him to let the mailbox incident go, but one evening he hears the Walker gang's hounds and the click of dog paws on his porch. As he investigates, he discovers a wolf and takes her to the pound. He removes her collar and flings it on the Walker's dooryard while driving home. The reader begins to suspect that the Walker gang is not entirely at fault. The narrator then relates his thoughts on the Walker gang's sort of people:

I never gave it too much thought but must
have figured right along that they belonged
to that great crowd of folks who *don't* belong.
Their children wear their marks right on them: speech

you hardly understand, a rock and sway
where a normal boy would take an easy stride.
And in and out of jail. If they can't find
another bunch to fight with, why they'll fight

with one another. . . .

The narrator's superficial comments about the Walkers reveal a judgmental and self-righteous character. He says, "Is it any wonder, / then, I didn't make a special point / of mixing with them? No more than I would / with any crowd that filthed itself that way." He proceeds to bolt his own dogs shut in their houses in anticipation of the retaliation to follow. The narrator admits, "The only thing I knew for sure they'd done / was leave a mess of guts out on my lawn." However, he justifies his actions:

For all we either knew, the Boss was making
visions in our eyes which, feeling righteous,
we took upon our *selves* to figure out.
And since, between the parties, I guessed *I*

had better claim to righteousness than they did,
I'm the one who—thinking back—began
to read the signs according to my will.

The feud continues in escalating fashion as the narrator finds all four of his summer tires on his new pickup have been slashed. He immediately assumes the Walkers are at fault. After debating whether or not to exact revenge, he decides to poison their hog with an apple filled with rat pellets. He watches the hog die, and on the way home he sings "Old Rugged Cross," "Onward Christian Soldiers," and "Amazing Grace." He says, "I slept two righteous hours." The next day he is terribly sick with pneumonia, apparently from paddling through a brook the previous evening while going to and from the Walkers' house. He proceeds to go to the clinic twenty miles away. On his way home, he sees "Above the ridge / the sky was copper orange, and thick black smoke / was flying up to heaven." He realizes that his house is on fire. When he arrives home, he attempts to free a ladder that is stuck in a puddle of ice but is unsuccessful. Meanwhile, his son is yelling for him from upstairs behind a storm window. The reader is overcome with anxiety as the parents attempt to free their trapped child:

And so my wife began to call the boy,
"Throw something through the window and jump out!"

He threw a model boat, a book, a drumstick.
He couldn't make a crack. I flung the ax.
It missed by half a mile. I threw again
And broke a hole, and scared the boy back in.

That was the last I saw of him.

Lea's use of short sentences intensifies the drama. The subject/verb repetitions—"He threw," "I flung," "I missed," "I threw again"—occur in rapid succession and heighten the action before the reader realizes the futility of the narrator's actions. The narrator recalls slapping Lemmie Watson thirty years ago, his punishment for doing so, and his teacher asking if "one small paddle wheel / was worth all this? I had to answer No." The narrator says that he will let it go, but the reader knows this decision has come too late. The narrator finally leaves revenge to God, but the reader ponders, along with the narrator, what kind of God exacts this kind of revenge:

For me, it was revenge. And what to do
right now? The house is gone, the boy, and I
believe I know just how they came to be.
But do I? Do I know what led to what

or who's to blame? This time I'll let it go.
No man can find revenge for a thing like this.
They say revenge is something for the Lord.
And let Him have it. Him, such as He is.

The narrator's "namelessness" portrays him as an Everyman. His judgmental attitudes are the stuff of society in general, in which people make surface judgments about others of whom they really know nothing. The story is also told as a warning; "No good can grow from any feud." Lea's use of iambic pentameter is unobtrusive and conversational, revealing that the line is apt for contemporary storytelling.

"The Ballad of Aunt Geneva" by Nelson, a poem in her collection *The Homeplace* (1990) and also reprinted in the anthology *Rebel Angels,* is primarily narrative. *The Homeplace* recreates several generations of Nelson's family. The story is told in eleven quatrains written mainly in trimeters, but occasionally it includes a tetrameter line. Nelson regularly rhymes the second and fourth lines and sometimes the first and fourth. The ballad is a form used liberally in popular music, but contemporary "literary" poets generally ignore it, although the form has been used for centuries. In fact, according to Joseph Addison, Ben Jonson is recorded as saying that he would rather have been the author of the ballad "Chevy Chase" than all of his own works.

"The Ballad of Aunt Geneva" is about headstrong, passionate Geneva, who is a black woman, and her love affair with a white man:

> Geneva was the wild one.
> Geneva was a tart.
> Geneva met a blue-eyed boy
> and gave away her heart.

Aunt Geneva appears to be the black sheep of the family because she is not given the same rewards as "the others." Pomp fathered five daughters, one of whom is Geneva. She has inherited her father's prideful nature, and her lips are "pursed into hardness" as she cooks on a riverboat. Geneva is tough and does not weep over her situation. In fact, she is rumored to have killed a woman:

> They say she killed a woman
> over a good black man
> by braining the jealous heifer
> with an iron frying pan.

Then, as with most ballads, there is a jump in time followed by dwelling on an incident, a technique known as "leaping and lingering," and the reader hears Geneva's voice for the first time:

> They say, when she was eighty,
> she got up late at night
> and sneaked her old, white lover in
> to make love, and to fight.
> . . . .
> *then Geneva's voice rang out:*
> *I need to buy some things,*
>
> *So next time, bring more money.*
> *And bring more moxie, too.*
> *I ain't got no time to waste*
> *on limp white mens like you.*
>
> *Oh yeah? Well, Mister White Man,*
> *it sure might be stone-white,*
> *but my thing's white as it is.*
> *And you know damn well I'm right.*

Geneva appears to have fun verbally chastising her white lover. Though no response is given by him in the story, one is able to infer that he has told Geneva that though he is flaccid, at least he is white. And she responds "but my thing's white as it is." The argumentative tone changes in the next stanza:

> Now listen: take your heart pills
> and pay the doctor mind.
> If you up and die on me,
> I'll whip your white behind.

Geneva's love for her white lover is shown through her concern for his health, and they have both grown old with "time-slowed feet." After they clandestinely cross the parlor, she longingly watches him as he leaves. Though it is never explicitly stated, one is left to wonder if it was her love for the white man that caused all of her suffering to begin with. The poem ends as it begins:

> Geneva was a wild one.
> Geneva was a tart.
> Geneva met a blue-eyed boy
> and gave away her heart.

The ballad tradition is distinguished from other narrative poems by its focus on the crucial situation and letting the action unfold itself in event and speech. The narrative is presented not as a seamless and continuous sequence of events, but as a series of flashbacks and leaps forward. It has its origins as an oral art, stories related among a community by word of mouth, as is much of African American literature, a tradition that includes poets from Francis Harper to Langston Hughes. "The Ballad of Aunt Geneva" is told in the third person, which gives the author distance, but it is also told as if the author received the story second- or thirdhand with the repetitive "They say" and "they heard." In addition, ballads are usually told objectively with little comment or intrusion. The first and last stanzas appear to break that rule; yet, since it is a story that is passed down, apparently attitudes about Geneva have been passed down as well, and the reader realizes that she is more than this. The story moves forward in bounds, and it is the stanzaic patterns and rhymes that it is set against that provide counterpoint and tension. The story is made more striking specifically because of the formality and the music.

Gioia's mid-length narrative "The Homecoming" first appeared in *Crosscurrents* and was later made part 4 in his collection *The Gods of Winter* (1991). The section begins with an epigraph by Donald Justice: "How shall I speak of doom, and ours in special, / But as of something altogether common?" Divided into eight parts,

"The Homecoming" is a story told in blank verse about an escaped convict's return to the home where he grew up. The poem is a dramatic monologue told from the perspective of the convict. The first section opens with the convict at home having already escaped prison and the headlights of the police coming up the drive. The convict says, "'Thank God it's over.' Do you know / I waited up all night for you." He has spent the time remembering "what it was like to grow up in this house." He then tells the reader, "But there's something else you need to know. / Look in the other room. No need to hurry."

The second section begins with a history of the convict's childhood. The reader learns that his father left when he was three years old and his mother took off soon after. The convict was raised by a foster mother who forced him to go to church every Sunday. One Sunday, though, when he was twelve, the convict went to the State Fair instead of to church. He says, "I couldn't stand / another dreary day of Jesus." By accident, at the fair he encountered his birth mother:

> Then suddenly I saw her at a booth,
> my mother, talking to some man, and she,
> was holding a stuffed animal they'd won,
> . . . .
> . . . I started to call out,
> but then she noticed I was watching her.
>
> And for an instant we stood face to face.
> I knew from pictures it was her. And she
> paused for a moment, staring absently,
> . . . .
> She smiled and winked at me, the intimacy
> of strangers at a summer fair, a smile
> without the slightest trace of recognition.

This sweet, tender meeting between mother and son is immediately followed by a dark, metaphysical meditation on the convict's destiny. He begins the third section:

> God didn't care. He saw where I belonged.
> She told me years ago how everyone
> would either go to Heaven or to Hell.
> . . . .
> . . . I asked her how
> a person knew where he was chosen for.
> She said, "A person always knows inside."

The convict looks inside as his foster mother tells him. All he finds is a heart like an empty shell, "And now it lies / forgotten in a cluttered dresser drawer." The word "lies," appearing at that crucial line break, is at once cruel and sad. Later, the convict concludes, "That night I knew that I would go to Hell." In part 4, the convict runs away from home. He slips into a ditch beside a cornfield and has a portentous meeting with a crow. The convict swears never to be afraid again. Eventually he is found and brought back home, and that is when he begins to get into trouble at school.

Section 5 begins with the convict revealing his love for adventure stories. He relates how he steals books from the local library so no one else can read them. He arrives at some Machiavellian conclusions:

> The more I read the more I realized
> how power was the only thing that mattered.
> The weak made up the rules to penalize
> the strong, but if the strong were smart enough,
> they always found another way to win.

Some nights he would sneak out of the house to go to his "special hiding place," a dilapidated farmhouse and a boarded-up old well. He tells the reader, "I knew there was a boy who'd fallen there," and the convict begins to talk to the dead boy.

> One night I started whispering down the well.
> . . . .
> Of course he didn't answer me. The dead
> never do. Not him. Not even Jesus.
> Only a razor's edge of moonlight gleaming,
> silent at the bottom of the well.

Referring to the dead boy, he asks, "How was I any different from him?" He then has a dark religious experience that leads him to a sinister realization:

> That was the night that I was born again,
> not out of death, but into it—with him,
> my poor unwitting Savior in the well.

He initiates himself into his "new life" by killing the neighbors' pets. Later, he starts to pull petty robberies, "And things went on like that until one night / they caught me cold, and I still had the gun."

In section 6, the convict is in prison. He makes up games to pass the time. His favorite is Roommates. He takes a cockroach or horsefly and puts it in a jar with a spider to see what will happen. He learns that "The spider always wins." After seven years in jail, he grows restless. He thinks of his foster mother:

> I looked into my heart and heard a voice.
> It told me what I must have known for years—
> That when they let me out, I had to kill her.

Section 7 begins with his escape. He proceeds straight home. He hitches a ride, and a lady picks him up. She dies at his hand: "I ditched the car at nightfall in a field, / and walked the six miles home. I knew the way." He enters his house and finds his foster mother preparing supper. The convict questions whether or not he should proceed with his revenge, realizing his childhood cannot be given back.

In the final section, the foster mother tells him she will set another place for supper, and the convict changes his mind about killing her: "She had a way about her, see?" He goes to wash up for supper and meets a boy who lives there now. "He had the wisdom of the unloved child / who knew he had been damned by being born." He gives the boy some money he had stolen from a guard and asks the boy to leave him alone with the foster mother. The convict returns to the kitchen and kills her as she is working at the sink. At first, he feels sheer delight, as if a weight has been suddenly lifted from him. By killing her, he has his freedom; however, his attitude soon changes, and he realizes the futility in murdering her:

> But as I stood there gloating, gradually
> the darkness and the walls closed in again.
> . . . .
> I saw her body lying on the floor
> And knew that we would always be together.
> All I could do was wait for the police.

During the story, the reader senses the convict's powerlessness; yet, even as he gains power, one realizes he is inevitably doomed, that power is a "phoney high."

Throughout "The Homecoming," Gioia presents a variety of emotional tones. Both tender and brutal, the story of this nameless convict reveals the common bond between all people, especially family. In addition, the persona of the convict allows Gioia to explore issues of mortality, loss, and family in a complex and substantial way. Gioia's use of the iambic pentameter line provides momentum and structure. Gioia is able to slow the lines during moments of contemplation and then rush headlong in anticipation of events to come.

With these few examples, one can begin developing an idea of what these poets consider a narrative poem. In an issue of *The Reaper,* McDowell and Jarman provided a checklist on how to write a narrative poem, which was later included in a collection of essays known as *The Reaper Essays* (1996). To be considered a narrative poem, the work must be more than just a journalistic report or merely anecdotal; it must imply a belief or an idea that the poet deems necessary for the reader to understand. There must be a beginning, middle, and an end, though not necessarily in that order. There must be dramatic action, and there must be dramatic resolution. The action must be compressed, and time must be controlled. In addition, the story should take place in an identifiable region, and the subjects and the characters must be compelling and memorable.

Paperback cover for a 1997 verse novel about a young couple living on the streets of San Francisco (Richland County Public Library)

Whether narrative poems are told in traditional forms or free verse, they must maintain the integrity of the poetic line; otherwise, the author risks losing the rhythm and becoming prosaic. A mysterious connection occurs between an idea and the form in which it is told. A narrative poem is not simply an idea or experience rendered into metrical language; it is something in which ideas, experiences, and emotions move rhythmically in significant arrangements or forms. The poet must choose the form in which meaning and sound coalesce. Neither meaning nor sound can operate independently. The articulations of sound in temporal sequences, rhythms and meters, present the "aesthetic surface" of a poem. All visual elements are, indeed, contributors to rhythmic effect; yet, they should be secondary. Elements other than just form are needed to tell a story, but the form of the poem is the means by which the passage of time is evoked. By ignoring form, poets reject rhythm and time; any possibility for a story dies. These have been the typical elements of narrative poetry since *Gilgamesh,* Homer, and the Bible. These elements, however, are not intended to be constraining and in no way limit the multifarious subjects that are possible nor the author's individual stylistic techniques. Paradoxically, the forms and techniques for poetry and fiction are not oppressive but, rather, are elastic and infinitely generative. To paraphrase John Gardner from the *Art of Fiction* (1984), if a work of art has no laws, or if its laws are incoherent, it fails—usually—on that basis.

For the New Narrative poets, narrative poetry is an art of inclusion and should not be restricted to some literary coterie. Any realm of human experience can be expressed in verse storytelling. Science, religion, philosophy, popular culture, politics, social issues, family relationships, and marriage are areas that poets have at their disposal. These New Narrative poems also include some of the most intense lyrical and meditative passages in American poetry, lyrical and meditative passages that are in service to the story rather than being the focus of the poem. In fact, complex figurative language and syntax, handled skillfully, can add force to narrative. Along with the speaker's subjective voice, a dynamic tension is created. New Narrative poems are as entertaining and as accessible as the best contemporary short stories and novels. They have the pace and appeal of motion pictures, yet maintain the intensity of the language and imagery of lyric poetry. The verse forms used are as various as the subjects, forms that intensify the drama and make them more compelling and memorable.

Since the first collection of essays on the New Narrative and the New Formalism appeared in 1989, many important anthologies and book-length studies have been published. Timothy Steele published his critical book *Missing Measures: Modern Poetry and the Revolt against Meter* in 1990, a study that endeavors to reveal the effects of Modern poetry on contemporary verse. Annie Finch's 1994 anthology *A Formal Feeling Comes: Poems in Form by Contemporary Women* is a collection devoted solely to women writing in form. Thomas M. Disch's collected essays and reviews, *The Castle of Indolence,* published in 1995, provides critical insight into several New Narrative poets and their work. Mark Jarman and David Mason edited the anthology *Rebel Angels: 25 Poets of the New Formalism,* published in 1996, which also presents several narrative poems. In 1998 Kevin Walzer published *The Ghost of Tradition: Expansive Poetry and Postmodernism,* which is "the first book-length study of the Expansive poetry movement, devoted to restoring traditional rhyme, meter and narrative to contemporary poetry." The third edition of Lewis Turco's *Book of Forms,* published in 2000, is considered an important book for those writing in form and narrative. Robert McDowell edited an anthology titled *Cowboy Poetry Matters: From Abilene to the Mainstream,* published in 2000, which includes poetry and essays from a wide range of contributors.

After twenty years, the Expansive poetry movement has produced an impressive body of poetry and has achieved what it initially set out to do—to expand the possibilities of form and narrative. By renewing interest in neglected forms and reviving storytelling in poetry, Expansive poetry has opened the imaginative realms of style and subject matter; it has also established legitimacy for poets who wish to work in form and narrative. The future direction of Expansive poetry is difficult to predict, though many younger poets have drawn from its example. In any case, this movement has made an indelible mark on the landscape of American poetry.

Presses of the New Formalism and the New Narrative

April Lindner
Saint Joseph's University

SELECTED BIBLIOGRAPHY:
Aralia Press:
BOOKS BY INDIVIDUAL AUTHORS
Bawer, Bruce. *Innocence*. 1988.
Cope, Wendy. *Being Boring*. 1998.
Davis, Dick. *Four Visitations*. 1984.
Dove, Rita. *Evening Primrose*. 1998.
Finch, Annie. *Catching the Mer-Mother*. 1995.
Gioia, Dana. *For the Birth of Christ*. 1985.
Gioia. *The Litany*. Aralia Solo Voices Series. 1999.
Gioia. *Planting a Sequoia*. 1991.
Gioia. *A Remembrance: Michael Jasper Gioia*. 1988.
Gioia. *Summer*. 1983.
Gwynn, R. S. *The Area Code of God*. 1993.
Hix, H. L. *Intellectual Pleasures*. 1998.
Justice, Donald. *Ralph: A Love Story*. Aralia Solo Voices Series. 1999.
Justice and Robert Mezey. *The Ballad of Charles Starkweather*. 1997.
Kees, Weldon. *Contributor's Note*. 1999.
Kees. *Two Prose Sketches*. 1984.
Kees. *Weldon Kees vs. The New Yorker*. 1988.
Krisak, Len. *Fugitive Child*. 1999.
Mason, David. *Blackened Peaches*. 1989.
Mirollo, Gabriella. *Shadow of a Child*. 1997.
Monsour, Leslie. *Indelibility*. 1999.
Murphy, Timothy. *Bedrock*. 1998.
Nelson, Marilyn. *She-Devil Circus*. 2001.
Northrup, Kate. *Evening*. 1999.
Salter, Mary Jo. *Wreckage*. Aralia Solo Voices Series. 1999.
Seneca. *Juno Plots Her Revenge*. Trans. Dana Gioia. 1992.
Thiel, Diane. *Cleft in the Wall*. 1999.
Tufariello, Catherine. *Annunciations*. 2001.
Wilbur, Richard. *Bone Key and Other Poems*. 1997.
Wilbur. *A Digression*. 1995.
ANTHOLOGIES
An Aralia Commonplace. Ed. Michael Peich. 1983.
Formal Introductions: An Investigative Anthology. Ed. Dana Gioia. 1994.
Intelligence There With Passion: A Festschrift in Honor of Frederick Morgan's Fiftieth Anniversary at The Hudson Review. Ed. Peich. 1998.
A Miscellany of Aralia Keepsakes. Ed. Peich. 1988.

Graywolf Press:
Gallagher, Tess. *Amplitude: New & Selected Poems*. 1987.
Gallagher. *Instructions to the Double*. 1976.
Gallagher. *Moon Crossing Bridge*. 1992.
Gallagher. *Under Stars*. 1978.
Gioia, Dana. *Can Poetry Matter?: Essays on Poetry and American Culture*. 1992.
Gioia. *Daily Horoscope*. 1986.
Gioia. *The Gods of Winter*. 1991.
Gioia. *Interrogations at Noon*. 2001.
Gioia. *Nosferatu: An Opera Libretto*. 2001.
Goldbarth, Albert. *Many Circles: New & Selected Essays*. 2001.
Gregg, Linda. *Chosen by the Lion*. 1994.
Gregg. *The Sacraments of Desire*. 1991.
Gregg. *Things and Flesh*. 1999.
Grennan, Eamon. *As If It Matters*. 1992.
Grennan. *Relations: New & Selected Poems*. 1998.
Grennan. *So It Goes*. 1995.
Haines, John. *The Owl in the Mask of the Dreamer: Collected Poems*. 1993.
Haines. *The Stars, the Snow, the Fire: Twenty-five Years in the Northern Wilderness: A Memoir*. 1989.
Hoagland, Tony. *Donkey Gospel*. 1998.
Kenyon, Jane. *Boat of Quiet Hours*. 1986.
Kenyon. *Constance*. 1993.
Kenyon. *A Hundred White Daffodils: Essays, the Akhmatova Translations, Newspaper Columns, Notes, Interviews, and One Poem*. 1999.
Kenyon. *Let Evening Come*. 1990.
Kenyon. *Otherwise: New and Selected Poems*. 1996.
Montale Eugenio. *Mottetti: Poems of Love*. Trans. Gioia. 1990.

Phillips, Carl. *Cortège*. 1995.
Phillips. *From the Devotions*. 1998.

Johns Hopkins University Press:
Bricuth, John. *The Heisenberg Variations*. 1981.
Burt, John. *Work Without Hope*. 1996.
Carper, Thomas. *Fiddle Lane*. 1991.
Carper. *From Nature*. 1995.
Dacey, Philip. *The Boy under the Bed*. 1981.
Disch, Thomas M. *Dark Verses and Light*. 1991.
Disch. *Yes, Let's. New and Selected Poems*. 1989.
Grosholz, Emily. *Eden*. 1992.
Hearne, Vicki. *The Parts of Light*. 1994.
Hollander, John. *Blue Wine and Other Poems*. 1979.
Hollander. *In Time and Place*. 1986.
Jacobsen, Josephine. *In the Crevice of Time: New and Collected Poems*. 2000.
Kennedy, X. J. *Dark Horses*. 1992.
Kennedy. *The Lords of Misrule: Poems 1992-2001*. 2002.
Martin, Charles. *Steal the Bacon*. 1987.
Martin. *What the Darkness Proposes*. 1996.
Pack, Robert. *Waking to My Name: New and Selected Poems*. 1980.
Phillips, Robert. *Breakdown Lane*. 1994.
Phillips. *Spinach Days*. 2000.
Prunty, Wyatt. *Balance as Belief*. 1989.
Prunty. *The Run of the House*. 1993.
Prunty. *Since the Noon Mail Stopped*. 1997.
Prunty. *The Times Between*. 1982.
Prunty. *Unarmed and Dangerous: New and Selected Poems*. 2000.
Prunty. *What Women Know, What Men Believe*. 1986.
Ruark, Gibbons. *Keeping Company*. 1983.
Smith, William Jay. *The World below the Window: Poems 1937-1997*. 1998.
Spacks, Barry. *Spacks Street, New and Selected Poems*. 1982.
Steele, Timothy. *The Color Wheel*. 1994.

Story Line Press:
BOOKS BY INDIVIDUAL AUTHORS
Alpaugh, David. *Counterpoint*. 1994.
Anderson, Daniel. *January Rain*. 1997.
Andrews, Ginger. *An Honest Answer*. 1999.
Barr, John. *Grace: An Epic Poem*. 1999.
Barr. *The Hundred Fathom Curve*. 1997.
Bawer, Bruce. *Coast to Coast*. 1993.
Blakely, Diann. *Farewell, My Lovelies*. 2000.
Budy, Andrea Hollander. *House Without a Dreamer*. 1993.
Canavan, Rosemary. *The Island*. 1994.
Curtis, Tony. *Poems: Selected & New*. 1986.
Djerassi, Carl. *The Clock Runs Backward*. 1991.
Dooley, David. *The Volcano Inside*. 1988.
Dove, Rita. *The Darker Face of the Earth: A Verse Play in Fourteen Scenes*. 1994.
Driscoll, Jeremy. *Some Other Morning*. 1992.
Fanthorpe, U. A. *Safe as Houses*. 1995.
Feirstein, Frederick. *City Life*. 1991.
Feirstein. *New and Selected Poems*. 1998.
Finch, Annie. *Eve*. 1997.
Fitzmaurice, Gabriel. *The Father's Part*. 1992.
Gery, John. *The Enemies of Leisure*. 1995.
Gwynn, R. S. *No Word of Farewell: Selected Poems 1970-2000*. 2001.
Haines, John. *New Poems: 1980-88*. 1992.
Hall, James B. *Bereavements: Selected and Collected Poems*. 1991.
Harris, MacDonald. *Glad Rags*. 1991.
Haskins, Lola. *Extranjera*. 1998.
Haskins. *Hunger*. Second edition. 1996.
Haxton, Brooks. *Dead Reckoning*. 1989.
Inez, Colette. *Family Life*. 1988.
Inez. *Getting Under Way: New and Selected Poems*. 1993.
Jarman, Mark. *Iris*. 1992.
Jarman. *Questions for Ecclesiastes*. 1997.
Joselow, Beth. *Broad Daylight*. 1989.
Kees, Weldon. *Fall Quarter*. Ed. James Reidel. 1990.
Keithley, George. *Earth's Eye*. 1994.
Lake, Paul. *Walking Backward*. 1999.
Lea, Sydney. *The Blainville Testament*. 1992.
Light, Kate. *The Laws of Falling Bodies*. 1997.
Mason, David. *The Buried Houses*. 1991.
Mason. *The Country I Remember*. 1996.
McBreen, Joan. *A Walled Garden in Moylough*. 1995.
McBreen. *The Wind beyond the Wall*. 1990.
McCarthy, Lee. *Desire's Door*. 1991.
McDonald, Ian. *Essequibo*. 1992.
McElroy, Colleen J. *Travelling Music*. 1998.
Meyer, Bruce. *The Presence*. 1999.
Morgan, Frederick. *Poems for Paula*. 1995.
Murphy, Timothy. *The Deed of Gift*. 1998.
Ochester, Ed. *The Land of Cockaigne*. 2001.
Paschen, Elise. *Infidelities*. 1996.
Pedersen, Laura. *Going Away Party: A Novel*. 2001.
Pollack, Frederick. *The Adventure*. 1986.
Pollack. *Happiness*. 1998.
Ransom, Jane. *Scene of the Crime*. 1997.
Ransom. *Without Asking*. 1989.
Rector, Liam. *American Prodigal*. 1994.
Rutsala, Vern. *Backtracking*. 1985.
Rutsala. *Selected Poems*. 1991.
Sampson, Dennis. *The Double Genesis*. 1985.
Semansky, Chris. *Death, But at a Good Price*. 1990.
Simmons, Diane. *Dreams Like Thunder*. 1995.
Simpson, Louis. *There You Are*. 1995.
Skloot, Floyd. *The Evening Light*. 2001.
Slaughter, Adèle. *What the Body Remembers*. 1994.

Starck, Clemens. *Journeyman's Wages*. 1995.
Stefanile, Felix. *The Dance at St. Gabriel's*. 1995.
Thiel, Diane. *Echolocations*. 2000.
Tillinghast, Richard. *Six Mile Mountain*. 2000.
Turner, Frederick. *Hadean Eclogues*. 1999.
Uyematsu, Amy. *Nights of Fire, Nights of Rain*. 1998.
Uyematsu. *30 Miles from J-Town*. 1992.
Vial, Noelle. *Promiscuous Winds*. 1995.
Williamson, Greg. *The Silent Partner*. 1995.
Wiman, Christian. *The Long Home*. 1998.
Winch, Terence. *The Great Indoors*. 1995.

POETRY ANTHOLOGIES

Cowboy Poetry Matters: From Abilene to the Mainstream, Contemporary Cowboy Writing. Ed. Robert McDowell. 2000.
A Formal Feeling Comes: Poems in Form by Contemporary Women. Ed. Annie Finch. 1994.
The Imagist Poem. Ed. William Pratt. 2001.
Modern Poets of France: A Bilingual Anthology. Ed. Louis Simpson. 1997.
The Muse Strikes Back: A Poetic Response by Women to Men. Ed. Katherine McAlpine and Gail White. 1997.
Place of Passage: Contemporary Catholic Poetry. Ed. David Craig and Janet McCann. 2000.
Rebel Angels: 25 Poets of the New Formalism. Ed. Mark Jarman and David Mason. 1996.
Turning Tides: Modern Dutch & Flemish Verse in English Versions by Irish Poets. Ed. Peter Van de Kamp and Frank van Meurs. 1994.

CRITICAL VOLUMES BY INDIVIDUAL AUTHORS

Bawer, Bruce. *Prophets & Professors: Essays on the Lives and Works of Modern Poets*. 1995.
Justice, Donald. *Oblivion: On Writers and Writing*. 1998.
Karman, James. *Robinson Jeffers: Poet of California*. 1994.
Mason, David. *The Poetry of Life and the Life of Poetry*. 2000.
Rudman, Mark. *Diverse Voices: Essays on Poets and Poetry*. 1992.
Walzer, Kevin. *The Ghost of Tradition: Expansive Poetry and Post-modernism*. 1998.
Wilbur, Richard. *Responses: Prose Pieces, 1953–1976*, expanded edition. 1999.

CRITICAL ANTHOLOGIES

After New Formalism: Poets on Form, Narrative, and Tradition. Ed. Annie Finch. 1999.
The Day I Was Older: On the Poetry of Donald Hall. Ed. Liam Rector. 1989.
Expansive Poetry: Essays on the New Formalism & The New Narrative. Ed. Frederick Feirstein. 1989.
New Expansive Poetry: Theory, Criticism, History. Ed. R. S. Gwynn. 1999.
Poetry After Modernism. Ed. Robert McDowell. 1991. Revised and expanded, 1998.
The Wilderness of Vision: On the Poetry of John Haines. Ed. Kevin Bezner and Kevin Walzer. 1996.

WRITER'S GUIDES

Bugeja, Michael J. *Poet's Guide: How to Publish and Perform Your Work*. 1995.
Corn, Alfred. *The Poem's Heartbeat*. 1997.
Joselow, Beth Baruch. *Writing Without the Muse: 50 Beginning Exercises for the Creative Writer*. 1995.

Swallow Press/Ohio University Press:
Carson, Meredith. *Infinite Morning*. 1997.
Cassity, Turner. *The Destructive Element: New and Selected Poems*. 1998.
Cassity. *No Second Eden*. 2002.
Cunningham, J. V. *The Poems of J. V. Cunningham*. Ed. Timothy Steele. 1997.
Dawes, Kwame. *Midland*. 2000.
Jenks, Allison Eir. *The Palace of Bones*. 2002.
Lewis, Janet. *The Selected Poems of Janet Lewis*. Ed. R. L. Barth. 2000.
Pelizzon, V. Penelope. *Nostos*. 2000.
Steele, Timothy. *All the Fun's in How You Say a Thing: An Explanation of Meter and Versification*. 1999.
Tucker, Memye Curtis. *The Watchers*. 1998.
Winters, Yvor. *Selected Letters of Yvor Winters*. Ed. Barth. 2000.
Winters. *Selected Poems of Yvor Winters*. Ed. Barth. 1999.

Truman State University Press:
Baer, William. *The Unfortunates*. 1997.
Bakken, Christopher. *After Greece*. 2001.
Espaillat, Rhina P. *Where Horizons Go*. 1998.
Hix, H. L. *Rational Numbers*. 2000.
Keplinger, David. *The Rose Inside*. 1999.
Maio, Samuel. *The Burning of Los Angeles*. 1997.
Nick, Dagmar. *Numbered Days*. Trans. Jim Barnes. 1998.

University of Arkansas Press:
POETRY
Baker, David. *After the Reunion*. 1994.
Baker. *Changeable Thunder*. 2001.
Baker. *Sweet Home, Saturday Night*. 1991.
Baker. *The Truth about Small Towns*. 1998.
Bond, Bruce. *The Throats of Narcissus*. 2001.
Bugeja, Michael. *Talk*. 1997.
Ciardi, John. *The Birds of Pompeii*. 1985.
Ciardi. *The Collected Poems of John Ciardi*. Ed. Edward M. Cifelli. 1997.
Ciardi. *Echoes: Poems Left Behind*. 1989.
Ciardi. *Poems of Love and Marriage*. 1988.
Collins, Billy. *The Apple that Astonished Paris*. 2001.
Coulette, Henri. *The Collected Poems of Henri Coulette*. 1991.
Dickey, William. *In the Dreaming: Selected Poems*. 1994.
Holden, Jonathan. *Knowing*. 2000.
Howes, Barbara. *Collected Poems, 1945–1990*. 1995.

Koertge, Ron. *Geography of the Forehead*. 2000.

Koertge. *Life on the Edge of the Continent: Selected Poems of Ronald Koertge*. 1982.

Koertge. *Making Love to Roget's Wife: Poems New and Selected*. 1997.

Lammon, Martin. *News From Where I Live*. 1998.

Lieberman, Laurence. *Compass of the Dying*. 1998.

Lieberman. *Dark Songs: Slave House and Synagogue*. 1996.

Lieberman. *Flight from the Mother Stone*. 2000.

McAuley, James J. *Meditations with Distractions: Poems, 1988–98*. 2001.

McDougall, Jo. *From Darkening Porches*. 1996.

McDougall. *Towns Facing Railroads*. 1991.

Mezey, Robert. *Collected Poems 1952–1999*. 2000.

Nims, John Frederick. *Sappho to Valery: Poems in Translation*. 1990.

Shomer, Enid. *Black Drum*. 1997.

Shomer. *Stars at Noon: Poems from the Life of Jacqueline Cochran*. 2001.

Shomer. *This Close to the Earth*. 1992.

Steele, Timothy. *Sapphics and Uncertainties: Poems, 1970–1986*. 1995.

Stokesbury, Leon. *Autumn Rhythm: New and Selected Poems*. 1996.

Stokesbury. *The Drifting Away*. 1986.

Trowbridge, William. *Enter Dark Stranger*. 1989.

Trowbridge. *Flickers*. 2000.

Trowbridge. *O Paradise*. 1995.

Turco, Lewis. *The Shifting Web: New and Selected Poems*. 1989.

Zimmer, Paul. *Big Blue Train*. 1993.

NONFICTION

Baker, David, ed. *Meter in English: A Critical Engagement*. 1996.

Ciardi, John. *Ciardi Himself: Fifteen Essays on the Reading, Writing and Teaching of Poetry*. 1989.

Ciardi. *Saipan: The War Diary of John Ciardi*. 1988.

Ciardi. *The Selected Letters of John Ciardi*. Ed. Edward M. Cifelli. 1991.

Cifelli, Edward M. *John Ciardi: A Biography*. 1997.

Gioia, Dana, and William Logan, eds. *Certain Solitudes: Essays on the Poetry of Donald Justice*. 1997.

Gwynn, R. S., ed. *The Advocates of Poetry: A Reader of American Poet-Critics of the Modernist Era*. 1996.

Holden, Jonathan. *The Old Formalism: Character and Contemporary American Poetry*. 1999.

Steele, Timothy. *Missing Measures: Modern Poetry and the Revolt Against Meter*. 1992.

Turco, Lewis. *Visions and Revisions of American Poetry*. 1986.

The major works of the New Formalist and New Narrative poetry movements have, perhaps not surprisingly, been published mostly by a handful of presses willing to take a chance on what began as an unfashionable approach to versification. Two of these presses–Aralia and Story Line–promoted the work of poets working in form and narrative as an early and central part of their missions. Though less inextricably linked with the New Formalist movement, the Poetry and Fiction Series of the Johns Hopkins University Press has long been open to the work of poets actively interested in formalism. Swallow Press, an imprint of Ohio University Press, historically has supported the followers of poet/critic Yvor Winters who make up an important strain of the New Formalism. Other small presses–including Graywolf Press and the University of Arkansas Press–simply are more catholic in their tastes than most presses and, as a result, publish both free verse and poetry in received forms. Finally, Truman State University Press, based in Kirksville, Missouri, has awarded its T. S. Eliot Prize for a full-length poetry book to a string of emerging formalists, enlarging the focus of its poetry list. These literary ventures stand out among the nation's many small independent and university presses for their willingness to make available a significant body of work in received and experimental forms. Although mainstream literary magazines are increasingly likely to publish formal verse, and longtime free-verse practitioners are dabbling more often in traditional forms, poets working in form are still published and promoted by relatively few presses.

Called "one of the most significant literary ventures in the United States" by David Mason, Aralia Press was an early promoter of Expansive poetry and has maintained ardent support for the movement. However, Aralia Press was founded with another goal: to uphold the tradition of the book as a work of fine art. Founder Michael Peich is a professor of English at West Chester University in Pennsylvania, where he offers one of the nation's few opportunities to make books by hand. Peich named his fledgling press for *Acanthopanax sieboldianus*, the "Five-leaf Aralia," a shrub with palmately compound leaves. Since 1983, he and his students have produced limited-edition books distinctive for their graceful design and consistently good poetry. The look of Aralia Press books is inspired by such noteworthy fine-arts presses as Stone Wall, Prairie, and Windhover; its books are produced from hand-set types and printed letterpress on quality paper. Peich's work has won the press many awards, including recognition in the American Institute of Graphic Arts' 50 Best Books Competition in 1996. Bruce Meyer has praised the distinctive look of Aralia's books: "There is a restrained elegance to the Aralia Press works, a formality that bespeaks the highest form of understatement where the printer raises his craft to the level of transparency in order to let the text speak for itself." Aralia's aesthetic is straightfor-

The founders of Story Line Press, Robert McDowell and Mark Jarman (photographs by Bruce Meyer [left] and Amy Jarman)

ward: "Design is intended to make the reading experience a pleasure," says Peich. The resulting books and broadsides encourage the reader to linger with reverence over the poems within. As Mason has observed, "The purpose of such publications is not to reach a mass audience, but to make books that give tactile and visual as well as intellectual and auditory pleasure."

Aralia's distinctive look is matched by its equally distinctive verse. The critic Robert McPhillips has noted in *Bookways* (1993) Aralia's "remarkable integrity in the quality of the verse it has published," referring to Peich's consistent preference for the carefully crafted, classically transparent poem. From its inception, Aralia has published the work of established formal poets, including Richard Wilbur, Donald Justice, Anthony Hecht, Frederick Morgan, Anne Stevenson, and James Merrill. *The Ballad of Charles Starkweather,* a collaborative work by Justice and Robert Mezey, was published in 1997 with a frontispiece drawn by Justice. Wendy Cope, a British poet with an enormous popular readership, published the chapbook *Being Boring* (1998) with Aralia. The press also has served as a venue for a younger generation of formalists, publishing early works by Dana Gioia, Mark Jarman, Marilyn Nelson, Molly Peacock, and R. S. Gwynn; Gioia's *Summer* (1983) was the first title published by the press. Moreover, Aralia stands alone among literary fine presses for its willingness to publish first books by emerging poets. Mason, Diane Thiel, Bruce Bawer, Annie Finch, Timothy Murphy, Gabriella Mirollo, Catherine Tufariello, Wilmer Mills, and Kate Northrop have published first books with Peich. The press also seeks to right critical oversights. Early on, Peich championed the work of the undervalued late poet Weldon Kees, publishing *Two Prose Sketches* (1984) and a previously undiscovered Kees poem, *Contributor's Note* (1999).

Aralia also has distinguished itself by producing anthologies and specialty publications, beginning with *Formal Introductions: An Investigative Anthology* (1994). Edited by Gioia, this limited-edition sampler was the first anthology of New Formalist verse. *Formal Introductions* includes work by several poets associated with the New Formalist and New Narrative movements, including Peacock, Vikram Seth, Timothy Steele, Frederick

Feirstein, and Wyatt Prunty. Peich also edited and published *Intelligence There With Passion: A Festschrift in Honor of Frederick Morgan's Fiftieth Anniversary at The Hudson Review,* which includes poetry by Dick Allen, Hayden Carruth, Alfred Corn, Tom Disch, Emily Grosholz, John Haines, Daniel Hoffman, Maxine Kumin, Philip Levine, W. S. Merwin, Charles Tomlinson, and Louis Simpson. Aralia also produces literary keepsakes or broadsides–single poems on loose, framable sheets of fine paper, often in honor of special occasions. In 1988 the press issued *A Miscellany of Aralia Keepsakes,* a collection of poems by Bawer, Gioia, Disch, Len Roberts, Gary Soto, and Jon Veinberg. The Solo Voices Series features chapbooks of single poems by contemporary American poets. The series includes poems by Gioia, Jarman, Justice, Thiel, and Mary Jo Salter.

In 1995 Peich and Gioia founded the West Chester Poetry Conference, the first and only ongoing conference wholly devoted to teaching poetic forms. The synergy between the conference and Aralia Press has benefited both; Aralia writers often teach at or otherwise take part in the conference, and the conference regularly features a session at which Peich demonstrates the all-but-lost art of literary fine printing by making a broadside. Since its inception, the conference has doubled its attendance, indicating strong interest in received forms and narrative.

Of all presses large and small, Story Line Press has been the most effective in promoting narrative and formal poetry to a wide audience. Perhaps Story Line's most important contribution to poetry was the publication of *Rebel Angels: 25 Poets of the New Formalism* (1996), the definitive anthology of the movement. *Rebel Angels* features the most visible New Formalists, among them Jarman, Gioia, Nelson, Steele, Mason, Salter, Peacock, Andrew Hudgins, Marilyn Hacker, Brad Leithauser, and Raphael Campo. While hard-line formalists such as T. L. Ponick of *The Edge City Review* have criticized the anthology for its inclusion of poets who work in freer metrics as well as for its efforts toward multiculturalism, *Rebel Angels* illustrates that there is no one New Formalism: a poet such as Peacock, who often subverts the reader's expectations by establishing and then departing from regular iambics, is as representative of the New Formalism as Steele, whose rhymes are full and whose meter is meticulously regular. Moreover, *Rebel Angels* features the formal work of poets who fall in the center of this spectrum, such as Gioia, Nelson, and Hudgins, who choose free verse as a medium at least as often as they choose rhyme and regular meter. *Rebel Angels* is valuable precisely because it offers a sense of the range of poets loosely grouped together under the less-than-perfect rubric "New Formalists" and the slightly more accurate but less catchy name, the Expansive poets.

Beyond *Rebel Angels,* the contributions of Story Line Press to contemporary poetry have been legion. Story Line's ambitious list includes anthologies such as *A Formal Feeling Comes: Poems in Form by Contemporary Women* (1994), edited by Finch; *Cowboy Poetry Matters: From Abilene to the Mainstream, Contemporary Cowboy Writing* (2000), edited by McDowell; *Place of Passage: Contemporary Catholic Poetry* (2000), edited by David Craig and Janet McCann; and *The Muse Strikes Back: A Poetic Response by Women to Men* (1997), edited by Katherine McAlpine and Gail White. Story Line also has published several groundbreaking critical volumes, among them *After New Formalism: Poets on Form, Narrative, and Tradition* (1999), edited by Finch, and *Poetry After Modernism* (1991, expanded 1998), edited by Story Line publisher McDowell. Its single-author critical volumes include Mason's *The Poetry of Life and the Life of Poetry* (2000) and Kevin Walzer's *The Ghost of Tradition: Expansive Poetry and Post-modernism* (1998). Also in the press's catalogue are writer's guides such as Corn's *The Poem's Heartbeat* (1997) and Michael J. Bugeja's *Poet's Guide: How to Publish and Perform Your Work* (1995). Finally, Story Line has published poetry collections by a long list of important poets writing both in received forms and free verse. Among them are Jarman, Corn, Finch, Gwynn, Justice, Kumin, Simpson, Wilbur, Rita Dove, Sydney Lea, Vern Rutsala, and Liam Rector.

Story Line Press grew out of a collaboration between McDowell and Jarman, both champions of narrative poetry. The writers met as undergraduates at the University of California at Santa Cruz and went on to found *The Reaper,* a literary magazine whose main purpose was to argue the superiority of narrative poetry over the free-verse, semi-autobiographical lyric that has been the main mode of contemporary American poetry. *The Reaper* ran for ten years and folded in part because of the difficulty of finding narrative poetry that lived up to their demands.

In 1984 the Nicholas Roerich Museum in New York offered to fund an annual series of poetry books, to be chosen and published by Jarman and McDowell, and Story Line Press was created. Four years later, the press established the Nicholas Roerich Poetry Prize, one of the largest first-book competitions in the United States; the first winner was David Dooley, whose book *The Volcano Inside* (1988) was made up of free-verse meditations and narratives. Since then, the Roerich Prize–which honors the work of Russian philosopher, painter, poet, and peace advocate Nicholas Roerich–has often gone to promising poets working in form, including Mason, Thiel, Kate Light, and Christian Wiman.

In 1989, when *The Reaper* ceased publication, Jarman relinquished his duties at Story Line, but McDowell continued as publisher. The press grew to produce more than a dozen books each year, and the catalogue expanded to include fiction, writer's guides, criticism, memoirs, essays, and translations. However, the main focus of the press remains its poetry books. These attractively designed commercial volumes have enabled Story Line to win a wider audience for Expansive poetry.

Like Aralia and Story Line, the Johns Hopkins University Press Fiction and Poetry Series has long featured the work of poets interested in received forms. Founded in 1979 as a joint venture between the Johns Hopkins writing seminars and Johns Hopkins University Press, the series has since been in continuous operation under the guidance of editor John T. Irwin, who dedicated his attention to short fiction and poetry because he felt these two genres were in danger of being neglected by commercial presses. The series publishes poets at all stages of their careers; its catalogue features first and midcareer collections as well as selected volumes by poets in their fifties and sixties. Books in the Fiction and Poetry Series include Steele's *The Color Wheel* (1994); William Jay Smith's *The World below the Window: Poems 1937–1997* (1998); several of Prunty's books, from *The Times Between* (1982) to *Unarmed and Dangerous: New and Selected Poems* (2000); and Josephine Jacobsen's *In the Crevice of Time: New and Collected Poems* (2000). Irwin, who has always been partial to the work of an older generation of formalists, among them Hecht, John Hollander, and Mona Van Duyn, has been particularly open to poets interested in formality since the mid 1980s, when, he said in an e-mail interview, "It was my sense that there was a swinging back of the pendulum toward people who were more and more interested in meter, regular stanza, rhyme. Till then, I had felt that American poetry had simply given up too many of the things it could do." Citing the increasing number of poets writing in forms, Irwin feels that the state of American poetry in the twenty-first century is more interesting than it was in the 1970s. The Hopkins poetry series shows every sign of continuing its support of poets and readers interested in the variety of forms open to poets.

An imprint of Ohio University Press, Swallow Press has published such works as Steele's *All the Fun's in How You Say a Thing: An Explanation of Meter and Versification* (1999) and *The Poems of J. V. Cunningham* (1997), edited by Steele, as well as Turner Cassity's *The Destructive Element: New and Selected Poems* (1998). Steele and Cassity are among the chief literary heirs of Yvor Winters, who advocated logic and plain speech in poetry and whose adherents tend to be formal purists, eschewing free verse altogether in favor of full rhyme and strict meter. Swallow Press, founded in the 1940s by poet and publisher Alan Swallow, has a long history of working with formalists, particularly those of the Winters circle. Its focus became broader after Swallow's death in 1966; the press became affiliated with Ohio University Press, which has a license to acquire, market, and distribute its books, in 1979. When David Sanders became director in 1996, he rejuvenated the commitment of the press to supporting formalist poetry.

Swallow has published Winters's *Selected Poems* (1999) and his *Selected Letters* (2000), as well as the *Selected Poems* (2000) of distinguished poet and novelist Janet Lewis, Winters's wife. All three volumes were edited by R. L. Barth. Ohio University Press/Swallow Press also runs the Hollis Summers Poetry Prize, an annual competition founded in 1997.

While some presses have been created with the primary mission of changing the face of American verse by promoting narrative and traditional forms, other presses that have no such overt interest have nevertheless helped to promote contemporary formalism by publishing noteworthy books by emerging and established writers working in received and experimental forms. One such press is Truman State University Press in Kirksville, Missouri. Since 1997 the press has sponsored the T. S. Eliot Prize, an annual competition for the best unpublished book-length collection of poetry (which the press then publishes). Partly because the press has chosen dedicated formalists as judges for the prize, winners have included some of the most promising emerging formalists. In 1997, judge Samuel Maio chose *The Unfortunates* by William Baer for the first Eliot Prize. Baer is best known as the founding editor of *The Formalist,* a journal that, as its name indicates, is dedicated exclusively to verse in traditional forms. Judge X. J. Kennedy's chosen manuscript in 1998 was *Where Horizons Go* by Rhina P. Espaillat, an adept formalist. Judge Gioia's choice for the 2000 prize was H. L. Hix's *Rational Numbers,* written in experimental form. Truman State University Press also publishes poetry collections outside of the Eliot Prize; among these is Maio's *The Burning of Los Angeles* (1997). Jim Barnes, editor of the Truman State University poetry list, said in an e-mail interview that the emphasis of the press on formal poetry is not the result of a calculated effort. "Truman State University Press has been an advocate of the well-made poem, the well-made book," he says. "Form has a lot to do with the making of course." He adds, "TSUP actively supports the cause of good poetry. If more of our books are formal . . . it must be because form and content work together in the best possible ways."

Founded in 1980 by the poet Miller Williams, the University of Arkansas Press has published strong formal poets of two generations, among them John Frederick Nims, John Ciardi, Lewis Turco, and Steele. Williams ran the press until 1998; after his departure, the press was shut down briefly, then reopened with Larry Malley as director. The press plans to publish four books of poetry per year; one title each year will be a first book chosen by an established poet. Malley expects the press will publish work in a wide variety of poetic styles and might devote each year to a different style.

Among small presses, Graywolf Press is noteworthy for publishing the work of one particular poet whose criticism and creative work have been a cornerstone of the New Formalism. In publishing the book-length version of Gioia's first poetry collection, *Daily Horoscope,* in 1986, Graywolf proved itself willing to go out on a limb at a time when new poetry in received forms was regarded with suspicion and when formal poets were widely reviled as reactionary neoconservatives. Graywolf has published subsequent volumes by Gioia, including *The Gods of Winter* (1991) and *Interrogations at Noon* (2001), his libretto *Nosferatu* (2001), his translation of Eugenio Montale's *Mottetti: Poems of Love* (1990), and his essay collection *Can Poetry Matter?* (1992). Graywolf Press was founded in 1976 by Scott Walker, who originally worked in a space provided by Copper Canyon Press. Later, Walker moved the shop into what he called the "print shack," a small building in his backyard. Graywolf's early books were hand-set and hand-printed on machines operated by treadle. The first book published by the press, Tess Gallagher's *Instructions to the Double* (1976), sold out its small run in four months. Over the next few years, Graywolf published poetry collections by John Haines, Jane Kenyon, and Carl Phillips, establishing itself as a strong independent literary press. After Walker's resignation in 1994, Fiona McCrae was appointed director, and Graywolf became the first nonprofit literary press to survive the departure of its founder. Graywolf publishes sixteen books a year, including poetry, novels, essays, literary criticism, and memoir.

Despite the inroads Expansive poetry has made since the 1990s, younger poets interested in form and narrative may still have trouble placing their first books. While it has become easier to place sonnets and villanelles in certain mainstream journals, placing a first manuscript with a prestigious press almost always involves catching the eye of an established poet judging a first-book contest—and edging out the competition, which often amounts to hundreds of manuscripts. Judges frequently choose winning manuscripts from contest entrants whose aesthetic approach approximates their own; and most first-book contests are judged by poets from the literary mainstream. Moreover, since a greater than average number of established poets writing in regular forms make their livings outside the academy, talented younger poets working in form are relatively isolated from like-minded mentors—and contest judges are known to favor their most promising former students. These conditions tend to stack the already steep odds against budding formalists trying to break into print.

While contest judges might not find formally regular verse the anathema it once was, it is still true that a first book written mainly in traditional forms is likely to face certain residual prejudices. For New Formalism to reach an ever-wider audience, it is essential that more contest judges and more presses prove willing to take on emerging formalists.

The Prosody of the New Formalism

Thomas Cable
University of Texas at Austin

Whether New Formalism has been the cause of more writing in meter during the last quarter of the twentieth century, or simply the frame that has selected and displayed it, is hard to know. Meter would be, of course, an essential part of any poetic movement involving formalism, though even in the richness of a movement, some meters appear constantly while others appear seldom or never. A survey of poems within the New Formalist tradition reveals a division between iambic meters and all others. Periodically, such a division is made by prosodists on theoretical grounds, but no two prosodists agree about theory. To be empirical will best serve present purposes.

As in English poetry, historically the iamb reigns. For example, Annie Finch's anthology, *A Formal Feeling Comes: Poems in Form by Contemporary Women* (1994), has a handy index of metrical forms. Of the 124 poems that are in an identifiable meter, 106 are iambic pentameter, tetrameter, trimeter, or dimeter. Similar proportions are found in other New Formalist collections. Despite its popularity, however, iambic poetry has its hazards. Even after the culling effects of anthologies and periodicals, craftily written iambic poems with effective modulations are flanked on one side by verse that suffers from excessive regularity and on the other by verse that appears superficially to be metrical but turns out not to be—"pseudo-formal" verse as Dana Gioia terms it. The idea of pseudoformal, or unmetrical, poetry brings up the practical and philosophical division between poetry in meter and free verse, and the present survey works toward this division. Along the way something will be said also about the noniambic meters that have sporadically appeared in recent writing—especially "accentual" or "strong-stress" meters, and anapestic, trochaic, and dipodic meters.

Iambic Meters

To begin in the center of things, with poetry that is firmly a part of the iambic pentameter tradition from Sir Philip Sidney to Robert Frost, Timothy Steele displays in his own writing the structures that he analyzes in his prosodical scholarship. Few poets are more self-consciously and explicitly knowledgeable about the devices that are used, and though a practice based on such knowledge could be pedantic, his is an art that conceals art. For example, in "The Wartburg 1521–22," with the subtitle "where Luther hides for ten months after the Diet of Worms," many metrists will immediately understand what is happening in the four italicized syllables in each line:

The hare the two dogs sav*age is frail man* (line 9)
Or will *descry false gods* when history slips (line 17)
And thus he justifies *as he works out* (line 27)
Till one gray dawn in early March he leaves (line 30)

Each syllable in each series of four is more heavily stressed than the syllable that precedes it. The effect is of a rising contour through four levels of stress, and yet each series includes two iambic feet, as required by the meter:

x \ | / //
descry false gods

Connoisseurs of meter will recognize the pattern as the one occurring in such much-discussed lines as those that begin William Shakespeare's Sonnet 30:

When to the ses*sions of sweet si*lent thought,
I summon up remem*brance of things past*.

The pattern modulates the iambic pentameter by letting it progress incrementally and climb slowly, without abrupt shifts of stress between syllables that bear ictus and those that do not.

Much harder to see is the tradition in which metrical stress appears to fall on an unlikely word such as the definite article *the*, not at all an obvious candidate to carry one of the five beats, as in these lines from the same poem by Steele:

x / x \ x \ x / x /
Imperatives of *the* Almighty's Word (line 6)
x / x / x / x \ x /
While far below the fortress, *the* cascade (line 23)

Yet, recent technical research in linguistic prosody has revealed that this pattern is probably one that Shakespeare used: in line 6 *the* receives more stress than *of;* in line 23 *the* receives more than *-tress.*

Harder still to analyze metrically is this line in Steele's poem:

> He hears the pure truth the first angels chorused (line 12)

Yet, one has confidence that Steele knows the tradition and that he probably has in mind a precedent for subordinating the noun *truth* to the article *the,* or another way of reducing the apparent six metrical stresses to five. Steele never makes these variations whimsically.

A formalist poet, of course, does not have to be a technical prosodist to use patterns such as these. Rachel Hadas is a critic as well as a poet, though her criticism generally deals with matters other than meter. A poem that she published in *The New Yorker,* "The Red Hat," uses traditional variations in a way that is completely contemporary. Its twenty-two lines describe a new family routine—the young son's walking to school alone but under the watchful eye of one parent or the other:

> He walks up on the east side of West End,
> we on the west side. Glances can extend
> (and do) across the street; not eye contact.
> Already ties are feeling and not fact.
> Straus Park is where these parallel paths part.

The lines are perfectly regular in the sense of being perfectly metrical, and yet they are constantly varied by substitutions for the iambic foot that any poet in the year 1600 could have used: "West End" and "Straus Park" are obvious examples of spondaic feet, and there are more subtle modulations in the two series of four syllables, "-ing and not fact" and "-allel paths part." These are the patterns of rising stress in Steele's poem on Martin Luther and in Shakespeare's sonnets.

Hadas's technique also makes use of standard variations such as the "inverted first foot," or "initial trochee":

> holding a hand, he'd dawdle, dreamy, slow (line 14)

In this line the trochaic patterns of the words "dawdle" and "dreamy" offer a counterpoint to the metrical template, retarding the forward movement of the iambic line and causing the line itself to dawdle.

Less obvious but even more interesting is a pattern that is more characteristic of the inverted first foot in "The Red Hat"—a word stressed as a trochee, / x, followed by a word stressed wholly as an iamb or beginning as an iamb, x /:

> Semi-aloud it's accurate to say (line 3)
> stretches, elastic in its love and fear (line 11)
> empty, unanchored, perilously light (line 21)

This pattern of word division is used by earlier poets, including Shakespeare and Alexander Pope, but relatively rarely. For example, although the "inverted first foot" is one of Pope's favorite metrical variations, he seldom uses it in this two-word configuration. In the 794 lines of *The Rape of the Lock,* it occurs only four times, as in 5.8:

> Silence ensued, and thus the nymph began

Why this particular instantiation of the inverted first foot should be so infrequent does not have an obvious answer. A contemporary use of a structure, however, can throw light back on the tradition and raise new questions about older metrical style. In unexpected ways a line can be completely traditional by the usual measures and yet not sound derivatively so.

An earlier formalist, Howard Nemerov, once stated succinctly the challenge of writing in meter: "I have only two rules in prosody. One is, it goes ta dum ta dum ta dum ta dum ta dum, and the second is, try not to sound like that." At the beginning of the twenty-first century, after the predominance of free verse since the 1960s, the mastery of meter by some poets has advanced only to the first of Nemerov's prescriptions. In a fair and balanced survey, Keith Maillard noted that issues of *The Formalist* include "an unpleasantly large number of metrical poems so mediocre that they are scarcely a cut above greeting card verse." There is no need to pick on poems that are boring for being too regular.

More interesting are those poems on the other side of the divide—those that use the tradition but violate it consciously. Molly Peacock chooses to write poems that cross over the line of metricality—"sonnets" that run beyond fourteen lines, or a rhyme scheme that goes awry. She speaks of a "tolerance of imperfection in technique that I sense is particularly female" and suggests, without insisting on it, that men admire rigor more than she does. Peacock does not value the strict constraints of metrical rules as highly as some other readers of poetry do. Opinions on this matter will probably always be divided.

Strong-Stress Meter

An interesting question is whether strong-stress, or accentual, meter is a workable option as it is usually understood in contemporary poetry. The ancestors of this form were the alliterative meters of Old and Middle English, though as the term "alliterative" suggests, cues to the stress patterns in the older poetry existed beyond the grammar of the stress patterns themselves. Gioia has commented that he intended "Words," the opening poem of *Interrogations at Noon*, to be in strong-stress meter—that is, a meter in which only the metrically stressed syllables counted, and the unstressed syllables fell freely, now more, now fewer. However, without alliteration or a half-line structure with precise constraints to organize the metrical stresses, as Old and Middle English had, the reader sometimes has difficulty knowing which syllables bear metrical stress.

In reviewing Gioia's volume, Arthur Mortensen is uncertain about the first line of "Words":

The world does not need words. It articulates itself.

Mortensen writes, "The line itself, as many of those following, is difficult to measure metrically, as though the first half-lines are iambic feet and the second free verse, but too much muddles the sound." Readers are confronted with an epistemological and an ontological problem at once. A strong-stress tune seems to have played in the author's head and let him organize the lines in a certain way, and yet some of the lines do not point unambiguously to the strong-stress tune. Despite the handbook histories that trace strong-stress meter from *Beowulf* and *Piers Plowman* through Edmund Spenser's *February Eclogue* (1579) to Samuel Taylor Coleridge's *Christabel* (1816), Gerard Manley Hopkins's "The Windhover" (composed in 1877), and T. S. Eliot's *Four Quartets* (1943), these poems—all presumably in strong-stress meter—are as different metrically from each other as any one of them is from the iambic pentameter. Without the external cues that medieval poetry had, there might always be a gulf of metrical indeterminacy between the author and the reader.

Poems that make use of these cues—especially half-line structure and alliteration—are usually clear in their stress patterns. Richard Wilbur's "Junk," which begins by quoting five half-lines of Old English poetry, is a famous example. Similarly, Alan Sullivan and Timothy Murphy's translation of *Beowulf* is perspicuous in its metrical structure and can readily be scanned, as in the passage describing the hero's low point in his fight with Grendel's mother:

> Weary, the warrior   stumbled and slipped;
> the strongest foot-soldier   fell to the foe.
> Astraddle the hall-guest,   she drew her dagger,
> broad and bright-bladed,   bent on avenging
> her only offspring.

Much in this passage has the feel of Anglo-Saxon poetry: the compound words with clashing stress (*foot-soldier, hall-guest, bright-bladed*), the syntactic structure of the half-lines, the alliteration.

Yet, two important points stand out. First, this mode is most often found in translations of medieval poetry—as by Ezra Pound and Seamus Heaney—and not generally elsewhere. And then, despite the archaic quality and superficial resemblances to Old English meter, the modern versions are never really like the older meter at all. From the view of the Anglo-Saxon poet, the modern versions are essentially free verse.

For example, Sullivan and Murphy's meter has a definite trisyllabic lilt, whether considered anapestic or dactylic. Half-lines such as *stumbled and slipped* or *fell to the foe* would be unmetrical in Old English poetry, in which the unstressed syllables are tightly controlled. Thus, the last two half-lines in the original are

> x x x x /   / x
> wolde hire bearn wrecan
> 'would her son avenge'

Four consecutive unstressed syllables do not occur in the 254 lines of Sullivan and Murphy's excerpt in *The Dark Horse*. Such a sequence points to a different principle of meter that might or might not be viable in Modern English. It has not yet been tried.

Dipodic Meter

A completely different kind of meter that is often classed as accentual or strong-stress is *dipodic meter,* though in the most important way it is just the opposite of accentual meter. Dipodic meters are unworkable unless they assume an underlying template of stressed and unstressed syllables, whereas a basic principle of all the accentual texts above, both medieval and modern, is lack of a template. One cannot guess even the approximate stress pattern of an accentual half-line until it is realized, after the fact.

Gioia's *Interrogations at Noon* includes a poem in dipodic meter—a rare species in contemporary poetry, even among New Formalists—though a staple in the Victorian period when Rudyard Kipling's dipodic poetry was familiar, and George Meredith's was brilliantly, quirkily musical. "At the Waterfront Café" begins

> Docked beside the quiet river, yachts are rocking in the sun
> While their skippers stop for cocktails to replay the race they've run.
> Military in their khakis, they invade the chic café
> Smirnoff tinkles in their tumblers. No one's drinking Perrier.

The key to this meter is that it can be heard two ways, like the rabbit and the duck of a line drawing, and both flicker in the perception. There can be a metrical stress on every odd-numbered syllable beginning with *Docked, -side, qui-, riv-,* and so on. But there is also the possibility of a heavier stress every fourth syllable on *-side, riv-, rock-, sun*. This meter was used by Robert Browning in "A Toccato of Galuppi's," but the fact that a Victorian reference point is so clear makes one realize the rarity of the form and wonder why. This meter is one that could repay more attention.

Ballad and Related Meters

Dipodic meters are actually the most complex manifestations of a whole family of meters that again are usually lumped together with medieval accentual meters. These are formed on the basis of four feet to the line, four lines to the stanza, or in Derek Attridge's phrase, "4 x 4 structure." In some of the derivative meters, one of the four beats can be replaced by a pause, and in some, two of the lines can be combined into one, to give, in various combinations, such meters as ballad meter, hymn meter, fourteeners, poulter's measure, and limericks. The stanza from "At the Waterfront Café" includes lines of eight beats that can readily be divided into short lines of four beats, usually at a punctuation mark.

Marilyn Nelson's "The Ballad of Aunt Geneva" shows the relationship between ballad meter (with feet-per-line counts of 4.3.4.3) and dipodic meter:

> Geneva was the wild one.
> Geneva was a tart.
> Geneva met a blue-eyed boy
> and gave away her heart.

Among the syllables bearing metrical ictus, the alternation between primary stress (Ge*ne*va, *wild*) and secondary stress *(was)* gives the dipodic lilt that is familiar in nursery rhymes and folk poetry:

> Taffy was a Welshman,
> Taffy was a thief;
> Taffy came to my house
> And stole a piece of beef.

This same pattern underlies "Sing a song of sixpence." Murphy divides the lines of the 4 x 4 structure to get 8 x 2 and, with liberal anapestic substitutions, obtains a completely different effect:

> When willows yellow
> in the windy hollows,
> we butcher the barrows
> and fallow the prairies.

> The silo swallows
> a harvest of sorrows;
> the ploughshare buries
> a farmer's worries.

The feminine endings are an important part of the effect, as can be seen by comparing other two-stress lines with consistent or occasional masculine endings: Bottom's verses in *A Midsummer Night's Dream* (1.2.33–40), for example, or George Gordon, Lord Byron's "Stanzas: Could Love for ever."

Triple Meters

The noniambic meters considered to this point are based on a count of four and are divisible by two into half-lines or hemistichs. The triple meters, anapestic and dactylic (if one believes there is a difference) are not a completely separate species, because trisyllabic substitutions are frequent in iambic meter and vice versa. Sometimes lines in isolation are ambiguous between iambic with anapestic substitutions and anapestic with iambic substitutions.

Still, there is a definite feel to poems that are largely in triple meter. Annie Finch intended her "Running in Church" to be anapestic, though it could equally be scanned dactylic:

> Then, you were a hot-thinking, thin-lidded tinderbox.
> Losing your balance meant nothing at all. You would
> pour through the aisles in the highest cathedrals,
> careening deftly as patriarchs brooded.

The three compounds in the first line have the dactylic pattern / x x (ignoring secondary stress), and the second line could be read wholly as dactylic tetrameter. In any event, the rhythmical effect is mainly determined by the disyllabic dips, which in triple meter always have a marked power to demote syllables bearing secondary and primary stress (*-think, -lid,* and *-box* in line 1, *meant* in line 2).

As the tradition of temporal metrists has long argued, whether the disyllabic dip is construed with the stressed syllable to the left or to the right matters less than that it occurs regularly. In this instance the poet (also a conscious, technical prosodist) is surely correct in identifying a rising, anapestic rhythm, even as it cuts across line ends *(You would / pour)*.

This rising rhythm is probably a specific instance of the more general principle that triple meters are nearly always perceived as rising, even when the author thinks otherwise. What may be true is that dactylic meter does not exist in English, or exists only under highly constrained circumstances, as in Henry Wadsworth Longfellow's *Evangeline*. Longfellow anglicized the classical meter by using trochees in place of spondees and allowing analogous substitutions in specific parts of the hexameter line. With this kind of precision, there is a dactylic feel, though how to fit the form into a typology of meter is hard to know. A full and persuasive analysis of the presumed anapestic-dactylic distinction has yet to be made.

Things As Yet Unattempted

In 1930 George R. Stewart predicted that dipodic verse would be an area of fruitful prosodic exploration for twentieth-century poets. That, of course, did not happen. The familiar account is that the Modernism of Pound and Eliot, and William Carlos Williams's style of free verse, supplanted a mode of Victorian and Edwardian versifying that was, on the one hand, exhausted and, on the other, too self-consciously musical to express the sensibilities, concerns, and anxieties of the new century. A better story might be that nothing was intrinsically inadequate or depleted or too musical in the works of A. C. Swinburne or Meredith but that the developments that might have happened were cut short by the extraordinary technical successes of the Modernist poets and the intellectual achievements of their endorsing critics.

In the smartest essay on English prosody written in the twentieth century, William K. Wimsatt Jr. and Monroe C. Beardsley called Meredith's "Love in the Valley" (1851, revised 1878) a "pleasant little monstrosity." Yet, its particular form of dipodic meter is fascinating, a meter that deserves to be explored for its clues to verbal magic–if not necessarily adopted entire:

> Lovely are the curves of the white owl sweeping
>   Wavy in the dusk lit by one large star.
> Lone on the fir-branch, his rattle-note unvaried,
>   Brooding o'er the gloom, spins the brown evejar.

No New Formalist has worked with anything approaching this seven-foot line that constantly incorporates substitutions and stress clashes and yet sustains the double-jump rhythm–not even W. H. Auden.

Similarly, no New Formalist has come close to Swinburne's haunting anapestic heptameter in "Hymn to Proserpine" with its medial rhyme and end rhyme between lines:

> I have lived long enough, having seen one thing, that love hath an end;
> Goddess and maiden and queen, be near me now and befriend.
> Thou art more than the day or the morrow, the seasons that laugh or that weep;
> For these give joy and sorrow; but thou, Proserpina, sleep.
> Sweet is the treading of wine, and sweet the feet of the dove;
> But a goodlier gift is thine than foam of the grapes or love.

There is no problem in this poem with the notorious "anapestic gallop."

No New Formalist has worked to any extent either with true trochaic verse, the line ending with an unstressed syllable. The "catalectic" form of trochaic verse, as the meter of William Blake's "The Tyger" is often called, is quite common, though it raises a question similar to that raised in the presumed distinction between anapestic and dactylic. However, the "acatalectic trochaic tetrameter"–the normal form of / x / x / x / x–may have a claim to be separate from the iambic. Longfellow's *Hiawatha* is written in this meter; it is certainly, distinctively monotonous; and the poets of the New Formalism have probably done well in avoiding it. Ways to adapt the metrical tricks of Meredith, Swinburne, and Kipling to the ears of the twenty-first century may exist, but the *Hiawatha* meter can be adapted only by making it something other than what it is.

References:

Derek Attridge, *The Rhythms of English Poetry* (London: Longman, 1982);

Annie Finch, *Eve* (Brownsville, Ore.: Story Line Press, 1997);

Finch, ed., *A Formal Feeling Comes: Poems in Form by Contemporary Women* (Brownsville, Ore.: Story Line Press, 1994);

Dana Gioia, *Interrogations at Noon* (St. Paul, Minn.: Graywolf Press, 2001);

Mark Jarman and David Mason, *Rebel Angels: 25 Poets of the New Formalism* (Ashville, Ore.: Story Line Press, 1998);

Keith Maillard, "The New Formalism and the Return of Prosody," *Antigonish Review*, 100 (Winter 1995): 163–183;

Arthur Mortensen, Review of *Interrogations at Noon*, by Dana Gioia, *Expansive Poetry & Music Online* (29 May 2001);

Timothy Murphy, *The Deed of Gift* (Ashville, Ore.: Story Line Press, 1998);

Howard Nemerov, "Prosody," *Formalist*, 3, no. 1 (1992): 71;

Timothy Steele, *All the Fun's in How You Say a Thing* (Athens: Ohio University Press, 1999);

George R. Stewart Jr., *The Technique of English Verse* (New York: Holt, 1930);

Alan Sullivan and Timothy Murphy, "Blood in the Lake: Lines 1397–1650 from *Beowulf*," *Dark Horse*, 9–10 (Summer 2000): 98–104;

W. K. Wimsatt Jr. and Monroe C. Beardsley, "The Concept of Meter: An Exercise in Abstraction," *Publications of the Modern Language Association*, 74 (1959): 585–598.

Younger Women Poets of the New Formalism

April Lindner
Saint Joseph's University

In the second half of the last century, many women poets were prone to be suspicious of received poetic forms, to view them as relics of a patriarchal past that excluded women, gays, blacks, and other minorities. Since the 1980s New Formalist revolution, however, some women poets have worked to theorize their attraction to such forms as the sonnet, despite its reputation as a "gilded cage" for women. Julia Alvarez has written, "My idea of traditional forms is that as women much of our heritage is trapped in them. But the cage can turn into a house if you housekeep it the right way" ("Housekeeping Cages"). Though clearly interested in reconnecting with literary tradition, some women formalists, Alvarez among them, have chosen to enact an ambivalence toward tradition in their approach to form. Alvarez explains that she has chosen to remake the gilded cage into something more distinctly her own by taking a looser approach to form, setting up formal expectations, and then subverting them:

> I wanted to go in that heavily mined and male labyrinth with the string of my own voice. I wanted to explore it and explode it too. I call my sonnets free verse sonnets. They have ten syllables per line, and the lines are in a loose iambic pentameter. But they are heavily enjambed and the rhymes are often slant-rhymes and the rhyme scheme is peculiar to each sonnet. One friend read them and said, "I didn't know they were sonnets. They sounded like you talking!["]
>
> –from "Housekeeping Cages"

Molly Peacock's poetry enacts a similar ambivalence toward the strictures of form. She theorizes as feminist her looser approach to formalism in the essay "From Gilded Cage to Rib Cage," in which she writes,

> Women poets show a marked preference for an "informal" use of form. What women seem to appropriate for themselves in the realm of traditional prosody are general methods they can put to the organic purposes, or the psychological shape, of what is the attempt to convey or say or even, perhaps, be. They have not seemed to have aspired toward the perfect sonnet, the perfect villanelle, the perfect quatrain, although they have shown themselves to be linguistically virtuosic in so many ways that we must assume that they are perfectly capable of such "perfection." Poets from Emily Dickinson to Marianne Moore to Elizabeth Bishop to Mona van Duyn have appropriated formal gestures but have used these gestures inside a personally constructed poetic....

Clearly, some women have opted to stretch the definition of formal verse, to break its rules in pursuit of a "personally constructed poetic." Apart from eschewing the "perfect" sonnet, villanelle, quatrain, or blank-verse line, however, a feminist poetics can coexist with form in other ways. Elsewhere in her essay, Alvarez hints that the act of choosing to write in a traditional form is a subversive act for a non-Anglo woman: "See, I feel subversive in formal verse. A voice is going to inhabit that form that was barred from entering it before!" And elsewhere in *her* essay, Peacock sees value in the rigor of form: she argues that traditional form is by its nature personally freeing. In concentrating on fulfilling the formal strictures, a writer can lighten up on the self-censorship, free to explore difficult–and possibly even subversive–subject matter.

A less ambivalent stance toward form is taken by the poet Marilyn Nelson, who has used regular rhyme and meter to write movingly about the African American experience. Nelson makes a compelling case that regular forms are too powerful a tool for any writer to abandon. In her essay "Owning the Masters," Nelson explains her choice to embrace literary history and received poetic form despite its associations with racism and misogyny: "'The master's tools will never dismantle the master's house,' writes Audre Lorde in *Sister Outsider*. But why should we dismantle the house? Why toss the baby over the porch railing, with its bassinetteful of soapy water? Why don't we instead take possession of, why don't we own the tradition? Own the masters, all of them."

Nelson, who often opts to write in free verse, is nonetheless unambivalent about the value of traditional form, and in this belief, she is followed by many emerging women poets who strictly adhere to the constraints of form. Poets such as A. E. Stallings, Catherine Tufariello, Leslie Monsour, and Suzanne Noguerre consistently write in received forms and bring to their sonnets and blank verse a clear and classical eye and a belief that experience can be understood and transmitted. Others—among them Diane Thiel and Chryss Yost—choose free verse at least as often as they do formal. Annie Finch, whose poetic agenda is clearly feminist, frequently uses form to catalogue the tradition of goddess worship across cultures. Finally, Beth Gylys and Kate Light have conducted extended explorations of, respectively, the villanelle and the sonnet, undermining expectations of these forms. These varied strategies thwart any critic who might want to make a sweeping generalization about how emerging women formalists navigate the tension between order and freedom.

Formal Purists: Stallings, Tufariello, Noguerre, and Monsour

The winner of the 1999 Richard Wilbur Award, A. E. Stallings's artful and original *Archaic Smile* (1999) is written exclusively in received forms. The dramatic monologues that make up a significant portion of the book include more vigor and humor than most contemporary takes on classical mythology. Readers hear from, among others, Persephone, Daphne, and Penelope. In "Hades Welcomes His Bride," the underworld and its overlord spring into life:

> Come now, child, adjust your eyes, for sight
> Is here a lesser sense. Here you must learn
> Directions through your fingertips and feet
> And map them in your mind. I think some shapes
> Will gradually appear. The pale things twisting
> Overhead are mostly roots, although some worms
> Arrive here clinging to their dead. Turn here.
> Ah. And in this hall will sit our thrones,
> And here you shall be queen, my dear, the queen
> Of all men ever to be born. No smile?
> Well, some solemnity befits a queen.

Persephone's tour continues.

> . . . Come, come. This is the greatest room;
> I had it specially made after great thought
> So you would feel at home. I had the ceiling
> Painted to recall some evening sky–
> But without the garish stars and lurid moon.
> What? That stark shape crouching in the corner?
> Sweet, that is to be our bed. Our bed.
> Ah! Your hand is trembling! I fear
> There is, as yet, too much pulse in it.

While her dramatic monologues consistently manage to be both moving and funny, Stallings proves equally skilled at the lyric. "The Tantrum" describes a four-year-old distraught when she learns her mother has "cut her mermaid hair / And [stands] a stranger, smiling at the door." Though the adults around the child scold her for her "willful, cruel despair," the child remains inconsolable:

> . . . You wept down on the floor;
> She wept up in her room. They told you this:
> That she could grow it back, and just as long,
> They told you, lying always about loss,
>
> For you know she never did. And they were wrong.

Another standout, the villanelle "Study in White" treats a complicated subject, the dilemma of a painter who must choose between the integrity of her art and the health of the children she hopes to conceive someday. As a woman the poet's subject must choose whether or not to forgo the superior quality of lead-based paint, which "gets in the flesh and in the bone." She knows well that she "may be reviled / Because [she] lack[s] the seriousness bred / For art in men–or else how could [she] think / Of compromise in this." Serious lyrics such as this one are balanced with lighter ones–for example, "RepRoach," which seeks to explain its speaker's particular revulsion for cockroaches:

> I shrink from nothing else that crawls.
> It is their elegance appalls:
> Tapping away into the bruise
> Of dark like patent leather shoes.

A deft and playful intellect runs through even the darkest of Stallings's poems. The result is a voice distinctive for its marriage of lyricism and wit.

Like *Archaic Smile,* Catherine Tufariello's slender debut volume *Annunciations* (2001) is made up exclusively of formal poems, many of them retellings of myths. The centerpiece of this volume is "No Angel," a series of Petrarchan sonnets in which Tufariello retells the Old Testament story of Ruth and Naomi. The poem explores the strangeness of the bond between Naomi, the Jewish mother-in-law, and Ruth, the pagan widow of Naomi's son. Escaping on foot from a famine, the two women must determine a strategy for survival. Tufariello's retelling seeks to come to terms with the sacrifice of Ruth, who must marry the old farmer Boaz, "a human and unlikely savior," in order to provide for her mother-in-law. In the end, both Ruth and Naomi are rewarded:

> In nine months more, Naomi was to dandle
> Fat Obed on her lap–the squalling, messy
> Grandson who would grow up to father Jesse.
> Good rabbis, later on, quailed at the scandal:

Chryss Yost, who writes formal and free verse with confessional themes (photograph by Dave Prine; courtesy of the author)

King David's great-grandma was not a Jew.
So strange, the story almost must be true.

The poem draws much of its energy from the poet's curiosity about the strangeness of the story she is retelling, and, finally, from her doubts about the plausibility of the story. Ruth's devotion to Naomi feels startling to a contemporary reader, and the narrative is driven by this strangeness, even as the poet seeks to make the story feel believable.

Tufariello's interest in seeing Christian myth through the eyes of a contemporary woman is established in the opening poem of the volume, "Lorenzo Lotto's *Annunciation*," another sonnet. In this poem the author seeks to understand what makes Lotto's version of the Annunciation distinctive:

Other approaching Gabriels offer the lily
In a ceremonial hush to humble girls
Who bow their heads or touch their breasts. She whirls
Away as the angel runs in willy-nilly
And sinks to one knee, hair streaming . . .

The line "Away as the angel runs in willy-nilly" uses metric irregularity onomatopoetically, re-creating the confusion of the moment. The ambivalence—possibly even the resistance—of this particular Mary appeals to the poet over the passive reverence of others who accept their fate without question or even surprise. To a contemporary viewer, she seems more flawed and thus more human in her reaction to "the divine turned terribly real." This interest in finding contemporary relevance in the past runs through the poems that make up *Annunciations*.

Among those formalists whose poems evince a classical reliance on reason and clarity is Suzanne Noguerre, whose *Whirling Round the Sun* (1996) is dense with ideas, wordplay, and elevated diction. Noguerre published her first volume of poetry relatively late in her life, at least in comparison with the many contemporary poets who bring out first collections in their twenties. This relative maturity is reflected in both technique and thematics. The sonnet "Pervigilium Veneris" asks, "When is the year I shall be as the swallow / that I may sing my one specific song?" And the poem "The

Scribes" looks at patience and restraint, and how absence can inform presence:

> ... It is the space
> inside the vessel, said Lao-tzu,
> that is its usefulness. It is the space
> inside the u that gives it life. And where
> the leaflets of the white ash meet the stalk,
> not sessile but set a space apart, the air
> moves in between them in the give and take
> of interpretation, as nearing
> the end, the poem itself comes to a clearing.

A sonnet, "The Scribes" delineates the special virtues of that form: compression, and an ending that gives closure and stasis. This celebration of the logic of the sonnet points toward a key element of Noguerre's aesthetic. While her approach to the iambic line is sometimes fluid, she is a formal purist in the emphasis of her poems on lucidity and logic. This classical sensibility links Noguerre to Stallings and to another emerging woman formalist, Leslie Monsour.

Monsour has devoted her poetic career to traditional form. While she has yet to publish a full-length collection, she has produced three chapbooks of great maturity and promise–*Earth's Beauty, Desire, & Loss* (1998), *Indelibility* (1999), and *Travel Plans* (2001). As critic Jack Foley has pointed out in his review of *Travel Plans*, Monsour's consistently elegant and restrained poetry often takes restraint itself as its subject matter, drawing energy from the tension between an idealized life of the mind and the physical world with its crassness, violence, and unfulfilled desire. Monsour's sonnet "Emily's Words," for example, explores how Dickinson's choice to live a solitary life caused her pain but was the source of her power as a poet:

> Unsquandered, sure and quiet as a root,
>   She stayed at home all dressed in pleated white,
>   And accurately weighed the brain of God,
>   The sum of acts not carried out. Unwed,
>   That she not be divided, she stayed whole,
> And heard the sound the tooth makes in the soul.

To keep removed from the world is less possible for the speaker of a related sonnet, "Parking Lot," in which a contemporary woman strains to find beauty and order in the utterly prosaic:

> It's true that billboard silhouettes and power
> Lines rebuke dusk's fair and fragile fire,
> As those who go on living have to prowl
> And watch for someone leaving down each aisle.
> While this takes place, a tender moon dips toward
> The peach and blood horizon, pale, ignored.

The speaker's musings are ended by a driver in a Camaro who waits impatiently for her parking space. The driver's car, which "glistens, mean and earthly, like a heart," embodies the restless and predatory driver, who plainly is better suited for this particular landscape than the speaker. Poetic meditations are out of place in a parking lot, as they would be in most of the workaday world, but such landscapes are nonetheless what the contemporary poet has to write about. Because Monsour has turned exurban dissonance into a meditative and measured sonnet, the poem embodies a small triumph of poet over world.

In the witty "Nimis Compos Mentis" (a phrase Monsour translates as "too sound of mind"), the intellect vies with the body and triumphs, to the protagonist's regret. Over coffee, the speaker in the poem unexpectedly finds herself attracted to a male acquaintance:

> Never mind the coffee we were drinking,
> Whatever I said was not what I was thinking.
> I wanted to become his mandolin,
>
>   And lie across his lap, a dainty lute,
>   And sing to him and feed him ripened fruit,
>   While light upon the sea turned opaline.
>
>   Instead, this conversation about art
>   And formal education–God, he's smart!
>   Such rationality should be a sin.

By the end of the lunch date, the gorgeous, unruly sea has taken on a different cast for the speaker: "Outside, the sea was gray and dull as tin; / It ruled the shore with tedious discipline." The speaker in the poem comports herself as she knows she should, limiting her physical contact with her friend to a parting "handshake and a peck of shy remorse." She sees the need for discipline, even if she cannot help sometimes longing to break the rules. Monsour's love of traditional form–her reaping of the rewards afforded by discipline–underscores her interest in the tension between restraint and freedom.

Choosing Freely: Thiel and Yost

In contrast to formal purists such as Stallings, Noguerre, Monsour, and Tufariello, many emerging women poets move freely between free and formal verse. One of the best of these is Diane Thiel, whose stunning debut volume, *Echolocations* (2000), received the Nicholas Roerich Poetry Prize and who recently has brought out a book on craft, *Writing Your Rhythm: Using Nature, Culture, Form & Myth* (2001). *Echolocations*, which covers a wide emotional range, opens with its darkest poems. These treat the protagonist's complicated relationship with her father, a German émigré scarred by his childhood experience of World War II. In "Changeling," the poet imagines the devastation of firebombed Dresden through the eyes of a child:

> The heat melted all it touched,
> bodies before the stones,
> carving out the Frauenkirche
> down to her catacombs.

One of the few survivors, the boy searches for his family. The poem expresses his dispossession with graceful understatement:

> Alone in the hollowed city, Father
> Wrote on the church in chalk:
> Where are you, Paul and Hedel Thiel?
>
> I live. Bernhard

In other related poems, a father's childhood trauma shapes his child's worldview. In "The Minefield" the poet recounts these aftereffects:

> He brought them with him—the minefields.
> He carried them underneath his good intentions.
> He gave them to us—in the volume of his anger,
> in the bruises we covered up with sleeves.
> In the way he threw anything against the wall—
> a radio, that wasn't even ours,
> a melon, once, that opened like a head.
> In the way we still expect, years later and continents away,
> that anything might explode at any time . . .

Elsewhere, readers learn that the sensibility of the protagonist also has been shaped by having read the Brothers Grimm in their original language, an experience both chilling and comforting. Bilingual, she's torn between her mother's English and her father's German. In her sestina "Love Letters," Thiel recounts how the protagonist's American mother practices her German by writing love letters to her husband, who grades them in red ink. The poem is genuinely touching and avoids the pitfalls of the sestina, which so often can seem like a mere poetic exercise.

Thiel also makes good use of the sonnet, reserving it mostly for her lighter subject matter. In "Bedside Reader," for example, she pokes fun at commitment-phobic men who keep Charles Bukowski's *Love Is a Dog from Hell* (1977) by their beds. "At the Mailbox" considers the point of view of a lizard living inside the speaker's mailbox, asking, "What would I do, if every day / *my* little house would open and receive / a mountain, where my living room once stood?" "Tea" explores the mysterious strength of romantic desire and mingles the small and intimate with the Leviathan. The poem begins,

> My love reminds me of a great blue whale.
> He moves like honey in this cup of tea,
> his motions nearly imperceptible,
> and yet he reaches both ends of the sea.

Though her lover is far away, the speaker still finds herself shaken by longing. As the title of the book indicates, these poems explore the echoes of experience, how history sends aftershocks through the present, and how people—even at a distance—may experience connection.

Like Thiel, California poet Chryss Yost is as adept in free verse as in formal. Though her work has yet to be published in a full-length collection, her chapbooks—*La Jolla Boys* (2000) and *Escaping from Autopia* (1998)—reveal a distinctive sensibility. Yost is frequently and unabashedly confessional, as when she takes on the most private of subjects in her rhymed sestina "Advice for Women," which begins

> Keep focused on the ceiling and you might
> not bite your cheek too hard at the tresspass
> of cold metal sliding in. And you're right
> to feel so pale and exposed (no master of your body now!) Clinical light
> keeps you composed here, but beyond the glass
>
> window, in the lab next door, a glass
> dish cultivates the worst in you

Thematically and formally, "Advice for Women" enacts a struggle for control, as its persona struggles to be master of her body, despite the indignities of the gynecologist's table and her genetic tendency toward cancer. The poem draws power from the tension between restraint and confession, between control and chaos. The best of Yost's poems work to reconcile opposites. "Last Night," which has appeared in *The Hudson Review* and the website *Poetry Daily*, pits its protagonist's need to believe in her errant beloved against his human fallibility:

> Once you believe in finding gods in mortal men
> You understand their restlessness as faith;
>
> The way she feels his truth against her skin,
> The rough edge of a matchbook, while she grieves
> To see her saviors lost, and lost again.

The poem ends by simultaneously pitying its protagonist and critiquing her desperate belief in her beloved:

> God save the church that she takes refuge in,
> The sanctuary given fools and thieves,
> This silent girl who loves a man who leaves.

The protagonist's need to see her beloved in religious terms, as a savior, coexists uncomfortably with her need to see his "restlessness as faith." This uncomfortable reconciliation of opposites is also an important feature in the poem "La Jolla Boys," whose fifteen-year-old protagonists embody both innocence and a steely determination to grow up. This tension culminates in the unsettling final lines of the poem:

> We practice doing runway walks
> And suck on popsicles like cocks
> And build sandcastles as we talk
> Of rich La Jolla Boys.

While the adult reader may be able to identify with the adolescents' desire to become sexually viable women, she cannot help seeing what will be lost when the sandcastles are outgrown. The poem is typical of Yost's work in marrying the jolt of the confessional with a welcome ironic distance from the merely personal.

Recovering Traditions: Annie Finch

As a critic, Annie Finch has edited several definitive volumes on postmodern poetics, among them the groundbreaking anthology *A Formal Feeling Comes: Poems in Form by Contemporary Women* (1994). In the introduction to the anthology, Finch makes a case for a formalist female poetic tradition that persisted in the late twentieth century despite the widespread sense that traditional forms were politically regressive. She claims that women poets are "reclaiming a formal inheritance more openly than women have done in many decades, and their work demonstrates that the long tradition of women's formal poetry is evolving once again."

This interest in continuity between the present and the past is enacted in *Eve* (1997), Finch's debut collection, which uses traditional form and free verse to re-envision ancient traditions of goddess worship. Finch takes as her subjects the Welsh goddess Rhiannon, the Apache earth-goddess Changing Woman, Celtic Brigid, and pre-Columbian Coatique, as well as biblical figures. The strongest of these revisionist poems is "Nut," Finch's version of the ancient African and Egyptian goddess of that name, who is envisioned as arching over the earth, with only her hands and feet touching ground:

> I cry for my lost days, I cry for my childhood,
> I cry for the goddess coming down from the sky.
> I cry for a place on the ground for my feet
> and I call for a place on the ground for my hands

Many of the poems in the volume are directly addressed to goddesses and appear in italics, giving the impression that they are spoken by personae. "Nut" is one of these poems. The speaker who cries "for the goddess" *must* be human; however, the reader cannot help but associate the speaker, who cries "for a place on the ground for my [her] feet," with Nut herself, who can be imagined as homesick for Earth even as her presence accounts for much of its beauty. The elision in the poem of the human and the divine accounts for much of its power. The strongest poems in *Eve* find humanity in the divine and transcendence in the human. "Being a Constellation," for example, explains the need for and logic of matriarchal religion by envisioning a nursing mother as goddess:

> If, looking up, you recognize
> the shadowing of curves that casts
> toward my belly, and the way
> my nipples travel, like two stars
>
> twinned by your eyesight; if my arms
> take night, and keep it from the sky,
> if my night voice can stop your cry,
> I'll be the Mother over you.

To the infant, the mother is a powerful and benevolent goddess; the nipples which provide a breast-feeding child with sustenance take on the mythic dimensions of stars. This poem, like most of Finch's work, builds meaning primarily through imagery. Other poems in the volume, however, have a more classically rhetorical feel. Both are about poetic influences. One, addressed to Emily Dickinson, is titled "Tribute"; the other is a retort. In "Coy Mistress," Finch imagines the response Andrew Marvell's "coy mistress" might have made to her importunate suitor. She asks,

> How could we two write lines of rhyme
> were we not fond of numbered Time
> and grateful to the vast and sweet
> trials his days will make us meet?

Practical and clever, the speaker insists upon her suitor's patience and, implicitly, his fidelity: "You've praised my eyes, forehead, breast: / you've all our lives to praise the rest." Finch's response to Marvell's poem turns object to subject and envisions the mistress as far more sensible than coy.

Pushing Limits: Light and Gylys

Finally, two emerging poets are engaged in testing the limitations of a particular form. In the case of Kate Light's *The Laws of Falling Bodies* (1997) that form is the sonnet. While Light makes use of other forms, her first

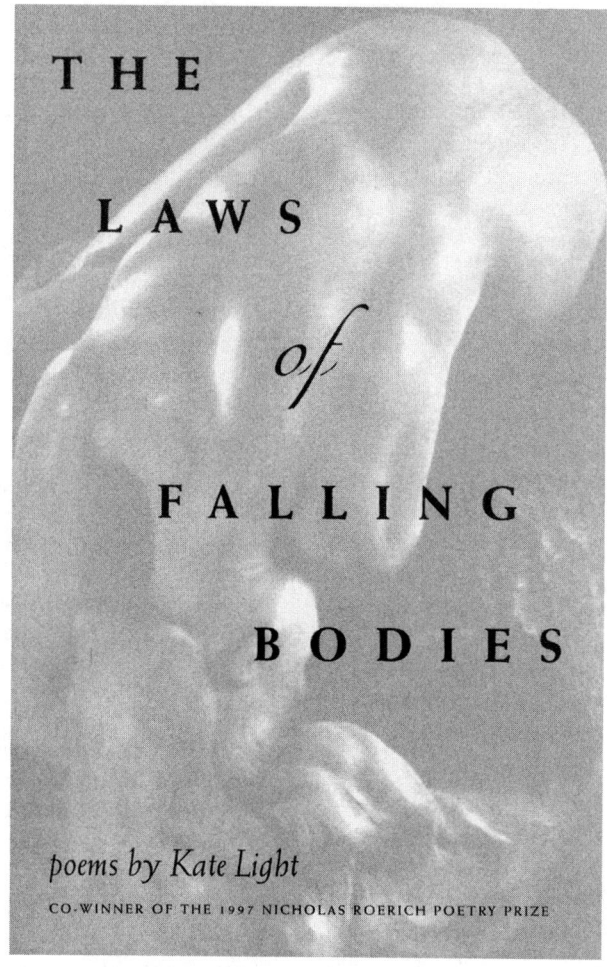

Paperback cover for the first book (1997) by a poet known for her experiments with the sonnet form (Bruccoli Clark Layman Archives)

collection takes its distinctive feel from the sonnet; though some of her poems are thirteen or seventeen lines long, they function as sonnets, making their arguments in rhymed iambic pentameter. The lyric poems that predominate in the volume are arranged in a dramatic arc: the protagonist falls in love, struggles to hold on to her beloved, loses him, and begins tentatively to imagine life without him. These poems are delicate and luminous. Many of them seem spoken, abounding as they do with parenthetical asides; they re-create the process of thought and of emotional adjustment to new love and the loss thereof. Light's real achievement is the way in which these poems manage to be simultaneously crafted and spontaneous, witty and deeply felt. In the second of a series, "Five Urban Love Songs," for example, the speaker, dining out with her beloved, finds herself repelled, fascinated, and threatened by her waitress's pierced tongue. The poem re-creates the speaker's struggle to work through these feelings:

Pierced tongue. Do-it-yourself lisp.
What is this? Penitence? Native wisdom?
Mutilation? or signal: *I'll do anything*.
Was it a dare? or a careful plan? Did it sting–
or ache–and does the food get caught–
and should such a person *work* in a restaurant?

The speaker's musings turn eventually toward her beloved and his overly lively interest in the waitress; then the poem turns toward a weightier subject–sexual jealousy. The speaker of the poem strives for a resolution to this unsettling feeling, insisting "I am here. / This is my body; eat. Unwrap. Disappear"–but there can be no mutually satisfying solution for this mismatched couple. Identified as love songs, the poems that make up the sequence are really about the failures of love. The fourth poem compares the beloved to Safe-T-Man–an inflatable life-sized male doll designed to deter criminals from targeting single women–finding the beloved just as incapable of love and filled with "hotter air." Though labeled "urban," these poems do not focus mainly on re-creating the dissonance of contemporary urban life. While Light writes at times of the detritus of postmodern culture–pierced tongues and refrigerator magnets in the likeness of Michelangelo's *David*–her poems register an impatience with the artifacts of consumerism. Light, who makes her living as a violinist in the New York City Opera and is active in the worlds of modern dance and theater, is more interested in high art than in pop culture. She is preoccupied with the concerns of the working artist. In her *ars poetica*, "How Sonnets Are Like Bungee Jumping," she describes how formal demands can allow for thematic daring:

> It's the calculated danger–leap! The form will hold
> you–will be as arms around you–ropes–
> so when you say: *If I could be so bold . . .*
> it says, *Okay, then, go! Spew out in hopes!*
> There's safety in measure. . .

While extolling the virtues of the sonnet, Light nonetheless frequently pushes its limits, eschewing the traditional neatness of the form–its closure and clear synthesis of opposing ideas–with open endings and uncertainty. The stasis of the sonnet is replaced by a feel of tentativeness, of arriving at conclusions that might be revised at any time.

Just as Light's first collection, like her second, *Open Slowly* (2003), is informed by the sonnet, Beth Gylys's debut collection, *Bodies that Hum* (1999), is preoccupied with pushing the limits of the villanelle, a form usually characterized by its mournful, haunted feeling. Traditionally, the repetition dictated by the form creates a mood of reverence, but Gylys's villanelles are startlingly irreverent. Frank and conversational, these poems are confessional, but one feels that the speaker is confessing not to her priest or psychiatrist as much as to her trusted girlfriends after a glass or two of wine. The predominant subject matter is sex and how it often falls short of the protagonist's expectations. The villanelles explore infidelity, disconnection, divorce, kinks, and predatory men. "Desire," for example, begins, "Your penis fits quite fine between my thighs. / Come lie with me awhile; this life is hell. / We're nothing but our bodies. Close your eyes." "The Spectator" explores the point of view of the voyeur: "He loved to look at bodies, so he said. / His high-rise faced another just as tall. / He didn't care for women in his bed." "Marriage Song" states that "Some have affairs. They never stop to think / until they're begging for a second chance. / We love and learn we sometimes need a drink." In "Personal" the speaker says, "I want a man whose body makes mine hum, / who when he looks my way the sky goes hazy. / Don't call me if you're boring, crude or dumb."

While the voice that speaks these villanelles is often deeply cynical, the volume does include a few rare moments of romantic wistfulness, as in the free-verse poem "Why I Like to Lie Awhile Longer," about the moments just after sex: "I know / the sense of blending's false–we break / so easily apart–but still, I love you / soft inside me and us not quite alone." Even in this poem, however, the speaker's declaration of love–underscored by the line break after "I love you"–is conditional; she loves her partner, but possibly only in the fleeting afterglow. Moreover, such serene moments are the exception. Real, lasting connection between a man and a woman seems impossible. One of the strongest poems in the volume, "Dynamics," explores a couple's clashing expectations of intimacy:

> He imagines her greeting him at the door in nothing
> but silk stockings. She thinks they ought
> to go out and look at the stars, drink a bottle
> of French Bordeaux on the roof of his Honda.
>
> When he wonders whether to stroke her breasts,
> she has to water the dying plant and balance
> her checkbook. She's tired, but he wants
> to lie awake all night, her skin pulsing next to his.

The humorous disconnect between these two people is made more poignant by his thinking maybe they need to get married, while she already has made up her mind to leave him. An even darker view of heterosexual romance is presented by "Not an Affair, a Sestina," in which a man rebuffs his lover, trying to deny the importance of their affair, or even that it counts as an affair:

> You're crazy if you called this an affair.
> We slept together, and I made you come.
> No big deal. You've got a lot of strange
> ideas. You think you know so much about me,
> think because you've seen me naked that counts
> for something . . .

Apart from being a sustained critique of romantic love, *Bodies that Hum* also provides a new way of seeing the villanelle. In Gylys's hands, the obsessive refrain of that form becomes an incessant complaint, the *cris de coeur* (crisis of the heart) of the wrongheaded lover.

A Post-Feminist Poetic?

Considering the range of work produced by this group of poets, to overgeneralize about the direction in which women formalists are heading would be dangerous, just as to claim that this brief survey is exhaustive would be a mistake. One point is clear, though: emerging poets are dabbling in form more freely than they have in decades, and many are choosing to conduct sustained formal experiments. Women are no exception. Moreover, while the spirit of Peacock's "personally constructed poetic" can be seen in the idiosyncratic approach poets such as Gylys and Light take to form, their respective approaches have less to do with setting up and thwarting metrical expectations than with diverging from the moods traditionally associated with particular forms. For a woman–Latina, African American, or Anglo–to choose traditional form over free verse to describe the experience of being a woman in America no longer feels particularly subversive or surprising. That so many emerging women poets are drawing freely from Western literary tradition and are doing so with decreasing ambivalence can be read as a sign that poetic formalism has moved into a post-feminist era. But that newer women poets feel increasingly free to embrace the Western literary tradition without apology is nonetheless a tribute to an earlier generation of women formalists–including Peacock, Alvarez, Nelson, Marilyn Hacker, Mary Jo Salter, Gjertrud Schnackenberg, and Rachel Hadas.

References:

Julia Alvarez, "Housekeeping Cages," in *A Formal Feeling Comes: Poems in Form by Contemporary Women,* edited by Annie Finch (Brownsville, Ore.: Story Line Press, 1994), pp. 16–18;

Annie Finch, *Eve* (Brownsville, Ore.: Story Line Press, 1997);

Finch, ed., *After New Formalism: Poets on Form, Narrative, and Tradition* (Ashland, Ore.: Story Line Press, 1999);

Finch, ed., *A Formal Feeling Comes* (Brownsville, Ore.: Story Line Press, 1994);

Jack Foley, A Review of Leslie Monsour, *Travel Plans, Alsop Review* <http://www.alsopreview.com/foley/jfmonsour.html>;

Beth Gylys, *Bodies that Hum* (Eugene, Ore.: Silverfish Review Press, 1999);

Kate Light, *The Laws of Falling Bodies* (Brownsville, Ore.: Story Line Press, 1997);

Light, *Open Slowly* (Lincoln, Neb.: Zoo Press, 2003);

Leslie Monsour, *Earth's Beauty, Desire, & Loss* (Edgewood, Ky.: Barth, 1998);

Monsour, *Indelibility* (West Chester, Pa.: Aralia Press, 1999);

Monsour, "Notes on Contemporary Formalism," in *A Formal Feeling Comes,* edited by Finch (Brownsville, Ore.: Story Line Press, 1994), pp. 157–159;

Monsour, *Travel Plans* (Edgewood, Ky.: Barth, 2001);

Marilyn Nelson, "Owning the Masters," in *After New Formalism,* edited by Finch (Ashland, Ore.: Story Line Press, 1999), pp. 8–17;

Suzanne Noguerre, "A Living Thing," in *A Formal Feeling Comes,* edited by Finch (Brownsville, Ore.: Story Line Press, 1994), p. 166;

Noguerre, *Whirling Round the Sun* (New York: Midmarch Arts Press, 1996);

Carole Oles and Hilda Raz, "The Feminist Literary Movement," in *Poetry After Modernism,* second edition, edited by Robert McDowell (Brownsville, Ore.: Story Line Press, 1998);

Molly Peacock, "From Gilded Cage to Rib Cage," in *After New Formalism,* edited by Finch (Ashland, Ore.: Story Line Press, 1999), pp. 70–78;

A. E. Stallings, *Archaic Smile* (Evansville, Ind.: University of Evansville Press, 1999);

Stallings, "Crooked Roads without Improvement: Some Thoughts on Formal Verse," *Alsop Review* <http://www.alsopreview.com/aside/stallings/aesthoughts.html>;

Diane Thiel, *Echolocations* (Ashland, Ore.: Story Line Press, 2000);

Thiel, *Writing Your Rhythm: Using Nature, Culture, Form & Myth* (Ashland, Ore.: Story Line Press, 2001);

Catherine Tufariello, *Annunciations* (West Chester, Pa.: Aralia Press, 2001);

Chryss Yost, *Escaping from Autopia* (West Chester, Pa.: Oberon Press, 1998);

Yost, *La Jolla Boys* (Santa Barbara, Cal.: Mille Grazie Press, 2000);

Yost, "Last Night," *Hudson Review,* 54, no. 2 (Summer 2001): 258.

Books For Further Reading

Attridge, Derek. *Poetic Rhythm: An Introduction.* Cambridge: Cambridge University Press, 1995.

Baker, David. *Meter in English: A Critical Engagement.* Fayetteville: University of Arkansas Press, 1996.

Corn, Alfred. *The Poem's Heartbeat: A Manual of Prosody.* Brownsville, Ore.: Story Line Press, 1997.

Dacey, Philip, and David Jauss. *Strong Measures: Contemporary American Poetry in Traditional Forms.* New York: Harper & Row, 1986.

Feirstein, Frederick, ed. *Expansive Poetry: Essays on the New Narrative and the New Formalism.* Santa Cruz, Cal.: Story Line Press, 1989.

Finch, Annie, ed. *After New Formalism: Poets on Form, Narrative, and Tradition.* Ashland, Ore.: Story Line Press, 1999.

Finch, ed. *A Formal Feeling Comes: Poems in Form by Contemporary Women.* Brownsville, Ore.: Story Line Press, 1994.

Finch and Kathrine Varnes, eds. *An Exaltation of Forms: Contemporary Poets Celebrate the Diversity of Their Art.* Ann Arbor: University of Michigan Press, 2002.

Foley, Jack, ed. *The "Fallen Western Star" Wars.* Oakland, Cal.: Scarlett Tanager Books, 2001.

Gioia, Dana. *Can Poetry Matter: Essays on Poetry and American Culture.* St. Paul, Minn.: Graywolf Press, 1992.

Gwynn, R. S., ed. *New Expansive Poetry: Theory, Criticism, History.* Ashland, Ore.: Story Line Press, 1999.

Hirsch, Edward. *How to Read a Poem: And Fall in Love with Poetry.* New York: Harcourt Brace, 1999.

Jarman, Mark, and David Mason, eds. *Rebel Angels: 25 Poets of the New Formalism.* Brownsville, Ore.: Story Line Press, 1996.

Jarman and Robert McDowell. *The Reaper Essays.* Brownsville, Ore.: Story Line Press, 1996.

Lehman, David, ed. *Ecstatic Occasions, Expedient Forms: 85 Leading Contemporary Poets Select and Comment on Their Poems.* Ann Arbor: University of Michigan Press, 1996.

Mason. *The Poetry of Life and the Life of Poetry: Essays and Reviews.* Ashland, Ore.: Story Line Press, 2000.

McDowell, ed. *Poetry After Modernism.* Ashland, Ore.: Story Line Press, 1998.

Peacock, Molly. *How to Read a Poem . . . and Start a Poetry Circle.* Toronto: McClelland & Stewart Limited, 1999.

Prunty, Wyatt. *"Fallen from the Symboled World:" Precedents for the New Formalism.* New York: Oxford University Press, 1990.

Books For Further Reading

Steele, Timothy. *All the Fun's in How You Say a Thing: An Explanation of Meter and Versification.* Athens: Ohio University Press, 1999.

Steele. *Missing Measures: Modern Poetry and the Revolt Against Meter.* Fayetteville: University of Arkansas Press, 1990.

Turco, Lewis. *The New Book of Forms: A Handbook of Poetics.* Hanover, Mass.: University Press of New England, 1986.

Walzer, Kevin. *The Ghost of Tradition: Expansive Poetry and Postmodernism.* Ashland, Ore.: Story Line Press, 1998.

Contributors

Joseph O. Aimone . . . . *Santa Clara University*
Daniel Anderson . . . . *The University of the South*
Jonathan N. Barron . . . . *University of Southern Mississippi*
D. Creason Bartlett . . . . *University of Texas at Dallas*
R. A. Benthall . . . . *University of North Carolina at Chapel Hill*
Thomas Cable . . . . *University of Texas at Austin*
David Caplan . . . . *Ohio Wesleyan University*
Jennifer Factor . . . . *Pasadena, California*
Paul A. Griffith . . . . *Lamar University*
Kymberly Taylor Haywood . . . . *University of Notre Dame*
H. L. Hix . . . . *Cleveland Institute of Art*
Mark Jarman . . . . *Vanderbilt University*
Len Krisak . . . . *Stonehill College*
Paul Lake . . . . *Arkansas Tech University*
April Lindner . . . . *Saint Joseph's University*
Charles Martin . . . . *Queensborough Community College, CUNY*
David Mason . . . . *Colorado College*
Robert McPhillips . . . . *Iona College*
Carolyn Meyer . . . . *University of Toronto School of Continuing Studies*
Bruce Meyer . . . . *University of Toronto School of Continuing Studies*
F. S. Ponick . . . . *Music Educators National Conference (MENC)*
T. L. Ponick . . . . *Washington Times*
Steven P. Schneider . . . . *University of Texas Pan American*
Jason Schneiderman . . . . *Hofstra University*
Meg Schoerke . . . . *San Francisco State University*
Ernest J. Smith . . . . *University of Central Florida*
N. S. Thompson . . . . *Christ Church, University of Oxford*
Catherine Tufariello . . . . *Brooklyn, New York*
Kathrine Varnes . . . . *University of Missouri–Columbia*
Sonny Williams . . . . *University of New Orleans*
Terri Witek . . . . *Stetson University*
David Yezzi . . . . *San Francisco, California*

Cumulative Index

Dictionary of Literary Biography, Volumes 1-282
Dictionary of Literary Biography Yearbook, 1980-2002
Dictionary of Literary Biography Documentary Series, Volumes 1-19
Concise Dictionary of American Literary Biography, Volumes 1-7
Concise Dictionary of British Literary Biography, Volumes 1-8
Concise Dictionary of World Literary Biography, Volumes 1-4

Cumulative Index

DLB before number: *Dictionary of Literary Biography,* Volumes 1-282
Y before number: *Dictionary of Literary Biography Yearbook,* 1980-2002
DS before number: *Dictionary of Literary Biography Documentary Series,* Volumes 1-19
CDALB before number: *Concise Dictionary of American Literary Biography,* Volumes 1-7
CDBLB before number: *Concise Dictionary of British Literary Biography,* Volumes 1-8
CDWLB before number: *Concise Dictionary of World Literary Biography,* Volumes 1-4

A

Aakjær, Jeppe 1866-1930 .... DLB-214
Abbey, Edward 1927-1989 .... DLB-256, 275
Abbey, Edwin Austin 1852-1911 .... DLB-188
Abbey, Maj. J. R. 1894-1969 .... DLB-201
Abbey Press DLB-49
The Abbey Theatre and Irish Drama,
   1900-1945 .... DLB-10
Abbot, Willis J. 1863-1934 .... DLB-29
Abbott, Jacob 1803-1879 .... DLB-1, 42, 243
Abbott, Lee K. 1947- DLB-130
Abbott, Lyman 1835-1922 .... DLB-79
Abbott, Robert S. 1868-1940 .... DLB-29, 91
Abe Kōbō 1924-1993 .... DLB-182
Abelard, Peter circa 1079-1142? DLB-115, 208
Abelard-Schuman DLB-46
Abell, Arunah S. 1806-1888 .... DLB-43
Abell, Kjeld 1901-1961 .... DLB-214
Abercrombie, Lascelles 1881-1938 .... DLB-19
Aberdeen University Press Limited DLB-106
Abish, Walter 1931- DLB-130, 227
Ablesimov, Aleksandr Onisimovich
   1742-1783 .... DLB-150
Abraham à Sancta Clara 1644-1709 ...... DLB-168
Abrahams, Peter
   1919- DLB-117, 225; CDWLB-3
Abrams, M. H. 1912- DLB-67
Abramson, Jesse 1904-1979 .... DLB-241
Abrogans circa 790-800 .... DLB-148
Abschatz, Hans Aßmann von
   1646-1699 .... DLB-168
Abse, Dannie 1923- DLB-27, 245
Abutsu-ni 1221-1283 .... DLB-203
Academy Chicago Publishers DLB-46
Accius circa 170 B.C.-circa 80 B.C. DLB-211
Accrocca, Elio Filippo 1923- DLB-128
Ace Books DLB-46
Achebe, Chinua 1930- DLB-117; CDWLB-3
Achtenberg, Herbert 1938- DLB-124
Ackerman, Diane 1948- DLB-120
Ackroyd, Peter 1949- DLB-155, 231

Acorn, Milton 1923-1986 .... DLB-53
Acosta, Oscar Zeta 1935?- DLB-82
Acosta Torres, José 1925- DLB-209
Actors Theatre of Louisville DLB-7
Adair, Gilbert 1944- DLB-194
Adair, James 1709?-1783? DLB-30
Adam, Graeme Mercer 1839-1912 .... DLB-99
Adam, Robert Borthwick, II 1863-1940 .. DLB-187
Adame, Leonard 1947- DLB-82
Adameșteanu, Gabriel 1942- DLB-232
Adamic, Louis 1898-1951 .... DLB-9
Adams, Abigail 1744-1818 .... DLB-200
Adams, Alice 1926-1999 .... DLB-234; Y-86
Adams, Bertha Leith (Mrs. Leith Adams,
   Mrs. R. S. de Courcy Laffan)
   1837?-1912 .... DLB-240
Adams, Brooks 1848-1927 .... DLB-47
Adams, Charles Francis, Jr. 1835-1915 .... DLB-47
Adams, Douglas 1952- DLB-261; Y-83
Adams, Franklin P. 1881-1960 .... DLB-29
Adams, Hannah 1755-1832 .... DLB-200
Adams, Henry 1838-1918 .... DLB-12, 47, 189
Adams, Herbert Baxter 1850-1901 .... DLB-47
Adams, J. S. and C. [publishing house] DLB-49
Adams, James Truslow 1878-1949 ... DLB-17; DS-17
Adams, John 1735-1826 .... DLB-31, 183
Adams, John 1735-1826 and
   Adams, Abigail 1744-1818 .... DLB-183
Adams, John Quincy 1767-1848 .... DLB-37
Adams, Léonie 1899-1988 .... DLB-48
Adams, Levi 1802-1832 .... DLB-99
Adams, Richard 1920- DLB-261
Adams, Samuel 1722-1803 .... DLB-31, 43
Adams, Sarah Fuller Flower 1805-1848 ... DLB-199
Adams, Thomas 1582 or 1583-1652 ..... DLB-151
Adams, William Taylor 1822-1897 .... DLB-42
Adamson, Sir John 1867-1950 .... DLB-98
Adamson, Harold 1906-1980 .... DLB-265
Adcock, Arthur St. John 1864-1930 ..... DLB-135
Adcock, Betty 1938- DLB-105
"Certain Gifts" DLB-105

Adcock, Fleur 1934- DLB-40
Addison, Joseph 1672-1719 ... DLB-101; CDBLB-2
Ade, George 1866-1944 .... DLB-11, 25
Adeler, Max (see Clark, Charles Heber)
Adlard, Mark 1932- DLB-261
Adler, Richard 1921- and
   Ross, Jerry 1926-1955 .... DLB-265
Adonias Filho 1915-1990 .... DLB-145
Adorno, Theodor W. 1903-1969 .... DLB-242
Advance Publishing Company DLB-49
Ady, Endre 1877-1919 ...... DLB-215; CDWLB-4
AE 1867-1935 .... DLB-19; CDBLB-5
Ælfric circa 955-circa 1010 .... DLB-146
Aeschines
   circa 390 B.C.-circa 320 B.C. DLB-176
Aeschylus 525-524 B.C.-456-455 B.C.
   .... DLB-176; CDWLB-1
Afro-American Literary Critics:
   An Introduction DLB-33
After Dinner Opera Company Y-92
Agassiz, Elizabeth Cary 1822-1907 ...... DLB-189
Agassiz, Louis 1807-1873 .... DLB-1, 235
Agee, James 1909-1955 ... DLB-2, 26, 152; CDALB-1
The Agee Legacy: A Conference at the University
   of Tennessee at Knoxville Y-89
Aguilera Malta, Demetrio 1909-1981 .... DLB-145
Ahlin, Lars 1915-1997 .... DLB-257
Ai 1947- DLB-120
Aichinger, Ilse 1921- DLB-85
Aickman, Robert 1914-1981 .... DLB-261
Aidoo, Ama Ata 1942- DLB-117; CDWLB-3
Aiken, Conrad
   1889-1973 .... DLB-9, 45, 102; CDALB-5
Aiken, Joan 1924- DLB-161
Aikin, Lucy 1781-1864 .... DLB-144, 163
Ainsworth, William Harrison 1805-1882 .. DLB-21
Aistis, Jonas 1904-1973 ..... DLB-220; CDWLB-4
Aitken, George A. 1860-1917 .... DLB-149
Aitken, Robert [publishing house] DLB-49
Akenside, Mark 1721-1770 .... DLB-109
Akins, Zoë 1886-1958 .... DLB-26
Aksahov, Ivan Sergeevich 1823-1826 .... DLB-277

Cumulative Index

Aksahov, Sergei Timofeevich 1791-1859 .... DLB-198

Akutagawa, Ryūnsuke 1892-1927 ...... DLB-180

Alabaster, William 1568-1640 .... DLB-132

Alain de Lille circa 1116-1202/1203 ..... DLB-208

Alain-Fournier 1886-1914 .... DLB-65

Alanus de Insulis (see Alain de Lille)

Alarcón, Francisco X. 1954- DLB-122

Alarcón, Justo S. 1930- DLB-209

Alba, Nanina 1915-1968 .... DLB-41

Albee, Edward 1928- DLB-7, 266; CDALB-1

Albert the Great circa 1200-1280 .... DLB-115

Albert, Octavia 1853-ca. 1889 .... DLB-221

Alberti, Rafael 1902-1999 .... DLB-108

Albertinus, Aegidius circa 1560-1620 .... DLB-164

Alcaeus born circa 620 B.C. DLB-176

Alcott, Bronson 1799-1888 .... DLB-1, 223

Alcott, Louisa May 1832-1888
 ... DLB-1, 42, 79, 223, 239; DS-14; CDALB-3

Alcott, William Andrus 1798-1859 .... DLB-1, 243

Alcuin circa 732-804 .... DLB-148

Alden, Beardsley and Company DLB-49

Alden, Henry Mills 1836-1919 .... DLB-79

Alden, Isabella 1841-1930 .... DLB-42

Alden, John B. [publishing house] DLB-49

Aldington, Richard
 1892-1962 .... DLB-20, 36, 100, 149

Aldis, Dorothy 1896-1966 .... DLB-22

Aldis, H. G. 1863-1919 .... DLB-184

Aldiss, Brian W. 1925- DLB-14, 261, 271

Aldrich, Thomas Bailey
 1836-1907 .... DLB-42, 71, 74, 79

Alegría, Ciro 1909-1967 .... DLB-113

Alegría, Claribel 1924- DLB-145

Aleixandre, Vicente 1898-1984 .... DLB-108

Aleksandravičius, Jonas (see Aistis, Jonas)

Aleksandrov, Aleksandr Andreevich
 (see Durova, Nadezhda Andreevna)

Aleramo, Sibilla 1876-1960 .... DLB-114, 264

Alexander, Cecil Frances 1818-1895 ..... DLB-199

Alexander, Charles 1868-1923 .... DLB-91

Alexander, Charles Wesley
 [publishing house] DLB-49

Alexander, James 1691-1756 .... DLB-24

Alexander, Lloyd 1924- DLB-52

Alexander, Sir William, Earl of Stirling
 1577?-1640 .... DLB-121

Alexie, Sherman 1966- DLB-175, 206, 278

Alexis, Willibald 1798-1871 .... DLB-133

Alfred, King 849-899 .... DLB-146

Alger, Horatio, Jr. 1832-1899 .... DLB-42

Algonquin Books of Chapel Hill DLB-46

Algren, Nelson
 1909-1981 .....DLB-9; Y-81, Y-82; CDALB-1

Nelson Algren: An International
 Symposium Y-00

"All the Faults of Youth and Inexperience":
 A Reader's Report on
 Thomas Wolfe's *O Lost* Y-01

Allan, Andrew 1907-1974 .... DLB-88

Allan, Ted 1916-1995 .... DLB-68

Allbeury, Ted 1917- DLB-87

Alldritt, Keith 1935- DLB-14

Allen, Dick 1939- DLB-282

Allen, Ethan 1738-1789 .... DLB-31

Allen, Frederick Lewis 1890-1954 ... DLB-137

Allen, Gay Wilson 1903-1995 .....DLB-103; Y-95

Allen, George 1808-1876 .... DLB-59

Allen, George [publishing house] DLB-106

Allen, George, and Unwin Limited DLB-112

Allen, Grant 1848-1899 ....DLB-70, 92, 178

Allen, Henry W. 1912- Y-85

Allen, Hervey 1889-1949 .... DLB-9, 45

Allen, James 1739-1808 .... DLB-31

Allen, James Lane 1849-1925 .... DLB-71

Allen, Jay Presson 1922- DLB-26

Allen, John, and Company DLB-49

Allen, Paula Gunn 1939- DLB-175

Allen, Samuel W. 1917- DLB-41

Allen, Woody 1935- DLB-44

Allende, Isabel 1942- DLB-145; CDWLB-3

Alline, Henry 1748-1784 .... DLB-99

Allingham, Margery 1904-1966 .... DLB-77

Allingham, William 1824-1889 .... DLB-35

Allison, W. L. [publishing house] DLB-49

The *Alliterative Morte Arthure and the Stanzaic
 Morte Arthur* circa 1350-1400 .... DLB-146

Allott, Kenneth 1912-1973 .... DLB-20

Allston, Washington 1779-1843 ...... DLB-1, 235

Almon, John [publishing house] DLB-154

Alonzo, Dámaso 1898-1990 .... DLB-108

Alsop, George 1636-post 1673 .... DLB-24

Alsop, Richard 1761-1815 .... DLB-37

Altemus, Henry, and Company DLB-49

Altenberg, Peter 1885-1919 .... DLB-81

Althusser, Louis 1918-1990 .... DLB-242

Altolaguirre, Manuel 1905-1959 .... DLB-108

Aluko, T. M. 1918- DLB-117

Alurista 1947- DLB-82

Alvarez, A. 1929- DLB-14, 40

Alvarez, Julia 1950- DLB-282

Alvaro, Corrado 1895-1956 .... DLB-264

Alver, Betti 1906-1989 ..... DLB-220; CDWLB-4

Amadi, Elechi 1934- DLB-117

Amado, Jorge 1912- DLB-113

Ambler, Eric 1909-1998 .... DLB-77

The Library of America DLB-46

The Library of America: An Assessment
 After Two Decades Y-02

American Conservatory Theatre DLB-7

American Fiction and the 1930s DLB-9

American Humor: A Historical Survey
 East and Northeast
 South and Southwest
 Midwest
 West DLB-11

Studies in American Jewish Literatue Y-02

The American Library in Paris Y-93

American News Company DLB-49

A Century of Poetry, a Lifetime of Collecting:
 J. M. Edelstein's Collection of Twentieth-
 Century American Poetry Y-02

The American Poets' Corner: The First
 Three Years (1983-1986) Y-86

American Publishing Company DLB-49

American Stationers' Company DLB-49

American Sunday-School Union DLB-49

American Temperance Union DLB-49

American Tract Society DLB-49

The American Trust for the
 British Library Y-96

The American Writers Congress
 (9-12 October 1981) Y-81

The American Writers Congress: A Report
 on Continuing Business Y-81

Ames, Fisher 1758-1808 .... DLB-37

Ames, Mary Clemmer 1831-1884 .... DLB-23

Ames, William 1576-1633 .... DLB-281

Amiel, Henri-Frédéric 1821-1881 ....DLB-217

Amini, Johari M. 1935- DLB-41

Amis, Kingsley 1922-1995
 .... DLB-15, 27, 100, 139, Y-96; CDBLB-7

Amis, Martin 1949- DLB-194

Ammianus Marcellinus
 circa A.D. 330-A.D. 395 .... DLB-211

Ammons, A. R. 1926- DLB-5, 165

Amory, Thomas 1691?-1788 .... DLB-39

Anania, Michael 1939- DLB-193

Anaya, Rudolfo A. 1937- DLB-82, 206, 278

Ancrene Riwle circa 1200-1225 .... DLB-146

Andersch, Alfred 1914-1980 .... DLB-69

Andersen, Benny 1929- DLB-214

Anderson, Alexander 1775-1870 .... DLB-188

Anderson, David 1929- DLB-241

Anderson, Frederick Irving 1877-1947 ... DLB-202

Anderson, Margaret 1886-1973 .... DLB-4, 91

Anderson, Maxwell 1888-1959 ....DLB-7, 228

Anderson, Patrick 1915-1979 .... DLB-68

Anderson, Paul Y. 1893-1938 .... DLB-29

Anderson, Poul 1926- DLB-8

Anderson, Robert 1750-1830 .... DLB-142

Anderson, Robert 1917- DLB-7

Anderson, Sherwood
 1876-1941 ..... DLB-4, 9, 86; DS-1; CDALB-4

Andreae, Johann Valentin 1586-1654 .... DLB-164

Andreas Capellanus
 flourished circa 1185 .... DLB-208

Andreas-Salomé, Lou 1861-1937 .... DLB-66

Andres, Stefan 1906-1970 .... DLB-69

Andreu, Blanca 1959- DLB-134

Andrewes, Lancelot 1555-1626 . . . . . DLB-151, 172
Andrews, Charles M. 1863-1943 . . . . DLB-17
Andrews, Miles Peter ?-1814 . . . . DLB-89
Andrews, Stephen Pearl 1812-1886 . . . . . . DLB-250
Andrian, Leopold von 1875-1951 . . . . DLB-81
Andrić, Ivo 1892-1975 . . . . . . DLB-147; CDWLB-4
Andrieux, Louis (see Aragon, Louis)
Andrus, Silas, and Son DLB-49
Andrzejewski, Jerzy 1909-1983 . . . . DLB-215
Angell, James Burrill 1829-1916 . . . . DLB-64
Angell, Roger 1920- DLB-171, 185
Angelou, Maya 1928- DLB-38; CDALB-7
Anger, Jane flourished 1589 . . . . DLB-136
Angers, Félicité (see Conan, Laure)
Anglo-Norman Literature in the Development
 of Middle English Literature DLB-146
The Anglo-Saxon Chronicle circa 890-1154 . . . DLB-146
The "Angry Young Men" DLB-15
Angus and Robertson (UK) Limited DLB-112
Anhalt, Edward 1914-2000 . . . . DLB-26
Annenkov, Pavel Vasil'evich
 1813?-1887 . . . . DLB-277
Anners, Henry F. [publishing house] DLB-49
Annolied between 1077 and 1081 . . . . DLB-148
Annual Awards for *Dictionary of Literary Biography*
 Editors and
 Contributors Y-98, Y-99, Y-00, Y-01, Y-02
Anscombe, G. E. M. 1919-2001 . . . . DLB-262
Anselm of Canterbury 1033-1109 . . . . DLB-115
Anstey, F. 1856-1934 . . . . DLB-141, 178
Anthologizing New Formalism DLB-282
Anthony, Michael 1932- DLB-125
Anthony, Piers 1934- DLB-8
Anthony, Susanna 1726-1791 . . . . DLB-200
Antin, David 1932- DLB-169
Antin, Mary 1881-1949 . . . . DLB-221; Y-84
Anton Ulrich, Duke of Brunswick-Lüneburg
 1633-1714 . . . . DLB-168
Antschel, Paul (see Celan, Paul)
Anyidoho, Kofi 1947- DLB-157
Anzaldúa, Gloria 1942- DLB-122
Anzengruber, Ludwig 1839-1889 . . . . DLB-129
Apess, William 1798-1839 . . . . DLB-175, 243
Apodaca, Rudy S. 1939- DLB-82
Apollinaire, Guillaume 1880-1918 . . . . DLB-258
Apollonius Rhodius third century B.C. . . . DLB-176
Apple, Max 1941- DLB-130
Appleton, D., and Company DLB-49
Appleton-Century-Crofts DLB-46
Applewhite, James 1935- DLB-105
Applewood Books DLB-46
April, Jean-Pierre 1948- DLB-251
Apukhtin, Aleksei Nikolaevich
 1840-1893 . . . . DLB-277
Apuleius circa A.D. 125-post A.D. 164
 . . . . DLB-211; CDWLB-1

Aquin, Hubert 1929-1977 . . . . DLB-53
Aquinas, Thomas 1224 or 1225-1274 . . . . DLB-115
Aragon, Louis 1897-1982 . . . . DLB-72, 258
Aralica, Ivan 1930- DLB-181
Aratus of Soli
 circa 315 B.C.-circa 239 B.C. DLB-176
Arbasino, Alberto 1930- DLB-196
Arbor House Publishing Company DLB-46
Arbuthnot, John 1667-1735 . . . . DLB-101
Arcadia House DLB-46
Arce, Julio G. (see Ulica, Jorge)
Archer, William 1856-1924 . . . . DLB-10
Archilochhus
 mid seventh century B.C.E. DLB-176
The Archpoet circa 1130?-? DLB-148
Archpriest Avvakum (Petrovich)
 1620?-1682 . . . . DLB-150
Arden, John 1930- DLB-13, 245
Arden of Faversham DLB-62
Ardis Publishers Y-89
Ardizzone, Edward 1900-1979 . . . . DLB-160
Arellano, Juan Estevan 1947- DLB-122
The Arena Publishing Company DLB-49
Arena Stage DLB-7
Arenas, Reinaldo 1943-1990 . . . . DLB-145
Arendt, Hannah 1906-1975 . . . . DLB-242
Arensberg, Ann 1937- Y-82
Arghezi, Tudor 1880-1967 . . . DLB-220; CDWLB-4
Arguedas, José María 1911-1969 . . . . DLB-113
Argueta, Manlio 1936- DLB-145
Arias, Ron 1941- DLB-82
Arishima, Takeo 1878-1923 . . . . DLB-180
Aristophanes circa 446 B.C.-circa 386 B.C.
 . . . . DLB-176; CDWLB-1
Aristotle 384 B.C.-322 B.C.
 . . . . DLB-176; CDWLB-1
Ariyoshi Sawako 1931-1984 . . . . DLB-182
Arland, Marcel 1899-1986 . . . . DLB-72
Arlen, Michael 1895-1956 . . . . DLB-36, 77, 162
Armah, Ayi Kwei 1939- . . . DLB-117; CDWLB-3
Armantrout, Rae 1947- DLB-193
Der arme Hartmann ?-after 1150 . . . . DLB-148
Armed Services Editions DLB-46
Armitage, G. E. (Robert Edric) 1956- . . DLB-267
Armstrong, Martin Donisthorpe
 1882-1974 . . . . DLB-197
Armstrong, Richard 1903- DLB-160
Armstrong, Terence Ian Fytton (see Gawsworth, John)
Arnauld, Antoine 1612-1694 . . . . DLB-268
Arndt, Ernst Moritz 1769-1860 . . . . DLB-90
Arnim, Achim von 1781-1831 . . . . DLB-90
Arnim, Bettina von 1785-1859 . . . . DLB-90
Arnim, Elizabeth von (Countess Mary
 Annette Beauchamp Russell)
 1866-1941 . . . . DLB-197
Arno Press DLB-46
Arnold, Edward [publishing house] DLB-112

Arnold, Edwin 1832-1904 . . . . DLB-35
Arnold, Edwin L. 1857-1935 . . . . DLB-178
Arnold, Matthew
 1822-1888 . . . . DLB-32, 57; CDBLB-4
Preface to *Poems* (1853) DLB-32
Arnold, Thomas 1795-1842 . . . . DLB-55
Arnott, Peter 1962- DLB-233
Arnow, Harriette Simpson 1908-1986 . . . . . . DLB-6
Arp, Bill (see Smith, Charles Henry)
Arpino, Giovanni 1927-1987 . . . . DLB-177
Arreola, Juan José 1918- DLB-113
Arrian circa 89-circa 155 . . . . DLB-176
Arrowsmith, J. W. [publishing house] DLB-106
The Art and Mystery of Publishing:
 Interviews Y-97
Artaud, Antonin 1896-1948 . . . . DLB-258
Arthur, Timothy Shay
 1809-1885 . . . . . . DLB-3, 42, 79, 250; DS-13
The Arthurian Tradition and
 Its European Context DLB-138
Artmann, H. C. 1921-2000 . . . . DLB-85
Arvin, Newton 1900-1963 . . . . DLB-103
Asch, Nathan 1902-1964 . . . . DLB-4, 28
Nathan Asch Remembers Ford Madox Ford,
 Sam Roth, and Hart Crane Y-02
Ascham, Roger 1515 or 1516-1568 . . . . . . DLB-236
Ash, John 1948- DLB-40
Ashbery, John 1927- DLB-5, 165; Y-81
Ashbridge, Elizabeth 1713-1755 . . . . DLB-200
Ashburnham, Bertram Lord
 1797-1878 . . . . DLB-184
Ashendene Press DLB-112
Asher, Sandy 1942- Y-83
Ashton, Winifred (see Dane, Clemence)
Asimov, Isaac 1920-1992 . . . . DLB-8; Y-92
Askew, Anne circa 1521-1546 . . . . DLB-136
Aspazija 1865-1943 . . . . DLB-220; CDWLB-4
Asselin, Olivar 1874-1937 . . . . DLB-92
The Association of American Publishers Y-99
The Association for Documentary Editing . . Y-00
Astell, Mary 1666-1731 . . . . DLB-252
Astley, William (see Warung, Price)
Asturias, Miguel Angel
 1899-1974 . . . . DLB-113; CDWLB-3
At Home with Albert Erskine Y-00
Atava, S. (see Terpigorev, Sergei Nikolaevich)
Atheneum Publishers DLB-46
Atherton, Gertrude 1857-1948 . . . . . DLB-9, 78, 186
Athlone Press DLB-112
Atkins, Josiah circa 1755-1781 . . . . DLB-31
Atkins, Russell 1926- DLB-41
Atkinson, Kate 1951- DLB-267
Atkinson, Louisa 1834-1872 . . . . DLB-230
The Atlantic Monthly Press DLB-46
Attaway, William 1911-1986 . . . . DLB-76
Atwood, Margaret 1939- DLB-53, 251

Cumulative Index

Aubert, Alvin 1930- DLB-41

Aubert de Gaspé, Phillipe-Ignace-François
1814-1841..................... DLB-99

Aubert de Gaspé, Phillipe-Joseph
1786-1871..................... DLB-99

Aubin, Napoléon 1812-1890........... DLB-99

Aubin, Penelope 1685-circa 1731 .... DLB-39

Preface to *The Life of Charlotta
du Pont* (1723) DLB-39

Aubrey-Fletcher, Henry Lancelot (see Wade, Henry)

Auchincloss, Louis 1917- DLB-2, 244; Y-80

Auction of Jack Kerouac's *On the Road* Scroll .. Y-01

Auden, W. H. 1907-1973 .. DLB-10, 20; CDBLB-6

Audio Art in America: A Personal Memoir ... Y-85

Audubon, John James 1785-1851 .... DLB-248

Audubon, John Woodhouse
1812-1862..................... DLB-183

Auerbach, Berthold 1812-1882......... DLB-133

Auernheimer, Raoul 1876-1948 .... DLB-81

Augier, Emile 1820-1889 .... DLB-192

Augustine 354-430 .... DLB-115

Responses to Ken Auletta................. Y-97

Aulnoy, Marie-Catherine Le Jumel de
Barneville, comtesse d'
1650 or 1651-1705................ DLB-268

Aulus Cellius
circa A.D. 125-circa A.D. 180?..... DLB-211

Austen, Jane 1775-1817 .... DLB-116; CDBLB-3

Auster, Paul 1947- DLB-227

Austin, Alfred 1835-1913 .... DLB-35

Austin, J. L. 1911-1960................ DLB-262

Austin, Jane Goodwin 1831-1894....... DLB-202

Austin, John 1790-1859................ DLB-262

Austin, Mary Hunter
1868-1934.......DLB-9, 78, 206, 221, 275

Austin, William 1778-1841 .... DLB-74

Australie (Emily Manning)
1845-1890 .... DLB-230

Author-Printers, 1476–1599 .... DLB-167

Author Websites..................... Y-97

Authors and Newspapers Association..... DLB-46

Authors' Publishing Company DLB-49

Avallone, Michael 1924-1999 .... Y-99

Avalon Books DLB-46

Avancini, Nicolaus 1611-1686 .... DLB-164

Avendaño, Fausto 1941- DLB-82

Averroës 1126-1198 .... DLB-115

Avery, Gillian 1926- DLB-161

Avicenna 980-1037 .... DLB-115

Avison, Margaret 1918- DLB-53

Avon Books DLB-46

Avyžius, Jonas 1922-1999.............. DLB-220

Awdry, Wilbert Vere 1911-1997........ DLB-160

Awoonor, Kofi 1935- DLB-117

Ayckbourn, Alan 1939- DLB-13, 245

Ayer, A. J. 1910-1989 .... DLB-262

Aymé, Marcel
1902-1967 .... DLB-72

Aytoun, Sir Robert
1570-1638..................... DLB-121

Aytoun, William Edmondstoune
1813-1865 .... DLB-32, 159

B

B. V. (see Thomson, James)

Babbitt, Irving 1865-1933.............. DLB-63

Babbitt, Natalie 1932- DLB-52

Babcock, John [publishing house]........ DLB-49

Babel, Isaak Emmanuilovich 1894-1940...DLB-272

Babits, Mihály 1883-1941... DLB-215; CDWLB-4

Babrius circa 150-200 .... DLB-176

Babson, Marion 1929- DLB-276

Baca, Jimmy Santiago 1952- DLB-122

Bacchelli, Riccardo 1891-1985 .... DLB-264

Bache, Benjamin Franklin 1769-1798 ..... DLB-43

Bacheller, Irving 1859-1950 .... DLB-202

Bachmann, Ingeborg 1926-1973 .... DLB-85

Bačinskaitė-Bučienė, Salomėja (see Nėris, Salomėja)

Bacon, Delia 1811-1859 .... DLB-1, 243

Bacon, Francis
1561-1626 .... DLB-151, 236, 252; CDBLB-1

Bacon, Sir Nicholas circa 1510-1579..... DLB-132

Bacon, Roger circa 1214/1220-1292..... DLB-115

Bacon, Thomas circa 1700-1768 .... DLB-31

Bacovia, George
1881-1957........... DLB-220; CDWLB-4

Badger, Richard G., and Company DLB-49

Bagaduce Music Lending Library Y-00

Bage, Robert 1728-1801 .... DLB-39

Bagehot, Walter 1826-1877 .... DLB-55

Bagley, Desmond 1923-1983 .... DLB-87

Bagley, Sarah G. 1806-1848 .... DLB-239

Bagnold, Enid 1889-1981 ...DLB-13, 160, 191, 245

Bagryana, Elisaveta
1893-1991 ....DLB-147; CDWLB-4

Bahr, Hermann 1863-1934......... DLB-81, 118

Bailey, Abigail Abbot 1746-1815........ DLB-200

Bailey, Alfred Goldsworthy 1905- DLB-68

Bailey, Francis [publishing house]........ DLB-49

Bailey, H. C. 1878-1961 .... DLB-77

Bailey, Jacob 1731-1808 .... DLB-99

Bailey, Paul 1937- DLB-14, 271

Bailey, Philip James 1816-1902......... DLB-32

Baillargeon, Pierre 1916-1967.......... DLB-88

Baillie, Hugh 1890-1966.............. DLB-29

Baillie, Joanna 1762-1851 .... DLB-93

Bailyn, Bernard 1922- DLB-17

Bainbridge, Beryl 1933- DLB-14, 231

Baird, Irene 1901-1981 .... DLB-68

Baker, Augustine 1575-1641 .... DLB-151

Baker, Carlos 1909-1987 .... DLB-103

Baker, David 1954- DLB-120

Baker, George Pierce 1866-1935 .... DLB-266

Baker, Herschel C. 1914-1990 .... DLB-111

Baker, Houston A., Jr. 1943- DLB-67

Baker, Nicholson 1957- DLB-227

Baker, Samuel White 1821-1893 .... DLB-166

Baker, Thomas 1656-1740 .... DLB-213

Baker, Walter H., Company
("Baker's Plays") DLB-49

The Baker and Taylor Company........ DLB-49

Bakhtin, Mikhail Mikhailovich
1895-1975..................... DLB-242

Bakunin, Mikhail Aleksandrovich
1814-1876..................... DLB-277

Balaban, John 1943- DLB-120

Bald, Wambly 1902- DLB-4

Balde, Jacob 1604-1668 .... DLB-164

Balderston, John 1889-1954 ....DLB-26

Baldwin, James 1924-1987
...... DLB-2, 7, 33, 249, 278; Y-87; CDALB-1

Baldwin, Joseph Glover
1815-1864 .... DLB-3, 11, 248

Baldwin, Louisa (Mrs. Alfred Baldwin)
1845-1925 .... DLB-240

Baldwin, Richard and Anne
[publishing house] DLB-170

Baldwin, William circa 1515-1563 ...... DLB-132

Bale, John 1495-1563 .... DLB-132

Balestrini, Nanni 1935- DLB-128, 196

Balfour, Sir Andrew 1630-1694 .... DLB-213

Balfour, Arthur James 1848-1930....... DLB-190

Balfour, Sir James 1600-1657 .... DLB-213

Ballantine Books..................... DLB-46

Ballantyne, R. M. 1825-1894 .... DLB-163

Ballard, J. G. 1930- DLB-14, 207, 261

Ballard, Martha Moore 1735-1812 ...... DLB-200

Ballerini, Luigi 1940- DLB-128

Ballou, Maturin Murray
1820-1895 ....DLB-79, 189

Ballou, Robert O. [publishing house] DLB-46

Balzac, Guez de 1597?-1654.............DLB-268

Balzac, Honoré de 1799-1855.......... DLB-119

Bambara, Toni Cade
1939- DLB-38, 218; CDALB-7

Bamford, Samuel 1788-1872........... DLB-190

Bancroft, A. L., and Company.......... DLB-49

Bancroft, George 1800-1891... DLB-1, 30, 59, 243

Bancroft, Hubert Howe 1832-1918 ...DLB-47, 140

Bandelier, Adolph F. 1840-1914........ DLB-186

Bangs, John Kendrick 1862-1922......DLB-11, 79

Banim, John 1798-1842..........DLB-116, 158, 159

Banim, Michael 1796-1874 .... DLB-158, 159

Banks, Iain 1954- DLB-194, 261

Banks, John circa 1653-1706............ DLB-80

Banks, Russell 1940- DLB-130, 278

Bannerman, Helen 1862-1946 .... DLB-141

Bantam Books DLB-46

Banti, Anna 1895-1985................DLB-177

Banville, John 1945- DLB-14, 271
Banville, Théodore de 1823-1891 . . . . DLB-217
Baraka, Amiri
 1934- DLB-5, 7, 16, 38; DS-8; CDALB-1
Barańczak, Stanisław 1946- DLB-232
Baratynsky, Evgenii Abramovich
 1800-1844 . . . . DLB-205
Barbauld, Anna Laetitia
 1743-1825 . . . . DLB-107, 109, 142, 158
Barbeau, Marius 1883-1969 . . . . DLB-92
Barber, John Warner 1798-1885 . . . . DLB-30
Bàrberi Squarotti, Giorgio 1929- DLB-128
Barbey d'Aurevilly, Jules-Amédée
 1808-1889 . . . . DLB-119
Barbier, Auguste 1805-1882 . . . . DLB-217
Barbilian, Dan (see Barbu, Ion)
Barbour, John circa 1316-1395 . . . . DLB-146
Barbour, Ralph Henry 1870-1944 . . . . DLB-22
Barbu, Ion 1895-1961 . . . . . . DLB-220; CDWLB-4
Barbusse, Henri 1873-1935 . . . . DLB-65
Barclay, Alexander circa 1475-1552 . . . . . DLB-132
Barclay, E. E., and Company DLB-49
Bardeen, C. W. [publishing house] DLB-49
Barham, Richard Harris 1788-1845 . . . . . DLB-159
Barich, Bill 1943- DLB-185
Baring, Maurice 1874-1945 . . . . DLB-34
Baring-Gould, Sabine
 1834-1924 . . . . DLB-156, 190
Barker, A. L. 1918- DLB-14, 139
Barker, Arthur, Limited DLB-112
Barker, Clive 1952- DLB-261
Barker, George 1913-1991 . . . . DLB-20
Barker, Harley Granville 1877-1946 . . . . . . DLB-10
Barker, Howard 1946- DLB-13, 233
Barker, James Nelson 1784-1858 . . . . DLB-37
Barker, Jane 1652-1727 . . . . DLB-39, 131
Barker, Lady Mary Anne 1831-1911 . . . . . DLB-166
Barker, Pat 1943- DLB-271
Barker, William circa 1520-after 1576 . . . . DLB-132
Barkov, Ivan Semenovich 1732-1768 . . . . . DLB-150
Barks, Coleman 1937- DLB-5
Barlach, Ernst 1870-1938 . . . . DLB-56, 118
Barlow, Joel 1754-1812 . . . . DLB-37
The Prospect of Peace (1778) DLB-37
Barnard, John 1681-1770 . . . . DLB-24
Barnard, Marjorie 1879-1987 and Eldershaw, Flora
 (M. Barnard Eldershaw) 1897-1956 . . . DLB-260
Barnard, Robert 1936- DLB-276
Barne, Kitty (Mary Catherine Barne)
 1883-1957 . . . . DLB-160
Barnes, A. S., and Company DLB-49
Barnes, Barnabe 1571-1609 . . . . DLB-132
Barnes, Djuna 1892-1982 . . . . DLB-4, 9, 45
Barnes, Jim 1933- DLB-175
Barnes, Julian 1946- DLB-194; Y-93
Julian Barnes Checklist Y-01

Barnes, Margaret Ayer 1886-1967 . . . . DLB-9
Barnes, Peter 1931- DLB-13, 233
Barnes, William 1801-1886 . . . . DLB-32
Barnes and Noble Books DLB-46
Barnet, Miguel 1940- DLB-145
Barney, Natalie 1876-1972 . . . . DLB-4
Barnfield, Richard 1574-1627 . . . . DLB-172
Baron, Richard W.,
 Publishing Company DLB-46
Barr, Amelia Edith Huddleston
 1831-1919 . . . . DLB-202, 221
Barr, Robert 1850-1912 . . . . DLB-70, 92
Barral, Carlos 1928-1989 . . . . DLB-134
Barrax, Gerald William 1933- DLB-41, 120
Barrès, Maurice 1862-1923 . . . . DLB-123
Barrett, Eaton Stannard 1786-1820 . . . . . . DLB-116
Barrie, J. M.
 1860-1937 . . . . . DLB-10, 141, 156; CDBLB-5
Barrie and Jenkins DLB-112
Barrio, Raymond 1921- DLB-82
Barrios, Gregg 1945- DLB-122
Barry, Philip 1896-1949 . . . . DLB-7, 228
Barry, Robertine (see Françoise)
Barry, Sebastian 1955- DLB-245
Barse and Hopkins DLB-46
Barstow, Stan 1928- DLB-14, 139
Barth, John 1930- DLB-2, 227
Barthelme, Donald
 1931-1989 . . . . DLB-2, 234; Y-80, Y-89
Barthelme, Frederick 1943- DLB-244; Y-85
Bartholomew, Frank 1898-1985 . . . . DLB-127
Bartlett, John 1820-1905 . . . . DLB-1, 235
Bartol, Cyrus Augustus 1813-1900 . . . . DLB-1, 235
Barton, Bernard 1784-1849 . . . . DLB-96
Barton, John ca. 1610-1675 . . . . DLB-236
Barton, Thomas Pennant 1803-1869 . . . . . DLB-140
Bartram, John 1699-1777 . . . . DLB-31
Bartram, William 1739-1823 . . . . DLB-37
Barykova, Anna Pavlovna 1839-1893 . . . . DLB-277
Basic Books DLB-46
Basille, Theodore (see Becon, Thomas)
Bass, Rick 1958- DLB-212, 275
Bass, T. J. 1932- Y-81
Bassani, Giorgio 1916- DLB-128, 177
Basse, William circa 1583-1653 . . . . DLB-121
Bassett, John Spencer 1867-1928 . . . . DLB-17
Bassler, Thomas Joseph (see Bass, T. J.)
Bate, Walter Jackson 1918-1999 . . . . . DLB-67, 103
Bateman, Christopher
 [publishing house] DLB-170
Bateman, Stephen circa 1510-1584 . . . . . . DLB-136
Bates, H. E. 1905-1974 . . . . DLB-162, 191
Bates, Katharine Lee 1859-1929 . . . . DLB-71
Batiushkov, Konstantin Nikolaevich
 1787-1855 . . . . DLB-205
Batsford, B. T. [publishing house] DLB-106

Battiscombe, Georgina 1905- DLB-155
The Battle of Maldon circa 1000 . . . . DLB-146
Baudelaire, Charles 1821-1867 . . . . DLB-217
Bauer, Bruno 1809-1882 . . . . DLB-133
Bauer, Wolfgang 1941- DLB-124
Baum, L. Frank 1856-1919 . . . . DLB-22
Baum, Vicki 1888-1960 . . . . DLB-85
Baumbach, Jonathan 1933- Y-80
Bausch, Richard 1945- DLB-130
Bausch, Robert 1945- DLB-218
Bawden, Nina 1925- DLB-14, 161, 207
Bax, Clifford 1886-1962 . . . . DLB-10, 100
Baxter, Charles 1947- DLB-130
Bayer, Eleanor (see Perry, Eleanor)
Bayer, Konrad 1932-1964 . . . . DLB-85
Bayle, Pierre 1647-1706 . . . . DLB-268
Bayley, Barrington J. 1937- DLB-261
Baynes, Pauline 1922- DLB-160
Baynton, Barbara 1857-1929 . . . . DLB-230
Bazin, Hervé 1911-1996 . . . . DLB-83
The BBC Four Samuel Johnson Prize
 for Non-fiction Y-02
Beach, Sylvia 1887-1962 . . . . DLB-4; DS-15
Beacon Press DLB-49
Beadle and Adams DLB-49
Beagle, Peter S. 1939- Y-80
Beal, M. F. 1937- Y-81
Beale, Howard K. 1899-1959 . . . . DLB-17
Beard, Charles A. 1874-1948 . . . . DLB-17
A Beat Chronology: The First Twenty-five
 Years, 1944-1969 . . . . DLB-16
Periodicals of the Beat Generation DLB-16
The Beats in New York City DLB-237
The Beats in the West DLB-237
Beattie, Ann 1947- DLB-218, 278; Y-82
Beattie, James 1735-1803 . . . . DLB-109
Beatty, Chester 1875-1968 . . . . DLB-201
Beauchemin, Nérée 1850-1931 . . . . DLB-92
Beauchemin, Yves 1941- DLB-60
Beaugrand, Honoré 1848-1906 . . . . DLB-99
Beaulieu, Victor-Lévy 1945- DLB-53
Beaumont, Francis circa 1584-1616
 and Fletcher, John 1579-1625
 . . . . DLB-58; CDBLB-1
Beaumont, Sir John 1583?-1627 . . . . DLB-121
Beaumont, Joseph 1616-1699 . . . . DLB-126
Beauvoir, Simone de 1908-1986 . . . . DLB-72; Y-86
Becher, Ulrich 1910- DLB-69
Becker, Carl 1873-1945 . . . . DLB-17
Becker, Jurek 1937-1997 . . . . DLB-75
Becker, Jurgen 1932- DLB-75
Beckett, Samuel 1906-1989
 . . . . DLB-13, 15, 233; Y-90; CDBLB-7
Beckford, William 1760-1844 . . . . DLB-39
Beckham, Barry 1944- DLB-33
Becon, Thomas circa 1512-1567 . . . . DLB-136

Cumulative Index

Becque, Henry 1837-1899 .... DLB-192
Beddoes, Thomas 1760-1808 .... DLB-158
Beddoes, Thomas Lovell 1803-1849 ..... DLB-96
Bede circa 673-735 .... DLB-146
Bedford-Jones, H. 1887-1949 .... DLB-251
Beebe, William 1877-1962 .... DLB-275
Beecher, Catharine Esther 1800-1878 .. DLB-1, 243
Beecher, Henry Ward 1813-1887 .. DLB-3, 43, 250
Beer, George L. 1872-1920 .... DLB-47
Beer, Johann 1655-1700 .... DLB-168
Beer, Patricia 1919-1999 .... DLB-40
Beerbohm, Max 1872-1956 .... DLB-34, 100
Beer-Hofmann, Richard 1866-1945 ...... DLB-81
Beers, Henry A. 1847-1926 .... DLB-71
Beeton, S. O. [publishing house] DLB-106
Bégon, Elisabeth 1696-1755 .... DLB-99
Behan, Brendan
    1923-1964 .... DLB-13, 233; CDBLB-7
Behn, Aphra 1640?-1689 .... DLB-39, 80, 131
Behn, Harry 1898-1973 .... DLB-61
Behrman, S. N. 1893-1973 .... DLB-7, 44
Beklemishev, Iurii Solomonvich
    (see Krymov, Iurii Solomonovich)
Belaney, Archibald Stansfeld (see Grey Owl)
Belasco, David 1853-1931 .... DLB-7
Belford, Clarke and Company DLB-49
Belinksy, Vissarion Grigor'evich
    1811-1848 .... DLB-198
Belitt, Ben 1911- DLB-5
Belknap, Jeremy 1744-1798 .... DLB-30, 37
Bell, Adrian 1901-1980 .... DLB-191
Bell, Clive 1881-1964 .... DS-10
Bell, Daniel 1919- DLB-246
Bell, George, and Sons DLB-106
Bell, Gertrude Margaret Lowthian
    1868-1926 .... DLB-174
Bell, James Madison 1826-1902 .... DLB-50
Bell, Madison Smartt 1957- DLB-218, 278
Bell, Marvin 1937- DLB-5
Bell, Millicent 1919- DLB-111
Bell, Quentin 1910-1996 .... DLB-155
Bell, Robert [publishing house] DLB-49
Bell, Vanessa 1879-1961 .... DS-10
Bellamy, Edward 1850-1898 .... DLB-12
Bellamy, John [publishing house] DLB-170
Bellamy, Joseph 1719-1790 .... DLB-31
La Belle Assemblée 1806-1837 .... DLB-110
Bellezza, Dario 1944-1996 .... DLB-128
Belloc, Hilaire 1870-1953 .... DLB-19, 100, 141, 174
Belloc, Madame (see Parkes, Bessie Rayner)
Bellonci, Maria 1902-1986 .... DLB-196
Bellow, Saul
    1915- DLB-2, 28; Y-82; DS-3; CDALB-1
Belmont Productions DLB-46
Bels, Alberts 1938- DLB-232
Belševica, Vizma 1931- ... DLB-232; CDWLB-4

Bemelmans, Ludwig 1898-1962 .... DLB-22
Bemis, Samuel Flagg 1891-1973 .... DLB-17
Bemrose, William [publishing house] DLB-106
Ben no Naishi 1228?-1271? DLB-203
Benchley, Robert 1889-1945 .... DLB-11
Bencúr, Matej (see Kukučin, Martin)
Benedetti, Mario 1920- DLB-113
Benedict, Pinckney 1964- DLB-244
Benedict, Ruth 1887-1948 .... DLB-246
Benedictus, David 1938- DLB-14
Benedikt, Michael 1935- DLB-5
Benediktov, Vladimir Grigor'evich
    1807-1873 .... DLB-205
Benét, Stephen Vincent
    1898-1943 .... DLB-4, 48, 102, 249
Benét, William Rose 1886-1950 .... DLB-45
Benford, Gregory 1941- Y-82
Benjamin, Park 1809-1864 ..... DLB-3, 59, 73, 250
Benjamin, S. G. W. 1837-1914 .... DLB-189
Benjamin, Walter 1892-1940 .... DLB-242
Benlowes, Edward 1602-1676 .... DLB-126
Benn Brothers Limited DLB-106
Benn, Gottfried 1886-1956 .... DLB-56
Bennett, Arnold
    1867-1931 .... DLB-10, 34, 98, 135; CDBLB-5
Bennett, Charles 1899-1995 .... DLB-44
Bennett, Emerson 1822-1905 .... DLB-202
Bennett, Gwendolyn 1902- DLB-51
Bennett, Hal 1930- DLB-33
Bennett, James Gordon 1795-1872 ...... DLB-43
Bennett, James Gordon, Jr. 1841-1918 .... DLB-23
Bennett, John 1865-1956 .... DLB-42
Bennett, Louise 1919- DLB-117; CDWLB-3
Benni, Stefano 1947- DLB-196
Benoit, Jacques 1941- DLB-60
Benson, A. C. 1862-1925 .... DLB-98
Benson, E. F. 1867-1940 .... DLB-135, 153
Benson, Jackson J. 1930- DLB-111
Benson, Robert Hugh 1871-1914 .... DLB-153
Benson, Stella 1892-1933 .... DLB-36, 162
Bent, James Theodore 1852-1897 .... DLB-174
Bent, Mabel Virginia Anna ?-? DLB-174
Bentham, Jeremy 1748-1832 .... DLB-107, 158, 252
Bentley, E. C. 1875-1956 .... DLB-70
Bentley, Phyllis 1894-1977 .... DLB-191
Bentley, Richard 1662-1742 .... DLB-252
Bentley, Richard [publishing house] DLB-106
Benton, Robert 1932- and Newman,
    David 1937- DLB-44
Benziger Brothers DLB-49
Beowulf circa 900-1000 or 790-825
    .... DLB-146; CDBLB-1
Berent, Wacław 1873-1940 .... DLB-215
Beresford, Anne 1929- DLB-40
Beresford, John Davys
    1873-1947 .... DLB-162, 178, 197

"Experiment in the Novel" (1929) DLB-36
Beresford-Howe, Constance 1922- DLB-88
Berford, R. G., Company DLB-49
Berg, Stephen 1934- DLB-5
Bergengruen, Werner 1892-1964 .... DLB-56
Berger, John 1926- DLB-14, 207
Berger, Meyer 1898-1959 .... DLB-29
Berger, Thomas 1924- DLB-2; Y-80
Bergman, Hjalmar 1883-1931 .... DLB-259
Bergman, Ingmar 1918- DLB-257
Berkeley, Anthony 1893-1971 .... DLB-77
Berkeley, George 1685-1753 ..... DLB-31, 101, 252
The Berkley Publishing Corporation DLB-46
Berlin, Irving 1888-1989 .... DLB-265
Berlin, Lucia 1936- DLB-130
Berman, Marshall 1940- DLB-246
Bernal, Vicente J. 1888-1915 .... DLB-82
Bernanos, Georges 1888-1948 .... DLB-72
Bernard, Catherine 1663?-1712 .... DLB-268
Bernard, Harry 1898-1979 .... DLB-92
Bernard, John 1756-1828 .... DLB-37
Bernard of Chartres circa 1060-1124? ... DLB-115
Bernard of Clairvaux 1090-1153 .... DLB-208
The Bernard Malamud Archive at the
    Harry Ransom Humanities
    Research Center Y-00
Bernard, Richard 1568-1641 .... DLB-281
Bernard Silvestris
    flourished circa 1130-1160 .... DLB-208
Bernari, Carlo 1909-1992 .... DLB-177
Bernhard, Thomas
    1931-1989 .... DLB-85, 124; CDWLB-2
Bernières, Louis de 1954- DLB-271
Bernstein, Charles 1950- DLB-169
Berriault, Gina 1926-1999 .... DLB-130
Berrigan, Daniel 1921- DLB-5
Berrigan, Ted 1934-1983 .... DLB-5, 169
Berry, Wendell 1934- DLB-5, 6, 234, 275
Berryman, John 1914-1972 .... DLB-48; CDALB-1
Bersianik, Louky 1930- DLB-60
Berthelet, Thomas [publishing house] DLB-170
Berto, Giuseppe 1914-1978 .... DLB-177
Bertocci, Peter Anthony 1910-1989 ...... DLB-279
Bertolucci, Attilio 1911- DLB-128
Berton, Pierre 1920- DLB-68
Bertrand, Louis "Aloysius"
    1807-1841 .... DLB-217
Besant, Sir Walter 1836-1901 .... DLB-135, 190
Bessette, Gerard 1920- DLB-53
Bessie, Alvah 1904-1985 .... DLB-26
Bester, Alfred 1913-1987 .... DLB-8
Besterman, Theodore 1904-1976 .... DLB-201
Beston, Henry 1888-1968 .... DLB-275
The Bestseller Lists: An Assessment Y-84
Bestuzhev, Aleksandr Aleksandrovich
    (Marlinsky) 1797-1837 .... DLB-198

Bestuzhev, Nikolai Aleksandrovich
1791-1855 . . . . DLB-198

Betham-Edwards, Matilda Barbara (see Edwards, Matilda Barbara Betham-)

Betjeman, John
1906-1984 . . . . DLB-20; Y-84; CDBLB-7

Betocchi, Carlo 1899-1986. . . . . DLB-128

Bettarini, Mariella 1942- DLB-128

Betts, Doris 1932- DLB-218; Y-82

Beùkoviù, Matija 1939- DLB-181

Beveridge, Albert J. 1862-1927. . . . . DLB-17

Beverley, Robert circa 1673-1722. . . . . . DLB-24, 30

Bevilacqua, Alberto 1934- DLB-196

Bevington, Louisa Sarah 1845-1895 . . . . . DLB-199

Beyle, Marie-Henri (see Stendhal)

Białoszewski, Miron 1922-1983 . . . . DLB-232

Bianco, Margery Williams 1881-1944 . . . . DLB-160

Bibaud, Adèle 1854-1941. . . . . DLB-92

Bibaud, Michel 1782-1857 . . . . DLB-99

Bibliographical and Textual Scholarship
Since World War II Y-89

The Bicentennial of James Fenimore Cooper:
An International Celebration Y-89

Bichsel, Peter 1935- DLB-75

Bickerstaff, Isaac John 1733-circa 1808 . . . . DLB-89

Biddle, Drexel [publishing house] DLB-49

Bidermann, Jacob
1577 or 1578-1639. . . . . DLB-164

Bidwell, Walter Hilliard 1798-1881 . . . . DLB-79

Bienek, Horst 1930- DLB-75

Bierbaum, Otto Julius 1865-1910. . . . . DLB-66

Bierce, Ambrose 1842-1914?
. . . . . . DLB-11, 12, 23, 71, 74, 186; CDALB-3

Bigelow, William F. 1879-1966 . . . . DLB-91

Biggle, Lloyd, Jr. 1923- DLB-8

Bigiaretti, Libero 1905-1993 . . . . DLB-177

Bigland, Eileen 1898-1970 . . . . DLB-195

Biglow, Hosea (see Lowell, James Russell)

Bigongiari, Piero 1914- DLB-128

Bilenchi, Romano 1909-1989. . . . . DLB-264

Billinger, Richard 1890-1965 . . . . DLB-124

Billings, Hammatt 1818-1874 . . . . DLB-188

Billings, John Shaw 1898-1975 . . . . DLB-137

Billings, Josh (see Shaw, Henry Wheeler)

Binding, Rudolf G. 1867-1938 . . . . DLB-66

Bingay, Malcolm 1884-1953 . . . . DLB-241

Bingham, Caleb 1757-1817. . . . . DLB-42

Bingham, George Barry 1906-1988 . . . . . . DLB-127

Bingham, Sallie 1937- DLB-234

Bingley, William [publishing house] DLB-154

Binyon, Laurence 1869-1943. . . . . DLB-19

Biographia Brittanica. DLB-142

Biographical Documents I Y-84

Biographical Documents II Y-85

Bioren, John [publishing house] DLB-49

Bioy Casares, Adolfo 1914- DLB-113

Bird, Isabella Lucy 1831-1904 . . . . DLB-166

Bird, Robert Montgomery 1806-1854 . . . . DLB-202

Bird, William 1888-1963 . . . . DLB-4; DS-15

Birken, Sigmund von 1626-1681 . . . . DLB-164

Birney, Earle 1904-1995 . . . . DLB-88

Birrell, Augustine 1850-1933 . . . . DLB-98

Bisher, Furman 1918- DLB-171

Bishop, Elizabeth
1911-1979 . . . . DLB-5, 169; CDALB-6

Bishop, John Peale 1892-1944 . . . . DLB-4, 9, 45

Bismarck, Otto von 1815-1898 . . . . DLB-129

Bisset, Robert 1759-1805 . . . . DLB-142

Bissett, Bill 1939- DLB-53

Bitzius, Albert (see Gotthelf, Jeremias)

Bjørnvig, Thorkild 1918- DLB-214

Black, David (D. M.) 1941- DLB-40

Black, Gavin 1913-1998. . . . . DLB-276

Black, Lionel 1910-1980 . . . . DLB-276

Black, Walter J. [publishing house] DLB-46

Black, Winifred 1863-1936 . . . . DLB-25

The Black Aesthetic: Background DS-8

The Black Arts Movement,
by Larry Neal DLB-38

Black Theaters and Theater Organizations in
America, 1961-1982:
A Research List. DLB-38

Black Theatre: A Forum [excerpts] DLB-38

Blackamore, Arthur 1679-? DLB-24, 39

Blackburn, Alexander L. 1929- Y-85

Blackburn, John 1923- DLB-261

Blackburn, Paul 1926-1971 . . . . DLB-16; Y-81

Blackburn, Thomas 1916-1977 . . . . DLB-27

Blacker, Terence 1948- DLB-271

Blackmore, R. D. 1825-1900 . . . . DLB-18

Blackmore, Sir Richard 1654-1729. . . . . . . DLB-131

Blackmur, R. P. 1904-1965 . . . . DLB-63

Blackwell, Basil, Publisher DLB-106

Blackwood, Algernon Henry
1869-1951 . . . . DLB-153, 156, 178

Blackwood, Caroline 1931-1996 . . . . . DLB-14, 207

Blackwood, William, and Sons, Ltd. DLB-154

Blackwood's Edinburgh Magazine
1817-1980 . . . . DLB-110

Blades, William 1824-1890 . . . . DLB-184

Blaga, Lucian 1895-1961 . . . . DLB-220

Blagden, Isabella 1817?-1873 . . . . DLB-199

Blair, Eric Arthur (see Orwell, George)

Blair, Francis Preston 1791-1876 . . . . DLB-43

Blair, James circa 1655-1743 . . . . DLB-24

Blair, John Durburrow 1759-1823 . . . . DLB-37

Blais, Marie-Claire 1939- DLB-53

Blaise, Clark 1940- DLB-53

Blake, George 1893-1961. . . . . DLB-191

Blake, Lillie Devereux 1833-1913 . . . DLB-202, 221

Blake, Nicholas 1904-1972 . . . . DLB-77
(see Day Lewis, C.)

Blake, William
1757-1827 . . . . DLB-93, 154, 163; CDBLB-3

The Blakiston Company DLB-49

Blanchard, Stephen 1950- DLB-267

Blanchot, Maurice 1907- DLB-72

Blanckenburg, Christian Friedrich von
1744-1796 . . . . DLB-94

Blandiana, Ana 1942- DLB-232; CDWLB-4

Blanshard, Brand 1892-1987 . . . . DLB-279

Blaser, Robin 1925- DLB-165

Blaumanis, Rudolfs 1863-1908 . . . . DLB-220

Bleasdale, Alan 1946- DLB-245

Bledsoe, Albert Taylor 1809-1877 . . DLB-3, 79, 248

Bleecker, Ann Eliza 1752-1783 . . . . DLB-200

Blelock and Company DLB-49

Blennerhassett, Margaret Agnew
1773-1842 . . . . DLB-99

Bles, Geoffrey [publishing house] DLB-112

Blessington, Marguerite, Countess of
1789-1849 . . . . DLB-166

Blew, Mary Clearman 1939- DLB-256

The Blickling Homilies circa 971 . . . . DLB-146

Blind, Mathilde 1841-1896 . . . . DLB-199

Blish, James 1921-1975 . . . . DLB-8

Bliss, E., and E. White
[publishing house] DLB-49

Bliven, Bruce 1889-1977 . . . . DLB-137

Blixen, Karen 1885-1962 . . . . DLB-214

Bloch, Robert 1917-1994 . . . . DLB-44

Block, Lawrence 1938- DLB-226

Block, Rudolph (see Lessing, Bruno)

Blondal, Patricia 1926-1959. . . . . DLB-88

Bloom, Harold 1930- DLB-67

Bloomer, Amelia 1818-1894 . . . . DLB-79

Bloomfield, Robert 1766-1823 . . . . DLB-93

Bloomsbury Group DS-10

Blotner, Joseph 1923- DLB-111

Blount, Thomas 1618?-1679 . . . . DLB-236

Bloy, Léon 1846-1917 . . . . DLB-123

Blume, Judy 1938- DLB-52

Blunck, Hans Friedrich 1888-1961 . . . . DLB-66

Blunden, Edmund 1896-1974 . . . DLB-20, 100, 155

Blundeville, Thomas 1522?-1606 . . . . DLB-236

Blunt, Lady Anne Isabella Noel
1837-1917 . . . . DLB-174

Blunt, Wilfrid Scawen 1840-1922 . . . . DLB-19, 174

Bly, Nellie (see Cochrane, Elizabeth)

Bly, Robert 1926- DLB-5

Blyton, Enid 1897-1968 . . . . DLB-160

Boaden, James 1762-1839 . . . . DLB-89

Boas, Frederick S. 1862-1957. . . . . DLB-149

The Bobbs-Merrill Archive at the
Lilly Library, Indiana University Y-90

Boborykin, Petr Dmitrievich 1836-1921 . . DLB-238

The Bobbs-Merrill Company DLB-46

Bobrov, Semen Sergeevich
1763?-1810 . . . . DLB-150

Cumulative Index

Bobrowski, Johannes 1917-1965 .... DLB-75

The Elmer Holmes Bobst Awards in Arts and Letters Y-87

Bodenheim, Maxwell 1892-1954 ...... DLB-9, 45

Bodenstedt, Friedrich von 1819-1892 .... DLB-129

Bodini, Vittorio 1914-1970 .... DLB-128

Bodkin, M. McDonnell 1850-1933 ...... DLB-70

Bodley, Sir Thomas 1545-1613 .... DLB-213

Bodley Head DLB-112

Bodmer, Johann Jakob 1698-1783 .... DLB-97

Bodmershof, Imma von 1895-1982 ..... DLB-85

Bodsworth, Fred 1918- DLB-68

Boehm, Sydney 1908- DLB-44

Boer, Charles 1939- DLB-5

Boethius circa 480-circa 524 .... DLB-115

Boethius of Dacia circa 1240-? DLB-115

Bogan, Louise 1897-1970 .... DLB-45, 169

Bogarde, Dirk 1921- DLB-14

Bogdanovich, Ippolit Fedorovich circa 1743-1803 .... DLB-150

Bogue, David [publishing house] DLB-106

Böhme, Jakob 1575-1624 .... DLB-164

Bohn, H. G. [publishing house] DLB-106

Bohse, August 1661-1742 .... DLB-168

Boie, Heinrich Christian 1744-1806 ...... DLB-94

Boileau-Despréaux, Nicolas 1636-1711 ... DLB-268

Bok, Edward W. 1863-1930 ...... DLB-91; DS-16

Boland, Eavan 1944- DLB-40

Boldrewood, Rolf (Thomas Alexander Browne) 1826?-1915 .... DLB-230

Bolingbroke, Henry St. John, Viscount 1678-1751 .... DLB-101

Böll, Heinrich 1917-1985 .... DLB-69; Y-85; CDWLB-2

Bolling, Robert 1738-1775 .... DLB-31

Bolotov, Andrei Timofeevich 1738-1833 .... DLB-150

Bolt, Carol 1941- DLB-60

Bolt, Robert 1924-1995 .... DLB-13, 233

Bolton, Herbert E. 1870-1953 .... DLB-17

Bonaventura DLB-90

Bonaventure circa 1217-1274 .... DLB-115

Bonaviri, Giuseppe 1924- DLB-177

Bond, Edward 1934- DLB-13

Bond, Michael 1926- DLB-161

Boni, Albert and Charles [publishing house] DLB-46

Boni and Liveright DLB-46

Bonnefoy, Yves 1923- DLB-258

Bonner, Marita 1899-1971 .... DLB-228

Bonner, Paul Hyde 1893-1968 .... DS-17

Bonner, Sherwood (see McDowell, Katharine Sherwood Bonner)

Robert Bonner's Sons DLB-49

Bonnin, Gertrude Simmons (see Zitkala-Ša)

Bonsanti, Alessandro 1904-1984 .... DLB-177

Bontempelli, Massimo 1878-1960 ...... DLB-264

Bontemps, Arna 1902-1973 .... DLB-48, 51

The Book Arts Press at the University of Virginia Y-96

The Book League of America DLB-46

Book Publishing Accounting: Some Basic Concepts Y-98

Book Reviewing in America: I Y-87

Book Reviewing in America: II Y-88

Book Reviewing in America: III Y-89

Book Reviewing in America: IV Y-90

Book Reviewing in America: V Y-91

Book Reviewing in America: VI Y-92

Book Reviewing in America: VII Y-93

Book Reviewing in America: VIII Y-94

Book Reviewing in America and the Literary Scene Y-95

Book Reviewing and the Literary Scene Y-96, Y-97

Book Supply Company DLB-49

The Book Trade History Group Y-93

The Book Trade and the Internet Y-00

The Booker Prize Y-96

Address by Anthony Thwaite, Chairman of the Booker Prize Judges Comments from Former Booker Prize Winners Y-86

The Books of George V. Higgins: A Checklist of Editions and Printings Y-00

Boorde, Andrew circa 1490-1549 .... DLB-136

Boorstin, Daniel J. 1914- DLB-17

Booth, Franklin 1874-1948 .... DLB-188

Booth, Mary L. 1831-1889 .... DLB-79

Booth, Philip 1925- Y-82

Booth, Wayne C. 1921- DLB-67

Booth, William 1829-1912 .... DLB-190

Borchardt, Rudolf 1877-1945 .... DLB-66

Borchert, Wolfgang 1921-1947 ...... DLB-69, 124

Borel, Pétrus 1809-1859 .... DLB-119

Borges, Jorge Luis 1899-1986 .... DLB-113; Y-86; CDWLB-3

Borgese, Giuseppe Antonio 1882-1952 ... DLB-264

Börne, Ludwig 1786-1837 .... DLB-90

Bornstein, Miriam 1950- DLB-209

Borowski, Tadeusz 1922-1951 .... DLB-215; CDWLB-4

Borrow, George 1803-1881 ..... DLB-21, 55, 166

Bosanquet, Bernard 1848-1923 .... DLB-262

Bosch, Juan 1909- DLB-145

Bosco, Henri 1888-1976 .... DLB-72

Bosco, Monique 1927- DLB-53

Bosman, Herman Charles 1905-1951 .... DLB-225

Bossuet, Jacques-Bénigne 1627-1704 ...... DLB-268

Bostic, Joe 1908-1988 .... DLB-241

Boston, Lucy M. 1892-1990 .... DLB-161

Boswell, James 1740-1795 .... DLB-104, 142; CDBLB-2

Boswell, Robert 1953- DLB-234

Bote, Hermann circa 1460-circa 1520 .... DLB-179

Botev, Khristo 1847-1876 .... DLB-147

Botkin, Vasilii Petrovich 1811-1869 ...... DLB-277

Botta, Anne C. Lynch 1815-1891 ..... DLB-3, 250

Botto, Ján (see Krasko, Ivan)

Bottome, Phyllis 1882-1963 .... DLB-197

Bottomley, Gordon 1874-1948 .... DLB-10

Bottoms, David 1949- DLB-120; Y-83

Bottrall, Ronald 1906- DLB-20

Bouchardy, Joseph 1810-1870 .... DLB-192

Boucher, Anthony 1911-1968 .... DLB-8

Boucher, Jonathan 1738-1804 .... DLB-31

Boucher de Boucherville, Georges 1814-1894 .... DLB-99

Boudreau, Daniel (see Coste, Donat)

Bouhours, Dominic 1626-1702 .... DLB-268

Bourassa, Napoléon 1827-1916 .... DLB-99

Bourget, Paul 1852-1935 .... DLB-123

Bourinot, John George 1837-1902 .... DLB-99

Bourjaily, Vance 1922- DLB-2, 143

Bourne, Edward Gaylord 1860-1908 .... DLB-47

Bourne, Randolph 1886-1918 .... DLB-63

Bousoño, Carlos 1923- DLB-108

Bousquet, Joë 1897-1950 .... DLB-72

Bova, Ben 1932- Y-81

Bovard, Oliver K. 1872-1945 .... DLB-25

Bove, Emmanuel 1898-1945 .... DLB-72

Bowen, Elizabeth 1899-1973 .... DLB-15, 162; CDBLB-7

Bowen, Francis 1811-1890 .... DLB-1, 59, 235

Bowen, John 1924- DLB-13

Bowen, Marjorie 1886-1952 .... DLB-153

Bowen-Merrill Company DLB-49

Bowering, George 1935- DLB-53

Bowers, Bathsheba 1671-1718 .... DLB-200

Bowers, Claude G. 1878-1958 .... DLB-17

Bowers, Edgar 1924-2000 .... DLB-5

Bowers, Fredson Thayer 1905-1991 .... DLB-140; Y-80, 91

Bowles, Paul 1910-1999 ...... DLB-5, 6, 218; Y-99

Bowles, Samuel, III 1826-1878 .... DLB-43

Bowles, William Lisle 1762-1850 .... DLB-93

Bowman, Louise Morey 1882-1944 ...... DLB-68

Bowne, Borden Parker 1847-1910 .... DLB-270

Boyd, James 1888-1944 .... DLB-9; DS-16

Boyd, John 1919- DLB-8

Boyd, Martin 1893-1972 .... DLB-260

Boyd, Thomas 1898-1935 .... DLB-9; DS-16

Boyd, William 1952- DLB-231

Boye, Karin 1900-1941 .... DLB-259

Boyesen, Hjalmar Hjorth 1848-1895 .... DLB-12, 71; DS-13

Boylan, Clare 1948- DLB-267

Boyle, Kay 1902-1992 ..... DLB-4, 9, 48, 86; Y-93

Boyle, Roger, Earl of Orrery 1621-1679 ...DLB-80
Boyle, T. Coraghessan
    1948- DLB-218, 278; Y-86
Božić, Mirko 1919- DLB-181
Brackenbury, Alison 1953- DLB-40
Brackenridge, Hugh Henry
    1748-1816 ....DLB-11, 37
Brackett, Charles 1892-1969 ....DLB-26
Brackett, Leigh 1915-1978 ....DLB-8, 26
Bradburn, John [publishing house] DLB-49
Bradbury, Malcolm 1932-2000 ......DLB-14, 207
Bradbury, Ray 1920- DLB-2, 8; CDALB-6
Bradbury and Evans DLB-106
Braddon, Mary Elizabeth
    1835-1915 ....DLB-18, 70, 156
Bradford, Andrew 1686-1742.........DLB-43, 73
Bradford, Gamaliel 1863-1932...........DLB-17
Bradford, John 1749-1830 ....DLB-43
Bradford, Roark 1896-1948..............DLB-86
Bradford, William 1590-1657 ....DLB-24, 30
Bradford, William, III 1719-1791......DLB-43, 73
Bradlaugh, Charles 1833-1891...........DLB-57
Bradley, David 1950- DLB-33
Bradley, F. H. 1846-1924..............DLB-262
Bradley, Ira, and Company DLB-49
Bradley, J. W., and Company DLB-49
Bradley, Katherine Harris (see Field, Michael)
Bradley, Marion Zimmer 1930-1999.......DLB-8
Bradley, William Aspenwall 1878-1939.....DLB-4
Bradshaw, Henry 1831-1886...........DLB-184
Bradstreet, Anne
    1612 or 1613-1672....... DLB-24; CDABL-2
Bradūnas, Kazys 1917- DLB-220
Bradwardine, Thomas circa
    1295-1349 ....DLB-115
Brady, Frank 1924-1986 ....DLB-111
Brady, Frederic A. [publishing house] DLB-49
Bragg, Melvyn 1939- DLB-14, 271
Brainard, Charles H. [publishing house] ...DLB-49
Braine, John 1922-1986 ..DLB-15; Y-86; CDBLB-7
Braithwait, Richard 1588-1673 ....DLB-151
Braithwaite, William Stanley
    1878-1962 ....DLB-50, 54
Bräker, Ulrich 1735-1798................DLB-94
Bramah, Ernest 1868-1942 ....DLB-70
Branagan, Thomas 1774-1843 ....DLB-37
Brancati, Vitaliano 1907-1954 ....DLB-264
Branch, William Blackwell 1927- DLB-76
Brand, Christianna 1907-1988 ....DLB-276
Brand, Max (see Faust, Frederick Schiller)
Branden Press DLB-46
Branner, H.C. 1903-1966 ....DLB-214
Brant, Sebastian 1457-1521 ....DLB-179
Brassey, Lady Annie (Allnutt)
    1839-1887 ....DLB-166
Brathwaite, Edward Kamau
    1930- DLB-125; CDWLB-3

Brault, Jacques 1933- DLB-53
Braun, Matt 1932- DLB-212
Braun, Volker 1939- DLB-75
Brautigan, Richard
    1935-1984 .... DLB-2, 5, 206; Y-80, Y-84
Braxton, Joanne M. 1950- DLB-41
Bray, Anne Eliza 1790-1883.............DLB-116
Bray, Thomas 1656-1730...............DLB-24
Brazdžionis, Bernardas 1907- DLB-220
Braziller, George [publishing house] DLB-46
The Bread Loaf Writers' Conference 1983 ... Y-84
Breasted, James Henry 1865-1935.......DLB-47
Brecht, Bertolt
    1898-1956 .... DLB-56, 124; CDWLB-2
Bredel, Willi 1901-1964.................DLB-56
Bregendahl, Marie 1867-1940 ....DLB-214
Breitinger, Johann Jakob 1701-1776 ....DLB-97
Bremser, Bonnie 1939- DLB-16
Bremser, Ray 1934- DLB-16
Brennan, Christopher 1870-1932........DLB-230
Brentano, Bernard von 1901-1964........DLB-56
Brentano, Clemens 1778-1842 ....DLB-90
Brentano's DLB-49
Brenton, Howard 1942- DLB-13
Breslin, Jimmy 1929-1996 ....DLB-185
Breton, André 1896-1966 ....DLB-65, 258
Breton, Nicholas circa 1555-circa 1626 ...DLB-136
The Breton Lays
    1300-early fifteenth century.........DLB-146
Brett, Simon 1945- DLB-276
Brewer, Luther A. 1858-1933 ....DLB-187
Brewer, Warren and Putnam DLB-46
Brewster, Elizabeth 1922- DLB-60
Breytenbach, Breyten 1939- DLB-225
Bridge, Ann (Lady Mary Dolling Sanders
    O'Malley) 1889-1974.................DLB-191
Bridge, Horatio 1806-1893 ....DLB-183
Bridgers, Sue Ellen 1942- DLB-52
Bridges, Robert
    1844-1930 ....DLB-19, 98; CDBLB-5
The Bridgewater Library...............DLB-213
Bridie, James 1888-1951 ....DLB-10
Brieux, Eugene 1858-1932..............DLB-192
Brigadere, Anna 1861-1933...........DLB-220
Briggs, Charles Frederick
    1804-1877 .... DLB-3, 250
Brighouse, Harold 1882-1958 ....DLB-10
Bright, Mary Chavelita Dunne (see Egerton, George)
Brightman, Edgar S. 1884-1953.........DLB-270
Brimmer, B. J., Company DLB-46
Brines, Francisco 1932- DLB-134
Brink, André 1935- DLB-225
Brinley, George, Jr. 1817-1875 ....DLB-140
Brinnin, John Malcolm 1916-1998........DLB-48
Brisbane, Albert 1809-1890 ....DLB-3, 250
Brisbane, Arthur 1864-1936 ....DLB-25

British Academy DLB-112
The British Critic 1793-1843...........DLB-110
The British Library and the Regular
    Readers' Group...................... Y-91
British Literary Prizes Y-98
*The British Review and London Critical
    Journal 1811-1825*..................DLB-110
British Travel Writing, 1940-1997.......DLB-204
Brito, Aristeo 1942- DLB-122
Brittain, Vera 1893-1970 ....DLB-191
Brizeux, Auguste 1803-1858 ....DLB-217
Broadway Publishing Company DLB-46
Broch, Hermann
    1886-1951 .... DLB-85, 124; CDWLB-2
Brochu, André 1942- DLB-53
Brock, Edwin 1927- DLB-40
Brockes, Barthold Heinrich 1680-1747 ...DLB-168
Brod, Max 1884-1968 ....DLB-81
Brodber, Erna 1940- DLB-157
Brodhead, John R. 1814-1873 ....DLB-30
Brodkey, Harold 1930-1996 ....DLB-130
Brodsky, Joseph 1940-1996................Y-87
Brodsky, Michael 1948- DLB-244
Broeg, Bob 1918- DLB-171
Brøgger, Suzanne 1944- DLB-214
Brome, Richard circa 1590-1652 ....DLB-58
Brome, Vincent 1910- DLB-155
Bromfield, Louis 1896-1956 ....DLB-4, 9, 86
Bromige, David 1933- DLB-193
Broner, E. M. 1930- DLB-28
Bronk, William 1918-1999 ....DLB-165
Bronnen, Arnolt 1895-1959............DLB-124
Brontë, Anne 1820-1849 ....DLB-21, 199
Brontë, Charlotte
    1816-1855 ......DLB-21, 159, 199; CDBLB-4
Brontë, Emily
    1818-1848 ...... DLB-21, 32, 199; CDBLB-4
Brook, Stephen 1947- DLB-204
Brook Farm 1841-1847 ....DLB-223
Brooke, Frances 1724-1789 ....DLB-39, 99
Brooke, Henry 1703?-1783 ....DLB-39
Brooke, L. Leslie 1862-1940 ....DLB-141
Brooke, Margaret, Ranee of Sarawak
    1849-1936...................... DLB-174
Brooke, Rupert
    1887-1915 ....DLB-19, 216; CDBLB-6
Brooker, Bertram 1888-1955............DLB-88
Brooke-Rose, Christine 1923- DLB-14, 231
Brookner, Anita 1928- DLB-194; Y-87
Brooks, Charles Timothy 1813-1883 ..DLB-1, 243
Brooks, Cleanth 1906-1994 .... DLB-63; Y-94
Brooks, Gwendolyn
    1917-2000 ......DLB-5, 76, 165; CDALB-1
Brooks, Jeremy 1926- DLB-14
Brooks, Mel 1926- DLB-26
Brooks, Noah 1830-1903.........DLB-42; DS-13
Brooks, Richard 1912-1992 ....DLB-44

Brooks, Van Wyck 1886-1963 .... DLB-45, 63, 103
Brophy, Brigid 1929-1995 .... DLB-14, 70, 271
Brophy, John 1899-1965. .... DLB-191
Brossard, Chandler 1922-1993 .... DLB-16
Brossard, Nicole 1943- DLB-53
Broster, Dorothy Kathleen 1877-1950.... DLB-160
Brother Antoninus (see Everson, William)
Brotherton, Lord 1856-1930. .... DLB-184
Brougham and Vaux, Henry Peter Brougham, Baron 1778-1868 .... DLB-110, 158
Brougham, John 1810-1880 .... DLB-11
Broughton, James 1913-1999 .... DLB-5
Broughton, Rhoda 1840-1920 .... DLB-18
Broun, Heywood 1888-1939 ......DLB-29, 171
Brown, Alice 1856-1948 .... DLB-78
Brown, Bob 1886-1959. .... DLB-4, 45
Brown, Cecil 1943- DLB-33
Brown, Charles Brockden 1771-1810 .... DLB-37, 59, 73; CDALB-2
Brown, Christy 1932-1981 .... DLB-14
Brown, Dee 1908- Y-80
Brown, Frank London 1927-1962. .... DLB-76
Brown, Fredric 1906-1972 .... DLB-8
Brown, George Mackay 1921-1996 .... DLB-14, 27, 139, 271
Brown, Harry 1917-1986 .... DLB-26
Brown, Larry 1951- DLB-234
Brown, Lew (see DeSylva, Buddy)
Brown, Marcia 1918- DLB-61
Brown, Margaret Wise 1910-1952 .... DLB-22
Brown, Morna Doris (see Ferrars, Elizabeth)
Brown, Oliver Madox 1855-1874. .... DLB-21
Brown, Sterling 1901-1989 .... DLB-48, 51, 63
Brown, T. E. 1830-1897 .... DLB-35
Brown, Thomas Alexander (see Boldrewood, Rolf)
Brown, Warren 1894-1978 .... DLB-241
Brown, William Hill 1765-1793 .... DLB-37
Brown, William Wells 1815-1884. .... DLB-3, 50, 183, 248
Browne, Charles Farrar 1834-1867. ...... DLB-11
Browne, Frances 1816-1879 .... DLB-199
Browne, Francis Fisher 1843-1913 .... DLB-79
Browne, Howard 1908-1999 .... DLB-226
Browne, J. Ross 1821-1875. .... DLB-202
Browne, Michael Dennis 1940- DLB-40
Browne, Sir Thomas 1605-1682. .... DLB-151
Browne, William, of Tavistock 1590-1645 .... DLB-121
Browne, Wynyard 1911-1964 ...... DLB-13, 233
Browne and Nolan DLB-106
Brownell, W. C. 1851-1928 .... DLB-71
Browning, Elizabeth Barrett 1806-1861 .... DLB-32, 199; CDBLB-4
Browning, Robert 1812-1889. .... DLB-32, 163; CDBLB-4

Introductory Essay: *Letters of Percy Bysshe Shelley* (1852) DLB-32
Brownjohn, Allan 1931- DLB-40
Brownson, Orestes Augustus 1803-1876. .... DLB-1, 59, 73, 243
Bruccoli, Matthew J. 1931- DLB-103
Bruce, Charles 1906-1971. .... DLB-68
John Edward Bruce: Three Documents ... DLB-50
Bruce, Leo 1903-1979. .... DLB-77
Bruce, Mary Grant 1878-1958 .... DLB-230
Bruce, Philip Alexander 1856-1933 ...... DLB-47
Bruce Humphries [publishing house] DLB-46
Bruce-Novoa, Juan 1944- DLB-82
Bruckman, Clyde 1894-1955 .... DLB-26
Bruckner, Ferdinand 1891-1958. .... DLB-118
Brundage, John Herbert (see Herbert, John)
Brunner, John 1934-1995 .... DLB-261
Brutus, Dennis 1924- DLB-117, 225; CDWLB-3
Bryan, C. D. B. 1936- DLB-185
Bryant, Arthur 1899-1985 .... DLB-149
Bryant, William Cullen 1794-1878 .... DLB-3, 43, 59, 189, 250; CDALB-2
Bryce Echenique, Alfredo 1939- DLB-145; CDWLB-3
Bryce, James 1838-1922 .... DLB-166, 190
Bryden, Bill 1942- DLB-233
Brydges, Sir Samuel Egerton 1762-1837 ...DLB-107
Bryskett, Lodowick 1546?-1612 .... DLB-167
Buchan, John 1875-1940. ....DLB-34, 70, 156
Buchanan, George 1506-1582 .... DLB-132
Buchanan, Robert 1841-1901. .... DLB-18, 35
"The Fleshly School of Poetry and Other Phenomena of the Day" (1872), by Robert Buchanan DLB-35
"The Fleshly School of Poetry: Mr. D. G. Rossetti" (1871), by Thomas Maitland (Robert Buchanan). DLB-35
Buchler, Justus 1914-1991 .... DLB-279
Buchman, Sidney 1902-1975. .... DLB-26
Buchner, Augustus 1591-1661 .... DLB-164
Büchner, Georg 1813-1837. .... DLB-133; CDWLB-2
Bucholtz, Andreas Heinrich 1607-1671 ... DLB-168
Buck, Pearl S. 1892-1973 .. DLB-9, 102; CDALB-7
Bucke, Charles 1781-1846 .... DLB-110
Bucke, Richard Maurice 1837-1902 ...... DLB-99
Buckingham, Joseph Tinker 1779-1861 and Buckingham, Edwin 1810-1833 ...... DLB-73
Buckler, Ernest 1908-1984 .... DLB-68
Buckley, William F., Jr. 1925- DLB-137; Y-80
Buckminster, Joseph Stevens 1784-1812. .... DLB-37
Buckner, Robert 1906- DLB-26
Budd, Thomas ?-1698 .... DLB-24
Budrys, A. J. 1931- DLB-8
Buechner, Frederick 1926- Y-80
Buell, John 1927- DLB-53

Bufalino, Gesualdo 1920-1996 .... DLB-196
Buffum, Job [publishing house]. DLB-49
Bugnet, Georges 1879-1981 .... DLB-92
Buies, Arthur 1840-1901 .... DLB-99
Building the New British Library at St Pancras. Y-94
Bukowski, Charles 1920-1994 ....DLB-5, 130, 169
Bulatović, Miodrag 1930-1991 .... DLB-181; CDWLB-4
Bulgakov, Mikhail Afanas'evich 1891-1940 .... DLB-272
Bulgarin, Faddei Venediktovich 1789-1859 .... DLB-198
Bulger, Bozeman 1877-1932 ....DLB-171
Bullein, William between 1520 and 1530-1576....... DLB-167
Bullins, Ed 1935- DLB-7, 38, 249
Bulwer, John 1606-1656. .... DLB-236
Bulwer-Lytton, Edward (also Edward Bulwer) 1803-1873. .... DLB-21
"On Art in Fiction "(1838) DLB-21
Bumpus, Jerry 1937- Y-81
Bunce and Brother DLB-49
Bunner, H. C. 1855-1896 ....DLB-78, 79
Bunting, Basil 1900-1985 .... DLB-20
Buntline, Ned (Edward Zane Carroll Judson) 1821-1886 .... DLB-186
Bunyan, John 1628-1688 ..... DLB-39; CDBLB-2
Burch, Robert 1925- DLB-52
Burciaga, José Antonio 1940- DLB-82
Burdekin, Katharine 1896-1963 .... DLB-255
Bürger, Gottfried August 1747-1794 ...... DLB-94
Burgess, Anthony 1917-1993 .... DLB-14, 194, 261; CDBLB-8
The Anthony Burgess Archive at the Harry Ransom Humanities Research Center. Y-98
Anthony Burgess's 99 Novels: An Opinion Poll. Y-84
Burgess, Gelett 1866-1951 .... DLB-11
Burgess, John W. 1844-1931 .... DLB-47
Burgess, Thornton W. 1874-1965 .... DLB-22
Burgess, Stringer and Company. DLB-49
Burick, Si 1909-1986 ....DLB-171
Burk, John Daly circa 1772-1808 .... DLB-37
Burk, Ronnie 1955- DLB-209
Burke, Edmund 1729?-1797 .... DLB-104, 252
Burke, James Lee 1936- DLB-226
Burke, Johnny 1908-1964. .... DLB-265
Burke, Kenneth 1897-1993 .... DLB-45, 63
Burke, Thomas 1886-1945 ....DLB-197
Burley, Dan 1907-1962. .... DLB-241
Burley, W. J. 1914- DLB-276
Burlingame, Edward Livermore 1848-1922 .... DLB-79
Burman, Carina 1960- DLB-257
Burnet, Gilbert 1643-1715 .... DLB-101

Burnett, Frances Hodgson
 1849-1924 . . . . DLB-42, 141; DS-13, 14
Burnett, W. R. 1899-1982 . . . . DLB-9, 226
Burnett, Whit 1899-1973 and
 Martha Foley 1897-1977 . . . . DLB-137
Burney, Fanny 1752-1840 . . . . DLB-39
Dedication, *The Wanderer* (1814) DLB-39
Preface to *Evelina* (1778) DLB-39
Burns, Alan 1929- DLB-14, 194
Burns, John Horne 1916-1953 . . . . Y-85
Burns, Robert 1759-1796 . . . . . DLB-109; CDBLB-3
Burns and Oates DLB-106
Burnshaw, Stanley 1906- DLB-48
James Dickey and Stanley
 Burnshaw Correspondence Y-02
Review of Stanley Burnshaw: The Collected
 Poems and Selected Prose Y-02
Burr, C. Chauncey 1815?-1883 . . . . DLB-79
Burr, Esther Edwards 1732-1758 . . . . DLB-200
Burroughs, Edgar Rice 1875-1950 . . . . DLB-8
Burroughs, John 1837-1921 . . . . DLB-64, 275
Burroughs, Margaret T. G. 1917- DLB-41
Burroughs, William S., Jr. 1947-1981 . . . . . . DLB-16
Burroughs, William Seward 1914-1997
 . . . . DLB-2, 8, 16, 152, 237; Y-81, Y-97
Burroway, Janet 1936- DLB-6
Burt, Maxwell Struthers
 1882-1954 . . . . DLB-86; DS-16
Burt, A. L., and Company DLB-49
Burton, Hester 1913- DLB-161
Burton, Isabel Arundell 1831-1896 . . . . . . DLB-166
Burton, Miles (see Rhode, John)
Burton, Richard Francis
 1821-1890 . . . . DLB-55, 166, 184
Burton, Robert 1577-1640 . . . . DLB-151
Burton, Virginia Lee 1909-1968 . . . . DLB-22
Burton, William Evans 1804-1860 . . . . DLB-73
Burwell, Adam Hood 1790-1849 . . . . DLB-99
Bury, Lady Charlotte 1775-1861 . . . . DLB-116
Busch, Frederick 1941- DLB-6, 218
Busch, Niven 1903-1991 . . . . DLB-44
Bushnell, Horace 1802-1876 . . . . DS-13
Bussières, Arthur de 1877-1913 . . . . DLB-92
Butler, Charles ca. 1560-1647 . . . . DLB-236
Butler, Guy 1918- DLB-225
Butler, E. H., and Company DLB-49
Butler, Joseph 1692-1752 . . . . DLB-252
Butler, Josephine Elizabeth 1828-1906 . . . . DLB-190
Butler, Juan 1942-1981 . . . . DLB-53
Butler, Judith 1956- DLB-246
Butler, Octavia E. 1947- DLB-33
Butler, Pierce 1884-1953 . . . . DLB-187
Butler, Robert Olen 1945- DLB-173
Butler, Samuel 1613-1680 . . . . DLB-101, 126
Butler, Samuel 1835-1902 . . . . . . DLB-18, 57, 174
Butler, William Francis 1838-1910 . . . . DLB-166

Butor, Michel 1926- DLB-83
Butter, Nathaniel [publishing house] DLB-170
Butterworth, Hezekiah 1839-1905 . . . . DLB-42
Buttitta, Ignazio 1899- DLB-114
Butts, Mary 1890-1937 . . . . DLB-240
Buzzati, Dino 1906-1972 . . . . DLB-177
Byars, Betsy 1928- DLB-52
Byatt, A. S. 1936- DLB-14, 194
Byles, Mather 1707-1788 . . . . DLB-24
Bynneman, Henry [publishing house] DLB-170
Bynner, Witter 1881-1968 . . . . DLB-54
Byrd, William circa 1543-1623 . . . . DLB-172
Byrd, William, II 1674-1744 . . . . DLB-24, 140
Byrne, John Keyes (see Leonard, Hugh)
Byron, George Gordon, Lord
 1788-1824 . . . . DLB-96, 110; CDBLB-3
Byron, Robert 1905-1941 . . . . DLB-195

C

Caballero Bonald, José Manuel
 1926- DLB-108
Cabañero, Eladio 1930- DLB-134
Cabell, James Branch 1879-1958 . . . . DLB-9, 78
Cabeza de Baca, Manuel 1853-1915 . . . . . DLB-122
Cabeza de Baca Gilbert, Fabiola
 1898- DLB-122
Cable, George Washington
 1844-1925 . . . . DLB-12, 74; DS-13
Cable, Mildred 1878-1952 . . . . DLB-195
Cabrera, Lydia 1900-1991 . . . . DLB-145
Cabrera Infante, Guillermo
 1929- DLB-113; CDWLB-3
Cadell [publishing house] DLB-154
Cady, Edwin H. 1917- DLB-103
Caedmon flourished 658-680 . . . . DLB-146
Caedmon School circa 660-899 . . . . DLB-146
Caesar, Irving 1895-1996 . . . . DLB-265
Cafés, Brasseries, and Bistros DS-15
Cage, John 1912-1992 . . . . DLB-193
Cahan, Abraham 1860-1951 . . . . DLB-9, 25, 28
Cahn, Sammy 1913-1993 . . . . DLB-265
Cain, George 1943- DLB-33
Cain, James M. 1892-1977 . . . . DLB-226
Caird, Edward 1835-1908 . . . . DLB-262
Caird, Mona 1854-1932 . . . . DLB-197
Čaks, Aleksandrs
 1901-1950 . . . . DLB-220; CDWLB-4
Caldecott, Randolph 1846-1886 . . . . DLB-163
Calder, John (Publishers), Limited DLB-112
Calderón de la Barca, Fanny
 1804-1882 . . . . DLB-183
Caldwell, Ben 1937- DLB-38
Caldwell, Erskine 1903-1987 . . . . DLB-9, 86
Caldwell, H. M., Company DLB-49
Caldwell, Taylor 1900-1985 . . . . DS-17
Calhoun, John C. 1782-1850 . . . . DLB-3, 248

Călinescu, George 1899-1965 . . . . DLB-220
Calisher, Hortense 1911- DLB-2, 218
Calkins, Mary W. 1863-1930 . . . . DLB-270
A Call to Letters and an Invitation
 to the Electric Chair,
 by Siegfried Mandel DLB-75
Callaghan, Mary Rose 1944- DLB-207
Callaghan, Morley 1903-1990 . . . . DLB-68
Callahan, S. Alice 1868-1894 . . . . . . DLB-175, 221
Callaloo Y-87
Callimachus circa 305 B.C.-240 B.C. . . . DLB-176
Calmer, Edgar 1907- DLB-4
Calverley, C. S. 1831-1884 . . . . DLB-35
Calvert, George Henry
 1803-1889 . . . . DLB-1, 64, 248
Calvino, Italo 1923-1985 . . . . DLB-196
Cambridge, Ada 1844-1926 . . . . DLB-230
Cambridge Press DLB-49
Cambridge Songs (Carmina Cantabrigiensia)
 circa 1050 . . . . DLB-148
Cambridge University Press DLB-170
Camden, William 1551-1623 . . . . DLB-172
Camden House: An Interview with
 James Hardin Y-92
Cameron, Eleanor 1912- DLB-52
Cameron, George Frederick
 1854-1885 . . . . DLB-99
Cameron, Lucy Lyttelton 1781-1858 . . . . . DLB-163
Cameron, Peter 1959- DLB-234
Cameron, William Bleasdell 1862-1951 . . . DLB-99
Camm, John 1718-1778 . . . . DLB-31
Camon, Ferdinando 1935- DLB-196
Camp, Walter 1859-1925 . . . . DLB-241
Campana, Dino 1885-1932 . . . . DLB-114
Campbell, Bebe Moore 1950- DLB-227
Campbell, David 1915-1979 . . . . DLB-260
Campbell, Gabrielle Margaret Vere
 (see Shearing, Joseph, and Bowen, Marjorie)
Campbell, James Dykes 1838-1895 . . . . . . DLB-144
Campbell, James Edwin 1867-1896 . . . . . . DLB-50
Campbell, John 1653-1728 . . . . DLB-43
Campbell, John W., Jr. 1910-1971 . . . . DLB-8
Campbell, Ramsey 1946- DLB-261
Campbell, Roy 1901-1957 . . . . DLB-20, 225
Campbell, Thomas 1777-1844 . . . . DLB-93, 144
Campbell, William Wilfred 1858-1918 . . . DLB-92
Campion, Edmund 1539-1581 . . . . DLB-167
Campion, Thomas
 1567-1620 . . . . DLB-58, 172; CDBLB-1
Campo, Rafael 1964- DLB-282
Campton, David 1924- DLB-245
Camus, Albert 1913-1960 . . . . DLB-72
Camus, Jean-Pierre 1584-1652 . . . . DLB-268
The Canadian Publishers' Records
 Database Y-96
Canby, Henry Seidel 1878-1961 . . . . DLB-91
Candelaria, Cordelia 1943- DLB-82

Candelaria, Nash 1928- DLB-82
Canetti, Elias
   1905-1994 .... DLB-85, 124; CDWLB-2
Canham, Erwin Dain 1904-1982 ...... DLB-127
Canitz, Friedrich Rudolph Ludwig von
   1654-1699 .... DLB-168
Cankar, Ivan 1876-1918 ..... DLB-147; CDWLB-4
Cannan, Gilbert 1884-1955 .... DLB-10, 197
Cannan, Joanna 1896-1961 .... DLB-191
Cannell, Kathleen 1891-1974 .... DLB-4
Cannell, Skipwith 1887-1957........... DLB-45
Canning, George 1770-1827 .... DLB-158
Cannon, Jimmy 1910-1973 .... DLB-171
Cano, Daniel 1947- DLB-209
Old Dogs / New Tricks? New Technologies,
   the Canon, and the Structure
   of the Profession.................... Y-02
Cantú, Norma Elia 1947- DLB-209
Cantwell, Robert 1908-1978............ DLB-9
Cape, Jonathan, and Harrison Smith
   [publishing house] DLB-46
Cape, Jonathan, Limited............ DLB-112
Čapek, Karel 1890-1938 .... DLB-215; CDWLB-4
Capen, Joseph 1658-1725 .... DLB-24
Capes, Bernard 1854-1918 .... DLB-156
Capote, Truman 1924-1984
   ...... DLB-2, 185, 227; Y-80, Y-84; CDALB-1
Capps, Benjamin 1922- DLB-256
Caproni, Giorgio 1912-1990........... DLB-128
Caragiale, Mateiu Ioan 1885-1936 ...... DLB-220
Cardarelli, Vincenzo 1887-1959 .... DLB-114
Cárdenas, Reyes 1948- DLB-122
Cardinal, Marie 1929- DLB-83
Carew, Jan 1920- DLB-157
Carew, Thomas 1594 or 1595-1640 .... DLB-126
Carey, Henry circa 1687-1689-1743 ...... DLB-84
Carey, M., and Company............... DLB-49
Carey, Mathew 1760-1839 .... DLB-37, 73
Carey and Hart DLB-49
Carlell, Lodowick 1602-1675 .... DLB-58
Carleton, William 1794-1869 .... DLB-159
Carleton, G. W. [publishing house] DLB-49
Carlile, Richard 1790-1843 .... DLB-110, 158
Carlson, Ron 1947- DLB-244
Carlyle, Jane Welsh 1801-1866 .... DLB-55
Carlyle, Thomas
   1795-1881.......... DLB-55, 144; CDBLB-3
"The Hero as Man of Letters: Johnson,
   Rousseau, Burns" (1841) [excerpt].... DLB-57
The Hero as Poet. Dante;
   Shakspeare (1841) DLB-32
Carman, Bliss 1861-1929 .... DLB-92
Carmina Burana circa 1230............. DLB-138
Carnap, Rudolf 1891-1970 .... DLB-270
Carnero, Guillermo 1947- DLB-108
Carossa, Hans 1878-1956............. DLB-66

Carpenter, Humphrey
   1946- DLB-155; Y-84, Y-99
The Practice of Biography III: An Interview
   with Humphrey Carpenter Y-84
Carpenter, Stephen Cullen ?-1820? DLB-73
Carpentier, Alejo
   1904-1980 .... DLB-113; CDWLB-3
Carr, Marina 1964- DLB-245
Carrier, Roch 1937- DLB-53
Carrillo, Adolfo 1855-1926............ DLB-122
Carroll, Gladys Hasty 1904- DLB-9
Carroll, John 1735-1815 .... DLB-37
Carroll, John 1809-1884............... DLB-99
Carroll, Lewis
   1832-1898 ...... DLB-18, 163, 178; CDBLB-4
The Lewis Carroll Centenary Y-98
Carroll, Paul 1927- DLB-16
Carroll, Paul Vincent 1900-1968 .... DLB-10
Carroll and Graf Publishers DLB-46
Carruth, Hayden 1921- DLB-5, 165
Carryl, Charles E. 1841-1920........... DLB-42
Carson, Anne 1950- DLB-193
Carson, Rachel 1907-1964 .... DLB-275
Carswell, Catherine 1879-1946.......... DLB-36
Cărtărescu, Mirea 1956- DLB-232
Carter, Angela 1940-1992....... DLB-14, 207, 261
Carter, Elizabeth 1717-1806 .... DLB-109
Carter, Henry (see Leslie, Frank)
Carter, Hodding, Jr. 1907-1972......... DLB-127
Carter, Jared 1939- DLB-282
Carter, John 1905-1975............... DLB-201
Carter, Landon 1710-1778............. DLB-31
Carter, Lin 1930- Y-81
Carter, Martin 1927-1997 .... DLB-117; CDWLB-3
Carter, Robert, and Brothers DLB-49
Carter and Hendee.................... DLB-49
Cartwright, Jim 1958- DLB-245
Cartwright, John 1740-1824 .... DLB-158
Cartwright, William circa 1611-1643 .... DLB-126
Caruthers, William Alexander
   1802-1846 .... DLB-3, 248
Carver, Jonathan 1710-1780 .... DLB-31
Carver, Raymond
   1938-1988 .... DLB-130; Y-83, Y-88
First Strauss "Livings" Awarded to Cynthia
   Ozick and Raymond Carver
   An Interview with Raymond Carver..... Y-83
Carvic, Heron 1917?-1980 .... DLB-276
Cary, Alice 1820-1871 .... DLB-202
Cary, Joyce 1888-1957 ... DLB-15, 100; CDBLB-6
Cary, Patrick 1623?-1657 .... DLB-131
Case, John 1540-1600................ DLB-281
Casey, Gavin 1907-1964 .... DLB-260
Casey, Juanita 1925- DLB-14
Casey, Michael 1947- DLB-5
Cassady, Carolyn 1923- DLB-16
Cassady, Neal 1926-1968.......... DLB-16, 237

Cassell and Company................ DLB-106
Cassell Publishing Company DLB-49
Cassill, R. V. 1919-2002........ DLB-6, 218; Y-02
Cassity, Turner 1929-2002........ DLB-105, Y-02
Cassius Dio circa 155/164-post 229 ...... DLB-176
Cassola, Carlo 1917-1987 .... DLB-177
The Castle of Perseverance circa 1400-1425 . DLB-146
Castellano, Olivia 1944- DLB-122
Castellanos, Rosario
   1925-1974............. DLB-113; CDWLB-3
Castillo, Ana 1953- DLB-122, 227
Castillo, Rafael C. 1950- DLB-209
Castlemon, Harry (see Fosdick, Charles Austin)
Čašule, Kole 1921- DLB-181
Caswall, Edward 1814-1878............ DLB-32
Catacalos, Rosemary 1944- DLB-122
Cather, Willa 1873-1947
   .... DLB-9, 54, 78, 256; DS-1; CDALB-3
Catherine II (Ekaterina Alekseevna), "The Great,"
   Empress of Russia 1729-1796....... DLB-150
Catherwood, Mary Hartwell 1847-1902... DLB-78
Catledge, Turner 1901-1983 .... DLB-127
Catlin, George 1796-1872 .... DLB-186, 189
Cato the Elder 234 B.C.-149 B.C. DLB-211
Cattafi, Bartolo 1922-1979 .... DLB-128
Catton, Bruce 1899-1978 .... DLB-17
Catullus circa 84 B.C.-54 B.C.
   .... DLB-211; CDWLB-1
Caubraith, Robert (see Galbraith, Robert)
Causley, Charles 1917- DLB-27
Caute, David 1936- DLB-14, 231
Cavendish, Duchess of Newcastle, Margaret
   Lucas 1623?-1673........ DLB-131, 252, 281
Cawein, Madison 1865-1914 .... DLB-54
Caxton, William [publishing house]...... DLB-170
The Caxton Printers, Limited DLB-46
Caylor, O. P. 1849-1897............... DLB-241
Cayrol, Jean 1911- DLB-83
Cecil, Lord David 1902-1986.......... DLB-155
Cela, Camilo José 1916- Y-89
Celan, Paul 1920-1970 ...... DLB-69; CDWLB-2
Celati, Gianni 1937- DLB-196
Celaya, Gabriel 1911-1991............ DLB-108
A Celebration of Literary Biography Y-98
Céline, Louis-Ferdinand 1894-1961 ...... DLB-72
The Celtic Background to Medieval English
   Literature..................... DLB-146
Celtis, Conrad 1459-1508............. DLB-179
Cendrars, Blaise 1887-1961 .... DLB-258
The Steinbeck Centennial.................. Y-02
Center for Bibliographical Studies and
   Research at the University of
   California, Riverside Y-91
The Center for the Book in the Library
   of Congress Y-93
Center for the Book Research Y-84
Centlivre, Susanna 1669?-1723.......... DLB-84

The Centre for Writing, Publishing and
   Printing History at the University
   of Reading........................ Y-00

The Century Company............... DLB-49

A Century of Poetry, a Lifetime of Collecting:
   J. M. Edelstein's Collection of
   Twentieth-Century American Poetry Y-02

Cernuda, Luis 1902-1963 .... DLB-134

Cervantes, Lorna Dee 1954- DLB-82

de Céspedes, Alba 1911-1997 .... DLB-264

Ch., T. (see Marchenko, Anastasiia Iakovlevna)

Chaadaev, Petr Iakovlevich
   1794-1856 .... DLB-198

Chabon, Michael 1963- DLB-278

Chacel, Rosa 1898- DLB-134

Chacón, Eusebio 1869-1948 .... DLB-82

Chacón, Felipe Maximiliano 1873-?...... DLB-82

Chadwick, Henry 1824-1908........... DLB-241

Chadwyck-Healey's Full-Text Literary Databases:
   Editing Commercial Databases of
   Primary Literary Texts Y-95

Challans, Eileen Mary (see Renault, Mary)

Chalmers, George 1742-1825........... DLB-30

Chaloner, Sir Thomas 1520-1565 ..... DLB-167

Chamberlain, Samuel S. 1851-1916...... DLB-25

Chamberland, Paul 1939- DLB-60

Chamberlin, William Henry 1897-1969.... DLB-29

Chambers, Charles Haddon 1860-1921 ... DLB-10

Chambers, María Cristina (see Mena, María Cristina)

Chambers, Robert W. 1865-1933 .... DLB-202

Chambers, W. and R.
   [publishing house]................ DLB-106

Chamisso, Adelbert von 1781-1838...... DLB-90

Champfleury 1821-1889 .... DLB-119

Chandler, Harry 1864-1944 .... DLB-29

Chandler, Norman 1899-1973......... DLB-127

Chandler, Otis 1927- DLB-127

Chandler, Raymond
   1888-1959 .... DLB-226, 253; DS-6; CDALB-5

Raymond Chandler Centenary Tributes
   from Michael Avallone, James Ellroy,
   Joe Gores, and William F. Nolan Y-88

Channing, Edward 1856-1931........... DLB-17

Channing, Edward Tyrrell
   1790-1856 ....DLB-1, 59, 235

Channing, William Ellery
   1780-1842 ....DLB-1, 59, 235

Channing, William Ellery, II
   1817-1901 ....DLB-1, 223

Channing, William Henry
   1810-1884 ....DLB-1, 59, 243

Chapelain, Jean 1595-1674........... DLB-268

Chaplin, Charlie 1889-1977............ DLB-44

Chapman, George
   1559 or 1560-1634 ....DLB-62, 121

Chapman, John DLB-106

Chapman, Olive Murray 1892-1977 ...... DLB-195

Chapman, R. W. 1881-1960........... DLB-201

Chapman, William 1850-1917........... DLB-99

Chapman and Hall DLB-106

Chappell, Fred 1936- DLB-6, 105

   "A Detail in a Poem" DLB-105

Chappell, William 1582-1649 .... DLB-236

Char, René 1907-1988 .... DLB-258

Charbonneau, Jean 1875-1960.......... DLB-92

Charbonneau, Robert 1911-1967........ DLB-68

Charles, Gerda 1914- DLB-14

Charles, William [publishing house]..... DLB-49

Charles d'Orléans 1394-1465 .... DLB-208

Charley (see Mann, Charles)

Charteris, Leslie 1907-1993 .... DLB-77

Chartier, Alain circa 1385-1430......... DLB-208

Charyn, Jerome 1937- Y-83

Chase, Borden 1900-1971 .... DLB-26

Chase, Edna Woolman 1877-1957 ...... DLB-91

Chase, James Hadley 1906-1985 .... DLB-276

Chase, Mary Coyle 1907-1981.......... DLB-228

Chase-Riboud, Barbara 1936- DLB-33

Chateaubriand, François-René de
   1768-1848 .... DLB-119

Chatterton, Thomas 1752-1770 .... DLB-109

Essay on Chatterton (1842), by
   Robert Browning................. DLB-32

Chatto and Windus................. DLB-106

Chatwin, Bruce 1940-1989 .... DLB-194, 204

Chaucer, Geoffrey
   1340?-1400 .... DLB-146; CDBLB-1

Chaudhuri, Amit 1962- DLB-267

Chauncy, Charles 1705-1787 .... DLB-24

Chauveau, Pierre-Joseph-Olivier
   1820-1890 .... DLB-99

Chávez, Denise 1948- DLB-122

Chávez, Fray Angélico 1910- DLB-82

Chayefsky, Paddy 1923-1981 .... DLB-7, 44; Y-81

Cheesman, Evelyn 1881-1969 .... DLB-195

Cheever, Ezekiel 1615-1708............ DLB-24

Cheever, George Barrell 1807-1890...... DLB-59

Cheever, John 1912-1982
   ..... DLB-2, 102, 227; Y-80, Y-82; CDALB-1

Cheever, Susan 1943- Y-82

Cheke, Sir John 1514-1557 .... DLB-132

Chekhov, Anton Pavlovich 1860-1904 ... DLB-277

Chelsea House..................... DLB-46

Chênedollé, Charles de 1769-1833 ...... DLB-217

Cheney, Ednah Dow 1824-1904 ..... DLB-1, 223

Cheney, Harriet Vaughan 1796-1889 ..... DLB-99

Chénier, Marie-Joseph 1764-1811 ...... DLB-192

Chernyshevsky, Nikolai Gavrilovich
   1828-1889 .... DLB-238

Cherry, Kelly 1940 .... Y-83

Cherryh, C. J. 1942- Y-80

Chesebro', Caroline 1825-1873 .... DLB-202

Chesney, Sir George Tomkyns
   1830-1895 .... DLB-190

Chesnut, Mary Boykin 1823-1886 ...... DLB-239

Chesnutt, Charles Waddell
   1858-1932 .... DLB-12, 50, 78

Chesson, Mrs. Nora (see Hopper, Nora)

Chester, Alfred 1928-1971 .... DLB-130

Chester, George Randolph 1869-1924.... DLB-78

The Chester Plays circa 1505-1532;
   revisions until 1575 .... DLB-146

Chesterfield, Philip Dormer Stanhope,
   Fourth Earl of 1694-1773............ DLB-104

Chesterton, G. K. 1874-1936
  .. DLB-10, 19, 34, 70, 98, 149, 178; CDBLB-6

Chettle, Henry circa 1560-circa 1607..... DLB-136

Cheuse, Alan 1940- DLB-244

Chew, Ada Nield 1870-1945 .... DLB-135

Cheyney, Edward P. 1861-1947 .... DLB-47

Chiara, Piero 1913-1986 .... DLB-177

Chicano History DLB-82

Chicano Language..................... DLB-82

Child, Francis James 1825-1896..... DLB-1, 64, 235

Child, Lydia Maria 1802-1880 .... DLB-1, 74, 243

Child, Philip 1898-1978............... DLB-68

Childers, Erskine 1870-1922 .... DLB-70

Children's Book Awards and Prizes DLB-61

Children's Illustrators, 1800-1880 .... DLB-163

Childress, Alice 1916-1994 .... DLB-7, 38, 249

Childs, George W. 1829-1894........... DLB-23

Chilton Book Company DLB-46

Chin, Frank 1940- DLB-206

Chinweizu 1943- DLB-157

Chitham, Edward 1932- DLB-155

Chittenden, Hiram Martin 1858-1917..... DLB-47

Chivers, Thomas Holley 1809-1858 ... DLB-3, 248

Cholmondeley, Mary 1859-1925........ DLB-197

Chomsky, Noam 1928- DLB-246

Chopin, Kate 1850-1904 ... DLB-12, 78; CDALB-3

Chopin, René 1885-1953.............. DLB-92

Choquette, Adrienne 1915-1973 .... DLB-68

Choquette, Robert 1905- DLB-68

Choyce, Lesley 1951- DLB-251

Chrétien de Troyes
   circa 1140-circa 1190.............. DLB-208

Christensen, Inger 1935- DLB-214

The Christian Publishing Company DLB-49

Christie, Agatha
   1890-1976 .... DLB-13, 77, 245; CDBLB-6

Christine de Pizan
   circa 1365-circa 1431............... DLB-208

Christopher, John 1922- DLB-255

Christus und die Samariterin circa 950 ...... DLB-148

Christy, Howard Chandler 1873-1952 ... DLB-188

Chulkov, Mikhail Dmitrievich
   1743?-1792..................... DLB-150

Church, Benjamin 1734-1778........... DLB-31

Church, Francis Pharcellus 1839-1906 ... DLB-79

Church, Peggy Pond 1903-1986 .... DLB-212

Church, Richard 1893-1972........... DLB-191

Church, William Conant 1836-1917 .... DLB-79

Churchill, Caryl 1938- DLB-13
Churchill, Charles 1731-1764 .... DLB-109
Churchill, Winston 1871-1947 .... DLB-202
Churchill, Sir Winston
  1874-1965 .... DLB-100; DS-16; CDBLB-5
Churchyard, Thomas 1520?-1604 ...... DLB-132
Churton, E., and Company DLB-106
Chute, Marchette 1909-1994 .... DLB-103
Ciardi, John 1916-1986 .... DLB-5; Y-86
Cibber, Colley 1671-1757 .... DLB-84
Cicero
  106 B.C.-43 B.C. DLB-211, CDWLB-1
Cima, Annalisa 1941- DLB-128
Čingo, Živko 1935-1987 .... DLB-181
Cioran, E. M. 1911-1995 .... DLB-220
Čipkus, Alfonsas (see Nyka-Niliūnas, Alfonsas)
Cirese, Eugenio 1884-1955 .... DLB-114
Cīrulis, Jānis (see Bels, Alberts)
Cisneros, Sandra 1954- DLB-122, 152
City Lights Books DLB-46
Cixous, Hélène 1937- DLB-83, 242
The Claims of Business and Literature:
  An Undergraduate Essay by
  Maxwell Perkins Y-01
Clampitt, Amy 1920-1994 .... DLB-105
Clancy, Tom 1947- DLB-227
Clapper, Raymond 1892-1944 .... DLB-29
Clare, John 1793-1864 .... DLB-55, 96
Clarendon, Edward Hyde, Earl of
  1609-1674 .... DLB-101
Clark, Alfred Alexander Gordon (see Hare, Cyril)
Clark, Ann Nolan 1896- DLB-52
Clark, C. E. Frazer, Jr. 1925- DLB-187; Y-01
Clark, C. M., Publishing Company DLB-46
Clark, Catherine Anthony 1892-1977 .... DLB-68
Clark, Charles Heber 1841-1915 .... DLB-11
Clark, Davis Wasgatt 1812-1871 .... DLB-79
Clark, Douglas 1919-1993 .... DLB-276
Clark, Eleanor 1913- DLB-6
Clark, J. P. 1935- DLB-117; CDWLB-3
Clark, Lewis Gaylord
  1808-1873 .... DLB-3, 64, 73, 250
Clark, Walter Van Tilburg
  1909-1971 .... DLB-9, 206
Clark, William (see Lewis, Meriwether)
Clark, William Andrews, Jr. 1877-1934 .. DLB-187
Clarke, Sir Arthur C. 1917- DLB-261
Clarke, Austin 1896-1974 .... DLB-10, 20
Clarke, Austin C. 1934- DLB-53, 125
Clarke, Gillian 1937- DLB-40
Clarke, James Freeman
  1810-1888 .... DLB-1, 59, 235
Clarke, John circa 1596-1658 .... DLB-281
Clarke, Lindsay 1939- DLB-231
Clarke, Marcus 1846-1881 .... DLB-230
Clarke, Pauline 1921- DLB-161
Clarke, Rebecca Sophia 1833-1906 ...... DLB-42

Clarke, Robert, and Company DLB-49
Clarke, Samuel 1675-1729 .... DLB-252
Clarkson, Thomas 1760-1846 .... DLB-158
Claudel, Paul 1868-1955 .... DLB-192, 258
Claudius, Matthias 1740-1815 .... DLB-97
Clausen, Andy 1943- DLB-16
Clawson, John L. 1865-1933 .... DLB-187
Claxton, Remsen and Haffelfinger DLB-49
Clay, Cassius Marcellus 1810-1903 ...... DLB-43
Cleage, Pearl 1948- DLB-228
Cleary, Beverly 1916- DLB-52
Cleary, Kate McPhelim 1863-1905 ...... DLB-221
Cleaver, Vera 1919- and
  Cleaver, Bill 1920-1981 .... DLB-52
Cleeve, Brian 1921- DLB-276
Cleland, John 1710-1789 .... DLB-39
Clemens, Samuel Langhorne (Mark Twain)
  1835-1910 .... DLB-11, 12, 23, 64, 74,
                            186, 189; CDALB-3
Mark Twain on Perpetual Copyright Y-92
Clement, Hal 1922- DLB-8
Clemo, Jack 1916- DLB-27
Clephane, Elizabeth Cecilia
  1830-1869 .... DLB-199
Cleveland, John 1613-1658 .... DLB-126
Cliff, Michelle 1946- DLB-157; CDWLB-3
Clifford, Lady Anne 1590-1676 .... DLB-151
Clifford, James L. 1901-1978 .... DLB-103
Clifford, Lucy 1853?-1929 ..... DLB-135, 141, 197
Clift, Charmian 1923-1969 .... DLB-260
Clifton, Lucille 1936- DLB-5, 41
Clines, Francis X. 1938- DLB-185
Clive, Caroline (V) 1801-1873 .... DLB-199
Clode, Edward J. [publishing house] DLB-46
Clough, Arthur Hugh 1819-1861 .... DLB-32
Cloutier, Cécile 1930- DLB-60
Clouts, Sidney 1926-1982 .... DLB-225
Clutton-Brock, Arthur 1868-1924 .... DLB-98
Coates, Robert M. 1897-1973 ...... DLB-4, 9, 102
Coatsworth, Elizabeth 1893- DLB-22
Cobb, Charles E., Jr. 1943- DLB-41
Cobb, Frank I. 1869-1923 .... DLB-25
Cobb, Irvin S. 1876-1944 .... DLB-11, 25, 86
Cobbe, Frances Power 1822-1904 ...... DLB-190
Cobbett, William 1763-1835 .... DLB-43, 107
Cobbledick, Gordon 1898-1969 .... DLB-171
Cochran, Thomas C. 1902- DLB-17
Cochrane, Elizabeth 1867-1922 ..... DLB-25, 189
Cockerell, Sir Sydney 1867-1962 .... DLB-201
Cockerill, John A. 1845-1896 .... DLB-23
Cocteau, Jean 1889-1963 .... DLB-65, 258
Coderre, Emile (see Jean Narrache)
Cody, Liza 1944- DLB-276
Coe, Jonathan 1961- DLB-231
Coetzee, J. M. 1940- DLB-225

Coffee, Lenore J. 1900?-1984 .... DLB-44
Coffin, Robert P. Tristram 1892-1955 .... DLB-45
Coghill, Mrs. Harry (see Walker, Anna Louisa)
Cogswell, Fred 1917- DLB-60
Cogswell, Mason Fitch 1761-1830 .... DLB-37
Cohan, George M. 1878-1942 .... DLB-249
Cohen, Arthur A. 1928-1986 .... DLB-28
Cohen, Leonard 1934- DLB-53
Cohen, Matt 1942- DLB-53
Cohen, Morris Raphael 1880-1947 ..... DLB-270
Colbeck, Norman 1903-1987 .... DLB-201
Colden, Cadwallader 1688-1776 ... DLB-24, 30, 270
Colden, Jane 1724-1766 .... DLB-200
Cole, Barry 1936- DLB-14
Cole, George Watson 1850-1939 ...... DLB-140
Colegate, Isabel 1931- DLB-14, 231
Coleman, Emily Holmes 1899-1974 ..... DLB-4
Coleman, Wanda 1946- DLB-130
Coleridge, Hartley 1796-1849 .... DLB-96
Coleridge, Mary 1861-1907 .... DLB-19, 98
Coleridge, Samuel Taylor
  1772-1834 .... DLB-93, 107; CDBLB-3
Coleridge, Sara 1802-1852 .... DLB-199
Colet, John 1467-1519 .... DLB-132
Colette 1873-1954 .... DLB-65
Colette, Sidonie Gabrielle (see Colette)
Colinas, Antonio 1946- DLB-134
Coll, Joseph Clement 1881-1921 .... DLB-188
A Century of Poetry, a Lifetime of Collecting:
  J. M. Edelstein's Collection of Twentieth-
  Century American Poetry Y-02
Collier, John 1901-1980 .... DLB-77, 255
Collier, John Payne 1789-1883 .... DLB-184
Collier, Mary 1690-1762 .... DLB-95
Collier, P. F. [publishing house] DLB-49
Collier, Robert J. 1876-1918 .... DLB-91
Collin and Small DLB-49
Collingwood, R. G. 1889-1943 .... DLB-262
Collingwood, W. G. 1854-1932 .... DLB-149
Collins, An floruit circa 1653 .... DLB-131
Collins, Anthony 1676-1729 .... DLB-252
Collins, Isaac [publishing house] DLB-49
Collins, Merle 1950- DLB-157
Collins, Michael 1964- DLB-267
Collins, Mortimer 1827-1876 .... DLB-21, 35
Collins, Tom (see Furphy, Joseph)
Collins, Wilkie
  1824-1889 .... DLB-18, 70, 159; CDBLB-4
Collins, William 1721-1759 .... DLB-109
Collins, William, Sons and Company ... DLB-154
Collis, Maurice 1889-1973 .... DLB-195
Collyer, Mary 1716?-1763? DLB-39
Colman, Benjamin 1673-1747 .... DLB-24
Colman, George, the Elder 1732-1794 ... DLB-89
Colman, George, the Younger
  1762-1836 .... DLB-89

Colman, S. [publishing house] DLB-49
Colombo, John Robert 1936- DLB-53
Colquhoun, Patrick 1745-1820 ....DLB-158
Colter, Cyrus 1910- DLB-33
Colum, Padraic 1881-1972..............DLB-19
Columella fl. first century A.D..........DLB-211
Colvin, Sir Sidney 1845-1927 ....DLB-149
Colwin, Laurie 1944-1992........DLB-218; Y-80
Comden, Betty 1919- and
  Green, Adolph 1918- DLB-44, 265
Come to Papa Y-99
Comi, Girolamo 1890-1968............DLB-114
The Comic Tradition Continued
  [in the British Novel]...............DLB-15
Comisso, Giovanni 1895-1969..........DLB-264
Commager, Henry Steele 1902-1998......DLB-17
The Commercialization of the Image of
  Revolt, by Kenneth Rexroth..........DLB-16
Community and Commentators: Black
  Theatre and Its Critics.............DLB-38
Commynes, Philippe de
  circa 1447-1511...................DLB-208
Compton, D. G. 1930- DLB-261
Compton-Burnett, Ivy 1884?-1969 ......DLB-36
Conan, Laure (Félicité Angers)
  1845-1924 ....DLB-99
Concord History and Life DLB-223
Concord Literary History of a Town DLB-223
Conde, Carmen 1901- DLB-108
Conference on Modern Biography Y-85
Congreve, William
  1670-1729 .... DLB-39, 84; CDBLB-2
Preface to *Incognita* (1692)...............DLB-39
Conkey, W. B., Company.............DLB-49
Conn, Stewart 1936- DLB-233
Connell, Evan S., Jr. 1924- DLB-2; Y-81
Connelly, Marc 1890-1980 ....DLB-7; Y-80
Connolly, Cyril 1903-1974.............DLB-98
Connolly, James B. 1868-1957..........DLB-78
Connor, Ralph (Charles William Gordon)
  1860-1937 ....DLB-92
Connor, Tony 1930- DLB-40
Conquest, Robert 1917- DLB-27
Conrad, John, and Company DLB-49
Conrad, Joseph
  1857-1924 ....DLB-10, 34, 98, 156; CDBLB-5
Conroy, Jack 1899-1990 ....Y-81
Conroy, Pat 1945- DLB-6
Considine, Bob 1906-1975............DLB-241
The Consolidation of Opinion: Critical
  Responses to the Modernists.........DLB-36
Consolo, Vincenzo 1933- DLB-196
Constable, Archibald, and Company.....DLB-154
Constable, Henry 1562-1613..........DLB-136
Constable and Company Limited DLB-112
Constant, Benjamin 1767-1830.........DLB-119
Constant de Rebecque, Henri-Benjamin de
  (see Constant, Benjamin)

Constantine, David 1944- DLB-40
Constantin-Weyer, Maurice 1881-1964....DLB-92
Contempo Caravan: Kites in a Windstorm....Y-85
A Contemporary Flourescence of Chicano
  Literature Y-84
Continental European Rhetoricians,
  1400-1600 ....DLB-236
The Continental Publishing Company DLB-49
A Conversation between William Riggan
  and Janette Turner Hospital Y-02
Conversations with Editors Y-95
Conversations with Publishers I: An Interview
  with Patrick O'Connor Y-84
Conversations with Publishers II: An Interview
  with Charles Scribner III Y-94
Conversations with Publishers III: An Interview
  with Donald Lamm.................Y-95
Conversations with Publishers IV: An Interview
  with James Laughlin Y-96
Conversations with Rare Book Dealers I: An
  Interview with Glenn Horowitz Y-90
Conversations with Rare Book Dealers II: An
  Interview with Ralph Sipper Y-94
Conversations with Rare Book Dealers
  (Publishers) III: An Interview with
  Otto Penzler Y-96
The Conversion of an Unpolitical Man,
  by W. H. Bruford.................DLB-66
Conway, Anne 1631-1679 ....DLB-252
Conway, Moncure Daniel
  1832-1907 ....DLB-1, 223
Cook, David C., Publishing Company DLB-49
Cook, Ebenezer circa 1667-circa 1732 .....DLB-24
Cook, Edward Tyas 1857-1919.........DLB-149
Cook, Eliza 1818-1889................DLB-199
Cook, George Cram 1873-1924.........DLB-266
Cook, Michael 1933-1994 ....DLB-53
Cooke, George Willis 1848-1923........DLB-71
Cooke, Increase, and Company DLB-49
Cooke, John Esten 1830-1886........DLB-3, 248
Cooke, Philip Pendleton
  1816-1850 ....DLB-3, 59, 248
Cooke, Rose Terry 1827-1892........DLB-12, 74
Cook-Lynn, Elizabeth 1930- DLB-175
Coolbrith, Ina 1841-1928..........DLB-54, 186
Cooley, Peter 1940- DLB-105
"Into the Mirror"....................DLB-105
Coolidge, Clark 1939- DLB-193
Coolidge, George [publishing house]......DLB-49
Coolidge, Susan (see Woolsey, Sarah Chauncy)
Cooper, Anna Julia 1858-1964 ....DLB-221
Cooper, Edith Emma (see Field, Michael)
Cooper, Giles 1918-1966...............DLB-13
Cooper, J. California 19??- DLB-212
Cooper, James Fenimore
  1789-1851 ......DLB-3, 183, 250; CDALB-2
Cooper, Kent 1880-1965 ....DLB-29
Cooper, Susan 1935- DLB-161, 261
Cooper, Susan Fenimore 1813-1894 .....DLB-239

Cooper, William [publishing house] DLB-170
Coote, J. [publishing house]............DLB-154
Coover, Robert 1932- DLB-2, 227; Y-81
Copeland and Day....................DLB-49
Ćopić, Branko 1915-1984 ....DLB-181
Copland, Robert 1470?-1548..........DLB-136
Coppard, A. E. 1878-1957 ....DLB-162
Coppée, François 1842-1908 ....DLB-217
Coppel, Alfred 1921- Y-83
Coppola, Francis Ford 1939- DLB-44
Copway, George (Kah-ge-ga-gah-bowh)
  1818-1869 ....DLB-175, 183
Editorial: The Extension of Copyright Y-02
Corazzini, Sergio 1886-1907 ....DLB-114
Corbett, Richard 1582-1635 ....DLB-121
Corbière, Tristan 1845-1875 ....DLB-217
Corcoran, Barbara 1911- DLB-52
Cordelli, Franco 1943- DLB-196
Corelli, Marie 1855-1924..........DLB-34, 156
Corle, Edwin 1906-1956 ....Y-85
Corman, Cid 1924- DLB-5, 193
Cormier, Robert 1925-2000....DLB-52; CDALB-6
Corn, Alfred 1943- DLB-120, 282; Y-80
Corneille, Pierre 1606-1684 ....DLB-268
Cornford, Frances 1886-1960 ....DLB-240
Cornish, Sam 1935- DLB-41
Cornish, William circa 1465-circa 1524...DLB-132
Cornwall, Barry (see Procter, Bryan Waller)
Cornwallis, Sir William, the Younger
  circa 1579-1614 ....DLB-151
Cornwell, David John Moore (see le Carré, John)
Corpi, Lucha 1945- DLB-82
Corrington, John William
  1932-1988 ....DLB-6, 244
Corriveau, Monique 1927-1976.........DLB-251
Corrothers, James D. 1869-1917 ....DLB-50
Corso, Gregory 1930- DLB-5, 16, 237
Cortázar, Julio 1914-1984 ...DLB-113; CDWLB-3
Cortéz, Carlos 1923- DLB-209
Cortez, Jayne 1936- DLB-41
Corvinus, Gottlieb Siegmund
  1677-1746......................DLB-168
Corvo, Baron (see Rolfe, Frederick William)
Cory, Annie Sophie (see Cross, Victoria)
Cory, Desmond 1928- DLB-276
Cory, William Johnson 1823-1892 ....DLB-35
Coryate, Thomas 1577?-1617 ......DLB-151, 172
Ćosić, Dobrica 1921- DLB-181; CDWLB-4
Cosin, John 1595-1672............DLB-151, 213
Cosmopolitan Book Corporation DLB-46
The Cost of *The Cantos*: William Bird
  to Ezra Pound Y-01
Costain, Thomas B. 1885-1965...........DLB-9
Coste, Donat (Daniel Boudreau)
  1912-1957 ....DLB-88
Costello, Louisa Stuart 1799-1870 ....DLB-166

Cota-Cárdenas, Margarita 1941- DLB-122
Côté, Denis 1954- DLB-251
Cotten, Bruce 1873-1954 .... DLB-187
Cotter, Joseph Seamon, Sr. 1861-1949 .... DLB-50
Cotter, Joseph Seamon, Jr. 1895-1919 .... DLB-50
Cottle, Joseph [publishing house] DLB-154
Cotton, Charles 1630-1687............ DLB-131
Cotton, John 1584-1652.............. DLB-24
Cotton, Sir Robert Bruce 1571-1631..... DLB-213
Coulter, John 1888-1980 .... DLB-68
Cournos, John 1881-1966............. DLB-54
Courteline, Georges 1858-1929 .... DLB-192
Cousins, Margaret 1905-1996 .... DLB-137
Cousins, Norman 1915-1990 .... DLB-137
Couvreur, Jessie (see Tasma)
Coventry, Francis 1725-1754 .... DLB-39
Dedication, *The History of Pompey the Little* (1751) DLB-39
Coverdale, Miles 1487 or 1488-1569 .... DLB-167
Coverly, N. [publishing house].......... DLB-49
Covici-Friede DLB-46
Cowan, Peter 1914- DLB-260
Coward, Noel
 1899-1973.......... DLB-10, 245; CDBLB-6
Coward, McCann and Geoghegan....... DLB-46
Cowles, Gardner 1861-1946............ DLB-29
Cowles, Gardner "Mike", Jr.
 1903-1985 .... DLB-127, 137
Cowley, Abraham 1618-1667...... DLB-131, 151
Cowley, Hannah 1743-1809............ DLB-89
Cowley, Malcolm
 1898-1989 .... DLB-4, 48; Y-81, Y-89
Cowper, Richard 1926-2002........... DLB-261
Cowper, William 1731-1800....... DLB-104, 109
Cox, A. B. (see Berkeley, Anthony)
Cox, James McMahon 1903-1974....... DLB-127
Cox, James Middleton 1870-1957....... DLB-127
Cox, Leonard circa 1495-circa 1550..... DLB-281
Cox, Palmer 1840-1924 .... DLB-42
Coxe, Louis 1918-1993................ DLB-5
Coxe, Tench 1755-1824 .... DLB-37
Cozzens, Frederick S. 1818-1869 .... DLB-202
Cozzens, James Gould
 1903-1978..... DLB-9; Y-84; DS-2; CDALB-1
James Gould Cozzens—A View from Afar Y-97
James Gould Cozzens Case Re-opened Y-97
James Gould Cozzens: How to Read Him Y-97
Cozzens's *Michael Scarlett*................ Y-97
James Gould Cozzens Symposium and
 Exhibition at the University of
 South Carolina, Columbia........... Y-00
Crabbe, George 1754-1832........... DLB-93
Crace, Jim 1946- DLB-231
Crackanthorpe, Hubert 1870-1896...... DLB-135
Craddock, Charles Egbert (see Murfree, Mary N.)
Cradock, Thomas 1718-1770 .... DLB-31

Craig, Daniel H. 1811-1895 .... DLB-43
Craik, Dinah Maria 1826-1887...... DLB-35, 136
Cramer, Richard Ben 1950- DLB-185
Cranch, Christopher Pearse
 1813-1892 .... DLB-1, 42, 243
Crane, Hart 1899-1932..... DLB-4, 48; CDALB-4
Nathan Asch Remembers Ford Madox Ford,
 Sam Roth, and Hart Crane Y-02
Crane, R. S. 1886-1967................ DLB-63
Crane, Stephen
 1871-1900........ DLB-12, 54, 78; CDALB-3
Crane, Walter 1845-1915.............. DLB-163
Cranmer, Thomas 1489-1556 ..... DLB-132, 213
Crapsey, Adelaide 1878-1914.......... DLB-54
Crashaw, Richard 1612 or 1613-1649 ... DLB-126
Craven, Avery 1885-1980.............. DLB-17
Crawford, Charles 1752-circa 1815 ..... DLB-31
Crawford, F. Marion 1854-1909........ DLB-71
Crawford, Isabel Valancy 1850-1887..... DLB-92
Crawley, Alan 1887-1975 .... DLB-68
Crayon, Geoffrey (see Irving, Washington)
Crayon, Porte (see Strother, David Hunter)
Creamer, Robert W. 1922- DLB-171
Creasey, John 1908-1973 .... DLB-77
Creative Age Press DLB-46
Creative Nonfiction Y-02
Creech, William [publishing house] DLB-154
Creede, Thomas [publishing house]......DLB-170
Creel, George 1876-1953 .... DLB-25
Creeley, Robert 1926- DLB-5, 16, 169; DS-17
Creelman, James 1859-1915............ DLB-23
Cregan, David 1931- DLB-13
Creighton, Donald 1902-1979 .... DLB-88
Crémazie, Octave 1827-1879........... DLB-99
Crémer, Victoriano 1909?- DLB-108
Crescas, Hasdai circa 1340-1412?....... DLB-115
Crespo, Angel 1926- DLB-134
Cresset Press..................... DLB-112
Cresswell, Helen 1934- DLB-161
Crèvecoeur, Michel Guillaume Jean de
 1735-1813..................... DLB-37
Crewe, Candida 1964- DLB-207
Crews, Harry 1935- DLB-6, 143, 185
Crichton, Michael 1942- Y-81
A Crisis of Culture: The Changing Role
 of Religion in the New Republic DLB-37
Crispin, Edmund (Robert Bruce
 Montgomery) 1921-1978 .... DLB-87
Cristofer, Michael 1946- DLB-7
Crnjanski, Miloš
 1893-1977..............DLB-147; CDWLB-4
Crocker, Hannah Mather 1752-1829 .... DLB-200
Crockett, David (Davy)
 1786-1836.............DLB-3, 11, 183, 248
Croft-Cooke, Rupert (see Bruce, Leo)
Crofts, Freeman Wills 1879-1957 .... DLB-77
Croker, John Wilson 1780-1857 .... DLB-110

Croly, George 1780-1860 .... DLB-159
Croly, Herbert 1869-1930 .... DLB-91
Croly, Jane Cunningham 1829-1901 ..... DLB-23
Crompton, Richmal 1890-1969 .... DLB-160
Cronin, A. J. 1896-1981 .... DLB-191
Cros, Charles 1842-1888 ....DLB-217
Crosby, Caresse 1892-1970 .... DLB-48
Crosby, Caresse 1892-1970
 and Crosby, Harry
 1898-1929 .... DLB-4; DS-15
Crosby, Harry 1898-1929 .... DLB-48
Crosland, Camilla Toulmin
 (Mrs. Newton Crosland)
 1812-1895 .... DLB-240
Cross, Gillian 1945- DLB-161
Cross, Victoria 1868-1952 ....DLB-135, 197
Crossley-Holland, Kevin 1941- DLB-40, 161
Crothers, Rachel 1870-1958 ....DLB-7, 266
Crowell, Thomas Y., Company......... DLB-49
Crowley, John 1942- Y-82
Crowley, Mart 1935- DLB-7, 266
Crown Publishers.................. DLB-46
Crowne, John 1641-1712 .... DLB-80
Crowninshield, Edward Augustus
 1817-1859..................... DLB-140
Crowninshield, Frank 1872-1947 .... DLB-91
Croy, Homer 1883-1965 .... DLB-4
Crumley, James 1939- DLB-226; Y-84
Cruse, Mary Anne 1825?-1910 .... DLB-239
Cruz, Migdalia 1958- DLB-249
Cruz, Victor Hernández 1949- DLB-41
Csokor, Franz Theodor 1885-1969 ...... DLB-81
Csoóri, Sándor 1930- DLB-232; CDWLB-4
Cuala Press..................... DLB-112
Cudworth, Ralph 1617-1688........... DLB-252
Cugoano, Quobna Ottabah 1797-?......... Y-02
Cullen, Countee
 1903-1946 .... DLB-4, 48, 51; CDALB-4
Culler, Jonathan D. 1944- DLB-67, 246
Cullinan, Elizabeth 1933- DLB-234
The Cult of Biography
 Excerpts from the Second Folio Debate:
 "Biographies are generally a disease of
 English Literature" – Germaine Greer,
 Victoria Glendinning, Auberon Waugh,
 and Richard Holmes Y-86
Culverwel, Nathaniel 1619?-1651?...... DLB-252
Cumberland, Richard 1732-1811 .... DLB-89
Cummings, Constance Gordon
 1837-1924......................DLB-174
Cummings, E. E.
 1894-1962 .... DLB-4, 48; CDALB-5
Cummings, Ray 1887-1957............. DLB-8
Cummings and Hilliard DLB-49
Cummins, Maria Susanna
 1827-1866.................... DLB-42
Cumpián, Carlos 1953- DLB-209
Cunard, Nancy 1896-1965............ DLB-240
Cundall, Joseph [publishing house] DLB-106

Cuney, Waring 1906-1976................DLB-51
Cuney-Hare, Maude 1874-1936..........DLB-52
Cunningham, Allan 1784-1842.....DLB-116, 144
Cunningham, J. V. 1911- DLB-5
Cunningham, Peter 1947- DLB-267
Cunningham, Peter F.
  [publishing house].................DLB-49
Cunqueiro, Alvaro 1911-1981..........DLB-134
Cuomo, George 1929- Y-80
Cupples, Upham and Company DLB-49
Cupples and Leon DLB-46
Cuppy, Will 1884-1949.................DLB-11
Curiel, Barbara Brinson 1956- DLB-209
Curll, Edmund [publishing house].......DLB-154
Currie, James 1756-1805 ....DLB-142
Currie, Mary Montgomerie Lamb Singleton,
  Lady Currie
  (see Fane, Violet)
Cursor Mundi circa 1300 ....DLB-146
Curti, Merle E. 1897- DLB-17
Curtis, Anthony 1926- DLB-155
Curtis, Cyrus H. K. 1850-1933 ....DLB-91
Curtis, George William
  1824-1892................DLB-1, 43, 223
Curzon, Robert 1810-1873...............DLB-166
Curzon, Sarah Anne 1833-1898...........DLB-99
Cusack, Dymphna 1902-1981..............DLB-260
Cushing, Eliza Lanesford 1794-1886......DLB-99
Cushing, Harvey 1869-1939 ....DLB-187
Custance, Olive (Lady Alfred Douglas)
  1874-1944 ....DLB-240
Cynewulf circa 770-840 ....DLB-146
Cyrano de Bergerac, Savinien de
  1619-1655........................DLB-268
Czepko, Daniel 1605-1660..............DLB-164
Czerniawski, Adam 1934- DLB-232

D

Dabit, Eugène 1898-1936................DLB-65
Daborne, Robert circa 1580-1628 ....DLB-58
Dąbrowska, Maria
  1889-1965 ....DLB-215; CDWLB-4
Dacey, Philip 1939- DLB-105
"Eyes Across Centuries: Contemporary
  Poetry and 'That Vision Thing,'"....DLB-105
Dach, Simon 1605-1659.................DLB-164
Dagerman, Stig 1923-1954...............DLB-259
Daggett, Rollin M. 1831-1901 ....DLB-79
D'Aguiar, Fred 1960- DLB-157
Dahl, Roald 1916-1990 ....DLB-139, 255
Dahlberg, Edward 1900-1977.............DLB-48
Dahn, Felix 1834-1912.................DLB-129
Dal', Vladimir Ivanovich (Kazak Vladimir
  Lugansky) 1801-1872 ....DLB-198
Dale, Peter 1938- DLB-40
Daley, Arthur 1904-1974 ....DLB-171
Dall, Caroline Healey 1822-1912......DLB-1, 235

Dallas, E. S. 1828-1879 ....DLB-55
From *The Gay Science* (1866)..........DLB-21
The Dallas Theater Center DLB-7
D'Alton, Louis 1900-1951 ....DLB-10
Daly, Carroll John 1889-1958 ....DLB-226
Daly, T. A. 1871-1948..................DLB-11
Damon, S. Foster 1893-1971 ....DLB-45
Damrell, William S. [publishing house]....DLB-49
Dana, Charles A. 1819-1897 ......DLB-3, 23, 250
Dana, Richard Henry, Jr.
  1815-1882................DLB-1, 183, 235
Dandridge, Ray Garfield DLB-51
Dane, Clemence 1887-1965 ....DLB-10, 197
Danforth, John 1660-1730 ....DLB-24
Danforth, Samuel, I 1626-1674 ....DLB-24
Danforth, Samuel, II 1666-1727.........DLB-24
Dangerous Years: London Theater,
  1939-1945 ....DLB-10
Daniel, John M. 1825-1865 ....DLB-43
Daniel, Samuel 1562 or 1563-1619 ......DLB-62
Daniel Press..........................DLB-106
Daniells, Roy 1902-1979 ....DLB-68
Daniels, Jim 1956- DLB-120
Daniels, Jonathan 1902-1981 ....DLB-127
Daniels, Josephus 1862-1948 ....DLB-29
Daniels, Sarah 1957- DLB-245
Danilevsky, Grigorii Petrovich
  1829-1890 ....DLB-238
Dannay, Frederic 1905-1982 and
  Manfred B. Lee 1905-1971 ....DLB-137
Danner, Margaret Esse 1915- DLB-41
Danter, John [publishing house].........DLB-170
Dantin, Louis (Eugène Seers) 1865-1945...DLB-92
Danto, Arthur C. 1924- DLB-279
Danzig, Allison 1898-1987..............DLB-171
D'Arcy, Ella circa 1857-1937 ....DLB-135
Dark, Eleanor 1901-1985................DLB-260
Darke, Nick 1948- DLB-233
Darley, Felix Octavious Carr 1822-1888...DLB-188
Darley, George 1795-1846...............DLB-96
Darmesteter, Madame James
  (see Robinson, A. Mary F.)
Darwin, Charles 1809-1882..........DLB-57, 166
Darwin, Erasmus 1731-1802 ....DLB-93
Daryush, Elizabeth 1887-1977 ....DLB-20
Dashkova, Ekaterina Romanovna
  (née Vorontsova) 1743-1810 ....DLB-150
Dashwood, Edmée Elizabeth Monica de la Pasture
  (see Delafield, E. M.)
Daudet, Alphonse 1840-1897............DLB-123
d'Aulaire, Edgar Parin 1898- and
  d'Aulaire, Ingri 1904- DLB-22
Davenant, Sir William 1606-1668 ....DLB-58, 126
Davenport, Guy 1927- DLB-130
Davenport, Marcia 1903-1996............DS-17
Davenport, Robert ?-? DLB-58
Daves, Delmer 1904-1977 ....DLB-26

Davey, Frank 1940- DLB-53
Davidson, Avram 1923-1993..............DLB-8
Davidson, Donald 1893-1968 ....DLB-45
Davidson, Donald 1917- DLB-279
Davidson, John 1857-1909...............DLB-19
Davidson, Lionel 1922- DLB-14, 276
Davidson, Robyn 1950- DLB-204
Davidson, Sara 1943- DLB-185
Davie, Donald 1922- DLB-27
Davie, Elspeth 1919- DLB-139
Davies, Sir John 1569-1626 ....DLB-172
Davies, John, of Hereford 1565?-1618....DLB-121
Davies, Peter, Limited DLB-112
Davies, Rhys 1901-1978 ....DLB-139, 191
Davies, Robertson 1913-1995 ....DLB-68
Davies, Samuel 1723-1761 ....DLB-31
Davies, Thomas 1712?-1785 ....DLB-142, 154
Davies, W. H. 1871-1940.........DLB-19, 174
Davin, Nicholas Flood 1840?-1901 ......DLB-99
Daviot, Gordon 1896?-1952 ....DLB-10
  (see also Tey, Josephine)
Davis, Arthur Hoey (see Rudd, Steele)
Davis, Charles A. 1795-1867 ....DLB-11
Davis, Clyde Brion 1894-1962 ....DLB-9
Davis, Dick 1945- DLB-40, 282
Davis, Frank Marshall 1905-? DLB-51
Davis, H. L. 1894-1960................DLB-9, 206
Davis, John 1774-1854..................DLB-37
Davis, Lydia 1947- DLB-130
Davis, Margaret Thomson 1926- DLB-14
Davis, Ossie 1917- DLB-7, 38, 249
Davis, Owen 1874-1956..................DLB-249
Davis, Paxton 1925-1994................Y-89
Davis, Rebecca Harding 1831-1910...DLB-74, 239
Davis, Richard Harding 1864-1916
  ....DLB-12, 23, 78, 79, 189; DS-13
Davis, Samuel Cole 1764-1809 ....DLB-37
Davis, Samuel Post 1850-1918...........DLB-202
Davison, Frank Dalby 1893-1970 ....DLB-260
Davison, Peter 1928- DLB-5
Davydov, Denis Vasil'evich
  1784-1839 ....DLB-205
Davys, Mary 1674-1732..................DLB-39
  Preface to *The Works of
    Mrs. Davys* (1725)...................DLB-39
DAW Books............................DLB-46
Dawson, Ernest 1882-1947 ....DLB-140
Dawson, Fielding 1930-2002 ......DLB-130; Y-02
Dawson, Sarah Morgan 1842-1909......DLB-239
Dawson, William 1704-1752 ....DLB-31
Day, Angel flourished 1583-1599 ...DLB-167, 236
Day, Benjamin Henry 1810-1889 ....DLB-43
Day, Clarence 1874-1935................DLB-11
Day, Dorothy 1897-1980................DLB-29
Day, Frank Parker 1881-1950 ....DLB-92

Day, John circa 1574-circa 1640 .... DLB-62
Day, John [publishing house] DLB-170
Day, The John, Company DLB-46
Day Lewis, C. 1904-1972 .... DLB-15, 20
(see also Blake, Nicholas)
Day, Mahlon [publishing house]......... DLB-49
Day, Thomas 1748-1789 .... DLB-39
Dazai Osamu 1909-1948 .... DLB-182
Deacon, William Arthur 1890-1977 ..... DLB-68
Deal, Borden 1922-1985................ DLB-6
de Angeli, Marguerite 1889-1987 .... DLB-22
De Angelis, Milo 1951- DLB-128
De Bow, J. D. B.
 1820-1867.................. DLB-3, 79, 248
de Bruyn, Günter 1926- DLB-75
de Camp, L. Sprague 1907-2000 .... DLB-8
De Carlo, Andrea 1952- DLB-196
De Casas, Celso A. 1944- DLB-209
Dechert, Robert 1895-1975............ DLB-187
Dedications, Inscriptions,
 and Annotations................ Y-01, Y-02
Dee, John 1527-1608 or 1609 ...... DLB-136, 213
Deeping, George Warwick 1877-1950 ... DLB 153
Defoe, Daniel
 1660-1731....... DLB-39, 95, 101; CDBLB-2
Preface to *Colonel Jack* (1722)............ DLB-39
Preface to *The Farther Adventures of
 Robinson Crusoe* (1719) DLB-39
Preface to *Moll Flanders* (1722)........... DLB-39
Preface to *Robinson Crusoe* (1719) DLB-39
Preface to *Roxana* (1724) DLB-39
de Fontaine, Felix Gregory 1834-1896 .... DLB-43
De Forest, John William 1826-1906 .. DLB-12, 189
DeFrees, Madeline 1919- DLB-105
"The Poet's Kaleidoscope: The Element
 of Surprise in the Making of
 the Poem" DLB-105
DeGolyer, Everette Lee 1886-1956...... DLB-187
de Graff, Robert 1895-1981 .... Y-81
de Graft, Joe 1924-1978 .... DLB-117
De Heinrico circa 980? DLB-148
Deighton, Len 1929- DLB-87; CDBLB-8
DeJong, Meindert 1906-1991 .... DLB-52
Dekker, Thomas
 circa 1572-1632 ..... DLB-62, 172; CDBLB-1
Delacorte, George T., Jr. 1894-1991...... DLB-91
Delafield, E. M. 1890-1943 .... DLB-34
Delahaye, Guy (Guillaume Lahaise)
 1888-1969..................... DLB-92
de la Mare, Walter 1873-1956
 .... DLB-19, 153, 162, 255; CDBLB-6
Deland, Margaret 1857-1945 .... DLB-78
Delaney, Shelagh 1939- DLB-13; CDBLB-8
Delano, Amasa 1763-1823 .... DLB-183
Delany, Martin Robinson 1812-1885..... DLB-50
Delany, Samuel R. 1942- DLB-8, 33
de la Roche, Mazo 1879-1961........... DLB-68

Delavigne, Jean François Casimir
 1793-1843..................... DLB-192
Delbanco, Nicholas 1942- DLB-6, 234
Delblanc, Sven 1931-1992 .... DLB-257
Del Castillo, Ramón 1949- DLB-209
Deledda, Grazia 1871-1936............ DLB-264
De León, Nephtal 1945- DLB-82
Delfini, Antonio 1907-1963............ DLB-264
Delgado, Abelardo Barrientos 1931- DLB-82
Del Giudice, Daniele 1949- DLB-196
De Libero, Libero 1906-1981 .... DLB-114
DeLillo, Don 1936- DLB-6, 173
de Lint, Charles 1951- DLB-251
de Lisser H. G. 1878-1944 ....DLB-117
Dell, Floyd 1887-1969................. DLB-9
Dell Publishing Company DLB-46
delle Grazie, Marie Eugene 1864-1931.... DLB-81
Deloney, Thomas died 1600 .... DLB-167
Deloria, Ella C. 1889-1971 ....DLB-175
Deloria, Vine, Jr. 1933- DLB-175
del Rey, Lester 1915-1993 .... DLB-8
Del Vecchio, John M. 1947- DS-9
Del'vig, Anton Antonovich 1798-1831 ... DLB-205
de Man, Paul 1919-1983 .... DLB-67
DeMarinis, Rick 1934- DLB-218
Demby, William 1922- DLB-33
De Mille, James 1833-1880......... DLB-99, 251
de Mille, William 1878-1955........... DLB-266
Deming, Philander 1829-1915 .... DLB-74
Deml, Jakub 1878-1961............... DLB-215
Demorest, William Jennings 1822-1895... DLB-79
De Morgan, William 1839-1917........ DLB-153
Demosthenes 384 B.C.-322 B.C. DLB-176
Denham, Henry [publishing house] DLB-170
Denham, Sir John 1615-1669 .... DLB-58, 126
Denison, Merrill 1893-1975 .... DLB-92
Denison, T. S., and Company DLB-49
Dennery, Adolphe Philippe 1811-1899... DLB-192
Dennie, Joseph 1768-1812...... DLB-37, 43, 59, 73
Dennis, C. J. 1876-1938 .... DLB-260
Dennis, John 1658-1734 .... DLB-101
Dennis, Nigel 1912-1989 .... DLB-13, 15, 233
Denslow, W. W. 1856-1915 .... DLB-188
Dent, J. M., and Sons DLB-112
Dent, Tom 1932-1998 .... DLB-38
Denton, Daniel circa 1626-1703 .... DLB-24
DePaola, Tomie 1934- DLB-61
Department of Library, Archives, and Institutional
 Research, American Bible Society Y-97
De Quille, Dan 1829-1898 .... DLB-186
De Quincey, Thomas
 1785-1859........ DLB-110, 144; CDBLB-3
"Rhetoric" (1828; revised, 1859)
 [excerpt]..................... DLB-57
Derby, George Horatio 1823-1861....... DLB-11

Derby, J. C., and Company DLB-49
Derby and Miller DLB-49
De Ricci, Seymour 1881-1942 .... DLB-201
Derleth, August 1909-1971.........DLB-9; DS-17
Derrida, Jacques 1930- DLB-242
The Derrydale Press.................. DLB-46
Derzhavin, Gavriil Romanovich
 1743-1816..................... DLB-150
Desai, Anita 1937- DLB-271
Desaulniers, Gonzalve 1863-1934 .... DLB-92
Desbordes-Valmore, Marceline
 1786-1859.....................DLB-217
Descartes, René 1596-1650 ....DLB-268
Deschamps, Emile 1791-1871 ....DLB-217
Deschamps, Eustache 1340?-1404 ...... DLB-208
Desbiens, Jean-Paul 1927- DLB-53
des Forêts, Louis-Rene 1918- DLB-83
Desiato, Luca 1941- DLB-196
Desjardins, Marie-Catherine
 (see Villedieu, Madame de)
Desnica, Vladan 1905-1967 .... DLB-181
Desnos, Robert 1900-1945 .... DLB-258
DesRochers, Alfred 1901-1978.......... DLB-68
Desrosiers, Léo-Paul 1896-1967 .... DLB-68
Dessaulles, Louis-Antoine 1819-1895..... DLB-99
Dessì, Giuseppe 1909-1977............DLB-177
Destouches, Louis-Ferdinand
 (see Céline, Louis-Ferdinand)
DeSylva, Buddy 1895-1950 and
 Brown, Lew 1893-1958 .... DLB-265
De Tabley, Lord 1835-1895............ DLB-35
Deutsch, André, Limited DLB-112
Deutsch, Babette 1895-1982........... DLB-45
Deutsch, Niklaus Manuel (see Manuel, Niklaus)
Devanny, Jean 1894-1962............. DLB-260
Deveaux, Alexis 1948- DLB-38
The Development of the Author's Copyright
 in Britain DLB-154
The Development of Lighting in the Staging
 of Drama, 1900-1945 .... DLB-10
"The Development of Meiji Japan" DLB-180
De Vere, Aubrey 1814-1902............ DLB-35
Devereux, second Earl of Essex, Robert
 1565-1601 .... DLB-136
The Devin-Adair Company DLB-46
De Vinne, Theodore Low
 1828-1914 ....DLB-187
Devlin, Anne 1951- DLB-245
De Voto, Bernard 1897-1955 .... DLB-9, 256
De Vries, Peter 1910-1993 ....DLB-6; Y-82
Dewart, Edward Hartley 1828-1903 ..... DLB-99
Dewdney, Christopher 1951- DLB-60
Dewdney, Selwyn 1909-1979 .... DLB-68
Dewey, John 1859-1952...........DLB-246, 270
Dewey, Orville 1794-1882 .... DLB-243
Dewey, Thomas B. 1915-1981 .... DLB-226
DeWitt, Robert M., Publisher DLB-49

DeWolfe, Fiske and Company DLB-49
Dexter, Colin 1930- DLB-87
de Young, M. H. 1849-1925 ....DLB-25
Dhlomo, H. I. E. 1903-1956 ...... DLB-157, 225
Dhuoda circa 803-after 843 ....DLB-148
The Dial 1840-1844 ....DLB-223
The Dial Press DLB-46
Diamond, I. A. L. 1920-1988 ....DLB-26
Dibble, L. Grace 1902-1998...........DLB-204
Dibdin, Thomas Frognall
 1776-1847......................DLB-184
Di Cicco, Pier Giorgio 1949- DLB-60
Dick, Philip K. 1928-1982 ....DLB-8
Dick and Fitzgerald DLB-49
Dickens, Charles 1812-1870
 ....DLB-21, 55, 70, 159, 166; CDBLB-4
Dickey, James 1923-1997
 .... DLB-5, 193; Y-82, Y-93, Y-96;
 DS-7, DS-19; CDALB-6
James Dickey and Stanley
 Burnshaw Correspondence............ Y-02
James Dickey Tributes................... Y-97
The Life of James Dickey: A Lecture to
 the Friends of the Emory Libraries,
 by Henry Hart Y-98
Dickey, William 1928-1994..............DLB-5
Dickinson, Emily
 1830-1886..........DLB-1, 243; CDWLB-3
Dickinson, John 1732-1808 ....DLB-31
Dickinson, Jonathan 1688-1747 ....DLB-24
Dickinson, Patric 1914- DLB-27
Dickinson, Peter 1927- DLB-87, 161, 276
Dicks, John [publishing house].........DLB-106
Dickson, Gordon R. 1923- DLB-8
Dictionary of Literary Biography Yearbook Awards
 .Y-92, Y-93, Y-97, Y-98, Y-99, Y-00, Y-01, Y-02
The Dictionary of National Biography........DLB-144
Didion, Joan 1934-
 .... DLB-2, 173, 185; Y-81, Y-86; CDALB-6
Di Donato, Pietro 1911- DLB-9
Die Fürstliche Bibliothek Corvey........... Y-96
Diego, Gerardo 1896-1987.............DLB-134
Dietz, Howard 1896-1983 ....DLB-265
Digby, Everard 1550?-1605............DLB-281
Digges, Thomas circa 1546-1595........DLB-136
The Digital Millennium Copyright Act:
 Expanding Copyright Protection in
 Cyberspace and Beyond Y-98
Diktonius, Elmer 1896-1961 ....DLB-259
Dillard, Annie 1945- DLB-275, 278; Y-80
Dillard, R. H. W. 1937- DLB-5, 244
Dillingham, Charles T., Company DLB-49
The Dillingham, G. W., Company DLB-49
Dilly, Edward and Charles
 [publishing house] DLB-154
Dilthey, Wilhelm 1833-1911 ....DLB-129
Dimitrova, Blaga 1922- ...DLB-181; CDWLB-4
Dimov, Dimitr 1909-1966 ....DLB-181

Dimsdale, Thomas J. 1831?-1866 ....DLB-186
Dinescu, Mircea 1950- DLB-232
Dinesen, Isak (see Blixen, Karen)
Dingelstedt, Franz von 1814-1881 ....DLB-133
Dintenfass, Mark 1941- Y-84
Diogenes, Jr. (see Brougham, John)
Diogenes Laertius circa 200............DLB-176
DiPrima, Diane 1934- DLB-5, 16
Disch, Thomas M. 1940- DLB-8, 282
Diski, Jenny 1947- DLB-271
Disney, Walt 1901-1966 ....DLB-22
Disraeli, Benjamin 1804-1881 ....DLB-21, 55
D'Israeli, Isaac 1766-1848 ....DLB-107
DLB Award for Distinguished
 Literary Criticism Y-02
Ditlevsen, Tove 1917-1976.............DLB-214
Ditzen, Rudolf (see Fallada, Hans)
Dix, Dorothea Lynde 1802-1887......DLB-1, 235
Dix, Dorothy (see Gilmer, Elizabeth Meriwether)
Dix, Edwards and Company............DLB-49
Dix, Gertrude circa 1874-?.............DLB-197
Dixie, Florence Douglas 1857-1905 ......DLB-174
Dixon, Ella Hepworth
 1855 or 1857-1932................DLB-197
Dixon, Paige (see Corcoran, Barbara)
Dixon, Richard Watson 1833-1900.......DLB-19
Dixon, Stephen 1936- DLB-130
DLB Award for Distinguished
 Literary Criticism Y-02
Dmitriev, Ivan Ivanovich 1760-1837 .....DLB-150
Do They Or Don't They?
 Writers Reading Book Reviews Y-01
Dobell, Bertram 1842-1914 ....DLB-184
Dobell, Sydney 1824-1874.............DLB-32
Dobie, J. Frank 1888-1964.............DLB-212
Döblin, Alfred 1878-1957.....DLB-66; CDWLB-2
Dobroliubov, Nikolai Aleksandrovich
 1836-1861 ....DLB-277
Dobson, Austin 1840-1921 ....DLB-35, 144
Dobson, Rosemary 1920- DLB-260
Doctorow, E. L.
 1931- DLB-2, 28, 173; Y-80; CDALB-6
Documents on Sixteenth-Century
 Literature DLB-167, 172
Dodd, Anne [publishing house].........DLB-154
Dodd, Mead and Company............DLB-49
Dodd, Susan M. 1946- DLB-244
Dodd, William E. 1869-1940...........DLB-17
Doderer, Heimito von 1896-1966 ....DLB-85
Dodge, B. W., and Company DLB-46
Dodge, Mary Abigail 1833-1896 ....DLB-221
Dodge, Mary Mapes
 1831?-1905 .... DLB-42, 79; DS 13
Dodge Publishing Company DLB-49
Dodgson, Charles Lutwidge (see Carroll, Lewis)
Dodsley, R. [publishing house] DLB-154
Dodsley, Robert 1703-1764 ....DLB-95

Dodson, Owen 1914-1983..............DLB-76
Dodwell, Christina 1951- DLB-204
Doesticks, Q. K. Philander, P. B.
 (see Thomson, Mortimer)
Doheny, Carrie Estelle 1875-1958.......DLB-140
Doherty, John 1798?-1854.............DLB-190
Doig, Ivan 1939- DLB-206
Doinaș, Ștefan Augustin 1922- DLB-232
Domínguez, Sylvia Maida 1935- DLB-122
Donaghy, Michael 1954- DLB-282
Donahoe, Patrick [publishing house]......DLB-49
Donald, David H. 1920- DLB-17
The Practice of Biography VI: An
 Interview with David Herbert Donald Y-87
Donaldson, Scott 1928- DLB-111
Doni, Rodolfo 1919- DLB-177
Donleavy, J. P. 1926- DLB-6, 173
Donnadieu, Marguerite (see Duras, Marguerite)
Donne, John
 1572-1631 ....DLB-121, 151; CDBLB-1
Donnelley, R. R., and Sons Company.....DLB-49
Donnelly, Ignatius 1831-1901 ....DLB-12
Donoghue, Emma 1969- DLB-267
Donohue and Henneberry.............DLB-49
Donoso, José 1924-1996 .... DLB-113; CDWLB-3
Doolady, M. [publishing house].........DLB-49
Dooley, Ebon (see Ebon)
Doolittle, Hilda 1886-1961 ....DLB-4, 45
Doplicher, Fabio 1938- DLB-128
Dor, Milo 1923- DLB-85
Doran, George H., Company DLB-46
Dorgelès, Roland 1886-1973 ....DLB-65
Dorn, Edward 1929-1999 ....DLB-5
Dorr, Rheta Childe 1866-1948 ....DLB-25
Dorris, Michael 1945-1997 ....DLB-175
Dorset and Middlesex, Charles Sackville,
 Lord Buckhurst, Earl of 1643-1706 ....DLB-131
Dorsey, Candas Jane 1952- DLB-251
Dorst, Tankred 1925- DLB-75, 124
Dos Passos, John 1896-1970
 ...... DLB-4, 9, 274; DS-1, DS-15; CDALB-5
John Dos Passos: Artist Y-99
John Dos Passos: A Centennial
 Commemoration.................... Y-96
Dostoevsky, Fyodor 1821-1881........DLB-238
Doubleday and Company.............DLB-49
Dougall, Lily 1858-1923 ....DLB-92
Doughty, Charles M.
 1843-1926.................DLB-19, 57, 174
Douglas, Lady Alfred (see Custance, Olive)
Douglas, Gavin 1476-1522.............DLB-132
Douglas, Keith 1920-1944 ....DLB-27
Douglas, Norman 1868-1952.........DLB-34, 195
Douglass, Frederick 1818-1895
 ....DLB-1, 43, 50, 79, 243; CDALB-2
Frederick Douglass Creative Arts CenterY-01
Douglass, William circa 1691-1752 ....DLB-24

Cumulative Index

Dourado, Autran 1926- DLB-145
Dove, Arthur G. 1880-1946 .... DLB-188
Dove, Rita 1952- DLB-120; CDALB-7
Dover Publications DLB-46
Doves Press DLB-112
Dowden, Edward 1843-1913 .... DLB-35, 149
Dowell, Coleman 1925-1985 .... DLB-130
Dowland, John 1563-1626 .... DLB-172
Downes, Gwladys 1915- DLB-88
Downing, J., Major (see Davis, Charles A.)
Downing, Major Jack (see Smith, Seba)
Dowriche, Anne
    before 1560-after 1613 .... DLB-172
Dowson, Ernest 1867-1900 .... DLB-19, 135
Doxey, William [publishing house] DLB-49
Doyle, Sir Arthur Conan
    1859-1930 ...DLB-18, 70, 156, 178; CDBLB-5
Doyle, Kirby 1932- DLB-16
Doyle, Roddy 1958- DLB-194
Drabble, Margaret
    1939- DLB-14, 155, 231; CDBLB-8
Drach, Albert 1902- DLB-85
Dragojević, Danijel 1934- DLB-181
Drake, Samuel Gardner 1798-1875 ...... DLB-187
The Dramatic Publishing Company DLB-49
Dramatists Play Service DLB-46
Drant, Thomas early 1540s?-1578 ...... DLB-167
Draper, John W. 1811-1882 .... DLB-30
Draper, Lyman C. 1815-1891 .... DLB-30
Drayton, Michael 1563-1631 .... DLB-121
Dreiser, Theodore 1871-1945
    .... DLB-9, 12, 102, 137; DS-1; CDALB-3
Dresser, Davis 1904-1977 .... DLB-226
Drewitz, Ingeborg 1923-1986 .... DLB-75
Drieu La Rochelle, Pierre 1893-1945 ..... DLB-72
Drinker, Elizabeth 1735-1807 .... DLB-200
Drinkwater, John
    1882-1937 ....DLB-10, 19, 149
Droste-Hülshoff, Annette von
    1797-1848 .... DLB-133; CDWLB-2
The Drue Heinz Literature Prize
    Excerpt from "Excerpts from a Report
    of the Commission," in David
    Bosworth's *The Death of Descartes*
    An Interview with David Bosworth Y-82
Drummond, William, of Hawthornden
    1585-1649 .... DLB-121, 213
Drummond, William Henry
    1854-1907 .... DLB-92
Druzhinin, Aleksandr Vasil'evich
    1824-1864 .... DLB-238
Dryden, Charles 1860?-1931 .... DLB-171
Dryden, John
    1631-1700 ...... DLB-80, 101, 131; CDBLB-2
Držić, Marin
    circa 1508-1567 .... DLB-147; CDWLB-4
Duane, William 1760-1835 .... DLB-43
Dubé, Marcel 1930- DLB-53
Dubé, Rodolphe (see Hertel, François)

Dubie, Norman 1945- DLB-120
Dubin, Al 1891-1945 .... DLB-265
Dubois, Silvia
    1788 or 1789?-1889 .... DLB-239
Du Bois, W. E. B.
    1868-1963 ....DLB-47, 50, 91, 246; CDALB-3
Du Bois, William Pène 1916-1993 ...... DLB-61
Dubrovina, Ekaterina Oskarovna
    1846-1913 .... DLB-238
Dubus, Andre 1936-1999 .... DLB-130
Ducange, Victor 1783-1833 .... DLB-192
Du Chaillu, Paul Belloni 1831?-1903 .... DLB-189
Ducharme, Réjean 1941- DLB-60
Dučić, Jovan
    1871-1943 ....DLB-147; CDWLB-4
Duck, Stephen 1705?-1756 .... DLB-95
Duckworth, Gerald, and Company
    Limited DLB-112
Duclaux, Madame Mary (see Robinson, A. Mary F.)
Dudek, Louis 1918- DLB-88
Duell, Sloan and Pearce DLB-46
Duerer, Albrecht 1471-1528 ....DLB-179
Duff Gordon, Lucie 1821-1869 .... DLB-166
Dufferin, Helen Lady, Countess of Gifford
    1807-1867 .... DLB-199
Duffield and Green DLB-46
Duffy, Maureen 1933- DLB-14
Dufief, Nicholas Gouin 1776-1834 ...... DLB-187
Dugan, Alan 1923- DLB-5
Dugard, William 1606-1662 ....DLB-170, 281
Dugard, William [publishing house] DLB-170
Dugas, Marcel 1883-1947 .... DLB-92
Dugdale, William [publishing house] DLB-106
Duhamel, Georges 1884-1966 .... DLB-65
Dujardin, Edouard 1861-1949 .... DLB-123
Dukes, Ashley 1885-1959 .... DLB-10
Dumas, Alexandre *père* 1802-1870 ..... DLB-119, 192
Dumas, Alexandre *fils*
    1824-1895 .... DLB-192
Dumas, Henry 1934-1968 .... DLB-41
du Maurier, Daphne 1907-1989 .... DLB-191
Du Maurier, George
    1834-1896 ....DLB-153, 178
Dummett, Michael 1925- DLB-262
Dunbar, Paul Laurence
    1872-1906 .... DLB-50, 54, 78; CDALB-3
Dunbar, William
    circa 1460-circa 1522 .... DLB-132, 146
Duncan, Dave 1933- DLB-251
Duncan, David James 1952- DLB-256
Duncan, Norman 1871-1916 .... DLB-92
Duncan, Quince 1940- DLB-145
Duncan, Robert 1919-1988 .... DLB-5, 16, 193
Duncan, Ronald 1914-1982 .... DLB-13
Duncan, Sara Jeannette 1861-1922 .... DLB-92
Dunigan, Edward, and Brother DLB-49
Dunlap, John 1747-1812 .... DLB-43

Dunlap, William 1766-1839 ....DLB-30, 37, 59
Dunlop, William "Tiger" 1792-1848 ..... DLB-99
Dunmore, Helen 1952- DLB-267
Dunn, Douglas 1942- DLB-40
Dunn, Harvey Thomas 1884-1952 ..... DLB-188
Dunn, Stephen 1939- DLB-105
"The Good, The Not So Good" DLB-105
Dunne, Finley Peter 1867-1936 .... DLB-11, 23
Dunne, John Gregory 1932- Y-80
Dunne, Philip 1908-1992 .... DLB-26
Dunning, Ralph Cheever 1878-1930 ...... DLB-4
Dunning, William A. 1857-1922 ....DLB-17
Dunsany, Lord (Edward John Moreton
    Drax Plunkett, Baron Dunsany)
    1878-1957 .... DLB-10, 77, 153, 156, 255
Duns Scotus, John
    circa 1266-1308 .... DLB-115
Dunton, John [publishing house] DLB-170
Dunton, W. Herbert 1878-1936 .... DLB-188
Dupin, Amantine-Aurore-Lucile (see Sand, George)
Dupuy, Eliza Ann 1814-1880 .... DLB-248
Durack, Mary 1913-1994 .... DLB-260
Durand, Lucile (see Bersianik, Louky)
Duranti, Francesca 1935- DLB-196
Duranty, Walter 1884-1957 .... DLB-29
Duras, Marguerite 1914-1996 .... DLB-83
Durfey, Thomas 1653-1723 .... DLB-80
Durova, Nadezhda Andreevna
    (Aleksandr Andreevich Aleksandrov)
    1783-1866 .... DLB-198
Durrell, Lawrence 1912-1990
    .... DLB-15, 27, 204; Y-90; CDBLB-7
Durrell, William [publishing house] DLB-49
Dürrenmatt, Friedrich
    1921-1990 ....DLB-69, 124; CDWLB-2
Duston, Hannah 1657-1737 .... DLB-200
Dutt, Toru 1856-1877 .... DLB-240
Dutton, E. P., and Company DLB-49
Duvoisin, Roger 1904-1980 .... DLB-61
Duyckinck, Evert Augustus
    1816-1878 .... DLB-3, 64, 250
Duyckinck, George L.
    1823-1863 .... DLB-3, 250
Duyckinck and Company DLB-49
Dwight, John Sullivan 1813-1893 ..... DLB-1, 235
Dwight, Timothy 1752-1817 .... DLB-37
Dybek, Stuart 1942- DLB-130
Dyer, Charles 1928- DLB-13
Dyer, Sir Edward 1543-1607 .... DLB-136
Dyer, George 1755-1841 .... DLB-93
Dyer, John 1699-1757 .... DLB-95
Dyk, Viktor 1877-1931 .... DLB-215
Dylan, Bob 1941- DLB-16

E

Eager, Edward 1911-1964 .... DLB-22
Eagleton, Terry 1943- DLB-242

Eames, Wilberforce 1855-1937 . . . . DLB-140

Earle, Alice Morse 1853-1911 . . . . DLB-221

Earle, James H., and Company DLB-49

Earle, John 1600 or 1601-1665 . . . . DLB-151

Early American Book Illustration,
by Sinclair Hamilton DLB-49

Eastlake, William 1917-1997 . . . . DLB-6, 206

Eastman, Carol ?- DLB-44

Eastman, Charles A. (Ohiyesa)
1858-1939 . . . . DLB-175

Eastman, Max 1883-1969 . . . . DLB-91

Eaton, Daniel Isaac 1753-1814 . . . . DLB-158

Eaton, Edith Maude 1865-1914 . . . . DLB-221

Eaton, Winnifred 1875-1954 . . . . DLB-221

Eberhart, Richard 1904- DLB-48; CDALB-1

Ebner, Jeannie 1918- DLB-85

Ebner-Eschenbach, Marie von
1830-1916 . . . . DLB-81

Ebon 1942- DLB-41

E-Books' Second Act in Libraries Y-02

E-Books Turn the Corner Y-98

Ecbasis Captivi circa 1045 . . . . DLB-148

Ecco Press DLB-46

Eckhart, Meister circa 1260-circa 1328 . . . DLB-115

The Eclectic Review 1805-1868 . . . . DLB-110

Eco, Umberto 1932- DLB-196, 242

Eddison, E. R. 1882-1945 . . . . DLB-255

Edel, Leon 1907-1997 . . . . DLB-103

Edelfeldt, Inger 1956- DLB-257

A Century of Poetry, a Lifetime of Collecting:
J. M. Edelstein's Collection of Twentieth-
Century American Poetry Y-02

Edes, Benjamin 1732-1803 . . . . DLB-43

Edgar, David 1948- DLB-13, 233

Edgerton, Clyde 1944- DLB-278

Edgeworth, Maria
1768-1849 . . . . DLB-116, 159, 163

The Edinburgh Review 1802-1929 . . . . DLB-110

Edinburgh University Press DLB-112

The Editor Publishing Company DLB-49

Editorial Institute at Boston University Y-00

Editorial Statements DLB-137

Editorial: The Extension of Copyright Y-02

Edmonds, Randolph 1900- DLB-51

Edmonds, Walter D. 1903-1998 . . . . DLB-9

Edric, Robert (see Armitage, G. E.)

Edschmid, Kasimir 1890-1966 . . . . DLB-56

Edson, Margaret 1961- DLB-266

Edson, Russell 1935- DLB-244

Edwards, Amelia Anne Blandford
1831-1892 . . . . DLB-174

Edwards, Dic 1953- DLB-245

Edwards, Edward 1812-1886 . . . . DLB-184

Edwards, James [publishing house] DLB-154

Edwards, Jonathan 1703-1758 . . . . . . DLB-24, 270

Edwards, Jonathan, Jr. 1745-1801 . . . . DLB-37

Edwards, Junius 1929- DLB-33

Edwards, Matilda Barbara Betham
1836-1919 . . . . DLB-174

Edwards, Richard 1524-1566 . . . . DLB-62

Edwards, Sarah Pierpont 1710-1758 . . . . . DLB-200

Effinger, George Alec 1947- DLB-8

Egerton, George 1859-1945 . . . . DLB-135

Eggleston, Edward 1837-1902 . . . . DLB-12

Eggleston, Wilfred 1901-1986 . . . . DLB-92

Eglītis, Anšlavs 1906-1993 . . . . DLB-220

Ehrenreich, Barbara 1941- DLB-246

Ehrenstein, Albert 1886-1950 . . . . DLB-81

Ehrhart, W. D. 1948- DS-9

Ehrlich, Gretel 1946- DLB-212, 275

Eich, Günter 1907-1972 . . . . DLB-69, 124

Eichendorff, Joseph Freiherr von
1788-1857 . . . . DLB-90

Eifukumon'in 1271-1342 . . . . DLB-203

1873 Publishers' Catalogues DLB-49

Eighteenth-Century Aesthetic
Theories DLB-31

Eighteenth-Century Philosophical
Background DLB-31

Eigner, Larry 1926-1996 . . . . DLB-5, 193

Eikon Basilike 1649 . . . . DLB-151

Eilhart von Oberge
circa 1140-circa 1195 . . . . DLB-148

Einhard circa 770-840 . . . . DLB-148

Eiseley, Loren 1907-1977 . . . . DLB-275, DS-17

Eisenberg, Deborah 1945- DLB-244

Eisenreich, Herbert 1925-1986 . . . . DLB-85

Eisner, Kurt 1867-1919 . . . . DLB-66

Ekelöf, Gunnar 1907-1968 . . . . DLB-259

Eklund, Gordon 1945- Y-83

Ekman, Kerstin 1933- DLB-257

Ekwensi, Cyprian
1921- DLB-117; CDWLB-3

Elaw, Zilpha circa 1790-? DLB-239

Eld, George [publishing house] DLB-170

Elder, Lonne, III 1931- DLB-7, 38, 44

Elder, Paul, and Company DLB-49

The Electronic Text Center and the Electronic
Archive of Early American Fiction at the
University of Virginia Library Y-98

Eliade, Mircea 1907-1986 . . . . DLB-220; CDWLB-4

Elie, Robert 1915-1973 . . . . DLB-88

Elin Pelin 1877-1949 . . . . DLB-147; CDWLB-4

Eliot, George
1819-1880 . . . . DLB-21, 35, 55; CDBLB-4

Eliot, John 1604-1690 . . . . DLB-24

Eliot, T. S. 1888-1965
. . . . DLB-7, 10, 45, 63, 245; CDALB-5

T. S. Eliot Centennial Y-88

Eliot's Court Press DLB-170

Elizabeth I 1533-1603 . . . . DLB-136

Elizabeth of Nassau-Saarbrücken
after 1393-1456 . . . . DLB-179

Elizondo, Salvador 1932- DLB-145

Elizondo, Sergio 1930- DLB-82

Elkin, Stanley
1930-1995 . . . . . . DLB-2, 28, 218, 278; Y-80

Elles, Dora Amy (see Wentworth, Patricia)

Ellet, Elizabeth F. 1818?-1877 . . . . DLB-30

Elliot, Ebenezer 1781-1849 . . . . DLB-96, 190

Elliot, Frances Minto (Dickinson)
1820-1898 . . . . DLB-166

Elliott, Charlotte 1789-1871 . . . . DLB-199

Elliott, George 1923- DLB-68

Elliott, George P. 1918-1980 . . . . DLB-244

Elliott, Janice 1931- DLB-14

Elliott, Sarah Barnwell 1848-1928 . . . . . . DLB-221

Elliott, Thomes and Talbot DLB-49

Elliott, William, III 1788-1863 . . . . DLB-3, 248

Ellis, Alice Thomas (Anna Margaret Haycraft)
1932- DLB-194

Ellis, Edward S. 1840-1916 . . . . DLB-42

Ellis, Frederick Staridge
[publishing house] DLB-106

The George H. Ellis Company DLB-49

Ellis, Havelock 1859-1939 . . . . DLB-190

Ellison, Harlan 1934- DLB-8

Ellison, Ralph
1914-1994 . . . DLB-2, 76, 227; Y-94; CDALB-1

Ellmann, Richard 1918-1987 . . . . . . DLB-103; Y-87

Ellroy, James 1948- DLB-226; Y-91

Eluard, Paul 1895-1952 . . . . DLB-258

Elyot, Thomas 1490?-1546 . . . . DLB-136

Emanuel, James Andrew 1921- DLB-41

Emecheta, Buchi 1944- . . . DLB-117; CDWLB-3

Emendations for Look Homeward, Angel Y-00

The Emergence of Black Women Writers . . . DS-8

Emerson, Ralph Waldo 1803-1882
. . . . . DLB-1, 59, 73, 183, 223, 270; CDALB-2

Ralph Waldo Emerson in 1982 . . . . Y-82

Emerson, William 1769-1811 . . . . DLB-37

Emerson, William 1923-1997 . . . . Y-97

Emin, Fedor Aleksandrovich
circa 1735-1770 . . . . DLB-150

Emmanuel, Pierre 1916-1984 . . . . DLB-258

Empedocles fifth century B.C. DLB-176

Empson, William 1906-1984 . . . . DLB-20

Enchi Fumiko 1905-1986 . . . . DLB-182

"Encounter with the West" DLB-180

The End of English Stage Censorship,
1945-1968 . . . . DLB-13

Ende, Michael 1929-1995 . . . . DLB-75

Endō Shūsaku 1923-1996 . . . . DLB-182

Engel, Marian 1933-1985 . . . . DLB-53

Engel'gardt, Sof'ia Vladimirovna
1828-1894 . . . . DLB-277

Engels, Friedrich 1820-1895 . . . . DLB-129

Engle, Paul 1908- DLB-48

English, Thomas Dunn 1819-1902 . . . . . . DLB-202

English Composition and Rhetoric (1866),
by Alexander Bain [excerpt] DLB-57

The English Language: 410 to 1500..... DLB-146
Ennius 239 B.C.-169 B.C............. DLB-211
Enquist, Per Olov 1934-............ DLB-257
Enright, Anne 1962-................ DLB-267
Enright, D. J. 1920-................ DLB-27
Enright, Elizabeth 1909-1968.......... DLB-22
Epic and Beast Epic................ DLB-208
Epictetus circa 55-circa 125-130........DLB-176
Epicurus 342/341 B.C.-271/270 B.C......DLB-176
Epps, Bernard 1936-................ DLB-53
Epstein, Julius 1909- and
    Epstein, Philip 1909-1952........... DLB-26
Equiano, Olaudah
    circa 1745-1797........ DLB-37, 50; DWLB-3
Olaudah Equiano and Unfinished Journeys:
    The Slave-Narrative Tradition and
    Twentieth-Century Continuities, by
    Paul Edwards and Pauline T.
    Wangman.................... DLB-117
The E-Researcher: Possibilities and Pitfalls... Y-00
Eragny Press..................... DLB-112
Erasmus, Desiderius 1467-1536......... DLB-136
Erba, Luciano 1922-................ DLB-128
Erdman, Nikolai Robertovich
    1900-1970..................... DLB-272
Erdrich, Louise
    1954-........DLB-152, 175, 206; CDALB-7
Erenburg, Il'ia Grigor'evich 1891-1967.. DLB-272
Erichsen-Brown, Gwethalyn Graham
    (see Graham, Gwethalyn)
Eriugena, John Scottus circa 810-877.... DLB-115
Ernst, Paul 1866-1933............. DLB-66, 118
Ershov, Petr Pavlovich 1815-1869...... DLB-205
Erskine, Albert 1911-1993................Y-93
Erskine, John 1879-1951............DLB-9, 102
Erskine, Mrs. Steuart ?-1948........... DLB-195
Ertel', Aleksandr Ivanovich
    1855-1908..................... DLB-238
Ervine, St. John Greer 1883-1971........ DLB-10
Eschenburg, Johann Joachim 1743-1820... DLB-97
Escoto, Julio 1944-................. DLB-145
Esdaile, Arundell 1880-1956........... DLB-201
Eshleman, Clayton 1935-............... DLB-5
Espaillat, Rhina P. 1932-............. DLB-282
Espriu, Salvador 1913-1985............ DLB-134
Ess Ess Publishing Company.......... DLB-49
Essex House Press.................. DLB-112
Esson, Louis 1878-1993............... DLB-260
Essop, Ahmed 1931-................. DLB-225
Esterházy, Péter 1950-.... DLB-232; CDWLB-4
Estes, Eleanor 1906-1988............. DLB-22
Estes and Lauriat................... DLB-49
Estleman, Loren D. 1952-............. DLB-226
Eszterhas, Joe 1944-................. DLB-185
Etherege, George 1636-circa 1692....... DLB-80
Ethridge, Mark, Sr. 1896-1981......... DLB-127
Ets, Marie Hall 1893-................ DLB-22

Etter, David 1928-................. DLB-105
Ettner, Johann Christoph 1654-1724.... DLB-168
Eudora Welty Remembered in Two Exhibits. Y-02
Eugene Gant's Projected Works........... Y-01
Eupolemius flourished circa 1095....... DLB-148
Euripides circa 484 B.C.-407/406 B.C.
    ....DLB-176; CDWLB-1
Evans, Augusta Jane 1835-1909........ DLB-239
Evans, Caradoc 1878-1945............ DLB-162
Evans, Charles 1850-1935............ DLB-187
Evans, Donald 1884-1921.............. DLB-54
Evans, George Henry 1805-1856........ DLB-43
Evans, Hubert 1892-1986.............. DLB-92
Evans, M., and Company............. DLB-46
Evans, Mari 1923-................... DLB-41
Evans, Mary Ann (see Eliot, George)
Evans, Nathaniel 1742-1767........... DLB-31
Evans, Sebastian 1830-1909........... DLB-35
Evans, Ray 1915- and
    Livingston, Jay 1915-2001......... DLB-265
Evaristi, Marcella 1953-............. DLB-233
Everett, Alexander Hill 1790-1847...... DLB-59
Everett, Edward 1794-1865...... DLB-1, 59, 235
Everson, R. G. 1903-................ DLB-88
Everson, William 1912-1994..... DLB-5, 16, 212
Ewart, Gavin 1916-1995.............. DLB-40
Ewing, Juliana Horatia 1841-1885... DLB-21, 163
The Examiner 1808-1881............. DLB-110
Exley, Frederick 1929-1992........DLB-143; Y-81
Editorial: The Extension of Copyright....... Y-02
von Eyb, Albrecht 1420-1475.........DLB-179
Eyre and Spottiswoode.............. DLB-106
Ezera, Regīna 1930-................. DLB-232
Ezzo ?-after 1065................... DLB-148

F

Faber, Frederick William 1814-1863..... DLB-32
Faber and Faber Limited............. DLB-112
Faccio, Rena (see Aleramo, Sibilla)
Fadeev, Aleksandr Aleksandrovich
    1901-1956.....................DLB-272
Fagundo, Ana María 1938-.......... DLB-134
Fainzil'berg, Il'ia Arnol'dovich
    (see Il'f, Il'ia and Evgenii Petrov)
Fair, Ronald L. 1932-................ DLB-33
Fairfax, Beatrice (see Manning, Marie)
Fairlie, Gerard 1899-1983............. DLB-77
Fallada, Hans 1893-1947.............. DLB-56
Fancher, Betsy 1928-.................. Y-83
Fane, Violet 1843-1905............... DLB-35
Fanfrolico Press................... DLB-112
Fanning, Katherine 1927............ DLB-127
Fanshawe, Sir Richard 1608-1666...... DLB-126
Fantasy Press Publishers.............. DLB-46
Fante, John 1909-1983............DLB-130; Y-83

Al-Farabi circa 870-950.............. DLB-115
Farabough, Laura 1949-............. DLB-228
Farah, Nuruddin 1945-....DLB-125; CDWLB-3
Farber, Norma 1909-1984............. DLB-61
Fargue, Léon-Paul 1876-1947......... DLB-258
Farigoule, Louis (see Romains, Jules)
Farjeon, Eleanor 1881-1965.......... DLB-160
Farley, Harriet 1812-1907............ DLB-239
Farley, Walter 1920-1989............. DLB-22
Farmborough, Florence 1887-1978..... DLB-204
Farmer, Penelope 1939-.............. DLB-161
Farmer, Philip José 1918-.............. DLB-8
Farnaby, Thomas 1575?-1647......... DLB-236
Farningham, Marianne (see Hearn, Mary Anne)
Farquhar, George circa 1677-1707....... DLB-84
Farquharson, Martha (see Finley, Martha)
Farrar, Frederic William 1831-1903..... DLB-163
Farrar and Rinehart................. DLB-46
Farrar, Straus and Giroux............. DLB-46
Farrell, J. G. 1935-1979.............DLB-14, 271
Farrell, James T. 1904-1979... DLB-4, 9, 86; DS-2
Fast, Howard 1914-.................. DLB-9
Faulkner, George [publishing house]..... DLB-154
Faulkner, William 1897-1962
    ....DLB-9, 11, 44, 102; DS-2; Y-86; CDALB-5
William Faulkner Centenary............ Y-97
"Faulkner 100–Celebrating the Work,"
    University of South Carolina, Columbia.. Y-97
Impressions of William Faulkner........... Y-97
Faulkner and Yoknapatawpha Conference,
    Oxford, Mississippi.................. Y-97
Faulks, Sebastian 1953-.............. DLB-207
Fauset, Jessie Redmon 1882-1961........ DLB-51
Faust, Frederick Schiller (Max Brand)
    1892-1944..................... DLB-256
Faust, Irvin 1924-.... DLB-2, 28, 218, 278; Y-80
Fawcett, Edgar 1847-1904............ DLB-202
Fawcett, Millicent Garrett 1847-1929.... DLB-190
Fawcett Books..................... DLB-46
Fay, Theodore Sedgwick 1807-1898..... DLB-202
Fearing, Kenneth 1902-1961............ DLB-9
Federal Writers' Project.............. DLB-46
Federman, Raymond 1928-.............. Y-80
Fedin, Konstantin Aleksandrovich
    1892-1977.....................DLB-272
Fedorov, Innokentii Vasil'evich
    (see Omulevsky, Innokentii Vasil'evich)
Feiffer, Jules 1929-.................DLB-7, 44
Feinberg, Charles E. 1899-1988....DLB-187; Y-88
Feind, Barthold 1678-1721........... DLB-168
Feinstein, Elaine 1930-.............DLB-14, 40
Feirstein, Frederick 1940-............ DLB-282
Feiss, Paul Louis 1875-1952...........DLB-187
Feldman, Irving 1928-............... DLB-169
Felipe, Léon 1884-1968.............. DLB-108
Fell, Frederick, Publishers............. DLB-46

Felltham, Owen 1602?-1668 . . . . DLB-126, 151
Felman, Soshana 1942- DLB-246
Fels, Ludwig 1946- DLB-75
Felton, Cornelius Conway 1807-1862 . . DLB-1, 235
Mothe-Fénelon, François de Salignac de La
   1651-1715 . . . . DLB-268
Fenn, Harry 1837-1911 . . . . DLB-188
Fennario, David 1947- DLB-60
Fenner, Dudley 1558?-1587? DLB-236
Fenno, Jenny 1765?-1803 . . . . DLB-200
Fenno, John 1751-1798 . . . . DLB-43
Fenno, R. F., and Company DLB-49
Fenoglio, Beppe 1922-1963 . . . . DLB-177
Fenton, Geoffrey 1539?-1608 . . . . DLB-136
Fenton, James 1949- DLB-40
The Hemingway/Fenton Correspondence Y-02
Ferber, Edna 1885-1968 . . . . DLB-9, 28, 86, 266
Ferdinand, Vallery, III (see Salaam, Kalamu ya)
Ferguson, Sir Samuel 1810-1886 . . . . DLB-32
Ferguson, William Scott 1875-1954 . . . . . . DLB-47
Fergusson, Robert 1750-1774 . . . . DLB-109
Ferland, Albert 1872-1943 . . . . DLB-92
Ferlinghetti, Lawrence
   1919- DLB-5, 16; CDALB-1
Fermor, Patrick Leigh 1915- DLB-204
Fern, Fanny (see Parton, Sara Payson Willis)
Ferrars, Elizabeth (Morna Doris Brown)
   1907- DLB-87
Ferré, Rosario 1942- DLB-145
Ferret, E., and Company DLB-49
Ferrier, Susan 1782-1854 . . . . DLB-116
Ferril, Thomas Hornsby 1896-1988 . . . . . . DLB-206
Ferrini, Vincent 1913- DLB-48
Ferron, Jacques 1921-1985 . . . . DLB-60
Ferron, Madeleine 1922- DLB-53
Ferrucci, Franco 1936- DLB-196
Fet, Afanasy Afanas'evich (Shenshin)
   1820-1892 . . . . DLB-277
Fetridge and Company DLB-49
Feuchtersleben, Ernst Freiherr von
   1806-1849 . . . . DLB-133
Feuchtwanger, Lion 1884-1958 . . . . DLB-66
Feuerbach, Ludwig 1804-1872 . . . . DLB-133
Feuillet, Octave 1821-1890 . . . . DLB-192
Feydeau, Georges 1862-1921 . . . . DLB-192
Fichte, Johann Gottlieb 1762-1814 . . . . . . DLB-90
Ficke, Arthur Davison 1883-1945 . . . . DLB-54
Fiction Best-Sellers, 1910-1945 . . . . DLB-9
Fiction into Film, 1928-1975: A List of Movies
   Based on the Works of Authors in
   British Novelists, 1930-1959 . . . . DLB-15
Fiedler, Leslie A. 1917- DLB-28, 67
Field, Barron 1789-1846 . . . . DLB-230
Field, Edward 1924- DLB-105
Field, Joseph M. 1810-1856 . . . . DLB-248
Field, Eugene
   1850-1895 . . . . DLB-23, 42, 140; DS-13

Field, John 1545?-1588 . . . . DLB-167
Field, Marshall, III 1893-1956 . . . . DLB-127
Field, Marshall, IV 1916-1965 . . . . DLB-127
Field, Marshall, V 1941- DLB-127
Field, Michael
   (Katherine Harris Bradley [1846-1914]
   and Edith Emma Cooper
   [1862-1913]) DLB-240
"The Poetry File" DLB-105
Field, Nathan 1587-1619 or 1620 . . . . DLB-58
Field, Rachel 1894-1942 . . . . DLB-9, 22
A Field Guide to Recent Schools of American
   Poetry Y-86
Fielding, Helen 1958- DLB-231
Fielding, Henry
   1707-1754 . . . . DLB-39, 84, 101; CDBLB-2
"Defense of Amelia" (1752) DLB-39
From The History of the Adventures of
   Joseph Andrews (1742) DLB-39
Preface to Joseph Andrews (1742) DLB-39
Preface to Sarah Fielding's The Adventures
   of David Simple (1744) DLB-39
Preface to Sarah Fielding's Familiar Letters
   (1747) [excerpt] DLB-39
Fielding, Sarah 1710-1768 . . . . DLB-39
Preface to The Cry (1754) DLB-39
Fields, Annie Adams 1834-1915 . . . . DLB-221
Fields, Dorothy 1905-1974 . . . . DLB-265
Fields, James T. 1817-1881 . . . . DLB-1, 235
Fields, Julia 1938- DLB-41
Fields, Osgood and Company DLB-49
Fields, W. C. 1880-1946 . . . . DLB-44
Fierstein, Harvey 1954- DLB-266
Fifty Penguin Years Y-85
Figes, Eva 1932- DLB-14, 271
Figuera, Angela 1902-1984 . . . . DLB-108
Filmer, Sir Robert 1586-1653 . . . . DLB-151
Filson, John circa 1753-1788 . . . . DLB-37
Finch, Anne, Countess of Winchilsea
   1661-1720 . . . . DLB-95
Finch, Annie 1956- DLB-282
Finch, Robert 1900- DLB-88
Findley, Timothy 1930- DLB-53
Finlay, Ian Hamilton 1925- DLB-40
Finley, Martha 1828-1909 . . . . DLB-42
Finn, Elizabeth Anne (McCaul)
   1825-1921 . . . . DLB-166
Finnegan, Seamus 1949- DLB-245
Finney, Jack 1911-1995 . . . . DLB-8
Finney, Walter Braden (see Finney, Jack)
Firbank, Ronald 1886-1926 . . . . DLB-36
Firmin, Giles 1615-1697 . . . . DLB-24
First Edition Library/Collectors'
   Reprints, Inc. Y-91
Fischart, Johann
   1546 or 1547-1590 or 1591 . . . . DLB-179
Fischer, Karoline Auguste Fernandine
   1764-1842 . . . . DLB-94

Fischer, Tibor 1959- DLB-231
Fish, Stanley 1938- DLB-67
Fishacre, Richard 1205-1248 . . . . DLB-115
Fisher, Clay (see Allen, Henry W.)
Fisher, Dorothy Canfield 1879-1958 . . . DLB-9, 102
Fisher, Leonard Everett 1924- DLB-61
Fisher, Roy 1930- DLB-40
Fisher, Rudolph 1897-1934 . . . . DLB-51, 102
Fisher, Steve 1913-1980 . . . . DLB-226
Fisher, Sydney George 1856-1927 . . . . DLB-47
Fisher, Vardis 1895-1968 . . . . DLB-9, 206
Fiske, John 1608-1677 . . . . DLB-24
Fiske, John 1842-1901 . . . . DLB-47, 64
Fitch, Thomas circa 1700-1774 . . . . DLB-31
Fitch, William Clyde 1865-1909 . . . . DLB-7
FitzGerald, Edward 1809-1883 . . . . DLB-32
Fitzgerald, F. Scott 1896-1940
   . . . . DLB-4, 9, 86, 219, 273; Y-81, Y-92;
   DS-1, 15, 16; CDALB-4
F. Scott Fitzgerald Centenary
   Celebrations Y-96
F. Scott Fitzgerald: A Descriptive Bibliography,
   Supplement (2001) Y-01
F. Scott Fitzgerald Inducted into the American
   Poets' Corner at St. John the Divine;
   Ezra Pound Banned Y-99
"F. Scott Fitzgerald: St. Paul's Native Son
   and Distinguished American Writer":
   University of Minnesota Conference,
   29-31 October 1982 . . . . Y-82
First International F. Scott Fitzgerald
   Conference Y-92
Fitzgerald, Penelope 1916- DLB-14, 194
Fitzgerald, Robert 1910-1985 . . . . Y-80
FitzGerald, Robert D. 1902-1987 . . . . DLB-260
Fitzgerald, Thomas 1819-1891 . . . . DLB-23
Fitzgerald, Zelda Sayre 1900-1948 . . . . Y-84
Fitzhugh, Louise 1928-1974 . . . . DLB-52
Fitzhugh, William circa 1651-1701 . . . . DLB-24
Flagg, James Montgomery 1877-1960 . . . . DLB-188
Flanagan, Thomas 1923- Y-80
Flanner, Hildegarde 1899-1987 . . . . DLB-48
Flanner, Janet 1892-1978 . . . . DLB-4
Flannery, Peter 1951- DLB-233
Flaubert, Gustave 1821-1880 . . . . DLB-119
Flavin, Martin 1883-1967 . . . . DLB-9
Fleck, Konrad
   (flourished circa 1220) DLB-138
Flecker, James Elroy 1884-1915 . . . . . . DLB-10, 19
Fleeson, Doris 1901-1970 . . . . DLB-29
Fleißer, Marieluise 1901-1974 . . . . DLB-56, 124
Fleischer, Nat 1887-1972 . . . . DLB-241
Fleming, Abraham 1552?-1607 . . . . DLB-236
Fleming, Ian 1908-1964 . . . DLB-87, 201; CDBLB-7
Fleming, Joan Margaret 1908-1980 . . . . . DLB-276
Fleming, Mary Agnes 1840-1880 . . . . DLB-99
Fleming, Paul 1609-1640 . . . . DLB-164
Fleming, Peter 1907-1971 . . . . DLB-195

Cumulative Index

Fletcher, Giles, the Elder 1546-1611 ..... DLB-136
Fletcher, Giles, the Younger
    1585 or 1586-1623 .... DLB-121
Fletcher, J. S. 1863-1935 .... DLB-70
Fletcher, John (see Beaumont, Francis)
Fletcher, John Gould 1886-1950 .... DLB-4, 45
Fletcher, Phineas 1582-1650 .... DLB-121
Flieg, Helmut (see Heym, Stefan)
Flint, F. S. 1885-1960 .... DLB-19
Flint, Timothy 1780-1840 .... DLB-73, 186
Flores-Williams, Jason 1969- DLB-209
Florio, John 1553?-1625 .... DLB-172
Fludd, Robert 1574-1637 .... DLB-281
Fo, Dario 1926- Y-97
Foden, Giles 1967- DLB-267
Fofanov, Konstantin Mikhailovich
    1862-1911 .... DLB-277
Foix, J. V. 1893-1987 .... DLB-134
Foley, Martha (see Burnett, Whit, and Martha Foley)
Folger, Henry Clay 1857-1930 .... DLB-140
Folio Society DLB-112
Follain, Jean 1903-1971 .... DLB-258
Follen, Charles 1796-1840 .... DLB-235
Follen, Eliza Lee (Cabot) 1787-1860 ... DLB-1, 235
Follett, Ken 1949- DLB-87; Y-81
Follett Publishing Company DLB-46
Folsom, John West [publishing house] DLB-49
Folz, Hans
    between 1435 and 1440-1513 .... DLB-179
Fontane, Theodor
    1819-1898 .... DLB-129; CDWLB-2
Fontenelle, Bernard Le Bovier de
    1657-1757 .... DLB-268
Fontes, Montserrat 1940- DLB-209
Fonvisin, Denis Ivanovich
    1744 or 1745-1792 .... DLB-150
Foote, Horton 1916- DLB-26, 266
Foote, Mary Hallock
    1847-1938 .... DLB-186, 188, 202, 221
Foote, Samuel 1721-1777 .... DLB-89
Foote, Shelby 1916- DLB-2, 17
Forbes, Calvin 1945- DLB-41
Forbes, Ester 1891-1967 .... DLB-22
Forbes, Rosita 1893?-1967 .... DLB-195
Forbes and Company DLB-49
Force, Peter 1790-1868 .... DLB-30
Forché, Carolyn 1950- DLB-5, 193
Ford, Charles Henri 1913- DLB-4, 48
Ford, Corey 1902-1969 .... DLB-11
Ford, Ford Madox
    1873-1939 .... DLB-34, 98, 162; CDBLB-6
Ford, J. B., and Company DLB-49
Ford, Jesse Hill 1928-1996 .... DLB-6
Ford, John 1586-? DLB-58; CDBLB-1
Ford, R. A. D. 1915- DLB-88
Ford, Richard 1944- DLB-227
Ford, Worthington C. 1858-1941 .... DLB-47

Nathan Asch Remembers Ford Madox Ford,
    Sam Roth, and Hart Crane Y-02
Fords, Howard, and Hulbert DLB-49
Foreman, Carl 1914-1984 .... DLB-26
Forester, C. S. 1899-1966 .... DLB-191
Forester, Frank (see Herbert, Henry William)
Anthologizing New Formalism DLB-282
The Little Magazines of the
    New Formalism DLB-282
The New Narrative Poetry DLB-282
Presses of the New Formalism and
    the New Narrative DLB-282
The Prosody of the New Formalism DLB-282
Younger Women Poets of the
    New Formalism DLB-282
Forman, Harry Buxton 1842-1917 ...... DLB-184
Fornés, María Irene 1930- DLB-7
Forrest, Leon 1937-1997 .... DLB-33
Forsh, Ol'ga Dmitrievna 1873-1961 .... DLB-272
Forster, E. M. 1879-1970
    ..DLB-34, 98, 162, 178, 195; DS-10; CDBLB-6
Forster, Georg 1754-1794 .... DLB-94
Forster, John 1812-1876 .... DLB-144
Forster, Margaret 1938- DLB-155, 271
Forsyth, Frederick 1938- DLB-87
Forten, Charlotte L. 1837-1914 ..... DLB-50, 239
Charlotte Forten: Pages from
    her Diary DLB-50
Fortini, Franco 1917- DLB-128
Fortune, Mary ca. 1833-ca. 1910 ...... DLB-230
Fortune, T. Thomas 1856-1928 .... DLB-23
Fosdick, Charles Austin 1842-1915 .... DLB-42
Foster, Genevieve 1893-1979 .... DLB-61
Foster, Hannah Webster 1758-1840 ... DLB-37, 200
Foster, John 1648-1681 .... DLB-24
Foster, Michael 1904-1956 .... DLB-9
Foster, Myles Birket 1825-1899 .... DLB-184
Foucault, Michel 1926-1984 .... DLB-242
Foulis, Robert and Andrew / R. and A.
    [publishing house] DLB-154
Fouqué, Caroline de la Motte
    1774-1831 .... DLB-90
Fouqué, Friedrich de la Motte
    1777-1843 .... DLB-90
Four Seas Company DLB-46
Four Winds Press DLB-46
Fournier, Henri Alban (see Alain-Fournier)
Fowler, Christopher 1953- DLB-267
Fowler and Wells Company DLB-49
Fowles, John
    1926- DLB-14, 139, 207; CDBLB-8
Fox, John 1939- DLB-245
Fox, John, Jr. 1862 or 1863-1919 ... DLB-9; DS-13
Fox, Paula 1923- DLB-52
Fox, Richard K. [publishing house] DLB-49
Fox, Richard Kyle 1846-1922 .... DLB-79
Fox, William Price 1926- DLB-2; Y-81

Foxe, John 1517-1587 .... DLB-132
Fraenkel, Michael 1896-1957 .... DLB-4
France, Anatole 1844-1924 .... DLB-123
France, Richard 1938- DLB-7
Francis, C. S. [publishing house] DLB-49
Francis, Convers 1795-1863 .... DLB-1, 235
Francis, Dick 1920- DLB-87
Francis, Sir Frank 1901-1988 .... DLB-201
Francis, Jeffrey, Lord 1773-1850 .... DLB-107
Françoise (Robertine Barry) 1863-1910 ... DLB-92
François, Louise von 1817-1893 .... DLB-129
Franck, Sebastian 1499-1542 .... DLB-179
Francke, Kuno 1855-1930 .... DLB-71
Frank, Bruno 1887-1945 .... DLB-118
Frank, Leonhard 1882-1961 .... DLB-56, 118
Frank, Melvin (see Panama, Norman)
Frank, Waldo 1889-1967 .... DLB-9, 63
Franken, Rose 1895?-1988 ...... DLB-228, Y-84
Franklin, Benjamin
    1706-1790 .... DLB-24, 43, 73, 183; CDALB-2
Franklin, James 1697-1735 .... DLB-43
Franklin, John 1786-1847 .... DLB-99
Franklin, Miles 1879-1954 .... DLB-230
Franklin Library DLB-46
Frantz, Ralph Jules 1902-1979 .... DLB-4
Franzos, Karl Emil 1848-1904 .... DLB-129
Fraser, Antonia 1932- DLB-276
Fraser, G. S. 1915-1980 .... DLB-27
Fraser, Kathleen 1935- DLB-169
Frattini, Alberto 1922- DLB-128
Frau Ava ?-1127 .... DLB-148
Fraunce, Abraham 1558?-1592 or 1593 ... DLB-236
Frayn, Michael 1933- DLB-13, 14, 194, 245
Fréchette, Louis-Honoré 1839-1908 .... DLB-99
Frederic, Harold
    1856-1898 .... DLB-12, 23; DS-13
Freed, Arthur 1894-1973 .... DLB-265
Freeling, Nicolas 1927- DLB-87
Freeman, Douglas Southall
    1886-1953 .... DLB-17; DS-17
Freeman, Judith 1946- DLB-256
Freeman, Legh Richmond 1842-1915 .... DLB-23
Freeman, Mary E. Wilkins
    1852-1930 .... DLB-12, 78, 221
Freeman, R. Austin 1862-1943 .... DLB-70
Freidank circa 1170-circa 1233 .... DLB-138
Freiligrath, Ferdinand 1810-1876 ..... DLB-133
Fremlin, Celia 1914- DLB-276
Frémont, John Charles 1813-1890 ..... DLB-186
Frémont, John Charles 1813-1890 and
    Frémont, Jessie Benton 1834-1902 ... DLB-183
French, Alice 1850-1934 .... DLB-74; DS-13
French Arthurian Literature DLB-208
French, David 1939- DLB-53
French, Evangeline 1869-1960 .... DLB-195
French, Francesca 1871-1960 .... DLB-195

French, James [publishing house]..........DLB-49
French, Samuel [publishing house].........DLB-49
Samuel French, Limited.....................DLB-106
Freneau, Philip 1752-1832............DLB-37, 43
Freni, Melo 1934-..........................DLB-128
Freshfield, Douglas W. 1845-1934..........DLB-174
Freytag, Gustav 1816-1895..................DLB-129
Fridegård, Jan 1897-1968...................DLB-259
Fried, Erich 1921-1988......................DLB-85
Friedan, Betty 1921-........................DLB-246
Friedman, Bruce Jay 1930-......DLB-2, 28, 244
Friedrich von Hausen circa 1171-1190....DLB-138
Friel, Brian 1929-...........................DLB-13
Friend, Krebs 1895?-1967?....................DLB-4
Fries, Fritz Rudolf 1935-...................DLB-75
Fringe and Alternative Theater in
    Great Britain...........................DLB-13
Frisch, Max
    1911-1991.........DLB-69, 124; CDWLB-2
Frischlin, Nicodemus 1547-1590..........DLB-179
Frischmuth, Barbara 1941-..................DLB-85
Fritz, Jean 1915-...........................DLB-52
Froissart, Jean circa 1337-circa 1404......DLB-208
From John Hall Wheelock's Oral Memoir....Y-01
Fromentin, Eugene 1820-1876................DLB-123
Frontinus circa A.D. 35-A.D. 103/104.....DLB-211
Frost, A. B. 1851-1928..........DLB-188; DS-13
Frost, Robert
    1874-1963........DLB-54; DS-7; CDALB-4
Frostenson, Katarina 1953-................DLB-257
Frothingham, Octavius Brooks
    1822-1895...........................DLB-1, 243
Froude, James Anthony
    1818-1894..................DLB-18, 57, 144
Fruitlands 1843-1844......................DLB-223
Fry, Christopher 1907-.....................DLB-13
Fry, Roger 1866-1934..........................DS-10
Fry, Stephen 1957-.........................DLB-207
Frye, Northrop 1912-1991.......DLB-67, 68, 246
Fuchs, Daniel 1909-1993
    ....DLB-9, 26, 28; Y-93
Fuentes, Carlos 1928-......DLB-113; CDWLB-3
Fuertes, Gloria 1918-.....................DLB-108
Fugard, Athol 1932-........................DLB-225
The Fugitives and the Agrarians:
    The First Exhibition.......................Y-85
Fujiwara no Shunzei 1114-1204............DLB-203
Fujiwara no Tameaki 1230s?-1290s?......DLB-203
Fujiwara no Tameie 1198-1275.............DLB-203
Fujiwara no Teika 1162-1241..............DLB-203
Fulbecke, William 1560-1603?.............DLB-172
Fuller, Charles H., Jr. 1939-........DLB-38, 266
Fuller, Henry Blake 1857-1929..............DLB-12
Fuller, John 1937-.........................DLB-40
Fuller, Margaret (see Fuller, Sarah)
Fuller, Roy 1912-1991..................DLB-15, 20

Fuller, Samuel 1912-........................DLB-26
Fuller, Sarah 1810-1850
    .....DLB-1, 59, 73, 183, 223, 239; CDALB-2
Fuller, Thomas 1608-1661..................DLB-151
Fullerton, Hugh 1873-1945.................DLB-171
Fullwood, William flourished 1568........DLB-236
Fulton, Alice 1952-.......................DLB-193
Fulton, Len 1934-............................Y-86
Fulton, Robin 1937-.........................DLB-40
Furbank, P. N. 1920-......................DLB-155
Furetière, Antoine 1619-1688..............DLB-268
Furman, Laura 1945-...........................Y-86
Furmanov, Dmitrii Andreevich
    1891-1926..............................DLB-272
Furness, Horace Howard
    1833-1912...............................DLB-64
Furness, William Henry
    1802-1896..........................DLB-1, 235
Furnivall, Frederick James
    1825-1910..............................DLB-184
Furphy, Joseph
    (Tom Collins) 1843-1912..............DLB-230
Furthman, Jules 1888-1966..................DLB-26
Shakespeare and Montaigne: A Symposium
    by Jules Furthman.........................Y-02
Furui Yoshikichi 1937-....................DLB-182
Fushimi, Emperor 1265-1317................DLB-203
Futabatei, Shimei
    (Hasegawa Tatsunosuke)
    1864-1909..............................DLB-180
The Future of the Novel (1899), by
    Henry James............................DLB-18
Fyleman, Rose 1877-1957...................DLB-160

G

Gadallah, Leslie 1939-....................DLB-251
Gadda, Carlo Emilio 1893-1973............DLB-177
Gaddis, William 1922-1998.....DLB-2, 278; Y-99
Gág, Wanda 1893-1946........................DLB-22
Gagarin, Ivan Sergeevich 1814-1882......DLB-198
Gagnon, Madeleine 1938-....................DLB-60
Gaiman, Neil 1960-........................DLB-261
Gaine, Hugh 1726-1807......................DLB-43
Gaine, Hugh [publishing house].............DLB-49
Gaines, Ernest J.
    1933-.....DLB-2, 33, 152; Y-80; CDALB-6
Gaiser, Gerd 1908-1976.....................DLB-69
Gaitskill, Mary 1954-.....................DLB-244
Galarza, Ernesto 1905-1984................DLB-122
Galaxy Science Fiction Novels..............DLB-46
Galbraith, Robert (or Caubraith)
    circa 1483-1544.......................DLB-281
Gale, Zona 1874-1938...........DLB-9, 228, 78
Galen of Pergamon 129-after 210..........DLB-176
Gales, Winifred Marshall 1761-1839......DLB-200
Gall, Louise von 1815-1855................DLB-133
Gallagher, Tess 1943-.......DLB-120, 212, 244
Gallagher, Wes 1911-......................DLB-127

Gallagher, William Davis 1808-1894.......DLB-73
Gallant, Mavis 1922-........................DLB-53
Gallegos, María Magdalena 1935-..........DLB-209
Gallico, Paul 1897-1976...............DLB-9, 171
Gallop, Jane 1952-........................DLB-246
Galloway, Grace Growden 1727-1782......DLB-200
Gallup, Donald 1913-......................DLB-187
Galsworthy, John 1867-1933
    .....DLB-10, 34, 98, 162; DS-16; CDBLB-5
Galt, John 1779-1839.................DLB-99, 116
Galton, Sir Francis 1822-1911............DLB-166
Galvin, Brendan 1938-.......................DLB-5
Gambit.....................................DLB-46
Gamboa, Reymundo 1948-...................DLB-122
Gammer Gurton's Needle....................DLB-62
Gan, Elena Andreevna (Zeneida R-va)
    1814-1842..............................DLB-198
Gannett, Frank E. 1876-1957................DLB-29
Gao Xingjian 1940-...........................Y-00
Gaos, Vicente 1919-1980...................DLB-134
García, Andrew 1854?-1943.................DLB-209
García, Lionel G. 1935-....................DLB-82
García, Richard 1941-.....................DLB-209
García-Camarillo, Cecilio 1943-...........DLB-209
García Lorca, Federico 1898-1936.........DLB-108
García Márquez, Gabriel
    1928-.........DLB-113; Y-82; CDWLB-3
Gardam, Jane 1928-..........DLB-14, 161, 231
Gardell, Jonas 1963-......................DLB-257
Garden, Alexander circa 1685-1756........DLB-31
Gardiner, John Rolfe 1936-...............DLB-244
Gardiner, Margaret Power Farmer
    (see Blessington, Marguerite, Countess of)
Gardner, John
    1933-1982.........DLB-2; Y-82; CDALB-7
Garfield, Leon 1921-1996..................DLB-161
Garis, Howard R. 1873-1962.................DLB-22
Garland, Hamlin 1860-1940..DLB-12, 71, 78, 186
Garneau, François-Xavier 1809-1866.......DLB-99
Garneau, Hector de Saint-Denys
    1912-1943...............................DLB-88
Garneau, Michel 1939-......................DLB-53
Garner, Alan 1934-................DLB-161, 261
Garner, Hugh 1913-1979.....................DLB-68
Garnett, David 1892-1981...................DLB-34
Garnett, Eve 1900-1991....................DLB-160
Garnett, Richard 1835-1906................DLB-184
Garrard, Lewis H. 1829-1887...............DLB-186
Garraty, John A. 1920-.....................DLB-17
Garrett, George
    1929-.........DLB-2, 5, 130, 152; Y-83
Fellowship of Southern Writers..............Y-98
Garrett, John Work 1872-1942..............DLB-187
Garrick, David 1717-1779............DLB-84, 213
Garrison, William Lloyd
    1805-1879........DLB-1, 43, 235; CDALB-2
Garro, Elena 1920-1998....................DLB-145

Garshin, Vsevolod Mikhailovich 1855-1888 .... DLB-277
Garth, Samuel 1661-1719 .... DLB-95
Garve, Andrew 1908- DLB-87
Gary, Romain 1914-1980 .... DLB-83
Gascoigne, George 1539?-1577 .... DLB-136
Gascoyne, David 1916- DLB-20
Gash, Jonathan 1933- DLB-276
Gaskell, Elizabeth Cleghorn 1810-1865 ...... DLB-21, 144, 159; CDBLB-4
Gaskell, Jane 1941- DLB-261
Gaspey, Thomas 1788-1871 .... DLB-116
Gass, William H. 1924- DLB-2, 227
Gates, Doris 1901- DLB-22
Gates, Henry Louis, Jr. 1950- DLB-67
Gates, Lewis E. 1860-1924 .... DLB-71
Gatto, Alfonso 1909-1976 .... DLB-114
Gault, William Campbell 1910-1995 .... DLB-226
Gaunt, Mary 1861-1942 .... DLB-174, 230
Gautier, Théophile 1811-1872 .... DLB-119
Gauvreau, Claude 1925-1971 .... DLB-88
The *Gawain*-Poet flourished circa 1350-1400 .... DLB-146
Gawsworth, John (Terence Ian Fytton Armstrong) 1912-1970 .... DLB-255
Gay, Ebenezer 1696-1787 .... DLB-24
Gay, John 1685-1732 .... DLB-84, 95
Gayarré, Charles E. A. 1805-1895 .... DLB-30
Gaylord, Charles [publishing house] DLB-49
Gaylord, Edward King 1873-1974 ...... DLB-127
Gaylord, Edward Lewis 1919- DLB-127
Gébler, Carlo 1954- DLB-271
Geda, Sigitas 1943- DLB-232
Geddes, Gary 1940- DLB-60
Geddes, Virgil 1897- DLB-4
Gedeon (Georgii Andreevich Krinovsky) circa 1730-1763 .... DLB-150
Gee, Maggie 1948- DLB-207
Gee, Shirley 1932- DLB-245
Geibel, Emanuel 1815-1884 .... DLB-129
Geiogamah, Hanay 1945- DLB-175
Geis, Bernard, Associates DLB-46
Geisel, Theodor Seuss 1904-1991 ... DLB-61; Y-91
Gelb, Arthur 1924- DLB-103
Gelb, Barbara 1926- DLB-103
Gelber, Jack 1932- DLB-7, 228
Gélinas, Gratien 1909- DLB-88
Gellert, Christian Fuerchtegott 1715-1769 .... DLB-97
Gellhorn, Martha 1908-1998 .... Y-82, Y-98
Gems, Pam 1925- DLB-13
Genet, Jean 1910-1986 .... DLB-72; Y-86
Genette, Gérard 1930- DLB-242
Genevoix, Maurice 1890-1980 .... DLB-65
Genovese, Eugene D. 1930- DLB-17
Gent, Peter 1942- Y-82

Geoffrey of Monmouth circa 1100-1155 .... DLB-146
George, Henry 1839-1897 .... DLB-23
George, Jean Craighead 1919- DLB-52
George, W. L. 1882-1926 .... DLB-197
George III, King of Great Britain and Ireland 1738-1820 .... DLB-213
George V. Higgins to Julian Symons Y-99
Georgslied 896? DLB-148
Gerber, Merrill Joan 1938- DLB-218
Gerhardie, William 1895-1977 .... DLB-36
Gerhardt, Paul 1607-1676 .... DLB-164
Gérin, Winifred 1901-1981 .... DLB-155
Gérin-Lajoie, Antoine 1824-1882 .... DLB-99
German Drama 800-1280 .... DLB-138
German Drama from Naturalism to Fascism: 1889-1933 .... DLB-118
German Literature and Culture from Charlemagne to the Early Courtly Period DLB-148; CDWLB-2
German Radio Play, The DLB-124
German Transformation from the Baroque to the Enlightenment, The DLB-97
The Germanic Epic and Old English Heroic Poetry: *Widsith, Waldere,* and *The Fight at Finnsburg* DLB-146
Germanophilism, by Hans Kohn DLB-66
Gernsback, Hugo 1884-1967 .... DLB-8, 137
Gerould, Katharine Fullerton 1879-1944 .... DLB-78
Gerrish, Samuel [publishing house] DLB-49
Gerrold, David 1944- DLB-8
Gershwin, Ira 1896-1983 .... DLB-265
The Ira Gershwin Centenary Y-96
Gerson, Jean 1363-1429 .... DLB-208
Gersonides 1288-1344 .... DLB-115
Gerstäcker, Friedrich 1816-1872 .... DLB-129
Gerstenberg, Heinrich Wilhelm von 1737-1823 .... DLB-97
Gervinus, Georg Gottfried 1805-1871 .... DLB-133
Gery, John 1953- DLB-282
Geßner, Solomon 1730-1788 .... DLB-97
Geston, Mark S. 1946- DLB-8
Al-Ghazali 1058-1111 .... DLB-115
Gibbings, Robert 1889-1958 .... DLB-195
Gibbon, Edward 1737-1794 .... DLB-104
Gibbon, John Murray 1875-1952 .... DLB-92
Gibbon, Lewis Grassic (see Mitchell, James Leslie)
Gibbons, Floyd 1887-1939 .... DLB-25
Gibbons, Reginald 1947- DLB-120
Gibbons, William ?-? DLB-73
Gibson, Charles Dana 1867-1944 .... DLB-188; DS-13
Gibson, Graeme 1934- DLB-53
Gibson, Margaret 1944- DLB-120
Gibson, Margaret Dunlop 1843-1920 ..... DLB-174
Gibson, Wilfrid 1878-1962 .... DLB-19

Gibson, William 1914- DLB-7
Gibson, William 1948- DLB-251
Gide, André 1869-1951 .... DLB-65
Giguère, Diane 1937- DLB-53
Giguère, Roland 1929- DLB-60
Gil de Biedma, Jaime 1929-1990 .... DLB-108
Gil-Albert, Juan 1906- DLB-134
Gilbert, Anthony 1899-1973 .... DLB-77
Gilbert, Sir Humphrey 1537-1583 ...... DLB-136
Gilbert, Michael 1912- DLB-87
Gilbert, Sandra M. 1936- DLB-120, 246
Gilchrist, Alexander 1828-1861 .... DLB-144
Gilchrist, Ellen 1935- DLB-130
Gilder, Jeannette L. 1849-1916 .... DLB-79
Gilder, Richard Watson 1844-1909 .... DLB-64, 79
Gildersleeve, Basil 1831-1924 .... DLB-71
Giles of Rome circa 1243-1316 .... DLB-115
Giles, Henry 1809-1882 .... DLB-64
Gilfillan, George 1813-1878 .... DLB-144
Gill, Eric 1882-1940 .... DLB-98
Gill, Sarah Prince 1728-1771 .... DLB-200
Gill, William F., Company DLB-49
Gillespie, A. Lincoln, Jr. 1895-1950 .... DLB-4
Gillespie, Haven 1883-1975 .... DLB-265
Gilliam, Florence ?-? DLB-4
Gilliatt, Penelope 1932-1993 .... DLB-14
Gillott, Jacky 1939-1980 .... DLB-14
Gilman, Caroline H. 1794-1888 .... DLB-3, 73
Gilman, Charlotte Perkins 1860-1935 ... DLB-221
Gilman, W. and J. [publishing house] DLB-49
Gilmer, Elizabeth Meriwether 1861-1951 .. DLB-29
Gilmer, Francis Walker 1790-1826 .... DLB-37
Gilmore, Mary 1865-1962 .... DLB-260
Gilroy, Frank D. 1925- DLB-7
Gimferrer, Pere (Pedro) 1945- DLB-134
Gingrich, Arnold 1903-1976 .... DLB-137
Ginsberg, Allen 1926-1997 .... DLB-5, 16, 169, 237; CDALB-1
Ginzburg, Natalia 1916-1991 .... DLB-177
Ginzkey, Franz Karl 1871-1963 .... DLB-81
Gioia, Dana 1950- DLB-120, 282
Giono, Jean 1895-1970 .... DLB-72
Giotti, Virgilio 1885-1957 .... DLB-114
Giovanni, Nikki 1943- ... DLB-5, 41; CDALB-7
Gipson, Lawrence Henry 1880-1971 ...... DLB-17
Girard, Rodolphe 1879-1956 .... DLB-92
Giraudoux, Jean 1882-1944 .... DLB-65
Gissing, George 1857-1903 ...... DLB-18, 135, 184
The Place of Realism in Fiction (1895) DLB-18
Giudici, Giovanni 1924- DLB-128
Giuliani, Alfredo 1924- DLB-128
Glackens, William J. 1870-1938 .... DLB-188
Gladkov, Fedor Vasil'evich 1883-1958 .... DLB-272
Gladstone, William Ewart 1809-1898 .... DLB-57, 184

Glaeser, Ernst 1902-1963.................DLB-69
Glancy, Diane 1941- DLB-175
Glanvill, Joseph 1636-1680 ....DLB-252
Glanville, Brian 1931- DLB-15, 139
Glapthorne, Henry 1610-1643?.........DLB-58
Glasgow, Ellen 1873-1945 ....DLB-9, 12
Glasier, Katharine Bruce 1867-1950.....DLB-190
Glaspell, Susan 1876-1948 ...... DLB-7, 9, 78, 228
Glass, Montague 1877-1934 ....DLB-11
Glassco, John 1909-1981 ....DLB-68
Glauser, Friedrich 1896-1938............DLB-56
F. Gleason's Publishing Hall DLB-49
Gleim, Johann Wilhelm Ludwig
    1719-1803 ....DLB-97
Glendinning, Victoria 1937- DLB-155
The Cult of Biography
    Excerpts from the Second Folio Debate:
    "Biographies are generally a disease of
    English Literature" Y-86
Glidden, Frederick Dilley (Luke Short)
    1908-1975 ....DLB-256
Glinka, Fedor Nikolaevich 1786-1880 ....DLB-205
Glover, Keith 1966- DLB-249
Glover, Richard 1712-1785..............DLB-95
Glück, Louise 1943- DLB-5
Glyn, Elinor 1864-1943.................DLB-153
Gnedich, Nikolai Ivanovich 1784-1833 ...DLB-205
Gobineau, Joseph-Arthur de
    1816-1882 ....DLB-123
Godber, John 1956- DLB-233
Godbout, Jacques 1933- DLB-53
Goddard, Morrill 1865-1937 ....DLB-25
Goddard, William 1740-1817............DLB-43
Godden, Rumer 1907-1998 ....DLB-161
Godey, Louis A. 1804-1878..............DLB-73
Godey and McMichael DLB-49
Godfrey, Dave 1938- DLB-60
Godfrey, Thomas 1736-1763 ....DLB-31
Godine, David R., Publisher DLB-46
Godkin, E. L. 1831-1902................DLB-79
Godolphin, Sidney 1610-1643 ....DLB-126
Godwin, Gail 1937- DLB-6, 234
Godwin, M. J., and Company DLB-154
Godwin, Mary Jane Clairmont
    1766-1841 ....DLB-163
Godwin, Parke 1816-1904 ....DLB-3, 64, 250
Godwin, William 1756-1836 .... DLB-39, 104,
    .... 142, 158, 163, 262; CDBLB-3
Preface to *St. Leon* (1799) DLB-39
Goering, Reinhard 1887-1936 ....DLB-118
Goes, Albrecht 1908- DLB-69
Goethe, Johann Wolfgang von
    1749-1832 ....DLB-94; CDWLB-2
Goetz, Curt 1888-1960 ....DLB-124
Goffe, Thomas circa 1592-1629..........DLB-58
Goffstein, M. B. 1940- DLB-61
Gogarty, Oliver St. John 1878-1957....DLB-15, 19

Gogol, Nikolai Vasil'evich 1809-1852 ....DLB-198
Goines, Donald 1937-1974 ....DLB-33
Gold, Herbert 1924- DLB-2; Y-81
Gold, Michael 1893-1967..........DLB-9, 28
Goldbarth, Albert 1948- DLB-120
Goldberg, Dick 1947- DLB-7
Golden Cockerel Press DLB-112
Golding, Arthur 1536-1606 ....DLB-136
Golding, Louis 1895-1958 ....DLB-195
Golding, William 1911-1993
    ....DLB-15, 100, 255; Y-83; CDBLB-7
Goldman, Emma 1869-1940 ....DLB-221
Goldman, William 1931- DLB-44
Goldring, Douglas 1887-1960 ....DLB-197
Goldsmith, Oliver 1730?-1774
    ....DLB-39, 89, 99, 104, 109, 142; CDBLB-2
Goldsmith, Oliver 1794-1861............DLB-99
Goldsmith Publishing Company DLB-46
Goldstein, Richard 1944- DLB-185
Gollancz, Sir Israel 1864-1930 ....DLB-201
Gollancz, Victor, Limited................DLB-112
Gomberville, Marin LeRoy de
    1600?-1674 ....DLB-268
Gombrowicz, Witold
    1904-1969 ....DLB-215; CDWLB-4
Gómez-Quiñones, Juan 1942- DLB-122
Gomme, Laurence James
    [publishing house]..................DLB-46
Goncharov, Ivan Aleksandrovich
    1812-1891 ....DLB-238
Goncourt, Edmond de 1822-1896.......DLB-123
Goncourt, Jules de 1830-1870 ....DLB-123
Gonzales, Rodolfo "Corky" 1928- DLB-122
González, Angel 1925- DLB-108
Gonzalez, Genaro 1949- DLB-122
Gonzalez, Ray 1952- DLB-122
Gonzales-Berry, Erlinda 1942- DLB-209
    "Chicano Language" DLB-82
González de Mireles, Jovita
    1899-1983 ....DLB-122
González-T., César A. 1931- DLB-82
Goodbye, Gutenberg? A Lecture at the
    New York Public Library,
    18 April 1995, by Donald Lamm Y-95
Goodis, David 1917-1967...............DLB-226
Goodison, Lorna 1947- DLB-157
Goodman, Allegra 1967- DLB-244
Goodman, Nelson 1906-1998 ....DLB-279
Goodman, Paul 1911-1972........DLB-130, 246
The Goodman Theatre DLB-7
Goodrich, Frances 1891-1984 and
    Hackett, Albert 1900-1995 ....DLB-26
Goodrich, Samuel Griswold
    1793-1860 ....DLB-1, 42, 73, 243
Goodrich, S. G. [publishing house]........DLB-49
Goodspeed, C. E., and Company DLB-49
Goodwin, Stephen 1943- Y-82
Googe, Barnabe 1540-1594 ....DLB-132

Gookin, Daniel 1612-1687...............DLB-24
Goran, Lester 1928- DLB-244
Gordimer, Nadine 1923- DLB-225; Y-91
Gordon, Adam Lindsay 1833-1870 ......DLB-230
Gordon, Caroline
    1895-1981 .... DLB-4, 9, 102; DS-17; Y-81
Gordon, Charles F. (see OyamO)
Gordon, Charles William (see Connor, Ralph)
Gordon, Giles 1940- DLB-14, 139, 207
Gordon, Helen Cameron, Lady Russell
    1867-1949 ....DLB-195
Gordon, Lyndall 1941- DLB-155
Gordon, Mack 1904-1959 ....DLB-265
Gordon, Mary 1949- DLB-6; Y-81
Gordone, Charles 1925-1995..............DLB-7
Gore, Catherine 1800-1861 ....DLB-116
Gore-Booth, Eva 1870-1926 ....DLB-240
Gores, Joe 1931- DLB-226; Y-02
Gorey, Edward 1925-2000 ....DLB-61
Gorgias of Leontini
    circa 485 B.C.-376 B.C. DLB-176
Görres, Joseph 1776-1848 ....DLB-90
Gosse, Edmund 1849-1928 ..... DLB-57, 144, 184
Gosson, Stephen 1554-1624..............DLB-172
    The Schoole of Abuse (1579)................DLB-172
Gotanda, Philip Kan 1951- DLB-266
Gotlieb, Phyllis 1926- DLB-88, 251
Go-Toba 1180-1239....................DLB-203
Gottfried von Straßburg
    died before 1230 ....DLB-138; CDWLB-2
Gotthelf, Jeremias 1797-1854 ....DLB-133
Gottschalk circa 804/808-869 ....DLB-148
Gottsched, Johann Christoph
    1700-1766 ....DLB-97
Götz, Johann Nikolaus 1721-1781 ....DLB-97
Goudge, Elizabeth 1900-1984 ....DLB-191
Gough, John B. 1817-1886..............DLB-243
Gould, Wallace 1882-1940 ....DLB-54
Govoni, Corrado 1884-1965 ....DLB-114
Gower, John circa 1330-1408 ....DLB-146
Goyen, William 1915-1983 ..... DLB-2, 218; Y-83
Goytisolo, José Augustín 1928- DLB-134
Gozzano, Guido 1883-1916 ....DLB-114
Grabbe, Christian Dietrich 1801-1836....DLB-133
Gracq, Julien 1910- DLB-83
Grady, Henry W. 1850-1889 ....DLB-23
Graf, Oskar Maria 1894-1967 ....DLB-56
Graf Rudolf
    between circa 1170 and circa 1185 ...DLB-148
Graff, Gerald 1937- DLB-246
Grafton, Richard [publishing house] DLB-170
Grafton, Sue 1940- DLB-226
Graham, Frank 1893-1965.............DLB-241
Graham, George Rex 1813-1894.........DLB-73
Graham, Gwethalyn (Gwethalyn Graham
    Erichsen-Brown) 1913-1965 ....DLB-88

Graham, Jorie 1951- DLB-120
Graham, Katharine 1917- DLB-127
Graham, Lorenz 1902-1989 .... DLB-76
Graham, Philip 1915-1963 .... DLB-127
Graham, R. B. Cunninghame
    1852-1936 .... DLB-98, 135, 174
Graham, Shirley 1896-1977 .... DLB-76
Graham, Stephen 1884-1975 .... DLB-195
Graham, W. S. 1918- DLB-20
Graham, William H. [publishing house] ... DLB-49
Graham, Winston 1910- DLB-77
Grahame, Kenneth
    1859-1932 .... DLB-34, 141, 178
Grainger, Martin Allerdale 1874-1941 .... DLB-92
Gramatky, Hardie 1907-1979 .... DLB-22
Grand, Sarah 1854-1943 .... DLB-135, 197
Grandbois, Alain 1900-1975 .... DLB-92
Grandson, Oton de circa 1345-1397 ..... DLB-208
Grange, John circa 1556-? DLB-136
Granger, Thomas 1578-1627 .... DLB-281
Granich, Irwin (see Gold, Michael)
Granovsky, Timofei Nikolaevich
    1813-1855 .... DLB-198
Grant, Anne MacVicar 1755-1838 ..... DLB-200
Grant, Duncan 1885-1978 .... DS-10
Grant, George 1918-1988 .... DLB-88
Grant, George Monro 1835-1902 .... DLB-99
Grant, Harry J. 1881-1963 .... DLB-29
Grant, James Edward 1905-1966 .... DLB-26
War of the Words (and Pictures): The Creation
    of a Graphic Novel Y-02
Grass, Günter 1927- ...DLB-75, 124; CDWLB-2
Grasty, Charles H. 1863-1924 .... DLB-25
Grau, Shirley Ann 1929- DLB-2, 218
Graves, John 1920- Y-83
Graves, Richard 1715-1804 .... DLB-39
Graves, Robert 1895-1985
    ....DLB-20, 100, 191; DS-18; Y-85; CDBLB-6
Gray, Alasdair 1934- DLB-194, 261
Gray, Asa 1810-1888 .... DLB-1, 235
Gray, David 1838-1861 .... DLB-32
Gray, Simon 1936- DLB-13
Gray, Thomas 1716-1771 .... DLB-109; CDBLB-2
Grayson, Richard 1951- DLB-234
Grayson, William J. 1788-1863.... DLB-3, 64, 248
The Great Bibliographers Series Y-93
The Great Modern Library Scam Y-98
The Great War and the Theater, 1914-1918
    [Great Britain] DLB-10
The Great War Exhibition and Symposium at
    the University of South Carolina Y-97
"The Greatness of Southern Literature":
    League of the South Institute for the
    Study of Southern Culture and History
    .... Y-02
Grech, Nikolai Ivanovich 1787-1867 ..... DLB-198
Greeley, Horace 1811-1872 .. DLB-3, 43, 189, 250

Green, Adolph (see Comden, Betty)
Green, Anna Katharine
    1846-1935 .... DLB-202, 221
Green, Duff 1791-1875 .... DLB-43
Green, Elizabeth Shippen 1871-1954 .... DLB-188
Green, Gerald 1922- DLB-28
Green, Henry 1905-1973 .... DLB-15
Green, Jonas 1712-1767 .... DLB-31
Green, Joseph 1706-1780 .... DLB-31
Green, Julien 1900-1998 .... DLB-4, 72
Green, Paul 1894-1981 .... DLB-7, 9, 249; Y-81
Green, T. and S. [publishing house] DLB-49
Green, T. H. 1836-1882 .... DLB-262
Green, Terence M. 1947- DLB-251
Green, Thomas Hill 1836-1882 .... DLB-190, 262
Green, Timothy [publishing house] DLB-49
Greenaway, Kate 1846-1901 .... DLB-141
Greenberg: Publisher DLB-46
Green Tiger Press DLB-46
Greene, Asa 1789-1838 .... DLB-11
Greene, Belle da Costa 1883-1950 ...... DLB-187
Greene, Benjamin H.
    [publishing house] DLB-49
Greene, Graham 1904-1991
    .... DLB-13, 15, 77, 100, 162, 201, 204;
    Y-85, Y-91; CDBLB-7
Greene, Robert 1558-1592 .... DLB-62, 167
Greene, Robert Bernard (Bob), Jr.
    1947- DLB-185
Greenfield, George 1917-2000 .... Y-00
Derek Robinson's Review of
    George Greenfield's Rich Dust Y-02
Greenhow, Robert 1800-1854 .... DLB-30
Greenlee, William B. 1872-1953 .... DLB-187
Greenough, Horatio 1805-1852 ...... DLB-1, 235
Greenwell, Dora 1821-1882 .... DLB-35, 199
Greenwillow Books DLB-46
Greenwood, Grace (see Lippincott, Sara Jane Clarke)
Greenwood, Walter 1903-1974 ..... DLB-10, 191
Greer, Ben 1948- DLB-6
Greflinger, Georg 1620?-1677 .... DLB-164
Greg, W. R. 1809-1881 .... DLB-55
Greg, W. W. 1875-1959 .... DLB-201
Gregg, Josiah 1806-1850 .... DLB-183, 186
Gregg Press DLB-46
Gregory, Isabella Augusta Persse, Lady
    1852-1932 .... DLB-10
Gregory, Horace 1898-1982 .... DLB-48
Gregory of Rimini circa 1300-1358 ..... DLB-115
Gregynog Press DLB-112
Greiffenberg, Catharina Regina von
    1633-1694 .... DLB-168
Greig, Noël 1944- DLB-245
Grenfell, Wilfred Thomason
    1865-1940 .... DLB-92
Gress, Elsa 1919-1988 .... DLB-214
Greve, Felix Paul (see Grove, Frederick Philip)

Greville, Fulke, First Lord Brooke
    1554-1628 .... DLB-62, 172
Grey, Sir George, K.C.B. 1812-1898 ... DLB-184
Grey, Lady Jane 1537-1554 .... DLB-132
Grey Owl (Archibald Stansfeld Belaney)
    1888-1938 .... DLB-92; DS-17
Grey, Zane 1872-1939 .... DLB-9, 212
Grey Walls Press DLB-112
Griboedov, Aleksandr Sergeevich
    1795?-1829 .... DLB-205
Grice, Paul 1913-1988 .... DLB-279
Grier, Eldon 1917- DLB-88
Grieve, C. M. (see MacDiarmid, Hugh)
Griffin, Bartholomew flourished 1596 ... DLB-172
Griffin, Gerald 1803-1840 .... DLB-159
The Griffin Poetry Prize Y-00
Griffith, Elizabeth 1727?-1793 .... DLB-39, 89
    Preface to The Delicate Distress (1769) DLB-39
Griffith, George 1857-1906 .... DLB-178
Griffiths, Ralph [publishing house] DLB-154
Griffiths, Trevor 1935- DLB-13, 245
Griggs, S. C., and Company DLB-49
Griggs, Sutton Elbert 1872-1930 .... DLB-50
Grignon, Claude-Henri 1894-1976 ...... DLB-68
Grigor'ev, Apollon Aleksandrovich
    1822-1864 .... DLB-277
Grigorovich, Dmitrii Vasil'evich
    1822-1899 .... DLB-238
Grigson, Geoffrey 1905- DLB-27
Grillparzer, Franz
    1791-1872 .... DLB-133; CDWLB-2
Grimald, Nicholas
    circa 1519-circa 1562 .... DLB-136
Grimké, Angelina Weld 1880-1958 ... DLB-50, 54
Grimké, Sarah Moore 1792-1873 .... DLB-239
Grimm, Hans 1875-1959 .... DLB-66
Grimm, Jacob 1785-1863 .... DLB-90
Grimm, Wilhelm
    1786-1859 .... DLB-90; CDWLB-2
Grimmelshausen, Johann Jacob Christoffel von
    1621 or 1622-1676 ...... DLB-168; CDWLB-2
Grimshaw, Beatrice Ethel 1871-1953 ..... DLB-174
Grin, Aleksandr Stepanovich
    1880-1932 .... DLB-272
Grindal, Edmund 1519 or 1520-1583 ... DLB-132
Gripe, Maria (Kristina) 1923- DLB-257
Griswold, Rufus Wilmot
    1815-1857 .... DLB-3, 59, 250
Grosart, Alexander Balloch 1827-1899 ... DLB-184
Grosholz, Emily 1950- DLB-282
Gross, Milt 1895-1953 .... DLB-11
Grosset and Dunlap DLB-49
Grossman, Allen 1932- DLB-193
Grossman Publishers DLB-46
Grossman, Vasilii Semenovich
    1905-1964 .... DLB-272
Grosseteste, Robert circa 1160-1253 ..... DLB-115
Grosvenor, Gilbert H. 1875-1966 .... DLB-91

Groth, Klaus 1819-1899.................DLB-129

Groulx, Lionel 1878-1967.............DLB-68

Grove, Frederick Philip (Felix Paul Greve)
    1879-1948.......................DLB-92

Grove Press..........................DLB-46

Grubb, Davis 1919-1980..............DLB-6

Gruelle, Johnny 1880-1938..........DLB-22

von Grumbach, Argula
    1492-after 1563?................DLB-179

Grymeston, Elizabeth
    before 1563-before 1604.........DLB-136

Gryphius, Andreas
    1616-1664............DLB-164; CDWLB-2

Gryphius, Christian 1649-1706......DLB-168

Guare, John 1938-..............DLB-7, 249

Guerra, Tonino 1920-...............DLB-128

Guest, Barbara 1920-..............DLB-5, 193

Guèvremont, Germaine 1893-1968....DLB-68

Guglielminetti, Amalia 1881-1941....DLB-264

Guidacci, Margherita 1921-1992....DLB-128

Guide to the Archives of Publishers, Journals,
    and Literary Agents in North American
    Libraries........................Y-93

Guillén, Jorge 1893-1984............DLB-108

Guilloux, Louis 1899-1980............DLB-72

Guilpin, Everard
    circa 1572-after 1608?...........DLB-136

Guiney, Louise Imogen 1861-1920....DLB-54

Guiterman, Arthur 1871-1943........DLB-11

Günderrode, Caroline von
    1780-1806........................DLB-90

Gundulić, Ivan
    1589-1638..........DLB-147; CDWLB-4

Gunesekera, Romesh 1954-...........DLB-267

Gunn, Bill 1934-1989................DLB-38

Gunn, James E. 1923-................DLB-8

Gunn, Neil M. 1891-1973.............DLB-15

Gunn, Thom 1929-........DLB-27; CDBLB-8

Gunnars, Kristjana 1948-............DLB-60

Günther, Johann Christian
    1695-1723........................DLB-168

Gurik, Robert 1932-.................DLB-60

Gurney, A. R. 1930-.................DLB-266

Gurney, Ivor 1890-1937...............Y-02

Gustafson, Ralph 1909-1995..........DLB-88

Gustafsson, Lars 1936-..............DLB-257

Gütersloh, Albert Paris 1887-1973...DLB-81

Guthrie, A. B., Jr. 1901-1991.....DLB-6, 212

Guthrie, Ramon 1896-1973............DLB-4

The Guthrie Theater.................DLB-7

Guthrie, Thomas Anstey (see Anstey, FC)

Gutzkow, Karl 1811-1878.............DLB-133

Guy, Ray 1939-......................DLB-60

Guy, Rosa 1925-.....................DLB-33

Guyot, Arnold 1807-1884.............DS-13

Gwynn, R. S. 1948-..................DLB-282

Gwynne, Erskine 1898-1948...........DLB-4

Gyles, John 1680-1755...............DLB-99

Gyllensten, Lars 1921-..............DLB-257

Gysin, Brion 1916-..................DLB-16

H

H.D. (see Doolittle, Hilda)

Habermas, Jürgen 1929-..............DLB-242

Habington, William 1605-1654........DLB-126

Hacker, Marilyn 1942-............DLB-120, 282

Hackett, Albert (see Goodrich, Frances)

Hacks, Peter 1928-..................DLB-124

Hadas, Rachel 1948-.............DLB-120, 282

Hadden, Briton 1898-1929............DLB-91

Hagedorn, Friedrich von 1708-1754....DLB-168

Hagelstange, Rudolf 1912-1984.......DLB-69

Haggard, H. Rider
    1856-1925........DLB-70, 156, 174, 178

Haggard, William 1907-1993....DLB-276; Y-93

Hagy, Alyson 1960-..................DLB-244

Hahn-Hahn, Ida Gräfin von
    1805-1880........................DLB-133

Haig-Brown, Roderick 1908-1976......DLB-88

Haight, Gordon S. 1901-1985.........DLB-103

Hailey, Arthur 1920-............DLB-88; Y-82

Haines, John 1924-...............DLB-5, 212

Hake, Edward flourished 1566-1604...DLB-136

Hake, Thomas Gordon 1809-1895.......DLB-32

Hakluyt, Richard 1552?-1616.........DLB-136

Halas, František 1901-1949..........DLB-215

Halbe, Max 1865-1944................DLB-118

Halberstam, David 1934-.............DLB-241

Haldane, J. B. S. 1892-1964.........DLB-160

Haldeman, Joe 1943-.................DLB-8

Haldeman-Julius Company.............DLB-46

Haldone, Charlotte 1894-1969........DLB-191

Hale, E. J., and Son................DLB-49

Hale, Edward Everett
    1822-1909............DLB-1, 42, 74, 235

Hale, Janet Campbell 1946-..........DLB-175

Hale, Kathleen 1898-................DLB-160

Hale, Leo Thomas (see Ebon)

Hale, Lucretia Peabody 1820-1900....DLB-42

Hale, Nancy
    1908-1988......DLB-86; DS-17; Y-80, Y-88

Hale, Sarah Josepha (Buell)
    1788-1879............DLB-1, 42, 73, 243

Hale, Susan 1833-1910...............DLB-221

Hales, John 1584-1656...............DLB-151

Halévy, Ludovic 1834-1908...........DLB-192

Haley, Alex 1921-1992........DLB-38; CDALB-7

Haliburton, Thomas Chandler
    1796-1865........................DLB-11, 99

Hall, Adam 1920-1995................DLB-276

Hall, Anna Maria 1800-1881..........DLB-159

Hall, Donald 1928-..................DLB-5

Hall, Edward 1497-1547..............DLB-132

Hall, Halsey 1898-1977..............DLB-241

Hall, James 1793-1868............DLB-73, 74

Hall, Joseph 1574-1656..........DLB-121, 151

Hall, Radclyffe 1880-1943...........DLB-191

Hall, Samuel [publishing house].....DLB-49

Hall, Sarah Ewing 1761-1830.........DLB-200

Hall, Stuart 1932-..................DLB-242

Hallam, Arthur Henry 1811-1833......DLB-32

On Some of the Characteristics of Modern
    Poetry and On the Lyrical Poems of
    Alfred Tennyson (1831)..........DLB-32

Halleck, Fitz-Greene 1790-1867....DLB-3, 250

Haller, Albrecht von 1708-1777......DLB-168

Halliday, Brett (see Dresser, Davis)

Halliwell-Phillipps, James Orchard
    1820-1889........................DLB-184

Hallmann, Johann Christian
    1640-1704 or 1716?...............DLB-168

Hallmark Editions...................DLB-46

Halper, Albert 1904-1984............DLB-9

Halperin, John William 1941-........DLB-111

Halstead, Murat 1829-1908...........DLB-23

Hamann, Johann Georg 1730-1788.....DLB-97

Hamburger, Michael 1924-............DLB-27

Hamilton, Alexander 1712-1756.......DLB-31

Hamilton, Alexander 1755?-1804......DLB-37

Hamilton, Cicely 1872-1952......DLB-10, 197

Hamilton, Edmond 1904-1977..........DLB-8

Hamilton, Elizabeth 1758-1816....DLB-116, 158

Hamilton, Gail (see Corcoran, Barbara)

Hamilton, Gail (see Dodge, Mary Abigail)

Hamilton, Hamish, Limited...........DLB-112

Hamilton, Hugo 1953-................DLB-267

Hamilton, Ian 1938-.............DLB-40, 155

Hamilton, Janet 1795-1873...........DLB-199

Hamilton, Mary Agnes 1884-1962......DLB-197

Hamilton, Patrick 1904-1962......DLB-10, 191

Hamilton, Virginia 1936-2002.....DLB-33, 52

Hamilton-Paterson, James 1941-......DLB-267

Hamilton, Sir William 1788-1856.....DLB-262

Hammerstein, Oscar, II 1895-1960....DLB-265

Hammett, Dashiell
    1894-1961....DLB-226, 280; DS-6; CDALB-5

The Glass Key and Other Dashiell Hammett
    Mysteries........................Y-96

Dashiell Hammett: An Appeal in TAC..Y-91

Hammon, Jupiter 1711-died between
    1790 and 1806................DLB-31, 50

Hammond, John ?-1663................DLB-24

Hamner, Earl 1923-..................DLB-6

Hampson, John 1901-1955.............DLB-191

Hampton, Christopher 1946-..........DLB-13

Handel-Mazzetti, Enrica von 1871-1955..DLB-81

Handke, Peter 1942-.............DLB-85, 124

Handlin, Oscar 1915-................DLB-17

Hankin, St. John 1869-1909..........DLB-10

Cumulative Index

Hanley, Clifford 1922- DLB-14
Hanley, James 1901-1985 .... DLB-191
Hannah, Barry 1942- DLB-6, 234
Hannay, James 1827-1873 .... DLB-21
Hano, Arnold 1922- DLB-241
Hansberry, Lorraine
   1930-1965 .... DLB-7, 38; CDALB-1
Hansen, Martin A. 1909-1955 .... DLB-214
Hansen, Thorkild 1927-1989 .... DLB-214
Hanson, Elizabeth 1684-1737 .... DLB-200
Hapgood, Norman 1868-1937 .... DLB-91
Happel, Eberhard Werner 1647-1690.... DLB-168
Harbach, Otto 1873-1963 .... DLB-265
The Harbinger 1845-1849 .... DLB-223
Harburg, E. Y. "Yip" 1896-1981 .... DLB-265
Harcourt Brace Jovanovich DLB-46
Hardenberg, Friedrich von (see Novalis)
Harding, Walter 1917- DLB-111
Hardwick, Elizabeth 1916- DLB-6
Hardy, Alexandre 1572?-1632 .... DLB-268
Hardy, Frank 1917-1994................ DLB-260
Hardy, Thomas
   1840-1928 ...... DLB-18, 19, 135; CDBLB-5
"Candour in English Fiction" (1890) DLB-18
Hare, Cyril 1900-1958 .... DLB-77
Hare, David 1947- DLB-13
Hare, R. M. 1919-2002................. DLB-262
Hargrove, Marion 1919- DLB-11
Häring, Georg Wilhelm Heinrich
   (see Alexis, Willibald)
Harington, Donald 1935- DLB-152
Harington, Sir John 1560-1612......... DLB-136
Harjo, Joy 1951- DLB-120, 175
Harkness, Margaret (John Law)
   1854-1923 .... DLB-197
Harley, Edward, second Earl of Oxford
   1689-1741..................... DLB-213
Harley, Robert, first Earl of Oxford
   1661-1724..................... DLB-213
Harlow, Robert 1923- DLB-60
Harman, Thomas flourished 1566-1573.. DLB-136
Harness, Charles L. 1915- DLB-8
Harnett, Cynthia 1893-1981............ DLB-161
Harnick, Sheldon 1924- DLB-265
Harper, Edith Alice Mary (see Wickham, Anna)
Harper, Fletcher 1806-1877 .... DLB-79
Harper, Frances Ellen Watkins
   1825-1911................... DLB-50, 221
Harper, Michael S. 1938- DLB-41
Harper and Brothers.................. DLB-49
Harpur, Charles 1813-1868 .... DLB-230
Harraden, Beatrice 1864-1943 .... DLB-153
Harrap, George G., and Company
   Limited..................... DLB-112
Harriot, Thomas 1560-1621............ DLB-136
Harris, Alexander 1805-1874 .... DLB-230
Harris, Benjamin ?-circa 1720........ DLB-42, 43

Harris, Christie 1907- DLB-88
Harris, Errol E. 1908- DLB-279
Harris, Frank 1856-1931 ....DLB-156, 197
Harris, George Washington
   1814-1869 .... DLB-3, 11, 248
Harris, Joanne 1964- DLB-271
Harris, Joel Chandler
   1848-1908 ....DLB-11, 23, 42, 78, 91
Harris, Mark 1922- DLB-2; Y-80
Harris, William Torrey 1835-1909.......DLB-270
Harris, Wilson 1921- DLB-117; CDWLB-3
Harrison, Mrs. Burton
   (see Harrison, Constance Cary)
Harrison, Charles Yale 1898-1954....... DLB-68
Harrison, Constance Cary 1843-1920 ... DLB-221
Harrison, Frederic 1831-1923........DLB-57, 190
"On Style in English Prose" (1898) DLB-57
Harrison, Harry 1925- DLB-8
Harrison, James P., Company DLB-49
Harrison, Jim 1937- Y-82
Harrison, M. John 1945- DLB-261
Harrison, Mary St. Leger Kingsley
   (see Malet, Lucas)
Harrison, Paul Carter 1936- DLB-38
Harrison, Susan Frances 1859-1935...... DLB-99
Harrison, Tony 1937- DLB-40, 245
Harrison, William 1535-1593.......... DLB-136
Harrison, William 1933- DLB-234
Harrisse, Henry 1829-1910 .... DLB-47
The Harry Ransom Humanities
   Research Center at the University
   of Texas at Austin Y-00
Harryman, Carla 1952- DLB-193
Harsdörffer, Georg Philipp 1607-1658 ... DLB-164
Harsent, David 1942- DLB-40
Hart, Albert Bushnell 1854-1943 .... DLB-17
Hart, Anne 1768-1834 .... DLB-200
Hart, Elizabeth 1771-1833............. DLB-200
Hart, Julia Catherine 1796-1867 .... DLB-99
Hart, Lorenz 1895-1943 .... DLB-265
The Lorenz Hart Centenary............... Y-95
Hart, Moss 1904-1961 ....DLB-7, 266
Hart, Oliver 1723-1795................ DLB-31
Hart-Davis, Rupert, Limited.......... DLB-112
Harte, Bret 1836-1902
   ....DLB-12, 64, 74, 79, 186; CDALB-3
Harte, Edward Holmead 1922- DLB-127
Harte, Houston Harriman 1927- DLB-127
Hartlaub, Felix 1913-1945 .... DLB-56
Hartleben, Otto Erich 1864-1905....... DLB-118
Hartley, David 1705-1757 .... DLB-252
Hartley, L. P. 1895-1972............ DLB-15, 139
Hartley, Marsden 1877-1943 .... DLB-54
Hartling, Peter 1933- DLB-75
Hartman, Geoffrey H. 1929- DLB-67
Hartmann, Sadakichi 1867-1944......... DLB-54

Hartmann von Aue
   circa 1160-circa 1205 ....DLB-138; CDWLB-2
Hartshorne, Charles 1897- DLB-270
Harvey, Gabriel
   1550?-circa 1631 ....DLB-167, 213, 281
Harvey, Jack (see Rankin, Ian)
Harvey, Jean-Charles 1891-1967 .... DLB-88
Harvill Press Limited DLB-112
Harwood, Lee 1939- DLB-40
Harwood, Ronald 1934- DLB-13
Hašek, Jaroslav 1883-1923 ...DLB-215; CDWLB-4
Haskins, Charles Homer 1870-1937...... DLB-47
Haslam, Gerald 1937- DLB-212
Hass, Robert 1941- DLB-105, 206
Hasselstrom, Linda M. 1943- DLB-256
Hastings, Michael 1938- DLB-233
Hatar, Győző 1914- DLB-215
The Hatch-Billops Collection DLB-76
Hathaway, William 1944- DLB-120
Hauff, Wilhelm 1802-1827............. DLB-90
A Haughty and Proud Generation (1922),
   by Ford Madox Hueffer........... DLB-36
Haugwitz, August Adolph von
   1647-1706..................... DLB-168
Hauptmann, Carl 1858-1921 .... DLB-66, 118
Hauptmann, Gerhart
   1862-1946 ....DLB-66, 118; CDWLB-2
Hauser, Marianne 1910- Y-83
Havel, Václav 1936- DLB-232; CDWLB-4
Haven, Alice B. Neal 1827-1863 .... DLB-260
Havergal, Frances Ridley 1836-1879 .... DLB-199
Hawes, Stephen 1475?-before 1529 ..... DLB-132
Hawker, Robert Stephen 1803-1875...... DLB-32
Hawkes, John
   1925-1998 .... DLB-2, 7, 227; Y-80, Y-98
John Hawkes: A Tribute Y-98
Hawkesworth, John 1720-1773 .... DLB-142
Hawkins, Sir Anthony Hope (see Hope, Anthony)
Hawkins, Sir John 1719-1789 ....DLB-104, 142
Hawkins, Walter Everette 1883-? DLB-50
Hawthorne, Nathaniel 1804-1864
   ....DLB-1, 74, 183, 223, 269; CDALB-2
Hawthorne, Nathaniel 1804-1864 and
   Hawthorne, Sophia Peabody
   1809-1871..................... DLB-183
Hawthorne, Sophia Peabody
   1809-1871................... DLB-183, 239
Hay, John 1835-1905 ....DLB-12, 47, 189
Hay, John 1915- DLB-275
Hayashi, Fumiko 1903-1951........... DLB-180
Haycox, Ernest 1899-1950............ DLB-206
Haycraft, Anna Margaret (see Ellis, Alice Thomas)
Hayden, Robert
   1913-1980 .... DLB-5, 76; CDALB-1
Haydon, Benjamin Robert
   1786-1846..................... DLB-110
Hayes, John Michael 1919- DLB-26
Hayley, William 1745-1820 .... DLB-93, 142

Haym, Rudolf 1821-1901 ....DLB-129

Hayman, Robert 1575-1629.............DLB-99

Hayman, Ronald 1932- DLB-155

Hayne, Paul Hamilton
  1830-1886 ....DLB-3, 64, 79, 248

Hays, Mary 1760-1843.............DLB-142, 158

Hayward, John 1905-1965.............DLB-201

Haywood, Eliza 1693?-1756.............DLB-39

From the Dedication, *Lasselia* (1723) DLB-39

From *The Tea-Table* *DLB-39*

From the Preface to *The Disguis'd
  Prince* (1723).............DLB-39

Hazard, Willis P. [publishing house].............DLB-49

Hazlitt, William 1778-1830.............DLB-110, 158

Hazzard, Shirley 1931- Y-82

Head, Bessie
  1937-1986 ....DLB-117, 225; CDWLB-3

Headley, Joel T. 1813-1897 ....DLB-30, 183; DS-13

Heaney, Seamus
  1939- DLB-40; Y-95; CDBLB-8

Heard, Nathan C. 1936- DLB-33

Hearn, Lafcadio 1850-1904 ....DLB-12, 78, 189

Hearn, Mary Anne (Marianne Farningham,
  Eva Hope) 1834-1909 ....DLB-240

Hearne, John 1926- DLB-117

Hearne, Samuel 1745-1792.............DLB-99

Hearne, Thomas 1678?-1735.............DLB-213

Hearst, William Randolph 1863-1951.............DLB-25

Hearst, William Randolph, Jr.
  1908-1993 ....DLB-127

Heartman, Charles Frederick
  1883-1953 ....DLB-187

Heath, Catherine 1924- DLB-14

Heath, James Ewell 1792-1862.............DLB-248

Heath, Roy A. K. 1926- DLB-117

Heath-Stubbs, John 1918- DLB-27

Heavysege, Charles 1816-1876 ....DLB-99

Hebbel, Friedrich
  1813-1863 ....DLB-129; CDWLB-2

Hebel, Johann Peter 1760-1826 ....DLB-90

Heber, Richard 1774-1833 ....DLB-184

Hébert, Anne 1916-2000 ....DLB-68

Hébert, Jacques 1923- DLB-53

Hecht, Anthony 1923- DLB-5, 169

Hecht, Ben 1894-1964 ....DLB-7, 9, 25, 26, 28, 86

Hecker, Isaac Thomas 1819-1888 ....DLB-1, 243

Hedge, Frederic Henry
  1805-1890 ....DLB-1, 59, 243

Hefner, Hugh M. 1926- DLB-137

Hegel, Georg Wilhelm Friedrich
  1770-1831 ....DLB-90

Heide, Robert 1939- DLB-249

Heidish, Marcy 1947- Y-82

Heißenbüttel, Helmut 1921-1996.............DLB-75

Heike monogatari DLB-203

Hein, Christoph 1944- DLB-124; CDWLB-2

Hein, Piet 1905-1996.............DLB-214

Heine, Heinrich 1797-1856.............DLB-90; CDWLB-2

Heinemann, Larry 1944- DS-9

Heinemann, William, Limited.............DLB-112

Heinesen, William 1900-1991 ....DLB-214

Heinlein, Robert A. 1907-1988.............DLB-8

Heinrich Julius of Brunswick
  1564-1613 ....DLB-164

Heinrich von dem Türlîn
  flourished circa 1230.............DLB-138

Heinrich von Melk
  flourished after 1160 ....DLB-148

Heinrich von Veldeke
  circa 1145-circa 1190.............DLB-138

Heinrich, Willi 1920- DLB-75

Heinse, Wilhelm 1746-1803.............DLB-94

Heinz, W. C. 1915- DLB-171

Heiskell, John 1872-1972 ....DLB-127

Hejinian, Lyn 1941- DLB-165

Heliand circa 850 ....DLB-148

Heller, Joseph
  1923-1999 ....DLB-2, 28, 227; Y-80, Y-99, Y-02

Heller, Michael 1937- DLB-165

Hellman, Lillian 1906-1984 ....DLB-7, 228; Y-84

Hellwig, Johann 1609-1674 ....DLB-164

Helprin, Mark 1947- Y-85; CDALB-7

Helwig, David 1938- DLB-60

Hemans, Felicia 1793-1835.............DLB-96

Hemenway, Abby Maria 1828-1890 ....DLB-243

Hemingway, Ernest 1899-1961
  .....DLB-4, 9, 102, 210; Y-81, Y-87, Y-99;
  DS-1, DS-15, DS-16; CDALB-4

The Hemingway Centenary Celebration at the
  JFK Library.............Y-99

Ernest Hemingway: A Centennial
  Celebration Y-99

The Ernest Hemingway Collection at the
  John F. Kennedy Library Y-99

Ernest Hemingway Declines to Introduce
  War and Peace.............Y-01

The Hemingway Letters Project
  Finds an Editor Y-02

The Hemingway/Fenton Correspondence.............Y-02

Ernest Hemingway's Reaction to James Gould
  Cozzens.............Y-98

Ernest Hemingway's Toronto Journalism
  Revisited: With Three Previously
  Unrecorded Stories Y-92

Falsifying Hemingway Y-96

Hemingway: Twenty-Five Years Later Y-85

Not Immediately Discernible . . . but Eventually
  Quite Clear: The *First Light* and *Final Years*
  of Hemingway's Centenary Y-99

Hemingway Salesmen's Dummies.............Y-00

Second International Hemingway Colloquium:
  Cuba.............Y-98

Hémon, Louis 1880-1913 ....DLB-92

Hempel, Amy 1951- DLB-218

Hempel, Carl G. 1905-1997.............DLB-279

Hemphill, Paul 1936- Y-87

Hénault, Gilles 1920- DLB-88

Henchman, Daniel 1689-1761 ....DLB-24

Henderson, Alice Corbin 1881-1949.............DLB-54

Henderson, Archibald 1877-1963.............DLB-103

Henderson, David 1942- DLB-41

Henderson, George Wylie 1904- DLB-51

Henderson, Zenna 1917-1983 ....DLB-8

Henighan, Tom 1934- DLB-251

Henisch, Peter 1943- DLB-85

Henley, Beth 1952- Y-86

Henley, William Ernest 1849-1903.............DLB-19

Henning, Rachel 1826-1914 ....DLB-230

Henningsen, Agnes 1868-1962 ....DLB-214

Henniker, Florence 1855-1923.............DLB-135

Henry, Alexander 1739-1824.............DLB-99

Henry, Buck 1930- DLB-26

Henry VIII of England 1491-1547 ....DLB-132

Henry of Ghent
  circa 1217-1229 - 1293.............DLB-115

Henry, Marguerite 1902-1997 ....DLB-22

Henry, O. (see Porter, William Sydney)

Henry, Robert Selph 1889-1970.............DLB-17

Henry, Will (see Allen, Henry W.)

Henryson, Robert
  1420s or 1430s-circa 1505.............DLB-146

Henschke, Alfred (see Klabund)

Hensher, Philip 1965- DLB-267

Hensley, Sophie Almon 1866-1946 ....DLB-99

Henson, Lance 1944- DLB-175

Henty, G. A. 1832?-1902.............DLB-18, 141

Hentz, Caroline Lee 1800-1856.............DLB-3, 248

Heraclitus
  flourished circa 500 B.C. DLB-176

Herbert, Agnes circa 1880-1960 ....DLB-174

Herbert, Alan Patrick 1890-1971 ....DLB-10, 191

Herbert, Edward, Lord, of Cherbury
  1582-1648 ....DLB-121, 151, 252

Herbert, Frank 1920-1986 ....DLB-8; CDALB-7

Herbert, George 1593-1633 ....DLB-126; CDBLB-1

Herbert, Henry William 1807-1858.............DLB-3, 73

Herbert, John 1926- DLB-53

Herbert, Mary Sidney, Countess of Pembroke
  (see Sidney, Mary)

Herbert, Xavier 1901-1984 ....DLB-260

Herbert, Zbigniew
  1924-1998 ....DLB-232; CDWLB-4

Herbst, Josephine 1892-1969 ....DLB-9

Herburger, Gunter 1932- DLB-75, 124

Hercules, Frank E. M. 1917-1996 ....DLB-33

Herder, Johann Gottfried 1744-1803 ....DLB-97

Herder, B., Book Company.............DLB-49

Heredia, José-María de 1842-1905.............DLB-217

Herford, Charles Harold 1853-1931 ....DLB-149

Hergesheimer, Joseph 1880-1954 ....DLB-9, 102

Heritage Press DLB-46

Hermann the Lame 1013-1054 ....DLB-148

Cumulative Index

Hermes, Johann Timotheus
1738-1821.....................DLB-97

Hermlin, Stephan 1915-1997..........DLB-69

Hernández, Alfonso C. 1938-........DLB-122

Hernández, Inés 1947-...............DLB-122

Hernández, Miguel 1910-1942.........DLB-134

Hernton, Calvin C. 1932-............DLB-38

Herodotus circa 484 B.C.-circa 420 B.C.
................DLB-176; CDWLB-1

Heron, Robert 1764-1807.............DLB-142

Herr, Michael 1940-..................DLB-185

Herrera, Juan Felipe 1948-..........DLB-122

Herrick, E. R., and Company.........DLB-49

Herrick, Robert 1591-1674...........DLB-126

Herrick, Robert 1868-1938.........DLB-9, 12, 78

Herrick, William 1915-..............Y-83

Herrmann, John 1900-1959............DLB-4

Hersey, John
1914-1993......DLB-6, 185, 278; CDALB-7

Hertel, François 1905-1985..........DLB-68

Hervé-Bazin, Jean Pierre Marie (see Bazin, Hervé)

Hervey, John, Lord 1696-1743........DLB-101

Herwig, Georg 1817-1875.............DLB-133

Herzen, Aleksandr Ivanovich
1812-1870....................DLB-277

Herzog, Emile Salomon Wilhelm
(see Maurois, André)

Hesiod eighth century B.C............DLB-176

Hesse, Hermann
1877-1962............DLB-66; CDWLB-2

Hessus, Helius Eobanus 1488-1540......DLB-179

Heureka! (see Kertész, Imre and Nobel Prize
in Literature: 2002)..............Y-02

Hewat, Alexander circa 1743-circa 1824...DLB-30

Hewitt, John 1907-..................DLB-27

Hewlett, Maurice 1861-1923.......DLB-34, 156

Heyen, William 1940-................DLB-5

Heyer, Georgette 1902-1974........DLB-77, 191

Heym, Stefan 1913-..................DLB-69

Heyse, Paul 1830-1914...............DLB-129

Heytesbury, William
circa 1310-1372 or 1373..........DLB-115

Heyward, Dorothy 1890-1961.........DLB-7, 249

Heyward, DuBose 1885-1940....DLB-7, 9, 45, 249

Heywood, John 1497?-1580?..........DLB-136

Heywood, Thomas
1573 or 1574-1641...............DLB-62

Hibbs, Ben 1901-1975................DLB-137

Hichens, Robert S. 1864-1950........DLB-153

Hickey, Emily 1845-1924.............DLB-199

Hickman, William Albert 1877-1957...DLB-92

Hicks, Granville 1901-1982..........DLB-246

Hidalgo, José Luis 1919-1947........DLB-108

Hiebert, Paul 1892-1987.............DLB-68

Hieng, Andrej 1925-.................DLB-181

Hierro, José 1922-..................DLB-108

Higgins, Aidan 1927-................DLB-14

Higgins, Colin 1941-1988............DLB-26

Higgins, George V.
1939-1999.........DLB-2; Y-81, Y-98, Y-99

George V. Higgins in Class..........Y-02

George V. Higgins to Julian Symons.....Y-99

Higginson, Thomas Wentworth
1823-1911.................DLB-1, 64, 243

Highwater, Jamake 1942?-........DLB-52; Y-85

Hijuelos, Oscar 1951-..............DLB-145

Hildegard von Bingen 1098-1179......DLB-148

Das Hildebrandslied
circa 820...............DLB-148; CDWLB-2

Hildesheimer, Wolfgang
1916-1991....................DLB-69, 124

Hildreth, Richard 1807-1865...DLB-1, 30, 59, 235

Hill, Aaron 1685-1750...............DLB-84

Hill, Geoffrey 1932-..........DLB-40; CDBLB-8

Hill, George M., Company............DLB-49

Hill, "Sir" John 1714?-1775.........DLB-39

Hill, Lawrence, and Company,
Publishers......................DLB-46

Hill, Leslie 1880-1960..............DLB-51

Hill, Reginald 1936-................DLB-276

Hill, Susan 1942-...............DLB-14, 139

Hill, Walter 1942-..................DLB-44

Hill and Wang.......................DLB-46

Hillberry, Conrad 1928-.............DLB-120

Hillerman, Tony 1925-...............DLB-206

Hilliard, Gray and Company..........DLB-49

Hills, Lee 1906-....................DLB-127

Hillyer, Robert 1895-1961...........DLB-54

Hilton, James 1900-1954..........DLB-34, 77

Hilton, Walter died 1396............DLB-146

Hilton and Company..................DLB-49

Himes, Chester 1909-1984....DLB-2, 76, 143, 226

Hindmarsh, Joseph [publishing house]....DLB-170

Hine, Daryl 1936-...................DLB-60

Hingley, Ronald 1920-...............DLB-155

Hinojosa-Smith, Rolando 1929-.......DLB-82

Hinton, S. E. 1948-.................CDALB-7

Hippel, Theodor Gottlieb von
1741-1796........................DLB-97

Hippocrates of Cos flourished circa 425 B.C.
..........................DLB-176; CDWLB-1

Hirabayashi, Taiko 1905-1972........DLB-180

Hirsch, E. D., Jr. 1928-............DLB-67

Hirsch, Edward 1950-................DLB-120

Hoagland, Edward 1932-..............DLB-6

Hoagland, Everett H., III 1942-.....DLB-41

Hoban, Russell 1925-............DLB-52; Y-90

Hobbes, Thomas
1588-1679................DLB-151, 252, 281

Hobby, Oveta 1905-..................DLB-127

Hobby, William 1878-1964............DLB-127

Hobsbaum, Philip 1932-..............DLB-40

Hobson, Laura Z. 1900-..............DLB-28

Hobson, Sarah 1947-.................DLB-204

Hoby, Thomas 1530-1566..............DLB-132

Hoccleve, Thomas
circa 1368-circa 1437............DLB-146

Hochhuth, Rolf 1931-................DLB-124

Hochman, Sandra 1936-...............DLB-5

Hocken, Thomas Morland
1836-1910.......................DLB-184

Hocking, William E. 1873-1966.......DLB-270

Hodder and Stoughton, Limited.......DLB-106

Hodgins, Jack 1938-.................DLB-60

Hodgman, Helen 1945-................DLB-14

Hodgskin, Thomas 1787-1869..........DLB-158

Hodgson, Ralph 1871-1962............DLB-19

Hodgson, William Hope
1877-1918...............DLB-70, 153, 156, 178

Hoe, Robert, III 1839-1909..........DLB-187

Hoeg, Peter 1957-...................DLB-214

Højholt, Per 1928-..................DLB-214

Hoffenstein, Samuel 1890-1947.......DLB-11

Hoffman, Charles Fenno 1806-1884...DLB-3, 250

Hoffman, Daniel 1923-...............DLB-5

Hoffmann, E. T. A.
1776-1822................DLB-90; CDWLB-2

Hoffman, Frank B. 1888-1958.........DLB-188

Hoffman, William 1925-..............DLB-234

Hoffmanswaldau, Christian Hoffman von
1616-1679.......................DLB-168

Hofmann, Michael 1957-..............DLB-40

Hofmannsthal, Hugo von
1874-1929.............DLB-81, 118; CDWLB-2

Hofstadter, Richard 1916-1970.....DLB-17, 246

Hogan, Desmond 1950-................DLB-14

Hogan, Linda 1947-..................DLB-175

Hogan and Thompson..................DLB-49

Hogarth Press.......................DLB-112

Hogg, James 1770-1835...........DLB-93, 116, 159

Hohberg, Wolfgang Helmhard Freiherr von
1612-1688.......................DLB-168

von Hohenheim, Philippus Aureolus
Theophrastus Bombastus (see Paracelsus)

Hohl, Ludwig 1904-1980..............DLB-56

Holbrook, David 1923-............DLB-14, 40

Holcroft, Thomas 1745-1809....DLB-39, 89, 158

Preface to *Alwyn* (1780)...........DLB-39

Holden, Jonathan 1941-..............DLB-105

"Contemporary Verse Story-telling"....DLB-105

Holden, Molly 1927-1981.............DLB-40

Hölderlin, Friedrich
1770-1843............DLB-90; CDWLB-2

Holdstock, Robert 1948-.............DLB-261

Holiday House.......................DLB-46

Holinshed, Raphael died 1580........DLB-167

Holland, J. G. 1819-1881............DS-13

Holland, Norman N. 1927-............DLB-67

Hollander, John 1929-...............DLB-5

Holley, Marietta 1836-1926..........DLB-11

Hollinghurst, Alan 1954-............DLB-207

Hollingsworth, Margaret 1940- DLB-60
Hollo, Anselm 1934- DLB-40
Holloway, Emory 1885-1977..........DLB-103
Holloway, John 1920- DLB-27
Holloway House Publishing Company....DLB-46
Holme, Constance 1880-1955...........DLB-34
Holmes, Abraham S. 1821?-1908........DLB-99
Holmes, John Clellon 1926-1988.....DLB-16, 237
"Four Essays on the Beat Generation".....DLB-16
Holmes, Mary Jane 1825-1907......DLB-202, 221
Holmes, Oliver Wendell
 1809-1894.......DLB-1, 189, 235; CDALB-2
Holmes, Richard 1945- DLB-155
The Cult of Biography
 Excerpts from the Second Folio Debate:
 "Biographies are generally a disease of
 English Literature"................... Y-86
Holmes, Thomas James 1874-1959......DLB-187
Holroyd, Michael 1935- DLB-155; Y-99
Holst, Hermann E. von 1841-1904........DLB-47
Holt, Henry, and Company.........DLB-49, 280
Holt, John 1721-1784..................DLB-43
Holt, Rinehart and Winston............DLB-46
Holtby, Winifred 1898-1935............DLB-191
Holthusen, Hans Egon 1913- DLB-69
Hölty, Ludwig Christoph Heinrich
 1748-1776........................DLB-94
Holub, Miroslav
 1923-1998............DLB-232; CDWLB-4
Holz, Arno 1863-1929.................DLB-118
Home, Henry, Lord Kames
 (see Kames, Henry Home, Lord)
Home, John 1722-1808..................DLB-84
Home, William Douglas 1912- DLB-13
Home Publishing Company DLB-49
Homer circa eighth-seventh centuries B.C.
 ....DLB-176; CDWLB-1
Homer, Winslow 1836-1910............DLB-188
Homes, Geoffrey (see Mainwaring, Daniel)
Honan, Park 1928- DLB-111
Hone, William 1780-1842.........DLB-110, 158
Hongo, Garrett Kaoru 1951- DLB-120
Honig, Edwin 1919- DLB-5
Hood, Hugh 1928- DLB-53
Hood, Mary 1946- DLB-234
Hood, Thomas 1799-1845..............DLB-96
Hook, Sidney 1902-1989..............DLB-279
Hook, Theodore 1788-1841............DLB-116
Hooker, Jeremy 1941- DLB-40
Hooker, Richard 1554-1600...........DLB-132
Hooker, Thomas 1586-1647............DLB-24
hooks, bell 1952- DLB-246
Hooper, Johnson Jones
 1815-1862................DLB-3, 11, 248
Hope, Anthony 1863-1933........DLB-153, 156
Hope, Christopher 1944- DLB-225
Hope, Eva (see Hearn, Mary Anne)

Hope, Laurence (Adela Florence
 Cory Nicolson) 1865-1904.........DLB-240
Hopkins, Ellice 1836-1904............DLB-190
Hopkins, Gerard Manley
 1844-1889..........DLB-35, 57; CDBLB-5
Hopkins, John (see Sternhold, Thomas)
Hopkins, John H., and Son DLB-46
Hopkins, Lemuel 1750-1801............DLB-37
Hopkins, Pauline Elizabeth 1859-1930....DLB-50
Hopkins, Samuel 1721-1803............DLB-31
Hopkinson, Francis 1737-1791.........DLB-31
Hopkinson, Nalo 1960- DLB-251
Hopper, Nora (Mrs. Nora Chesson)
 1871-1906.......................DLB-240
Hoppin, Augustus 1828-1896..........DLB-188
Hora, Josef 1891-1945........DLB-215; CDWLB-4
Horace 65 B.C.-8 B.C......DLB-211; CDWLB-1
Horgan, Paul 1903-1995......DLB-102, 212; Y-85
Horizon Press DLB-46
Hornby, C. H. St. John 1867-1946......DLB-201
Hornby, Nick 1957- DLB-207
Horne, Frank 1899-1974................DLB-51
Horne, Richard Henry (Hengist)
 1802 or 1803-1884.................DLB-32
Horne, Thomas 1608-1654.............DLB-281
Horney, Karen 1885-1952.............DLB-246
Hornung, E. W. 1866-1921.............DLB-70
Horovitz, Israel 1939- DLB-7
Horton, George Moses 1797?-1883?......DLB-50
Horváth, Ödön von 1901-1938.....DLB-85, 124
Horwood, Harold 1923- DLB-60
Hosford, E. and E. [publishing house].....DLB-49
Hoskens, Jane Fenn 1693-1770?........DLB-200
Hoskyns, John circa 1566-1638.....DLB-121, 281
Hosokawa Yūsai 1535-1610............DLB-203
Hospers, John 1918- DLB-279
Hostovský, Egon 1908-1973...........DLB-215
Hotchkiss and Company...............DLB-49
Hough, Emerson 1857-1923.........DLB-9, 212
Houghton, Stanley 1881-1913..........DLB-10
Houghton Mifflin Company DLB-49
Household, Geoffrey 1900-1988........DLB-87
Housman, A. E. 1859-1936....DLB-19; CDBLB-5
Housman, Laurence 1865-1959.........DLB-10
Houston, Pam 1962- DLB-244
Houwald, Ernst von 1778-1845.........DLB-90
Hovey, Richard 1864-1900.............DLB-54
Howard, Donald R. 1927-1987.........DLB-111
Howard, Maureen 1930- Y-83
Howard, Richard 1929- DLB-5
Howard, Roy W. 1883-1964............DLB-29
Howard, Sidney 1891-1939......DLB-7, 26, 249
Howard, Thomas, second Earl of Arundel
 1585-1646......................DLB-213
Howe, E. W. 1853-1937............DLB-12, 25
Howe, Henry 1816-1893................DLB-30

Howe, Irving 1920-1993...............DLB-67
Howe, Joseph 1804-1873...............DLB-99
Howe, Julia Ward 1819-1910....DLB-1, 189, 235
Howe, Percival Presland 1886-1944....DLB-149
Howe, Susan 1937- DLB-120
Howell, Clark, Sr. 1863-1936..........DLB-25
Howell, Evan P. 1839-1905.............DLB-23
Howell, James 1594?-1666.............DLB-151
Howell, Soskin and Company..........DLB-46
Howell, Warren Richardson
 1912-1984......................DLB-140
Howells, William Dean 1837-1920
 ....DLB-12, 64, 74, 79, 189; CDALB-3
Introduction to Paul Laurence Dunbar,
 Lyrics of Lowly Life (1896) DLB-50
Howitt, Mary 1799-1888.........DLB-110, 199
Howitt, William 1792-1879 and
 Howitt, Mary 1799-1888...........DLB-110
Hoyem, Andrew 1935- DLB-5
Hoyers, Anna Ovena 1584-1655........DLB-164
Hoyle, Fred 1915-2001...............DLB-261
Hoyos, Angela de 1940- DLB-82
Hoyt, Henry [publishing house] DLB-49
Hoyt, Palmer 1897-1979...............DLB-127
Hrabal, Bohumil 1914-1997............DLB-232
Hrabanus Maurus 776?-856............DLB-148
Hronský, Josef Cíger 1896-1960 ....DLB-215
Hrotsvit of Gandersheim
 circa 935-circa 1000................DLB-148
Hubbard, Elbert 1856-1915.............DLB-91
Hubbard, Kin 1868-1930...............DLB-11
Hubbard, William circa 1621-1704.......DLB-24
Huber, Therese 1764-1829.............DLB-90
Huch, Friedrich 1873-1913.............DLB-66
Huch, Ricarda 1864-1947..............DLB-66
Huck at 100: How Old Is
 Huckleberry Finn?.................. Y-85
Huddle, David 1942- DLB-130
Hudgins, Andrew 1951- DLB-120, 282
Hudson, Henry Norman 1814-1886......DLB-64
Hudson, Stephen 1868?-1944..........DLB-197
Hudson, W. H. 1841-1922......DLB-98, 153, 174
Hudson and Goodwin..................DLB-49
Huebsch, B. W. [publishing house].......DLB-46
Oral History: B. W. Huebsch Y-99
Hueffer, Oliver Madox 1876-1931.......DLB-197
Hugh of St. Victor circa 1096-1141......DLB-208
Hughes, David 1930- DLB-14
Hughes, Dusty 1947- DLB-233
Hughes, Hatcher 1881-1945...........DLB-249
Hughes, John 1677-1720...............DLB-84
Hughes, Langston 1902-1967
 ....DLB-4, 7, 48, 51, 86, 228; CDALB-5
Hughes, Richard 1900-1976.........DLB-15, 161
Hughes, Ted 1930-1998............DLB-40, 161
Hughes, Thomas 1822-1896.........DLB-18, 163

Hugo, Richard 1923-1982 .... DLB-5, 206
Hugo, Victor 1802-1885 .... DLB-119, 192, 217
Hugo Awards and Nebula Awards DLB-8
Hull, Richard 1896-1973 .... DLB-77
Hulme, T. E. 1883-1917 .... DLB-19
Hulton, Anne ?-1779? DLB-200
Humboldt, Alexander von 1769-1859 ..... DLB-90
Humboldt, Wilhelm von 1767-1835 ...... DLB-90
Hume, David 1711-1776 .... DLB-104, 252
Hume, Fergus 1859-1932 .... DLB-70
Hume, Sophia 1702-1774 .... DLB-200
Hume-Rothery, Mary Catherine
   1824-1885 .... DLB-240
Humishuma (see Mourning Dove)
Hummer, T. R. 1950- DLB-120
Humorous Book Illustration DLB-11
Humphrey, Duke of Gloucester
   1391-1447 .... DLB-213
Humphrey, William
   1924-1997 .... DLB-6, 212, 234, 278
Humphreys, David 1752-1818 .... DLB-37
Humphreys, Emyr 1919- DLB-15
Huncke, Herbert 1915-1996 .... DLB-16
Huneker, James Gibbons
   1857-1921 .... DLB-71
Hunold, Christian Friedrich
   1681-1721 .... DLB-168
Hunt, Irene 1907- DLB-52
Hunt, Leigh 1784-1859 .... DLB-96, 110, 144
Hunt, Violet 1862-1942 .... DLB-162, 197
Hunt, William Gibbes 1791-1833 .... DLB-73
Hunter, Evan 1926- Y-82
Hunter, Jim 1939- DLB-14
Hunter, Kristin 1931- DLB-33
Hunter, Mollie 1922- DLB-161
Hunter, N. C. 1908-1971 .... DLB-10
Hunter-Duvar, John 1821-1899 .... DLB-99
Huntington, Henry E. 1850-1927 .... DLB-140
Huntington, Susan Mansfield
   1791-1823 .... DLB-200
Hurd and Houghton DLB-49
Hurst, Fannie 1889-1968 .... DLB-86
Hurst and Blackett DLB-106
Hurst and Company DLB-49
Hurston, Zora Neale
   1901?-1960 .... DLB-51, 86; CDALB-7
Husson, Jules-François-Félix (see Champfleury)
Huston, John 1906-1987 .... DLB-26
Hutcheson, Francis 1694-1746 ...... DLB-31, 252
Hutchinson, Ron 1947- DLB-245
Hutchinson, R. C. 1907-1975 .... DLB-191
Hutchinson, Thomas
   1711-1780 .... DLB-30, 31
Hutchinson and Company
   (Publishers) Limited DLB-112
Huth, Angela 1938- DLB-271
Hutton, Richard Holt 1826-1897 .... DLB-57

von Hutton, Ulrich 1488-1523 .... DLB-179
Huxley, Aldous 1894-1963
   ..... DLB-36, 100, 162, 195, 255; CDBLB-6
Huxley, Elspeth Josceline
   1907-1997 .... DLB-77, 204
Huxley, T. H. 1825-1895 .... DLB-57
Huyghue, Douglas Smith 1816-1891 ..... DLB-99
Huysmans, Joris-Karl 1848-1907 .... DLB-123
Hwang, David Henry 1957- DLB-212, 228
Hyde, Donald 1909-1966 and
   Hyde, Mary 1912- DLB-187
Hyman, Trina Schart 1939- DLB-61

I

Iavorsky, Stefan 1658-1722 .... DLB-150
Iazykov, Nikolai Mikhailovich
   1803-1846 .... DLB-205
Ibáñez, Armando P. 1949- DLB-209
Ibn Bajja circa 1077-1138 .... DLB-115
Ibn Gabirol, Solomon
   circa 1021-circa 1058 .... DLB-115
Ibuse, Masuji 1898-1993 .... DLB-180
Ichijō Kanera
   (see Ichijō Kaneyoshi)
Ichijō Kaneyoshi (Ichijō Kanera)
   1402-1481 .... DLB-203
The Iconography of Science-Fiction Art DLB-8
Iffland, August Wilhelm 1759-1814 ...... DLB-94
Ignatieff, Michael 1947- DLB-267
Ignatow, David 1914-1997 .... DLB-5
Ike, Chukwuemeka 1931- DLB-157
Ikkyū Sōjun 1394-1481 .... DLB-203
Iles, Francis (see Berkeley, Anthony)
Il'f, Il'ia (Il'ia Arnol'dovich Fainzil'berg) 1897-1937
   and Evgenii Petrov (Evgenii Petrovich Kataev)
   1903-1942 .... DLB-272
Illich, Ivan 1926- DLB-242
The Illustration of Early German Literar
   Manuscripts, circa 1150-circa 1300 .. DLB-148
Illyés, Gyula 1902-1983 .... DLB-215; CDWLB-4
Imbs, Bravig 1904-1946 .... DLB-4
Imbuga, Francis D. 1947- DLB-157
Immermann, Karl 1796-1840 .... DLB-133
Inchbald, Elizabeth 1753-1821 .... DLB-39, 89
Indiana University Press Y-02
Ingamells, Rex 1913-1955 .... DLB-260
Inge, William 1913-1973 ... DLB-7, 249; CDALB-1
Ingelow, Jean 1820-1897 .... DLB-35, 163
Ingersoll, Ralph 1900-1985 .... DLB-127
The Ingersoll Prizes Y-84
Ingoldsby, Thomas (see Barham, Richard Harris)
Ingraham, Joseph Holt 1809-1860 .... DLB-3, 248
Inman, John 1805-1850 .... DLB-73
Innerhofer, Franz 1944- DLB-85
Innes, Michael 1906-1994 .... DLB-276
Innis, Harold Adams 1894-1952 .... DLB-88
Innis, Mary Quayle 1899-1972 .... DLB-88

Inō Sōgi 1421-1502 .... DLB-203
Inoue Yasushi 1907-1991 .... DLB-181
"The Greatness of Southern Literature":
   League of the South Institute for the
   Study of Southern Culture and History
   .... Y-02
International Publishers Company DLB-46
Interviews:
   Adoff, Arnold and Virginia Hamilton Y-01
   Anastas, Benjamin Y-98
   Baker, Nicholson Y-00
   Bank, Melissa Y-98
   Bernstein, Harriet Y-82
   Betts, Doris Y-82
   Bosworth, David Y-82
   Bottoms, David Y-83
   Bowers, Fredson Y-80
   Burnshaw, Stanley Y-97
   Carpenter, Humphrey Y-84, Y-99
   Carr, Virginia Spencer Y-00
   Carver, Raymond Y-83
   Cherry, Kelly Y-83
   Coppel, Alfred Y-83
   Cowley, Malcolm Y-81
   Davis, Paxton Y-89
   De Vries, Peter Y-82
   Dickey, James Y-82
   Donald, David Herbert Y-87
   Ellroy, James Y-91
   Fancher, Betsy Y-83
   Faust, Irvin Y-00
   Fulton, Len Y-86
   Furst, Alan Y-01
   Garrett, George Y-83
   Gores, Joe Y-02
   Greenfield, George Y-91
   Griffin, Bryan Y-81
   Groom, Winston Y-01
   Guilds, John Caldwell Y-92
   Hardin, James Y-92
   Harrison, Jim Y-82
   Hazzard, Shirley Y-82
   Herrick, William Y-01
   Higgins, George V Y-98
   Hoban, Russell Y-90
   Holroyd, Michael Y-99
   Horowitz, Glen Y-90
   Iggulden, John Y-01
   Jakes, John Y-83
   Jenkinson, Edward B. Y-82
   Jenks, Tom Y-86
   Kaplan, Justin Y-86
   King, Florence Y-85
   Klopfer, Donald S. Y-97
   Krug, Judith Y-82

Lamm, Donald. Y-95	Isaksson, Ulla 1916-2000. . . . . DLB-257	Jahier, Piero 1884-1966 . . . . DLB-114, 264
Laughlin, James Y-96	Iser, Wolfgang 1926- DLB-242	Jahnn, Hans Henny 1894-1959 . . . . . . DLB-56, 124
Lindsay, Jack Y-84	Isherwood, Christopher 1904-1986 . . . . DLB-15, 195; Y-86	Jakes, John 1932- DLB-278; Y-83
Mailer, Norman. Y-97		Jakobson, Roman 1896-1982. . . . . DLB-242
Manchester, William Y-85	The Christopher Isherwood Archive, The Huntington Library Y-99	James, Alice 1848-1892 . . . . DLB-221
McCormack, Thomas Y-98	Ishiguro, Kazuo 1954- DLB-194	James, C. L. R. 1901-1989. . . . . DLB-125
McNamara, Katherine Y-97	Ishikawa Jun 1899-1987. . . . . DLB-182	James, George P. R. 1801-1860 . . . . DLB-116
McTaggart, J. M. E. 1866-1925 . . . . DLB-262	The Island Trees Case: A Symposium on School Library Censorship An Interview with Judith Krug An Interview with Phyllis Schlafly An Interview with Edward B. Jenkinson An Interview with Lamarr Mooneyham An Interview with Harriet Bernstein. Y-82	James, Henry 1843-1916 . . . . . . DLB-12, 71, 74, 189; DS-13; CDALB-3
Mellen, Joan. Y-94		
Menaher, Daniel Y-97		James, John circa 1633-1729 . . . . DLB-24
Mooneyham, Lamarr. Y-82		James, M. R. 1862-1936. . . . . DLB-156, 201
Murray, Les. Y-01		James, Naomi 1949- DLB-204
Nosworth, David Y-82	Islas, Arturo 1938-1991 . . . . DLB-122	James, P. D. (Phyllis Dorothy James White) 1920- DLB-87, 276; DS-17; CDBLB-8
O'Connor, Patrick Y-84, Y-99		
Ozick, Cynthia. Y-83	Issit, Debbie 1966- DLB-233	James VI of Scotland, I of England 1566-1625 . . . . DLB-151, 172
Penner, Jonathan Y-83	Ivanišević, Drago [1907-1981 . . . . DLB-181	
Pennington, Lee. Y-82		*Ane Schort Treatise Conteining Some Revlis and Cautelis to Be Obseruit and Eschewit in Scottis Poesi* (1584). DLB-172
Penzler, Otto Y-96	Ivanov, Vsevolod Viacheslavovich 1895-1963 . . . . DLB-272	
Plimpton, George. Y-99		
Potok, Chaim. Y-84	Ivaska, Astrīde 1926- DLB-232	James, Thomas 1572?-1629 . . . . DLB-213
Powell, Padgett Y-01	Ivers, M. J., and Company. DLB-49	James, U. P. [publishing house] DLB-49
Prescott, Peter S. Y-86	Iwaniuk, Wacław 1915- DLB-215	James, Will 1892-1942. . . . . DS-16
Rabe, David. Y-91	Iwano, Hōmei 1873-1920. . . . . DLB-180	James, William 1842-1910 . . . . DLB-270
Rallyson, Carl Y-97	Iwaszkiewicz, Jarosław 1894-1980 . . . . . . DLB-215	Jameson, Anna 1794-1860 . . . . DLB-99, 166
Rechy, John Y-82	Iyayi, Festus 1947- DLB-157	Jameson, Fredric 1934- DLB-67
Reid, B. L. Y-83	Izumi, Kyōka 1873-1939 . . . . DLB-180	Jameson, J. Franklin 1859-1937 . . . . DLB-17
Reynolds, Michael Y-95, Y-99	# J	Jameson, Storm 1891-1986 . . . . DLB-36
Robinson, Derek Y-02		Jančar, Drago 1948- DLB-181
Rosset, Barney. Y-02	Jackmon, Marvin E. (see Marvin X)	Janés, Clara 1940- DLB-134
Schlafly, Phyllis Y-82	Jacks, L. P. 1860-1955 . . . . DLB-135	Janevski, Slavko 1920- DLB-181; CDWLB-4
Schroeder, Patricia Y-99	Jackson, Angela 1951- DLB-41	Jansson, Tove 1914-2001. . . . . DLB-257
Schulberg, Budd. Y-81, Y-01	Jackson, Charles 1903-1968. . . . . DLB-234	Janvier, Thomas 1849-1913. . . . . DLB-202
Scribner, Charles, III Y-94	Jackson, Helen Hunt 1830-1885 . . . . DLB-42, 47, 186, 189	Jaramillo, Cleofas M. 1878-1956 . . . . DLB-122
Sipper, Ralph Y-94		Jarman, Mark 1952- DLB-120, 282
Staley, Thomas F. Y-00	Jackson, Holbrook 1874-1948 . . . . DLB-98	Jarrell, Randall 1914-1965 . . DLB-48, 52; CDALB-1
Styron, William Y-80	Jackson, Laura Riding 1901-1991 . . . . DLB-48	Jarrold and Sons DLB-106
Toth, Susan Allen Y-86	Jackson, Shirley 1916-1965 . . . . DLB-6, 234; CDALB-1	Jarry, Alfred 1873-1907 . . . . DLB-192, 258
Tyler, Anne. Y-82		Jarves, James Jackson 1818-1888 . . . . DLB-189
Vaughan, Samuel. Y-97	Jacob, Max 1876-1944 . . . . DLB-258	Jasmin, Claude 1930- DLB-60
Von Ogtrop, Kristin Y-92	Jacob, Naomi 1884?-1964 . . . . DLB-191	Jaunsudrabiņš, Jānis 1877-1962 . . . . DLB-220
Wallenstein, Barry. Y-92	Jacob, Piers Anthony Dillingham (see Anthony, Piers)	Jay, John 1745-1829 . . . . DLB-31
Weintraub, Stanley Y-82		Jean de Garlande (see John of Garland)
Williams, J. Chamberlain. Y-84	Jacob, Violet 1863-1946. . . . . DLB-240	Jefferies, Richard 1848-1887 . . . . DLB-98, 141
Editors, Conversations with. Y-95	Jacobi, Friedrich Heinrich 1743-1819. . . . . DLB-94	Jeffers, Lance 1919-1985 . . . . DLB-41
Interviews on E-Publishing Y-00	Jacobi, Johann Georg 1740-1841 . . . . DLB-97	Jeffers, Robinson 1887-1962 . . . . DLB-45, 212; CDALB-4
Into the Past: William Jovanovich's Reflections in Publishing. Y-02	Jacobs, George W., and Company DLB-49	
	Jacobs, Harriet 1813-1897 . . . . DLB-239	Jefferson, Thomas 1743-1826 . . . . DLB-31, 183; CDALB-2
The National Library of Ireland's New James Joyce Manuscripts Y-02	Jacobs, Joseph 1854-1916. . . . . DLB-141	
	Jacobs, W. W. 1863-1943 . . . . DLB-135	Jégé 1866-1940. . . . . DLB-215
Irving, John 1942- DLB-6, 278; Y-82	Jacobsen, Jørgen-Frantz 1900-1938 . . . . . . DLB-214	Jelinek, Elfriede 1946- DLB-85
Irving, Washington 1783-1859 . . . . DLB-3, 11, 30, 59, 73, 74, 183, 186, 250; CDALB-2	Jacobsen, Josephine 1908- DLB-244	Jellicoe, Ann 1927- DLB-13, 233
	Jacobson, Dan 1929- DLB-14, 207, 225	Jemison, Mary circa 1742-1833 . . . . DLB-239
	Jacobson, Howard 1942- DLB-207	Jenkins, Dan 1929- DLB-241
	Jacques de Vitry circa 1160/1170-1240 . . . DLB-208	Jenkins, Elizabeth 1905- DLB-155
Irwin, Grace 1907- DLB-68	Jæger, Frank 1926-1977 . . . . DLB-214	Jenkins, Robin 1912- DLB-14, 271
Irwin, Will 1873-1948 . . . . DLB-25	Jaggard, William [publishing house] DLB-170	Jenkins, William Fitzgerald (see Leinster, Murray)

Cumulative Index

Jenkins, Herbert, Limited DLB-112
Jennings, Elizabeth 1926- DLB-27
Jens, Walter 1923- DLB-69
Jensen, Johannes V. 1873-1950......... DLB-214
Jensen, Merrill 1905-1980.............. DLB-17
Jensen, Thit 1876-1957 .... DLB-214
Jephson, Robert 1736-1803............. DLB-89
Jerome, Jerome K. 1859-1927 .... DLB-10, 34, 135
Jerome, Judson 1927-1991............. DLB-105
Jerrold, Douglas 1803-1857 .... DLB-158, 159
Jersild, Per Christian 1935- DLB-257
Jesse, F. Tennyson 1888-1958.......... DLB-77
Jewel, John 1522-1571................. DLB-236
Jewett, John P., and Company DLB-49
Jewett, Sarah Orne 1849-1909 .... DLB-12, 74, 221
The Jewish Publication Society......... DLB-49
Studies in American Jewish Literature Y-02
Jewitt, John Rodgers 1783-1821 .... DLB-99
Jewsbury, Geraldine 1812-1880 .... DLB-21
Jewsbury, Maria Jane 1800-1833 .... DLB-199
Jhabvala, Ruth Prawer 1927- DLB-139, 194
Jiménez, Juan Ramón 1881-1958 .... DLB-134
Jimmy, Red, and Others: Harold Rosenthal
  Remembers the Stars of the Press Box.... Y-01
Jin, Ha 1956- DLB-244
Joans, Ted 1928- DLB-16, 41
Jōha 1525-1602....................... DLB-203
Johannis de Garlandia (see John of Garland)
John, Errol 1924-1988 .... DLB-233
John, Eugenie (see Marlitt, E.)
John of Dumbleton
  circa 1310-circa 1349 .... DLB-115
John of Garland (Jean de Garlande, Johannis de
  Garlandia) circa 1195-circa 1272 .... DLB-208
Johns, Captain W. E. 1893-1968 .... DLB-160
Johnson, Mrs. A. E. ca. 1858-1922...... DLB-221
Johnson, Amelia (see Johnson, Mrs. A. E.)
Johnson, B. S. 1933-1973 .... DLB-14, 40
Johnson, Benjamin [publishing house] DLB-49
Johnson, Benjamin, Jacob, and
  Robert [publishing house] DLB-49
Johnson, Charles 1679-1748 .... DLB-84
Johnson, Charles R. 1948- DLB-33, 278
Johnson, Charles S. 1893-1956........ DLB-51, 91
Johnson, Denis 1949- DLB-120
Johnson, Diane 1934- Y-80
Johnson, Dorothy M. 1905–1984....... DLB-206
Johnson, E. Pauline (Tekahionwake)
  1861-1913........................DLB-175
Johnson, Edgar 1901-1995 .... DLB-103
Johnson, Edward 1598-1672............ DLB-24
Johnson, Eyvind 1900-1976 .... DLB-259
Johnson, Fenton 1888-1958 .... DLB-45, 50
Johnson, Georgia Douglas
  1877?-1966.................... DLB-51, 249
Johnson, Gerald W. 1890-1980 .... DLB-29

Johnson, Greg 1953- DLB-234
Johnson, Helene 1907-1995 .... DLB-51
Johnson, Jacob, and Company DLB-49
Johnson, James Weldon
  1871-1938.............. DLB-51; CDALB-4
Johnson, John H. 1918- DLB-137
Johnson, Joseph [publishing house] DLB-154
Johnson, Linton Kwesi 1952- DLB-157
Johnson, Lionel 1867-1902 .... DLB-19
Johnson, Nunnally 1897-1977........... DLB-26
Johnson, Owen 1878-1952 .... Y-87
Johnson, Pamela Hansford 1912- DLB-15
Johnson, Pauline 1861-1913 .... DLB-92
Johnson, Ronald 1935-1998 .... DLB-169
Johnson, Samuel 1696-1772 ... DLB-24; CDBLB-2
Johnson, Samuel
  1709-1784.........DLB-39, 95, 104, 142, 213
Johnson, Samuel 1822-1882 .... DLB-1, 243
The BBC Four Samuel Johnson Prize
  for Non-fiction Y-02
Johnson, Susanna 1730-1810 .... DLB-200
Johnson, Terry 1955- DLB-233
Johnson, Uwe 1934-1984 ..... DLB-75; CDWLB-2
Johnston, Annie Fellows 1863-1931 ...... DLB-42
Johnston, Basil H. 1929- DLB-60
Johnston, David Claypole 1798?-1865 ... DLB-188
Johnston, Denis 1901-1984............. DLB-10
Johnston, Ellen 1835-1873 .... DLB-199
Johnston, George 1912-1970........... DLB-260
Johnston, George 1913- DLB-88
Johnston, Sir Harry 1858-1927.........DLB-174
Johnston, Jennifer 1930- DLB-14
Johnston, Mary 1870-1936 .... DLB-9
Johnston, Richard Malcolm 1822-1898 ... DLB-74
Johnstone, Charles 1719?-1800? DLB-39
Johst, Hanns 1890-1978 .... DLB-124
Jolas, Eugene 1894-1952............. DLB-4, 45
Jones, Alice C. 1853-1933.............. DLB-92
Jones, Charles C., Jr. 1831-1893.......... DLB-30
Jones, D. G. 1929- DLB-53
Jones, David 1895-1974 .. DLB-20, 100; CDBLB-7
Jones, Diana Wynne 1934- DLB-161
Jones, Ebenezer 1820-1860............. DLB-32
Jones, Ernest 1819-1868................ DLB-32
Jones, Gayl 1949- DLB-33, 278
Jones, George 1800-1870 .... DLB-183
Jones, Glyn 1905- DLB-15
Jones, Gwyn 1907- DLB-15, 139
Jones, Henry Arthur 1851-1929 .... DLB-10
Jones, Hugh circa 1692-1760 .... DLB-24
Jones, James 1921-1977........DLB-2, 143; DS-17
James Jones Papers in the Handy Writers'
  Colony Collection at the University of
  Illinois at Springfield Y-98
The James Jones Society................. Y-92
Jones, Jenkin Lloyd 1911- DLB-127

Jones, John Beauchamp 1810-1866...... DLB-202
Jones, LeRoi (see Baraka, Amiri)
Jones, Lewis 1897-1939................ DLB-15
Jones, Madison 1925- DLB-152
Jones, Major Joseph
  (see Thompson, William Tappan)
Jones, Marie 1951- DLB-233
Jones, Preston 1936-1979 .... DLB-7
Jones, Rodney 1950- DLB-120
Jones, Thom 1945- DLB-244
Jones, Sir William 1746-1794 .... DLB-109
Jones, William Alfred
  1817-1900...................... DLB-59
Jones's Publishing House DLB-49
Jong, Erica 1942- DLB-2, 5, 28, 152
Jonke, Gert F. 1946- DLB-85
Jonson, Ben 1572?-1637 .. DLB-62, 121; CDBLB-1
Jordan, June 1936- DLB-38
Joseph and George Y-99
Joseph, Jenny 1932- DLB-40
Joseph, Michael, Limited DLB-112
Josephson, Matthew 1899-1978 .... DLB-4
Josephus, Flavius 37-100...............DLB-176
Josiah Allen's Wife (see Holley, Marietta)
Josipovici, Gabriel 1940- DLB-14
Josselyn, John ?-1675 .... DLB-24
Joudry, Patricia 1921- DLB-88
Jouve, Pierre-Jean 1887-1976.......... DLB-258
Jovanovich, William 1920-2001 .... Y-01
Into the Past: William Jovanovich's
  Reflections on Publishing............. Y-02
The Temper of the West: William Jovanovich ... Y-02
Jovine, Francesco 1902-1950 .... DLB-264
Jovine, Giuseppe 1922- DLB-128
Joyaux, Philippe (see Sollers, Philippe)
Joyce, Adrien (see Eastman, Carol)
Joyce, James 1882-1941
  ....DLB-10, 19, 36, 162, 247; CDBLB-6
James Joyce Centenary: Dublin, 1982 .... Y-82
James Joyce Conference Y-85
A Joyce (Con)Text: Danis Rose and the
  Remaking of *Ulysses* Y-97
The New *Ulysses* Y-84
The National Library of Ireland's
  New James Joyce Manuscripts........... Y-02
Jozsef, Attila 1905-1937......DLB-215; CDWLB-4
Judd, Orange, Publishing Company...... DLB-49
Judd, Sylvester 1813-1853 .... DLB-1, 243
Judith circa 930..................... DLB-146
Julian Barnes Checklist.................... Y-01
Julian of Norwich
  1342-circa 1420 .... DLB-1146
Julius Caesar
  100 B.C.-44 B.C. DLB-211; CDWLB-1
June, Jennie (see Croly,
  Jane Cunningham)
Jung, Franz 1888-1963 .... DLB-118

Jünger, Ernst 1895- DLB-56; CDWLB-2
Der jüngere Titurel circa 1275 .... DLB-138
Jung-Stilling, Johann Heinrich
   1740-1817 .... DLB-94
Justice, Donald 1925- Y-83
Juvenal circa A.D. 60-circa A.D. 130
   .... DLB-211; CDWLB-1
The Juvenile Library (see Godwin, M. J.,
   and Company)

K

Kacew, Romain (see Gary, Romain)
Kafka, Franz 1883-1924 ...... DLB-81; CDWLB-2
Kahn, Gus 1886-1941 .... DLB-265
Kahn, Roger 1927- DLB-171
Kaikō Takeshi 1939-1989 .... DLB-182
Kaiser, Georg 1878-1945 .... DLB-124; CDWLB-2
Kaiserchronik circca 1147 .... DLB-148
Kaleb, Vjekoslav 1905- DLB-181
Kalechofsky, Roberta 1931- DLB-28
Kaler, James Otis 1848-1912 .... DLB-12
Kalmar, Bert 1884-1947 .... DLB-265
Kames, Henry Home, Lord
   1696-1782 .... DLB-31, 104
Kamo no Chōmei (Kamo no Nagaakira)
   1153 or 1155-1216 .... DLB-203
Kamo no Nagaakira (see Kamo no Chōmei)
Kampmann, Christian 1939-1988 .... DLB-214
Kandel, Lenore 1932- DLB-16
Kanin, Garson 1912-1999 .... DLB-7
Kant, Hermann 1926- DLB-75
Kant, Immanuel 1724-1804 .... DLB-94
Kantemir, Antiokh Dmitrievich
   1708-1744 .... DLB-150
Kantor, MacKinlay 1904-1977 .... DLB-9, 102
Kanze Kōjirō Nobumitsu 1435-1516 ..... DLB-203
Kanze Motokiyo (see Zeimi)
Kaplan, Fred 1937- DLB-111
Kaplan, Johanna 1942- DLB-28
Kaplan, Justin 1925- DLB-111; Y-86
The Practice of Biography V:
   An Interview with Justin Kaplan Y-86
Kaplinski, Jaan 1941- DLB-232
Kapnist, Vasilii Vasilevich 1758?-1823 ... DLB-150
Karadžić, Vuk Stefanović
   1787-1864 .... DLB-147; CDWLB-4
Karamzin, Nikolai Mikhailovich
   1766-1826 .... DLB-150
Karinthy, Frigyes 1887-1938 .... DLB-215
Karsch, Anna Louisa 1722-1791 .... DLB-97
Kasack, Hermann 1896-1966 .... DLB-69
Kasai, Zenzō 1887-1927 .... DLB-180
Kaschnitz, Marie Luise 1901-1974 ...... DLB-69
Kassák, Lajos 1887-1967 .... DLB-215
Kaštelan, Jure 1919-1990 .... DLB-147
Kästner, Erich 1899-1974 .... DLB-56

Kataev, Evgenii Petrovich
   (see Il'f, Il'ia and Evgenii Petrov)
Kataev, Valentin Petrovich 1897-1986 .... DLB-272
Katenin, Pavel Aleksandrovich
   1792-1853 .... DLB-205
Kattan, Naim 1928- DLB-53
Katz, Steve 1935- Y-83
Kauffman, Janet 1945- DLB-218; Y-86
Kauffmann, Samuel 1898-1971 .... DLB-127
Kaufman, Bob 1925- DLB-16, 41
Kaufman, George S. 1889-1961 .... DLB-7
Kaufmann, Walter 1921-1980 .... DLB-279
Kavan, Anna 1901-1968 .... DLB-255
Kavanagh, P. J. 1931- DLB-40
Kavanagh, Patrick 1904-1967 .... DLB-15, 20
Kaverin, Veniamin Aleksandrovich
   (Veniamin Aleksandrovich Zil'ber)
   1902-1989 .... DLB-272
Kawabata, Yasunari 1899-1972 .... DLB-180
Kay, Guy Gavriel 1954- DLB-251
Kaye-Smith, Sheila 1887-1956 .... DLB-36
Kazin, Alfred 1915-1998 .... DLB-67
Keane, John B. 1928- DLB-13
Keary, Annie 1825-1879 .... DLB-163
Keary, Eliza 1827-1918 .... DLB-240
Keating, H. R. F. 1926- DLB-87
Keatley, Charlotte 1960- DLB-245
Keats, Ezra Jack 1916-1983 .... DLB-61
Keats, John 1795-1821 .... DLB-96, 110; CDBLB-3
Keble, John 1792-1866 .... DLB-32, 55
Keckley, Elizabeth 1818?-1907 .... DLB-239
Keeble, John 1944- Y-83
Keeffe, Barrie 1945- DLB-13, 245
Keeley, James 1867-1934 .... DLB-25
W. B. Keen, Cooke and Company DLB-49
The Mystery of Carolyn Keene Y-02
Keillor, Garrison 1942- Y-87
Keith, Marian (Mary Esther MacGregor)
   1874?-1961 .... DLB-92
Keller, Gary D. 1943- DLB-82
Keller, Gottfried 1819-1890 ... DLB-129; CDWLB-2
Kelley, Edith Summers 1884-1956 .... DLB-9
Kelley, Emma Dunham ?-? DLB-221
Kelley, William Melvin 1937- DLB-33
Kellogg, Ansel Nash 1832-1886 .... DLB-23
Kellogg, Steven 1941- DLB-61
Kelly, George E. 1887-1974 .... DLB-7, 249
Kelly, Hugh 1739-1777 .... DLB-89
Kelly, Piet and Company DLB-49
Kelly, Robert 1935- DLB-5, 130, 165
Kelman, James 1946- DLB-194
Kelmscott Press DLB-112
Kelton, Elmer 1926- DLB-256
Kemble, E. W. 1861-1933 .... DLB-188
Kemble, Fanny 1809-1893 .... DLB-32
Kemelman, Harry 1908- DLB-28

Kempe, Margery circa 1373-1438 .... DLB-146
Kempner, Friederike 1836-1904 .... DLB-129
Kempowski, Walter 1929- DLB-75
Kendall, Claude [publishing company] DLB-46
Kendall, Henry 1839-1882 .... DLB-230
Kendall, May 1861-1943 .... DLB-240
Kendell, George 1809-1867 .... DLB-43
Kenedy, P. J., and Sons DLB-49
Kenkō circa 1283-circa 1352 .... DLB-203
Kennan, George 1845-1924 .... DLB-189
Kennedy, A. L. 1965- DLB-271
Kennedy, Adrienne 1931- DLB-38
Kennedy, John Pendleton 1795-1870 ... DLB-3, 248
Kennedy, Leo 1907- DLB-88
Kennedy, Margaret 1896-1967 .... DLB-36
Kennedy, Patrick 1801-1873 .... DLB-159
Kennedy, Richard S. 1920-2002 ... DLB-111; Y-02
Kennedy, William 1928- DLB-143; Y-85
Kennedy, X. J. 1929- DLB-5
Kennelly, Brendan 1936- DLB-40
Kenner, Hugh 1923- DLB-67
Kennerley, Mitchell [publishing house] DLB-46
Kenny, Maurice 1929- DLB-175
Kent, Frank R. 1877-1958 .... DLB-29
Kenyon, Jane 1947-1995 .... DLB-120
Keough, Hugh Edmund 1864-1912 ...... DLB-171
Keppler and Schwartzmann DLB-49
Ker, John, third Duke of Roxburghe
   1740-1804 .... DLB-213
Ker, N. R. 1908-1982 .... DLB-201
Kerlan, Irvin 1912-1963 .... DLB-187
Kermode, Frank 1919- DLB-242
Kern, Jerome 1885-1945 .... DLB-187
Kernaghan, Eileen 1939- DLB-251
Kerner, Justinus 1786-1862 .... DLB-90
Kerouac, Jack
   1922-1969 ... DLB-2, 16, 237; DS-3; CDALB-1
The Jack Kerouac Revival Y-95
"Re-meeting of Old Friends":
   The Jack Kerouac Conference Y-82
Auction of Jack Kerouac's *On the Road* Scroll .. Y-01
Kerouac, Jan 1952-1996 .... DLB-16
Kerr, Charles H., and Company DLB-49
Kerr, Orpheus C. (see Newell, Robert Henry)
Kersh, Gerald 1911-1968 .... DLB-255
Kertész, Imre Y-02
Kesey, Ken 1935-2001 ... DLB-2, 16, 206; CDALB-6
Kessel, Joseph 1898-1979 .... DLB-72
Kessel, Martin 1901- DLB-56
Kesten, Hermann 1900- DLB-56
Keun, Irmgard 1905-1982 .... DLB-69
Key, Ellen 1849-1926 .... DLB-259
Key and Biddle DLB-49
Keynes, Sir Geoffrey 1887-1982 .... DLB-201
Keynes, John Maynard 1883-1946 .... DS-10

Keyserling, Eduard von 1855-1918 ...... DLB-66
Khan, Ismith 1925- DLB-125
Khaytov, Nikolay 1919- DLB-181
Khemnitser, Ivan Ivanovich
 1745-1784 .... DLB-150
Kheraskov, Mikhail Matveevich
 1733-1807 .... DLB-150
Khomiakov, Aleksei Stepanovich
 1804-1860 .... DLB-205
Khristov, Boris 1945- DLB-181
Khvoshchinskaia, Nadezhda Dmitrievna
 1824-1889 .... DLB-238
Khvostov, Dmitrii Ivanovich
 1757-1835 .... DLB-150
Kidd, Adam 1802?-1831............ DLB-99
Kidd, William [publishing house]...... DLB-106
Kidder, Tracy 1945- DLB-185
Kiely, Benedict 1919- DLB-15
Kieran, John 1892-1981 .... DLB-171
Kies, Marietta 1853-1899 ....DLB-270
Kiggins and Kellogg DLB-49
Kiley, Jed 1889-1962.................. DLB-4
Kilgore, Bernard 1908-1967 .... DLB-127
Kilian, Crawford 1941- DLB-251
Killens, John Oliver 1916- DLB-33
Killigrew, Anne 1660-1685........... DLB-131
Killigrew, Thomas 1612-1683 .... DLB-58
Kilmer, Joyce 1886-1918.............. DLB-45
Kilroy, Thomas 1934- DLB-233
Kilwardby, Robert circa 1215-1279 .... DLB-115
Kilworth, Garry 1941- DLB-261
Kimball, Richard Burleigh 1816-1892 ... DLB-202
Kincaid, Jamaica 1949-
 ....DLB-157, 227; CDALB-7; CDWLB-3
King, Charles 1844-1933 .... DLB-186
King, Clarence 1842-1901 .... DLB-12
King, Florence 1936 .... Y-85
King, Francis 1923- DLB-15, 139
King, Grace 1852-1932............. DLB-12, 78
King, Harriet Hamilton 1840-1920...... DLB-199
King, Henry 1592-1669 .... DLB-126
King, Solomon [publishing house] DLB-49
King, Stephen 1947- DLB-143; Y-80
King, Susan Petigru 1824-1875......... DLB-239
King, Thomas 1943- DLB-175
King, Woodie, Jr. 1937- DLB-38
Kinglake, Alexander William
 1809-1891 .... DLB-55, 166
Kingsbury, Donald 1929- DLB-251
Kingsley, Charles
 1819-1875.........DLB-21, 32, 163, 178, 190
Kingsley, Henry 1830-1876 ..... DLB-21, 230
Kingsley, Mary Henrietta 1862-1900 .....DLB-174
Kingsley, Sidney 1906- DLB-7
Kingsmill, Hugh 1889-1949 .... DLB-149
Kingsolver, Barbara 1955- .. DLB-206; CDALB-7

Kingston, Maxine Hong
 1940- DLB-173, 212; Y-80; CDALB-7
Kingston, William Henry Giles
 1814-1880 .... DLB-163
Kinnan, Mary Lewis 1763-1848 .... DLB-200
Kinnell, Galway 1927- DLB-5; Y-87
Kinsella, Thomas 1928- DLB-27
Kipling, Rudyard 1865-1936
 .... DLB-19, 34, 141, 156; CDBLB-5
Kipphardt, Heinar 1922-1982.......... DLB-124
Kirby, William 1817-1906............. DLB-99
Kircher, Athanasius 1602-1680......... DLB-164
Kireevsky, Ivan Vasil'evich 1806-1856... DLB-198
Kireevsky, Petr Vasil'evich 1808-1856... DLB-205
Kirk, Hans 1898-1962 .... DLB-214
Kirk, John Foster 1824-1904........... DLB-79
Kirkconnell, Watson 1895-1977 .... DLB-68
Kirkland, Caroline M.
 1801-1864 ....DLB-3, 73, 74, 250; DS-13
Kirkland, Joseph 1830-1893 .... DLB-12
Kirkman, Francis [publishing house] DLB-170
Kirkpatrick, Clayton 1915- DLB-127
Kirkup, James 1918- DLB-27
Kirouac, Conrad (see Marie-Victorin, Frère)
Kirsch, Sarah 1935- DLB-75
Kirst, Hans Hellmut 1914-1989 .... DLB-69
Kiš, Danilo 1935-1989 ..... DLB-181; CDWLB-4
Kita Morio 1927- DLB-182
Kitcat, Mabel Greenhow 1859-1922..... DLB-135
Kitchin, C. H. B. 1895-1967............ DLB-77
Kittredge, William 1932- DLB-212, 244
Kiukhel'beker, Vil'gel'm Karlovich
 1797-1846 .... DLB-205
Kizer, Carolyn 1925- DLB-5, 169
Klabund 1890-1928 .... DLB-66
Klaj, Johann 1616-1656 .... DLB-164
Klappert, Peter 1942- DLB-5
Klass, Philip (see Tenn, William)
Klein, A. M. 1909-1972................ DLB-68
Kleist, Ewald von 1715-1759............ DLB-97
Kleist, Heinrich von
 1777-1811 .... DLB-90; CDWLB-2
Klinger, Friedrich Maximilian 1752-1831... DLB-94
Klíma, Ivan 1931- DLB-232; CDWLB-4
Klimentev, Andrei Platonovic (see Platonov, Andrei
 Platonovich)
Kliushnikov, Viktor Petrovich
 1841-1892 .... DLB-238
Oral History Interview with Donald S.
 Klopfer.......................... Y-97
Klopstock, Friedrich Gottlieb 1724-1803 .. DLB-97
Klopstock, Meta 1728-1758............ DLB-97
Kluge, Alexander 1932- DLB-75
Kluge, P. F. 1942- Y-02
Knapp, Joseph Palmer 1864-1951........ DLB-91
Knapp, Samuel Lorenzo 1783-1838 ...... DLB-59

Knapton, J. J. and P.
 [publishing house] DLB-154
Kniazhnin, Iakov Borisovich 1740-1791 ... DLB-150
Knickerbocker, Diedrich (see Irving, Washington)
Knigge, Adolph Franz Friedrich Ludwig,
 Freiherr von 1752-1796 .... DLB-94
Knight, Charles, and Company DLB-106
Knight, Damon 1922- DLB-8
Knight, Etheridge 1931-1992 .... DLB-41
Knight, John S. 1894-1981 .... DLB-29
Knight, Sarah Kemble 1666-1727 .... DLB-24, 200
Knight-Bruce, G. W. H. 1852-1896 ......DLB-174
Knister, Raymond 1899-1932........... DLB-68
Knoblock, Edward 1874-1945 .... DLB-10
Knopf, Alfred A. 1892-1984............. Y-84
Knopf, Alfred A. [publishing house]...... DLB-46
Knopf to Hammett: The Editoral
 Correspondence..................... Y-00
Knorr von Rosenroth, Christian
 1636-1689 .... DLB-168
"Knots into Webs: Some Autobiographical
 Sources," by Dabney Stuart........ DLB-105
Knowles, John 1926- DLB-6; CDALB-6
Knox, Frank 1874-1944 .... DLB-29
Knox, John circa 1514-1572 .... DLB-132
Knox, John Armoy 1850-1906........... DLB-23
Knox, Lucy 1845-1884............... DLB-240
Knox, Ronald Arbuthnott 1888-1957..... DLB-77
Knox, Thomas Wallace 1835-1896 ..... DLB-189
Kobayashi Takiji 1903-1933........... DLB-180
Kober, Arthur 1900-1975 .... DLB-11
Kobiakova, Aleksandra Petrovna
 1823-1892 .... DLB-238
Kocbek, Edvard 1904-1981 ...DLB-147; CDWB-4
Koch, Howard 1902- DLB-26
Koch, Kenneth 1925- DLB-5
Kōda, Rohan 1867-1947............. DLB-180
Koehler, Ted 1894-1973 .... DLB-265
Koenigsberg, Moses 1879-1945 .... DLB-25
Koeppen, Wolfgang 1906-1996 .... DLB-69
Koertge, Ronald 1940- DLB-105
Koestler, Arthur 1905-1983 ......Y-83; CDBLB-7
Kohn, John S. Van E. 1906-1976 and
 Papantonio, Michael 1907-1978 ......DLB-187
Kokhanovskaia (see, Sokhanskaia,
 Nadezhda Stepanova)
Kokoschka, Oskar 1886-1980 .... DLB-124
Kolb, Annette 1870-1967 .... DLB-66
Kolbenheyer, Erwin Guido
 1878-1962.................. DLB-66, 124
Kolleritsch, Alfred 1931- DLB-85
Kolodny, Annette 1941- DLB-67
Kol'tsov, Aleksei Vasil'evich
 1809-1842 .... DLB-205
Komarov, Matvei circa 1730-1812 ...... DLB-150
Komroff, Manuel 1890-1974............ DLB-4
Komunyakaa, Yusef 1947- DLB-120

Kondoleon, Harry 1955-1994 ....DLB-266
Koneski, Blaže 1921-1993 ...DLB-181; CDWLB-4
Konigsburg, E. L. 1930- DLB-52
Konparu Zenchiku 1405-1468?.........DLB-203
Konrád, György 1933- DLB-232; CDWLB-4
Konrad von Würzburg circa 1230-1287 ....DLB-138
Konstantinov, Aleko 1863-1897........DLB-147
Konwicki, Tadeusz 1926- DLB-232
Kooser, Ted 1939- DLB-105
Kopit, Arthur 1937- DLB-7
Kops, Bernard 1926?- DLB-13
Kornbluth, C. M. 1923-1958.............DLB-8
Körner, Theodor 1791-1813 ....DLB-90
Kornfeld, Paul 1889-1942 ....DLB-118
Korolenko, Vladimir Galaktionovich 1853-1921 ....DLB-277
Kosinski, Jerzy 1933-1991 ....DLB-2; Y-82
Kosmač, Ciril 1910-1980 ....DLB-181
Kosovel, Srečko 1904-1926 ....DLB-147
Kostrov, Ermil Ivanovich 1755-1796 .....DLB-150
Kotzebue, August von 1761-1819.........DLB-94
Kotzwinkle, William 1938- DLB-173
Kovačić, Ante 1854-1889...............DLB-147
Kovalevskaia, Sof'ia Vasil'evna 1850-1891 ....DLB-277
Kovič, Kajetan 1931- DLB-181
Kozlov, Ivan Ivanovich 1779-1840.......DLB-205
Kraf, Elaine 1946- Y-81
Kramer, Jane 1938- DLB-185
Kramer, Larry 1935- DLB-249
Kramer, Mark 1944- DLB-185
Kranjčević, Silvije Strahimir 1865-1908 ....DLB-147
Krasko, Ivan 1876-1958................DLB-215
Krasna, Norman 1909-1984..............DLB-26
Kraus, Hans Peter 1907-1988............DLB-187
Kraus, Karl 1874-1936.................DLB-118
Krause, Herbert 1905-1976 ....DLB-256
Krauss, Ruth 1911-1993 ....DLB-52
Kreisel, Henry 1922- DLB-88
Krestovsky V. (see Khvoshchinskaia, Nadezhda Dmitrievna)
Krestovsky, Vsevolod Vladimirovich 1839-1895 ....DLB-238
Kreuder, Ernst 1903-1972 ....DLB-69
Krėvė-Mickevičius, Vincas 1882-1954....DLB-220
Kreymborg, Alfred 1883-1966.........DLB-4, 54
Krieger, Murray 1923- DLB-67
Krim, Seymour 1922-1989...............DLB-16
Kripke, Saul 1940- DLB-279
Kristensen, Tom 1893-1974 ....DLB-214
Kristeva, Julia 1941- DLB-242
Kritzer, Hyman W. 1918-2002 ....Y-02
Krleža, Miroslav 1893-1981..DLB-147; CDWLB-4
Krock, Arthur 1886-1974................DLB-29

Kroetsch, Robert 1927- DLB-53
Kropotkin, Petr Alekseevich 1842-1921 ..DLB-277
Kross, Jaan 1920- DLB-232
Krúdy, Gyula 1878-1933 ....DLB-215
Krutch, Joseph Wood 1893-1970 ....DLB-63, 206, 275
Krylov, Ivan Andreevich 1769-1844 .....DLB-150
Krymov, Iurii Solomonovich (Iurii Solomonovich Beklemishev) 1908-1941 ....DLB-272
Kubin, Alfred 1877-1959 ....DLB-81
Kubrick, Stanley 1928-1999.............DLB-26
Kudrun circa 1230-1240 ....DLB-138
Kuffstein, Hans Ludwig von 1582-1656 ....DLB-164
Kuhlmann, Quirinus 1651-1689 ....DLB-168
Kuhn, Thomas S. 1922-1996.............DLB-279
Kuhnau, Johann 1660-1722 ....DLB-168
Kukol'nik, Nestor Vasil'evich 1809-1868 ....DLB-205
Kukučín, Martin 1860-1928 ....DLB-215; CDWLB-4
Kumin, Maxine 1925- DLB-5
Kuncewicz, Maria 1895-1989 ....DLB-215
Kundera, Milan 1929- DLB-232; CDWLB-4
Kunene, Mazisi 1930- DLB-117
Kunikida, Doppo 1869-1908............DLB-180
Kunitz, Stanley 1905- DLB-48
Kunjufu, Johari M. (see Amini, Johari M.)
Kunnert, Gunter 1929- DLB-75
Kunze, Reiner 1933- DLB-75
Kupferberg, Tuli 1923- DLB-16
Kurahashi Yumiko 1935- DLB-182
Kureishi, Hanif 1954- DLB-194, 245
Kürnberger, Ferdinand 1821-1879.......DLB-129
Kurz, Isolde 1853-1944 ....DLB-66
Kusenberg, Kurt 1904-1983.............DLB-69
Kushchevsky, Ivan Afanas'evich 1847-1876......................DLB-238
Kushner, Tony 1956- DLB-228
Kuttner, Henry 1915-1958................DLB-8
Kyd, Thomas 1558-1594................DLB-62
Kyffin, Maurice circa 1560?-1598 .....DLB-136
Kyger, Joanne 1934- DLB-16
Kyne, Peter B. 1880-1957 ....DLB-78
Kyōgoku Tamekane 1254-1332 ....DLB-203
Kyrklund, Willy 1921- DLB-257

L

L. E. L. (see Landon, Letitia Elizabeth)
Laberge, Albert 1871-1960..............DLB-68
Laberge, Marie 1950- DLB-60
Labiche, Eugène 1815-1888............DLB-192
Labrunie, Gerard (see Nerval, Gerard de)
La Bruyère, Jean de 1645-1696 ....DLB-268
La Calprenède 1609?-1663 ....DLB-268

La Capria, Raffaele 1922- DLB-196
Lacombe, Patrice (see Trullier-Lacombe, Joseph Patrice)
Lacretelle, Jacques de 1888-1985.........DLB-65
Lacy, Ed 1911-1968...................DLB-226
Lacy, Sam 1903- DLB-171
Ladd, Joseph Brown 1764-1786 ....DLB-37
La Farge, Oliver 1901-1963.............DLB-9
La Fayette, Marie-Madeleine Pioche de La Vergne, comtesse de 1634-1696 ....DLB-268
Laffan, Mrs. R. S. de Courcy (see Adams, Bertha Leith)
Lafferty, R. A. 1914- DLB-8
La Flesche, Francis 1857-1932 ....DLB-175
La Fontaine, Jean de 1621-1695..........DLB-268
Laforge, Jules 1860-1887 ....DLB-217
Lagerkvist, Pär 1891-1974 ....DLB-259
Lagerlöf, Selma 1858-1940 ....DLB-259
Lagorio, Gina 1922- DLB-196
La Guma, Alex 1925-1985 ....DLB-117, 225; CDWLB-3
Lahaise, Guillaume (see Delahaye, Guy)
Lahontan, Louis-Armand de Lom d'Arce, Baron de 1666-1715?...............DLB-99
Laing, Kojo 1946- DLB-157
Laird, Carobeth 1895- Y-82
Laird and Lee DLB-49
Lake, Paul 1951- DLB-282
Lalić, Ivan V. 1931-1996................DLB-181
Lalić, Mihailo 1914-1992................DLB-181
Lalonde, Michèle 1937- DLB-60
Lamantia, Philip 1927- DLB-16
Lamartine, Alphonse de 1790-1869 .....DLB-217
Lamb, Lady Caroline 1785-1828 ....DLB-116
Lamb, Charles 1775-1834 ......DLB-93, 107, 163; CDBLB-3
Lamb, Mary 1764-1874 ....DLB-163
Lambert, Angela 1940- DLB-271
Lambert, Betty 1933-1983 ....DLB-60
Lamming, George 1927- ...DLB-125; CDWLB-3
La Mothe Le Vayer 1588-1672 ....DLB-268
L'Amour, Louis 1908-1988 ....DLB-206; Y-80
Lampman, Archibald 1861-1899 ....DLB-92
Lamson, Wolffe and Company..........DLB-49
Lancer Books.........................DLB-46
Lanchester, John 1962- DLB-267
Landesman, Jay 1919- and Landesman, Fran 1927- DLB-16
Landolfi, Tommaso 1908-1979 ....DLB-177
Landon, Letitia Elizabeth 1802-1838.....DLB-96
Landor, Walter Savage 1775-1864....DLB-93, 107
Landry, Napoléon-P. 1884-1956 ....DLB-92
Lane, Charles 1800-1870 ....DLB-1, 223
Lane, F. C. 1885-1984..................DLB-241
Lane, John, Company DLB-49
Lane, Laurence W. 1890-1967 ....DLB-91

Lane, M. Travis 1934- DLB-60	Lauremberg, Johann 1590-1658 .... DLB-164	Leavitt and Allen DLB-49
Lane, Patrick 1939- DLB-53	Laurence, Margaret 1926-1987.......... DLB-53	Le Blond, Mrs. Aubrey 1861-1934.......DLB-174
Lane, Pinkie Gordon 1923- DLB-41	Laurentius von Schnüffis 1633-1702..... DLB-168	le Carré, John (David John Moore Cornwell)1931- DLB-87; CDBLB-8
Laney, Al 1896-1988 ....DLB-4, 171	Laurents, Arthur 1918- DLB-26	
Lang, Andrew 1844-1912...... DLB-98, 141, 184	Laurie, Annie (see Black, Winifred)	Lécavelé, Roland (see Dorgeles, Roland)
Langer, Susanne K. 1895-1985.........DLB-270	Laut, Agnes Christiana 1871-1936 .... DLB-92	Lechlitner, Ruth 1901- DLB-48
Langevin, André 1927- DLB-60	Lauterbach, Ann 1942- DLB-193	Leclerc, Félix 1914- DLB-60
Langford, David 1953- DLB-261	Lautreamont, Isidore Lucien Ducasse, Comte de 1846-1870..................... DLB-217	Le Clézio, J. M. G. 1940- DLB-83
Langgässer, Elisabeth 1899-1950 .... DLB-69		Lectures on Rhetoric and Belles Lettres (1783), by Hugh Blair [excerpts] DLB-31
Langhorne, John 1735-1779 .... DLB-109	Lavater, Johann Kaspar 1741-1801....... DLB-97	
Langland, William circa 1330-circa 1400 .... DLB-146	Lavin, Mary 1912-1996 .... DLB-15	Leder, Rudolf (see Hermlin, Stephan)
	Law, John (see Harkness, Margaret)	Lederer, Charles 1910-1976 .... DLB-26
Langton, Anna 1804-1893 .... DLB-99	Lawes, Henry 1596-1662 .... DLB-126	Ledwidge, Francis 1887-1917 .... DLB-20
Lanham, Edwin 1904-1979............. DLB-4	Lawless, Anthony (see MacDonald, Philip)	Lee, Dennis 1939- DLB-53
Lanier, Sidney 1842-1881........ DLB-64; DS-13	Lawless, Emily (The Hon. Emily Lawless) 1845-1913 DLB-240	Lee, Don L. (see Madhubuti, Haki R.)
Lanyer, Aemilia 1569-1645........... DLB-121		Lee, George W. 1894-1976............ DLB-51
Lapointe, Gatien 1931-1983 .... DLB-88	Lawrence, D. H. 1885-1930 ..... DLB-10, 19, 36, 98, 162, 195; CDBLB-6	Lee, Harper 1926- DLB-6; CDALB-1
Lapointe, Paul-Marie 1929- DLB-88		Lee, Harriet (1757-1851) and Lee, Sophia (1750-1824)............ DLB-39
Larcom, Lucy 1824-1893 .... DLB-221, 243	Lawrence, David 1888-1973 .... DLB-29	
Lardner, John 1912-1960 ....DLB-171	Lawrence, Jerome 1915- and Lee, Robert E. 1918-1994 .... DLB-228	Lee, Laurie 1914-1997 .... DLB-27
Lardner, Ring 1885-1933 ....DLB-11, 25, 86, 171; DS-16; CDALB-4		Lee, Leslie 1935- DLB-266
	Lawrence, Seymour 1926-1994 .... Y-94	Lee, Li-Young 1957- DLB-165
Lardner 100: Ring Lardner Centennial Symposium Y-85	Lawrence, T. E. 1888-1935 .... DLB-195	Lee, Manfred B. (see Dannay, Frederic, and Manfred B. Lee)
	Lawson, George 1598-1678 .... DLB-213	
Lardner, Ring, Jr. 1915-2000 ......DLB-26, Y-00	Lawson, Henry 1867-1922 .... DLB-230	Lee, Nathaniel circa 1645-1692 .... DLB-80
Larkin, Philip 1922-1985 ..... DLB-27; CDBLB-8	Lawson, John ?-1711.................. DLB-24	Lee, Sir Sidney 1859-1926 .... DLB-149, 184
La Roche, Sophie von 1730-1807 .... DLB-94	Lawson, John Howard 1894-1977 ..... DLB-228	Lee, Sir Sidney, "Principles of Biography," in Elizabethan and Other Essays DLB-149
La Rochefoucauld, François VI de 1613-1680.....................DLB-268	Lawson, Louisa Albury 1848-1920...... DLB-230	
	Lawson, Robert 1892-1957............ DLB-22	Lee, Tanith 1947- DLB-261
La Rocque, Gilbert 1943-1984 .... DLB-60	Lawson, Victor F. 1850-1925 .... DLB-25	Lee, Vernon 1856-1935 ....DLB-57, 153, 156, 174, 178
Laroque de Roquebrune, Robert (see Roquebrune, Robert de)	Layard, Sir Austen Henry 1817-1894.................... DLB-166	
		Lee and Shepard..................... DLB-49
Larrick, Nancy 1910- DLB-61	Layton, Irving 1912- DLB-88	Le Fanu, Joseph Sheridan 1814-1873............DLB-21, 70, 159, 178
Larsen, Nella 1893-1964............... DLB-51	LaZamon flourished circa 1200 .... DLB-146	
Larson, Clinton F. 1919-1994 .... DLB-256	Lazarević, Laza K. 1851-1890.......... DLB-147	Leffland, Ella 1931- Y-84
La Sale, Antoine de circa 1386-1460/1467 .... DLB-208	Lazarus, George 1904-1997 .... DLB-201	le Fort, Gertrud von 1876-1971.......... DLB-66
	Lazhechnikov, Ivan Ivanovich 1792-1869 .... DLB-198	Le Gallienne, Richard 1866-1947......... DLB-4
Lasch, Christopher 1932-1994 .... DLB-246		Legaré, Hugh Swinton 1797-1843 ....DLB-3, 59, 73, 248
Lasker-Schüler, Else 1869-1945 ..... DLB-66, 124	Lea, Henry Charles 1825-1909 .... DLB-47	
Lasnier, Rina 1915- DLB-88	Lea, Sydney 1942- DLB-120, 282	Legaré, James Mathewes 1823-1859... DLB-3, 248
Lassalle, Ferdinand 1825-1864 .... DLB-129	Lea, Tom 1907- DLB-6	The Legends of the Saints and a Medieval Christian Worldview............. DLB-148
Latham, Robert 1912-1995............ DLB-201	Leacock, John 1729-1802 .... DLB-31	
Lathrop, Dorothy P. 1891-1980 .... DLB-22	Leacock, Stephen 1869-1944 .... DLB-92	Léger, Antoine-J. 1880-1950 .... DLB-88
Lathrop, George Parsons 1851-1898 ..... DLB-71	Lead, Jane Ward 1623-1704 .... DLB-131	Leggett, William 1801-1839............ DLB-250
Lathrop, John, Jr. 1772-1820........... DLB-37	Leadenhall Press..................... DLB-106	Le Guin, Ursula K. 1929- DLB-8, 52, 256, 275; CDALB-6
Latimer, Hugh 1492?-1555............ DLB-136	"The Greatness of Southern Literature": League of the South Institute for the Study of Southern Culture and History Y-02	
Latimore, Jewel Christine McLawler (see Amini, Johari M.)		Lehman, Ernest 1920- DLB-44
		Lehmann, John 1907- DLB-27, 100
La Tour du Pin, Patrice de 1911-1975 ... DLB-258	Leakey, Caroline Woolmer 1827-1881... DLB-230	Lehmann, John, Limited.............. DLB-112
Latymer, William 1498-1583 .... DLB-132	Leapor, Mary 1722-1746............. DLB-109	Lehmann, Rosamond 1901-1990 .... DLB-15
Laube, Heinrich 1806-1884 .... DLB-133	Lear, Edward 1812-1888 ...... DLB-32, 163, 166	Lehmann, Wilhelm 1882-1968.......... DLB-56
Laud, William 1573-1645 .... DLB-213	Leary, Timothy 1920-1996............. DLB-16	Leiber, Fritz 1910-1992 .... DLB-8
Laughlin, James 1914-1997....... DLB-48; Y-96	Leary, W. A., and Company DLB-49	Leibniz, Gottfried Wilhelm 1646-1716 ... DLB-168
James Laughlin Tributes................. Y-97	Léautaud, Paul 1872-1956 .... DLB-65	Leicester University Press DLB-112
Conversations with Publishers IV: An Interview with James Laughlin....... Y-96	Leavis, F. R. 1895-1978................ DLB-242	Leigh, Carolyn 1926-1983 .... DLB-265
		Leigh, W. R. 1866-1955............... DLB-188
Laumer, Keith 1925- DLB-8	Leavitt, David 1961- DLB-130	Leinster, Murray 1896-1975............. DLB-8

Leiser, Bill 1898-1965 . . . . DLB-241	Lessing, Doris 1919- DLB-15, 139; Y-85; CDBLB-8	Lewis, Wyndham 1882-1957 . . . . DLB-15
Leisewitz, Johann Anton 1752-1806 . . . . DLB-94	Lessing, Gotthold Ephraim 1729-1781 . . . . DLB-97; CDWLB-2	Lewisohn, Ludwig 1882-1955 . . . DLB-4, 9, 28, 102
Leitch, Maurice 1933- DLB-14	Lettau, Reinhard 1929- DLB-75	Leyendecker, J. C. 1874-1951 . . . . DLB-188
Leithauser, Brad 1953- DLB-120, 282	Letter from Japan Y-94, Y-98	Lezama Lima, José 1910-1976 . . . . DLB-113
Leland, Charles G. 1824-1903 . . . . DLB-11	Letter from London Y-96	L'Heureux, John 1934- DLB-244
Leland, John 1503?-1552 . . . . DLB-136	Letter to [Samuel] Richardson on *Clarissa* (1748), by Henry Fielding DLB-39	Libbey, Laura Jean 1862-1924 . . . . DLB-221
Lemay, Pamphile 1837-1918 . . . . DLB-99	A Letter to the Editor of *The Irish Times* Y-97	Libedinsky, Iurii Nikolaevich 1898-1959 . . . . DLB-272
Lemelin, Roger 1919-1992 . . . . DLB-88	The Hemingway Letters Project Finds an Editor Y-02	E-Books' Second Act in Libraries Y-02
Lemercier, Louis-Jean-Népomucène 1771-1840 . . . . DLB-192	Lever, Charles 1806-1872 . . . . DLB-21	Library History Group Y-01
Le Moine, James MacPherson 1825-1912 . . . . DLB-99	Lever, Ralph ca. 1527-1585 . . . . DLB-236	The Library of America DLB-46
Lemon, Mark 1809-1870 . . . . DLB-163	Leverson, Ada 1862-1933 . . . . DLB-153	The Library of America: An Assessment After Two Decades Y-02
Le Moyne, Jean 1913-1996 . . . . DLB-88	Levertov, Denise 1923-1997 . . . . DLB-5, 165; CDALB-7	The Licensing Act of 1737 . . . . DLB-84
Lemperly, Paul 1858-1939 . . . . DLB-187	Levi, Peter 1931- DLB-40	Lichfield, Leonard I [publishing house] . . . DLB-170
L'Engle, Madeleine 1918- DLB-52	Levi, Primo 1919-1987 . . . . DLB-177	Lichtenberg, Georg Christoph 1742-1799 . . DLB-94
Lennart, Isobel 1915-1971 . . . . DLB-44	Lévi-Strauss, Claude 1908- DLB-242	The Liddle Collection Y-97
Lennox, Charlotte 1729 or 1730-1804 . . . . DLB-39	Levien, Sonya 1888-1960 . . . . DLB-44	Lidman, Sara 1923- DLB-257
Lenox, James 1800-1880 . . . . DLB-140	Levin, Meyer 1905-1981 . . . . DLB-9, 28; Y-81	Lieb, Fred 1888-1980 . . . . DLB-171
Lenski, Lois 1893-1974 . . . . DLB-22	Levin, Phillis 1954- DLB-282	Liebling, A. J. 1904-1963 . . . . DLB-4, 171
Lentricchia, Frank 1940- DLB-246	Levine, Norman 1923- DLB-88	Lieutenant Murray (see Ballou, Maturin Murray)
Lenz, Hermann 1913-1998 . . . . DLB-69	Levine, Philip 1928- DLB-5	Lighthall, William Douw 1857-1954 . . . . . . DLB-92
Lenz, J. M. R. 1751-1792 . . . . DLB-94	Levis, Larry 1946- DLB-120	Lilar, Françoise (see Mallet-Joris, Françoise)
Lenz, Siegfried 1926- DLB-75	Levitov, Aleksandr Ivanovich 1835?-1877 . . . . DLB-277	Lili'uokalani, Queen 1838-1917 . . . . DLB-221
Leonard, Elmore 1925- DLB-173, 226	Levy, Amy 1861-1889 . . . . DLB-156, 240	Lillo, George 1691-1739 . . . . DLB-84
Leonard, Hugh 1926- DLB-13	Levy, Benn Wolfe 1900-1973 . . . . . . DLB-13; Y-81	Lilly, J. K., Jr. 1893-1966 . . . . DLB-140
Leonard, William Ellery 1876-1944 . . . . DLB-54	Lewald, Fanny 1811-1889 . . . . DLB-129	Lilly, Wait and Company DLB-49
Leonov, Leonid Maksimovich 1899-1994 . . . . DLB-272	Lewes, George Henry 1817-1878 . . . . . DLB-55, 144	Lily, William circa 1468-1522 . . . . DLB-132
Leonowens, Anna 1834-1914 . . . . DLB-99, 166	"Criticism In Relation To Novels" (1863) DLB-21	Limited Editions Club DLB-46
Leont'ev, Konstantin Nikolaevich 1831-1891 . . . . DLB-277	*The Principles of Success in Literature* (1865) [excerpt] DLB-57	Limón, Graciela 1938- DLB-209
Leopold, Aldo 1887-1948 . . . . DLB-275	Lewis, Agnes Smith 1843-1926 . . . . DLB-174	Lincoln and Edmands DLB-49
LePan, Douglas 1914- DLB-88	Lewis, Alfred H. 1857-1914 . . . . DLB-25, 186	Lindesay, Ethel Forence (see Richardson, Henry Handel)
Lepik, Kalju 1920-1999 . . . . DLB-232	Lewis, Alun 1915-1944 . . . . DLB-20, 162	Lindgren, Astrid 1907-2002 . . . . DLB-257
Leprohon, Rosanna Eleanor 1829-1879 . . . . DLB-99	Lewis, C. Day (see Day Lewis, C.)	Lindgren, Torgny 1938- DLB-257
Le Queux, William 1864-1927 . . . . DLB-70	Lewis, C. I. 1883-1964 . . . . DLB-270	Lindsay, Alexander William, Twenty-fifth Earl of Crawford 1812-1880 . . . . DLB-184
Lermontov, Mikhail Iur'evich 1814-1841 . . . . DLB-205	Lewis, C. S. 1898-1963 . . . . DLB-15, 100, 160, 255; CDBLB-7	Lindsay, Sir David circa 1485-1555 . . . . . . DLB-132
Lerner, Alan Jay 1918-1986 . . . . DLB-265	Lewis, Charles B. 1842-1924 . . . . DLB-11	Lindsay, David 1878-1945 . . . . DLB-255
Lerner, Max 1902-1992 . . . . DLB-29	Lewis, David 1941-2001 . . . . DLB-279	Lindsay, Jack 1900- Y-84
Lernet-Holenia, Alexander 1897-1976 . . . . . DLB-85	Lewis, Henry Clay 1825-1850 . . . . DLB-3, 248	Lindsay, Lady (Caroline Blanche Elizabeth Fitzroy Lindsay) 1844-1912 . . . . DLB-199
Le Rossignol, James 1866-1969 . . . . DLB-92	Lewis, Janet 1899-1999 . . . . Y-87	Lindsay, Norman 1879-1969 . . . . DLB-260
Lescarbot, Marc circa 1570-1642 . . . . DLB-99	Lewis, Matthew Gregory 1775-1818 . . . . DLB-39, 158, 178	Lindsay, Vachel 1879-1931 . . . . DLB-54; CDALB-3
LeSeur, William Dawson 1840-1917 . . . . DLB-92	Lewis, Meriwether 1774-1809 and Clark, William 1770-1838 . . . . . . DLB-183, 186	Linebarger, Paul Myron Anthony (see Smith, Cordwainer)
LeSieg, Theo. (see Geisel, Theodor Seuss)	Lewis, Norman 1908- DLB-204	Link, Arthur S. 1920-1998 . . . . DLB-17
Leskov, Nikolai Semenovich 1831-1895 . . DLB-238	Lewis, R. W. B. 1917- DLB-111	Linn, Ed 1922-2000 . . . . DLB-241
Leslie, Doris before 1902-1982 . . . . DLB-191	Lewis, Richard circa 1700-1734 . . . . DLB-24	Linn, John Blair 1777-1804 . . . . DLB-37
Leslie, Eliza 1787-1858 . . . . DLB-202	Lewis, Sinclair 1885-1951 . . . . . . DLB-9, 102; DS-1; CDALB-4	Lins, Osman 1924-1978 . . . . DLB-145
Leslie, Frank 1821-1880 . . . . DLB-43, 79	Sinclair Lewis Centennial Conference Y-85	Linton, Eliza Lynn 1822-1898 . . . . DLB-18
Leslie, Frank, Publishing House DLB-49	Lewis, Wilmarth Sheldon 1895-1979 . . . . . DLB-140	Linton, William James 1812-1897 . . . . DLB-32
Leśmian, Bolesław 1878-1937 . . . . DLB-215		Lintot, Barnaby Bernard [publishing house] DLB-170
Lesperance, John 1835?-1891 . . . . DLB-99		Lion Books DLB-46
Lessing, Bruno 1870-1940 . . . . DLB-28		Lionni, Leo 1910-1999 . . . . DLB-61

Cumulative Index

Lippard, George 1822-1854 .... DLB-202

Lippincott, J. B., Company DLB-49

Lippincott, Sara Jane Clarke 1823-1904 ... DLB-43

Lippmann, Walter 1889-1974 .... DLB-29

Lipton, Lawrence 1898-1975 .... DLB-16

Liscow, Christian Ludwig 1701-1760 ..... DLB-97

Lish, Gordon 1934- DLB-130

Lisle, Charles-Marie-René Leconte de 1818-1894 .... DLB-217

Lispector, Clarice 1925-1977 .... DLB-113; CDWLB-3

LitCheck Website Y-01

A Literary Archaeologist Digs On: A Brief Interview with Michael Reynolds by Michael Rogers Y-99

Literary Awards and Honors Announced in 2002 .... Y-02

The Literary Chronicle and Weekly Review 1819-1828 .... DLB-110

DLB Award for Distinguished Literary Criticism Y-02

Literary Documents: William Faulkner and the People-to-People Program Y-86

Literary Documents II: *Library Journal* Statements and Questionnaires from First Novelists Y-87

Literary Effects of World War II [British novel] DLB-15

Literary Prizes Y-00

Literary Prizes [British] DLB-15

Literary Research Archives: The Humanities Research Center, University of Texas Y-82

Literary Research Archives II: Berg Collection of English and American Literature of the New York Public Library Y-83

Literary Research Archives III: The Lilly Library Y-84

Literary Research Archives IV: The John Carter Brown Library Y-85

Literary Research Archives V: Kent State Special Collections Y-86

Literary Research Archives VI: The Modern Literary Manuscripts Collection in the Special Collections of the Washington University Libraries Y-87

Literary Research Archives VII: The University of Virginia Libraries Y-91

Literary Research Archives VIII: The Henry E. Huntington Library Y-92

Literary Research Archives IX: Special Collections at Boston University . . Y-99

The Literary Scene and Situation and . . . Who (Besides Oprah) Really Runs American Literature? Y-99

The Literary Scene 2002: Publishing, Book Reviewing, and Literary Journalism Y-02

Literary Societies Y-98, Y-99, Y-00, Y-01, Y-02

"Literary Style" (1857), by William Forsyth [excerpt] DLB-57

Literatura Chicanesca: The View From Without DLB-82

Literature at Nurse, or Circulating Morals (1885), by George Moore DLB-18

The Literature of Boxing in England through Arthur Conan Doyle Y-01

The Literature of the Modern Breakthrough DLB-259

"The Greatness of Southern Literature": League of the South Institute for the Study of Southern Culture and History Y-02

Litt, Toby 1968- DLB-267

Littell, Eliakim 1797-1870 .... DLB-79

Littell, Robert S. 1831-1896 .... DLB-79

Little, Brown and Company DLB-49

Little Magazines and Newspapers DS-15

The Little Magazines of the New Formalism DLB-282

The Little Review 1914-1929 .... DS-15

Littlewood, Joan 1914- DLB-13

Lively, Penelope 1933- DLB-14, 161, 207

Liverpool University Press DLB-112

The Lives of the Poets DLB-142

Livesay, Dorothy 1909- DLB-68

Livesay, Florence Randall 1874-1953 ..... DLB-92

"Living in Ruin," by Gerald Stern DLB-105

Livings, Henry 1929-1998 .... DLB-13

Livingston, Anne Howe 1763-1841 ... DLB-37, 200

Livingston, Jay (see Evans, Ray)

Livingston, Myra Cohn 1926-1996 ..... DLB-61

Livingston, William 1723-1790 .... DLB-31

Livingstone, David 1813-1873 .... DLB-166

Livingstone, Douglas 1932-1996 .... DLB-225

Livy 59 B.C.-A.D. 17 ...... DLB-211; CDWLB-1

Liyong, Taban lo (see Taban lo Liyong)

Lizárraga, Sylvia S. 1925- DLB-82

Llewellyn, Richard 1906-1983 .... DLB-15

Lloyd, Edward [publishing house] DLB-106

Lobel, Arnold 1933- DLB-61

Lochridge, Betsy Hopkins (see Fancher, Betsy)

Locke, David Ross 1833-1888 .... DLB-11, 23

Locke, John 1632-1704 ..... DLB-31, 101, 213, 252

Locke, Richard Adams 1800-1871 .... DLB-43

Locker-Lampson, Frederick 1821-1895 .... DLB-35, 184

Lockhart, John Gibson 1794-1854 .... DLB-110, 116 144

Lockridge, Ross, Jr. 1914-1948 ..... DLB-143; Y-80

Locrine and Selimus DLB-62

Lodge, David 1935- DLB-14, 194

Lodge, George Cabot 1873-1909 .... DLB-54

Lodge, Henry Cabot 1850-1924 .... DLB-47

Lodge, Thomas 1558-1625 .... DLB-172

From *Defence of Poetry* (1579) DLB-172

Loeb, Harold 1891-1974 .... DLB-4

Loeb, William 1905-1981 .... DLB-127

Loesser, Frank 1919-1986 .... DLB-265

Lofting, Hugh 1886-1947 .... DLB-160

Logan, Deborah Norris 1761-1839 ...... DLB-200

Logan, James 1674-1751 .... DLB-24, 140

Logan, John 1923- DLB-5

Logan, Martha Daniell 1704?-1779 ...... DLB-200

Logan, William 1950- DLB-120

Logau, Friedrich von 1605-1655 .... DLB-164

Logue, Christopher 1926- DLB-27

Lohenstein, Daniel Casper von 1635-1683 .... DLB-168

Lo-Johansson, Ivar 1901-1990 .... DLB-259

Lokert, George circa 1485-1547 .... DLB-281

Lomonosov, Mikhail Vasil'evich 1711-1765 .... DLB-150

London, Jack 1876-1916 ...... DLB-8, 12, 78, 212; CDALB-3

The London Magazine 1820-1829 .... DLB-110

Long, David 1948- DLB-244

Long, H., and Brother DLB-49

Long, Haniel 1888-1956 .... DLB-45

Long, Ray 1878-1935 .... DLB-137

Longfellow, Henry Wadsworth 1807-1882 .... DLB-1, 59, 235; CDALB-2

Longfellow, Samuel 1819-1892 .... DLB-1

Longford, Elizabeth 1906- DLB-155

Longinus circa first century DLB-176

Longley, Michael 1939- DLB-40

Longman, T. [publishing house] DLB-154

Longmans, Green and Company DLB-49

Longmore, George 1793?-1867 .... DLB-99

Longstreet, Augustus Baldwin 1790-1870 .... DLB-3, 11, 74, 248

Longworth, D. [publishing house] DLB-49

Lonsdale, Frederick 1881-1954 .... DLB-10

A Look at the Contemporary Black Theatre Movement DLB-38

Loos, Anita 1893-1981 ..... DLB-11, 26, 228; Y-81

Lopate, Phillip 1943- Y-80

Lopez, Barry 1945- DLB-256, 275

López, Diana (see Isabella, Ríos)

López, Josefina 1969- DLB-209

Loranger, Jean-Aubert 1896-1942 .... DLB-92

Lorca, Federico García 1898-1936 ..... DLB-108

Lord, John Keast 1818-1872 .... DLB-99

The Lord Chamberlain's Office and Stage Censorship in England DLB-10

Lorde, Audre 1934-1992 .... DLB-41

Lorimer, George Horace 1867-1937 ..... DLB-91

Loring, A. K. [publishing house] DLB-49

Loring and Mussey DLB-46

Lorris, Guillaume de (see *Roman de la Rose*)

Lossing, Benson J. 1813-1891 .... DLB-30

Lothar, Ernst 1890-1974 .... DLB-81

Lothrop, D., and Company DLB-49

Lothrop, Harriet M. 1844-1924 .... DLB-42

Loti, Pierre 1850-1923 .... DLB-123

Lotichius Secundus, Petrus 1528-1560 .... DLB-179

Lott, Emeline ?-? DLB-166

Louisiana State University Press Y-97

The Lounger, no. 20 (1785), by Henry
    Mackenzie.........................DLB-39
Lounsbury, Thomas R. 1838-1915.......DLB-71
Louÿs, Pierre 1870-1925..............DLB-123
Lovejoy, Arthur O. 1873-1962..........DLB-270
Lovelace, Earl 1935-........DLB-125; CDWLB-3
Lovelace, Richard 1618-1657...........DLB-131
Lovell, Coryell and Company............DLB-49
Lovell, John W., Company..............DLB-49
Lover, Samuel 1797-1868..........DLB-159, 190
Lovesey, Peter 1936-..................DLB-87
Lovinescu, Eugen
    1881-1943............DLB-220; CDWLB-4
Lovingood, Sut
    (see Harris, George Washington)
Low, Samuel 1765-?....................DLB-37
Lowell, Amy 1874-1925............DLB-54, 140
Lowell, James Russell 1819-1891
    ......DLB-1, 11, 64, 79, 189, 235; CDALB-2
Lowell, Robert 1917-1977...DLB-5, 169; CDALB-7
Lowenfels, Walter 1897-1976............DLB-4
Lowndes, Marie Belloc 1868-1947........DLB-70
Lowndes, William Thomas 1798-1843...DLB-184
Lownes, Humphrey [publishing house]...DLB-170
Lowry, Lois 1937-.....................DLB-52
Lowry, Malcolm 1909-1957...DLB-15; CDBLB-7
Lowther, Pat 1935-1975................DLB-53
Loy, Mina 1882-1966................DLB-4, 54
Lozeau, Albert 1878-1924..............DLB-92
Lubbock, Percy 1879-1965.............DLB-149
Lucan A.D. 39-A.D. 65................DLB-211
Lucas, E. V. 1868-1938........DLB-98, 149, 153
Lucas, Fielding, Jr. [publishing house].....DLB-49
Luce, Clare Booth 1903-1987..........DLB-228
Luce, Henry R. 1898-1967..............DLB-91
Luce, John W., and Company............DLB-46
Lucian circa 120-180.................DLB-176
Lucie-Smith, Edward 1933-.............DLB-40
Lucilius circa 180 B.C.-102/101 B.C......DLB-211
Lucini, Gian Pietro 1867-1914.........DLB-114
Lucretius circa 94 B.C.-circa 49 B.C.
    ....DLB-211; CDWLB-1
Luder, Peter circa 1415-1472..........DLB-179
Ludlam, Charles 1943-1987............DLB-266
Ludlum, Robert 1927-.....................Y-82
Ludus de Antichristo circa 1160........DLB-148
Ludvigson, Susan 1942-...............DLB-120
Ludwig, Jack 1922-....................DLB-60
Ludwig, Otto 1813-1865...............DLB-129
Ludwigslied 881 or 882..............DLB-148
Luera, Yolanda 1953-.................DLB-122
Luft, Lya 1938-......................DLB-145
Lugansky, Kazak Vladimir
    (see Dal', Vladimir Ivanovich)
Lugn, Kristina 1948-.................DLB-257
Lukács, Georg (see Lukács, György)

Lukács, György
    1885-1971.......DLB-215, 242; CDWLB-4
Luke, Peter 1919-.....................DLB-13
Lummis, Charles F. 1859-1928.........DLB-186
Lundkvist, Artur 1906-1991...........DLB-259
Lunts, Lev Natanovich 1901-1924......DLB-272
Lupton, F. M., Company................DLB-49
Lupus of Ferrières
    circa 805-circa 862................DLB-148
Lurie, Alison 1926-....................DLB-2
Lussu, Emilio 1890-1975..............DLB-264
Lustig, Arnošt 1926-.................DLB-232
Luther, Martin 1483-1546...DLB-179; CDWLB-2
Luzi, Mario 1914-....................DLB-128
L'vov, Nikolai Aleksandrovich 1751-1803..DLB-150
Lyall, Gavin 1932-....................DLB-87
Lydgate, John circa 1370-1450........DLB-146
Lyly, John circa 1554-1606........DLB-62, 167
Lynch, Patricia 1898-1972............DLB-160
Lynch, Richard flourished 1596-1601...DLB-172
Lynd, Robert 1879-1949...............DLB-98
Lyon, Matthew 1749-1822...............DLB-43
Lyotard, Jean-François 1924-1998.....DLB-242
Lyric Poetry........................DLB-268
Lysias circa 459 B.C.-circa 380 B.C.....DLB-176
Lytle, Andrew 1902-1995..........DLB-6; Y-95
Lytton, Edward
    (see Bulwer-Lytton, Edward)
Lytton, Edward Robert Bulwer
    1831-1891........................DLB-32

M

Maass, Joachim 1901-1972..............DLB-69
Mabie, Hamilton Wright 1845-1916......DLB-71
Mac A'Ghobhainn, Iain (see Smith, Iain Crichton)
MacArthur, Charles 1895-1956.....DLB-7, 25, 44
Macaulay, Catherine 1731-1791........DLB-104
Macaulay, David 1945-.................DLB-61
Macaulay, Rose 1881-1958..............DLB-36
Macaulay, Thomas Babington
    1800-1859.............DLB-32, 55; CDBLB-4
Macaulay Company.....................DLB-46
MacBeth, George 1932-.................DLB-40
Macbeth, Madge 1880-1965..............DLB-92
MacCaig, Norman 1910-1996.............DLB-27
MacDiarmid, Hugh
    1892-1978..............DLB-20; CDBLB-7
MacDonald, Cynthia 1928-.............DLB-105
MacDonald, George 1824-1905....DLB-18, 163, 178
MacDonald, John D. 1916-1986......DLB-8; Y-86
MacDonald, Philip 1899?-1980..........DLB-77
Macdonald, Ross (see Millar, Kenneth)
Macdonald, Sharman 1951-.............DLB-245
MacDonald, Wilson 1880-1967...........DLB-92
Macdonald and Company (Publishers)...DLB-112
MacEwen, Gwendolyn 1941-1987....DLB-53, 251

Macfadden, Bernarr 1868-1955.......DLB-25, 91
MacGregor, John 1825-1892............DLB-166
MacGregor, Mary Esther (see Keith, Marian)
Machado, Antonio 1875-1939...........DLB-108
Machado, Manuel 1874-1947............DLB-108
Machar, Agnes Maule 1837-1927.........DLB-92
Machaut, Guillaume de
    circa 1300-1377...................DLB-208
Machen, Arthur Llewelyn Jones
    1863-1947...............DLB-36, 156, 178
MacIlmaine, Roland 1550?-?...........DLB-281
MacInnes, Colin 1914-1976.............DLB-14
MacInnes, Helen 1907-1985.............DLB-87
Mac Intyre, Tom 1931-................DLB-245
Mačiulis, Jonas (see Maironis, Jonas)
Mack, Maynard 1909-..................DLB-111
Mackall, Leonard L. 1879-1937........DLB-140
MacKay, Isabel Ecclestone 1875-1928....DLB-92
MacKaye, Percy 1875-1956..............DLB-54
Macken, Walter 1915-1967..............DLB-13
Mackenzie, Alexander 1763-1820........DLB-99
Mackenzie, Alexander Slidell
    1803-1848........................DLB-183
Mackenzie, Compton 1883-1972....DLB-34, 100
Mackenzie, Henry 1745-1831............DLB-39
Mackenzie, Kenneth (Seaforth)
    1913-1955........................DLB-260
Mackenzie, William 1758-1828.........DLB-187
Mackey, Nathaniel 1947-..............DLB-169
Mackey, Shena 1944-..................DLB-231
Mackey, William Wellington
    1937-............................DLB-38
Mackintosh, Elizabeth (see Tey, Josephine)
Mackintosh, Sir James 1765-1832......DLB-158
Maclaren, Ian (see Watson, John)
Macklin, Charles 1699-1797............DLB-89
MacLaverty, Bernard 1942-............DLB-267
MacLean, Allistair 1922-1987..........DLB-276
MacLean, Katherine Anne 1925-..........DLB-8
Maclean, Norman 1902-1990............DLB-206
MacLeish, Archibald 1892-1982
    ....DLB-4, 7, 45, 228; Y-82; CDALB-7
MacLennan, Hugh 1907-1990............DLB-68
MacLeod, Alistair 1936-...............DLB-60
Macleod, Fiona (see Sharp, William)
Macleod, Norman 1906-1985.............DLB-4
Mac Low, Jackson 1922-...............DLB-193
Macmillan and Company...............DLB-106
The Macmillan Company................DLB-49
Macmillan's English Men of Letters,
    First Series (1878-1892).............DLB-144
MacNamara, Brinsley 1890-1963.........DLB-10
MacNeice, Louis 1907-1963.........DLB-10, 20
Macphail, Andrew 1864-1938............DLB-92
Macpherson, James 1736-1796..........DLB-109
Macpherson, Jay 1931-.................DLB-53

Cumulative Index

Macpherson, Jeanie 1884-1946 . . . . DLB-44
Macrae Smith Company DLB-46
MacRaye, Lucy Betty (see Webling, Lucy)
Macrone, John [publishing house] DLB-106
MacShane, Frank 1927-1999 . . . . DLB-111
Macy-Masius DLB-46
Madden, David 1933- DLB-6
Madden, Sir Frederic 1801-1873 . . . . DLB-184
Maddow, Ben 1909-1992 . . . . DLB-44
Maddux, Rachel 1912-1983 . . . . . . DLB-234; Y-93
Madgett, Naomi Long 1923- DLB-76
Madhubuti, Haki R. 1942- DLB-5, 41; DS-8
Madison, James 1751-1836 . . . . DLB-37
Madsen, Svend Åge 1939- DLB-214
Maeterlinck, Maurice 1862-1949 . . . . DLB-192
Mafūz, Najīb 1911- Y-88
The Little Magazines of the New Formalism DLB-282
Magee, David 1905-1977 . . . . DLB-187
Maginn, William 1794-1842 . . . . . . DLB-110, 159
Magoffin, Susan Shelby 1827-1855 . . . . . . DLB-239
Mahan, Alfred Thayer 1840-1914 . . . . DLB-47
Maheux-Forcier, Louise 1929- DLB-60
Mahin, John Lee 1902-1984 . . . . DLB-44
Mahon, Derek 1941- DLB-40
Maikov, Apollon Nikolaevich 1821-1897 . . . . DLB-277
Maikov, Vasilii Ivanovich 1728-1778 . . . . DLB-150
Mailer, Norman 1923- DLB-2, 16, 28, 185, 278; Y-80, Y-83, Y-97; DS-3; CDALB-6
Maillart, Ella 1903-1997 . . . . DLB-195
Maillet, Adrienne 1885-1963 . . . . DLB-68
Maillet, Antonine 1929- DLB-60
Maillu, David G. 1939- DLB-157
Maimonides, Moses 1138-1204 . . . . DLB-115
Main Selections of the Book-of-the-Month Club, 1926-1945 . . . . DLB-9
Main Trends in Twentieth-Century Book Clubs DLB-46
Mainwaring, Daniel 1902-1977 . . . . DLB-44
Mair, Charles 1838-1927 . . . . DLB-99
Mair, John circa 1467-1550 . . . . DLB-281
Maironis, Jonas 1862-1932 . . . . DLB-220; CDWLB-4
Mais, Roger 1905-1955 . . . . . DLB-125; CDWLB-3
Maitland, Sara 1950- DLB-271
Major, Andre 1942- DLB-60
Major, Charles 1856-1913 . . . . DLB-202
Major, Clarence 1936- DLB-33
Major, Kevin 1949- DLB-60
Major Books DLB-46
Makarenko, Anton Semenovich 1888-1939 . . . . DLB-272
Makemie, Francis circa 1658-1708 . . . . . . DLB-24
The Making of Americans Contract Y-98

The Making of a People, by J. M. Ritchie DLB-66
Maksimović, Desanka 1898-1993 . . . . DLB-147; CDWLB-4
Malamud, Bernard 1914-1986 . . . . . . DLB-2, 28, 152; Y-80, Y-86; CDALB-1
Mălăncioiu, Ileana 1940- DLB-232
Malaparte, Curzio 1898-1957 . . . . DLB-264
Malerba, Luigi 1927- DLB-196
Malet, Lucas 1852-1931 . . . . DLB-153
Mallarmé, Stéphane 1842-1898 . . . . DLB-217
Malleson, Lucy Beatrice (see Gilbert, Anthony)
Mallet-Joris, Françoise 1930- DLB-83
Mallock, W. H. 1849-1923 . . . . .DLB-18, 57
"Every Man His Own Poet; or, The Inspired Singer's Recipe Book" (1877) DLB-35
Malone, Dumas 1892-1986 . . . . DLB-17
Malone, Edmond 1741-1812 . . . . DLB-142
Malory, Sir Thomas circa 1400-1410 - 1471 . . . DLB-146; CDBLB-1
Malpede, Karen 1945- DLB-249
Malraux, André 1901-1976 . . . . DLB-72
Malthus, Thomas Robert 1766-1834 . . . . DLB-107, 158
Maltz, Albert 1908-1985 . . . . DLB-102
Malzberg, Barry N. 1939- DLB-8
Mamet, David 1947- DLB-7
Mamin, Dmitrii Narkisovich 1852-1912 . . DLB-238
Manaka, Matsemela 1956- DLB-157
Manchester University Press DLB-112
Mandel, Eli 1922-1992 . . . . DLB-53
Mandeville, Bernard 1670-1733 . . . . DLB-101
Mandeville, Sir John mid fourteenth century DLB-146
Mandiargues, André Pieyre de 1909- . . . DLB-83
Manea, Norman 1936- DLB-232
Manfred, Frederick 1912-1994 . . . . DLB-6, 212, 227
Manfredi, Gianfranco 1948- DLB-196
Mangan, Sherry 1904-1961 . . . . DLB-4
Manganelli, Giorgio 1922-1990 . . . . DLB-196
Manilius fl. first century A.D. DLB-211
Mankiewicz, Herman 1897-1953 . . . . DLB-26
Mankiewicz, Joseph L. 1909-1993 . . . . . . DLB-44
Mankowitz, Wolf 1924-1998 . . . . DLB-15
Manley, Delarivière 1672?-1724 . . . . . . DLB-39, 80
Preface to *The Secret History, of Queen Zarah, and the Zarazians* (1705) DLB-39
Mann, Abby 1927- DLB-44
Mann, Charles 1929-1998 . . . . Y-98
Mann, Emily 1952- DLB-266
Mann, Heinrich 1871-1950 . . . . DLB-66, 118
Mann, Horace 1796-1859 . . . . DLB-1, 235
Mann, Klaus 1906-1949 . . . . DLB-56
Mann, Mary Peabody 1806-1887 . . . . DLB-239
Mann, Thomas 1875-1955 . . . DLB-66; CDWLB-2
Mann, William D'Alton 1839-1920 . . . . . DLB-137

Mannin, Ethel 1900-1984 . . . . DLB-191, 195
Manning, Emily (see Australie)
Manning, Frederic 1882-1935 . . . . DLB-260
Manning, Laurence 1899-1972 . . . . DLB-251
Manning, Marie 1873?-1945 . . . . DLB-29
Manning and Loring DLB-49
Mannyng, Robert flourished 1303-1338 . . . . DLB-146
Mano, D. Keith 1942- DLB-6
Manor Books DLB-46
Mansfield, Katherine 1888-1923 . . . . DLB-162
Mantel, Hilary 1952- DLB-271
Manuel, Niklaus circa 1484-1530 . . . . . . .DLB-179
Manzini, Gianna 1896-1974 . . . . .DLB-177
Mapanje, Jack 1944- DLB-157
Maraini, Dacia 1936- DLB-196
Marcel Proust at 129 and the Proust Society of America Y-00
Marcel Proust's *Remembrance of Things Past*: The Rediscovered Galley Proofs Y-00
March, William (William Edward Campbell) 1893-1954 . . . . DLB-9, 86
Marchand, Leslie A. 1900-1999 . . . . DLB-103
Marchant, Bessie 1862-1941 . . . . DLB-160
Marchant, Tony 1959- DLB-245
Marchenko, Anastasiia Iakovlevna 1830-1880 . . . . DLB-238
Marchessault, Jovette 1938- DLB-60
Marcinkevičius, Justinas 1930- DLB-232
Marcus, Frank 1928- DLB-13
Marcuse, Herbert 1898-1979 . . . . DLB-242
Marden, Orison Swett 1850-1924 . . . . . . .DLB-137
Marechera, Dambudzo 1952-1987 . . . . . . .DLB-157
Marek, Richard, Books DLB-46
Mares, E. A. 1938- DLB-122
Margulies, Donald 1954- DLB-228
Mariani, Paul 1940- DLB-111
Marie de France flourished 1160-1178 . . . DLB-208
Marie-Victorin, Frère (Conrad Kirouac) 1885-1944 . . . . DLB-92
Marin, Biagio 1891-1985 . . . . DLB-128
Marincovič, Ranko 1913- DLB-147; CDWLB-4
Marinetti, Filippo Tommaso 1876-1944 . . . . DLB-114, 264
Marion, Frances 1886-1973 . . . . DLB-44
Marius, Richard C. 1933-1999 . . . . Y-85
Markevich, Boleslav Mikhailovich 1822-1884 . . . . DLB-238
Markfield, Wallace 1926-2002 . . . .DLB-2, 28; Y-02
Wallace Markfield's "Steeplechase" Y-02
Markham, Edwin 1852-1940 . . . . DLB-54, 186
Markle, Fletcher 1921-1991 . . . . .DLB-68; Y-91
Marlatt, Daphne 1942- DLB-60
Marlitt, E. 1825-1887 . . . . DLB-129
Marlowe, Christopher 1564-1593 . . . . DLB-62; CDBLB-1

Marlyn, John 1912- DLB-88
Marmion, Shakerley 1603-1639..........DLB-58
Der Marner before 1230-circa 1287......DLB-138
Marnham, Patrick 1943- DLB-204
The *Marprelate Tracts* 1588-1589 ....DLB-132
Marquand, John P. 1893-1960........DLB-9, 102
Marqués, René 1919-1979 ....DLB-113
Marquis, Don 1878-1937 ....DLB-11, 25
Marriott, Anne 1913- DLB-68
Marryat, Frederick 1792-1848 .....DLB-21, 163
Marsh, Capen, Lyon and Webb DLB-49
Marsh, George Perkins
 1801-1882 ....DLB-1, 64, 243
Marsh, James 1794-1842 ....DLB-1, 59
Marsh, Narcissus 1638-1713 ....DLB-213
Marsh, Ngaio 1899-1982................DLB-77
Marshall, Alan 1902-1984 ....DLB-260
Marshall, Edison 1894-1967 ....DLB-102
Marshall, Edward 1932- DLB-16
Marshall, Emma 1828-1899 ....DLB-163
Marshall, James 1942-1992 ....DLB-61
Marshall, Joyce 1913- DLB-88
Marshall, Paule 1929- DLB-33, 157, 227
Marshall, Tom 1938-1993 ....DLB-60
Marsilius of Padua
 circa 1275-circa 1342.............DLB-115
Mars-Jones, Adam 1954- DLB-207
Marson, Una 1905-1965 ....DLB-157
Marston, John 1576-1634............DLB-58, 172
Marston, Philip Bourke 1850-1887 ....DLB-35
Martens, Kurt 1870-1945...............DLB-66
Martial circa A.D. 40-circa A.D. 103
 ....DLB-211; CDWLB-1
Martien, William S. [publishing house] DLB-49
Martin, Abe (see Hubbard, Kin)
Martin, Catherine ca. 1847-1937 ....DLB-230
Martin, Charles 1942- DLB-120, 282
Martin, Claire 1914- DLB-60
Martin, David 1915-1997................DLB-260
Martin, Jay 1935- DLB-111
Martin, Johann (see Laurentius von Schnüffis)
Martin, Thomas 1696-1771 ....DLB-213
Martin, Violet Florence (see Ross, Martin)
Martin du Gard, Roger 1881-1958 ....DLB-65
Martineau, Harriet
 1802-1876 ....DLB-21, 55, 159, 163, 166, 190
Martínez, Demetria 1960- DLB-209
Martínez, Eliud 1935- DLB-122
Martínez, Max 1943- DLB-82
Martínez, Rubén 1962- DLB-209
Martinson, Harry 1904-1978 ....DLB-259
Martinson, Moa 1890-1964 ....DLB-259
Martone, Michael 1955- DLB-218
Martyn, Edward 1859-1923 ....DLB-10
Marvell, Andrew
 1621-1678 ....DLB-131; CDBLB-2

Marvin X 1944- DLB-38
Marx, Karl 1818-1883 ....DLB-129
Marzials, Theo 1850-1920.............DLB-35
Masefield, John
 1878-1967 ...DLB-10, 19, 153, 160; CDBLB-5
Masham, Damaris Cudworth Lady
 1659-1708 ....DLB-252
Masino, Paola 1908-1989..............DLB-264
Mason, A. E. W. 1865-1948 ....DLB-70
Mason, Bobbie Ann
 1940- DLB-173; Y-87; CDALB-7
Mason, David 1954- DLB-282
Mason, William 1725-1797.............DLB-142
Mason Brothers.....................DLB-49
Massey, Gerald 1828-1907.............DLB-32
Massey, Linton R. 1900-1974 ....DLB-187
Massie, Allan 1938- DLB-271
Massinger, Philip 1583-1640 ....DLB-58
Masson, David 1822-1907.............DLB-144
Masters, Edgar Lee
 1868-1950 ....DLB-54; CDALB-3
Masters, Hilary 1928- DLB-244
Mastronardi, Lucio 1930-1979..........DLB-177
Matevski, Mateja 1929- ...DLB-181; CDWLB-4
Mather, Cotton
 1663-1728 ....DLB-24, 30, 140; CDALB-2
Mather, Increase 1639-1723............DLB-24
Mather, Richard 1596-1669............DLB-24
Matheson, Annie 1853-1924 ....DLB-240
Matheson, Richard 1926- DLB-8, 44
Matheus, John F. 1887- DLB-51
Mathews, Cornelius 1817?-1889 ...DLB-3, 64, 250
Mathews, Elkin [publishing house] DLB-112
Mathews, John Joseph 1894-1979 ......DLB-175
Mathias, Roland 1915- DLB-27
Mathis, June 1892-1927...............DLB-44
Mathis, Sharon Bell 1937- DLB-33
Matković, Marijan 1915-1985 ....DLB-181
Matoš, Antun Gustav 1873-1914........DLB-147
Matsumoto Seichō 1909-1992 ....DLB-182
The Matter of England 1240-1400 ......DLB-146
The Matter of Rome early twelfth to late
 fifteenth century DLB-146
Matthew of Vendôme
 circa 1130-circa 1200..............DLB-208
Matthews, Brander
 1852-1929 ....DLB-71, 78; DS-13
Matthews, Jack 1925- DLB-6
Matthews, Victoria Earle 1861-1907 .....DLB-221
Matthews, William 1942-1997...........DLB-5
Matthiessen, F. O. 1902-1950 ....DLB-63
Matthiessen, Peter 1927- DLB-6, 173, 275
Maturin, Charles Robert 1780-1824 .....DLB-178
Maugham, W. Somerset 1874-1965
 ....DLB-10, 36, 77, 100, 162, 195; CDBLB-6
Maupassant, Guy de 1850-1893 ....DLB-123
Maupin, Armistead 1944- DLB-278

Mauriac, Claude 1914-1996 ....DLB-83
Mauriac, François 1885-1970...........DLB-65
Maurice, Frederick Denison
 1805-1872 ....DLB-55
Maurois, André 1885-1967 ....DLB-65
Maury, James 1718-1769 ....DLB-31
Mavor, Elizabeth 1927- DLB-14
Mavor, Osborne Henry (see Bridie, James)
Maxwell, Gavin 1914-1969 ....DLB-204
Maxwell, H. [publishing house]..........DLB-49
Maxwell, John [publishing house] DLB-106
Maxwell, William
 1908-2000 ....DLB-218, 278; Y-80
May, Elaine 1932- DLB-44
May, Karl 1842-1912..................DLB-129
May, Thomas 1595 or 1596-1650 ....DLB-58
Mayer, Bernadette 1945- DLB-165
Mayer, Mercer 1943- DLB-61
Mayer, O. B. 1818-1891 ....DLB-3, 248
Mayes, Herbert R. 1900-1987 ....DLB-137
Mayes, Wendell 1919-1992............DLB-26
Mayfield, Julian 1928-1984 ....DLB-33; Y-84
Mayhew, Henry 1812-1887......DLB-18, 55, 190
Mayhew, Jonathan 1720-1766 ....DLB-31
Mayne, Ethel Colburn 1865-1941.......DLB-197
Mayne, Jasper 1604-1672...............DLB-126
Mayne, Seymour 1944- DLB-60
Mayor, Flora Macdonald 1872-1932 .....DLB-36
Mayröcker, Friederike 1924- DLB-85
Mazrui, Ali A. 1933- DLB-125
Mažuranić, Ivan 1814-1890 ....DLB-147
Mazursky, Paul 1930- DLB-44
McAlmon, Robert 1896-1956 ...DLB-4, 45; DS-15
Robert McAlmon's "A Night at Bricktop's" .. Y-01
McArthur, Peter 1866-1924............DLB-92
McAuley, James 1917-1976 ....DLB-260
McBride, Robert M., and Company DLB-46
McCabe, Patrick 1955- DLB-194
McCaffrey, Anne 1926- DLB-8
McCann, Colum, 1965- DLB-267
McCarthy, Cormac 1933- DLB-6, 143, 256
McCarthy, Mary 1912-1989 ....DLB-2; Y-81
McCay, Winsor 1871-1934 ....DLB-22
McClane, Albert Jules 1922-1991 ....DLB-171
McClatchy, C. K. 1858-1936............DLB-25
McClellan, George Marion 1860-1934 ....DLB-50
McCloskey, Robert 1914- DLB-22
McClung, Nellie Letitia 1873-1951 ......DLB-92
McClure, James 1939- DLB-276
McClure, Joanna 1930- DLB-16
McClure, Michael 1932- DLB-16
McClure, Phillips and Company.........DLB-46
McClure, S. S. 1857-1949..............DLB-91
McClurg, A. C., and Company.........DLB-49
McCluskey, John A., Jr. 1944- DLB-33

Cumulative Index

McCollum, Michael A. 1946 .... Y-87
McConnell, William C. 1917- DLB-88
McCord, David 1897-1997 .... DLB-61
McCord, Louisa S. 1810-1879 .... DLB-248
McCorkle, Jill 1958- DLB-234; Y-87
McCorkle, Samuel Eusebius
   1746-1811 .... DLB-37
McCormick, Anne O'Hare 1880-1954 .... DLB-29
Kenneth Dale McCormick Tributes Y-97
McCormick, Robert R. 1880-1955 .... DLB-29
McCourt, Edward 1907-1972 .... DLB-88
McCoy, Horace 1897-1955 .... DLB-9
McCrae, Hugh 1876-1958 .... DLB-260
McCrae, John 1872-1918 .... DLB-92
McCullagh, Joseph B. 1842-1896 .... DLB-23
McCullers, Carson
   1917-1967 ...... DLB-2, 7, 173, 228; CDALB-1
McCulloch, Thomas 1776-1843 .... DLB-99
McDonald, Forrest 1927- DLB-17
McDonald, Walter 1934- DLB-105, DS-9
"Getting Started: Accepting the Regions
   You Own–or Which Own You," ... DLB-105
McDougall, Colin 1917-1984 .... DLB-68
McDowell, Katharine Sherwood Bonner
   1849-1883 .... DLB-202, 239
McDowell, Obolensky DLB-46
McDowell, Robert 1953- DLB-282
McEwan, Ian 1948- DLB-14, 194
McFadden, David 1940- DLB-60
McFall, Frances Elizabeth Clarke
   (see Grand, Sarah)
McFarlane, Leslie 1902-1977 .... DLB-88
McFarland, Ronald 1942- DLB-256
McFee, William 1881-1966 .... DLB-153
McGahern, John 1934- DLB-14, 231
McGee, Thomas D'Arcy 1825-1868 ..... DLB-99
McGeehan, W. O. 1879-1933 .... DLB-25, 171
McGill, Ralph 1898-1969 .... DLB-29
McGinley, Phyllis 1905-1978 .... DLB-11, 48
McGinniss, Joe 1942- DLB-185
McGirt, James E. 1874-1930 .... DLB-50
McGlashan and Gill DLB-106
McGough, Roger 1937- DLB-40
McGrath, John 1935- DLB-233
McGrath, Patrick 1950- DLB-231
McGraw-Hill DLB-46
McGuane, Thomas 1939- DLB-2, 212; Y-80
McGuckian, Medbh 1950- DLB-40
McGuffey, William Holmes 1800-1873 ... DLB-42
McGuinness, Frank 1953- DLB-245
McHenry, James 1785-1845 .... DLB-202
McIlvanney, William 1936- DLB-14, 207
McIlwraith, Jean Newton 1859-1938 ..... DLB-92
McIntosh, Maria Jane 1803-1878 ... DLB-239, 248
McIntyre, James 1827-1906 .... DLB-99
McIntyre, O. O. 1884-1938 .... DLB-25

McKay, Claude 1889-1948 ..... DLB-4, 45, 51, 117
The David McKay Company DLB-49
McKean, William V. 1820-1903 .... DLB-23
McKenna, Stephen 1888-1967 .... DLB-197
The McKenzie Trust Y-96
McKerrow, R. B. 1872-1940 .... DLB-201
McKinley, Robin 1952- DLB-52
McKnight, Reginald 1956- DLB-234
McLachlan, Alexander 1818-1896 ..... DLB-99
McLaren, Floris Clark 1904-1978 .... DLB-68
McLaverty, Michael 1907- DLB-15
McLean, Duncan 1964- DLB-267
McLean, John R. 1848-1916 .... DLB-23
McLean, William L. 1852-1931 .... DLB-25
McLennan, William 1856-1904 .... DLB-92
McLoughlin Brothers DLB-49
McLuhan, Marshall 1911-1980 .... DLB-88
McMaster, John Bach 1852-1932 .... DLB-47
McMurtry, Larry 1936-
   ...... DLB-2, 143, 256; Y-80, Y-87; CDALB-6
McNally, Terrence 1939- DLB-7, 249
McNeil, Florence 1937- DLB-60
McNeile, Herman Cyril 1888-1937 ..... DLB-77
McNickle, D'Arcy 1904-1977 .... DLB-175, 212
McPhee, John 1931- DLB-185, 275
McPherson, James Alan 1943- DLB-38, 244
McPherson, Sandra 1943- Y-86
McTaggart, J. M. E. 1866-1925 .... DLB-262
McWhirter, George 1939- DLB-60
McWilliam, Candia 1955- DLB-267
McWilliams, Carey 1905-1980 .... DLB-137
Mda, Zakes 1948- DLB-225
Mead, George Herbert 1863-1931 .... DLB-270
Mead, L. T. 1844-1914 .... DLB-141
Mead, Matthew 1924- DLB-40
Mead, Taylor ?- DLB-16
Meany, Tom 1903-1964 .... DLB-171
Mechthild von Magdeburg
   circa 1207-circa 1282 .... DLB-138
Medieval French Drama DLB-208
Medieval Travel Diaries DLB-203
Medill, Joseph 1823-1899 .... DLB-43
Medoff, Mark 1940- DLB-7
Meek, Alexander Beaufort
   1814-1865 .... DLB-3, 248
Meeke, Mary ?-1816? DLB-116
Mei, Lev Aleksandrovich 1822-1862 ..... DLB-277
Meinke, Peter 1932- DLB-5
Mejia Vallejo, Manuel 1923- DLB-113
Melanchthon, Philipp 1497-1560 .... DLB-179
Melançon, Robert 1947- DLB-60
Mell, Max 1882-1971 .... DLB-81, 124
Mellow, James R. 1926-1997 .... DLB-111
Mel'nikov, Pavel Ivanovich 1818-1883 .. DLB-238
Meltzer, David 1937- DLB-16

Meltzer, Milton 1915- DLB-61
Melville, Elizabeth, Lady Culross
   circa 1585-1640 .... DLB-172
Melville, Herman
   1819-1891 .... DLB-3, 74, 250; CDALB-2
Memoirs of Life and Literature (1920),
   by W. H. Mallock [excerpt] DLB-57
Melville, James 1931- DLB-276
Mena, María Cristina 1893-1965 ... DLB-209, 221
Menander 342-341 B.C.-circa 292-291 B.C.
   .... DLB-176; CDWLB-1
Menantes (see Hunold, Christian Friedrich)
Mencke, Johann Burckhard
   1674-1732 .... DLB-168
Mencken, H. L. 1880-1956
   .... DLB-11, 29, 63, 137, 222; CDALB-4
H. L. Mencken's "Berlin, February, 1917" Y-00
Mencken and Nietzsche: An Unpublished
   Excerpt from H. L. Mencken's *My Life
   as Author and Editor* Y-93
Mendelssohn, Moses 1729-1786 .... DLB-97
Mendes, Catulle 1841-1909 .... DLB-217
Méndez M., Miguel 1930- DLB-82
Mens Rea (or Something) Y-97
The Mercantile Library of New York Y-96
Mercer, Cecil William (see Yates, Dornford)
Mercer, David 1928-1980 .... DLB-13
Mercer, John 1704-1768 .... DLB-31
Mercer, Johnny 1909?-1976 .... DLB-265
Meredith, George
   1828-1909 .... DLB-18, 35, 57, 159; CDBLB-4
Meredith, Louisa Anne 1812-1895 .. DLB-166, 230
Meredith, Owen
   (see Lytton, Edward Robert Bulwer)
Meredith, William 1919- DLB-5
Mergerle, Johann Ulrich
   (see Abraham à Sancta Clara)
Mérimée, Prosper 1803-1870 .... DLB-119, 192
Merivale, John Herman 1779-1844 ...... DLB-96
Meriwether, Louise 1923- DLB-33
Merlin Press DLB-112
Merriam, Eve 1916-1992 .... DLB-61
The Merriam Company DLB-49
Merril, Judith 1923-1997 .... DLB-251
Merrill, James 1926-1995 .... DLB-5, 165; Y-85
Merrill and Baker DLB-49
The Mershon Company DLB-49
Merton, Thomas 1915-1968 .... DLB-48; Y-81
Merwin, W. S. 1927- DLB-5, 169
Messner, Julian [publishing house] DLB-46
Mészöly, Miklós 1921- DLB-232
Metcalf, J. [publishing house] DLB-49
Metcalf, John 1938- DLB-60
The Methodist Book Concern DLB-49
Methuen and Company DLB-112
Meun, Jean de (see *Roman de la Rose*)
Mew, Charlotte 1869-1928 .... DLB-19, 135
Mewshaw, Michael 1943- Y-80

Meyer, Bruce 1957- DLB-282	Miller, Eugene Ethelbert 1950- DLB-41	Mitchell, Ken 1940- DLB-60
Meyer, Conrad Ferdinand 1825-1898 ....DLB-129	Miller, Heather Ross 1939- DLB-120	Mitchell, Langdon 1862-1935 ....DLB-7
Meyer, E. Y. 1946- DLB-75	Miller, Henry 1891-1980 ....DLB-4, 9; Y-80; CDALB-5	Mitchell, Loften 1919- DLB-38
Meyer, Eugene 1875-1959 ....DLB-29	Miller, Hugh 1802-1856 ....DLB-190	Mitchell, Margaret 1900-1949 ...DLB-9; CDALB-7
Meyer, Michael 1921-2000 ....DLB-155	Miller, J. Hillis 1928- DLB-67	Mitchell, S. Weir 1829-1914 ....DLB-202
Meyers, Jeffrey 1939- DLB-111	Miller, James [publishing house] DLB-49	Mitchell, W. J. T. 1942- DLB-246
Meynell, Alice 1847-1922............DLB-19, 98	Miller, Jason 1939- DLB-7	Mitchell, W. O. 1914- DLB-88
Meynell, Viola 1885-1956 ....DLB-153	Miller, Joaquin 1839-1913 ....DLB-186	Mitchison, Naomi Margaret (Haldane) 1897-1999 ....DLB-160, 191, 255
Meyrink, Gustav 1868-1932 ....DLB-81	Miller, May 1899- DLB-41	Mitford, Mary Russell 1787-1855.... DLB-110, 116
Mézières, Philipe de circa 1327-1405 .....DLB-208	Miller, Paul 1906-1991 ....DLB-127	Mitford, Nancy 1904-1973............DLB-191
Michael, Ib 1945- DLB-214	Miller, Perry 1905-1963............ DLB-17, 63	Mittelholzer, Edgar 1909-1965............ DLB-117; CDWLB-3
Michael, Livi 1960- DLB-267	Miller, Sue 1943- DLB-143	Mitterer, Erika 1906- DLB-85
Michaëlis, Karen 1872-1950...........DLB-214	Miller, Vassar 1924-1998..............DLB-105	Mitterer, Felix 1948- DLB-124
Michaels, Leonard 1933- DLB-130	Miller, Walter M., Jr. 1923- DLB-8	Mitternacht, Johann Sebastian 1613-1679 ....DLB-168
Michaux, Henri 1899-1984 ....DLB-258	Miller, Webb 1892-1940 ....DLB-29	Miyamoto, Yuriko 1899-1951 ....DLB-180
Micheaux, Oscar 1884-1951 ....DLB-50	Millett, Kate 1934- DLB-246	Mizener, Arthur 1907-1988 ....DLB-103
Michel of Northgate, Dan circa 1265-circa 1340..............DLB-146	Millhauser, Steven 1943- DLB-2	Mo, Timothy 1950- DLB-194
Micheline, Jack 1929-1998.............DLB-16	Millican, Arthenia J. Bates 1920- DLB-38	Moberg, Vilhelm 1898-1973 ....DLB-259
Michener, James A. 1907?-1997..........DLB-6	Milligan, Alice 1866-1953 ....DLB-240	Modern Age Books DLB-46
Micklejohn, George circa 1717-1818 ....DLB-31	Mills and Boon DLB-112	"Modern English Prose" (1876), by George Saintsbury DLB-57
Middle English Literature: An Introduction..................DLB-146	Mills, Magnus 1954- DLB-267	Some Basic Notes on Three Modern Genres: Interview, Blurb, and Obituary......... Y-02
The Middle English Lyric DLB-146	Milman, Henry Hart 1796-1868 ....DLB-96	The Modern Language Association of America Celebrates Its Centennial Y-84
Middle Hill Press..................DLB-106	Milne, A. A. 1882-1956 ..... DLB-10, 77, 100, 160	The Modern Library..................DLB-46
Middleton, Christopher 1926- DLB-40	Milner, Ron 1938- DLB-38	"Modern Novelists – Great and Small" (1855), by Margaret Oliphant..............DLB-21
Middleton, Richard 1882-1911 ....DLB-156	Milner, William [publishing house] DLB-106	"Modern Style" (1857), by Cockburn Thomson [excerpt] DLB-57
Middleton, Stanley 1919- DLB-14	Milnes, Richard Monckton (Lord Houghton) 1809-1885 ....DLB-32, 184	The Modernists (1932), by Joseph Warren Beach............DLB-36
Middleton, Thomas 1580-1627 ....DLB-58	Milton, John 1608-1674 .....DLB-131, 151, 281; CDBLB-2	Modiano, Patrick 1945- DLB-83
Miegel, Agnes 1879-1964..............DLB-56	Miłosz, Czesław 1911- DLB-215; CDWLB-4	Moffat, Yard and Company DLB-46
Miežalaitis, Eduardas 1919-1997........DLB-220	Minakami Tsutomu 1919- DLB-182	Moffet, Thomas 1553-1604............DLB-136
Mihailović, Dragoslav 1930- DLB-181	Minamoto no Sanetomo 1192-1219......DLB-203	Mohr, Nicholasa 1938- DLB-145
Mihalić, Slavko 1928- DLB-181	The Minerva Press DLB-154	Moix, Ana María 1947- DLB-134
Mikhailov, A. (see Sheller, Aleksandr Konstantinovich)	Minnesang circa 1150-1280 ....DLB-138	Molesworth, Louisa 1839-1921 ....DLB-135
Mikhailov, Mikhail Larionovich 1829-1865 ....DLB-238	Minns, Susan 1839-1938 ....DLB-140	Molière (Jean-Baptiste Poquelin) 1622-1673 ....DLB-268
Mikhailovsky, Nikolai Konstantinovich 1842-1904 ....DLB-277	Minor, Wendell 1944- Y-02	Möllhausen, Balduin 1825-1905 ....DLB-129
Miles, Josephine 1911-1985 ....DLB-48	Minor Illustrators, 1880-1914 ....DLB-141	Molnár, Ferenc 1878-1952 ....DLB-215; CDWLB-4
Miles, Susan (Ursula Wyllie Roberts) 1888-1975 ....DLB-240	Minor Poets of the Earlier Seventeenth Century.......................DLB-121	Molnár, Miklós (see Mészöly, Miklós)
Miliković, Branko 1934-1961 ....DLB-181	Minton, Balch and Company DLB-46	Momaday, N. Scott 1934- DLB-143, 175, 256; CDALB-7
Milius, John 1944- DLB-44	Mirbeau, Octave 1848-1917........DLB-123, 192	Monkhouse, Allan 1858-1936 ....DLB-10
Mill, James 1773-1836 .... DLB-107, 158, 262	Mirk, John died after 1414?...........DLB-146	Monro, Harold 1879 1932..............DLB-19
Mill, John Stuart 1806-1873 ......DLB-55, 190, 262; CDBLB-4	Miron, Gaston 1928- DLB-60	Monroe, Harriet 1860-1936..........DLB-54, 91
Millar, Andrew [publishing house].......DLB-154	A Mirror for Magistrates DLB-167	Monsarrat, Nicholas 1910-1979..........DLB-15
Millar, Kenneth 1915-1983 ....DLB-2, 226; Y-83; DS-6	Mishima Yukio 1925-1970............DLB-182	Montagu, Lady Mary Wortley 1689-1762 ....DLB-95, 101
Millay, Edna St. Vincent 1892-1950 ....DLB-45, 249; CDALB-4	Mitchel, Jonathan 1624-1668 ....DLB-24	Montague, C. E. 1867-1928 ....DLB-197
Millen, Sarah Gertrude 1888-1968 ......DLB-225	Mitchell, Adrian 1932- DLB-40	Montague, John 1929- DLB-40
Miller, Andrew 1960- DLB-267	Mitchell, Donald Grant 1822-1908 ....DLB-1, 243; DS-13	Shakespeare and Montaigne: A Symposium by Jules Furthman Y-02
Miller, Arthur 1915- DLB-7, 266; CDALB-1	Mitchell, Gladys 1901-1983 ....DLB-77	
	Mitchell, James Leslie 1901-1935.........DLB-15	
Miller, Caroline 1903-1992 ....DLB-9	Mitchell, John (see Slater, Patrick)	
	Mitchell, John Ames 1845-1918.........DLB-79	
	Mitchell, Joseph 1908-1996 .... DLB-185; Y-96	
	Mitchell, Julian 1935- DLB-14	

Montale, Eugenio 1896-1981 .... DLB-114
Montalvo, José 1946-1994 .... DLB-209
Monterroso, Augusto 1921- DLB-145
Montesquiou, Robert de 1855-1921 ..... DLB-217
Montgomerie, Alexander
  circa 1550?-1598 .... DLB-167
Montgomery, James 1771-1854 ...... DLB-93, 158
Montgomery, John 1919- DLB-16
Montgomery, Lucy Maud
  1874-1942 .... DLB-92; DS-14
Montgomery, Marion 1925- DLB-6
Montgomery, Robert Bruce (see Crispin, Edmund)
Montherlant, Henry de 1896-1972 ...... DLB-72
The Monthly Review 1749-1844 .... DLB-110
Montigny, Louvigny de 1876-1955 ...... DLB-92
Montoya, José 1932- DLB-122
Moodie, John Wedderburn Dunbar
  1797-1869 .... DLB-99
Moodie, Susanna 1803-1885 .... DLB-99
Moody, Joshua circa 1633-1697 .... DLB-24
Moody, William Vaughn 1869-1910 ....DLB-7, 54
Moorcock, Michael 1939- DLB-14, 231, 261
Moore, Alan 1953- DLB-261
Moore, Brian 1921-1999 .... DLB-251
Moore, Catherine L. 1911- DLB-8
Moore, Clement Clarke 1779-1863 ...... DLB-42
Moore, Dora Mavor 1888-1979 .... DLB-92
Moore, G. E. 1873-1958 .... DLB-262
Moore, George 1852-1933 .... DLB-10, 18, 57, 135
Moore, Lorrie 1957- DLB-234
Moore, Marianne
  1887-1972 .... DLB-45; DS-7; CDALB-5
Moore, Mavor 1919- DLB-88
Moore, Richard 1927- DLB-105
Moore, T. Sturge 1870-1944 .... DLB-19
Moore, Thomas 1779-1852 .... DLB-96, 144
Moore, Ward 1903-1978 .... DLB-8
Moore, Wilstach, Keys and Company DLB-49
Moorehead, Alan 1901-1983 .... DLB-204
Moorhouse, Geoffrey 1931- DLB-204
The Moorland-Spingarn Research
  Center DLB-76
Moorman, Mary C. 1905-1994 .... DLB-155
Mora, Pat 1942- DLB-209
Moraga, Cherríe 1952- DLB-82, 249
Morales, Alejandro 1944- DLB-82
Morales, Mario Roberto 1947- DLB-145
Morales, Rafael 1919- DLB-108
Morality Plays: *Mankind* circa 1450-1500 and
  Everyman circa 1500 .... DLB-146
Morante, Elsa 1912-1985 ....DLB-177
Morata, Olympia Fulvia 1526-1555 .....DLB-179
Moravia, Alberto 1907-1990 ....DLB-177
Mordaunt, Elinor 1872-1942 ....DLB-174
Mordovtsev, Daniil Lukich 1830-1905 ... DLB-238

More, Hannah
  1745-1833 .... DLB-107, 109, 116, 158
More, Henry 1614-1687 .... DLB-126, 252
More, Sir Thomas
  1477 or 1478-1535 .... DLB-136, 281
Moreno, Dorinda 1939- DLB-122
Morency, Pierre 1942- DLB-60
Moretti, Marino 1885-1979 .... DLB-114, 264
Morgan, Berry 1919- DLB-6
Morgan, Charles 1894-1958 .... DLB-34, 100
Morgan, Edmund S. 1916- DLB-17
Morgan, Edwin 1920- DLB-27
Morgan, John Pierpont 1837-1913 ..... DLB-140
Morgan, John Pierpont, Jr. 1867-1943 ... DLB-140
Morgan, Robert 1944- DLB-120
Morgan, Sydney Owenson, Lady
  1776?-1859 .... DLB-116, 158
Morgner, Irmtraud 1933- DLB-75
Morhof, Daniel Georg 1639-1691 ...... DLB-164
Mori, Ōgai 1862-1922 .... DLB-180
Móricz, Zsigmond 1879-1942 .... DLB-215
Morier, James Justinian
  1782 or 1783?-1849 .... DLB-116
Mörike, Eduard 1804-1875 .... DLB-133
Morin, Paul 1889-1963 .... DLB-92
Morison, Richard 1514?-1556 .... DLB-136
Morison, Samuel Eliot 1887-1976 ...... DLB-17
Morison, Stanley 1889-1967 .... DLB-201
Moritz, Karl Philipp 1756-1793 .... DLB-94
Moriz von Craûn circa 1220-1230 .... DLB-138
Morley, Christopher 1890-1957 .... DLB-9
Morley, John 1838-1923 .... DLB-57, 144, 190
Morris, George Pope 1802-1864 .... DLB-73
Morris, James Humphrey (see Morris, Jan)
Morris, Jan 1926- DLB-204
Morris, Lewis 1833-1907 .... DLB-35
Morris, Margaret 1737-1816 .... DLB-200
Morris, Richard B. 1904-1989 .... DLB-17
Morris, William 1834-1896
  ..... DLB-18, 35, 57, 156, 178, 184; CDBLB-4
Morris, Willie 1934-1999 .... Y-80
Morris, Wright
  1910-1998 .... DLB-2, 206, 218; Y-81
Morrison, Arthur 1863-1945 ....DLB-70, 135, 197
Morrison, Charles Clayton 1874-1966 .... DLB-91
Morrison, John 1904-1988 .... DLB-260
Morrison, Toni 1931-
  .... DLB-6, 33, 143; Y-81, Y-93; CDALB-6
Morrissy, Mary 1957- DLB-267
Morrow, William, and Company DLB-46
Morse, James Herbert 1841-1923 .... DLB-71
Morse, Jedidiah 1761-1826 .... DLB-37
Morse, John T., Jr. 1840-1937 .... DLB-47
Morselli, Guido 1912-1973 ....DLB-177
Mortimer, Favell Lee 1802-1878 .... DLB-163
Mortimer, John
  1923- ... DLB-13, 245, 254, 271; CDBLB-8

Morton, Carlos 1942- DLB-122
Morton, H. V. 1892-1979 .... DLB-195
Morton, John P., and Company DLB-49
Morton, Nathaniel 1613-1685 .... DLB-24
Morton, Sarah Wentworth 1759-1846 .... DLB-37
Morton, Thomas circa 1579-circa 1647 ... DLB-24
Moscherosch, Johann Michael
  1601-1669 .... DLB-164
Moseley, Humphrey
  [publishing house] DLB-170
Möser, Justus 1720-1794 .... DLB-97
Mosley, Nicholas 1923- DLB-14, 207
Moss, Arthur 1889-1969 .... DLB-4
Moss, Howard 1922-1987 .... DLB-5
Moss, Thylias 1954- DLB-120
The Most Powerful Book Review
  in America
  [*New York Times Book Review*] Y-82
Motion, Andrew 1952- DLB-40
Motley, John Lothrop
  1814-1877 .... DLB-1, 30, 59, 235
Motley, Willard 1909-1965 ....DLB-76, 143
Mott, Lucretia 1793-1880 .... DLB-239
Motte, Benjamin, Jr. [publishing house] .. DLB-154
Motteux, Peter Anthony 1663-1718 ...... DLB-80
Mottram, R. H. 1883-1971 .... DLB-36
Mount, Ferdinand 1939- DLB-231
Mouré, Erin 1955- DLB-60
Mourning Dove (Humishuma) between
  1882 and 1888?-1936 ....DLB-175, 221
Movies from Books, 1920-1974 .... DLB-9
Mowat, Farley 1921- DLB-68
Mowbray, A. R., and Company,
  Limited DLB-106
Mowrer, Edgar Ansel 1892-1977 .... DLB-29
Mowrer, Paul Scott 1887-1971 .... DLB-29
Moxon, Edward [publishing house] DLB-106
Moxon, Joseph [publishing house] DLB-170
Moyes, Patricia 1923-2000 ....DLB-276
Mphahlele, Es'kia (Ezekiel)
  1919- DLB-125; CDWLB-3
Mrożek, Sławomir 1930- .. DLB-232; CDWLB-4
Mtshali, Oswald Mbuyiseni 1940- DLB-125
Mucedorus DLB-62
Mudford, William 1782-1848 .... DLB-159
Mueller, Lisel 1924- DLB-105
Muhajir, El (see Marvin X)
Muhajir, Nazzam Al Fitnah (see Marvin X)
Mühlbach, Luise 1814-1873 .... DLB-133
Muir, Edwin 1887-1959 ....DLB-20, 100, 191
Muir, Helen 1937- DLB-14
Muir, John 1838-1914 ....DLB-186, 275
Muir, Percy 1894-1979 .... DLB-201
Mujū Ichien 1226-1312 .... DLB-203
Mukherjee, Bharati 1940- DLB-60, 218
Mulcaster, Richard
  1531 or 1532-1611 .... DLB-167

Muldoon, Paul 1951- DLB-40
Müller, Friedrich (see Müller, Maler)
Müller, Heiner 1929-1995 ....DLB-124
Müller, Maler 1749-1825 ....DLB-94
Muller, Marcia 1944- DLB-226
Müller, Wilhelm 1794-1827 ....DLB-90
Mumford, Lewis 1895-1990 ....DLB-63
Munby, A. N. L. 1913-1974............DLB-201
Munby, Arthur Joseph 1828-1910.......DLB-35
Munday, Anthony 1560-1633 ......DLB-62, 172
Mundt, Clara (see Mühlbach, Luise)
Mundt, Theodore 1808-1861 ....DLB-133
Munford, Robert circa 1737-1783.......DLB-31
Mungoshi, Charles 1947- DLB-157
Munk, Kaj 1898-1944 ....DLB-214
Munonye, John 1929- DLB-117
Munro, Alice 1931- DLB-53
Munro, George [publishing house] DLB-49
Munro, H. H.
 1870-1916 ....DLB-34, 162; CDBLB-5
Munro, Neil 1864-1930................DLB-156
Munro, Norman L.
 [publishing house].................DLB-49
Munroe, James, and Company DLB-49
Munroe, Kirk 1850-1930...............DLB-42
Munroe and Francis...................DLB-49
Munsell, Joel [publishing house] DLB-49
Munsey, Frank A. 1854-1925 ....DLB-25, 91
Munsey, Frank A., and Company........DLB-49
Murakami Haruki 1949- DLB-182
Murav'ev, Mikhail Nikitich
 1757-1807 ....DLB-150
Murdoch, Iris 1919-1999
 ....DLB-14, 194, 233; CDBLB-8
Murdoch, Rupert 1931- DLB-127
Murfree, Mary N. 1850-1922 ....DLB-12, 74
Murger, Henry 1822-1861..............DLB-119
Murger, Louis-Henri (see Murger, Henry)
Murner, Thomas 1475-1537 ....DLB-179
Muro, Amado 1915-1971...............DLB-82
Murphy, Arthur 1727-1805 ....DLB-89, 142
Murphy, Beatrice M. 1908- DLB-76
Murphy, Dervla 1931- DLB-204
Murphy, Emily 1868-1933..............DLB-99
Murphy, Jack 1923-1980 ....DLB-241
Murphy, John, and Company DLB-49
Murphy, John H., III 1916- DLB-127
Murphy, Richard 1927-1993 ....DLB-40
Murray, Albert L. 1916- DLB-38
Murray, Gilbert 1866-1957 ....DLB-10
Murray, Jim 1919-1998 ....DLB-241
Murray, John [publishing house] DLB-154
Murry, John Middleton 1889-1957 ......DLB-149
"The Break-Up of the Novel" (1922)......DLB-36
Murray, Judith Sargent
 1751-1820 ....DLB-37, 200

Murray, Pauli 1910-1985...............DLB-41
Musäus, Johann Karl August 1735-1787 ...DLB-97
Muschg, Adolf 1934- DLB-75
The Music of *Minnesang*................DLB-138
Musil, Robert
 1880-1942 ....DLB-81, 124; CDWLB-2
Muspilli circa 790-circa 850...........DLB-148
Musset, Alfred de 1810-1857 ......DLB-192, 217
Mussey, Benjamin B., and Company DLB-49
Mutafchieva, Vera 1929- DLB-181
Mwangi, Meja 1948- DLB-125
My Summer Reading Orgy: Reading for Fun
 and Games: One Reader's Report
 on the Summer of 2001................Y-01
Myers, Frederic W. H. 1843-1901.......DLB-190
Myers, Gustavus 1872-1942 ....DLB-47
Myers, L. H. 1881-1944 ....DLB-15
Myers, Walter Dean 1937- DLB-33
Myerson, Julie 1960- DLB-267
Mykolaitis-Putinas, Vincas
 1893-1967 ....DLB-220
Myles, Eileen 1949- DLB-193
Myrdal, Jan 1927- DLB-257
The Mystery of Carolyn Keene............Y-02

N

Na Prous Boneta circa 1296-1328 ....DLB-208
Nabl, Franz 1883-1974.................DLB-81
Nabokov, Vladimir 1899-1977 .. DLB-2, 244, 278;
 Y-80, Y-91; DS-3; CDALB-1
The Vladimir Nabokov Archive
 in the Berg Collection Y-91
Nabokov Festival at Cornell Y-83
Nádaši, Ladislav (see Jégé)
Naden, Constance 1858-1889 ....DLB-199
Nadezhdin, Nikolai Ivanovich
 1804-1856 ....DLB-198
Nadson, Semen Iakovlevich 1862-1887... DLB-277
Naevius circa 265 B.C.-201 B.C..........DLB-211
Nafis and Cornish DLB-49
Nagai, Kafū 1879-1959.................DLB-180
Nagel, Ernest 1901-1985 ....DLB-279
Naipaul, Shiva 1945-1985 ...... DLB-157; Y-85
Naipaul, V. S. 1932-
 ....DLB-125, 204, 207; Y-85, Y-01;
 CDBLB-8; CDWLB-3
Nakagami Kenji 1946-1992 ....DLB-182
Nakano-in Masatada no Musume (see Nijō, Lady)
Nałkowska, Zofia 1884-1954...........DLB-215
Nancrede, Joseph [publishing house]......DLB-49
Naranjo, Carmen 1930- DLB-145
Narezhny, Vasilii Trofimovich
 1780-1825 ....DLB-198
Narrache, Jean (Emile Coderre)
 1893-1970 ....DLB-92
The New Narrative Poetry DLB-282
Nasby, Petroleum Vesuvius (see Locke, David Ross)
Nash, Eveleigh [publishing house].......DLB-112

Nash, Ogden 1902-1971 ....DLB-11
Nashe, Thomas 1567-1601?............DLB-167
Nason, Jerry 1910-1986................DLB-241
Nasr, Seyyed Hossein 1933- DLB-279
Nast, Condé 1873-1942 ....DLB-91
Nast, Thomas 1840-1902...............DLB-188
Nastasijević, Momčilo 1894-1938 ....DLB-147
Nathan, George Jean 1882-1958 ....DLB-137
Nathan, Robert 1894-1985 ....DLB-9
National Book Critics Circle Awards....Y-00; Y-01
The National Jewish Book Awards Y-85
The National Library of Ireland's
 New James Joyce Manuscripts Y-02
The National Theatre and the Royal
 Shakespeare Company: The
 National Companies DLB-13
Natsume, Sōseki 1867-1916 ....DLB-180
Naughton, Bill 1910- DLB-13
Navarro, Joe 1953- DLB-209
Naylor, Gloria 1950- DLB-173
Nazor, Vladimir 1876-1949 ....DLB-147
Ndebele, Njabulo 1948- DLB-157
Neagoe, Peter 1881-1960................DLB-4
Neal, John 1793-1876............DLB-1, 59, 243
Neal, Joseph C. 1807-1847 ....DLB-11
Neal, Larry 1937-1981 ....DLB-38
The Neale Publishing Company DLB-49
Nebel, Frederick 1903-1967 ....DLB-226
Neely, F. Tennyson [publishing house] DLB-49
Negoițescu, Ion 1921-1993 ....DLB-220
Negri, Ada 1870-1945 ....DLB-114
"The Negro as a Writer," by
 G. M. McClellan...................DLB-50
"Negro Poets and Their Poetry," by
 Wallace Thurman...................DLB-50
Neidhart von Reuental
 circa 1185-circa 1240..............DLB-138
Neihardt, John G. 1881-1973......DLB-9, 54, 256
Neilson, John Shaw 1872-1942 ....DLB-230
Nekrasov, Nikolai Alekseevich
 1821-177 ....DLB-277
Neledinsky-Meletsky, Iurii Aleksandrovich
 1752-1828 ....DLB-150
Nelligan, Emile 1879-1941..............DLB-92
Nelson, Alice Moore Dunbar 1875-1935 ...DLB-50
Nelson, Antonya 1961- DLB-244
Nelson, Kent 1943- DLB-234
Nelson, Marilyn 1946- DLB-120, 282
Nelson, Richard K. 1941- DLB-275
Nelson, Thomas, and Sons [U.K.].......DLB-106
Nelson, Thomas, and Sons [U.S.] DLB-49
Nelson, William 1908-1978 ....DLB-103
Nelson, William Rockhill 1841-1915......DLB-23
Nemerov, Howard 1920-1991......DLB-5, 6; Y-83
Németh, László 1901-1975..............DLB-215
Nepos circa 100 B.C.-post 27 B.C........DLB-211

401

Nėris, Salomėja 1904-1945 .... DLB-220; CDWLB-4
Nerval, Gerard de 1808-1855 .... DLB-217
Nesbit, E. 1858-1924 .... DLB-141, 153, 178
Ness, Evaline 1911-1986 .... DLB-61
Nestroy, Johann 1801-1862 .... DLB-133
Nettleship, R. L. 1846-1892 .... DLB-262
Neugeboren, Jay 1938- DLB-28
Neukirch, Benjamin 1655-1729 .... DLB-168
Neumann, Alfred 1895-1952 .... DLB-56
Neumann, Ferenc (see Molnár, Ferenc)
Neumark, Georg 1621-1681 .... DLB-164
Neumeister, Erdmann 1671-1756 .... DLB-168
Nevins, Allan 1890-1971 .... DLB-17; DS-17
Nevinson, Henry Woodd 1856-1941 .... DLB-135
The New American Library DLB-46
New Approaches to Biography: Challenges from Critical Theory, USC Conference on Literary Studies, 1990 .... Y-90
New Directions Publishing Corporation... DLB-46
A New Edition of *Huck Finn* Y-85
New Forces at Work in the American Theatre: 1915-1925 .... DLB-7
Anthologizing New Formalism DLB-282
The Little Magazines of the New Formalism DLB-282
The New Narrative Poetry DLB-282
Presses of the New Formalism and the New Narrative DLB-282
The Prosody of the New Formalism DLB-282
Younger Women Poets of the New Formalism DLB-282
New Literary Periodicals: A Report for 1987 .... Y-87
New Literary Periodicals: A Report for 1988 .... Y-88
New Literary Periodicals: A Report for 1989 .... Y-89
New Literary Periodicals: A Report for 1990 .... Y-90
New Literary Periodicals: A Report for 1991 .... Y-91
New Literary Periodicals: A Report for 1992 .... Y-92
New Literary Periodicals: A Report for 1993 .... Y-93
The New Monthly Magazine 1814-1884 .... DLB-110
The New Narrative Poetry DLB-282
Presses of the New Formalism and the New Narrative DLB-282
The New Variorum Shakespeare Y-85
A New Voice: The Center for the Book's First Five Years Y-83
The New Wave [Science Fiction] DLB-8
New York City Bookshops in the 1930s and 1940s: The Recollections of Walter Goldwater... Y-93
Newbery, John [publishing house] DLB-154
Newbolt, Henry 1862-1938 .... DLB-19
Newbound, Bernard Slade (see Slade, Bernard)

Newby, Eric 1919- DLB-204
Newby, P. H. 1918- DLB-15
Newby, Thomas Cautley [publishing house] DLB-106
Newcomb, Charles King 1820-1894... DLB-1, 223
Newell, Peter 1862-1924 .... DLB-42
Newell, Robert Henry 1836-1901 .... DLB-11
Newhouse, Samuel I. 1895-1979 .... DLB-127
Newman, Cecil Earl 1903-1976 .... DLB-127
Newman, David (see Benton, Robert)
Newman, Frances 1883-1928 .... Y-80
Newman, Francis William 1805-1897.... DLB-190
Newman, John Henry 1801-1890 .... DLB-18, 32, 55
Newman, Mark [publishing house] DLB-49
Newmarch, Rosa Harriet 1857-1940 ..... DLB-240
Newnes, George, Limited DLB-112
Newsome, Effie Lee 1885-1979 .... DLB-76
Newspaper Syndication of American Humor DLB-11
Newton, A. Edward 1864-1940 .... DLB-140
Newton, Sir Isaac 1642-1727 .... DLB-252
Nexø, Martin Andersen 1869-1954 ..... DLB-214
Nezval, Vítěslav 1900-1958 .... DLB-215; CDWLB-4
Ngugi wa Thiong'o 1938- DLB-125; CDWLB-3
Niatum, Duane 1938- DLB-175
The *Nibelungenlied* and the *Klage* circa 1200 .... DLB-138
Nichol, B. P. 1944-1988 .... DLB-53
Nicholas of Cusa 1401-1464 .... DLB-115
Nicole, Pierre 1625-1695 .... DLB-268
Nichols, Ann 1891?-1966 .... DLB-249
Nichols, Beverly 1898-1983 .... DLB-191
Nichols, Dudley 1895-1960 .... DLB-26
Nichols, Grace 1950- DLB-157
Nichols, John 1940- Y-82
Nichols, Mary Sargeant (Neal) Gove 1810-1884 .... DLB-1, 243
Nichols, Peter 1927- DLB-13, 245
Nichols, Roy F. 1896-1973 .... DLB-17
Nichols, Ruth 1948- DLB-60
Nicholson, Edward Williams Byron 1849-1912 .... DLB-184
Nicholson, Geoff 1953- DLB-271
Nicholson, Norman 1914- DLB-27
Nicholson, William 1872-1949 .... DLB-141
Ní Chuilleanáin, Eiléan 1942- DLB-40
Nicol, Eric 1919- DLB-68
Nicolai, Friedrich 1733-1811 .... DLB-97
Nicolas de Clamanges circa 1363-1437... DLB-208
Nicolay, John G. 1832-1901 and Hay, John 1838-1905 .... DLB-47
Nicole, Pierre 1625-1695 .... DLB-268
Nicolson, Adela Florence Cory (see Hope, Laurence)
Nicolson, Harold 1886-1968 .... DLB-100, 149

Nicolson, Harold, "The Practice of Biography," in *The English Sense of Humour and Other Essays* DLB-149
Nicolson, Nigel 1917- DLB-155
Niebuhr, Reinhold 1892-1971 ...... DLB-17; DS-17
Niedecker, Lorine 1903-1970 .... DLB-48
Nieman, Lucius W. 1857-1935 .... DLB-25
Nietzsche, Friedrich 1844-1900 .... DLB-129; CDWLB-2
Nievo, Stanislao 1928- DLB-196
Niggli, Josefina 1910- Y-80
Nightingale, Florence 1820-1910 ...... DLB-166
Nijō, Lady (Nakano-in Masatada no Musume) 1258-after 1306 .... DLB-203
Nijō Yoshimoto 1320-1388 .... DLB-203
Nikitin, Ivan Savvich 1824-1861 .... DLB-277
Nikitin, Nikolai Nikolaevich 1895-1963 .... DLB-272
Nikolev, Nikolai Petrovich 1758-1815 .... DLB-150
Niles, Hezekiah 1777-1839 .... DLB-43
Nims, John Frederick 1913-1999 .... DLB-5
Nin, Anaïs 1903-1977 .... DLB-2, 4, 152
1985: The Year of the Mystery: A Symposium Y-85
The 1997 Booker Prize Y-97
The 1998 Booker Prize Y-98
Niño, Raúl 1961- DLB-209
Nissenson, Hugh 1933- DLB-28
Niven, Frederick John 1878-1944 .... DLB-92
Niven, Larry 1938- DLB-8
Nixon, Howard M. 1909-1983 .... DLB-201
Nizan, Paul 1905-1940 .... DLB-72
Njegoš, Petar II Petrović 1813-1851 .... DLB-147; CDWLB-4
Nkosi, Lewis 1936- DLB-157
"The No Self, the Little Self, and the Poets," by Richard Moore DLB-105
Noah, Mordecai M. 1785-1851 .... DLB-250
Noailles, Anna de 1876-1933 .... DLB-258
Nobel Peace Prize
The 1986 Nobel Peace Prize: Elie Wiesel Y-86
The Nobel Prize and Literary Politics Y-88
Nobel Prize in Literature
The 1982 Nobel Prize in Literature: Gabriel García Márquez Y-82
The 1983 Nobel Prize in Literature: William Golding Y-83
The 1984 Nobel Prize in Literature: Jaroslav Seifert Y-84
The 1985 Nobel Prize in Literature: Claude Simon Y-85
The 1986 Nobel Prize in Literature: Wole Soyinka Y-86
The 1987 Nobel Prize in Literature: Joseph Brodsky Y-87
The 1988 Nobel Prize in Literature: Najīb Mahfūz Y-88
The 1989 Nobel Prize in Literature: Camilo José Cela Y-89

The 1990 Nobel Prize in Literature:
    Octavio Paz.....................Y-90
The 1991 Nobel Prize in Literature:
    Nadine Gordimer.................Y-91
The 1992 Nobel Prize in Literature:
    Derek Walcott...................Y-92
The 1993 Nobel Prize in Literature:
    Toni Morrison...................Y-93
The 1994 Nobel Prize in Literature:
    Kenzaburō Ōe....................Y-94
The 1995 Nobel Prize in Literature:
    Seamus Heaney...................Y-95
The 1996 Nobel Prize in Literature:
    Wisława Szymborsha..............Y-96
The 1997 Nobel Prize in Literature:
    Dario Fo........................Y-97
The 1998 Nobel Prize in Literature:
    José Saramago...................Y-98
The 1999 Nobel Prize in Literature:
    Günter Grass....................Y-99
The 2000 Nobel Prize in Literature:
    Gao Xingjian....................Y-00
The 2001 Nobel Prize in Literature:
    V. S. Naipaul...................Y-01
The 2002 Nobel Prize in Literature:
    Imre Kertész....................Y-02
Nodier, Charles 1780-1844...........DLB-119
Noël, Marie 1883-1967...............DLB-258
Noel, Roden 1834-1894...............DLB-35
Nogami, Yaeko 1885-1985.............DLB-180
Nogo, Rajko Petrov 1945-............DLB-181
Nolan, William F. 1928-.............DLB-8
Noland, C. F. M. 1810?-1858.........DLB-11
Noma Hiroshi 1915-1991..............DLB-182
Nonesuch Press......................DLB-112
Creative Nonfiction.................Y-02
Noon, Jeff 1957-....................DLB-267
Noonan, Robert Phillipe (see Tressell, Robert)
Noonday Press.......................DLB-46
Noone, John 1936-...................DLB-14
Nora, Eugenio de 1923-..............DLB-134
Nordan, Lewis 1939-.................DLB-234
Nordbrandt, Henrik 1945-............DLB-214
Nordhoff, Charles 1887-1947.........DLB-9
Norén, Lars 1944-...................DLB-257
Norfolk, Lawrence 1963-.............DLB-267
Norman, Charles 1904-1996...........DLB-111
Norman, Marsha 1947-........DLB-266; Y-84
Norris, Charles G. 1881-1945........DLB-9
Norris, Frank
    1870-1902.......DLB-12, 71, 186; CDALB-3
Norris, John 1657-1712..............DLB-252
Norris, Leslie 1921-...........DLB-27, 256
Norse, Harold 1916-.................DLB-16
Norte, Marisela 1955-...............DLB-209
North, Marianne 1830-1890...........DLB-174
North Point Press...................DLB-46
Nortje, Arthur 1942-1970............DLB-125
Norton, Alice Mary (see Norton, Andre)

Norton, Andre 1912-.................DLB-8, 52
Norton, Andrews 1786-1853...........DLB-1, 235
Norton, Caroline 1808-1877....DLB-21, 159, 199
Norton, Charles Eliot 1827-1908...DLB-1, 64, 235
Norton, John 1606-1663..............DLB-24
Norton, Mary 1903-1992..............DLB-160
Norton, Thomas (see Sackville, Thomas)
Norton, W. W., and Company..........DLB-46
Norwood, Robert 1874-1932...........DLB-92
Nosaka Akiyuki 1930-................DLB-182
Nossack, Hans Erich 1901-1977.......DLB-69
Not Immediately Discernible . . . but Eventually
    Quite Clear: The *First Light* and *Final Years*
    of Hemingway's Centenary........Y-99
A Note on Technique (1926), by
    Elizabeth A. Drew [excerpts]....DLB-36
Notes from the Underground
    of *Sister Carrie*..............Y-01
Notker Balbulus circa 840-912.......DLB-148
Notker III of Saint Gall
    circa 950-1022..................DLB-148
Notker von Zweifalten ?-1095........DLB-148
Nourse, Alan E. 1928-...............DLB-8
Novak, Slobodan 1924-...............DLB-181
Novak, Vjenceslav 1859-1905.........DLB-147
Novakovich, Josip 1956-.............DLB-244
Novalis 1772-1801.........DLB-90; CDWLB-2
Novaro, Mario 1868-1944.............DLB-114
Novás Calvo, Lino
    1903-1983.......................DLB-145
"The Novel in [Robert Browning's]
    'The Ring and the Book'" (1912),
    by Henry James..................DLB-32
The Novel of Impressionism,
    by Jethro Bithell...............DLB-66
Novel-Reading: *The Works of
    Charles Dickens, The Works of
    W. Makepeace Thackeray*
    (1879), by Anthony Trollope.....DLB-21
Novels for Grown-Ups................Y-97
The Novels of Dorothy Richardson (1918),
    by May Sinclair.................DLB-36
Novels with a Purpose (1864), by
    Justin M'Carthy.................DLB-21
Noventa, Giacomo 1898-1960..........DLB-114
Novikov, Nikolai
    Ivanovich 1744-1818.............DLB-150
Novomeský, Laco 1904-1976...........DLB-215
Nowlan, Alden 1933-1983.............DLB-53
Noyes, Alfred 1880-1958.............DLB-20
Noyes, Crosby S. 1825-1908..........DLB-23
Noyes, Nicholas 1647-1717...........DLB-24
Noyes, Theodore W. 1858-1946........DLB-29
Nozick, Robert 1938-2002............DLB-279
N-Town Plays circa 1468 to early
    sixteenth century...............DLB-146
Nugent, Frank 1908-1965.............DLB-44
Nugent, Richard Bruce 1906-.........DLB-151
Nušić, Branislav 1864-1938...DLB-147; CDWLB-4

Nutt, David [publishing house]......DLB-106
Nwapa, Flora
    1931-1993...........DLB-125; CDWLB-3
Nye, Bill 1850-1896.................DLB-186
Nye, Edgar Wilson (Bill)
    1850-1896.......................DLB-11, 23
Nye, Naomi Shihab 1952-.............DLB-120
Nye, Robert 1939-...................DLB-14, 271
Nyka-Niliūnas, Alfonsas
    1919-...........................DLB-220

O

Oakes Smith, Elizabeth
    1806-1893...........DLB-1, 239, 243
Oakes, Urian circa 1631-1681........DLB-24
Oakley, Violet 1874-1961............DLB-188
Oates, Joyce Carol 1938-...DLB-2, 5, 130; Y-81
Ōba Minako 1930-....................DLB-182
Ober, Frederick Albion 1849-1913....DLB-189
Ober, William 1920-1993.............Y-93
Oberholtzer, Ellis Paxson 1868-1936.....DLB-47
The Obituary as Literary Form.......Y-02
Obradović, Dositej 1740?-1811.......DLB-147
O'Brien, Charlotte Grace 1845-1909.....DLB-240
O'Brien, Edna 1932-....DLB-14, 231; CDBLB-8
O'Brien, Fitz-James 1828-1862.......DLB-74
O'Brien, Flann (see O'Nolan, Brian)
O'Brien, Kate 1897-1974.............DLB-15
O'Brien, Tim
    1946-.......DLB-152; Y-80; DS-9; CDALB-7
O'Casey, Sean 1880-1964......DLB-10; CDBLB-6
Occom, Samson 1723-1792.............DLB-175
Ochs, Adolph S. 1858-1935...........DLB-25
Ochs-Oakes, George Washington
    1861-1931.......................DLB-137
O'Connor, Flannery 1925-1964
    ....DLB-2, 152; Y-80; DS-12; CDALB-1
O'Connor, Frank 1903-1966...........DLB-162
O'Connor, Joseph 1963-..............DLB-267
Octopus Publishing Group............DLB-112
Oda Sakunosuke 1913-1947............DLB-182
Odell, Jonathan 1737-1818...........DLB-31, 99
O'Dell, Scott 1903-1989.............DLB-52
Odets, Clifford 1906-1963...........DLB-7, 26
Odhams Press Limited................DLB-112
Odoevsky, Aleksandr Ivanovich
    1802-1839.......................DLB-205
Odoevsky, Vladimir Fedorovich
    1804 or 1803-1869...............DLB-198
O'Donnell, Peter 1920-..............DLB-87
O'Donovan, Michael (see O'Connor, Frank)
O'Dowd, Bernard 1866-1953...........DLB-230
Ōe Kenzaburō 1935-..........DLB-182; Y-94
O'Faolain, Julia 1932-..............DLB-14, 231
O'Faolain, Sean 1900-...............DLB-15, 162
Off Broadway and Off-Off Broadway......DLB-7
Off-Loop Theatres...................DLB-7

Offord, Carl Ruthven 1910- DLB-76
O'Flaherty, Liam 1896-1984. ...DLB-36, 162; Y-84
Ogarev, Nikolai Platonovich 1813-1877 ...DLB-277
Ogilvie, J. S., and Company DLB-49
Ogilvy, Eliza 1822-1912 .... DLB-199
Ogot, Grace 1930- DLB-125
O'Grady, Desmond 1935- DLB-40
Ogunyemi, Wale 1939- DLB-157
O'Hagan, Howard 1902-1982 .... DLB-68
O'Hara, Frank 1926-1966. .... DLB-5, 16, 193
O'Hara, John
 1905-1970 .... DLB-9, 86; DS-2; CDALB-5
John O'Hara's Pottsville Journalism Y-88
O'Hegarty, P. S. 1879-1955 .... DLB-201
Okara, Gabriel 1921- DLB-125; CDWLB-3
O'Keeffe, John 1747-1833 .... DLB-89
Okes, Nicholas [publishing house] DLB-170
Okigbo, Christopher
 1930-1967. .... DLB-125; CDWLB-3
Okot p'Bitek 1931-1982 .... DLB-125; CDWLB-3
Okpewho, Isidore 1941- DLB-157
Okri, Ben 1959- DLB-157, 231
Olaudah Equiano and Unfinished Journeys:
 The Slave-Narrative Tradition and
 Twentieth-Century Continuities, by
 Paul Edwards and Pauline T.
 Wangman DLB-117
Old Dogs / New Tricks? New Technologies,
 the Canon, and the Structure of
 the Profession. Y-02
Old English Literature:
 An Introduction DLB-146
Old English Riddles
 eighth to tenth centuries DLB-146
Old Franklin Publishing House DLB-49
Old German Genesis and *Old German Exodus*
 circa 1050-circa 1130 .... DLB-148
Old High German Charms and
 Blessings. DLB-148; CDWLB-2
The *Old High German Isidor*
 circa 790-800 .... DLB-148
The Old Manse DLB-223
Older, Fremont 1856-1935 .... DLB-25
Oldham, John 1653-1683 .... DLB-131
Oldman, C. B. 1894-1969. .... DLB-201
Olds, Sharon 1942- DLB-120
Olearius, Adam 1599-1671 .... DLB-164
O'Leary, Ellen 1831-1889. .... DLB-240
Olesha, Iurii Karlovich 1899-1960 ..... DLB-272
Oliphant, Laurence 1829?-1888 ..... DLB-18, 166
Oliphant, Margaret 1828-1897 .. DLB-18, 159, 190
Oliver, Chad 1928- DLB-8
Oliver, Mary 1935- DLB-5, 193
Ollier, Claude 1922- DLB-83
Olsen, Tillie 1912 or 1913-
 .... DLB-28, 206; Y-80; CDALB-7
Olson, Charles 1910-1970. .... DLB-5, 16, 193
Olson, Elder 1909- DLB-48, 63
Olson, Sigurd F. 1899-1982 ....DLB-275

Omotoso, Kole 1943- DLB-125
Omulevsky, Innokentii Vasil'evich
 1836 [or 1837]-1883 .... DLB-238
On Learning to Write. Y-88
Ondaatje, Michael 1943- DLB-60
O'Neill, Eugene 1888-1953. .... DLB-7; CDALB-5
Eugene O'Neill Memorial Theater
 Center DLB-7
Eugene O'Neill's Letters: A Review Y-88
Onetti, Juan Carlos
 1909-1994 .... DLB-113; CDWLB-3
Onions, George Oliver 1872-1961 ...... DLB-153
Onofri, Arturo 1885-1928 .... DLB-114
O'Nolan, Brian 1911-1966 .... DLB-231
Opie, Amelia 1769-1853 .... DLB-116, 159
Opitz, Martin 1597-1639. .... DLB-164
Oppen, George 1908-1984 .... DLB-5, 165
Oppenheim, E. Phillips 1866-1946 ...... DLB-70
Oppenheim, James 1882-1932 .... DLB-28
Oppenheimer, Joel 1930-1988 .... DLB-5, 193
Optic, Oliver (see Adams, William Taylor)
Oral History: B. W. Huebsch. Y-99
Oral History Interview with Donald S.
 Klopfer. Y-97
Orczy, Emma, Baroness 1865-1947 ...... DLB-70
Oregon Shakespeare Festival Y-00
Origo, Iris 1902-1988 .... DLB-155
Orlovitz, Gil 1918-1973 .... DLB-2, 5
Orlovsky, Peter 1933- DLB-16
Ormond, John 1923- DLB-27
Ornitz, Samuel 1890-1957 .... DLB-28, 44
O'Riordan, Kate 1960- DLB-267
O'Rourke, P. J. 1947- DLB-185
Orten, Jiří 1919-1941 .... DLB-215
Ortese, Anna Maria 1914- DLB-177
Ortiz, Simon J. 1941- DLB-120, 175, 256
Ortnit and *Wolfdietrich* circa 1225-1250.... DLB-138
Orton, Joe 1933-1967 .... DLB-13; CDBLB-8
Orwell, George (Eric Arthur Blair)
 1903-1950 .. DLB-15, 98, 195, 255; CDBLB-7
The Orwell Year. Y-84
(Re-)Publishing Orwell Y-86
Ory, Carlos Edmundo de 1923- DLB-134
Osbey, Brenda Marie 1957- DLB-120
Osbon, B. S. 1827-1912. .... DLB-43
Osborn, Sarah 1714-1796 .... DLB-200
Osborne, John 1929-1994. .... DLB-13; CDBLB-7
Osgood, Frances Sargent 1811-1850. .... DLB-250
Osgood, Herbert L. 1855-1918. .... DLB-47
Osgood, James R., and Company DLB-49
Osgood, McIlvaine and Company DLB-112
O'Shaughnessy, Arthur 1844-1881. ...... DLB-35
O'Shea, Patrick [publishing house] DLB-49
Osipov, Nikolai Petrovich
 1751-1799 .... DLB-150
Oskison, John Milton 1879-1947 ....DLB-175

Osler, Sir William 1849-1919 .... DLB-184
Osofisan, Femi 1946- DLB-125; CDWLB-3
Ostenso, Martha 1900-1963 .... DLB-92
Ostrauskas, Kostas 1926- DLB-232
Ostriker, Alicia 1937- DLB-120
Ostrovsky, Aleksandr Nikolaevich
 1823-1886 ....DLB-277
Ostrovsky, Nikolai Alekseevich
 1904-1936 ....DLB-272
Osundare, Niyi
 1947- DLB-157; CDWLB-3
Oswald, Eleazer 1755-1795 .... DLB-43
Oswald von Wolkenstein
 1376 or 1377-1445 ....DLB-179
Otero, Blas de 1916-1979 .... DLB-134
Otero, Miguel Antonio 1859-1944 ...... DLB-82
Otero, Nina 1881-1965. .... DLB-209
Otero Silva, Miguel 1908-1985. .... DLB-145
Otfried von Weißenburg
 circa 800-circa 875? DLB-148
Otis, Broaders and Company.......... DLB-49
Otis, James (see Kaler, James Otis)
Otis, James, Jr. 1725-1783 .... DLB-31
Ottaway, James 1911- DLB-127
Ottendorfer, Oswald 1826-1900. .... DLB-23
Ottieri, Ottiero 1924- DLB-177
Otto-Peters, Louise 1819-1895 .... DLB-129
Otway, Thomas 1652-1685 .... DLB-80
Ouellette, Fernand 1930- DLB-60
Ouida 1839-1908 .... DLB-18, 156
Outing Publishing Company DLB-46
Outlaw Days, by Joyce Johnson DLB-16
Overbury, Sir Thomas
 circa 1581-1613 .... DLB-151
The Overlook Press DLB-46
Overview of U.S. Book Publishing,
 1910-1945 .... DLB-9
Ovid 43 B.C.-A.D. 17........DLB-211; CDWLB-1
Owen, Guy 1925- DLB-5
Owen, John 1564-1622. .... DLB-121
Owen, John [publishing house]. DLB-49
Owen, Peter, Limited DLB-112
Owen, Robert 1771-1858 .... DLB-107, 158
Owen, Wilfred
 1893-1918 .... DLB-20; DS-18; CDBLB-6
The Owl and the Nightingale
 circa 1189-1199 .... DLB-146
Owsley, Frank L. 1890-1956 ....DLB-17
Oxford, Seventeenth Earl of, Edward
 de Vere 1550-1604. ....DLB-172
OyamO (Charles F. Gordon
 1943- DLB-266
Ozerov, Vladislav Aleksandrovich
 1769-1816. .... DLB-150
Ozick, Cynthia 1928- DLB-28, 152; Y-83
First Strauss "Livings" Awarded to Cynthia
 Ozick and Raymond Carver
 An Interview with Cynthia Ozick Y-83

P

Pace, Richard 1482?-1536 ....DLB-167
Pacey, Desmond 1917-1975 ....DLB-88
Pack, Robert 1929- DLB-5
Packaging Papa: *The Garden of Eden* Y-86
Padell Publishing Company.............DLB-46
Padgett, Ron 1942- DLB-5
Padilla, Ernesto Chávez 1944- DLB-122
Page, L. C., and Company DLB-49
Page, Louise 1955- DLB-233
Page, P. K. 1916- DLB-68
Page, Thomas Nelson
 1853-1922 ....DLB-12, 78; DS-13
Page, Walter Hines 1855-1918 ....DLB-71, 91
Paget, Francis Edward 1806-1882 ....DLB-163
Paget, Violet (see Lee, Vernon)
Pagliarani, Elio 1927- DLB-128
Pain, Barry 1864-1928...........DLB-135, 197
Pain, Philip ?-circa 1666................DLB-24
Paine, Robert Treat, Jr. 1773-1811........DLB-37
Paine, Thomas
 1737-1809.....DLB-31, 43, 73, 158; CDALB-2
Painter, George D. 1914- DLB-155
Painter, William 1540?-1594 ....DLB-136
Palazzeschi, Aldo 1885-1974 ....DLB-114, 264
Paley, Grace 1922- DLB-28, 218
Paley, William 1743-1805 ....DLB-251
Palfrey, John Gorham 1796-1881...DLB-1, 30, 235
Palgrave, Francis Turner 1824-1897 ......DLB-35
Palmer, Joe H. 1904-1952 ....DLB-171
Palmer, Michael 1943- DLB-169
Palmer, Nettie 1885-1964 ....DLB-260
Palmer, Vance 1885-1959 ....DLB-260
Paltock, Robert 1697-1767 ....DLB-39
Paludan, Jacob 1896-1975 ....DLB-214
Pan Books Limited....................DLB-112
Panama, Norman 1914- and
 Frank, Melvin 1913-1988 ....DLB-26
Panaev, Ivan Ivanovich 1812-1862 .....DLB-198
Panaeva, Avdot'ia Iakovlevna
 1820-1893 ....DLB-238
Pancake, Breece D'J 1952-1979 ....DLB-130
Panduro, Leif 1923-1977 ....DLB-214
Panero, Leopoldo 1909-1962...........DLB-108
Pangborn, Edgar 1909-1976............DLB-8
"Panic Among the Philistines": A Postscript,
 An Interview with Bryan Griffin........ Y-81
Panizzi, Sir Anthony 1797-1879 ....DLB-184
Panneton, Philippe (see Ringuet)
Panshin, Alexei 1940- DLB-8
Pansy (see Alden, Isabella)
Pantheon Books.....................DLB-46
Papadat-Bengescu, Hortensia
 1876-1955 ....DLB-220
Papantonio, Michael (see Kohn, John S. Van E.)

Paperback Library DLB-46
Paperback Science Fiction DLB-8
Papini, Giovanni 1881-1956 ....DLB-264
Paquet, Alfons 1881-1944 ....DLB-66
Paracelsus 1493-1541..................DLB-179
Paradis, Suzanne 1936- DLB-53
Páral, Vladimír, 1932- DLB-232
Pardoe, Julia 1804-1862.................DLB-166
Paredes, Américo 1915-1999 ....DLB-209
Pareja Diezcanseco, Alfredo 1908-1993...DLB-145
Parents' Magazine Press..................DLB-46
Parfit, Derek 1942- DLB-262
Parise, Goffredo 1929-1986..............DLB-177
Parisian Theater, Fall 1984: Toward
 A New Baroque....................Y-85
Parish, Mitchell 1900-1993 ....DLB-265
Parizeau, Alice 1930-....................DLB-60
Park, Ruth 1923- DLB-260
Parke, John 1754-1789 ....DLB-31
Parker, Dan 1893-1967 ....DLB-241
Parker, Dorothy 1893-1967........DLB-11, 45, 86
Parker, Gilbert 1860-1932 ....DLB-99
Parker, J. H. [publishing house].........DLB-106
Parker, James 1714-1770.................DLB-43
Parker, John [publishing house]..........DLB-106
Parker, Matthew 1504-1575..............DLB-213
Parker, Stewart 1941-1988...............DLB-245
Parker, Theodore 1810-1860.........DLB-1, 235
Parker, William Riley 1906-1968 ....DLB-103
Parkes, Bessie Rayner (Madame Belloc)
 1829-1925 ....DLB-240
Parkman, Francis
 1823-1893 ....DLB-1, 30, 183, 186, 235
Parks, Gordon 1912-....................DLB-33
Parks, Tim 1954-.......................DLB-231
Parks, William 1698-1750 ....DLB-43
Parks, William [publishing house].........DLB-49
Parley, Peter (see Goodrich, Samuel Griswold)
Parmenides
 late sixth-fifth century B.C..........DLB-176
Parnell, Thomas 1679-1718 ....DLB-95
Parnicki, Teodor 1908-1988 ....DLB-215
Parr, Catherine 1513?-1548..............DLB-136
Parrington, Vernon L. 1871-1929 .....DLB-17, 63
Parrish, Maxfield 1870-1966 ....DLB-188
Parronchi, Alessandro 1914- DLB-128
Parton, James 1822-1891................DLB-30
Parton, Sara Payson Willis
 1811-1872 ....DLB-43, 74, 239
Partridge, S. W., and Company DLB-106
Parun, Vesna 1922- DLB-181; CDWLB-4
Pascal, Blaise 1623-1662................DLB-268
Pasinetti, Pier Maria 1913- DLB-177
Pasolini, Pier Paolo 1922- DLB-128, 177
Pastan, Linda 1932- DLB-5

Paston, George (Emily Morse Symonds)
 1860-1936 ....DLB-149, 197
The Paston Letters 1422-1509 ....DLB-146
Pastorius, Francis Daniel
 1651-circa 1720 ....DLB-24
Patchen, Kenneth 1911-1972 ....DLB-16, 48
Pater, Walter
 1839-1894.........DLB-57, 156; CDBLB-4
 Aesthetic Poetry (1873) DLB-35
Paterson, A. B. "Banjo" 1864-1941 ......DLB-230
Paterson, Katherine 1932- DLB-52
Patmore, Coventry 1823-1896 ....DLB-35, 98
Paton, Alan 1903-1988 .... DS-17
Paton, Joseph Noel 1821-1901...........DLB-35
Paton Walsh, Jill 1937- DLB-161
Patrick, Edwin Hill ("Ted") 1901-1964...DLB-137
Patrick, John 1906-1995.................DLB-7
Pattee, Fred Lewis 1863-1950 ....DLB-71
Pattern and Paradigm: History as
 Design, by Judith Ryan DLB-75
Patterson, Alicia 1906-1963.............DLB-127
Patterson, Eleanor Medill 1881-1948......DLB-29
Patterson, Eugene 1923-...............DLB-127
Patterson, Joseph Medill 1879-1946.......DLB-29
Pattillo, Henry 1726-1801 ....DLB-37
Paul, Elliot 1891-1958..................DLB-4
Paul, Jean (see Richter, Johann Paul Friedrich)
Paul, Kegan, Trench, Trubner and
 Company Limited.................DLB-106
Paul, Peter, Book Company DLB-49
Paul, Stanley, and Company Limited DLB-112
Paulding, James Kirke
 1778-1860 ....DLB-3, 59, 74, 250
Paulin, Tom 1949- DLB-40
Pauper, Peter, Press..................DLB-46
Paustovsky, Konstantin Georgievich
 1892-1968 ....DLB-272
Pavese, Cesare 1908-1950 .... DLB-128, 177
Pavić, Milorad 1929- DLB-181; CDWLB-4
Pavlov, Konstantin 1933- DLB-181
Pavlov, Nikolai Filippovich 1803-1864.....DLB-198
Pavlova, Karolina Karlovna 1807-1893 ....DLB-205
Pavlović, Miodrag
 1928- DLB-181; CDWLB-4
Paxton, John 1911-1985................DLB-44
Payn, James 1830-1898 ....DLB-18
Payne, John 1842-1916 ....DLB-35
Payne, John Howard 1791-1852 ....DLB-37
Payson and Clarke DLB-46
Paz, Octavio 1914-1998..............Y-90, Y-98
Pazzi, Roberto 1946- DLB-196
Pea, Enrico 1881-1958.................DLB-264
Peabody, Elizabeth Palmer 1804-1894..DLB-1, 223
Peabody, Elizabeth Palmer
 [publishing house].................DLB-49
Peabody, Josephine Preston 1874-1922 ...DLB-249

Peabody, Oliver William Bourn 1799-1848 .... DLB-59
Peace, Roger 1899-1968 .... DLB-127
Peacham, Henry 1578-1644? DLB-151
Peacham, Henry, the Elder 1547-1634 .... DLB-172, 236
Peachtree Publishers, Limited DLB-46
Peacock, Molly 1947- DLB-120, 282
Peacock, Thomas Love 1785-1866 ... DLB-96, 116
Pead, Deuel ?-1727 .... DLB-24
Peake, Mervyn 1911-1968 ..... DLB-15, 160, 255
Peale, Rembrandt 1778-1860 .... DLB-183
Pear Tree Press DLB-112
Pearce, Philippa 1920- DLB-161
Pearson, H. B. [publishing house] DLB-49
Pearson, Hesketh 1887-1964 .... DLB-149
Peattie, Donald Culross 1898-1964 ...... DLB-275
Pechersky, Andrei (see Mel'nikov, Pavel Ivanovich)
Peck, George W. 1840-1916 .... DLB-23, 42
Peck, H. C., and Theo. Bliss [publishing house] DLB-49
Peck, Harry Thurston 1856-1914 ..... DLB-71, 91
Peden, William 1913-1999 .... DLB-234
Peele, George 1556-1596 .... DLB-62, 167
Pegler, Westbrook 1894-1969 .... DLB-171
Péguy, Charles Pierre 1873-1914 .... DLB-258
Peirce, Charles Sanders 1839-1914 .... DLB-270
Pekić, Borislav 1930-1992 ... DLB-181; CDWLB-4
Pellegrini and Cudahy DLB-46
Pelletier, Aimé (see Vac, Bertrand)
Pelletier, Francine 1959- DLB-251
Pemberton, Sir Max 1863-1950 .... DLB-70
de la Peña, Terri 1947- DLB-209
Penfield, Edward 1866-1925 .... DLB-188
Penguin Books [U.K.] DLB-112
Penguin Books [U.S.] DLB-46
Penn Publishing Company DLB-49
Penn, William 1644-1718 .... DLB-24
Penna, Sandro 1906-1977 .... DLB-114
Pennell, Joseph 1857-1926 .... DLB-188
Penner, Jonathan 1940- Y-83
Pennington, Lee 1939- Y-82
Penton, Brian 1904-1951 .... DLB-260
Pepper, Stephen C. 1891-1972 .... DLB-270
Pepys, Samuel 1633-1703 .... DLB-101, 213; CDBLB-2
Percy, Thomas 1729-1811 .... DLB-104
Percy, Walker 1916-1990 ..... DLB-2; Y-80, Y-90
Percy, William 1575-1648 .... DLB-172
Perec, Georges 1936-1982 .... DLB-83
Perelman, Bob 1947- DLB-193
Perelman, S. J. 1904-1979 ..... DLB-11, 44
Perez, Raymundo "Tigre" 1946- DLB-122
Peri Rossi, Cristina 1941- DLB-145
Perkins, Eugene 1932- DLB-41

Perkins, William 1558-1602 .... DLB-281
Perkoff, Stuart Z. 1930-1974 .... DLB-16
Perley, Moses Henry 1804-1862 .... DLB-99
Permabooks DLB-46
Perovsky, Aleksei Alekseevich (Antonii Pogorel'sky) 1787-1836 .... DLB-198
Perrault, Charles 1628-1703 .... DLB-268
Perri, Henry 1561-1617 .... DLB-236
Perrin, Alice 1867-1934 .... DLB-156
Perry, Anne 1938- DLB-276
Perry, Bliss 1860-1954 .... DLB-71
Perry, Eleanor 1915-1981 .... DLB-44
Perry, Henry (see Perri, Henry)
Perry, Matthew 1794-1858 .... DLB-183
Perry, Sampson 1747-1823 .... DLB-158
Perse, Saint-John 1887-1975 .... DLB-258
Persius A.D. 34-A.D. 62 .... DLB-211
Perutz, Leo 1882-1957 .... DLB-81
Pesetsky, Bette 1932- DLB-130
Pestalozzi, Johann Heinrich 1746-1827 .... DLB-94
Peter, Laurence J. 1919-1990 .... DLB-53
Peter of Spain circa 1205-1277 .... DLB-115
Peterkin, Julia 1880-1961 .... DLB-9
Peters, Ellis 1913-1995 .... DLB-276
Peters, Lenrie 1932- DLB-117
Peters, Robert 1924- DLB-105
"Foreword to Ludwig of Baviria" DLB-105
Petersham, Maud 1889-1971 and Petersham, Miska 1888-1960 .... DLB-22
Peterson, Charles Jacobs 1819-1887 ...... DLB-79
Peterson, Len 1917- DLB-88
Peterson, Levi S. 1933- DLB-206
Peterson, Louis 1922-1998 .... DLB-76
Peterson, T. B., and Brothers DLB-49
Petitclair, Pierre 1813-1860 .... DLB-99
Petrescu, Camil 1894-1957 .... DLB-220
Petronius circa A.D. 20-A.D. 66 .... DLB-211; CDWLB-1
Petrov, Aleksandar 1938- DLB-181
Petrov, Evgenii (see Il'f, Il'ia and Evgenii Petrov)
Petrov, Gavriil 1730-1801 .... DLB-150
Petrov, Valeri 1920- DLB-181
Petrov, Vasilii Petrovich 1736-1799 ..... DLB-150
Petrović, Rastko 1898-1949 .... DLB-147; CDWLB-4
Petruslied circa 854? DLB-148
Petry, Ann 1908-1997 .... DLB-76
Pettie, George circa 1548-1589 .... DLB-136
Peyton, K. M. 1929- DLB-161
Pfaffe Konrad flourished circa 1172 ..... DLB-148
Pfaffe Lamprecht flourished circa 1150 .. DLB-148
Pfeiffer, Emily 1827-1890 .... DLB-199
Pforzheimer, Carl H. 1879-1957 .... DLB-140
Phaedrus circa 18 B.C.-circa A.D. 50 .... DLB-211
Phaer, Thomas 1510?-1560 .... DLB-167

Phaidon Press Limited DLB-112
Pharr, Robert Deane 1916-1992 .... DLB-33
Phelps, Elizabeth Stuart 1815-1852 ...... DLB-202
Phelps, Elizabeth Stuart 1844-1911 .... DLB-74, 221
Philander von der Linde (see Mencke, Johann Burckhard)
Philby, H. St. John B. 1885-1960 .... DLB-195
Philip, Marlene Nourbese 1947- DLB-157
Philippe, Charles-Louis 1874-1909 ...... DLB-65
Philips, John 1676-1708 .... DLB-95
Philips, Katherine 1632-1664 .... DLB-131
Phillipps, Sir Thomas 1792-1872 .... DLB-184
Phillips, Caryl 1958- DLB-157
Phillips, David Graham 1867-1911 ..... DLB-9, 12
Phillips, Jayne Anne 1952- Y-80
Phillips, Robert 1938- DLB-105
"Finding, Losing, Reclaiming: A Note on My Poems" DLB-105
Phillips, Sampson and Company DLB-49
Phillips, Stephen 1864-1915 .... DLB-10
Phillips, Ulrich B. 1877-1934 .... DLB-17
Phillips, Wendell 1811-1884 .... DLB-235
Phillips, Willard 1784-1873 .... DLB-59
Phillips, William 1907- DLB-137
Phillpotts, Adelaide Eden (Adelaide Ross) 1896-1993 .... DLB-191
Phillpotts, Eden 1862-1960 .. DLB-10, 70, 135, 153
Philo circa 20-15 B.C.-circa A.D. 50 ...... DLB-176
Philosophical Library DLB-46
Phinney, Elihu [publishing house] DLB-49
Phoenix, John (see Derby, George Horatio)
PHYLON (Fourth Quarter, 1950), The Negro in Literature: The Current Scene DLB-76
Physiologus circa 1070-circa 1150 .... DLB-148
Piccolo, Lucio 1903-1969 .... DLB-114
Pickard, Tom 1946- DLB-40
Pickering, William [publishing house] ... DLB-106
Pickthall, Marjorie 1883-1922 .... DLB-92
Pictorial Printing Company DLB-49
Pielmeier, John 1949- DLB-266
Piercy, Marge 1936- DLB-120, 227
Pierro, Albino 1916- DLB-128
Pignotti, Lamberto 1926- DLB-128
Pike, Albert 1809-1891 .... DLB-74
Pike, Zebulon Montgomery 1779-1813 .... DLB-183
Pillat, Ion 1891-1945 .... DLB-220
Pil'niak, Boris Andreevich (Boris Andreevich Vogau) 1894-1938 .... DLB-272
Pilon, Jean-Guy 1930- DLB-60
Pinckney, Eliza Lucas 1722-1793 .... DLB-200
Pinckney, Josephine 1895-1957 .... DLB-6
Pindar circa 518 B.C.-circa 438 B.C. DLB-176; CDWLB-1
Pindar, Peter (see Wolcot, John)
Pineda, Cecile 1942- DLB-209

Pinero, Arthur Wing 1855-1934 ....DLB-10
Piñero, Miguel 1946-1988 ....DLB-266
Pinget, Robert 1919-1997................DLB-83
Pinkney, Edward Coote 1802-1828......DLB-248
Pinnacle Books......................DLB-46
Piñon, Nélida 1935- DLB-145
Pinsky, Robert 1940- Y-82
Robert Pinsky Reappointed Poet Laureate ... Y-98
Pinter, Harold 1930- DLB-13; CDBLB-8
Piontek, Heinz 1925- DLB-75
Piozzi, Hester Lynch [Thrale]
  1741-1821 ....DLB-104, 142
Piper, H. Beam 1904-1964................DLB-8
Piper, Watty DLB-22
Pirandello, Luigi 1868-1936............DLB-264
Pirckheimer, Caritas 1467-1532 ....DLB-179
Pirckheimer, Willibald 1470-1530 ......DLB-179
Pisar, Samuel 1929- Y-83
Pisarev, Dmitrii Ivanovich 1840-1868 ....DLB-277
Pisemsky, Aleksei Feofilaktovich
  1821-1881 ....DLB-238
Pitkin, Timothy 1766-1847 ....DLB-30
The Pitt Poetry Series: Poetry Publishing
  Today Y-85
Pitter, Ruth 1897- DLB-20
Pix, Mary 1666-1709 ....DLB-80
Pixerécourt, René Charles Guilbert de
  1773-1844 ....DLB-192
Plaatje, Sol T. 1876-1932 ....DLB-125, 225
Plante, David 1940- Y-83
Platen, August von 1796-1835 ....DLB-90
Plath, Sylvia
  1932-1963 ....DLB-5, 6, 152; CDALB-1
Plantinga, Alvin 1932- DLB-279
Plato circa 428 B.C.-348-347 B.C.
  .... DLB-176; CDWLB-1
Plato, Ann 1824?-?..................DLB-239
Platon 1737-1812 ....DLB-150
Platonov, Andrei Platonovich (Andrei
  Platonovic Klimentev) 1899-1951 ....DLB-272
Platt, Charles 1945- DLB-261
Platt and Munk Company..............DLB-46
Plautus circa 254 B.C.-184 B.C.
  .... DLB-211; CDWLB-1
Playboy Press.......................DLB-46
Playford, John [publishing house] DLB-170
Plays, Playwrights, and Playgoers DLB-84
Playwrights on the Theater DLB-80
Der Pleier flourished circa 1250.........DLB-138
Pleijel, Agneta 1940- DLB-257
Plenzdorf, Ulrich 1934- DLB-75
Pleshcheev, Aleksei Nikolaevich
  1823?-1893 ....DLB-277
Plessen, Elizabeth 1944- DLB-75
Pletnev, Petr Aleksandrovich
  1792-1865 ....DLB-205
Pliekšāne, Elza Rozenberga (see Aspazija)

Pliekšāns, Jānis (see Rainis, Jānis)
Plievier, Theodor 1892-1955............DLB-69
Plimpton, George 1927- DLB-185, 241; Y-99
Pliny the Elder A.D. 23/24-A.D. 79......DLB-211
Pliny the Younger
  circa A.D. 61-A.D. 112 ....DLB-211
Plomer, William
  1903-1973 ....DLB-20, 162, 191, 225
Plotinus 204-270.......... DLB-176; CDWLB-1
Plowright, Teresa 1952- DLB-251
Plume, Thomas 1630-1704 ....DLB-213
Plumly, Stanley 1939- DLB-5, 193
Plumpp, Sterling D. 1940- DLB-41
Plunkett, James 1920- DLB-14
Plutarch
  circa 46-circa 120....... DLB-176; CDWLB-1
Plymell, Charles 1935- DLB-16
Pocket Books......................DLB-46
Poe, Edgar Allan 1809-1849
  ....DLB-3, 59, 73, 74, 248; CDALB-2
Poe, James 1921-1980 ....DLB-44
The Poet Laureate of the United States
  Statements from Former Consultants
  in Poetry Y-86
The New Narrative Poetry DLB-282
A Century of Poetry, a Lifetime of Collecting:
  J. M. Edelstein's Collection of Twentieth-
  Century American Poetry............Y-02
Younger Women Poets of the
  New Formalism.................DLB-282
Pogodin, Mikhail Petrovich
  1800-1875 ....DLB-198
Pogorel'sky, Antonii
  (see Perovsky, Aleksei Alekseevich)
Pohl, Frederik 1919- DLB-8
Poirier, Louis (see Gracq, Julien)
Poláček, Karel 1892-1945 ...DLB-215; CDWLB-4
Polanyi, Michael 1891-1976.............DLB-100
Pole, Reginald 1500-1558 ....DLB-132
Polevoi, Nikolai Alekseevich
  1796-1846 ....DLB-198
Polezhaev, Aleksandr Ivanovich
  1804-1838 ....DLB-205
Poliakoff, Stephen 1952- DLB-13
Polidori, John William 1795-1821 ....DLB-116
Polite, Carlene Hatcher 1932- DLB-33
Pollard, Alfred W. 1859-1944 ....DLB-201
Pollard, Edward A. 1832-1872...........DLB-30
Pollard, Graham 1903-1976 ....DLB-201
Pollard, Percival 1869-1911 ....DLB-71
Pollard and Moss....................DLB-49
Pollock, Sharon 1936- DLB-60
Polonsky, Abraham 1910-1999 ....DLB-26
Polonsky, Iakov Petrovich 1819-1898....DLB-277
Polotsky, Simeon 1629-1680 ....DLB-150
Polybius circa 200 B.C.-118 B.C........DLB-176
Pomialovsky, Nikolai Gerasimovich
  1835-1863 ....DLB-238
Pomilio, Mario 1921-1990.............DLB-177

Ponce, Mary Helen 1938- DLB-122
Ponce-Montoya, Juanita 1949- DLB-122
Ponet, John 1516?-1556................DLB-132
Ponge, Francis 1899-1988 ....DLB-258; Y-02
Poniatowski, Elena
  1933- DLB-113; CDWLB-3
Ponsard, François 1814-1867...........DLB-192
Ponsonby, William [publishing house] ...DLB-170
Pontiggia, Giuseppe 1934- DLB-196
Pony Stories.......................DLB-160
Poole, Ernest 1880-1950 ....DLB-9
Poole, Sophia 1804-1891 ....DLB-166
Poore, Benjamin Perley 1820-1887 ....DLB-23
Popa, Vasko 1922-1991.....DLB-181; CDWLB-4
Pope, Abbie Hanscom 1858-1894 ....DLB-140
Pope, Alexander
  1688-1744 ......DLB-95, 101, 213; CDBLB-2
Popov, Aleksandr Serafimovich
  (see Serafimovich, Aleksandr Serafimovich)
Popov, Mikhail Ivanovich
  1742-circa 1790 ....DLB-150
Popović, Aleksandar 1929-1996 ....DLB-181
Popper, Sir Karl R. 1902-1994..........DLB-262
Popular Library.....................DLB-46
Poquelin, Jean-Baptiste (see Molière)
Porete, Marguerite ?-1310 ....DLB-208
Porlock, Martin (see MacDonald, Philip)
Porpoise Press DLB-112
Porta, Antonio 1935-1989 ....DLB-128
Porter, Anna Maria 1780-1832 .....DLB-116, 159
Porter, Cole 1891-1964 ....DLB-265
Porter, David 1780-1843 ....DLB-183
Porter, Eleanor H. 1868-1920 ....DLB-9
Porter, Gene Stratton (see Stratton-Porter, Gene)
Porter, Hal 1911-1984 ....DLB-260
Porter, Henry ?-?.....................DLB-62
Porter, Jane 1776-1850............DLB-116, 159
Porter, Katherine Anne 1890-1980
  ......DLB-4, 9, 102; Y-80; DS-12; CDALB-7
Porter, Peter 1929- DLB-40
Porter, William Sydney
  1862-1910 ....DLB-12, 78, 79; CDALB-3
Porter, William T. 1809-1858 .....DLB-3, 43, 250
Porter and Coates DLB-49
Portillo Trambley, Estela 1927-1998 .....DLB-209
Portis, Charles 1933- DLB-6
Posey, Alexander 1873-1908 ....DLB-175
Postans, Marianne circa 1810-1865......DLB-166
Postgate, Raymond 1896-1971..........DLB-276
Postl, Carl (see Sealsfield, Carl)
Poston, Ted 1906-1974 ....DLB-51
Potekhin, Aleksei Antipovich 1829-1908..DLB-238
Potok, Chaim 1929- DLB-28, 152
A Conversation with Chaim Potok Y-84
Potter, Beatrix 1866-1943 ....DLB-141
Potter, David M. 1910-1971.............DLB-17

Potter, Dennis 1935-1994 . . . . DLB-233	Prescott, William Hickling 1796-1859 . . . . DLB-1, 30, 59, 235	Prunty, Wyatt 1947- DLB-282
The Harry Potter Phenomenon Y-99	The Present State of the English Novel (1892), by George Saintsbury DLB-18	Prutkov, Koz'ma Petrovich 1803-1863 . . . . DLB-277
Potter, John E., and Company DLB-49		Prynne, J. H. 1936- DLB-40
Pottle, Frederick A. 1897-1987 . . . . . DLB-103; Y-87	Prešeren, Francè 1800-1849 . . . . DLB-147; CDWLB-4	Przybyszewski, Stanislaw 1868-1927 . . . . . DLB-66
Poulin, Jacques 1937- DLB-60	Preston, Margaret Junkin 1820-1897 . . . . DLB-239, 248	Pseudo-Dionysius the Areopagite floruit circa 500 . . . . DLB-115
Pound, Ezra 1885-1972 . . . . DLB-4, 45, 63; DS-15; CDALB-4		Public Domain and the Violation of Texts Y-97
Poverman, C. E. 1944- DLB-234	Presses of the New Formalism and the New Narrative DLB-282	The Public Lending Right in America Statement by Sen. Charles McC. Mathias, Jr. PLR and the Meaning of Literary Property Statements on PLR by American Writers Y-83
Povich, Shirley 1905-1998 . . . . DLB-171	Preston, May Wilson 1873-1949 . . . . . . DLB-188	
Powell, Anthony 1905-2000 . . . DLB-15; CDBLB-7	Preston, Thomas 1537-1598 . . . . DLB-62	
The Anthony Powell Society: Powell and the First Biennial Conference Y-01	Prévert, Jacques 1900-1977 . . . . DLB-258	The Public Lending Right in the United Kingdom Public Lending Right: The First Year in the United Kingdom Y-83
	Prichard, Katharine Susannah 1883-1969 . . . . DLB-260	
Dawn Powell, Where Have You Been All Our Lives? Y-97	Price, Anthony 1928- DLB-276	The Publication of English Renaissance Plays DLB-62
Powell, John Wesley 1834-1902 . . . . DLB-186	Price, Reynolds 1933- DLB-2, 218, 278	Publications and Social Movements [Transcendentalism] DLB-1
Powell, Padgett 1952- DLB-234	Price, Richard 1723-1791 . . . . DLB-158	
Powers, J. F. 1917-1999 . . . . DLB-130	Price, Richard 1949- Y-81	Publishers and Agents: The Columbia Connection Y-87
Powers, Jimmy 1903-1995 . . . . DLB-241	Prideaux, John 1578-1650 . . . . DLB-236	
Pownall, David 1938- DLB-14	Priest, Christopher 1943- DLB-14, 207, 261	The Literary Scene 2002: Publishing, Book Reviewing, and Literary Journalism Y-02
Powys, John Cowper 1872-1963 . . . . . DLB-15, 255	Priestley, J. B. 1894-1984 . . . . DLB-10, 34, 77, 100, 139; Y-84; CDBLB-6	
Powys, Llewelyn 1884-1939 . . . . DLB-98		Publishing Fiction at LSU Press Y-87
Powys, T. F. 1875-1953 . . . . DLB-36, 162	Priestley, Joseph 1733-1804 . . . . DLB-252	The Publishing Industry in 1998: Sturm-und-drang.com Y-98
Poynter, Nelson 1903-1978 . . . . DLB-127	Primary Bibliography: A Retrospective Y-95	
The Practice of Biography: An Interview with Stanley Weintraub Y-82	Prime, Benjamin Young 1733-1791 . . . . . . DLB-31	The Publishing Industry in 1999 . . . . Y-99
	Primrose, Diana floruit circa 1630 . . . . . . DLB-126	Pückler-Muskau, Hermann von 1785-1871 . . . . DLB-133
The Practice of Biography II: An Interview with B. L. Reid Y-83	Prince, F. T. 1912- DLB-20	
	Prince, Nancy Gardner 1799-? DLB-239	Pufendorf, Samuel von 1632-1694 . . . . . . DLB-168
The Practice of Biography III: An Interview with Humphrey Carpenter Y-84	Prince, Thomas 1687-1758 . . . . DLB-24, 140	Pugh, Edwin William 1874-1930 . . . . DLB-135
The Practice of Biography IV: An Interview with William Manchester Y-85	Pringle, Thomas 1789-1834 . . . . DLB-225	Pugin, A. Welby 1812-1852 . . . . DLB-55
	Printz, Wolfgang Casper 1641-1717 . . . . . DLB-168	Puig, Manuel 1932-1990 . . . . . DLB-113; CDWLB-3
The Practice of Biography VI: An Interview with David Herbert Donald Y-87	Prior, Matthew 1664-1721 . . . . DLB-95	Pulitzer, Joseph 1847-1911 . . . . DLB-23
	Prisco, Michele 1920- DLB-177	Pulitzer, Joseph, Jr. 1885-1955 . . . . DLB-29
The Practice of Biography VII: An Interview with John Caldwell Guilds Y-92	Prishvin, Mikhail Mikhailovich 1873-1954 . . . . DLB-272	Pulitzer Prizes for the Novel, 1917-1945 . . . . DLB-9
The Practice of Biography VIII: An Interview with Joan Mellen Y-94	Pritchard, William H. 1932- DLB-111	Pulliam, Eugene 1889-1975 . . . . DLB-127
	Pritchett, V. S. 1900-1997 . . . . DLB-15, 139	Purcell, Deirdre 1945- DLB-267
The Practice of Biography IX: An Interview with Michael Reynolds Y-95	Probyn, May 1856 or 1857-1909 . . . . DLB-199	Purchas, Samuel 1577?-1626 . . . . DLB-151
Prados, Emilio 1899-1962 . . . . DLB-134	Procter, Adelaide Anne 1825-1864 . . . DLB-32, 199	Purdy, Al 1918-2000 . . . . DLB-88
Praed, Mrs. Caroline (see Praed, Rosa)	Procter, Bryan Waller 1787-1874 . . . . DLB-96, 144	Purdy, James 1923- DLB-2, 218
Praed, Rosa (Mrs. Caroline Praed) 1851-1935 . . . . DLB-230	Proctor, Robert 1868-1903 . . . . DLB-184	Purdy, Ken W. 1913-1972 . . . . DLB-137
	Producing Dear Bunny, Dear Volodya: The Friendship and the Feud Y-97	Pusey, Edward Bouverie 1800-1882 . . . . . . DLB-55
Praed, Winthrop Mackworth 1802-1839 . . DLB-96		Pushkin, Aleksandr Sergeevich 1799-1837 . . . . DLB-205
Praeger Publishers DLB-46	The Profession of Authorship: Scribblers for Bread Y-89	
Praetorius, Johannes 1630-1680 . . . . DLB-168		Pushkin, Vasilii L'vovich 1766-1830 . . . . DLB-205
Pratolini, Vasco 1913-1991 . . . . DLB-177	Prokopovich, Feofan 1681?-1736 . . . . DLB-150	
Pratt, E. J. 1882-1964 . . . . DLB-92	Prokosch, Frederic 1906-1989 . . . . DLB-48	Putnam, George Palmer 1814-1872 . . . . DLB-3, 79, 250, 254
Pratt, Samuel Jackson 1749-1814 . . . . DLB-39	The Proletarian Novel DLB-9	
Preciado Martin, Patricia 1939- DLB-209	Pronzini, Bill 1943- DLB-226	G. P. Putnam [publishing house] DLB-254
Preface to The History of Romances (1715), by Pierre Daniel Huet [excerpts] DLB-39	Propertius circa 50 B.C.-post 16 B.C. DLB-211; CDWLB-1	G. P. Putnam's Sons [U.K.] DLB-106
		G. P. Putnam's Sons [U.S.] DLB-49
Préfontaine, Yves 1937- DLB-53	Propper, Dan 1937- DLB-16	A Publisher's Archives: G. P. Putnam Y-92
Prelutsky, Jack 1940- DLB-61	Prose, Francine 1947- DLB-234	Putnam, Hilary 1926- DLB-279
Premisses, by Michael Hamburger DLB-66	The Prosody of the New Formalism DLB-282	Putnam, Samuel 1892-1950 . . . . DLB-4
Prentice, George D. 1802-1870 . . . . DLB-43	Protagoras circa 490 B.C.-420 B.C. DLB-176	Puttenham, George 1529?-1590 . . . . DLB-281
Prentice-Hall DLB-46	Proud, Robert 1728-1813 . . . . DLB-30	Puzo, Mario 1920-1999 . . . . DLB-6
Prescott, Orville 1906-1996 . . . . Y-96	Proust, Marcel 1871-1922 . . . . DLB-65	Pyle, Ernie 1900-1945 . . . . DLB-29
		Pyle, Howard 1853-1911 . . . . DLB-42, 188; DS-13

Pyle, Robert Michael 1947- DLB-275
Pym, Barbara 1913-1980 ..... DLB-14, 207; Y-87
Pynchon, Thomas 1937- DLB-2, 173
Pyramid Books DLB-46
Pyrnelle, Louise-Clarke 1850-1907 .... DLB-42
Pythagoras circa 570 B.C.-? DLB-176

Q

Quad, M. (see Lewis, Charles B.)
Quaritch, Bernard 1819-1899 .... DLB-184
Quarles, Francis 1592-1644 .... DLB-126
The Quarterly Review 1809-1967 .... DLB-110
Quasimodo, Salvatore 1901-1968 .... DLB-114
Queen, Ellery (see Dannay, Frederic, and Manfred B. Lee)
Queen, Frank 1822-1882 .... DLB-241
The Queen City Publishing House DLB-49
Queneau, Raymond 1903-1976 ..... DLB-72, 258
Quennell, Sir Peter 1905-1993 ..... DLB-155, 195
Quesnel, Joseph 1746-1809 .... DLB-99
The Question of American Copyright
  in the Nineteenth Century
    Preface, by George Haven Putnam
    The Evolution of Copyright, by
      Brander Matthews
    Summary of Copyright Legislation in
      the United States, by R. R. Bowker
    Analysis of the Provisions of the
      Copyright Law of 1891, by
      George Haven Putnam
    The Contest for International Copyright,
      by George Haven Putnam
    Cheap Books and Good Books,
      by Brander Matthews DLB-49
Quiller-Couch, Sir Arthur Thomas
  1863-1944 .... DLB-135, 153, 190
Quin, Ann 1936-1973 .... DLB-14, 231
Quinault, Philippe 1635-1688 .... DLB-268
Quincy, Samuel, of Georgia ?-? DLB-31
Quincy, Samuel, of Massachusetts
  1734-1789 .... DLB-31
Quine, W. V. 1908-2000 .... DLB-279
Quinn, Anthony 1915- DLB-122
The Quinn Draft of James Joyce's
  Circe Manuscript Y-00
Quinn, John 1870-1924 .... DLB-187
Quiñónez, Naomi 1951- DLB-209
Quintana, Leroy V. 1944- DLB-82
Quintana, Miguel de 1671-1748
  A Forerunner of Chicano Literature .. DLB-122
Quintillian
  circa A.D. 40-circa A.D. 96 .... DLB-211
Quintus Curtius Rufus fl. A.D. 35 .... DLB-211
Quist, Harlin, Books DLB-46
Quoirez, Françoise (see Sagan, Françoise)

R

R-va, Zeneida (see Gan, Elena Andreevna)
Raabe, Wilhelm 1831-1910 .... DLB-129
Raban, Jonathan 1942- DLB-204
Rabe, David 1940- DLB-7, 228

Raboni, Giovanni 1932- DLB-128
Rachilde 1860-1953 .... DLB-123, 192
Racin, Kočo 1908-1943 .... DLB-147
Racine, Jean 1639-1699 .... DLB-268
Rackham, Arthur 1867-1939 .... DLB-141
Radauskas, Henrikas
  1910-1970 .... DLB-220; CDWLB-4
Radcliffe, Ann 1764-1823 .... DLB-39, 178
Raddall, Thomas 1903-1994 .... DLB-68
Radford, Dollie 1858-1920 .... DLB-240
Radichkov, Yordan 1929- DLB-181
Radiguet, Raymond 1903-1923 .... DLB-65
Radishchev, Aleksandr Nikolaevich
  1749-1802 .... DLB-150
Radnóti, Miklós
  1909-1944 .... DLB-215; CDWLB-4
Radványi, Netty Reiling (see Seghers, Anna)
Rahv, Philip 1908-1973 .... DLB-137
Raich, Semen Egorovich 1792-1855 ..... DLB-205
Raičković, Stevan 1928- DLB-181
Raimund, Ferdinand Jakob 1790-1836 ... DLB-90
Raine, Craig 1944- DLB-40
Raine, Kathleen 1908- DLB-20
Rainis, Jānis 1865-1929 ..... DLB-220; CDWLB-4
Rainolde, Richard
  circa 1530-1606 .... DLB-136, 236
Rainolds, John 1549-1607 .... DLB-281
Rakić, Milan 1876-1938 ..... DLB-147; CDWLB-4
Rakosi, Carl 1903- DLB-193
Ralegh, Sir Walter
  1554?-1618 .... DLB-172; CDBLB-1
Ralin, Radoy 1923- DLB-181
Ralph, Julian 1853-1903 .... DLB-23
Ramat, Silvio 1939- DLB-128
Rambler, no. 4 (1750), by Samuel Johnson
  [excerpt] DLB-39
Ramée, Marie Louise de la (see Ouida)
Ramírez, Sergío 1942- DLB-145
Ramke, Bin 1947- DLB-120
Ramler, Karl Wilhelm 1725-1798 .... DLB-97
Ramon Ribeyro, Julio 1929- DLB-145
Ramos, Manuel 1948- DLB-209
Ramous, Mario 1924- DLB-128
Rampersad, Arnold 1941- DLB-111
Ramsay, Allan 1684 or 1685-1758 .... DLB-95
Ramsay, David 1749-1815 .... DLB-30
Ramsay, Martha Laurens 1759-1811 ..... DLB-200
Ramsey, Frank P. 1903-1930 .... DLB-262
Ranck, Katherine Quintana 1942- DLB-122
Rand, Avery and Company DLB-49
Rand, Ayn 1905-1982 ... DLB-227, 279; CDALB-7
Rand McNally and Company DLB-49
Randall, David Anton 1905-1975 .... DLB-140
Randall, Dudley 1914- DLB-41
Randall, Henry S. 1811-1876 .... DLB-30
Randall, James G. 1881-1953 .... DLB-17

The Randall Jarrell Symposium:
  A Small Collection of Randall Jarrells
  Excerpts From Papers Delivered at the
  Randall Jarrel Symposium Y-86
Randall, John Herman Jr. 1899-1980 .... DLB-279
Randolph, A. Philip 1889-1979 .... DLB-91
Randolph, Anson D. F.
  [publishing house] DLB-49
Randolph, Thomas 1605-1635 ...... DLB-58, 126
Random House DLB-46
Rankin, Ian (Jack Harvey) 1960- DLB-267
Ranlet, Henry [publishing house] DLB-49
Ransom, Harry 1908-1976 .... DLB-187
Ransom, John Crowe
  1888-1974 .... DLB-45, 63; CDALB-7
Ransome, Arthur 1884-1967 .... DLB-160
Raphael, Frederic 1931- DLB-14
Raphaelson, Samson 1896-1983 .... DLB-44
Rashi circa 1040-1105 .... DLB-208
Raskin, Ellen 1928-1984 .... DLB-52
Rastell, John 1475?-1536 .... DLB-136, 170
Rattigan, Terence
  1911-1977 .... DLB-13; CDBLB-7
Raven, Simon 1927-2001 .... DLB-271
Rawlings, Marjorie Kinnan 1896-1953
  .... DLB-9, 22, 102; DS-17; CDALB-7
Rawlinson, Richard 1690-1755 .... DLB-213
Rawlinson, Thomas 1681-1725 .... DLB-213
Rawls, John 1921-2002 .... DLB-279
Raworth, Tom 1938- DLB-40
Ray, David 1932- DLB-5
Ray, Gordon Norton 1915-1986 .... DLB-103, 140
Ray, Henrietta Cordelia 1849-1916 .... DLB-50
Raymond, Ernest 1888-1974 .... DLB-191
Raymond, Henry J. 1820-1869 .... DLB-43, 79
Razaf, Andy 1895-1973 .... DLB-265
Michael M. Rea and the Rea Award for the
  Short Story Y-97
Reach, Angus 1821-1856 .... DLB-70
Read, Herbert 1893-1968 .... DLB-20, 149
Read, Martha Meredith DLB-200
Read, Opie 1852-1939 .... DLB-23
Read, Piers Paul 1941- DLB-14
Reade, Charles 1814-1884 .... DLB-21
Reader's Digest Condensed Books DLB-46
Readers Ulysses Symposium Y-97
Reading, Peter 1946- DLB-40
Reading Series in New York City Y-96
The Reality of One Woman's Dream:
  The de Grummond Children's
  Literature Collection Y-99
Reaney, James 1926- DLB-68
Rebhun, Paul 1500?-1546 .... DLB-179
Rèbora, Clemente 1885-1957 .... DLB-114
Rebreanu, Liviu 1885-1944 .... DLB-220
Rechy, John 1931- DLB-122, 278; Y-82
The Recovery of Literature:
  Criticism in the 1990s: A Symposium Y-91

Cumulative Index

Redding, J. Saunders 1906-1988 ...... DLB-63, 76
Redfield, J. S. [publishing house] DLB-49
Redgrove, Peter 1932- DLB-40
Redmon, Anne 1943- Y-86
Redmond, Eugene B. 1937- DLB-41
Redpath, James [publishing house] DLB-49
Reed, Henry 1808-1854 .... DLB-59
Reed, Henry 1914- DLB-27
Reed, Ishmael
 1938- DLB-2, 5, 33, 169, 227; DS-8
Reed, Rex 1938- DLB-185
Reed, Sampson 1800-1880 .... DLB-1, 235
Reed, Talbot Baines 1852-1893 .... DLB-141
Reedy, William Marion 1862-1920 ..... DLB-91
Reese, Lizette Woodworth 1856-1935 .... DLB-54
Reese, Thomas 1742-1796. .... DLB-37
Reeve, Clara 1729-1807 .... DLB-39
Preface to *The Old English Baron* (1778) DLB-39
The Progress of Romance (1785) [excerpt] DLB-39
Reeves, James 1909-1978 .... DLB-161
Reeves, John 1926- DLB-88
Reeves-Stevens, Garfield 1953- DLB-251
"Reflections: After a Tornado,"
 by Judson Jerome................. DLB-105
Regnery, Henry, Company DLB-46
Rehberg, Hans 1901-1963 .... DLB-124
Rehfisch, Hans José 1891-1960. .... DLB-124
Reich, Ebbe Kløvedal 1940- DLB-214
Reid, Alastair 1926- DLB-27
Reid, B. L. 1918-1990. .... DLB-111; Y-83
The Practice of Biography II:
 An Interview with B. L. Reid........... Y-83
Reid, Christopher 1949- DLB-40
Reid, Forrest 1875-1947 .... DLB-153
Reid, Helen Rogers 1882-1970 .... DLB-29
Reid, James ?-? DLB-31
Reid, Mayne 1818-1883 .... DLB-21, 163
Reid, Thomas 1710-1796 .... DLB-31, 252
Reid, V. S. (Vic) 1913-1987 .... DLB-125
Reid, Whitelaw 1837-1912 .... DLB-23
Reilly and Lee Publishing Company DLB-46
Reimann, Brigitte 1933-1973 .... DLB-75
Reinmar der Alte
 circa 1165-circa 1205 .... DLB-138
Reinmar von Zweter
 circa 1200-circa 1250 .... DLB-138
Reisch, Walter 1903-1983 .... DLB-44
Reizei Family DLB-203
Remarks at the Opening of "The Biographical
 Part of Literature" Exhibition, by
 William R. Cagle................... Y-98
Remarque, Erich Maria
 1898-1970............. DLB-56; CDWLB-2
Remington, Frederic
 1861-1909 .... DLB-12, 186, 188
Reminiscences, by Charles Scribner, Jr. DS-17
Renaud, Jacques 1943- DLB-60

Renault, Mary 1905-1983 .... Y-83
Rendell, Ruth 1930- DLB-87, 276
Rensselaer, Maria van Cortlandt van
 1645-1689 .... DLB-200
Repplier, Agnes 1855-1950 .... DLB-221
Representative Men and Women: A Historical
 Perspective on the British Novel,
 1930-1960 .... DLB-15
Research in the American Antiquarian Book
 Trade Y-97
Reshetnikov, Fedor Mikhailovich
 1841-1871..................... DLB-238
Rettenbacher, Simon 1634-1706 .... DLB-168
Retz, Jean-François-Paul de Gondi, cardinal de
 1613-1679 .... DLB-268
Reuchlin, Johannes 1455-1522 .... DLB-179
Reuter, Christian 1665-after 1712 .... DLB-168
Revell, Fleming H., Company DLB-49
Reverdy, Pierre 1889-1960............ DLB-258
Reuter, Fritz 1810-1874............... DLB-129
Reuter, Gabriele 1859-1941 .... DLB-66
Reventlow, Franziska Gräfin zu
 1871-1918..................... DLB-66
Review of Nicholson Baker's *Double Fold:
 Libraries and the Assault on Paper* Y-00
Review of Reviews Office............. DLB-112
Review of [Samuel Richardson's] *Clarissa* (1748),
 by Henry Fielding DLB-39
The Revolt (1937), by Mary Colum
 [excerpts] DLB-36
Rexroth, Kenneth 1905-1982
 .... DLB-16, 48, 165, 212; Y-82; CDALB-1
Rey, H. A. 1898-1977................. DLB-22
Reynal and Hitchcock DLB-46
Reynolds, G. W. M. 1814-1879 .... DLB-21
Reynolds, John Hamilton 1794-1852 ..... DLB-96
Reynolds, Sir Joshua 1723-1792 .... DLB-104
Reynolds, Mack 1917- DLB-8
A Literary Archaeologist Digs On: A Brief
 Interview with Michael Reynolds by
 Michael Rogers Y-99
Reznikoff, Charles 1894-1976........ DLB-28, 45
Rhett, Robert Barnwell 1800-1876 .... DLB-43
Rhode, John 1884-1964 .... DLB-77
Rhodes, Eugene Manlove 1869-1934.... DLB-256
Rhodes, James Ford 1848-1927......... DLB-47
Rhodes, Richard 1937- DLB-185
Rhys, Jean 1890-1979
 ..... DLB-36, 117, 162; CDBLB-7; CDWLB-3
Ricardo, David 1772-1823 .... DLB-107, 158
Ricardou, Jean 1932- DLB-83
Rice, Elmer 1892-1967 .... DLB-4, 7
Rice, Grantland 1880-1954.......... DLB-29, 171
Rich, Adrienne 1929- DLB-5, 67; CDALB-7
Richard de Fournival
 1201-1259 or 1260................ DLB-208
Richard, Mark 1955- DLB-234
Richards, David Adams 1950- DLB-53
Richards, George circa 1760-1814 .... DLB-37

Richards, Grant [publishing house] DLB-112
Richards, I. A. 1893-1979 .... DLB-27
Richards, Laura E. 1850-1943 .... DLB-42
Richards, William Carey 1818-1892 .... DLB-73
Richardson, Charles F. 1851-1913 ...... DLB-71
Richardson, Dorothy M. 1873-1957 ..... DLB-36
Richardson, Henry Handel
 (Ethel Florence Lindesay
 Robertson) 1870-1946 .... DLB-197, 230
Richardson, Jack 1935- DLB-7
Richardson, John 1796-1852............ DLB-99
Richardson, Samuel
 1689-1761.......... DLB-39, 154; CDBLB-2
Introductory Letters from the Second
 Edition of *Pamela* (1741) DLB-39
Postscript to [the Third Edition of]
 Clarissa (1751) DLB-39
Preface to the First Edition of
 Pamela (1740) DLB-39
Preface to the Third Edition of
 Clarissa (1751) [excerpt] DLB-39
Preface to Volume 1 of *Clarissa* (1747) DLB-39
Preface to Volume 3 of *Clarissa* (1748) DLB-39
Richardson, Willis 1889-1977........... DLB-51
Riche, Barnabe 1542-1617 .... DLB-136
Richepin, Jean 1849-1926............. DLB-192
Richler, Mordecai 1931- DLB-53
Richter, Conrad 1890-1968 .... DLB-9, 212
Richter, Hans Werner 1908- DLB-69
Richter, Johann Paul Friedrich
 1763-1825............. DLB-94; CDWLB-2
Rickerby, Joseph [publishing house]..... DLB-106
Rickword, Edgell 1898-1982 .... DLB-20
Riddell, Charlotte 1832-1906......... DLB-156
Riddell, John (see Ford, Corey)
Ridge, John Rollin 1827-1867.......... DLB-175
Ridge, Lola 1873-1941 .... DLB-54
Ridge, William Pett 1859-1930....... DLB-135
Riding, Laura (see Jackson, Laura Riding)
Ridler, Anne 1912- DLB-27
Ridruejo, Dionisio 1912-1975 .... DLB-108
Riel, Louis 1844-1885................ DLB-99
Riemer, Johannes 1648-1714 .... DLB-168
Rifbjerg, Klaus 1931- DLB-214
Riffaterre, Michael 1924- DLB-67
A Conversation between William Riggan
 and Janette Turner Hospital Y-02
Riggs, Lynn 1899-1954 .... DLB-175
Riis, Jacob 1849-1914................ DLB-23
Riker, John C. [publishing house]........ DLB-49
Riley, James 1777-1840 .... DLB-183
Riley, John 1938-1978................ DLB-40
Rilke, Rainer Maria
 1875-1926............. DLB-81; CDWLB-2
Rimanelli, Giose 1926- DLB-177
Rimbaud, Jean-Nicolas-Arthur
 1854-1891....................... DLB-217
Rinehart and Company DLB-46

Ringuet 1895-1960..................DLB-68
Ringwood, Gwen Pharis 1910-1984.......DLB-88
Rinser, Luise 1911- DLB-69
Ríos, Alberto 1952- DLB-122
Ríos, Isabella 1948- DLB-82
Ripley, Arthur 1895-1961..............DLB-44
Ripley, George 1802-1880.....DLB-1, 64, 73, 235
The Rising Glory of America:
    Three Poems...................DLB-37
The Rising Glory of America:
    Written in 1771 (1786),
    by Hugh Henry Brackenridge and
    Philip Freneau..................DLB-37
Riskin, Robert 1897-1955..............DLB-26
Risse, Heinz 1898- DLB-69
Rist, Johann 1607-1667................DLB-164
Ristikivi, Karl 1912-1977..............DLB-220
Ritchie, Anna Mowatt 1819-1870......DLB-3, 250
Ritchie, Anne Thackeray 1837-1919......DLB-18
Ritchie, Thomas 1778-1854.............DLB-43
Rites of Passage [on William Saroyan].......Y-83
The Ritz Paris Hemingway Award Y-85
Rivard, Adjutor 1868-1945.............DLB-92
Rive, Richard 1931-1989..........DLB-125, 225
Rivera, José 1955- DLB-249
Rivera, Marina 1942- DLB-122
Rivera, Tomás 1935-1984..............DLB-82
Rivers, Conrad Kent 1933-1968.........DLB-41
Riverside Press......................DLB-49
Rivington, Charles [publishing house]....DLB-154
Rivington, James circa 1724-1802........DLB-43
Rivkin, Allen 1903-1990...............DLB-26
Roa Bastos, Augusto 1917- DLB-113
Robbe-Grillet, Alain 1922- DLB-83
Robbins, Tom 1936- Y-80
Roberts, Charles G. D. 1860-1943........DLB-92
Roberts, Dorothy 1906-1993............DLB-88
Roberts, Elizabeth Madox
    1881-1941..................DLB-9, 54, 102
Roberts, James [publishing house].......DLB-154
Roberts, Keith 1935-2000..............DLB-261
Roberts, Kenneth 1885-1957.............DLB-9
Roberts, Michèle 1949- DLB-231
Roberts, Theodore Goodridge
    1877-1953.....................DLB-92
Roberts, Ursula Wyllie (see Miles, Susan)
Roberts, William 1767-1849............DLB-142
Roberts Brothers....................DLB-49
Robertson, A. M., and Company DLB-49
Robertson, Ethel Florence Lindesay
    (see Richardson, Henry Handel)
Robertson, William 1721-1793.........DLB-104
Robin, Leo 1895-1984.................DLB-265
Robins, Elizabeth 1862-1952...........DLB-197
Robinson, A. Mary F. (Madame James
    Darmesteter, Madame Mary
    Duclaux) 1857-1944..............DLB-240

Robinson, Casey 1903-1979.............DLB-44
Robinson, Derek Y-02
Review by Derek Robinson of George Greenfield's
    Rich Dust Y-02
Robinson, Edwin Arlington
    1869-1935.............DLB-54; CDALB-3
Robinson, Henry Crabb 1775-1867......DLB-107
Robinson, James Harvey 1863-1936......DLB-47
Robinson, Lennox 1886-1958............DLB-10
Robinson, Mabel Louise 1874-1962......DLB-22
Robinson, Marilynne 1943- DLB-206
Robinson, Mary 1758-1800..............DLB-158
Robinson, Richard circa 1545-1607......DLB-167
Robinson, Therese 1797-1870.......DLB-59, 133
Robison, Mary 1949- DLB-130
Roblès, Emmanuel 1914-1995............DLB-83
Roccatagliata Ceccardi, Ceccardo
    1871-1919.....................DLB-114
Roche, Billy 1949- DLB-233
Rochester, John Wilmot, Earl of
    1647-1680.....................DLB-131
Rochon, Esther 1948- DLB-251
Rock, Howard 1911-1976...............DLB-127
Rockwell, Norman Perceval 1894-1978...DLB-188
Rodgers, Carolyn M. 1945- DLB-41
Rodgers, W. R. 1909-1969..............DLB-20
Rodney, Lester 1911- DLB-241
Rodríguez, Claudio 1934-1999..........DLB-134
Rodríguez, Joe D. 1943- DLB-209
Rodríguez, Luis J. 1954- DLB-209
Rodriguez, Richard 1944- DLB-82, 256
Rodríguez Julia, Edgardo 1946- DLB-145
Roe, E. P. 1838-1888..................DLB-202
Roethke, Theodore
    1908-1963..........DLB-5, 206; CDALB-1
Rogers, Jane 1952- DLB-194
Rogers, Pattiann 1940- DLB-105
Rogers, Samuel 1763-1855..............DLB-93
Rogers, Will 1879-1935................DLB-11
Rohmer, Sax 1883-1959.................DLB-70
Roiphe, Anne 1935- Y-80
Rojas, Arnold R. 1896-1988............DLB-82
Rolfe, Frederick William
    1860-1913.................DLB-34, 156
Rolland, Romain 1866-1944.............DLB-65
Rolle, Richard circa 1290-1300 - 1340....DLB-146
Rölvaag, O. E. 1876-1931...........DLB-9, 212
Romains, Jules 1885-1972..............DLB-65
Roman, A., and Company...............DLB-49
Roman de la Rose: Guillaume de Lorris
    1200 to 1205-circa 1230, Jean de Meun
    1235-1240-circa 1305 ....DLB-208
Romano, Lalla 1906- DLB-177
Romano, Octavio 1923- DLB-122
Rome, Harold 1908-1993...............DLB-265
Romero, Leo 1950- DLB-122
Romero, Lin 1947- DLB-122

Romero, Orlando 1945- DLB-82
Rook, Clarence 1863-1915.............DLB-135
Roosevelt, Theodore 1858-1919 ..DLB-47, 186, 275
Root, Waverley 1903-1982..............DLB-4
Root, William Pitt 1941- DLB-120
Roquebrune, Robert de 1889-1978.......DLB-68
Rorty, Richard 1931- DLB-246, 279
Rosa, João Guimarães 1908-1967.......DLB-113
Rosales, Luis 1910-1992...............DLB-134
Roscoe, William 1753-1831.............DLB-163
Danis Rose and the Rendering of Ulysses......Y-97
Rose, Reginald 1920- DLB-26
Rose, Wendy 1948- DLB-175
Rosegger, Peter 1843-1918.............DLB-129
Rosei, Peter 1946- DLB-85
Rosen, Norma 1925- DLB-28
Rosenbach, A. S. W. 1876-1952........DLB-140
Rosenbaum, Ron 1946- DLB-185
Rosenberg, Isaac 1890-1918 ....DLB-20, 216
Rosenfeld, Isaac 1918-1956............DLB-28
Rosenthal, Harold 1914-1999..........DLB-241
Jimmy, Red, and Others: Harold Rosenthal
    Remembers the Stars of the Press Box... Y-01
Rosenthal, M. L. 1917-1996.............DLB-5
Rosenwald, Lessing J. 1891-1979.......DLB-187
Ross, Alexander 1591-1654............DLB-151
Ross, Harold 1892-1951...............DLB-137
Ross, Jerry (see Adler, Richard)
Ross, Leonard Q. (see Rosten, Leo)
Ross, Lillian 1927- DLB-185
Ross, Martin 1862-1915................DLB-135
Ross, Sinclair 1908-1996..............DLB-88
Ross, W. W. E. 1894-1966..............DLB-88
Rosselli, Amelia 1930-1996...........DLB-128
Rossen, Robert 1908-1966..............DLB-26
Rosset, Barney.......................Y-02
Rossetti, Christina 1830-1894...DLB-35, 163, 240
Rossetti, Dante Gabriel
    1828-1882...............DLB-35; CDBLB-4
Rossner, Judith 1935- DLB-6
Rostand, Edmond 1868-1918 ....DLB-192
Rosten, Leo 1908-1997................DLB-11
Rostenberg, Leona 1908- DLB-140
Rostopchina, Evdokiia Petrovna
    1811-1858.....................DLB-205
Rostovsky, Dimitrii 1651-1709.........DLB-150
Rota, Bertram 1903-1966..............DLB-201
    Bertram Rota and His Bookshop.........Y-91
Roth, Gerhard 1942- DLB-85, 124
Roth, Henry 1906?-1995................DLB-28
Roth, Joseph 1894-1939................DLB-85
Roth, Philip 1933-
    ....DLB-2, 28, 173; Y-82; CDALB-6
Nathan Asch Remembers Ford Madox Ford,
    Sam Roth, and Hart Crane Y-02
Rothenberg, Jerome 1931- DLB-5, 193

Rothschild Family................... DLB-184
Rotimi, Ola 1938- DLB-125
Rotrou, Jean 1609-1650................ DLB-268
Routhier, Adolphe-Basile 1839-1920 ..... DLB-99
Routier, Simone 1901-1987 .... DLB-88
Routledge, George, and Sons DLB-106
Roversi, Roberto 1923- DLB-128
Rowe, Elizabeth Singer 1674-1737 .... DLB-39, 95
Rowe, Nicholas 1674-1718 .... DLB-84
Rowlands, Samuel circa 1570-1630...... DLB-121
Rowlandson, Mary
    circa 1637-circa 1711........... DLB-24, 200
Rowley, William circa 1585-1626....... DLB-58
Rowse, A. L. 1903-1997 .... DLB-155
Rowson, Susanna Haswell
    circa 1762-1824................ DLB-37, 200
Roy, Camille 1870-1943 .... DLB-92
Roy, Gabrielle 1909-1983.............. DLB-68
Roy, Jules 1907- DLB-83
The G. Ross Roy Scottish Poetry Collection
    at the University of South Carolina...... Y-89
The Royal Court Theatre and the English
    Stage Company DLB-13
The Royal Court Theatre and the New
    Drama DLB-10
The Royal Shakespeare Company
    at the Swan...................... Y-88
Royall, Anne Newport 1769-1854 ... DLB-43, 248
Royce, Josiah 1855-1916............... DLB-270
The Roycroft Printing Shop DLB-49
Royde-Smith, Naomi 1875-1964........ DLB-191
Royster, Vermont 1914- DLB-127
Royston, Richard [publishing house].....DLB-170
Różewicz, Tadeusz 1921- DLB-232
Ruark, Gibbons 1941- DLB-120
Ruban, Vasilii Grigorevich 1742-1795 ... DLB-150
Rubens, Bernice 1928- DLB-14, 207
Rudd and Carleton.................... DLB-49
Rudd, Steele (Arthur Hoey Davis) DLB-230
Rudkin, David 1936- DLB-13
Rudnick, Paul 1957- DLB-266
Rudolf von Ems circa 1200-circa 1254 ... DLB-138
Ruffin, Josephine St. Pierre
    1842-1924 .... DLB-79
Ruganda, John 1941- DLB-157
Ruggles, Henry Joseph 1813-1906 .... DLB-64
Ruiz de Burton, María Amparo
    1832-1895 .... DLB-209, 221
Rukeyser, Muriel 1913-1980 .... DLB-48
Rule, Jane 1931- DLB-60
Rulfo, Juan 1918-1986 ..... DLB-113; CDWLB-3
Rumaker, Michael 1932- DLB-16
Rumens, Carol 1944- DLB-40
Rummo, Paul-Eerik 1942- DLB-232
Runyon, Damon 1880-1946......DLB-11, 86, 171
Ruodlieb circa 1050-1075 .... DLB-148
Rush, Benjamin 1746-1813 .... DLB-37

Rush, Rebecca 1779-? DLB-200
Rushdie, Salman 1947- DLB-194
Rusk, Ralph L. 1888-1962 .... DLB-103
Ruskin, John
    1819-1900....... DLB-55, 163, 190; CDBLB-4
Russ, Joanna 1937- DLB-8
Russell, B. B., and Company DLB-49
Russell, Benjamin 1761-1845 .... DLB-43
Russell, Bertrand 1872-1970 .... DLB-100, 262
Russell, Charles Edward 1860-1941...... DLB-25
Russell, Charles M. 1864-1926......... DLB-188
Russell, Eric Frank 1905-1978 .... DLB-255
Russell, Fred 1906- DLB-241
Russell, George William (see AE)
Russell, Countess Mary Annette Beauchamp
    (see Arnim, Elizabeth von)
Russell, R. H., and Son............... DLB-49
Russell, Willy 1947- DLB-233
Rutebeuf flourished 1249-1277......... DLB-208
Rutherford, Mark 1831-1913 .... DLB-18
Ruxton, George Frederick
    1821-1848 .... DLB-186
Ryan, James 1952- DLB-267
Ryan, Kay 1945- DLB-282
Ryan, Michael 1946- Y-82
Ryan, Oscar 1904- DLB-68
Ryder, Jack 1871-1936 .... DLB-241
Ryga, George 1932- DLB-60
Rylands, Enriqueta Augustina Tennant
    1843-1908 .... DLB-184
Rylands, John 1801-1888 .... DLB-184
Ryle, Gilbert 1900-1976 .... DLB-262
Ryleev, Kondratii Fedorovich
    1795-1826....................... DLB-205
Rymer, Thomas 1643?-1713............ DLB-101
Ryskind, Morrie 1895-1985 .... DLB-26
Rzhevsky, Aleksei Andreevich
    1737-1804 .... DLB-150

S

The Saalfield Publishing Company DLB-46
Saba, Umberto 1883-1957 .... DLB-114
Sábato, Ernesto 1911- DLB-145; CDWLB-3
Saberhagen, Fred 1930- DLB-8
Sabin, Joseph 1821-1881............... DLB-187
Sacer, Gottfried Wilhelm 1635-1699 .... DLB-168
Sachs, Hans 1494-1576......DLB-179; CDWLB-2
Sack, John 1930- DLB-185
Sackler, Howard 1929-1982 .... DLB 7
Sackville, Lady Margaret 1881-1963 .... DLB-240
Sackville, Thomas 1536-1608.......... DLB-132
Sackville, Thomas 1536-1608
    and Norton, Thomas 1532-1584 ..... DLB-62
Sackville-West, Edward 1901-1965 ..... DLB-191
Sackville-West, V. 1892-1962....... DLB-34, 195
Sadlier, D. and J., and Company DLB-49

Sadlier, Mary Anne 1820-1903.......... DLB-99
Sadoff, Ira 1945- DLB-120
Sadoveanu, Mihail 1880-1961 .... DLB-220
Sáenz, Benjamin Alire 1954- DLB-209
Saenz, Jaime 1921-1986 .... DLB-145
Saffin, John circa 1626-1710 .... DLB-24
Sagan, Françoise 1935- DLB-83
Sage, Robert 1899-1962 .... DLB-4
Sagel, Jim 1947- DLB-82
Sagendorph, Robb Hansell 1900-1970 ....DLB-137
Sahagún, Carlos 1938- DLB-108
Sahkomaapii, Piitai (see Highwater, Jamake)
Sahl, Hans 1902- DLB-69
Said, Edward W. 1935- DLB-67
Saigyō 1118-1190 .... DLB-203
Saiko, George 1892-1962 .... DLB-85
St. Dominic's Press................... DLB-112
Saint-Exupéry, Antoine de 1900-1944 .... DLB-72
St. John, J. Allen 1872-1957........... DLB-188
St John, Madeleine 1942- DLB-267
St. Johns, Adela Rogers 1894-1988....... DLB-29
The St. John's College Robert Graves Trust .. Y-96
St. Martin's Press DLB-46
St. Omer, Garth 1931- DLB-117
Saint Pierre, Michel de 1916-1987 .... DLB-83
Sainte-Beuve, Charles-Augustin
    1804-1869 ....DLB-217
Saints' Lives DLB-208
Saintsbury, George 1845-1933 ....DLB-57, 149
Saiokuken Sōchō 1448-1532............ DLB-203
Saki (see Munro, H. H.)
Salaam, Kalamu ya 1947- DLB-38
Šalamun, Tomaž 1941- DLB-181; CDWLB-4
Salas, Floyd 1931- DLB-82
Sálaz-Marquez, Rubén 1935- DLB-122
Salemson, Harold J. 1910-1988 .... DLB-4
Salesbury, William 1520?-1584? DLB-281
Salinas, Luis Omar 1937- DLB-82
Salinas, Pedro 1891-1951 .... DLB-134
Salinger, J. D.
    1919- DLB-2, 102, 173; CDALB-1
Salkey, Andrew 1928- DLB-125
Sallust circa 86 B.C.-35 B.C.
    ....DLB-211; CDWLB-1
Salt, Waldo 1914- DLB-44
Salter, James 1925- DLB-130
Salter, Mary Jo 1954- DLB-120, 282
Saltus, Edgar 1855-1921.............. DLB-202
Saltykov, Mikhail Evgrafovich
    1826-1889 .... DLB-238
Salustri, Carlo Alberto (see Trilussa)
Salverson, Laura Goodman 1890-1970.... DLB-92
Samain, Albert 1858-1900 ....DLB-217
Sampson, Richard Henry (see Hull, Richard)
Samuels, Ernest 1903-1996............ DLB-111

Sanborn, Franklin Benjamin 1831-1917 .... DLB-1, 223
Sánchez, Luis Rafael 1936- DLB-145
Sánchez, Philomeno "Phil" 1917- DLB-122
Sánchez, Ricardo 1941-1995 .... DLB-82
Sánchez, Saúl 1943- DLB-209
Sanchez, Sonia 1934- DLB-41; DS-8
Sand, George 1804-1876 .... DLB-119, 192
Sandburg, Carl 1878-1967 .... DLB-17, 54; CDALB-3
Sanders, Edward 1939- DLB-16, 244
Sanderson, Robert 1587-1663 .... DLB-281
Sandoz, Mari 1896-1966 .... DLB-9, 212
Sandwell, B. K. 1876-1954 .... DLB-92
Sandy, Stephen 1934- DLB-165
Sandys, George 1578-1644 .... DLB-24, 121
Sangster, Charles 1822-1893 .... DLB-99
Sanguineti, Edoardo 1930- DLB-128
Sanjōnishi Sanetaka 1455-1537 .... DLB-203
Sansay, Leonora ?-after 1823 .... DLB-200
Sansom, William 1912-1976 .... DLB-139
Santayana, George 1863-1952 .... DLB-54, 71, 246, 270; DS-13
Santiago, Danny 1911-1988 .... DLB-122
Santmyer, Helen Hooven 1895-1986 .... Y-84
Sanvitale, Francesca 1928- DLB-196
Sapidus, Joannes 1490-1561 .... DLB-179
Sapir, Edward 1884-1939 .... DLB-92
Sapper (see McNeile, Herman Cyril)
Sappho circa 620 B.C.-circa 550 B.C. DLB-176; CDWLB-1
Saramago, José 1922- Y-98
Sarban (John F. Wall) 1910-1989 .... DLB-255
Sardou, Victorien 1831-1908 .... DLB-192
Sarduy, Severo 1937- DLB-113
Sargent, Pamela 1948- DLB-8
Saro-Wiwa, Ken 1941- DLB-157
Saroyan, William 1908-1981 .... DLB-7, 9, 86; Y-81; CDALB-7
Sarraute, Nathalie 1900-1999 .... DLB-83
Sarrazin, Albertine 1937-1967 .... DLB-83
Sarris, Greg 1952- DLB-175
Sarton, May 1912-1995 .... DLB-48; Y-81
Sartre, Jean-Paul 1905-1980 .... DLB-72
Sassoon, Siegfried 1886-1967 .... DLB-20, 191; DS-18
Siegfried Loraine Sassoon: A Centenary Essay Tributes from Vivien F. Clarke and Michael Thorpe Y-86
Sata, Ineko 1904- DLB-180
Saturday Review Press DLB-46
Saunders, James 1925- DLB-13
Saunders, John Monk 1897-1940 .... DLB-26
Saunders, Margaret Marshall 1861-1947 .... DLB-92
Saunders and Otley DLB-106

Saussure, Ferdinand de 1857-1913 .... DLB-242
Savage, James 1784-1873 .... DLB-30
Savage, Marmion W. 1803?-1872 .... DLB-21
Savage, Richard 1697?-1743 .... DLB-95
Savard, Félix-Antoine 1896-1982 .... DLB-68
Savery, Henry 1791-1842 .... DLB-230
Saville, (Leonard) Malcolm 1901-1982 .... DLB-160
Savinio, Alberto 1891-1952 .... DLB-264
Sawyer, Robert J. 1960- DLB-251
Sawyer, Ruth 1880-1970 .... DLB-22
Sayers, Dorothy L. 1893-1957 .... DLB-10, 36, 77, 100; CDBLB-6
Sayle, Charles Edward 1864-1924 .... DLB-184
Sayles, John Thomas 1950- DLB-44
Sbarbaro, Camillo 1888-1967 .... DLB-114
Scalapino, Leslie 1947- DLB-193
Scannell, Vernon 1922- DLB-27
Scarry, Richard 1919-1994 .... DLB-61
Schaefer, Jack 1907-1991 .... DLB-212
Schaeffer, Albrecht 1885-1950 .... DLB-66
Schaeffer, Susan Fromberg 1941- DLB-28
Schaff, Philip 1819-1893 .... DS-13
Schaper, Edzard 1908-1984 .... DLB-69
Scharf, J. Thomas 1843-1898 .... DLB-47
Schede, Paul Melissus 1539-1602 .... DLB-179
Scheffel, Joseph Viktor von 1826-1886 .... DLB-129
Scheffler, Johann 1624-1677 .... DLB-164
Schelling, Friedrich Wilhelm Joseph von 1775-1854 .... DLB-90
Scherer, Wilhelm 1841-1886 .... DLB-129
Scherfig, Hans 1905-1979 .... DLB-214
Schickele, René 1883-1940 .... DLB-66
Schiff, Dorothy 1903-1989 .... DLB-127
Schiller, Friedrich 1759-1805 .... DLB-94; CDWLB-2
Schirmer, David 1623-1687 .... DLB-164
Schlaf, Johannes 1862-1941 .... DLB-118
Schlegel, August Wilhelm 1767-1845 .... DLB-94
Schlegel, Dorothea 1763-1839 .... DLB-90
Schlegel, Friedrich 1772-1829 .... DLB-90
Schleiermacher, Friedrich 1768-1834 .... DLB-90
Schlesinger, Arthur M., Jr. 1917- DLB-17
Schlumberger, Jean 1877-1968 .... DLB-65
Schmid, Eduard Hermann Wilhelm (see Edschmid, Kasimir)
Schmidt, Arno 1914-1979 .... DLB-69
Schmidt, Johann Kaspar (see Stirner, Max)
Schmidt, Michael 1947- DLB-40
Schmidtbonn, Wilhelm August 1876-1952 .... DLB-118
Schmitz, Aron Hector (see Svevo, Italo)
Schmitz, James H. 1911- DLB-8
Schnabel, Johann Gottfried 1692-1760 .... DLB-168
Schnackenberg, Gjertrud 1953- DLB-120, 282

Schnitzler, Arthur 1862-1931 .... DLB-81, 118; CDWLB-2
Schnurre, Wolfdietrich 1920-1989 .... DLB-69
Schocken Books DLB-46
Scholartis Press DLB-112
Scholderer, Victor 1880-1971 .... DLB-201
The Schomburg Center for Research in Black Culture DLB-76
Schönbeck, Virgilio (see Giotti, Virgilio)
Schönherr, Karl 1867-1943 .... DLB-118
Schoolcraft, Jane Johnston 1800-1841 .... DLB-175
School Stories, 1914-1960 .... DLB-160
Schopenhauer, Arthur 1788-1860 .... DLB-90
Schopenhauer, Johanna 1766-1838 .... DLB-90
Schorer, Mark 1908-1977 .... DLB-103
Schottelius, Justus Georg 1612-1676 .... DLB-164
Schouler, James 1839-1920 .... DLB-47
Schoultz, Solveig von 1907-1996 .... DLB-259
Schrader, Paul 1946- DLB-44
Schreiner, Olive 1855-1920 .... DLB-18, 156, 190, 225
Schroeder, Andreas 1946- DLB-53
Schubart, Christian Friedrich Daniel 1739-1791 .... DLB-97
Schubert, Gotthilf Heinrich 1780-1860 .... DLB-90
Schücking, Levin 1814-1883 .... DLB-133
Schulberg, Budd 1914- DLB-6, 26, 28; Y-81
Schulte, F. J., and Company DLB-49
Schulz, Bruno 1892-1942 .... DLB-215; CDWLB-4
Schulze, Hans (see Praetorius, Johannes)
Schupp, Johann Balthasar 1610-1661 .... DLB-164
Schurz, Carl 1829-1906 .... DLB-23
Schuyler, George S. 1895-1977 .... DLB-29, 51
Schuyler, James 1923-1991 .... DLB-5, 169
Schwartz, Delmore 1913-1966 .... DLB-28, 48
Schwartz, Jonathan 1938- Y-82
Schwartz, Lynne Sharon 1939- DLB-218
Schwarz, Sibylle 1621-1638 .... DLB-164
Schwerner, Armand 1927-1999 .... DLB-165
Schwob, Marcel 1867-1905 .... DLB-123
Sciascia, Leonardo 1921-1989 .... DLB-177
Science Fantasy DLB-8
Science-Fiction Fandom and Conventions DLB-8
Science-Fiction Fanzines: The Time Binders DLB-8
Science-Fiction Films DLB-8
Science Fiction Writers of America and the Nebula Awards DLB-8
Scot, Reginald circa 1538-1599 .... DLB-136
Scotellaro, Rocco 1923-1953 .... DLB-128
Scott, Alicia Anne (Lady John Scott) 1810-1900 .... DLB-240
Scott, Catharine Amy Dawson 1865-1934 .... DLB-240
Scott, Dennis 1939-1991 .... DLB-125
Scott, Dixon 1881-1915 .... DLB-98
Scott, Duncan Campbell 1862-1947 .... DLB-92

Scott, Evelyn 1893-1963 . . . . DLB-9, 48
Scott, F. R. 1899-1985. . . . . DLB-88
Scott, Frederick George 1861-1944. . . . . . . DLB-92
Scott, Geoffrey 1884-1929 . . . . DLB-149
Scott, Harvey W. 1838-1910 . . . . DLB-23
Scott, Lady Jane (see Scott, Alicia Anne)
Scott, Paul 1920-1978 . . . . DLB-14, 207
Scott, Sarah 1723-1795 . . . . DLB-39
Scott, Tom 1918- DLB-27
Scott, Sir Walter 1771-1832
 . . . . . . DLB-93, 107, 116, 144, 159; CDBLB-3
Scott, Walter, Publishing
 Company Limited DLB-112
Scott, William Bell 1811-1890 . . . . DLB-32
Scott, William R. [publishing house]. DLB-46
Scott-Heron, Gil 1949- DLB-41
Scribe, Eugene 1791-1861 . . . . DLB-192
Scribner, Arthur Hawley 1859-1932. . . . . DS-13, 16
Scribner, Charles 1854-1930. . . . . DS-13, 16
Scribner, Charles, Jr. 1921-1995 . . . . Y-95
Reminiscences. DS-17
Charles Scribner's Sons DLB-49; DS-13, 16, 17
Scripps, E. W. 1854-1926 . . . . DLB-25
Scudder, Horace Elisha 1838-1902. . . . DLB-42, 71
Scudder, Vida Dutton 1861-1954. . . . . DLB-71
Scudéry, Madeleine de 1607-1701 . . . . DLB-268
Scupham, Peter 1933- DLB-40
Seabrook, William 1886-1945 . . . . DLB-4
Seabury, Samuel 1729-1796 . . . . DLB-31
Seacole, Mary Jane Grant 1805-1881 . . . . DLB-166
The Seafarer circa 970. . . . . DLB-146
Sealsfield, Charles (Carl Postl)
 1793-1864. . . . . DLB-133, 186
Searle, John R. 1932- DLB-279
Sears, Edward I. 1819?-1876. . . . . DLB-79
Sears Publishing Company. DLB-46
Seaton, George 1911-1979 . . . . DLB-44
Seaton, William Winston 1785-1866 . . . . . DLB-43
Secker, Martin [publishing house]. DLB-112
Secker, Martin, and Warburg Limited . . . DLB-112
The Second Annual New York Festival
 of Mystery Y-00
Second-Generation Minor Poets of the
 Seventeenth Century. DLB-126
Sedgwick, Arthur George 1844-1915 . . . . . DLB-64
Sedgwick, Catharine Maria
 1789-1867. . . . . DLB-1, 74, 183, 239, 243
Sedgwick, Ellery 1872-1960 . . . . DLB-91
Sedgwick, Eve Kosofsky 1950- DLB-246
Sedley, Sir Charles 1639-1701. . . . . DLB-131
Seeberg, Peter 1925-1999 . . . . DLB-214
Seeger, Alan 1888-1916 . . . . DLB-45
Seers, Eugene (see Dantin, Louis)
Segal, Erich 1937- Y-86
Šegedin, Petar 1909- DLB-181
Seghers, Anna 1900-1983 . . . . DLB-69; CDWLB-2

Seid, Ruth (see Sinclair, Jo)
Seidel, Frederick Lewis 1936- Y-84
Seidel, Ina 1885-1974 . . . . DLB-56
Seifert, Jaroslav
 1901-1986 . . . . DLB-215; Y-84; CDWLB-4
Seifullina, Lidiia Nikolaevna 1889-1954 . . . DLB-272
Seigenthaler, John 1927- DLB-127
Seizin Press DLB-112
Séjour, Victor 1817-1874. . . . . DLB-50
Séjour Marcou et Ferrand, Juan Victor
 (see Séjour, Victor)
Sekowski, Józef-Julian, Baron Brambeus
 (see Senkovsky, Osip Ivanovich)
Selby, Bettina 1934- DLB-204
Selby, Hubert, Jr. 1928- DLB-2, 227
Selden, George 1929-1989 . . . . DLB-52
Selden, John 1584-1654 . . . . DLB-213
Selected English-Language Little Magazines
 and Newspapers [France, 1920-1939]. . . DLB-4
Selected Humorous Magazines
 (1820-1950) DLB-11
Selected Science-Fiction Magazines and
 Anthologies DLB-8
Selenić, Slobodan 1933-1995 . . . . DLB-181
Self, Edwin F. 1920- DLB-137
Self, Will 1961- DLB-207
Seligman, Edwin R. A. 1861-1939 . . . . DLB-47
Selimović, Meša
 1910-1982 . . . . DLB-181; CDWLB-4
Sellars, Wilfrid 1912-1989 . . . . DLB-279
Sellings, Arthur 1911-1968 . . . . DLB-261
Selous, Frederick Courteney
 1851-1917. . . . . DLB-174
Seltzer, Chester E. (see Muro, Amado)
Seltzer, Thomas [publishing house] DLB-46
Selvon, Sam 1923-1994 . . . . DLB-125; CDWLB-3
Semmes, Raphael 1809-1877 . . . . DLB-189
Senancour, Etienne de 1770-1846 . . . . DLB-119
Sendak, Maurice 1928- DLB-61
Seneca the Elder
 circa 54 B.C.-circa A.D. 40. . . . . DLB-211
Seneca the Younger
 circa 1 B.C.-A.D. 65. . . . . DLB-211; CDWLB-1
Senécal, Eva 1905- DLB-92
Sengstacke, John 1912- DLB-127
Senior, Olive 1941- DLB-157
Senkovsky, Osip Ivanovich
 (Józef-Julian Sekowski, Baron Brambeus)
 1800-1858 . . . . DLB-198
Šenoa, August 1838-1881 . . . . DLB-147; CDWLB-4
"Sensation Novels" (1863), by
 H. L. Manse. DLB-21
Sepamla, Sipho 1932- DLB-157, 225
Serafimovich, Aleksandr Serafimovich
 (Aleksandr Serafimovich Popov)
 1863-1949 . . . . DLB-272
Serao, Matilde 1856-1927 . . . . DLB-264
Seredy, Kate 1899-1975 . . . . DLB-22
Sereni, Vittorio 1913-1983 . . . . DLB-128

Seres, William [publishing house]. DLB-170
Sergeev-Tsensky, Sergei Nikolaevich (Sergei
 Nikolaevich Sergeev) 1875-1958 . . . . . DLB-272
Serling, Rod 1924-1975. . . . . DLB-26
Sernine, Daniel 1955- DLB-251
Serote, Mongane Wally 1944- . . . DLB-125, 225
Serraillier, Ian 1912-1994 . . . . DLB-161
Serrano, Nina 1934- DLB-122
Service, Robert 1874-1958 . . . . DLB-92
Sessler, Charles 1854-1935 . . . . DLB-187
Seth, Vikram 1952- DLB-120, 271, 282
Seton, Elizabeth Ann 1774-1821 . . . . DLB-200
Seton, Ernest Thompson
 1860-1942 . . . . DLB-92; DS-13
Seton, John circa 1509-1567 . . . . DLB-281
Setouchi Harumi 1922- DLB-182
Settle, Mary Lee 1918- DLB-6
Seume, Johann Gottfried 1763-1810 . . . . . DLB-94
Seuse, Heinrich 1295?-1366 . . . . DLB-179
Seuss, Dr. (see Geisel, Theodor Seuss)
"The Greatness of Southern Literature":
 League of the South Institute for the
 Study of Southern Culture and History
 . . . . Y-02
The Seventy-fifth Anniversary of the Armistice:
 The Wilfred Owen Centenary and
 the Great War Exhibit
 at the University of Virginia Y-93
Severin, Timothy 1940- DLB-204
Sévigné, Marie de Rabutin Chantal,
 Madame de 1626-1696 . . . . DLB-268
Sewall, Joseph 1688-1769 . . . . DLB-24
Sewall, Richard B. 1908- DLB-111
Sewell, Anna 1820-1878 . . . . DLB-163
Sewell, Samuel 1652-1730. . . . . DLB-24
Sex, Class, Politics, and Religion [in the
 British Novel, 1930-1959] DLB-15
Sexton, Anne 1928-1974. . . DLB-5, 169; CDALB-1
Seymour-Smith, Martin 1928-1998 . . . . . DLB-155
Sgorlon, Carlo 1930- DLB-196
Shaara, Michael 1929-1988 . . . . Y-83
Shabel'skaia, Aleksandra Stanislavovna
 1845-1921 . . . . DLB-238
Shadwell, Thomas 1641?-1692. . . . . DLB-80
Shaffer, Anthony 1926- DLB-13
Shaffer, Peter 1926- DLB-13, 233; CDBLB-8
Shaftesbury, Anthony Ashley Cooper,
 Third Earl of 1671-1713 . . . . DLB-101
Shaginian, Marietta Sergeevna
 1888-1982 . . . . DLB-272
Shairp, Mordaunt 1887-1939 . . . . DLB-10
Shakespeare, Nicholas 1957- DLB-231
Shakespeare, William
 1564-1616 . . . . . DLB-62, 172, 263; CDBLB-1
Shakespeare and Montaigne: A Symposium
 by Jules Furthman Y-02
$6,166,000 for a *Book!* Observations on
 *The Shakespeare First Folio: The History
 of the Book* Y-01
The Shakespeare Globe Trust Y-93

Shakespeare Head Press DLB-112
Shakhova, Elizaveta Nikitichna
    1822-1899 ....DLB-277
Shakhovskoi, Aleksandr Aleksandrovich
    1777-1846.......................DLB-150
Shange, Ntozake 1948- DLB-38, 249
Shapiro, Karl 1913-2000 ....DLB-48
Sharon Publications DLB-46
Sharp, Margery 1905-1991 ....DLB-161
Sharp, William 1855-1905 ....DLB-156
Sharpe, Tom 1928- DLB-14, 231
Shaw, Albert 1857-1947 ....DLB-91
Shaw, George Bernard
    1856-1950 .... DLB-10, 57, 190, CDBLB-6
Shaw, Henry Wheeler 1818-1885 ....DLB-11
Shaw, Joseph T. 1874-1952 ....DLB-137
Shaw, Irwin
    1913-1984 ...... DLB-6, 102; Y-84; CDALB-1
Shaw, Mary 1854-1929 ....DLB-228
Shaw, Robert 1927-1978............DLB-13, 14
Shaw, Robert B. 1947- DLB-120
Shawn, Wallace 1943- DLB-266
Shawn, William 1907-1992 ....DLB-137
Shay, Frank [publishing house] DLB-46
Shchedrin, N. (see Saltykov, Mikhail Evgrafovich)
Shcherbina, Nikolai Fedorovich
    1821-1869 ....DLB-277
Shea, John Gilmary 1824-1892 ....DLB-30
Sheaffer, Louis 1912-1993 ....DLB-103
Shearing, Joseph 1886-1952.........DLB-70
Shebbeare, John 1709-1788..........DLB-39
Sheckley, Robert 1928- DLB-8
Shedd, William G. T. 1820-1894........DLB-64
Sheed, Wilfred 1930- DLB-6
Sheed and Ward [U.S.] DLB-46
Sheed and Ward Limited [U.K.] DLB-112
Sheldon, Alice B. (see Tiptree, James, Jr.)
Sheldon, Edward 1886-1946 ....DLB-7
Sheldon and Company DLB-49
Sheller, Aleksandr Konstantinovich
    1838-1900 ....DLB-238
Shelley, Mary Wollstonecraft 1797-1851
    .... DLB-110, 116, 159, 178; CDBLB-3
Shelley, Percy Bysshe
    1792-1822 ...... DLB-96, 110, 158; CDBLB-3
Shelnutt, Eve 1941- DLB-130
Shenshin (see Fet, Afanasy Afanas'evich)
Shenstone, William 1714-1763 ....DLB-95
Shepard, Clark and Brown DLB-49
Shepard, Ernest Howard 1879-1976......DLB-160
Shepard, Sam 1943- DLB-7, 212
Shepard, Thomas I, 1604 or 1605-1649 ...DLB-24
Shepard, Thomas, II, 1635-1677 ......DLB-24
Shepherd, Luke
    flourished 1547-1554 ....DLB-136
Sherburne, Edward 1616-1702........DLB-131
Sheridan, Frances 1724-1766 ......DLB-39, 84

Sheridan, Richard Brinsley
    1751-1816 .... DLB-89; CDBLB-2
Sherman, Francis 1871-1926 ....DLB-92
Sherman, Martin 1938- DLB-228
Sherriff, R. C. 1896-1975 .... DLB-10, 191, 233
Sherrod, Blackie 1919- DLB-241
Sherry, Norman 1935- DLB-155
Sherry, Richard 1506-1551 or 1555......DLB-236
Sherwood, Mary Martha 1775-1851 .....DLB-163
Sherwood, Robert E. 1896-1955 ... DLB-7, 26, 249
Shevyrev, Stepan Petrovich
    1806-1864 ....DLB-205
Shiel, M. P. 1865-1947...............DLB-153
Shiels, George 1886-1949 ....DLB-10
Shiga, Naoya 1883-1971..............DLB-180
Shiina Rinzō 1911-1973 ....DLB-182
Shikishi Naishinnō 1153?-1201 ....DLB-203
Shillaber, Benjamin Penhallow
    1814-1890 .... DLB-1, 11, 235
Shimao Toshio 1917-1986 ....DLB-182
Shimazaki, Tōson 1872-1943 ....DLB-180
Shine, Ted 1931- DLB-38
Shinkei 1406-1475 ....DLB-203
Ship, Reuben 1915-1975 ....DLB-88
Shirer, William L. 1904-1993 ....DLB-4
Shirinsky-Shikhmatov, Sergii Aleksandrovich
    1783-1837 ....DLB-150
Shirley, James 1596-1666...............DLB-58
Shishkov, Aleksandr Semenovich
    1753-1841 ....DLB-150
Shockley, Ann Allen 1927- DLB-33
Sholokhov, Mikhail Aleksandrovich
    1905-1984 ....DLB-272
Shōno Junzō 1921- DLB-182
Shore, Arabella 1820?-1901 and
    Shore, Louisa 1824-1895...........DLB-199
Short, Luke (see Glidden, Frederick Dilley)
Short, Peter [publishing house] DLB-170
Shorter, Dora Sigerson 1866-1918......DLB-240
Shorthouse, Joseph Henry 1834-1903 .....DLB-18
Shōtetsu 1381-1459 ....DLB-203
Showalter, Elaine 1941- DLB-67
Shulevitz, Uri 1935- DLB-61
Shulman, Max 1919-1988 ....DLB-11
Shute, Henry A. 1856-1943..............DLB-9
Shute, Nevil 1899-1960 ....DLB-255
Shuttle, Penelope 1947- DLB-14, 40
Shvarts, Evgenii L'vovich 1896-1958......DLB-272
Sibbes, Richard 1577-1635 ....DLB-151
Sibiriak, D. (see Mamin, Dmitrii Narkisovich)
Siddal, Elizabeth Eleanor 1829-1862 ....DLB-199
Sidgwick, Ethel 1877-1970 ....DLB-197
Sidgwick, Henry 1838-1900...........DLB-262
Sidgwick and Jackson Limited DLB-112
Sidney, Margaret (see Lothrop, Harriet M.)
Sidney, Mary 1561-1621 ....DLB-167

Sidney, Sir Philip
    1554-1586 .... DLB-167; CDBLB-1
An Apologie for Poetrie (the Olney
    edition, 1595, of Defence of Poesie)......DLB-167
Sidney's Press DLB-49
Sierra, Rubén 1946- DLB-122
Sierra Club Books DLB-49
Siger of Brabant circa 1240-circa 1284....DLB-115
Sigourney, Lydia Huntley
    1791-1865 ...... DLB-1, 42, 73, 183, 239, 243
Silkin, Jon 1930- DLB-27
Silko, Leslie Marmon
    1948- DLB-143, 175, 256, 275
Silliman, Benjamin 1779-1864 ....DLB-183
Silliman, Ron 1946- DLB-169
Silliphant, Stirling 1918- DLB-26
Sillitoe, Alan 1928- DLB-14, 139; CDBLB-8
Silman, Roberta 1934- DLB-28
Silone, Ignazio (Secondino Tranquilli)
    1900-1978 ....DLB-264
Silva, Beverly 1930- DLB-122
Silverberg, Robert 1935- DLB-8
Silverman, Kaja 1947- DLB-246
Silverman, Kenneth 1936- DLB-111
Simak, Clifford D. 1904-1988 ....DLB-8
Simcoe, Elizabeth 1762-1850 ....DLB-99
Simcox, Edith Jemima 1844-1901 ....DLB-190
Simcox, George Augustus 1841-1905 .....DLB-35
Sime, Jessie Georgina 1868-1958 ....DLB-92
Simenon, Georges 1903-1989 ...... DLB-72; Y-89
Simic, Charles 1938- DLB-105
    "Images and 'Images,'"..............DLB-105
Simionescu, Mircea Horia 1928- DLB-232
Simmel, Johannes Mario 1924- DLB-69
Simmes, Valentine [publishing house] DLB-170
Simmons, Ernest J. 1903-1972 ....DLB-103
Simmons, Herbert Alfred 1930- DLB-33
Simmons, James 1933- DLB-40
Simms, William Gilmore
    1806-1870 .... DLB-3, 30, 59, 73, 248
Simms and M'Intyre DLB-106
Simon, Claude 1913- DLB-83; Y-85
Simon, Neil 1927- DLB-7, 266
Simon and Schuster DLB-46
Simons, Katherine Drayton Mayrant
    1890-1969 ....Y-83
Simović, Ljubomir 1935- DLB-181
Simpkin and Marshall
    [publishing house] DLB-154
Simpson, Helen 1897-1940............DLB-77
Simpson, Louis 1923- DLB-5
Simpson, N. F. 1919- DLB-13
Sims, George 1923- DLB-87; Y-99
Sims, George Robert 1847-1922... DLB-35, 70, 135
Sinán, Rogelio 1904- DLB-145
Sinclair, Andrew 1935- DLB-14
Sinclair, Bertrand William 1881-1972 .....DLB-92

Sinclair, Catherine 1800-1864 . . . . DLB-163	Sluchevsky, Konstantin Konstantinovich 1837-1904 . . . . DLB-277	Smith, John 1580-1631 . . . . DLB-24, 30
Sinclair, Jo 1913-1995 . . . . DLB-28	Small, Maynard and Company DLB-49	Smith, John 1618-1652 . . . . DLB-252
Sinclair, Lister 1921- DLB-88	Small Presses in Great Britain and Ireland, 1960-1985 . . . . DLB-40	Smith, John fl. 1657 . . . . DLB-281
Sinclair, May 1863-1946 . . . . DLB-36, 135		Smith, Josiah 1704-1781 . . . . DLB-24
Sinclair, Upton 1878-1968 . . . . . DLB-9; CDALB-5	Small Presses I: Jargon Society Y-84	Smith, Ken 1938- DLB-40
Sinclair, Upton [publishing house] DLB-46	Small Presses II: The Spirit That Moves Us Press Y-85	Smith, Lee 1944- DLB-143; Y-83
Singer, Isaac Bashevis 1904-1991 . . . . DLB-6, 28, 52, 278; Y-91; CDALB-1	Small Presses III: Pushcart Press Y-87	Smith, Logan Pearsall 1865-1946 . . . . DLB-98
	Smart, Christopher 1722-1771 . . . . DLB-109	Smith, Margaret Bayard 1778-1844 . . . . . DLB-248
Singer, Mark 1950- DLB-185	Smart, David A. 1892-1957 . . . . DLB-137	Smith, Mark 1935- Y-82
Singmaster, Elsie 1879-1958 . . . . DLB-9	Smart, Elizabeth 1913-1986 . . . . DLB-88	Smith, Michael 1698-circa 1771 . . . . DLB-31
Sinisgalli, Leonardo 1908-1981 . . . . DLB-114	Smart, J. J. C. 1920- DLB-262	Smith, Pauline 1882-1959 . . . . DLB-225
Siodmak, Curt 1902-2000 . . . . DLB-44	Smedley, Menella Bute 1820?-1877 . . . . . DLB-199	Smith, Red 1905-1982 . . . . DLB-29, 171
Sîrbu, Ion D. 1919-1989 . . . . DLB-232	Smellie, William [publishing house] DLB-154	Smith, Roswell 1829-1892 . . . . DLB-79
Siringo, Charles A. 1855-1928 . . . . DLB-186	Smiles, Samuel 1812-1904 . . . . DLB-55	Smith, Samuel Harrison 1772-1845 . . . . . DLB-43
Sissman, L. E. 1928-1976 . . . . DLB-5	Smiley, Jane 1949- DLB-227, 234	Smith, Samuel Stanhope 1751-1819 . . . . . DLB-37
Sisson, C. H. 1914- DLB-27	Smith, A. J. M. 1902-1980 . . . . DLB-88	Smith, Sarah (see Stretton, Hesba)
Sitwell, Edith 1887-1964 . . . . . . DLB-20; CDBLB-7	Smith, Adam 1723-1790 . . . . DLB-104, 252	Smith, Sarah Pogson 1774-1870 . . . . DLB-200
Sitwell, Osbert 1892-1969 . . . . DLB-100, 195	Smith, Adam (George Jerome Waldo Goodman) 1930- DLB-185	Smith, Seba 1792-1868 . . . . DLB-1, 11, 243
Skácel, Jan 1922-1989 . . . . DLB-232		Smith, Stevie 1902-1971 . . . . DLB-20
Skalbe, Kārlis 1879-1945 . . . . DLB-220	Smith, Alexander 1829-1867 . . . . DLB-32, 55	Smith, Sydney 1771-1845 . . . . DLB-107
Skármeta, Antonio 1940- DLB-145; CDWLB-3	"On the Writing of Essays" (1862) DLB-57	Smith, Sydney Goodsir 1915-1975 . . . . . . DLB-27
	Smith, Amanda 1837-1915 . . . . DLB-221	Smith, Sir Thomas 1513-1577 . . . . DLB-132
Skavronsky, A. (see Danilevsky, Grigorii Petrovich)	Smith, Betty 1896-1972 . . . . Y-82	Smith, W. B., and Company DLB-49
Skeat, Walter W. 1835-1912 . . . . DLB-184	Smith, Carol Sturm 1938- Y-81	Smith, W. H., and Son DLB-106
Skeffington, William [publishing house] DLB-106	Smith, Charles Henry 1826-1903 . . . . DLB-11	Smith, Wendell 1914-1972 . . . . DLB-171
	Smith, Charlotte 1749-1806 . . . . DLB-39, 109	Smith, William flourished 1595-1597 . . . . DLB-136
Skelton, John 1463-1529 . . . . DLB-136	Smith, Chet 1899-1973 . . . . DLB-171	Smith, William 1727-1803 . . . . DLB-31
Skelton, Robin 1925- DLB-27, 53	Smith, Cordwainer 1913-1966 . . . . DLB-8	*A General Idea of the College of Mirania* (1753) [excerpts] DLB-31
Škėma, Antanas 1910-1961 . . . . DLB-220	Smith, Dave 1942- DLB-5	
Skinner, Constance Lindsay 1877-1939 . . . . DLB-92	Smith, Dodie 1896- DLB-10	Smith, William 1728-1793 . . . . DLB-30
	Smith, Doris Buchanan 1934- DLB-52	Smith, William Gardner 1927-1974 . . . . . DLB-76
Skinner, John Stuart 1788-1851 . . . . DLB-73	Smith, E. E. 1890-1965 . . . . DLB-8	Smith, William Henry 1808-1872 . . . . DLB-159
Skipsey, Joseph 1832-1903 . . . . DLB-35	Smith, Elder and Company DLB-154	Smith, William Jay 1918- DLB-5
Skou-Hansen, Tage 1925- DLB-214	Smith, Elihu Hubbard 1771-1798 . . . . DLB-37	Smithers, Leonard [publishing house] . . . DLB-112
Škvorecký, Josef 1924- DLB-232; CDWLB-4		Smollett, Tobias 1721-1771 . . . . DLB-39, 104; CDBLB-2
Slade, Bernard 1930- DLB-53	Smith, Elizabeth Oakes (Prince) (see Oakes Smith, Elizabeth)	
Slamnig, Ivan 1930- DLB-181	Smith, Eunice 1757-1823 . . . . DLB-200	Dedication, *Ferdinand Count Fathom* (1753) DLB-39
Slančeková, Božena (see Timrava)	Smith, F. Hopkinson 1838-1915 . . . . DS-13	
Slataper, Scipio 1888-1915 . . . . DLB-264	Smith, George D. 1870-1920 . . . . DLB-140	Preface to *Ferdinand Count Fathom* (1753) . . . DLB-39
Slater, Patrick 1880-1951 . . . . DLB-68	Smith, George O. 1911-1981 . . . . DLB-8	Preface to *Roderick Random* (1748) . . . DLB-39
Slaveykov, Pencho 1866-1912 . . . . DLB-147	Smith, Goldwin 1823-1910 . . . . DLB-99	Smythe, Francis Sydney 1900-1949 . . . . . DLB-195
Slaviček, Milivoj 1929- DLB-181	Smith, H. Allen 1907-1976 . . . . DLB-11, 29	Snelling, William Joseph 1804-1848 . . . . . DLB-202
Slavitt, David 1935- DLB-5, 6	Smith, Harrison, and Robert Haas [publishing house] DLB-46	Snellings, Rolland (see Touré, Askia Muhammad)
Sleigh, Burrows Willcocks Arthur 1821-1869 . . . . DLB-99		Snodgrass, W. D. 1926- DLB-5
	Smith, Harry B. 1860-1936 . . . . DLB-187	Snow, C. P. 1905-1980 . . . . DLB-15, 77; DS-17; CDBLB-7
A Slender Thread of Hope: The Kennedy Center Black Theatre Project DLB-38	Smith, Hazel Brannon 1914- DLB-127	
	Smith, Henry circa 1560-circa 1591 . . . . . DLB-136	Snyder, Gary 1930- DLB-5, 16, 165, 212, 237, 275
Sleptsov, Vasilii Alekseevich 1836-1878 . . . DLB-277	Smith, Horatio (Horace) 1779-1849 . . . . . DLB-116	
Slesinger, Tess 1905-1945 . . . . DLB-102	Smith, Horatio (Horace) 1779-1849 and James Smith 1775-1839 . . . . DLB-96	Sobiloff, Hy 1912-1970 . . . . DLB-48
Slessor, Kenneth 1901-1971 . . . . DLB-260		The Society for Textual Scholarship and *TEXT* Y-87
Slick, Sam (see Haliburton, Thomas Chandler)	Smith, Iain Crichton 1928- DLB-40, 139	
Sloan, John 1871-1951 . . . . DLB-188	Smith, J. Allen 1860-1924 . . . . DLB-47	The Society for the History of Authorship, Reading and Publishing Y-92
Sloane, William, Associates DLB-46	Smith, J. Stilman, and Company DLB-49	Söderberg, Hjalmar 1869-1941 . . . . DLB-259
Slonimsky, Mikhail Leonidovich 1897-1972 . . . . DLB-272	Smith, Jessie Willcox 1863-1935 . . . . DLB-188	Södergran, Edith 1892-1923 . . . . DLB-259
		Soffici, Ardengo 1879-1964 . . . . DLB-114, 264

Sofola, 'Zulu 1938- DLB-157
Sokhanskaia, Nadezhda Stepanova
 (Kokhanovskaia) 1823-1884 ....DLB-277
Solano, Solita 1888-1975 ....DLB-4
Soldati, Mario 1906-1999...............DLB-177
Šoljan, Antun 1932-1993 ....DLB-181
Sollers, Philippe 1936- DLB-83
Sollogub, Vladimir Aleksandrovich
 1813-1882 ....DLB-198
Sollors, Werner 1943- DBL-246
Solmi, Sergio 1899-1981 ....DLB-114
Solomon, Carl 1928- DLB-16
Solway, David 1941- DLB-53
Solzhenitsyn and America Y-85
Some Basic Notes on Three Modern Genres:
 Interview, Blurb, and Obituary.........Y-02
Somerville, Edith Œnone 1858-1949.....DLB-135
Somov, Orest Mikhailovich
 1793-1833 ....DLB-198
Sønderby, Knud 1909-1966..........DLB-214
Song, Cathy 1955- DLB-169
Sonnevi, Göran 1939- DLB-257
Sono Ayako 1931- DLB-182
Sontag, Susan 1933- DLB-2, 67
Sophocles 497/496 B.C.-406/405 B.C.
 ....DLB-176; CDWLB-1
Šopov, Aco 1923-1982................DLB-181
Sorel, Charles ca.1600-1674.............DLB-268
Sørensen, Villy 1929- DLB-214
Sorensen, Virginia 1912-1991 ....DLB-206
Sorge, Reinhard Johannes 1892-1916 ....DLB-118
Sorrentino, Gilbert 1929-   DLB-5, 173; Y-80
Sotheby, James 1682-1742.............DLB-213
Sotheby, John 1740-1807 ....DLB-213
Sotheby, Samuel 1771-1842 ....DLB-213
Sotheby, Samuel Leigh 1805-1861.......DLB-213
Sotheby, William 1757-1833.........DLB-93, 213
Soto, Gary 1952- DLB-82
Sources for the Study of Tudor and Stuart
 Drama.................................DLB-62
Soueif, Ahdaf 1950- DLB-267
Souster, Raymond 1921- DLB-88
The *South English Legendary* circa thirteenth-fifteenth
 centuries.............................DLB-146
Southerland, Ellease 1943- DLB-33
Southern, Terry 1924-1995 ....DLB-2
Southern Illinois University Press Y-95
"The Greatness of Southern Literature":
 League of the South Institute for the
 Study of Southern Culture and History
 ....Y-02
Southern Writers Between the Wars.......DLB-9
Southerne, Thomas 1659-1746 ....DLB-80
Southey, Caroline Anne Bowles
 1786-1854 ....DLB-116
Southey, Robert 1774-1843 .....DLB-93, 107, 142
Southwell, Robert 1561?-1595..........DLB-167
Southworth, E. D. E. N. 1819-1899......DLB-239

Sowande, Bode 1948- DLB-157
Sowle, Tace [publishing house] DLB-170
Soyfer, Jura 1912-1939...............DLB-124
Soyinka, Wole
 1934- ... DLB-125; Y-86, Y-87; CDWLB-3
Spacks, Barry 1931- DLB-105
Spalding, Frances 1950- DLB-155
Spark, Muriel 1918- DLB-15, 139; CDBLB-7
Sparke, Michael [publishing house] DLB-170
Sparks, Jared 1789-1866.........DLB-1, 30, 235
Sparshott, Francis 1926- DLB-60
Späth, Gerold 1939- DLB-75
Spatola, Adriano 1941-1988............DLB-128
Spaziani, Maria Luisa 1924- DLB-128
Special Collections at the University of Colorado
 at Boulder Y-98
The Spectator 1828- DLB-110
Spedding, James 1808-1881............DLB-144
Spee von Langenfeld, Friedrich
 1591-1635 ....DLB-164
Speght, Rachel 1597-after 1630 ....DLB-126
Speke, John Hanning 1827-1864 ....DLB-166
Spellman, A. B. 1935- DLB-41
Spence, Catherine Helen 1825-1910 ....DLB-230
Spence, Thomas 1750-1814 ....DLB-158
Spencer, Anne 1882-1975.............DLB-51, 54
Spencer, Charles, third Earl of Sunderland
 1674-1722 ....DLB-213
Spencer, Elizabeth 1921- DLB-6, 218
Spencer, George John, Second Earl Spencer
 1758-1834 ....DLB-184
Spencer, Herbert 1820-1903 ....DLB-57, 262
 "The Philosophy of Style" (1852) DLB-57
Spencer, Scott 1945- Y-86
Spender, J. A. 1862-1942..............DLB-98
Spender, Stephen 1909-1995 .. DLB-20; CDBLB-7
Spener, Philipp Jakob 1635-1705 ....DLB-164
Spenser, Edmund
 circa 1552-1599.........DLB-167; CDBLB-1
 Envoy from *The Shepheardes Calender* DLB-167
 "The Generall Argument of the
  Whole Booke," from
  The Shepheardes Calender DLB-167
 "A Letter of the Authors Expounding
  His Whole Intention in the Course
  of this Worke: Which for that It Giueth
  Great Light to the Reader, for the Better
  Vnderstanding Is Hereunto Annexed,"
  from *The Faerie Queene* (1590)........DLB-167
 "To His Booke," from
  The Shepheardes Calender (1579)......DLB-167
 "To the Most Excellent and Learned Both
  Orator and Poete, Mayster Gabriell Haruey,
  His Verie Special and Singular Good Frend
  E. K. Commendeth the Good Lyking of
  This His Labour, and the Patronage of
  the New Poete," from
  The Shepheardes Calender DLB-167
Sperr, Martin 1944- DLB-124
Spewack, Samuel 1899-1971 and
 Bella 1899-1990..................DLB-266

Spicer, Jack 1925-1965...........DLB-5, 16, 193
Spielberg, Peter 1929- Y-81
Spielhagen, Friedrich 1829-1911 ....DLB-129
"Spielmannsepen" (circa 1152-circa 1500) ...DLB-148
Spier, Peter 1927- DLB-61
Spillane, Mickey 1918- DLB-226
Spink, J. G. Taylor 1888-1962..........DLB-241
Spinrad, Norman 1940- DLB-8
Spires, Elizabeth 1952- DLB-120
Spitteler, Carl 1845-1924..............DLB-129
Spivak, Lawrence E. 1900- DLB-137
Spofford, Harriet Prescott
 1835-1921 ....DLB-74, 221
Sprigge, T. L. S. 1932- DLB-262
Spring, Howard 1889-1965 ....DLB-191
Squibob (see Derby, George Horatio)
Squier, E. G. 1821-1888................DLB-189
Stableford, Brian 1948- DLB-261
Stacpoole, H. de Vere 1863-1951 ......DLB-153
Staël, Germaine de 1766-1817 ......DLB-119, 192
Staël-Holstein, Anne-Louise Germaine de
 (see Staël, Germaine de)
Stafford, Jean 1915-1979 ....DLB-2, 173
Stafford, William 1914-1993 ....DLB-5, 206
Stage Censorship: "The Rejected Statement"
 (1911), by Bernard Shaw [excerpts] ...DLB-10
Stallings, Laurence 1894-1968 ....DLB-7, 44
Stallworthy, Jon 1935- DLB-40
Stampp, Kenneth M. 1912- DLB-17
Stănescu, Nichita 1933-1983 ....DLB-232
Stanev, Emiliyan 1907-1979 ....DLB-181
Stanford, Ann 1916- DLB-5
Stangerup, Henrik 1937-1998 ....DLB-214
Stanihurst, Richard 1547-1618.........DLB-281
Stanitsky, N. (see Panaeva, Avdot'ia Iakovlevna)
Stankevich, Nikolai Vladimirovich
 1813-1840 ....DLB-198
Stanković, Borisav ("Bora")
 1876-1927 ....DLB-147; CDWLB-4
Stanley, Henry M. 1841-1904 ....DLB-189; DS-13
Stanley, Thomas 1625-1678............DLB-131
Stannard, Martin 1947- DLB-155
Stansby, William [publishing house] DLB-170
Stanton, Elizabeth Cady 1815-1902.......DLB-79
Stanton, Frank L. 1857-1927 ....DLB-25
Stanton, Maura 1946- DLB-120
Stapledon, Olaf 1886-1950 ....DLB-15, 255
Star Spangled Banner Office DLB-49
Stark, Freya 1893-1993 ....DLB-195
Starkey, Thomas circa 1499-1538 ....DLB-132
Starkie, Walter 1894-1976 ....DLB-195
Starkweather, David 1935- DLB-7
Starrett, Vincent 1886-1974 ....DLB-187
The State of Publishing Y-97
Statements on the Art of Poetry..........DLB-54
Stationers' Company of London, The.... DLB-170

Cumulative Index

Statius circa A.D. 45-A.D. 96 .... DLB-211
Stead, Christina 1902-1983............ DLB-260
Stead, Robert J. C. 1880-1959 .... DLB-92
Steadman, Mark 1930- DLB-6
The Stealthy School of Criticism (1871), by
    Dante Gabriel Rossetti................ DLB-35
Stearns, Harold E. 1891-1943.......... DLB-4
Stebnitsky, M. (see Leskov, Nikolai Semenovich)
Stedman, Edmund Clarence 1833-1908 ... DLB-64
Steegmuller, Francis 1906-1994 .... DLB-111
Steel, Flora Annie 1847-1929........ DLB-153, 156
Steele, Max 1922- Y-80
Steele, Richard
    1672-1729.......... DLB-84, 101; CDBLB-2
Steele, Timothy 1948- DLB-120, 282
Steele, Wilbur Daniel 1886-1970 .... DLB-86
Wallace Markfield's "Steeplechase" Y-02
Steere, Richard circa 1643-1721 .... DLB-24
Stefanovski, Goran 1952- DLB-181
Stegner, Wallace
    1909-1993 .... DLB-9, 206, 275; Y-93
Stehr, Hermann 1864-1940 .... DLB-66
Steig, William 1907- DLB-61
Stein, Gertrude 1874-1946
    .... DLB-4, 54, 86, 228; DS-15; CDALB-4
Stein, Leo 1872-1947................. DLB-4
Stein and Day Publishers DLB-46
Steinbeck, John 1902-1968
    ....DLB-7, 9, 212, 275; DS-2; CDALB-5
John Steinbeck Research Center........... Y-85
The Steinbeck Centennial................. Y-02
Steinem, Gloria 1934- DLB-246
Steiner, George 1929- DLB-67
Steinhoewel, Heinrich 1411/1412-1479....DLB-179
Steloff, Ida Frances 1887-1989.......... DLB-187
Stendhal 1783-1842................ DLB-119
Stephen Crane: A Revaluation Virginia
    Tech Conference, 1989 .... Y-89
Stephen, Leslie 1832-1904 ......DLB-57, 144, 190
Stephen Vincent Benét Centenary Y-97
Stephens, A. G. 1865-1933............. DLB-230
Stephens, Alexander H. 1812-1883....... DLB-47
Stephens, Alice Barber 1858-1932 ...... DLB-188
Stephens, Ann 1810-1886........ DLB-3, 73, 250
Stephens, Charles Asbury 1844?-1931 .... DLB-42
Stephens, James 1882?-1950.... DLB-19, 153, 162
Stephens, John Lloyd 1805-1852 ... DLB-183, 250
Stephens, Michael 1946- DLB-234
Stephenson, P. R. 1901-1965 .... DLB-260
Sterling, George 1869-1926 .... DLB-54
Sterling, James 1701-1763 .... DLB-24
Sterling, John 1806-1844.............. DLB-116
Stern, Gerald 1925- DLB-105
Stern, Gladys B. 1890-1973............ DLB-197
Stern, Madeleine B. 1912- DLB-111, 140
Stern, Richard 1928- DLB-218; Y-87

Stern, Stewart 1922- DLB-26
Sterne, Laurence
    1713-1768 .... DLB-39; CDBLB-2
Sternheim, Carl 1878-1942 .... DLB-56, 118
Sternhold, Thomas ?-1549 and
    John Hopkins ?-1570 .... DLB-132
Steuart, David 1747-1824 .... DLB-213
Stevens, Henry 1819-1886 .... DLB-140
Stevens, Wallace 1879-1955 ... DLB-54; CDALB-5
Stevenson, Anne 1933- DLB-40
Stevenson, D. E. 1892-1973 .... DLB-191
Stevenson, Lionel 1902-1973 .... DLB-155
Stevenson, Robert Louis
    1850-1894 ....DLB-18, 57, 141, 156, 174;
                             DS-13; CDBLB-5
"On Style in Literature:
    Its Technical Elements" (1885) DLB-57
Stewart, Donald Ogden
    1894-1980 .... DLB-4, 11, 26
Stewart, Douglas 1913-1985........... DLB-260
Stewart, Dugald 1753-1828............. DLB-31
Stewart, George, Jr. 1848-1906......... DLB-99
Stewart, George R. 1895-1980 .... DLB-8
Stewart, Harold 1916-1995............ DLB-260
Stewart, Maria W. 1803?-1879 .... DLB-239
Stewart, Randall 1896-1964 .... DLB-103
Stewart, Sean 1965- DLB-251
Stewart and Kidd Company........... DLB-46
Stickney, Trumbull 1874-1904 .... DLB-54
Stieler, Caspar 1632-1707 .... DLB-164
Stifter, Adalbert
    1805-1868 .... DLB-133; CDWLB-2
Stiles, Ezra 1727-1795 .... DLB-31
Still, James 1906- DLB-9; Y01
Stirling, S. M. 1954- DLB-251
Stirner, Max 1806-1856 .... DLB-129
Stith, William 1707-1755 .... DLB-31
Stock, Elliot [publishing house]......... DLB-106
Stockton, Frank R.
    1834-1902 ....DLB-42, 74; DS-13
Stockton, J. Roy 1892-1972............ DLB-241
Stoddard, Ashbel [publishing house] DLB-49
Stoddard, Charles Warren
    1843-1909 .... DLB-186
Stoddard, Elizabeth 1823-1902......... DLB-202
Stoddard, Richard Henry
    1825-1903 .... DLB-3, 64, 250; DS-13
Stoddard, Solomon 1643-1729 .... DLB-24
Stoker, Bram
    1847-1912.......DLB-36, 70, 178; CDBLB-5
Stokes, Frederick A., Company DLB-49
Stokes, Thomas L. 1898-1958 .... DLB-29
Stokesbury, Leon 1945- DLB-120
Stolberg, Christian Graf zu 1748-1821 .... DLB-94
Stolberg, Friedrich Leopold Graf zu
    1750-1819....................... DLB-94
Stone, Herbert S., and Company DLB-49
Stone, Lucy 1818-1893........... DLB-79, 239

Stone, Melville 1848-1929 .... DLB-25
Stone, Robert 1937- DLB-152
Stone, Ruth 1915- DLB-105
Stone, Samuel 1602-1663 .... DLB-24
Stone, William Leete 1792-1844........ DLB-202
Stone and Kimball DLB-49
Stoppard, Tom
    1937- DLB-13, 233; Y-85; CDBLB-8
Playwrights and Professors............. DLB-13
Storey, Anthony 1928- DLB-14
Storey, David 1933- DLB-13, 14, 207, 245
Storm, Theodor 1817-1888...DLB-129; CDWLB-2
Story, Thomas circa 1670-1742.......... DLB-31
Story, William Wetmore 1819-1895 .. DLB-1, 235
Storytelling: A Contemporary Renaissance ... Y-84
Stoughton, William 1631-1701.......... DLB-24
Stow, John 1525-1605................ DLB-132
Stow, Randolph 1935- DLB-260
Stowe, Harriet Beecher 1811-1896
    ...DLB-1, 12, 42, 74, 189, 239, 243; CDALB-3
Stowe, Leland 1899- DLB-29
Stoyanov, Dimitr Ivanov (see Elin Pelin)
Strabo 64 or 63 B.C.-circa A.D. 25.......DLB-176
Strachey, Lytton 1880-1932 ..... DLB-149; DS-10
Strachey, Lytton, Preface to Eminent
    Victorians...................... DLB-149
Strahan, William [publishing house]..... DLB-154
Strahan and Company DLB-106
Strand, Mark 1934- DLB-5
The Strasbourg Oaths 842 .... DLB-148
Stratemeyer, Edward 1862-1930 .... DLB-42
Strati, Saverio 1924- DLB-177
Stratton and Barnard DLB-49
Stratton-Porter, Gene
    1863-1924 .... DLB-221; DS-14
Straub, Peter 1943- Y-84
Strauß, Botho 1944- DLB-124
Strauß, David Friedrich 1808-1874...... DLB-133
The Strawberry Hill Press DLB-154
Strawson, P. F. 1919- DLB-262
Streatfeild, Noel 1895-1986 .... DLB-160
Street, Cecil John Charles (see Rhode, John)
Street, G. S. 1867-1936 .... DLB-135
Street and Smith..................... DLB-49
Streeter, Edward 1891-1976 .... DLB-11
Streeter, Thomas Winthrop 1883-1965 .. DLB-140
Stretton, Hesba 1832-1911 .... DLB-163, 190
Stribling, T. S. 1881-1965 .... DLB-9
Der Stricker circa 1190-circa 1250 ..... DLB-138
Strickland, Samuel 1804-1867.......... DLB-99
Strindberg, August 1849-1912 .... DLB-259
Stringer, Arthur 1874-1950............ DLB-92
Stringer and Townsend DLB-49
Strittmatter, Erwin 1912- DLB-69
Strniša, Gregor 1930-1987 .... DLB-181

Strode, William 1630-1645 .... DLB-126
Strong, L. A. G. 1896-1958 .... DLB-191
Strother, David Hunter (Porte Crayon)
    1816-1888 .... DLB-3, 248
Strouse, Jean 1945- DLB-111
Stuart, Dabney 1937- DLB-105
Stuart, Jesse 1906-1984 ..... DLB-9, 48, 102; Y-84
Stuart, Lyle [publishing house] DLB-46
Stuart, Ruth McEnery 1849?-1917 .... DLB-202
Stubbs, Harry Clement (see Clement, Hal)
Stubenberg, Johann Wilhelm von
    1619-1663 .... DLB-164
Studebaker, William V. 1947- DLB-256
Studies in American Jewish Literature Y-02
Studio DLB-112
The Study of Poetry (1880), by
    Matthew Arnold DLB-35
Stump, Al 1916-1995 .... DLB-241
Sturgeon, Theodore 1918-1985 ...... DLB-8; Y-85
Sturges, Preston 1898-1959 .... DLB-26
"Style" (1840; revised, 1859), by
    Thomas de Quincey [excerpt] DLB-57
"Style" (1888), by Walter Pater DLB-57
Style (1897), by Walter Raleigh
    [excerpt] DLB-57
"Style" (1877), by T. H. Wright
    [excerpt] DLB-57
"Le Style c'est l'homme" (1892), by
    W. H. Mallock DLB-57
Styron, William
    1925- DLB-2, 143; Y-80; CDALB-6
Suárez, Mario 1925- DLB-82
Such, Peter 1939- DLB-60
Suckling, Sir John 1609-1641? DLB-58, 126
Suckow, Ruth 1892-1960 .... DLB-9, 102
Sudermann, Hermann 1857-1928 .... DLB-118
Sue, Eugène 1804-1857 .... DLB-119
Sue, Marie-Joseph (see Sue, Eugène)
Suetonius circa A.D. 69-post A.D. 122 ... DLB-211
Suggs, Simon (see Hooper, Johnson Jones)
Sui Sin Far (see Eaton, Edith Maude)
Suits, Gustav 1883-1956 .... DLB-220; CDWLB-4
Sukenick, Ronald 1932- DLB-173; Y-81
Sukhovo-Kobylin, Aleksandr Vasil'evich
    1817-1903 .... DLB-277
Suknaski, Andrew 1942- DLB-53
Sullivan, Alan 1868-1947 .... DLB-92
Sullivan, C. Gardner 1886-1965 .... DLB-26
Sullivan, Frank 1892-1976 .... DLB-11
Sulte, Benjamin 1841-1923 .... DLB-99
Sulzberger, Arthur Hays 1891-1968 ..... DLB-127
Sulzberger, Arthur Ochs 1926- DLB-127
Sumarokov, Aleksandr Petrovich
    1717-1777 .... DLB-150
Summers, Hollis 1916- DLB-6
A Summing Up at Century's End Y-99
Sumner, Charles 1811-1874 .... DLB-235

Sumner, Henry A. [publishing house] DLB-49
Sumner, William Graham 1840-1910 .... DLB-270
Sundman, Per Olof 1922-1992 .... DLB-257
Supervielle, Jules 1884-1960 .... DLB-258
Surtees, Robert Smith 1803-1864 .... DLB-21
Survey of Literary Biographies Y-00
A Survey of Poetry Anthologies,
    1879-1960 .... DLB-54
Surveys: Japanese Literature,
    1987-1995 .... DLB-182
Sutcliffe, Matthew 1550?-1629 .... DLB-281
Sutcliffe, William 1971- DLB-271
Sutherland, Efua Theodora
    1924-1996 .... DLB-117
Sutherland, John 1919-1956 .... DLB-68
Sutro, Alfred 1863-1933 .... DLB-10
Svendsen, Hanne Marie 1933- DLB-214
Svevo, Italo (Aron Hector Schmitz)
    1861-1928 .... DLB-264
Swados, Harvey 1920-1972 .... DLB-2
Swain, Charles 1801-1874 .... DLB-32
Swallow Press DLB-46
Swan Sonnenschein Limited DLB-106
Swanberg, W. A. 1907- DLB-103
Swenson, May 1919-1989 .... DLB-5
Swerling, Jo 1897- DLB-44
Swift, Graham 1949- DLB-194
Swift, Jonathan
    1667-1745 .... DLB-39, 95, 101; CDBLB-2
Swinburne, A. C.
    1837-1909 .... DLB-35, 57; CDBLB-4
Swineshead, Richard floruit circa 1350 ... DLB-115
Swinnerton, Frank 1884-1982 .... DLB-34
Swisshelm, Jane Grey 1815-1884 .... DLB-43
Swope, Herbert Bayard 1882-1958 .... DLB-25
Swords, T. and J., and Company DLB-49
Swords, Thomas 1763-1843 and
    Swords, James ?-1844 .... DLB-73
Swynnerton, Thomas
    early 16th century-1554 .... DLB-281
Sykes, Ella C. ?-1939 .... DLB-174
Sylvester, Josuah 1562 or 1563-1618 ..... DLB-121
Symonds, Emily Morse (see Paston, George)
Symonds, John Addington
    1840-1893 .... DLB-57, 144
"Personal Style" (1890) DLB-57
Symons, A. J. A. 1900-1941 .... DLB-149
Symons, Arthur 1865-1945 ..... DLB-19, 57, 149
Symons, Julian
    1912-1994 .... DLB-87, 155; Y-92
Julian Symons at Eighty Y-92
Symons, Scott 1933- DLB-53
A Symposium on The Columbia History of
    the Novel Y-92
Synge, John Millington
    1871-1909 .... DLB-10, 19; CDBLB-5
Synge Summer School: J. M. Synge and the
    Irish Theater, Rathdrum, County Wiclow,
    Ireland Y-93

Syrett, Netta 1865-1943 .... DLB-135, 197
Szabó, Lőrinc 1900-1957 .... DLB-215
Szabó, Magda 1917- DLB-215
Szymborska, Wisława
    1923- DLB-232, Y-96; CDWLB-4

T

Taban lo Liyong 1939?- DLB-125
Tabori, George 1914- DLB-245
Tabucchi, Antonio 1943- DLB-196
Taché, Joseph-Charles 1820-1894 .... DLB-99
Tachihara Masaaki 1926-1980 .... DLB-182
Tacitus circa A.D. 55-circa A.D. 117
    .... DLB-211; CDWLB-1
Tadijanović, Dragutin 1905- DLB-181
Tafdrup, Pia 1952- DLB-214
Tafolla, Carmen 1951- DLB-82
Taggard, Genevieve 1894-1948 .... DLB-45
Taggart, John 1942- DLB-193
Tagger, Theodor (see Bruckner, Ferdinand)
Taiheiki late fourteenth century DLB-203
Tait, J. Selwin, and Sons DLB-49
Tait's Edinburgh Magazine 1832-1861 ..... DLB-110
The Takarazaka Revue Company Y-91
Talander (see Bohse, August)
Talese, Gay 1932- DLB-185
Talev, Dimitr 1898-1966 .... DLB-181
Taliaferro, H. E. 1811-1875 .... DLB-202
Tallent, Elizabeth 1954- DLB-130
TallMountain, Mary 1918-1994 .... DLB-193
Talvj 1797-1870 .... DLB-59, 133
Tamási, Áron 1897-1966 .... DLB-215
Tammsaare, A. H.
    1878-1940 .... DLB-220; CDWLB-4
Tan, Amy 1952- DLB-173; CDALB-7
Tandori, Dezső 1938- DLB-232
Tanner, Thomas 1673/1674-1735 .... DLB-213
Tanizaki Jun'ichirō 1886-1965 .... DLB-180
Tapahonso, Luci 1953- DLB-175
The Mark Taper Forum DLB-7
Taradash, Daniel 1913- DLB-44
Tarasov-Rodionov, Aleksandr Ignat'evich
    1885-1938 .... DLB-272
Tarbell, Ida M. 1857-1944 .... DLB-47
Tardivel, Jules-Paul 1851-1905 .... DLB-99
Targan, Barry 1932- DLB-130
Tarkington, Booth 1869-1946 .... DLB-9, 102
Tashlin, Frank 1913-1972 .... DLB-44
Tasma (Jessie Couvreur) 1848-1897 ..... DLB-230
Tate, Allen 1899-1979 ...... DLB-4, 45, 63; DS-17
Tate, James 1943- DLB-5, 169
Tate, Nahum circa 1652-1715 .... DLB-80
Tatian circa 830 .... DLB-148
Taufer, Veno 1933- DLB-181
Tauler, Johannes circa 1300-1361 ...... DLB-179

Cumulative Index

Tavčar, Ivan 1851-1923 . . . . DLB-147
Taverner, Richard ca. 1505-1575 . . . . DLB-236
Taylor, Ann 1782-1866 . . . . DLB-163
Taylor, Bayard 1825-1878 . . . . . . DLB-3, 189, 250
Taylor, Bert Leston 1866-1921 . . . . DLB-25
Taylor, Charles H. 1846-1921 . . . . DLB-25
Taylor, Edward circa 1642-1729 . . . . DLB-24
Taylor, Elizabeth 1912-1975 . . . . DLB-139
Taylor, Henry 1942- DLB-5
Taylor, Sir Henry 1800-1886 . . . . DLB-32
Taylor, Jane 1783-1824 . . . . DLB-163
Taylor, Jeremy circa 1613-1667 . . . . DLB-151
Taylor, John 1577 or 1578 - 1653 . . . . DLB-121
Taylor, Mildred D. ?- DLB-52
Taylor, Peter 1917-1994 . DLB-218, 278; Y-81, Y-94
Taylor, Susie King 1848-1912 . . . . DLB-221
Taylor, William Howland 1901-1966 . . . DLB-241
Taylor, William, and Company DLB-49
Taylor-Made Shakespeare? Or Is "Shall I Die?" the Long-Lost Text of Bottom's Dream? Y-85
Teale, Edwin Way 1899-1980 . . . . DLB-275
Teasdale, Sara 1884-1933 . . . . DLB-45
Old Dogs / New Tricks? New Technologies, the Canon, and the Structure of the Profession Y-02
Telles, Lygia Fagundes 1924- DLB-113
The Temper of the West: William Jovanovich Y-02
Temple, William 1555?-1627 . . . . DLB-281
Temple, Sir William 1628-1699 . . . . DLB-101
Temple, William F. 1914-1989 . . . . DLB-255
Temrizov, A. (see Marchenko, Anastasia Iakovlevna)
Tench, Watkin ca. 1758-1833 . . . . DLB-230
Tenn, William 1919- DLB-8
Tennant, Emma 1937- DLB-14
Tenney, Tabitha Gilman 1762-1837 . . . . DLB-37, 200
Tennyson, Alfred 1809-1892 . . . . DLB-32; CDBLB-4
Tennyson, Frederick 1807-1898 . . . . DLB-32
Tenorio, Arthur 1924- DLB-209
Tepliakov, Viktor Grigor'evich 1804-1842 . . . . DLB-205
Terence circa 184 B.C.-159 B.C. or after DLB-211; CDWLB-1
Terhune, Albert Payson 1872-1942 . . . . . . DLB-9
Terhune, Mary Virginia 1830-1922 . . . . DS-13, DS-16
Terpigorev, Sergei Nikolaevich(S. Atava) 1841-1895 . . . . DLB-277
Terry, Megan 1932- DLB-7, 249
Terson, Peter 1932- DLB-13
Tesich, Steve 1943-1996 . . . . Y-83
Tessa, Delio 1886-1939 . . . . DLB-114
Testori, Giovanni 1923-1993 . . . . DLB-128, 177
Tey, Josephine 1896?-1952 . . . . DLB-77
Thacher, James 1754-1844 . . . . DLB-37
Thacher, John Boyd 1847-1909 . . . . DLB-187

Thackeray, William Makepeace 1811-1863 . . DLB-21, 55, 159, 163; CDBLB-4
Thames and Hudson Limited DLB-112
Thanet, Octave (see French, Alice)
Thaxter, Celia Laighton 1835-1894 . . . . . DLB-239
Thayer, Caroline Matilda Warren 1785-1844 . . . . DLB-200
Thayer, Douglas 1929- DLB-256
The Theatre Guild DLB-7
The Theater in Shakespeare's Time DLB-62
Thegan and the Astronomer flourished circa 850 . . . . DLB-148
Thelwall, John 1764-1834 . . . . DLB-93, 158
Theocritus circa 300 B.C.-260 B.C. . . . DLB-176
Theodorescu, Ion N. (see Arghezi, Tudor)
Theodulf circa 760-circa 821 . . . . DLB-148
Theophrastus circa 371 B.C.-287 B.C. . . DLB-176
Thériault, Yves 1915-1983 . . . . DLB-88
Thério, Adrien 1925- DLB-53
Theroux, Paul 1941- DLB-2, 218; CDALB-7
Thesiger, Wilfred 1910- DLB-204
They All Came to Paris DS-15
Thibaudeau, Colleen 1925- DLB-88
Thielen, Benedict 1903-1965 . . . . DLB-102
Thiong'o Ngugi wa (see Ngugi wa Thiong'o)
Third-Generation Minor Poets of the Seventeenth Century DLB-131
This Quarter 1925-1927, 1929-1932 . . . . DS-15
Thoma, Ludwig 1867-1921 . . . . DLB-66
Thoma, Richard 1902- DLB-4
Thomas, Audrey 1935- DLB-60
Thomas, D. M. 1935- . . DLB-40, 207; CDBLB-8
D. M. Thomas: The Plagiarism Controversy Y-82
Thomas, Dylan 1914-1953 . . . . . . DLB-13, 20, 139; CDBLB-7
The Dylan Thomas Celebration Y-99
Thomas, Edward 1878-1917 . . . . DLB-19, 98, 156, 216
Thomas, Frederick William 1806-1866 . . DLB-202
Thomas, Gwyn 1913-1981 . . . . DLB-15, 245
Thomas, Isaiah 1750-1831 . . . . . . DLB-43, 73, 187
Thomas, Isaiah [publishing house] DLB-49
Thomas, Johann 1624-1679 . . . . DLB-168
Thomas, John 1900-1932 . . . . DLB-4
Thomas, Joyce Carol 1938- DLB-33
Thomas, Lewis 1913-1993 . . . . DLB-275
Thomas, Lorenzo 1944- DLB-41
Thomas, R. S. 1915-2000 . . . . . DLB-27; CDBLB-8
Thomasîn von Zerclære circa 1186-circa 1259 . . . . DLB-138
Thomasius, Christian 1655-1728 . . . . DLB-168
Thompson, Daniel Pierce 1795-1868 . . . . DLB-202
Thompson, David 1770-1857 . . . . DLB-99
Thompson, Dorothy 1893-1961 . . . . DLB-29
Thompson, E. P. 1924-1993 . . . . DLB-242
Thompson, Flora 1876-1947 . . . . DLB-240

Thompson, Francis 1859-1907 . . . . DLB-19; CDBLB-5
Thompson, George Selden (see Selden, George)
Thompson, Henry Yates 1838-1928 . . . . DLB-184
Thompson, Hunter S. 1939- DLB-185
Thompson, Jim 1906-1977 . . . . DLB-226
Thompson, John 1938-1976 . . . . DLB-60
Thompson, John R. 1823-1873 . . . . DLB-3, 73, 248
Thompson, Lawrance 1906-1973 . . . . . . DLB-103
Thompson, Maurice 1844-1901 . . . . . . DLB-71, 74
Thompson, Ruth Plumly 1891-1976 . . . . . DLB-22
Thompson, Thomas Phillips 1843-1933 . . DLB-99
Thompson, William 1775-1833 . . . . DLB-158
Thompson, William Tappan 1812-1882 . . . . DLB-3, 11, 248
Thomson, Edward William 1849-1924 . . . DLB-92
Thomson, James 1700-1748 . . . . DLB-95
Thomson, James 1834-1882 . . . . DLB-35
Thomson, Joseph 1858-1895 . . . . DLB-174
Thomson, Rupert 1955- DLB-267
Thomson, Mortimer 1831-1875 . . . . DLB-11
Thon, Melanie Rae 1957- DLB-244
Thoreau, Henry David 1817-1862 . . . . DLB-1, 183, 223, 270; CDALB-2
The Thoreauvian Pilgrimage: The Structure of an American Cult DLB-223
Thorne, William 1568?-1630 . . . . DLB-281
Thorpe, Adam 1956- DLB-231
Thorpe, Thomas Bangs 1815-1878 . . . . DLB-3, 11, 248
Thorup, Kirsten 1942- DLB-214
Thoughts on Poetry and Its Varieties (1833), by John Stuart Mill DLB-32
Thrale, Hester Lynch (see Piozzi, Hester Lynch [Thrale])
Some Basic Notes on Three Modern Genres: Interview, Blurb, and Obituary Y-02
Thubron, Colin 1939- DLB-204, 231
Thucydides circa 455 B.C.-circa 395 B.C. DLB-176
Thulstrup, Thure de 1848-1930 . . . . DLB-188
Thümmel, Moritz August von 1738-1817 . . . . DLB-97
Thurber, James 1894-1961 . . . . DLB-4, 11, 22, 102; CDALB-5
Thurman, Wallace 1902-1934 . . . . DLB-51
Thwaite, Anthony 1930- DLB-40
The Booker Prize Address by Anthony Thwaite, Chairman of the Booker Prize Judges Comments from Former Booker Prize Winners Y-86
Thwaites, Reuben Gold 1853-1913 . . . . . . DLB-47
Tibullus circa 54 B.C.-circa 19 B.C. DLB-211
Ticknor, George 1791-1871 . . . DLB-1, 59, 140, 235
Ticknor and Fields DLB-49
Ticknor and Fields (revived) DLB-46
Tieck, Ludwig 1773-1853 . . . . DLB-90; CDWLB-2
Tietjens, Eunice 1884-1944 . . . . DLB-54

Tikkanen, Märta 1935- DLB-257
Tilghman, Christopher circa 1948.......DLB-244
Tilney, Edmund circa 1536-1610..........DLB-136
Tilt, Charles [publishing house].........DLB-106
Tilton, J. E., and Company DLB-49
Time and Western Man (1927), by Wyndham Lewis [excerpts]..................DLB-36
Time-Life Books DLB-46
Times Books DLB-46
Timothy, Peter circa 1725-1782 ....DLB-43
Timrava 1867-1951 ....DLB-215
Timrod, Henry 1828-1867..........DLB-3, 248
Tindal, Henrietta 1818?-1879 ....DLB-199
Tinker, Chauncey Brewster 1876-1963 ...DLB-140
Tinsley Brothers DLB-106
Tiptree, James, Jr. 1915-1987............DLB-8
Tišma, Aleksandar 1924- DLB-181
Titus, Edward William 1870-1952 ....DLB-4; DS-15
Tiutchev, Fedor Ivanovich 1803-1873 ....DLB-205
Tlali, Miriam 1933- DLB-157, 225
Todd, Barbara Euphan 1890-1976.......DLB-160
Todorov, Tzvetan 1939- DLB-242
Tofte, Robert 1561 or 1562-1619 or 1620.........DLB-172
Tóibín, Colm 1955- DLB-271
Toklas, Alice B. 1877-1967..............DLB-4
Tokuda, Shūsei 1872-1943.............DLB-180
Toland, John 1670-1722...............DLB-252
Tolkien, J. R. R. 1892-1973 ......DLB-15, 160, 255; CDBLB-6
Toller, Ernst 1893-1939................DLB-124
Tollet, Elizabeth 1694-1754 ....DLB-95
Tolson, Melvin B. 1898-1966........DLB-48, 76
Tolstoy, Aleksei Konstantinovich 1817-1875......................DLB-238
Tolstoy, Aleksei Nikolaevich 1883-1945 ..DLB-272
Tolstoy, Leo 1828-1910...............DLB-238
Tom Jones (1749), by Henry Fielding [excerpt]......................DLB-39
Tomalin, Claire 1933- DLB-155
Tomasi di Lampedusa, Giuseppe 1896-1957 ....DLB-177
Tomlinson, Charles 1927- DLB-40
Tomlinson, H. M. 1873-1958 ...DLB-36, 100, 195
Tompkins, Abel [publishing house].......DLB-49
Tompson, Benjamin 1642-1714..........DLB-24
Tomson, Graham R. (see Watson, Rosamund Marriott)
Ton'a 1289-1372 ....DLB-203
Tondelli, Pier Vittorio 1955-1991 ....DLB-196
Tonks, Rosemary 1932- DLB-14, 207
Tonna, Charlotte Elizabeth 1790-1846 ..DLB-163
Tonson, Jacob the Elder [publishing house]................DLB-170
Toole, John Kennedy 1937-1969 ....Y-81
Toomer, Jean 1894-1967 ...DLB-45, 51; CDALB-4

Tor Books DLB-46
Torberg, Friedrich 1908-1979 ....DLB-85
Torrence, Ridgely 1874-1950.......DLB-54, 249
Torres-Metzger, Joseph V. 1933- DLB-122
Toth, Susan Allen 1940- Y-86
Tottell, Richard [publishing house] DLB-170
"The Printer to the Reader," (1557) by Richard Tottell................DLB-167
Tough-Guy Literature................DLB-9
Touré, Askia Muhammad 1938- DLB-41
Tourgée, Albion W. 1838-1905.........DLB-79
Tournemir, Elizaveta Sailhas de (see Tur, Evgeniia)
Tourneur, Cyril circa 1580-1626..........DLB-58
Tournier, Michel 1924- DLB-83
Tousey, Frank [publishing house].......DLB-49
Tower Publications DLB-46
Towne, Benjamin circa 1740-1793 ....DLB-43
Towne, Robert 1936- DLB-44
The Townely Plays fifteenth and sixteenth centuries DLB-146
Townsend, Sue 1946- DLB-271
Townshend, Aurelian by 1583-circa 1651 ....DLB-121
Toy, Barbara 1908- DLB-204
Tozzi, Federigo 1883-1920............DLB-264
Tracy, Honor 1913- DLB-15
Traherne, Thomas 1637?-1674 ....DLB-131
Traill, Catharine Parr 1802-1899........DLB-99
Train, Arthur 1875-1945 ....DLB-86; DS-16
Tranquilli, Secondino (see Silone, Ignazio)
The Transatlantic Publishing Company ...DLB-49
The Transatlantic Review 1924-1925 ....DS-15
The Transcendental Club 1836-1840 ....DLB-223
Transcendentalism...................DLB-223
Transcendentalists, American DS-5
A Transit of Poets and Others: American Biography in 1982..................Y-82
transition 1927-1938.....................DS-15
Translators of the Twelfth Century: Literary Issues Raised and Impact Created.........DLB-115
Tranströmer, Tomas 1931- DLB-257
Travel Writing, 1837-1875.............DLB-166
Travel Writing, 1876-1909 ....DLB-174
Travel Writing, 1910-1939 ....DLB-195
Traven, B. 1882? or 1890?-1969?......DLB-9, 56
Travers, Ben 1886-1980 ....DLB-10, 233
Travers, P. L. (Pamela Lyndon) 1899-1996....................DLB-160
Trediakovsky, Vasilii Kirillovich 1703-1769....................DLB-150
Treece, Henry 1911-1966 ....DLB-160
Treitel, Jonathan 1959- DLB-267
Trejo, Ernesto 1950- DLB-122
Trelawny, Edward John 1792-1881 ....DLB-110, 116, 144
Tremain, Rose 1943- DLB-14, 271
Tremblay, Michel 1942- DLB-60

Trends in Twentieth-Century Mass Market Publishing DLB-46
Trent, William P. 1862-1939............DLB-47
Trescot, William Henry 1822-1898.......DLB-30
Tressell, Robert (Robert Phillipe Noonan) 1870-1911 ....DLB-197
Trevelyan, Sir George Otto 1838-1928....................DLB-144
Trevisa, John circa 1342-circa 1402......DLB-146
Trevor, William 1928- DLB-14, 139
Trierer Floyris circa 1170-1180...........DLB-138
Trillin, Calvin 1935- DLB-185
Trilling, Lionel 1905-1975 ....DLB-28, 63
Trilussa 1871-1950...................DLB-114
Trimmer, Sarah 1741-1810 ....DLB-158
Triolet, Elsa 1896-1970 ....DLB-72
Tripp, John 1927- DLB-40
Trocchi, Alexander 1925- DLB-15
Troisi, Dante 1920-1989 ....DLB-196
Trollope, Anthony 1815-1882 ....DLB-21, 57, 159; CDBLB-4
Trollope, Frances 1779-1863 ....DLB-21, 166
Trollope, Joanna 1943- DLB-207
Troop, Elizabeth 1931- DLB-14
Trotter, Catharine 1679-1749........DLB-84, 252
Trotti, Lamar 1898-1952...............DLB-44
Trottier, Pierre 1925- DLB-60
Trotzig, Birgitta 1929- DLB-257
Troubadours, *Trobaíritz*, and Trouvères ..DLB-208
Troupe, Quincy Thomas, Jr. 1943- DLB-41
Trow, John F., and Company DLB-49
Trowbridge, John Townsend 1827-1916 ..DLB-202
Trudel, Jean-Louis 1967- DLB-251
Truillier-Lacombe, Joseph-Patrice 1807-1863....................DLB-99
Trumbo, Dalton 1905-1976 ....DLB-26
Trumbull, Benjamin 1735-1820..........DLB-30
Trumbull, John 1750-1831..............DLB-31
Trumbull, John 1756-1843..............DLB-183
Truth, Sojourner 1797?-1883...........DLB-239
Tscherning, Andreas 1611-1659 ....DLB-164
Tsubouchi, Shōyō 1859-1935...........DLB-180
Tucholsky, Kurt 1890-1935.............DLB-56
Tucker, Charlotte Maria 1821-1893................DLB-163, 190
Tucker, George 1775-1861........DLB-3, 30, 248
Tucker, James 1808?-1866?............DLB-230
Tucker, Nathaniel Beverley 1784-1851 ....DLB-3, 248
Tucker, St. George 1752-1827 ....DLB-37
Tuckerman, Frederick Goddard 1821-1873 ....DLB-243
Tuckerman, Henry Theodore 1813-1871 ....DLB-64
Tumas, Juozas (see Vaizgantas)
Tunis, John R. 1889-1975 ....DLB-22, 171
Tunstall, Cuthbert 1474-1559 ....DLB-132

Tunström, Göran 1937-2000 .... DLB-257
Tuohy, Frank 1925- DLB-14, 139
Tupper, Martin F. 1810-1889 .... DLB-32
Tur, Evgeniia 1815-1892 .... DLB-238
Turbyfill, Mark 1896- DLB-45
Turco, Lewis 1934- Y-84
Turgenev, Aleksandr Ivanovich
  1784-1845 .... DLB-198
Turgenev, Ivan Sergeevich
  1818-1883 .... DLB-238
Turnball, Alexander H. 1868-1918 ..... DLB-184
Turnbull, Andrew 1921-1970 .... DLB-103
Turnbull, Gael 1928- DLB-40
Turner, Arlin 1909-1980 .... DLB-103
Turner, Charles (Tennyson)
  1808-1879 .... DLB-32
Turner, Ethel 1872-1958 .... DLB-230
Turner, Frederick 1943- DLB-40, 282
Turner, Frederick Jackson
  1861-1932 .... DLB-17, 186
A Conversation between William Riggan
  and Janette Turner Hospital Y-02
Turner, Joseph Addison 1826-1868 ..... DLB-79
Turpin, Waters Edward 1910-1968 ..... DLB-51
Turrini, Peter 1944- DLB-124
Tutuola, Amos 1920-1997 .. DLB-125; CDWLB-3
Twain, Mark (see Clemens, Samuel Langhorne)
Tweedie, Ethel Brilliana
  circa 1860-1940 .... DLB-174
The 'Twenties and Berlin, by Alex Natan . DLB-66
A Century of Poetry, a Lifetime of Collecting:
  J. M. Edelstein's Collection of Twentieth-
  Century American Poetry YB-02
Two Hundred Years of Rare Books and
  Literary Collections at the
  University of South Carolina Y-00
Twombly, Wells 1935-1977 .... DLB-241
Twysden, Sir Roger 1597-1672 .... DLB-213
Tyler, Anne
  1941- DLB-6, 143; Y-82; CDALB-7
Tyler, Mary Palmer 1775-1866 .... DLB-200
Tyler, Moses Coit 1835-1900 .... DLB-47, 64
Tyler, Royall 1757-1826 .... DLB-37
Tylor, Edward Burnett 1832-1917 ...... DLB-57
Tynan, Katharine 1861-1931 ...... DLB-153, 240
Tyndale, William circa 1494-1536 ...... DLB-132

U

Uchida, Yoshika 1921-1992 .... CDALB-7
Udall, Nicholas 1504-1556 .... DLB-62
Ugrešić, Dubravka 1949- DLB-181
Uhland, Ludwig 1787-1862 .... DLB-90
Uhse, Bodo 1904-1963 .... DLB-69
Ujević, Augustin ("Tin") 1891-1955 ..... DLB-147
Ulenhart, Niclas flourished circa 1600 ... DLB-164
Ulibarrí, Sabine R. 1919- DLB-82
Ulica, Jorge 1870-1926 .... DLB-82
Ulivi, Ferruccio 1912- DLB-196

Ulizio, B. George 1889-1969 .... DLB-140
Ulrich von Liechtenstein
  circa 1200-circa 1275 .... DLB-138
Ulrich von Zatzikhoven
  before 1194-after 1214 .... DLB-138
Ulysses, Reader's Edition Y-97
Unaipon, David 1872-1967 .... DLB-230
Unamuno, Miguel de 1864-1936 .... DLB-108
Under, Marie 1883-1980
  .... DLB-220; CDWLB-4
Under the Microscope (1872), by
  A. C. Swinburne DLB-35
Underhill, Evelyn
  1875-1941 .... DLB-240
Ungaretti, Giuseppe 1888-1970 .... DLB-114
Unger, Friederike Helene 1741-1813 ..... DLB-94
United States Book Company DLB-49
Universal Publishing and Distributing
  Corporation DLB-46
Indiana University Press Y-02
The University of Iowa
  Writers' Workshop Golden Jubilee Y-86
University of Missouri Press Y-01
The University of South Carolina Press Y-94
University of Wales Press DLB-112
University Press of Florida Y-00
University Press of Kansas Y-98
University Press of Mississippi Y-99
"The Unknown Public" (1858), by
  Wilkie Collins [excerpt] DLB-57
Uno, Chiyo 1897-1996 .... DLB-180
Unruh, Fritz von 1885-1970 .... DLB-56, 118
Unspeakable Practices II:
  The Festival of Vanguard
  Narrative at Brown University Y-93
Unsworth, Barry 1930- DLB-194
Unt, Mati 1944- DLB-232
The Unterberg Poetry Center of the
  92nd Street Y Y-98
Unwin, T. Fisher [publishing house] DLB-106
Upchurch, Boyd B. (see Boyd, John)
Updike, John 1932- DLB-2, 5, 143, 218, 227;
  Y-80, Y-82; DS-3; CDALB-6
John Updike on the Internet Y-97
Upīts, Andrejs 1877-1970 .... DLB-220
Upton, Bertha 1849-1912 .... DLB-141
Upton, Charles 1948- DLB-16
Upton, Florence K. 1873-1922 .... DLB-141
Upward, Allen 1863-1926 .... DLB-36
Urban, Milo 1904-1982 .... DLB-215
Urfé, Honoré d' 1567-1625 .... DLB-268
Urista, Alberto Baltazar (see Alurista)
Urquhart, Fred 1912- DLB-139
Urrea, Luis Alberto 1955- DLB-209
Urzidil, Johannes 1896-1970 .... DLB-85
The Uses of Facsimile Y-90
Usk, Thomas died 1388 .... DLB-146
Uslar Pietri, Arturo 1906- DLB-113

Uspensky, Gleb Ivanovich 1843-1902 ....DLB-277
Ussher, James 1581-1656 .... DLB-213
Ustinov, Peter 1921- DLB-13
Uttley, Alison 1884-1976 .... DLB-160
Uz, Johann Peter 1720-1796 .... DLB-97

V

Vac, Bertrand (Aimé Pelletier)
  1914- DLB-88
Vācietis, Ojārs 1933-1983 .... DLB-232
Vaičiulaitis, Antanas 1906-1992 .... DLB-220
Vaculík, Ludvík 1926- DLB-232
Vaičiūnaite, Judita 1937- DLB-232
Vail, Laurence 1891-1968 .... DLB-4
Vailland, Roger 1907-1965 .... DLB-83
Vaižgantas 1869-1933 .... DLB-220
Vajda, Ernest 1887-1954 .... DLB-44
Valdés, Gina 1943- DLB-122
Valdez, Luis Miguel 1940- DLB-122
Valduga, Patrizia 1953- DLB-128
Valente, José Angel 1929-2000 .... DLB-108
Valenzuela, Luisa 1938- ...DLB-113; CDWLB-3
Valeri, Diego 1887-1976 .... DLB-128
Valerius Flaccus fl. circa A.D. 92 .... DLB-211
Valerius Maximus fl. circa A.D. 31 ..... DLB-211
Valéry, Paul 1871-1945 .... DLB-258
Valesio, Paolo 1939- DLB-196
Valgardson, W. D. 1939- DLB-60
Valle, Víctor Manuel 1950- DLB-122
Valle-Inclán, Ramón del 1866-1936 ..... DLB-134
Vallejo, Armando 1949- DLB-122
Vallès, Jules 1832-1885 .... DLB-123
Vallette, Marguerite Eymery (see Rachilde)
Valverde, José María 1926-1996 ...... DLB-108
Van Allsburg, Chris 1949- DLB-61
Van Anda, Carr 1864-1945 .... DLB-25
van der Post, Laurens 1906-1996 ...... DLB-204
Van Dine, S. S. (see Wright, Williard Huntington)
Van Doren, Mark 1894-1972 .... DLB-45
van Druten, John 1901-1957 .... DLB-10
Van Duyn, Mona 1921- DLB-5
Van Dyke, Henry 1852-1933 ......DLB-71; DS-13
Van Dyke, Henry 1928- DLB-33
Van Dyke, John C. 1856-1932 .... DLB-186
van Gulik, Robert Hans 1910-1967 ..... DS-17
van Itallie, Jean-Claude 1936- DLB-7
Van Loan, Charles E. 1876-1919 .... DLB-171
Van Rensselaer, Mariana Griswold
  1851-1934 .... DLB-47
Van Rensselaer, Mrs. Schuyler
  (see Van Rensselaer, Mariana Griswold)
Van Vechten, Carl 1880-1964 .... DLB-4, 9
van Vogt, A. E. 1912-2000 .... DLB-8, 251
Vanbrugh, Sir John 1664-1726 .... DLB-80
Vance, Jack 1916?- DLB-8

Vančura, Vladislav
   1891-1942 . . . . DLB-215; CDWLB-4
Vane, Sutton 1888-1963 . . . . DLB-10
Vanguard Press DLB-46
Vann, Robert L. 1879-1940 . . . . DLB-29
Vargas Llosa, Mario
   1936- DLB-145; CDWLB-3
Varley, John 1947- Y-81
Varnhagen von Ense, Karl August
   1785-1858 . . . . DLB-90
Varnhagen von Ense, Rahel
   1771-1833 . . . . DLB-90
Varro 116 B.C.-27 B.C. DLB-211
Vasiliu, George (see Bacovia, George)
Vásquez, Richard 1928- DLB-209
Vásquez Montalbán, Manuel 1939- DLB-134
Vassa, Gustavus (see Equiano, Olaudah)
Vassalli, Sebastiano 1941- DLB-128, 196
Vaugelas, Claude Favre de 1585-1650 . . . . DLB-268
Vaughan, Henry 1621-1695 . . . . DLB-131
Vaughan, Thomas 1621-1666 . . . . DLB-131
Vaughn, Robert 1592?-1667 . . . . DLB-213
Vaux, Thomas, Lord 1509-1556 . . . . DLB-132
Vazov, Ivan 1850-1921 . . . . . DLB-147; CDWLB-4
Véa, Alfredo, Jr. 1950- DLB-209
Veblen, Thorstein 1857-1929 . . . . DLB-246
Vega, Janine Pommy 1942- DLB-16
Veiller, Anthony 1903-1965 . . . . DLB-44
Velásquez-Trevino, Gloria 1949- DLB-122
Veley, Margaret 1843-1887 . . . . DLB-199
Velleius Paterculus
   circa 20 B.C.-circa A.D. 30 . . . . DLB-211
Veloz Maggiolo, Marcio 1936- DLB-145
Vel'tman, Aleksandr Fomich
   1800-1870 . . . . DLB-198
Venegas, Daniel ?-? DLB-82
Venevitinov, Dmitrii Vladimirovich
   1805-1827 . . . . DLB-205
Vergil, Polydore circa 1470-1555 . . . . DLB-132
Veríssimo, Erico 1905-1975 . . . . DLB-145
Verlaine, Paul 1844-1896 . . . . DLB-217
Verne, Jules 1828-1905 . . . . DLB-123
Verplanck, Gulian C. 1786-1870 . . . . DLB-59
Very, Jones 1813-1880 . . . . DLB-1, 243
Vian, Boris 1920-1959 . . . . DLB-72
Viazemsky, Petr Andreevich
   1792-1878 . . . . DLB-205
Vicars, Thomas 1591-1638 . . . . DLB-236
Vickers, Roy 1888?-1965 . . . . DLB-77
Vickery, Sukey 1779-1821 . . . . DLB-200
Victoria 1819-1901 . . . . DLB-55
Victoria Press DLB-106
Vidal, Gore 1925- DLB-6, 152; CDALB-7
Vidal, Mary Theresa 1815-1873 . . . . DLB-230
Vidmer, Richards 1898-1978 . . . . DLB-241
Viebig, Clara 1860-1952 . . . . DLB-66

Viereck, George Sylvester
   1884-1962 . . . . DLB-54
Viereck, Peter 1916- DLB-5
Viets, Roger 1738-1811 . . . . DLB-99
Viewpoint: Politics and Performance, by
   David Edgar DLB-13
Vigil-Piñon, Evangelina 1949- DLB-122
Vigneault, Gilles 1928- DLB-60
Vigny, Alfred de
   1797-1863 . . . . DLB-119, 192, 217
Vigolo, Giorgio 1894-1983 . . . . DLB-114
The Viking Press DLB-46
Vilde, Eduard 1865-1933 . . . . DLB-220
Vilinskaia, Mariia Aleksandrovna
   (see Vovchok, Marko)
Villanueva, Alma Luz 1944- DLB-122
Villanueva, Tino 1941- DLB-82
Villard, Henry 1835-1900 . . . . DLB-23
Villard, Oswald Garrison
   1872-1949 . . . . DLB-25, 91
Villarreal, Edit 1944- DLB-209
Villarreal, José Antonio 1924- DLB-82
Villaseñor, Victor 1940- DLB-209
Villedieu, Madame de (Marie-Catherine
   Desjardins) 1640?-1683 . . . . DLB-268
Villegas de Magnón, Leonor
   1876-1955 . . . . DLB-122
Villehardouin, Geoffroi de
   circa 1150-1215 . . . . DLB-208
Villemaire, Yolande 1949- DLB-60
Villena, Luis Antonio de 1951- DLB-134
Villiers, George, Second Duke
   of Buckingham 1628-1687 . . . . DLB-80
Villiers de l'Isle-Adam, Jean-Marie Mathias
   Philippe-Auguste, Comte de
   1838-1889 . . . . DLB-123, 192
Villon, François 1431-circa 1463? DLB-208
Vine Press DLB-112
Viorst, Judith ?- DLB-52
Vipont, Elfrida (Elfrida Vipont Foulds,
   Charles Vipont) 1902-1992 . . . . DLB-160
Viramontes, Helena María 1954- DLB-122
Virgil 70 B.C.-19 B.C. DLB-211; CDWLB-1
Virtual Books and Enemies of Books Y-00
Vischer, Friedrich Theodor 1807-1887 . . . DLB-133
Vitruvius circa 85 B.C.-circa 15 B.C. DLB-211
Vitry, Philippe de 1291-1361 . . . . DLB-208
Vittorini, Elio 1908-1966 . . . . DLB-264
Vivanco, Luis Felipe 1907-1975 . . . . DLB-108
Vivian, E. Charles 1882-1947 . . . . DLB-255
Viviani, Cesare 1947- DLB-128
Vivien, Renée 1877-1909 . . . . DLB-217
Vizenor, Gerald 1934- DLB-175, 227
Vizetelly and Company DLB-106
Voaden, Herman 1903- DLB-88
Voß, Johann Heinrich 1751-1826 . . . . DLB-90
Vogau, Boris Andreevich (see Pil'niak,
   Boris Andreevich)

Voigt, Ellen Bryant 1943- DLB-120
Vojnović, Ivo 1857-1929 . . . . DLB-147; CDWLB-4
Volkoff, Vladimir 1932- DLB-83
Volland, P. F., Company DLB-46
Vollbehr, Otto H. F.
   1872?-1945 or 1946 . . . . DLB-187
Vologdin (see Zasodimsky,
   Pavel Vladimirovich)
Volponi, Paolo 1924- DLB-177
Vonarburg, Élisabeth 1947- DLB-251
von der Grün, Max 1926- DLB-75
Vonnegut, Kurt 1922-
   . . . . DLB-2, 8, 152; Y-80; DS-3; CDALB-6
Voranc, Prežihov 1893-1950 . . . . DLB-147
Voronsky, Aleksandr Konstantinovich
   1884-1937 . . . . DLB-272
Vovchok, Marko 1833-1907 . . . . DLB-238
Voynich, E. L. 1864-1960 . . . . DLB-197
Vroman, Mary Elizabeth
   circa 1924-1967 . . . . DLB-33

W

Wace, Robert ("Maistre")
   circa 1100-circa 1175 . . . . DLB-146
Wackenroder, Wilhelm Heinrich
   1773-1798 . . . . DLB-90
Wackernagel, Wilhelm 1806-1869 . . . . . . DLB-133
Waddell, Helen 1889-1965 . . . . DLB-240
Waddington, Miriam 1917- DLB-68
Wade, Henry 1887-1969 . . . . DLB-77
Wagenknecht, Edward 1900- DLB-103
Wägner, Elin 1882-1949 . . . . DLB-259
Wagner, Heinrich Leopold 1747-1779 . . . . DLB-94
Wagner, Henry R. 1862-1957 . . . . DLB-140
Wagner, Richard 1813-1883 . . . . DLB-129
Wagoner, David 1926- DLB-5, 256
Wah, Fred 1939- DLB-60
Waiblinger, Wilhelm 1804-1830 . . . . DLB-90
Wain, John
   1925-1994 . . . DLB-15, 27, 139, 155; CDBLB-8
Wainwright, Jeffrey 1944- DLB-40
Waite, Peirce and Company DLB-49
Wakeman, Stephen H. 1859-1924 . . . . . . DLB-187
Wakoski, Diane 1937- DLB-5
Walahfrid Strabo circa 808-849 . . . . DLB-148
Walck, Henry Z. DLB-46
Walcott, Derek
   1930- DLB-117; Y-81, Y-92; CDWLB-3
Waldegrave, Robert [publishing house] . . . DLB-170
Waldman, Anne 1945- DLB-16
Waldrop, Rosmarie 1935- DLB-169
Walker, Alice 1900-1982 . . . . DLB-201
Walker, Alice
   1944- DLB-6, 33, 143; CDALB-6
Walker, Annie Louisa (Mrs. Harry Coghill)
   circa 1836-1907 . . . . DLB-240
Walker, George F. 1947- DLB-60
Walker, John Brisben 1847-1931 . . . . DLB-79

Walker, Joseph A. 1935- DLB-38
Walker, Margaret 1915- DLB-76, 152
Walker, Obadiah 1616-1699 .... DLB-281
Walker, Ted 1934- DLB-40
Walker and Company DLB-49
Walker, Evans and Cogswell Company... DLB-49
Wall, John F. (see Sarban)
Wallace, Alfred Russel 1823-1913 ...... DLB-190
Wallace, Dewitt 1889-1981 and
 Lila Acheson Wallace 1889-1984.... DLB-137
Wallace, Edgar 1875-1932 .... DLB-70
Wallace, Lew 1827-1905.............. DLB-202
Wallace, Lila Acheson
 (see Wallace, Dewitt, and Lila Acheson Wallace)
Wallace, Naomi 1960- DLB-249
Wallace Markfield's "Steeplechase" Y-02
Wallant, Edward Lewis
 1926-1962 .... DLB-2, 28, 143
Waller, Edmund 1606-1687 .... DLB-126
Walpole, Horace 1717-1797..... DLB-39, 104, 213
Preface to the First Edition of
 The Castle of Otranto (1764)........... DLB-39
Preface to the Second Edition of
 The Castle of Otranto (1765)........... DLB-39
Walpole, Hugh 1884-1941 .... DLB-34
Walrond, Eric 1898-1966 .... DLB-51
Walser, Martin 1927- DLB-75, 124
Walser, Robert 1878-1956 .... DLB-66
Walsh, Ernest 1895-1926 .... DLB-4, 45
Walsh, Robert 1784-1859 .... DLB-59
Walters, Henry 1848-1931 .... DLB-140
Waltharius circa 825................. DLB-148
Walther von der Vogelweide
 circa 1170-circa 1230 .... DLB-138
Walton, Izaak
 1593-1683 .... DLB-151, 213; CDBLB-1
Wambaugh, Joseph 1937- DLB-6; Y-83
Wand, Alfred Rudolph 1828-1891...... DLB-188
Waniek, Marilyn Nelson 1946- DLB-120
Wanley, Humphrey 1672-1726. .... DLB-213
War of the Words (and Pictures): The Creation
 of a Graphic Novel................... Y-02
Warburton, William 1698-1779 .... DLB-104
Ward, Aileen 1919- DLB-111
Ward, Artemus (see Browne, Charles Farrar)
Ward, Arthur Henry Sarsfield (see Rohmer, Sax)
Ward, Douglas Turner 1930- DLB-7, 38
Ward, Mrs. Humphry 1851-1920 .... DLB-18
Ward, James 1843-1925.............. DLB-262
Ward, Lynd 1905-1985 .... DLB-22
Ward, Lock and Company DLB-106
Ward, Nathaniel circa 1578-1652 .... DLB-24
Ward, Theodore 1902-1983 .... DLB-76
Wardle, Ralph 1909-1988 .... DLB-103
Ware, Henry, Jr. 1794-1843 .... DLB-235
Ware, William 1797-1852 .... DLB-1, 235
Warfield, Catherine Ann 1816-1877 ...... DLB-248

Waring, Anna Letitia 1823-1910 .... DLB-240
Warne, Frederick, and Company [U.K.]... DLB-106
Warne, Frederick, and Company [U.S.]... DLB-49
Warner, Anne 1869-1913 .... DLB-202
Warner, Charles Dudley 1829-1900 ..... DLB-64
Warner, Marina 1946- DLB-194
Warner, Rex 1905- DLB-15
Warner, Susan 1819-1885 ... DLB-3, 42, 239, 250
Warner, Sylvia Townsend
 1893-1978................... DLB-34, 139
Warner, William 1558-1609............DLB-172
Warner Books DLB-46
Warr, Bertram 1917-1943............. DLB-88
Warren, John Byrne Leicester (see De Tabley, Lord)
Warren, Lella 1899-1982 .... Y-83
Warren, Mercy Otis 1728-1814 ..... DLB-31, 200
Warren, Robert Penn 1905-1989
 ....DLB-2, 48, 152; Y-80, Y-89; CDALB-6
Warren, Samuel 1807-1877 .... DLB-190
Die Wartburgkrieg circa 1230-circa 1280... DLB-138
Warton, Joseph 1722-1800 ....DLB-104, 109
Warton, Thomas 1728-1790........DLB-104, 109
Warung, Price (William Astley)
 1855-1911 .... DLB-230
Washington, George 1732-1799 .... DLB-31
Washington, Ned 1901-1976 .... DLB-265
Wassermann, Jakob 1873-1934 .... DLB-66
Wasserstein, Wendy 1950- DLB-228
Wasson, David Atwood 1823-1887 ... DLB-1, 223
Watanna, Onoto (see Eaton, Winnifred)
Waterhouse, Keith 1929- DLB-13, 15
Waterman, Andrew 1940- DLB-40
Waters, Frank 1902-1995.........DLB-212; Y-86
Waters, Michael 1949- DLB-120
Watkins, Tobias 1780-1855 .... DLB-73
Watkins, Vernon 1906-1967 .... DLB-20
Watmough, David 1926- DLB-53
Watson, Colin 1920-1983..............DLB-276
Watson, Ian 1943- DLB-261
Watson, James Wreford (see Wreford, James)
Watson, John 1850-1907 .... DLB-156
Watson, Rosamund Marriott
 (Graham R. Tomson) 1860-1911.... DLB-240
Watson, Sheila 1909- DLB-60
Watson, Thomas 1545?-1592........... DLB-132
Watson, Wilfred 1911- DLB-60
Watt, W. J., and Company DLB-46
Watten, Barrett 1948- DLB-193
Watterson, Henry 1840-1921 .... DLB-25
Watts, Alan 1915-1973 .... DLB-16
Watts, Franklin [publishing house]........ DLB-46
Watts, Isaac 1674-1748 .... DLB-95
Waugh, Alec 1898-1981............... DLB-191
Waugh, Auberon 1939-2000 ...DLB-14, 194; Y-00
The Cult of Biography
 Excerpts from the Second Folio Debate:

"Biographies are generally a disease of
 English Literature"................. Y-86
Waugh, Evelyn
 1903-1966 ..... DLB-15, 162, 195; CDBLB-6
Way and Williams DLB-49
Wayman, Tom 1945- DLB-53
We See the Editor at Work Y-97
Weatherly, Tom 1942- DLB-41
Weaver, Gordon 1937- DLB-130
Weaver, Robert 1921- DLB-88
Webb, Beatrice 1858-1943 and
 Webb, Sidney 1859-1947.......... DLB-190
Webb, Francis 1925-1973 .... DLB-260
Webb, Frank J. ?-? DLB-50
Webb, James Watson 1802-1884........ DLB-43
Webb, Mary 1881-1927 .... DLB-34
Webb, Phyllis 1927- DLB-53
Webb, Walter Prescott 1888-1963 ....DLB-17
Webbe, William ?-1591 .... DLB-132
Webber, Charles Wilkins 1819-1856?... DLB-202
Webling, Lucy (Lucy Betty MacRaye)
 1877-1952..................... DLB-240
Webling, Peggy (Arthur Weston)
 1871-1949..................... DLB-240
Webster, Augusta 1837-1894 .... DLB-35, 240
Webster, Charles L., and Company...... DLB-49
Webster, John
 1579 or 1580-1634?...... DLB-58; CDBLB-1
John Webster: The Melbourne
 Manuscript....................... Y-86
Webster, Noah
 1758-1843......... DLB-1, 37, 42, 43, 73, 243
Webster, Paul Francis 1907-1984 .... DLB-265
Weckherlin, Georg Rodolf 1584-1653 ... DLB-164
Wedekind, Frank
 1864-1918 .... DLB-118; CDBLB-2
Weeks, Edward Augustus, Jr.
 1898-1989 ....DLB-137
Weeks, Stephen B. 1865-1918 ....DLB-187
Weems, Mason Locke 1759-1825...DLB-30, 37, 42
Weerth, Georg 1822-1856 .... DLB-129
Weidenfeld and Nicolson............ DLB-112
Weidman, Jerome 1913-1998 .... DLB-28
Weiß, Ernst 1882-1940................ DLB-81
Weigl, Bruce 1949- DLB-120
Weinbaum, Stanley Grauman 1902-1935 .. DLB-8
Weiner, Andrew 1949- DLB-251
Weintraub, Stanley 1929- DLB-111; Y82
The Practice of Biography: An Interview
 with Stanley Weintraub................Y-82
Weise, Christian 1642-1708 .... DLB-168
Weisenborn, Gunther 1902-1969.... DLB-69, 124
Weiss, John 1818-1879 .... DLB-1, 243
Weiss, Paul 1901-2002................DLB-279
Weiss, Peter 1916-1982 .... DLB-69, 124
Weiss, Theodore 1916- DLB-5
Weiße, Christian Felix 1726-1804........ DLB-97
Weitling, Wilhelm 1808-1871.......... DLB-129

Welch, James 1940- DLB-175, 256
Welch, Lew 1926-1971? DLB-16
Weldon, Fay 1931- DLB-14, 194; CDBLB-8
Wellek, René 1903-1995 .... DLB-63
Wells, Carolyn 1862-1942 .... DLB-11
Wells, Charles Jeremiah circa 1800-1879 ... DLB-32
Wells, Gabriel 1862-1946 .... DLB-140
Wells, H. G.
 1866-1946 ... DLB-34, 70, 156, 178; CDBLB-6
Wells, Helena 1758?-1824 .... DLB-200
Wells, Robert 1947- DLB-40
Wells-Barnett, Ida B. 1862-1931 ..... DLB-23, 221
Welsh, Irvine 1958- DLB-271
Welty, Eudora 1909- DLB-2, 102, 143;
 .... Y-87, Y-01; DS-12; CDALB-1
Eudora Welty: Eye of the Storyteller Y-87
Eudora Welty Newsletter Y-99
Eudora Welty Remembered in Two Exhibits . Y-02
Eudora Welty's Funeral Y-01
Eudora Welty's Ninetieth Birthday Y-99
Wendell, Barrett 1855-1921 .... DLB-71
Wentworth, Patricia 1878-1961 .... DLB-77
Wentworth, William Charles
 1790-1872 .... DLB-230
Werder, Diederich von dem 1584-1657 ... DLB-164
Werfel, Franz 1890-1945 .... DLB-81, 124
Werner, Zacharias 1768-1823 .... DLB-94
The Werner Company DLB-49
Wersba, Barbara 1932- DLB-52
Wescott, Glenway 1901-1987 .... DLB-4, 9, 102
Wesker, Arnold 1932- DLB-13; CDBLB-8
Wesley, Charles 1707-1788 .... DLB-95
Wesley, John 1703-1791 .... DLB-104
Wesley, Mary 1912- DLB-231
Wesley, Richard 1945- DLB-38
Wessels, A., and Company DLB-46
Wessobrunner Gebet circa 787-815 .... DLB-148
West, Anthony 1914-1988 .... DLB-15
West, Cheryl L. 1957- DLB-266
West, Cornel 1953- DLB-246
West, Dorothy 1907-1998 .... DLB-76
West, Jessamyn 1902-1984 .... DLB-6; Y-84
West, Mae 1892-1980 .... DLB-44
West, Michelle Sagara 1963- DLB-251
West, Nathanael
 1903-1940 .... DLB-4, 9, 28; CDALB-5
West, Paul 1930- DLB-14
West, Rebecca 1892-1983 .... DLB-36; Y-83
West, Richard 1941- DLB-185
West and Johnson DLB-49
Westcott, Edward Noyes 1846-1898 ..... DLB-202
The Western Messenger 1835-1841 .... DLB-223
Western Publishing Company DLB-46
Western Writers of America Y-99
The Westminster Review 1824-1914 .... DLB-110

Weston, Arthur (see Webling, Peggy)
Weston, Elizabeth Jane circa 1582-1612 .. DLB-172
Wetherald, Agnes Ethelwyn 1857-1940 .... DLB-99
Wetherell, Elizabeth (see Warner, Susan)
Wetherell, W. D. 1948- DLB-234
Wetzel, Friedrich Gottlob 1779-1819 ...... DLB-90
Weyman, Stanley J. 1855-1928 ...... DLB-141, 156
Wezel, Johann Karl 1747-1819 .... DLB-94
Whalen, Philip 1923- DLB-16
Whalley, George 1915-1983 .... DLB-88
Wharton, Edith 1862-1937
 .... DLB-4, 9, 12, 78, 189; DS-13; CDALB-3
Wharton, William 1920s?- Y-80
"What You Lose on the Swings You Make Up
 on the Merry-Go-Round" Y-99
Whately, Mary Louisa 1824-1889 .... DLB-166
Whately, Richard 1787-1863 .... DLB-190
From *Elements of Rhetoric* (1828;
 revised, 1846) DLB-57
What's Really Wrong With Bestseller Lists .. Y-84
Wheatley, Dennis 1897-1977 .... DLB-77, 255
Wheatley, Phillis
 circa 1754-1784 .... DLB-31, 50; CDALB-2
Wheeler, Anna Doyle 1785-1848? DLB-158
Wheeler, Charles Stearns 1816-1843 ... DLB-1, 223
Wheeler, Monroe 1900-1988 .... DLB-4
Wheelock, John Hall 1886-1978 .... DLB-45
From John Hall Wheelock's Oral Memoir ... Y-01
Wheelwright, J. B. 1897-1940 .... DLB-45
Wheelwright, John circa 1592-1679 ...... DLB-24
Whetstone, George 1550-1587 .... DLB-136
Whetstone, Colonel Pete (see Noland, C. F. M.)
Whewell, William 1794-1866 .... DLB-262
Whichcote, Benjamin 1609?-1683 .... DLB-252
Whicher, Stephen E. 1915-1961 .... DLB-111
Whipple, Edwin Percy 1819-1886 ...... DLB-1, 64
Whitaker, Alexander 1585-1617 .... DLB-24
Whitaker, Daniel K. 1801-1881 .... DLB-73
Whitcher, Frances Miriam
 1812-1852 .... DLB-11, 202
White, Andrew 1579-1656 .... DLB-24
White, Andrew Dickson 1832-1918 ...... DLB-47
White, E. B. 1899-1985 .... DLB-11, 22; CDALB-7
White, Edgar B. 1947- DLB-38
White, Edmund 1940- DLB-227
White, Ethel Lina 1887-1944 .... DLB-77
White, Hayden V. 1928- DLB-246
White, Henry Kirke 1785-1806 .... DLB-96
White, Horace 1834-1916 .... DLB-23
White, James 1928-1999 .... DLB-261
White, Patrick 1912-1990 .... DLB-260
White, Phyllis Dorothy James (see James, P. D.)
White, Richard Grant 1821-1885 .... DLB-64
White, T. H. 1906-1964 .... DLB-160, 255
White, Walter 1893-1955 .... DLB-51
White, William, and Company DLB-49

White, William Allen 1868-1944 .... DLB-9, 25
White, William Anthony Parker
 (see Boucher, Anthony)
White, William Hale (see Rutherford, Mark)
Whitchurch, Victor L. 1868-1933 .... DLB-70
Whitehead, Alfred North 1861-1947 ..... DLB-100
Whitehead, James 1936- Y-81
Whitehead, William 1715-1785 ...... DLB-84, 109
Whitfield, James Monroe 1822-1871 ..... DLB-50
Whitfield, Raoul 1898-1945 .... DLB-226
Whitgift, John circa 1533-1604 .... DLB-132
Whiting, John 1917-1963 .... DLB-13
Whiting, Samuel 1597-1679 .... DLB-24
Whitlock, Brand 1869-1934 .... DLB-12
Whitman, Albert, and Company DLB-46
Whitman, Albery Allson 1851-1901 ..... DLB-50
Whitman, Alden 1913-1990 .... Y-91
Whitman, Sarah Helen (Power)
 1803-1878 .... DLB-1, 243
Whitman, Walt
 1819-1892 .... DLB-3, 64, 224, 250; CDALB-2
Whitman Publishing Company DLB-46
Whitney, Geoffrey 1548 or 1552?-1601 .. DLB-136
Whitney, Isabella flourished 1566-1573 ... DLB-136
Whitney, John Hay 1904-1982 .... DLB-127
Whittemore, Reed 1919-1995 .... DLB-5
Whittier, John Greenleaf
 1807-1892 .... DLB-1, 243; CDALB-2
Whittlesey House DLB-46
Who Runs American Literature? Y-94
Whose *Ulysses?* The Function of Editing Y-97
Wickham, Anna (Edith Alice Mary Harper)
 1884-1947 .... DLB-240
Wicomb, Zoë 1948- DLB-225
Wideman, John Edgar 1941- DLB-33, 143
Widener, Harry Elkins 1885-1912 ...... DLB-140
Wiebe, Rudy 1934- DLB-60
Wiechert, Ernst 1887-1950 .... DLB-56
Wied, Martina 1882-1957 .... DLB-85
Wiehe, Evelyn May Clowes (see Mordaunt, Elinor)
Wieland, Christoph Martin 1733-1813 .... DLB-97
Wienbarg, Ludolf 1802-1872 .... DLB-133
Wieners, John 1934- DLB-16
Wier, Ester 1910- DLB-52
Wiesel, Elie
 1928- DLB-83; Y-86, 87; CDALB-7
Wiggin, Kate Douglas 1856-1923 .... DLB-42
Wigglesworth, Michael 1631-1705 .... DLB-24
Wilberforce, William 1759-1833 .... DLB-158
Wilbrandt, Adolf 1837-1911 .... DLB-129
Wilbur, Richard
 1921- DLB-5, 169; CDALB-7
Wild, Peter 1940- DLB-5
Wilde, Lady Jane Francesca Elgee
 1821?-1896 .... DLB-199
Wilde, Oscar 1854-1900
 .... DLB-10, 19, 34, 57, 141, 156, 190;

CDBLB-5	Williams, Joe 1889-1972 . . . . DLB-241	Wilson, Robert McLiam 1964- DLB-267
"The Critic as Artist" (1891) DLB-57	Williams, John A. 1925- DLB-2, 33	Wilson, Robley 1930- DLB-218
Oscar Wilde Conference at Hofstra University Y-00	Williams, John E. 1922-1994 . . . . DLB-6	Wilson, Romer 1891-1930 . . . . DLB-191
From "The Decay of Lying" (1889) DLB-18	Williams, Jonathan 1929- DLB-5	Wilson, Thomas 1524-1581 . . . . DLB-132, 236
"The English Renaissance of Art" (1908) DLB-35	Williams, Miller 1930- DLB-105	Wilson, Woodrow 1856-1924 . . . . DLB-47
	Williams, Nigel 1948- DLB-231	Wimsatt, William K., Jr. 1907-1975 . . . . . DLB-63
"L'Envoi" (1882) DLB-35	Williams, Raymond 1921- . . . DLB-14, 231, 242	Winchell, Walter 1897-1972 . . . . DLB-29
Wilde, Richard Henry 1789-1847 . . . . . . DLB-3, 59	Williams, Roger circa 1603-1683 . . . . DLB-24	Winchester, J. [publishing house] DLB-49
Wilde, W. A., Company DLB-49	Williams, Rowland 1817-1870 . . . . DLB-184	Winckelmann, Johann Joachim 1717-1768 . . . . DLB-97
Wilder, Billy 1906- DLB-26	Williams, Samm-Art 1946- DLB-38	
Wilder, Laura Ingalls 1867-1957 . . . . . DLB-22, 256	Williams, Sherley Anne 1944-1999 . . . . . . DLB-41	Winckler, Paul 1630-1686 . . . . DLB-164
Wilder, Thornton 1897-1975 . . . . DLB-4, 7, 9, 228; CDALB-7	Williams, T. Harry 1909-1979 . . . . DLB-17	Wind, Herbert Warren 1916- DLB-171
	Williams, Tennessee 1911-1983 . . . . DLB-7; Y-83; DS-4; CDALB-1	Windet, John [publishing house] DLB-170
Thornton Wilder Centenary at Yale Y-97		Windham, Donald 1920- DLB-6
Wildgans, Anton 1881-1932 . . . . DLB-118	Williams, Terry Tempest 1955- . . .DLB-206, 275	Wing, Donald Goddard 1904-1972 . . . . . .DLB-187
Wiley, Bell Irvin 1906-1980 . . . . DLB-17	Williams, Ursula Moray 1911- DLB-160	Wing, John M. 1844-1917 . . . . .DLB-187
Wiley, John, and Sons DLB-49	Williams, Valentine 1883-1946 . . . . DLB-77	Wingate, Allan [publishing house] DLB-112
Wilhelm, Kate 1928- DLB-8	Williams, William Appleman 1921- DLB-17	Winnemucca, Sarah 1844-1921 . . . . . . .DLB-175
Wilkes, Charles 1798-1877 . . . . DLB-183	Williams, William Carlos 1883-1963 . . . . . DLB-4, 16, 54, 86; CDALB-4	Winnifrith, Tom 1938- DLB-155
Wilkes, George 1817-1885 . . . . DLB-79		Winning an Edgar Y-98
Wilkins, John 1614-1672 . . . . DLB-236	Williams, Wirt 1921- DLB-6	Winsloe, Christa 1888-1944 . . . . DLB-124
Wilkinson, Anne 1910-1961 . . . . DLB-88	Williams Brothers DLB-49	Winslow, Anna Green 1759-1780 . . . . DLB-200
Wilkinson, Eliza Yonge 1757-circa 1813 . . . . DLB-200	Williamson, Henry 1895-1977 . . . . DLB-191	Winsor, Justin 1831-1897 . . . . DLB-47
	Williamson, Jack 1908- DLB-8	John C. Winston Company DLB-49
Wilkinson, Sylvia 1940- Y-86	Willingham, Calder Baynard, Jr. 1922-1995 . . . . DLB-2, 44	Winters, Yvor 1900-1968 . . . . DLB-48
Wilkinson, William Cleaver 1833-1920 . . . DLB-71		Winterson, Jeanette 1959- DLB-207, 261
Willard, Barbara 1909-1994 . . . . DLB-161	Williram of Ebersberg circa 1020-1085 . . DLB-148	Winthrop, John 1588-1649 . . . . DLB-24, 30
Willard, Emma 1787-1870 . . . . DLB-239	Willis, John circa 1572-1625 . . . . DLB-281	Winthrop, John, Jr. 1606-1676 . . . . DLB-24
Willard, Frances E. 1839-1898 . . . . DLB-221	Willis, Nathaniel Parker 1806-1867 . . . . DLB-3, 59, 73, 74, 183, 250; DS-13	Winthrop, Margaret Tyndal 1591-1647 . . DLB-200
Willard, L. [publishing house] DLB-49		Winthrop, Theodore 1828-1861 . . . . DLB-202
Willard, Nancy 1936- DLB-5, 52	Willkomm, Ernst 1810-1886 . . . . DLB-133	Wirt, William 1772-1834 . . . . DLB-37
Willard, Samuel 1640-1707 . . . . DLB-24	Willumsen, Dorrit 1940- DLB-214	Wise, John 1652-1725 . . . . DLB-24
Willeford, Charles 1919-1988 . . . . DLB-226	Wills, Garry 1934- DLB-246	Wise, Thomas James 1859-1937 . . . . DLB-184
William of Auvergne 1190-1249 . . . . DLB-115	Willson, Meredith 1902-1984 . . . . DLB-265	Wiseman, Adele 1928-1992 . . . . DLB-88
William of Conches circa 1090-circa 1154 . . . . DLB-115	Wilmer, Clive 1945- DLB-40	Wishart and Company DLB-112
	Wilson, A. N. 1950- DLB-14, 155, 194	Wisner, George 1812-1849 . . . . DLB-43
William of Ockham circa 1285-1347 . . . . DLB-115	Wilson, Angus 1913-1991 . . . . . .DLB-15, 139, 155	Wister, Owen 1860-1938 . . . . . . .DLB-9, 78, 186
William of Sherwood 1200/1205-1266/1271 . . . . DLB-115	Wilson, Arthur 1595-1652 . . . . DLB-58	Wister, Sarah 1761-1804 . . . . DLB-200
	Wilson, August 1945- DLB-228	Wither, George 1588-1667 . . . . DLB-121
The William Chavrat American Fiction Collection at the Ohio State University Libraries Y-92	Wilson, Augusta Jane Evans 1835-1909 . . . DLB-42	Witherspoon, John 1723-1794 . . . . DLB-31
	Wilson, Colin 1931- DLB-14, 194	Withrow, William Henry 1839-1908 . . . . . DLB-99
Williams, A., and Company DLB-49	Wilson, Edmund 1895-1972 . . . . DLB-63	Witkacy (see Witkiewicz, Stanisław Ignacy)
Williams, Ben Ames 1889-1953 . . . . DLB-102	Wilson, Effingham [publishing house] . . . DLB-154	Witkiewicz, Stanisław Ignacy 1885-1939 . . . . .DLB-215; CDWLB-4
Williams, C. K. 1936- DLB-5	Wilson, Ethel 1888-1980 . . . . DLB-68	
Williams, Chancellor 1905- DLB-76	Wilson, F. P. 1889-1963 . . . . DLB-201	Wittgenstein, Ludwig 1889-1951 . . . . DLB-262
Williams, Charles 1886-1945 . . .DLB-100, 153, 255	Wilson, Harriet E. 1827/1828?-1863? DLB-50, 239, 243	Wittig, Monique 1935- DLB-83
Williams, Denis 1923-1998 . . . . DLB-117		Wodehouse, P. G. 1881-1975 . . . . DLB-34, 162; CDBLB-6
Williams, Emlyn 1905-1987 . . . . .DLB-10, 77	Wilson, Harry Leon 1867-1939 . . . . DLB-9	
Williams, Garth 1912-1996 . . . . DLB-22	Wilson, John 1588-1667 . . . . DLB-24	Wohmann, Gabriele 1932- DLB-75
Williams, George Washington 1849-1891 . . . . DLB-47	Wilson, John 1785-1854 . . . . DLB-110	Woiwode, Larry 1941- DLB-6
	Wilson, John Dover 1881-1969 . . . . DLB-201	Wolcot, John 1738-1819 . . . . DLB-109
Williams, Heathcote 1941- DLB-13	Wilson, Lanford 1937- DLB-7	Wolcott, Roger 1679-1767 . . . . DLB-24
Williams, Helen Maria 1761-1827 . . . . . . DLB-158	Wilson, Margaret 1882-1973 . . . . DLB-9	Wolf, Christa 1929- DLB-75; CDWLB-2
Williams, Hugo 1942- DLB-40	Wilson, Michael 1914-1978 . . . . DLB-44	
Williams, Isaac 1802-1865 . . . . DLB-32	Wilson, Mona 1872-1954 . . . . DLB-149	Wolf, Friedrich 1888-1953 . . . . DLB-124
Williams, Joan 1928- DLB-6	Wilson, Robert Charles 1953- DLB-251	Wolfe, Gene 1931- DLB-8

Wolfe, John [publishing house] DLB-170

Wolfe, Reyner (Reginald)
 [publishing house] DLB-170

Wolfe, Thomas
 1900-1938 ....DLB-9, 102, 229; Y-85;
  DS-2, DS-16; CDALB-5

"All the Faults of Youth and Inexperience":
 A Reader's Report on
 Thomas Wolfe's *O Lost* Y-01

Eugene Gant's Projected Works Y-01

The Thomas Wolfe Collection at the University
 of North Carolina at Chapel Hill Y-97

Thomas Wolfe Centennial
 Celebration in Asheville Y-00

Fire at Thomas Wolfe Memorial...........Y-98

The Thomas Wolfe Society................Y-97

Wolfe, Tom 1931- DLB-152, 185

Wolfenstein, Martha 1869-1906 ....DLB-221

Wolff, Helen 1906-1994 .... Y-94

Wolff, Tobias 1945- DLB-130

Wolfram von Eschenbach
 circa 1170-after 1220 ....DLB-138; CDWLB-2

Wolfram von Eschenbach's *Parzival*:
 Prologue and Book 3................DLB-138

Wolker, Jiří 1900-1924 ....DLB-215

Wollstonecraft, Mary 1759-1797
 ....DLB-39, 104, 158, 252; CDBLB-3

Younger Women Poets of the
 New Formalism....................DLB-282

Wondratschek, Wolf 1943- DLB-75

Wong, Elizabeth 1958- DLB-266

Wood, Anthony à 1632-1695 ....DLB-213

Wood, Benjamin 1820-1900 ....DLB-23

Wood, Charles 1932- DLB-13

Wood, Mrs. Henry 1814-1887............DLB-18

Wood, Joanna E. 1867-1927..............DLB-92

Wood, Sally Sayward Barrell Keating
 1759-1855 ....DLB-200

Wood, Samuel [publishing house] DLB-49

Wood, William ?-?....................DLB-24

The Charles Wood Affair:
 A Playwright Revived Y-83

Woodberry, George Edward
 1855-1930 ....DLB-71, 103

Woodbridge, Benjamin 1622-1684 ....DLB-24

Woodbridge, Frederick J. E. 1867-1940...DLB-270

Woodcock, George 1912-1995 ....DLB-88

Woodhull, Victoria C. 1838-1927 ....DLB-79

Woodmason, Charles circa 1720-?........DLB-31

Woodress, Jr., James Leslie 1916- DLB-111

Woods, Margaret L. 1855-1945.........DLB-240

Woodson, Carter G. 1875-1950..........DLB-17

Woodward, C. Vann 1908-1999.........DLB-17

Woodward, Stanley 1895-1965 ....DLB-171

Woodworth, Samuel 1785-1842.........DLB-260

Wooler, Thomas 1785 or 1786-1853 .....DLB-158

Woolf, David (see Maddow, Ben)

Woolf, Douglas 1922-1992 ....DLB-244

Woolf, Leonard 1880-1969 .....DLB-100; DS-10

Woolf, Virginia 1882-1941
 ....DLB-36, 100, 162; DS-10; CDBLB-6

Woolf, Virginia, "The New Biography," *New York
 Herald Tribune*, 30 October 1927 ....DLB-149

Woollcott, Alexander 1887-1943 ....DLB-29

Woolman, John 1720-1772..............DLB-31

Woolner, Thomas 1825-1892 ....DLB-35

Woolrich, Cornell 1903-1968 ....DLB-226

Woolsey, Sarah Chauncy 1835-1905 ......DLB-42

Woolson, Constance Fenimore
 1840-1894 ....DLB-12, 74, 189, 221

Worcester, Joseph Emerson
 1784-1865 ....DLB-1, 235

Worde, Wynkyn de [publishing house]...DLB-170

Wordsworth, Christopher 1807-1885 ....DLB-166

Wordsworth, Dorothy 1771-1855 ....DLB-107

Wordsworth, Elizabeth 1840-1932 ....DLB-98

Wordsworth, William
 1770-1850 ....DLB-93, 107; CDBLB-3

Workman, Fanny Bullock 1859-1925 ....DLB-189

The Works of the Rev. John Witherspoon
 (1800-1801) [excerpts]..............DLB-31

A World Chronology of Important Science
 Fiction Works (1818-1979) DLB-8

World Literatue Today: A Journal for the
 New Millennium................... Y-01

World Publishing Company DLB-46

World War II Writers Symposium
 at the University of South Carolina,
 12–14 April 1995..................... Y-95

Worthington, R., and Company DLB-49

Wotton, Sir Henry 1568-1639..........DLB-121

Wouk, Herman 1915- Y-82; CDALB-7

Wreford, James 1915- DLB-88

Wren, Sir Christopher 1632-1723 ....DLB-213

Wren, Percival Christopher 1885-1941...DLB-153

Wrenn, John Henry 1841-1911.........DLB-140

Wright, C. D. 1949- DLB-120

Wright, Charles 1935- DLB-165; Y-82

Wright, Charles Stevenson 1932- DLB-33

Wright, Chauncey 1830-1875 ....DLB-270

Wright, Frances 1795-1852 ....DLB-73

Wright, Harold Bell 1872-1944 ....DLB-9

Wright, James 1927-1980....DLB-5, 169; CDALB-7

Wright, Jay 1935- DLB-41

Wright, Judith 1915-2000 ....DLB-260

Wright, Louis B. 1899-1984 ....DLB-17

Wright, Richard
 1908-1960 .....DLB-76, 102; DS-2; CDALB-5

Wright, Richard B. 1937- DLB-53

Wright, S. Fowler 1874-1965 ....DLB-255

Wright, Sarah Elizabeth 1928- DLB-33

Wright, Willard Huntington
 ("S. S. Van Dine") 1888-1939 .... DS-16

Wrigley, Robert 1951- DLB-256

A Writer Talking: A Collage............ Y-00

Writers and Politics: 1871-1918,
 by Ronald Gray DLB-66

Writers and their Copyright Holders:
 the WATCH Project................. Y-94

Writers' Forum Y-85

Writing for the Theatre,
 by Harold Pinter...................DLB-13

A Writing Life......................... Y-02

Wroth, Lawrence C. 1884-1970 ....DLB-187

Wroth, Lady Mary 1587-1653..........DLB-121

Wurlitzer, Rudolph 1937- DLB-173

Wyatt, Sir Thomas circa 1503-1542 .....DLB-132

Wycherley, William
 1641-1715 ....DLB-80; CDBLB-2

Wyclif, John
 circa 1335-31 December 1384.......DLB-146

Wyeth, N. C. 1882-1945.........DLB-188; DS-16

Wylie, Elinor 1885-1928 ....DLB-9, 45

Wylie, Philip 1902-1971................DLB-9

Wyllie, John Cook 1908-1968..........DLB-140

Wyman, Lillie Buffum Chace
 1847-1929 ....DLB-202

Wymark, Olwen 1934- DLB-233

Wyndham, John 1903-1969 ....DLB-255

Wynne-Tyson, Esmé 1898-1972 ....DLB-191

X

Xenophon circa 430 B.C.-circa 356 B.C....DLB-176

Y

Yasuoka Shōtarō 1920- DLB-182

Yates, Dornford 1885-1960 ....DLB-77, 153

Yates, J. Michael 1938- DLB-60

Yates, Richard 1926-1992 .DLB-2, 234; Y-81, Y-92

Yau, John 1950- DLB-234

Yavorov, Peyo 1878-1914 ....DLB-147

The Year in Book Publishing Y-86

The Year in Book Reviewing and
 the Literary Situation Y-98

The Year in British and Irish Novels........ Y-02

The Year in British Drama Y-99, Y-00, Y-01

The Year in British Fiction Y-99, Y-00, Y-01

The Year in Children's
 Books Y-92–Y-96, Y-98, Y-99, Y-00, Y-01

The Year in Children's Literature....... Y-97, Y-02

The Year in Drama Y-82-Y-85, Y-87–Y-96

The Year in Fiction
 ....Y-84–Y-86, Y-89, Y-94–Y-99, Y-02

The Year in Fiction: A Biased View Y-83

The Year in Literary
 Biography Y-83–Y-98, Y-00, Y-01, Y-02

The Year in Literary Theory...........Y-92–Y-93

The Year in London Theatre Y-92

The Year in the Novel......Y-87, Y-88, Y-90–Y-93

The Year in Poetry .. Y-83–Y-92, Y-94, Y-95, Y-96,
 ....Y-97, Y-98, Y-99, Y-00, Y-01, Y-02

The Year in Science Fiction
 and Fantasy.................Y-00, Y-01, Y-02

The Year in Short Stories Y-87

The Year in the Short Story...... Y-88, Y-90–Y-93

The Year in Texas Literature Y-98

The Year in U.S. Drama Y-00

The Year in U.S. Fiction Y-00, Y-01

The Year's Work in American Poetry....... Y-82

The Year's Work in Fiction: A Survey Y-82

Yearsley, Ann 1753-1806..............DLB-109

Yeats, William Butler 1865-1939 ... DLB-10, 19, 98, 156; CDBLB-5

Yellen, Jack 1892-1991 .... DLB-265

Yep, Laurence 1948- DLB-52

Yerby, Frank 1916-1991 .... DLB-76

Yezierska, Anzia 1880-1970 .... DLB-28, 221

Yolen, Jane 1939- DLB-52

Yonge, Charlotte Mary 1823-1901 ... DLB-18, 163

The York Cycle circa 1376-circa 1569 ... DLB-146

A Yorkshire Tragedy DLB-58

Yoseloff, Thomas [publishing house] DLB-46

Young, A. S. "Doc" 1919-1996 .... DLB-241

Young, Al 1939- DLB-33

Young, Arthur 1741-1820 .... DLB-158

Young, Dick 1917 or 1918 - 1987 .... DLB-171

Young, Edward 1683-1765 .... DLB-95

Young, Frank A. "Fay" 1884-1957 ..... DLB-241

Young, Francis Brett 1884-1954 .... DLB-191

Young, Gavin 1928- DLB-204

Young, Stark 1881-1963 ...... DLB-9, 102; DS-16

Young, Waldeman 1880-1938 .... DLB-26

Young, William publishing house] DLB-49

Young Bear, Ray A. 1950- DLB-175

Younger Women Poets of the New Formalism DLB-282

Yourcenar, Marguerite 1903-1987 ....DLB-72; Y-88

"You've Never Had It So Good," Gusted by "Winds of Change": British Fiction in the 1950s, 1960s, and After DLB-14

Yovkov, Yordan 1880-1937 ..DLB-147; CDWLB-4

Z

Zachariä, Friedrich Wilhelm 1726-1777 ... DLB-97

Zagajewski, Adam 1945- DLB-232

Zagoskin, Mikhail Nikolaevich 1789-1852 DLB-198

Zajc, Dane 1929- DLB-181

Zālīte, Māra 1952- DLB-232

Zamiatin, Evgenii Ivanovich 1884-1937 ...DLB-272

Zamora, Bernice 1938- DLB-82

Zand, Herbert 1923-1970 .... DLB-85

Zangwill, Israel 1864-1926 ...... DLB-10, 135, 197

Zanzotto, Andrea 1921- DLB-128

Zapata Olivella, Manuel 1920- DLB-113

Zasodimsky, Pavel Vladimirovich 1843-1912 .... DLB-238

Zebra Books DLB-46

Zebrowski, George 1945- DLB-8

Zech, Paul 1881-1946 .... DLB-56

Zeidner, Lisa 1955- DLB-120

Zeidonis, Imants 1933- DLB-232

Zeimi (Kanze Motokiyo) 1363-1443 ..... DLB-203

Zelazny, Roger 1937-1995 .... DLB-8

Zenger, John Peter 1697-1746 .... DLB-24, 43

Zepheria DLB-172

Zesen, Philipp von 1619-1689 .... DLB-164

Zhadovskaia, Iuliia Valerianovna 1824-1883 .... DLB-277

Zhukova, Mar'ia Semenovna 1805-1855 ..DLB-277

Zhukovsky, Vasilii Andreevich 1783-1852 .... DLB-205

Zieber, G. B., and Company DLB-49

Ziedonis, Imants 1933- CDWLB-4

Zieroth, Dale 1946- DLB-60

Zigler und Kliphausen, Heinrich Anshelm von 1663-1697 .... DLB-168

Zil'ber, Veniamin Aleksandrovich (see Kaverin, Veniamin Aleksandrovich)

Zimmer, Paul 1934- DLB-5

Zinberg, Len (see Lacy, Ed)

Zindel, Paul 1936- DLB-7, 52; CDALB-7

Zingref, Julius Wilhelm 1591-1635 ...... DLB-164

Zinnes, Harriet 1919- DLB-193

Zinzendorf, Nikolaus Ludwig von 1700-1760 .... DLB-168

Zitkala-Ša 1876-1938 ....DLB-175

Zīverts, Mārtiņš 1903-1990 .... DLB-220

Zlatovratsky, Nikolai Nikolaevich 1845-1911 .... DLB-238

Zola, Emile 1840-1902 .... DLB-123

Zolla, Elémire 1926- DLB-196

Zolotow, Charlotte 1915- DLB-52

Zoshchenko, Mikhail Mikhailovich 1895-1958 .... DLB-272

Zschokke, Heinrich 1771-1848 .... DLB-94

Zubly, John Joachim 1724-1781 .... DLB-31

Zu-Bolton, Ahmos, II 1936- DLB-41

Zuckmayer, Carl 1896-1977 .... DLB-56, 124

Zukofsky, Louis 1904-1978 .... DLB-5, 165

Zupan, Vitomil 1914-1987 .... DLB-181

Župančič, Oton 1878-1949 ...DLB-147; CDWLB-4

zur Mühlen, Hermynia 1883-1951 .... DLB-56

Zweig, Arnold 1887-1968 .... DLB-66

Zweig, Stefan 1881-1942 .... DLB-81, 118

Zwinger, Ann 1925- DLB-275

ISBN 0-7876-6819-2